BEA WebLogic Server 8.1

UNLEASHED

Mark Artiges, Gupreet Singh Bhasin, Bernard Ciconte,
Malcolm Garland, Saranathan Govindarajan, James Huang,
Subramanian Kovilmadam, Kunal Mittal, Paul J. Perrone,
Tom Schwenk, Steve Steffen

800 East 96th Street, Indianapolis, Indiana 46240

BEA WebLogic Server 8.1 Unleashed

International Standard Book Number: 0-672-32487-3

Library of Congress Catalog Card Number: 2003092628

Printed in the United States of America

First Printing: November 2003

06 05 04 03 4 3 2 1

Sams Publishing offers excellent discounts on this book when ordered in quantity for bulk purchases or special sales. For more information, please contact

U.S. Corporate and Government Sales
1-800-382-3419
corpsales@pearsontechgroup.com

For sales outside of the U.S., please contact

International Sales
1-317-428-3341
international@pearsontechgroup.com

Trademarks

All terms mentioned in this book that are known to be trademarks or service marks have been appropriately capitalized. Sams Publishing cannot attest to the accuracy of this information. Use of a term in this book should not be regarded as affecting the validity of any trademark or service mark.

Warning and Disclaimer

Every effort has been made to make this book as complete and as accurate as possible, but no warranty or fitness is implied. The information provided is on an "as is" basis. The authors and the publisher shall have neither liability nor responsibility to any person or entity with respect to any loss or damages arising from the information contained in this book or from the use of the CD or programs accompanying it.

Associate Publisher
Michael Stephens

Acquisitions Editor
Todd Green

Development Editor
Songlin Qiu

Managing Editor
Charlotte Clapp

Project Editor
George E. Nedeff

Copy Editor
Mike Henry

Indexer
Heather McNeill

Proofreader
Carla Lewis

Technical Editors
Emmanuel Proulx
Chris Madrid
Michael Abbott
Luis Felipe Pantoja García
Steve Heckler
Ramanjeet Johar

Team Coordinator
Cindy Teeters

Multimedia Developer
Dan Scherf

Interior Designer
Gary Adair

Cover Designer
Alan Clements

Page Layout
Eric S. Miller
Michelle Mitchell

Contents at a Glance

Table of Contents

Foreword

When I joined the WebLogic founders in 1996, it was a small company with some excellent JDBC drivers and a rudimentary Java server with events, servlets, rowsets, and remoting. This book describes the culmination of the original vision: to create a distributed systems development platform in Java that would replace the existing enterprise infrastructure. Even one of our first advertising slogans now appears prophetic: "Elevating Java to the Enterprise."

Although WebLogic was acquired in 1998 by BEA Systems, the WebLogic Server engineers share a special bond with one another and with their product. This explains the extremely small attrition in the engineering organization and why the product has such continuity from release to release. With the release of WebLogic 8.1, nearly everything that can be built-in to the server is there. The focus for BEA is now on the products and platform that are built on top of this stable, scalable, and well-performing infrastructure. This book describes this infrastructure in great detail and is an excellent guide to the problems and solutions for large-scale distributed systems development using WebLogic Server.

WebLogic Server's development was most often directed by the engineers and the choices they made were often answers to the question, "How would I want it to work?" Everything from being able to download the server directly from the Web site to being able to install it and run it without a lot of tedious setup was a result of this question. Most critically, the engineers did not want to learn proprietary APIs nor maintain those APIs if it could be helped. Carefully implementing each API from Sun and combining them into a single package helped create the Java Application Server and, soon after that, the J2EE standard. Our focus at the 1998 JavaOne conference was a checklist of standard APIs that your Java server should have. This list soon became a standard unto itself along with all its advantages from a developer perspective. Whereas CORBA created a vast library of APIs, few people had built them all and integrated them into a single platform, let alone made them interoperable at the binary level. The grand vision of Java had not been implemented on the client, but on the server instead.

The real revelation that we had while working at WebLogic is that our value would come to the table in a very concrete, verifiable way. We would build our server to exacting specifications and at the same time make applications written to the other side of those standards more scalable and better performing than when they are run on another server. We would not achieve vendor lock-in through tricks and proprietary APIs, but we would instead just be better than the competition. That's a hard road to follow, but it's a very fulfilling one. Giving people the opportunity to "learn once, write everywhere" is just another way of looking at the fundamental tenet of Java.

One thing that I noticed while reviewing this book is that the authors have a deep understanding of the software development process and all the details that are sometimes overlooked. All aspects of enterprise software development are treated and then framed within WebLogic Server so that you know not only what to do, but why you're doing it. Sitting down with this book you should come away not only an expert on WebLogic software, but also a more effective enterprise software engineer.

Sam Pullara
WebLogic Server Architect

About Gamma Enterprise Technologies

Gamma Enterprise Technologies has been helping WebLogic developers get BEA-certified for years. Employees of Gamma Enterprise Technologies have collaborated with leading WebLogic consultants, trainers, and authors to write the most comprehensive book on WebLogic Server: *BEA WebLogic Server 8.1 Unleashed.*

Each Gamma author involved in this book has extensive field experience implementing WebLogic Server solutions across a vast number of industries including the financial, industrial, and insurance markets. In addition to offering J2EE and WebLogic-based services and products, Gamma's other focal point is SAP where they have a special expertise in integrating WebLogic Server and other J2EE application servers and applications to SAP R/3 instances.

About the Authors

Mark Artiges is an independent consultant currently working as a Lead Software Engineer for Tepik Systems. During his 18-plus years in the computer industry, Mark has been involved in a wide range of data processing initiatives and development methodologies. He has worked as a system architect and lead developer on large application development efforts aimed at transitioning core legacy systems to WebLogic Platform at companies such as AT&T, US Search, and Public Storage.

Gurpreet Singh Bhasin is an architect, designer, and developer with certifications from BEA, Sun, and Microsoft. He has more than five years of experience in design, development, testing, and maintenance of n-tier e-commerce and enterprise information systems using J2EE and Microsoft technologies. Most recently, Gurpreet was Module Leader on an Internet-based system for DIRECTV allowing over 10 million customers enhanced account access. He holds a bachelor's degree in electronics and communication engineering from Kurukshetra University, India.

To my parents and sisters: Thank you for all your love and support.

—Gurpreet Bhasin

Bernard Ciconte is a software engineer for Blair Computing Systems, Inc. (BCSI). As an employee of BCSI since 1989, he has worked as a contractor for DuPont, Sterling Diagnostic Imaging, and Agfa Corporation. His technical expertise is in distributed computing and image processing for radiographical medical devices. Previously Bernard contributed to Sams' book *BEA WebLogic Platform 7.0.*

Bernard would like to thank his wife Cheryl, daughter Courtney Huff, and dog Minx, for the sacrifices and support they made while he dedicated so much of his time and effort towards this book. He would also like to thank Todd Green and Sams Publishing for inviting him to be a co-author with such a talented group of individuals. Finally, he would like to thank Mark Blair and all his co-workers for the interesting and challenging career they share at Blair Computing Systems, Inc.

—Bernard Ciconte

Malcolm Garland has more than ten years of experience in the field of software development and has received certifications from BEA and Sun. He was recently CM Lead and systems analyst on an integration project in J2EE and WebLogic, developed for DIRECTV, for which he advised on architectural design, testing, configuration, and component development. Currently, he is a Senior Systems Analyst with Zenith National Insurance.

Saranathan Govindarajan is a key member of DIRECTV's Enterprise Architecture Team responsible for the design and development of infrastructure services using BEA WebLogic Server and Tuxedo. Saranathan has more than 8 years of experience in designing and implementing mission-critical systems using BEA's flagship products: WebLogic Server, Tuxedo, and Jolt/WTC. Saranathan holds a MSc(Tech) and M.S(Software Systems) from Birla Institute of Technology and Sciences(BITS) in Pilani, India.

To my parents and Deepa, for their love, support, and inspiration.

—Saranathan Govindarajan

James Huang is currently an IT Developer with BEA Systems. A veteran software developer, James has handled numerous J2EE, Web application, and database development projects. In a previous life, he was a lecturer in the Department of Electric and Computer Engineering at East China Normal University. James is the primary designer and developer of JudoScript, a project to bring the functionality of scripting and shell programming to Java.

Subramanian Kovilmadam is a BEA and Sun Certified Developer, and currently serves as an Enterprise Application Integration Systems Architect with DIRECTV, responsible for the design and development of integration infrastructure strategies using XML-based services, J2EE, BEA WebLogic, and BEA Tuxedo.

I wish to thank my family, especially my dear wife, Amudha, for being patient with me and encouraging me all the way during this process. Their constant backing and encouragement proved to be a huge source of inspiration for me.

—Subramanian Kovilmadam

Kunal Mittal, is a Solutions Engineer at Wakesoft, Inc. and a consultant for implementation and strategy for Web Services and Services Oriented Architectures. He has co-authored and contributed to several books on Java, WebLogic, and Web Services. Over the past several years, Kunal has worked on numerous projects using different BEA products, ranging from WebLogic Server 4.5 to 8.1, BEA Portal, BEA Integration, Liquid Data for WebLogic, and WebLogic Workshop. His projects have ranged in verticals such as finance, real estate, supply chain, broadband, entertainment, and ISVs in the Web Services space.

I would like to thank my wife, Neeta, and dog, Dusty, for being patient as I put in those extra hours and weekends on this book. I would also like to thank the Sams team (Todd Green, Songlin Qiu, and George Nedeff) for their patience with me (especially my email problems).

—Kunal Mittal

Paul J. Perrone is the Founder, President, and CTO at Assured Technologies, Inc. Through Assured Technologies (`www.assuredtech.com`), Paul provides software architecture and development consulting, mentoring, and training related to J2EE, XML, Web Services, and object-oriented technologies. Paul has been involved with the architecture, design, and development of numerous large-scale enterprise systems and products for both Fortune 500 and medium-sized organizations. Paul also has co-authored *J2EE Developer's Handbook, Building Java Enterprise Systems with J2EE,* and *Java Security Handbook*; has published articles on Java; and has spoken at conferences such as JavaOne and Web Services Edge. He has an MS from the University of Virginia and a BS from Rutgers University. He is a member of the IEEE and ACM, has served as chapter chair for the Northern Virginia IEEE Computer Society, has helped in the startup of the Northern Virginia Java User's Group (NOVAJUG), and chairs the NOVAJUG's enterprise SIG. Paul is also an avid Java-based robot and AI tinkerer.

To Stax Dooley's Irish Pub (aka "Crack Shack") patrons.

—Paul J. Perrone

I'd like to acknowledge my wife, parents, parents-in-law, brother, sister-in-law, nieces (Allison, Julia, & Nina), extended family, friends, Cappy, and my robots.

Tom Schwenk is a Senior Software Consultant with Assured Technologies, Inc. Since 1995, he has been working with Java, specializing in highly scalable, distributed application design and development. He has been involved in the design and implementation of Java enterprise and e-commerce applications for both Fortune 500 and smaller companies. He holds a BS in Electrical Engineering and an ME in Biomedical Engineering, both from the University of Virginia. Previously Tom co-authored *J2EE Developer's Handbook.*

I would like to thank all of my family, friends, and colleagues that have given me the advice, assistance, opportunities, and support to accomplish this goal.

—Tom Schwenk

Steve Steffen is part of Gamma's highly regarded Java-SAP team and brings to it a strong combination of knowledge and experience in corporate computing. Prior to joining Gamma, Steve was called to consult Fortune 500 companies including Lucent Technologies, Bridgestone/Firestone, Mercury Marine, and Kubota Engine America. His area of specialization since the lat 1990's has been integration technologies for SAP and Java using WebLogic Server. He developed his training expertise at Lucent Technologies, where he created and delivered Java and Internet classes.

To my wife, April, my companion for life; my parents, for a job well done; and my three sisters for support and inspiration.

—Steve Steffen

Dedication

This book is dedicated to my friend Matt Green, who ran the BEA Worldwide Sales Organization for many years and who provided me with an introduction to BEA before it became a recognized industry leader, and to the authors, whose expertise continues to be an invaluable contribution to Gamma and its customers.

Matthew Minkovsky—President and CEO, Gamma Enterprise Technologies.

We Want to Hear from You!

As the reader of this book, *you* are our most important critic and commentator. We value your opinion and want to know what we're doing right, what we could do better, what areas you'd like to see us publish in, and any other words of wisdom you're willing to pass our way.

As an associate publisher for Sams Publishing, I welcome your comments. You can email or write me directly to let me know what you did or didn't like about this book—as well as what we can do to make our books better.

Please note that I cannot help you with technical problems related to the *topic* of this book. We do have a User Services group, however, where I will forward specific technical questions related to the book.

When you write, please be sure to include this book's title and author as well as your name, email address, and phone number. I will carefully review your comments and share them with the author and editors who worked on the book.

Email: `feedback@samspublishing.com`

Mail: Michael Stephens
Associate Publisher
Sams Publishing
800 East 96th Street
Indianapolis, Indiana 46240 USA

For more information about this book or another Sams Publishing title, visit our Web site at `www.samspublishing.com`. Type the ISBN (excluding hyphens) or the title of a book in the Search field to find the page you're looking for.

Introduction

Welcome to *BEA WebLogic Server 8.1 Unleashed*. Developers from Gamma Enterprise Technologies have collaborated with a group of leading WebLogic consultants, developers, and authors to make this the most comprehensive developer's guide to WebLogic Server 8.1 available. Inside this book you'll find a wealth of useful information on developing and administering scalable and secure enterprise Java applications using WebLogic Server 8.1.

Who Should Read This Book?

This book is designed to be comprehensive with regard to BEA WebLogic Server. Even if you've never developed for WebLogic, you should be comfortable here. However, we assume that you have some previous Java and distributed application development experience. Although many J2EE technologies are explained in the context of WebLogic development, readers with no previous exposure to J2EE might benefit from a refresher, either online at `http://java.sun.com/j2ee` or from another book, such as *Sams Teach Yourself J2EE in 21 Days*.

Which Version of J2EE?

This book covers Java 2 Enterprise Edition (J2EE) version 1.3, which is supported by BEA WebLogic Server 8.1. J2EE 1.3 includes many technologies such as JavaServer Pages 1.2, Java Servlets 2.3, and Enterprise JavaBeans 2.0. Sun has just released J2EE version 1.4, and subsequent versions of WebLogic might support it.

How This Book Is Organized

Part I, "Getting Started with WebLogic Server," introduces WebLogic Server and discusses the necessary skills, hardware and software configuration, and design methodologies required to build WebLogic applications.

To get the most from this book, you should have BEA WebLogic Server 8.1—part of BEA WebLogic Platform 8.1—ready to install. We've included a developer edition of WebLogic Platform 8.1 on this book's accompanying CD-ROM, and we cover WebLogic Server installation in Chapter 2.

Part II, "WebLogic Server Web Applications," discusses the physical structure of J2EE Web applications and how to use WebLogic Builder to deploy them.

Part III, "Using J2EE Technologies in WebLogic Applications," covers the core J2EE APIs that WebLogic leverages: Java Naming and Directory Interface (JNDI), Java Transaction API (JTA), Java Transaction Service (JTS), Java Database Connectivity (JDBC), Remote Method Invocation (RMI), Java Message Service (JMS), and JavaMail.

Part IV, "Using Web Technologies in WebLogic Applications," discusses JavaServer Pages (JSPs) and Java servlets for developing presentation layers. This section includes chapters on working with JSP tag libraries and building applications using the Apache Jakarta Struts framework.

Part V, "Using Enterprise JavaBeans in WebLogic Applications," covers Session, Entity, and Message-Driven beans, including best practices and design patterns for each.

Part VI, "Working with WebLogic Server Applications," discusses testing, debugging, and optimizing WebLogic applications, using tools such as JUnit, JProbe, and JMeter.

Part VII, "WebLogic Server Security," first covers Web application security issues in general, and then discusses WebLogic's security implementation and the specific WebLogic features designed to ensure it.

Part VIII, "Integrating the Enterprise with WebLogic Applications," brings in integration technologies and tools including XML, Web services, the J2EE Connector Architecture, SAP's Java Connector, jCOM, CORBA, and BEA Tuxedo. We provide techniques and ideas for connecting WebLogic applications in real-world enterprise systems for each of those technologies.

Finally, in Part IX, "Administering WebLogic Applications," we discuss the WebLogic Administration Console, working with clusters, Java Management Extensions, and using the command-line interface commands for administration.

At the end of the book, appendices provide a reference for common tasks and insightful advice for migrating from previous versions of WebLogic. The last appendix details WebLogic development with WebLogic Workshop, improved in version 8.1 to enable developers to build J2EE applications on WebLogic Server.

Source Code and Updates

Source code for all the examples discussed in this book is included on this book's accompanying CD-ROM. You'll find detailed instructions for installing the CD-ROM and a list of the CD-ROM's other contents in the back of the book.

If we discover any errors in the book after publication, errata will be posted at this book's page at Sams' Web site. Please visit `www.samspublishing.com`, type this book's ISBN (0672324873) into the search window, press Enter, and you'll be taken to a page with links to errata and updates to the book.

Conventions Used in This Book

The following conventions are used in this book:

- Code lines, commands, statements, and any other code-related terms appear in a `monospace` typeface.
- When a line of code is too long to fit on one line of this book, it is broken at a convenient place and continued to the next line. The continuation is preceded by a special code continuation character (➥).

NOTE

A note presents interesting information related to the discussion—a little more insight or a pointer to some new technique.

TIP

A tip offers advice or shows you an easier way of doing something.

CAUTION

A caution alerts you to a possible problem and gives you advice on how to avoid it.

PART I

Getting Started with WebLogic Server

IN THIS PART

CHAPTER 1

Introduction to WebLogic Server

by Jeff Marin and Steve Steffen

IN THIS CHAPTER

- The Need for WebLogic Server
- Brief Overview of WebLogic Server
- How WebLogic Server Fits in an Organization
- BEA's Product Line
- What's New with WebLogic Server 8.1

WebLogic Server 8.1 is BEA's market leading Web application server, an enterprise-level application server that is a highly scalable, secure application server that provides the location to deploy and manage J2EE and standalone applications both locally and remotely. WebLogic 8.1 is fully compliant with the Sun J2EE 1.3 specification providing the containers to run JavaServer Pages and servlets, Enterprise JavaBeans, J2EE connector architecture resource adapters, and much more. This chapter gives an overview of why we need application servers, what WebLogic 8.1 supports, additions and changes to WebLogic 8.1, and a brief history of WebLogic.

The Need for WebLogic Server

Although the Internet has been around for more than 30 years, the last 7 years have revolutionized how people obtain many services. During this time, Web applications have gone through distinct phases. Initially, Web sites were informational, providing content that changed occasionally. Companies were able to provide product support through online manuals and frequently asked questions. Being a brand-new method of communication, customers were very happy to have an alternative to busy signals and long wait times when attempting to call companies directly.

Over time, customers expected more (as users often do!) and interactive Web sites started springing up. They provided forms that users could fill out to request customer service, search Web sites, and take company surveys. As these Web applications became more powerful, the developers creating them became overwhelmed with the number of issues involved with creating applications on the Internet. Issues such as security and scalability had never been dealt with on the level required for these new kinds of applications.

Once again, users are expecting more and companies are required to meet their demands. Customers want to be able to bank online, buy and sell stock through their Web browser, and see their account information in real time. To create these kinds of applications, developers must connect to existing mainframe applications, corporate databases, and enterprise information systems (EIS). They must be able to create applications that span multiple machines containing diverse operating systems and hardware architectures. Companies need to create Web applications that are always available to their customers despite hardware failures and scheduled maintenance. Not only do these applications have to be accessed from a Web browser, but must now be accessed by various clients running on different platforms written in several languages from small devices such as cell phones to nongraphical aggregator applications not intended for humans.

Many firms have had Internet divisions for some time—groups of developers and engineers assigned to creating Internet content and keeping the Web site running. These groups operate autonomously from the corporate IT division responsible for internal information management. These two groups of individuals have historically co-existed without having to utilize each other's resources.

Today's Web applications require these groups to work together to provide internal corporate information to customers, suppliers, and partners in a secure, user friendly, and stable environment. Providing services such as e-commerce, supply chain management, customer relationship management, and personalization is causing IT departments around the world to reorganize and reassess their internal skill sets.

In addition to providing services to their customers, companies are realizing the power of the Internet for their own internal uses. Enabling their employees to use the Web for common tasks such as entering work requests, signing up for upcoming educational classes, and checking on health benefits have saved companies millions of dollars.

What originally began as an ad hoc method of providing services over the Internet has now become the standard way of doing business for many companies. BEA WebLogic Server was created to power this new breed of Web applications and to assist developers in their efforts to deliver on the expectations of their company's customers, employees, partners, and suppliers.

Brief Overview of WebLogic Server

WebLogic Server 8.1 is based on providing support and handling issues such as security, fault tolerance, and implementing the J2EE technology from the Sun specifications. This section gives an overview of WebLogic for different areas, such as the J2EE specifications supported, WebLogic framework, security, and handling traffic.

The J2EE Specification

The Java 2 Enterprise Edition (J2EE) specification was created to address the needs of these new multi-tiered Web applications. This specification comes from the Java Community Process, a group of more than 100 companies that meet to form open computing standards for information technology problems such as database connectivity and the generation of dynamic HTML.

The latest version of the J2EE specification, 1.3, contains many new features, especially in the areas of enterprise integration. WebLogic Server 8.1 fully supports the entire J2EE 1.3 spec and in doing so, provides developers with the engine, tools, and APIs to build secure, enterprise-level applications that can scale with user load, connect to legacy systems, and provide the high availability that your customers expect.

BEA WebLogic Server has always been a world-class, enterprise-level J2EE application server that has focused on open standards, high performance, and time-to-market features. By being a J2EE application server, WebLogic Server has passed the rigorous J2EE Compatibility Test Suite, containing more than 5,000 tests for J2EE compliance.

Because WebLogic Server is entirely written in Java (except for native drivers for performance purposes), it is available for many platforms including Unix, Windows, and the mainframe. Companies can upgrade their hardware as their needs change without having to worry about their software infrastructure.

Companies using WebLogic Server can hire experienced J2EE developers and be sure that can be productive from the first day. They can also utilize existing J2EE in-house or third-party application components with minimal effort.

The full list of technologies in the J2EE 1.3 specification is the following:

- Java Authentication and Authorization Service (JAAS) 1.0
- Java Transaction API (JTA) 1.0.1b
- Java Database Connectivity (JDBC) 2.0
- Enterprise JavaBeans (EJB) 2.0
- JavaServer Pages (JSP) 1.2
- Java Servlet 2.3
- Java Messaging Service (JMS) 1.0.2b
- Java API for XML Parsing (JAXP) 1.1
- Remote Method Invocation (RMI)/Internet Inter-Orb Protocol (IIOP) 1.0

- J2EE Connector Architecture (J2EE-CA) 1.0
- Java Naming and Directory Interface (JNDI) 1.2

BEA WebLogic Server provides a framework on which to build today's technically demanding Internet-based applications. It supplies tools to make building these applications easier. After these applications are built, WebLogic Server provides the engine to run them.

The WebLogic Server Framework

Building applications that span multiple machines, connect legacy systems, and service the multitudes of users on the Internet can be a nightmare for developers. Thankfully, WebLogic Server provides building blocks for the

- Presentation layer—JavaServer Pages and servlets
- Business layer—EJBs and Web Services
- Back-end layer—JDBC and J2EE Connector Architecture

This gives developers a head start in the development process.

Presentation Layer

Currently, the Internet browser is the most common way that customers connect to Web applications. Therefore, the capability to deliver customized, dynamic HTML is critical in the overall acceptance and usage of Web applications. WebLogic Server offers two options for creating this presentation layer: JavaServer Pages and Java servlets.

WebLogic Server also supports thick clients such as Java standalone applications and applications written in Visual Basic and Visual C++. These clients can connect using many communication methods such as CORBA, RMI, SOAP, and COM+.

Although customers using devices such as PDAs and wireless phones are in the minority, their numbers are growing. WebLogic Server can handle their needs by dynamically rendering JavaServer Pages and servlets to communicate in their language, Wireless Markup Language (WML) or any other WAP compatible language, much as it dynamically creates HTML pages for Web browsers on personal computers.

Business Layer

To support the presentation layer, WebLogic Server provides a strong, stable business layer through the use of Enterprise JavaBeans (EJB). EJBs provide reusable scalable business objects that supply business logic and access to EIS and database information. By implementing the J2EE EJB 2.0 specification, WebLogic Server enables developers to create three different types of EJBs: Session, Entity, and Message-Driven.

- Session beans represent workers that can perform business processes, such as determining the sales tax of a purchase, determining the risk of insuring an automobile driver, and transferring funds between accounts.
- Entity beans represent data within a business process, such as a customer, an account, or an insurance policy. WebLogic Server helps developers by automating code generation for this type of EJB to save itself to and retrieve itself from a database.
- Message-Driven beans work with message queues that receive and hold messages from other applications or other parts of the same application. For instance, a queue can be set up to receive requests for information. Message-Driven beans remove messages from their assigned queue and process them according to the business logic within them.

Also contained in the business layer are Web Services. Although Web Services are in their infancy, many industry experts agree that their usage will grow tremendously in the next several years. The technologies behind Web Services include Universal Description, Discovery and Integration (UDDI) and Web Services Description Language (WSDL). Not only does WebLogic Server come with all the technologies and tools required for Web Services, it also provides an incredible way for creating them from existing application components without requiring any new code to be written.

The Back-End Layer

WebLogic Server provides many options for connecting to legacy systems and databases across vendor, hardware, and operating system chasms. Creating applications comprising data and program logic from various ERP, CRM, and mainframe applications has never been easier. Other services provided by the back-end layer including creating and maintaining topics and queues to hold messages, sending email messages, and connecting to native applications such as Microsoft COM programs and BEA Tuxedo.

By supporting Java Database Connectivity (JDBC), WebLogic Server can connect to every major database on the planet. Database vendors supply JDBC drivers that hide their implementation details, and developers can write code that connects to databases without being concerned with low-level communication details.

WebLogic Server implements the J2EE Connector Architecture (J2EE-CA) and thus supports J2EE-CA resources adapters from EIS vendors such as SAP, PeopleSoft, SeeBeyond, and JD Edwards. Java developers can connect to and communicate with these systems without having to understand their whole infrastructure. Transactional integrity and security credentials can span between WebLogic Server and these EIS systems as if they were all one big application.

The WebLogic Server Engine

When WebLogic Server executes Web applications, it provides a multitude of services for

- Security
- Handling traffic
- Keeping the application server running
- Improving run time

This means that developers do not have to write these services and administrators merely have to configure them. These services let Web applications handle large amounts of Internet traffic, keep the application running despite hardware and software failures, and improve their response time to customer requests.

Security

Security is becoming the number one concern for companies doing business on the Internet and WebLogic Server provides many mechanisms for securing access to the applications it's running. WebLogic Server can work with your existing security infrastructure or provide one for your Web applications and possibly the rest of your IT infrastructure.

WebLogic Server employs security at many levels such as how customers log on to a Web site, who can access a Web page, and when can these pages be accessed. The WebLogic Server plug-and-play security model makes it simple to introduce third-party modules that perform security-specific tasks and thus expand Weblogic Server's already rich set of security functionality.

Handling the Traffic

When developers write code, they're usually concerned about business logic, which keeps them quite busy. Having to consider varying amounts of web traffic at different times of the day, week, and year, could be overwhelming.

With WebLogic Server, developers can create Web applications for a single machine and these applications can be recompiled at a later time to run on a cluster of machines. By splitting the work among many machines, response times will be greatly improved.

WebLogic Server handles clustering at the application component level by providing services for clustering EJBs and JMS queues and destination. WebLogic Server supports commonly used load balancers, but a Web server can act as a proxy to redirect customer requests to the instances of WebLogic Server running in your cluster.

Clustering is not your only option. However, WebLogic allows even a single server to handle high traffic by adding processors or configuring worker threads.

Keeping the Application Running

Web applications can go down because of hardware and software failures or because of negligent coding. In all cases, WebLogic Server does its best to keep things running by providing features such as hardware clustering, clustering of application components, and transparent failover.

Clustering not only improves performance, it also provides redundancy in the infrastructure. If an instance of WebLogic Server that's servicing a customer request fails, it will transparently failover to another instance in the cluster.

WebLogic can also be enabled to restart based on health monitoring configuration. This enables the administrator to configure a health check interval that checks for the server's availability. If there's a problem, WebLogic automatically restarts to avoid long periods of downtime.

Improving Response Time

WebLogic Server employs many methods for increasing performance that reduces response time for Web application customers. Caching of often-used resources occurs with EJBs, servlets, and JSPs. Connections to EIS systems and databases are pooled and reused as needed, avoiding the overhead of constantly reconnecting.

How WebLogic Server Fits in an Organization

Because WebLogic Server can be used in many ways, its fit is determined by its purpose. No matter how your company plans to use WebLogic Server, you'll most likely want to have it as the engine behind one or more Web sites.

WebLogic Server comes with its own Web server out of the box. This Web server works with the application server, and caches client information that changes infrequently for increased performance. Additionally, WebLogic Server has plug-ins to work with the most popular Web servers: Apache, Microsoft IIS, and iPlanet.

In its simplest form, WebLogic Server will be used in conjunction with your Web server to deliver dynamic HTML to your customers, partners, and staff. As the needs of your company grow, WebLogic Server accommodates them by providing excellent scalability, extensive security options, and comprehensive administrative monitoring tools to ensure that the needs of your customers are being met.

With its excellent integration services, your Web applications can grow to include data and functionality from multiple relational database management systems (RDBMS), enterprise integration systems (EIS), customer relationship management (CRM) systems, and legacy systems including mainframe applications.

WebLogic Server can also be used to create Web Services whereby your company, your customers, partners, and suppliers can communicate using XML over the Internet. With its incredible new built-in developer tools and full implementation of Web Services technologies, WebLogic Server is the best application server for the creation and execution of Web Services.

Companies That Are Using WebLogic Server

There is no one vertical market for WebLogic Server. Companies from all industries looking for a strong Internet presence have Web sites powered by WebLogic Server. They turn to WebLogic Server because of its proven track record as a high-performance, scalable, latest-standards-compliant, and reliable application server. Here are some of the companies that are using WebLogic Server and BEA products. Their case studies can be found at `http://www.bea.com/ framework.jsp?CNT=index.htm&FP=/content/customers`.

- **Banking**

  Chase Manhattan Bank

- **Brokerage**

  Charles Schwab Corporation

- **Airlines**

  British Airways

  Delta Airlines

  Northwest Airlines

  United Airlines

BEA's Product Line

Building on the functionality of WebLogic Server, BEA has created the following four software solutions that provide out-of-the-box functionality and, together with WebLogic Server, make up the WebLogic Platform.

BEA WebLogic Portal

Provides a foundation for Web applications, business processes, and information to work together to provide business functionality through a Web site. These Web applications are referred to as *portlets*. BEA WebLogic Portal provides a portlet foundation for developers to build on and offers many services to portlets including personalization, administration, and integration.

BEA WebLogic Integration

Provides both a GUI and an application framework to enable nonprogrammers to define business processes through workflows. When executed, these workflows invoke the services of existing application components such as Enterprise JavaBeans. After these business processes are modeled in its user-friendly GUI, BEA WebLogic Integration allows them to be executed manually, in response to an application-specific event, or through a configurable schedule.

BEA WebLogic JRockit

In February 2002, BEA acquired Appeal Virtual Systems AB, a company that creates Java Virtual Machines (JVM). In doing so, BEA now owns JRockit, a high-speed JVM created specifically for server-side Java applications. Server-side JVMs know that the applications they execute will run for long periods of time. Knowing this, the JVM spends time analyzing and optimizing the code it's executing. BEA ships a copy of JRockit with WebLogic Server 8.1 to ensure better performance over previous releases and other application servers.

BEA WebLogic Workshop

WebLogic Workshop is BEA's integrated development environment focused on building Web Services applications. The new version of Workshop, version 8.1, expands on the usability of Workshop to create Web services to all parts of enterprise application development. It contains graphical tools for creating PageFlow-modeled applications, BEA's version of the Model-View-Controller architecture, similar to Struts (covered in Chapter 19, "Working with Struts"). Features include a What-You-See-Is-What-You-Get (WYSIWYG) JSP editor and the ability to create your own custom controls. To learn more about WebLogic Workshop, log on to `http://edocs.bea.com/workshop/docs81/index.html`.

What's New with WebLogic Server 8.1

If you're already a user of WebLogic Server, you might be wondering what new features are in version 8.1. BEA WebLogic Server is already the leading J2EE application server by market share and version 8.1 has many added features that make the best application server even better. These include vastly improved support for Web Services, security, developer tools, performance and administration enhancements, and extensions to the J2EE specification.

Web Services Support

These days, Web Services are on everybody's mind and WebLogic 8.1, in conjunction with WebLogic Workshop, provides the simplest and most powerful way for developers to create them. This standalone GUI tool connects to WebLogic and enables developers and nonprogrammers to create Web Services based on existing application components such as EJBs, Java classes, and other Web Services. Web Services built can be synchronous or conversational.

WebLogic Server 8.1 provides improvements in Web Services themselves. In addition to supporting SOAP 1.2, WebLogic Server 8.1 adds the capability to add digital signatures and encryption to Web Services. It's also possible to use JMS as the transport protocol over HTTP/S and invoke asynchronous web services.

New Security Model

Version 8.1 expands on WebLogic Server 7.x security architecture and improves the functionality for creating security roles and policies. Version 8.1 features improved key store and SSL configuration support and adds the support for Java Cryptography Extension (JCE) packages. JCE is a set of packages from Sun that gives a framework to construct strong cipher encryption, key generation and agreement, and message authentication code algorithms.

In general, version 8.1 provides JAAS as an alternative to JNDI authentication. Version 8.1 implements and surpasses the J2EE 1.3 specification for single sign-on by supporting failover and load balancing of this feature in a cluster. It also comes with a rules-driven graphical Security Policies Editor that's integrated into the WebLogic Administration Console and is used to create a mapping between a WebLogic resource and users, groups, and security roles.

Developer Tools

Version 8.1 updates and adds tools to help developers create and deploy Web applications. The new appc compiler replaces the ejbc and jspc compilers and adds features to enable developers to generate and compile classes needed to deploy EJBs and JSPs to WebLogic Server.

WebLogic 8.1 also comes with new client JAR files that are much smaller then the required `weblogic.jar` and `weblogicaux.jar` files required for client applications in 7.x.

The EJBGen tool enables developers to create remote and home interfaces and deployment descriptors by adding Javadoc tags to their bean class file. Instead of creating and maintaining five or more files per EJB, this tool reduces the number to one.

WebLogic Builder provides a GUI for editing application deployment files. It works with JAR, EAR, and WAR files, including those created for other application servers.

Ant, the Java-based build tool from the Apache Group, is now deeply embedded within WebLogic Server. Ant tasks have been created for compiling and deploying EJBs and working with Web Services.

To help with the creation and editing of XML, WebLogic Server now includes an XML editor. The BEA XML Editor can also validate XML code against a DTD or XML Schema.

BEA has worked closely with its partners to ensure tighter integration between WebLogic Server and many IDEs, including Borland JBuilder and Visual Café.

Performance Enhancements

BEA continues to improve the performance of WebLogic Server with each new release, and version 8.1 is no exception. It is in the top ten application server configurations as measured by Ecperf. Ecperf is a benchmark for measuring the performance and scalability of Enterprise JavaBeans on J2EE application servers. The URL for Ecperf is `http://ecperf.theserverside.com/ecperf/`.

BEA is now including its own high-performance JVM, JRockit, with WebLogic Server on the Windows and Linux platforms. Although JRockit out-performs most other JVMs, BEA includes it with WebLogic Server at no extra cost.

Some other performance enhancements in WebLogic Server 8.1 include improved JSP string handling and compilation time, overall application deployment performance, and three new algorithms to improve client load balancing through affinity policies. Those algorithms are

- Round-robin affinity—This algorithm cycles through a list of WebLogic Servers in order.
- Weight-based-affinity—This algorithm works by the assignment of a weight of 1 to 100 to each server. The weight corresponds to the proportion of work that the server will bear.
- Random affinity—Applies only to EJB and RMI object clustering; in random load balancing, the requests are assigned to each server at random.

Administration Enhancements

With WebLogic Server 8.1, system administrators now have many tools to help them with a variety of tasks, including

- Configuring clusters and domains
- Deploying applications
- Monitoring the health of servers in a cluster

Another feature that will benefit system administrators is that WebLogic Server 8.1 can respond to events such as server failures and take corrective action automatically.

The Admin Console has improved both visually and functionally. BEA has enhanced the configuration wizards and reorganized the server configuration tabs, the SSL and Key Store tabs, and added deployment and JDBC assistants. There are now many more parameters that can be viewed and modified on the Admin Console. This includes JRockit JVM monitoring and a new timer service to send notifications at certain dates, times, or intervals.

Additionally, the functionality of the Admin Console can be extended with custom code that utilizes the Sun Microsystems Java Management Extensions (JMX) specification. This enables third parties to create custom screens to monitor and control the software packages they're selling. Companies can also choose to build Admin Console extensions to improve their capability to monitor and control their own applications.

WebLogic also includes Node Manager for management of distributed managed WebLogic instances. Version 8.1 enhances Node Manager by improving logging and monitoring capabilities and the capability to configure a managed server during the installation process.

Extensions to the J2EE Specification

BEA has never stopped at merely being J2EE compliant, and WebLogic Server provides many services above and beyond the specification. These extensions are discussed throughout the book.

As an example, the messaging services provided by WebLogic Server extend the JMS 1.0.2 specification with features such as clustered JMS connection factories and JMS destinations, using multicasting to deliver messages, and asynchronous sending of messages to improve performance.

Summary

This chapter introduced some of the features and benefits of WebLogic 8.1. WebLogic 8.1 exemplifies BEA's commitment to improving and enhancing this product to keep it in the forefront of the application server market. This chapter gave a brief overview of WebLogic 8.1, including what current J2EE technologies it works with, where it fits into the organization, what other BEA products work with it, and what new features it includes. Enjoy unleashing WebLogic Server 8.1!

CHAPTER **2**

Installing WebLogic Server

by Malcolm Garland

IN THIS CHAPTER

The objective of this chapter is to get you started using WebLogic Server. Various ways and aspects of installing the server are discussed for both Windows and Unix operating systems. Creating start scripts, along with starting and stopping the server, are also discussed. WebLogic Server 8 comes as an individual distribution and also bundled within the WebLogic Platform distribution. The WebLogic Platform distribution includes WebLogic Workshop, WebLogic Integration, WebLogic Portal, and WebLogic Platform Samples and Utilities (JRockit). Within this chapter, we address only the installation of WebLogic Server.

Windows Install

Installing WebLogic Server is a straightforward process. There are two installation options for Windows: Graphical mode (Java-based GUI interactive execution) and Silent mode (noninteractive command prompt execution). To begin, you must get the executable (`platform8x_win32.exe` or `server810_win32.exe`) from either the BEA-provided CD-ROM or download the file from the BEA downloads area at `http://bea.com`. Our example assumes that you're installing the server from the platform distribution. To ensure that you have the most current version of the software, downloading the executable is the preferred means of attaining the software.

The WebLogic Server installation program will create many folders. Table 2.1 will familiarize you with the end result WebLogic directory structure prior to beginning your installation.

TABLE 2.1 WebLogic Server 8 Directories

Directory	Contains	Default Location
BEA Home	License files, JDK, common files.	C:\bea
WebLogic Home	The WebLogic software packages and configuration files.	C:\bea\weblogic81
User Projects	The default location for new domains. A domain can be placed anywhere.	C:\bea\user_projects
Applications folder	The default location for installed applications. An application can be placed anywhere; the domain configuration points to its location.	C:\bea\user_projects*yourDomain*\applications

System Requirements

Prior to installation, ensure that you have sufficient disk space. The Windows install might require as much as 405MB. Additionally, the installer program requires 312MB in a temporary directory. This is a separate requirement from the 405MB, yielding a total of up to 717MB required to install the WebLogic Platform. A WebLogic Server–only installation requires at least 550MB. The temp directory defaults to `c:\temp`. You'll be prompted to change this directory if your C: drive does not have sufficient disk space available. For detailed system (platform and software) requirements, refer to the BEA documentation site at `http://edocs.beasys.com`.

Running platform8xx_win32.exe—Graphical Mode

After you've attained the software (approximately 300MB), run the executable to initiate the installation process as detailed later. If you have sufficient disk space, a welcome screen will be displayed as shown in Figure 2.1.

Continue negotiating through screens until you come to the BEA Home Directory screen. The BEA home directory will contain BEA common files, such as the JDK certified for use with this particular server release (JDK 1.4.1_02 for 8.1), WebLogic Server license, and other BEA utilities. Multiple BEA products deployed on the same box may use the one BEA home directory; that is, a WebLogic 8 series server can be deployed within a BEA home directory that hosts a WebLogic 7 or 6 series server. Earlier WebLogic Server versions (5 series and earlier) would not be deployed under this BEA home directory structure.

If this is an initial installation, accept the default of Create a New BEA Home as shown in Figure 2.2.

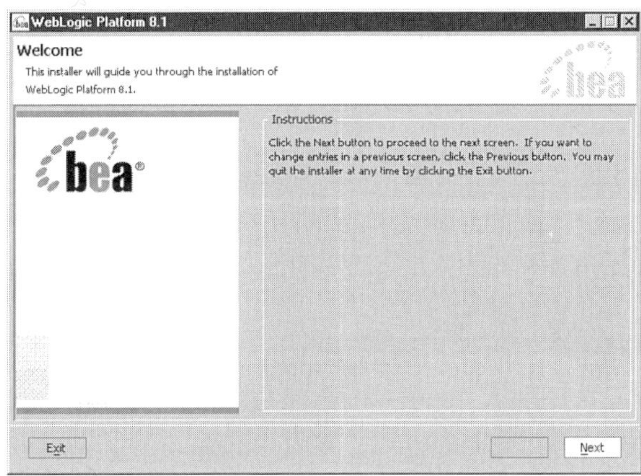

Figure 2.1 WebLogic Server 8 welcome screen.

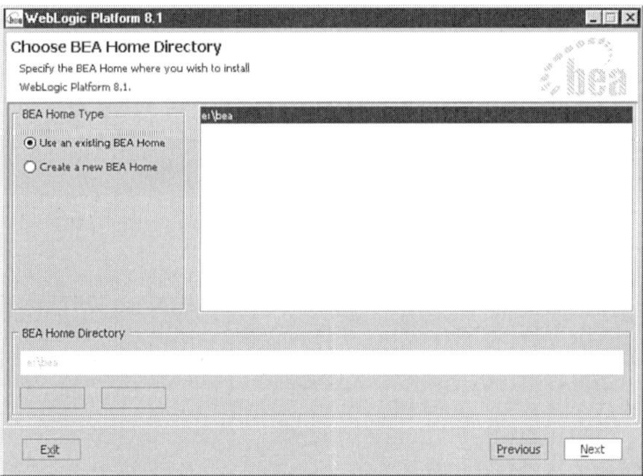

Figure 2.2 Creating a new BEA home directory.

If the BEA home directory exists, select Use an Existing BEA Home.

Both selections bring you to the Choose Install Type Screen. Selecting a typical install, as shown in Figure 2.3, will install the complete WebLogic Platform. To install only WebLogic Server, select Custom Install. For now, let's look quickly at a typical installation. The custom installation option is discussed later within this section.

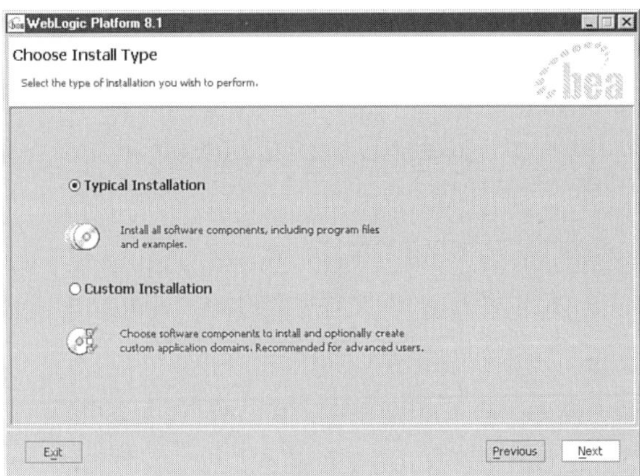

Figure 2.3 Selecting a typical WebLogic Platform installation.

Typical WebLogic Platform Installation

Selecting a typical install yields a default WebLogic Server install. This default install deploys all WebLogic Platform components (including WebLogic Server) with samples. There are no default `mydomain` or `myserver` server deployments, as was the case under WebLogic 6 series and earlier WebLogic Server installations. However, you can find functional server deployments with associated configuration files within `../bea/weblogic8x/samples/domains/`.

Following the selection of a typical installation, the next screen is Choose Product Directory. Here you select your WebLogic Platform deployment directory. The default directory name is `WebLogic8x`, as shown in Figure 2.4. This directory may be located anywhere on your system. There is no constraint or requirement that this directory be located under the BEA home directory.

The file copy routine now initiates; it terminates with an Install Complete screen.

Custom WebLogic 8 Installation

To install WebLogic Server only, you must select Custom Installation on the Choose Install Type screen shown earlier in Figure 2.3.

Selecting a custom installation gives you the option to specify which platform components to install, as shown in Figure 2.5. If you intend to install WebLogic Server, this is where you have the option of installing the functional samples that are included with the download.

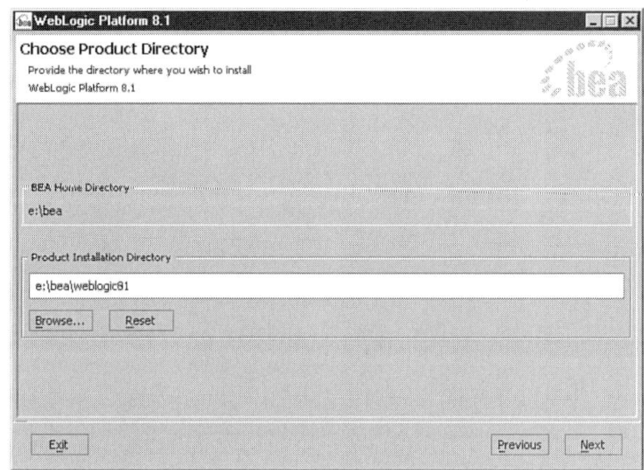

Figure 2.4 Accepting the WebLogic default production directory name.

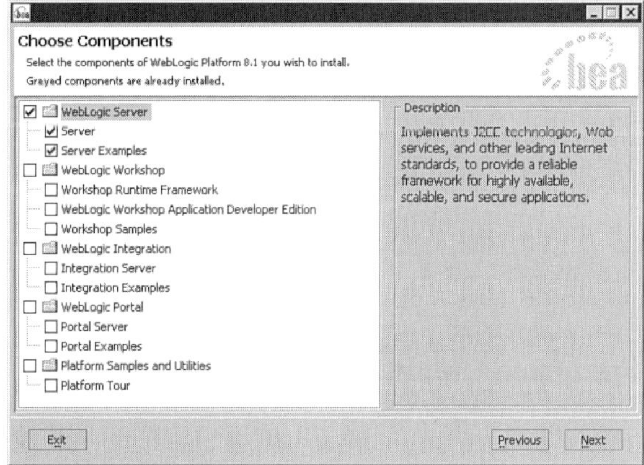

Figure 2.5 Choosing WebLogic Platform components for installation.

The next step in the custom installation process is to choose a production directory (the actual location of your WebLogic Server deployment) as you did earlier for the typical WebLogic installation. As before, you have the option to specify the location and name of this directory, as shown in Figure 2.4. Just as with the typical installation, there's no requirement in a custom installation to locate the production directory under the BEA home directory.

The next screen prompts whether to install WebLogic Node Manager as a Windows service, as shown in Figure 2.6.

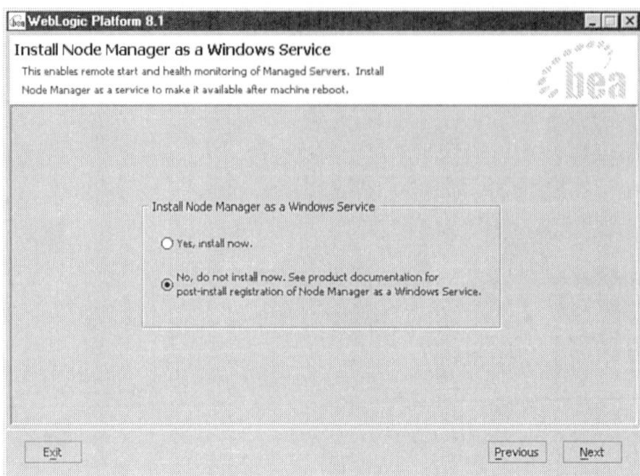

Figure 2.6 Installing Node Manager as a Windows service.

At this point within the custom installation process, assuming that you installed the server samples, you have two functional WebLogic domains (servers): `examples` and `medrec`. These domains are located under `../bea/weblogic8x/samples/domains/`.

Now you have the option of running the WebLogic Configuration Wizard to configure your custom domain, as shown in Figure 2.7. Simply check the Run the Configuration Wizard box to create an application domain. You may also install XML Spy from this window, as shown in Figure 2.7. XML Spy is an XML editing/development environment. For more information about this application, refer to the product's Web site at `http://www.xmlspy.com`.

Skipping the Configuration Wizard initiates a default WebLogic install using either your specified WebLogic production directory name or the default production directory name as mentioned in the earlier discussion of a typical WebLogic 8 installation.

WebLogic Domains and the Domain Configuration Wizard

A WebLogic *domain* is a related set of servers. A *server* is an instance of WebLogic Server where applications must run. There are various types of servers:

- Administration server—This is a configuration repository for the domain. There must be one administration server per domain. Applications may be deployed here within a development environment, but applications usually aren't deployed here within a production environment.
- Managed server—This is a "worker" server, which receives its configuration from an administration server. Applications are deployed here in a production environment.

* Clustered managed server—One or more managed servers working in unison. This is a special managed server that replicates its content to other clustered managed servers for load balancing and high availability.

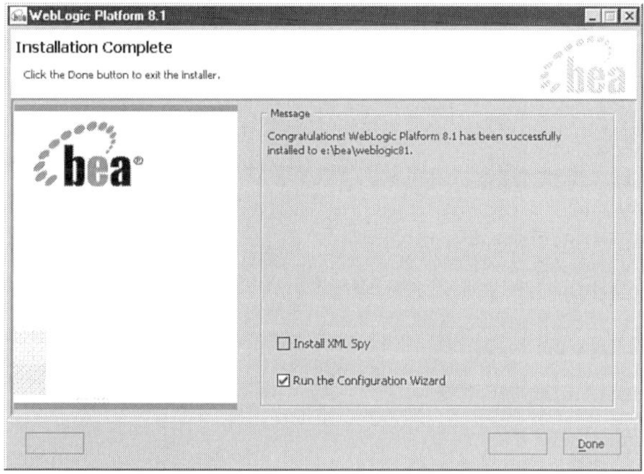

Figure 2.7 Opting to Run the WebLogic Domain Configuration Wizard.

A single WebLogic domain may therefore contain one or more servers and zero to more WebLogic clusters.

The Domain Configuration Wizard is a Java application that assists you in configuring the WebLogic domain to your specifications.

After you've selected the option to run the Configuration Wizard, you must specify whether to create a new domain configuration or add elements to an existing domain. For example, let's create a new domain as shown in Figure 2.8.

You must specify a domain name and the domain template to use as shown in Figure 2.9. The templates specify which canned WebLogic Server installation to deploy. Three templates are provided with your WebLogic Platform distribution. The WebLogic Server Examples and Avitek Medical Records Sample Domains create copies of the WebLogic Server Samples and Medrec applications, which are installed by default under a typical installation. The Basic WebLogic Server Domain template provides you a blank WebLogic Server domain without the samples. The selected domain name will be the directory name under which your servers will be deployed.

NOTE

Other BEA templates might be available within this window depending on your past BEA installations.

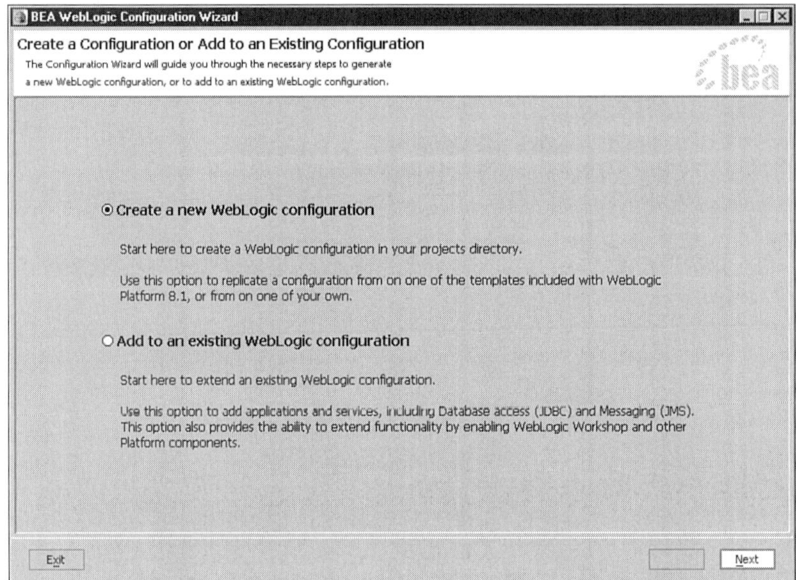

Figure 2.8 Creating a domain configuration.

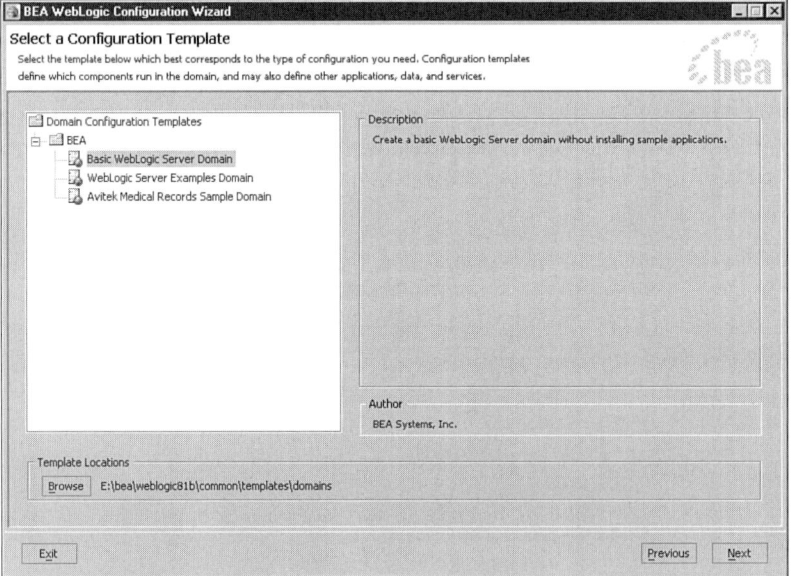

Figure 2.9 Selecting a domain template.

The next screen, shown in Figure 2.10, enables you to select the level of configuration. The Express Configuration option allows the adoption of preexisting domain configurations without modification. In contrast, the Custom Configuration option configures the specific character of servers within your domain; that is, whether your domain has a single server, an administration server with managed servers, an administration server with clustered managed servers, or a managed server under an existing administration server, along with individual server configuration parameters.

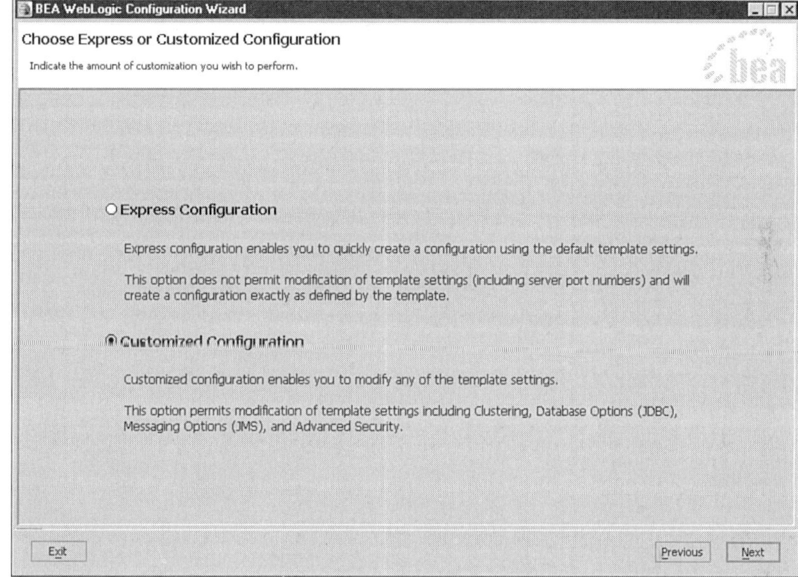

Figure 2.10 Selecting the level of domain configuration.

Your domain must include at least one administration server that is configured first, as shown in Figure 2.11. If you're running only one WebLogic Server, this server must be an administration server that may host applications. Our example will configure a single server. Other options are

- Administration server with managed servers—Creates an administration server and one or more managed server. Each managed server may host different applications. The administration server usually doesn't host any applications within this configuration.
- Administration server with clustered managed servers—Creates an administration server and one or more clustered managed server. All clustered managed servers usually host the same applications. The administration server usually doesn't host any applications within this configuration.

Regardless of the options selected, you must configure each individual server, as shown in Figure 2.11. The Server Name value is a unique server name within your domain; that is, you cannot have two servers with the same name within one domain. The Server Listen Address value is the unique IP address associated with this server. Listen Port numbers are integers in the range of 1 to 65535, but are typically four digits. The default values for Listen Address and Port are displayed in Figure 2.11.

CAUTION

For security reasons, you may choose not to use these default values for your custom server configurations, especially within a production environment.

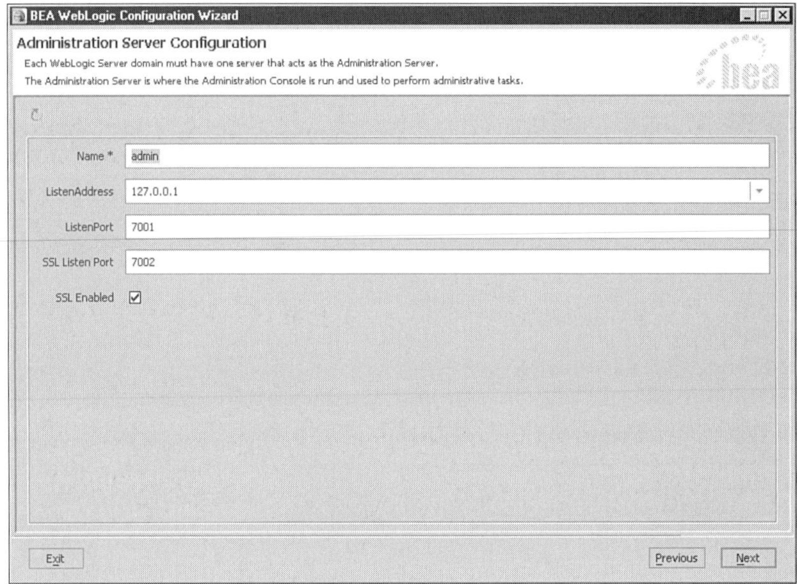

Figure 2.11 Configuring the administration server.

The next screen enables you to install managed servers, clusters, or alter the current server to machine mapping. If you're installing a single server, select Skip as shown in Figure 2.12.

The following screens enable you to configure JDBC, JMS, and Advanced Security options, as shown in Figures 2.13–2.15.

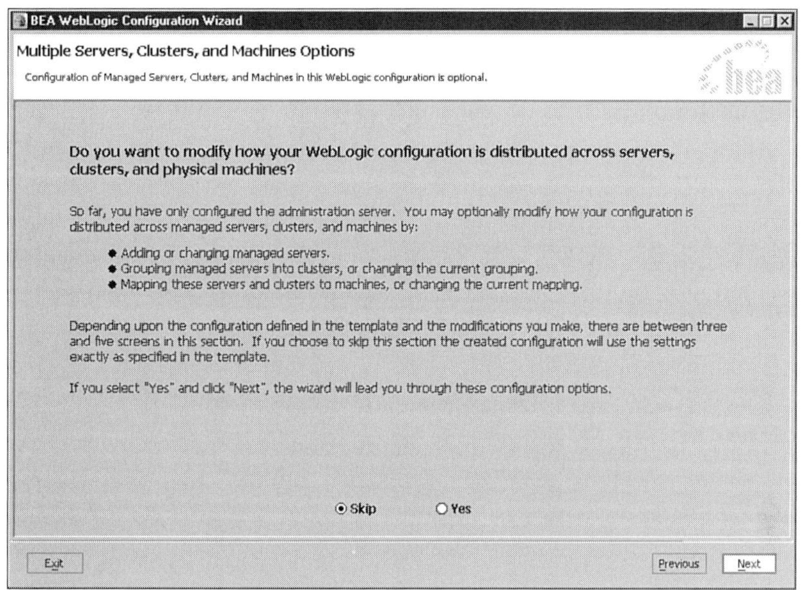

Figure 2.12 Installing multiple machines and clusters or altering machine options.

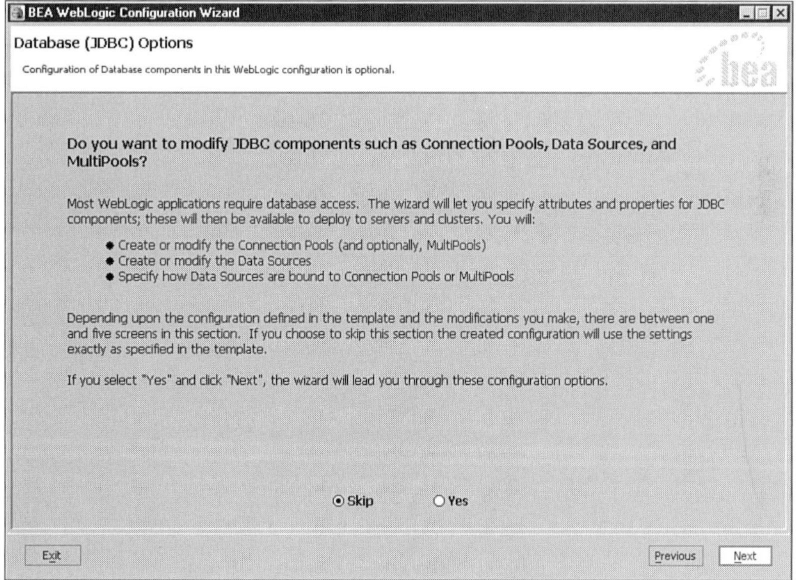

Figure 2.13 Configuring JDBC options.

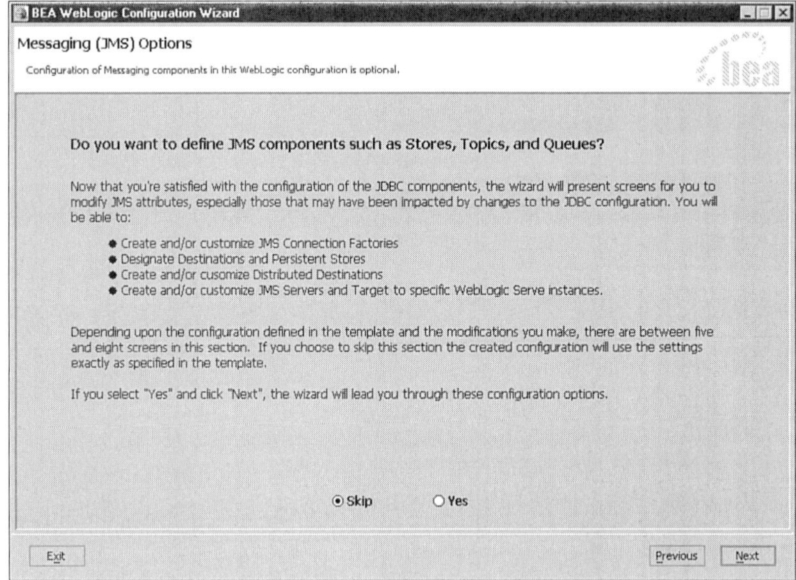

Figure 2.14 Configuring JMS options.

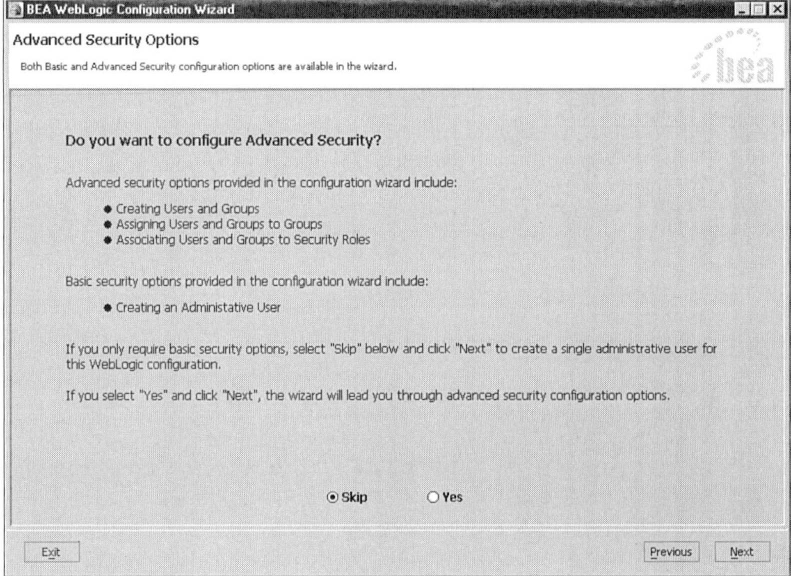

Figure 2.15 Configuring advanced security options.

After configuring servers within your domain, you must set the administrative username and password as shown in Figure 2.16. This username and password are needed to boot your server, connect to the administration server, and to access the WebLogic Console. After entering the information and selecting Next, you'll be prompted to confirm the password entered.

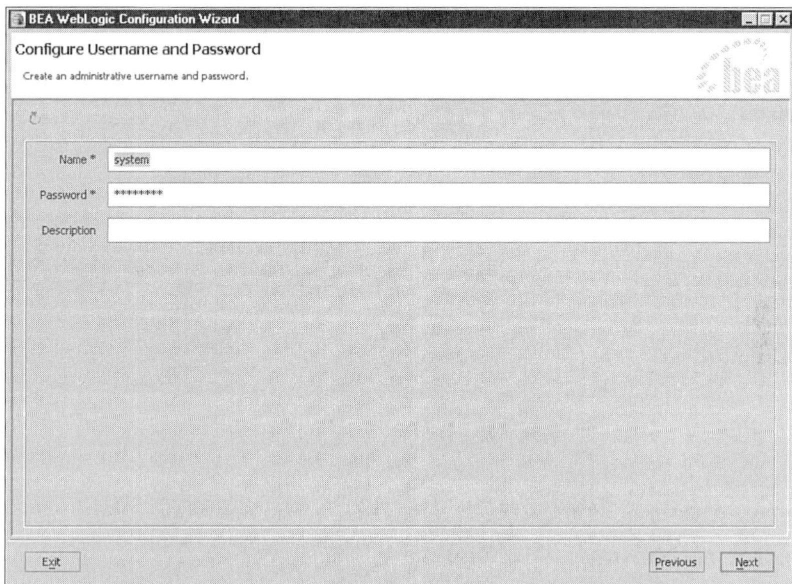

Figure 2.16 Designating system username/password.

CAUTION

The use of commonly used terms such as *system, admin, administrator, root, WebLogic,* and so on for username/password may compromise your server's security. Use uncommon usernames and passwords to further promote server security, especially within a production environment.

Next you're prompted to link your administration server's start script to your Windows Start menu. We'll do so. Lastly we're asked to install our WebLogic administration server (and associated domain) as a Windows service (our example does not select this option), as shown in Figure 2.17. This option will start your server at boot time. You must have administrator rights on your system to set up this option.

The next screen displays WebLogic shortcuts to be included in the Windows Start menu, as shown in Figure 2.18. There is one tab per shortcut in this dialog. The figure shows a single shortcut. You may delete unwanted shortcuts or add needed items.

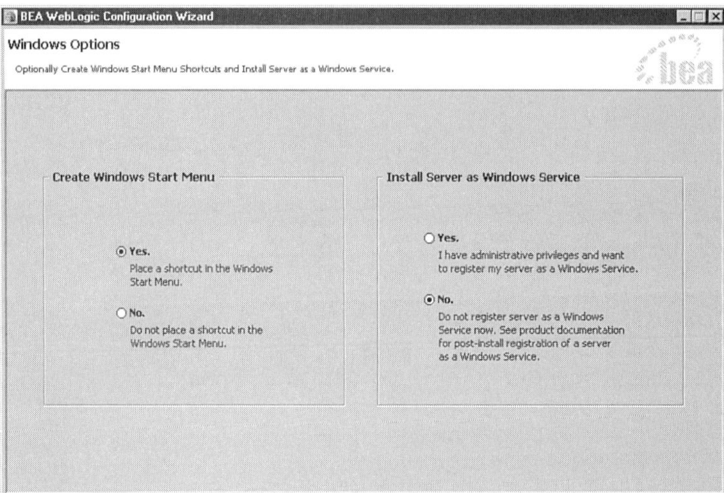

Figure 2.17 Including the Admin server in the Windows Start menu, and installing our domain as a Windows service.

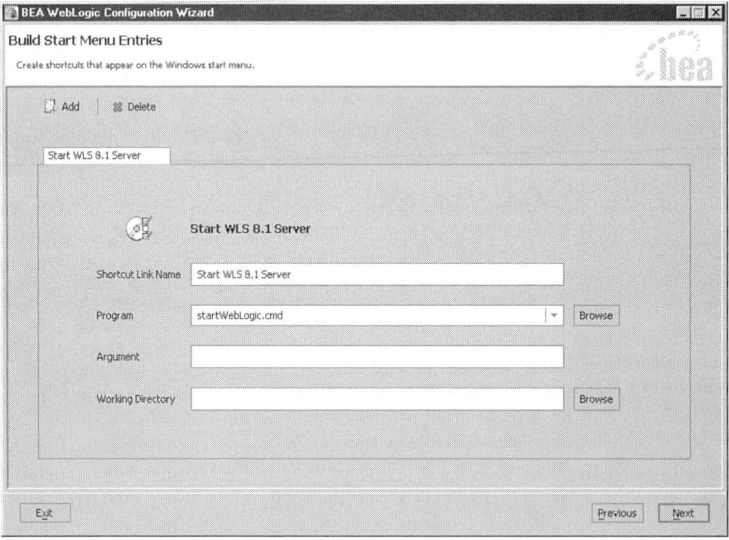

Figure 2.18 WebLogic Server shortcuts.

The next screen requires you to select the JDK to use and to specify the configuration environment as either development or production, as shown in Figure 2.19. Choose the Sun SDK and development mode.

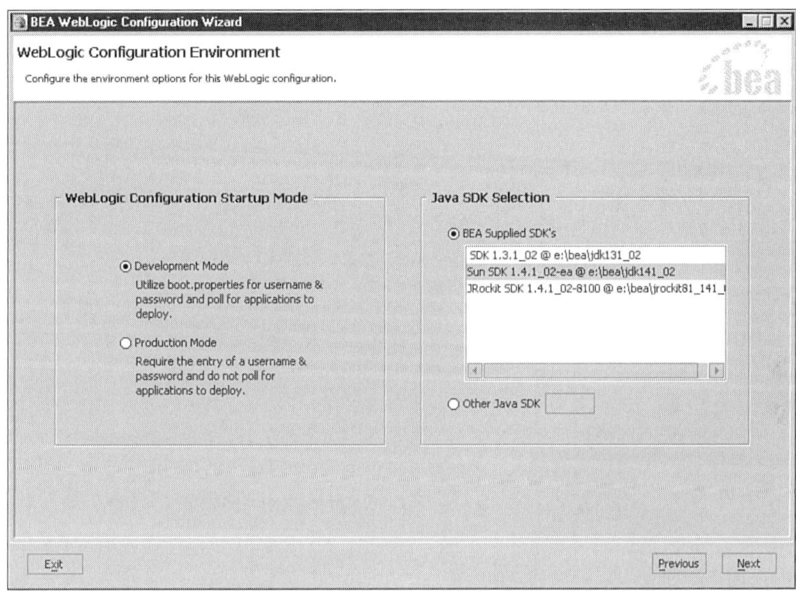

Figure 2.19 Selecting configuration environment and JDK.

The next screen displays a summary of your domain configuration selections, along with a prompt to create the domain at a specified location, as shown in Figure 2.20. As mentioned earlier, there's no requirement to locate the domain within BEA home directory, but we'll create our sample domain in the default location. Click the Create button to continue.

After creating the domain and selecting Done, you have the option to run the Configuration Wizard again, as shown in Figure 2.21.

If no further domain configurations are required, the custom installation process terminates.

The Configuration Wizard can be initiated directly from Windows by executing the command script at `..\bea\weblogic8x\common\bin\config.cmd`.

CAUTION

If you encounter problems running a command script such as `config.cmd` or `startWebLogic.cmd`, inspect the script for correct paths for JDK, BEA home, and so forth.

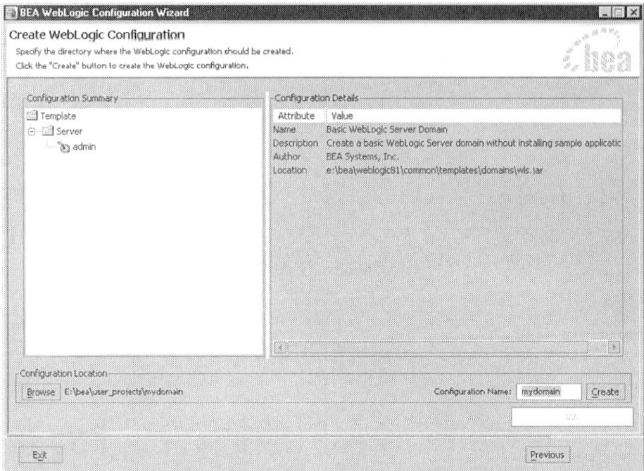

Figure 2.20 Specifying the domain location and creating the domain.

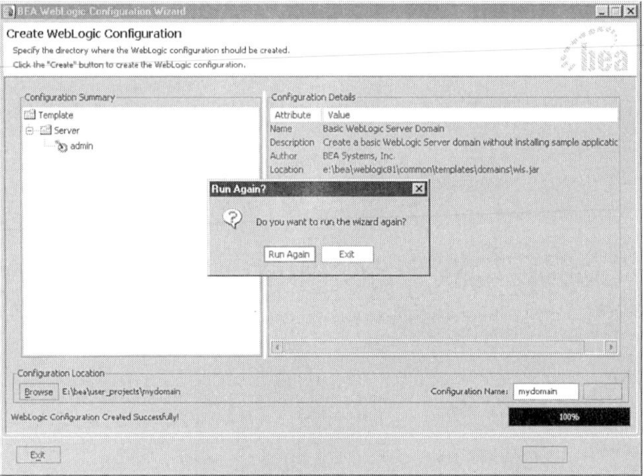

Figure 2.21 Terminating the Configuration Wizard.

Running WebLogic8xx_win32.exe—Silent Mode

The second method of installing WebLogic Server is the Silent mode. This entails passing an XML file, `silent.xml`, whose code sample is shown in Listing 2.1, as a parameter to the WebLogic executable. Silent mode installation is usually employed for a typical installation. In that case, only three parameters (BEA home, platform install directory, and whether to install Node Manager as a Windows service) are required, as shown in Listing 2.1. If additional configuration is desired for a silent installation, the Configuration Wizard can also be run in Silent mode. You need only execute the two commands within the same command script. For further information on running the Configuration Wizard within Silent mode, refer to `http://e-docs.bea.com/platform/docs81/confgwiz/`.

LISTING 2.1 Silent.xml Provided by BEA

```
<?xml version="1.0" encoding="UTF-8"?>
<!-- Silent installer option: -mode=silent -silent_xml=/home/me/silent.xml -->
<domain-template-descriptor>
  <input-fields>
   <data-value name="BEAHOME"           value="C:\bea" />
   <data-value name="USER_INSTALL_DIR"      value="C:\bea\weblogic81" />
   <data-value name="INSTALL_NODE_MANAGER_SERVICE"  value="no" />
  </input-fields>
</domain-template-descriptor>
```


CAUTION

XML syntax must be correct. The first line of the XML file must be as shown in Listing 2.1, without any preceding spaces or blank lines. The Silent mode installer does not conduct any XML verification checks, the install merely fails.

The command

```
weblogic8x_win32.exe -mode=silent -silent_xml=d:\temp\silent.xml
➥-log=d:\temp\logs\install.log
```

installs the WebLogic Platform using the configuration parameters located within the file `d:\temp\silent.xml`. An audit of the installation will be logged to file `d:\temp\logs\install.log`. Note that absolute filenames are required for XML and the log file. The `mode` and `silent_xml` options are required, but the `log` option is optional. The silent mode installation is not interactive. However, a processing screen is displayed.

The `Done` reported at the conclusion of the silent installation does not signify a successful installation. Conditions produced by incorrect parameters, insufficient system resources, or other issues will cause the installation to fail. You must vigorously investigate the installation log to identify these concerns. Additionally, the log file folder (`d:\temp\logs` in our example) must exist prior to initiating the silent mode installation. The silent mode installation process will not create the log file if its parent directory is nonexistent (the installation will fail without the benefit of an install log). The silent mode might not be your best option for installing the WebLogic Platform.

Unix Install

There are three installation options for a Unix install: Graphical mode (interactive Java GUI), Console mode (interactive text-based), and Silent mode (noninteractive command prompt execution). To begin, you must get the executable from the BEA-provided CD-ROM or download the file from the BEA downloads area at `http://bea.com`. Software downloads currently available (as of this printing) for WebLogic Server 8–certified Unix platforms are shown in Table 2.2. Refer to `http://bea.com` for current availability. Prior to installation, verify that your specific Unix platform is supported. Installation on a Unix system requires admin or root access.

TABLE 2.2 Certified Unix Downloads Currently Available from BEA

Unix OS	Filename	File Size
Sun Solaris 8, 9	server8x0_solaris32.bin	182MB
Red Hat Linux 2.1	server8x_linux32.bin	183MB

To ensure that you have the most current version, downloading the executable is the preferred means of attaining the software. You can contact a BEA representative for beta versions of WebLogic Server for Unix platforms that aren't currently supported. Note: You might encounter versions of these Unix installation files that end in `.jar`. These files do not contain a JDK; you must therefore manually update your `PATH` variable to include the JDK installed on your machine. As of this printing, you must use JDK1.4.1_02 or higher for WebLogic Server 8.

System Requirements

Prior to installation, ensure that you have sufficient disk space. A Unix install requires approximately 250MB, and the installer program requires an additional 200MB in a temporary directory. This is a separate requirement from the 250MB. The temp directory defaults to `/tmp`. You're prompted to change this directory if your system does not have sufficient disk space available. For detailed system (platform and software) requirements, refer to the BEA documentation site at
`http://edocs.beasys.com/wls/certifications/certifications/index.html`.

Unix Install—Graphical Mode

There are two files that you might encounter for WebLogic Server Unix distributions: BIN and JAR files. They both contain the WebLogic Server distribution; the difference is that the JAR file does contain a JDK. As mentioned earlier, you must provide the JDK and set any JDK-related path variables manually. Installing the WebLogic Server Unix distribution using the graphical mode is addressed within this section.

Running server8xx_OS32.bin

After you've attained the software, modify the executable rights to the file:

```
chmod a+x server8xx_OS32.bin
```

Then run the executable:

```
./server8xx_OS32.bin
```

Running server8xx_OS32.jar

When you've attained the software, ensure that a certified JDK is in your PATH variable. Then execute the Java option:

```
$ java -jar server8xx_OS32.jar
```

Unix Install—Console Mode

Installing the WebLogic Server Unix distribution within Console mode is addressed within this section.

Running server8xx_OS32.bin

After you've attained the software, modify the executable rights to the file:

```
chmod a+x server8xx_OS32.bin
```

Then run the executable:

```
./wserver8xx_OS32.bin -mode=console -log=install.log
```

Running server8xx_OS32.jar

When you've attained the software, ensure that a certified JDK is in your PATH variable. Then execute the Java option:

```
java -jar server8xx_OS32.jar -mode=console -log=install.log
```

Installing WebLogic Platform License

Your WebLogic Server will not initiate without a valid BEA license. If you received the current download from the BEA site (http://bea.com), your installation will deploy a one-year evaluation license. This license is contained in the file license.bea, located under your BEA home directory. A partial listing of this file is shown in Listing 2.2.

LISTING 2.2 Partial Listing of WebLogic Platform 8 License

```
<?xml version="1.0"?>
<bea-licenses>
  <license-group format="1.0" product="WebLogic Platform" release="8.1">
    <license
      component="2PC"
      cpus="1"
      expiration="2004-04-02"
      ip="any"
      licensee="BEA Evaluation Customer"
```

LISTING 2.2 Continued

```
      type="EVAL"
      units="5"
      signature="M+Qz+p2hFIbCIbFqKjM3rBSVZEw=0MC0CFAs3CO6iYAhh+
➥t5YOt8ND2ZaEXHlAhUAkf19nn/Dw4+wXmrsTqnmqlLMbbk="
    />
    <license
      component="AI"
      cpus="1"
      expiration="2004-04-02"
      ip="any"
      licensee="BEA Evaluation Customer"
      type="EVAL"
      units="5"
      signature="1NxSManISFSMo5Npm+fmFIrUUU8=0MC0CFQDIgzPDqiTTG5Gd29w3P6Nq6
➥4NIEwIURKEfPUCo2MIcsWEs2fhtZ33OuAs="
    />...
```

Long-term licenses with unlimited client connections must be purchased from BEA. These unlimited licenses are usually delivered via email. The evaluation license gives you access for at most 5 client and 15 database connections, which is sufficient for evaluation and most development purposes. WebLogic Server licenses older than 7 series (6 series and earlier) do not work with a WebLogic 8 series distribution.

Updating WebLogic 8 License

Before attempting to update your current BEA license file, change the name of your newly received `license.bea` file to avoid overwriting the current license file. Back up your old license and save the new license in your BEA home directory. If there's no current `license.bea` file in the BEA home directory, place the new license in the BEA home directory. Remember, in any case, always back up both the old and new licenses.

To update your current license file with the newly received WebLogic 8 series license, you must run the `UpdateLicense` script. The WebLogic 8 series installation provides a command script for Windows and a shell script for Unix. This script is found directly under your BEA home directory.

To run the script, verify that JDK1.4.1_02 or higher is in your `PATH` variable. Navigate to your BEA home directory and execute the command script, passing the new license file as a parameter, as shown in the following examples.

Windows

```
UpdateLicense.cmd newlicenseFileName.bea
```

Unix

```
UpdateLicense.sh newlicenseFileName.bea
```

In reference to the Unix shell script: Ensure that you have execute rights to the script. If you currently have a WebLogic 7.0 license, the license will be updated for WebLogic 8 use during install—all licenses will be merged into one document.

UPDATING LEGACY WEBLOGIC LICENSES (WEBLOGIC 6 AND EARLIER) FOR WEBLOGIC 8 USE

To update a WebLogic 6 or earlier license for use on an 8 platform, contact BEA customer support at `http://websupport.beasys.com/custsupp`.

Encryption Licensing

WebLogic Server 8 series comes with 56-bit encryption. If 128-bit encryption is desired, a 128-bit encryption license must be purchased from BEA. This license must be present in the BEA home directory before installation; otherwise, only 56-bit encryption is available for SSL. A 128-bit encryption allows both 128 and 56-bit encryption schemes. The WebLogic 8 series evaluation license supports only 56-bit encryption.

Installing WebLogic 8 Service Packs

WebLogic Server 8 series includes the Smart Update feature. This feature determines whether a service pack is available for your current WebLogic 8 series installation. Smart Update further prompts you with directions for installing the service pack. To activate the command, navigate to your BEA home directory and execute the `bsu` script as shown. The script is located within the `utils` directory under your BEA home directory.

Windows

```
.\utils\bsu.cmd
```

Unix

```
./utils/bsu.sh
```

For Unix, ensure that you have execute rights to the shell script.

Starting and Stopping WebLogic Server 8

Starting your WebLogic Server 8 is done differently depending on the type of server you want to start (administrative or managed). Let's look at two configurations: the typical WebLogic installation with the Examples Server (Admin server only) and a custom domain installation that contains two managed servers. (Note: Before starting the server using either method, ensure that your system CLASSPATH variable is scrubbed.)

Starting the WebLogic 8 Admin Server

Regardless of your configuration, the Admin server must be started first.

In Windows, there are two ways in which to start the Examples Server: the Start menu and command script (which is generated as part of the WebLogic 8 installation).

To start the Examples Server from the Windows Start menu, choose the sequence Start→BEA WebLogic Platform 8.1→Examples→WebLogic Server Examples→Launch Server Examples. This sequence is shown in Figure 2.22.

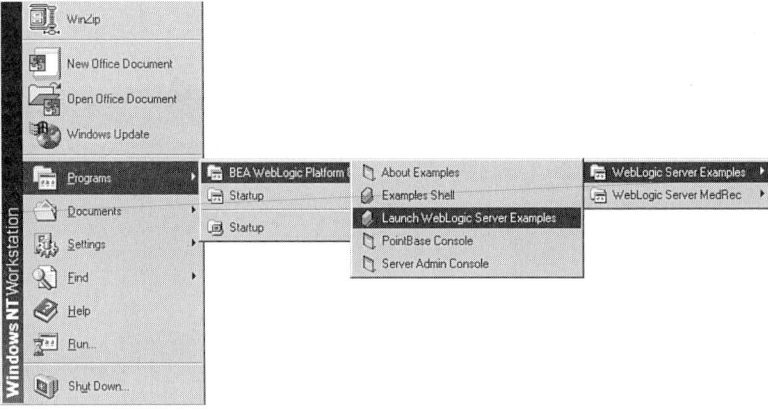

Figure 2.22 Starting the Examples Server from the Start menu.

> **CAUTION**
>
> When starting WebLogic Server, if the username and password weren't provided during installation, you will be prompted to enter them during the server start routine.

To start the Examples Server on Windows using the command script provided with your installation, open a DOS/command prompt window and navigate to the directory containing the file `startExamplesServer.cmd`. This should be the directory *`BEAHome`*`\`*`WebLogicHOME`*`\samples\domains\examples`. Execute the script as shown in Figure 2.23.

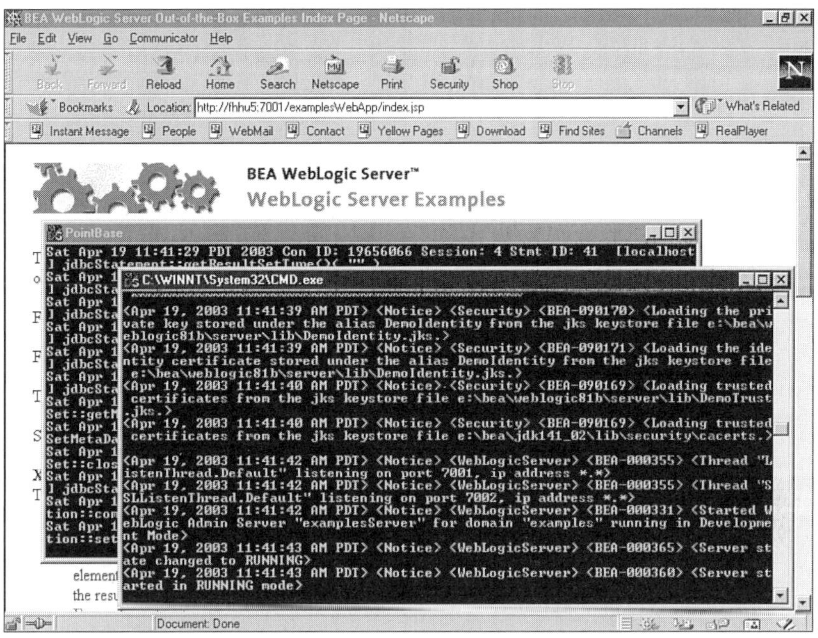

Figure 2.23 Starting the Examples Server from the command prompt.

When starting the WebLogic Examples Server, three applications are activated: your default Web browser, the PointBase database, and WebLogic Server. The default Web browser is initiated on a successful start of WebLogic Server.

The browser will open to the index page within the samples application. This index is a WebLogic Server Examples welcome page, which contains a link to the WebLogic Admin Console. The WebLogic console, which is discussed later within this book, enables you to administer your WebLogic domains.

The WebLogic Platform installation provides the PointBase database to use with your WebLogic Server examples. The PointBase database is a lightweight relational database suitable for evaluation or developmental use. A console window to the PointBase application will pop up. For details about the PointBase product, refer to the BEA documentation site at `http://e-docs.bea.com/workshop/docs81/doc/en/workshop/guide/howdoi/howAdministerTheDefaultPointbaseDatabase.html`. Additional documentation is available on the PointBase Web site at `http://www.pointbase.com/node.shtml?navHier=Support/Product+Docs&CF=support/docs/overview.html`.

WebLogic Server will activate a command prompt window (for Windows) or command-line output (for Unix—you may choose to redirect this output to a file and "tail" that file), which will display a series of server messages. Figure 2.23 displays the end text of a successful server start process. If you encounter problems with WebLogic Server, investigate this output along with the associated server log file, which is found under the domain's directory (in our example, `e:\bea\weblogic81\samples\domains\examples\examples.log`).

To start WebLogic Server on a Unix system, navigate to the directory containing the start script provided by your install: the file `startExamplesServer.sh`. This should be in the directory `BEAHome\WebLogicHOME\samples\domains\examples`. Ensure you've set execute permission on this script, and execute it as shown:

```
$ ./startExamplesServer.sh
```

Both start scripts (Windows and Unix versions) set environment variables and pass parameters to the Java class `weblogic.Server`, which configures a JVM suitable for the server and starts it. See the "Creating Your Own Start Scripts" section presented later in this chapter. You can also inspect the provided scripts on specific parameters used to start your server or refer to the BEA documentation on specific server start parameters at `http://e-docs.bea.com/wls/docs81/admin_ref/weblogicServer.html`.

Starting WebLogic 8 Managed Servers

Before starting a managed server, the associated parent Admin server must be started as detailed earlier. In our example, we have an Admin server containing two managed servers.

There are two general ways in which to start a managed server: the WebLogic 8 console and command scripts. The `weblogic.Server` command implemented within scripts may be manually executed on the command line, as mentioned earlier.

First, the Admin server must be running as previously detailed. To start the managed server after your Admin server is started, enter the Administration Console at `http://`*`yourURL`*`:`*`port`*`/console`. (Note that `console` is case-sensitive; that is, `Console` will not work.) After entering a username and password, start the specific managed server using the sequence *yourDomain*→Servers→server#→Control (TAB)→Start This Server as shown in Figure 2.24.

> **NOTE**
>
> The Administration Console is a browser-based tool used to manage your WebLogic Server configurations. Details about the use of the console occur throughout this book.

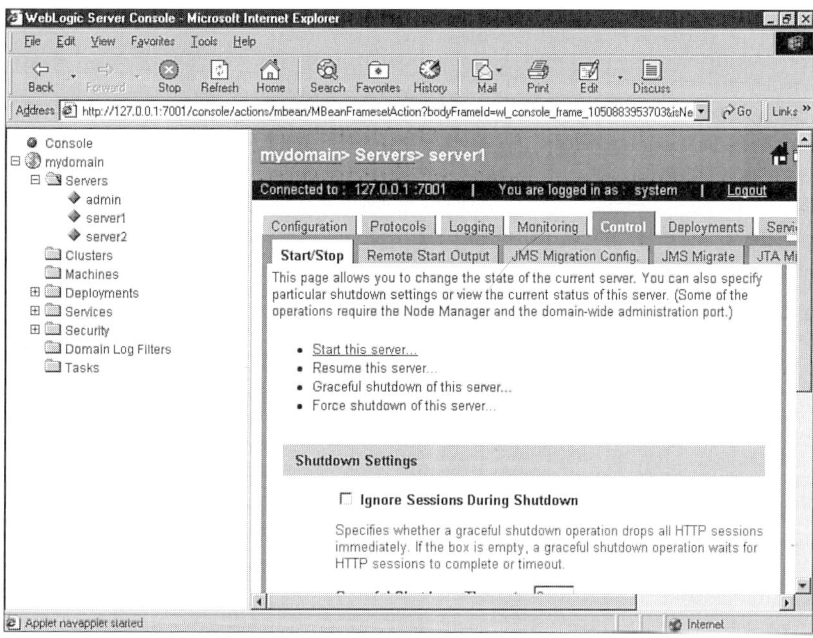

Figure 2.24 Starting a domain-managed server from the WebLogic Console.

> **NOTE**
>
> The WebLogic Server default setting for *`URL`*`:`*`port`* is `127.0.0.1:7001`, yielding an address of `http://localhost:7001/console`.

To start managed servers using command scripts after successfully initiating your Admin server, open a DOS/Command Prompt window and navigate to the directory containing the file `startManagedWebLogic.cmd`. This should be the directory `\\user_project_location\yourDomain`. Execute the script, passing the managed server's name and the Admin server's URL; for our example, that's `startManagedWeblogic server1 http://127.0.0.1:7001`, as shown in Figure 2.25. Note the command given on the first line.

On Unix, navigate to the directory containing the file `startManagedWebLogic.sh`. This should be the directory `BEAHome/user_project_location/yourDomain`. Ensure you've set execute permission and execute the script as shown:

```
$ ./startManagedWebLogic.sh server# admminServerURL:port
```

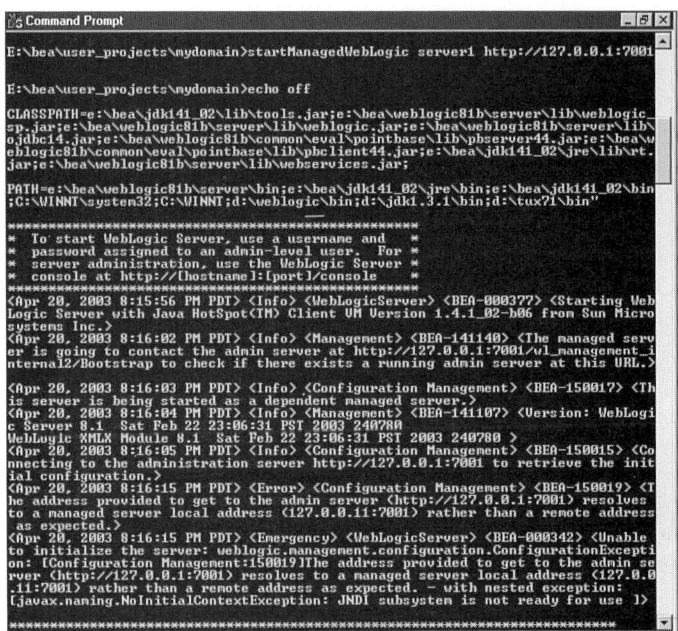

Figure 2.25 Starting a domain-managed server using a command script.

Successful Start Messages

All successful server start operations should display the WebLogic 8 standard output messages, indicating the type of server (admin or managed), IP address, port number, and server status (running) as shown here:

```
<Apr 20, 2003 5:07:47 PM PDT> <Notice> <WebLogicServer> <BEA-000365>
➥<Server state changed to RUNNING>
<Apr 20, 2003 5:07:47 PM PDT> <Notice> <WebLogicServer> <BEA-000360>
➥<Server started in RUNNING mode>
```

An example of the actual server window text is shown in Figure 2.23.

> **CAUTION**
>
> All errors reported in the server window (and associate server log)—especially errors involving RMI services on your Admin servers—should be corrected before continuing.

Graceful Termination of WebLogic Server 8

There are two means in which to terminate WebLogic Server gracefully: by using the Administration Console and by executing the `weblogic.Admin` utility. The Administration Console and the `weblogic.Admin` utility enable you to conduct graceful and forced shutdowns of WebLogic Server. A *graceful* shutdown allows all processes (including outstanding requests) to complete before the server initiates shutdown routines. A *forced* shutdown immediately terminates all server processes (dropping outstanding requests).

Terminating WebLogic Server 8 Using the Administration Console

Using your Administration Console, you can conduct either a graceful or a forced shutdown of the WebLogic Server 8 series. To shut down a server, enter your Admin server's console at `http://`*`yourURL`*`:`*`port`*`/console`. At the prompt screen, enter your username and password, and navigate to the specific server using the sequence *yourDomain*→Servers→*server#*→Control (TAB)→Shutdown This Server# (or Forced Shutdown of this Server#), as shown in Figure 2.24 earlier.

Terminating WebLogic Server 8 Using the weblogic.Admin Utility

The `weblogic.Admin` utility is a Java application that's included in your WebLogic 8 installation. Using this utility, you can conduct either a graceful or a forced shutdown of the WebLogic Server 8. To shut down a server using this utility, execute the Java application, passing the administration server URL (including port number), username, password, `SHUTDOWN` (or `FORCESHUTDOWN`) keyword, and name of server targeted for termination, as shown:

```
java webLogic.Admin -url http://127.0.0.1:7001 -username system
➥-password weblogic SHUTDOWN server1
```

or

```
java webLogic.Admin -url http://127.0.0.1:7001 -username system
➥-password weblogic FORCESHUTDOWN server1
```

The previous commands shuts down managed `server1`, controlled by an administration server located at `http://127.0.0.1:7001`.

Ungraceful Termination of WebLogic Server 8

Ungraceful termination of WebLogic Server entails terminating the process. On a Unix system, merely find the server's process ID (`ps -ef ¦ grep java`) and issue the `kill` command: `kill -PID`. On a Windows system, terminate the Windows process or merely kill the server's execution window. Obviously, no shutdown routines or classes will execute using this method.

Creating Your Own Startup Scripts

To start WebLogic Server, you can create your own startup scripts. When creating your scripts, use the generated default scripts as a guide. There are three issues to address when creating start scripts: classpath, `config.xml`, and `weblogic.Server` command.

Ensure that you set your classpath properly to include the JDK certified for use with the WebLogic 8 series server, currently JDK 1.4.1_02. Ensure that server name used within your start scripts is reflected in your `config.xml` file, which is generated during your installation. Finally, pass the proper parameters to the `weblogic.Server` Java application that actually starts WebLogic Server as shown here

Admin server

```
e:\bea\jdk141_02\bin\java" -client -Xms32m -Xmx200m -XX:MaxPermSize=128m
➥-Dweblogic.Name=admin -Dweblogic.management.username=<username>
➥-Dweblogic.management.password=<password> -Dweblogic.ProductionModeEnabled=false
➥-Djava.security.policy="e:\bea\weblogic81\server\lib\weblogic.policy"
➥weblogic.Server
```

Managed server

```
e:\bea\jdk141_02\bin\java" -client -Xms32m -Xmx200m -XX:MaxPermSize=128m
-Dweblogic.Name="server1" -Dweblogic.management.username=<username>
➥-Dweblogic.management.password=<password>
➥-Dweblogic.management.server="http://127.0.0.1:7001"
➥-Dweblogic.ProductionModeEnabled=false -Djava.security.policy="
➥e:\bea\weblogic81\server\lib\weblogic.policy" weblogic.Server
```

Refer to Table 2.3 for descriptions of commonly used `weblogic.Server` parameters.

TABLE 2.3 Key Java and weblogic.Admin Parameters

Parameter	Description
Xms	Minimum Java heap size. For better performance, make this the same as the maximum Java heap size; set it to some large amount that's available.
Xmx	Maximum Java heap size.
Dweblogic.Name	Target server name.
Dweblogic.management.username	Admin server's username.
Dweblogic.management.password	Admin server's password.
Dweblogic.management.server	Admin server's address.

Further details about `weblogic.Server` parameters can be found on the BEA documentation site at `http://e-docs.bea.com/wls/docs81/admin_ref/weblogicServer.html`.

Troubleshooting

Most problems you'll encounter when starting WebLogic Server will be attributable to your classpath. To avoid any problems with your classpath, clear or clean your system classpath prior to staring the server. I suggest that you do not set this environmental variable manually (Windows) and allow your start scripts to set all values. Another option is to allow the WebLogic settings to be first (first class wins in Java) in your classpath before any other items you want to include within the classpath.

Other common problems deal with starting managed servers once your Admin server is initiated. If you encounter problems starting your managed servers, verifying the configurations using your Admin Console is the BEA preferred method. You can also inspect configurations within your domain's `config.xml` file; however, any changes made there directly must be done with extreme caution. Ensure that there are no conflicts among server names or IP address/port designations. Also verify that your Admin server started cleanly; that is, there were no errors (log files can be found under domain and individual server directories). Note: An RMI error (RMI services not initiated) prevents any managed servers from initiating, even though the Admin server started successfully.

Summary

In this chapter, we discussed various ways of installing your WebLogic server on a Windows or Unix platform. We also discussed such terms as *WebLogic domain*, *cluster*, *server*, and *machine*, in addition to installing licenses and service packs. WebLogic startup scripts and how to start and stop your server were also addressed. The next chapter covers the human component of application development: assembling your development team.

CHAPTER 3

Skillset Required for WebLogic Application Development

by Steve Steffen

IN THIS CHAPTER

- Software and Hardware Administration
- Java Skills
- Visual Presentation Skills
- Database Skills
- Connectivity to Legacy Systems
- Testing and Quality Assurance
- Customer Support Specialists
- Software Development Phases

The skills needed to build an enterprise application with WebLogic Server 8.1 vary somewhat depending on what's being built. However, certain key roles must be covered. This chapter presents those roles, as well as others needed to perform virtually any development using WebLogic Server (WLS) 8.1.

When a significant software project is undertaken, it usually spans multiple groups of people and covers a vast array of knowledge. This knowledge must be managed in an effective way to keep the project on time and on budget. Managers must be knowledgeable in many different areas of the application to best use their resources. Although they might not need to perform this activity, a manager should know the reasoning behind it. At that point, project plans must be created and a division of labor set up. All projects must be

- Designed
- Implemented
- Administered
- Maintained

Each of these areas has skill sets that overlap. This chapter breaks down, identifies, and describes each needed skill, and then puts each skill into the correct categories.

Software and Hardware Administration

Software and hardware administration is an important part of any development environment. It encompasses designing, installing, maintaining, and supporting the entire software and hardware platform used by the development team or teams.

Hardware and Software Scalability Design

When a project is being designed, the scope of the hardware and software required to run the applications must be considered. How many users will it support? Can it easily support more users? What are the performance needs of the applications? What's the cost of the hardware? These are just some of the questions about hardware and software that must be answered.

Hardware Support

On any team, no matter how small, hardware support becomes an issue. Motherboards burn out, networks go down, the computer locks up, and those are just the start. The company technical support group usually handles these support issues. If it doesn't, someone must be able to handle the inevitable hardware failures that will occur over time. Certain hardware failures can cause the entire team to wait until the issue is fixed, which can be very expensive.

Operating System Maintenance

Operating system maintenance goes hand-in-hand with hardware support. In small shops, one person is usually responsible for maintaining the hardware, installing service packs, and installing new software. In large efforts in large companies, the maintenance team could span several states and have hundreds of employees. Operating system maintenance involves installing updates and patches, upgrading, and finding errors that inhibit the performance of any software running on the particular operating system.

WebLogic Server Administration

WebLogic Server administration is related to software administration, but is its own skill set. At least one person in the development team should understand how to configure, start, and optimize WLS on each platform it will be run on. This is critical in the implementation, administration, and maintenance phases. A properly set up server can make the development easier and progress smoothly. In the administration phase, responsibilities shift to focus on keeping the servers running, adjusting settings as performance issues arise, and checking logs for errors. During the maintenance phase, administrators' tasks include rebooting installing patches released by WebLogic and upgrading to new components.

Security Experts

Protecting data is a main concern for many companies. When access to data is available online, the concern grows. Security experts can design, analyze, and provide solutions for this protection. Systems can never be 100% secure, but a security expert can make hacking much more difficult.

Backup and Archiving Support

Just as important as security measures are backup and archiving measures. Data must be protected from system crashes, hardware failures, and network outages. A proper system has periodic backups scheduled to avoid the loss of data.

Java Skills

Java skills are, of course, the essence of WLS 8.1 development. Java skills are vastly different depending on what you're doing. A programmer used to doing small command-line programs in Java won't necessarily even know where to start developing an online application using WLS, or even a Swing GUI app connecting through JDBC to a database.

Because of this, assembling a team to build applications becomes more difficult. A manager cannot simply hire a Java programmer; she must know what underlying technologies the application will be using. This doesn't mean the employee can't learn the new technology, but a learning curve will be associated with doing so.

The norm in software development is to have one person wear many hats and do multiple things. This not only enables the developer to grow in his craft, but also saves on the overhead of hiring another person. A word of caution: A developer doing too many things at one time can directly relate to nothing getting done on time. A division of labor and a hierarchy of Java skills are what it takes to develop mission-critical software quickly, efficiently, and correctly.

A Java Architect

Software solutions are only as good or as bad as their design. Hence the importance of a good Java architect. A Java architect developing for WLS 8.1 must understand all the technologies available and choose the best ones for the solution. Most architects will use a design product to lay out the project—first at a high level, and then at a more detailed level, showing what technologies and classes are being used, extended, and created.

As the software cycle progresses, changes will ultimately come into play as new requirements and technical limitations are uncovered. A good Java architect will have years of experience in software design and an excellent understanding of not only OOP, but the J2EE architecture as well. The architect should also be aware of the features of WLS 8.1, which will enable him to take full advantage of its benefits. This experience, coupled with knowledge, enables managers and architects to work together to provide the leadership and direction for the software project.

JSPs and Servlets

Almost all applications running on WLS 8.1 will use either JavaServer Pages (JSP) or servlets. A servlet or JSP page must be run in a J2EE-compliant server, whereas other Java programs are standalone. JSPs include HTML with tags that denote Java coding, whereas servlets are a bit more involved because they're coded completely in Java.

JSPs are the easiest J2EE programs to write. A basic understanding of the Java programming language and certain J2EE-specific Web classes are all that's needed.

Another important part of writing JSPs is writing custom tag libraries to go along with them. Tag libraries enhance the ability of the JSP creator to create complex pages without writing any Java within the JSP file. Tag libraries are written completely in Java and have basic rules associated with them. Java developers should understand how tag libraries work and how to write them.

Servlets are slightly more difficult, but not much. Different levels of Java developers should exist here, with the more advanced programmers leading the entry level programmers.

JDBC and SQL

A J2EE application will usually connect to a database of some kind. This requires the use and set up of Java Database Connectivity (JDBC). JDBC enables Java programmers to connect, create, update, and retrieve information from databases that have JDBC drivers. Structured Query Language (SQL) statements are formed, and data is returned.

JDBC calls are an integral part of the J2EE framework. A developer who works with JDBC must understand SQL and how it operates because improperly designed SQL statements can have a huge affect on the runtime of an application—especially when the application is under heavy load. A developer experienced with connecting with databases is desired here, or a person who understands SQL is needed to properly formulate the SQL statements for the Java programmer.

> **NOTE**
>
> Developers can always get help with database administrators or designers when constructing SQL statements for a program. However, understanding SQL at a high level is always beneficial.

Beyond the Basics

The scalability of the J2EE architecture is a paramount reason why J2EE is the platform of choice to develop on. Certain technologies work together to give the application seamless integration, even though it might be across different networks on multitudes of separate platforms. The skill set needed for this type of application requires the knowledge of some of, if not all, the following technologies:

- EJB—Enterprise Java Beans, although not difficult to create or deploy, must be properly designed to fit into a framework.
- CMP—Container-managed persistence, which is extended with the EJB 2.0 specification, allows entity beans to have container-managed relationships. That means multiple beans can interact with each other based on the containers they're in. The container can then perform actions, such as interact with databases, independent from the entity beans contained within.
- BMP—Bean-managed persistence defines the persistence relationship at the bean level.
- JMS—Java Message Service allows asynchronous messages and events to be sent and received through out an environment.
- JTA and JTS—Java Transaction API and Java Transaction Service are related technologies that allow transactions to be managed by a transaction server instead of individual components.
- RMI—Remote Method Invocation is a powerful feature of Java that allows different virtual machines to invoke methods on each other.
- JNDI—Java Naming and Directory Interface enables programmers to access different directory interfaces, such as LDAP and DNS, seamlessly within Java.
- JMX—Java Management Extensions is an API that can be used by component developers to create management interfaces and tools.
- XML—Document Object Model (DOM) and Simple API for XML (SAX) parsers are two of the standard APIs used to create and parse XML documents in Java.
- XML Web Services—Program to program Web interfaces using standardized XML protocols to communicate and run different programs or services.
- JCOM—This is a Java connector for connecting to Microsoft COM components used in an environment in which both technologies are present.

These core technologies are advanced and are usually performed or directed by a senior Java developer. One person is usually not proficient in all the skills needed, but two or three developers with overlapping skills can work together to create and deploy these services.

Applets

Java applets are used to fill in the gaps between what HTML can do and what regular applications can do. Applets are graphical in nature, so they comprise a different skill set from J2EE. A J2EE programmer won't necessarily know even where to start when building an applet. Applets aren't used in all J2EE applications, but if dynamically displayed information is needed without requesting it from the server, this is a helpful skill.

Swing Components

Swing components are not usually thought of as being used in J2EE applications with WLS. Java Swing components are used to build fat graphical user interfaces in a standard environment such as Mac OS, KDE, or Windows 2000. Swing components can be used to design applets, but the primary focus is on developing utilities for managing Web applications.

Visual Presentation Skills

A picture might be worth more than 1000 words when putting together a Web site. Even if the Web site works properly, graphical enhancements and layouts attract new users and give a professional appearance to the site. Depending on what's being presented, many different skills are needed. The minimal skill set is HTML.

HTML Development

HTML development doesn't require the same technical expertise as coding in Java, but it isn't necessarily easy. J2EE applications have both dynamic and static pages. The dynamic pages are written in JSP and servlet format, whereas the static pages are plain HTML.

Dynamic HTML (DHTML) is an extension of the HTML scope. Using JavaScript, HTML objects can be manipulated to form menus, for example. Also, cascading style sheets (CSS) files can be used in conjunction with HTML to provide a changeable look and feel. A good HTML developer has experience in laying out forms, working with specific tag properties, working with DHTML, and knowledge of CSS tags. There's a difference in how different browsers and versions of browsers display information. A good HTML developer knows these differences and implements browser-neutral applications.

It's also necessary to point out that senior Java developers could have adequate skills for HTML and design, which is helpful. But in my experience, they don't necessarily create the most attractive sites using and watching out for any nuances the way a dedicated HTML person would.

JavaScript

Although they share a similar name, JavaScript is not Java. It's not even a subset of Java. JavaScript was created by Netscape to add scripting to HTML pages. JavaScript is useful in applications by providing a method to access form data and manipulate HTML objects. JavaScript was designed as an easy-to-use component for HTML developers. Consequently, most good HTML developers know this information.

GUI Design

Graphical user interface design is the key component to application usability. Most of the time, the designs change several times before a product is released. The actual programmers sometimes work with the users to find the screen layouts and functionality. This isn't always the best idea. Users are normally used to the old way they did things, so instead of improving the process or using a new layout that might be easier, they want exactly what they had before.

A better choice is to use a GUI designer who understands these concepts and components. Bigger application companies employ designers for this reason. Sometimes it's not feasible to hire one because of budget constraints. In that case, the developers must be trained in GUI development. Good GUI design can make or break an application because the GUI is what the customer sees first. The customer won't see all the work that was put into the back end of an application, and applaud you for that design, until he can easily learn, find, and use the application's front end.

Graphic Arts

The days of presenting green screens full of data are gone. The presentation of data is now expected to please the senses. In a WLS format, not only must data be created, but pictures, movies, sounds, and other multimedia must also be created and distributed. Engineers don't usually have the skills to create and manipulate this art (they're too busy reading technical manuals). A graphic artist is now becoming a must in the development of applications. The graphic artist works with the GUI designer to create visually appealing screens. The skill of the graphic artist obviously depends on the applications you're building. The more visually intensive your applications are, the better the artist must be.

Database Skills

Database skills are essential for almost any application using WebLogic. Information must be gathered, stored, and recalled on a moment's notice free from errors. Database specialists ensure that the system is scalable and has good performance for the application. This first step in this process is always database design.

Database Design

Database design encompasses knowledge of grouping related information. This enables information to be found and queried easily. Using certain rules such as third normal form, tables, fields, primary keys, foreign keys, and so on can be identified. A good database designer can make it easy for administration later on.

> **NOTE**
>
> A database designer can make the job of the entire team easy or near impossible. This can affect the entire project development process and even maintenance later on.

Database Development

Database developers take the design specifications and create the database, stored procedures, and views necessary for the application. Each database is slightly different in the features it supports, so database developers usually develop for only one database, such as Oracle or Microsoft SQL Server. This might not be true in all cases, but it's generally true that the larger the project, the more specialized the people.

Database Administration

Database administration is often overlooked when developing applications, but it's a crucial aspect of all areas of an application life cycle. Database administrators are responsible for analyzing database use to increase performance using database views, memory allocation, table size allocation, and stored procedures. These performance tweaks allow WLS applications to speed up the most time-consuming operation: waiting for data.

Connectivity to Legacy Systems

Over time, every system becomes a legacy system. Companies usually cannot afford to rewrite all their existing systems, so it becomes imperative that the new system be able to communicate with the old systems. This requires the people who know the older systems, both functionally and technically, to communicate what constitutes a logical transaction to the Java architects and programmers. Many legacy systems have already built adapters to work with Java, but if not, an interface might have to be written for the application to talk to Java. Most of the bigger ERP systems already have Java connectors, and with the release of the J2EE Connector Architecture (J2EE-CA) specification, they'll be coming out with J2EE-CA–compliant connectors in the near future. This enables Java programmers to spend less time learning a company's Java API, and more time working with the actual transaction needed.

Transactions with legacy systems become more complicated if two-phase commits are necessary. A two-phase commit ensures that an entire transaction, which might involve multiple systems, either entirely completes or rolls back and does not happen at all. Some systems don't have the capability to do this, which usually means it has to be built. As it stands right now, the skill sets for legacy systems require a Java programmer who knows the legacy Java API and a functional person who knows the transactions needed.

Testing and Quality Assurance

Testing the written application is a critical part of the development life cycle. Testing is done at a few different levels.

Functional testing is the first phase. This phase makes sure that all required functionality is not only in the application, but also works as designed. A developer should not do this testing because she has knowledge of the application and won't necessarily test all combinations of user input. Therefore, a third party who isn't related to the development should test the application or write the associated scripts to test it.

Load testing tests whether an application can handle the required transactions. This testing is usually performed by software. If the test comes back unsatisfactory, an engineer can analyze the results and point out the problem areas that then can be rewritten for the best performance.

A testing group skill set includes a wide array of skills from the general end user to an engineer capable of developing testing scripts for various software products such as JMeter.

Customer Support Specialists

Customer support specialists handle all the phone calls from end users using the actual product. This skill requires both technical knowledge of the application and good people skills. Depending on the number of users on the application, the support team can vary in size. There are usually different levels of support, from general questions to source code revisions.

Software Development Phases

There are four different distinct software development phases that occur in the lifespan of a software system. Those phases are

- Design
- Implementation
- Administration
- Maintenance

This section organizes the skills needed in each phase of software development. The number of skill sets to people isn't a 1-to-1 relationship. Individual people usually take on multiple roles. Depending on the project, the number of people could vary significantly.

Design Phase

The design phase entails planning and designing the application. This phase is the most critical in ensuring a successful project. Each skill set must gather requirements and then design a working operational system that suits the needs of the business both now and in the future. During this phase, a budget can usually be set and a time frame for implementation discussed. If the cost is too high, the project can be scaled back or implemented in phases. If the length of the project is too long, more resources can be allocated. The actual resources are then scheduled so that they're utilized when they're needed, and then can move on to another role or project.

- Project managers—Organize the project
- Hardware and software scalability designers—Perform analysis for the hardware and software needed
- Security experts—Help design an application that resists illicit activity
- Java architects—Work with the senior Java programmers to design the workflow and technical design to be implemented
- Senior Java programmers—Technical reference for the Java architects during the design
- Legacy functional analysts—Provide insight to the team about legacy requirements
- Database designers—Work with the design team to lay out a proper database schema
- GUI designers—Work with end users and functional analysts to design the screens and layouts
- Graphic arts developers—Work with designers to create images and buttons for site
- QA engineers—Prepare a test environment and write a test plan and test cases

Implementation Phase

During the implementation phase, the system and design specifications are being created. This part of the project requires the most resources and time. The actual needs vary as the project moves toward completion. Certain skills needed early in the plan won't be needed later and vice versa. These dependencies and resource management areas are worked out in the design phase.

- Project managers—Manage the implementation teams
- Hardware support engineers—Handle any and all hardware support issues
- WebLogic Server administrators—Install, configure, and administer the WLS software environment
- Security experts—Makes sure that data is safe and not vulnerable to attack
- Java architects—Manage any design changes made to the software during implementation
- JSP and servlet developers—Perform the work or building the application
- JDBC developers—Create the calls to databases on the Java side
- Advanced Java developers—Create the more advanced J2EE technologies

- Database developers—Create the database applications and write advanced SQL queries
- Database administrators—Administer the database
- Legacy system developers—Create any interfaces needed to connect to the legacy systems
- Legacy system functional analysts—Identify what information must be pushed and pulled from the old systems
- Testers—Verify that the newly built application works, using automatic or manual tests

Administration Phase

During the administration phase, all the work on the new application has been completed. It's now the responsibility of the various administrators to keep it running smoothly. This task requires rebooting servers, evaluating performance, combating attacks on the system, and handling any problems that inhibit the system from working properly.

- Hardware support—Correct any problems with hardware
- Operating system support—Administer the various operating systems
- WebLogic Server administrator—Handle starting and stopping the WLS servers and checking performance settings to allow for maximum transactions
- Web server administrator—Administers the server if a separate server is used for static HTML
- Security experts—Makes sure that data is secure and there are no attacks on the systems
- Database administrator—Makes sure that database is working properly and analyzes system for performance tuning
- Backup and archiving specialist—Manages the data backup and archiving to persist data in case of a system crash
- Help desk—Reports any problems end users are having with the developed application

Maintenance Phase

An implemented system will inevitably need maintenance. During the maintenance phase, service packs are installed, bugs fixed, and applications updated.

- Hardware support—Hardware is upgraded and checked for problems
- Operating system support—Operating systems are upgraded and support patches installed
- Java developers—Any reported bugs are fixed
- Database developers—System patches are applied and upgrades performed
- Testers—Changes are tested and bugs reported

Summary

The skills needed to design, implement, administer, and maintain a WLS 8.1 application can be diverse. These skills depend on the scope of project, and can be covered by a few individuals with a wide array of knowledge or many individuals with more specialized knowledge bases. This chapter outlined the important roles needed in a successful software implementation using the Web and WebLogic. These skills overlap and can be covered by one person or several, depending on the size of the project and the skills of the people involved.

CHAPTER 4

Hardware and Configuration Required for WebLogic Application Development

by Steve Steffen

IN THIS CHAPTER

Creating a development environment that meets the needs of the software managers, architects, developers, and testers in a production environment is a crucial step in developing rock-solid applications using WebLogic Server. Several tools must work together to model, develop, test, debug, deploy, and evaluate performance metrics for your application. These tools include

- Java compilers
- Integrated development environments (IDEs)
- Web browsers
- Version control software
- Modeling tools
- Testing software

Minimally, a Java compiler must be installed with a text editor, XML editor, an HTTP 1.1–compliant Web browser, and access to a local or server install of WebLogic Server 8.1. This is all right if it's a small project, but as the scope of a project grows, so must the development environment.

This chapter covers the software needed to begin development with WebLogic Server 8.1 and optional software that helps speed up the process and deliver a better software product.

Running WebLogic Server 8.1 in a Development Environment

If a developer wants to run WebLogic Server 8.1 as a local install, the machine should meet or exceed the minimum requirements discussed in Chapter 2, "Installing WebLogic Server." Development can slow to a crawl if the machine does not have enough processing power, memory, or even hard disk space to accommodate WebLogic Server. Besides WebLogic Server, most applications require database access. Databases that run locally can really tax the machine. Developers sometimes choose to run smaller or light versions of a testing database filled with a small subset of data or simply run a database on another machine.

In larger environments, WebLogic Server will run on its own machine and the developer will upload builds or changes during development and testing. Depending on the landscape, three or more servers could be required. A large-scale project requires at least a test system, and can contain a development system, integration system, and even a consolidation system. Most often each of these systems requires its own databases in addition to the WebLogic Server install. The development process for deployment is discussed later in the chapter in the "Packaging and Deploying Software" section.

Whichever way your specific environment is set up, it's crucial that the developer has hardware that allows the flexibility to run debuggers, compilers, IDEs, and other components easily without long waits because of insufficient memory. A significant amount of time can be wasted waiting for slow hardware to catch up with the software compilation and testing process. This is especially evident when debugging software is needed. The time wasted waiting usually far outweighs the cost of upgrading development hardware.

Java Compilers

To compile Java software into compatible byte code class files that WebLogic Server 8.1 can read, a Java compiler is required. There are many Java compilers available, but BEA strongly suggests using one of the compilers included in the Java Software Development Kits (SDK) that come with WebLogic Server 8.1 for Windows and Linux. The two SDKs are

- Sun Java 2 SDK
- BEA WebLogic JRockit SDK

The SDK by Sun is the standard compiler used in Java applications. The new JRockit SDK is developed by BEA and is written to optimize server-side applications. This product is fully certified and complies with Sun's Java 2 Standard Edition (J2SE) version 1.4.1.

For the compiler to work, it must be placed in your path statement or directly referenced every time it's used. This procedure varies depending on the operating system being used. If you're using an IDE to compile your applications, set the correct compiler settings within the IDE.

NOTE

JRockit and the Standard Sun JDK use the same names for their compilers. Remember to reference the correct one when compiling.

The `classpath` is the most important environment variable needed to compile and run files in Java. Countless errors can be avoided by setting up the `classpath` correctly in any development environment. All classes needed for compilation must be referenced in the `classpath`. If the classes aren't in the `classpath`, an error will be thrown at compile time. There are four ways to set this up in a system:

- Set a system variable that's set when the machine starts up
- Set it on a batch file
- Type it in on the command prompt
- Use an IDE to manage the compilation

Setting system variables in each operating system varies, so check your documentation or contact a system administrator. To set the `classpath` in a batch file or at the command prompt, use the javac program parameter `-classpath`. A developer will normally use a batch file to set up these variables or use an integrated development environment (IDE) to save project files. The following is a sample batch file used to compile several files on Windows 2000:

```
set CLASSPATH=%JAVA_HOME%\lib\tools.jar;%WL_HOME%\server\lib\weblogic.jar;
%CLASSPATH%
```

This classpath contains the minimal classes to compile a J2EE application for WebLogic Server. The most important JAR file is `weblogic.jar`. This file contains all the J2EE-specific classes for servlets, EJBs, and so forth. The `tools.jar` file contains the standard Java classes and libraries.

NOTE

When a WebLogic Server 8.1 service pack is installed, the service pack JAR needs to precede the `weblogic.jar` in the classpath.

Software Development

To write the actual Java code, all that's needed is a text editor, but it's a good idea to use an IDE. These programs can significantly reduce development time by generating skeleton code, arranging all your files into projects, allowing one-button compilation, providing support for debugging mechanisms, enabling rapid graphical user interface (GUI) design capabilities, and much more. BEA has introduced the WebLogic Workshop development environment, which is included with the WebLogic platform.

This tool enables a developer to quickly add components such as database access, hiding the complexity and tediousness of the actual code. You can view the source code and write special conditions, but the overhead of setting up the initial call is already taken care of. Other IDEs include IBM's WSAD, Borland's JBuilder, Oracle's JDeveloper, Eclipse, and NetBeans.

Each of these products offers slightly different benefits and continues to improve. NetBeans is open source and provides many updateable modules including modules for JSPs, Struts, and modeling, and also has links to third-party modules that aren't free. Borland is partnering with BEA and provides a WebLogic edition of JBuilder. This enables the programmer to develop, build, and deploy applications to WebLogic Server 8.1 right from the IDE without having to transfer files directly to the server. Some other popular IDEs include the Eclipse platform. This gives developers the ability to quickly integrate plug-ins to a standard GUI environment. It's open source and comes with a basic Java IDE with no Web application support. Borland, IBM, and Oracle are the leaders in the IDE market. There are other products that work well for J2SE and J2EE development and new versions come out constantly (about every 6 months). It's a good idea to download the trial versions of other software as they come out to see the benefits. Each company usually allows you to try out its development environment for 30 days before you have to buy it, giving you time to learn how to use it effectively.

Here is one of the arguments against using an IDE. People opposed to using an IDE say that instead of learning the how the software runs, a developer simply learns how to use his IDE more effectively. In turn, this renders him useless when he switches to a different IDE or doesn't have access to one. I believe it's the developer's responsibility to learn what the IDE is helping him do so that he fully understands the software code that's been generated. This enables the developer to not only use the time-saving shortcuts provided by the IDE, but also recognize problems with what he's trying to do and what was generated. The IDE then enables the developer to spend his time solving hard problems and not writing generic code that's more of a rote task especially error detection and correction features that save hours of debugging and produce code that can be compiled much sooner. Also beneficial is the ability to package and deploy the application from your IDE right to WebLogic.

Web Browser

Almost all WebLogic Server applications are deployed for use with a Web browser. The Web browser should be HTTP 1.1–compatible in order to display information properly. Any software you write should be tested on all browsers that you intend to support; there are slight differences in different browsers' JavaScript compatibility and overall display of a page. The common solution is to support Netscape 4.x and 6.x and Internet Explorer 4.x or later. But other browsers, such as Opera and Mozilla, are gaining acceptance. Opera provides solutions for eight different platforms and claims to be the fastest browser. There are slight display variations with this browser, too, so testing is definitely required.

Developers and Web designers should test the software as it's written in unit tests, and it should be tested in the functional tests by a third person who did not write the software. This will help alleviate most of the bugs before an end user views the software.

Other Helpful Software

This section covers other helpful software in detail normally used in a development environment. This normally used software includes version control software, modeling tools, testing software, and build and deployment tools. This section is meant to introduce you to such tools if you aren't currently using them.

Version Control Software

When several people are developing software over different releases, it becomes necessary to manage source code making up the project. Version control software such as Rational ClearCase, Merant PVCS, Microsoft SourceSafe, and Concurrent Versions System (CVS) helps manage this process. The main benefits of version control software are

- Organization of software resources—Allows the separation of projects into different categories and developers can retrieve and maintain files from one central repository.
- Track changes easily—All changes to the program are logged when the file the developer is working on is checked back in.
- File ownership tracking—If many developers are working on a project, tracking software can identify who is working on what files.
- Rollback changes—If a developer makes a change to the file that breaks the program in some way, all the changes he made can be rolled back.
- Parallel development—Two or more developers can work on the same project or files at the same time and version control software will merge the work and notify whether they modified the same lines of code.

Version control enables you to track software releases, changes made, and editors of project files. This prevents teams from overwriting files and allows previous versions to be debugged and replaced without installing the new release. Of the four mentioned previously, CVS is a leading alternative. It is open source, and therefore free. If you're not familiar with version control and want to try it, check out CVS on the Web at `www.cvshome.org`.

Modeling Tools

As software projects increase in size, efficient design and modeling becomes crucial. This is especially true in object-oriented programming (OOP). Implementing proper OOP technique isn't an easy task, but it's greatly facilitated using software tools.

Modeling is usually done in a graphical environment by creating models representing your software. The standard modeling language in use is Unified Modeling Language (UML). UML enables architects to detail system requirements, develop a solution, and implement that solution with a clear and concise roadmap. UML provides basic building blocks of software along with a way to express complex relationships among these blocks. Some of the more popular tools are Rational Rose, Borland JBuilder Enterprise, and Visio, which is a less expensive alternative to the more advanced tools.

The sample Rose model in Figure 4.1 shows a class-scheduling model. Software architects, designers, and developers have found UML to be useful planning, writing, and maintaining software. Pictures clarify and exemplify the software process, which is why design tools are being used more often. During the construction phase of a project, products such as Rose can create all the classes and methods for a developer. This enables the developer to start writing code immediately. The diagrams then serve as a map of the development effort and facilitate understanding of the system. After the system is finished, UML documents serve as support documentation, allowing maintenance to be performed quickly and efficiently.

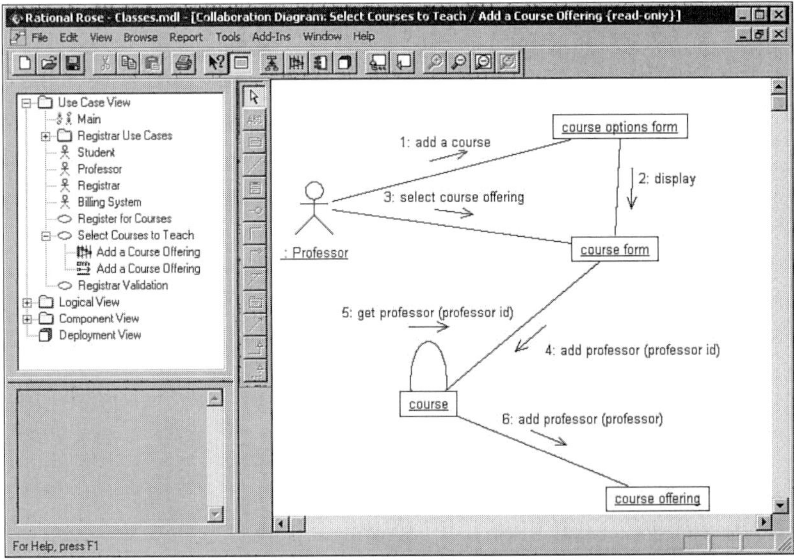

Figure 4.1 Rational Rose design software in action.

Testing Software

Testing is an important phase of any software project. When software isn't tested properly, the end product suffers tremendously in quality. Instead of finding bugs when the product is still in the developer's hands, the bugs are experienced by the end users, who then form a negative opinion of the product or Web site. Or the entire site goes down often, costing the company thousands of dollars in downtime.

Testing software can be an arduous task. Even a simple change could affect an entire application and render it useless. Developers never seem to have enough time to write test cases, and always leave it to functional testing to catch all the runtime bugs.

Testing can be performed manually or automatically. Testing manually is beneficial when initially testing random user errors. After these errors are quantified, an automated testing script can be created. That script can then be run on periodic basis such as nightly or weekly, and a report of failures can be diagnosed and fixed as they occur. One such scenario is a test after a nightly or weekly build. When the build is complete, the testing software is run and any bugs are found right away, while the code is still fresh to the developer. Some of the most common automated testing solutions include Rational TestStudio, Mercury Interactive WinRunner, Segue SilkTest, and JUnit, just to name a few.

Automated testing provides several benefits that include the following:

- Reduced testing time—An automated testing environment can run thousands of tests in a 24-hour period.
- Consistent testing procedures—The testing procedure is consistent and there won't be any skipped scenarios.
- Reduced QA costs—More bugs will be caught and fixed in development, which means less time analyzing software after it's released.
- Product quality improved—The overall benefit of automated testing is the enhanced quality of the final software product.

One product that is gaining popularity is JUnit. JUnit is a free testing framework for creating tests that call Java methods and classes with data. Writing an automated test in JUnit requires writing a Java class with a special, yet simple, syntax.

JUnit has a text or graphical suite-testing tool that runs every test in each test case and reports whether there's an error. Figure 4.2 shows the graphical test in progress. A test can be run every time a build is done to verify that methods still function properly. This saves countless hours of debugging and catches the easy mistakes. Implementing a testing framework is not nearly as difficult as maintaining the framework. The tests are easy to write, but deadlines are usually so tight on software projects that there isn't enough time to finish coding let alone write tests for the code. The best practice is to implement test cases first and then write the software. At the end, you can run the test and validate that your software works. Information about JUnit can be found on the Web at `www.junit.org`.

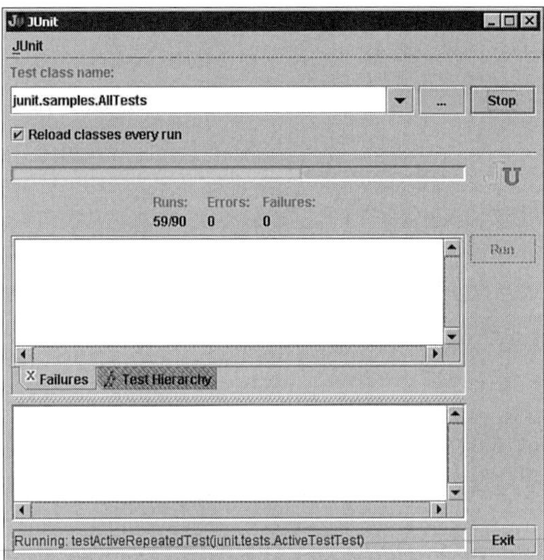

Figure 4.2 JUnit interface testing an application for errors.

Nightly or Weekly Builds

Nightly or weekly builds are important for maintaining a good testing environment. In large software applications, the application is built and tested nightly to catch any errors or prove the software's reliability. In a nightly build, the software source is retrieved from the version control repository, compiled, packaged, deployed, run, and tested.

WebLogic 8.1 is packaged with a tool named Ant that can greatly reduce this timeframe. Ant works with XML files that describe what files to compile and where to put them. It can be configured to use alternative Java compilers and to create applications in a variety of formats, including `.jar`, `.war`, and `.ear`. Many plug-ins are available for Ant, including ones to run JUnit tests. Ant works with both Windows and Unix, and is covered in depth in Chapter 7, "Deploying Web Applications."

Performance-Testing Tools

Performance testing is critical in delivering fast, reliable software in a scalable environment. Typically, there are three steps for performance testing: load testing, evaluating results, and optimization.

- Load Testing—Load testing ensures that the application will have good response times during different usages. Tests usually contain a low, medium, high, and maximum load. The number of concurrent hits for each category depends on your specific need.
- Evaluating Results—Once the testing results are in, evaluate the results to find and identify the problems.
- Optimization—Optimize the code as needed and test again. Repeat these procedures until the application runs as expected.

Performance testing is one of the last tests done before software is released, although it can be done periodically to catch bad algorithms and poor design choices early in development. These tests simulate real-world usage on the application. Performance-testing suites can cost thousands of dollars, but are worth every penny if the application being delivered will be subjected to high volumes. Some of the leaders in Java software performance testing are JProbe Suite by Quest Software, LoadRunner by Mercury Interactive, Optimizeit by Borland, and JMeter. JMeter is an alternative to high-cost suites. It's an all-Java testing tool that's available for download from `apache.org`. JMeter provides limited basic testing utilities, but setting up scripts and analyzing data is straightforward, and the tool is free.

Figure 4.3 shows a results screen of a test for speed on login. JMeter allows for multiple threads and infinite loop testing against the designated server. JMeter is a good basic step if a performance-testing suite isn't readily available. More information about JMeter can be found on the Web at `jakarta.apache.org/jmeter/`.

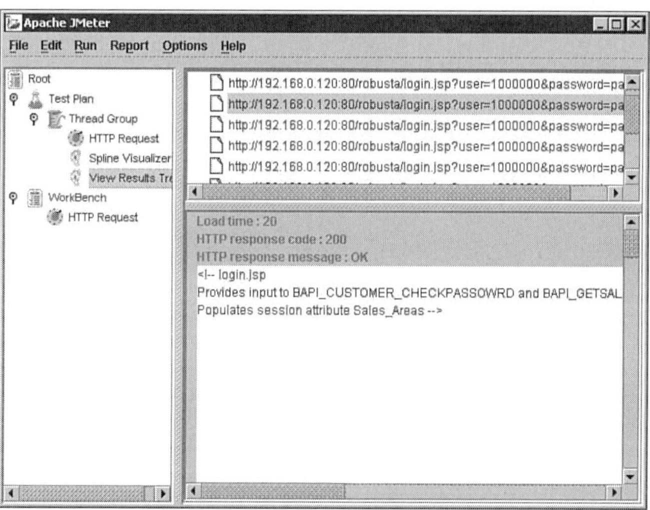

Figure 4.3 JMeter results screen for a simple HTML login test.

Packaging and Deploying Software

After the software has been built, it needs to be packaged and deployed. The first step is packaging.

A Java Web application is packaged in a Web archive file (`*.war`). If the application uses other J2EE components, such as Resource Adapters or EJBs, the `.war` file and the other components are packaged in an enterprise archive file (`*.ear`). Packaging on the command line or with simple batch scripts can be done using the Java `jar` command. Ant, as previously discussed, can do this for you when using WebLogic's Ant tasks. It's also possible to build and package applications from the IDE you are using. For example, JBuilder 8 has the option to package your application and EJBs in an `.ear` file. Of course, there's no need to package software when deploying on WebLogic—just a properly defined directory is required. However, it's much easier to move the application from one server to another because the application is self-contained. Chapter 7, "Deploying Web Applications," covers this in greater depth.

After the application is packaged, the next step is deployment. Software using WebLogic Server 8.1 can be deployed either locally on the same machine or remotely on a separate machine. Deployment can be done by using the WebLogic Administrator, the standalone deployment tool, an IDE, in Ant, or in a shell or batch script. Local deployments are easier because the Web application doesn't have to physically move locations. When remote deployment is required, a shared directory, FTP, or Web address that contains a link to the packaged application is required. An archived application can also be uploaded using the console.

In most large-scale applications, development work is done in the development system, and deployed and unit tested by individual developers. Then the application is transferred from development to a testing server, where full functional tests are performed by separate testers or by automated testing scripts. If everything is fine, the software can be moved to production or another development iteration can begin.

Team Development

Most of the time, software is written as a team effort, not individually. The process of handling many developers requires management software to keep track of the progress and source code as the project develops. Each individual developer has an environment for writing the software. When the software is written, each developer must merge his work with the rest of the team with version control software. As the project moves along, it's beneficial for each team member to have an individual server dedicated to testing that individual's changes. This can be accomplished with locally installed WebLogic Server servers or with multiple instances of WebLogic deployed on a development server or servers.

Managing many different developers in on project is a full-time job. A manager needs to keep track of the work to be done, resource allocation, progress, , and most importantly, verify that the application written by several developers works as intended. A big help is documentation. JavaDocs in the code and UML diagrams are beneficial in explaining what the application is supposed to do and what each part of the software does. This becomes especially important as team members leave and new programmers take their place, which is commonplace on large projects.

A typical implementation phase development environment has the following:

- Several developers with IDEs writing source code
- Administration system that has version control software and building and packaging tools on it
- Development system where developers can gain access to the build product for testing and debugging individually
- Test system where manual and automated testing is done both functional and performance wise

The first step is the developer writing his part of the application in Java. This is managed by the central version control repository where the developer checks out the code he's working on and checks it back in when he's done. The developer has access to a development system running WebLogic for testing the code he is writing. This is done by replacing or building the application with the new files he's working on and deploying it on an individual instance of WebLogic Server. After he has unit tested the application, he checks in his source code. The next build of the software contains his changes, which now affect the entire product. He then coordinates with the testing team and helps them write testing scenarios, either manual or automated, to test his new functionality. As bugs are found, they're reported and assigned to developers to fix. When all the software for a certain release is complete, additional tests might be performed and performance tests are completed. At that point, if the tests are all successful, the application is released into production and another iteration of implementation is started or continued. Figure 4.4 shows a typical team development environment using WebLogic Server.

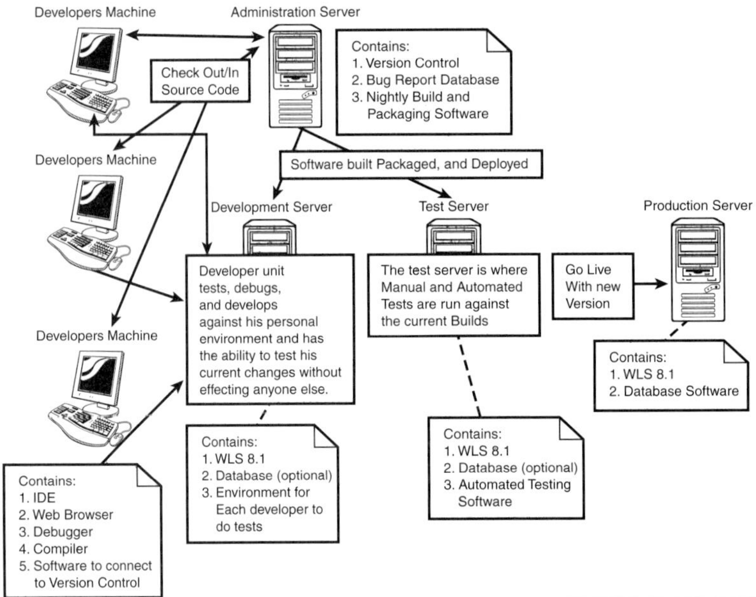

Figure 4.4 Diagram of a typical team WebLogic development environment.

Summary

Setting up a development environment can be different depending on the software being written and the personal choice of architects, developers, and testers. The tools available for the software development process continue to improve and expand. Tools, however, are no substitute for good design and coding practices. This chapter reiterated the importance of testing software for both function and performance to ensure the quality of the final product. It also showed standard practices for deployment and team development.

CHAPTER **5**

Enterprise Application Design with WebLogic Server

by Saranathan Govindarajan

IN THIS CHAPTER

- Understanding N-Tier Applications
- J2EE Platform
- Modeling Technique—UML
- Design Strategy—Model View Controller Pattern
- Development Methodologies

In this age of e-commerce revolution, most organizations want large-scale enterprise integration projects at Internet delivery time. Internet delivery time is driven by the day-to-day demand of the enterprise application to roll out into production at the shortest time possible, thereby enabling organizations to tap new markets, retain existing customers, and introduce innovative products and services ahead of the competition. Additionally, the products and services have to be delivered through multiple channels, such as Web-based systems and call center–based applications like automated interactive voice response system and a customer relationship system. The applications also require working with existing legacy applications and using the existing corporate data that resides in heterogeneous databases. As you can see, multichannel delivery coupled with Internet delivery time makes organizations concentrate a lot on architecting a suitable solution that's technically and financially viable.

In this chapter, we go over some of the common concepts for designing enterprise-class applications and how WebLogic Server can provide an effective and easy solution for the problems we face in enterprise application design and integration as mentioned here. Later in the chapter, we move on to discuss some of the design strategies and implementation methodologies available to J2EE architects. These are some of the best available and most adopted strategies for implementing the specific components that make up a multitier, multichannel enterprise application.

Understanding N-Tier Applications

The design and deployment of an application fulfilling all or some of the requirements discussed earlier needs a robust and proven platform that can integrate the data and the legacy applications and deliver it over multiple channels, and also make it scalable, portable, and reliable. In this customer-centric e-commerce age, enterprises should be able to update their systems to add new services and constantly work on improving the current services with no or negligible application downtime. All this has to be done to hold on to the customer base and expand it at the same time. It might seem a daunting task to achieve all this in every business application. To achieve these goals and make them easily manageable, applications are divided into multiple layers to perform different necessary functions, and in general can be grouped into the following tiers or layers:

- Backend tier—For integrating to existing or new corporate databases or to legacy applications
- Middle tier—For handling business logic and acting as the glue between the backend and the client tiers
- Client tier—For rendering the output in different channels, such as a Web browser, standalone client, mobile device, and so on

Figure 5.1 describes the three main tiers of an enterprise application.

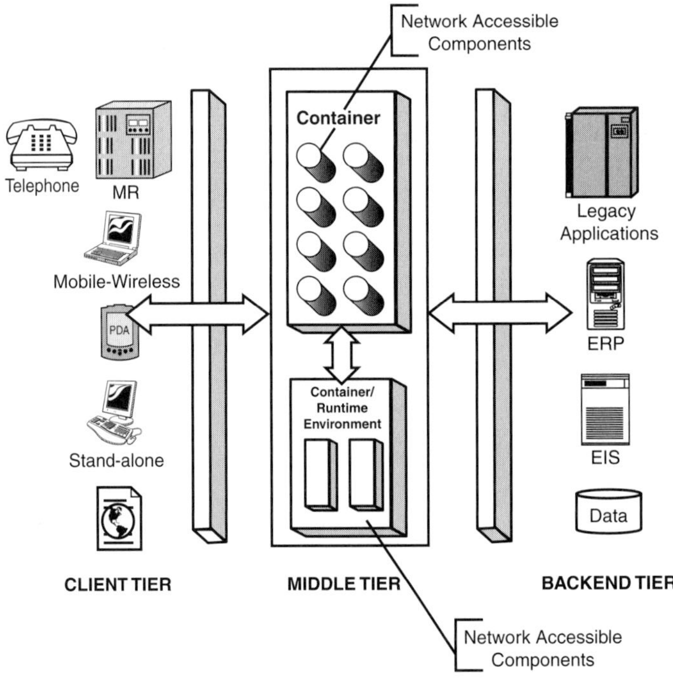

Figure 5.1 N-tier architecture.

The responsibilities of each of the tiers are clearly demarcated. As you can see, the application that performs the role of the middle tier has the most important role for making the entire application work in unison. It also serves as the right place for providing the services such as security, transaction, and resource management (that is, database connections), which are limited in most business cases.

To clearly understand the n-tier scenario described here, let's consider a common real-life example. By default, a banking system is expected to provide online banking, teller support in branches, and automated balance inquiry among many other customer-centric functions in order to provide the highest quality customer service. Additionally, those systems must be constantly updated to cater to changing business practices and to satisfy changing customer needs. All the systems need to talk to the same database to access the account information. The differences between the systems are the output rendered to the customer and the protocol they have to use to render them. It isn't advisable to develop separate applications to build up the functions offered through the many divisions of the bank. The middle tier helps manage the business logic in one place, thereby avoiding a duplication of effort in creating the different applications from scratch as required in this real-life scenario.

J2EE Platform

The Java 2 Platform, Enterprise Edition (J2EE) has emerged as a desired bleeding-edge technology that can provide the necessary infrastructure for developing distributed multitier applications. The J2EE framework is based on well-defined component models that conform to specific guidelines, are deployable in multiple server environments and, above all, can be reused to increase productivity. The J2EE platform defines the standards to server vendors and application developers alike for providing scalable, portable, secure, and reliable applications. These are the core factors in application development for enterprises that enable them to stay ahead of the competition.

Tiered Architecture Support

The J2EE platform is designed to address requirements in all the tiers, as described in Figure 5.1. The J2EE architecture defines the necessary protocols and standard API for developing and integrating the components that make up each of the tiers. Let's look at how J2EE addresses each tier's requirements and what components and services it provides for simplifying their development.

Client Tier

Most enterprise applications have to render the business function through multiple channels. The output rendered differs based on the client type; for example, an HTML page for Web browsers. HTML pages are normally generated dynamically using the JavaServer Pages (JSP) and servlet technologies. Web clients interact with the middle tier server using the HTTP protocol. XML is another common format in which the client and server interact.

Standalone clients written in Java or any other language can integrate with the middle tier server by using a standard socket library and implementing the connection protocol depending on the component being used; that is, HTTP for accessing servlets and JSPs, and RMI/RMI-IIOP for accessing Enterprise JavaBeans. The latest addition to the Java 2 platform—J2ME (Java 2 Platform, Micro Edition)—extends the middle tier services to other client models such as mobile devices, PDAs, and so forth.

Middle Tier

This tier represents the business logic components that take care of implementing the business function. One of the common components used to implement business logic is the Enterprise JavaBeans technology. EJB technology enables a developer to concentrate on the business logic and leave primary services such as life cycle management, naming, and transactions to the runtime environment, which holds the EJBs. The runtime environment is known as the *container*. The middle tier provides other services, such as messaging services using Java Messaging Service (JMS), naming services using the Java Naming and Directory Interface (JNDI), database connectivity using the JDBC (Java Database Connectivity) API, and much more.

Backend Tier

The components and applications that constitute the backend tier are critical to every enterprise business application because in most cases they represent the corporate data or legacy application or an enterprise information system. These components and applications form the backbone of the enterprise business. The J2EE platform provides the enabling technologies (that is, Java Connector Architecture [J2EE-CA]) for integrating existing enterprise legacy applications with the middle tier as described earlier. The JDBC API coupled with application server–specific connection pools provides an excellent infrastructure for database connectivity.

> **NOTE**
>
> Although Java is the language used in J2EE (why not—J2EE stands for Java 2 Platform, Enterprise Edition), the platform provides the ability to support other complementary technology components (namely CORBA and XML Web Services) written in any language. The J2EE application can also be used by heterogeneous clients.

We've briefly gone through the different tiers that make up an n-tier application and the responsibilities associated with them. It's evident from the discussion that the middle tier has to be robust and extensible to successfully manage the business it models. Changing business needs have to be addressed almost immediately and without affecting the quality of service. The J2EE platform and the architecture it supports (with the help of the different components and services they offer) make the enterprise application development much easier. Let's now look at some key features of the J2EE platform in the next section. Let's also examine how WebLogic Server, built on the J2EE platform, provides a robust platform for implementing portable, distributed, n-tier enterprise applications.

Component Model Architecture

The cornerstone of the J2EE platform is the simplified architecture focused on a component-based development model. Some of the benefits it offers directly affect delivery time, which is one of the major concerns for large organizations deploying enterprise applications. The component model enables parallel development of the different components that make up the application. Figure 5.2 zooms in on the middle tier described in Figure 5.1 and illustrates the services and components supported by a fully compliant J2EE application server such as WebLogic Server. Most of the components and services described in Figure 5.2 are essential components in conforming to the J2EE platform specifications. Some of the services might be proprietary and this gives the application server vendor the ability to add value to its product. Almost all commercially available J2EE-compliant application servers, including WebLogic Server, stay on top of the current version of the specifications. This enables them to provide their customer/business with the maximum value that can be leveraged from the J2EE platform.

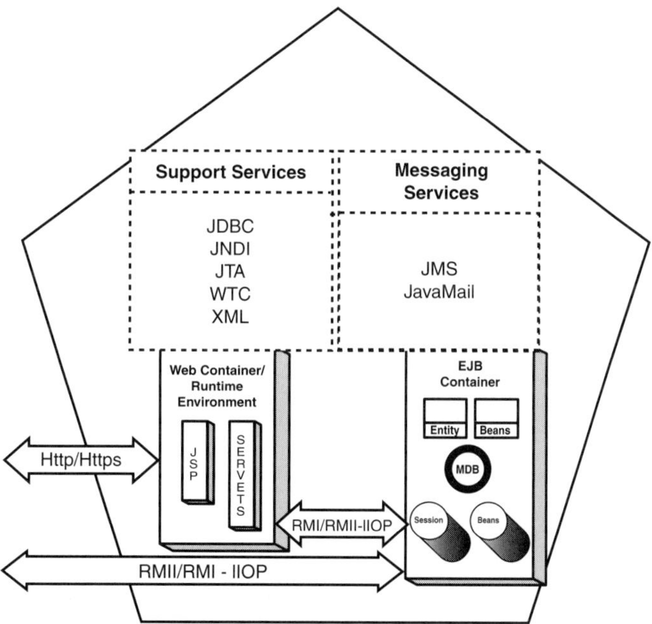

Figure 5.2 J2EE platform infrastructure—WebLogic Server.

As you can see in Figure 5.2, there are multiple containers within the J2EE environment. These containers are runtime environments for different components of the platform. For example, Web applications are managed in a different runtime environment within the server (Web container) from that of the business domain environment like the EJBs (EJB container). This enables Web developers to create HTML/JSP templates, which can be used by application designers to incorporate the application behavior. In parallel, functional experts in collaboration with component developers (such as EJB developers) can create the business logic components. An application assembler can assemble all the application components that can then can be bundled with the configuration files and deployed by a deployer. Assembling an application is also done using standardized file formats (for example, `*.jar`, `*.war`, and `*.ear` files), depending on the application component. The deployment-time behaviors of the application are controlled by a set of deployment descriptors and configuration files. After the application is deployed, it can be managed by a maintenance team. Figure 5.3 illustrates the different parties involved in a component-based development model using WebLogic Server.

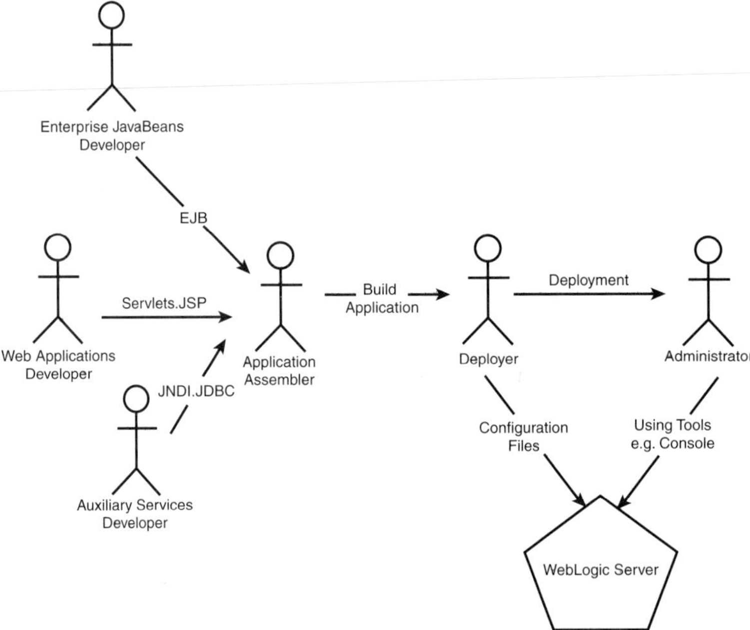

Figure 5.3 J2EE application development parties.

The J2EE specifications provide guidelines for the roles that a developer or set of developers may perform, including the ones specified in Figure 5.3 (that is, application component developer, assembler, deployer, and so forth). There are no hard-and-fast rules as to who should perform each of the functions. This is a logical demarcation because development teams might assign multiple roles to a developer. In very large-scale projects, it's possible that these roles could be split up into more specific functional areas, such as user interface designers, business data mappers, application logic developers, and so on.

COMPONENT-APPLICATION MAPPING

J2EE provides different types of components for translating the real-world requirements into an enterprise application. A J2EE-platform–enabled server such as WebLogic Server provides a rich set of API and integration mechanisms for simultaneously delivering enterprise solutions to multiple client types, reusing the components for delivering the same functionality for each type. For example, an EJB can be invoked from a JSP/servlet (serving HTML or even WML), from a J2ME client, from a standalone Java client, from a C++ application (using CORBA or via an XML Web Service), and so on.

Infrastructure and Services

The component model architecture addresses some of the main requirements leading to the development and deployment of enterprise systems in current technology scenarios. With Internet delivery time as a major requirement, most systems don't have time to concentrate on the development of auxiliary services such as security and making the system highly available. They depend on the application server vendors to provide the necessary infrastructure for these services and allow the enterprise systems the capability to configure them according to their business needs. We'll now look at some of the important infrastructure components and services that are part of the J2EE platform and that help in simplifying the design and development of enterprise systems.

Integration Services

As you saw in Figure 5.2, the J2EE platform provides the necessary infrastructure and well-defined APIs for integrating to existing enterprise applications and to external services such as directory services. Table 5.1 lists the different J2EE standard/framework services along with their uses in the J2EE-based enterprise development model.

TABLE 5.1 J2EE Platform Integration Services

J2EE Standard/Framework	Description
J2EE Connector Architecture (J2EE-CA)	Provides a portable framework for integrating applications such as ERP, CRM, and mainframe applications
Java Naming and Directory Interface (JNDI)	API for accessing enterprise naming and directory services
Java Database Connectivity (JDBC)	API set for accessing relational databases
Java Messaging Service (JMS)	Enterprise messaging infrastructure with a rich set of APIs for implementing standard, portable messaging applications, and asynchronous request-response model applications

TABLE 5.1 Continued

J2EE Standard/Framework	Description
Java Transaction (JTA)	API set for implementing transactional systems
XML API (JAXP)	Java API for XML provides support for XML-based application framework such as XML Web services
JavaMail	API set for sending and receiving mails
JavaIDL	Provides support for integrating CORBA services

Scalability and High Availability

Most J2EE application servers support clustering of services, which provides simplified distributed application scalability with absolutely no special code. An applications server cluster (for example, a WebLogic Server cluster) contains two or more instances of the application server providing the same kind of services to all clients. This provides increased scalability and high availability. All server instances in the cluster are equal and are transparent to the client making the request. The server instances can be distributed across different machines or in one big powerful machine. The cluster capacity can be increased easily just by adding new servers. These servers can be hosted on new machines or on the machines that are already part of the cluster.

The clusters are designed to address scalability requirements of the different services that are offered by the server; that is, transactions and resource management services such as connection pooling. These services impact performance and are the best candidates for clustering. The benefits of application server clustering can be summarized in two categories:

- Scalability—As the number of servers in a cluster increases, it directly affects the application's capacity positively. Additionally, new server instances can be added to a cluster without bringing down the application server environment, so there's no interruption of service for the end users.

  There's an auxiliary benefit to this because the application server automatically takes care of load balancing in response to fluctuating demand. For example, WebLogic Server provides the capability to specify an algorithm for load balancing that can be used to spread the client requests based on many factors such as machine's available memory, clock speed, and so on.

- High availability—Because deployed components run in multiple instances of the server grouped in a WebLogic Server cluster, a single server instance failure does not cause a request to fail. Request processing can continue with the help of another server instance. WebLogic Server automatically takes care of migrating the request to the server instance designated as the backup for the server that went down.

Security Framework

One of the key concerns for any enterprise architect is how to secure an application. The J2EE security framework eases this concern by the simple unified security model, which is adapted well by WebLogic Server. The granularity of the security framework provided as part of the J2EE platform is at the component method level. Component developers have the option to specify who should be able to execute a particular component method. The most common security mechanism is the role-based security mechanism in which users with the same privileges are grouped together. This is entirely configurable, enabling component developers not to worry about securing applications through code. But technologies such as Enterprise JavaBeans and servlets also provide APIs for programmatic security. All this provides for both greater flexibility and sophisticated security control for all the parties involved in the J2EE enterprise application development.

WebLogic Server and J2EE

WebLogic Server is built on the J2EE platform, thereby making it a robust platform for implementing portable, distributed, n-tier enterprise applications. WebLogic Server provides all the services for the J2EE components advocated by the specifications. The specifications are developed by the Java community, which includes many software vendors such as Sun Microsystems and BEA Systems.

Being an application server, WebLogic Server provides a perfect environment for implementing the middle tier described in Figure 5.1. WebLogic Server provides all services relating to Web clients, container services for business logic components implemented in EJB, JMS, and so on, and efficient resource management using connection pooling mechanisms. WebLogic Server leverages the component model very well. WebLogic Server also provides a proprietary application framework for seamless integration of WebLogic Server applications with BEA Tuxedo/CORBA services using WebLogic to Tuxedo Connecter (WTC). This is in addition to the Jolt API that also gives access to remote Tuxedo applications.

Development Aids—Tools and Components

WebLogic Server is bundled with its own set of tools that help develop, configure, deploy, and maintain applications. These tools are a mixture of GUI-based tools (such as the WebLogic Console and WebLogic Builder) and command-line based tools (such as EJBGen). WebLogic Console is used for managing the WebLogic Server environment. WebLogic Builder is used for building enterprise applications. EJBGen is used for generating the necessary component classes based on the business methods defined in the user-written Enterprise Java Beans.

The J2EE standard created a marketplace for development tools for different phases of the enterprise application developed on the J2EE platform. These third-party tools can be used during development, packaging, and configuration of Web applications and EJBs. Most of the tools are compatible with all J2EE application servers. WebLogic Server is part of the J2EE family so, of course, these tools can be used with WebLogic Server as well.

Apart from the tools, component-based architecture and design has enabled third parties to develop standard, reusable components using J2EE technologies such as servlets, JSPs, and EJBs that can be deployed in a J2EE-compliant application server such as WebLogic Server with no or little modifications. This eases the task of enterprises that are under constant pressure to roll out new functions as part of enterprise applications just to be part of the competition. For example, a component such as shopping cart can be used in wide a range of applications: an online bookstore and a grocery store, to name just two examples. Buying that component instead of developing it can save precious time.

Other Considerations

WebLogic Server has built on the J2EE security standard with additional features such as the Security Service Provider Interfaces (SSPI) for authentication, authorization, and role and credential mapping as well as auditing purposes. WebLogic Server allows third parties to develop security modules that can integrate seamlessly into the WebLogic runtime environment. Additionally, third-party administration tools can be integrated with the WebLogic Administration Console.

WebLogic Server clustering fully echoes the scalability and failover attributes that were explained earlier. Clustering is not mandatory for all J2EE components according to specifications. Not all components can be clustered in the current release of WebLogic Server. Table 5.2 lists the objects that can be clustered and provides information that's replicated among the servers in the cluster.

TABLE 5.2 WebLogic Server Clusterable Components

Component Type	Clustering Type
Servlets and JSPs	Maintains HTTP session states in memory, a file system, or a database.
EJB and RMI objects	Replica-aware stubs that can locate the bean instance anywhere in the cluster.
JDBC	Datasources, connection pools are clusterable and these objects should exist in all server instances.
JMS	JMS destinations are clusterable.
JNDI	Some cluster support (for example, RMI stubs and replicated trees).

WebLogic Server now provides improved availability for nonclustered services. An administrator can migrate a nonclustered service from one server instance to another server instance in the same cluster. This can be used when the server instance fails or for a scheduled maintenance.

So far, we've looked at the J2EE platform benefits and how WebLogic Server provides an effective J2EE-based enterprise solution. Now we move on to applying these concepts in architecting an enterprise application.

Architecting a J2EE Application

We've just scratched the surface of the J2EE and WebLogic Server platform and the benefits it offers when used to implement a large-scale enterprise application. We briefly covered some of the components (that is, EJB, servlets, JSP, and JMS) that were shown as part of Figure 5.2. But some of the most important constituents of the J2EE environment are the different containers that provide the runtime environment for specific components. For example, the Web container manages the Web application environment that contains the servlet and JSP components, and the EJB container provides the runtime environment for Enterprise JavaBeans.

Not all components are necessary for architecting a business solution. The programming model is flexible enough to support multiple channels of delivery as shown in Figure 5.1. For instance, certain client types don't require Web containers and the associated components, and some other clients might not require an EJB container and the beans deployed in it. The J2EE environment does not enforce the use of certain components in all application designs. This opens up a wide range of options when designing an application on WebLogic Server. Let's look at some architectures using some real-life examples.

Web Application Scenario

Consider the case of XYZ Pizza Company, which specializes in pizza delivery and is building a Web site to enable customers to order pizza online. The business function is limited to constructing your favorite pizza by specifying the type of crust (thick or thin) and adding the toppings and sides required. The customer has to specify the delivery address along with payment method, such as a credit card. Figure 5.4 gives a possible architecture for designing a Web site for the XYZ Pizza Company.

The servlets and JSPs listed inside the Web container might be the only functions for a fully functional online pizza ordering system. The servlets perform the dual functions of both the presentation layer and the business logic layer (which is bad practice). The database connectivity can be managed using JDBC, and integration with the credit card system can be achieved with either the help of a proprietary solution or a more portable Java connector architecture.

N-Tier Scenario

The Web application scenario explained in the preceding section will not work for more complex scenarios, which might involve multiple client types and many more business functions. Consider a banking system trying to extend all of its services (that is, account management, loans, and so forth) through multiple channels. Some of the common channels are an online system, an automated call center powered by an interactive voice response system, and a customer service department powered by customer-relationship management application (CRM). This is in addition to traditional branches with their own teller-system applications. In this business case, the business services offered are more complex than the XYZ Pizza Company.

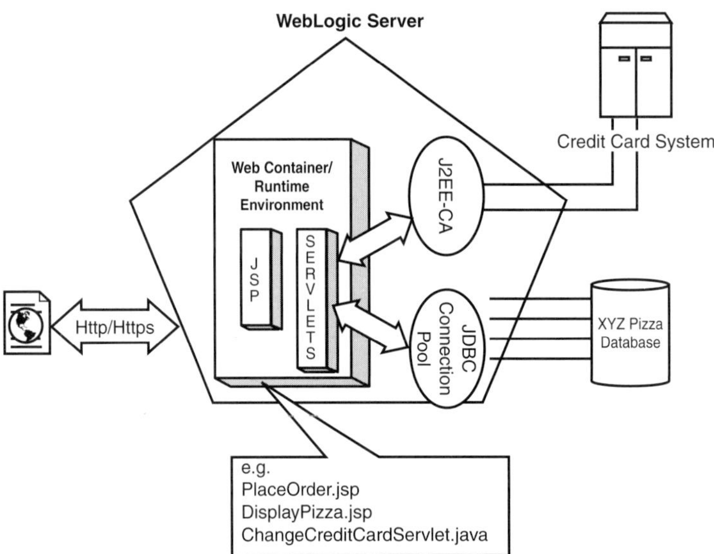

Figure 5.4 XYZ Pizza—Web application scenario.

The banking application architecture is driven by many factors apart from the number of services that are offered as part of the application. Let's look at some of them:

- Multiple client types such as IVR, Web, and so on that understand different protocols.
- Rapid application design leveraging off-the shelf business logic components. As you can see, some of the entities involved in the business case—including customer, account, products the bank offers—are common across many other horizontal businesses and might be available as ready-made components.
- Modular development to enable multiple teams to work on different aspects of the application. The most evident is splitting the presentation and business logic components so that Web designers and domain experts can work simultaneously.
- Enterprise information system integration and the options available for integrating the new application with the existing corporate data and legacy systems. The options may be custom built or well-defined products that can be integrated seamlessly with the new application.

Keeping in view of the some of these requirements, a bird's eye view of the application architecture for the banking system is illustrated in Figure 5.5.

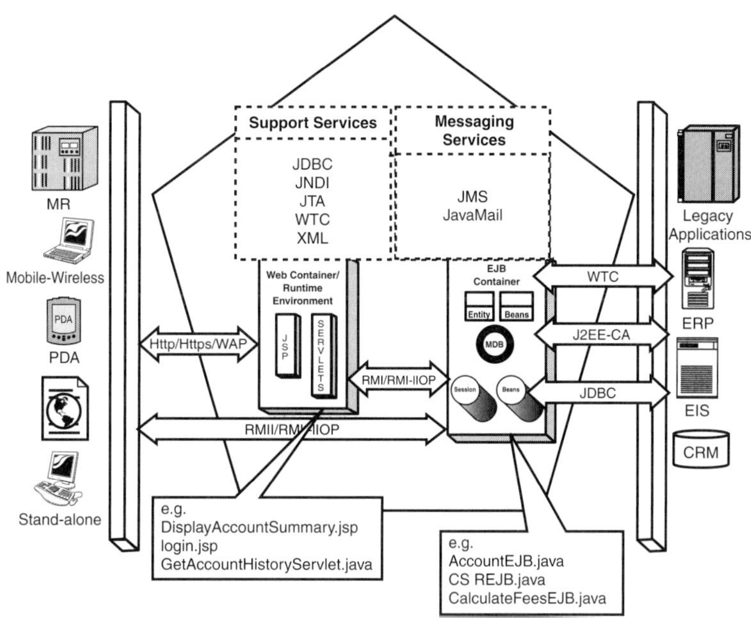

Figure 5.5 N-tier application scenario.

The other consideration during the design of complex enterprise applications in WebLogic Server is the use of XML for data transformation. Java and XML are complementary technologies. Java's popularity is driven by the Write Once, Run Everywhere concept, and in a similar fashion, XML provides portability for data. It isn't the most important choice for data exchange and doesn't necessarily impact the overall architecture. But the data portability definitely simplifies data transformation, especially when dealing with heterogeneous rendering depending on the client types. For example, the XML data messages between the different client types and their server components make it easy to integrate the different channels with one enterprise application sharing the business logic components. In fact, the use of XML is not limited to this, but can be used anywhere in the application; namely, between the server components in the middle tier.

Global Auctions—Case Study

Now let's look at a global auctions system in the light of the N-tier scenario we discussed earlier. The Global Auctions Management Systems may involve interactions with external systems, such as a credit card company, an accounting system, and the global auctions database that stores the users (buyer and seller) and their interactions. Figure 5.6 illustrates the architecture for the global auctions system along with some of the components involved in the interactions between the different users—guests, sellers, and buyers.

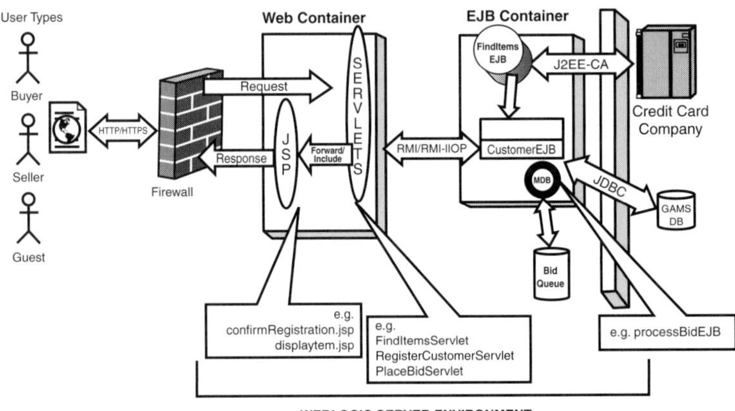

Figure 5.6 Global auctions architecture.

So far, we've gone through what is needed for an n-tier application and how J2EE helps solve these business problems in an effective manner. We've also gone over how to architect some of the common business problems. In getting an enterprise application to work as relates to the needs of the business, there must be coordination between the different communities that make up the enterprise application team. This coordination can be achieved if all of the communities can speak in a common language. But the skill sets don't necessarily match, which makes things difficult for effective communication. For instance, the user community, with its expertise in the functional knowledge of the business, is responsible for providing the application inputs—in other words, what they want from the enterprise application. The application designers are responsible for translating those requirements into meaningful representation that can be understood and reviewed by the user community. After making sure that the application design truly reflects the users' requirements, the architects have to come up with a viable technical solution. They're responsible for coming up with a high-level design strategy and choosing the different J2EE components that match the technical solution. Finally, the identified components must be represented in a way so that they can be communicated to the developers. The level of communication and disparate skill sets make it difficult to implement an enterprise application.

We'll now look at how we can address these problems effectively with the help of some strategies and techniques that have evolved over the years. We'll also look at a modeling technique, the MVC pattern, and two of the most-adopted development strategies available.

Modeling Technique—UML

The Unified Modeling Language (UML) has evolved into an industry standard for documenting the components of an object-oriented system. The construction of a model that maps to the real-world object is half the solution to the problem. The model abstracts the necessary details of the software problem and maps the real-world objects to their corresponding software system artifacts. This section gives a short introduction of UML.

Because UML is a language itself, it provides its own set of rules, notations, and syntax. The notations are used in a set of specialized software diagrams that represent different facets of the solution. The notations are governed by a set of rules and the diagrams are created by combining the shapes to conform to the UML syntax. UML is managed by the Object Management Group (OMG) and was greatly influenced by other object-oriented analysis and design techniques. Most of the notations have been adopted from two of the most popular techniques: Rumbaugh's object modeling technique (OMT) and Booch's object-oriented design (OOD). For a full specification of UML, refer to the OMG's site at `http://www.omg.org/uml`.

Now let's take a brief look at the different notations available as part of UML.

UML Diagrams—Overview

Each of the UML diagrams is designed to give a different perspective to the different parties involved in a software solution. The degree of abstraction also varies from diagram to diagram. UML defines the diagrams representing the different perspective of the problem as grouped in the following major categories. There is no hard-and-fast rule on the category because these diagrams can be subcategorized even further. Table 5.3 summarizes the UML diagrams.

TABLE 5.3 UML Diagrams

Category	Diagram	Description
Structural	Class	Models class structure and contents using design elements such as classes, packages, and objects. This diagram is also used to depict relationships between the elements, such as containment, inheritance, associations, and so forth.
	Object	Represents a static picture of the system at a given time in the life of the system.
	Component	Represents the different components organized in a high-level packaged structure. The components represented include source code components, binary code components, and executable components. It also reflects the dependencies among components.
	Deployment	Represents the physical links between the different elements in the software solution. The elements include software and hardware components.

TABLE 5.3 Continued

Category	Diagram	Description
Behavioral	Use Case	Describes the relationship among the different actors and the associated use cases.
	Sequence	Displays the different interactions between the objects over the period of the execution of a business function. The horizontal dimension represents the different object(s) and the vertical dimension represents time.
	Activity	Represents the flows involved in a single process and how they depend on each other. This can be seen as an advanced flowchart, and most of the transitions are a result of finishing a particular action.
	Collaboration	Represents interactions between the objects. Resembles sequence diagrams.
	State Chart	Represents the status conditions and component responses. In the lifetime of an object, it undergoes changes, moving from one state to another, and the sequence of object state is displayed using this diagram.

Apart from those listed in Table 5.3, there are model management diagrams that include packages, subsystems, and models. Creating these diagrams appears to be a lot of work, but UML has evolved into a popular standard and the number of tools that help create these diagrams has increased. Now let's see some of the diagrams in detail with the help of the global auctions management system described earlier in the chapter.

Use Case Diagram

This diagram describes what a system does. A use case is a summary of all the scenarios for completing a task. Let's take the case of the global auctions system in which a one-time user (guest) is one of the actors. Figure 5.7 illustrates all the communications between the guest and the related use cases.

As you can see, these diagrams are an effective way of representing the functionality and communicating the business process to clients.

Class Diagram

As Figure 5.8 illustrates, class diagrams are an effective way of representing a system overview with its classes and the relationships among them.

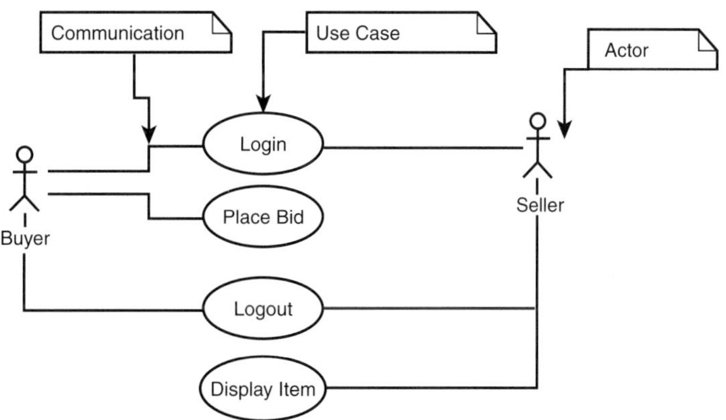

Figure 5.7 Use case diagram.

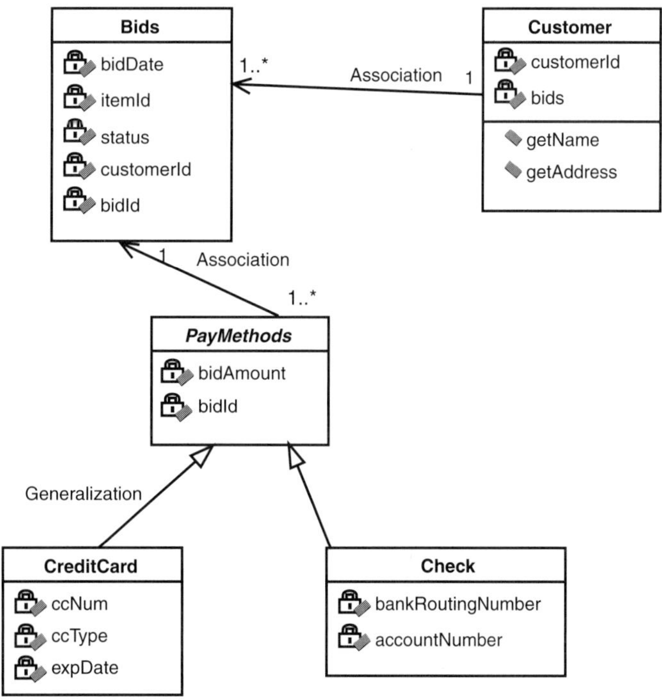

Figure 5.8 Class diagram.

5

Package Diagram

Packages organize the classes into well-defined groups. Figure 5.9 illustrates part of the sample package structure for the global auctions application.

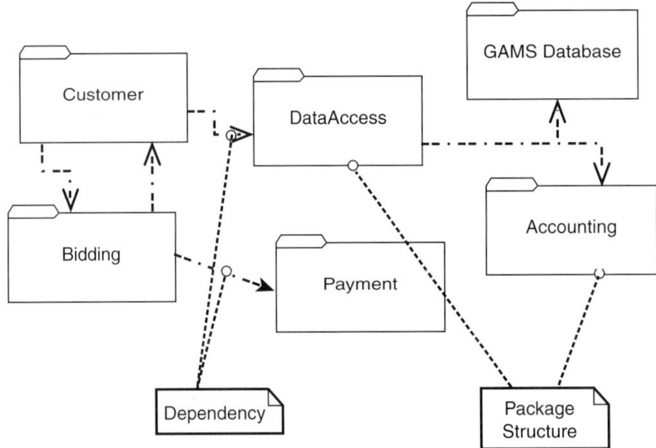

Figure 5.9 Package diagram.

Sequence Diagram

A sequence diagram is an interaction map that represents how operations are executed over time. Figure 5.10 illustrates part of the sample sequence diagram for the customer registration process.

Collaboration Diagram

The collaboration diagram is an interaction chart similar to the sequence diagram, but the focus is on the object roles instead of the times that messages are sent. Figure 5.11 illustrates part of the sample collaboration diagram for the customer registration process.

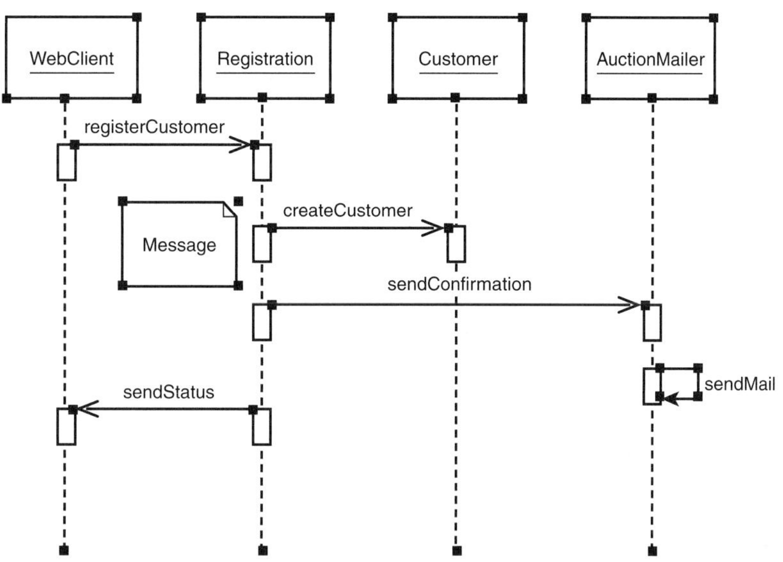

Figure 5.10 Sequence diagram.

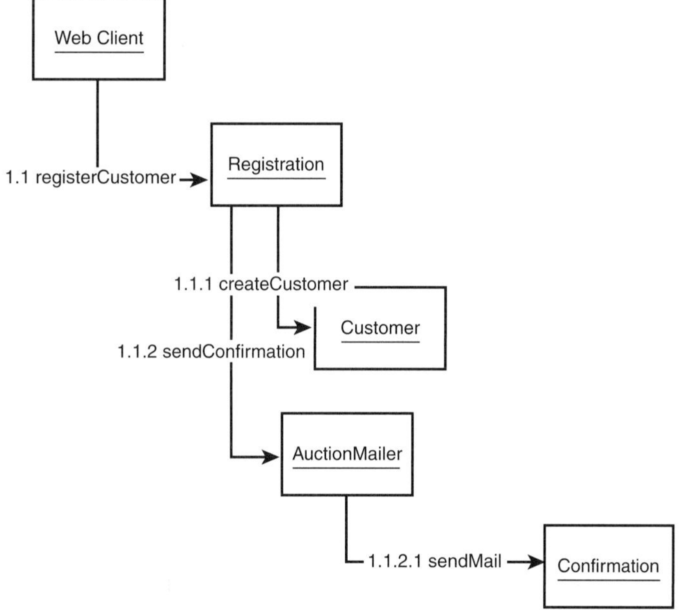

Figure 5.11 Collaboration diagram.

5

Activity Diagram

The activity diagram is a sophisticated flowchart and it shows how the different activities are interdependent. Figure 5.12 illustrates part of the sample activity diagram for the auction closing process.

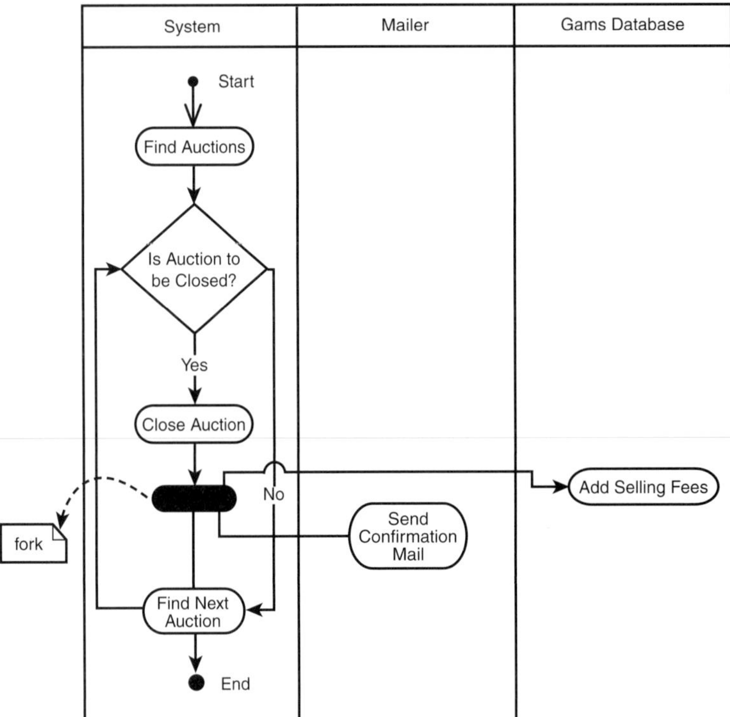

Figure 5.12 Activity diagram.

Deployment Diagram

A deployment diagram represents the physical configurations of the system. Figure 5.13 illustrates the deployment diagram for part of the global auctions system.

We just saw some of the different UML diagrams that give different users their perspective of the system. Now let's move on to the MVC pattern, which gives an effective design strategy for the enterprise applications we discussed earlier.

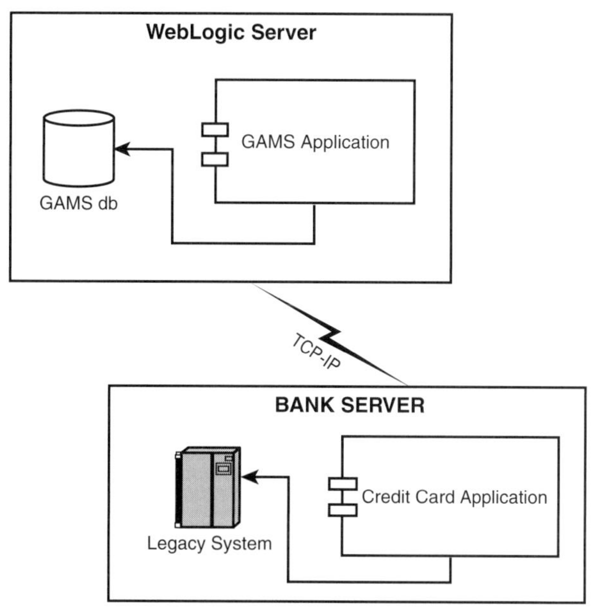

Figure 5.13 Deployment diagram.

Design Strategy—Model View Controller Pattern

In the current competitive climate, most enterprises need to cater to customers using different channels of delivery. We saw a sample business case in a banking system illustrated in Figure 5.5. All the different client types use different interfaces, but execute the same business function. This leads to multiple views of the same data depending on the client type accessing it. For example, a Web customer needs the data in an HTML format, a wireless customer needs data in a WML format, and B2B (business-to-business) customers increasingly want XML-based Web Services for integrating businesses.

In a classic single-customer view, as illustrated in Figure 5.4 with the XYZ Pizza Company business case, the business logic, the data access layer, and the presentation view are bundled into one component. This approach will not work well with a complex multiple-client–type scenario. The developer would end up creating multiple clients to service the different client types. There will be a lot of duplication of the same code in different clients because the business logic remains the same for any given business function irrespective of the client type. The duplication of effort involves recurring costs when it comes to maintaining the same code when it's replicated over different clients. As more and more business functions evolve, applications with the same core functionality develop into separate applications, which leads to a maintenance nightmare.

One of the most common solutions to this problem is the Model View Controller design pattern. This pattern breaks the application into three logical layers: data access layer, business logic layer, and data presentation and user interaction. By applying the MVC pattern to a J2EE enterprise application like our banking system business case, it's possible to decouple the core business functionality from that of the presentation component that uses the business function. The decoupling allows the multiple client types to share the business and data access layer, thereby solving the biggest issues we talked about earlier: development, testing, and maintenance of the application.

Structure of MVC

Now let's look at the participants in the MVC pattern and their responsibilities. The advantages of this pattern lie in the clear demarcation of the responsibilities between the different components that constitute the pattern.

Table 5.4 summarizes the different entities and their responsibilities based on the discussion so far. We cover this in great detail in Chapter 16.

TABLE 5.4 MVC Pattern Participants

Participant	Responsibility
Model	Abstracts application state, exposing application functionality. This is the heart of the enterprise application.
View	Abstracts presentation. This is responsible for accessing the enterprise data with the help of model and rendering model's contents.
Controller	Abstracts application behavior. The controller, based on user actions, triggers the model updates. There is usually a single controller for each business function.

Applying MVC

The banking system business case (as illustrated in Figure 5.5) can use JSP pages as a view, with servlets as controllers, and Enterprise JavaBeans to represent the model. There are variations to this strategy in which the enterprise architect might decide to use a single servlet as controller (known as the *front* controller). The XYZ Pizza Company is a good candidate for implementing the front controller pattern in which one servlet does the job of the controller and other servlets can serve as models. This enables easier introduction of new client types by simplifying writing a new view and adding some logic into the controller to manage the new view.

Development Methodologies

In most real-world problems, the requirements of a system are never complete at the start of the solution. Customers always want changes to be incorporated during the life cycle of the project development and beyond. This often leads to chaos right through the different phases of the software and continues into production. Methodologies have evolved to discipline the software development process and make software development more manageable, resulting in a predictable solution. But most of the methodologies are heavy in nature and don't solve the problem of software development effectively. Most of the methodologies are predictive in nature (that is, all parts of the software are planned to minute detail), which involves a lot of time. This works fine until the changes to the requirements start rolling into software development. Apart from being predictive, most heavy methodologies are process oriented.

The lightweight methodologies work toward eliminating these deficiencies. In the next section, we go over one of the most popular lightweight methodologies that's evolved in the last few years: extreme programming or XP. Following that, we discuss the Rational Unified Process (RUP) methodology, which might not be categorized as *light*, but answers some of the questions posed by the heavyweight methodologies. RUP is extensive in nature, but at the same time it can be used in parts, too.

Extreme Programming—Core Practices

Extreme programming (XP) was developed in response to the situations mentioned earlier. XP gives an effective solution to all systems in which a change in requirements is a routine affair. XP is adaptive in nature, accepting changes throughout the development life cycle. The foundation of XP is based on the following values: simplicity, communication, feedback, and courage. Based on these four values, the XP outlines 12 core practices for a successful execution of a project. Most of these practices are time tested but are often forgotten. XP makes the most of these core practices by integrating them intelligently. The core practices advocated by XP are as follows:

- Emphasis on teamwork—XP, unlike heavy methodologies, is people oriented rather than process oriented. The emphasis is on every contributor being part of the team, including the customer, who oversees the entire development. The presence of an onsite customer improves communication because he can address the requirement questions as and when they appear.
- Planning game—Also known as the planning *process*, this helps to steer the project to be on time and cost effective. This stage determines what will be achieved and in what timeframe. The planning game may involve multiple plans; that is, a release plan and multiple iteration plans. A release plan may contain the software features to be delivered and the total time for delivering them, whereas a iteration plan outlines short-term goals; that is, those on a weekly or biweekly basis.
- Testing—XP believes in continuous testing for keeping the developed software in a stable condition right through the development stage. It forms the foundation of development and all programmers are responsible for writing test cases for their code. The XP customer defines the acceptance tests that the developers have to take into consideration.

- Small releases—Because iteration planning forms the core of the planning game, it allows XP projects to roll out releases at regular intervals. There are frequent builds, as frequent as daily, through the development life cycle and these builds are also made for the end user.
- Simple design—XP emphasizes a simple design that conforms to current user requirements without much thought about what the customer's future needs would be. XP believes in evolution of the software through refactoring.
- Refactoring—This provides design improvement and accommodating new business requirements, thereby adding business value in every iteration. This is complemented by continuous testing.
- Continuous integration—XP advocates multiple builds during the course of development, and this is made possible by continuous integration of the components developed by the team. This keeps the team in sync and helps developers find out about loose ends between them at a very early stage.
- Metaphor—This is a common vocabulary for system names for effective communication within the team.
- Code ownership—There's no single owner for a piece of code and more than one programmer is aware of every single piece of code. This enables changes to be incorporated at the earliest possible time without waiting for the original developer.
- Pair programming—XP advocates using two programmers for developing a business function. This improves every facet of the development life cycle—better design, better testing, and better code.
- Coding standard—This facilitates easier development and maintenance. It complements collective code ownership.
- No overworking—XP emphasizes regular working hours over a long period of time, which sustains the same zeal in the entire development effort.

As you can see, some of the steps have been adapted from other methodologies. The software evolves through the many steps, relying on simple design and improvements through the many cycles of re-factoring and adding business value in every iteration. This helps to build a very disciplined and adaptive design methodology for complex enterprise problems.

TIP

The disciplined approach has been well adapted by the J2EE development community. The Java community has developed tools through community processes that have aided the J2EE application development. Some of the tools are

- Ant (`http://jakarta.apache.org/ant/`). This is an XML-based open source utility that aids in continuous integration.
- EJBgen (EJB component classes generator shipped with WebLogic Server). It also comes with several other utilities that aid in development and deployment.
- JUnit (`http://www.junit.org/`). This is a unit-testing tool.
- JMeter (`http://jakarta.apache.org/jmeter/`). This is for doing performance testing.

Rational Unified Process

The Rational Unified Process (RUP), as its name suggests, was developed at Rational. It complements the Unified Modeling Language (UML). This process is a framework that can be used to model different processes that constitute the software system. Table 5.5 lists the fundamental workflow processes that govern the RUP.

TABLE 5.5 RUP Workflow Processes

Process	Description
Business Modeling	Understanding the business needs
Requirements	Translating the business needs identified into well-defined requirements that identify a possible software system
Analysis and Design	Translating the requirements into a system architecture
Implementation	Translating the design into software that conforms to the requirements
Testing	Validating the software against the requirements
Configuration Management	Maintaining versions of the different elements that constitute the software solution
Project Management	Managing the different teams through the development life cycle
Environment	Runtime environment maintenance
Deployment	Rolling out the software for production use

These processes are not governed by time. They extend during the different phases of the project. RUP defines four phases through which the processes in Table 5.5 are executed. The phases identified by the RUP are

- Inception—Determines the project objectives
- Elaboration—Helps in a complete understanding of the problem at hand
- Construction—Builds software artifacts
- Transition—Adds improvements to the developed software

RUP helps manage projects through the many iterations of the processes listed in Table 5.5 from inception to the transition phase. The four phases help to define milestones during the software development and also define a boundary for producing different artifacts. The biggest advantage of this process is its capability to respond to changes in the business needs.

RUP, similar to XP, provides an excellent process framework for developing J2EE applications. For a detailed discussion of RUP and the tool support for incorporating in WebLogic Server development, refer to the Web site `http://www.rational.com/products/rup/index.jsp`.

Summary

In this chapter, we looked at some of the basic concepts governing an n-tier application and possible architectural options for solving a complex enterprise problem. We also covered what WebLogic Server, as a J2EE-compliant application server, provides for solving the various problems software architects face in the age of the Internet economy. We covered one of the most common design techniques used in J2EE applications: UML. Finally, we covered some of the effective methodologies for designing an effective J2EE solution.

PART II

WebLogic Server Web Applications

IN THIS PART

CHAPTER 6

Introduction to WebLogic Web Applications

IN THIS CHAPTER

- Web Applications Defined
- Web Applications and Request-Response Model
- Creating a Web Application

By Saranathan Govindarajan

The J2EE application model supported by the associated specifications as part of the J2EE platform provides an architecture that enables designing scalable, maintainable, *n*-tier applications. The application model helps to overcome the traditional problems that arise from the complexities involved in developing and deploying multitier applications and simultaneously leveraging the benefits of *n*-tier applications; for example, scalability, manageability. In this chapter, we take a first look at one of the main J2EE component: Web applications. We start with defining what Web applications are. We then cover some basic elements of a Web application and its runtime environment: the Web container. We then move on to the relationship of Web applications to the request-response model. Finally, we look at the development strategy for creating and configuring a simple Web application. All components of the J2EE platform, including Web applications, are well supported by specifications for development and deployment of the related components.

Web Applications Defined

Web applications were originally introduced in the Servlet 2.2 specification, and are currently defined as follows by the Servlet 2.3 specification:

"A Web application is a collection of servlets, HTML pages, classes, and other resources that make up a complete application on a Web server."

In other terms, a Web application is usually the layer between the Web client and the business layer, and acts as a bridge between them by passing the user requests to the business components and the processed response to the Web client.

A typical Web application consists of one or more of the following components:

- Servlets—Read the input and perform simple operations, such as login and logout
- JavaServer Pages—Used as presentation components
- Static resources—HTML pages, graphics, CSS and JavaScript files
- Utility and helper classes—For example, might include JavaBeans that can be used in the JSPs
- Libraries—For example, Java classes bundled together as a JAR file that make up the tag library that contains the custom JSP tags
- Any client-related classes, such as applets

Apart from the preceding components, a Web application contains configuration files containing the metadata that describes the application.

The clients to Web-based applications are categorized as *thin* clients, as opposed to traditional application clients, which are characterized as *fat* clients. In a traditional application, such as a three-tier application framework, the client layer is responsible for user interaction as well as some of the application logic, which makes it fat. In a Web-based application, the client is driven from within a browser that manages the user interaction in a way similar to that of the fat clients, but the application logic is completely embedded in the server components that make up the Web applications defined earlier.

The Web client user interface is usually defined using HTML, variations of it (for example, DHTML), or an XML/XSL combination. There are clearly defined protocols for data exchange between the client layer and the Web application, depending on the server components serving the client requests. But the most popular and widely used protocol is the HTTP/HTTPS protocol. HTTPS is a secure flavor of HTTP protocol for information exchange between Web applications (for example, servlets and JSP) and Web clients. Before we look at some of the key elements of the Web application, let's look at the environment in which Web applications run.

Web Container

The J2EE platform provides the necessary infrastructure for servicing client requests. These client requests might come from traditional clients or from Web clients. An application server such as WebLogic Server, providing the J2EE infrastructure, has one or more of the specific runtime environments that form the core of the product. These runtime environments are responsible for providing the services necessary for the different J2EE components such as servlets and EJBs. These are called *containers*. The most important of them are the Web container for Web applications and the EJB container for Enterprise JavaBeans. Figure 6.1 gives an idea of what each of the runtime environments hosts and the type of client requests they handle.

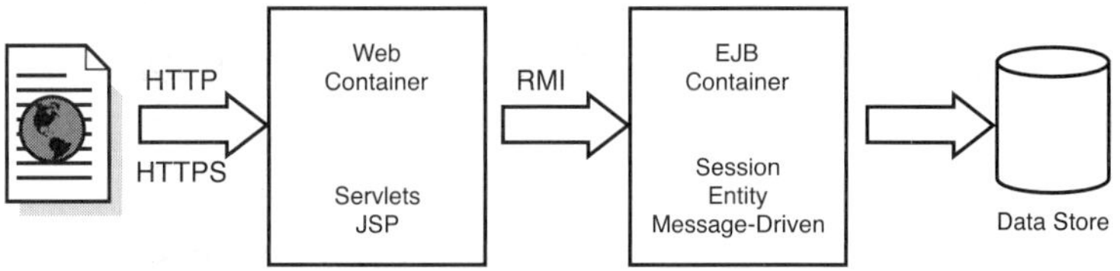

FIGURE 6.1 Anatomy of an application server.

Let's look at the need for these containers and benefit they offer to the components running within their environment. One of the fundamental goals of the J2EE application server framework is to provide the basic operating environment for all applications running within it. In other words, a business application such as an airline reservation system should concentrate on providing the business functions necessary to run the business, such as reservation, cancellation, flight status, and so on. Such an application should not be worried about transaction and state management, resource pooling, and other services. These services are common to most business applications. The different containers that are bundled as part of the application server provide the operating environment. Now let's look at the basic services offered by the Web container that is the runtime environment for the Web applications.

6

Web Container Services

The Web container is the interface between the J2EE components, such as servlets, and the low-level, platform-dependent functionality that's needed for the execution of the business function embedded in the component. There are certain rules of engagement for the container to provide the services to these components. The components are bundled into a well-defined package as specified by the J2EE specification and deployed into the Web container. The package contains application code as well as J2EE and vendor-specific configuration files that describe the application. The configuration parameters that are described using the XML-based configuration files specify certain container settings for every Web component and also specify settings for the Web application in totality. In short, these container settings help configure the basic support provided by the J2EE server as needed by the Web application. The support includes providing services such as security, transaction, JNDI lookup, and external resource mapping, to name a few.

A host of configurable services makes the life of the application deployer much easier. In most cases, a Web application can be deployed to heterogeneous environments with changes only to the configuration. For example, a Web component might have relaxed security settings in the development environment, whereas this would have to change when it's rolled into a production environment. Alternatively, the requirements might include that the application allow for a certain level of access to database data in one production environment and another level of database access in another production environment. All these are possible without change in the underlying application code with the help of the configuration files and the basic services offered by the container.

Let's look at the some of benefits that the WebLogic Server offers for the Web container:

- The WebLogic Server security model helps the application deployer to secure the Web component so that the application and system resources are available only for the authorized users.
- In accordance with the J2EE specifications, WebLogic Server also provides a unified access to the naming and directory services that enable Web components to access other enterprise components, such as EJBs, through the JNDI APIs.
- In addition to the configurable services, some of which we touched on, WebLogic Server also manages some non-configurable services such as servlet/JSP life cycle, access to the J2EE platform APIs related to all Web components, and so on.

Web Application Components

As mentioned earlier in the chapter, the components that make up a Web application include servlets, JavaServer Pages, and their associated libraries and classes; specifically, the JSP tag library, JavaBeans, and so on. Let's look at each of these components in detail:

- Servlets—These are Java classes that interact with Web clients to access server-side applications and that also can generate dynamic pages, thereby serving as an efficient server-side functional extension.
- JSP (JavaServer Pages)—It is the enabling technology that enables you to combine the power of static HTML with dynamically generated content. JSPs enable the embedding of Java code in regular HTML-based Web pages. Additionally, JSP specifications allow for defining custom tags driven by Java classes called as taglibs, thereby enabling the encapsulation of complex server-side logic into simple tags that can be used in the JSP pages.

NOTE

We'll have a detailed discussion of the development of each of the preceding elements in Part IV, "Using Web Technologies in WebLogic Applications."

- JavaBeans—An API standard defined for Java classes, JavaBeans is one of the key technologies used in JSP and forms a part of the Web application. This concept is covered in detail in Chapter 16, "JavaBeans and Model-View-Controller (MVC) Architecture." For further information, look at `http://java.sun.com/beans/docs/`.

Web Application Configuration

Apart from one or more of the key components, a Web application contains configuration-related information in a set of XML files that describes the Web application. These configuration files contain entries that are used by the Web container to provide the configurable services needed by the application, such as security and so on.

- `Web.xml`—This is the Web application deployment descriptor that describes the contents of the Web application defined by J2EE standard as part of the specifications.
- `Weblogic.xml`—This configuration file contains WebLogic Server–specific elements that describe the Web applications.

The configuration elements of `web.xml` are governed by the DTD (`http://java.sun.com/dtd/web-app_2_3.dtd`) defined as part of the J2EE Servlet Specification (V 2.3). The elements defined in `web.xml` can be grouped into the following types:

- Servlet definitions—Defines the logical name for the servlet/JSP that maps to the implementing class
- Servlet/JSP mappings—Help the Web container to map Web client requests to the corresponding servlet by using a defined URL pattern.
- JSP tag library definition.
- `ServletContext` parameters—Initialization parameters.
- Session configuration.
- Default welcome page for the Web application. For example, `index.html` and `index.htm`.
- Error pages for defined error code or exception types.
- Security-related parameters.
- Filters and filter mappings that define the filter resources and filters that must be applied for the request types, respectively.

NOTE

Similar to `web.xml`, the configuration elements of `weblogic.xml` are controlled by the following DTD `http://www.bea.com/servers/wls810/dtd/weblogic810-web-jar.dtd`.

Some of the most important elements defined in `weblogic.xml` are

- The session descriptor, which defines servlet session-related parameters such as URL rewriting and cookie parameters
- The JSP descriptor, which defines the compile options for the JSP such as the compile command, flags, pre-compiler, and working directory
- The security role assignment for the security options defined in `web.xml`
- The reference descriptors that define the resources referenced in the Web application

Figure 6.2 summarizes the discussion in this section and also touches on the deployment descriptors that make up the Web application.

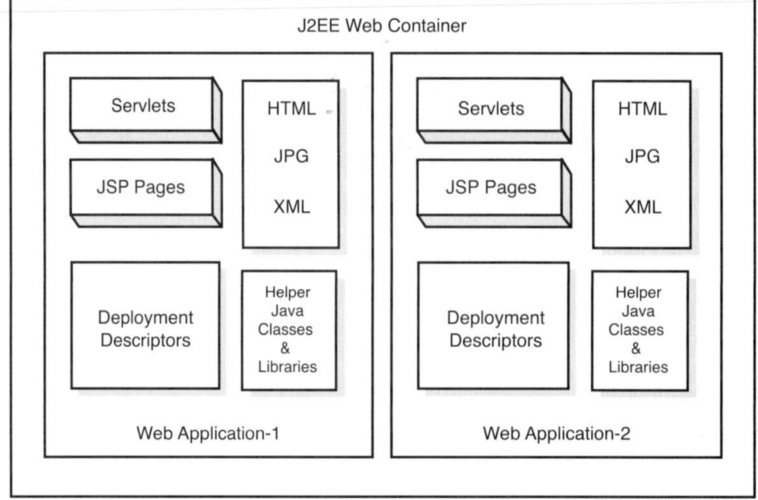

FIGURE 6.2 Web application and containers.

In Figure 6.2, Web Application-1 and Web Application-2 represent two distinct applications that may be based on functionality, for example. In an airline reservation system, one Web application could cater to administrative functions executed by supervisors and another Web application could be related to customer-centric functions such as reservations, and so forth. As you can see from Figure 6.2, Web components are building blocks of all Web applications. The supporting cast for these applications includes other Java classes and static documents that can be in HTML and JPG file formats.

Web Applications and Request-Response Model

One of the most important concepts for understanding Web applications is to know how the client's request is processed and how responses are produced as the client needs it. When we covered the important components of the Web application earlier in the chapter, we learned that the J2EE platform provides multiple flavors of servlets to cater to different protocols. One of the most popular and widely used servlet types in the Web application model is based on the HTTP protocol. The Servlet specification provides the necessary infrastructure in terms of APIs and other services for implementing this type of servlet. We'll use this servlet type to understand the request-response model as implemented for Web applications and different parties involved in making this client-server conversation happen. We don't have to know much about the classes and APIs that make up the servlet infrastructure at this time. We'll go into that when we get to Chapter 14, "Writing WebLogic Server Servlets."

The different parties involved in the HTTP-based request response model are as follows:

- The Web browser that provides the runtime environment for the Web client
- The Web server that listens to the incoming requests from different clients and also has the responsibility of serving some static resources, such as HTML pages
- The application server with a Web container built into it
- The Web applications that include components as described in Figure 6.2

Figure 6.3 describes the entire request-response cycle in HTTP-based servlets. With the help of Figure 6.3, let's look at the steps involved.

- The Web browser sends the client request to the Web server.
- The Web server sorts out the requests, identifies the ones that have to be serviced by a business Web application, and passes them on to the Web container. The Web server itself services some other requests by delivering some static resources, such as HTML pages, to the client.
- The Web container determines the Web component to invoke based on the deployment information and the input request. The Web component invoked may be a servlet, JSP, or a static resource.

- The Web container passes objects that map to the Web client request and response streams for use by the invoked component. The request stream is used to get the parameters from the user, and the response stream is used to pass the formatted response back to the client.

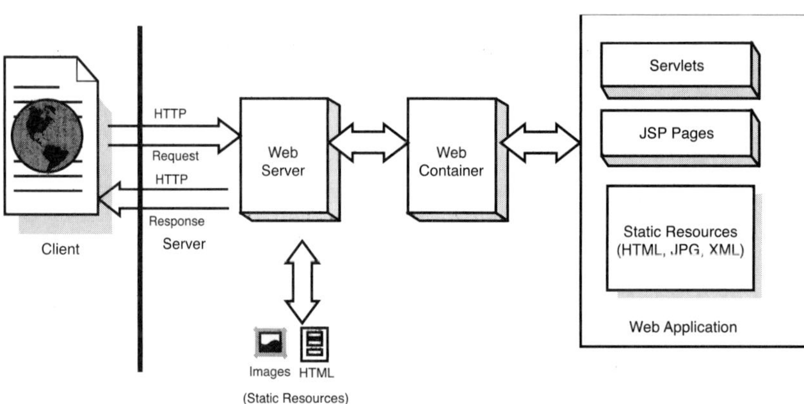

FIGURE 6.3 Request-response model.

The Web server and the application server containing the Web applications need not be different processes. In the case of WebLogic Server, it serves as the Web server and as a J2EE-compliant application server with a built-in Web and EJB container, among other features. The Web browser is the most common client for Web applications, but the user is free to access the Web applications from other client types, including PDA, mobile, and so on. The Web application component should be enabled to deliver the response according to the client that sent the request.

Creating a Web Application

So far, we've gone through the essentials of a Web application and how client requests are processed. Now let's go over some of the development strategies and common concepts that encompass Web application development. As with most application development, Web application development can also be categorized into multiple stages as described in Figure 6.4. The life cycle described in Figure 6.4 looks similar to the classic spiral model of software development. There are distinct outputs from each of the steps described. Let's look at some of the important artifacts that are produced as part of the Web application development process. We already mentioned some of the elements that make up the Web application in the previous section.

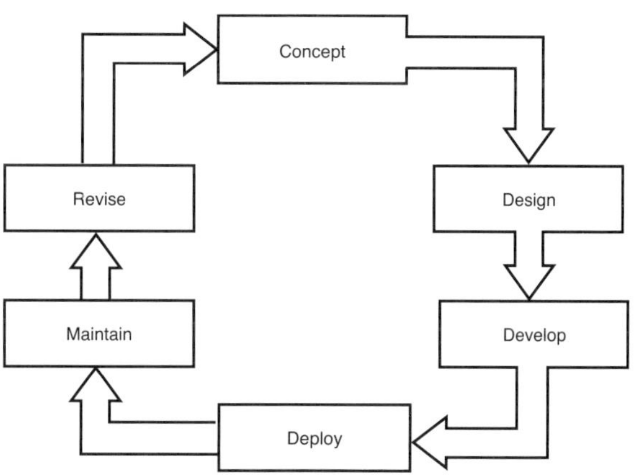

FIGURE 6.4 Web application development life cycle.

Development Life Cycle

The conceptual and design phase are similar to any application development, and Web application development is no different. The artifacts of these phases include UML diagrams (as covered in Chapter 5, "Enterprise Application Design with WebLogic Server") and user specifications document. The artifacts of the development include static resources (such as images, HTML, and so forth) that make up the Web application as well as servlets and JSPs. We'll look at developing these components in detail later in the book when we cover servlets and JSP in detail.

But before we go into the deployment phase of the development life cycle, we need to take a look at the special packaging needs of Web applications.

WEB APPLICATION PACKAGING

The Servlet specifications define the directory structure for organizing the elements of a Web application. The directory structure is hierarchical in nature. Most Web servers, including WebLogic Server, implement the specification in this regard even though it isn't a required format but is merely a recommended format. The following directory listing explains the directory structure for a Web application:

```
/defaultWebApp (document/context root)
  jsps(subdirectories as needed)
  htmls      "
  etc.      "
   /WEB-INF
    web.xml
```

```
weblogic.xml
/classes
 servlets and
 supporting java classes
/lib
 supporting java classes in a jar file
```

The root of the directory structure hierarchy is called the *document root* for the Web application. For example, in the Web application defined as part of the default WebLogic domain, `mydomain`, the document root is `defaultWebApp`. The document root (also known as the *context path*) of an application defines the URL namespace for the Web application components; that is, the servlets, static pages, and so on. WebLogic Server does not allow duplicate Web application names in the same WebLogic Server instance. All static files, such as images and welcome files (for example, `index.html`), must be placed somewhere under the document root.

Alternatively, static files can be placed in directories under the document root. As a convention, images are placed under a subdirectory (for example, `\images`) in the same level as of that of the `\WEB-INF` directory. The files can be referred to using the relative path with respect to the document root in the referenced files. All files under the document root (except for the special directory `WEB-INF`) are public and will be served to the clients. Although the files under `WEB_INF/` aren't accessible for the client, the servlets in the Web application can get access to these using the servlet context-related API. We'll cover that when we discuss servlets in detail in Chapter 14. The Web application can take advantage of this restricted access and use the `WEB-INF` directory to store application-specific files that aren't served to the client but must be accessed from the servlets. The `WEB-INF/classes` directory contains the classes used by the Web application; for example, servlet, helper, and utility classes. The `WEB-INF/lib` directory contains the archived class files (JAR files) that contain other helper classes and utility classes. For example, this directory can contain the custom tag libraries.

The following listing is a partial listing of the examples Web application that is packaged along with WebLogic Server:

```
examplesWebApp\index.jsp
examplesWebApp\SurveyExample.html
examplesWebApp\images\built_on_bea.gif
examplesWebApp\WEB-INF\web.xml
examplesWebApp\WEB-INF\weblogic.xml
examplesWebApp\WEB-INF\classes\examples\servlets\HelloWorldServlet.class
examplesWebApp\WEB-INF\classes\lib\utils_common.jar
```

If a Web application is packaged and deployed in the recommended format as described here, it can be ported to any other J2EE-compliant server with little or no modifications. In the case of `examplesWebApp` described earlier, `weblogic.xml` must be converted to another J2EE-compliant application server format.

Web application can be deployed on the target J2EE server (for example, WebLogic Server) using different techniques depending on the application development phase (that is, development and testing) and requirement of the Web application. Because the source code undergoes frequent changes during the development phase, the Web application can be deployed in an exploded directory format that follows the directory structure listed earlier. Alternatively, all components of Web application can be bundled into a single unit, known as a *Web application archive* file (WAR), and deployed to the server. Alternatively, Web applications can be packaged into a Web Archive format (war) file. A WAR file is a JAR file that contains a Web application with the same content as the exploded directory. Enterprise archive file deployment provides another option for deploying Web applications in conjunction with other J2EE applications that include EJBs and other Web applications. In the next chapter, we'll take a detailed look at creating WAR and EAR files using the different tools available and deploying them to the WebLogic Server environment.

The last phases in the development life cycle are to make sure that the application conforms to the business requirements. Additionally, these phases can be used to tune the Web application as well as it works in unison with other components of the business application.

Development Strategy

As described in Figure 6.4, building a deployable Web application involves multiple steps, and it's possible for different resource groups to work in tandem to complete a Web application. Figure 6.4 indicates the steps involved in development of the Web application, but does not tell you about the optimal way of going about implementing the different life-cycle processes. In this section, we look at an efficient way of accomplishing each of those tasks. The elements that form the Web application defined earlier, along with the development life cycle, help to define the roles of the Web application developer. The development roles and the corresponding functions can be defined as follows:

- Web design—Web designers create the static HTML pages and the images required for the Web application.
- Java development—Java developers create the servlet classes and the tag library associated with the JSPs. Along with the Web designers, developers are involved in the development of JSPs.

The development tasks defined earlier can be carried out in parallel. After the development is done, the application must be assembled to conform to the specifications.

- Configuration—The configuration files `web.xml` (contains the servlet mapping) and `weblogic.xml` (if needed) have to be written or generated using the tools such as WebLogic Builder, which is described in the next chapter.
- Application assembly—Application assemblers place the compiled sources, along with configuration files (`web.xml` and `weblogic.xml`), in the directory structure described

- Packaging—The packager bundles the Web application into a Web archive (WAR format). If the Web application forms a part of an enterprise application, it can added to an enterprise archive (EAR format).
- Deployment—The packaged Web application is deployed to WebLogic Server.

Figure 6.5 summarizes the steps involved in the creation of a Web application.

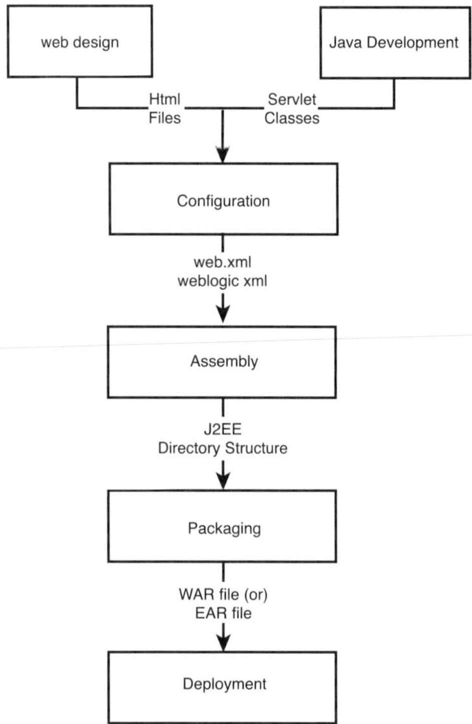

FIGURE 6.5 Web application role-based development.

Configuring Web Applications

Earlier in the chapter, we took a brief look at the configuration elements (that is, `web.xml` and `weblogic.xml`) associated with the Web application. Let's look at configuring a simple Web application (zoo) that maintains animal groups based on the type of food each group eats. The Web application contains the carnivores and herbivores servlets to handle the different types of animals. The zoo Web application is organized in the same structure as described earlier for `examplesWebApp`.

Listing 6.1 describes the whole simple Web deployment descriptor describing the zoo web application. This provides a working example of how the tags defined in Table 6.1 are used in `web.xml`.

LISTING 6.1 Zoo Web Application—web.xml

```
<?xml version="1.0" ?>
<!DOCTYPE web-app PUBLIC "-//Sun Microsystems, Inc.//DTD Web Application 2.3//EN"
"http://java.sun.com/dtd/web-app_2_3.dtd">
<web-app>
<welcome-file-list>
 <welcome-file>index.jsp</welcome-file>
</welcome-file-list>
<error-page>
 <exception-type>
  wlsunleashed.zoo.exception.AnimalNotFoundException
  </exception-type>
  <location>animalNotFound.jsp</location>
 </error-page>
 <servlet>
  <servlet-name> carnivores </servlet-name>
  <servlet-class> wlsunleashed.zoo.CarnivoresServlet </servlet-class>
  <init-param>
   <param-name>KingOftheZoo</param-name>
   <param-value>lion</param-value>
  </init-param>
 </servlet>
 <servlet>
  <servlet-name> herbivores </servlet-name>
  <servlet-class> wlsunleashed.zoo.HerbivoresServlet</servlet-class>
  <init-param>
   <param-name>StapleDiet</param-name>
   <param-value>grass</param-value>
  </init-param>
 </servlet>
  <servlet-mapping>
  <servlet-name>carnivores</servlet-name>
  <url-pattern>/carnivores/*</url-pattern>
 </servlet-mapping>
<servlet-mapping>
  <servlet-name>herbivores</servlet-name>
  <url-pattern>/herbivores/*</url-pattern>
 </servlet-mapping>
```

LISTING 6.1 Continued

```
39<servlet-mapping>
40   <servlet-name>carnivores</servlet-name>
41   <url-pattern>/king</url-pattern>
42 </servlet-mapping>
43 <servlet-mapping>
44   <servlet-name>herbivores</servlet-name>
45   <url-pattern>/mammals</url-pattern>
46 </servlet-mapping>
47 <servlet-mapping>
48   <servlet-name>carnivores</servlet-name>
49   <url-pattern>/cats</url-pattern>
50 </servlet-mapping>
51 <servlet-mapping>
52   <servlet-name>carnivores</servlet-name>
53   <url-pattern>/mammals/*<url-pattern>
54 </servlet-mapping>
55 </web-app>
```

The main elements in Listing 6.1 are the <servlet> and <servlet-mapping> tags. Lines 15 to 22 define a <servlet> tag for specifying the logical name mapping for wlsunleashed.zoo.CarnivoresServlet. They also define the initialization parameters for this servlet. Similarly, lines 23 to 30 define the logical name mapping for wlsunleashed.zoo.HerbivoresServlet. The logical names defined by the <servlet-name> along with the <servlet-mapping> elements (lines 31–54) are the key to accessing servlets in a Web application. The servlet-mapping element helps to identify URL requests based on a pattern to a mapped servlet. Now we need to understand how these tag values (servlet and servlet-mapping) are used in responding to a client request. Table 6.1 helps to understand the servlet mapping better for the configuration shown in Listing 6.1.

ACCESSING WEB APPLICATIONS COMPONENTS

The Servlet specifications define the URL pattern to use for accessing servlets defined in a Web application. Let's consider CarnivoresServlet of the zoo Web application. To access this servlet from a Web browser, we use the following URL:

```
http://zoo:7001/zooWebApp/carnivores
```

The URL corresponds to the following pattern:

```
http://machineName:portno/webapp/mapping/resourcename
```

where

- *machineName* is the name of the machine where the WebLogic Server is running; for example, localhost.
- *portno* is port at which the WebLogic Server is listening, usually 7001

- *webapp* is the Web application name or the context root
- *resourcename* is the name of the servlet or JSP as defined in the Web deployment descriptor. Alternatively, the resource name can be divided into the following components: *servletpath/pathinfo* (where *servletpath* is the servlet that's mapped to a servlet path) and *pathinfo* (which is the remaining portion of the URL). Resources can also be static files such as HTML and graphics.

TABLE 6.1 Servlet Mapping Rules

URL Pattern	Servlet
http://zooserver:7001/zoo/mammals	Herbivores
http://zooserver:7001/zoo/mammals/lion	Carnivores
http://zooserver:7001/zoo/king	Carnivores
http://zooserver:7001/zoo/cats	Carnivores

In addition to the servlet configuration, we must configure the JSP-specific configuration parameters related to WebLogic Server in the WebLogic-specific deployment descriptor briefly described earlier in the chapter. Listing 6.2 describes the simple `weblogic.xml` file that defines the basic JSP specific elements such as the compile command, working directory, and so on.

LISTING 6.2 Zoo Web Application—weblogic.xml

```
<!DOCTYPE weblogic-web-app PUBLIC "-//BEA
Systems, Inc.//DTD Web Application 7.0//EN"
"http://www.bea.com/servers/wls810/dtd/weblogic810-web-jar.dtd">

<weblogic-web-app>
   <jsp-descriptor>
    <jsp-param>
     <param-name>
      pageCheckSeconds
     </param-name>
     <param-value>
      30
     </param-value>
    </jsp-param>
    <jsp-param>
     <param-name>
      compileCommand
     </param-name>
     <param-value>
      javac
```

6

LISTING 6.2 Continued

```
      </param-value>
    </jsp-param>
  </jsp-descriptor>
</weblogic-web-app>
```

The `pagecheckseconds` defined as a JSP `param` tag instructs the Web container to check for the changes in the JSP file every 30 seconds. Listing 6.2 lists only some of the settings that can be defined as `<jsp-param>` element. For a full list of elements, refer to the following URL: `http://edocs.bea.com/wls/docs81/webapp/weblogic_xml.html`.

Summary

In this chapter, we discussed the basics of a Web application including the definition of a Web application and had a short discussion of the key elements that make up a Web application: servlets, JSP, `web.xml`, and so on. This is just the tip of the iceberg; we dive deep into the intricacies of the different elements that make up Web applications later in the book. Servlets and JSP development, along with tag libraries, are covered in great detail in Part IV, "Using Web Technologies in WebLogic Applications." Web application packaging and deployment are dealt with in detail in the next chapter.

CHAPTER 7

Deploying Web Applications

by Malcolm Garland

IN THIS CHAPTER

- Application Packaging and Predeployment
- Methods of Deploying Applications
- Deployment Issues with WebLogic Server
- Deployment Best Practices

All components developed for WebLogic Server must be executed within the greater context of a J2EE application. This chapter covers deploying applications on WebLogic Server. Application packaging, deployment, deployment issues, and WebLogic deployment tools are discussed.

Application Packaging and Predeployment

Deployment is the process of placing and activating applications within WebLogic Server or cluster configurations. Prior to deployment, applications must be packaged. Packaging entails staging, creating deployment descriptors, and archiving the application. We'll discuss packaging Web and enterprise applications.

Packaging Web Applications

As detailed in Chapter 6, "Introduction to WebLogic Web Applications," Web applications are packaged within WAR files. WAR files are created using the Java archive utility `jar` command and designating a `.war` extension for the archive. WAR files contain all files necessary to execute the Web application, which may include JSP(s), JSP tag libraries, servlets (see Chapter 14, "Writing WebLogic Server Servlets," for details on servlet registrations), other supporting Java classes, HTML(s), image files, and so on. To package a Web application, you must assemble the target application files (HTMLs,

JSPs, servlets, and so forth) within a staging directory. All servlets and supporting Java class files should be marshaled under the Web application's `WEB-INF/classes` directory. JSP and HTML files are placed within the applications top-level staging directory. The Web application's deployment descriptors must be created and placed under the directory `WEB-INF`, as shown here:

```
/WebAppName (staging directory)
  JSP(s) (subdirectories allowed)
  HTML(s)       "
  images        "
  non-Java files  "
 /WEB_INF
  web.xml
  weblogic.xml
  /Classes
    Servlets
    Other Java Classes
  /lib
    JSP Tag Libraries
```

There are two deployment descriptors for a Web application: `web.xml` and `weblogic.xml`. The `web.xml` is the J2EE standard for defining a Web application. This descriptor defines non-server-specific items such as servlet mappings, deployment-time attributes, context parameters, filters, filter mappings, listeners, MIME mappings, welcome pages, error pages, JSP tag libraries mappings, security, and other non-server-specific items. A partial listing of a `web.xml` that can be used for the global auctions application is shown in Listing 7.1.

LISTING 7.1 Partial Web.xml

```
<?xml version="1.0" ?>
<!DOCTYPE web-app PUBLIC "-//Sun Microsystems, Inc.//DTD Web
➥Application 2.3//EN" "http://java.sun.com/dtd/web-app_2_3.dtd">
<web-app>
 <welcome-file-list>
  <welcome-file>index.jsp</welcome-file>
 </welcome-file-list>

 <servlet>
  <servlet-name>FindItemsServlet</servlet-name>
  <servlet-class>com.gams.servlets.system.FindItemsServlet</servlet
➥-class>
 </servlet>
```

LISTING 7.1 Continued

```
<security-constraint>
 <web-resource-collection>
 <web-resource-name>MySecureBit0</web-resource-name>
  <url-pattern>/AdminRequestProcessor</url-pattern>
  <http-method>GET</http-method>
  <http-method>POST</http-method>
 </web-resource-collection>
 <auth-constraint>
  <role-name>administrator</role-name>
 </auth-constraint>
 <user-data-constraint>
  <transport-guarantee>NONE</transport-guarantee>
 </user-data-constraint>
</security-constraint>

<login-config>
 <auth-method>FORM</auth-method>
 <realm-name>default</realm-name>
 <form-login-config>
  <form-login-page>/login.jsp</form-login-page>
  <form-error-page>/error.jsp</form-error-page>
 </form-login-config>
</login-config>

<security-role>
 <role-name>administrator</role-name>
</security-role>

<ejb-ref>
 <ejb-ref-name>ejb/opcadminfacade</ejb-ref-name>
 <ejb-ref-type>Session</ejb-ref-type>
 <home>com.sun.j2ee.blueprints.opc.admin.ejb.OPCAdminFacadeHome</home>
 <remote>com.sun.j2ee.blueprints.opc.admin.ejb.OPCAdminFacade</remote>
</ejb-ref>
...
<taglib>
 <taglib-uri>
  itemDisplay.tld
 </taglib-uri>
 <taglib-location>
   /WEB-INF/lib/itemDisplay-tags.jar
```

7

LISTING 7.1 Continued

```
   </taglib-location>
 </taglib>
</web-app>
```

The `weblogic.xml` deployment descriptor contains WebLogic-specific connectivity items such as HTTP session or cookie parameters, JSP parameters, resource references (for `DataSources`, EJBs, security realm), security role assignments, character set mappings, and container attributes. A partial listing of a `weblogic.xml` that can be used for the global auctions application is shown in Listing 7.2.

LISTING 7.2 Partial `Weblogic.xml`

```
<!DOCTYPE weblogic-web-app PUBLIC "-//BEA
Systems, Inc.//DTD Web Application 7.0//EN"
"http://www.bea.com/servers/wls700/dtd/weblogic700-web-jar.dtd">

<weblogic-web-app>
 <description>WebLogic Descriptor</description>
  <security-role-assignment>
  <role-name>administrator</role-name>
  <principal-name>admin</principal-name>
 </security-role-assignment>
 <session-descriptor>
  <session-param>
   <param-name>PersistentStoreType</param-name>
   <param-value>replicated</param-value>
  </session-param>
 </session-descriptor>
 <reference-descriptor>
  <ejb-reference-description>
   <ejb-ref-name>ejb/opcadminfacade</ejb-ref-name>
    <jndi-name>ejb/remote/opcApplication/opcadminfacade</jndi-name>
  </ejb-reference-description>
 </reference-descriptor>
 <jsp-descriptor>
   <jsp-param>
    <param-name>
     pageCheckSeconds
    </param-name>
    <param-value>
     1
    </param-value>
```

LISTING 7.2 Continued

```
    </jsp-param>
    <jsp-param>
     <param-name>
      verbose
     </param-name>
     <param-value>
      true
     </param-value>
    </jsp-param>
  </jsp-descriptor>
</weblogic-web-app>
```

After the Web application's files are properly arrayed, the application should be archived within a WAR (Web Archive) file, as shown here:

```
$ jar cv0f gams.war *.html *.jsp WEB-INF
```

Note the `0` option in the preceding line. Some HTMLs or JSPs might not function if compressed.

Packaging Enterprise Applications

Enterprise applications contain Web modules, Web applications, EJBs (see Chapter 20, "Enterprise JavaBeans and WebLogic Server," for information on packaging EJBs), and other Web modules and files required to execute the enterprise-level application. To package an enterprise application, you must assemble the target application files (WAR files, EJB JAR files, deployment descriptor, and so on) within a staging directory. The enterprise application's deployment descriptor must be created and placed under directory `META-INF`, as shown here:

```
/EntAppName (staging directory)
  EJB.jar
  WebApp.war
  /APP-INF
   SharedFiles.jar
  /META_INF
   application.xml
   weblogic-application.xml
```

> **NOTE**
>
> If your Web application accesses EJBs using local interfaces, you must package the modules (Web app and EJB) within the same EAR file.

There are two deployment descriptors for an enterprise application: `weblogic-application.xml` and `application.xml`. The `weblogic-application.xml` specifies WebLogic-specific application deployment information, such as classpath hierarchies, which are discussed later within this section. The `application.xml` file is the J2EE standard for identifying modules and defining security roles to be used within the enterprise application. A sample listing of an `application.xml` file that can be used for the global auctions application is shown in Listing 7.3.

LISTING 7.3 Sample application.xml

```
<?xml version="1.0" encoding="UTF-8"?>

<!DOCTYPE application PUBLIC '-//Sun Microsystems, Inc.//DTD J2EE
➥Application 1.3//EN' 'http://java.sun.com/dtd/application_1_3.dtd'>

<application>
 <display-name>gams</display-name>
 <description>Global Auctions Management Systems</description>
 <module>
  <ejb>customer.jar</ejb>
 </module>
  <module>
   <ejb>item.jar</ejb>
 </module>
  <module>
   <ejb>processbid.jar</ejb>
 </module>
 <module>
  <web>
   <web-uri>gams.war</web-uri>
   <context-root>gams</context-root>
  </web>
 </module>
 <security-role>
  <role-name>administrator</role-name>
 </security-role>
</application>
```

After the enterprise application's files are properly arrayed, the application should be archived within an EAR (Enterprise Archive) file, as shown here:

```
$ jar cv0f gams.ear *.war *.jar META-INF
```

In reference to deploying enterprise applications on WebLogic Server: To facilitate hot deployments, WebLogic uses separate class loaders for Web modules deployed within the enterprise application. Therefore, individual Web components cannot see each other's class files. If your Web components (modules) are using the same files, there are three general strategies to employ using WebLogic Server 8.1:

- Place the common or shared files within an archive (JAR file) at the enterprise application level, within `APP-INF/lib`. Any archives placed here are automatically added to the application's classpath, which is visible to all application modules (see `item_A.ear`—included in your distribution).
- Place the common or shared files within an archive at the enterprise application level. You must reference that archive within the manifest files of the application module archives. For example, within our example GAMS application, we have a Web application (`item.war`) that uses some of the same classes that an EJB module (`item.jar`) does. To avoid class loader/classpath issues, we've moved the common files from each module and placed these files within a shared JAR file called `itemUtil.jar`. This file is placed under the enterprise application root directory. Then the `manifest.mf` file of each module's archive is updated to reference the shared JAR file, using its `Class-Path` attribute as shown here:

  ```
  Class-Path: itemUtil.jar
  ```

  To execute this update, place the `Class-Path` reference within a text file. Then, using the `jar` command, execute the following command:

  ```
  $jar umf myTextFile WebApp.war (or EJB.jar)
  ```

  The target module's archive manifest file will be updated with the classpath attribute. This should be done to all enterprise application modules that use any of the common files (see `item_B.ear`—included in your distribution).
- Define a `classloader`-structure within the application's `weblogic-application.xml`. The following `classloader`-structure (an excerpt from `weblogic-application.xml`) will make our utility JAR, `itemUtil.jar`, available to all modules within our item application (`item.jar` and `item.war`):

  ```
  <classloader-structure>
   <module-ref>
    <module-uri>itemUtil.jar</module-uri>
   </module-ref>
   <classloader-structure>
    <module-ref>
     <module-uri>item.jar</module-uri>
    </module-ref>
    <module-ref>
  ```

7

```
      <module-uri>item.war</module-uri>
    </module-ref>
  </classloader-structure>
</classloader-structure>
```

CAUTION

Failure to address this common/shared file issue will result in `NoClassDefFoundError`(s).

For more detailed information on WebLogic class loading, refer to `http://e-docs.bea.com/wls/docs81/programming/classloading.html`.

NOTE

There are two other types of applications that may be deployed to WebLogic Server—client applications and resource adaptors—each with associated deployment descriptors. Refer to the BEA documentation site at `http://edocs.beasys.com/wls/docs81/programming/packaging.html` for details on packaging and deploying these types of applications.

Creating and Editing Application Deployment Descriptors

Deployment descriptors may be generated automatically using the WebLogic `DDInit` utility as shown here:

```
$ java weblogic.ant.taskdefs.war.DDInit c:\...\stagingDirectory
➥(for Web Applications)
$ java weblogic.ant.taskdefs.ear DDInit c:\...\stagingDirectory
➥(for Enterprise Applications)
```

Existing deployment descriptors can be edited using the WebLogic Builder application.

NOTE

Editing deployment descriptors with the WebLogic Administration Console, although still commonly used, has been deprecated in WebLogic 8.1. WebLogic Builder is currently the BEA recommended tool for editing deployment descriptors.

Start WebLogic Builder as detailed later in the section "Deploying Applications Using WebLogic Builder." Navigate to and open an application archive. Edit selected elements as shown in Figure 7.1.

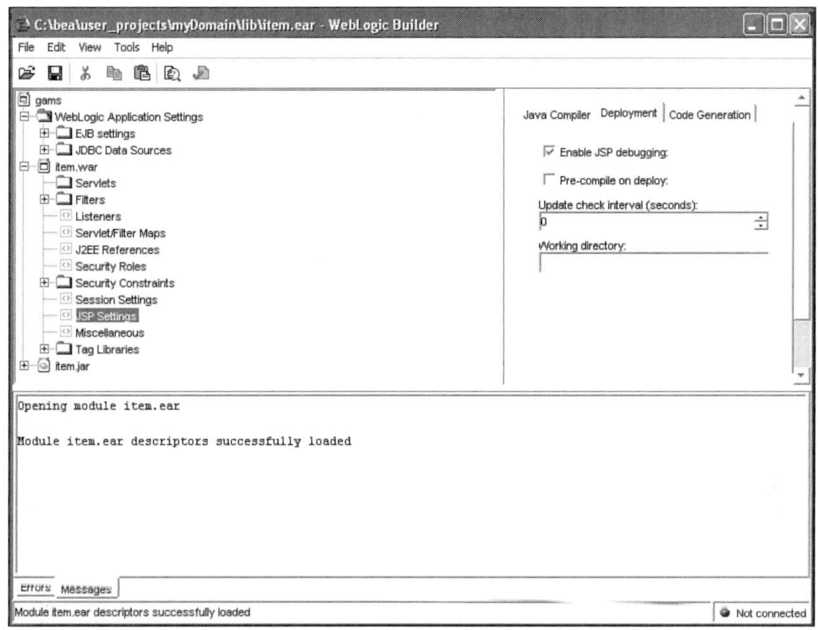

FIGURE 7.1 Editing application deployment descriptors.

Deployment descriptors may also be edited manually using any text editor or the provided BEA XML editor. For more information about creating or editing deployment descriptors refer to the BEA documentation site at `http://edocs.beasys.com/wls/docs81/programming/packaging.html` or `http://e-docs.bea.com/wls/docs81/webapp/deployment.html`.

Deployment Descriptor Security Elements

To promote application security, the `web.xml` and `weblogic.xml` files provide security implementation elements.

web.xml Security Elements

Within the `web.xml` file, the `<security-constraint>` tag (refer to Listing 7.1) is used to protect specific resources based on a URL pattern and an HTTP action. This tag may appear zero or more times within a `web.xml` file. An excerpt from `web-app2_3.dtd` regarding this tag is shown here:

```
<!ELEMENT security-constraint (display-name?, web-resource-collection+,
auth-constraint?, user-data-constraint?)>
```

Within each `<security-constraint>` tag, the `<display-name>` tag is optional. The `<web-resource-collection>` may appear one or more times. The `<auth-constraint>` tag is optional, as is the `<user-data-constraint>` tag.

The `<web-resource-collection>` tag restricts specified resources. Both the `<url-pattern>` and the `<http-method>` tags may appear one or more times. The `url-pattern` may refer to a directory, filename, or servlet mapping. In the following example, all resources in the `admin` directory are specified as restricted and available only with the HTTP `POST` method:

```
<web-resource-collection>
    <web-resource-name>Admin Pages</web-resource-name>
    <description>Only accessible by authorized administrators</description>
    <url-pattern>/admin/*</url-pattern>
    <http-method>POST</http-method>
</web-resource-collection>
```

The `<auth-constraint>` tag as shown in the following snippet defines roles that may access restricted resources. One or more roles may be assigned access. In the following example, the roles of `admin` and `backoffice` are specified to have access to resources:

```
<auth-constraint>
    <description>These are the roles who have access</description>
    <role-name>admin users</role-name>
    <role-name>back office users</role-name>
</auth-constraint>
```

The `<user-data-constraint>` shown in the following snippet may be used to indicate that this collection of Web resources should be communicated between the client and the server using no guarantees (`NONE`), certify that information cannot be changed in transit (`INTEGRAL`), or encrypted (`CONFIDENTIAL`). In most cases, the presence of the `INTEGRAL` or `CONFIDENTIAL` flag indicates that the use of SSL is required. If the `<user-data-constraint>` tag isn't present, these Web resources will not rely on SSL for communication.

```
<user-data-constraint>
    <description>This is how the user data must be transmitted</description>
    <transport-guarantee>CONFIDENTIAL</transport-guarantee>
</user-data-constraint>
```

Each `<security-constraint>` tag and its inner tags within a `web.xml` indicate one or more sets of protected resources as specified by URL patterns and HTTP methods, the roles that can access them, and whether or not SSL is required for access.

The roles mentioned within the `<auth-constraint>` tag must be declared within `<security-role>` tags in the following manner:

```
<security-role>
    <description>admin</description>
    <role-name>admin users</role-name>
</security-role>
<security-role>
    <description>backoffice</description>
    <role-name>back office users</role-name>
</security-role>
```

The `web.xml` file is also used to specify login behavior as shown here:

```
<login-config>
  <auth-method>BASIC</auth-method>
</login-config>
<login-config>
  <auth-method>FORM</auth-method>
  <form-login-config>
   <form-login-page>login.jsp</form-login-page>
   <form-error-page>error.jsp</form-error-page>
  </form-login-config>
 </login-config>
<login-config>
  <auth-method>CLIENT-CERT</auth-method>
</login-config>
```

weblogic.xml Security Elements

The roles specified in `web.xml` are abstract; they must be mapped to actual WebLogic Server users and groups. This occurs within the `weblogic.xml` file. The `<security-role-assignment>` tag (refer to Listing 7.2) is used to map a J2EE role to WebLogic Server users and groups. In the following example, the user `jeffm` and the group `Managers` are tied to the role called `admin users`:

```
<security-role-assignment>
    <role-name>admin users</role-name>
    <principal-name>jeffm</principal-name>
    <principal-name>Managers</principal-name>
</security-role-assignment>
```

Editing Security Elements

To edit security elements, use WebLogic Builder as shown in Figure 7.1. Click on the application name at the top of the directory tree. In the right pane (editing panel), select the Security Roles tab and enter role names and descriptions as needed. Next, select the target

Web application (`item.war` in Figure 7.1) from the directory tree and select Security Constraints. In the editing panel, click the Add button (a new window appears) and populate security elements as needed.

For example, to create a new security constraint, select the Resources/Pages tab. Enter a Web resource name. This equates to the `<display-name>` tag. Then add constraints and other security elements as needed. Be sure to add the appropriate security roles (Roles tab). When you're finished, click the OK button in the lower right corner. This will write the modified information back to the `web.xml` or `weblogic.xml` file as needed.

Methods of Deploying Applications

There are six ways in which you can deploy applications on WebLogic Server: auto-deployment, the `weblogic.Deployer` utility, the WebLogic Server Administration Console, the WebLogic Builder application, the popular Ant Java-based utility, and by manually modifying the domain `config.xml` file.

Auto-Deployment

Auto-deployment, used during development mode only, merely entails placing the application (archived or exploded) into the domain's `./applications` directory.

> **CAUTION**
>
> Beginning with WebLogic Server 8.1 , only one J2EE module may be posted within a directory without an associated `application.xml` that defines the application's modules.

The server will self-discover the application. This development mode is set in your administration server start script by passing parameter `-Dweblogic.ProductionModeEnabeled=false`. The default setting for this parameter is false; that is, auto-deployment/development mode is the default behavior. Due to security and configuration management concerns, auto-deployment is not advised for production environments.

> **NOTE**
>
> Setting auto-deployment affects the other deployment methods. For example, using the `weblogic.Deployer` to activate an application also targets the application to the administration server.

To redeploy an application after making changes, simply deposit the updated archive into the `applications` directory mentioned earlier. To redeploy an exploded application, WebLogic Server checks the timestamp on the marker file `REDEPLOY`. Create this file (an empty text file) and deposit it within the exploded application's `WEB-INF` directory for Web applications and `META-INF` directory for EJBs and enterprise applications. Deposit your updated files within the exploded directory structure and modify the `REDEPLOY` file to alter its timestamp. The administration server will detect the change in the timestamp and redeploy the exploded application. To undeploy an application (archived or exploded) remove the archive or exploded files from the `applications` directory.

Deploying Applications Using the WebLogic Server Administration Console

To deploy an application using the WebLogic Administration Console, enter the Administration console at `http://yourURL:port/console`. The default is `http://localhost:7001/console`. Entering the system username and password, deploy the application using the sequence yourDomain→Deployments→Applications→Deploy a New Application as shown in Figure 7.2.

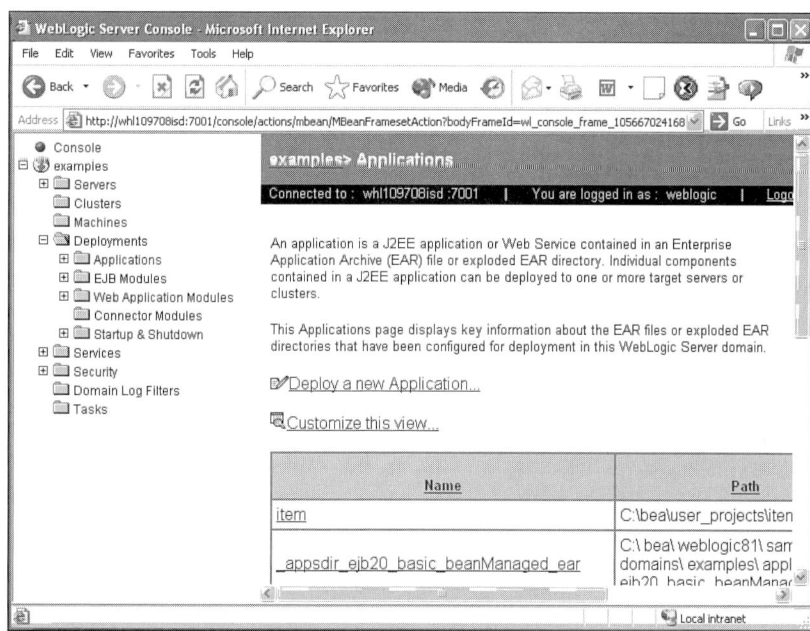

FIGURE 7.2 Deploying a new application.

To configure an application within its current folder, navigate to the application's folder and select the application as shown in Figure 7.3.

NOTE

If you don't navigate to the application's folder—away from the initial folder—using the Upload it Through Your Browser link copies the selected application to your domain's directory. If more than one application is available, you must select either Target Application or Target Each (application) to continue. In our example, for clarity, we have only one application available.

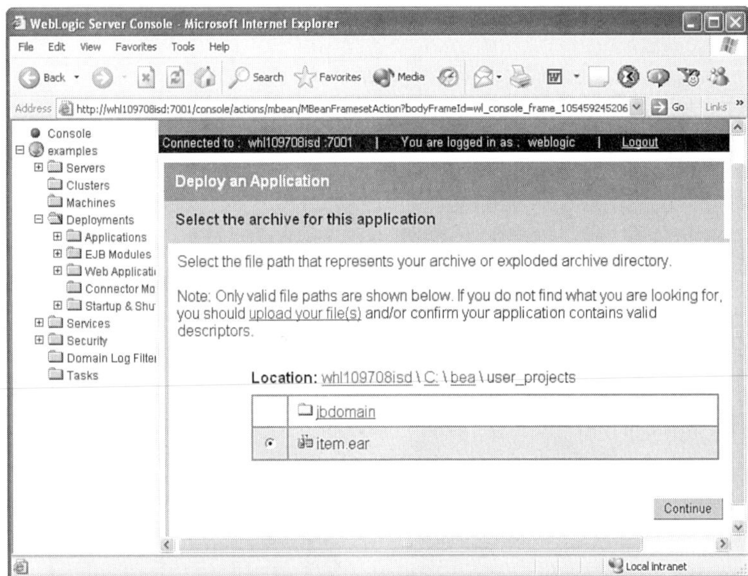

FIGURE 7.3 Selecting an application for deployment.

Next, select the target servers (and/or cluster(s)) for deployment and deploy the application as shown in Figures 7.4 and 7.5.

Any errors will be reported in the Administration Console and the WebLogic Server execution window. Deployment status is also reflected in the Administration Console as shown in Figure 7.5. Also note the Stop Application button within Figure 7.5. Click that button to undeploy any previously deployed application.

You can also deploy an exploded (nonarchived) application by navigating to and selecting the exploded application directory as you would an archived application.

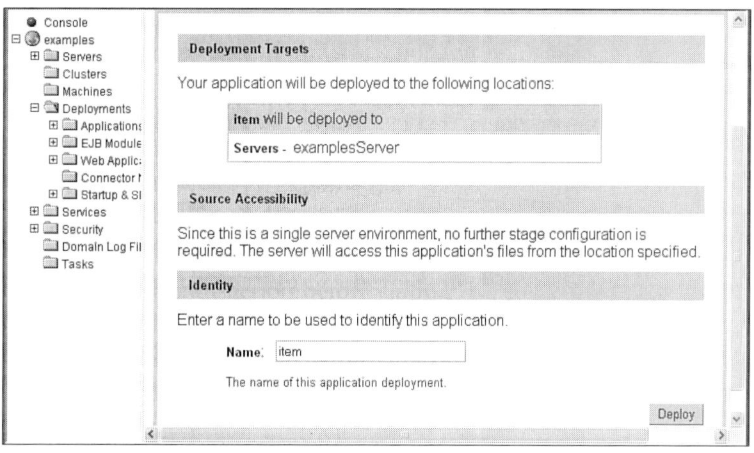

FIGURE 7.4 Selecting target servers.

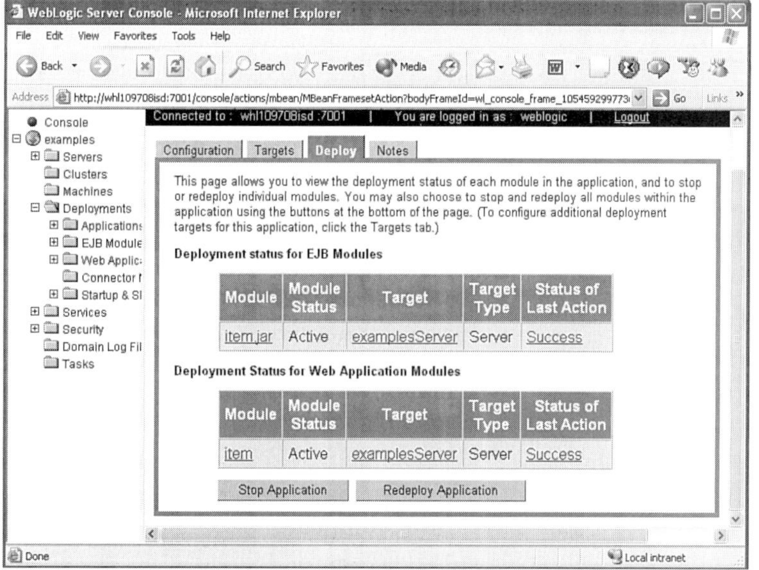

FIGURE 7.5 Deploying the application.

Deploying Applications Using the weblogic.Deployer Utility

The `weblogic.Deployer` utility is a Java application that's included in your WebLogic Server installation. With this utility you can deploy or redeploy an application, deactivate or unprepare an application, remove an application, cancel a pending deployment task, and list all deployment tasks. `weblogic.Deployer` uses a series of options and actions to complete deployment tasks. Some commonly used `weblogic.Deployer` options and actions are presented in Tables 7.1 and 7.2, respectively.

TABLE 7.1 weblogic.Deployer Options

Option	Description
-adminurl	URL to WebLogic Administration server; syntax: http://*serverName*:*port*
-id	Task identifier
-username	Administrator user's name
-password	Administrator user's password; if this option isn't used, the user will be prompted for the password
-name	Application name
-source	Archive location and name
-targets	Target WebLogic Server instance(s)

TABLE 7.2 weblogic.Deployer Actions

Action	Description
-cancel	Cancels task initiated. Use the -id option to specify which task to cancel.
-deploy	Deploys the application. If currently deployed, application is redeployed.
-distribute	Activates only. Application is copied to target servers' staging. Application is ready but not available.
-redeploy	Redeploys application.
-start	Activates available application. Follows -distribute or -deploy action.
-stop	Deactivates application and makes it unavailable to client. Deployment remains in target servers' staging.
-undeploy	Stops application and removes files from target server(s).

For a complete listing of `weblogic.Deployer` options and actions, refer to `http://e-docs.bea.com/wls/docs81/deployment/tools.html#999152`.

To deploy an application using the `weblogic.Deployer` utility, use the format:

```
$ java weblogic.Deployer [options] [actions]
```

To deploy/redeploy our global auction application, use the following command:

```
$java weblogic.Deployer -adminurl http://127.0.0.1:7001 -name globalAuctions
➥-deploy -user weblogic
➥ -source e:\bea\user_projects\yourDomain\applications\globalAuctions.ear
➥ ( options "-password PWD" may be used, especially when
➥writing deployment scripts )
```

To deactivate our global auction application, use the command

```
$ java weblogic.Deployer -adminurl http://127.0.0.1:7001 -name globalAuctions -stop
```

To remove our global auction application, use the command

```
$ java weblogic.Deployer -adminurl http://127.0.0.1:7001 -name globalAuctions
➥-targets server1, server2 -undeploy -id tag
```

To cancel a deployment task, use the command

```
$ java weblogic.Deployer -adminurl http://127.0.0.1:7001 -cancel -id tag
```

NOTE

The `-id` tag may be declared when using `-deploy`, `-redeploy`, or `-undeploy` because these tasks may be canceled or listed.

To list all unfinished deployment tasks, use this command:

```
$ java weblogic.Deployer -adminurl http://127.0.0.1:7001 -list
```


To add a module to our already deployed global auction application (after updating our WAR file), use the following command:

```
$ java weblogic.Deployer -start -name globalAuctions -source
➥e:\bea\user_projects\yourDomain\applications\globalAuctions.ear
```

Deploying Applications Using WebLogic Builder

WebLogic Builder is a GUI-based tool intended for use as an application builder; that is, generating, editing, compiling, and validating deployment descriptors for Web applications. You can use this tool to deploy applications to a single server.

To deploy an application to a single server using WebLogic Builder, start the GUI using the script `startWLBuilder.cmd` (Windows) or `startWLBuilder.sh` (Unix), or from the Windows start menu by using the sequence start→BEA WebLogic Platform 8.1→Other Development Tools→WebLogic Builder, as shown in Figure 7.6.

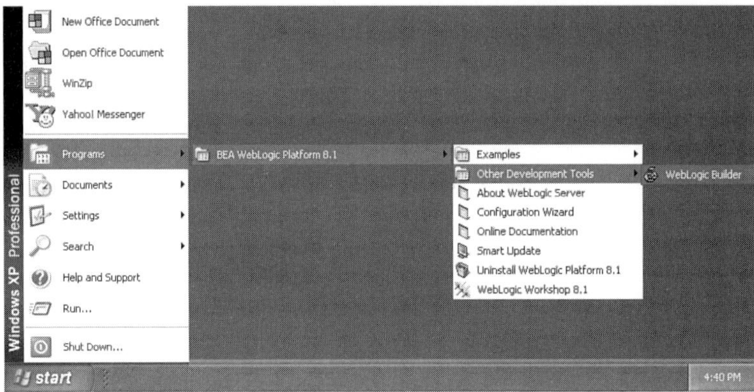

FIGURE 7.6 Starting WebLogic Builder.

From the File menu, select Open to open the module slated for deployment as shown in Figure 7.7.

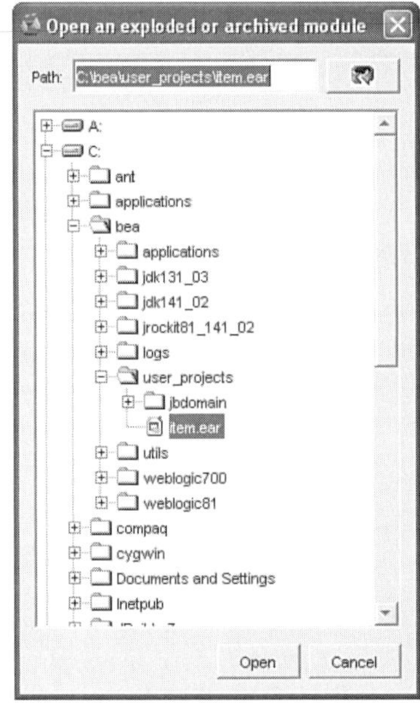

FIGURE 7.7 Opening a module slated for deployment.

From the Tools menu, select Connect to Server and connect to the target server as shown in Figure 7.8.

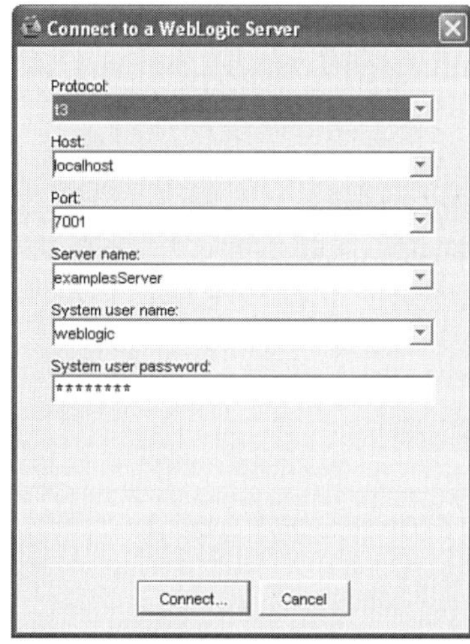

FIGURE 7.8 Connecting to target server.

From the Tools menu, select Deploy Module to deploy the module as shown in Figure 7.9.

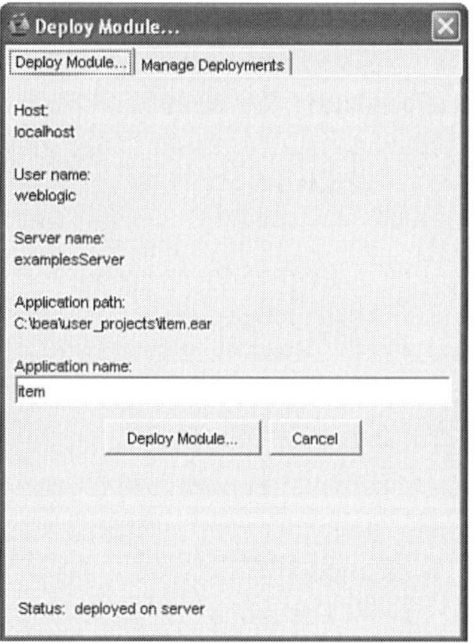

FIGURE 7.9 Deploying the module.

Deploying Applications Using the Ant Utility

The Ant utility provides a `ServerDeploy` task that includes a `weblogic` element. Use of this `weblogic` element implements *hot* deployment (that is, deployment while the server is running) of an application or application component to WebLogic Server. The Ant build file presented in Listing 7.4 implements deployment and a component redeployment of an application named gams.

CAUTION

Hot deployments are not written or persisted to server configuration files (`config.xml`). If the server is restarted, application deployments made via hot deployment are not retained.

LISTING 7.4 Ant Build File wlDeploy.xml

```
<?xml version="1.0"?>
<project name="WLDeploy" default="deploy" basedir=".">
<!--
    =================================================================
     Set properties related to weblogic deployment
    =================================================================
  -->
     <property name="weblogic.home" value="C:/bea/weblogic81/server" />
     <property name="java.home" value="C:/bea/jdk141_02" />
     <property name="lib.dir" value="C:/bea/user_projects/myDomain/lib" />
     <property name="username" value="weblogic" />
     <property name="password" value="weblogic" />
     <property name="wl.classpath" value="${weblogic.home}/lib/weblogic.jar" />

<!--
    =================================================================
     deploy application / application component to weblogic server
    =================================================================
  -->
    <target name="deploy">
        <serverdeploy action="deploy" source="${lib.dir}/item.ear">
         <weblogic application="gams" server="t3://localhost:7001"
            classpath="${wl.classpath}"
            username="${username}" password="${password}"
            component="item:examplesServer" debug="true"
        />
        </serverdeploy>
    </target>
<!--
```

LISTING 7.4 Continued

```
    ==================================================================
     Undeploy application / application component from weblogic server
    ==================================================================
  -->
    <target name="redeploy">
        <serverdeploy action="redeploy" source="${lib.dir}/item.jar" >
        <weblogic application="gams" server="t3://localhost:7001"
            classpath="${wl.classpath}"
            username="${username}" password="${password}"
        />
        </serverdeploy>
    </target>
</project>
```

A WebLogic application deployment can be executed using the build file as shown here:

```
ant -buildfile wlDeploy.xml deploy
```

A WebLogic component redeployment can be executed using the build file as shown here:

```
ant -buildfile wlDeploy.xml redeploy
```

Ant also includes tasks for JAR, WAR, and WebLogic EJB generation that may be useful during deployment operations. For detailed instructions and examples on using Ant WebLogic and other tasks, visit the Apache Web site at `http://jakarta.apache.org/ant`.

Deploying Applications by Manually Modifying config.xml

> **CAUTION**
>
> Take special care when manually editing the `config.xml` or any other XML files associated with WebLogic Server. Direct editing should be limited to small modifications. Make a backup copy of the file before modifying it.

One last means of deploying an application is to manually modify the domain's `config.xml`. For simple deployments, this can be the most efficient means of deploying your application. This approach requires knowledge of XML and the WebLogic tag library. When making manual modifications, ensure that your servers' names (for example, server1, server2, and so on) are included in the resources' (such as application, database connection pool, and so forth) `Target` listing, as shown in Listing 7.5.

LISTING 7.5 Partial Config.xml

```
<Application Deployed="true" Name="globalAuctions"
    Path="e:\bea\user_projects\yourDomain\globalAuctions.ear"
    StagedTargets="server1, server2" TwoPhase="true">
    <EJBComponent Name="findItemsEjb.jar" Targets="server1, server2"
➥URI="asyncSenderEjb.jar"/>
    <EJBComponent Name="closeAuctionEJB.jar" Targets="server1, server2"
➥URI="cartEjb.jar"/>
    <EJBComponent Name="ItemEjb.jar" Targets="server1, server2"
➥URI="catalogEjb.jar"/>
    <EJBComponent Name="customerEjb.jar" Targets="server1, server2"
➥URI="customerEjb.jar"/>
    <WebAppComponent Name="globalAuctions.war" Targets="server1, server2"
➥URI="globalAuctions.war"/>
</Application>

<JDBCConnectionPool CapacityIncrement="1"
    DriverName="com.pointbase.jdbc.jdbcUniversalDriver"
    InitialCapacity="1" MaxCapacity="10" Name="globalAuctionsPool"
    Password=""
    Properties="user=globalAuctions" RefreshMinutes="0"
    ShrinkPeriodMinutes="15" ShrinkingEnabled="true"
    Targets="server1, server2" TestConnectionsOnRelease="false"
    TestConnectionsOnReserve="false"
➥URL="jdbc:pointbase:server://localhost/demo"/>
```

Deployment Issues with WebLogic Server

The key issues with deployment involve consistency across clustered domains with multiple instances of WebLogic Server running the same application. More specifically, consistency means ensuring that all servers within the domain and/or cluster represent the same state of the application.

WebLogic Server addresses this issue by implementing a two-phase deployment model. Within the first phase, called the *prepare phase,* the application is copied across the domain/clusters and validated. Unless this phase is completed successfully, deployment is terminated. In the second phase, called the *activate phase,* the application is made available to clients. Within this two-phase model, the second phase is not implemented unless the first phase is implemented. The first phase is not implemented unless all servers within the domain are successfully prepared. This model ensures consistent deployment states across the domain.

Hot deployment (deploying or redeploying an application while the server is running) is also implemented in WebLogic Server. Hot deployment is desirable in situations in which WebLogic Server must remain active and changes or updates are required within an active application.

Deployment Best Practices

The following are suggested practices when deploying applications to WebLogic Server. Deployment methodology should provide deployment procedures that are orderly (to avoid development team confusion) and repeatable (to guarantee application state).

Archived Versus Exploded Applications

We recommend that, when deploying applications, it's best to deploy archived applications rather than exploded applications. This facilitates transport and management of the application; that is, controlling one `.ear` file as opposed to controlling 100 individual files of various types. We further suggest that all application modules (EJB applications, Web applications, supporting JARs) be packaged within one `.ear` file. For example, our global auctions application contains 13 JSPs, 10 servlets, 4 EJBs, and other support files. We would package the EJBs within one EJB `.jar` file (see Chapter 20 for EJB packaging); servlets, JSPs, and JSP tag libraries and all other files supporting the Web application within a separate `.war` file (refer to Chapter 6 for Web application packaging). All archives (EJB JAR, Web application WAR files, and support enterprise application–level JAR files) would then be packaged within the one `.ear` file for deployment.

Exploded Applications

However, if you choose to deploy an exploded application, ensure that your file structure facilitates WebLogic Server implementation; that is, modules should be deployed under a top-level source or staging directory. Each individual application should reside within a separate subdirectory as shown:

```
/sourceDirectory
  /module1
   /WEB_INF
    web.xml
    module1Files
  /module2
   /WEB-INF
    ejb-jar.xml
    module2Files
```

Development

During development, it's best to work in a single server environment until your application is stable enough for multiserver testing. This single server should be an administration server, set to auto-deployment to facilitate changes. When you're ready to test your application on multiple servers, either modify the application's targets using the Administration Console or use `weblogic.Deployer` as discussed earlier.

Staging Modes

WebLogic Server gives you the flexibility to determine where application files are located. There are three options: `nostage` (administration server default; application files are maintained on the administration server and not copied to managed servers), `stage` (managed server default; application files are copied to domain's managed servers), and `external_stage` (files are expected in a staging directory but the user, not WebLogic, posts the files to the target staging location).

Use the system defaults for staging mode, `nostage` for administration servers, and `stage` for managed servers. Two exceptions would be if you're using a third-party application to implement your deployments or if you're using a shared file system across managed servers. Use the `external_stage` mode for these exceptions. To set the staging mode using the WebLogic Administration Console, start the console as discussed earlier, navigate to the target Web application under Deployments→Web Application. Select the target Web application and then select the desired staging option, as shown in Figure 7.10.

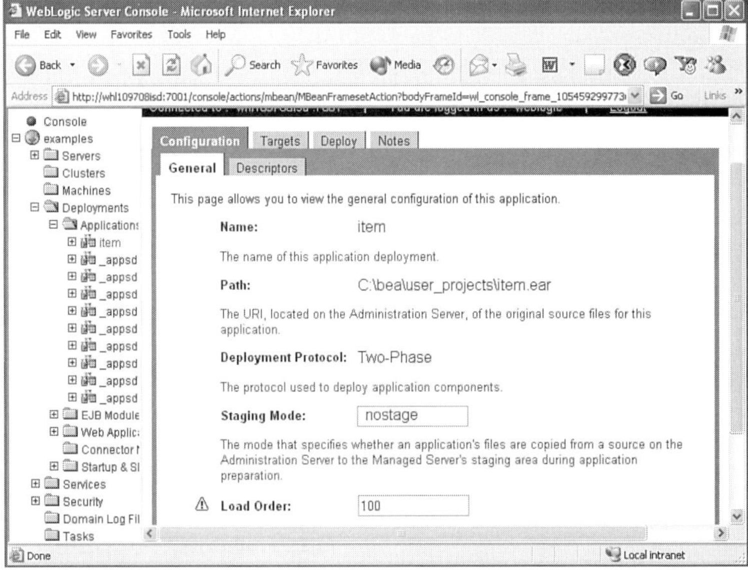

FIGURE 7.10 Setting the stage mode.

NOTE

You can also set the deployment order for a Web application within the screen in Figure 7.10. To force an application to deploy first, simply set a lower number than other components. This targets the application for deployment before higher-ordered counterparts. This is useful in situations in which one Web application or module sets conditions for follow-on modules.

To set the staging mode manually, adjust the staging mode attribute within the domain's `config.xml` file as shown here:

```
<Application Name="gams" Path="E:\bea\user_projects\gams.ear" TwoPhase="true"
  StagedTargets="" StagingMode="nostage" TwoPhase="true">
  <EJBComponent Name="customer.jar" Targets="adminServer" URI="customer.jar"/>
  <EJBComponent Name="item.jar" Targets="adminServer" URI="item.jar"/>
  <EJBComponent Name="processbid.jar" Targets="adminServer"
➥URI="processbid.jar"/>
  <WebAppComponent Name="gams.war" Targets="adminServer" URI="gams.war"/>
</Application>
```

Summary

In this chapter, we discussed deployment of WebLogic applications. We discussed application packaging, security constructs, deployment issues, deployment descriptors, various deployment tools provided by BEA, and deployment techniques to assist you in your deployment tasks. At this point, you should be able to package and deploy an application to WebLogic Server.

PART III

Using J2EE Technologies in WebLogic Applications

IN THIS PART

CHAPTER 8

Naming and Directory Services with JNDI

by Subramanian Kovilmadam

IN THIS CHAPTER

- Naming Services
- Java Naming and Directory Interface
- JNDI and WebLogic Server
- JNDI Best Practices

Walk into your local library and chances are you'll run into a card-based catalog system. This is a useful mechanism to look up the precise location of the book that you need, instead of browsing through the several racks of books without having a clue where to look. Modern libraries offer the same convenience by using a computer. The catalog provides us with several advantages. It makes accessing the book very easy, just by knowing the name of the book and/or the author. It also allows the library the flexibility to move the book from one rack to another with the guarantee that its customers can still find the book the next time they look for it—the library can simply update the new location information on the catalog card.

As a concept, the card-catalog system is still in use in our day-to-day life in the field of technology. There are catalog services available that let us look up objects or object references on the network—be it a LAN, a WAN, or the Internet—just by knowing their names. We look at a few types of such catalog systems—known as *naming services*—in the following sections.

Naming Services

A *naming service* is a mechanism in which complex data objects (or references to these objects) can be associated with well-known names that follow standard naming conventions. These names can then be published, and clients can use these names to look up the data objects associated with them. Each naming service has its own naming conventions.

Names can be *atomic* (an indivisible component of a name) or *compound* (a sequence of zero or more atomic names, such as `/usr/bin` in a file namespace). Names can also be composite; enterprises use composite namespaces a lot. For example, a name such as `http://www.getgamma.com/newsletter/archives/index.html` typically accesses a DNS (Internet naming) facility to first resolve the `www.getgamma.com` part. Following this, it accesses the file namespace to resolve the `index.html` file, stored under the `<wwwroot>/newsletter/archives/` directory. From a user's perspective, however, there's a single namespace consisting of composite names.

Associations between the names and objects are known as *bindings*. Naming services usually integrate with another service such as a file system, a directory, a database, and so on, to provide these bindings.

A directory can be compared to a database to the extent that it's used to store and organize data. A directory contains descriptive, attribute-based information about the stored objects. Directories are meant to be queried far many times more than they're meant to be updated. For this reason, they're built and indexed to handle large amounts of high-volume queries, thus allowing for fast queries but slower updates. For the same reason, directories don't usually implement transaction or rollback schemes like databases typically do.

The naming service allows for different components of the enterprise to work with each other without knowing their physical location, but only the name under which they are advertised. This enables the system administrators to move these objects around if necessary, without breaking any dependencies, as long as the naming service reflects the object's correct location at all times.

Several types of naming and directory services are available in the market. We'll take a look at a few of them here:

- *LDAP: Lightweight Directory Access Protocol*—A lightweight protocol, typically used in a LAN environment where the number of users isn't usually too high.
- *DNS: Domain Naming Service*—The distributed naming service for the Internet. It enables you to map well-known names to IP addresses of the servers. DNS enables you to remember `http://www.getgamma.com`, instead of `http://209.15.74.241`.
- *COS: Common Object Services*—The naming service for CORBA applications.
- *NIS: Network Information System*—A network naming service that enables users to access files on any host using a single ID and password.
- *NDS: The NDS Naming Adapter*—An adapter that enables you use native NDS naming conventions to connect to an Oracle database on a Novell NDS-enabled network.

Understanding the Differences in Naming Services

All the naming services allow for data bindings, which is the minimum requirement to qualify as a naming service. However, there are inherent differences between these services in the way the data is stored and looked up. For instance, consider the DNS naming service. To look up IP addresses, you would use the standard naming convention, which is `<sub domain>.<domain-name>.<top-level domain>` (for example, `www.getgamma.com`). To use LDAP to look up the phone number of John Smith, who works for Gamma Enterprise Technologies in United States, you would formulate the name using name-value pairs, separated by commas (,): `cn=John Smith, o=Gamma, c=US`.

With so many naming systems in the market, along with their different implementation artifacts, there's an obvious need for a common interface to access them all in a uniform manner from an application. This is where the Java Naming and Directory Interface (JNDI) comes into the picture.

WebLogic Server now ships with a private LDAP server, which is used by the LDAP security realm.

Java Naming and Directory Interface

Sun Microsystems defines JNDI as *"a standard extension to the Java platform, which provides Java technology-enabled applications with a unified interface to multiple naming and directory services in the enterprise. As part of the Java Enterprise API set, JNDI enables seamless connectivity to heterogeneous enterprise naming and directory services."* JNDI has been designed especially for Java. A Java application can use JNDI to retrieve Java objects. JNDI also provides for performing standard directory operations, such as associating attributes with objects and searching for objects using their attributes.

JNDI is an interface, not an implementation. It can be used to seamlessly integrate with different, possibly multiple, implementations (such as LDAP, DNS, and so on). You must still understand certain basics of the underlying implementations (such as their naming convention) to enable JNDI to connect to them, although you aren't required to understand their implementation artifacts.

Overview of the JNDI Architecture

JNDI is comprised of the JNDI SPI (service provider interface), which is used by service providers to JNDI-enable their products and the JNDI API (application programming interface), which is used by clients to connect to these service providers. Figure 8.1 describes the architecture and how clients can use the different service providers using JNDI.

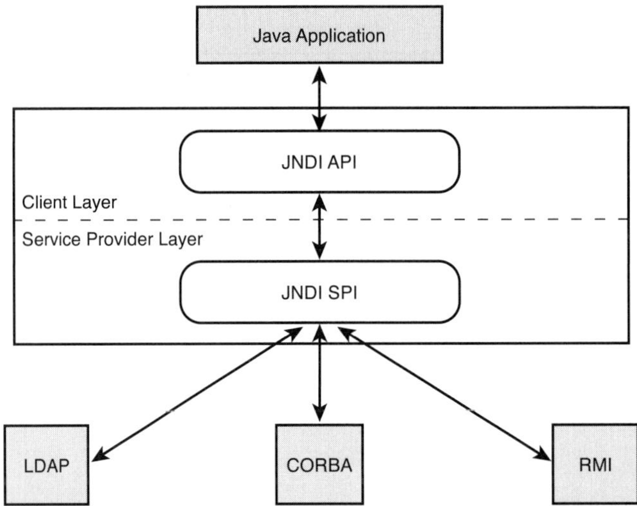

Figure 8.1 JNDI architecture.

In this chapter, you'll see how to use the JNDI API to access WebLogic's implementation of JNDI. Because this chapter discusses the usage of JNDI from your J2EE application, rather than writing a JNDI service provider, a discussion of the JNDI SPI is beyond the scope of this book.

Overview of the JNDI 1.2.1 Specification

WebLogic Server 8.1 fully supports JNDI version 1.2.1. Some of the features of this version of JNDI are

- Event notification—With JNDI 1.2.1, clients can register to receive events, which can make the client aware of changes to the naming service as well as the bound objects.
- LDAPv3 extensions and controls—Applications and service providers can now work with LDAPv3 extended operations and controls using the classes and interfaces in the `javax.naming.ldap` package.
- Resource file support—The JNDI environment can be created using resource files.
- The functionality provided by the `javax.naming.spi` package for service provider support has been enhanced in JNDI 1.2.1.

The following sections discuss the highlights of the packages that the JNDI 1.2.1 specification provides for.

javax.naming

The javax.naming package consists of classes and interfaces that enable the user to communicate with the different naming services. It provides the ability to perform several operations such as

- Adding or removing a name to object binding
- Creating or destroying subcontexts
- Looking up the object bound to a given name
- Listing the bindings in the namespace

The following are some of the key components of this package:

- Context—A naming system can be seen as a hierarchy of nodes. Each nonterminal node is represented by the Context interface. The naming system is a connected set of contexts, each of which follows the same naming convention. It defines basic operations on the naming system such as looking up an object bound to a name, listing the bindings, creating and destroying subcontexts, adding a new binding, removing an existing binding, and so forth. Thus, in JNDI, every name is relative to a context—there's no notion of an absolute name.
- InitialContext—Because a naming system is a connected set of contexts, an application can begin using a naming system by getting its first context of type InitialContext. After getting the InitialContext, you can then access all its subcontexts by using names relative to the initial context.
- Bindings—A binding is a mapping between a logical name with its object inside a naming service. The Context interface allows applications to access these bindings by using several of its methods. For example, Context.lookup() returns a handle to the object that is bound to the name, which is passed as its parameter, whereas Context.list() returns an enumeration of all the name-to-object bindings present in the naming system.

javax.naming.directory

A directory object is a particular type of object that holds several attributes of a computing environment, thus describing it at an atomic level. The classes and interfaces in the javax.naming.directory package allow the application to access attributes associated with directory objects. This package also provides the application with the capability to search through directory objects by passing in their attributes using the DirContext interface.

javax.naming.event

The classes and interfaces in the javax.naming.event package allow the application to be notified of several changes to the naming service as well as to the objects bound inside.

For example, events (called NamingEvents) are generated when adding a new object, changing the name (binding) of an object, and so on.

The NamingEvent's type attribute identifies the type of the event. The NamingEvent class defines four types of events, indicating different operations performed on objects (add, remove, rename, or change). Applications may register to receive one or both types of events (that is, namespace changes and object changes) by using either the EventContext or the EventDirContext interface.

You can learn more about JNDI events in the tutorial posted by Sun Microsystems at the URL http://java.sun.com/products/jndi/tutorial/index.html.

javax.naming.ldap

The javax.naming.ldap package allows the application to use LDAP v3–specific features including extensions and controls, which cannot be achieved using the javax.naming.directory package.

You can learn more about JNDI LDAP support in the tutorial posted by Sun Microsystems at the URL http://java.sun.com/products/jndi/tutorial/index.html.

javax.naming.spi

The javax.naming.spi package allows different naming/directory service providers to provide implementation hooks to their facilities so that applications using the JNDI API can have access to those facilities. This package also provides support for the case in which one service provider implementation must access other implementations to complete a client's JNDI operations, thus providing support for composite namespaces.

You can learn more about the JNDI SPI in the tutorial posted by Sun Microsystems at the URL http://java.sun.com/products/jndi/tutorial/index.html.

JNDI and WebLogic Server

WebLogic 8.1 provides a SPI implementation as specified in JNDI Specification 1.2.1. This enables Java clients to connect to WebLogic Server using standard JNDI calls. Clients can get access to WebLogic name services and make objects available, as well as retrieve them, in the WebLogic namespace. The naming service implementation of WebLogic uses a JNDI tree. Each WebLogic Server instance maintains its own copy of the JNDI tree where the object bindings that resolve into this server and other servers in the cluster are stored.

A Java client that wants to access services of an object that's already been loaded into a WebLogic Server's JNDI tree would typically perform the following tasks:

- Establish a context with the server
- Perform queries or updates on the JNDI tree using the API

Establishing an InitialContext to the WebLogic Server

This is the first step in accessing a bound object in a WebLogic namespace. The bootstrap context that an application will obtain is known as the InitialContext. The InitialContext is obtained from an InitialContext factory. This factory uses a few properties to identify the WebLogic Server that the context needs to point to. Some important properties that are used to customize the InitialContext for connecting to a WebLogic Server are as follows:

- Context.INITIAL_CONTEXT_FACTORY—This property identifies the factory that has to be used for creating the InitialContext object. To use WebLogic's JNDI implementation, this property must be set to weblogic.jndi.WLInitialContextFactory.
- Context.PROVIDER_URL—This provides the URL of the WebLogic Server, which provides the naming service.
- Context.SECURITY_PRINCIPAL—This value is used for authentication purposes. This specifies the identity of the user, which is defined in the WebLogic security realm. The default value depends on whether the current thread is already associated with a user. If it is, this value defaults to the current user. If not, this property defaults to the guest user.
- Context.SECURITY_CREDENTIALS—This can contain either the password of the user specified in the Context.SECURITY_PRINCIPAL property or an object that implements the weblogic.security.acl.UserInfo interface. Similar to Context.SECURITY_PRINCIPAL, this property defaults to the guest user unless the current thread is already associated with a user defined in the WebLogic security realm. If the password is incorrect, a javax.naming.NoPermissionException is thrown back to the client.

You can look up the InitialContext by setting the properties using a Hashtable, by using the environment where the client is executing, or by using a WebLogic environment object. We look at these three mechanisms in the following subsections.

8

Obtaining the InitialContext Using a Hashtable

To create an InitialContext object using a Hashtable, identify the various properties discussed in the previous section in a Hashtable instance, and pass it as a parameter to the constructor to the InitialContext. The following code snippet illustrates such use:

```
Hashtable props = new Hashtable () ;
props.put( Context.INITIAL_CONTEXT_FACTORY,
           "weblogic.jndi.WLInitialContextFactory" ) ;
props.put( Context.PROVIDER_URL,
           "t3://localhost:7001" ) ;
Context ctx = null ;
boolean contextInitialized = false ;
try {
```

```
        ctx = new InitialContext( props );
        contextInitialized = true ;
}
catch ( NamingException ne ) {
        // Unable to obtain InitialContext.
        // handle the NamingException here.
        ne.printStackTrace( );
}

// The initial context can be used here.
```

You can find this example in `ch08/com/wlsunleashed/jndi/Example1.java`. This example obtains the `InitialContext` object from WebLogic Server and then looks up `javax.transaction.UserTransaction`. To execute this example, start the WebLogic Server instance in your local host, listen in port 7001, and execute the corresponding class.

Obtaining the InitialContext Using the Client's Environment

The properties can be initialized in the client's environment, thus avoiding the need to hardcode the values for these properties inside the client's code. To do this, the following environment variables must be set. If any of the properties isn't set, its default value (if any) is assumed:

- `java.naming.factory.initial`—Provides the value for `Context.INITIAL_CONTEXT_FACTORY`
- `java.naming.provider.url`—Provides the value for `Context.PROVIDER_URL`
- `java.naming.security.principal`—Provides the value for `Context.SECURITY_PRINCIPAL`
- `java.naming.security.credentials`—Provides the value for `Context.SECURITY_CREDENTIALS`

These properties may be set in the Java runtime's system properties, or in cases of an applet, in the applet's parameter list.

Another way of setting these properties in the JNDI environment is by the use of resource files. A *resource file* is a flat file containing key-value pairs that define the JNDI's environment. The keys are the different properties that have been discussed in this section. This file should be named `jndi.properties` and should be available in the application's class path. In addition to this, JNDI also looks for the `jndi.properties` file under the `lib/` subdirectory under `java.home`. All the readable resource files are loaded into the application's environment. In most cases, if the same property is defined in different resources, the first value found is used. In a few other cases, where it makes sense, the values found in the different resource files are concatenated.

After these properties have been set, you can initialize the `InitialContext` simply by invoking its default constructor:

```
Context ctx = new InitialContext() ;
```

You can find this example in `ch08/com/wlsunleashed/jndi/Example2.java`. This example obtains the `InitialContext` object from the WebLogic Server and tries to looks up `javax.transaction.UserTransaction`. To execute this example, start the WebLogic Server instance in your local host, listen in port 7001, and execute the corresponding class. Pass in the different fields discussed in this section as command-line parameters. For example, you can execute the class file using the following command line:

```
C:> java -Djava.naming.factory.initial=
            weblogic.jndi.WLInitialContextFactory
            -Djava.naming.provider.url=t3://localhost:7001
            com.wlsunleashed.jndi.Example2
```

Experiment with this example a little more by creating a `jndi.properties` file and putting it in your classpath. Now execute this class without the command-line arguments. You'll get the same results. Perform the test again, but this time provide the command-line arguments along with the `jndi.properties` file. Make the port number in the command line incorrect. You'll notice that the value provided in the command line is used, and the class file errors out. It's quite easy to notice that the command line gets precedence over the `jndi.properties` file.

Obtaining the InitialContext Using WebLogic's Environment Object

WebLogic provides a `weblogic.jndi.Environment` class, which can be used to obtain the `InitialContext`. This method offers certain advantages, at the expense of making the code specific to WebLogic. It provides with convenient `set()` methods to set the various properties. This ensures type safety and identifies problems during compile time. This class also provides default values to several properties, and predefined constants for certain values.

- If the `Context.INITIAL_CONTEXT_FACTORY` property isn't set, this object defaults it to `WebLogic.jndi.WLInitialContextFactory`.
- If the `Context.PROVIDER_URL` property isn't set, this object defaults it to `t3://localhost:7001`.
- If either or both of the `Context.SECURITY_PRINCIPAL` and the `Context.SECURITY_CREDENTIALS` properties weren't provided, they would default to the guest user, unless the current thread is already associated with a WebLogic user.

This enables the programmer to create a default `Environment` object and modify only the values for which the defaults won't work. After setting the appropriate values, the `Environment` object can be requested to provide the `InitialContext` for further use.

The following code snippet can be used to create an `InitialContext` object using WebLogic's `Environment` object:

```
Environment env = new Environment () ;
env.setInitialContextFactory( Environment.DEFAULT_INITIAL_CONTEXT_FACTORY );
env.setProviderURL("t3://localhost:7021") ;
env.setSecurityPrincipal( "johnny" );
env.setSecurityCredentials( "begood" );
Context ctx = env.getInitialContext () ;
```

You can find this example in `ch08/com/wlsunleashed/jndi/Example3.java`. This example obtains the `InitialContext` object from the WebLogic Server and looks up `javax.transaction.UserTransaction`. To execute this example, start the WebLogic Server instance in your local host, listen in port 7001, and execute the corresponding class.

Precedence of the Various Mechanisms of Creating InitialContext

In the preceding few subsections, we saw three mechanisms for creating the `InitialContext` object. So, how do these mechanisms play out as far as their precedence goes? Passing in a `Hashtable` or an `Environment` object always takes first precedence. If neither of these is passed in, command-line properties are considered, and if passed, are used. If command-line properties are not present, the `jndi.properties` file in the classpath and then in `${JAVA_HOME}/lib` is looked up and used. If none of these mechanisms are available, the default values, if any, are used.

Obtaining the InitialContext from a Server-Side Object

It's often necessary to access the WebLogic JNDI tree from objects that have been instantiated inside the server JVM. This use can be seen while accessing EJB instances from within a servlet, for instance. To do this, you don't need to specify the `INITIAL_CONTEXT_FACTORY` or the `PROVIDER_URL` property. The `InitialContext` is built to the server where it's being requested. `SECURITY_PRINCIPAL` and `SECURITY_CREDENTIALS` must be provided only if you want to sign in as a specific user.

To create an `InitialContext` from within WebLogic Server, you can simply do the following:

```
Context ctx = new InitialContext ();
```

The correct `InitialContext` for WebLogic Server is returned.

Querying the WebLogic JNDI Tree

After the `InitialContext` has been established, the client application can now query from WebLogic's JNDI tree. To do this, the object should already be available in the tree. To query a named object, use the `Context.lookup()` method and pass the name of the binding to it:

```
AccountBean anAccountBean = null ;
try {
        // Obtain the InitialContext first
        Context ctx = getInitialContext() ;
        anAccountBean = ctx.lookup( "java:comp/env/ejb/AccountBean" );
}
catch ( NameNotFoundException nfe ) {
        // there is no object bound under the given name
}
catch ( NamingException ne ) {
        // there has been a failure while doing this operation.
}
// continue to use the anAccountBean here.
```

Examples 1, 2, and 3 in the directory `ch08/com/wlsunleashed/jndi` demonstrate such a lookup.

You can also list the contents of the JNDI tree or a subtree using the `Context` interface. `Context.listBindings()` method accepts the name of a context, and returns an `Enumeration` containing the bindings in the context:

```
try {
        // Obtain the InitialContext first
        Context ctx = getInitialContext() ;
        System.out.println("Listing Bindings under javax.transaction");
        NamingEnumeration enum = ctx.listBindings("javax.transaction");
        while (enum.hasMore())
        {
            System.out.println( enum.next() );
        }
        System.out.println("listing done");
}
catch ( NameNotFoundException nfe ) {
        // there is no object bound under the given name
}
catch ( NamingException ne ) {
        // there has been a failure while doing this operation.
}
```

This code snippet, when executed, produces the following output:

```
Listing Bindings under javax.transaction
UserTransaction: weblogic.transaction.internal.ClientTransaction
➥ManagerImpl:ClientTM[myserver+192.168.1.102:7001+mydomain+t3+]
```

8

```
TransactionManager: weblogic.transaction.internal.ClientTransaction
➥ManagerImpl:ClientTM[myserver+192.168.1.102:7001+mydomain+t3+]
listing done
```

This example can be found in `ch08/com/wlsunleashed/jndi/Example4.java`.

Updating the WebLogic JNDI Tree

Using the `Context` interface, you can also perform several operations apart from a lookup. This section discusses a few of these update operations.

While reading this part of the chapter, keep in mind that as a J2EE developer, one rarely if ever performs these kinds of updates on the JNDI tree. WebLogic performs these updates automatically when resources are deployed, and are destroyed when the server (and hence the JNDI tree) shuts down. All you have to do is to configure these resources in the appropriate configuration descriptor. If you find yourselves in a situation where you have to store data somewhere, you'll be better off considering the use of a database to store your data. Also remember that the objects that are typically stored on the JNDI tree have a small footprint.

Create New Bindings

To create a new binding in the WebLogic JNDI tree, use the `Context.bind()` method. This method accepts the name of the new binding, along with an object that has to be bound to this name. Note that the object passed in must be serializable; that is, the class representing the object should implement the `java.io.Serializable` tagging interface. This interface does not contain any methods that the class needs to implement—it simply tells the VM that objects of this class can be serialized.

The following code snippet creates an object of type `SimpleObject` and binds it under the name `TestBinding`:

```
SimpleObject myObject = new SimpleObject();
Context c = getInitialContext();
System.out.println("Binding "+ myObject + " to " + getName() );
c.bind(name, myObject);
System.out.println ("Bind : Done" );
```

Delete an Existing Binding (unbind)

Now let's delete the binding that we created in the previous section. To do this, use the `Context.unbind()` method. This operation removes the binding on the JNDI tree and the object is no longer accessible from this tree.

```
Context c = getInitialContext();
c.unbind(getName());
```

The sample program `ch08/com/wlsunleashed/jndi/Example5.java` demonstrates how to create and delete object bindings.

Create a Subcontext

It's often useful to bind objects under subcontexts rather than under the root context. This allows the JNDI tree to be organized. For example, consider the two bindings that you may find in the JNDI tree of your WebLogic installation: `weblogic.jms.ConnectionFactory` handles JMS connections to your WebLogic Server instance, whereas `weblogic.transaction.UserTransaction` enables you to manage transactions using JTA. These are two noticeably different operations, and thus are stored in different subcontexts: `weblogic.jms` and `weblogic.transaction`.

To create a subcontext for the use of your application, use the `Context.createSubContext()` method. The following code snippet creates a subcontext named `wlsunleashed` under the root context:

```
Context ctx = getInitialContext();
ctx.createSubcontext("wlsunleashed");
```

> **NOTE**
>
> Creating a subcontext named `wlsunleashed.examples` is a two-step process. You must first create the subcontext `wlsunleashed`, followed by the subcontext `wlsunleashed.examples`.

Destroying a Subcontext

Just as subcontexts can be created, they can be destroyed. To do this, you use the `Context.destroySubcontext()` method. The following code snippet destroys the `wlsunleashed` subcontext:

```
Context ctx = getInitialContext();
ctx.destroySubcontext("wlsunleashed");
```

8

Remember that the destroySubContext method is not recursive. In other words, if a subcontext has bindings or other subcontexts within, the destroy operation fails with a `ContextNotEmptyException`.

The sample program `ch08/com/wlsunleashed/jndi/Example6.java` demonstrates how to create and destroy a subcontext.

Closing the Context

After the `InitialContext` has been used, the context isn't necessary any more. It's recommended that you close the context at this point. Closing the context simply releases any resources that have been allocated while opening and using the context.

```
if ( ctx != null && contextInitialized ) {
        ctx.close () ;
        contextInitialized = false;
}
```

Browsing the JNDI Tree from the WebLogic Console

WebLogic Server enables you to browse through its JNDI tree. This can be useful while debugging your application, especially if your application needs to create bindings. You can access the tree using the command line as well as using the administration console. To access the JNDI tree using the command line, invoke the `weblogic.Admin` Java class, with the operation `LIST`.

```
java weblogic.Admin -username system -password password LIST
```

To view the JNDI tree using the console, log on to the WebLogic Server console. Assuming that WebLogic Server is running in your localhost at port 7001, you can access the console by typing in `http://localhost:7001/console` in your Web browser. If you have a different server name and/or port number, modify the URL accordingly.

Navigate to the link mydomain→Servers→myserver. (If you have different names for your domain and/or server, modify the link accordingly.) Right-click the server name node (`myserver`) and click on View JNDI Tree. You can see a screenshot of this menu in Figure 8.2.

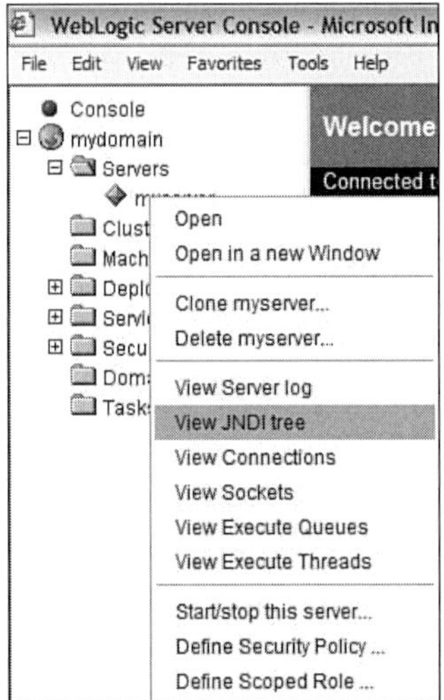

Figure 8.2 Click on View JNDI Tree to browse the JNDI tree.

This opens the JNDI tree of the server in a second browser window. The subcontexts are listed in a tree-like structure on the left pane, with the leaf-nodes representing the names of the bindings. If you have subtrees without bindings, the leaf nodes will not represent bindings. Clicking a binding name displays information about the object bound to this name on the right panel. This includes a `String` representation of this object. Figure 8.3 shows a sample screenshot of the JNDI tree.

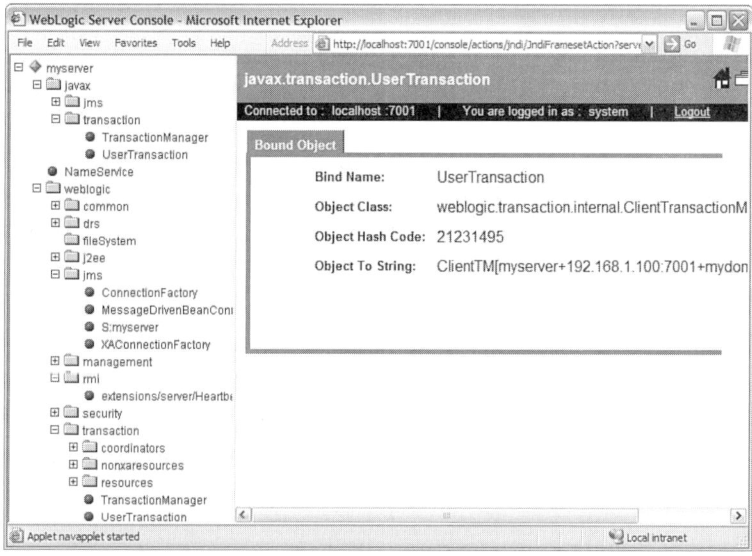

Figure 8.3 Browsing the JNDI tree of a WebLogic server.

If you've configured a J2EE component and service such as EJBs, JMS, JDBC, or RMI in the appropriate screens on the console, you'll be able to see that binding here. As you'll notice, the name of the binding you see here is the same name that you specified for the JNDI `Name` parameter while creating the component or service.

Note that you cannot add objects directly to the JNDI tree through this screen.

Private JNDI Tree

WebLogic Server also uses a private JNDI tree, which is visible only for certain components. This tree cannot be browsed using the WebLogic Server console. Only the target component has permissions to access this tree. For example, an EJB may refer to a `DataSource` object to access data from the database. To provide a level of abstraction, the EJB implementation itself will use a JNDI name such as `java:comp/env/jdbc/DataSourceName`. However, your `DataSource` object might have been loaded onto the JNDI tree under the name `com.company.data.DataSourceName`. The mapping between the internal name and the actual JNDI name is done in the configuration files for the EJB. Such JNDI bindings are present in the private tree of that EJB. No other object will have access to this binding. Any time a JNDI context begins with `java:comp/env`, that binding is present in a private tree.

You'll learn more about the use of such private trees in Part V, "Using Enterprise JavaBeans in WebLogic Applications," in this book.

JNDI and WebLogic Clusters

WebLogic clusters are used to provide high performance and fault tolerance. Several servers may participate in a WebLogic cluster. For clients to access the cluster's services, they first access the clusterwide JNDI tree. However, in practice, the clusterwide JNDI tree is not a single tree. Each server in the cluster maintains its own copy of the JNDI tree. The clustered bindings from different servers are replicated across to all the servers, keeping them in sync.

This way of maintaining the clusterwide tree offers better performance and transparency. To a client, each naming service is identical, regardless of which clustered server it's connected to—hence the concept of a single clusterwide JNDI tree.

When the servers start, the local implementations of the services (EJB, JMS, and so on) are bound to the local JNDI tree. After this, the RMI stubs of the services are sent to the other servers in the cluster by way of IP multicast. Using IP multicast ensures that all servers are updated using a single network message. When a server receives the message, it updates its copy of the JNDI tree with the received information. The RMI stub is cluster-aware; that is, it has information about which servers this service has been deployed to. When the service is deployed to one of the servers, the stub is updated with information about that server, and another multicast message is sent out, enabling the updates to the other servers. This enables the cluster to pick a server when the service is requested. Figure 8.4 shows the JNDI tree aggregation process.

Because of this mechanism, it's possible for the JNDI tree of a server to get out of sync with the other servers for a brief period of time. This can happen when an object is added to a server's tree, but the information has not yet been propagated to the other servers. But this should not pose a major problem because JNDI tree updates must be sent only in cases of a bind, rebind, or an unbind, and these operations are, and should be, relatively rare during the normal operations of the server. These operations are normally performed at server startup.

Replicated Versus Nonreplicated Bindings

RMI objects (such as EJBs) are usually deployed as replicated objects, which ensures that any server can act as the naming server for the service, whether or not that service is deployed in that server. If the service is deployed in several servers in the cluster under the same name, the cluster can choose any of the servers to service client requests. This provides for high performance and fault tolerance (only for idempotent services) in the cluster. When such objects are bound to a name in the JNDI tree, the information is propagated to the other servers in the cluster, updating their copies of the JNDI tree.

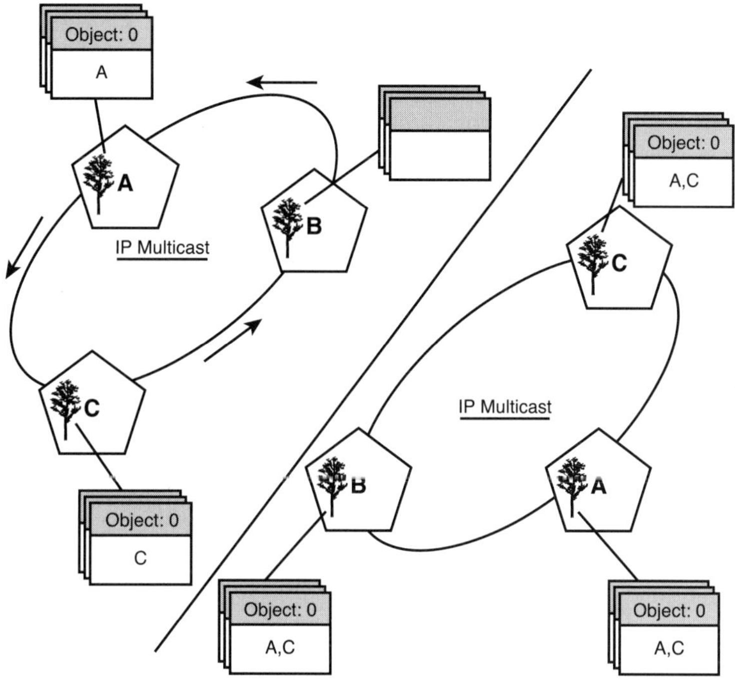

Figure 8.4 JNDI binding propagation between servers in a WebLogic cluster.

At the same time, it's possible for you to bind an object into the server's JNDI tree without replicating this information. This is quite useful in situations in which you want applications residing in each of the servers to have their own versions of objects bound in their respective JNDI trees, but you do not want them to share the data among the application instances. For example, an EJB application might want to read some server-specific properties out of a flat file and load them into the JNDI tree for later use. Here each deployment would use the same JNDI name, but bind its own `Properties` object into the JNDI tree of its server. These are known as *non-replicated bindings*.

Unless you choose the object not to be clustered, the binding is replicated across to the other servers. To tag a binding as a non-replicated, set the value of the `WLContext.REPLICATE_BINDINGS` property to `false` while creating the context. Alternatively, you can also use WebLogic's `Environment` object, and use the method `setReplicateBindings(boolean)` while creating the `InitialContext`, to achieve the same result.

Naming Conflicts in a Cluster

Imagine that two servers participate in a cluster. First, you bind an object of type A to server-1 under the name `MyObject`. This object is bound as nonreplicated, therefore, by definition, the binding information is not sent to all other servers.

In the meantime, you bind a second RMI object of type B to server-2, under the name `MyObject`. Let's make this binding replicated. Server-2 sends out a multicast message to server-1 saying that it has received a new binding of type B under the name `MyObject`. Server-1 is now confused because the object type that's already bound under the name `MyObject` (A) is different from the one that's being bound to server-2. This situation is known as a *conflict*. Obviously, there's nothing that the server can do to work around such a conflict. WebLogic Server detects such conflicts and prints out messages to the system log files. Such a condition typically implies that WebLogic Server has been configured incorrectly.

However, while using only nonreplicated bindings, there will not be any naming conflicts; that is, two servers in the cluster can have different objects using the same name bound to their JNDI trees.

TIP

Alternatively, you can also use only replicated bindings, and completely avoid nonreplicated bindings, which is a best practice in JNDI usage.

JNDI Best Practices

In this section, we look at some tips that can be useful in improving performance while using JNDI.

Avoiding Storing Application Data in the JNDI Tree

The JNDI tree should normally be used only to store objects when WebLogic Server starts up. Like any other naming service, the JNDI tree should not be used for frequent updates because it isn't designed for such tasks. You must use `Session` objects, cookies, or even databases to store temporary application data. Any updates to the JNDI tree and the objects within it have to be propagated to the other servers in the cluster. This can be expensive, especially if the object is heavy.

Optimizing Lookups from Remote Clients

While inside the JVM of WebLogic Server, making JNDI lookups are highly optimized. This amounts to making a direct method call inside the JVM. Hence, you need not be too concerned about optimizing your code in this scenario. However, performing JNDI lookups from a remote client is another story. Consider each lookup operation as a round-trip between the client and the server over the network. You should therefore keep JNDI lookups from remote clients to the bare minimum because they can negatively affect performance.

So, how do you achieve this? One alternative is to cache the results of a lookup locally and reuse the cached contents rather than going back to the server every time. Such lookups can be performed in the initialization routines of the application.

However, you should understand that caching results isn't a viable solution all the time. In cases where data can change often, you usually won't want to use a cached copy because you can't be sure whether you have the latest data. In such cases, one option might be to group operations that require JNDI lookups within your application. However, consider that JNDI values are not supposed to change that often, so such a situation should rarely arise.

In cases where lookups cannot be performed in the initialization routine, consider caching the `InitialContext` locally. Looking up the `InitialContext` is a very expensive operation. You can cache the initial context locally and reuse it. It's normally a good idea to provide for a re-lookup of the initial context (refresh), if you encounter any errors while looking up an object using the cached `InitialContext` object.

Considering the Use of a Service Locator Pattern

An extension of the caching strategy discussed in the previous section is the Service Locator pattern. A service locator object gets rid of redundant and expensive JNDI lookups by caching the service objects after a first lookup. This technique maintains a cache of service objects and provides methods to access them. Different portions of your client application can use this service locator object to obtain the service objects as and when they need it. They don't make direct JNDI lookups; rather, they go through the service locator object. Therefore, the service locator serves as an interceptor object between the client and the JNDI tree. Service locator objects can be programmed to refresh the service objects at regular intervals. Streamlining JNDI lookups using a service locator object helps to reduce network traffic, and hence it increases performance. Figure 8.5 shows this pattern in use.

8

Trying to Avoid Nonreplicated Bindings

As discussed earlier, using nonreplicated bindings increases the possibility of conflicts within the JNDI tree. By not replicating the binding, you're also essentially reducing the effectiveness of the cluster; clients must connect to *that* server to be able to get hold of the bound object. This can be a performance bottleneck, and effectively nullifies the advantages of having a cluster. You must therefore avoid using nonreplicated bindings unless you're absolutely convinced about the need for them.

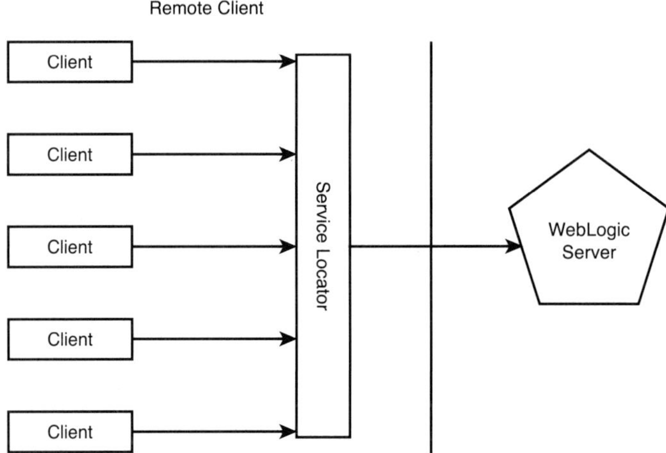

Figure 8.5 Service Locator pattern in use in a remote client.

Summary

JNDI provides your application with the capability to connect and use several object catalogs that exist in the enterprise in a standard uniform way. WebLogic Server provides an implementation of the JNDI SPI to which clients can connect seamlessly. The same clients can also connect to other naming services such as LDAP, DNS, and so on using JNDI APIs. WebLogic Server utilizes the JNDI tree extensively for its normal functioning. If your application uses an EJB, that EJB is published on the JNDI tree. Similarly, other resources such as `DataSource` objects, transaction objects, and so on are all published on the JNDI tree. The WebLogic JNDI tree is mainly useful for performing lookups of such resources within and outside of the server context. However, it isn't meant to be used for storing application data. Also keep in mind that while using JNDI from remote clients, you're essentially sending requests over the wire. Therefore, optimizing your code to improve the overall performance of your system is a must.

CHAPTER 9

Processing Transactions with the Java Transaction API

by Kunal Mittal and Joe McGuire

IN THIS CHAPTER

Distributed computing environments involve multiple components and operations working concurrently in a system. With multiple users for a single service, conflicts could occur. If two users change the same piece of data at the same time, which operation prevails? Luckily, we have transactions to coordinate the operations.

This chapter introduces you to the essential concepts of transactions. It then explains the Java Transaction API (JTA) and how to use it in the context of WebLogic Server 8.1.

WebLogic Server 8.1 supports Sun's Java Transaction API specification 1.0.1a and contains its own extensions to Sun's JTA, which enhance and extend its functionality. You'll also appreciate the ease with which transactions can be configured and monitored through WebLogic's Web-based Administration Console.

Transactions Overview

This section lays the foundation for understanding transactions in a distributed environment. Knowledge of transactional properties and how transactions are managed is essential to understanding the JTA and creating your own transaction-aware applications.

So, before we get into the definition of what makes up a transaction, let's first define the concept of *application state*. An application's state is made up of all of the data the application "knows." Application state may be stored in memory, in files (such as a text file or an XML file), or in a database. In the event of a system failure, such as a power outage, hardware failure, or system crash, we want to ensure that all the data can be restored exactly as it was before the outage, thereby restoring its state.

Now that we have a definition of state, we can define a *transaction* to be a related set of operations on an application's state. Transactions help bring order to the enterprise by combining multiple operations into a single, atomic action. Either all the individual operations complete or none of them complete. Transactions also lay out some ground rules, or *protocols*, by which all concurrent transactions abide to communicate with the data stores and ensure that no one steps on another's toes.

ACID Transactions

There are four basic properties that govern transactions, commonly referred to by the acronym ACID:

- **A**tomicity—A transaction is atomic. All the individual actions that make up a transaction are encapsulated into a single unit of work. Either all the actions occur or none of them occur. The granularity of these operations is up to the developer.
- **C**onsistency—Any alteration that a transaction makes to the data always abides by and fulfills the rules of the data store. When it ends, it leaves the data in the same consistent state. If the transaction fails, the data is in the same state it was when the transaction began.
- **I**solation—The transaction operates independent of and isolated from any other concurrent transactions on the data store. Only after the transaction has completed can its changes be viewed by other applications and transactions.
- **D**urability—The transaction's alterations persist, or are durable. After the transaction has completed, the updated (or rolled back) data is written securely to the data store. In the event of any future system failure, the data can be restored.

Consider the example of an ATM bank machine user who wants to transfer $500 from her checking account into her savings account. Atomicity assures us that either all the actions to complete her transfer commit successfully or none of them does. There are many individual actions that encapsulate the transfer transaction. You can identify the following three high-level actions:

1. Her checking account is verified to hold at least $500.
2. The $500 is subtracted from her checking account.
3. The $500 is added to her savings account.

Should there be a failure in any one of these individual actions to commit (for example, insufficient funds found, power failure, savings account invalid, and so on), they're all rolled back to their original pre-transaction states.

Consistency ensures that all the data is updated appropriately and resources are released back to the system. Our ATM user can be sure that each time she transfers funds from one account to the other, the numerical amounts are updated in the correct format required by the database. Let's assume that the transaction fails after step 2 and before step 3 can complete. In this case, the $500 must be put back into the user's checking account.

Isolation ensures that while the transaction is in process, no unexpected changes can occur in the data store. Suppose that the user's spouse attempts to make a withdrawal from the same checking account at the same time, but at a different ATM location. Isolation ensures that the first transaction (the transfer) is insulated from the second transaction (the withdrawal). The withdrawal transaction cannot access the checking account data until the transfer transaction completes. As we'll see, there are a few varying degrees of isolation that may be configured programmatically.

Durability ensures that if the user has transferred $500, she'll see that change the next time she checks her accounts, regardless of any power outages or database failures that might occur before that time.

Local Versus Global Transactions

A transaction is often classified as being either *local* or *global*, depending on its management and the number of resources it may alter.

Each participant in a transaction is called a *resource*. A resource can be a database system, persistent messaging store, or any other transaction-enabled entity. Resource managers are in charge of managing these resources. For a resource to support transactions, it must have a transaction-aware resource manager associated with it. A resource manager can be a driver, such as a transaction-aware JDBC driver, or it can be integrated into the resource itself, as is the case with WebLogic JMS resources.

Local Transactions

A local transaction involves a single resource and is restricted to a single process (all updates to the resource are committed at the end of that process). In Java, local transactions are normally managed by the objects used to access a resource. For example, a JDBC database's transactions are handled by objects that implement the `java.sql.Connection` interface. And a JMS server's transactions are handled by objects that implement the `javax.jms.Session` interface.

Global Transactions

Sometimes referred to as a *distributed* transaction, a global transaction differs from a local transaction in that it may update across two or more resource managers and JVMs. It also employs a transaction manager to manage those changes. Global transactions are usually managed by implementing the JTA `javax.transaction.UserTransaction` interface or through the transaction manager on the container.

WebLogic's global transactional support is based on The Open Group's X/Open Distributed Transactional Processing (DTP) model. DTP is the most widely adopted model for building global transactional applications. This is the same concept as XA-distributed transactions. It defines the transactional participants and the interfaces used to communicate between them. Almost all vendors developing transactional-related products, such as RDBMs, message queuing, and component containers, support the interfaces defined in the DTP model.

Global Transaction Participants

Global transactions may involve the following participants:

- Application server—The application server hosts the application by providing the infrastructure required to support the server (for example, BEA WebLogic Server).
- Application program—The application program is a component-based transactional application that has its transaction boundaries controlled through either the JTA interface or the transaction manager (examples include an EJB component, a JMS client, and a standalone Java client).
- Transaction manager—Sometimes referred to as a *transaction process monitor* (*TPM*), the transaction manager manages transactions for the application program. It communicates with all resource managers participating in a transaction and acts as a liaison between them and the application program. Based on those communications, the transaction manager can then tell the resource managers whether to commit or roll back. It then communicates the outcome back to the application program (examples are BEA WebLogic Server, BEA Tuxedo, and CICS).

The Two-Phase Commit Protocol

A transaction often manipulates data among multiple data stores. In a distributed environment there may be, and often are, many transactions occurring simultaneously, all trying to access and alter the same data on those data stores. How can these resources be coordinated to ensure data integrity? The answer comes in the form of the two-phase commit protocol. The two-phase commit protocol puts a lock on all the resources participating in a single transaction and coordinates all the resource managers to commit simultaneously. This all happens in an instant. There are two distinct phases in the global transaction process: a prepare phase and a commit phase.

1. Prepare phase—In the first phase, the resource manager attempts to record the original and the updated information (usually to a transaction log file). If successful, the resource then indicates to its resource manager that it's ready to make the changes.

This indication is a pledge that the operation *will* happen. Resources can then send their vote to the transaction manager whether to commit or roll back the transaction.

2. Commit phase—In the second phase, based on the votes sent in from all the participating resource managers, the transaction manager decides whether to commit the transaction. If all resources have voted to commit, all the resources are updated. If one or more of the resources votes to abort, all the resources are returned to their previous state.

How All the Participants Work Together to Manage a Transaction

Assume that we have a transactional application hosted on the application server and application data stored in a relational database. All the resource managers declare themselves by contacting the local transaction manager (known as *enlisting*), and then wait for an execution request from the application program. A typical request might be to insert, update, and delete records in the database.

The application program sends a commit request that updates records in two databases. The transaction manager initiates the two-phase commit protocol to communicate with each resource manager. First, the transaction manager queries each resource manager and asks whether it's prepared to commit the transaction. Based on the votes of all the participating resource managers, the transaction manager makes the decision whether to commit or roll back the transaction. It is the job of each resource manager to retain its data (both the original and the changed) pending the outcome of the global transaction. When the resource manager is holding this information, it is in the prepare phase. While in the prepare phase, the resource manager locks the data modified by the transaction to isolate these changes from any other transactions. It remains in this locked state (and thus locks the databases) until it receives a commit (or roll back) message from the transaction manager.

After receiving all the resource managers' votes, the transaction manager decides whether to commit the transaction. If all the resource managers vote to commit, the transaction goes to the commit phase, and each resource manager receives the message to update its resource. If there is at least one vote to abort, the transaction manager sends the message to abort all operations.

Finally, the application program is notified via the transaction manager whether the commit was successful.

The Java Transaction Service

When reading about transactions you are bound to come across the term *Java Transaction Service* (or *JTS*). What exactly is JTS?

Simply stated, JTS is an implementation of the transaction processing monitor paradigm. Shortly after The Open Group released its DTP model, the Object Management Group (OMG) released its own Object Transaction Service (OTS). Although based on the X/Open model, OTS replaces the DTP interfaces with CORBA IDL-aware interfaces. In this model, objects can communicate via CORBA method calls over IIOP. It was at about this time that specifications were being drawn up for the J2EE implementation of transactional services. Not surprisingly, the design of J2EE's transaction support is heavily influenced by OTS. In fact, JTS implements OTS and acts as an interface between JTA and OTS.

Recall that we defined a transaction manager as a kind of transaction process monitor (or TPM) that coordinates the execution of transactions on behalf of the application program. Transaction process monitors first appeared *en masse* with IBM's CICS in the 1960s. TPM-managed transactions were written to perform as procedural events on the database. The 1990s brought distributed object protocols such as CORBA and RMI to the scene. A new component-oriented implementation of the TPM was needed to manage those objects' transactions. The Java Transaction Service is that component-based implementation of the TPM: a component transaction-process monitor (or CTM). It is this component-oriented JTS model that WebLogic implements for its transaction management.

Transaction Isolation Level

Transactions in a distributed environment may have varying degrees of isolation, and as previously mentioned, they can be set programmatically. The degree to which those concurrent transactions can interface with one another is set by the transaction isolation level. The `java.sql.Connection` interface identifies five levels of isolation defined by integer constants. Not coincidentally, the names of those constants are the same ones used to set the isolation level of EJBs demarcated by the container, except for `TRANSACTION NONE`, which is not used by EJBs.

The isolation levels are designed to address specific data inconsistency scenarios defined by the ANSI/ISO 92 standard. Let's explore those scenarios in more detail.

Dirty Read

A *dirty read* occurs when a transaction is allowed to read data affected by another transaction before the other transaction commits. For example, assume you have a reservation system that shows all seats available in an amphitheater. Mr. X reserves four seats and pays with his credit card. Mr. Y wants to buy these same four seats, but they show up as being taken. Meanwhile, the credit card verification rejects the transaction and the seats are freed. This situation is acceptable, so dirty reads are allowed in this system.

Nonrepeatable Read

A nonrepeatable read occurs when a transaction attempts to select the same row twice, but a second transaction has modified or deleted the row in the interim. This situation might lead to unpredictable or incorrect results in the first transaction. In an auction Web site, a buyer sees that the last bid was $5. Another buyer posts a bid for $10 and commits. The first buyer posts a bid for $6, but this bid is rejected right away because there's already a higher bid in the system. During the second transaction, we checked the last bid and got the new value, although the transaction wasn't committed yet. There were two queries, yielding two different results, in the same transaction. This situation could cause trouble in other systems, but is required in the case of a bidding system. This is different from dirty reads because the buyers cannot see any bids that are not finalized (committed).

Phantom Read

A phantom read occurs when a transaction reads all rows that meet certain criteria, but a second transaction inserts a new row that meets the same criteria. If the first transaction rereads the rows, the new phantom row appears in the results. In an online bookstore, a client is searching for books by topic. At the same time, an employee is updating the book database with new books. The employee enters the ISBN of a book and its quantity, but doesn't commit (there are other books to enter). The book appears in the search results of the client. This situation is wanted; we want the clients to be able to order the book as soon as possible. Later on, the employee sees that he entered the wrong ISBN, so he erases the book from the database. The client cannot see it anymore. This is different from dirty and nonrepeatable read because the records are added, not modified. The client wouldn't see modified records until his transaction ends.

TRANSACTION_READ_UNCOMMITTED

The `TRANSACTION_READ_UNCOMMITTED` attribute gives a transaction the capability to read uncommitted data. This is the lowest level of isolation (that is, the least isolated from other transactions). Although this is certainly unacceptable for mission-critical applications, it's a good choice for read-often, update-rarely components. The payoff for data integrity is high performance and low interference. This suffers from the problems of nonrepeatable reads, phantom reads, and dirty reads.

TRANSACTION_READ_COMMITTED

The `TRANSACTION_READ_COMMITTED` attribute offers the next lowest level of transaction isolation. It denies a transaction to read uncommitted data, but allows a nonrepeatable read as well as phantom reads.

TRANSACTION_REPEATABLE_READ

The `TRANSACTION_REPEATABLE_READ` attribute offers the third level of transaction isolation. It denies a transaction the capability to read uncommitted or updated data, but allows added rows—the phantom read.

TRANSACTION_SERIALIZABLE

The `TRANSACTION_SERIALIZABLE` attribute offers the highest level of transaction isolation. While the first transaction is running, any modifications from other transactions are prevented from occurring. The transaction runs in a vacuum, insulated from all outside transactions. Although this might be good where data integrity is critical, the high overhead has a negative impact on performance. It's important to note that not all databases support serializable transactions; Oracle is one such example. An example of a situation in which a serializable behavior is required: Imagine a system that stores cars for a car dealer. Then someone wants to buy a car. While that person is looking at the car's description, nobody should be able to change the price (no dirty reads or nonrepeatable reads). Nor should anyone be able to add items to the list of previous owners (no phantom reads). We don't want to see other people modifying, adding, or removing data until the current transaction is finished.

One thing worth noting is the fact that the word *serializable* has nothing to do with Java's serialization mechanism. It merely means that transactions are performed one at a time.

TRANSACTION_NONE

The `TRANSACTION_NONE` attribute indicates that transactions are not supported. Trying to do so throws an exception. This can be used in three places:

- In the resource itself (in the database). This is the default transaction isolation level when none is provided.
- In the resource manager objects. For example, in the JDBC `Connection` object, you can set the transaction isolation level by calling (set programmatically).
- In the container configuration files. For example, in EJBs, you can set the isolation level using the `<isolation-level>` tag of `weblogic-ejb-jar.xml` (set declaratively).

Table 9.1 summarizes the isolation levels and what problems they do and do not address.

TABLE 9.1 Transaction Isolation Levels

Isolation Level	Dirty Read	Nonrepeatable Read	Phantom Read
TRANSACTION_READ_UNCOMMITTED	YES	YES	YES
TRANSACTION_READ_COMMITTED	NO	YES	YES
TRANSACTION_REPEATABLE_READ	NO	NO	YES
TRANSACTION_SERIALIZABLE	NO	NO	NO
TRANSACTION_NONE	N/A	N/A	N/A

How Transactions Are Performed by WebLogic Server

WebLogic Server can serve as both the application server and transaction manager. It also provides extensions to the JTA and an array configuration and management utilities. Those available to you depend on which type of transaction you're programming.

There are three different approaches to transaction management. The approach to be used depends on whether the transaction is local or global and, in some cases, the type of component:

- Local transactions—Resource managers can manage local transactions themselves, which is sufficient in nondistributed applications that utilize a single resource. For example, in JDBC, demarcation is easily managed with the `commit` and `rollback` methods of the `java.sql.Connection` interface.
- JTA programmatic transactions—In distributed environments with global transactions, servlets, RMI applications, MDBs, JavaBeans, and Session EJBs may be managed through the Java Transaction API. Demarcation is managed with the `begin`, `commit`, and `rollback` methods of the `javax.transaction.UserTransaction` interface.
- Container-managed transactions—Demarcation for EJBs may also be managed through the container (as we'll see, all Entity EJBs' transactions must be managed through the container). With container-managed demarcation, the transaction attributes are specified in the deployment descriptor. A transaction is rolled back via the `setRollbackOnly` method of the `javax.ejb.EJBContext` interface.

Transaction Scope

The *scope* of a transaction refers to the environment in which the transaction is performed. In WebLogic Server 8.1, transactions can execute on a standalone server or between clustered servers within a single domain or in multiple domains. Transactions also can occur between nonclustered servers. This is done using common credentials configured through the Administration Console.

The Java Transaction API and WebLogic

JTA specifies local, high-level Java interfaces between a transaction manager and the other parties involved in a distributed transactional system. The JTA package, `javax.transaction`, contains three core interfaces:

- `UserTransaction`
- `TransactionManager`
- `Transaction`

The UserTransaction Interface

The `UserTransaction` interface is implemented for bean-managed transaction boundaries. It defines six methods that allow an application to explicitly manage transaction boundaries:

- `begin`—Creates a new transaction associated with the current thread
- `commit`—Commits a transaction
- `getStatus`—Returns the status of a transaction as an integer
- `rollback`—Immediately rolls back the transaction associated with the current thread
- `setRollbackOnly`—Does not immediately roll back the transaction, but sets a flag that calls the `rollback` method after the current operation has completed
- `setTransactionTimeout`—Sets the time in seconds in which a transaction associated with the current thread will time out if not completed

  The following code is a high-level example of how to use the `UserTransaction` API:

```
// create a JNDI Initial context
Context ctx = new InitialContext();
// obtain the UserTransaction
UserTransaction utx = (UserTransaction) ctx.lookup
                                        ("java:comp/UserTransaction");
// begin the transaction
utx.begin();
//  . work.......
utx.commit();
```

With regular Java applications, such as servlets, RMI applications, JavaBeans, MDBs, and session EJBs, the `UserTransaction` interface is implemented explicitly in the source code of the application.

However, enterprise components (session beans and MDBs) may use the `TX_BEAN_MANAGED` transaction attribute, which is set in the bean's deployment descriptor, to implement the `UserTransaction` interface. In this manner, the application does not directly interface with the transaction manager, but relies on the EJB server to provide support for all of its transaction work. JTA transactions are automatically transferred from the client side to the server side when using RMI (and EJB). So, a server component can participate in a transaction and force it to roll back. However, it cannot commit or roll back; only the participant who started the transaction can finish it.

The TransactionManager Interface

The `TransactionManager` interface is the interface intended for the application server to manage transaction boundaries on behalf of the application being managed (that is, container-managed transactions). An example of using the `TransactionManager` interface follows:

```
Transaction tx = TransactionManager.suspend ();
. . .
TransactionManager.resume (tx);
```

WebLogic's `weblogic.transaction.TransactionManager` interface extends the `javax.transaction.TransactionManager` interface, allowing components using bean-managed transactions to suspend and resume their own transactions.

The Transaction Interface

The `Transaction` interface is intended for use by a resource manager to participate in and perform operations on the transaction itself. The following code snippet shows how the `Transaction` interface can be used:

```
Transaction tx = null;
      TransactionManager tm = getTransactionManager ();
  try
  {
      tx = tm.getTransaction();
  }
  catch(SystemException e)
  {
  }
  if (tx == null)
  {
      try
      {
          tm.begin();
      }
      catch(NotSupportedException e)
      {  }
      catch(SystemException e)
      {  }
  }
```

A resource manager could use this interface to enlist or delist resources, register for synchronization callbacks, commit or roll back a transaction, and obtain the status of a transaction.

NOTE

WebLogic's `weblogic.transaction.Transaction` interface extends the `javax.transaction.Transaction` interface, allowing components using bean-managed transactions to get and set transaction properties.

Other JTA Interfaces

JTA also includes the interfaces described in the next sections, which provide status and synchronization information and allow a transaction manager to work with resource managers.

NOTE

These interfaces are accessed by *only* the transaction manager.

The Status Interface

The `Status` interface (`javax.transaction.Status`) provides real-time transaction status. It enables you to specify the exact status of the transaction; for example, whether the transaction should be committed or rolled back.

The Synchronization Interface

The `Synchronization` interface (`javax.transaction.Synchronization`) provides notification with a registered listener before and after a transaction completes. You can register a transaction callback listener for each transaction that is invoked by the transaction manager.

The XAResource Interface

The `XAResource` interface (`javax.transaction.xa.XAResource`) is used by only the transaction manager to work with resource managers of XA-compliant resources. The industry-standard XA interface is based on the X/Open CAE specification.

The Xid Interface

The `Xid` interface (`javax.transaction.xa.Xid`) is also used by only the transaction manager to retrieve transaction identifiers from the X/Open transaction identifier (XID) structure. The XID is rarely if ever accessed by an application server in the context of transactional processing. The `Xid` interface provides methods that provide the transaction's format ID, a global transaction ID, and a branch qualifier.

WebLogic Extensions to the JTA

WebLogic provides the `weblogic.transaction` package to build on the Sun JTA specification and provide additional functionality.

The WebLogic TransactionManager Interface

As we saw earlier, the `javax.transaction.TransactionManager` interface is to be used exclusively by an application server to manage container-managed transactions. The WebLogic extension `weblogic.transaction.TransactionManager` permits access to the transaction manager from components using bean-managed transactions through a JNDI lookup. The bean-managed components can then suspend and resume transactions on their own behalf. The extension can also be used to allow XA resources to register and unregister themselves with the transaction manager on startup.

The WebLogic Transaction Interface

Recall that the `javax.transaction.Transaction` interface is to be used exclusively by a resource manager. The WebLogic extension `weblogic.transaction.Transaction` interface allows clients using bean-managed transactions to get and set their own transaction properties.

The WebLogic TxHelper Class

The `weblogic.transaction.TxHelper` class is a convenience wrapper to gain access to the current transaction manager and transaction. It provides the ability to get the transaction using the transaction manager and to check the status of the transaction.

The WebLogic XAResource Interface

The WebLogic `XAResource` interface extends the `javax.transaction.xa.XAResource` interface. It provides the XA resource provider with the capability to delist XA resources.

Configuring Container-Managed Enterprise Components

Unlike regular client applications, enterprise components (EJBs) provide support for declarative transactions. Transactional attributes are associated with the component methods at deployment time, rather than being explicitly demarcated in the code.

The Declarative Transaction Model

In the declarative transaction model, it is the application server's responsibility to demarcate and manage the transaction based on the values declared in the deployment descriptors.

Container-Managed Transaction Attributes

Six transactional attributes may be assigned to an enterprise component:

- `NotSupported`
- `Supports`
- `Mandatory`
- `Required`
- `RequiresNew`
- `Never`

These transaction attributes are configured in the enterprise component's `ejb-jar.xml` deployment descriptor, such as

```
<transaction-type>Container or Bean</transaction-type>
<trans-attribute>Mandatory or Supports or
Required or Requires New or Never or Not Supported</trans-attribute>
```

Transactional attributes can be configured to apply to the entire component or to a single method in the component's remote interface.

> **CAUTION**
>
> If attributes are specified at both the component and method levels, the method-level value takes precedence over the component-level value.

Let's look at each of these attributes in a little more detail, paying attention to what happens to a method call to a component when a transaction does or does not exist.

NotSupported

The `NotSupported` attribute ensures that the underlying component instance does not operate within a global transaction:

- If a method is called from within a transaction, the container suspends the transaction before calling the component's method. When the component method returns, the container resumes the client's transaction before returning control to the client.
- If a method is not called from within any transaction, the method will be called successfully.

NOTE

This is not supported for Entity EJBs because all Entity EJB transactions *must* be managed by the container!

Supports

The `Supports` attribute ensures that the underlying component instance is included in any client-started transaction. However, the container will not start a transaction for the client. If the client does not start a transaction before calling the component's method, the component won't take part in any subsequent transactions. This mechanism allows a component to operate only within the client demarcation boundaries: Whether or not the method is called from within a global transaction, the method will always be called successfully.

Mandatory

The `Mandatory` attribute ensures that the component's method can be invoked by a client only if the client passes a global transaction to that component. This mechanism thereby forces the client program to always demarcate its own transaction boundaries:

- If a method is called from within a transaction, the method call returns from the component successfully.
- If a method is not called from within any transaction, the container does not start a transaction and a `TransactionRequiredException` is thrown because there must already be an underlying transaction.

Required

The `Required` attribute forces a method call on a component to be always executed within a transaction started by either the client or the container:

- If a method is called from within a transaction, the method call to the component returns successfully.
- If a method is not called from within a transaction, the container first starts one, and then the method call returns from the component successfully.

RequiresNew

The `RequiresNew` attribute ensures that the container always starts a transaction. It forces the component to execute within a new transaction that is to be started by the container only. The container always starts a localized transaction before calling any of the EJB's methods:

- If a method is called from within a transaction, the client's transaction is suspended for the duration of the call to the component. The container starts its own localized transaction.

CAUTION

This scenario should be avoided because if an error occurs within the EJB, the error localization is the container only, even when the client might need to know about it!

- If a method is not called from within any transaction, the container starts a localized transaction, and then the method call returns from the component successfully.

Never

The `Never` attribute ensures that a method call to a component is never to take place within a transaction:

- If a method is called from within a transaction, a `RemoteException` exception is thrown.
- If a method is not called from within any transaction, the method call to the component is returned successfully.

JTA Properties in the Administration Console

The Administration Console is an excellent tool with which you can dynamically configure and monitor your transactions in real-time. In this section, we examine some of the more remarkable features of JTA management through the Administration Console.

Transaction Configuration

The Administration Console enables you to define defaults for transaction timeouts, limits, and transaction manager behavior. The default behavior can be overridden by settings in the `weblogic-ejb-jar.xml` file or programmatically. Let's take a look at the JTA page in the Administration Console. If you haven't already done so, start WebLogic Server and log in to the Administration Console.

Click on the JTA icon in the left panel to display the Transaction Management page of the Administration Console, as shown in Figure 9.1. It's here that you'll turn when you want to change transaction management settings.

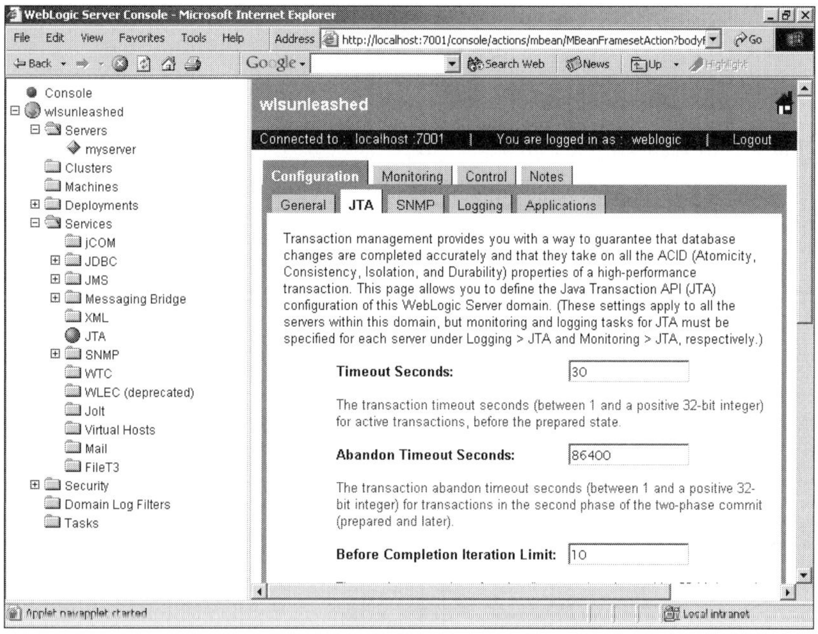

FIGURE 9.1 The JTA Management page.

Let's take a look at each of the configurable fields and see what each one does:

- Timeout Seconds—The first field shows the time (in seconds) in which a transaction will timeout if uncommitted (default = 30 seconds).
- Abandon Timeout Seconds—Determines the transaction abandon timeout in seconds (default = 86400 seconds [24 hours]).
- Before Completion Iteration Limit—Sets the maximum number of cycles the transaction manager will call the `beforeCompletion` method on the `Synchronization` interface. `beforeCompletion` is a callback method called by the transaction manager at the start of the completion process (default = 10 seconds).
- Max Transactions—The maximum number of simultaneous, in progress, transactions allowed to run on a server at any given time (default = 10000 transactions).
- Max Unique Name Statistics—The maximum number of unique transaction names allowed for which statistics will be maintained (default = 1000 names).
- Checkpoint Interval Seconds—The interval at which the transaction manager creates a new transaction log file and checks all old transaction log files to see whether they're ready to be deleted (default = 300 seconds; minimum = 10 seconds; maximum = 1800 seconds).

- Forget Heuristics—Returns a Boolean indicating whether the transaction manager automatically performs a `forget` operation on the `XAResource` interface for transaction heuristic completions (default checked = true). By unchecking the box, context information for heuristic completions is saved and written to the server log. This can be helpful in resolving resource manager data inconsistencies.

Transaction Monitoring

WebLogic provides real-time transaction monitoring through the Administration Console. To access the Transaction Monitoring page, perform the following steps:

1. Start WebLogic Server for the domain that you want to monitor.
2. Log on to the Administration Console.
3. In the left panel, click the Servers icon to display all configured servers in the domain. Click on the server in which you want to monitor JTA.
4. In the right panel, first click on the Monitoring tab and then on the JTA tab. The JTA Monitoring page is displayed, as in Figure 9.2.

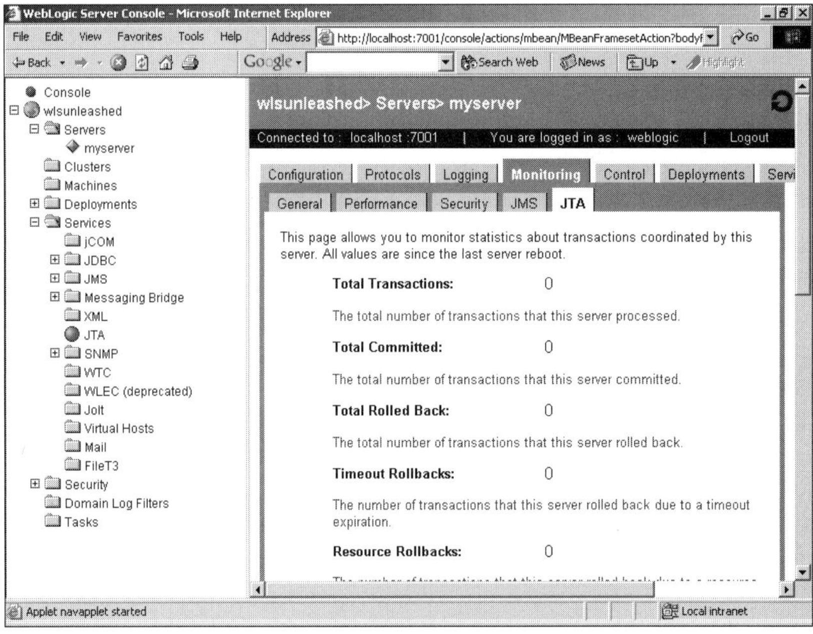

FIGURE 9.2 The Transaction Monitoring page.

The Transaction Monitoring page is a useful tool to see how your transactions are performing in the real world. It's also a good place to start debugging if there are problems. Let's take a look at some of the Transaction Monitoring fields and see what they mean:

- Total Transactions—The total number of transactions processed (includes committed, rolled back, and heuristic completions).
- Total Committed—The total number of committed transactions.
- Total Rolled Back—The total number of rolled back transactions.
- Timeout Rollbacks—The total number of transactions that were rolled back because the transaction Timeout Seconds expiration setting was reached.
- Resource Rollbacks—The total number of transactions that were rolled back because of a resource error.
- Application Rollbacks—The total number of transactions that were rolled back because of a application error.
- System Rollbacks—The total number of transactions that were rolled back because of an internal system error.
- Total Heuristics—The total number of transactions that completed with a heuristic status.
- Transaction Abandon Total Count—The total number of transactions that were abandoned.
- Average Commit Time—The average time, in milliseconds, for your transactions to complete.

You can also click on the links at the bottom of the page to monitor transactions by name or by resource, and *inflight transactions* (transactions that are in progress, but have not yet been committed).

Transaction Logging

Log files are another useful tool to see how your transactions are performing, and also a good place to debug if there are problems. They are the physical representation of the internal state of the transaction manager. Deleting a log file can cause the transaction manager to fail. These files must be backed up like the rest of the configuration files. If you're using a replication tool to keep a backup computer up-to-date, log files must be replicated, too. In case of a server failure, if you want to use the backup server, the transaction logs are necessary for the normal processing to go on.

Transaction logging is configured through the Administration Console.

To access the JTA Log File Configuration page, do the following:

1. Start WebLogic Server for the domain that you want to monitor.
2. Log on to the Administration Console.
3. In the left panel, click the Servers icon to display all configured servers in the domain. Click on the server in which you want to monitor JTA.
4. In the right panel, first click on the Logging tab, and then on the JTA tab. The JTA Log File Configuration page is displayed as shown in Figure 9.3.

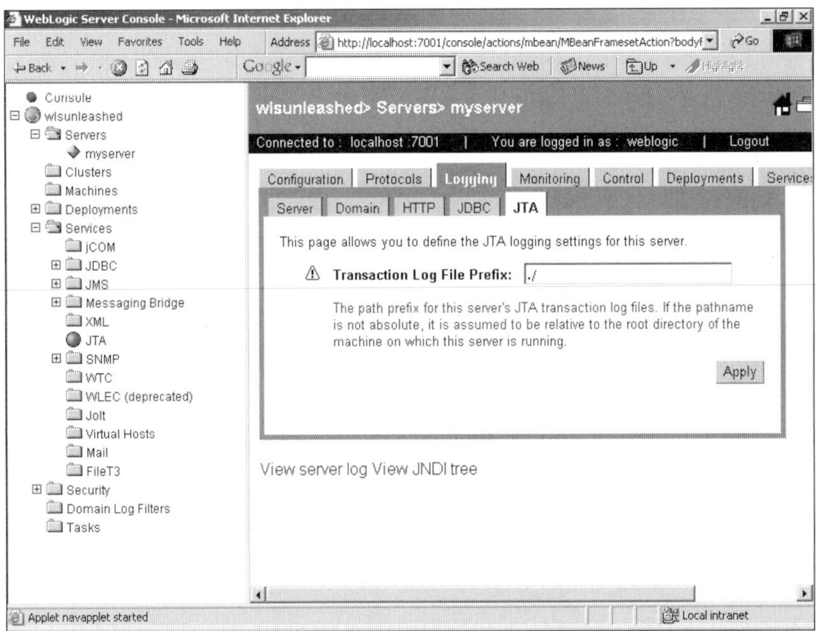

FIGURE 9.3 The Transaction Log File Configuration page.

Your JTA transaction Log files are normally written out to the root directory of your server, such as

```
C:/bea/user_projects/mydomain/myserver/myserver.0001.tlog
```

The Transaction Log File Configuration page enables you to configure a different pathname and prefix for the server's transaction log file output. The pathname is not absolute, and assumes the path entered to be relative to the root of the directory of the machine on which the server is running. For instance, if you enter the prefix `./Sunday/jun3002`, your JTA log files will create a subdirectory `/Sunday`, and add the `jun3002` prefix string to the front of your JTA log files, to be created as `C:/bea/user_projects/mydomain/myserver/Sunday/jun3002myserver.0000.tlog` where *myserver* is the name of your domain server. This can help keep your JTA log files organized when debugging.

Global Auctions Use of JTA

In the Global Auctions application, the `ProcessBidMDB` is the component used to process customers' bids. The MDB processes JMS messages received asynchronously, and notifications are returned to the user via an email sent through the `AuctionMailServlet`. The `ProcessBidMDB` can be used to read current bid information on an item, set a current bid, and close the bidding when the auction deadline has been met. Many different actors concurrently use the bean to read and update bid information on their item. This makes the `ProcessBidMDB` a good candidate for transaction management.

In this section, we'll configure the `ProcessBidMDB` to participate in a container-managed transaction. All that is required to configure the component for container-managed transactions is to modify the deployment descriptor file: `ejb-jar.xml`.

Specifying the Transaction Type

In a text editor (or, better yet, an XML editor), open the `ejb-jar.xml` file. Transaction type is defined as being either container managed or bean managed. You designate which by adding the transaction type element within the `<transaction-type>...</transaction-type>` tags. This can be either `Container` for container-managed or `Bean` for bean managed. Our `ProcessBidMDB` is going to be container managed, so we use the `Container` attribute. The `<transaction-type>...</transaction-type>` element tags lie between the `<message-driven>...</message-driven>` tags, as shown in Listing 9.1.

LISTING 9.1 ejb-jar.xml

```
<?xml version="1.0"?><!DOCTYPE ejb-jar PUBLIC "-//Sun Microsystems, Inc.
//DTD Enterprise JavaBeans 2.0//EN" "http://java.sun.com/dtds/ejb-jar_2_0.dtd">
<ejb-jar>
  <enterprise-beans>
    <message-driven>
      <ejb-name>EJB_Name</ejb-name>
      <ejb-class>com.wlsunleashed.EJB.ejbExample</ejb-class>
      <transaction-type>Container</transaction-type>
      <message-driven-destination>
         <destination-type>javax.jms.Queue</destination-type>
      </message-driven-destination>
</message-driven>
</enterprise-beans>
</ejb-jar>
```

9

After you've modified the `ejb-jar.xml` file, save it and close it.

> **NOTE**
>
> In this chapter, we've shown snippets of code and talked about various transaction APIs. The aim here is not to show complete code, but just to give you enough of an idea of how transactions work within Weblogic Server 8.1. Concepts such as EJBs will be explained in later chapters, and full code samples will be provided.

Specifying the Default Transaction Attribute

Recall that the transaction attribute defines how transactions are handled by the container. The default transaction attribute is also specified in the `ejb-jar.xml` file between the `<trans-attribute>...</trans-attribute>` element tags. These tags are between the `<message-driven>...</message-driven>` element tags.

There are six different transaction attributes that you can define in the deployment descriptor: `NotSupported`, `Required`, `Supports`, `RequiresNew`, `Mandatory`, or `Never`. The attributes were defined earlier in the chapter.

> **TIP**
>
> A transaction attribute may also be defined on the method level. When a client invokes a method on an enterprise component, the container checks the `trans-attribute` setting for that method. If found, that method-level transaction attribute is used; if not, the transaction attribute assigned to the entire bean is used.

Configuring a component for container-managed transactions is not hard at all. Bean-managed transactions are not that more difficult. Your bean just needs to obtain the `UserTransaction` interface and you handle the management methods with appropriate method calls. You set the transaction-type attribute to `Bean` and let WebLogic's JTS handle all the rest.

Best Practice for Choosing Transaction Attributes

In this section, we discuss the best practices for choosing the appropriate transaction attributes. The recommended choice for a transaction attribute is `Required` because it ensures that the methods of an enterprise bean are invoked under a JTA transaction. These EJBs can be made to perform work under the scope of a single transaction.

- If an enterprise bean method needs to commit its results unconditionally, the `RequiresNew` transaction attribute is the right choice. That attribute always creates a new transaction, regardless of whether another transaction is in progress—an example is logging. The appropriate method in the EJB that performs logging should be invoked with the `RequiresNew` attribute. This ensures that logging is performed regardless of whether other transactions complete or are rolled back.

- The `NotSupported` transaction attribute can be used when the resource being accessed for a transaction cannot be part of a JTA transaction. This is generally used when accessing external systems that do not support J2EE transactions. The J2EE server does not have any control over that system's transactions.
- The `Supports` transaction attribute is not recommended at all. `Supports` can lead to violations of the ACID properties because the EJB behaves differently based on the transaction context of the calling code.
- The transaction attributes `Mandatory` and `Never` can be used when it's necessary to verify the transaction association of the calling client. They put constraints on the transactionality of the calling components.

Summary

Transactions are an essential tool for maintaining data integrity in distributed computing systems. WebLogic's implementation of JTA gives Java programmers access to a robust transaction manager that supports manual or automatic transaction management in accordance with the J2EE specification. The WebLogic transaction manager also fully supports the EJB 2.0 specification, including container-managed transaction semantics for Session, Message-Driven, and Entity EJBs.

CHAPTER 10

Managing Database Connectivity Using JDBC

by Subramanian H Kovilmadam

IN THIS CHAPTER

- JDBC Architecture
- PointBase Database Server
- Basic JDBC Features
- Advanced JDBC Features
- WebLogic JDBC—Monitoring and Tuning
- JDBC—Best Practices
- JDBC and the Global Auctions Management System

The heart of any enterprise application is usually a database, where applications store and access data for providing business functionality. Several types of databases are available in the market. The same application often has to access more than one database to provide business functionality. Therefore, it is imperative for enterprise applications to have a standard, uniform mechanism of accessing a wide range of databases. Sun Microsystems' Java Database Connectivity API (JDBC) provides such a mechanism for Java-based applications that require access to the enterprise data. JDBC enables you to submit Structured Query Language (SQL) commands to any JDBC compliant database.

JDBC, like Microsoft's Open Database Connectivity (ODBC) standard, addresses the issue of a mechanism for uniform connectivity to databases. Both JDBC and ODBC are based on the Open Group (X/Open) SQL Call Level Interface (CLI) standard. Without these APIs, applications must use the APIs provided by the individual databases to access them. Using JDBC, you can code to a single standard API, and then plug-and-play different database drivers depending on which database you want to access. This mechanism clearly separates development and deployment activities, and also enables easy migration between databases.

Another advantage of using such a mechanism is that you no longer need to pre-compile embedded SQL statements in your code. If you have worked with a language such as Pro-C, you might be familiar with the requirement of pre-compiling your code, when the SQL statements are converted into native C language constructs. Because this is no longer necessary using JDBC, it makes your application more portable and also facilitates cleaner client/server relationships.

WebLogic Server 8.1 supports JDBC v2.0. In this chapter, we discuss some basic JDBC concepts and focus on the JDBC features provided by WebLogic Server 8.1.

JDBC Architecture

The protocol for communicating with a database normally is not compatible across different databases. Therefore, there is a need for a product, known as a *database driver*, to convert the JDBC calls into the native call for the particular database. Needless to say, each database requires a different driver. Applications that use JDBC communicate to the database by using drivers.

JDBC consists of two major sets of APIs: one for the application developers and another low-level JDBC driver API for driver developers. A discussion of the JDBC driver API is beyond the scope of this book. WebLogic supports any driver that conforms to the JDBC driver API.

JDBC drivers fit into four different categories. In this section, we discuss the different types of drivers and how they fit into the JDBC architecture.

- Type 1 drivers—The original JDBC implementation simply leveraged the features offered by ODBC drivers. Because ODBC had become quite popular, several ODBC drivers were already available in the market. Type 1 drivers use the existing ODBC drivers and provide a bridge, which converts the JDBC API calls to ODBC API calls. These are commonly referred to as the *JDBC-ODBC Bridge*. Obviously, using these drivers has performance implications because there is another layer (ODBC) to convert to. Another disadvantage is that the ODBC native code must be loaded on the client's machine. Because this type of driver uses native code, you cannot use them in an application such as an applet that works in the Java sandbox. Type 1 drivers are rarely used today. Figure 10.1 outlines a simple JDBC architecture using this type of driver.
- Type 2 drivers—A Type 2 driver converts JDBC calls directly into client APIs provided by the database, without the need for an intermediate ODBC layer. For this reason, these drivers offer better performance than Type 1 drivers. Such drivers are known as *native API partly Java drivers*. Type 2 drivers communicate with the database by using the native client library provided by the database. This library is required to be loaded on the client machine. Because of this, applets cannot use these types of drivers. This architecture can be seen in Figure 10.2.

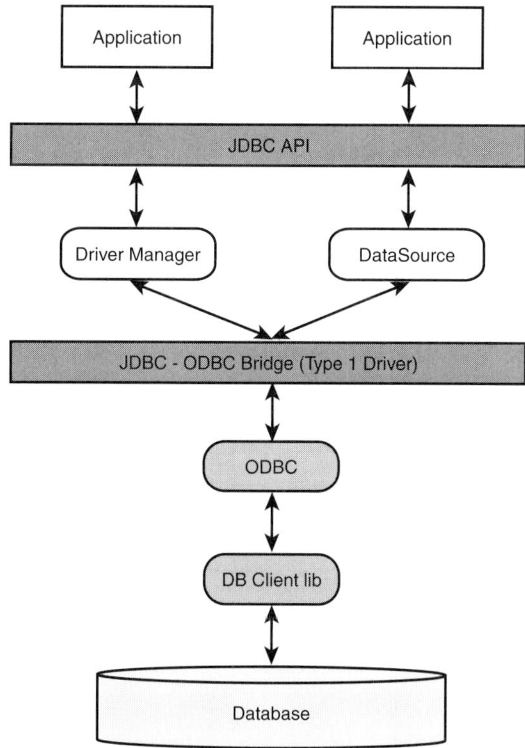

Figure 10.1 JDBC architecture—Type 1 drivers.

- Type 3 drivers—These drivers follow the three-tiered approach to client/server applications. The driver converts JDBC calls into the middleware's protocol and is sent to the server (middle tier). The calls are then converted to the DBMS protocol inside the middleware and sent to the database. The middleware usually supports several databases, thus providing access to different databases to the clients. Such drivers are usually referred to as the *Net protocol all-Java drivers*. This type of driver is useful for providing database access to applets directly. These drivers act as a proxy for database access by applets and other applications. Figure 10.3 represents a typical architecture using a Type 3 driver.

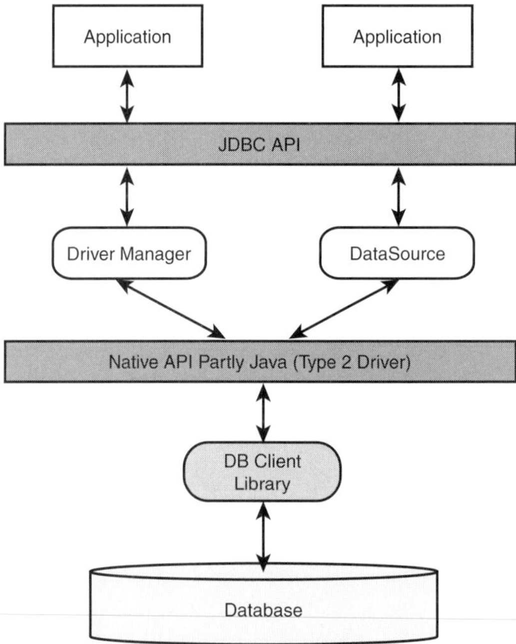

Figure 10.2 JDBC architecture—Type 2 drivers.

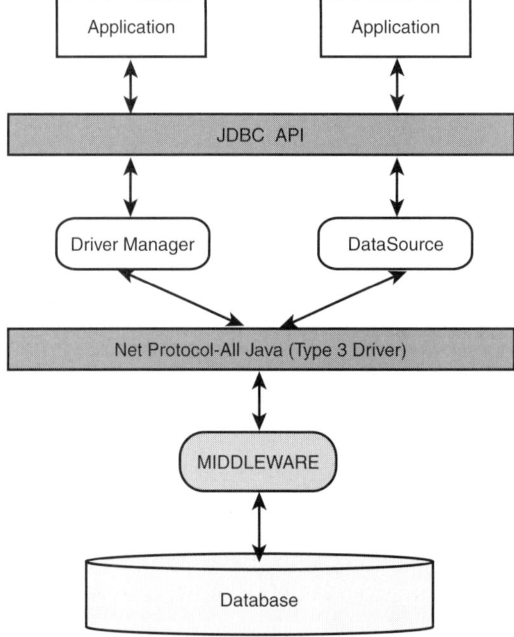

Figure 10.3 JDBC architecture—Type 3 drivers.

- Type 4 drivers—The *native protocol all-Java drivers* talk pure Java. They are aware of the underlying protocol used by the database, and they communicate directly with the database without the use of a middle layer. JDBC calls are converted into vendor-specific DBMS protocols. The difference between Type 4 and Type 2 drivers is that these drivers are implemented fully using Java, without the need for native libraries. Being pure Java provides very good performance compared to their mixed counterparts. Because no native code is used, these drivers may be used by applets. Your application obviously needs different drivers to communicate with different databases while using these types of drivers. Figure 10.4 represents a simple architecture using a Type 4 driver.

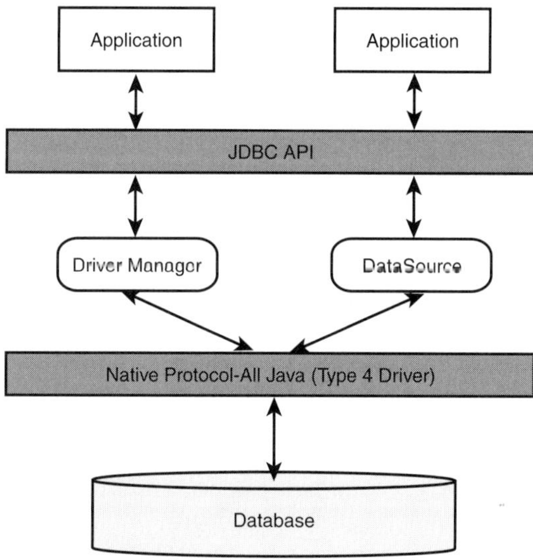

Figure 10.4 JDBC architecture—Type 4 drivers.

What Type of Driver Should I Use?

This is one question that probably has no definitive answer; it all depends on what your situation really is. Generally speaking, Types 1 and 2 should not be preferred, simply because they use native libraries. It's always preferable to reduce the number of components interacting with each other in your application in order to make it less complex and more maintainable. In the past, developers have used Type 2 drivers simply because native code tends to be faster. Type 2 drivers also have the advantage of being time-tested because they've been in use for quite a while. However, debugging your application does get rather tricky while using a native library. If you encounter a bug in your application, the error could very well be in the library, which is quite hard to track down. Again, with Type 2 drivers, you must have the native libraries installed on the client that requires the database access. There is no such requirement with Type 4 drivers. These drivers can be downloaded along with the other classes of your applet. With the new JVMs being rather advanced and fast, Type 4 drivers should be preferred over Type 2 for these reasons. If you want your client to access multiple databases, or if you want your applet to access a database that is hosted in a server other than your Web server, you'll want to go with Type 3 drivers.

Available JDBC Drivers with WebLogic Server

WebLogic ships with a few drivers that you can use with the server. This section discusses a few options that you have for using a driver with WebLogic Server. WebLogic supports both two-tier and multi-tier drivers.

NOTE

Be careful not to confuse the terms *Type 2 drivers* and *two-tier drivers*. Two-tier drivers provide database access without using a middle tier. You can and do have Type 4, two-tier drivers (for example, the WebLogic jDriver for Microsoft SQL Server).

WebLogic Server Two-Tier Drivers

Two-tier drivers provide database access directly between a connection pool and the database. WebLogic Server uses vendor-specific JDBC drivers, such as the WebLogic jDriver for Oracle and Microsoft SQL Server to connect to the respective databases. The following are some of the Type 2 and Type 4 two-tier drivers provided with WebLogic Server:

- WebLogic ships with a Type 2 native jDriver for Oracle. It also comes with an extension of this driver, which provides distributed transaction capability (XA Compliance). To use this driver, you must have a complete Oracle client installation on the workstation where you intend to run the application. Also, the Oracle client version must match the backend Oracle database. To learn more about configuring jDriver for Oracle and Oracle/XA, please refer to the WebLogic Server documentation available at `http://edocs.bea.com/wls/docs81/oracle/index.html`.
- WebLogic also ships with a pure-Java Type 4 jDriver for Microsoft SQL Server for providing connectivity to SQL Server databases. This driver has been deprecated with the 8.1 release of WebLogic Server. You must use the driver supplied by Microsoft instead of this driver. For more information about configuring and using this driver, please refer to the WebLogic server documentation at `http://edocs.bea.com/wls/docs81/mssqlserver4/index.html`. For more information about using the Microsoft driver, you can refer to `http://edocs.bea.com/wls/docs81/jdbc/thirdparty.html#1099135`.

WebLogic Server Multi-Tier Drivers

A multi-tier driver provides vendor-neutral database access. A Java application can use a multi-tier driver to access any database configured in WebLogic Server. Examples of multi-tier drivers supported by WebLogic are RMI, Pool, and JTS. Pool and JTS drivers are used only on the server-side. This section discusses the multi-tier driver options you have while using WebLogic Server.

- WebLogic RMI driver—RMI drivers are multi-tier Type 3 drivers that ship with WebLogic Server. Although these drivers can be used on remote clients, it's recommended that you look up a `DataSource` object from the JNDI tree and use that instead to get a database connection. The `DataSource` internally uses an RMI driver to get you the database connection. Because the `DataSource` object handles the details of RMI implementation internally, you don't need to worry about them. If you don't understand what a `DataSource` object is, don't fret; we look at it later in this chapter.
- WebLogic Pool driver—A server-side application such as a servlet or an EJB can use a Pool driver to obtain a connection from a connection pool. However, it is recommended that you look up a `DataSource` object from the JNDI tree and obtain the connection from that object. The `DataSource` object uses a Pool driver internally to get you the connection. Remote clients cannot use Pool drivers.
- WebLogic JTS driver—For cases in which you want to achieve distributed transaction support across multiple servers using one database instance, you can use a WebLogic JTS driver. This is a server-side JDBC driver that provides access to a connection pool as well as transactions for applications running in your server. Any application in the same thread that enters a transactional mode with this driver is assured to get the same connection to the database from the same connection pool. Once the transaction is committed or rolled back, the connection is returned to the connection pool. While working with a single instance of Oracle database, this driver is more efficient than the jDriver for Oracle XA because it avoids two-phase commits.

You can learn more about the uses of all these drivers in BEA WebLogic Server documentation, which can be found at `http://edocs.bea.com/wls/docs81/jdbc/rmidriver.html`.

PointBase Database Server

Before proceeding with the discussion on the features of JDBC, let's take a minute and talk about a pure-Java database server that we'll use in our examples.

PointBase is a pure-Java implementation of a relational database management system (RDBMS). You must have a JVM installed on your machine to use PointBase server, which you will if you have WebLogic Server installed. PointBase documentation says the server works on all platforms with a Java Virtual Machine. It has been tested on a variety of platforms including Microsoft Windows NT, Macintosh, Solaris, and Linux. It comes equipped with a graphical database management console to enable you to create and work with database schemas. PointBase comes in three different flavors:

- PointBase Micro Edition—Provides single connection to the database from one application running on the same JVM. This edition provides local access only.
- PointBase Embedded Edition—Provides multiple connections to the database from one application running on the same JVM. This edition provides local access only.
- PointBase Server Edition—Provides multiple connections to the database from multiple Java applications. Provides both local and network connection support. This edition is ideal for a server, such as an application server, serving multiple clients locally or over a network.

WebLogic Server 8.1 ships with an evaluation version of PointBase Server Edition. At the time this book is being written, the version shipping with WebLogic 8.1 is PointBase Server Edition 4.4. You can download an evaluation copy of a later version of PointBase (if available) from `http://www.pointbase.com`, although doing so isn't required for the purpose of this chapter. In this section, we discuss how to work with the PointBase server version 4.4 that ships with WebLogic 8.1.

Looking for PointBase Components in Your WebLogic Installation

The PointBase server components can be found under the subdirectory `common/eval/pointbase` (`${POINTBASE_HOME}`) under the WebLogic installation directory (`${WL_HOME}`) on your machine.

The `docs` subdirectory contains useful documentation for using the server and the console. The `lib` sub-directory contains the JAR files needed to use the database Server. The `tools` subdirectory contains scripts that you can use to start the default PointBase database instance and the console to connect to it.

Three JARs make up the PointBase database server. They are as follows:

- `pbserver.jar`—Contains the core PointBase database server, which will be used to start the PointBase server.
- `pbclient.jar`—Contains the class files that will be used by the clients connecting to the PointBase server.
- `pbtools.jar`—Contains some useful tools, including the classes that make up the PointBase server console.

> **NOTE**
>
> The names of the actual JAR files might include the version number (and perhaps also the build number); for example, the server JAR file might be named `pbserver44.jar`. In the following sections, we refer to the JAR files with their basic names (for example, `pbserver.jar`); you must substitute them with the actual filename if required. Also, any reference to these JAR files implies that the JAR files are present in the `${POINTBASE_HOME}/lib` subdirectory, unless otherwise specified.

Starting the PointBase Server

To start the PointBase server, set your `CLASSPATH` to include the JAR files `$JAVA_HOME/lib/tools.jar` and the full path to the `pbserver.jar`. Now execute the class file `com.pointbase.net.netServer`. Some of the command-line parameters used by this class are

- `/port:`*`nnnn`*—Where *`nnnn`* is a valid port number. By default, the PointBase server starts on port 9092. You need to specify this only if you want to change the default behavior.
- `/pointbase.ini=`*`<ini_file>`*—Where *`<ini_file>`* is a qualified filename of the PointBase server `.ini` filename. This file indicates several parameters to the server. One of the key parameters is the directory under which the databases must be created and found. A sample `.ini` file for PointBase comes with your WebLogic installation, and can be found under `${WL_HOME}/samples/domains/examples` and is named `pointbase.ini`.
- `/noconsole`—Starts the PointBase server as a background thread (on Unix and Solaris platforms) without the console window.

The class takes other command-line parameters, which can be found in the PointBase documentation.

> **NOTE**
>
> If you want to use the default database instance shipped with your WebLogic installation, you can simply use the scripts provided under the `${POINTBASE_HOME}/tools` subdirectory.

Starting the PointBase Console

To start the PointBase console, include the JAR files `pbclient.jar` and `pbtools.jar` in your `CLASSPATH`. Execute the class `com.pointbase.tools.toolsConsole` to bring up the PointBase console. The console uses Sun Microsystems' Swing library for its GUI. After it starts, you must provide four parameters in order to connect to the database:

- `Driver`—Specifies the driver to use to connect to the database. The value for this field is its default value: `com.pointbase.jdbc.jdbcUniversalDriver`. You should have no reason to change this.
- `URL`—The URL of the database to connect to. The URL is of the form `jdbc:pointbase:server://<host>[:<port>]/<db>` where *<host>* is the host name on which the server is running (for example, `localhost`). *<port>* is the port on which the server is listening. This is an optional value and must be specified only if the server was started on a port other than 9092. *<db>* is the name of your database (for example, `demo` in the case of the default instance).
- `User`—The user ID to use while connecting to the database. This field is not case sensitive. The default PointBase user ID is `PBPUBLIC`. The default system administrator user ID for PointBase is `PBSYSADMIN`.
- Password—The password of the user. This field is not case sensitive. The default password for the default user is `PBPUBLIC`. The password for the default system administrator login is `PBSYSADMIN`.

After you provide these values and click the OK button, the console will connect with the database server.

NOTE

You can use the scripts provided under the `${POINTBASE_HOME}/tools` subdirectory for starting the console.

Working with the PointBase Console

The PointBase Console has a self-descriptive GUI and you can access several of its features from its menu.

Clicking on the menu item Catalog, Catalog opens the catalog as a tree view and enables you to browse through the different schemas available in the current database. You can create a new schema by selecting the DBA, Create, Schema option. Right-clicking on a schema name in the tree view gives you the option of creating new tables. You may also create a new table by selecting the DBA, Create, Table menu option, which starts a wizard for creating new tables.

You may enter one or more SQL command in the Enter SQL Commands window on the main screen. The SQL commands can then be executed by selecting the SQL, Execute All menu item. The SQL menu also provides for mechanisms by which you can commit or rollback updates to the database. Right-clicking a table in the Catalog tree view also provides you with easy access to some simple predefined SQL statements.

You can perform several other tasks using the PointBase console, but it's beyond the scope of this chapter to discuss how to work with the console to perform those tasks.

> **NOTE**
>
> You can refer to the PointBase console documentation that ships with your WebLogic installation for working with the console. You can find the PDF files in the `docs` subdirectory of your `${POINTBASE_HOME}`.

The PointBase Database Driver

The PointBase driver is used to access PointBase databases using JDBC. The name of the PointBase driver that ships with the installation is `com.pointbase.jdbc.jdbcUniversalDriver`. (Sound familiar? The console uses JDBC behind the scenes to access the PointBase database.) The driver uses the parameters passed in while connecting to the server (such as URL, username, password, and so on) to connect to the PointBase database. This driver is a Type 4, or a native protocol all-Java driver, which directly accesses the PointBase database for servicing calls.

Case Study: XYZ Confectionaries

Now that we are familiar with the usage of the PointBase database server, let's create a schema for use in our examples. Let's take a simple case study and work with it as we discuss the features of JDBC.

We are building a schema for a billing system for a confectionary store, XYZ Confectionaries. The system must keep track of items and each item's unit price, as well as information about each sale.

When we model our case study, we'll have the following tables in our schema:

- The ITEM Table—This table stores a list of items that are present in the store, along with the stock quantity and unit price. Refer to Table 10.1 for the table definition.
- The BILL Table—This table maintains information about each generated bill—the bill ID and the total sale amount. Refer to Table 10.2 for the table definition.
- The BILL_ITEM Table—This table lists various items that are part of a bill, and the quantity of that item purchased. Refer to Table 10.3 for the table definition.

TABLE 10.1 The ITEM Table

Column Name	Type	Size
ITEM_ID	INTEGER	
ITEM_DESCRIPTION	VARCHAR2	100
STOCK_QTY	DOUBLE	
UNIT_PRICE	DOUBLE	

TABLE 10.2 The BILL Table

Column Name	Type	Size
BILL_ID	INTEGER	
SALE_AMOUNT	DOUBLE	

TABLE 10.3 The BILL_ITEM Table

Column Name	Type	Size
BILL_ID	INTEGER	
ITEM_ID	INTEGER	
QUANTITY	DOUBLE	

Create a schema called XYZCONF in the PointBase database. Then create the tables as described in this section under this schema. You can create the schema either by using the PointBase console Table Creation Wizard, or by executing the `schema.sql` that can be found along with the examples for this chapter. An easy way to execute the `schema.sql` file is to open the PointBase console and select `File, Open`. This enables you to pick the SQL file from your hard disk. Select the `schema.sql` file and open it. This will list the contents of this SQL file in the Enter SQL Commands window. You can then execute the commands by clicking the Execute All button.

NOTE

The schema contains `DROP TABLE` commands that attempt to drop the tables before creating them. This is useful if you want to re-create your schema in future for any reason. The first time you create the schema, these statements may generate errors because the tables do not exist yet. This should not cause any problem.

Basic JDBC Features

In this chapter, we look at the core functionality provided by JDBC. WebLogic Server 8.1 supports the JDBC Specification version 2.0. We look first at the basic features offered by JDBC, and then examine the advanced functions in the subsequent sections.

We'll be working with the PointBase database as we look at the features offered by JDBC.

Most of the classes and interfaces that constitute the JDBC API can be found under the package `java.sql`. In this section, we look at how to use some of these classes. Any classes that are referred in the following sections without being qualified by a package name should be assumed to be in the `java.sql` package; for example, references to `Connection` imply the interface `java.sql.Connection`.

Connecting to the Database

The first step in performing any database task is connecting to the database. The phrases *connecting to the database* and *obtaining a database connection* amount to obtaining an object that implements the interface `Connection` in your Java code. You can obtain database connections locally (on the client side) using the `DriverManager` object.

Getting a Connection Using the DriverManager

As part of the initialization process, the `DriverManager` tries to load the driver classes provided to it using an environment variable called `jdbc.drivers`. This variable can contain one or more drivers for use with multiple data sources if necessary. Each driver class is loaded by the `DriverManager` class, which uses the appropriate driver to issue connections when its `getConnection` method is called subsequently. The driver used will depend on the `url` string passed to the `DriverManager` when you request a connection.

```
jdbc.drivers=com.pointbase.jdbc.jdbcUniversalDriver:
➥jdbc.odbc.JdbcOdbcDriver
```

You may also load the driver object in your code by invoking the `Class.forName()` method and passing it the name of your driver class as a `String`. You don't need to instantiate the driver. The following line of code will initialize the `DriverManager` in your JVM with the driver for the PointBase database. For this to work, the driver class referenced should be available in your application `CLASSPATH`.

```
Class.forName( "com.pointbase.jdbc.jdbcUniversalDriver" );
```

As you can see, this call returns a class; however, you don't have to do anything with that returned class. Just by making the call, the driver class gets loaded into the JVM, and registers itself with the driver manager for the URL type that it can handle. In our case, the `jdbcUniversalDriver` class registers itself with the driver manager for all URLs beginning with `jdbc:pointbase:server`.

After the driver has been loaded, the `DriverManager` class can now be requested for the database connection by invoking its `getConnection` method. The `getConnection` method is provided three parameters: the URL to connect to, the user ID, and the password. The `getConnection` method signature is

```
public static Connection getConnection( String url,
➥                    String userId,
➥                    String password)
➥               throws SQLException;
```

10

The `url` parameter that's passed to this method is of the form `jdbc:`*`subprotocol`*`:`*`subname`*. The *`subprotocol`* part of the `url` identifies the driver that will be used to connect to the database. The driver documentation generally tells you what the *`subprotocol`* should be in your `url` string for the driver manager to use that driver. The driver manager uses this parameter to identify which driver will satisfy the request.

The *subname* part of the `url` will also depend on the driver being used. The *subname* is generally passed to the driver by the `DriverManager` while obtaining a connection, and will provide information to the driver about the database or the data source to connect to. For instance, while using the JDBC-ODBC Bridge, the *subprotocol* is `odbc`. While accessing a database registered under the name `test`, using this protocol, you would pass the `url` string as `jdbc:odbc:test`.

While connecting to a PointBase database server using the driver `com.pointbase.jdbc.jdbcUniversalDriver`, the *subprotocol* string passed should be `pointbase`. The *subname* part of the `url` string identifies the server to connect to by using a string of the form `server://<host>[:<port>]/<db>`. As discussed earlier in this chapter, `<host>` is the host on which the server is running (for example, `localhost`). `<port>` is the port on which the server is listening. This is an optional value and must be specified only if the server has been started on a port other than 9092. `<db>` is the name of your database (for example, `demo`). Therefore, a complete `url` string to connect to a PointBase database named `demo` using a PointBase database server running on the default port in your `localhost` would be `jdbc:pointbase:server://localhost/demo`. Note that your PointBase server must be running for a connection to be returned successfully. The `getConnection` method will throw an exception of type `SQLException` if for any reason a connection cannot be obtained.

The following code snippet will obtain a connection for the PointBase database, assuming that `host`, `port`, `dbName`, `userid`, and `password` are passed in as parameters to this function, and that the PointBase server is running in the specified host:

```
Connection conn = null;
try
{
 Class.forName( "com.pointbase.jdbc.jdbcUniversalDriver" );
 String url = "jdbc:pointbase:server://" + host + ":" +
           port + "/" + dbName ;
 System.out.println("Using url string " + url );
 conn = DriverManager.getConnection
             (url, userid, password);
 System.out.println("Connection Obtained");
}
catch (Throwable t)
{
  t.printStackTrace();
  conn = null;
}
```

The Connection Interface

So, what is this Connection interface after all? It's an interface that provides you with methods that represent the operations you can perform using a database connection. The Connection object is the core object that enables you to work with the database.

Using a Connection object, you can create a new SQL statement, commit or roll back your database updates, and get and set several attributes of the connection such as auto-commit, transaction isolation level, and so forth. While performing operations on a connection, the database might generate SQL warnings. You can get a hold of these warnings by using the appropriate methods in the Connection object. This object also enables you to close the connection when you're done with it, thereby releasing the connection for use by other clients. You can also access the database's schema (metadata) by using the Connection object.

The program com.wlsunleashed.jdbc.Example1.java demonstrates the process of opening a connection and printing a few basic parameters of the connection. You can execute this class in your command line after starting the PointBase database server. Make sure to include the pbclient.jar file in your CLASSPATH while executing this example. It contains the PointBase JDBC driver. Remember to bring up the PointBase server instance prior to executing this example! You can execute the startPointBase.cmd file present under ${POINTBASE_HOME}/tools to start the demo database packaged with WebLogic Server.

Executing SQL Statements in a Database

After you establish a connection with the database, you can execute SQL statements on the database. The database engine executes your SQL statements. To send a SQL statement to the database engine, you must create a Statement object. A Statement object can be created by using an active Connection object. The following code snippet creates a Statement from a Connection object, which has been obtained from the DriverManager as described in the previous section:

```
Statement stmt = aConnection.createStatement();
```

After a Statement object has been created, you can execute your SQL statement. A SQL statement can be of two types: queries and updates. Depending on the type of SQL statement, you will use the appropriate method in the Statement object to execute it.

NOTE

Inserts, deletes, and data definition language statements qualify as updates.

10

Updating the Database

Let's first try to insert a new row into the ITEM table with attributes ID = 1, description = "Candy", stock = 50, and unit price = 2.00. To do this, you have to execute the following SQL statement:

```
INSERT INTO "XYZCONF"."ITEM"
 VALUES ( 1, "Candy", 50, 2.0 )
```

This statement can be executed in the database by invoking the `executeUpdate` method of the `Statement` object. Note that SQL statements executed using this method should not be terminated with a semicolon (;). You can execute both data definition (`CREATE`, `ALTER TABLE`, and so on) as well as data manipulation (`INSERT`, `UPDATE`, `DELETE`, and so on) language statements using the `executeUpdate` method. Assuming that the SQL statement has been stored in the string variable named `anSQLStmt`, the following code snippet will insert the values into the ITEM table:

```
stmt.executeUpdate( anSQLStmt );
```

The `executeUpdate` method returns the number of database rows affected as a result of executing the given statement. While executing DDL statements or other statements that do not affect any row, this method returns a zero. This method throws an exception of type `SQLException` if anything fails while executing the update. Your program might also want to scan any `SQLWarnings` that might have been generated by looking for them in the `Connection` object.

The sample file `com.wlsunleashed.jdbc.Example2.java` demonstrates inserting rows into the ITEM table by using the `executeUpdate` method. This example inserts five rows into the ITEM table. Execute this class in the `XYZCONF` schema created earlier. Make sure to include the `pbclient.jar` in your `CLASSPATH` while executing this class. Remember, you must have already created the schema using the `schema.sql` file, and the PointBase server should be up and running before you can invoke this class.

Querying from the Database

Now let's try to query the data that we inserted into the ITEM table in the previous section. The `executeQuery` method of the `Statement` object is used to execute a query. The difference between a query and an update SQL statement is that the query SQL returns data. This data is returned by the `executeQuery` method as a `ResultSet`.

Let's try to query the ITEM table for all the records in the table. This can be done by using the following SQL statement:

```
SELECT * FROM XYZCONF.ITEM
```

You can execute this SQL statement and retrieve the results by using the following code snippet, assuming that the SQL Statement has been stored in the variable called `anSQLStmt`:

```
ResultSet rs = stmt.executeQuery( anSQLStmt );
```

The `executeQuery` method returns the result from the query as a `ResultSet`. Like the `executeUpdate` method, this method also throws an exception of type `SQLException` when it is unable to execute the query for some reason. We will look at manipulating data using a `ResultSet` in the following section.

Processing Results from a Query

When a query has been executed using the `executeQuery` method, you get an object of type `ResultSet` that contains the result of the query in a tabular format—meaning rows and columns. We use the `ResultSet` object to simply iterate through the rows. Later, you'll see how to access a row by its position and how to iterate backward.

The `ResultSet` has a cursor that's initially positioned *before* the first row. To read the next row in the result set, you must advance the cursor by calling the `next` method on the `ResultSet` object, thus allowing you to read that row. However, columns within a row may be read in any order.

In the previous section, we executed the `SELECT` statement that fetched all the items in the ITEM table. Let's try to iterate through the rows fetched as a result of this `SELECT` and print them out. We will assume that we've already obtained the connection and we have an active connection in the `conn` variable. Consider the following code snippet:

```
1. Statement stmt = conn.createStatement();
2. ResultSet rs = stmt.executeQuery(anSQLStmt);
3. int row=1;
4. while (rs.next())
5. {
6.   System.out.println( "Row #" + row++ +
7.   ➥         ", id = " + rs.getInt(1) +
8.   ➥         ", desc = " + rs.getString(2) +
9.   ➥         ", stock = " + rs.getDouble(3) +
10.  ➥         ", unit price = " + rs.getDouble(4));
11. }
12. stmt.close();
```

The output of this code snippet looks like this:

```
Row #1, id = 1, desc = Candy, stock = 50.0, unit price = 2.0
Row #2, id = 2, desc = Crunchies, stock = 24.0, unit price = 1.4
Row #3, id = 3, desc = Snickers, stock = 40.0, unit price = 2.3
Row #4, id = 4, desc = Polo, stock = 55.0, unit price = 2.0
Row #5, id = 5, desc = Wafers, stock = 40.0, unit price = 2.55
```


As you can see, there are five rows in the ITEM table, which has been printed out by this code. In line 2, we execute the query and accept the output of the execution in our local variable rs, which is of type ResultSet. In line 4, we advance the cursor of rs to the first row in order to access that row. We do this in a while loop to make sure that we get to each row in the ResultSet. The call to rs.next() is inside the conditional block of the while loop. This is because the next method returns a boolean, indicating whether the cursor was successfully positioned on the next row. If the ResultSet runs out of rows, the next method returns false, thereby quitting from the loop.

After advancing the cursor to the first row, you can access the columns by using a variety of get*XXX* methods offered by the ResultSet interface, passing to it the index of the column. Unlike Java arrays, this index starts from 1. This can be seen in lines 7 through 10 in the code block. These indexes are the column numbers in the ResultSet, and not in the original table. For instance, if you had constructed your SELECT clause to query only for ITEM_DESCRIPTION and the UNIT_PRICE, you would access the item description by calling getString(1) and the unit price by calling getDouble(2).

There's also a second flavor of each of these get*XXX* methods that can be accessed by passing in the names of the columns. The column names that you pass to these methods are not case sensitive. These forms of the methods are meant to be used when you explicitly specify the column names in your SELECT clause. Thus, line 8 in the code, which retrieves the Item description, can be rewritten as follows:

```
", desc = " + rs.getString("ITEM_DESCRIPTION");
```

NOTE

Sun Microsystems' documentation states that for maximum portability, you must access the ResultSet columns within each row in the left-to-right order, and each column should be read only once.

These get methods convert the database type into the requested Java data type; for example, the method getString converts the value stored in the field into a java.lang.String and returns the converted value. Similarly, getDouble converts the double value stored in the database column and returns it as Java's double data type.

The ResultSet interface offers several get methods. JDBC offers lots of flexibility on which flavor of the get method you use to retrieve the data. For instance, you can invoke the method getString on a column, which is defined in the database as a double. You can also invoke the getDouble method on a VARCHAR column in the database, provided the data stored in the column can be legally cast into a double. If the method is unable to cast it legally, it throws an SQLException. In cases where you attempt to down cast the data, which results in data loss (for example, using a getInt on a column of type double when the data stored in the column is too big to fit in an int), the method throws an exception. All the database data types (except the SQL3 data types) can be legally fetched as a String by using the getString method.

The ResultSet interface also provides with a wasNull method, which tells your program whether the last column read from the ResultSet using a getXXX method had a special value of SQL NULL. The ResultSet interface also provides you with a getMetaData method, which returns an object of type ResultSetMetaData that provides information about the number, types, and properties of the columns within this ResultSet.

The ResultSet interface provides you with a close method, which you can call to explicitly close the ResultSet when you're done with it. However, you aren't required to do so. The ResultSet is automatically closed when the Statement object is either closed or used to execute another SQL statement.

CAUTION

Because a ResultSet is closed automatically when a Statement object is closed, it is important to remember that a design that uses a generic method to execute an SQL statement passed to it and returns the ResultSet for processing outside that method will not work if the Statement object is closed within that method.

The class file com.wlsunleashed.jdbc.Example3.java demonstrates the process of querying from the ITEM table, scanning the ResultSet, and printing out the values as discussed in this section.

Using PreparedStatement for Faster SQL Executions

In earlier sections, we saw how to execute updates in the database table by calling the executeUpdate(String) method. When you execute this call, the SQL statement is sent into the database engine, which compiles the SQL to bring it to a format that it can understand. Obviously, this compilation process is an overhead. For updates that don't happen very often, this might not be too bad. Consider the scenario in which XYZ Confectionaries increases the stock of all its items at regular intervals. Obviously, in such a case, the overhead of SQL compilation will definitely be felt because we have to execute UPDATE statements for each item, every time new stock is brought in.

JDBC offers a solution to this problem by way of PreparedStatements. A PreparedStatement is a precompiled SQL statement that can be executed without the overhead of compilation. The DBMS simply executes the prepared statement, thus providing faster responses. Prepared statements enable you to provide parameters that will be plugged into the statement at runtime. You can also execute queries using PreparedStatements.

Creating a PreparedStatement

As with the Statement object, the PreparedStatement object is created using an active Connection object. The difference between creating the two objects is that in the case of the PreparedStatement, you must specify the SQL statement at the time of creation rather than execution. To do this, you'll use the prepareStatement method of the Connection object. The following code snippet shows how a `PreparedStatement` can be obtained from a `Connection` object. We first define an SQL statement to update the stock in the ITEM table and then prepare the statement in line 3.

```
1. String anSQLStmt = "UPDATE XYZCONF.ITEM SET STOCK_QTY = " +
2.             " STOCK_QTY + ? WHERE ITEM_ID = ? " ;
3. PreparedStatement prepStmt = aConnection.prepareStatement( anSQLStmt );
```

As you can see in line 2, we increment the `STOCK_QTY` by `?` for the item represented by `ITEM_ID ?`. So, what does that mean? This is how you tell the `PreparedStatement` object that you'll supply these values at runtime. The question mark (?) acts as a placeholder for the actual data, which will be supplied at runtime. When you call the `prepareStatement` method with this SQL, it provisions for the runtime data, compiles the SQL statement, and stores it in the `prepStmt` variable.

Executing a PreparedStatement

After a `PreparedStatement` has been created, you can execute it. But before you execute it, you must supply the actual data for the placeholders defined while creating the `PreparedStatement`. You can do so by calling corresponding `setXXX` methods in the `PreparedStatement` interface. If the value you want to substitute is an `int`, you'll call the `setInt` method of the interface. You'll normally find a `setXXX` method for each Java type. To substitute a placeholder with `SQL NULL`, you use the `setNull` method in the `PreparedStatement` interface.

Let's substitute the prepared statement stored in the variable `prepStmt` to increase the stock for the item with `ID = 1` by `7.0`. To do this, we'll use the following code fragment:

```
prepStmt.setDouble( 1, 7.0 ) ;
prepStmt.setInt( 2, 1 ) ;
```

The first argument to the `setXXX` method indicates the index of the placeholder that you want to replace. In the first line, we replaced the first placeholder to `7`. In the second line, we replaced the second placeholder to `1`. Now, the variable `prepStmt` represents the compiled version of the following SQL statement:

```
"UPDATE XYZCONF.ITEM SET STOCK_QTY = " +
" STOCK_QTY + 7.0 WHERE ITEM_ID = 1 " ;
```

All that's left is to execute this statement to send it to the RDBMS. This can be done by calling the `executeUpdate` method on the `PreparedStatement`. Unlike in the case of executing a `Statement`, we don't need to pass anything to the `executeUpdate` method. The following code fragment will execute this `PreparedStatement` for us:

```
prepStmt.executeUpdate() ;
```

Let's now increment the stock of item 3 by 7.0. Look at the following code fragment, which will do it for us:

```
prepStmt.setInt( 2, 3 ) ;
prepStmt.executeUpdate() ;
```

Notice in this code fragment that we didn't replace the placeholder for the STOCK_QTY field. This is because the prepared statement retains the value of each of the substitutions even after the statement has been executed. Because the increment value (7) was the same for item 3 as for item 1 earlier, we need not explicitly substitute the placeholder. In some cases, this behavior might not suit you. You can clear all the previous substitutions by calling the clearParameters method of the PreparedStatement interface.

The executeUpdate method returns the number of rows affected by executing the update. To execute a query using a PreparedStatement, use the executeQuery method. Again, this method takes no parameters and returns an object of type ResultSet. PreparedStatements need to be closed by calling the close method.

The following code fragment enables us to update the stock of each item in the ITEM table using a PreparedStatement. The array stockArray is passed as a parameter, which consists of the same number of rows as there are in the ITEM table. Each entry in this array is a double value. The stock of the item corresponding to the index of this value is incremented by this value.

```
String anSQLStmt = " UPDATE XYZCONF.ITEM SET " +
          " STOCK_QTY = STOCK_QTY + ? " +
          " WHERE ITEM_ID = ? " ;
try
{
   PreparedStatement stmt = conn.prepareStatement(anSQLStmt);
   for (int i = 0;i < stockArray.length; i++)
   {
     stmt.setDouble(1, stockArray[i]);
     stmt.setInt(2, i+1);
     System.out.println(" # Rows affected = " + stmt.executeUpdate());
   }
   stmt.close();
}
catch (SQLException t)
{
   t.printStackTrace();
}
```

Transactions

Assume that a customer walks into XYZ Confectionaries and wants to buy eight Snickers bars. Our billing system will check whether we have sufficient stock of this item to satisfy the customer's request. If the company has the stock, we'll enter a new bill in the system and reduce the stock of the item by eight. All these operations put together are known as a *transaction*. If any operation that's part of our transaction fails, we'll be unable to process the customer's request. In such a case, we'll have to undo any updates that we might have already made, and revert the data in the different tables to its original state to maintain integrity of the company's data.

A transaction is a set of one or more operations that are executed as an atomic unit so that we can guarantee that, at the end of the transaction, either all operations executed successfully or none of them did. In the case of the billing system for XYZ Confectionaries, we obviously don't want to reduce the stock of the item when the bill couldn't be entered into the system successfully, and vice versa.

Chapter 9, "Processing Transactions with the Java Transaction API," introduced you to the ACID properties of a transaction. These properties should be maintained at all times by any application that uses transactions. You can also read about local and global transactions in the same chapter.

JDBC provides mechanisms by which you can use transactions in your code while updating databases. As a matter of fact, no update operation that you perform in your code can be outside of a transaction. Of course, we didn't do anything in the inserts and updates in the previous sections that had anything to do with transactions—or did we?

When a connection to a database is created, the connection is set in what is known as an *auto-commit* mode; that is, each SQL statement that's executed using this connection is treated as a transaction in its own right and is committed after the statement has executed successfully. Thus, every insert or update that you execute is committed immediately, irrespective of what happens to any inserts or updates that might follow. However, as we've seen, this default behavior will not suit us all the time. To override this default behavior, we'll first have to disable the auto-commit mode of a connection before we can begin a transaction. This can be done by calling the `setAutoCommit` method on the `Connection` object as demonstrated in this code fragment:

```
aConnection.setAutoCommit( false );
```

This is technically the point at which your logical unit of work begins and you can continue to perform all the operations on the database that constitute your transaction. When you're done with all the operations, you can call the `commit` method on the `Connection` object if you're satisfied with the outcome of each participant of your transaction. If you feel any part of the transaction hasn't completed to satisfaction, you can rollback the entire transaction by calling the `rollback` method on the `Connection` object. After you either commit or roll back your transaction, the connection can be used to begin another transaction, if necessary. Irrespective of how the second transaction ends, the first transaction's changes are not affected.

NOTE

If you want to return the connection to auto-commit mode, you must explicitly call the `setAutoCommit` method and set it to true.

NOTE

The usage of `setAutoCommit` `commit` and `rollback` methods is sufficient for local transactions. However, for global transactions, you must use the JTA APIs. You can learn more about the JTA APIs in Chapter 9.

Thus, in our billing system example, the following code fragment will perform this transaction for us:

```
try
{
   aConnection.setAutoCommit( false );
   // check if we have sufficient stock of the item
   // insert a new bill
   // insert into the BILL_ITEM table
   // Update the stock of the item
   aConnection.commit();
}
catch (SQLException sqle)
{
   // handle the SQL exception
   aConnection.rollback();
}
finally
{
   // close the connection here
}
```

The source file `com.wlsunleashed.jdbc.Example4.java` demonstrates the process of adding a new bill into the billing system. It makes use of `PreparedStatements` for performing many of the updates. The items that are part of the bill are passed as parameters to the `buyItem` method of this class. The function checks the stock of each item, ensures enough quantity is available, inserts records into the BILL and BILL_ITEM tables, and finally updates the stock of each item by the quantity purchased.

Transaction Isolation Levels

The isolation property of transactions (the "I" in "ACID") warrants a little more discussion. There are a few scenarios that arise out of a database when multiple transactions are active at the same time. Let's take a look at these scenarios in this section.

- Dirty reads—Consider that new stock for several items arrives in XYZ Confectionaries. An employee is updating the stock for each item. In the meanwhile, the company owner is printing a report of the current stock of different items. At the same time, the new stock is found to have some problems and the Purchasing department decides to return the entire stock to the supplier. Because of this, the employee entering the new stock information rolls back the work by calling the `rollback` method on the `Connection` object. Now the owner's report can possibly indicate an incorrect stock of the items, based on whether the stock value was queried after it was updated, but before the rollback was issued. This is known as a *dirty read*.

- Nonrepeatable reads—Consider the following scenario. Two customers walk into XYZ Confectionaries and talk to two employees at the same time. Both require eight Snickers bars. Both employees begin their respective transactions and check the stock of Snickers bars, and find the stock to be 50. The first employee now enters the sale into the system and commits it. The second employee is still working on her transaction and queries the stock a second time. This time, she gets the stock as 42, which is different from the first time she queried the stock. Note that this is not a dirty read—the first employee has already committed her transaction. This is known as a *nonrepeatable read*.

- Phantom reads—Phantom reads occur when new rows are added or rows are deleted from the table, but the side effects are still seen by other transactions. The Finance department of XYZ Confectionaries is trying to tally the sale for the day of all items with the stock in the ITEM table. The transaction is done totaling the sale amount from the BILL_ITEMS table. In the meanwhile, another sale occurs. Now when the stock from the ITEM table is totaled, it falls short because the new sale doesn't show up in the total of the BILL_ITEMS table. This is known as a *phantom read*.

These situations are possible, but can be prevented by the database by using locks. These locks can be set at different levels based on a setting known as the *transaction isolation level*. You can set the transaction isolation level to five different values based on how you want the database to behave in such situations. All values of the transaction isolation levels might not be supported by all databases. You must refer to the documentation of your database to see which levels are supported.

- `TRANSACTION_NONE`—Transactions are not supported.

- TRANSACTION_READ_UNCOMMITTED—This is the lowest level of isolation for databases that support transactions. This level of isolation allows dirty reads, nonrepeatable reads, and phantom reads, but offers the highest performance.
- TRANSACTION_READ_COMMITTED—This guarantees that all queries return committed data (in other words, this level does not allow dirty reads). This level of transaction isolation is sufficient for most applications for normal functioning. This level of isolation does not guarantee repeatable reads and allows phantom reads.
- TRANSACTION_REPEATABLE_READ—This isolation level prevents dirty reads and guarantees repeatable reads. However, this level does not prevent phantom reads.
- TRANSACTION_SERIALIZABLE—This level of transaction isolation prevents dirty and phantom reads. It also guarantees repeatable reads. This offers the highest level of transaction isolation, but it also offers the lowest performance.

The transaction isolation level can be set in the Connection object by calling the method setTransactionIsolation as soon as you obtain the connection. You can also check the default value of the transaction isolation level for your database by calling the method getTransactionIsolation on the Connection object. The values of the different transaction isolation levels are available for use as public static constants in the Connection class. For example, the following code snippet sets the transaction isolation level to TRANSACTION_READ_COMMITTED:

```
aConnection.setTransactionIsolation( Connection.TRANSACTION_READ_COMMITTED );
```

SQL Error Handling

As you've already seen, any error that occurs while processing your SQL statements are reported to you as an SQLException. Each SQLException contains several pieces of information that can define the exact error for you. The SQLException object contains the following information:

- A string that describes the error. You can get this string by calling the getMessage method of the exception object.
- An SQLState string that follows the XOPEN SQLState specifications. You can access this string using the getSQLState method on the exception.
- A vendor-specific error code. This code is usually the actual error code that's returned from the underlying database. You can access this code by calling the getErrorCode method on the exception object.
- A chain to another SQLException object. You can access this exception by calling getNextException on the exception object. You can also set another SQLException object by calling the setNextException method to pass it up the call hierarchy.

Apart from exceptions, SQL executions can also result in warnings. For example, SQL can return a data truncation warning when data is truncated on an update or an insert. Such warnings indicate that the operation was successful, but the database wants you to be aware of something that happened that might affect your logic. These aren't reported as exceptions. These warnings are quietly tagged along with the appropriate object that caused this warning to be generated in the first place. Objects such as `Connection`, `Statement`, and `ResultSet` can all return `SQLWarnings`.

You can access the SQL warnings by calling the `getWarnings` method on the appropriate object. This returns the last created instance of `SQLWarning`. It's always a good idea to examine the warning list before you close the object. The `SQLWarning` class extends from `SQLException`; therefore, you have access to the same methods as when you get back exceptions. The only difference is that, in the case of warnings, you can get chained warnings by calling `getNextWarning` instead of the `getNextException` method.

Advanced JDBC Features

WebLogic Server 8.1 supports the 2.0 specification of JDBC. With this version, there have been several enhancements to the API. In this specification, the JDBC API has been separated into two parts: the core API and the standard extensions package. All the core classes and interfaces discussed as part of the basic JDBC features continue to remain in the `java.sql` package. Some new classes and interfaces have been added to this package with the 2.0 specification. Apart from this, the 2.0 specification introduces the `javax.sql` package, which is the JDBC Standard Extension API. In this section, we go over many of the enhancements of JDBC specification 2.0.

JDBC Extensions Package

One of the most important enhancements to JDBC 2.0 in terms of its relevance to using JDBC in application servers is the new extensions package that has made its way into the JDBC API specification. This package provides several classes that are closely related with other Java standard extensions, such as JNDI and JTA. One of the most important features that the extensions package offers is the way in which you connect with the database.

In a two-tier architecture, you obtain a connection to the database by using the `DriverManager` object. However, for a three-tier application that uses a middleware application server, you can connect to the database by using a `DataSource` object. Note that while using JDBC with WebLogic Server, the preferred way to obtain a connection is with the use of a `DataSource` object. In this section, we take a detailed look at the components that help us get a connection from a database by using the `DataSource` object. Wherever relevant, we'll also see how the particular concept applies in the world of WebLogic Server.

Connection Pools

Obtaining a connection to a database is often the most expensive part of the JDBC API. For applications that don't perform database operations often, it can be argued that this isn't a huge impact. However, in practice, most applications will access the database quite often. If a connection to the database is opened each time a database operation is made, it can cause a tremendous impact in performance.

Some programs might avoid this overhead by opening a connection at initialization time and holding on to the connection, and thus reusing the same connection over and over again for performing its SQL operations. Although this definitely addresses the issue of overhead while opening the connection, it introduces a second problem. Database licenses are usually based on the number of concurrent connections that operate on the databases. Therefore, if you want to have 50 threads servicing client requests with each thread holding onto its own connection, you need 50 concurrent connections to the database. Obviously, this isn't a very cost-effective alternative.

To address these two issues, the concept of connection pooling has been introduced. The idea of this concept is that every application thread will not be using its database connection at all times. It's therefore possible to share database connections across application threads. Several threads efficiently share limited resources, with no major impact on performance.

Using connection pooling enables you to perform initialization operations once and reuse the connections over and over again. This makes the database operations faster. Because a few connections are shared between many application threads, you can get away with having fewer database licenses, which makes this a very economical alternative. Because the connections are initialized at startup of your application, each request doesn't need to provide the database user ID and password. Those can be provided once, when the connections are established.

Using WebLogic Server, you can create connection pools using the server's console. You need to set up several properties of the connection pool, which are used by the server to initialize the pool. These pools are initialized, or in other words, the database connections are established at the server's startup time. Your applications (both client and server side) can borrow a connection from the connection pool, use it, and return it to the pool when the database operations are finished.

To create a connection pool, start WebLogic Server and access the console of the server. Make sure that you have the PointBase client library in your `CLASSPATH` when you start your server.

NOTE

You can access the WebLogic console by typing the URL `http://localhost:7001/console` in the address bar of a Web browser after bringing up WebLogic Server. You might have to substitute the hostname and port number according to your situation.

Remember that in order for WebLogic Server to use the driver and connect to the database, it should have the driver in its `CLASSPATH`. You should therefore make sure that you've changed the startup script of the WebLogic Server to include the `driver jar file` in its `CLASSPATH`. For PointBase Server, however, WebLogic Server 8.1 automatically includes the required JAR files in the `CLASSPATH`, so you don't have to change the script.

When you see the tree view that describes your domain on the left side, navigate to the link Services→JDBC→Connection Pools under the WebLogic domain. Right-click this link and select the menu item Configure a new `JDBCConnectionPool`. This starts an assistant (wizard) on the right side of the console, which will help you create your connection pool.

On the first screen, you can pick the type of database you want to connect to. There are several predefined database types in the choice box. We'll select the PointBase database type. As soon as you pick the type, the appropriate drivers are displayed in the Database Driver list. You will find that the assistant lists both a driver that's XA compliant, and one that isn't. Note that depending on what type of database you pick, the following screens will be different. In this section, we discuss all the steps only for a PointBase database. However, these steps are conceptually very similar for any given database type. This step is demonstrated in Figure 10.5.

Pick the non-XA-compliant driver and click Continue. This takes you to the Define Connection Properties step.

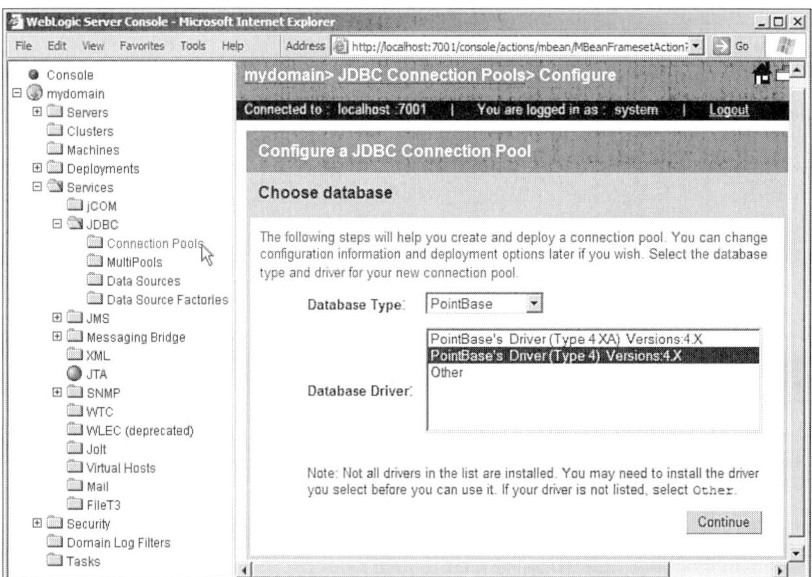

Figure 10.5 Creating a connection pool—Choose Database.

In the next screen of the assistant, you can specify the properties that will be used to connect to the database.

- The Name field identifies the connection pool. Provide a meaningful name that describes the connection pool. We're going to create the `XYZCONFConnectionPool`, which will provide our application with connections for the XYZCONF database.
- The Database Name field identifies the name of the PointBase database to connect to. If you are using the demo database, enter **`demo`** here. If you created a new database, you can enter that name here.
- The Hostname and Port fields identify the host and port to connect to. As you can see, these two fields are prefilled with default values (localhost and 9092). You'll have to change these if your values are different.
- The Database User Name field should be filled with the username to be used while connecting to the database. This username should be a valid username in the database. You can typically use PBSYSADMIN as the username—this user is the default system administrator for a PointBase database.
- The Password and the Confirm Password fields should be filled with the password for the user in the Database User Name field. The passwords entered in these two fields must match for the assistant to succeed.

This step of the Connection Pool assistant is shown in Figure 10.6.

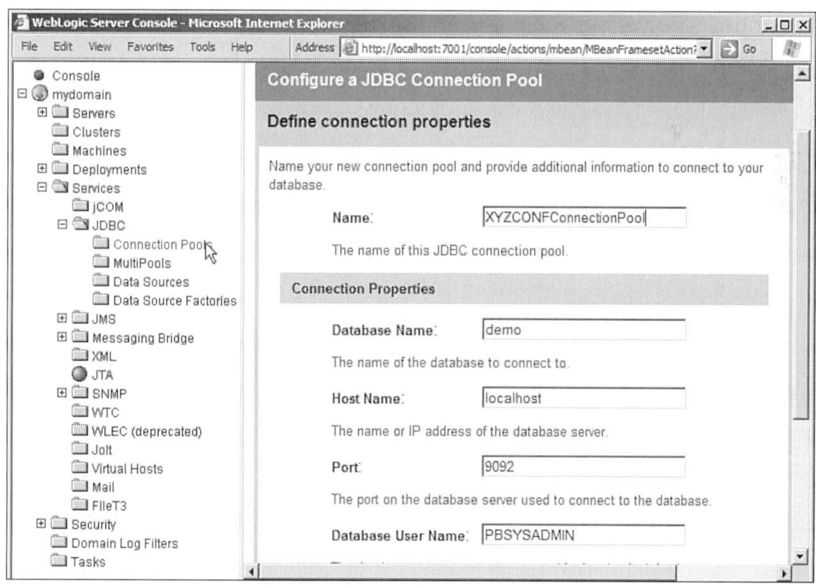

Figure 10.6 Creating a connection pool—Define Connection Properties.

After you click Continue on this screen, the assistant takes you to the Test Database Connection screen where you can optionally test the configuration. Here, you can see the driver class name, the URL, the database user name, the passwords, and any database-specific properties. All these values are prefilled with information that has been gathered by the assistant in the previous steps. If you want to change any of these values, you may do so in this step. Typically, if you've entered all the values in step 2 correctly, you shouldn't have to change these values.

At this point, you can either test the connection using these properties or skip the step. It is advisable to test the connection and make sure that all your configuration entries are working fine. You can see a screenshot of this step in Figure 10.7.

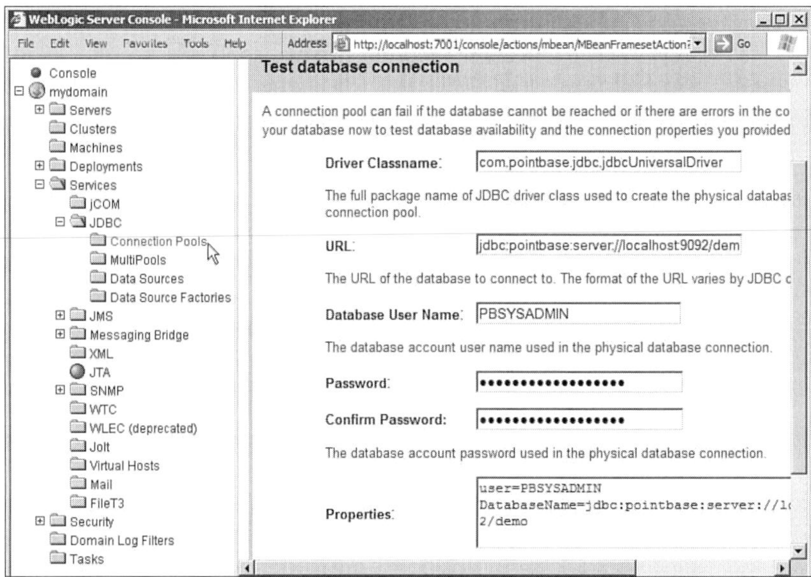

Figure 10.7 Creating a connection pool—Test Database Connection.

Once you click on the Test Connection button, if the connection could not be created successfully, the assistant remains on this screen and displays the error on the top of the screen. Make your changes and click the Test Connection button again. If the connection is successful, the assistant takes you to the Create and Deploy step. However, if you decide to skip the Test Database Connection step, you are still taken to the Create and Deploy screen.

This is the step in which you get to pick the clusters or the servers on which you want the connection pool to be deployed. If you have only one server in your domain, you aren't given an option to pick. The assistant automatically deploys the connection pool on that server. If you have more than one server, you can deploy the connection pool on more than one server. If you don't pick any server to deploy the connection pool, the pool will be created but won't be deployed on any server. You can change this deployment later by changing the properties of the pool. You can see a screenshot of this step in Figure 10.8.

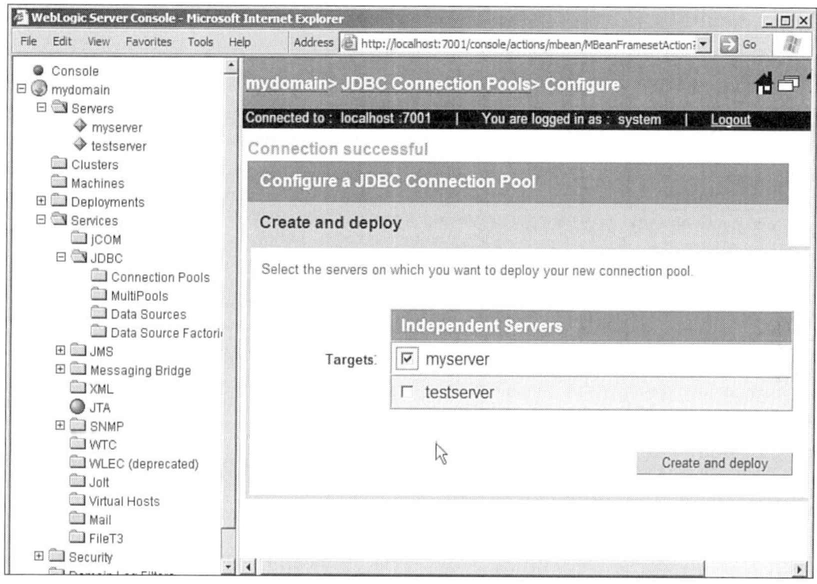

Figure 10.8 Creating a connection pool—Create and Deploy.

If you chose to skip the Test Database Connection step and create the connection pool, and if your configuration has any errors, the connection pool will be created but not deployed. You'll have to fix these errors and restart WebLogic Server before the connection pool can be deployed on the server(s).

After you've completed all the required steps in creating a connection pool, the wizard completes and takes you to the Connection Pool Configuration page. Here you can see all the configured connection pools and their deployment status. You'll also find the connection pool that we just created. Clicking on this will take you to the General tab of the Connection Pool Configuration page.

Here you can navigate to the Connections tab to change the maximum capacity of your connection pool. Capacity planning for a connection pool is an iterative process. By default, WebLogic Server sets this value to 15. If your connection pool has been targeted on a cluster, the number of connections in the pool depends on the number of servers in a cluster. For example, if a pool is configured with 5 connections and is targeted on a cluster with 3 servers, a total of 15 connections are produced.

You can also change other parameters of the connection pool in this screen. For a list and description of parameters that can be changed on this screen, see the "Tuning Your Connection Pool" section later in this chapter.

Multi-pools

Multi-pools are nothing but a pool of connection pools. Your application can get connections from any of the connection pools while using a multi-pool. Each connection within a connection pool that belongs to a multi-pool will be identical to the others; that is, all connections within a connection pool are made to the same database, using the same user ID and password. However, different connection pools within the multi-pool may be associated with different databases.

Multi-pools serve one of the following two purposes. You must determine which of these you need the most and must configure your multi-pool to use that algorithm.

- High availability—This configuration of a multi-pool assures high availability for your application. The first available connection pool normally services the connection requests. When a failure occurs for some reason, the next connection pool starts servicing client requests. Note that the term *failure* does not imply failure in executing SQL. It refers only to failures in the database connection itself. Also, capacity is not considered a failure because capacity is a configurable parameter. In other words, the fact that the first pool is busy doesn't trigger the next pool to service this request. Also, it's important to remember that this feature does not provide failover capabilities. In other words, if an error occurs as a result of a client request, that client will receive an error message. The client will then have to perform all the operations again, from the beginning of the transaction.
- Load balancing—The connection pool that services a client request is determined based on a round-robin algorithm. The pool next to the pool that serviced a request gets to service the next request. In this configuration, a multi-pool balances the load across different connection pools. It is obvious that each connection pool will provide connections to the same or similar databases. In other words, logically speaking, each connection pool should be identical to the others for your application to function correctly, although that is not technically a requirement.

You can create a multi-pool using the administration console by navigating to the link Services→JDBC→MultiPools under the domain. Right-clicking this link will give you an option to create a new multi-pool. Upon doing this, you'll be asked to enter the name for the multi-pool and the algorithm that you want to use. After the multi-pool has been created, you can associate connection pools to the multi-pool by switching to the `Pools` tab. You can then associate the multi-pool to the server by switching to the `Target and Deploy` tab.

Multi-pools can be targeted to a single WebLogic Server only. However, a `DataSource` that points to a multi-pool can be targeted to a cluster. Multi-pools also support only local—as opposed to distributed—transactions. Figure 10.9 shows the creation of a multi-pool using the WebLogic Server console.

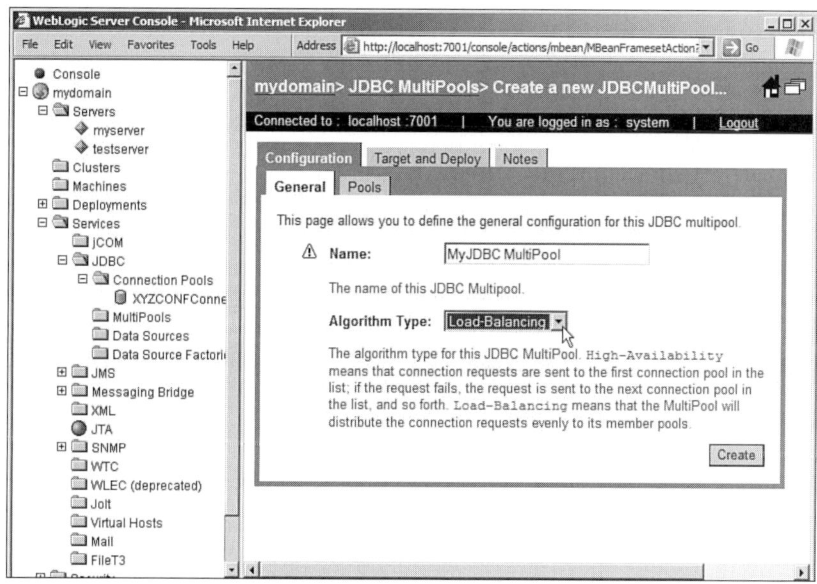

Figure 10.9 Creating a multi-pool using the WebLogic console.

DataSource

Now that we've created a connection pool, the next step is to actually pull out a connection from the pool and use it. This is where the `DataSource` object comes in. The `DataSource` is like a factory for server-side database connections. It's configured in the server console and it utilizes a single connection pool or a multi-pool. For this reason, you'll configure a `DataSource` after you configure the connection pool or a multi-pool. A connection pool or a multi-pool can be referred to by multiple `DataSources`. When a connection is requested from this factory, it returns a connection from the pool.

The `DataSource` object itself can be looked up from the JNDI tree of WebLogic Server. At the time of configuring a `DataSource` object, you can provide the name under which this object should be published in the JNDI tree.

WebLogic Server 8.1 includes an assistant (wizard) to configure a new `DataSource`. To kick off this assistant, navigate to the Services→JDBC→Data Sources link under the WebLogic domain on the console. Right-clicking this link will give you an option to configure a new `JDBCTxDataSource`. You may also click on the Configure a new JDBC Data Source link on the right side of the console. This displays the assistant on the right side of your console.

The first step is to configure the data source. In this screen, you can enter the name and the associated JNDI name for the `DataSource`. For our example, specify the name as `XYZCONFDataSource` and the JNDI name as `jdbc/XYZConfDataSource`.

You'll also find a check box, which is checked by default, that controls the behavior of the `DataSource` object to honor global transactions. In the early versions of WebLogic Server, transactional `DataSources` had to be created using what used to be known as *`TxDataSources`*. In this version of WebLogic Server, that's no longer necessary. By selecting the option to honor global transactions, you're essentially authorizing the `DataSource` to participate in existing global transactions. You should have no reason to uncheck this option because you would typically want your connections to be able to handle global transactions. When you're done, click the Continue button. The screen shot showing this step of the `DataSource` creation is shown in Figure 10.10.

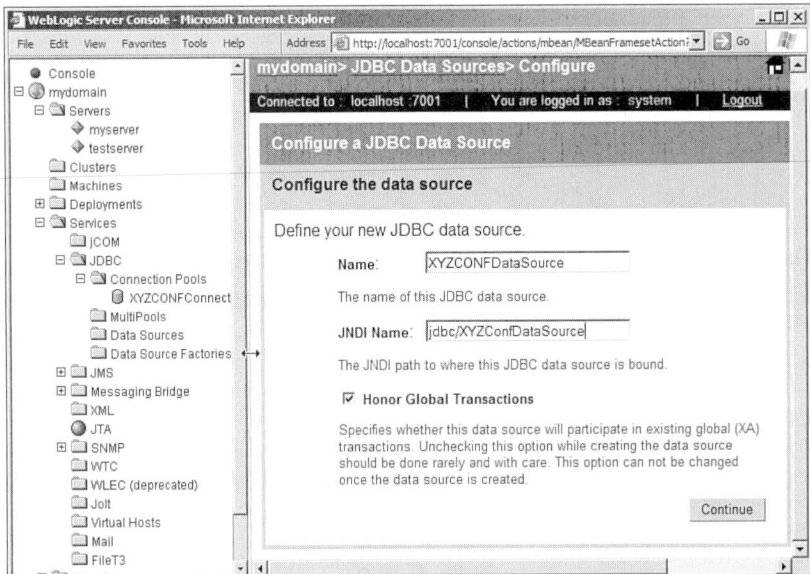

Figure 10.10 Creating a DataSource: Configure the Data Source

In the next screen, you can configure your `DataSource` to connect to a connection pool or a multi-pool. This can be seen in Figure 10.11. The drop-down box lists all the configured connection pools and multi-pools, and you can select the pool you're interested in. Click on Continue when you're done.

In the next screen, you can target your `DataSource` to a server or a cluster. If you have a cluster, you'll have an option of targeting your `DataSource` to the entire cluster or to some servers within the cluster. Select the server on which you want to target this `DataSource` object and click Create. The screen shot of this step is shown in Figure 10.12.

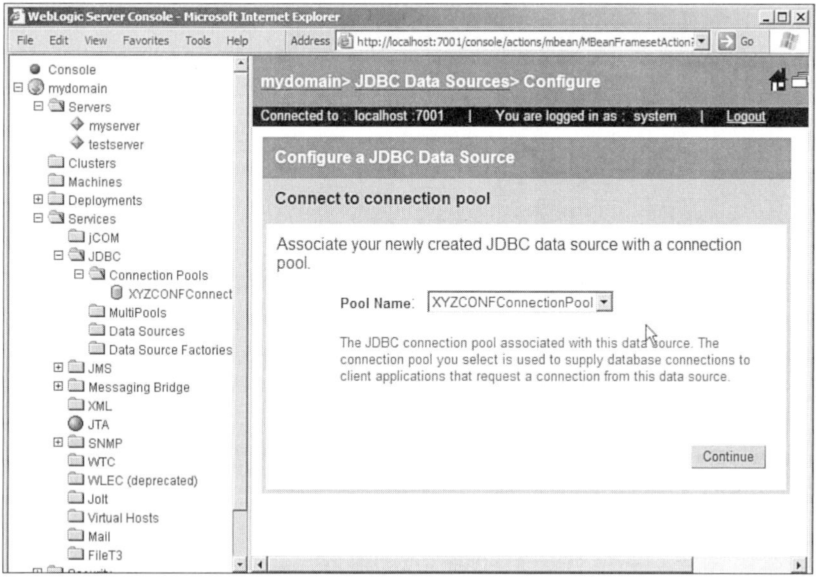

Figure 10.11 Creating a DataSource: Connect to a Connection Pool.

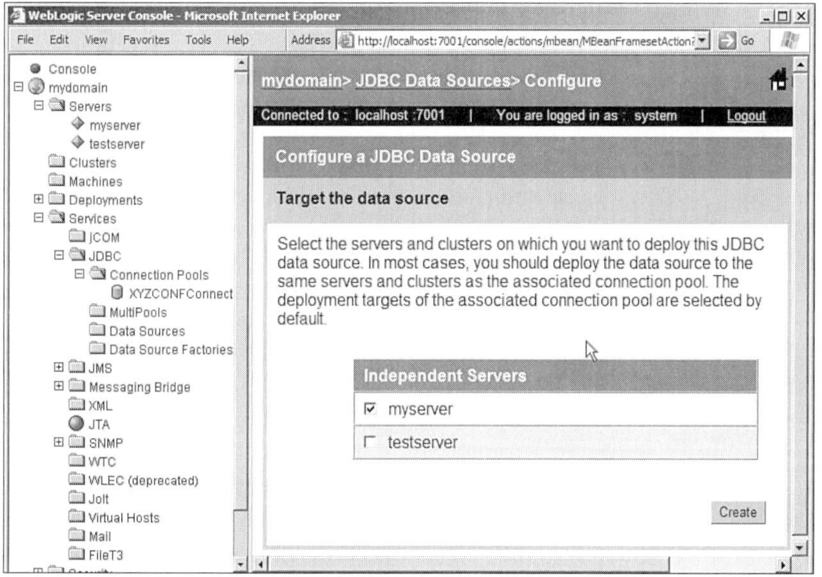

Figure 10.12 Creating a DataSource: Target the Data Source.

10

Now that we've created the DataSource, let's use it to get hold of a connection to the database. After you configure a DataSource and start WebLogic Server, the DataSource object is created and loaded in the JNDI tree under the given JNDI name. Your application can simply look up the DataSource object by using this published name and request a Connection from the object. The following code snippet obtains a Connection by using the DataSource object that we created earlier:

```
Context ctx = new InitialContext();
DataSource ds = (DataSource) ctx.lookup( "jdbc/XYZConfDataSource" );
Connection aConnection = ds.getConnection();
```

In the first line of this code, we create the InitialContext, which returns the initial context to the JNDI tree. For more information about JNDI, refer to Chapter 8, "Naming and Directory Services with JNDI." After we obtain an InitialContext, we can lookup the DataSource object by using the logical JNDI name that we provided while creating the DataSource. A Connection can now be obtained from the DataSource by using its getConnection method. When this method is called, the DataSource object contacts the connection pool, obtains a free connection, and returns it. After a connection is returned, you can use it to perform various database tasks such as creating a Statement, PreparedStatement, committing your updates, and so forth. When you invoke the close method on this connection, the physical connection is not closed, but the connection is returned back to the connection pool.

The advantage of using the DataSource to obtain a connection is that your program doesn't need to have any idea about the artifacts of connecting with the database. For example, in our earlier discussion of creating database connections for a two-tier application, we saw that while using the DriverManager to obtain a connection, we had to specify the URL, the user ID, and password in the program in order to connect to the database. This can make applications difficult to port.

By using the DataSource instead, you can separate the tasks of a developer and a deployer. The developer simply assumes the existence of a data source that will provide certain types of data. The deployer will configure this data source at a later time, while configuring the application. Moreover, the DriverManager class has the inherent disadvantage of being a synchronized class, which can potentially have performance problems for your application. Generally speaking, you can use a DataSource for a three-tiered application and a DriverManager for a two-tiered application.

You can use the DataSource to obtain connections from WebLogic Server from both client- and server-side applications. When you want to obtain the DataSource object from a server-side application, you can create the InitialContext with no parameters—the context to the JNDI tree present in the same JVM is returned automatically. While using it from a client context, you have to create the InitialContext, passing to it parameters that identify the server.

When you obtain a connection from the DataSource (and hence, from a connection pool), WebLogic provides you with a logical connection. But, in some cases, you might actually require the physical connection rather than the logical connection. You'll typically want to do this if you want to use extra functionality provided by the vendor's connection object, which isn't part of the standard JDBC specification. You can obtain the physical database connection by using a WebLogic Server extension: `weblogic.jdbc.extensions.WLConnection`. All connections returned by the connection pool are of this type. If you cast the connection into this type, you can then invoke the `getVendorConnection` method to return the physical vendor connection from the logical connection. Of course, you must be aware of the class that provides the vendor connection so that you can cast it appropriately and use it.

Using a physical connection has its disadvantages. The container will not provide any sort of connection management features, such as error handling, statement caching, and so on when you work with a physical connection. When you close the physical connection by invoking its `close` method, that connection is not reused. The connection pool replaces that connection with a new connection. A direct consequence of this is that the statement cache (if any) associated with that logical connection is also lost, not to mention the extra time involved in re-creating a new database connection. For these reasons, you're strongly discouraged from using physical connections.

The JSP `DisplayItemsTable.jsp` demonstrates the use of a `DataSource` to obtain a `Connection`. To execute this JSP, copy the directory `JDBCWebApp` that's packaged along with the sources in this book into the `applications` directory under the WebLogic domain (for example, `mydomain`). Make sure that the PointBase database server is up and running. After starting WebLogic, type the URL `http://localhost:7001/JDBCWebApp` into the address bar of your browser to execute the JSP. This server makes use of the `DataSource` under the name `jdbc/XYZConfDataSource` in the JNDI tree. So, remember to configure this `DataSource` and its associated connection pool before you attempt to deploy this application.

TxDataSource

Earlier in this chapter, we saw how to combine several tasks into logical transactions using JNDI. You may either use the auto-commit feature of JDBC (thus turning every call to the database into its own transaction), or you can turn this feature off and commit or roll back database operations at logical points. This will work fine with databases, but imagine if you want to include other tasks that do not involve a database inside your transaction. For instance, XYZ Confectionaries might want to send a message to a JMS queue whenever a customer purchases more than a preset quantity of an item. The Customer Service department might monitor this queue and send thank you letters to high-volume customers. So, how does this operation get rolled back if the database update rolls back? Obviously, it isn't possible to do this by using the transaction feature of JDBC without explicitly writing code to do it.

10

WebLogic Server enables you to work with transactions at a much higher level than by using JDBC. This is achieved by using JTA. When you use JTA, you can include several other WebLogic components in your transaction. Obviously, you can also include database operations in your transaction. The transaction commits or rollbacks are taken care of by the container. You can read more about JTA in Chapter 9.

To use JTA for transactions, you must select the Honor Global Transactions check box while creating your `DataSource`.

While using a global transaction–enabled `DataSource` (also known as a TxDataSource) in the context of a JTA transaction, the data source ensures that the same connection is returned to various parts of your application that are in the context of the same transaction. This way, all database operations are assured to be part of the transaction.

Advanced ResultSet

The class `java.sql.ResultSet` also contains two advanced features: the capability to scroll and update `ResultSets`.

Scrolling in a ResultSet

When iterating through a `ResultSet`, you were able to move in one direction—forward—by using its `next` method. However, you can also move backward within a `ResultSet` object. You can move to an absolute row within a `ResultSet` as well, thus providing random access to rows within it.

Not all `ResultSets` are scrollable—you'll have to specifically request the `Connection` to create a `Statement` that's capable of returning a scrollable `ResultSet`. This can be done by specifying a parameter in the `createStatement` method of the `Connection` object. This parameter identifies two things to the `Connection`: whether the `ResultSet` should be scrollable and whether any changes made to the underlying data store should be reflected back into the `ResultSet`. The `createStatement` method also takes a second parameter, which indicates whether you also want to update the rows in the `ResultSet`. We'll look more at updating `ResultSets` in the following section. The following code fragment creates a `Statement`, which will return a scrollable, nonupdateable `ResultSet` when the query is executed:

```
Statement stmt = aConnection.createStatement(
➥           ResultSet.TYPE_SCROLL_SENSITIVE,
➥           ResultSet.CONCUR_READ_ONLY );
ResultSet rs = stmt.executeQuery(" SELECT * FROM XYZCONF.ITEM ");
```

This code fragment is very similar to the one that we used in the previous chapter, except for the two parameters in the `createStatement` method. The first parameter can take three different values:

- `ResultSet.TYPE_FORWARD_ONLY`—Indicates a nonscrollable, `ResultSet`.
- `ResultSet.TYPE_SCROLL_INSENSITIVE`—Indicates a scrollable `ResultSet` that isn't sensitive to changes made by others to the database
- `ResultSet.TYPE_SCROLL_SENSITIVE`—Which is both scrollable and sensitive to the changes made by others

We look at this parameter in depth in the following sections. Apart from `ResultSet.CONCUR_READ_ONLY`, which indicates that the `ResultSet` isn't updateable, the second parameter can also take the value `ResultSet.CONCUR_UPDATABLE`, which indicates otherwise. These two parameters are optional, and you may continue to create a nonscrollable, read-only `ResultSet` using the same notation as used previously.

CAUTION

Remember that both the parameters are `int`s, so your compiler will not detect it if you switch these parameters around.

Like forward-only result sets, the cursor is initially positioned before the first row in a scrollable result set. Whereas calling the `next` method is the only way to move to a data row in a forward-only result set, you have a choice in the case of a scrollable result set. The `previous` method is complementary to the `next` method and can be used to move the cursor to the previous row relative to the current row in the `ResultSet`. Like the `next` method, this method also returns `false` when the boundary condition is reached—that is, when the cursor has reached the first row in the `ResultSet`—and can therefore be used in a `while` loop.

The methods `beforeFirst` and `afterLast` move the cursor before the first row and after the last row, respectively. The methods `first` and `last` move the cursor to the first and last row, respectively.

The `absolute` method moves the cursor to an absolute row number. The cursor moves from the beginning of the `ResultSet` for positive numbers, and from its end for negative numbers. Thus, the command `absolute(1)` will position the cursor at the first row, while `absolute(-1)` will position it at the last row. Note that any row numbers we talk about while discussing scrollable result sets are the row numbers within the result set as returned from the query. This is not the row number as stored within the database.

The `relative` method positions the cursor on a row that's relative to the current position of the cursor. Again, positive numbers advance the cursor, whereas negative numbers move the cursor back. For example, if the cursor is currently on the seventh row, the method `relative(-1)` moves the cursor to the sixth row, whereas `relative(1)` moves it to the eighth row.

You can get the current row in which the cursor is positioned by calling the `getRow` method. To verify whether the cursor is at a particular position in the `ResultSet`, you can use the methods `isBeforeFirst`, `isAfterLast`, `isFirst`, and `isLast`. These methods return `boolean` values and can be used to check for boundary conditions of the cursor.

The sample program `com.wlsunleashed.jdbc.Example5.java` demonstrates scrolling in a `ResultSet`. The JDBC 2.0 API also provides similar methods to create prepared statements to make them return scrollable and updateable result sets. Also, keep in mind that irrespective of what type of result set you want to use, the underlying database and the driver should support that type of result set. If a database or driver doesn't support scrollable result sets, you might be given a forward-only result set along with a `SQLWarning` indicating the same.

Updating Data Using a ResultSet

In the previous section, we saw that the `createStatement` method takes optional parameters indicating the type of `ResultSet` returned upon a successful database query. The second parameter that this method takes is called as the *concurrency type*, and determines whether the data in the result set can be updated directly. A value of `ResultSet.CONCUR_UPDATABLE` makes the `Statement` create an updateable result set. You can create result sets that are forward only, but updateable. Creating a scroll-sensitive result set will refresh the data in the result set after you update the data.

Updating data using a result set is a three-step process (after the query has been executed). The first step is to position the cursor on the row where you want to update the data. This can be done by using one of the positioning methods for scrollable result sets as discussed in the previous sections. For forward-only result sets, you can do this by repeatedly calling the `next` method until you reach the desired row.

Next, update the data in the columns. The `ResultSet` interface provides with several `updateXXX` methods that you can use to update the data. Like the `getXXX` methods discussed earlier, you'll find `updateXXX` methods for each Java data type. You can pass either the column index (within the `ResultSet`) or the column name to the `updateXXX` method, along with the data. For instance, to update the item stock of the first item queried, to fifty, you could use the following code fragment:

```
rs.first();
rs.updateDouble( "STOCK_QTY", 50.0 );
```

After all the updates have been performed on the row, the third step is to actually update the underlying database with the changes made to the `ResultSet`. This can be done by calling the `updateRow` method on the `ResultSet`. You can call more than one `updateXXX` method to update multiple columns before updating the entire row with a single call to `updateRow`. If you reposition the cursor to a different row after changing the data on a row but before calling the `updateRow` method, your changes will be lost. You can cancel all updates to a row before calling updateRow by calling the cancelRowUpdates method. The following code fragment updates the stock for the first item queried:

```
Statement stmt = aConnection.createStatement(
➥              ResultSet.TYPE_SCROLL_SENSITIVE,
➥              ResultSet.CONCUR_UPDATABLE );
ResultSet rs = stmt.executeQuery(" SELECT * FROM XYZCONF.ITEM ");
rs.first();
rs.updateDouble( "STOCK_QTY", 50.0 );
rs.updateRow();
```

The file com.wlsunleashed.jdbc.Example6.java demonstrates the process of updating data using an updateable result set.

Inserting Rows Using a ResultSet

It's possible to insert rows by calling the executeUpdate method on a Statement object and passing it an INSERT statement. It's also possible to insert rows using result sets. You have to create updateable result sets to be able to insert a new row.

The process of inserting a row involves moving to a buffer area within the result set that can hold the new row, updating the values of the new row within the buffer, and then inserting the row into the database. The first step is to move to the buffer area, which can be done by calling the special method moveToInsertRow. You can imagine that this method moves you into an empty row within the result set, which isn't really part of the result from the query. After moving into this empty row, you can update the fields in the row by calling the update*XXX* rows for all the fields. After all the field values have been entered, this row can be inserted into the database by calling the insertRow method. The following code snippet inserts a new item into the ITEM table:

```
Statement stmt = aConnection.createStatement(
➥              ResultSet.TYPE_SCROLL_SENSITIVE,
➥              ResultSet.CONCUR_UPDATABLE );
ResultSet rs = stmt.executeQuery(" SELECT * FROM XYZCONF.ITEM ");
rs.moveToInsertRow;
rs.updateInt( "ITEM_ID", 100 );
rs.updateString( "ITEM_DESCRIPTION", "Mayday" );
rs.updateDouble( "STOCK_QTY", 20.0 );
rs.updateDouble( "UNIT_PRICE", 1.99 );
rs.insertRow();
```

While inserting a row, if you don't supply values to a column by using an update*XXX* method, that field is set to SQL NULL. If the field in the database doesn't allow NULL values, you'll get an SQLException when the insertRow method is executed.

When the cursor is on the insert row, you can call any of the cursor-positioning methods discussed earlier, such as `previous`, `first`, `last`, and so on. When you're on the insert row, you can also use another positioning method—`moveToCurrentRow`, which positions the cursor to the current row in the result set. The current row is not the insert row—it's the row in which the cursor was positioned when you invoked the `moveToInsertRow` method.

Deleting Rows Using a ResultSet

You can also delete a row from an updateable result set. To do this, move to the row that has to be deleted and call the `deleteRow` method on the `ResultSet`. The following code snippet deletes the third row returned in the query:

```
rs.absolute(3);
rs.deleteRow();
```

CAUTION

Different database drivers behave differently when the `deleteRow` method is invoked. Some drivers will remove the row from the `ResultSet`, whereas others will leave a blank row where the row existed before deletion. Therefore, you'll need to keep this in mind while designing your application to work with multiple databases or drivers.

Reflecting Database Changes in a ResultSet

The data returned by a query is normally pretty much static until you run the query again. The consequence of this is that when the data changes in the data store—either because of an update that you executed or someone else did—the changes will not be visible to you until you re-execute the query. However, it's possible for you to refresh the data using certain types of result sets even while it is open. Of course, this will depend on whether the database and the driver that you use supports this behavior.

This can be done by using a scroll-sensitive result set by setting its type to `ResultSet.TYPE_SCROLL_SENSITIVE`. Note that just making the result set scroll sensitive does not automatically refresh the row when any changes occur. You must invoke a `refreshRow` method on the result set for it to refresh the row. This method actually performs a requery in the database under the covers, without using any data cache that the driver might use; therefore, this is one absolute way of ensuring that you have the current data in the database. But for this very same reason, this method is quite expensive and you should use it only if your application absolutely cannot do without the most recent data in the database. If your result set is not of the scroll-sensitive type, `refreshRow` method does nothing. You can use this feature of JDBC along with the appropriate transaction isolation level discussed earlier to determine what type of changes are visible to your code.

For example, consider a module that orders items in XYZ Confectionaries. This module initially checks for the stock of the item, and if it finds it, the module adds a new bill and bill item. Now, at this point, if we want to double-check whether we still have enough stock before we actually update the stock, the following code block will do it for us:

```
try
{
   Statement stmt = aConnection.createStatement(
                 ResultSet.TYPE_SCROLL_SENSITIVE,
                 ResultSet.CONCUR_UPDATABLE);
   ResultSet rs = stmt.executeQuery( "SELECT STOCK_QTY, UNIT_PRICE " +
                 " FROM XYZCONF.ITEM WHERE ITEM_ID = " +
                 itemToBuy );
   rs.next();
   if (rs.getDouble(1) > numRequested)
   {
     // add a new bill
     // add a new bill item
     // refresh the stock
     rs.refreshRow();
     // check for the stock one last time
     double newStock = rs.getDouble(1);
     if (newStock > numRequested)
     {
       rs.updateDouble(1, newStock - numRequested);
       rs.updateRow();
     }
     else
     {
       //rollback transaction here
     }
   }
}
catch (SQLException sqle)
{
   // rollback the transaction here
}
```

RowSets

`RowSets` enable easy transportation of tabular data over the network. They also help in providing scrollable and updateable result sets when the underlying database driver doesn't support these features. In this section, we briefly look at `RowSets` and some of the additional features provided by WebLogic in working with them.

10

RowSets can be of two types, depending on the implementation: connected and disconnected. While using disconnected RowSets, the user can modify the data contained in the RowSet in memory, as if she were modifying the underlying database. The changes aren't transmitted to the database immediately. When the user is satisfied with the changes, she can accept them, which then sends the changes over to the database. This is the behavior that makes disconnected RowSets a good choice to send data over the network. WebLogic Server provides an implementation of disconnected RowSets. It's important to remember that the following discussion of RowSets is very much dependent on the implementation of RowSets in WebLogic Server.

Creating RowSets

RowSets are created using the RowSetFactory. This class can be found in the package weblogic.jdbc.rowset. This factory returns a WebLogic implementation of the RowSet, which is represented by the interface weblogic.jdbc.rowset.WLCachedRowSet. The following code snippet creates a RowSet:

```
WLCachedRowSet rowSet = RowSetFactory.newInstance().newCachedRowSet();
```

Metadata

Each RowSet is associated with metadata that can be retrieved from the RowSet by using the getMetaData method. The interface that represents the WebLogic Server implementation of a RowSet metadata is weblogic.jdbc.rowset.WLRowSetMetaData, which extends the javax.sql.RowSetMetaData interface. You can use this object to get and set much useful information, such as concurrency policy, of the underlying database.

```
WLRowSetMetaData rowSetMetaData = (WLRowSetMetaData) aRowSet.getMetaData();
```

Populating a RowSet

RowSets may be populated either directly or using a ResultSet object. To populate the RowSet using a ResultSet object, use the populate method of the RowSet. The following code snippet assumes that we've already executed the query and obtained the ResultSet object:

```
rowSet.populate(myResultSet);
```

A second mechanism of populating RowSets is directly using the relevant database connection information and a query. The connection information can be passed in a couple of formats. They are

- A JNDI name resolving to a DataSource object
- A JDBC driver URL, which will be used by the DriverManager to obtain a connection

Needless to say, we recommend using the DataSource name because that's the way of getting database connections for a three-tiered application. After passing in the database connection information, you can set the command (the SQL statement) and the values and execute it. The following code snippet performs these operations. The first statement assumes the existence of a `DataSource` object under the JNDI name `jdbc/theDataSource`.

```
rowSet.setDataSourceName("jdbc/theDataSource");
rowSet.setCommand("SELECT * FROM BILL_ITEMS WHERE
➥           item_id = ?");
rowSet.setInt(1, 10);
rowSet.execute();
```

The `RowSet` interface provides several `setXXX` methods to set the values for various parameters. Each parameter is represented by a placeholder (the question mark in the SQL). The `setXXX` methods replace the parameter represented by the index with the value passed in. In this example, we replace the item ID with the number 10. After setting the value, we then execute the `RowSet` by invoking the `execute` method.

Reading from a RowSet

As in a `ResultSet` object, you can iterate through a `RowSet` using the `next` method. You can read the values of the columns using the `getXXX` methods defined in the interface. These methods take either the index of the column or the column name as a parameter. The following code snippet reads and prints the contents of the `RowSet` created earlier:

```
while (rowSet.next()) {
  System.out.println("bill id = " + rowSet.getInt("bill_id"));
  System.out.println("item id = " + rowSet.getInt("item_id"));
  System.out.println("quantity = " + rowSet.getDouble("quantity"));
}
```

Updating a RowSet

Before you update a row in the `RowSet`, you should first identify the primary key by invoking the `setPrimaryKeyColumn` method on the metadata.

```
WLRowSetMetaData rowSetMetaData = (WLRowSetMetaData) aRowSet.getMetaData();
rowSetMetaData.setPrimaryKeyColumn("ITEM_ID", true);
```

After you've done this, updating a `RowSet` is very similar to updating a scrollable `ResultSet`. As a matter of fact, the `RowSet` interface extends the `ResultSet` interface; therefore, you have access to all the methods in the `ResultSet`. Thus, you invoke various `updateXXX` methods on the `RowSet` object to update the columns. At the end of the updates, invoke the `updateRow` method to update the row.

The difference between updating the data using a `ResultSet` and a `RowSet` is that these updates are not reflected onto the database when you invoke the `updateRow` method. After you invoke all the `update` methods, you have to accept your changes. This can be done by invoking the acceptChanges method. You can invoke several updateRow or cancelRowUpdates methods before you accept the changes once.

```
rowSet.acceptChanges();
```

Deleting and Inserting a Row Using a RowSet

As with updates, you can delete or insert rows using a RowSet in exactly the same way as with ResultSets. Deleting a row requires that you first identify the primary key by invoking the setPrimaryKeyColumn method on the metadata. After you've done this, remember to invoke the acceptChanges method to commit the changes from memory into the database.

The file com.wlsunleashed.jdbc.Example7.java demonstrates the use of a RowSet to insert, update, and delete rows from a database. To use this, you *must* use the runtime JARs offered by JDK 1.4 or higher.

Concurrency Policy

As you know by now, RowSets implemented by WebLogic can be updated without being connected to the database (because they are disconnected). In many cases, the processes of reading the RowSet and updating it happen in two different transactions. So, it's quite possible that in between these two operations, the underlying data in the database will have been updated by other transactions, and thus the data in the RowSet might be outdated. WebLogic Server RowSet implementation uses optimistic concurrency policy to ensure data concurrency.

When you try to update or delete a row in the database using a RowSet, the implementation verifies whether the data in the database was modified after it was read into the RowSet. This is done by including the data that was read in the WHERE clause of the update or delete SQL statement. If the data has changed, the implementation raises an OptimisticConflictException. Applications can trap this exception and requery the RowSet before updating.

You have the ability to determine which fields of the table are used for checking for concurrency. You can set the concurrency strategy in the WLRowSetMetaData object obtained from the RowSet by invoking the setOptimisticPolicy method. This method takes an int. The various values that this method can take are defined as constants in the WLRowSetMetaData interface. These values and the concurrency mechanism they represent are described in Table 10.4.

TABLE 10.4 RowSet Concurrency Strategies

Concurrency Setting	Policy Adopted
VERIFY_READ_COLUMNS	This is the default policy. Includes all fields read from the database in the WHERE clause while updating or deleting the row.

TABLE 10.4 Continued

Concurrency Setting	Policy Adopted
VERIFY_MODIFIED_COLUMNS	Includes the primary key columns and the changed columns in the WHERE clause. Primary key columns must be identified by invoking the setPrimaryKeyColumn method on the metadata prior to updates or deletes.
VERIFY_SELECTED_COLUMNS	Includes the primary key columns and the columns you specify. You can specify columns using the setVerifySelectedColumn method. You can pick multiple columns to include in the WHERE clause.
VERIFY_NONE	Only includes the primary key columns in the WHERE clause.
VERIFY_AUTO_VERSION_COLUMNS	Includes the primary key columns and a version column in the WHERE clause. The version column should be an integer column defined in the database. Every time you update the row, the RowSet automatically increments the value of the version column.
VERIFY_VERSION_COLUMNS	Similar to the VERIFY_AUTO_VERSION strategy, but the RowSet does not automatically increment the version column. You must have some kind of trigger in the database that performs this task.

Executing Stored Procedures

Stored procedures are a very efficient way of performing tasks within a database. Because these are stored and executed within the database, there's very little data access overhead. As the name implies, these procedures are precompiled and stored within the database. Although a discussion of writing stored procedures is much beyond the scope of this chapter, it's important to remember that you should prefer writing stored procedures and accessing them for performing data intensive operations.

JDBC enables you to execute a stored procedure from within your Java application, pass values to it, and optionally obtain results in a standard way for all RDBMSs. To do that, you will use a `CallableStatement`. As usual, the `CallableStatement` object is also returned by the `Connection` object. To receive this object, invoke the `prepareCall` method of your `Connection` object. This method takes a `String`, which indicates the stored procedure to be invoked, using a special escape syntax. The syntax for invoking a stored procedure resembles the following if the procedure you're invoking does not return a result:

```
{call procedure_name[(?,?,...)]}
```

Here the question marks (?) indicate IN / OUT parameters of the procedure. As you can see, these are optional, and you can have a stored procedure that doesn't take any input and doesn't return any output. The *procedure_name* is the actual name of the procedure within the database. If your procedure returns data, the syntax would be

```
{? = call procedure_name[(?,?,...)]}
```

Needless to say, a stored procedure that doesn't have any IN / OUT parameters and does not return any output can be invoked using the syntax

```
{call procedure_name}
```

IN Parameters

After you create a `CallableStatement` with IN parameters, you can load the actual values by invoking the appropriate `setXXX` method on the `CallableStatement` object. These methods take the name of the IN parameter and its actual value as parameters. There are also alternative signatures that take the IN parameter index (which begins at 1). You can specify literal parameters, which are hard-coded values, in your escape syntax. The index obviously doesn't include these literal parameters.

For example, assume that there's a procedure for updating stocks in the XYZ Confectionary system. It takes an item ID and a stock quantity as input, and updates the corresponding records. To invoke this stored procedure, the following code snippet is to be used:

```
1. String sql = "{call updateStock(?,?}";
2. CallableStatement csmt = Connection.prepareCall(sql);
3. csmt.setInt( "item_id", 1 );
4. csmt.setDouble( 2, 10.0 );
5. csmt.executeUpdate();
```

In this code snippet, we first prepare a `CallableStatement` by invoking the `prepareCall` method and passing in the two parameter placeholders. In lines 3 and 4, we subsequently replace the placeholders with actual values. In line 3, we use the representation that takes the parameter name, and in line 4, we use the representation that takes the parameter index. After loading all the values, we execute the update by invoking the `executeUpdate` method.

OUT Parameters

Of course, your stored procedure can return values as output and you can have OUT parameters. To access these OUT parameters, you must first register those parameters as output parameters in your `CallableStatement` object. To do this, invoke the `registerOutParameter` method, which takes either the parameter index or the parameter name, along with other information about that parameter, such as the type of the parameter, its scale, and so on. The types of parameters are specified as integers, which are defined as constants in the class `java.sql.Types`. Remember that all OUT parameters in your stored procedure must be registered with the `CallableStatement` before you execute the procedure.

> **NOTE**
>
> You can learn more about the mapping between Java types and SQL types in the Sun documentation at the URL `http://java.sun.com/j2se/1.4.1/docs/guide/jdbc/getstart/mapping.html`.

For example, consider a procedure that returns a result set containing a list of all items that were purchased (from the BILL_ITEM table), as well as the total quantity of items, along with the total cost for all the purchases.

```
String sql = "{? = call getItemsPurchased(?, ?)}";
CallableStatement csmt = Connection.prepareCall(sql);
```

This procedure takes no inputs. Now we'll register the OUT parameters. As you can see from the escape syntax, this procedure contains two OUT parameters. We'll register this parameter as an output parameter with the `CallableStatement` object.

```
csmt.registerOutParameter(2, java.sql.Types.DOUBLE, 2);
csmt.registerOutParameter(2, java.sql.Types.INTEGER);
```

We've registered our first output parameter (`cost`) as a `Double`, with a scale of 2. This will return a double value with two decimal places. We then registered the second parameter as an `Integer`. This will return the total number of items purchased. You have to repeat this step for all the output parameters returned by your stored procedure.

After we do this, we can then execute the stored procedure by invoking the `executeQuery` method of the `CallableStatement` object. This method returns a `ResultSet`, which can then be processed as discussed in the earlier sections of this chapter. After processing the rows of the `ResultSet`, you can retrieve the OUT parameter values using appropriate `get`*`XXX`* methods present in the `CallableStatement` object. Remember that this is the recommended order of processing outputs from stored procedures (that is, OUT parameters are processed after the `ResultSet` is processed), owing to certain DBMS restrictions. If your procedure doesn't return a result set, you can invoke the `executeUpdate` method of the object. You can still access the OUT parameters by using the `CallableStatement` object.

INOUT Parameters

Stored procedures also allow you to define INOUT parameters, which act as both inputs and outputs from the stored procedure. The usage of these parameters is very similar to IN and OUT parameters, but in this case, you invoke both the appropriate `set`*`XXX`* method as well as the `registerOutParameter` method on this parameter.

Batch Updates

Applications are sometimes required to perform multiple updates of the same type. For instance, consider the Purchasing department of XYZ Confectionaries when new stocks of various items come in. The department must update the stock of all the items at this time. Another example is when the unit prices of different items go up. One way of to perform multiple updates of the same type is to call the `executeUpdate` method over and over again, once for each row. If you want to use updateable result sets, you still have to make multiple calls to `updateRow` method after updating each row. Obviously, this isn't very efficient because it amounts to many trips between your application and the database. You can avoid SQL compilation and improve performance by using a `PreparedStatement`, but that still doesn't avoid the problem of multiple database trips.

To address this issue, JDBC 2.0 introduced the concept of batch updates. A *batch update* is a set of SQL statements that's submitted to a database as one unit for batch processing. You may combine batch updates using a `Statement`, a `PreparedStatement`, or a `CallableStatement`.

For example, consider our requirement of updating the stock of several items in XYZ Confectionaries. The following code block will take care of creating a statement, adding three updates to a batch, and finally sending it to the database for processing. We look at what each line does after first looking at the code fragment. Assume that `items` is an array of item IDs, and `newStock` is an array containing new stock values for the corresponding items.

```
try
{
  aConnection.setAutoCommit( false );
  Statement stmt = aConnection.createStatement();
  for (int i = 0; i < items.length(); i++)
  {
    stmt.addBatch( "UPDATE XYZCONF.ITEM SET STOCK_QTY = " +
          newStock[i] + " WHERE ITEM_ID = " +
          items[i]);
  }
  int [] updateCounts = stmt.executeBatch();
  conn.commit();
}
catch (BatchUpdateException bue)
{
  System.out.println("SQLException: " + bue.getMessage());
  System.out.println("SQLState: " + bue.getSQLState());
  System.out.println("Code: " + bue.getErrorCode());
  System.err.print("Update counts: ");
  int [] updateCounts = bue.getUpdateCounts();
```

```
21.    for (int i = 0; i < updateCounts.length; i++)
22.    {
23.      System.out.println("oper : " + (i+1) + " = " + updateCounts[i]);
24.    }
25.    rollback(conn); //function that handles the rollback.
26. }
27. catch (SQLException sqle)
28. {
29.    sqle.printStackTrace();
30.    rollback(conn); //function that handles the rollback.
31. }
```

In line 3, we turn the auto-commit feature off. This ensures that each update is not independently committed to the database. This will allow for accurate checks for errors later in your code. As a reminder, if you have autocommit set to `true`, each operation within the batch transaction is considered a separate operation and is committed immediately. If you set it to `false`, you have control of whether to commit the entire batch transaction or roll it back.

In lines 7, 8, and 9, we add a batch operation to the `Statement` object by calling its `addBatch` method. This operation does not send the SQL command to the database—it merely registers the command as a part of a batch transaction within the statement object. This block of code will add as many SQL operations into the batch as there are items in the array passed to this code snippet.

After all the operations have been added successfully, we then send the batch to the database in line 11 by invoking the `executeBatch` method. This method does not take any parameters and can possibly send multiple SQL operations to the database, unlike the `executeUpdate` method, which sends in a single operation. The DBMS executes these operations in the same order they were added into the `Statement` object. If all operations succeed, the database returns update counts for each operation, which indicate the number of rows affected by each of these operations. These update counts are returned as an `int` array back to the calling method. Thus, after line 11 has been executed, we'll have as many items in the `updateCount` array as there are items, and each of the entry should be the value `1`—this is because each of our updates should affect a single row in the database table.

After executing the `executeUpdate` method, all the batch operations added earlier using the `addBatch` method are cleared from the `Statement` object. You can also manually clear the operations if you want to restart the transaction by calling the `clearBatch` method on the `Statement` object.

Batch updates can result in two kinds of exceptions. Like any other JDBC API, this method also throws an `SQLException` when there are any problems in accessing the database.

Apart from this, the executeBatch method also throws an SQLException when any operation in the batch requires that a ResultSet be returned to the calling process. For example, if you add a query in your batch processing, the executeBatch method will throw an SQLException back. You can execute only SQL commands (both DDLs and DMLs) that return an update count as a result of their execution in a batch transaction. Examples of such commands are INSERT, UPDATE, DELETE, CREATE TABLE, ALTER TABLE, and so on. The addBatch method won't result in an exception when you try to add queries using it because the statements aren't validated until you actually try to execute the batch.

If none of the preceding conditions occurs, you know that the method was able to successfully attempt to execute all the SQL statements. However, it's possible that one or more of the SQL statements within the batch transaction may have a syntax error, or there could be something else wrong with the statement. In such cases, this method throws a BatchUpdateException. This exception is a subclass of SQLException, and for this reason, you'll have to catch this type of exception before you catch SQLException. The BatchUpdateException object contains the same information as SQLException does. It also contains a method called getUpdateCounts, which returns the update count int array back to you. If the third operation in your batch failed, this array will now consist of two entries because only the first two operations would have been attempted. Each of these entries will give you the number of rows affected by the corresponding operations. If you had turned auto-commit off, you have the option of rolling back your entire batch operation at this point, if you so choose.

The file com.wlsunleashed.jdbc.Example8.java demonstrates a batch update. This process simply updates the stock of the first five items in the ITEM table to the passed values.

Statement Caching

Using PreparedStatement or CallableStatement increases performance considerably, but preparing these statements involves quite a processing overhead in communicating between the application server and the database. In cases in which you have to prepare these statements over and over, WebLogic Server provides an option to cache these prepared statements to minimize this overhead during subsequent calls. This is done using statement caching. Each connection maintains its own cache of statements, although the options of caching are specified at the connection pool level.

You can specify the caching options for a connection pool using the WebLogic Server console. In order to set up a statement cache, start the WebLogic Server console by typing in http://localhost:7001/console on your browser address bar. Navigate to the Services→JDBC→Connection Pools link on the left side of the console. Select the connection pool on which you want to create the cache. This opens the properties of that pool. Now, click the Connections tab. For a screenshot of this operation, refer to Figure 10.13, which appears later in this chapter.

Here you can create a cache and assign an algorithm to determine which statement is to be stored in the cache. The two algorithms that are available to you are

- LRU—When your application invokes a `prepareStatement` method call, the server first checks whether that statement already exists in the cache. If one is found, that statement is returned. If one isn't found and if the cache is full, the statement that is least recently used is removed from the cache, and a new statement is created and cached. Needless to say, if the cache is not full yet, no statement is removed.
- Fixed—The server caches statements as and when you invoke the `prepareStatement` method, until the cache size is reached. When the cache size is reached, the server stops caching statements.

You can also specify the cache size for each connection pool (and therefore every connection within it) using the console. You must determine this number very carefully because there's a potential downside to caching statements. Each open prepared or callable statement may potentially reserve DBMS cursors. Therefore, if your cache size is huge, it implies many open cursors, which might cause undesirable results. Remember that if you set the cache size to 10 on a connection pool with 10 connections deployed across two servers, the total number of statements cached is 2 servers×10 connections/server×10 statements/connection, which is 200 statements! Setting the cache size to 0 disables caching.

SQL3 Data Type Support

The next version of the ANSI/ISO SQL standard defines new data types that are commonly referred to as the SQL3 data types. JDBC 2.0 supports these very useful data types. It provides interfaces that represent these data types so that you can use them as if they were similar to other SQL data types.

There are five different interfaces that represent the various SQL3 data types. They are

- `BLOB`—Also known as a Binary Large OBject. It represents an SQL `BLOB`, which is used to store binary objects within a database. These objects can store very large amounts of data and are stored as raw bytes. This type can be very useful if you want to store images in your database.
- `CLOB`—A Character Large OBject represents an SQL `CLOB`, which can be used to store large amounts of data in character format.
- `Array`—Represents an SQL `Array` instance. You can use this to store an array as a column; for example, marks obtained stored as an array in a student table.
- `Struct`—Represents the SQL structured type. This enables you to store user-defined types (UDTs) in columns.
- Ref—Maps the `SQL REF` type, which serves as a reference to SQL data within a database.

`Arrays`, `BLOBs`, and `CLOBs` offer a very big advantage in terms of efficiency in storing large data. RDBMS are usually optimized to work well with these data types, and therefore offer better efficiency while using them as compared to breaking them down into multiple smaller columns. Also, the API itself does not always query these objects when you try to retrieve them. A query simply returns a reference to these objects, thus making your queries faster and more efficient. At the point when you need to actually use the data stored within the column, you would call appropriate methods defined by these interfaces to materialize the object.

You can retrieve and update these fields just as you would with any other regular SQL data type. These fields may be fetched using a `ResultSet` object or by invoking a `CallableStatement`. Both interfaces provide you with `getXXX` methods (`getBlob`, `getClob`, and so on) that enable you to work with these data types. For instance, the following code snippet reads the database for the image of the item from the ITEM table (after making appropriate changes to the database schema, of course):

```
ResultSet rs = stmt.executeQuery( " SELECT IMAGE FROM XYZCONF.ITEM " +
                " WHERE ITEM_ID = 1 " );
rs.next();
Blob myImage = rs.getBlob(1);
```

To update these types of fields, you would invoke the appropriate `setXXX` method (`setBlob`, `setClob`, and so on) of a `PreparedStatement`. For instance, the following code snippet updates the image of the item in the BILL_ITEM table with the image obtained in the previous code snippet:

```
PreparedStatement ps = aConn.prepareStatement( "
           " UPDATE XYZCONF.BILL_ITEM SET IMAGE = ? " +
           " WHERE ITEM_ID = 1 " ) ;
ps.setBlob(1, myImage);
```

As we discussed, `Arrays`, `BLOBs` and `CLOBs` are not queried from the database all the time, and only references are returned to your code. So, if you want to query the actual object, how do you do it? The interfaces have methods that enable you to materialize the stored data. For instance, the `BLOB` interface gives you a `getBinaryStream` method, whereas the `CLOB` interface provides you with a `getAsciiStream` method. Both these methods return an `InputStream`, which you can process as you would process a normal Java `InputStream` object. You can refer to the API documentation of JDBC 2.0 for a description of the different methods provided. You can find the documentation in Sun's Web site at the URL `http://java.sun.com/j2se/1.3/docs/api/java/sql/package-summary.html`.

The `Struct` data type behaves a little differently from what we've been discussing so far about other SQL3 data types. A `Struct` interface represents a user-defined type in SQL, also known as a UDT. Types can be created by using the `CREATE TYPE` SQL command and used as column data types. It's quite easy to notice that you don't have a `getStruct` method in either the `ResultSet` or the `CallableStatement` interface. The reason for this is that you will use the `getObject` method, and then cast the returned object to the `Struct` interface. You can then access the attributes of your UDT from within the `Struct` object. Similarly, you can update UDTs by calling the `setObject` method.

Apart from these SQL3 data types, JDBC 2.0 also enables you to work with SQL distinct types. *Distinct types* are user-defined types that are built based on existing data types. For instance, you could create a distinct type of `NUMERIC(16, 2)` and call it as `DECIMAL`. It's easy to see that the new type is based on the basic `NUMERIC` data type. Such types map to the same Java type as the underlying data type. For instance, in this example, `DECIMAL` maps to `java.math.BigDecimal` as its underlying data type. `NUMERIC` also maps to the same Java data type. Therefore, you'll use the `getBigDecimal` and `setBigDecimal` methods to work with this distinct type.

WebLogic JDBC—Monitoring and Tuning

WebLogic provides extensive monitoring capabilities for JDBC connections using the administration console. This section briefly describes the types of monitoring and tuning you can do with JDBC. Refer to the WebLogic administration guide for a detailed explanation of the various features offered.

Tuning Your Connection Pool

To tune your connection pool, start WebLogic Server and the console. Now navigate to your connection pool in the tree pane of the console and click it. This opens the properties of the connection pool on the right side of the connection pool. Click on the Connections tab. You can see this screenshot in Figure 10.13. On this screen, you can tune the connection pool by setting the following properties of the connection pool.

Some of the basic properties you can set are

- Initial Capacity—This is the number of connections to the database that are created when the JDBC connection pool is created at server startup. The default value is `1`.
- Maximum Capacity—The maximum number of connections that can be present in the pool. The default value is `15`.
- Capacity Increment—The number of connections that are added every time a connection is needed. Default value is `1`.
- Statement Cache Size—The number of statements that are cached per connection. By default, caching is not turned on; that is, the cache size is 0.

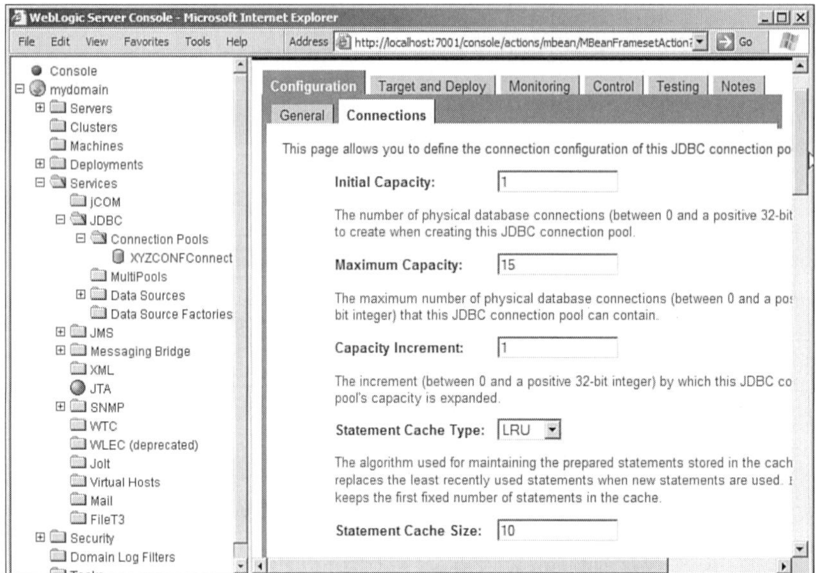

Figure 10.13 Tuning your connection pool.

You can also configure some advanced properties of the connection pool. To do this, click the Show link.

- Login Delay—The number of seconds to wait between creating two physical connections. The default is 0.
- Allow Shrinking—If the connections of the pool aren't being used, this property will determine whether the connection pool should give up those connections. By default, shrinking is allowed, and this is the recommended approach.
- Shrink Frequency—The number of seconds before which the server shrinks connections that aren't used. This property is used only if you've selected the Allow Shrinking property. The default value is 900 seconds.
- Enable Connection Leak Profiling—Indicates to the server that it should gather any leak information from JDBC connections. By default, this value is not set.
- Test Frequency—Indicates the number of seconds before which the server tests each unused connection. If a connection fails, that connection is given up and a new one is opened. By default, this property is set to 0, indicating testing isn't performed. If you set it to a positive value, you must also specify a valid Test Table Name value, as described later.

- Test Reserved Connections—Indicates to the server whether it has to test connections before handing them over to the client. By default, this value is not set. If you set this value, you must also specify a valid Test Table Name, as described later. Testing connections at reserve might cause a performance impact, but the client is assured of receiving a working connection.
- Test Released Connections—Indicates to the server whether it has to test connections that are released by clients. By default, this value is not set. If you set this value, you must also specify a valid Test Table Name value, as described later.
- Connection Reserve Timeout—The number of seconds after which the request to reserve a connection from the pool will timeout. By default, the value is set to 10 seconds. If you set this to –1, the request will never timeout.
- Connection Creation Retry Frequency—Indicates the number of seconds between retry attempts to create a connection. The default value is `0`.
- Inactive Connection Timeout—The number of seconds of inactivity on a connection after which the server reclaims the connection from the client and releases it back to the pool. The default is `0`.
- Maximum Waiting for Connection—Indicates the maximum number of requests that can wait for a connection to be handed out by the pool at any time. By default, this is a very high number.
- Maximum connections Made Unavailable—When the server tests or refreshes connections, they aren't available for clients. This parameter identifies the maximum number of such connections that can be made unavailable at any time.
- Test Table Name—Identifies the table to be used to test the physical connections at various points. At what points these connections are tested depends on other parameters on this screen, as discussed earlier. You can also put in an SQL code in this place for the server to execute that SQL on the connection. SQL code should begin with the word `SQL`, followed by a space. For instance, the values `TEST_TABLE` and `SQL SELECT COUNT(*) FROM TEST_TABLE` produce the same result.
- Init SQL—You can specify an SQL statement that will be executed on every connection that's created. This SQL code will typically be used to initialize the created connection. You may leave this field blank (which is the default behavior), and disable the server from running any SQL code. The SQL statement you put in here should begin with the word `SQL`, followed by a space.

Monitoring a Connection Pool

In the Connection Pool Properties page, you can also monitor the connection pool by clicking on the Monitoring tab. You can customize the properties of your connection pool that has to be displayed on this screen by clicking on the Customize This View link. Some of the fields that can be monitored using this screen are given in the following list. You can look at a screen shot of a sample monitoring page in Figure 10.14.

- Connections—The number of connections currently being used by clients.
- Connections High—The maximum number of connections that were used from this pool at any given time. It's a good idea to iteratively tune the `Maximum` Capacity property of the connection pool based on this parameter.
- Connections Total—Indicates the number of connections that are currently established within this pool. Initially, WebLogic Server starts with as many active connections as indicated by the Initial Capacity parameter. It subsequently adds active connections as and when required until it reaches the Maximum Capacity value. All connections that have been free for the number of minutes indicated by the Shrink Period parameter, and which are over and above the number indicated by Initial Capacity, can be shrunk. In other words, connections are closed at this time. This is done to conserve system resources. As discussed in the previous sections, it takes time to reconnect to the database, so you must configure the Initial Capacity and Shrink Period values based on the volume of database requests you expect.
- Wait Seconds High—The longest any client has had to wait before it has been serviced by this connection pool. Obviously, a big value in this field indicates a bottleneck in your application. You might want to increase the Maximum Capacity value of your connection pool if your resources permit. Tuning SQL statements also makes database access faster, thus making connections available faster for other clients.
- Waiters High—The maximum number of clients that have waited for a connection from this pool. Again, a high value in this field could indicate a bottleneck.

These parameters can also be monitored programmatically by using the `JDBCConnectionPoolRuntimeMBean`, which is the same management bean that enables you to monitor the connection pool using the console.

Controlling a Connection Pool

You can control a connection pool by clicking the Control tab of your connection pool configuration page. You can see a screen shot of this page in Figure 10.15. Here you can perform the following tasks on your pool. Note that you can also perform all of these operations using the `JDBCConnectionPoolRuntimeMBean` bean.

- Shrink—Shrinking a pool makes the server release unused connections from the pool that are over and above the initial capacity of the pool. Although the server does this automatically if you've enabled shrinking, this option is available for you if you want to perform this activity explicitly.

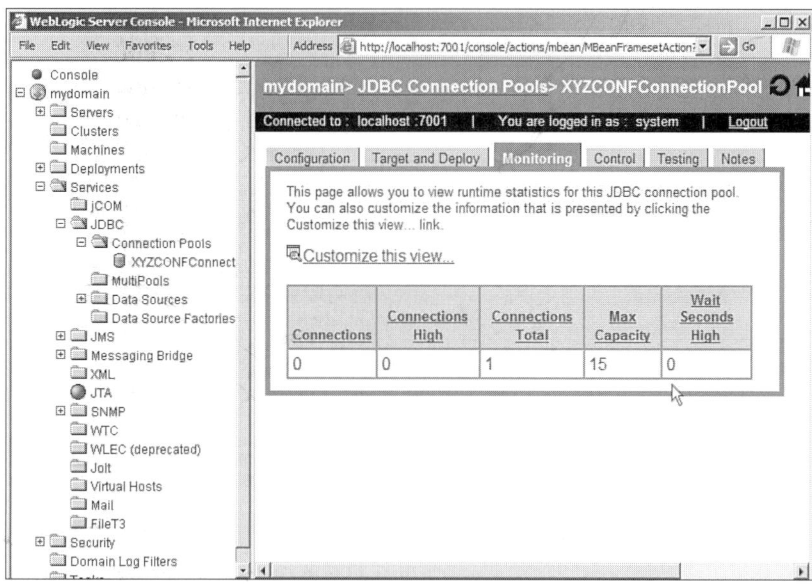

Figure 10.14 Monitoring a connection pool.

- Reset—Occasionally, you might want to force the server to reset the connection pool, which ensures that all connections are closed and reopened. For example, this might be required if you restart your database or if you feel that the connections are failing.
- Clear Statement Cache—This option enables you to clear the statement cache (if any) maintained for each connection within your connection pool.
- Suspend—This option enables you to suspend a connection pool, thus preventing clients from receiving connections out of this pool. If a client already has a connection reserved, executing any statement on this connection results in an exception.
- Force Suspend—This option enables the server to forcibly suspend all connections within the pool. Any transaction that's executing on the connection is rolled back, and all applications are disconnected. The connections are closed and reopened.
- Resume—Resumes the connection pool, and clients can now get connections from this pool.
- Destroy—Closes all connections from the pool, and the configuration is deleted from the configuration file. If any client is currently using a connection, this operation will fail.
- Force Destroy—All clients using the pool are disconnected and the connection pool is destroyed. The configuration is removed from the configuration file. You must have a very good reason to perform a Destroy or a Force Destroy operation.

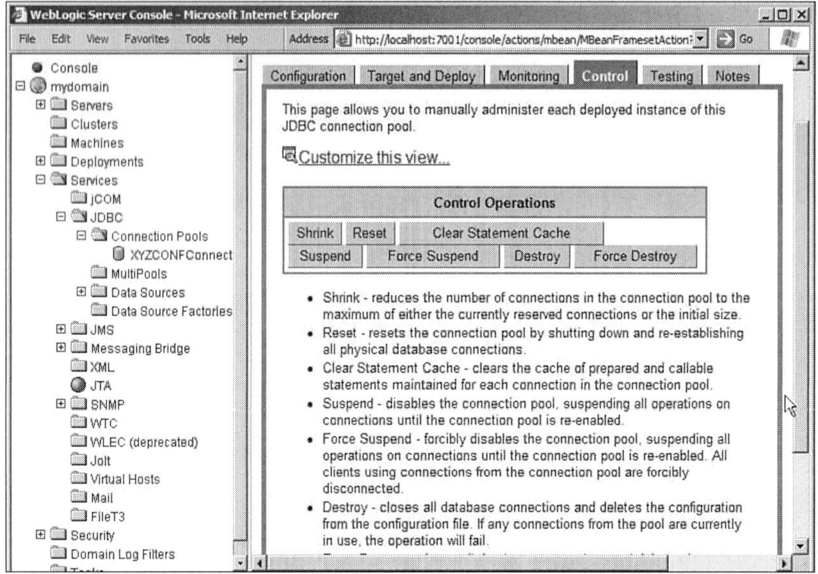

Figure 10.15 Controlling a connection pool.

Validating a Database Connection from the Command Line

WebLogic provides utilities with which you can test for a two-tier or a three-tier database connection to the database from the command line using the JDBC driver.

To test for a two-tier connection, use the class `utils.dbping`. This utility can work with WebLogic jDriver for Microsoft SQL Server, WebLogic jDriver for Oracle, Oracle thin driver, and Sybase jConnect driver. You specify the user ID, the password, and the database name (in the correct format for the appropriate driver) to the `dbping` utility.

You can test for a three-tier connection using the `utils.t3dbping` utility. You must first test for a two-tier connection using the `utils.dbping` utility and start WebLogic Server before using this tool. This utility also works with the same database drivers as the two-tier version. This utility takes the URL of WebLogic Server, the database user ID, the password, the database name, the driver class name, and the database URL for the driver.

JDBC—Best Practices

Most Web applications include some sort of a database access—thus making JDBC one of the most crucial components in an application. Therefore, it's important to take several factors into account while working with JDBC to improve performance of the overall application. In this section, we discuss some of the aspects that you must remember while programming with JDBC.

Use Smart Queries

Database queries can often be the most time-consuming aspect of your application. Make sure that you optimize your queries as much as possible. Never query more data than you require. This applies for columns, too. It's preferable to `SELECT` the fields that you need rather than performing a `SELECT *`. Avoid using database clauses such as `count(*)` and `sort by` because they might be resource intensive.

Combine Database Updates into a Transaction

Every database operation is treated as a transaction unless you explicitly specify the start and end of the transaction. Avoid the use of auto-commit feature while performing multiple database updates because it consumes time to commit each and every operation. Instead, try to combine database updates, inserts, and deletes into logical user transactions.

Don't Use Transactions That Span User Input

Transactions normally signify a single unit of work. Therefore, it's a very good practice to collect all user inputs prior to the beginning of the transaction. If transactions encompass user input, there's always the possibility that the user won't provide the input for a long time, thereby keeping the relevant locks in the database for that duration. This will obviously hamper other transactions, which might not start until these locks are released.

Design Your Application for Parallel Data Processing

Databases are much more than dumb file storage mechanisms. Most databases are tuned to perform better when several parallel tasks are running simultaneously, rather than a single process. Utilize this feature by "parallelizing" the data processing in your application.

Select an Optimal Isolation Level

The choice of isolation level will depend on the type of your application and the accuracy of the data it can work with in case of concurrent data access. An application is guaranteed the latest data in the database by using the isolation level `TRANSACTION_SERIALIZABLE`, but that's also the slowest in terms of performance. In most cases, `TRANSACTION_READ_COMMITTED` will work just fine, although this won't prevent nonrepeatable and phantom reads.

Use a Connection Pool

Always try to use a connection pool rather than attempting to create connections every time you need data access. Connection creation can be the most expensive operation in your application. Attempt to create connections at initialization time rather than at usage time. Using connection pools also uses fewer resources, and can make economic sense because it can make several application threads work with a limited number of connections.

Use the Appropriate Statement Object

While performing multiple database operations, such as inserting many rows at once, you should prefer the use of a `PreparedStatement` over a `Statement` object because the former supports precompiled SQL statements. You can simply change the input data every time you want to use this SQL and re-execute it. If your task involves the use of multiple different database operations, a `PreparedStatement` might not be very helpful. In such cases, consider the use of a stored procedure and localize the operations within the database. You can then invoke the stored procedure by using a `CallableStatement` object. Databases are often optimized to work very well with stored procedures.

Use Batch Processing

You might often want to perform a bunch of operations to the database at one time. In such cases, choose to use batch processing. The advantage of batch processing is that all the operations in the batch are sent to the database at once, thus making the performance better.

Use Data Caching

If you know some data won't change very often, and if you also know that you use this data quite often in your application, it's a very good idea to cache that data in memory. This is often very useful for dealing with lookup tables. Caching large amounts of data can obviously prove to be resource intensive. So, a decision of what to cache and what not to cache must be based on the type of data and the frequency of its use.

Use In-Place Updates Where Possible

Inserting and deleting records in a database can be very expensive, especially if several table indexes have to be updated because of this operation. Therefore, you must try to minimize such operations. Choose to use updates, rather than deletes and inserts.

Free Up JDBC Resources

JDBC objects such as `Connection`, `Statement`, and `ResultSet` utilize resources, which must be released appropriately. You can release these resources by simply invoking the `close` method in these objects. It's usually a good idea to invoke the `close` method in the `finally` block of your `try-catch` statement block so that you can ensure that the resources are freed whether or not an exception is thrown.

Release Connections When Done

Database connections that are obtained from a connection pool should be released as and when you are done with them. This is very important because you'll normally be working with a limited number of connections in the connection pool. By holding on to a connection, your application will not scale.

JDBC and the Global Auctions Management System

The global auctions management system uses a PointBase database to store information about customer registrations, auctions, and bids. This data is accessed using JDBC. In several cases, JDBC isn't directly used; instead, Entity EJBs that employ container-managed persistence (CMP) are used. In other cases, JDBC is used directly, either from an EJB that uses bean-managed persistence or directly from a JSP.

Summary

Considering that most Web applications require some sort of database access, JDBC aims at generalizing the way in which you can access these databases. It's powerful enough to handle most database access requirements. When used carefully, JDBC can provide good performance. Like any other component, the process of tuning a JDBC system has to be an iterative one. It's important for you to constantly monitor usage and increase or decrease the resources allocated to connection pools in order to keep your application performing at its best.

CHAPTER 11

Creating Distributed Applications with RMI

by Malcolm Garland

IN THIS CHAPTER

- Introduction to RMI
- When to Use RMI
- RMI Compiler
- Writing RMI Code
- Performance Issues
- WebLogic RMI Registry
- WebLogic RMI API
- WebLogic RMI Best Practices

This chapter discusses WebLogic Server's implementation of JavaSoft's Remote Method Invocation (RMI) and RMI over Internet Interop Orb Protocol (RMI-IIOP) API(s). The RMI paradigm enables Java developers to implement method calls on objects that live on remote servers. This ability to make remote method calls is the basis of distributed computing; that is, applications using the services (methods) of components that live across networks. WebLogic Server's implementation of RMI contains enhancements that provide an efficient and effective tool to employ in distributed computing. This chapter discusses WebLogic Server's enhancements to the generic RMI and how to develop an RMI application.

Introduction to RMI

RMI is a JavaSoft API, which provides for remote (across a network) method calls. RMI provides for location transparency by allowing client applications to access Java objects on remote servers by invoking similar syntax as they would to access local objects.

This RMI paradigm enables even entry-level programmers to easily develop distributed applications. Local applications are provided with a reference to objects that reside on remote servers, thus providing for remote method invocation as depicted in Figure 11.1.

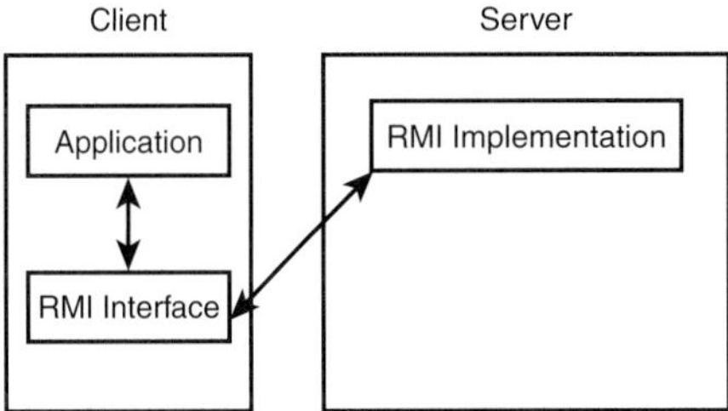

Figure 11.1 RMI architecture.

Notwithstanding transparency, there are some differences between using local and remote objects:

- Local objects are defined and implemented by local Java objects. However, remote objects are defined by local interfaces, but are implemented by remote objects that implement the local interfaces.
- Local objects are referenced directly via their objects' references; remote objects are referenced indirectly via local proxy stub references that contain instructions on how to connect to the remote object implementations.
- If implemented, local objects' `finalize()` methods are called before consideration for garbage collection as usual (assuming that all references to the local objects have been dropped). Remote objects may implement the `Unreferenced` interface, which is called when all references to the remote objects have been dropped. If all references to local objects are dropped and there are no further references to remote objects, the remote objects are then subject to garbage collection.
- Remote objects have a lease. If the specified leased time elapses, the lease expires, and references to remote objects are dropped, which qualifies the remote objects for garbage collection. Prudent developers should code for this situation; that is, a local object reference is available, but the associated remote object reference disappears.
- Local objects handle exceptions as usual; remote objects must also specifically handle `RemoteException`(s).

The methods of remote objects are defined within a Java remote interface that resides on the client side. *Implementation* classes, classes that implement methods of remote interfaces, reside on the server side.

The remote architecture is physically implemented by client-side proxy classes (stubs) that act as proxies for remote objects, and server-side implementation classes (skeletons) that implement the server-side code functionality. This stub-skeleton layer is depicted in Figure 11.2.

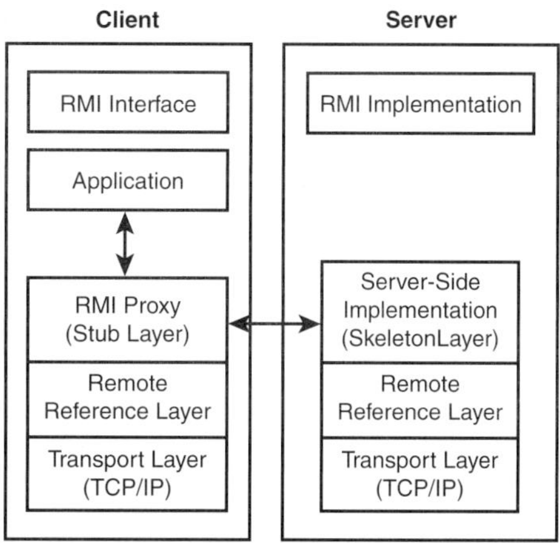

Figure 11.2 RMI architecture, proxy (stub)–server implementation (skeleton) layer.

Client-side applications issue method invocations on proxy classes, and proxy classes then send requests to remote server-side implementations. Those remote implementations invoke associated server-side methods and send any return values back to client-side proxies, which in turn provide results of these method invocations to the client-side applications.

These remote invocations are propagated over three layers. It is within the previous stub-skeleton layer that client-side (stub) method invocations are redirected to server-side (skeleton) remote objects. Beneath this layer is a remote reference layer that manages references and connections between clients and remote objects. The final layer within the physical implementation of the RMI architecture is the transport layer. The transport layer uses TCP/IP stream–based connections to provide network (or internal) connectivity between the client and remote hosts.

WebLogic's RMI Implementation

The WebLogic 8 series RMI implementation provides for client-side proxy classes and server-side objects (bytecode) as opposed to the client-side stub and server-side skeletons common in generic RMI implementations. The client executes method calls on client-side proxies; the requests are serialized and transported to WebLogic Server. In WebLogic Server, client requests are deserialized and processed against implementing objects. The results of the method invocations are then serialized and transported back to the client-side proxies. Client-side proxies then deserialize and forward results to the client.

WebLogic's implementation of JavaSoft's RMI API is a Java-to-Java remote method invocation solution. WebLogic's RMI implementation differs from the generic Sun RMI implementation by using proprietary features such as the WebLogic T3 protocol for communications (as opposed to the TCP/IP used in generic RMI solutions). Other WebLogic enhancements over the generic Sun RMI implementation are discussed throughout this chapter and especially under the "Performance Issues" section. RMI clients, coded in Java, must implement the RMI specification.

WebLogic's implementation of RMI-IIOP extends RMI object access to non-Java clients such as C, C++, Smalltalk, and COBOL, as depicted in Figure 11.3.

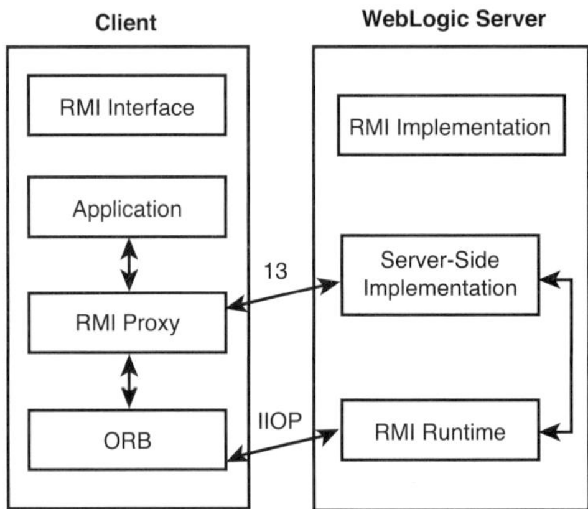

Figure 11.3 RMI architecture, IIOP client.

RMI-IIOP uses IIOP for communications, as opposed to the T3 protocol used for pure Java-Java RMI solutions. Clients must be a one of the following: a J2EE application thin client using CORBA 2.4; a J2EE non-thin client using CORBA 2.3; a Java client coded to the RMI-IIOP specification; a CORBA/IDL client (C, C++, Smalltalk, or COBOL) coded to the CORBA 2.3 or higher specification (using Interface Definition Language [IDL]); or a Tuxedo 8.0–compliant client (C, C++, COBOL, Java, or any language that Tuxedo can map to OMG IDL). The RMI-IIOP Tuxedo client uses the Tuxedo General Inter-Orb Protocol (TGIOP) for communications. The WebLogic 8.1 RMI-IIOP implementation supports any CORBA ORB that implements the Object Management Group's Objects-by-Value specification.

WebLogic 8 series implementation of RMI and RMI-IIOP assumes JDK 1.4.1_02 or higher. For further detailed information about WebLogic's implementation of the JavaSoft RMI API, refer to the BEA documentation site at `http://edocs.beasys.com/wls/docs81`.For JavaSoft RMI documentation, refer to the Sun documentation site at `http://java.sun.com/j2se/1.4/docs`.

When to Use RMI

RMI is applicable in situations in which local applications require services or methods available from remote locations.

You should use RMI in Java-to-Java architectures; that is, your local applications and the remote methods you want to invoke are both coded in Java. This strategy has the benefits of Java's inherent code portability and WebLogic's built-in security model, efficient garbage collection, thread management, and WebLogic Server's optimized t3–protocol-driven communications.

You should use RMI-IIOP in architectures if your local Java application must interface with applications coded in other languages. This strategy adds a degree of robustness and flexibility to your application.

If your applications are CORBA, you should create interfaces using IDL and implement Java client and server-side classes for deployment on your WebLogic Server 8 series server.

RMI Compiler

The WebLogic RMI compiler, `weblogic.rmic`, is used to generate the client-side proxy class and the server-side bytecode. The RMI complier takes as argument the class that implements your remote interface. For example, assume that you have an RMI solution that determines the current status of your application, with a remote interface named `BidStatus.class`, located in the package `com.utility`. The associated implementation class is named `BidStatusImpl.class`. You must run the RMI compiler against `BidStatusImpl.class` as such:

```
$ java weblogic.rmic com.utility.StatusImpl  [OPTION]
```

NOTE

You must use the *absolute* class name (the class name with the path) when submitting classes to the `rmic` compiler.

The WebLogic RMI compiler will produce a dynamic proxy class. WebLogic's hot code generation feature will create the server-side bytecode at runtime. The dynamic proxy is the client-side proxy (stub), and the server-side bytecode functions as the server-side implementation class (skeleton) as depicted in Figure 11.4.

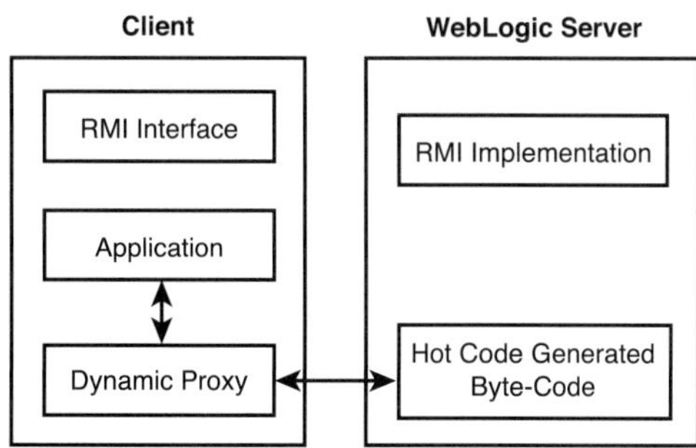

Figure 11.4 WebLogic RMI-generated classes.

RMI compilation is not required for Java-to-Java solutions. In this case, the proxy object communicates with WebLogic Server, which produces the skeleton dynamically. The default classes created are RMI-IIOP compliant. However, use of the -iiop option will generate the client proxy stub class and server-side tie class, as depicted in Figure 11.5.

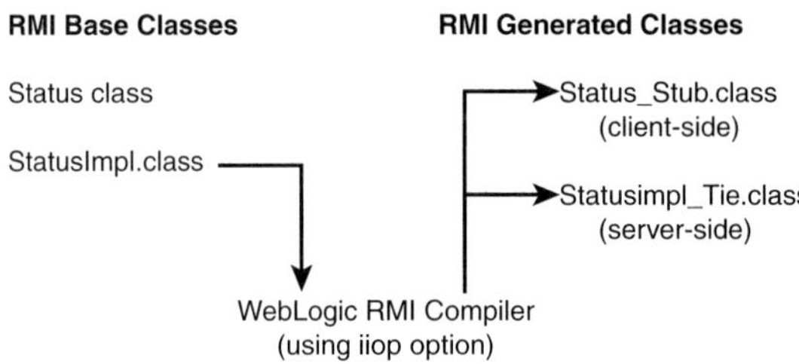

Figure 11.5 WebLogic RMI compiler-generated classes.

RMI compilation is required for the non-Java IIOP clients discussed earlier and clusterable stubs. Clusterable subs allow the RMI application to be used by all servers within a WebLogic *cluster* (a network of two or more WebLogic Servers). Clusterable stubs generated are *pinned*; that is, they aren't replicated within the cluster. Even though these clusterable stubs are available clusterwide through WebLogic JNDI, they reside only on the host in which they were registered. The WebLogic Server provides no failover or load balancing for clusterable RMI stubs. If the server on which the RMI is registered goes down, the cluster loses the services of that RMI. While the RMI is available, WebLogic Server does not balance the requests for the RMI evenly across the servers within the cluster. To create clusterable stubs, use the `rmic clusterable` option as shown here:

```
$ java weblogic.rmic com.utility.BidStatusImpl -clusterable
```

To gain a list of available options, use the `rmic help` option as shown here:

```
$ java weblogic.rmic com.utility.BidStatusImpl -help
```

To create IDLs for a remote interface, use the `rmic idl` option as shown here:

```
$ java weblogic.rmic com.utility.BidStatusImpl -idl
```

To create IIOP-compliant stubs, use the `rmic iiop` option as shown here:

```
$ java weblogic.rmic com.utility.BidStatusImpl -iiop
```

Writing RMI Code

To create a WebLogic RMI program, you must write a remote interface (client side), write the server-side implementation of the remote interface, compile (`javac`) the two classes, execute the `weblogic.rmic` compiler on the compiled implementation class, and write the

RMI client that uses the remote interface. The code listings in later sections are samples for the remote interface, implementation class, and RMI client. Note: The remote interface, implementation class, and `weblogic.rmic`-generated classes must be available to the WebLogic classpath for execution.

Writing the Remote Interface

Two points to remember when writing a WebLogic RMI remote interface: You must extend the interface `java.rm.Remote`, and the remote interface must be public. For our distributed computing example, we'll code an RMI that retrieves the bid status (item number, current date, and bid end date) of an auction item. The interface and the RMI client are available to the client box, but the implementation class lives only on the WebLogic Server across a network. Implement the remote interface as shown in Listing 11.1.

LISTING 11.1 Remote Interface

```
package your.package.structure;
/**
 * This interface is the remote interface.
 */
import java.rmi *;
import javax.ejb.*;

public interface BidStatus extends java.rmi.Remote {
  public String getBidStatus(Integer itemId)
➥throws javax.ejb.FinderException, java.rmi.RemoteException;
}
```

Implementing Your Remote Interface

To implement your remote interface, extend the remote interface and define the methods. For your implementing class name, use the name of the remote interface with the string `Impl` appended, as shown in Listing 11.2.

The `main()` method implemented in the sample code allows WebLogic Server to initiate the RMI class as a startup class. The `main()` method contains the code that registers the RMI class within the WebLogic Registry.

> **NOTE**
>
> A WebLogic startup class initializes at server startup. Startup classes are normally used to create conditions required at server startup, such as application initialization that might include the retrieving and setting of initial data. For more information about WebLogic startup classes, refer to `http://e-docs.bea.com/wls/docs81/ConsoleHelp/startup_shutdown.html`.

LISTING 11.2 Implementing Remote Interface

```
import javax.naming.*;
import java.util.*;
import weblogic.rmi.RMISecurityManager;
import java.rmi.RemoteException;
import javax.ejb.*;
import com.gams.ejbs.item.*;

public class BidStatusImpl implements BidStatus
{

  private Item item;
  private String BidStatus;
  private int itemIN;
  private ItemHome home;

 /**
  * Constructor.
  *
  * @param itemId         item id
  */
 public BidStatusImpl(Integer itemId) throws FinderException, RemoteException {
  super();
  try {
    findItem(itemId);
    }
  catch (Exception e) {
        System.out.println("BidStatusImpl.constructor: an exception occurred:");
        e.printStackTrace();
  }
 }

 /**
  *Method Find Item, returns item matching item id.
  *
  *@return item    item matching itemId
  */
 public Item findItem(Integer itemId) throws FinderException, RemoteException {
  try {
        Context ctx = new InitialContext();
        home = (ItemHome)ctx.lookup("ItemHome");
```

LISTING 11.2 Continued

```
        if (null != home)
          {item = (Item)home.findByPrimaryKey(itemId);}
        else {
           System.out.println("Item Matching ItemID Not Found");
            item=null;
        }
  }
  catch (Exception e) {
       System.out.println("BidStatusImpl.findItem: an exception occurred:");
       e.printStackTrace();
  }
  return item;
 }

 /**
  * Method Get Bid Status - Returns a string containing Bid status.
  *
  * @return          String Bid Status
  * @exception         java.rmi.RemoteException
  */
 public String getBidStatus(Integer inItemId) throws FinderException, RemoteExcep
➥tion {
 try {
    item = findItem(inItemId);
    if (null != item) {
      BidStatus = "Title: " + item.getTitle() + " ItemID: " + item.getItemId() +
➥" Curent Bid: " + item.getCurrentBid() + " Bid End Date: " +
item.getEndDate➥Time();
    }
    else {BidStatus = "No Bid Status Available For ItemID: " + inItemId;}
    }
  catch (Exception e) {
      System.out.println("BidStatusImpl.getBidStatus: an exception occurred:");
      e.printStackTrace();
  }
  return BidStatus;
 }

 /**
  * Allows the WebLogic Server to instantiate this implementation
  * and bind it in the registry. (allows rmi to run as a WebLogic startup class)
  */
```

LISTING 11.2 Continued

```
 public static void main(String args[]) {

  try {
       BidStatusImpl bidStatus = new BidStatusImpl(new Integer(12345));
       Context ctx = new InitialContext();
       ctx.bind("BidStatus", bidStatus);
       System.out.println("BidStatusImpl created and bound in registry
       ➥ to the WebLogic Server");
  }
  catch (Exception e) {
       System.out.println("BidStatusImpl.main: an exception occurred:");
       e.printStackTrace();
  }
 }

}
```

You can register startup classes manually by adding code to your `config.xml` as shown here:

```
<StartupClass ClassName="BidStatusImpl" Name="BidStatus" Targets="adminServer"/>
```

CAUTION

Take extra caution when manually editing the `config.xml` file. Ensure that you maintain a backup, even when making minor or routine modifications.

NOTE

An absolute pathname is not used for `ClassName` when registering a startup class within the `config.xml` file.

The formal method of registering a startup class is to use the WebLogic Administration Console. First ensure that the class is available to the server classpath. Enter the Administration Console at `http://`*`yourURL`*`:port/console`. Enter your username and password, and register the startup class using the sequence *yourDomain*→Deployments→Startup & Shutdown→Configure a New Startup Class as shown in Figure 11.6.

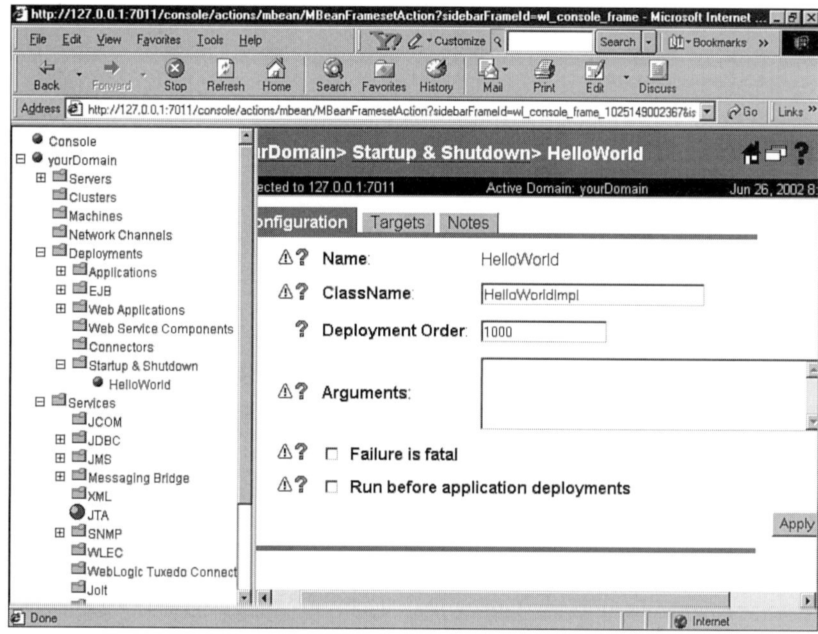

Figure 11.6 Configure the startup class.

Compiling the Interface and Implementation

Compile the remote interface and the implementation class using the `javac` command as shown here:

```
$ javac BidStatus.java
$ javac BidStatusImpl.java
```

Running the weblogic.rmic Compiler

Run the `weblogic.rmic` complier on the implementing class as shown here:

```
$ java weblogic.rmic package.structure.BidStatusmpl
```

To produce stub and tie classes, run

```
$ java weblogic.rmic package.structure.BidStatusImpl -iiop
```

NOTE

An absolute pathname is required when submitting an implementation class to the RMI compiler.

Writing the RMI Client

Writing the client code is straightforward. You need only get a context, lookup the RMI name in the Registry, and execute the method as shown in Listing 11.3. If you're developing an IIOP client, you must narrow your object after lookup, as shown in lines 26–28 of Listing 11.3.

LISTING 11.3 Writing RMI Client Code

```
1 import java.io.PrintStream;
2 import weblogic.utils.Debug;
3 import javax.naming.*;
4 import java.util.Hashtable;
5 import javax.rmi.*;
6
7
8 public class BidStatusClient {
9
10  public BidStatusClient() {}
11
12  public static void main(String[] argv) throws Exception {
13
14   try {
15
16       String host = argv[0];
17       String port = argv[1];
18       Integer itemId = new Integer(argv[2]);
19
20       InitialContext ctx = getInitialContext("t3://" + host + ":" + port);
21
22
23       BidStatus bStatus = (BidStatus)ctx.lookup("BidStatus");
24
25       //For IIOP Clients
26       //Context ctx = new InitialContext();
27       //Object home = ctx.lookup("BidStatus");
28       //BidStatus bStatus =
➥(BidStatus)PortableRemoteObject.narrow(home, BidStatus.class);
29
30    System.out.println("BidStatus RMIClient Successfully connected to
    ➥WebLogic Server:\n" + bStatus.getBidStatus(itemId) );
31   }
32   catch (Exception e) {
33    e.printStackTrace();
```

LISTING 11.3 Continued

```
   }
  }

  private static InitialContext getInitialContext(String url)
     throws NamingException
  {
   Hashtable env = new Hashtable();
   env.put(Context.INITIAL_CONTEXT_FACTORY,
  ➥"weblogic.jndi.WLInitialContextFactory");
   env.put(Context.PROVIDER_URL, url);
   return new InitialContext(env);
  }

}
```

This Java client can be executed as shown here:

```
$ java BidStatusClient localhost 7001 3456 (parameters are WebLogic host, port,
➥ and item ID)
```

Performance Issues

The following sections are areas where WebLogic's implementation of RMI has reportedly demonstrated marked enhancements in performance over generic RMI implementations.

Scalability

Scaling for RMI clients is linear. The WebLogic Server implementation of RMI, running on a small, single-processor, PC-class server can reportedly support more than 1,000 simultaneous RMI clients. If true, this is a marked improvement on the basic JavaSoft RMI implementation. See `http://e-docs.bea.com/wls/docs81/rmi/rmi_intro.html#852658`.

Thread/Socket Management

WebLogic RMI requests can be divided into a determinant number of threads. Multithread processing allows exploitation of latency times and available processors. WebLogic's implementation of RMI uses a single, bi-directional, asynchronous connection. WebLogic Server provides the connection; the client does not listen for connections, and there are no client server sockets. The same connection is also used for JDBC and other services, thereby reducing server overhead.

Serialization

WebLogic RMI uses greatly enhanced high-performance serialization, offering a performance gain even for one-time remote class use. WebLogic implements the `Externalizable` interface rather than the `Serializable` interface used in generic RMI implementation. This option saves overhead in the serialization process; that is, no super classes are serialized. The use of WebLogic's T3 protocol and a single asynchronous bi-directional connection in the serialization process also contributes to performance gains.

Supporting Services

WebLogic RMI uses WebLogic Registry services and WebLogic JNDI; both yield higher efficiencies than the generic versions. WebLogic's flavor of Java garbage collection is also optimized. WebLogic's T3 protocol greatly optimizes communications between remote components.

Distributed Garbage Collection

The distributed garbage collection mechanism, based on the Modula-3 Network Objects, works by requiring the server to track clients requesting the RMI. References to requested objects are flagged as *dirty* when the object is requested. The flag is removed (flagged as *clean*) when the client drops the reference and the object is eligible for server-side garbage collection. The client reference to the RMI object also has a lease. If the client does not refresh the remote object within the time limit of the lease, the object is then also eligible for server-side garbage collection.

The distributed garbage collection interface is `java.rmi.server.Unreferenced`. Implementing this interface provides notification when all clients have dropped references to the remote object. As mentioned earlier, due to the nature of distributed garbage collection, developers should code RMI clients to deal with the situation in which the server-side lease has expired while the clients still requires use of the remote object. WebLogic optimizes garbage collection by providing an option of implementing the Java HotSpot Server VM as opposed to the Java HotSpot Client or Classic Java VM(s). The Server version of the HotSpot VM provides for the fastest possible (long run) operating times that enhances garbage collection, as opposed to faster application startup times with slower operating times. This option is activated by passing the `-server` option at WebLogic Server startup.

WebLogic RMI Registry

The WebLogic RMI Registry allows applications to locate objects bound to WebLogic Server. This is critical in a distributed environment, where local clients must locate objects on remote servers. The WebLogic Registry is hosted by WebLogic Server and uses WebLogic's implementation of JNDI. Registry communications are conducted over the same single connection as RMI and JDBC transactions, thereby optimizing resources. The

RMI Registry is created at server startup. Objects bound to the Registry are accessed using several protocols, including `rmi://`, `http://`, `https://`, and `iiop`.

WebLogic RMI API

The WebLogic RMI API fully implements and supports the JavaSoft RMI API with the following: WebLogic implementation of RMI base classes; WebLogic Registry; WebLogic Server packages; WebLogic RMI compiler (covered previously); and WebLogic-provided supporting classes.

WebLogic Implementation of RMI API

Classes developed per the RMI specification, as demonstrated earlier in the "Writing the Remote Interface" section (refer to Listing 11.1), can be executed on WebLogic Server by extending the `java.rmi.Remote` class. To implement remote access within your RMI client, simply look up the remote object in the WebLogic Registry and execute target methods. The `java.rmi.Naming` class includes the methods for lookup and name binding within the WebLogic Registry. WebLogic JNDI provides the actual naming and lookup services.

All functionality of the `java.rmi` package is implemented in WebLogic's RMI implementation, with the exception of methods in the `jama.rmi.server.RMIClassLoader` class (implements dynamic class loading with RMI) and the `java.rmi.server.RemoteServer.getClientHost()` method (returns the client host for the remote method invocation being processed within the current thread).

WebLogic RMI Security Classes

The `rmi.RMISecurityManager` class is implemented as a nonfinal class with public methods. `RMISecurityManager` is a sample security manager for use by RMI applications that might use downloaded code. WebLogic RMI provides for Secure Sockets Layer (SSL) and access control lists (ACLs) to provide security during RMI processing; therefore, it does not use `RMISecurityManager`.

The `System.setSecurityManager(RMISecurityManager)` method is also provided. This method obviously sets `RMISecurityManager`. Within the WebLogic RMI implementation, no security is associated with this method. Use of this method is not recommended. WebLogic Server provides an internal security manager. You should use the WebLogic security model. Refer to Chapter 28, "Working with WebLogic Server Security Features," for details about security.

WebLogic RMI Registry Classes

The `rmi.registry.LocateRegistry` class is implemented as a nonfinal class with public methods. The `LocateRegistry` class obtains a reference to or creates an object registry on a local or remote system. A call to the `LocateRegisty.createRegisty(int port)` method allows the client to find the JNDI tree on WebLogic Server, but does not create a collocated Registry. The method returns a `java.rmi.registry.Registry`. This method could be useful when locating JNDI object entries on remote servers.

Other Useful WebLogic Server Classes

The `rmi.server.LogStream.write(byte[])` method logs messages through the WebLogic Server log file. The `UnicastRemoteObject` class defines a nonreplicated (not shared across a network) remote object whose references are only valid when the server is operational. This class is implemented as the WebLogic RMI base class. All associated methods are implemented in the WebLogic RMI base class stub. Therefore, there's no need to extend the `UnicastRemoteObject` class as required by the JavaSoft RMI specification. You merely write and implement your remote interface. WebLogic provides the `rmi.server.RemoteObject` class (base class for RMI objects; that is, implements `java.lang.Object`) to preserve the type equivalence of `UnicastRemoteObject`. For WebLogic Server development, it's not necessary to implement either of these classes (`UnicastRemoteObject` or `RemoteObject`).

Passing Parameters Within WebLogic RMI

Within WebLogic RMI, all parameters are passed by value unless the invoking object resides within the same JVM as the RMI object. In that case, the parameters are passed by reference. Any classes passed to the remote object must be available to the WebLogic Server's classpath.

CAUTION

Modifying parameters could possibly corrupt the caller's state (alter the value of the passed parameters). Critical applications should guard against this possibility.

Passing Java Primitive Data Types

Java primitive or simple data type parameters (`boolean`, `byte`, `short`, `int`, `long`, `char`, `float`, and `double`) are always passed by value. Passing by value protects data integrity from possible server-side corruption (a server-side implementation class can possibly modify a parameter passed by reference). When primitive data types are passed during a remote method call, a copy of the parameter is made, serialized across the network, deserialized, and made available to the remote method. If the remote method returns a Java primitive, the value is serialized, deserialized, and returned to the calling client.

Passing Java Objects

When a Java object is passed during a remote method call (nonlocal JVM), the *object* is passed by value, not just the reference to the object. Passing by value protects the object's data from corruption by the called remote object; that is, it's possible to implement methods within the server-side implementation class that can alter the value of the passed parameter. The passed object and all objects referenced by the passed object are serialized (via object serialization) across the network where they are deserialized by the remote JVM and made available to the remote object. Objects returned to the client are handled likewise. Only Java objects that implement the serializable interface may be passed as parameters.

Passing Remote Objects

RMI implementation also calls for passing remote objects (although returning is more commonly used), as presented in the previous RMI example and as used in EJB applications (see Part V, "Using Enterprise JavaBeans in WebLogic Applications"). If a method returns a local reference to a remote object, a copy of the object is not returned. Instead, a remote proxy class (client-side stub) is returned.

WebLogic RMI Best Practices

Use a Java client connecting to a Java implementation class when possible. Coding your RMI client applications in Java exploits both WebLogic's implementation of the JavaSoft RMI API (as discussed earlier) and the inherent strengths of Java to include, but not limited to, code portability, garbage collection, and security.

If you're developing a CORBA application, develop the Java remote interface and implementation class first, and then use IDL to create your client interfaces. You must determine whether your IDL client supports Objects-by-Value. If not, you can pass only other interfaces or CORBA primitive data types.

Design RMI systems to minimize remote method calls. Making few remote method calls that return larger data sets avoids the excessive overhead encountered when marshalling and unmarshalling objects. (Implementing the `Externalizable` interface versus the `Serializable` interface along with use of the `transient` keyword also reduces marshalling overhead.) Fewer method calls returning larger objects is more efficient than making many remote method calls returning many smaller objects. Designs should shun excessive object manipulation; that is, passing objects when only a few values are needed or returning objects when maintaining an object reference is unnecessary. Excessive method calls and coupled with excessive object manipulation can cause scalability and performance issues. If multiple remote method calls are unavoidable, try batching the remote method calls and combining method calls using a value object. Use of the Value Object design pattern allows for efficient transfer of finely grained data (many method calls) by providing a coarsely grained data view (batched method calls). Refer to Sun's documentation at `http://java.sun.com/blueprints/patterns/j2ee_patterns/catalog.html` for the details of the Value Object Design pattern.

Minimize distributed garbage collection by caching proxy stub classes. This strategy avoids unnecessary garbage collection. If used, you should implement a policy to delete unneeded or expired stubs from the cache.

In most cases, you should consider using session EJBs as opposed to pure RMI implementations. See Part V for detailed information on EJB implementation.

Summary

In this chapter, we discussed JavaSoft's RMI architecture and WebLogic's implementation of RMI. We addressed how to code, compile, and deploy an RMI application to include the various RMI clients and protocols supported by WebLogic Server. The next chapter covers WebLogic's implementation of enterprise messaging with JMS.

CHAPTER 12

Enterprise Messaging with JMS

by Paul J. Perrone

NOTE

This chapter is adapted from Sams Publishing's *J2EE Developer's Handbook* (ISBN 0-672-32348-6).

IN THIS CHAPTER

Passing messages between applications in a distributed system is a very common service for an enterprise information system. In an abstract sense, this is precisely what happens when you make a distributed object call using communication models such as CORBA, RMI, and Web Services using JAX-RPC. Messaging services can be distinguished from these remote procedure–oriented communication models by the added layer of abstraction that is provided above a communications paradigm to uncouple the connection between distributed message sender and receiver. Rather, an intermediate service exists between a message producer and a message consumer that handles the delivery of messages. Furthermore, producers do not block on messages they deliver. Instead, messages are sent asynchronously by the producer. This chapter describes the core concepts behind messaging services, the standard means for tapping into such services within Java and J2EE via the Java Message Service (JMS), and how such applications can be built using BEA WebLogic Server 8.1 as a messaging service provider as well as messaging client platform.

Brief Introduction to Enterprise Messaging

Enterprise messaging is one of the most widely used and most important technologies for integrating various disparate enterprise applications. The Java Message Service (JMS) API provides a standard interface for interacting with enterprise messaging services. The BEA WebLogic Server 8.1 provides an enterprise-class means for not only implementing such services, but also for configuring such services with your applications. Before we delve into the JMS API and how it is used inside of BEA WebLogic Server, it's important to have a foundation in enterprise messaging service concepts.

A *messaging service* is software that provides support for passing messages between distributed applications in a reliable, asynchronous, loosely coupled, language-independent, platform-independent, and often configurable fashion. Messaging services accomplish this task by encapsulating messages that are sent between a sender and a receiver and by providing a software layer that sits between distributed messaging clients. A messaging service also provides an interface for messaging clients to use that isolates the underlying message service implementation such that heterogeneous clients can communicate using a programmer-friendly interface. Such an infrastructure can also be viewed as an event notification type service in which messages are events, and the delivery of these messages between messaging clients acts as sort of an event notification mechanism. In this section, we explore the various facets of messaging services utilized by enterprise systems.

Message Service Locality

Figures 12.1 and 12.2 depict two types of messaging service implementations. Figure 12.1 shows the most common type of messaging service implementation, in which some middleware software implements the functionality of a messaging service to receive asynchronously generated messages from a message producer and route them to a message consumer. A messaging client utilizes the services of the centralized messaging service in a transparent fashion via a messaging client interface. Figure 12.2 depicts a messaging service implementation in which the messaging software is embedded directly into a thick messaging client.

Most of our discussions here assume the use of messaging middleware. Messaging middleware enhances the reliability and availability of a messaging service by virtue of a focus on the use of centrally managed persistent and redundant mechanisms in the middleware. Messaging middleware also alleviates the need for clients to manage connections to multiple messaging service endpoint locations by allowing a connection between a messaging client and a messaging service middleware server.

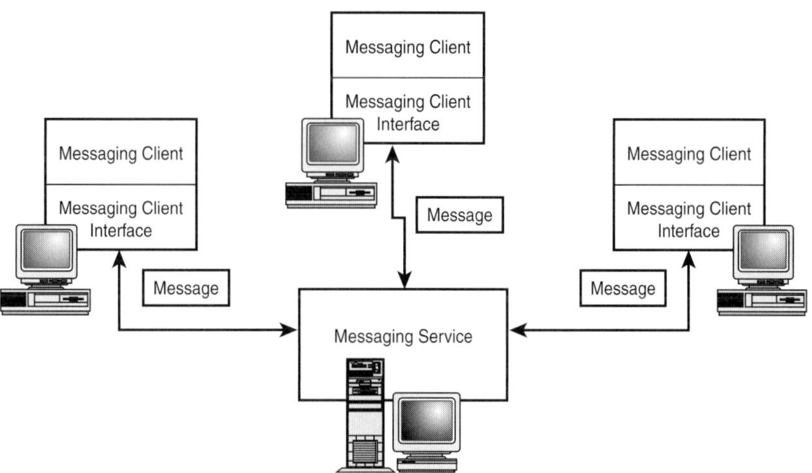

FIGURE 12.1 Messaging middleware.

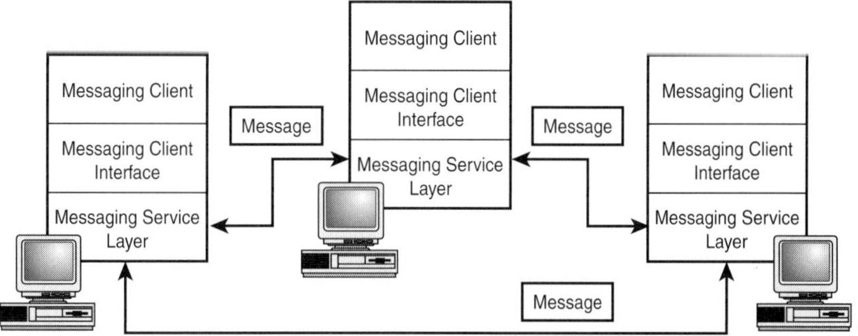

FIGURE 12.2 Messaging thick client software.

Point-to-Point Messaging

Figure 12.3 depicts one type of messaging service used for point-to-point communication between a message producer and a message consumer. A message producer sends a message to a particular consumer identified by some name (for example, "Foo"). This name actually corresponds to some queue in the message service used to store the message until it can deliver the message to the consumer associated with that queue. The queue may be persistent to help guarantee the delivery of a message even in the event of a message service failure. That is, a persistent queue can be read by a backup message service instance and used to deliver messages to a message consumer even if the primary message service fails.

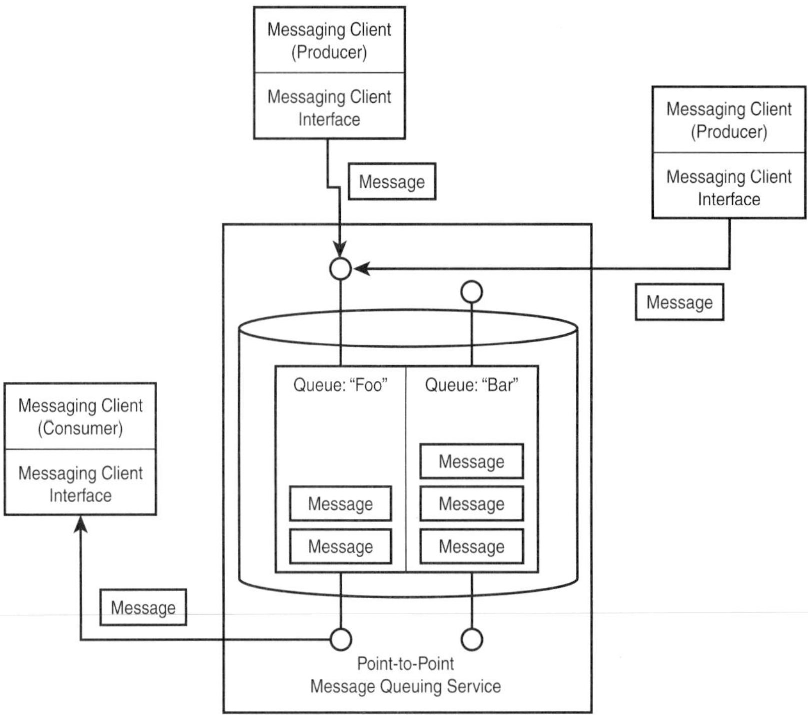

FIGURE 12.3 The point-to-point message queuing service.

Publish-Subscribe Messaging

Figure 12.4 depicts another popular model of messaging known as the *publish-subscribe* messaging service. With publish-subscribe, a message publisher publishes a message to a particular topic. Multiple subscribers can register to receive messages that have been published to a particular topic. Topics can be hierarchically arranged and can further enable the publication of messages and subscriptions to receive messages within a particular topic context. For example, we might subscribe to receive only those messages published specifically to the Stocks topic, or subscribe to receive all of those messages published to the Stocks topic and its subtopics, such as OTC.

Message Filtering, Synchronicity, and Quality

In the event that a message consumer desires to receive only certain messages based on some function of the message attributes, a message filtering scheme may be employed. Message filtering involves distinguishing between which messages should be delivered and which messages should not be delivered to a message consumer as a function of some filtering criteria. The filtering criteria are described in some language (for example, SQL) and can refer to attributes and values of a message. Thus, for example, you may subscribe to messages from a Stocks topic but filter out those messages whose StockSymbol attribute does not match the stock symbols in your stock portfolio.

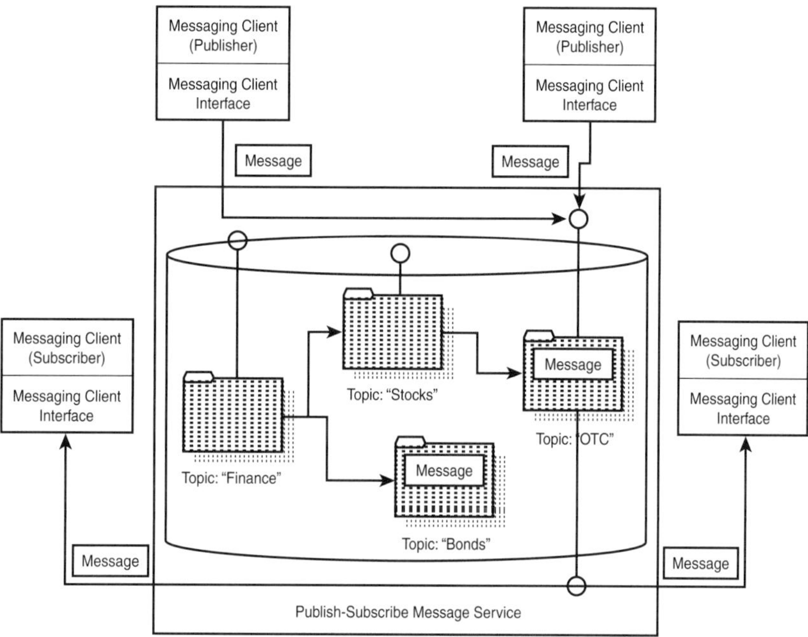

FIGURE 12.4 The publish-subscribe messaging service.

Although various models of messaging exist, all messaging services share a common attribute of asynchronicity. Messages are sent by message producers to message consumers and do not require that the message producer block processing until the message is received. However, typical remote method invocation protocols, such as RMI and CORBA, implement calls by default such that the distributed client does block until the call completes (that is, synchronous calls). Asynchronous calls thus offer a certain level of time-independence for the message producers and consumers.

As we've already alluded, a message service can also provide a certain level of assurance associated with message delivery. Reliability and availability of message delivery provide a Quality of Service (QoS) that can often be specified at various levels. Mission-critical messages must have a higher QoS than lower-priority messages. Many messaging services provide a means to designate the QoS at the connection, message type, and individual message levels.

MOM

The terms *Message-Oriented Middleware (MOM)* and *messaging service* are nearly synonymous. MOM is simply an implementation of a messaging service, albeit in a fashion that is standard for a particular type of MOM system. A MOM API defines how distributed applications should utilize an underlying MOM message channel or queue for communicating messages to one another. Messages are passed between applications via MOM in a way that does not block the sender of that message. That is, the sender can send a message and allow the MOM to ensure that it gets to the intended receiver without waiting for a response from the receiver.

MOM implementations can implement one or more types of messaging models. For example, one MOM implementation may employ simple point-to-point messaging. Another MOM implementation may implement a more sophisticated publish-and-subscribe model, and perhaps provide a server to manage message queuing in a centralized fashion and using redundant middleware server processes for enhanced reliability and availability.

MOM has historically been so popular that various organizations have been created and have gotten involved in providing standardization of MOM approaches. However, different underlying MOM implementations still abound. Because MOM is such a core part of an enterprise application, the Java Message Service was defined to provide a standard MOM API for Java-based applications usable in a J2EE context. As you'll see in the next section, JMS provides a standard means for interfacing with messaging systems and thus implements a standard Java-based interface to MOM.

Brief Introduction to JMS

The Java Message Service (JMS) is a Java API that defines how messaging clients can interface with underlying messaging service providers in a standard fashion. JMS also provides an interface that underlying messaging service providers implement to provide JMS services to clients. Thus, JMS follows the familiar model of providing both an application programmer interface and a service-provider interface to implement standard services akin to the model followed by JDBC, JNDI, and many other Java enterprise component interfaces.

JMS provides both a point-to-point and a publish-subscribe model of messaging. Such messaging models are also referred to as *messaging domains* within the JMS specification. Point-to-point messaging is accomplished by the implementation of message queues to which a producer writes a message to be received by a consumer. Publish-subscribe messaging is accomplished by the implementation of a hierarchy of topical nodes to which producers publish messages and to which consumers can subscribe.

JMS provides a core abstract messaging API that is extended by both the point-to-point message queuing model API and the publish-subscribe model API. In this chapter, we cover the core JMS architecture, basic point-to-point message queuing model, and basic publish-subscribe model. New to JMS v1.1 beyond JMS v1.0 is the unification of messaging domains such that the core JMS API can now be used to send and receive messages in either a point-to-point or a publish-subscribe fashion. Thus, in JMS v1.1, you can either use the core abstract and generic JMS APIs to send and receive messages or utilize the concrete point-to-point and publish-subscribe JMS APIs that subclass the generic JMS API.

The J2EE v1.3 specification requires that the JMS v1.0 API and an underlying service provider be included with a J2EE implementation. The J2EE v1.4 specification requires that the JMS v1.1 API and an underlying service provider be included with a J2EE implementation. However, BEA WebLogic Server 8.1 is geared only for J2EE v1.3 compliance. Hence, WebLogic Server 8.1 is equipped only with a JMS v1.0–compliant infrastructure. Nevertheless, a separate download of the JMS v1.1 API can offer JMS v1.1 functionality to your WebLogic Server 8.1.

Describing the JMS API and how it is used inside WebLogic Server is no simple task due to the rather large API embodied by JMS. Furthermore, a significant portion of the API is encapsulated inside of the core generic JMS API that is concretely extended by the publish-subscribe and point-to-point queuing APIs. We thus take the following approach toward describing JMS and its use within WebLogic Server 8.1 in the remainder of this chapter:

- Describe the *core generic JMS API*
- Describe the *concrete point-to-point queuing JMS API*, sample code, and how to configure and deploy inside of the WebLogic Server
- Describe the *concrete point-to-point queuing JMS API*, sample code, and how to configure and deploy inside of the WebLogic Server
- Describe the *unified domain model JMS API*, sample code, and how to configure and deploy inside of the WebLogic Server
- Describe advanced JMS configuration and deployment features embodied by WebLogic Server

JMS Core Architecture

The core architecture behind JMS is depicted in Figure 12.5. Here we see that JNDI is used to create an initial context to a JMS connection factory that is then used to create connections to JMS-based service providers. Given a JMS connection, a particular session context can be retrieved to create message producers and message consumers. Messages sent from a producer to a consumer are associated with a particular endpoint destination. At the consumer end of a messaging session, filtering of messages can be achieved using a message selector `String`.

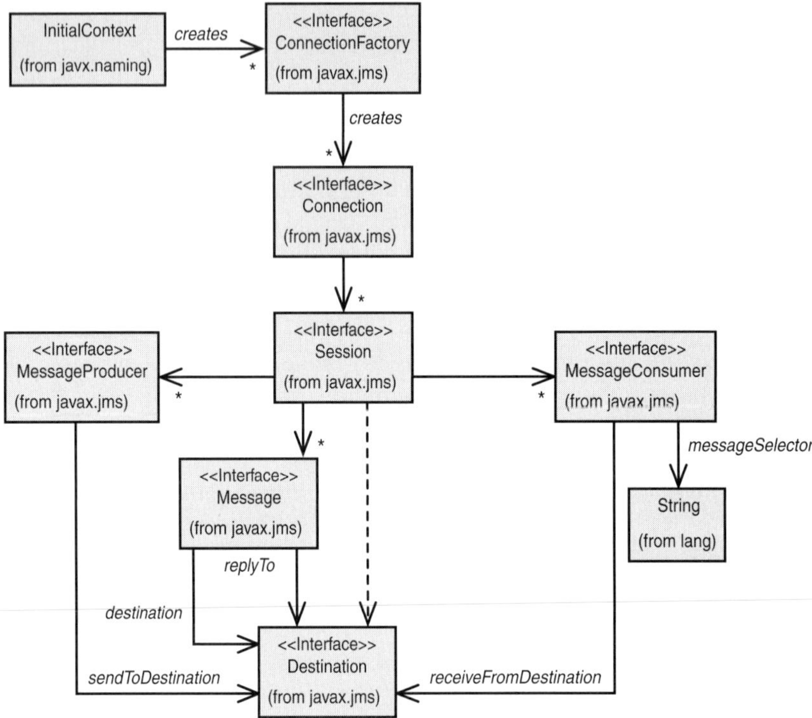

FIGURE 12.5 The JMS core architecture.

JMS Connections

Figure 12.6 depicts the detailed architecture behind JMS connections. JMS connections represent a connection between a JMS client and a JMS service provider's messaging server. The JMS connection-related interfaces shown here are base interfaces that are further extended for the two messaging domain models of JMS. JMS v1.1 also allows a JMS client to use the base interfaces directly in a more domain-independent fashion.

A `ConnectionFactory` interface is used to create a connection to a particular JMS service provider's message service. JNDI is used to look up a handle to an initial `ConnectionFactory` object managed by a JMS service provider. Sub-interfaces of `ConnectionFactory` and objects that implement the `ConnectionFactory` interface provide methods for returning specific `Connection` object instances. New to JMS v1.1, a JMS client can also use a base `ConnectionFactory` object directly to create handles to generic `Connection` objects that ultimately may encapsulate connections to either point-to-point or publish-subscribe messaging models. The `ConnectionFactory.createConnection()` method can be used to create handles to `Connection` objects either by using a default user identity or by passing in a username and password explicitly.

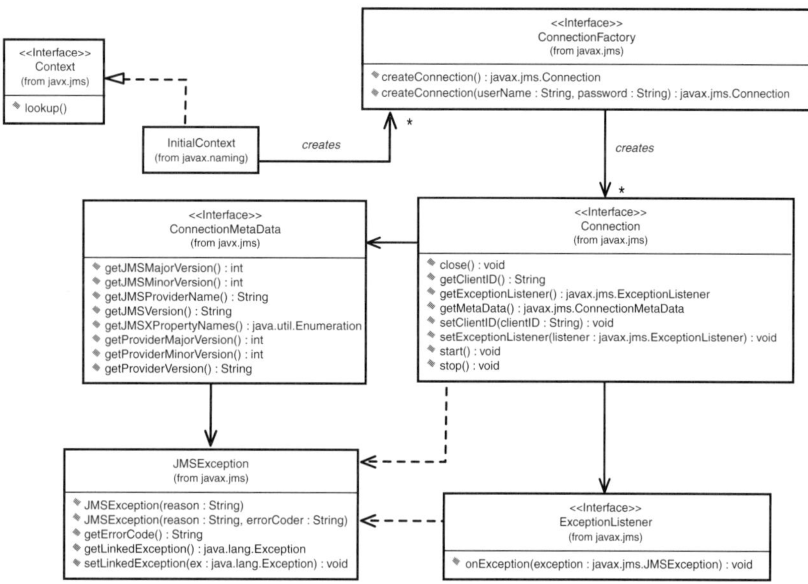

FIGURE 12.6 JMS connections.

A `Connection` interface encapsulates a JMS client's connection with a JMS service-provider instance. When a connection is created, it is in a stopped mode. That is, the consumers associated with the connection do not receive messages until `Connection.start()` is called. `Connection.stop()` can be used to return the connection to stopped mode. The `Connection.close()` method is called when the JMS client is finished with the connection and wants to clean up resources.

It should be noted that the `JMSException` class is an exception that is thrown by nearly every JMS API method call. It is also the root class for all other JMS exceptions. A `JMSException` can have a JMS service provider–specific error code `String` associated with it. A `JMSException` can also return its link to a lower-level exception that was responsible for the higher-level messaging exception. A JMS client can be notified of asynchronously occurring exceptions that are associated with the connection. The JMS client can register an object implementing the `ExceptionListener` interface with the connection by calling the `Connection.setExceptionListener()` method. The `ExceptionListener` implements the single `onException()` method to be notified of the `JMSException` occurring on the connection. As with any listener, the exception listener must be sure to provide an `onException()` implementation that can handle multiple client threads attempting to notify the listener. The listener may be retrieved by a call to `Connection.getExceptionListener()`.

A JMS service provider–specific client ID associated with a connection can be retrieved with `Connection.getClientID()` and set with `Connection.setClientID()`. The client ID will typically be associated with a connection by the JMS service provider when creating the connection using the `ConnectionFactory`. If the JMS client attempts to set the client ID using `setClientID()`, an `IllegalStateException` will be thrown in the event that the

ID set by the client is not permitted by the JMS service provider. If the client does attempt to set a client ID, it will be set immediately upon connection creation before any further actions are taken.

Metadata about the connection can also be returned from the `Connection` object using the `getMetaData()` call. The `ConnectionMetaData` object that is returned can provide the named version, major version numbers, and minor version numbers for both the JMS API and the service-provider code being used. Additionally, an enumeration of JMS properties associated with the connection can be returned from the `ConnectionMetaData` object.

JMS Sessions

Figure 12.7 depicts the core relations involved in JMS sessions. A JMS session is associated with a connection and represents a context within which messages are created. A session may be used to define a transaction within whose boundaries may exist a set of messages being sent and received within the transaction. Thus, all such messages may be contained within an atomic transaction.

The `Session` interface encapsulates the context within which JMS messages are created and received. The `Session` interface also extends the `java.lang.Runnable` interface, signifying that each session runs in the context of a single thread. The `Connection.createSession()` method can be used to create a handle to a `Session` object. A `boolean` parameter passed inside of the method indicates whether the session is to be transactional or not. As we'll discuss shortly, the mode for acknowledging received messages may also be specified in the `createSession()` when creating a `Session` object. The `Session.close()` method is used to close a session resource when the JMS client is finished with its use.

A set of `create`*`XXX`*`Message()` methods on the `Session` interface are used to create instances of messages that are to be associated with a session. Messages that are created using the same `Session` object are stored in the same session context until they're committed for delivery using the `Session.commit()` method if the particular `Session` object instance is transaction-sensitive. If `Session.rollback()` is called, the messages created within the context of this session are not sent. Such commit and rollback semantics ensure that messages created within the same session context are either all sent or that none is sent. The `Session.getTransacted()` method can be called to determine whether a session is transaction-aware via the return of a `boolean` value.

`Session` objects that are not transaction-aware require an acknowledgment that a message was received. Such messages are then marked as sent and will not be redelivered. Messages in transaction-aware sessions are delivered when they are sent and do not wait for a commit or rollback command to be issued on the session. Optionally, a `Session.recover()` method may be called to stop the current delivery of messages and to restart the message delivery process for all messages that have yet to be acknowledged as delivered. Three `static public` constants designate the mode in which messages are sent:

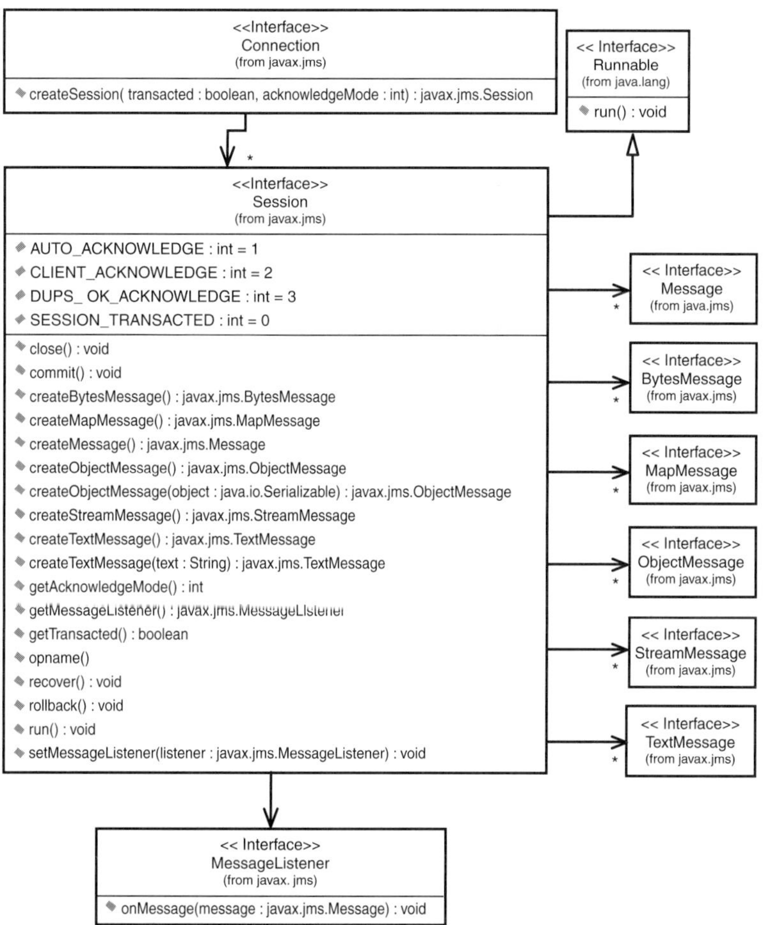

FIGURE 12.7 JMS sessions.

- `AUTO_ACKNOWLEDGE`—The session automatically acknowledges that a message was received by the client.
- `CLIENT_ACKNOWLEDGE`—The session requires that the client explicitly acknowledge that it has received a message.
- `DUPS_OK_ACKNOWLEDGE`—The session acknowledges that a message was received by a client, but the overhead that it assumes to ensure that duplicate messages were not delivered is relaxed. Thus, duplicate messages may be sent to the client in the event of some failure.

If the session is instead transactional, the `Session.SESSION_TRANSACTED` constant value is associated with the acknowledgment mode.

Listeners attached to sessions may also be used to enable more asynchronous callback behavior. A `MessageListener` interface implementation can be associated with a `Session` object to enable such behavior. The `MessageListener` implements an `onMessage()` method that takes a `Message` object as a parameter for any message that is received by this `Session` object. The `Session` object's `setMessageListener()` and `getMessageListener()` set and get the `MessageListener`, respectively.

JMS Session Pools

JMS also provides a set of standard abstractions that JMS messaging servers implement to manage a pool of JMS sessions. Figure 12.8 depicts such abstractions and relevant methods on other JMS classes. Here, a connection is used to create a handle to an object that encapsulates a consumer of messages. Such a consumer is associated with a pool of JMS sessions on the messaging server.

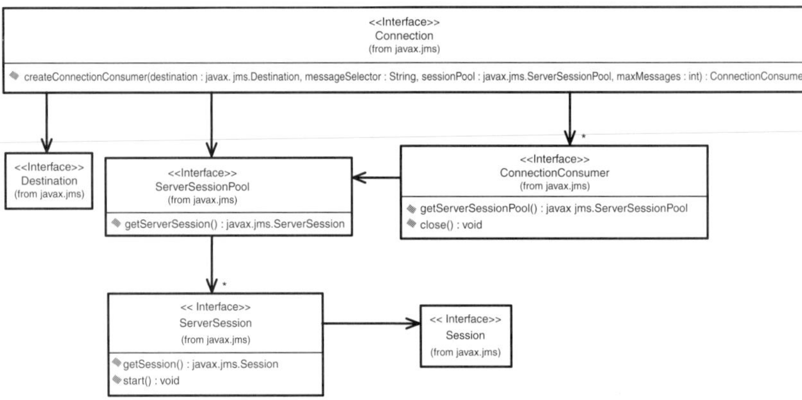

FIGURE 12.8 JMS session pools.

A `ServerSession` object is a wrapper object used by messaging server environments to wrap a handle to a JMS `Session` object. The `ServerSession.getSession()` method is used to retrieve the handle to the wrapped `Session` object. A `start()` method on the `ServerSession` object is used to ultimately induce the invocation of the `Session` object's `run()` method to start the thread associated with the session. A `ServerSessionPool` object encapsulates a managed collection of `ServerSession` objects in a messaging server's pool of such objects. The `ServerSessionPool.getServerSession()` returns a handle to one such `ServerSession` object from its pool.

The `ConnectionConsumer` interface encapsulates a consumer of messages associated with a particular connection. A `ConnectionConsumer` is associated with a particular destination point to which messages are delivered and as encapsulated by the `Destination` marker interface. Concrete implementations of such a `Destination` interface represent endpoints for the particular messaging domain model being used. A `ConnectionConsumer` is also associated with a `String` representation of a message selector which signals that only those messages with a particular message property are to be processed by the ConnectionConsumer, or indicates a null/empty-string if all messages are to be processed. A ConnectionConsumer also has a maximum bound for those messages that may be handled at one time by a ServerSession. Finally, an underlying ServerSessionPool is also associated with a ConnectionConsumer.

The Connection.createConnectionConsumer() method initializes and constructs a ConnectionConsumer given those attributes just described for a ConnectionConsumer, including the destination point, message filter, server session pool, and maximum number of messages processed. After a ConnectionConsumer handle has been created, the pool of sessions associated with the ConnectionConsumer may be gotten by invoking its getServerSessionPool() method. The close() method should be invoked by clients when use of the ConnectionConsumer is no longer needed by the client to ensure that resources allocated outside of the current JVM process are released and closed.

JMS Transactional Connections and Sessions

The JMS API also defines a set of interfaces depicted in Figure 12.9 that may optionally be implemented by JMS-based messaging servers to provide transactional functionality for JMS connections and sessions. Because coding JMS clients to talk directly to these interfaces is discouraged, we only briefly discuss their relevance here. In fact, JMS clients should use whatever transactional mechanisms (often declarative) are defined for the messaging environment in which they operate.

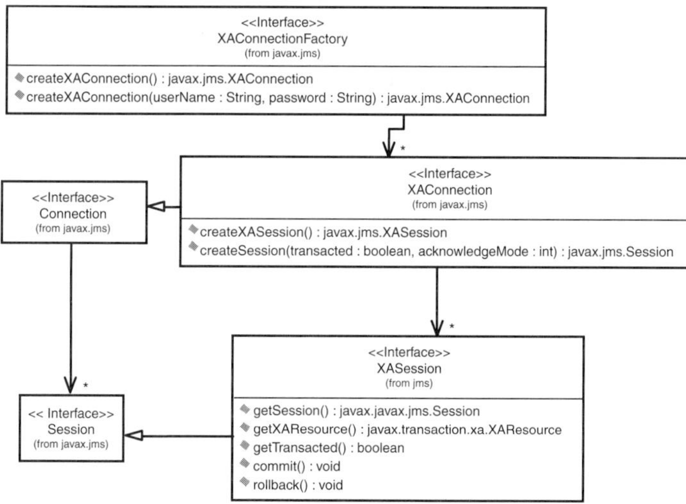

FIGURE 12.9 JMS XA-compliant connections and sessions.

Similar to the ConnectionFactory, the XAConnectionFactory is used to create a handle to an XAConnection object as opposed to a plain Connection object. The XAConnection object subclasses the Connection object to indicate that transactional support is implied by the particular JMS connection. Thus, messages sent and received as part of a session via such a connection are imbued with the basic transactional behavior via the Java Transaction API (JTA). In fact, the XAConnection object is used to create handles to XASession objects that subclass JMS Session objects. A JTA XAResource may be gotten from the XASession object and exposes other transactional management behavior.

JMS Generic Messages

Figure 12.10 depicts the core interfaces and conceptual relations of the base JMS Message type. The Message interface is the root interface for all messages that flow through a JMS-based messaging system. The Destination interface is a marker interface used to represent an endpoint of message delivery. Because Message objects may have relationships to a destination and reply-to location, conceptual relationships with a Destination interface are shown in the diagram. Similarly, because a delivery mode for a message also exists, a conceptual relationship to a DeliveryMode interface is also shown.

These are the major elements of a message encapsulated by the Message interface:

- Header—The header is a collection of control information items used for routing and identification of messages.
- Body—The actual data content of the message.
- Properties—Optional application-specific properties of a message used to support an extensible set of message types.

Header information can be gotten or set using a standard getter and setter syntax of get*XXX*() and set*XXX*(), where *XXX* is the name of a header property. Standard header properties defined as getters and setters on the Message interface are listed here:

- JMSMessageID—A unique ID associated with the message and beginning with the prefix ID:.
- JMSTimestamp—The time at which a message was sent.
- JMSCorrelationID—An identifier that can be used to link one message to another.
- JMSCorrelationIDAsBytes—A correlation identifier as an array of bytes.
- JMSReplyTo—A destination location to which a reply to this message should be sent.
- JMSDestination—A destination location to which a message is being sent.
- JMSDeliveryMode—The delivery mode of the message supported by the message service provider defined by DeliveryMode.PERSISTENT if the message is to be stored persistently during messaging, or by DeliveryMode.NON_PERSISTENT if the message is to be cached in memory during messaging.

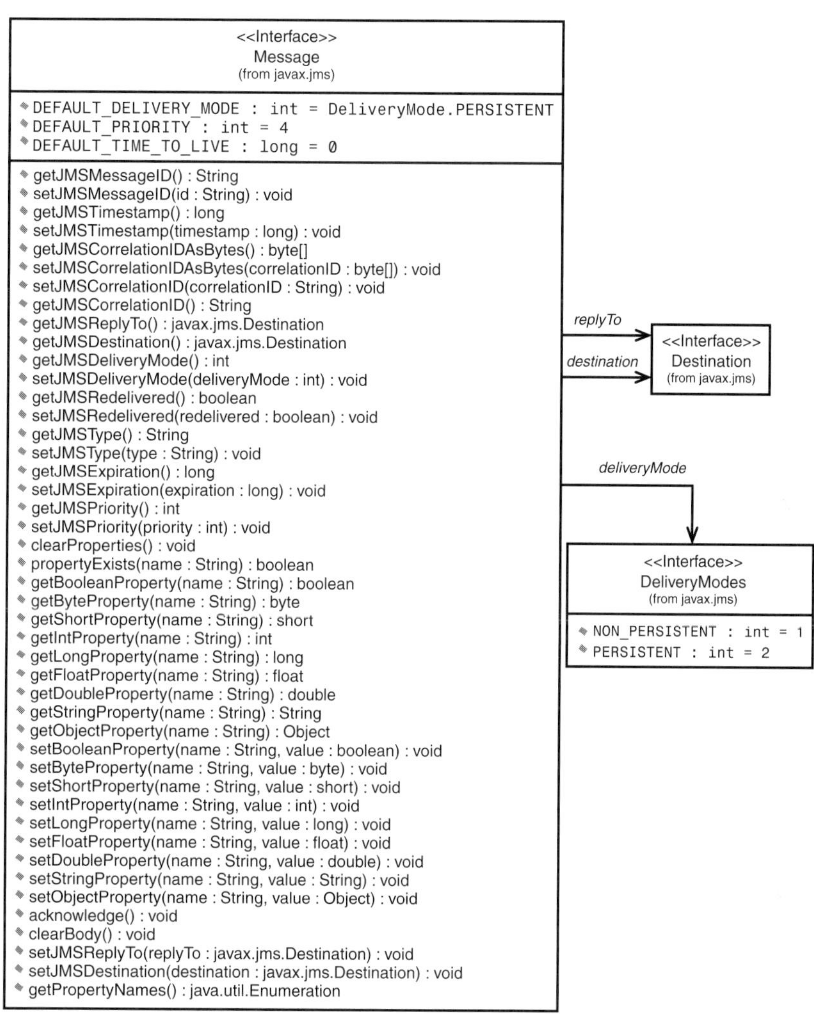

FIGURE 12.10 The JMS base message type.

- `JMSRedelivered`—Indicates whether the message was sent in a previous transmission but has not yet been acknowledged.
- `JMSType`—The type of message.
- `JMSExpiration`—The time at which the message is to be considered expired. A default value of `0` indicates no expiration.
- `JMSPriority`—The priority of a message with `0` as the lowest priority and `9` as the highest priority.

Provider-specific properties of a message can also be gotten and set onto a message using a host of `getXXXProperty()` and `setXXXProperty()` methods, respectively, where *XXX* specifies the property type. Each property has a name identified by a `String` and a value of its specific type. The existence of a named property can be tested using `Message.propertyExists(String)`. The `Message.getPropertyNames()` method returns an `Enumeration` of property names defined for this message. Property types supported are `boolean`, `byte`, `short`, `int`, `long`, `float`, `double`, and `String`.

This is the generic form of getter:

```
XXX getXXXProperty(String name) throws JMSException;
```

The `getObjectProperty()` method is the only exception to this rule. It allows retrieval of the types `Boolean`, `Byte`, `Short`, `Integer`, `Long`, `Float`, `Double`, and `String`.

This is the generic form of setter:

```
void setXXXProperty(String name, XXX value) throws JMSException;
```

The `setObjectProperty()` method is the only exception to this rule. It allows setting of the types `Boolean`, `Byte`, `Short`, `Integer`, `Long`, `Float`, `Double`, and `String`.

Property values are set before a message is sent and are in read-only mode when received by a client. A value written as a `byte`, `short`, `int`, or `long` can be read as a value of its own type or higher precision in the same type family. Thus, a `short`, for example, can be read as a `short`, an `int`, or a `long`. Values written as a `float` can be read as a `float` or `double`. All values can be read as a `String`, and `String` objects can possibly be read as another value of a particular type if they can be parsed into that type.

All properties can be removed from a message using the `Message.clearProperties()` method. When `clearProperties()` is called, the properties are no longer in read-only mode. If a client attempts to read a property when it is read-only, a `MessageNotWriteableException` is thrown.

Properties whose names begin with the `JMS_<provider_name>` prefix are reserved for the JMS service provider's defined properties. Properties whose names begin with the `JMSX` prefix are reserved for standard JMS properties. The properties `JMSXGroupID` and `JMSXGroupSeq` are required, but the remaining properties defined with the `JMSX` prefix are optional. The names of supported JMSX properties can be gotten from a call to `ConnectionMetaData.getJMSXPropertyNames()`. These are the standard JMSX properties:

- `JMSXGroupID`—Identifier for a group of messages.
- `JMSXGroupSeq`—Message sequence number for a message in a message group.
- `JMSXUserID`—User ID of the message sender.
- `JMSXAppID`—Identifier of the application that sent the message.
- `JMSXProducerTXID`—Identifier of the transaction that sent the message.

- JMSXConsumerTXID—Identifier of the transaction that received the message.
- JMSXDeliveryCount—Number of attempted deliveries of this message.
- JMSXRcvTimestamp—Time at which the message was sent to the consumer by the JMS service provider.
- JMSXState—Identifier for the state of a message in a service provider's message repository: waiting = 1, ready = 2, expired = 3, and retained = 4.

On a final note about generic JMS messages, sometimes it is important for a JMS client to know whether a message is received by its intended recipient. By calling Message.acknowledge(), a client can acknowledge that the associated message and all previous messages associated with a session were received. The last message in a group of messages that is acknowledged designates that all previous messages were received in that group.

JMS Specialized Messages

The generic JMS message interface just described offers a lot of generic functionality that any message inside a messaging system may expose. However, the JMS API also defines five additional types of messages that extend the Message interface and that correspond to five types of message body data, as shown in Figure 12.11. Byte data is encapsulated by the BytesMessage, a Serializable object is encapsulated by the ObjectMessage, a String message is encapsulated by the TextMessage, key and value pairs are encapsulated by the MapMessage, and I/O streams are encapsulated by the StreamMessage. Individual methods on the message sub-interfaces define getters and setters for the type-specific data body, but a generic clearBody() method to clear the data body of a message and place it in write-only mode exists on the base Message interface.

These are the various message body specialization types:

- BytesMessage—Interface encapsulates a message whose body is a collection of bytes. Various read*XXX*() and write*XXX*() methods defined in the BytesMessage interface are used to read and write specific types from and to the underlying byte stream, respectively. A BytesMessage.reset() call resets the pointer to the underlying byte stream and renders the object in read-only mode. Additionally, a getBodyLength() method may be used to retrieve the number of bytes associated with the message.
- StreamMessage—Interface encapsulates a message whose body is an underlying I/O stream of information. Various read*XXX*() and write*XXX*() methods also exist on the StreamMessage interface to read and write specific types from and to the underlying stream, respectively. A StreamMessage.reset() call resets the pointer to the underlying stream and renders the object in read-only mode.
- MapMessage—Interface encapsulates a message whose body is an underlying collection of key and value pairs. A collection of get*XXX*(String) methods returns a typed value

from the `MapMessage` given a particular `String` name. A collection of `setXXX(String, XXX)` methods sets a typed value into the `MapMessage` with a particular `String` name. The `getMapNames()` method returns an `Enumeration` of `String` key names associated with the `MapMessage`. The `itemExists(String)` method returns a `boolean` value indicating whether a particular `String` named value exists in the `MapMessage`.

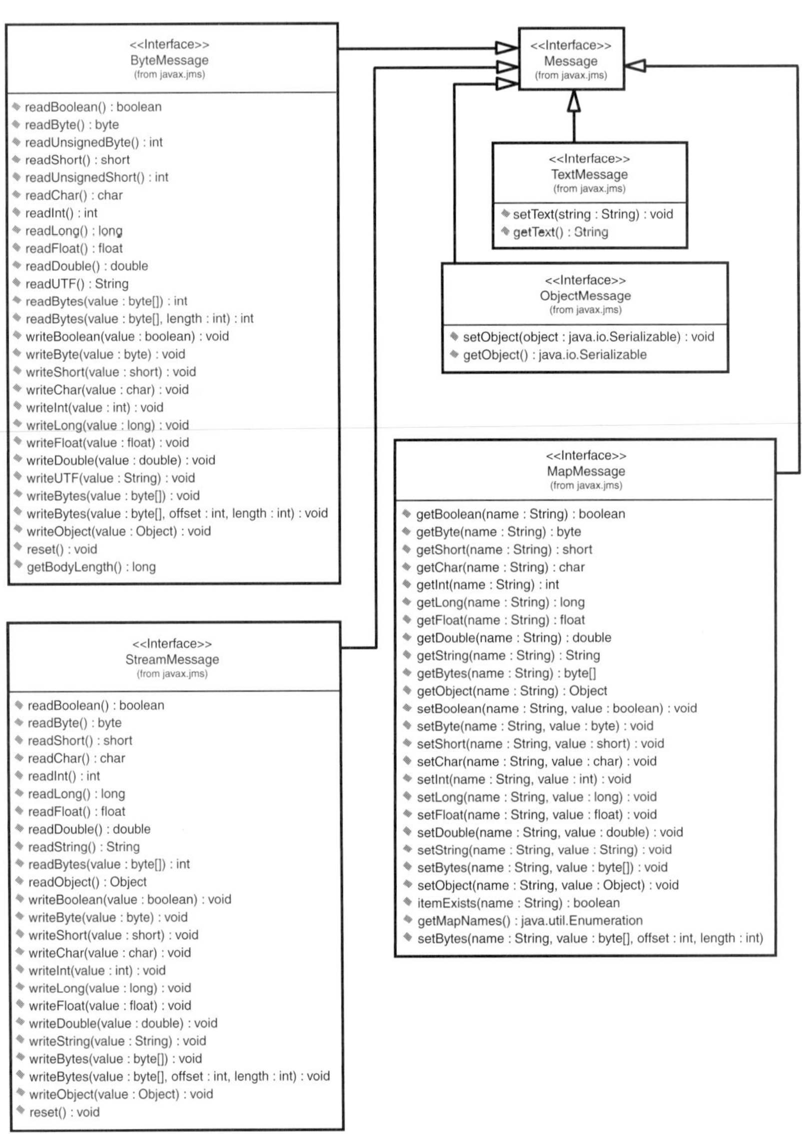

FIGURE 12.11 The JMS message body specialization types.

- `ObjectMessage`—Interface encapsulates a message whose body is an underlying `Serializable` object. Has `getObject()` and `setObject()` methods.

- `TextMessage`—Interface encapsulates a message whose body is an underlying `String` value. Has `getText()` and `setText()` methods.

Message Producers, Consumers, and Selectors

With all of this talk about JMS connections, sessions, and messages, you might be wondering when we'll finally get to the point of actually being able to send and receive these messages within such sessions and over such connections. Indeed, there are a lot of abstractions within JMS to enable the sending and receiving of messages. Although such abstractions are many, it does illustrate the well-thought-out object-oriented nature of the JMS API. Nevertheless, we have come to the point in our discussion where it becomes more apparent how messages are sent and received via JMS as described in this section.

JMS provides base encapsulations for message producers and consumers as shown in Figure 12.12. Message producers generate messages in a session context that are to be received by message consumers. Message consumers can filter which messages they receive by using a message selector.

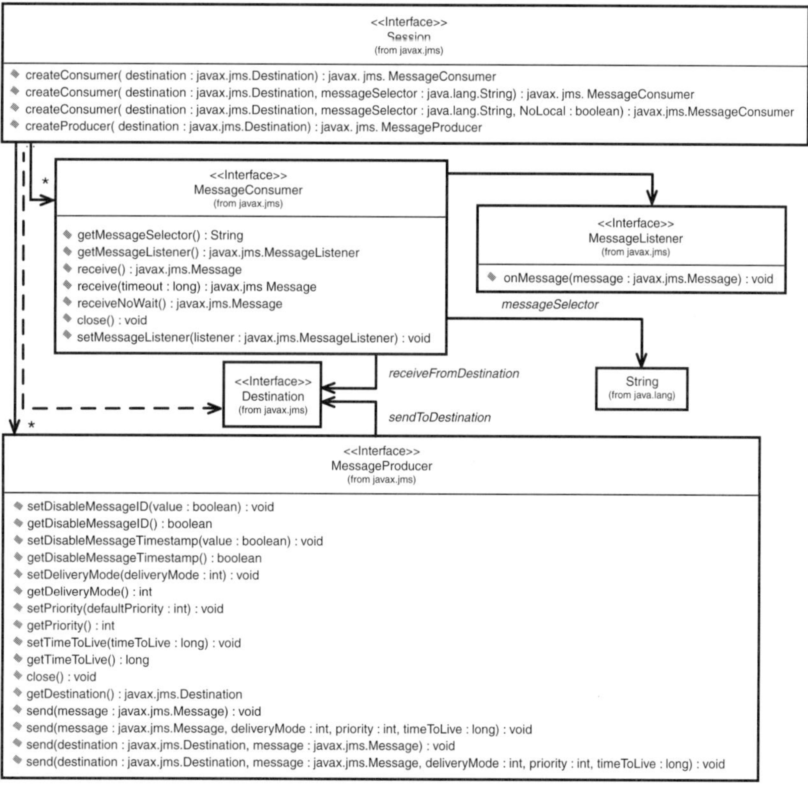

FIGURE 12.12 JMS message producers, consumers, and selectors.

The MessageProducer interface is the base interface for producers of messages. MessageProducer objects are created by passing a Destination for a message as an argument to a message producer creation method on a Session object. When utilizing the unified domain model of JMS v1.1, the Session.createProducer() method can be used to create a handle to a MessageProducer object. As you'll soon see, sub-interfaces of the Session interface that are specific to a particular messaging domain model also provide more concrete methods for returning messaging-domain–specific message producer object handles useable in a JMS v1.0 and JMS v1.1 context. Methods on the MessageProducer interface permit the setting and getting of a producer's default delivery mode, the associated message priority, and the time (in milliseconds) for which a message in the message system has to live. Setters also exist for disabling message ID and timestamps along with getters of these values. Finally, because the producer itself represents a destination point, its own Destination may be gotten using the getDestination() method.

Of primary importance when using a MessageProducer is to actually produce (that is, send) a message to a particular destination point. A series of MessageProducer.send() methods permit such behavior. If the destination is associated with a Message object, the MessageProducer object's send(Message) and send(Message, int, int, long) methods may be invoked to send that message to its intended destination. If default values for the Message object are undesirable, the message's priority number, time to live in milliseconds, and DeliveryMode setting may be submitted as parameters to the send() method. Alternatively, a Destination point may be explicitly identified by using the MessageProducer object's send(Destination, Message) or send(Destination, Message, int, int, long) methods.

The MessageConsumer interface is the base interface for consumers of messages. MessageConsumer objects are created using the unified domain model by invoking one of the createConsumer() methods on the Session object. Sub-interfaces of the Session object may also be used to create handles to domain-specific messaging model consumers, as we'll see later in this chapter. Regardless of the consumer creation method used, a Destination object must be passed as an input parameter to a message consumer creation method. The Destination object identifies that destination point with which the message consumer is associated to receive messages.

A MessageConsumer may also be created using a particular message selector String parameter passed into two of the Session.createConsumer() methods. Message selectors define a filter that is used to determine which messages should be routed to a message consumer. For example, a particular message consumer may be interested in receiving messages only from a system administrator with a JMSXUserID property of admin (for example, String exampleSelector = "JMSXUserID = admin"). A message selector String is expressed in a subset of SQL92 syntax and can refer only to header and property information in a message. A selector is expressed using the following types of expression elements:

- Literal—A String in single quotes, a numeral, and boolean identifiers.
- Identifier—A sequence of letters and digits beginning with a letter that refers to a header name or property name in a message.

- Whitespace—A space, a tab, a form feed, or an end of line.
- Expression—Conditional, arithmetic, and Boolean expressions.
- Brackets—The `()` brackets group elements.
- Operators—Logical operators `NOT`, `AND`, `OR`. Comparison operators `=`, `>`, `>=`, `<`, `<=`, `<>`. Arithmetic operators unary `+`, unary `-`, `*`, `/`, `+`, `-`.
- `BETWEEN`—Use of `BETWEEN` operator to specify a range using *`expression`* `[NOT] BETWEEN` *`expression`* `and` *`expression`*.
- `IN`—Use of `IN` to specify inclusion in a set using *`identifier`* `[NOT] IN (`*`literal`*`,` *`literal`*`, ...)`.
- `LIKE`—Use of `LIKE` to specify similarity in a pattern using *`identifier`* `[NOT] LIKE` *`pattern`*.
- `IS`—Use of `IS` for identifier `IS [NOT] NULL`.

The `MessageConsumer.getMessageSelector()` call returns the `String` object defining a message selector for that `MessageConsumer`.

Notice that one form of the `Session.createConsumer()` method also enables you to provide a `boolean` input parameter named `NoLocal`. This parameter enables you to specify whether a consumer sharing the same connection as the producer of a message should consume those messages sent to the consumer's destination point by that producer. By default, this value is `false`, indicating that a consumer will receive messages sent by a producer even if they share the same connection.

The `MessageConsumer` also allows a `MessageListener` to be registered with it to independently receive messages for the `MessageConsumer`. The `MessageConsumer.close()` method is used to close the resources used to implement the message consumer by the service provider. Various methods on the `MessageConsumer` are defined to receive messages from a destination. The `MessageConsumer.receive()` method blocks until a particular message is received for use by the consumer or until the `MessageConsumer` is closed. The `MessageConsumer.receive(long)` method can be used to specify a timeout in milliseconds for which the message consumer should wait to receive a message. `MessageConsumer.receiveNoWait()` can be called to receive a message only if it is immediately available and without blocking.

JMS Point-to-Point Queue Model

Figure 12.13 depicts the basic JMS architecture elements that support point-to-point message queuing. The message queuing architecture is really an extension of the core JMS architecture with features that specifically focus on message queuing behavior. Connection factories, connections, sessions, message producers, message consumers, and endpoint destinations are all extended with point-to-point message queuing model interfaces. Thus, by understanding the core JMS architecture presented earlier, you can most rapidly understand the specific point-to-point message queuing specializations presented here. As we'll also illustrate later in this chapter, new to JMS v1.1, the more generic JMS architecture may also be used to implement point-to-point messaging without much consideration for the messaging domain-specific APIs illustrated in Figure 12.13.

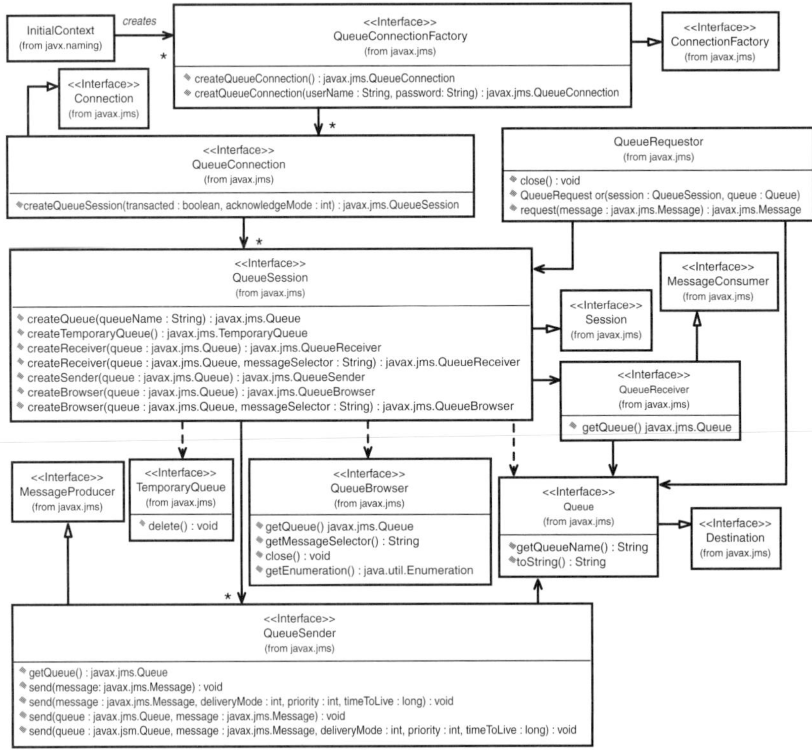

FIGURE 12.13 JMS point-to-point message queuing.

JMS clients may use JNDI to obtain an initial reference to a named `QueueConnectionFactory` object. One of the `QueueConnectionFactory.createQueueConnection()` methods is used to create an instance of a `QueueConnection` object. The `createQueueConnection()` method can be called with a username and password or by using the parameterless version of the method with a default user identity assumed.

The `QueueConnection` interface is a type of `Connection` interface that represents a connection to a JMS point-to-point messaging queue service. The `createQueueSession()` method is called by JMS clients to create a `QueueSession` instance. Whether or not transactions are to be implemented by the `QueueSession` object is designated by a `boolean` parameter to `createQueueSession()`. Also, the acknowledgment mode is specified in the call to `createQueueSession()` using one of the static session identifiers, such as `Session.AUTO_ACKNOWLEDGE`, `Session.CLIENT_ACKNOWLEDGE`, or

Session.DUPS_OK_ACKNOWLEDGE. The QueueSession interface extended from the Session interface implements various message-queuing–specific entity creation methods.

QueueSession.createQueue() creates an instance of a Queue object given a provider-specific name for that queue. Most service-provider implementations will provide other means for creating named queues, but this interface can be used by JMS clients for creating queues. The Queue interface encapsulates an interface to a queue destination using JMS's point-to-point messaging queue model and has a getQueueName() method to return the queue name. The QueueSession.createTemporaryQueue() method creates a TemporaryQueue object. The TemporaryQueue is deleted when its QueueConnection is closed.

The QueueSession.createBrowser() method creates an instance of a QueueBrowser object associated with a particular message queue. The QueueBrowser can be used to passively observe the live contents of a particular message queue without modifying the queue contents. If the QueueBrowser was created with a message selector, only those messages identified in the message selector expression will be viewable. The getEnumeration() method returns the list of messages associated with the queue and perhaps refined by the message selector.

The QueueSession.createSender() method creates a QueueSender message producer that is used to send messages to a Queue. Messages can be sent to a Queue using the various QueueSender.send() methods. Variations of these methods enable the delivery of messages to the QueueSender object's associated Queue or to a newly specified Queue object passed to the send() method. Delivery modes, priorities, and time to live for a message can also be specified during calls to QueueSender.send(). Messages to send to a Queue can be created using the various message-creation methods defined on the Session interface from which QueueSession extends.

The QueueSession.createReceiver() method creates a QueueReceiver message consumer used to receive messages from a Queue. A variation of the createReceiver() method also permits the specification of a message selector to filter out which messages are received by the QueueReceiver. Above and beyond the built-in message consuming methods provided by the QueueReceiver interface's base MessageConsumer interface, a QueueReceiver.getQueue() method returns a handle to the associated Queue.

A QueueRequestor helper class can also be used to simplify use of the JMS queue model for request and reply behavior. A QueueRequestor object is first created with a handle to a QueueSession and Queue object. The request method may then be used to send a Message to a queue destination and wait for a response in the form of a Message. To release and close any open distributed resources associated with the QueueRequestor and the underlying QueueSession, the JMS client invokes the close() method on the QueueRequestor.

Finally, as depicted in Figure 12.14, a set of interfaces exists to encapsulate transactional support for point-to-point message queuing. As mentioned before, the JMS client should not be coded to talk directly to such interfaces. Rather, the messaging server will use such interfaces to imbue a point-to-point message queue connection factory, connection, and session with JTA XA-compliant transaction management functionality. The interfaces in Figure 12.14 simply extend the interfaces presented in Figure 12.9 and provide method signatures specific to the message queue domain model.

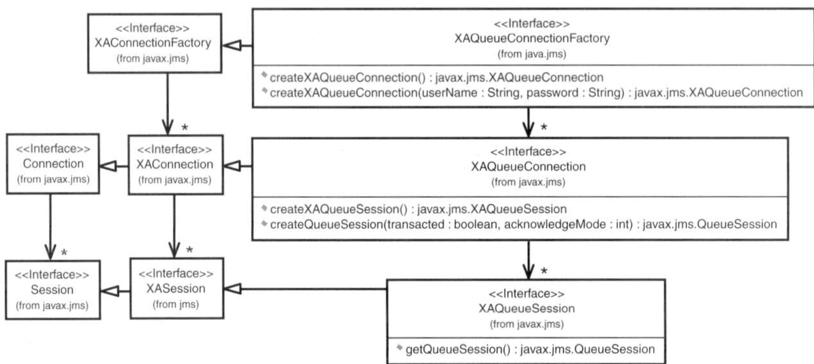

FIGURE 12.14 JMS transactional point-to-point message queuing.

Point-to-Point Message Queuing Sample Source Code

We present an example here to illustrate the use of JMS point-to-point message queuing. Our example implements a `QueueSupplier` that submits `OrderItem` objects to `Queue` objects managed by a WebLogic JMS service. A supplier implements a `QueueConsumer` that receives `OrderItem` objects from the `Queue`.

NOTE

The sample code throughout this section leaves out some exception handling and other nonessential features in the interest of simplifying the description. The `QueueManager`, `QueueSupplier`, `QueueConsumer`, and `MessageHandler` classes implement the core of this example, and `Props`, `OrderItem`, and `OrderManager` classes are also used.

You can use Ant (`ant.apache.org`) to execute the `build.xml` compilation script associated with this example in order to easily build this chapter's examples. You need to locate the `wlclient.jar` and `wljmsclient.jar` files associated with your BEA WebLogic installation (in `[WL_HOME]/server/lib`) and set the `jar.wlclient` and `jar.wlclientjms` variables in this chapter's sample `build.properties` file to those file locations, respectively.

After running the Ant script for this chapter's code, the generated `runqueue-supplier` and `runqueue-consumer` script files can be used for executing the example. Other properties inside of the local `build.properties` file are used to configure the example for use with the chapter's Ant script.

OrderItem

An `OrderItem` class implements a `Serializable` object encapsulating a simple order item request message. The `OrderItem` has an order identifier, order description, unit price, and an order quantity. Aside from a set of public attributes, an `OrderItem.toString()` prints the order request contents:

```
package com.wls8unleashed.jms;
 ...
public class OrderItem implements Serializable{
 private String itemID;
 private String itemDescription;
 private int quantity;
 private double price;

 public OrderItem( String itemID, String itemDescription,
            int quantity, double price){
  this.itemID = itemID;
  this.itemDescription = itemDescription;
  this.quantity = quantity;
  this.price = price;
 }

 public String toString(){
  return "OrderItem--> { "
      + "(ID, " + itemID + "), "
      + "(Description, " + itemDescription + "), "
      + "(Quantity, " + quantity + "), "
      + "(Price, $" + price + ") }";
 }

 public String getID(){ return itemID; }
 public String getDescription(){ return itemDescription;}
 public int getQuantity(){ return quantity;}
 public double getPrice(){ return price;}
}
```

OrderManager

The simple `OrderManager` class has a single `getOrders()` method that simply returns a `Collection` of `OrderItem` objects stubbed out for simplicity here as follows:

```
package com.wls8unleashed.jms;
 ...
public class OrderManager {
```

```
 public static Collection getOrders(){
  Vector dummyOrders = new Vector(2);

  OrderItem item1
   = new OrderItem("OID_2000", "Stale Yams", 20, 1.25);
  OrderItem item2
   = new OrderItem("OID_4000", "Elvis Wigs", 2, 19.95);

  dummyOrders.add(item1);
  dummyOrders.add(item2);

  return dummyOrders;
 }
}
```

Props

A special Props class is also used by these examples to read in information from the build.properties file for easy getter access by property name, as illustrated here:

```
package com.wls8unleashed.jms;
 ...
public class Props {
 private static String FILE_NAME = "build.properties";
 private static Properties props = null;

 private static void getInstance(){
  props = new Properties();
   ...
  props.load(new FileInputStream(FILE_NAME));
   ...
 }

 public static String get(String name){
  if(props == null){
   getInstance();
  }

  return (String) props.get(name);
 }

 public static Context getInitialContext(){
  Context ctx = null;
```

```
    // Get properties for naming service
    String jndiFactory = Props.get("jndi.factory");
    String providerURL = Props.get("jndi.provider.url");

    // Create hashtable of JNDI properties
    Hashtable env = new Hashtable();
    env.put(Context.INITIAL_CONTEXT_FACTORY, jndiFactory);
    env.put(Context.PROVIDER_URL, providerURL);

    // Return handle to JNDI context
     ...
    ctx = new InitialContext(env);
     ...

    return ctx;
  }
}
```

12

You'll note that the Props class also handles constructing a JNDI context for the sample code from within the getInitialContext() method by reading in JNDI properties from the build.properties file and constructing a handle to a JNDI InitialContext object. The JNDI properties of interest are the WebLogic JNDI factory class name and the URL of the WebLogic Server instance to which your JMS client examples will connect as exemplified by these entries in build.properties:

```
# JNDI Factory
jndi.factory=weblogic.jndi.WLInitialContextFactory

# JNDI Provider URL
jndi.provider.url=t3://localhost:7001/
```

QueueManager

A base QueueManager class is used by the QueueConsumer and QueueSupplier classes to encapsulate common JMS queue initialization functionality. The QueueManager constructor takes a JNDI Context object as an argument, looks up a handle to a JMS factory, creates JMS connections and sessions, looks up a handle to a queue name, and subsequently looks up a handle to a Queue object. As we'll see, the QueueConsumer and QueueSupplier inherit this behavior to initialize their handle to a Queue. The QueueManager class is illustrated here:

```
package com.wls8unleashed.jms;
 ...
public class QueueManager {
```

```
protected QueueConnectionFactory queueConnectionFactory;
protected QueueConnection queueConnection;
protected QueueSession queueSession;
protected Queue queue;

public QueueManager(Context context){
   ...
  // Get JMS factory JNDI name
  String jmsFactoryName = Props.get("jms.factory.for.queue");

  // Create queue connection factory
  System.out.println("Looking up factory name: " + jmsFactoryName);
  queueConnectionFactory =
   (QueueConnectionFactory) context.lookup(jmsFactoryName);

  // Create queue connection to the factory
  System.out.println("Creating queue connection...");
  queueConnection = queueConnectionFactory.createQueueConnection();

  // Create session to the connection
  System.out.println("Creating queue session...");
  queueSession = queueConnection.createQueueSession(
                false, Session.AUTO_ACKNOWLEDGE);

  // Get queue name
  String queueName = Props.get("queue.name");

  // Lookup handle to the Queue
  try {
   System.out.println("Looking up queue name: " + queueName);
   queue = (Queue) context.lookup(queueName);
  } catch (NamingException namingException) {
   // If not created, create new queue, and bind queue to name
   System.out.println("Didn't find the queue...so creating: " + queueName);
   queue = queueSession.createQueue(queueName);
   System.out.println("Binding queue: " + queueName);
   context.bind(queueName, queue);
  }
 }
 ...
 }
}
```

Note that the `QueueManager` reads the JMS factory and queue names passed into the JNDI lookup from the following properties set in the `build.properties` file:

```
# JMS Connection Factory for Queues
jms.factory.for.queue=UnleashedJMSFactory

# JMS Queue Name
queue.name=UnleashedQueue
```

We'll see shortly how such resources are established from within BEA WebLogic Server.

QueueSupplier

The `QueueSupplier` class extends the `QueueManager` class and implements a producer of a message to a queue. The `QueueSupplier.main()` method obtains a `Collection` of new BeeShirts.com order requests using the `OrderManager.getOrders()` call. For order `item` in the `Hashtable` of orders, an order request is sent within the `QueueSupplier.sendOrder()` method. The `QueueSupplier.main()` method is shown here:

```
public static void main(String[] args) {
    ...
   // Get some orders from the OrderManager class
   System.out.println("Getting a bunch of orders to send...");
   Collection orders = OrderManager.getOrders();

   // For each order, get order request and send to consumer
   Iterator it = orders.iterator();
   while (it.hasNext()) {
   // Get an OrderItem object to send
   OrderItem item = (OrderItem) it.next();

   // Create JNDI context
   Context context = Props.getInitialContext();

   // Create new QueueSupplier
   System.out.println("Creating new QueueSupplier...");
    QueueSupplier queueSupplier = new QueueSupplier(context);

    // Send the order
    System.out.println("Initiating order to send...");
    queueSupplier.sendOrder(item);

    // Close QueueSupplier
    System.out.println("Closing QueueSupplier...");
    queueSupplier.close();
   }
   ...
}
```

The QueueSupplier constructor is where all messaging queue initialization is performed on the supplier side. The QueueManager superclass constructor is first invoked to perform basic JMS queue object initialization. A QueueSender is then created from within the QueueSupplier. The QueueConnectionFactory, QueueConnection, QueueSession, Queue, and QueueSender objects are all saved as variables in either the QueueSupplier or base QueueManager class. The QueueSupplier constructor is shown here:

```
public QueueSupplier(Context context){
 // Call superclass QueueManager constructor
 super(context);
  ...
 // Create queue sender
 System.out.println("Creating queue sender...");
 queueSender = queueSession.createSender(queue);
   ...
}
```

The sendOrder() method called from main() first sends an object to a JMS queue. In our sample case, the object is always an OrderItem object. The sendOrder() method creates an ObjectMessage with the OrderItem object and sends it using a QueueSender:

```
public void sendOrder(OrderItem message) throws JMSException {
   System.out.println("Sending order message:" + message);

   // Create empty ObjectMessage on session
   System.out.println("Creating empty object message...");
   ObjectMessage sendingMessage = queueSession.createObjectMessage();

   // Start the queue connection
   System.out.println("Starting queue connection...");
   queueConnection.start();

   // Set the order object onto the message carrier
   System.out.println("Setting order item into message...");
   sendingMessage.setObject((Serializable) message);

   // Send the message
   System.out.println("Sending the order message...");
   queueSender.send(sendingMessage);
}
```

Finally, our QueueSupplier.close() method simply cleans up QueueSender, QueueSession, and QueueConnection resources:

```
public void close() throws JMSException{
 queueSender.close();
```

```
 queueSession.close();
 queueConnection.close();
}
```

QueueConsumer

Our sample QueueConsumer represents a vendor that the order producer application, represented by the QueueSupplier, talks to. The QueueConsumer has a queue that the QueueSupplier uses to place an order request with the vendor. The QueueConsumer.main() method first creates a JNDI context via a call to Props.getInitialContext(). The QueueConsumer is then constructed with the JNDI context as a parameter. The QueueConsumer then receives messages until the user exits the program. Finally, QueueConsumer.close resources are cleaned up, along with the JNDI context. The QueueConsumer.main() method is shown here:

```
public static void main(String[] args){
    ...
  // Create JNDI context
  Context context = Props.getInitialContext();

  // Create new QueueConsumer
  System.out.println("Creating new QueueConsumer...");
  QueueConsumer queueConsumer = new QueueConsumer(context);

  System.out.println("QueueConsumer is ready to receive messages...");

  // Receive messages until user quits from program or quit flags true.
  synchronized (queueConsumer) {
   while (!queueConsumer.quitFromReceiving) {
    try {
     // Wait for messages
     queueConsumer.wait();
    } catch (InterruptedException interruptedException) {
       System.out.println("Interruption!");
       interruptedException.printStackTrace();
    }
    }
   }

   // Close up resources when done and exit
   queueConsumer.close();
   context.close();
   System.exit(0);
   ...
}
```

The QueueConsumer constructor invokes its base class QueueManager constructor to perform the bulk of JMS queue object initialization. The QueueConsumer then creates a QueueReceiver and registers itself as a MessageListener with the QueueReceiver. The QueueConnection thread is then initialized to start receiving messages. The QueueConsumer constructor initialization is shown here:

```
public QueueConsumer(Context context)
  throws NamingException, JMSException {

 // Call superclass QueueManager constructor
 super(context);

 // Create queue receiver
 System.out.println("Creating queue receiver...");
 queueReceiver = queueSession.createReceiver(queue);

 // Register QueueConsumer as MessageListener
 System.out.println("Setting message listener...");
 queueReceiver.setMessageListener(this);

 // Start receiving messages
 System.out.println("Starting queue connection...");
 queueConnection.start();
}
```

Because the QueueConsumer is a message listener by virtue of implementing the MessageListener interface, it must implement the onMessage(Message) method. The QueueConsumer.onMessage() is called when the WebLogic JMS service provider receives an OrderItem from the QueueSupplier. The QueueConsumer object's onMessage() method delegates the handling of received messages to a MessageHandler object as illustrated here:

```
public void onMessage(Message message) {
 MessageHandler handler = new MessageHandler();
 handler.onMessage(message);
}
```

MessageHandler

The MessageHandler class implements one method: onMessage(Message). The onMessage() method will first display information from the received Message header and then display the message body information, depending on whether it is a TextMessage or an ObjectMessage as illustrated here:

```
public void onMessage(Message message) {
   ...
```

```
// Print information about the message
System.out.println("\nReceived message...");
System.out.println("MessageID :"
          + message.getJMSMessageID()
          + " for "
          + message.getJMSDestination());

System.out.print("Message expiration info: ");
if (message.getJMSExpiration() > 0) {
 System.out.println(new Date(message.getJMSExpiration()));
} else {
 System.out.println(" Never expires");
}

System.out.println("Priority :" + message.getJMSPriority());

System.out.println("Mode  : "
     + (message.getJMSDeliveryMode() == DeliveryMode.PERSISTENT
     ? "PERSISTENT"
     : "NON_PERSISTENT"));

System.out.println("Reply to :   " + message.getJMSReplyTo());

System.out.println("Message type : " + message.getJMSType());

if (message instanceof TextMessage) {
 String receivedMessage = ((TextMessage) message).getText();
 System.out.println("Received text message:" + receivedMessage);
} else if (message instanceof ObjectMessage) {
 String receivedMessage = message.toString();
 System.out.println("Received object message:" + receivedMessage);
}
 ...
}
```

WebLogic JMS Server Configuration

Now that we've seen the JMS source code that produces messages to a queue and consumes messages from a queue, let's examine how to configure WebLogic Server to manage such queues. The first step is to start the WebLogic Server administration console and step into the JMS servers configuration screen from within Services→JMS→Servers as shown in Figure 12.15.

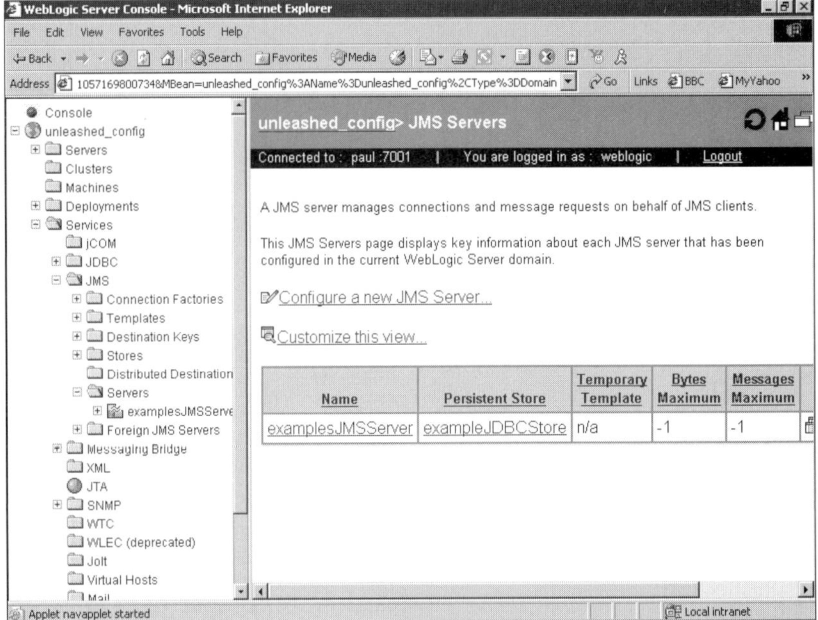

FIGURE 12.15 Admin console JMS server configuration.

You then must click on Configure a New JMS Server to begin configuring a new JMS server instance to run inside of your WebLogic instance. You then give the server a new name and click the Create button at the bottom of the screen, which results in the creation of a server configuration as illustrated in Figure 12.16. Note that we've created a server named `UnleashedJMS` for this example. A few other options may also be configured for your server at this stage. We'll discuss some of these options later in this section.

By clicking on the Thresholds and Quotas tab for your JMS server configuration, as illustrated ion Figure 12.17, you can also fine-tune how the server instance handles heavy load or large messages for your JMS server. Message and byte maximums and minimums for the JMS server can all be configured from this screen. In addition to helping with scalability, this also is useful for protecting against denial-of-service attacks.

At this point, you've only configured the JMS server but have yet to deploy it as an active server ready to manage JMS messages. By clicking on the JMS→Servers browser selection in the left browser pane, you can see those JMS servers that have been configured and are ready to deploy. To deploy your JMS server to the active state, the Target and Deploy screen is used. In Figure 12.18 we can select a particular WebLogic instance to which your JMS server is to be deployed. Upon deployment, you can verify that your JMS server is active by selecting your server's name in the left browser pane beneath the JMS→Servers browser selection, clicking on the server's Monitoring tab in the center pane, and then selecting Monitor Active JMS Servers to see that your JMS server is active and running.

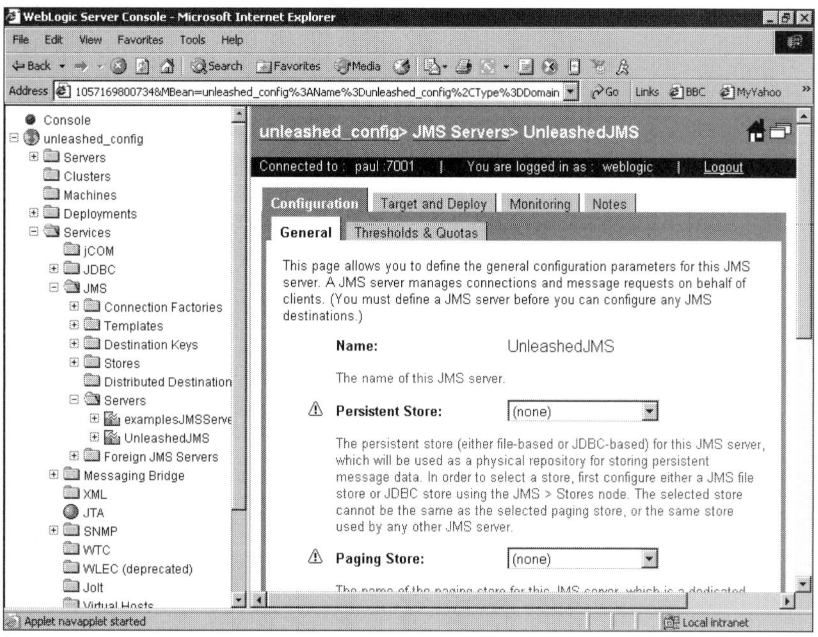

FIGURE 12.16 Create a JMS server configuration.

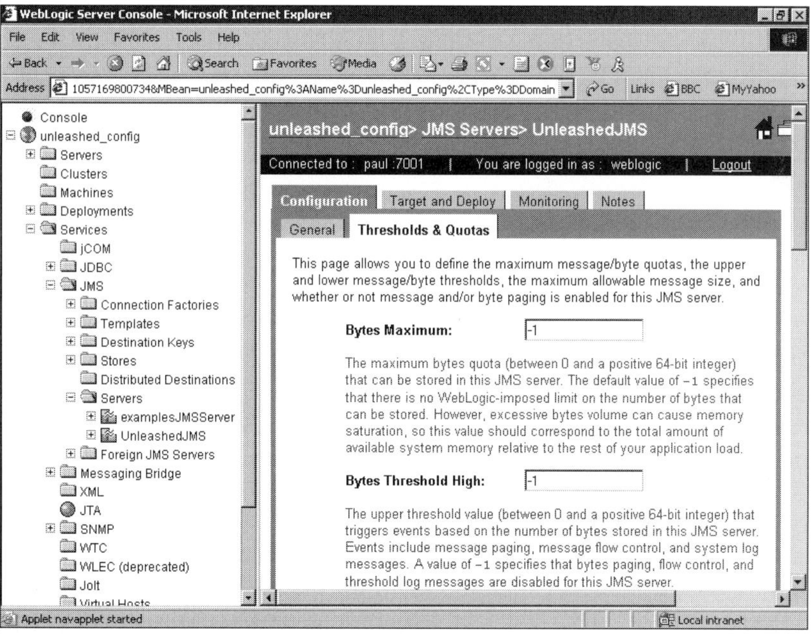

FIGURE 12.17 JMS server thresholds and quotas.

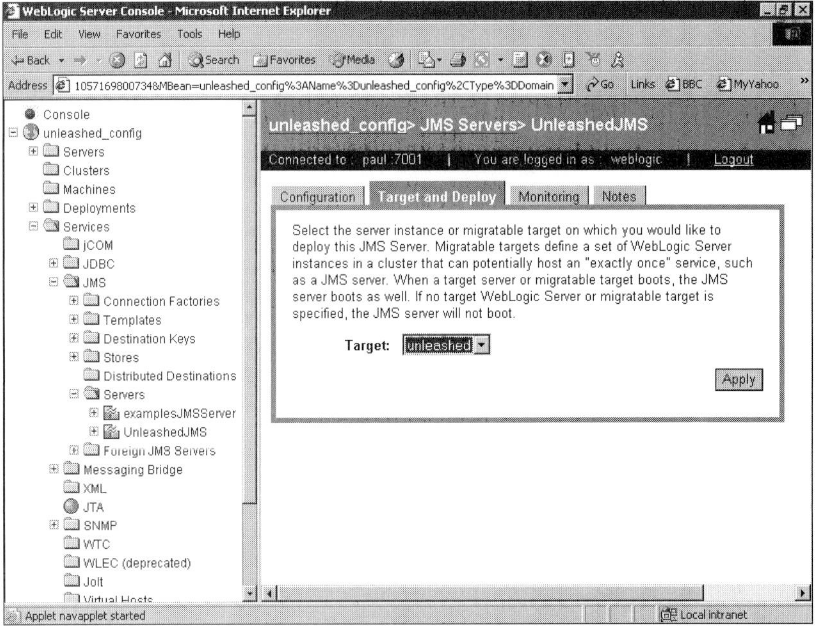

FIGURE 12.18 Deploying the JMS server.

WebLogic JMS Connection Factory Configuration

Recall from our JMS queue code example that we set the following factory name in our `build.properties` file used by the code to look up a handle to a `QueueConnectionFactory` object:

```
# JMS Connection Factory for Queues
jms.factory.for.queue=UnleashedJMSFactory
```

By default, WebLogic provides two default connection factories that can be used to look up connections: one for standard connections and one for XA-compliant connections. The `weblogic.jms.ConnectionFactory` and `weblogic.jms.XAConnectionFactory` JNDI names may be used to look up handles to these default connection factories. You may also configure your own connection factory, as we will do for our example. You begin this configuration process by clicking on the JMS→Connection Factories option in the left browser pane as illustrated in Figure 12.19.

You then select the Configure a New JMS Connection Factory option in the center pane, which yields the JMS connection factory configuration screen shown in Figure 12.20. Here we establish the name of our connection factory known to WebLogic Server and the JNDI name of the connection factory. The Transactions and Flow Control tabs associated with the JMS factory configuration screen also enable you to respectively specify transactional behavior and maximum rate at which messages can be produced via the connections created over the connection factory.

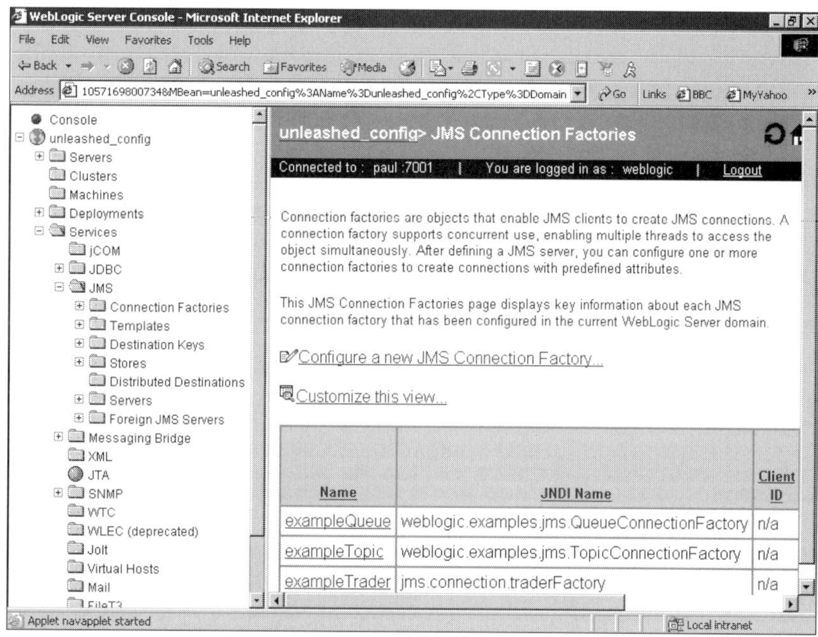

FIGURE 12.19 Viewing JMS connection factories.

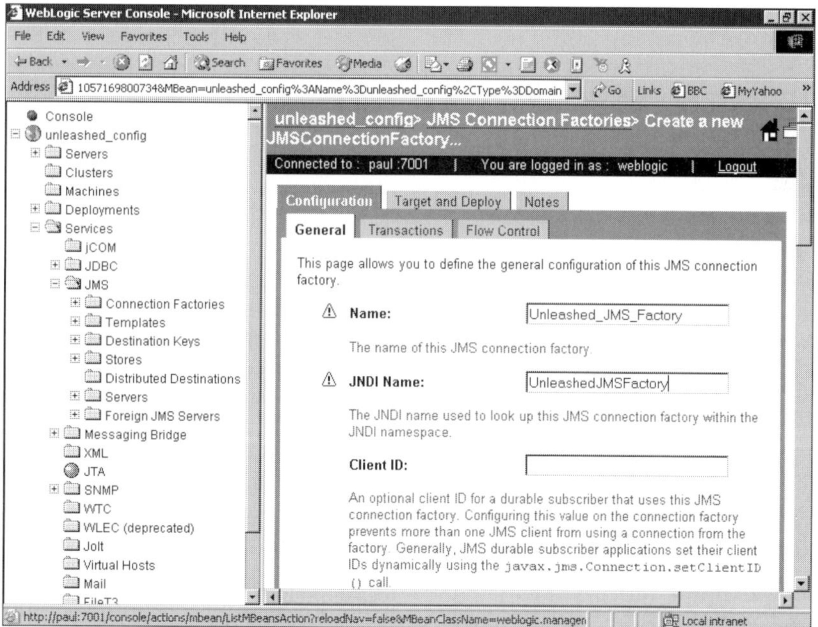

FIGURE 12.20 Configuring new JMS connection factories.

After configuring a JMS connection factory, you must generally then target a particular server or cluster to deploy the factory. The Target and Deploy tab shown in Figure 12.21 can be used to deploy active instances of the connection factories that you create. Note that whereas the JMS server can be targeted to a single WebLogic server instance, the connection factories can be targeted to many.

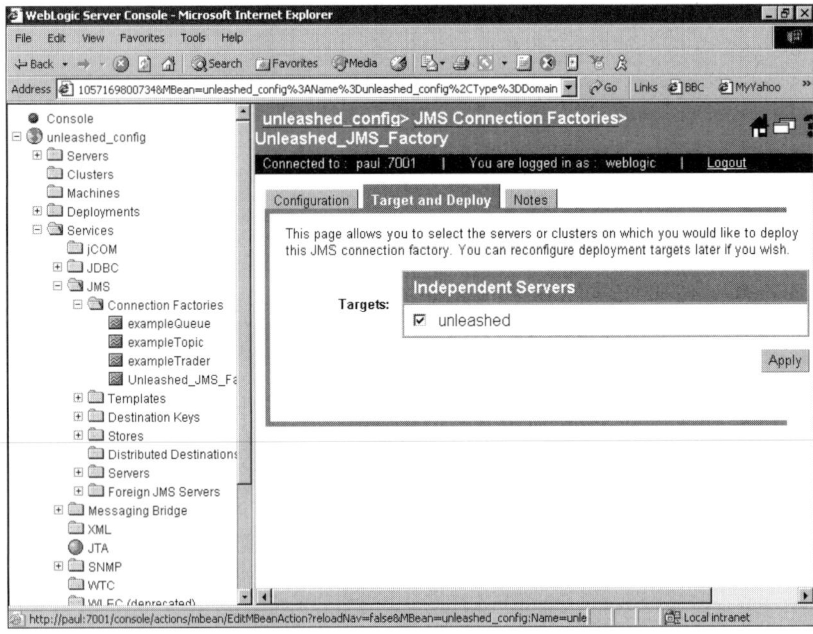

FIGURE 12.21 Deploying JMS connection factories.

WebLogic JMS Queue Configuration

After configuring a JMS server and connection factory, the next step in creating a concrete JMS application is to configure and deploy a JMS destination associated with a JMS server. In our first example, we use JMS queues to communicate between a consumer and producer. By clicking on the Destinations link in the left browser pane beneath a particular JMS server name in the JMS→Servers list, you yield the screen displayed in Figure 12.22.

For our first example, we want to click on Create a New JMS Queue in the center pane of the screen shown in Figure 12.22. The screen shown in Figure 12.23 is then used to perform the basic configuration for a queue. The queue name known to the JMS server and the JNDI name for the queue must be established along with other basic configuration information, such as the cluster-ability of the queue's JNDI name and the persistence of the queue. Note that we use the JNDI name `UnleashedQueue` in Figure 12.23 to be onsistent with the name we assume for our queue sample code as read in via the `build.properties` file:

```
# JMS Queue Name
queue.name=UnleashedQueue
```

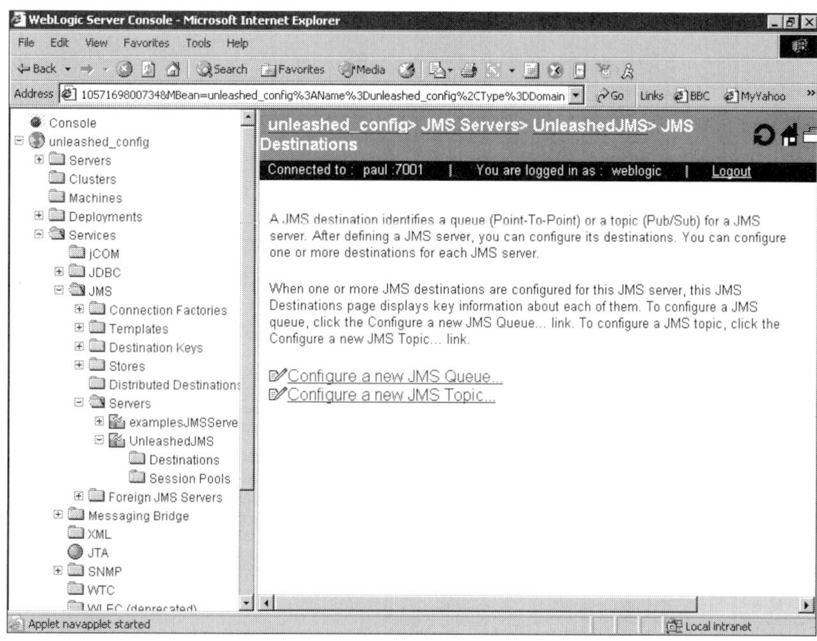

FIGURE 12.22 Viewing JMS server destinations.

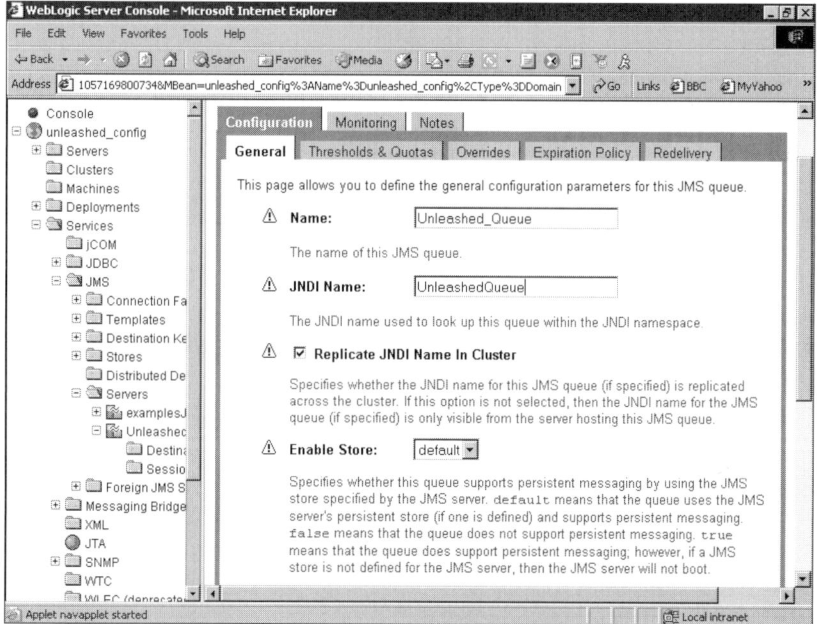

FIGURE 12.23 Configuring JMS queues.

A set of additional configuration screens also exists as tabs beneath the queue's configuration tab in the center pane. Configuration screens exist to define thresholds and quotas for message storage, override values for message priorities and delivery modes, message expiration policies, and message redelivery policies. The center pane also has a tab named Monitoring that enables you to monitor all active destinations, including the queue that we just created. Figure 12.24 demonstrates some of the useful information fields that can be observed for an active queue.

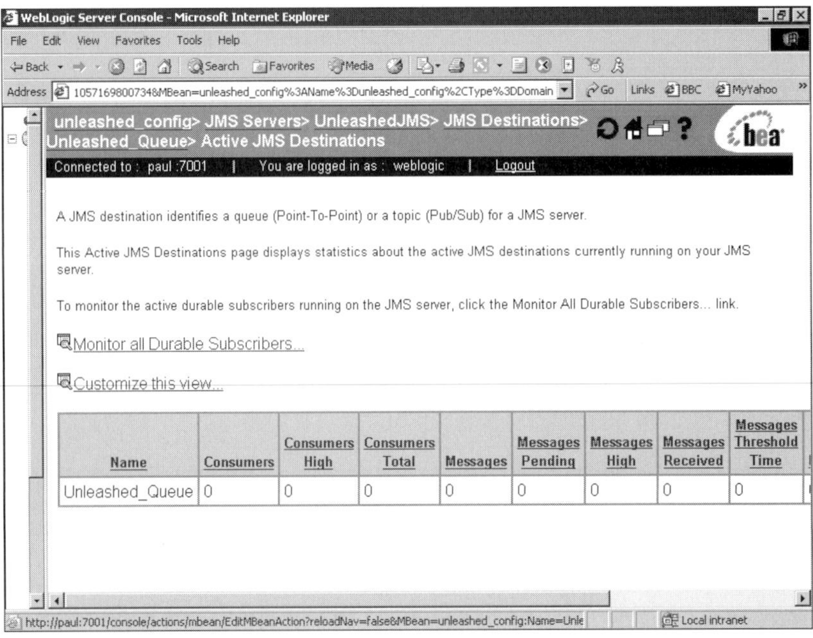

FIGURE 12.24 Monitoring JMS queues.

JMS Queue Sample Execution

Now that you have source code demonstrating a queue consumer and producer as well as a WebLogic Server instance hosting a queue, you're ready to execute the sample code presented earlier. The first step is to run the Ant script for this chapter's code by typing **`ant`** at the command line in the directory where you have deposited the source code. The default `all` Ant target will compile all the source code examples and generate two scripts: `runqueue-consumer` and `runqueue-supplier`. The scripts will have either a `.bat` or `.sh` extension depending on whether you are running the examples on a Windows or Unix platform, respectively.

Be sure to check the example's `build.properties` file as well. Aside from ensuring that the JMS libraries are properly referenced inside the `CLASSPATH` for the execution scripts, the JMS server URL, connection factory name, and queue name must all be set as you've configured for your WebLogic Server environment.

Then, in one command-line window, execute the `runqueue-consumer` script to start the sample `QueueConsumer`. In a separate window, you need to execute the `runqueue-supplier` script to start the `QueueSupplier`. The `QueueSupplier` publishes messages to the JMS queue that we configured. The messages are then asynchronously delivered to the `QueueConsumer` by the WebLogic JMS server.

Although this example illustrates how standalone J2SE clients using the JMS libraries can send and receive messages, the JMS producer code can also run inside of a J2EE container called from either a Java servlet, JavaServer Page (JSP), or Enterprise JavaBean (EJB). When calling JMS producer code from within a J2EE component, JNDI is used to look up handles to connection factories and destinations as with JMS producer code operating outside of a J2EE container. However, a call to the parameter-less form of the `InitialContext` constructor may be used to connect with the container's JMS managed resources. Furthermore, as we'll also see later in this book, message-driven EJBs can act as messaging consumers while leveraging the advantages of EJB life cycle management.

JMS Publish-Subscribe Model

Figure 12.25 depicts the basic JMS architecture elements that support publish-subscribe messaging. The publish-subscribe messaging architecture is an extension of the core JMS architecture with features specialized to suit a publish-subscribe messaging model. Connection factories, connections, sessions, message producers, message consumers, and endpoint destinations are all extended with publish-subscribe message model interfaces. As we'll also illustrate later in this chapter, new to JMS v1.1, the more generic JMS architecture may also be used to implement publish-subscribe messaging without much consideration for the messaging-domain–specific APIs illustrated in Figure 12.25.

JMS clients use JNDI to obtain an initial reference to a named `TopicConnectionFactory` object. The `TopicConnectionFactory.createTopicConnection()` methods are used to create an instance of a `TopicConnection` object. The `createTopicConnection()` method can be called with a username and password or by using the parameterless version of the method with a default user identity assumed.

The `TopicConnection` interface is a type of `Connection` interface that represents a connection to a JMS publish-subscribe messaging service. The `createConnectionConsumer()` and `createDurableConnectionConsumer()` methods are not used by regular JMS clients and are primarily used by a messaging server to manage publish-subscribe message service connections. The `createTopicSession()` method is called by JMS clients to create a `TopicSession` instance. Session transactions and acknowledgment mode are also established during the creation of a `TopicSession`.

`TopicSession.createTopic()` creates an instance of a `Topic` object given a provider-specific name for a topic. As with creating queues using `QueueSession`, the creation of named topics is something that will be provided using other means by most service-provider implementations. The `Topic` interface encapsulates a topic destination to which publishers publish messages and from which subscribers subscribe to receive messages. Different service providers will implement a hierarchy of topic names differently, but a

`Topic.getTopicName()` can be used to obtain the `String` representation of the topic. The `TopicSession.createTemporaryTopic()` method creates a `TemporaryTopic` object. The `TemporaryTopic` is deleted when its `TopicConnection` is closed.

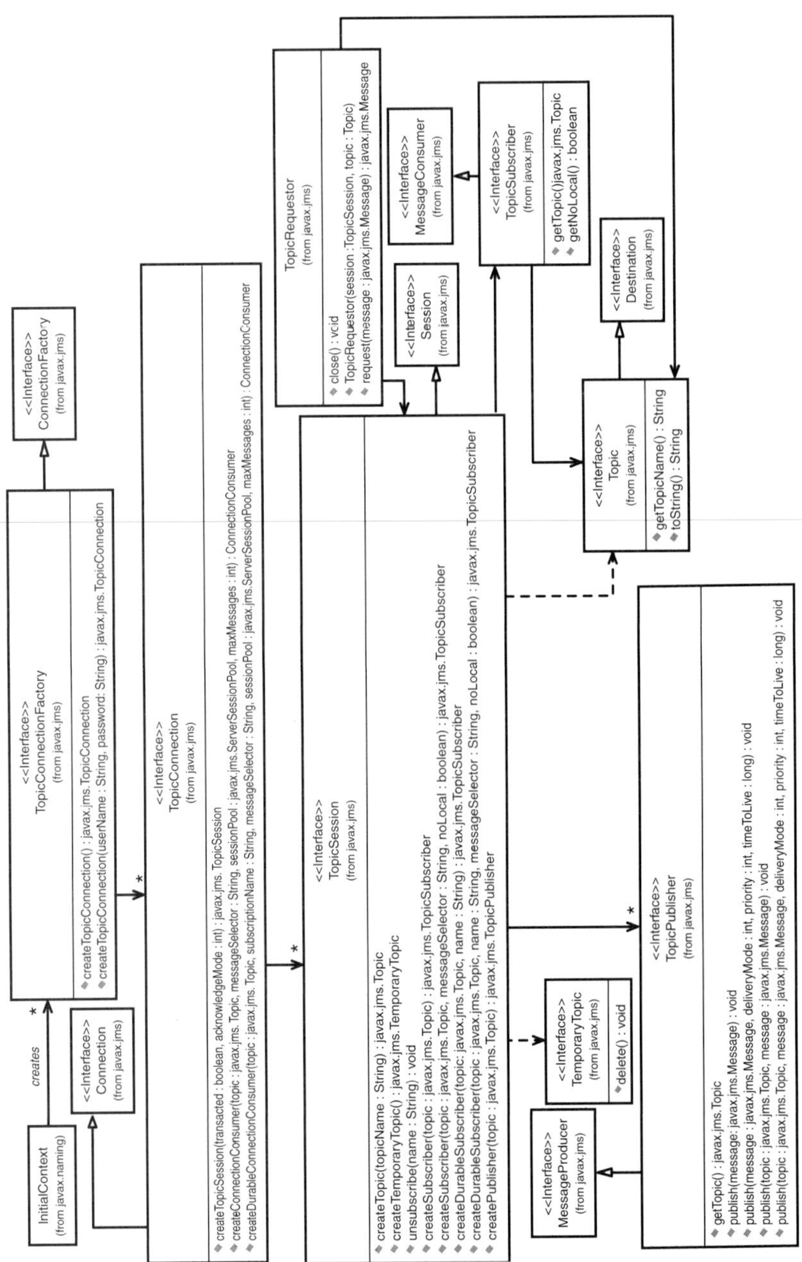

FIGURE 12.25 JMS publish-subscribe messaging.

The TopicSession.createPublisher() method creates a TopicPublisher message producer that is used to publish messages to a particular Topic. Messages can be published to a Topic using the various TopicPublisher.publish() methods. Variations of these methods enable the publishing of messages to a TopicPublisher object's associated Topic or to a newly specified Topic object passed to the publish() method. Delivery modes, priorities, and time to live for a message can also be specified during calls to TopicPublisher.publish(). Messages to publish to a Topic can be created using the various message-creation methods defined on the Session interface from which TopicSession extends.

Two types of TopicSubscriber creation methods exist on TopicSession. The TopicSession.createSubscriber() methods create nondurable TopicSubscriber instances. Nondurable TopicSubscribers are those subscribers who receive notification only of published messages to which they have subscribed while the subscriber is active. Durable subscribers are those who can receive messages later, even after they were temporarily unavailable; they can be created using the TopicSession.createDurableSubscriber() calls. Durable subscribers have a name associated with the published messages stored for their deferred notification. Versions of TopicSession.createSubscriber() and TopicSession.createDurableSubscriber() exist to also enable use of message selector filters, and with a boolean noLocal flag indicating that messages published by their own connection should be ignored.

A TopicRequestor helper class can also be used to simplify the use of the JMS publish-subscribe model for request and reply behavior. A TopicRequestor object is first created with a handle to a TopicSession and Topic object. The request() method may then be used to publish a Message to a topic destination and wait for a response in the form of a Message. To release and close any open distributed resources associated with the TopicRequestor and the underlying TopicSession, the JMS client invokes the close() method on the TopicRequestor.

Finally, as depicted in Figure 12.26, a set of interfaces exists to encapsulate transactional support for publish-subscribe messaging. As mentioned before, the JMS client should not be coded to talk directly to such interfaces. Rather, the messaging server will use such interfaces to imbue a publish-subscribe message connection factory, connection, and session with JTA XA-compliant transaction management functionality. The interfaces in Figure 12.26 simply extend the interfaces presented in Figure 12.9 and provide method signatures specific to the publish-subscribe message domain model.

Publish-Subscribe Sample Source Code

We present a brief example here to illustrate the use of JMS publish-subscribe messaging. Because our example here is very similar to the queue example presented earlier, we highlight only the core differences. This example implements a TopicSupplier to publish OrderItem objects to an UnleashedTopic topic name. A TopicConsumer mimics a simple topic subscriber that subscribes to receive OrderItem messages.

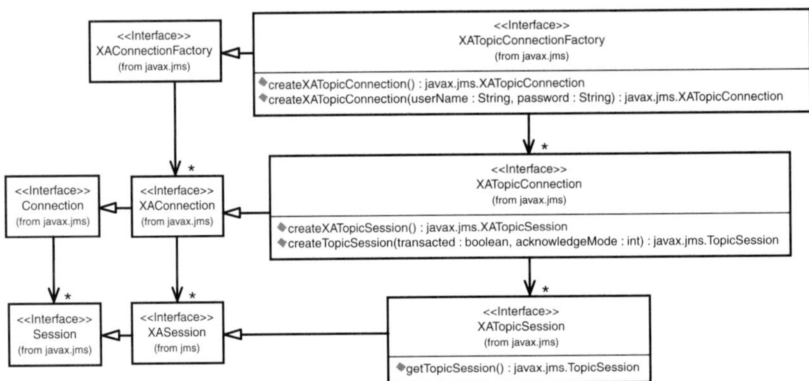

FIGURE 12.26 JMS transactional publish-subscribe messaging.

> **NOTE**
>
> The sample code strewn throughout this section leaves out some exception handling and other nonessential features in the interest of simplifying the description. The `TopicManager`, `TopicSupplier`, `TopicConsumer`, and `MessageHandler` classes implement the core of this example, and `Props`, `OrderItem`, and `OrderManager` classes are also used.
>
> As with the previous example, Ant can be used to execute the `build.xml` compilation script associated with this example. In fact, if you've already executed the Ant script for the last example, the code and execution scripts for this example will already have been generated. After running the Ant script, the generated `runtopic-supplier` and `runtopic-consumer` script files can be used for executing the example.

TopicManager

The `TopicManager` used with these examples serves as the base class for both the `TopicConsumer` and `TopicSupplier`. The constructor of the `TopicManager` performs all the necessary initialization steps for obtaining a `Topic` handle as illustrated here:

```
package com.wls8unleashed.jms;
 ...
public class TopicManager {

 protected TopicConnectionFactory topicConnectionFactory;
 protected TopicConnection topicConnection;
 protected TopicSession topicSession;
 protected Topic topic;

 public TopicManager(Context context){
    ...
   // Get JMS factory JNDI name
   String jmsFactoryName = Props.get("jms.factory.for.topic");
```

```
    // Create topic connection factory
    System.out.println("Looking up factory name: " + jmsFactoryName);
    topicConnectionFactory =
     (TopicConnectionFactory) context.lookup(jmsFactoryName);

    // Create topic connection to the factory
    System.out.println("Creating topic connection...");
    topicConnection = topicConnectionFactory.createTopicConnection();

    // Create session to the connection
    System.out.println("Creating topic session...");
    topicSession = topicConnection.createTopicSession(
                    false, Session.AUTO_ACKNOWLEDGE);

    // Get topic name
    String topicName = Props.get("topic.name");

    // Lookup handle to the Topic
    try {
     System.out.println("Looking up topic name: " + topicName);
     topic = (Topic) context.lookup(topicName);
    } catch (NamingException namingException) {
     // If not created, create new topic, and bind topic to name
     System.out.println("Didn't find the topic...so creating: " + topicName);
     topic = topicSession.createTopic(topicName);
     System.out.println("Binding topic: " + topicName);
     context.bind(topicName, topic);
    }
   }
   ...
  }
}
```

The topic connection factory JNDI name and topic JNDI name are read from the following `build.properties` file properties:

```
# JMS Connection Factory for Topics
jms.factory.for.topic=UnleashedJMSFactory

# JMS Topic Name
topic.name=UnleashedTopic
```

TopicConsumer

The sample TopicConsumer that extends the TopicManager represents a vendor that subscribes to receive orders from the UnleashedTopic topic. The TopicConsumer.main() method first creates a JNDI context with a call to Props.getInitialContext(). The TopicConsumer is then constructed with the JNDI context as an input parameter. The TopicConsumer receives messages until the user exits the program. Finally, TopicConsumer.close() ensures that all resources are cleaned up along with the JNDI context. The TopicConsumer.main() method is shown here:

```
public static void main(String[] args){
 try {
  // Create JNDI context
  Context context = Props.getInitialContext();

  // Create new TopicConsumer
  System.out.println("Creating new TopicConsumer...");
  TopicConsumer topicConsumer = new TopicConsumer(context);

  System.out.println(" TopicConsumer is ready to receive messages.");

  // Receive messages until user quits from program or quit flags true.
  synchronized (topicConsumer) {
   while (!topicConsumer.quitFromReceiving) {
    try {
    // Wait for messages
    topicConsumer.wait();
    } catch (InterruptedException interruptedException) {
     System.out.println("Interruption!");
     interruptedException.printStackTrace();
    }
   }
  }

  // Close up resources when done and exit
  topicConsumer.close();
  context.close();
  System.exit(0);
  ...
}
```

The TopicConsumer constructor first invokes its TopicManager superclass constructor, which looks up the TopicConnectionFactory, creates a TopicConnection, creates a TopicSession, and looks up or creates a Topic. The TopicConsumer then creates a

TopicSubscriber and registers itself as a MessageListener with the TopicSubscriber. The TopicConnection is then initialized to start receiving published messages. The TopicConsumer constructor initialization is shown here:

```
public TopicConsumer(Context context)
 throws NamingException, JMSException {

 // Call superclass constructor
 super(context);

 // Create subscriber
 System.out.println("Creating topic subscriber...");
 topicSubscriber = topicSession.createSubscriber(topic);

 // Register subscriber as a MessageListener
 System.out.println("Setting message listener...");
 topicSubscriber.setMessageListener(this);

 // Start the connection thread
 System.out.println("Starting connection thread...");
 topicConnection.start();
}
```

Because the TopicConsumer is a message listener implementing a MessageListener, it must implement the onMessage(Message) method. The TopicConsumer.onMessage() is called when the JMS service provider receives an OrderItem published by the TopicSupplier. The onMessage() method simply delegates its call to the MessageHandler implementation to display the information packed into a JMS message as illustrated here:

```
public void onMessage(Message message) {
 MessageHandler handler = new MessageHandler();
 handler.onMessage(message);
}
```

Finally, all TopicReceiver, TopicSession, and TopicConnection resources are closed in the close() method:

```
public void close() throws JMSException {
 topicSubscriber.close();
 this.topicSession.close();
 this.topicConnection.close();
}
```

TopicSupplier

The TopicSupplier class also extends the TopicManager class for basic topic resource initialization functionality. The TopicSupplier.main() method first retrieves the Collection of orders from the OrderManager.getOrders() call. For each OrderItem in the Collection, a call to sendOrder() is made on a TopicSupplier with an extracted OrderItem:

```
public static void main(String[] args) throws Exception {
 try {
  // Get some orders from the OrderManager class
  System.out.println("Getting a bunch of orders to send...");
  Collection orders = OrderManager.getOrders();

  // For each order, get order request and send to consumer
  Iterator it = orders.iterator();
  while (it.hasNext()) {
   // Get an OrderItem object to send
   OrderItem item = (OrderItem) it.next();

   // Create JNDI context
   Context context = Props.getInitialContext();

   // Create new TopicSupplier
   System.out.println("Creating new TopicSupplier...");
   TopicSupplier topicSupplier = new TopicSupplier(context);

   // Send the order
   System.out.println("Initiating order to send...");
   topicSupplier.sendOrder(item);

   // Close TopicSupplier
   System.out.println("Closing TopicSupplier...");
   topicSupplier.close();
  }
  ...
}
```

Inside the TopicSupplier constructor, a call is made to the TopicManager superclass constructor for topic resource initialization. A TopicPublisher is then created. The TopicSupplier constructor is shown here:

```
public TopicSupplier(Context context){

 // Call superclass TopicManager constructor
 super(context);
  ...
```

```
    // Create topic publisher
    System.out.println("Creating topic publisher...");
    topicPublisher = topicSession.createPublisher(topic);
     ...
  }
```

The TopicSupplier.sendOrder() method publishes a message containing an OrderItem to a topic as shown here:

```
public void sendOrder(OrderItem message) throws JMSException {
  System.out.println("Publishing order message:" + message);

  // Create empty ObjectMessage on session
  System.out.println("Creating empty object message...");
  ObjectMessage sendingMessage = topicSession.createObjectMessage();

  // Start the topicconnection
  System.out.println("Starting topic connection...");
  topicConnection.start();

  // Set the order object onto the message carrier
  System.out.println("Setting order item into message...");
  sendingMessage.setObject((Serializable) message);

  // Send the message
  System.out.println("Publishing the order message...");
  topicPublisher.publish(sendingMessage);
}
```

Finally, the TopicSupplier.close() method closes its TopicPublisher, TopicSession, and TopicConnection resources:

```
public void close() throws JMSException {
  topicPublisher.close();
  topicSession.close();
  topicConnection.close();
}
```

WebLogic JMS Topic Configuration

We've already seen earlier in this chapter how to configure a JMS server and connection factory inside of a WebLogic Server. We've also configured a JMS queue inside of the server. Configuring a JMS topic is almost identical to the configuration of a JMS queue. By clicking on the Destinations link in the left browser pane beneath a particular JMS server name in the JMS→Servers list, you yield the screen displayed in Figure 12.27.

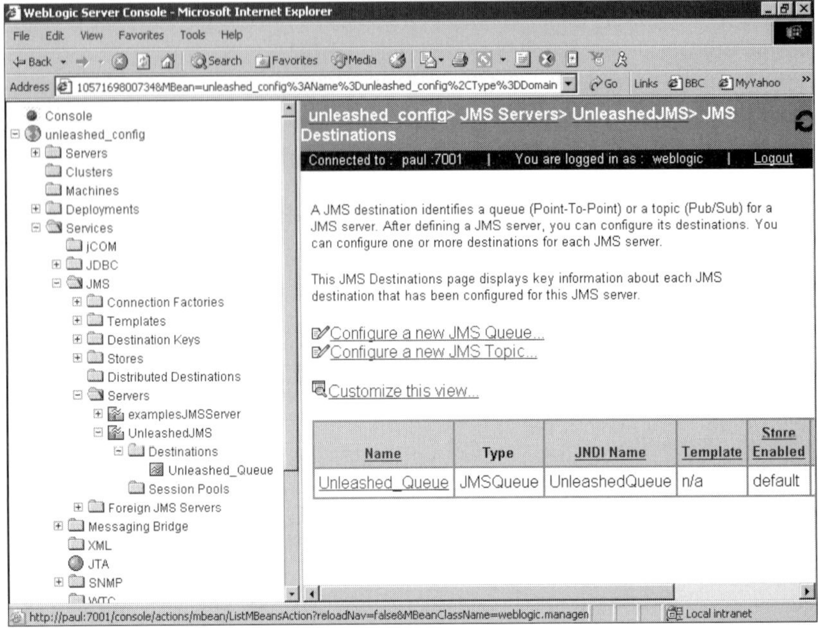

FIGURE 12.27 Viewing JMS server destinations.

For this example, we want to click on Create a New JMS Topic in the center pane of the screen shown in Figure 12.27. The screen shown in Figure 12.28 is then used to perform the basic configuration for a topic. The topic name known to the JMS server and the JNDI name for the topic must be established along with other basic configuration information such as the cluster-ability of the topic's JNDI name and the persistence of the topic. We use the JNDI name `UnleashedTopic` in Figure 12.28 to be consistent with the name we assume for our topic sample code as read in via the `build.properties` file:

```
# JMS Topic Name
topic.name=UnleashedTopic
```

As with JMS queue configuration, additional configuration screens also exist as tabs beneath the topic's configuration tab in the center pane. Configuration screens exist to define thresholds and quotas for message storage, override values for message priorities and delivery modes, message expiration policies, and message redelivery policies.

JMS Topic Sample Execution

As with the queue example, a set of execution scripts will be generated when you run the Ant script for this chapter's code by typing **`ant`** at the command line in the directory where you have deposited the source code. Ant will compile all the source code examples and generate two scripts named `runtopic-consumer` and `runtopic-supplier`. The scripts will have either a `.bat` or `.sh` extension, depending on whether you are running the examples on a Windows or Unix platform, respectively.

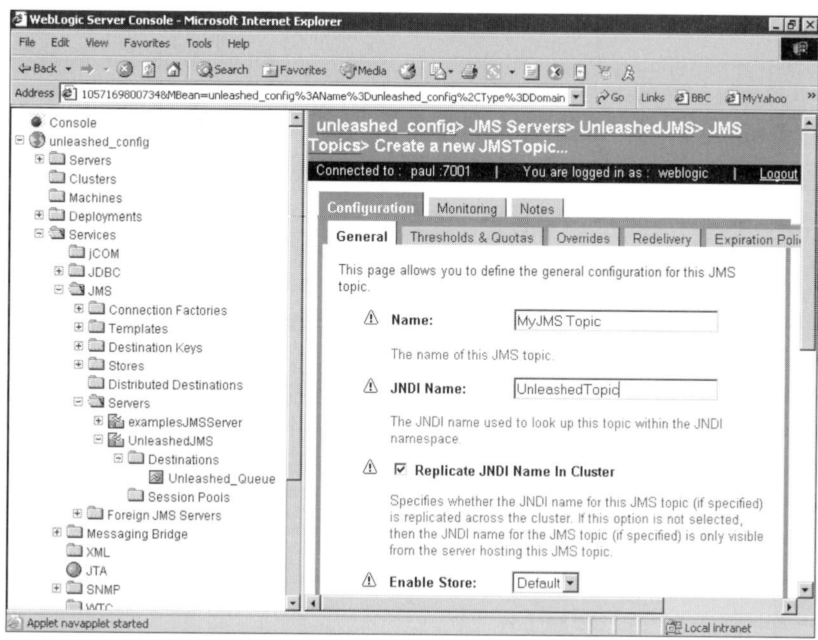

FIGURE 12.28 Configuring JMS topics.

In one command-line window, execute the `runtopic-consumer` script to start the sample `TopicConsumer`. In a separate window, you need to execute the `runtopic-supplier` script to start the `TopicSupplier`. The `TopicSupplier` publishes messages to the JMS topic that we configured. The messages are then asynchronously delivered to the `TopicConsumer` by the WebLogic JMS server.

JMS Unified Messaging Domain Model

Throughout this chapter, we have mentioned the fact that the core JMS API abstractions can now be used to support both the point-to-point queuing and publish-subscribe messaging models. Indeed, this unified messaging domain model is a feature new to JMS v1.1 and part of J2EE v1.4. In fact, the JMS v1.1 specification indicates that you should generally code JMS applications using this new unified model. The specification even hints that the JMS APIs that are specific to point-to-point queuing and publish-subscribe messaging might be deprecated in a future JMS specification version. Regardless, the domain-specific JMS APIs will still be used for some time because many legacy JMS-based applications already exist and because many developers still prefer the domain-specific model to the unified model. Furthermore, BEA WebLogic Server 8.1 is only geared for J2EE v1.3 compliance and thus can claim only JMS v1.0 compliance. However, as we'll see, it is a rather simple task to extend your applications to use the new JMS v1.1–compliant APIs.

We discuss the unified model in this section. In reality, you have already been introduced to this model by virtue of the fact that we've already examined the core JMS architecture earlier in this chapter and we've also discussed the types of domain-specific destinations and two models that the unified messaging model can support. Figure 12.29, in fact, depicts the main abstractions involved with the unified domain model. As you can see, the APIs involved in this diagram have already been introduced. Now let's discuss how they are used for unified domain messaging with a BEA WebLogic Server.

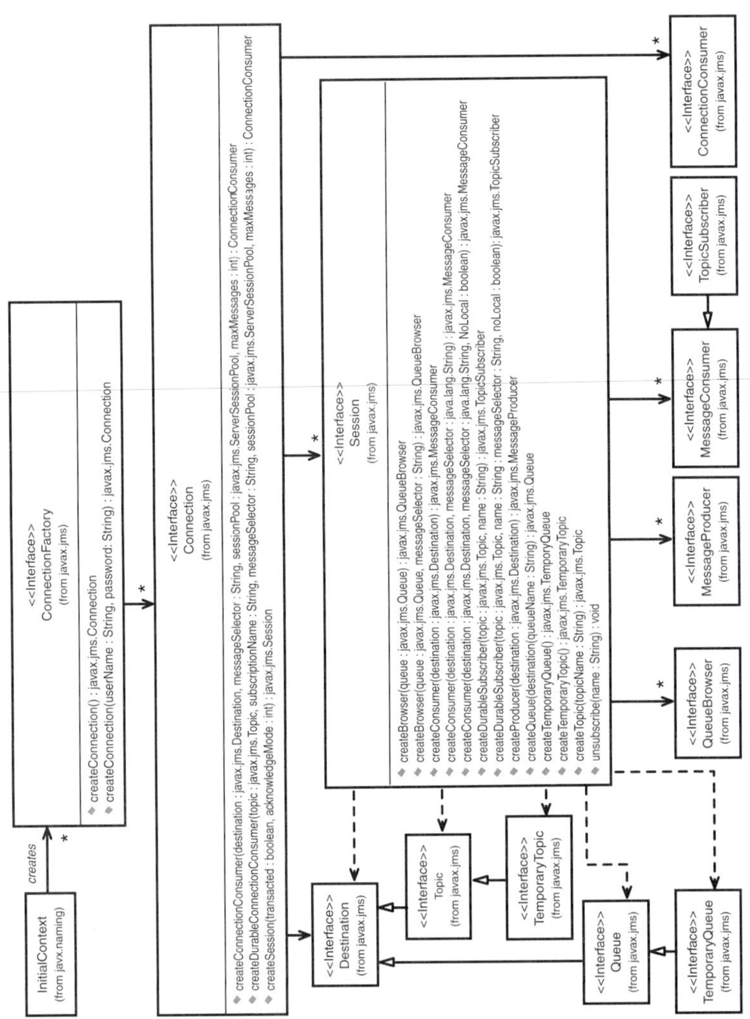

FIGURE 12.29 JMS unified domain messaging.

As depicted in Figure 12.29, a generic ConnectionFactory is looked up using JNDI and then the ConnectionFactory is used to create a Connection, which in turn is used to create a Session handle as before. The JMS v1.1 Session interface now offers a host of methods that enable us to create QueueBrowser, TopicSubscriber, Queue, TemporaryQueue, Topic, and TemporaryTopic objects. You've already seen all of these method signatures on the domain-specific QueueSession or TopicSession interfaces described earlier. The JMS v1.1 Session interface also now offers methods that allow us to create generic MessageConsumer and MessageProducer object handles that actually may implement domain-specific message consumer and message producer functionality, respectively. These methods are simply more generic forms of methods previously defined for the QueueSession and TopicSession interfaces.

In fact, using the generic methods on the core JMS APIs, you don't even have to code your JMS application to have any specific knowledge of queues or topics. This is because after you have a handle to a generic Session object, you can use JNDI to look up a handle to a Destination object when given a name for the destination. You can then use the generic createProducer() and createConsumer() methods on the Session interface to create handles to generic MessageProducer and MessageConsumer objects, respectively. Such object handles can then also be used to generically produce and consume JMS messages, respectively.

Unified Domain Messaging Sample Source Code

We present an example here to illustrate the use of JMS domain-independent messaging. Our example manifests itself in three core classes. A UnifyManager class implements generic initialization of JMS destination resources. A UnifySupplier class implements a generic message producer that sends a message to a destination. The message sent to the destination may then be read by the UnifyConsumer class. A UnifyConsumer class implements a generic message consumer that reads a message from a destination that is sent using the UnifySupplier class.

NOTE

The sample code strewn throughout this section leaves out some exception handling and other nonessential features in the interest of simplifying the description. The UnifyManager, UnifySupplier, UnifyConsumer, and MessageHandler classes implement the core of this example, and Props, OrderItem, and OrderManager classes are also used.

You must first download the JMS v1.1 API JAR file from http://java.sun.com/products/jms/docs.html and install it in a directory for your sample applications to use. You then need to set the location of this JAR file for the jar.jms1_1 property in the chapter's build.properties file. As with the previous examples, Ant can be used to execute the build.xml compilation script associated with this example. However, you must execute the jms11 target to build these JMS v1.1 examples along with the previous examples. That is, simply type **ant jms11** at the command line in the directory containing this chapter's sample source code. After running the Ant script, the generated rununify-supplier and rununify-consumer script files can be used to execute the example.

UnifyManager

The `UnifyManager` simply provides a constructor that initializes a set of generic JMS resources given a JNDI `Context` object. The JNDI context object is first used to look up a `ConnectionFactory` object in order for a `Connection` and then a `Session` object to be created. The JNDI context is then used to look up a handle to a generic `Destination` object as illustrated here:

```
package com.wls8unleashed.jms;
 ...
public class UnifyManager {
 protected ConnectionFactory connectionFactory;
 protected Connection connection;
 protected Session session;
 protected Destination destination;

 public UnifyManager(Context context){
  ...
  // Get JMS factory JNDI name
  String jmsFactoryName = Props.get("jms.factory.for.unify");

  // Create Generic Connection Factory
  System.out.println("Looking up factory name: " + jmsFactoryName);
  connectionFactory
   = (ConnectionFactory) context.lookup(jmsFactoryName);

  // Create Generic Connection to The Factory
  System.out.println("Creating generic JMS connection...");
  connection = connectionFactory.createConnection();

  // Create Session to the Connection
  System.out.println("Creating generic JMS session...");
  session
   = connection.createSession(false, Session.AUTO_ACKNOWLEDGE);

  // Get generic destination name
  String destinationName = Props.get("unify.name");

  // Get generic destination
  System.out.println("Looking up generic JMS destination name: "
           + destinationName);
  destination = (Destination) context.lookup(destinationName);
   ...
 }
}
```

The ConnectionFactory object looked up via JNDI uses whatever JNDI name is associated with jms.factory.for.unify in the build.properties file. For our example, we can simply use the same JNDI name for the UnleashedJMSFactory that we have already created as illustrated here:

```
# JMS Connection Factory for Unified JMS Model
jms.factory.for.unify=UnleashedJMSFactory
```


The Destination looked up via JNDI uses whatever JNDI name we've associated with unify.name in the build.properties file. For our example, we can use the name of the queue or topic that we've already created earlier in this chapter as illustrated here:

```
# JMS Unified Destination Name
unify.name=UnleashedQueue
```

UnifySupplier

There is nothing tremendously special about the UnifySupplier class aside from the fact that it uses generic JMS API calls. The UnifySupplier constructor simply delegates much of its work to its UnifyManager superclass constructor and then creates a generic MessageProducer as shown here:

```
public UnifySupplier(Context context){
 // Call superclass QueueManager constructor
 super(context);
  ...
 // Create generic producer
 System.out.println("Creating generic JMS producer...");
 producer = session.createProducer(destination);
  ...
}
```

When it comes time to send the message, the generic MessageProducer is used to send a JMS message as illustrated here:

```
public void sendOrder(OrderItem message) throws JMSException {
 System.out.println("Sending order message:" + message);

 // Create empty ObjectMessage on session
 System.out.println("Creating empty object message...");
 ObjectMessage sendingMessage = session.createObjectMessage();

 // Start the generic JMS connection
 System.out.println("Starting generic JMS connection...");
 connection.start();
```

```
  // Set the order object onto the message carrier
  System.out.println("Setting order item into message...");
  sendingMessage.setObject((Serializable) message);

  // Send the message
  System.out.println("Sending the order message...");
  producer.send(sendingMessage);
}
```

The UnifyConsumer class can be executed to receive the message sent by the UnifySupplier class. You can also use the QueueConsumer to receive the message sent by the UnifySupplier. Alternately, if you set the unify.name property in the build.properties file to UnleashedTopic, the UnifySupplier can act as a topic publisher and hence can be used with the TopicConsumer as well.

UnifyConsumer

There is also nothing tremendously special about the UnifyConsumer class aside from the fact that it also uses generic JMS API calls. The UnifyConsumer constructor simply delegates much of its work to the UnifyManager superclass constructor, creates a generic MessageConsumer, sets itself as a MessageListener on the MessageConsumer, and then starts receiving messages on the connection as shown here:

```
public UnifyConsumer(Context context)
  throws NamingException, JMSException {

  super(context);

  // Create Receiver
  System.out.println("Creating generic JMS consumer...");
  messageConsumer = session.createConsumer(destination);

  // Register QueueConsumer as Message Listener
  System.out.println("Setting message listener...");
  messageConsumer.setMessageListener(this);

  // Start Receiving Message
  System.out.println("Starting generic connection...");
  connection.start();
}
```

The UnifyConsumer.onMessage() method then receives and processes JMS messages as they are received from the JMS destination after they are sent to there by the UnifySupplier class or QueueSupplier class. The UnifyConsumer class can also act as a topic consumer if the unify.name in the build.properties file is set to UnleashedTopic and hence can also receive messages published by the TopicSupplier class.

Advanced WebLogic JMS Configuration

Thus far in this chapter we've learned about enterprise messaging, the JMS APIs, and how to configure BEA WebLogic Server as a JMS provider. Although the default configurations offered by WebLogic for JMS messaging are fine for many applications, WebLogic also offers a variety of other configuration options that allow for more sophisticated enterprise messaging applications. This section describes those additional features and how to configure WebLogic to use them. In addition to the features described in this section, WebLogic also provides support for clustered JMS services and message bridging between applications. Chapter 36, "Installing, Configuring, and Deploying WebLogic Server Clusters," discusses these more advanced features as other prerequisite features and concepts are introduced.

JMS Persistent Stores

The BEA WebLogic Server enables you to configure a persistent store for messages managed by a WebLogic JMS server. Such persistence increases the reliability of your messaging applications because message data will be persisted to a store, allowing for the recovery of messages even in the event of server and application failures. Durable topic subscribers and paging of messages can also leverage use of a persistent store. First you must open the Administration Console. By clicking on JMS→Stores in the left browser pane, you can opt to create a JDBC-based or file-based persistent store, as shown in Figure 12.30.

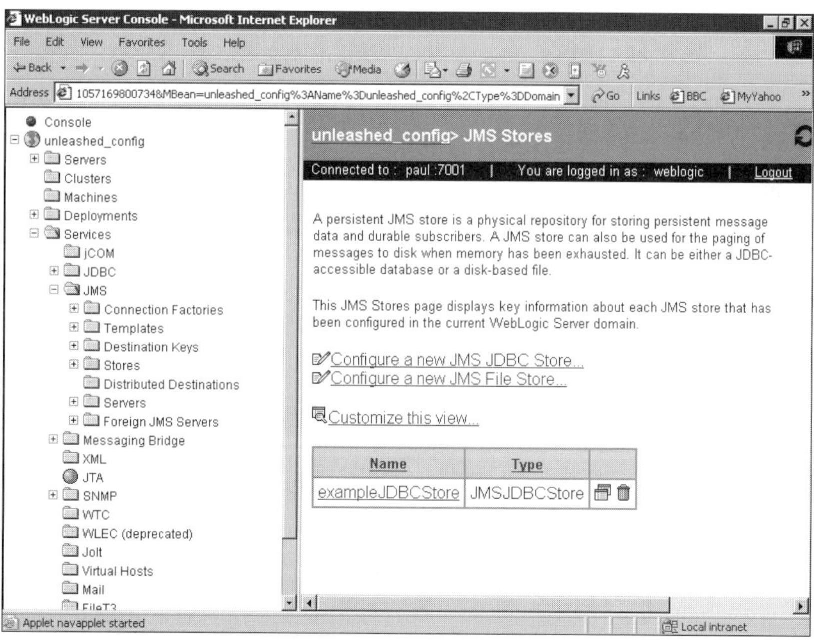

FIGURE 12.30 Administering JMS stores.

As an example, if you select Configure a New JMS JDBC Store, you are presented with the screen depicted in Figure 12.31. After entering a name for your JMS store, selecting a valid JDBC connection pool, and establishing any table prefixes, you then must click the Create button to establish the JMS store.

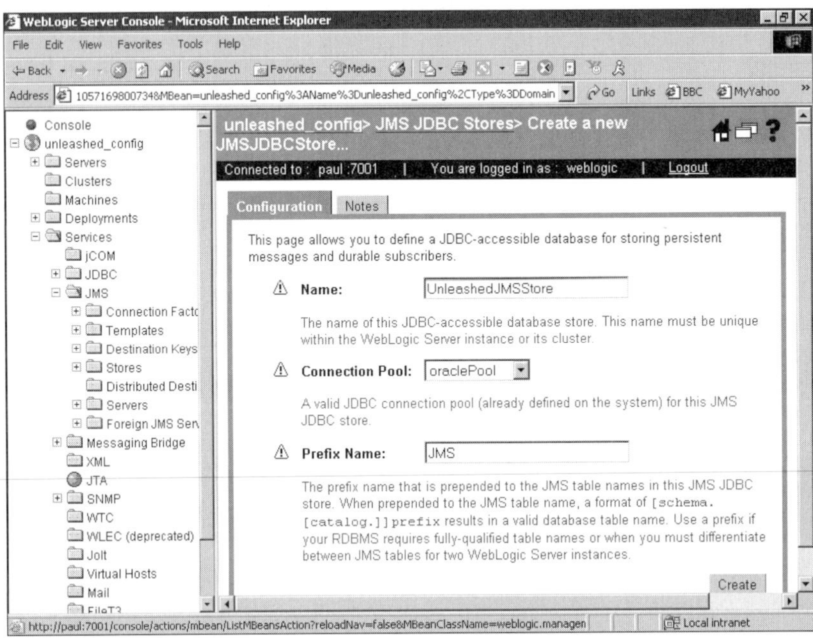

FIGURE 12.31 Configuring JMS stores.

As exemplified in Figure 12.32, you can then associate JMS servers with a particular JMS store such as the one we just created. By default, destinations within a particular JMS server use the default persistent store associated with the JMS server. Figure 12.32 illustrates the screen associated with configuring JMS destinations, whereby this default association can be overridden via the Enable Store option.

Messages are persisted for topics after the persistent store is configured. A subscriber can retrieve such messages if it has been created using the method `TopicSession.createDurableSubscriber()`.

Destination Keys

Although messaging is an asynchronous mechanism, a certain level of control might be desired for how messages are handled by WebLogic Server. In this consideration, WebLogic enables you to specify how messages are sorted within a particular JMS destination. This can be achieved by applying a destination key to a destination. Let's see how this is done. Figure 12.33 shows the screen that you are presented when you select JMS→Destination Keys in the left browser pane.

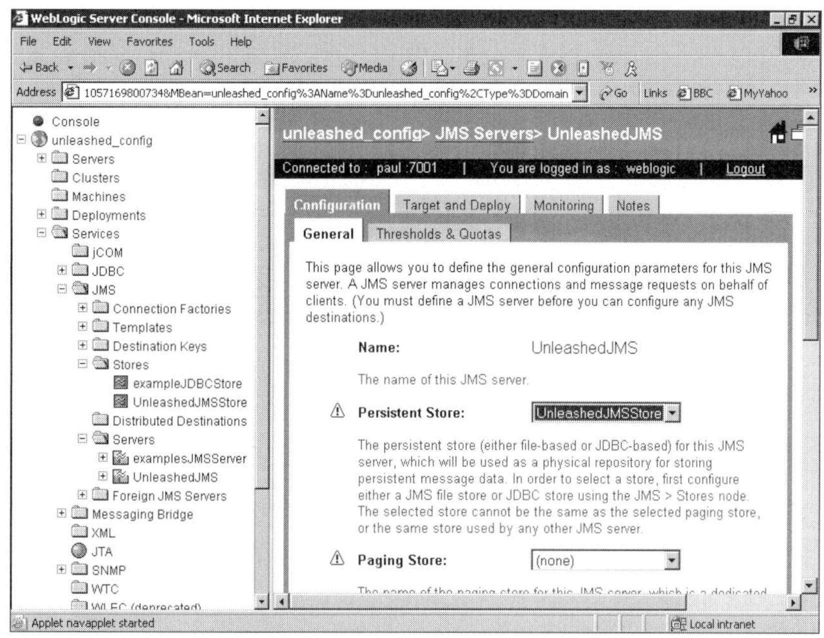

FIGURE 12.32 Associating JMS servers with JMS stores.

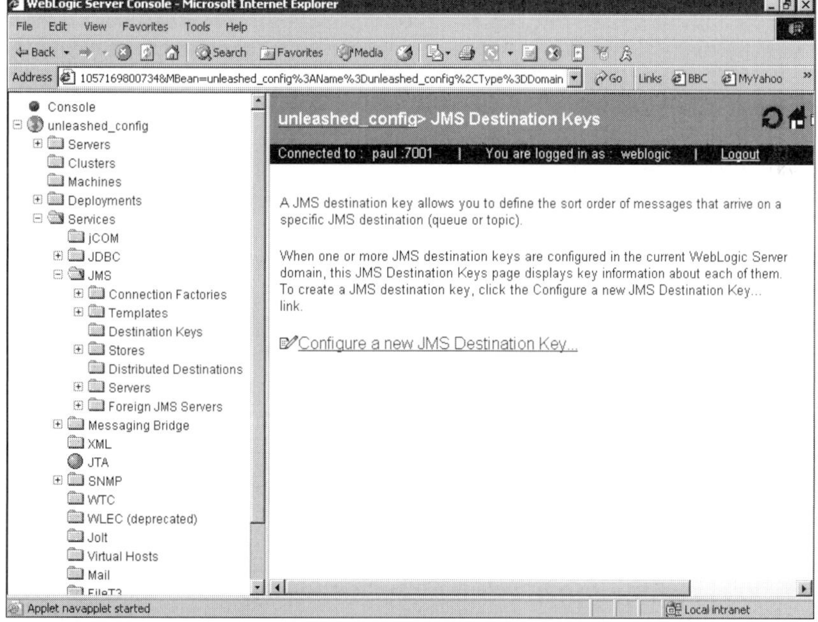

FIGURE 12.33 Administering JMS destination keys.

After selecting Configure a New JMS Destination Key, you are presented with the screen shown in Figure 12.34. The name of the key, message field by which sorting should occur, key type, and the direction of sort are all configured via this screen.

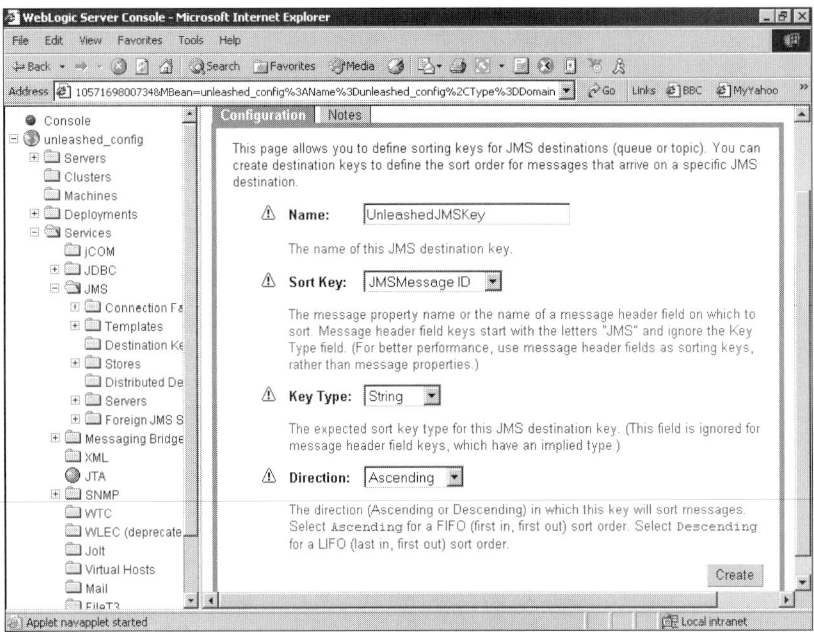

FIGURE 12.34 Configuring JMS destination keys.

After you select Create, the key will be available as an option for sorting via the destinations configuration screen as depicted in Figure 12.35.

Foreign JMS Servers

There might be times when your WebLogic applications will want to tap the resources of a third-party messaging service. Those external messaging services are referred to as *foreign JMS servers*. WebLogic provides a rather straightforward means to achieve this integration. Although any Java program can access a JMS server directly by accessing the JMS connection factory and destinations in the remote JNDI server, WebLogic Server provides an easier way of doing this for applications running inside of the server. In such a way, the foreign JMS provider's connection factories and destinations can be accessed by WebLogic applications as local JMS objects. Figure 12.36 depicts the initial screen presented to you when you select JMS→Foreign JMS Servers in the left browser pane.

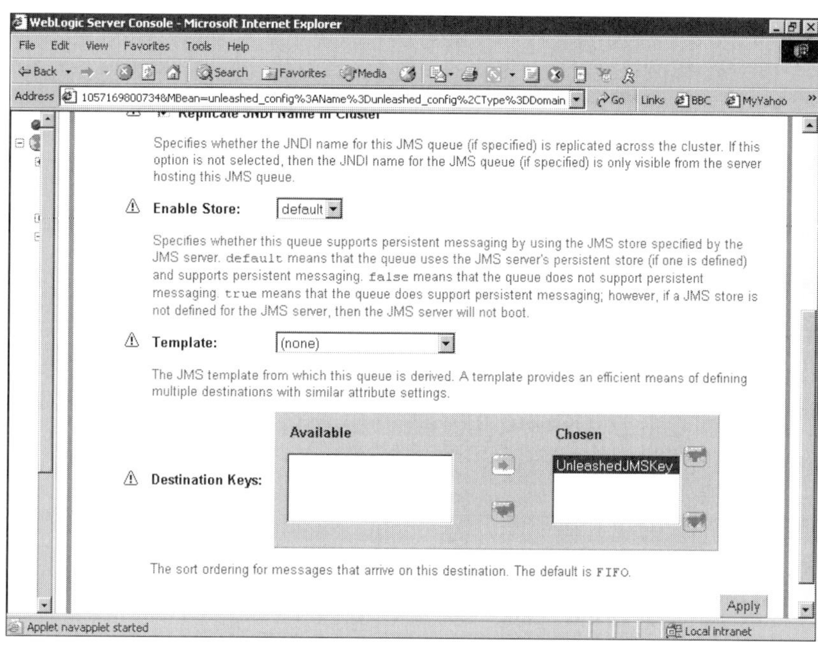

FIGURE 12.35 Associating JMS destination keys with destinations.

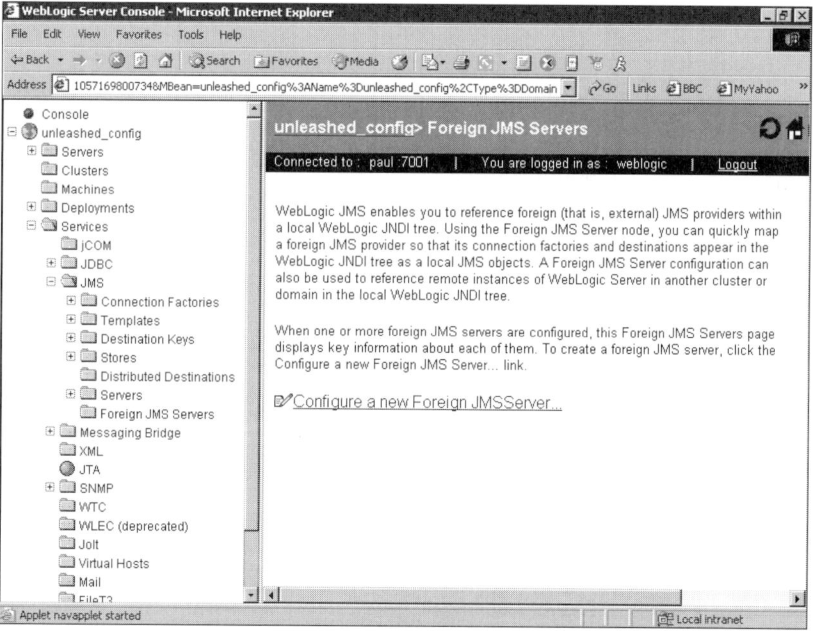

FIGURE 12.36 Administering foreign JMS servers.

After selecting Configure a New Foreign JMS Server, you are presented with a screen akin to Figure 12.37. Here you must enter a reference name for your foreign server, the JNDI factory class name, the JNDI URL, and any other JNDI properties to be passed to your foreign JMS service provider. After configuring your foreign service provider, you must select the Target and Deploy tab in the center pane for the foreign service provider and select a WebLogic Server or cluster to which you will deploy the provider.

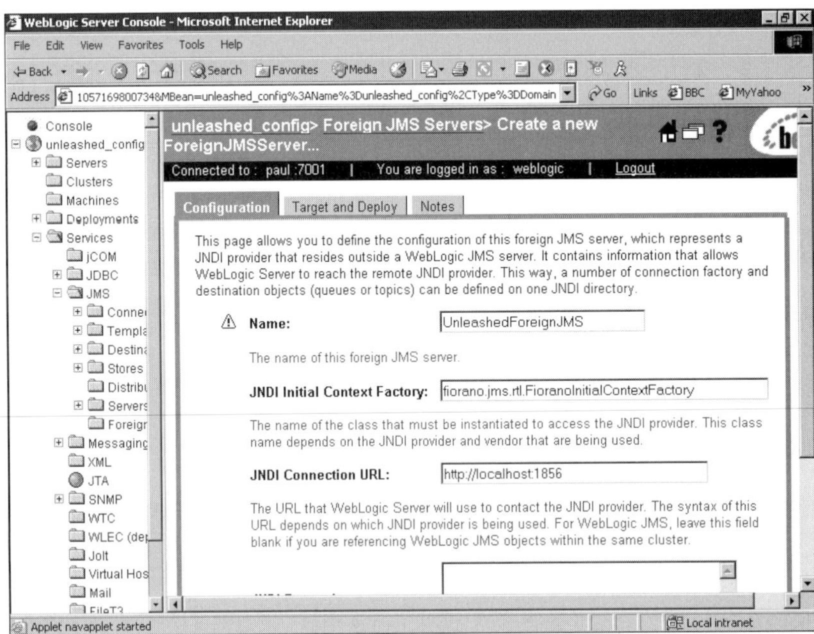

FIGURE 12.37 Configuring foreign JMS servers.

After deploying the foreign provider, connection factories and destinations associated with the service can be configured from within WebLogic. Figure 12.38 depicts a case in which a connection factory is being configured for a foreign JMS provider after selecting Foreign JMSConnection Factories beneath your foreign JMS provider listed in the left browser pane and then selecting Configure a New Foreign JMSConnection Factory in the center pane.

Figure 12.39 depicts the case in which a destination is being configured for a foreign JMS provider after selecting Foreign JMSDestinations beneath your foreign JMS provider listed in the left browser pane and then selecting Configure a New Foreign JMSDestination in the center pane.

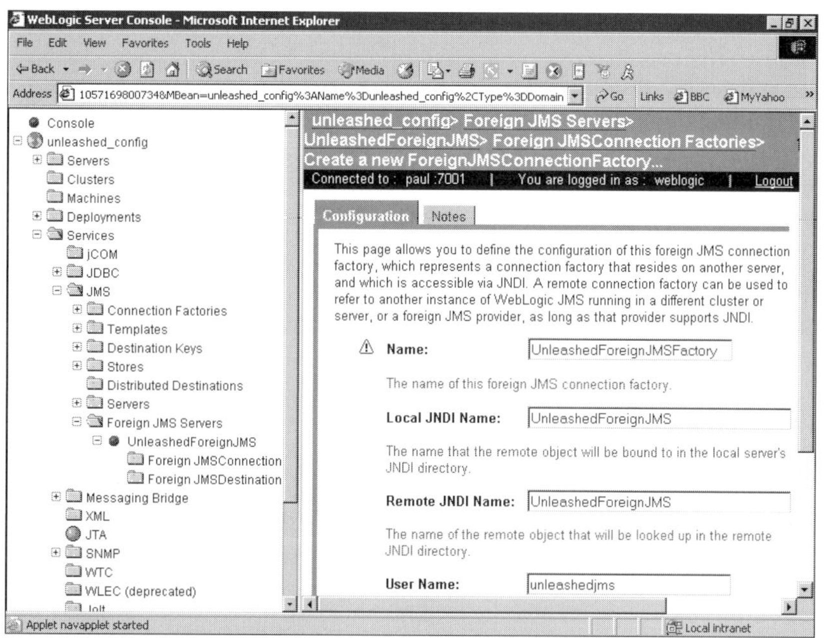

FIGURE 12.38 Configuring foreign JMS connection factories.

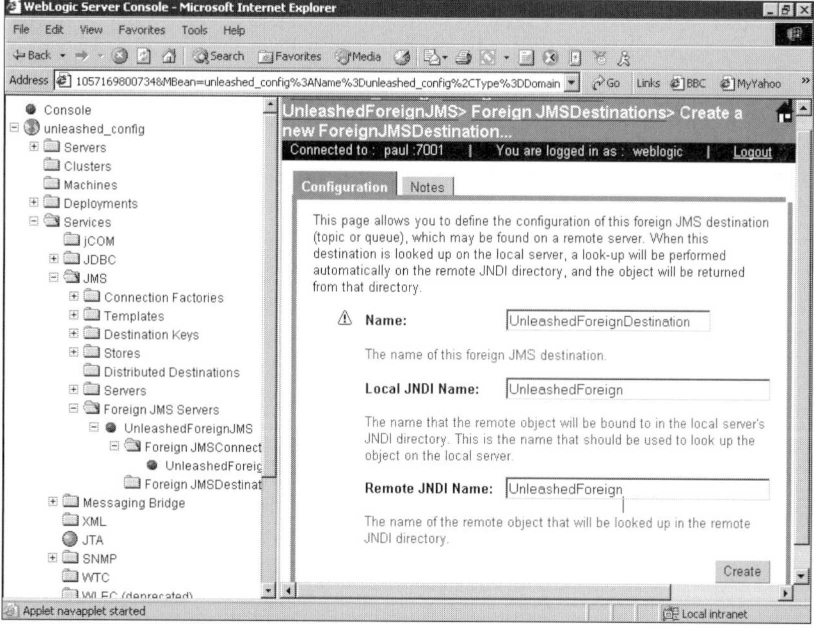

FIGURE 12.39 Configuring foreign JMS destination.

After configuring your foreign JMS provider with your WebLogic Server, your WebLogic applications can then send and receive messages through such a provider just as they would with the WebLogic JMS provider. WebLogic applications acting as message producers can use the same JMS APIs that they use to interact with the WebLogic JMS provider as they would use to interact with a foreign JMS provider. Message-driven EJBs can also act as message consumers for messages received by foreign JMS providers as they would for messages received by a WebLogic JMS provider.

JMS Templates

Throughout this chapter, we have examined various parameters that are entered into WebLogic's Administration Console and used to configure JMS applications. As you can probably imagine, when managing multiple JMS servers and destinations, the large number of parameters involved with such configuration may yield errors or affect repeatability of configuration. WebLogic Server enables you to create JMS configuration templates that contain common configuration values that can be applied to multiple JMS configurations. When you select JMS->Templates in the left browser pane, an initial template configuration screen is presented as illustrated in Figure 12.40.

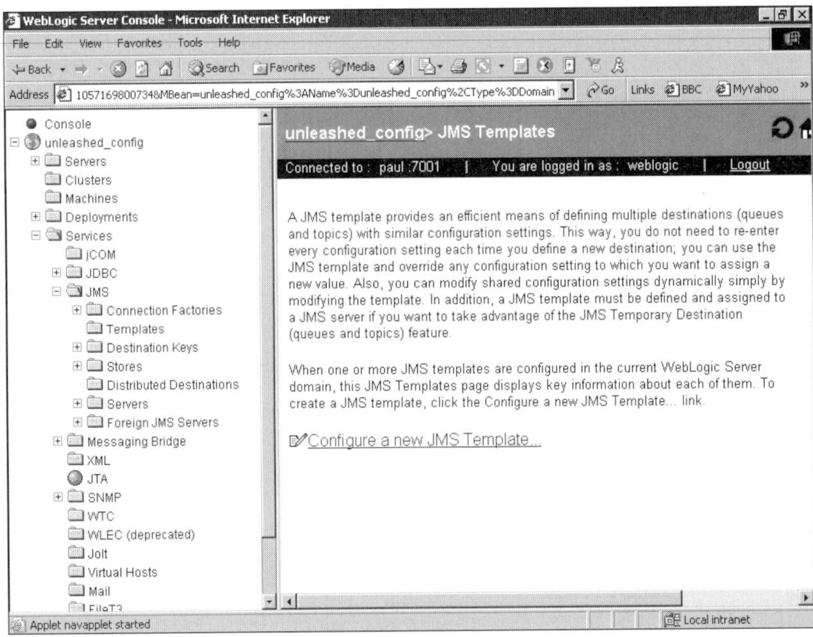

FIGURE 12.40 Administering JMS templates.

After selecting Configure a New JMS Template, you are presented with the basic configuration screen as illustrated in Figure 12.41. Tabs for basic configuration, thresholds and quotas, overrides, redelivery policies, and message expiration policies are all available for configuration.

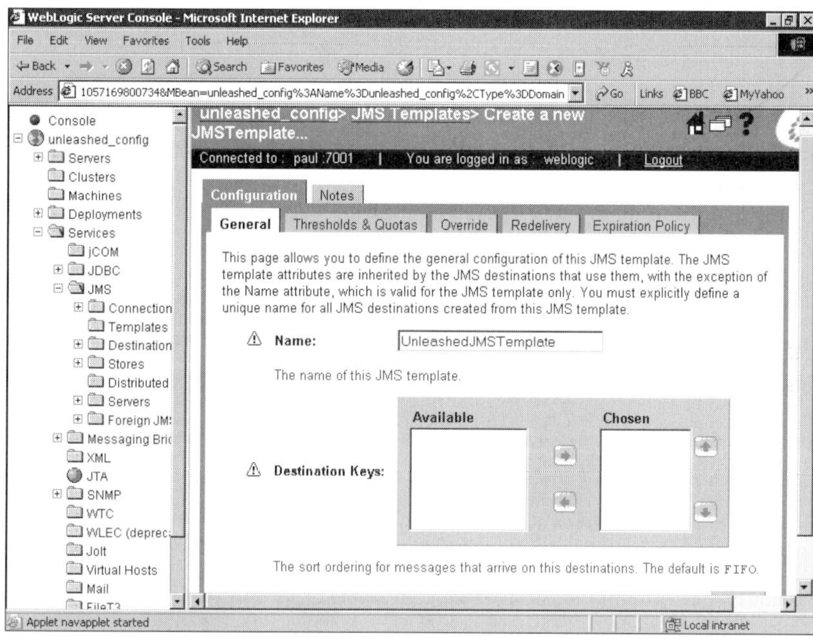

FIGURE 12.41 Configuring JMS templates.

After creating a JMS template, it may be associated with a JMS server (as depicted in Figure 12.42) or with a destination within a server (as depicted in Figure 12.43). Although such associations can be made with servers and destinations after they are created, such templates are most handy when initially configuring new servers and destinations.

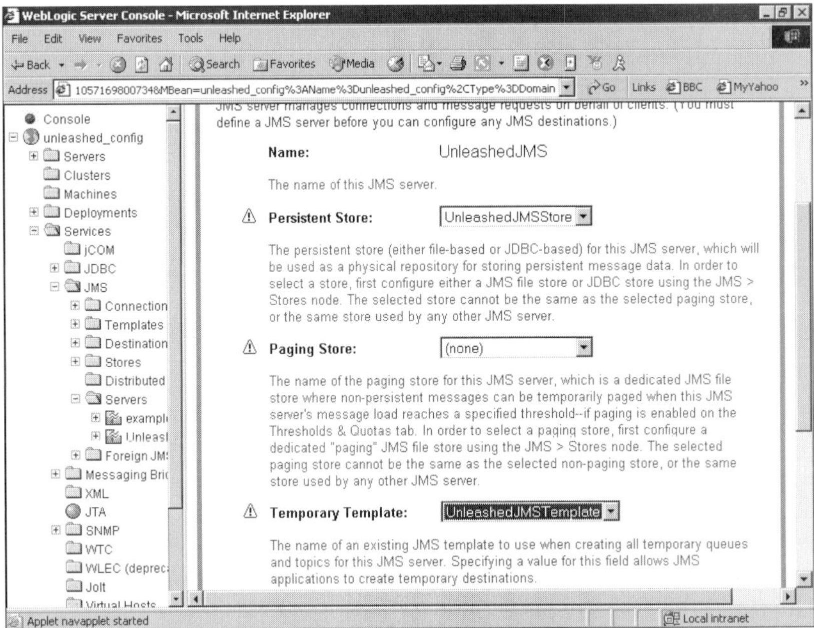

FIGURE 12.42 Associating JMS templates with JMS servers.

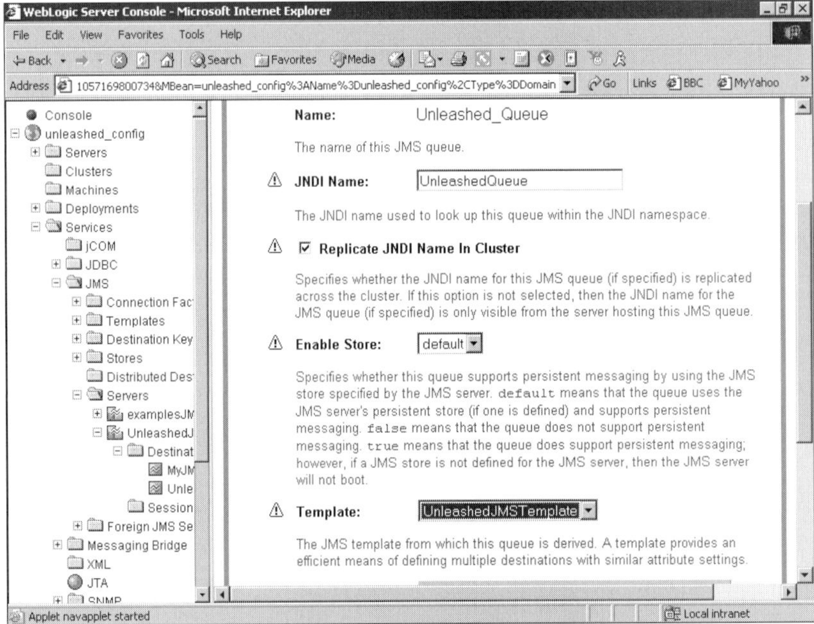

FIGURE 12.43 Associating JMS templates with JMS destinations.

Best Practices for Enterprise Messaging

Enterprise messaging is often a core part of an enterprise's infrastructure for connecting disparate systems together via a common messaging medium. Enterprise messaging can also involve overhead not only in terms of performance but also in establishing the infrastructure to support messaging. As such, it is thus important that enterprise messaging be done not only when appropriate but also implemented appropriately.

In terms of when it is appropriate to employ enterprise messaging, the asynchronous nature of messaging means that the applications sitting on each end of the producer-consumer spectrum need to be able to wait for messages to be delivered. Hence, applications connected via a messaging service often perform coarser-grained operations embodied by coarse-grained messages. You wouldn't want to be sending a user's last name in one message, and then a first name in another message, and then a username message, a password message, and so forth. You'd want to create messages that hold enough data to warrant the overhead involved with sending and receiving the message as well as the waiting that can be involved with its asynchronous delivery.

While a case can be made for using messaging to encapsulate more than just a minimal amount of data, there also might be a limit on the upper bound of a message size that you want to employ in your designs. This is most appropriately accomplished by thinking about the logical cohesiveness of the data inside of a message. If certain chunks of data are not logically related and can be processed separately without affecting the correctness of an application, such data may be encapsulated inside of separate messages. For example, if there exists an application to process a large amount of credit-related data for customers and that data is reasonably minimal, you might consider batching up chunks of that data into one message as it becomes available. However, if each individual amount of credit information is fairly large per customer, you might consider encapsulating the credit data in one message per customer.

The asynchronous nature of messaging also behooves you to warrant its use when the applications at each end of the producer-consumer spectrum are fairly disparate and logically operate independently as systems unto themselves. This is why messaging is used most often to integrate legacy and auxiliary applications.

Even though it is possible to do messaging over a wider area network, such as the Internet, messaging is most often used inside of a local area network or Intranet. The primary reason for this fact is that messaging often involves loosely coupled applications for which the enterprise's staff has control over the message interface definition among the applications. Over wider area networks, service-oriented architectures and Web Services are becoming the norm as opposed to traditional enterprise messaging. Additionally, many organizations also shy away from enterprise messaging over the Internet due to the fact that it requires potentially less secure and difficult to manage firewall configuration settings.

In terms of how to most appropriately implement messaging, the very fact that you will be using JMS gives you one huge advantage. The standard interface embodied by JMS enables you to learn how to implement messaging paradigms by learning one interface as opposed to understanding the many interfaces offered by various proprietary messaging providers. Use of BEA WebLogic also provides you with a simplified means to configure and deploy messaging applications either using WebLogic's built-in messaging provider or by connecting to an external messaging service.

Keeping in mind the aforementioned information about when it is appropriate to use messaging, you can map that to how you will implement your messaging solution using JMS and WebLogic. That is, the size of your JMS messages, coarse-grained nature of your JMS design, and use of JMS on local networks are all key implementation considerations.

Finally, following the examples in this book, you've seen how many JMS operations can be applied throughout your JMS applications in a reusable fashion. Many common JMS operations, such as establishing connection factories, creating connections, and creating destinations, can all be performed inside of reusable and generic code components that read in configuration data to adapt their behavior as needed. The new JMS v1.1 APIs take generic code components one step further by enabling you to create code completely independent of whether a topic- or queue-based messaging paradigm is employed. In such a way, you can create very robust and generic messaging applications using standard JMS APIs and quickly roll out new messaging applications via minimal effort in modifying configuration parameters.

Summary

We have explored the fundamental concepts involved with messaging services and examples in the context of BEA WebLogic JMS-based messaging services in this chapter. Messaging services provide a means for message producers to send messages to message consumers in an asynchronous and time-independent fashion. Message consumers can also pull messages from a messaging service at their convenience, receive messages directly queued to them from a messaging service, or receive messages to which they've subscribed based on a topic name. Messaging services provide all of this functionality in a manner that enhances the underlying reliability and availability of applications that tap their services.

Although various MOM implementations can be used for messaging in Java applications, JMS provides a standard Java-based messaging API and SPI framework that can be used to tap into different messaging implementations. Furthermore, JMS is part of the J2EE standard suite of enterprise components. JMS offers a core and generic API that can be used to send and receive messages in a generic fashion, independent of any particular messaging domain model. JMS also has APIs that are derived from the core and generic JMS API to provide domain-specific messaging behavior for point-to-point messaging via message queues and publish-subscribe messaging via message topics. JMS is clearly the most generic and standard way to infuse MOM functionality into your J2EE applications.

Finally, BEA WebLogic Server 8.1 not only provides the JMS API and a means for hooking into external JMS providers, but also provides an enterprise class JMS provider implementation itself. In addition to such rich support for JMS, WebLogic also provides an easy to use administration interface into the configuration and deployment of JMS servers and destinations. With BEA WebLogic Server 8.1, you are not only provided with a rich array of standard JMS-based enterprise messaging features, but also a messaging infrastructure that's ready to run and easy to configure straight out of the box.

CHAPTER 13

Handling Mail Services with JavaMail

by Joe McGuire and Gurpreet Singh Bhasin

IN THIS CHAPTER

- Email Protocols
- Extending the Capability to Your JavaMail API
- JavaBeans Activation Framework
- Core Classes of the JavaMail API
- JavaMail and WebLogic Server
- Creating Email Components
- JavaMail and the Global Auctions Application

You can add mail capabilities to your WebLogic Server applications with JavaMail. The JavaMail API provides access to the various mail protocols, enabling you to send, receive, reply to, and forward messages. You can also use it to develop fully functional email applications with capabilities similar to Eudora or MS Outlook. It does not, however, provide mail service functionality, so your applications must have access to a mail server to use JavaMail. That's not to say that you cannot develop your own SMTP or POP server, if you're so inclined, but you would need to use tools beyond the JavaMail API to do it.

If you've used JavaMail with WebLogic before, you know that you had to download and install the API as a separate package along with the JavaBeans Activation Framework extension (JAF). These would then be added to the WebLogic Server classpath and could then be accessed by your Java applications. WebLogic Server 8.1 now includes the JavaMail API and the JAF in the main WebLogic package `weblogic.jar`.

WebLogic Server 8.1 is compliant with the JavaMail 1.3 specification included with J2EE 1.3. However, WebLogic 8.1 ships with JavaMail implementation 1.1.3. The Post Office Protocol 3 (POP3) provider is not included in version 1.1.3, but is available in the following JavaMail API release (version 1.3). It's also available as a downloadable extension (more details on this are provided later in the chapter). The latest JavaMail implementation (1.3) can be downloaded from Sun's Web site at `http://java.sun.com/products/javamail/`.

This chapter is divided into two basic sections. The first part of the chapter provides an overview of the different mail protocols and the JavaMail API, and the second part shows you how to implement JavaMail into your own WebLogic applications.

Email Protocols

Electronic messaging systems require different standards, or protocols, for completing various tasks. Some are used to send messages (transfer protocols), whereas others are used to receive (store protocols). Still others are used to define attachments. If you've ever configured your own email applications, such as Eudora or MS Outlook, you know that you had to supply a POP3 provider address to receive messages, as well as an SMTP provider to send messages. Your WebLogic applications are no different, and will require a service provider for each protocol you're working with.

Let's clarify some terms here before continuing. An *electronic messaging protocol* can be defined as common language for performing certain tasks, such as sending or receiving a message. A *service provider* is the mail server, or *service*, hosting the protocol, such as an IMAP server running on your company's intranet, or the popular `smtp.mail.yahoo.com` or `pop.mail.yahoo.com` servers provided by Yahoo!. Your application functionality is limited to the functionality of the protocols it's using. This will become clearer as we take a look at each of the protocols in a little more detail:

- **SMTP**—The Simple Mail Transfer Protocol (SMTP) is a mechanism for the delivery of electronic messages. It sends mail and that's all it does. In the context of the JavaMail API, your application will communicate with your intranet or ISP's SMTP server to send messages to it.
- **POP**—The Post Office Protocol (POP) is a simple mechanism for retrieving (or *fetching*) electronic messages. It's currently in version 3, so it's often referred to as *POP3*.
- **IMAP**—The Internet Messaging Access Protocol (IMAP) is another mechanism for retrieving electronic messages. It's currently in version 4, so it's often referred to as *IMAP4*. IMAP has a few more capabilities than POP, such as the capability to assign multiple folders to users on the server and provide folder sharing among multiple users. It does have a few drawbacks, however, that keep it from replacing POP as the premier protocol for receiving messages. IMAP places a greater burden on the mail server in terms of both processing power and storage. Not only does it have to receive messages and deliver them to the proper recipients, it must also maintain shared folders and retain a copy of each message for each user on the server itself. Disk space on an IMAP server can get used up very quickly. POP servers, on the other hand, may delete messages from the server after they've been accessed by the POP client.
- **MIME**—The Multipurpose Internet Mail Extension (MIME) protocol is neither a transfer or store protocol, but rather a kind of content protocol. It defines how the

content of the message is transferred. For instance, your email message may be sent as text displayed in the body of the message, or perhaps it's an attachment that will be opened by another client application (such as an attached JPEG file or MS Word document).

As you can see, each protocol is pretty limited in what it can do. Features found in commercial email applications, such as capability to report new messages, send automated replies, apply filters, and automatically move messages to other folders, are actually programmed by the developer, and are *not* functions of the protocols. There also exist many extensions provided by third parties that can greatly enhance the capabilities and functions of your electronic messaging programs. We go over a few in the next section.

Extending the Capability to Your JavaMail API

The JavaMail API was designed to be as extensible as possible. Other protocols not supplied with WebLogic Server 8.1, such as the POP3 or the Network News Transfer Protocol (NNTP), can be implemented through various third-party providers.

The POP3 protocol in particular is a commonly used protocol not included in JavaMail version 1.1.3 and subsequently WebLogic Server 8.1. If you want to use it, you have three options: upgrade your JavaMail API to the latest version (recommended), use the Sun POP3 extension, or install a third-party extension.

Upgrading Your JavaMail API Version

If you're going to be using the POP3 protocol, I recommend you upgrade the JavaMail API to version 1.3. Users have reported bugs with certain methods of the POP3 extension, and because it's just as simple to upgrade the entire API as it is to add an extension, you might as well get the whole package with all its other enhancements. The following steps outline the procedure:

1. Download the latest JavaMail package (version 1.3 as of this writing) from Sun at:

   `http://java.sun.com/products/javamail/index.html`

   The JavaMail package is delivered as a Zip file, such as `javamail-1_3.zip` for version 1.3.

2. Extract the contents of the `javamail-1_3.zip` file to a temporary directory. This will create a `/javamail-1.3` subdirectory.

3. In the `/javamail-1.3` directory is the `mail.jar` file, which contains the class files for the API. This is the file you'll set in your WebLogic startup classpath. It can be referenced from anywhere on your hard drive, but to keep things organized, I recommend saving it to the same directory as your other WebLogic class files:

   `C:/bea/weblogic81/server/lib`

4. The final step is to reference the new package in your WebLogic startup classpath. This can be done in the `setWLSEnv.cmd` script that sets your environment (recommended), or the `StartWLS.cmd` script that starts WebLogic Server. Both scripts are located in WebLogic's binary directory:

   ```
   C:/bea/weblogic81/server/bin
   ```

   The `set CLASSPATH` statement in my `setWLSEnv.cmd` file looks like the following:

   ```
   set CLASSPATH=
   ➥%JAVA_HOME%\lib\tools.jar;
   ➥%WL_HOME%\server\lib\mail.jar;
   ➥%WL_HOME%\server\lib\weblogic_sp.jar;
   ➥%WL_HOME%\server\lib\weblogic.jar;
   ➥%WL_HOME%\server\lib\webservices.jar;
   ➥%CLASSPATH%
   ```

CAUTION

Make sure that `mail.jar` is referenced *before* `weblogic.jar` and `weblogic_sp.jar` in your `set CLASSPATH` statement! When an application program is searching the classpath for a JavaMail class, it will look in the `mail.jar` file first (holding JavaMail API version 1.3 classes) before the `weblogic.jar` file (holding JavaMail API version 1.1.3 classes).

Installing the Sun POP3 Extension

Sun provides a free extension to bring POP3 capability to JavaMail API versions 1.1.3 and earlier. If you have an aversion to upgrading your JavaMail API but want to use POP3, this is your next best option. The installation procedure is similar to that of upgrading the API:

1. Download the POP3 extension from Sun at `http://java.sun.com/products/javamail/pop3.html`. From there, you can obtain the package as a Zip file, `pop31_1_1.zip`.

2. Extract the contents of the `pop31_1_1.zip` file to a temporary directory. This will create the subdirectory `/pop3-1.1.1`.

3. In the `/pop3-1.1.1` directory is the `pop3.jar` file, which contains the class files for the POP3 provider. This is the file you will set in your WebLogic startup classpath. It can be referenced from anywhere on your hard drive, but to keep things organized, I recommend saving it to the same directory as your other WebLogic class files:

   ```
   C:/bea/weblogic81/server/lib
   ```

4. Finally, reference the `pop3.jar` file in your classpath. This can be done in the `setWLSEnv.cmd` script that sets your environment (recommended), or the `StartWLS.cmd` script that starts WebLogic Server. Both scripts are located in WebLogic binary directory:

   ```
   C:/bea/weblogic81/server/bin
   ```

   Add this `pop3.jar` before WebLogic Server libraries. The `set CLASSPATH` statement will resemble the following:

   ```
   set CLASSPATH=.;%JAVA_HOME%\lib\tools.jar;
   ➥%WL_HOME%\server\lib\pop3.jar;
   ➥%WL_HOME%\server\lib\weblogic.jar;%CLASSPATH%
   ```


Installing Third-Party Extensions

JavaMail extensions are constantly being developed by third parties to enhance and extend Java's email capabilities. Such extensions include support for Network News Transfer Protocol, additional MIME support, and JMS-to-email bridges, to name but a few. Sun maintains a list of third-party products on its Web site at

```
http://java.sun.com/products/javamail/Third_Party.html
```

The installation procedure for these extensions varies with each product, but most involve downloading the extension class files and making them available to the WebLogic startup classpath, as in the previous sections. Refer to the specific product you want to implement.

JavaBeans Activation Framework

Regardless of which JavaMail API version you use, they all require the JavaBeans Activation Framework (JAF) standard extension, which is now included in WebLogic Server 8.1 (`javax.activation`). The JAF gives your email applications the capability to recognize, display, and/or manipulate various types of MIME data, such as HTML pages and JPEG files. You don't really need to know how the API works because it's auto-enabled by the JavaMail API, but here are a few of the high-level details.

The framework provides classes that add MIME-type support to your applications. This is done by determining the type of an arbitrary piece of data, encapsulating access to it, discovering the operations available on it, and instantiating the appropriate bean to perform operations on it. For example, if an email application receives a message containing a JPEG image, the JAF enables the email application to identify that stream of data as an JPEG image, and from that type, the application can locate and instantiate an object that can manipulate or view that image.

Core Classes of the JavaMail API

The JavaMail API contains four packages: `javax.mail`, `javax.mail.event`, `javax.mail.internet`, and `javax.mail.search`, although all the core classes are found in the top-level `javax.mail` package.

The following sections outline the core classes of the `javax.mail` package.

Session

A `Session` object is both an object factory and a connection to the mail providers. It provides a hook on the security functionality, and is used to access the other objects of the mail API. The `Session` class is used to define a basic mail session and it's through the `Session` object that everything else works. You can use an instance of the `java.util.Properties` class to get information such as the mail server's name, the username, and the password. Setting up a Mail Session in the Administration Console creates an instance of the `javax.mail.session` class that you can use in all of your email components through a JNDI lookup (more about this in the next section).

Message

The `Message` class is an abstract class used to define a basic email message. It's used to set the recipient, subject, and content.

Address

The `Address` class is an abstract class used to define an email address. You'll most often use the subclass `InternetAddress` to define the recipients and senders.

Transport

The `Transport` class is an abstract class used to send messages via the SMTP protocol.

Authenticator

The `Authenticator` class is an abstract class used to obtain authentication to an SMTP host that requests it.

Store

The `Store` class is an abstract class that represents an email store. It's used to store and retrieve messages based on that store's protocol. The JavaMail API 1.1.3 implements the IMAP4 protocol, whereas later versions implement the IMAP4 and POP3 protocols.

Folder

The `Folder` class is an abstract class that represents a folder for mail messages.

JavaMail and WebLogic Server

The second half of this chapter focuses specifically with using JavaMail with WebLogic Server. We look first at configuring your WebLogic Server to use JavaMail, and then look at the details of building, sending, and receiving messages, and developing your own JavaMail applications.

Configuring WebLogic Server with a Mail Session

When writing email applications or components, you have a choice as to how you are going to define your `Session` object:

- You can create a new `Session` object and set all the session properties into the body of the code or in initialization parameters.
- You can create and define a Mail Session with the Administration Console. This is a universal `javax.mail.Session` object and is made available via a JNDI lookup to an email component that needs it.

Creating and using a WebLogic Server Mail Session greatly simplifies the construction and maintenance of mail applications and is the method we'll use in our examples. By configuring the Mail Session in WebLogic, you don't have to code the session parameters in the body of the code (or in servlet or EJB initialization parameters). You can make changes to the Mail Session's parameters on the fly within the Administration Console. Using a single Mail Session object also lowers overhead by removing the need to create a new Mail Session object for each client.

The following steps walk you through creating and configuring a Mail Session in the Administration Console:

1. Start WebLogic Server for the domain in which you're developing a JavaMail application.
2. Start the Administration Console.
3. In the Administration Console, click the Mail node in the left panel. The Mail Sessions page is displayed in the right panel, as shown in Figure 13.1.
4. Click the link to Configure a New Mail Session. The Create a new MailSession page is displayed, as shown in Figure 13.2.
5. Complete the form in the right panel, as shown in Figure 13.3.
    - In the Name field, enter a name for the new session. For illustrative purposes, we retain the default name and call this MyMail Session.
    - In the JNDIName field, enter a name that will be used as a JNDI lookup name. We call this MyMailSession (no spaces).

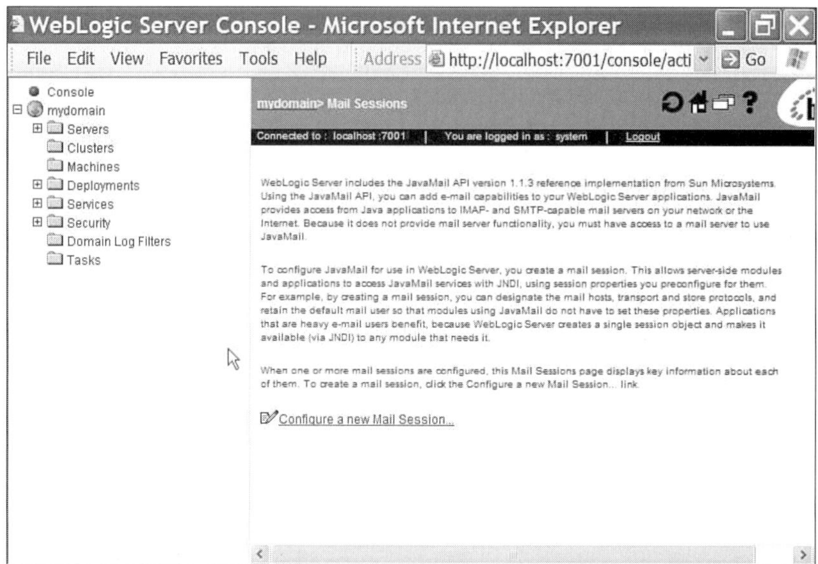

Figure 13.1 The Mail Session introduction page.

- In the Properties field, you may enter any properties to override the default settings of the JavaMail API. In the example, I've overridden the default store protocol IMAP to POP, with the statement `mail.transport.protocol=pop`. I'll also add the statement `mail.debug=true`, which will override the `false` setting and show JavaMail events in the WebLogic Server command window display.

NOTE

A complete list of the Mail Session property fields, their descriptions, key examples, and default values are listed in the following section.

NOTE

To use the POP protocol, you must have installed the POP3 extension or upgraded your JavaMail API to version 1.3, as previously explained in this chapter. Otherwise, leave the section blank to use the default IMAP protocol that comes with the `weblogic.jar` installation package. Click the Create button.

6. Finally, you must apply the Mail Session to a target server. Select the server myserver and click the Apply button as shown in Figure 13.4.

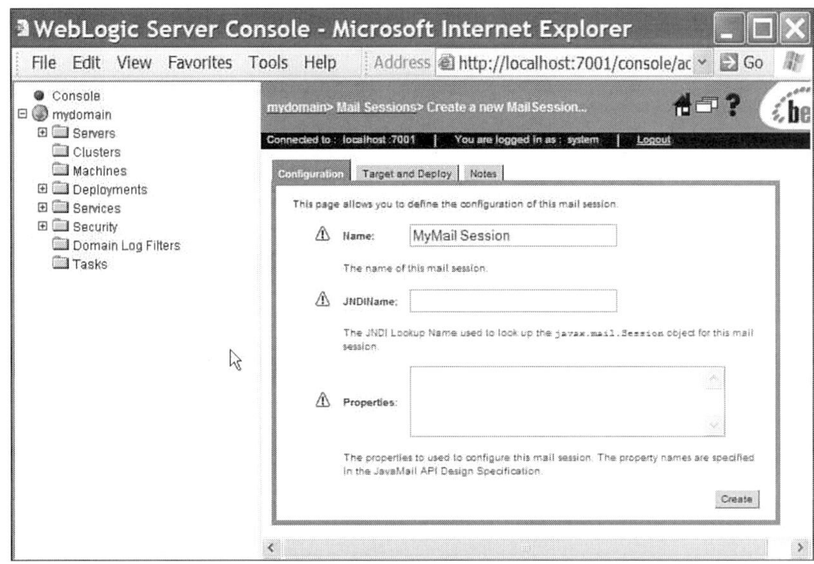

Figure 13.2 Enter the properties for your new Mail Session in the Create a New MailSession page.

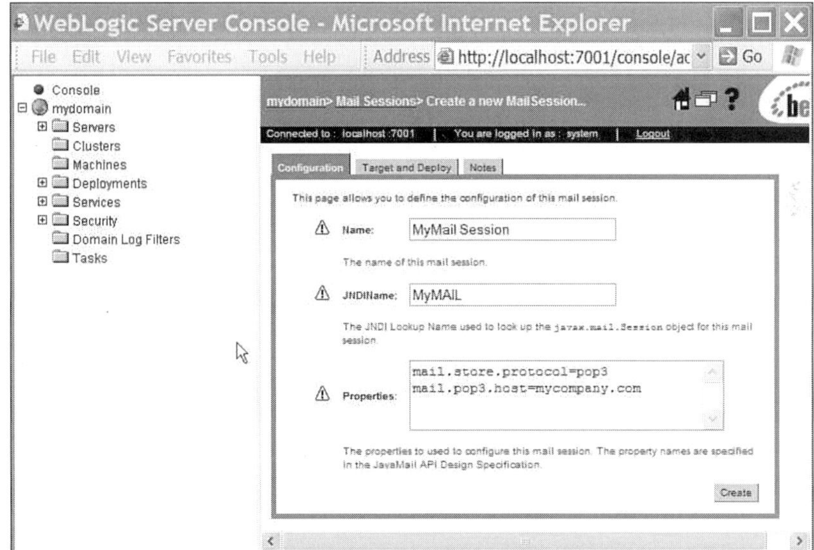

Figure 13.3 The completed Mail Session parameters page, which sets the store protocol as POP.

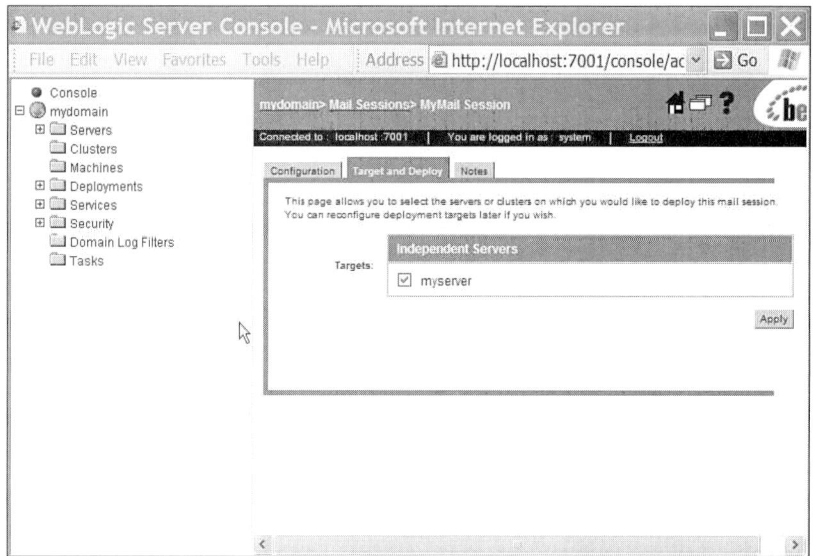

Figure 13.4 Assign the Mail Session to a server.

The new Mail Session, MyMail Session, is displayed under the Mail icon in the left panel. Clicking on the Mail Session icon in the left panel displays the configuration information in the right panel, as shown in Figure 13.5.

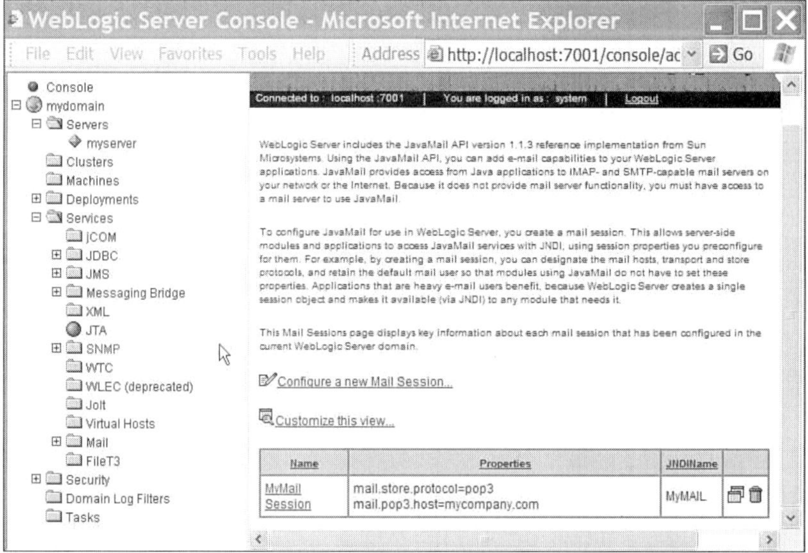

Figure 13.5 The MyMail Session page confirms all the configuration parameters for the MyMail Session Mail Session.

Mail Session Properties

The Mail Session object has default settings for all of its properties. This section outlines the more commonly used Mail Session properties that you can override when defining your own Mail Session object. An example will be provided, along with the default setting:

- `mail.host`—Name the mail server host machine.

  Example: `mail.host=myserver`

  Default value: Name of the local machine, such as localhost

- `mail.store.protocol`—Specify the mail store (retrieval) protocol.

  Example: `mail.store.protocol=pop`

  Default value: `IMAP`

- `mail.transport.protocol`—Specify the mail transport (send) protocol.

  Example: `mail.transport.protocol=smtp`

  Default value: `SMTP`

- `mail.user`—Name the default user for retrieving email.

  Example: `mail.user=postmaster`

  Default value: The value of the `user.name` Java system property

- `mail.`*`protocol`*`.host`—Specify the mail host for a specific protocol. For instance, you can set different mail services for your SMTP host and your IMAP host.

  Examples: `mail.smtp.host=smtp.mail.yahoo.com` and `mail.imap.host=localhost`

  Default value: The value of the `mail.host` property, such as `localhost`

- `mail.`*`protocol`*`.user`—Specify the username associated with a specific protocol for logging into a mailer server.

  Examples: `mail.smtp.user=myyahoousername` and `mail.imap.user=weblogic`

  Default value: The default value of the `mail.user` property

There are other Mail Session properties as well. Please refer to the following links for an exhaustive list:

- `http://java.sun.com/products/javamail/1.3/docs/javadocs/overview-summary.html`
- `http://java.sun.com/products/javamail/1.3/docs/javadocs/com/sun/mail/imap/package-summary.html`
- `http://java.sun.com/products/javamail/1.3/docs/javadocs/com/sun/mail/pop3/package-summary.html`

13

- http://java.sun.com/products/javamail/1.3/docs/javadocs/com/sun/mail/smtp/package-summary.html

Creating Email Components

Now that we've created and configured a Mail Session object to be used with our WebLogic Server installation, we can get into the business of creating email components that can send, retrieve, forward, and authenticate messages, and utilize attachments.

NOTE

All the examples presuppose that you've already configured a Mail Session in the Administration Console.

Sending Messages

Sending an email message in a WebLogic Server application involves three main steps:

1. Getting the mail session
2. Constructing the message
3. Sending the message

The following will walk you through each of these steps in putting together a simple program that sends a message with the SMTP protocol.

First, we must import the packages for JavaMail, JAF, and JNDI:

```
import javax.activation.*;
import javax.mail.*;
import javax.mail.internet.*;
import javax.naming.*;
```

Next, we obtain a `Session` object. There are two ways to do this. The first way is using the WebLogic Mail Session via JNDI. We'll use the MyMail `Session` object that we created in the previous section. This is done in the body of a `try/catch` block:

```
try{
 InitialContext ctx = new InitialContext();
 Session session = (Session)ctx.lookup("MyMail");
} catch (NamingException ne) {}
```

Please note that `javax.mail.Session` is not serializable. The preceding code is meant only for a server-side component such as a servlet, JSP, or EJB. A standalone Java client will not be able to look up the mail session from the JNDI tree on WebLogic Server. However, a standalone client can create its own `Session` directly, as shown in the following code snippet.

The second way to create a `Session` object is to create it from scratch by using the static `Session.getInstance()` or `Session.getDefaultInstance()` method. This can be used when no `Session` objects are declared in the server configuration or a standalone client uses JavaMail without using WebLogic Server. The following sample code snippet shows the usage for a standalone client that does not access the JNDI tree on WebLogic server:

```
Properties env = new Properties();
String host = "myCompany.com";
String username = "user";
String password = "pwd";
String protocol = "smtp";
env.put("mail.store.protocol", protocol);
env.put("mail.smtp.host", host);
Session session = Session.getInstance(env);
```

After we have the `Session`, we can construct a message to send. We'll create an instance of a subclass of the `Message` class: the `MimeMessage` class. The new `MimeMessage` is created by using its constructor and passing it in the current Mail Session object:

```
Message message = new MimeMessage(session);
```

Next we'll define some attributes for the message. The new Mail Message object is empty until we define its attributes, such as its subject, recipient, sender, and content.

To add the subject of the message, we use the `setSubject` method:

```
message.setSubject("Mail sent through Java Mail" );
```

Next we add the recipient of the message with the `addRecipient` method. This method takes a `Message.RecipientType` object and an `Address` object. The `Message.RecipientType` object can be `TO`, `CC` (carbon copy), or `BCC` (blind carbon copy), which are given as:

```
Message.RecipientType.TO
Message.RecipientType.CC
Message.RecipientType.BCC
```

In our example, we'll define two recipients: a `TO` and a `CC`. Recipients are defined by their email addresses, and these email addresses are given as a subclass of the `Address` class. So, before we can add the recipients, we must create objects that represent the recipients and then assign the recipient types.

The subclass of the Address class used to define email addresses is InternetAddress. To create a new instance of the InternetAddress class, we pass it one or two parameters to its constructor: a string of the actual email address and (optionally) a string that represents the name associated with the email address. The following code snippet creates two Address objects—one that will be for our message recipient type TO, and another that will be for the CC:

```
Address address1 = new
➥InternetAddress("wkidd@adventuregalley.com", "William Kidd");

Address address2 = new
➥InternetAddress("sbonnet@revenge.com", "Stede Bonnet");
```

Now that we've created the Address objects, we can go back and add them to our Message object with the addRecipient method:

```
message.addRecipient(Message.RecipientType.TO, address1);
message.addRecipient(Message.RecipientType.CC, address2);
```

If your application has a large number of recipients, the addRecipient method conveniently accepts an array of Address objects. The following code snippet defines a number of To recipients from the Address array spamlist:

```
Address [] spamlist = new Address[]( { address1, address2 } );
setRecipients(Message.RecipientType.TO, spamlist);
```

Now that we've defined to whom we're sending the message, we'll define who the message is from. The From is also defined by an InternetAddress object, and we'll pass it to the MimeMessage object's setFrom method. The following code snippet will create an Address object to be used as our From, and will then pass it to the setFrom method:

```
Address fromAddress = new
➥InternetAddress("broberts@royalfortune.com", "Black Bart");
message.setFrom(fromAddress);
```

If you want to show multiple From addresses, you can pass an array of Address objects to the addFrom method, as in the following:

```
Address spammersgroup[] = {fromAddress1, fromAddress2};
message.addFrom(spammersgroup);
```

The last part to constructing our message is to define some content. This is done with the setContent method of the MimeMessage object.

The `setContent` method takes a couple of different parameters, depending on the content of your message. If your message is of one object kind, say either text or an HTML document, you would pass in the content object as the first parameter, followed by a string describing the MIME type. For instance:

```
message.setContent("Hello dude!", "text/plain");
```

NOTE

The MIME type is used to help the client recognize and handle the attachment. The content of the `text/plain` type is usually displayed within the body of the client's email application. Other popular MIME types are `text/html` and `image/gif`. These are usually sent as attachments, which, depending on the client's associations, will open up in a browser or a graphic application when clicking on them. We'll see later how these MIME types can be defined to show up in the body of the email message, rather than as attachments.

A list of MIME media types can be found at `http://www.ltsw.se/knbase/internet/mime.htp`.

However, if your message consists of multiple parts, say a body of text, as well as an attachment, you must set the content with those body parts. This is done by creating a `MultiPart` object, which is a container for all the body parts, and then passing it to the `setContent` method. Let's look at an example to demonstrate this. We'll create a message that consists of a body of text and an attached JPEG file.

First, let's create objects for our two body parts. This is done by defining a subclass of the abstract `BodyPart` object, `MimeBodyPart`, as in the following:

```
BodyPart bp1 = new MimeBodyPart();
BodyPart bp2 = new MimeBodyPart();
```

To define the content of our `MimeBodyPart`, we can use its `setContent` method much like the `setContent` method of the `MimeMessage` object used for single-part messages.

Let's define the first body part as some text, as in the following:

```
bp1.setContent("Hello world.", "text/plain");
```

NOTE

There is a shortcut method you can substitute if the body part consists of plain text: the `setText` method (which you can also use with the `MimeMessage` object). You just pass in a string to `setText`, as in the following example:

```
bp1.setText("Hello world.");
```

Now let's define the second body part as a JPEG file attachment. To use an attachment, we must make use of the DataSource and DataHandler objects. These are two of those helper classes from the JavaBeans Activation Framework that are used to recognize and define how to handle different types of files. We don't need to go into the details of how each works to use them in our example, other than to say that they help to define and handle the attachment. Because our JPEG is a file, we'll use the file subclass FileDataSource and pass in the name of the file, vacation.jpg, as a string:

```
DataSource ds = new FileDataSource("vacation.jpg");
bp2.setDataHandler(new DataHandler(ds));
bp2.setFileName("vacation.jpg");
```

We have our two body parts, bp1 and bp2, which have their content wrapped inside. Recall that the setContent method of our message takes a MultiPart object, so we must first combine our body parts into a single MultiPart. To do so, we'll use the abstract MultiPart's subclass MimeMultiPart, and then add the body parts with the addBodyPart method:

```
MultiPart mp = new MimeMultiPart();
mp.addBodyPart(bp1);
mp.addBodyPart(bp2);
```

The last part to our message construction is to set the content of the message with our MimeMultiPart object, as in the following:

```
message.setContent(mp);
```

Our message is now completely defined and ready to send.

The Transport object is used to send messages. This is simply done by passing the message object to the send method, as in the following:

```
Transport.send(message);
```

A NOTE ABOUT JSP EXAMPLES IN THIS CHAPTER

In a Web application, JSPs should be concerned primarily with the GUI code. You'll notice that we've used JSP examples in the following examples to send and receive mails using JavaMail. We used JSPs instead of servlets/EJBs because they're easier to debug and modify. You can change code on the fly and refresh the page in your learning environment. However, as mentioned earlier, this should not be done in production code.

And those are the basics of creating and sending your bare-bones message. Altogether, our simple text message-sending program is shown in Listing 13.1.

LISTING 13.1 jspMailSender.jsp

```
<%@ page contentType="text/html;charset=UTF-8" language="java" %>
<%@ page import="javax.activation.*" %>
<%@ page import="javax.mail.*" %>
<%@ page import="javax.naming.*" %>
<%@ page import="javax.mail.internet.*" %>
<%
String host = "myCompany.com";
String username = "user";
String password = "pwd";
String protocol = "smtp";
String mailLookUp = "MyMail";
InitialContext ic = new InitialContext();
javax.mail.Session lookupMailSession = (javax.mail.Session)
          ➥ic.lookup(mailLookUp);

Properties env = new Properties();
env.put("mail.store.protocol", protocol);
env.put("mail.smtp.host", host);
javax.mail.Session mailSession= lookupMailSession.getInstance(env);

 Message message = new MimeMessage(mailSession);
//set the subject
message.setSubject("Mail sent through Java Mail");

//Construct and set the recipient addresses
Address address1 = new InternetAddress("wkidd@adventuregalley.com",
                    ➥"William Kidd");
Address address2 = new InternetAddress("sbonnet@revenge.com", "Stede Bonnet");

message.addRecipient(Message.RecipientType.TO, address1);
message.addRecipient(Message.RecipientType.CC, address2);

//construct and set the sender address
Address fromAddress = new InternetAddress("author@myCompany.com",
          ➥"Gurpreet Singh Bhasin");
message.setFrom(fromAddress);

//set the content of the message
 message.setContent("Hello dude!", "text/plain");
```

LISTING 13.1 Continued

```
//send the message
Transport.send(message);
%>
<html>
<HEAD>
<TITLE>Mailer
</TITLE></HEAD>
<BODY bgcolor=white TOPMARGIN="0" LEFTMARGIN="0" RIGHTMARGIN="0" MARGINWIDTH="0"
   ➥MARGINHEIGHT="0">
</BODY>
</html>
```

Listing 13.2 is a standalone JavaMail client. Note that in this listing no attempt is made to look up the JNDI tree.

LISTING 13.2 MailSender.java

```
/**
 * @author Gurpreet Singh Bhasin
 */

import java.util.*;
import javax.activation.*;
import javax.mail.*;
import javax.mail.internet.*;

public class MailSender {

  public static void main(String[] args) {
    try {
      Properties env = new Properties();
      String host = "myCompany.com";
      String username = "user";
      String password = "pwd";
      String protocol = "smtp";

      env.put("mail.store.protocol", protocol);
      env.put("mail.smtp.host", host);
      Session session = Session.getInstance(env);

      Message message = new MimeMessage(session);
      //set the subject
```

LISTING 13.2 Continued

```
      message.setSubject("Mail sent through Java Mail");
      Address address1 =
               new InternetAddress(
                 "wkidd@adventuregalley.com",
                 "William Kidd");

      Address address2 =
               new InternetAddress("sbonnet@revenge.com",
➥"Stede Bonnet");

      //construct and set the recipient addresses

      message.addRecipient(Message.RecipientType.TO, address1);
      message.addRecipient(Message.RecipientType.CC, address2);

      //construct and set the sender address
      Address fromAddress =
                new InternetAddress(
                  "author@myCompany.com",
                  "Gurpreet Singh Bhasin");

      message.setFrom(fromAddress);

      //set the content of the message
      message.setContent("Hello, dude!", "text/plain");

      //send the message
      Transport.send(message);
    } catch (Exception e) {
      System.out.println("Exception......");
      e.printStackTrace();
    }
  }
}
```

Retrieving Messages

Now that we know how to construct and send messages, let's take a look at retrieving messages. Retrieving an email message in a WebLogic Server application involves four main steps:

1. Getting the mail session
2. Connecting to the appropriate store
3. Opening the appropriate folder
4. Fetching the messages

The following walks you through each of these steps in putting together a simple program that retrieves messages from a POP server with the POP3 protocol.

NOTE

This example presupposes that the user has installed the POP3 extension or has upgraded to JavaMail 1.3.

First, we must import the packages for JavaMail, JAF, and JNDI:

```
import java.util.*;
import javax.activation.*;
import javax.mail.*;
import javax.mail.internet.*;
import javax.naming.*;
```

Next, we get the mail session via JNDI. This is done in the body of a `try/catch` block:

```
try{
 InitialContext ctx = new InitialContext();
 Session lookupMailSession = (Session)ctx.lookup("MyMail");
} catch (NamingException ne) {}
```

As with sending messages, if you need to override any properties defined in the WebLogic Mail Session, create a `Properties` object and add the properties you want to override. Then call the `getInstance` method to get a new `Session` object with the new properties, such as:

```
Properties env = new Properties();
String host = "mycompany.com";
String username = "userName";
String password = "pwd";
String protocol = "pop3";
env.put("mail.store.protocol", protocol);
env.put("mail.pop3.host", host);
Session session = Session.getInstance(env);
```

After we have the Mail Session, we can make a connection to the Store object with the getStore method:

```
Store store = session.getStore();
```

NOTE

The appropriate mail protocol for our server is passed to the Store, behind the scenes, from our Mail Session.

To connect to the store server, we call the connect method from the Store's parent class Service. Authenticating to the store is done by passing in the parameters for the mail-host, username, and password as String values, such as

```
store.connect(host, username, password);
```

where *host* is the name of the POP3 server, *username* is the username, and *password* is the password associated with that username.

Next, we connect to the default Folder object. In the case of POP mail, there's only one default folder, INBOX:

```
Folder folder = folder.getFolder("INBOX");
```

NOTE

As opposed to POP3, IMAP enables you to connect to any server folder you've created. Multiple clients can access the same mail folder on the server using IMAP. When mail messages are deleted by a client, they're no longer available on the server. Therefore, other clients cannot access them. The folder must be opened in READ_WRITE mode to be able to delete mails on the server. The following code snippet shows how to delete mail on the server:

```
Folder folder = folder.getFolder("INBOX");
Folder.open(FOLDER.READ_WRITE);
Message[] messages = folder.getMessages();
For (int count=0; count <messages.length, count++){
  Messages[i].setFlag(Flags.Flag.DELETED, true);
}
```

Next, we use the Folder's getMessages method to fetch the messages into an array of Message objects:

```
Message[] messages = folder.getMessages();
```

NOTE

With IMAP, you can use the Folder's `getNewMessageCount` method to return the number of new messages.

Now that we have our messages, we can perform operations on each, such as picking out the headers, content, subject, and to and from fields, and display them in some meaningful manner. For instance, the `Message` object's `getFrom` method returns the sender (as an array of `Address` objects), and the `getSubject` method returns the subject line of the message:

```
for (int i = 0, n = message.length; i < n; i++) {
  System.out.println(i + ": "+ message[i].getFrom()[0]
    + "\t" + message[i].getSubject());
}
```

Those are the basics of retrieving messages from a store. To finish up, remember to close the connection and resources:

```
folder.close(false);
store.close();
```

Altogether, our message-retrieval program is a JSP shown in Listing 13.3.

LISTING 13.3 jspMailReceiver.jsp

```
<%@ page contentType="text/html;charset=UTF-8" language="java" %>
<%@ page import="javax.activation.*" %>
<%@ page import="javax.mail.*" %>
<%@ page import="javax.naming.*" %>
<%
String host = "mycompany.com";
String username = "userName";
String password = "pwd";
String jndiMailName = "MyMail";
String protocol="pop3";
InitialContext ic = new InitialContext();
javax.mail.Session lookupMailSession = (javax.mail.Session)
          ➥ic.lookup(jndiMailName);

Store store = lookupMailSession.getStore("pop3");
store.connect(host, username, password);
Folder folder = store.getFolder("INBOX");
folder.open(Folder.READ_ONLY);
```

LISTING 13.3 Continued

```
// Get directory
Message message[] = folder.getMessages();
for (int i = 0, n = message.length; i < n; i++) {
  out.println(i+ ": " + message[i].getFrom()[0]
    + "\t" + message[i].getSubject());
  out.println("<br>");
}
// Close connection
folder.close(false);
store.close();
%>

<html>
<HEAD>
<TITLE>Mailer
</TITLE></HEAD>
<BODY bgcolor=white TOPMARGIN="0" LEFTMARGIN="0" RIGHTMARGIN="0"
   ➥MARGINWIDTH="0" MARGINHEIGHT="0">
</BODY>
</html>
```

We also list Java code to retrieve mail without using a JNDI tree. The source is as shown in Listing 13.4.

LISTING 13.4 MailReceiver.java

```
/**
 * @author Gurpreet Singh Bhasin
 */

import java.util.*;
import javax.activation.*;
import javax.mail.*;

public class MailReceiver {

  public static void main(String[] args) {
    try {
        Properties env = new Properties();
        String host = "mycompany.com";
        String username = "userName";
```

LISTING 13.4 Continued

```
        String password = "pwd";
        String protocol = "pop3";
        env.put("mail.store.protocol", protocol);
        env.put("mail.pop3.host", host);
        Session session = Session.getInstance(env);
        Store store = session.getStore(protocol);
        store.connect(host, username, password);
        Folder folder = store.getFolder("INBOX");
        folder.open(Folder.READ_ONLY);

        // Get directory
        Message message[] = folder.getMessages();

        for (int i = 0, n = message.length; i < n; i++) {
          System.out.println(i + ": " + message[i].getFrom()[0]
            + "\t" + message[i].getSubject());
        }

        // Close connection
        folder.close(false);
        store.close();

    } catch (Exception e) {
      System.out.println("Exception...............");
      e.printStackTrace();
    }
  }
}
```

User Authentication

Many SMTP servers require authentication to be able to send mail. If this is the case with your SMTP service provider, you must create and use your own authenticating mail session. To do this, we must make use of our own authentication object. The JavaMail API provides the abstract class `Authenticator` for just such purposes. The `Authenticator` defines a `getPasswordAuthentication` callback method, which when called by the session, returns a `PasswordAuthentication` object that's used by the session to authenticate against the SMTP host. The `PasswordAuthentication` object is itself just a wrapper for the username and password strings.

So, the first thing we must do is to create and define our own subclass of `Authenticator`. The session will use its `getPasswordAuthentication` method to return the username and password as strings wrapped in a `PasswordAuthentication` object. How do we get the username and password? The easiest thing to do is to pop up a little Swing pop-up box that takes both inputs delimited by a comma. Listing 13.5 defines a subclass of the `Authenticator` class, `UserAuthenticator.java`, which does this.

LISTING 13.5 UserAuthenticator.java

```
import javax.mail.*;
import javax.swing.*;
import java.util.*;

public class UserAuthenticator extends Authenticator
{
  private String username;
  private String password;

  public void setUser(String user)
  {
    username = user;
  }

  public String getUsername()
  {
    return username;
  }

  public void setPassword(String pword)
  {
    password = pword;
  }

  public String getPassword()
  {
    return password;
  }

  public PasswordAuthentication getPasswordAuthentication()
  {
    String input= JOptionPane.showInputDialog("Enter 'username,password'");
    StringTokenizer st = new StringTokenizer(input, ",");
    username = st.nextToken();
    password = st.nextToken();

    return new PasswordAuthentication(username, password);
  }
}
```

When the session calls the `getPasswordAuthentication` method to get the `PasswordAuthentication` object, a Swing pop-up box that looks like the one in Figure 13.6 is displayed to the user.

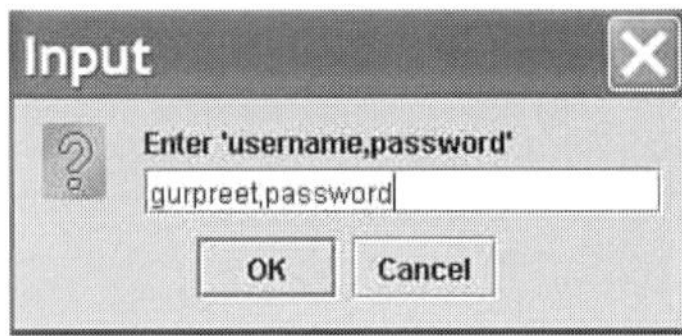

Figure 13.6 Authentication Pop-up box.

Okay, now that we have our authentication object, we can use it to create our authenticating mail session. We first define the environment properties of the session, and then create an instance of our authentication object, as in the following code snippet:

```
Properties env = new Properties();
env.put("mail.pop3.host", host);
Authenticator auth = new UserAuthenticator();
```

We can then create the mail session by passing the subclass object to the `getDefaultInstance` method of the `Session`:

```
Session session = Session.getDefaultInstance(env, auth);
```

When authentication is required, the session will invoke the `getPasswordAuthentication` method on the subclass. The pop-up is displayed, the username and password strings are submitted, and a `PasswordAuthentication` object is returned.

Please note that there is a another method to get an instance of a `Session` object, `getInstance()`, which takes the same arguments as the `getDefaultInstance()` method. The `getInstance()` method always gets a *new* instance of the `Session` object based on the parameters. On the other hand, the `getDefaultInstance()` method gets the default `Session` object. If no `Session` object exists, a new session is created and set as default.

Also note that the default `Session` object can contain security information pertaining to the session. Therefore, access to it is controlled. The `Authenticator` object passed as a parameter is used indirectly to validate access to the default `Session` object. On subsequent calls to the `getDefaultInstance()` method, the `Authenticator` object is compared to the `Authenticator` object passed in the very first time the method was invoked. Only if both objects are same or are loaded from the same class loader is the default `Session` object accessible.

Also beware that passing a null `Authenticator` object the first time while calling `getDefaultInstance()` leaves the door open for anyone to get access to the default

Session object. The current example just shows how to create a mail session. In the real world, caution must be observed when creating default Session objects.

After we have authentication, we can finally connect to the store:

```
Store store = session.getStore("pop3");
store.connect();
```

Replying to Messages

Before you can reply to a message, it's assumed that you've already established a mail session and have a retrieved message to which you're replying. The reply then involves the following steps:

1. Create a reply message object.
2. Define the subject, sender, and message body. You may add recipients, too.
3. Send the message.

We'll use the retrieved message to help create our reply message. Assume that the name of the retrieved object message is receivedMsg. A call to receivedMsg's reply method returns another Message object, but one in which the subject is set to the original message's but prefixed with Re:, and the To value is equal to the original message's From value. Other than that, the new reply message will be empty. We must still assign the From value and set the content. The following code snippet creates a new MimeMessage object replyMsg to illustrate this:

```
MimeMessage replyMsg = (MimeMessage)receivedMsg.reply(false);
```

NOTE

Note that we passed in a boolean parameter of false to the reply method, which indicates that we just want to reply to the sender. A true value would indicate a reply to all.

Okay, so now we have our empty reply message. Next, we'll use the setFrom method to set the From field. The setFrom method takes an InternetAddress object, which we can define in the parameter:

```
reply.setFrom(new InternetAddress(jrackham@treasure.com,
➥"Calico Jack"));
```

NOTE

It's interesting to note that you can set your From to be anything you like, so long as your mail server permits it.

13

To complete the message, we could add text or define some body parts. For our example, we'll just add some text content:

```
reply.setContent("Avast, ye!", "text/plain");
```

To include the original message, we can use the MimeBodyPart classes. This is covered later in the chapter when we send the input message as part of the reply.

Finally, we can use the Transport object to send our reply message:

```
Transport.send(reply);
```

Forwarding Messages

Forwarding a message is a little like sending a normal message, but we have to capture the content of the original message. Again, before you can reply to a message, it's assumed that you've already established a mail session, and have a retrieved message that you want to forward. The forward operation involves the following steps:

1. Create a forward message object.
2. Define the subject, recipient, and sender.
3. Get the content from the original message.
4. Send the message.

Let the received message be called recievedMessage. First we create a message object to be our forward message, as shown in the following code snippet:

```
Message forwardMsg = new MimeMessage(session);
```

The next step is to define the sender and recipient. The following snippet creates and assigns two InternetAddress objects for a sender and a recipient:

```
Address add1 = new
➥InternetAddress("abonney@treasure.com", "Anne Bonney");

Address add2 = new
➥InternetAddress("ttew@liberty.com", "Thomas Tew");

forwardMsg.addRecipient(Message.RecipientType.TO, add1);
forwardMsg.setFrom(add2);
```

To set our subject, we use the getSubject method on the received message:

```
forwardMsg.setSubject("Fwd: " + receivedMsg.getSubject());
```

> **NOTE**
>
> Note that unlike a message reply, we have to add the Fwd: prefix to the subject ourselves, if wanted.

The next step is to add the content. Content of the forwarding message can consist of the original message and attachments, as well as any additional text or attachments you want to add. Because we're dealing with multiple parts, we'll wrap those parts into `MimeBodyPart` objects, and then wrap those into a single `MultiPart` object, and finally assign the `MultiPart` to the forwarding message. For our example, we'll have two body parts: the first will be our added text message, and the second will be the content of the original message.

First, let's create the body part for our own content:

```
BodyPart addedPart = new MimeBodyPart();
addedPart.setContent("FYI...", "text/plain");
```

Next we capture the original message content into the second body part. The easiest way to do this is use to use the convenient `DataHandler` object from the JavaBeans Activation Framework:

```
BodyPart originalPart = new MimeBodyPart();
originalPart.setDataHandler(receivedMsg.getDataHandler());
```

Now we have our two body parts consisting of our added content and the forwarded content. Next, we'll wrap those into the `MultiPart` container:

```
Multipart multipart = new MimeMultipart();
multipart.addBodyPart(addedPart);
multipart.addBodyPart(originalPart);
```

Next we use the multipart object to the `setContent` method of the forwarding message:

```
forwardMsg.setContent(multipart);
```

Finally, we can send the message:

```
Transport.send(forwardMsg);
```

> **NOTE**
>
> To send the forwarded mail as an attachment, use the following:
>
> ```
> originalPart.setDisposition(Part.ATTACHMENT);
> ```
>
> The `setDisposition()` method is covered a little later in the chapter.

Working with Attachments

In the preceding sections, we introduced attachments by sending an attached JPEG file. Attachments are files associated with messages, such as an image or HTML file or perhaps a Word document.

Files can be embedded into the body of the message content, or may be attached to the message to be detached and saved or opened by another application. The MIME type association of the file helps the client recognize and handle the file.

To illustrate the differences between attaching and embedding, let's take a look at an example. We'll create and send a message with two body parts: a text message and an HTML file.

First, let's define our message object with the appropriate headers:

```
Message message = new MimeMessage(session);
message.setSubject("Visit the friendly South Pacific!");
Address add1 = new InternetAddress("wbligh@bounty.co.uk", "William Bligh");
Address add2 = new InternetAddress("jcook@resolution.co.uk", "James Cook");
message.addRecipient(Message.RecipinetType.TO, add1)
message.setFrom(add2);
```

Now let's build the content of the message. We'll need two body parts: one to hold the text message and one to hold the attached HTML file. Here we create the first body part:

```
BodyPart bp1 = new MimeBodyPart();
bp1.setText("Will return to this friendly island after Alaska.");
```

Next, let's create a second body part that we'll use to wrap the HTML file:

```
BodyPart bp2 = new MimeBodyPart();
```

Before we can wrap the HTML file into the body part, we first need an object of the `File` class that represents the HTML file:

```
File htmlFile = new File("hawaii.html");
```

where `Hawaii.html` is the name of the file we want to attach.

Next we need set a `DataHandler` object for the HTML file. We again turn to the JavaBeans Activation Framework—this time to the `FileDataSource` object, a subclass of `DataSource` that represents a file-based source:

```
FileDataSource fds= new FileDataSource(htmlFile);
DataHandler dh = new DataHandler(fds);
```

Next, pass the DataHandler object to the setDataHandler method of the body part:

```
bp2.setDataHandler(dh);
```

The following sets the filename and description of the attachment in the second body part's header:

```
bp2.setFileName(htmlFile.getName());
bp2.setDescription("Attached file: " + htmlFile.getName());
```

Now that we've completed both of our body parts, we'll wrap them into a MimeMultiPart:

```
MultiPart mp = new MimeMultiPart();
mp.addBodyPart(bp1);
mp.addBodyPart(bp2);
```

Finally the multipart can be added to the message and the message can be sent:

```
message.setContent(mp);
Transport.send(message);
```

The recipient of this message will see the text of the first body part in the body of the email message, and the attached file of second body part will appear, by default, as an outside attachment. The attachment will show the name of the file. Clicking on the attachment on the client side will either invoke the associated program to open the attachment or offer to save the file to a directory.

But what if you want the HTML message to be embedded into the body of the message? To do that, we need to set the disposition of the attachment's body part. The *disposition* determines whether the attachment is to be embedded into the body of the message or attached outside the body. This is done by passing in a String constant of the Part interface to the setDisposition method of the MimeBodyPart class. The Part interface defines the two as follows:

- ATTACHMENT—The part is to be presented as an attachment.
- INLINE—The part is to be presented inline (embedded).

So, to make the HTML page an embedded in the message, use the INLINE parameter:

```
bp2.setDisposition(Part.INLINE);
```

To make the HTML page an external attachment, use the ATTACHMENT parameter (the default, if no disposition is defined):

```
bp2.setDisposition(Part.INLINE);
```

13

JavaMail and the Global Auctions Application

The Global Auctions application makes use of JavaMail's functionality in a utility class that will send out an email to registered users notifying them when they have been outbid, or have won or lost on an item. It may also be used to send error messages to users.

The utility class makes use of the Mail Session configured in the Administration Console (defined earlier in this chapter). The class's constructor takes two parameters: a `String` of the recipient's email address and a `String` for the message.

Creating the AuctionMailer Utility Class

Now, let's get to the business of creating our utility class. In a text editor, create and save a new text file as `AuctionMailer.java`. First we import the classes needed:

```
import java.io.*;
import java.util.*;
import javax.activation.*;
import javax.mail.*;
import javax.mail.internet.*;
import javax.naming.*;
```

The `AuctionMailer`'s constructor takes two `String` parameters representing the recipient's address and the text message:

```
private String to;
private String emailText;

public AuctionMailer(String to, String emailText) {
  this.to = to;
  this.emailText = emailText;
}
```

Our class defines one method, `sendMail`, to send messages. In the body of this method, we'll obtain the Mail Session object via a JNDI lookup, construct our message, and send it out. In the Global Auctions application, the Mail Session's JNDI name is MyMail. The body of the `sendMail` method is done within a `try/catch` block (shown in the complete file contents, later in the chapter):

```
InitialContext ctx = new InitialContext();
Session serverSession = (Session)ctx.lookup("MyMail");
```

Next we pass our environment variables, such as the username, password, and so forth:

```
Properties env = new Properties();
String host = "mycompany.com";
String username = "webMaster";
String password = "pwd";
String protocol = "smtp";
env.put("mail.store.protocol", protocol);
env.put("mail. smtp.host", host);
javax.mail.Session session = serverSession.getInstance(env);
```


Note that this class should be deployed on WebLogic Server and can be called by either a JSP/servlet or an EJB. It cannot be used by a standalone Java client because the `Session` object is not serializable.

Then we'll construct the message and add the recipient with our `toAddress` value:

```
Message message = new MimeMessage(session);
message.setSubject("Message from Global Auctions");
message.addRecipient(Message.RecipientType.TO, toAddress);
```

We'll define and set the sender address:

```
Address fromAddress = new
➥InternetAddress("webmaster@globalauctions.com", "John Doe");
message.setFrom(fromAddress);
```

Here, we set the mail message:

```
message.setContent(emailText, "text/html");
```

Finally, we can send the message:

```
Transport.send(message);
```

Listing 13.6 outlines the entire contents of the `AuctionMailer` utility class.

LISTING 13.6 AuctionMailer.java

```
import java.util.*;
import javax.activation.*;
import javax.mail.*;
import javax.mail.internet.*;
import javax.naming.*;
```

LISTING 13.6 Continued

```
public class AuctionMailer {

  private String to;
  private String emailText;

  public AuctionMailer(String to, String emailText) {
    this.to = to;
    this.emailText = emailText;
  }

  public void sendMail() {
    try {
        Properties env = new Properties();
        String host = "mycompany.com";
        String username = "webMaster";
        String password = "pwd";
        String protocol = "smtp";
        env.put("mail.store.protocol", protocol);
        env.put("mail.smtp.host", host);
        //get passed parameters
        Address toAddress = new InternetAddress(to);

        //get the session
        InitialContext ctx = new InitialContext();
        Session serverSession = (Session) ctx.lookup("MyMail");
        javax.mail.Session session = serverSession.getInstance(env);
        //construct the message
        Message message = new MimeMessage(session);
        message.setSubject("Message from Global Auctions");
        message.addRecipient(Message.RecipientType.TO, toAddress);

        //define and set the sender address
        Address fromAddress =
          new InternetAddress("webmaster@globalauctions.com",
                  ➥"John Doe");
        message.setFrom(fromAddress);
        message.setContent(emailText, "text/html");

        //send the message
        Transport.send(message);
    } catch (NamingException ne) {
      ne.printStackTrace();
```

LISTING 13.6 Continued

```
    } catch (Exception e) {
      e.printStackTrace();
    }
  }
}
```

Summary

In this chapter, we covered the basics of Java's electronic messaging capabilities: sending, retrieving, replying to, and forwarding messages, and using attachments. We also mentioned how JavaMail works in the WebLogic environment and how to configure and use a WebLogic mail session. JavaMail's capabilities can be extended far beyond just sending and retrieving messages. There are add-ons for news protocols, store server protocols, and attachment handlers, just to name a few. You should now have no difficulties in adding email capabilities to your own WebLogic Server applications, and for the entrepreneurial developer this is just the starting point.

PART IV

Using Web Technologies in WebLogic Applications

IN THIS PART

CHAPTER 14

Writing WebLogic Server Servlets

by Saranathan Govindarajan

IN THIS CHAPTER

This chapter describes the key features that make up one of the core J2EE technologies: servlets. Servlets are one of the enabling technologies for Web clients to access server-side applications. They also generate dynamic pages, thereby serving as an efficient server-side functional extension. The integration of servlets with Web clients is based on a synchronous request-response approach. WebLogic Server 8.1 completely supports the servlets specification version 2.3 as defined by Sun Microsystems including the new features such as filters and events.

Servlet 2.3 Specification

The servlet 2.3 specification is a complete and clear explanation of the functions that make up the servlet technology. This is the bible for both developers of servlet containers such as WebLogic Server, and experienced web application developers who want to know the underlying implementation that makes up the servlet technology.

The specifications explain the following key components that form the core of the servlet implementation:

- Servlet container—Also referred to as the *servlet engine*. The servlet container enables request-response services, including decoding and encoding, to the corresponding formats and also manages the servlets configured through its life cycle.
- Servlet interface—The core interface of the Servlet API from which all other servlet types are derived, such as `GenericServlet` and `HttpServlet`.

- Servlet context interface—Web application environment attributes can be obtained through this interface.
- Request object—Encapsulates the user input.
- Response object—Encapsulates the server output back to the client.
- Filtering—Header and content modifier in both the request into and response from a resource. Common usage of filters includes logging, auditing, authentication, data conversion, and so on.
- Application event listener support—This feature enables better state management using `HttpSession` and `ServletContext` objects and also efficiently manages the application interactions with these objects.
- Sessions—Defines state management and implementation approaches for managing user sessions such as cookies and URL rewriting.
- `RequestDispatcher`—Helps forward requests to other servlets or include other servlets' output as part of the response.
- Web application—We went through the concept of Web applications in great detail in Chapters 6, "Introduction to WebLogic Web Applications," and 7, "Deploying Web Applications."
- Deployment descriptor—This depicts the Web application's configuration parameters that define the behavior of the application. It's also the contract between the different teams of the project, such as development, configuration, deployment, and so on.
- Web application security requirements and implementation—Security concepts are of the following types: *Declarative security* includes parameters such as roles and access control lists, which is external to the application and defined in configuration files. *Programmatic security* is defined in the application itself using specific methods defined in the servlet APIs, such as `getRemoteUser()`, `getRemotePrincipal()`, and so forth.

Finally, the specification describes the two core packages, `javax.servlet` and `javax.servlet.http`, that make the servlet implementation and HTTP servlet implementation, respectively. The core interface of the servlet API, `Servlet` is part of the `javax.servlet` package. Among other functions, this interface defines the `service` method for handling the client requests. The `javax.servlet.http` package contains, among other classes, `HttpServlet`, which implements the `Servlet` interface and provides the infrastructure for the Web application clients using HTTP protocol for request-response.

All changes made to the specifications based on the review of the earlier version (Servlet specification v2.2) are documented in the latest version of the specification. For complete reference of the specification, refer to the following Web site: `http://java.sun.com/j2ee/`.

Servlets and Alternatives

Traditional CGI (Common Gateway interface) and other proprietary technologies from Netscape (NSAPI) and Apache are some of the alternatives for extending the functions of the server into the presentation world. Servlets achieve the same basic goal as the other server extension mechanisms listed in Table 14.1, but the advantages of servlets outweigh the features of other alternatives. Some of the advantages are as follows:

- The traditional CGI process model in most Web servers (with the exception of some of them, such as `iTPWebServer` in Tandem platform) starts a new process for every invocation of a function. These are single-threaded processes with no caching abilities because the process is stopped once the service is finished. Servlets can be multithreaded and stay alive inside the Java Virtual Machine, thereby offering many advantages, such as data caching between requests, avoiding creation time for every request call, and more.
- Because servlets use the standard Java API defined in Sun's specification, they run on all leading Web servers that implement the specification with no change in code. In other words, servlets are highly portable.
- A well-defined and extensive API infrastructure and the Java programming language make servlets convenient and easy to use.
- The platform independence provided by the Java language, coupled with features that the specification provides, such as like session tracking, caching, and event filtering, make servlets a powerful server extension mechanism.
- Unlike traditional CGI programs, which were mostly developed as scripts, servlets have a well-defined set of security mechanisms, such as declarative and programmatic security as specified earlier.

14

Table 14.1 lists the alternatives, along with their disadvantages. It gives a better picture of what servlets bring to the table compared to the other options.

TABLE 14.1 Servlet Alternatives

Name	Disadvantages
CGI (Common Gateway Interface)	Performance limitations because it has to start a new process for every function invocation. No state maintenance. Not supported by well-defined API.
SSI (Server-Side Includes)	Simple but not powerful enough to address all dynamic content generation requirements.

TABLE 14.1 Continued

Name	Disadvantages
ISAPI	Implementation limitations because this can be written only in C or a C language derivative. Provides powerful API, but the programmer is responsible for handling all the application's thread requirements. Security is common to all applications running inside an ISAPI application server, making it inflexible.
NSAPI	Proprietary API. Similar to ISAPI, provides powerful API but the programmer is responsible for handling all the application's thread requirements.

Servlet Life Cycle

In this section, we look at the life cycle of the servlet from initialization to destruction and the functions that control it. The core abstract interface of the Servlet API, `Servlet`, defines the life cycle of a servlet using the `init()`, `service()`, and `destroy()` methods. All servlets are direct or indirect implementations of the `Servlet` interface, either through the protocol-independent `GenericServlet` interface or the HTTP protocol-based `HttpServlet`.

Configuration, Loading, and Instantiation

As a servlet container implementing the Sun Servlet specification, WebLogic Server is responsible for loading and instantiating the configured servlets at the user-configured time. The server provides the capability of loading the servlets at server startup time or at the first invocation of a request targeted at the servlet. The optional `load-on-startup` tag of the servlet element defined in the Web application deployment descriptor (`web.xml`) controls the loading sequence of servlets and also determines whether the servlet is to be loaded at startup time. The value of this optional element should be a positive integer indicating the order in which the servlet should be loaded starting with the lowest number. WebLogic Server determines the startup sequence if the value is not a positive integer or is intentionally left blank.

Initialization

Initialization of the servlet object follows the instantiation process defined earlier. WebLogic Server initializes the servlet instance using the `init()` method defined in the `Servlet` interface. This method is used for one-time initialization operations such as reading configuration parameters from a file, opening connections to expensive resources such as databases and legacy systems, and so on.

The `init` method comes in two flavors. The first version of the `init` method takes no arguments. This version is used when the servlet has no configuration parameters to read to initialize some basic settings to be used later. The following code snippet gives an example of such an init method. The servlet init method opens a configuration file and assigns it to a static variable, which may be used elsewhere in the servlet.

```
public void init() {

        try {
            configFile = new File("c:\\wlsunleashed\\config\\appconfig.xml");
            ....
        }
        catch (Exception ex) {
               System.out.println("init() failed:" + ex);
         }
}
```


The second version of the init method takes the ServletConfig object as an argument. The ServletConfig object is a configuration object that has the following functions:

- Aids servlets in accessing name-value configuration parameters defined in the Web application deployment configuration
- Provides access to the ServletContext object, which represents the servlet's runtime environment

The servlet can use the initialization parameters to define database connection properties, log file locations, and much more. The init function in the earlier example can be changed not to hard-code the name and location of the configuration file and instead read the same from the Web deployment descriptor. That version of the init method looks like this:

```
public void init(ServletConfig config) {
        super.init(config);
        // Initialize the class level config variable
        // Can be used later in the processing
        myConfig = config;
        String filename = getInitParameter("configFile");
        try {
            configFile = new File(filename);
            ....
        }
        catch (Exception ex) {
               System.out.println("init() failed:" + ex);
          }
}
```

The super.init is the first call that's made in the init method to ensure that the ServletConfig is registered before it's used. The initialization parameters are defined in the web.xml file as part of the servlet element. The initialization parameters for the earlier code snippet looks like the following:

```
<servlet>
    <servlet-name>InitServlet</servlet-name>
    <servlet-class>wlsunleashed.servlets..InitServlet</servlet-class>
    <init-param>
      <param-name>configFile</param-name>
      <param-value d:\\wlsunleashed\\config\\appconfig.xml </param-value>
    </init-param>
  </servlet>
```

The <init-param> tag defines the parameters that are read using the ServletConfig object passed in the init method. This tag is one of the many ways to initialize an application in the J2EE world. The tag is tied to a particular servlet as defined in the deployment descriptor, so the scope of this tag is limited to the configured servlet.

NOTE

Initialization parameters can be set up in a number of ways depending on the application scope requirements. The init-param is for a single servlet, whereas context-param is for all servlets and env-entry is for all components of the Web application. Additionally, custom properties files can be used to define parameters and read in the application. Also, if the parameters are to be shared to all server instances across the network, JNDI provides a viable option.

At this point, there's one outstanding question that must still be answered. The question that often comes up is, "Should I put my initialization code in init() or the constructor?"

Let's look at a reason why you would use the init() method rather than a constructor. The constructor is called sometime before the init() method is invoked. At the time the constructor is invoked, the container does not know about the initialization parameters that the developer is expecting as part of the servlet instance creation step. The container has to assume that the developer has added the no-argument default constructor that can be used for creating the default instance of the servlet. Any initialization parameters supplied to the servlet using the deployment descriptor will not be available in the constructor using ServletContext. In this case, other mechanisms may be used as noted earlier. This might not be construed as a major limitation, but it is a means of keeping the API and implementation as simple as possible.

Processing

All requests received by the servlet are processed by the servlet's service method using a new thread for every client request. The HttpServlet interface, a subinterface of the Servlet interface, is the most commonly used servlet interface for processing HTTP-based requests. The HttpServlet interface adds specialized methods that are automatically invoked by the service method. Table 14.2 summarizes the list of HTTP request-handling methods defined by this subinterface of Servlet.

TABLE 14.2 HTTPServlet Service Methods

Method Name	Request Type	Description
doDelete	HTTP DELETE requests	Removes a document or Web page from the server
doGet	HTTP GET requests	Handles client service requests (via the service method)
doHead	HTTP HEAD requests	Specialized GET request in which the client requires only the response headers
doOptions	HTTP OPTIONS requests	Determines the HTTP methods that are supported by the WebLogic Server
doPost	HTTP POST requests	Handles client service requests; similar to doGet
doPut	HTTP PUT requests	Used to execute FTP-type operations by allowing clients to place files on the server
doTrace	HTTP Trace requests	Useful in debugging

Unloading the Servlet

When the servlet is unloaded from the Web container, the servlet engine invokes the `destroy` method. This is the last method in the servlet life cycle. The `destroy` method can be used for closing out connections to resources such as databases and legacy applications, freeing up any other resources that can be connected and/or instantiated in the `init` method or later during the life of the servlet.

The `destroy` method does not take an argument. The `destroy` method for the simple servlet referenced earlier can be used to free the context that was initialized in the `init` method:

```
public void destroy() {
  // configFile is the configuration file handler
  // initialized in the init method
   configFile = null;
}
```

Figure 14.1 describes the typical life cycle of the servlet using the simple servlet mentioned earlier.

The programmer has to consider one important point when using the `destroy` method. This method should not be counted as the only mechanism for clean up, saving session data, and so forth because the container controls only this method invocation. Valuable data could be lost if there were a crash of the system or any other fatal error in which the `destroy` method may not be invoked by the container. So, it's prudent to store important data at the earliest possible opportunity and not wait for the `destroy` method.

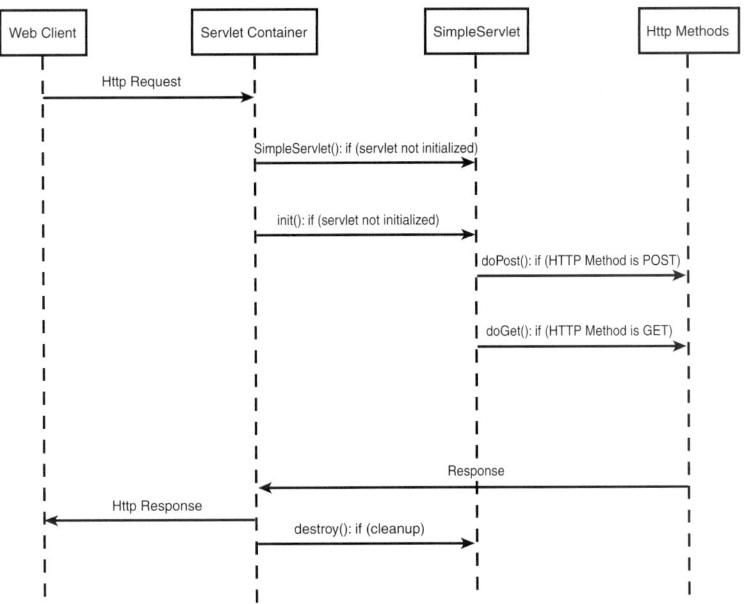

FIGURE 14.1 Servlet life cycle.

Writing Simple Servlets

At this time, we've learned enough to write a simple servlet. As mentioned earlier, the most popular servlet implementation is based on HTTP protocol, and we'll use this servlet type to write our first servlet. At this point, we won't go into details about the `Servlet` interface or the different auxiliary objects and interfaces available for the servlet developer to implement a servlet. We'll stick to the methods we've covered so far as part of the servlet life cycle.

Servlets could very well be used for other purposes, such as FTP, SMTP, and so on. These servers could be implemented using the protocol-independent `GenericServlet` or by directly implementing the `Servlet` interface. But the most important use of servlets is for handling HTTP requests in Web and application servers. `Generic Servlets` and custom implementation of the `Servlet` interface are very rarely done.

First Servlet

The simple servlet takes a string as input, converts it to uppercase letters, and prints it on the browser. Listing 14.1 lists the complete servlet.

LISTING 14.1 Simple Servlet

```
package wlsunleashed.servlets;

import javax.servlet.*;
import javax.servlet.http.*;
import java.io.*;

public class SimpleServlet extends HttpServlet
{
     private String defaultString="HELLO WORLD";

     public void service(HttpServletRequest req, HttpServletResponse res)
        throws IOException
    {

         String convertedString, inputString;

        //read the request parameter INPUT_STRING
       // If the input String is null
       // it returns "hello world" In uppercase

        if ((inputString = req.getParameter("INPUT_STRING"))
            != null) {
            convertedString = inputString.toUpperCase();
        }
        else {
            convertedString =defaultString.toUpperCase() ;
        }

        // Set the content type first
        res.setContentType("text/html");

        // get the PrintWriter
        PrintWriter out = res.getWriter();

        out.println("<html><head><title>SimpleServlet</title></head>");
        out.println("<body>");
        out.println("<h1>");

        out.println("The input string upper case(d):" + convertedString );
        out.println("</h1></body></html>");

    }
}
```

Anatomy of the Simple Servlet

The anatomy covers all the sections of the simple servlet from the package imports to the output of the converted string.

Package Imports

The package imports needed for the basic servlet are the following:

- `javax.servlet`—Defines among other classes; the core of the servlet API–servlet interface
- `javax.servlet.http`—Defines the classes related to the HTTP protocol
- `java.io`—Imports `IOException`, which is thrown in the service-processing methods

The Servlet Class

The `SimpleServlet` class is derived from the base class `HttpServlet`. In this servlet, the service method is used to handle the different kinds of HTTP requests. We'll go over that later in the chapter. All methods except the service method are default implementations defined in the `HttpServlet`.

Service Method

The service method in this servlet does all the processing; that is, it reads the input string given by the user, converts the string to uppercase letters, and flushes the output to the user output stream (that is usually the user browser).

Configuring the Simple Servlet

The last thing we have to know to use this servlet is about configuring this servlet. This is a basic servlet with no fancy requirements. Listing 14.2 gives the complete listing of the `web.xml` file for the simple servlet. The basic elements for configuring a servlet are the servlet and servlet mapping elements.

LISTING 14.2 Web Application Descriptor (web.xml)

```
<!DOCTYPE web-app PUBLIC "-//Sun Microsystems, Inc.//DTD Web Application 2.3//EN"
➥ "http://java.sun.com/dtd/web-app_2_3.dtd">
<web-app>
  <servlet>
    <servlet-name>SimpleServlet</servlet-name>
    <servlet-class>wlsunleashed.servlets.SimpleServlet</servlet-class>
    <init-param>
      <param-name>DEFAULT_STRING</param-name>
      <param-value>Hello World</param-value>
    </init-param>
  </servlet>
```

```
  <servlet-mapping>
    <servlet-name>SimpleServlet</servlet-name>
    <url-pattern>/SimpleServlet/*</url-pattern>
  </servlet-mapping>
</web-app>
```

Using the Init Method

As explained earlier, the `init` method can be used for reading any configuration parameters defined in the deployment descriptor. In the `SimpleServlet`, an `init` parameter can be used to read the default string to display on the user screen if the input string isn't given. By doing this, we can eliminate the need to hard-code a default value inside the code. The following code snippet implements the `init` method required for the simple servlet implementation:

```
public void init(ServletConfig config) throws ServletException
{
        super.init(config);

        // Check for all initialization parameters
        //Read the INPUT_STRING parameter.

        if ((defaultString= getInitParameter("DEFAULT_STRING")) == null)
            defaultString = "Hello World";

    }
```

The `init` parameter `DEFAULT_STRING` read in the method is defined in the Web deployment descriptor, `web.xml`. We've already declared `DEFAULT_STRING` previously, refer to Listing 14.2.

Executing the Simple Servlet

Servlets in WebLogic Server can be accessed from a Web browser using the following URL format:

http://*host*:*port*/*webApplicationName*/*mappedServletName*?*parameter*=*value*

where

- *host* is the machine name where the WebLogic Server instance is running.
- *port* is the port number where the WebLogic Server is listening for requests. By default, this is port 7001.
- *webApplicationName* is the name of the Web application where the accessed servlet is bundled.

- *mappedServletName* is the logical name given for the accessed servlet in the Web deployment descriptor.

All strings following the ? represent the input for the accessed servlet. If the earlier rule is translated to access the `SimpleServlet` described earlier, the URL will look like the following:

```
http://exampleServer:7001/servletExample/SimpleServlet?INPUT_STRING=helloWorld
```

Alternatively, the input can be obtained using form-based input designed using HTML. Listing 14.3 gives an idea of how this HTML will look like for our simple example.

LISTING 14.3 Input Form (simple.html)

```
<!DOCTYPE HTML PUBLIC "-//W3C//DTD HTML 4.0 Transitional//EN">
<HTML>
<HEAD>
<TITLE>A Sample FORM using POST</TITLE>
</HEAD>
<BODY BGCOLOR="#FDF5E6">
<H1 ALIGN="CENTER">A Sample FORM using POST</H1>
<FORM ACTION="/wlsUnleashed/SimpleServlet" METHOD="POST">
Input String: <INPUT TYPE="TEXT" NAME="INPUT_STRING"><BR>
</FORM>
</BODY>
</HTML>
```

The HTML file is to be placed under the root directory of the Web application. The directory structure was covered in detail in Chapters 5, “Enterprise Application Design with WebLogic Server,” and 6, “Introduction to WebLogic Web Applications.” The HTML has to be invoked in the same fashion as that used with the simple servlet shown earlier.

```
http://localhost:7001/wlsUnleashed/simple.html
```

Figure 14.2 displays the output from the `SimpleServlet`. You can note the link used to access the simple servlet in the address bar of the Web browser.

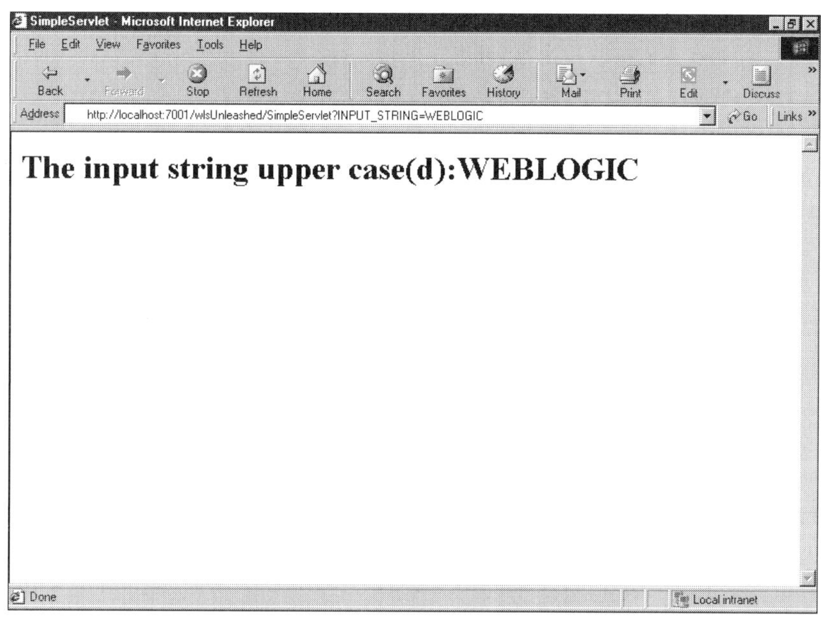

FIGURE 14.2 Simple servlet output.

When to Use Servlets

Servlets play an important role in providing the necessary infrastructure for integrating Web applications with enterprise components built using J2EE components such as EJBs, JMS, and so on. Servlets can be used on their own to implement small- to medium-scale applications.

HTTP servlets, the most popular implementation of servlets, provide the abstraction necessary for HTTP requests to access the underlying business components in an enterprise scenario. The HTTP servlets provide the framework for creating interactive applications for client presentation (usually in a Web browser), while other WebLogic Server components handle the necessary business logic. WebLogic Server HTTP servlets have access to the other components, such as JDBC connection pooling, Jolt connection pooling, EJBs, and JMS. Along with JSP, servlets can be effectively used to generate static or dynamic HTML, thereby providing an excellent application framework in an n-tier architecture.

As an MVC Controller

The Model-View-Controller (MVC) architecture extracts maximum benefits from the combined power of JavaServer Pages (JSP) and servlets. For example, Struts, an Apache Web application framework implementation, uses servlets as an effective controller and, with JSP, provides an excellent framework for developing Web applications. In the MVC design pattern, HTTP requests are sent to the servlet, which serves as the controller and dispatches the requests to the appropriate business handler that embeds the business logic. The controller receives the response from the handler when the request is processed, and again determines the appropriate view and displays it.

NOTE

As we go through one of the most important uses of servlet, it's good to note that servlets should not be used for producing a lot of HTML output. Servlets should be used in conjunction with JSP, which we'll cover later in the book in great detail. For now, because our servlets are small and simple, we'll use them to render the HTML output.

As a Session Tracker

HTTP servlets provide the necessary APIs for storing state management information for conversations between a client and the WebLogic Server, such as in a shopping cart example. The first invocation of a servlet from a client—for example, a login request—creates the session and the other application servlets used to update the session during the course of the conversation.

Servlet API

The `Servlet` API is a comprehensive set of functions which provides all the functions required for complex interactions between a Web client and a Web container, including session management, security, dispatching requests, and more.

Package Structure

All the servlet classes and interfaces are organized into the following packages:

- `javax.servlet`—Provides all the base interfaces needed for implementing generic servlets and HTTP servlets
- `javax.servlet.http`—Provides all the base interfaces and classes needed for implementing an HTTP servlet

In the following sections, we'll look at the important interfaces and classes that make up the servlet implementation, along with examples for each of the operations.

The Servlet Interface

The `Servlet` interface is the base interface for developing all servlets. The `GenericServlet` interface, described later, implements this interface. The interface defines the basic methods that a servlet running inside a servlet engine defines to process client requests. As explained earlier, the `Servlet` interface defines the following life cycle methods:

- `init()`—Servlet initialization routine
- `service()`—All-purpose routine to process client requests
- `destroy()`—Clean-up routine for freeing resources, storing state information, and so forth

The interface also defines the `getServletConfig()` method, which returns the `ServletConfig` object that holds the initialization parameters and other configuration of the servlet defined by the user. These parameters are usually defined in the deployment descriptor of the Web application. Developers who want to implement the `Servlet` interface should take care of storing the `ServletConfig` object passed to the `init` method if the `getServletConfig()` method has to return the object when the servlet needs the configuration object. This interface also provides a `getServletInfo()` method, which can return information about the servlet, such as its author, version, and copyright text.

ServletConfig Interface

This configuration object, which is passed into the servlet when it's instantiated (through the `init` method), provides user configuration information as name-value pairs. Table 14.3 lists the methods this object defines.

TABLE 14.3 ServletConfig Interface

Method	Description
getInitParameter	Takes a string representing the initialized parameter as argument and returns the value of the parameter.
getInitParameterNames	Returns all the names of the parameters.
getServletContext	Returns the ServletContext object, which represents the servlet's runtime environment. The ServletContext object is explained later.

The following snippet reads a list of initialization parameters. In this case, it reads logging-related parameters, such as the debug and threshold limit, and prints their values on the console. You can use the read values to turn on logging and the threshold level in a real-world scenario.

```
public void init(ServletConfig config) throws ServletException
{
       super.init(config);
       Enumeration params = getInitParameterNames();
       System.out.println("The init parameters are: ");
     while (params.hasMoreElements()) {
        String tempParam=(String)params.nextElement();
        String paramValue=(String)getInitParameter(tempParam);
        System.out.println(tempParam+"="+paramValue);
     }}
}
```

The configuration interface also provides the `getServletName()` function to return the name of the servlet instance. The servlet names are usually provided in the Web application deployment descriptor (`web.xml`). The following XML snippet provides an example of the initialization parameters and servlet name that are used by the functions we covered here:

```
<servlet>
  <servlet-name>SimpleServlet2</servlet-name>
  <servlet-class>wlsunleashed.servlets.SimpleServlet2</servlet-class>
    <init-param>
       <param-name>threshold</param-name>
       <param-value>1</param-value>
    </init-param>
    <init-param>
      <param-name>debug</param-name>
      <param-value>false</param-value>
    </init-param>
</servlet>
```

ServletContext Interface

The `ServletContext` interface is the servlet's view of the Web container. As mentioned earlier, the `getServletContext()` method of `ServletConfig` returns the `ServletContext` object. This interface provides a lot of methods, and for easier understanding we can classify the methods into the categories in the following sections.

Servlet Environment Properties

This interface provides the same methods defined in Table 14.3. Table 14.4 summarizes a list of additional methods defined in the `ServletContext` interface for obtaining the servlet and servlet's runtime environment properties along with the sample output for each of the methods

TABLE 14.4 ServletContext Environment Properties

Method	Sample Output
getMajorVersion	2; the major version of the Servlet API supported by the container.
getMinorVersion	3; the minor version of the Servlet API supported by the container.
getMimeType(String *file*)	Returns the MIME type of the file. text/html is one of the common MIME types.
getRealPath	For the SimpleServlet2 example, the path returned is c:\bea\user_projects\mydomain\applications\wlsUnleashed\SimpleServlet2. As you can see, it's with respect to the location of the file in the computer and the OS on which the WebLogic Server is running. This method will return null if WebLogic Server cannot translate the virtual path to a real path.

Method	Sample Output
getServerInfo	Returns the name and version of the servlet container. In our case, you'll an output similar to the following: WebLogic Server 8.1 Thu Mar 20 23:06:05 PST 2003 246620.

Servlet Forwarding and Including

One of the major functions of the servlet context object is to give access to `RequestDispatcher` objects. The `RequestDispatacher` objects are used to forward and/or include other resources in a servlet response. The dispatchers can be obtained by one of the following methods:

- `getRequestDispatcher()` takes as input the resource path with respect to the current context.
- `getNamedDispatcher()` takes as an argument the servlet name to be included. The servlet name can be obtained using the `ServletConfig.getServletName()` function described earlier.

`RequestDispatchers` are discussed in detail later in the chapter.

Resources and Contexts

The `ServletContext` object is also used to get the servlet context of a given URL that might correspond to another Web application in the Web container.

The ServletContext interface provides the following functions for getting the list of resources in a Web application. The resources returned are with respect to the specified paths.

- `getResource`—Returns the URL that maps to the given path. For example, `servletContext.getResource("/WEB-INF")` will return the URL `file:D:/bea/user_projects/mydomain/applications/wlsUnleashed/WEB-INF`.
- `getResourcePaths`—Returns all the resource paths with respect to the specified path. For example, in a simple Web application, using this function with `"/WEB-INF"` as the argument returns

```
/WEB-INF/web.xml
/WEB-INF/classes/
```

Additionally, this object provides the `getResourceAsStream()` method for obtaining the requested resource as an input stream object. Given the path, this method gives the servlet the power to access any resource at any location. These methods give the servlet container the capability to make a resource available to any servlet, irrespective of its location. Additionally, they don't use class loaders to perform this function because it's done with equivalent functions defined in the `java.lang.Class` definition.

Logging Routines

If a message has to be logged in the case of an exception, ServletContext provides a routine two flavors of log() functions. The first version takes a specified user message, and the second version takes a user message and a Throwable object as arguments. The detailed message and the exception are logged to the application log file. These log routines by no means represent a complete logging framework. Better logging capabilities have been introduced in JDK 1.4. You can refer to the related documentation at http://java.sun.com/j2se/1.4.1/docs/api/java/util/logging/package-summary.html.

Interservlet Communication Routines

Application objects can be handled as the ServletContext object using the getters and setters defined in the interface. ServletContext defines the getters (getAttribute() and getAttributeNames()) to get the value of a previously set attribute (using the setAttribute() method) or an enumeration containing the names supported in the context. The attributes set in the context can be removed using the removeAttribute() method.

Attributes can be used to exchange application objects between different parts of the Web application. For example, LoginServlet can set the name of the user logging into a system and this value can be also used in all other servlets during logging, authentication, and so forth.

The init() method of LoginServlet can be changed to include the attribute manipulation explained earlier:

```
public void init(ServletConfig config) throws ServletException
{
     super.init(config);
      //Other EJB Look code
      ServletContext ctx = config.getServletContext();
      ctx.setAttribute("com.username",
➥config.getInitParameter("def_username"));
}
```

The attribute com.username defined in the code snippet can be accessed by any other servlet in the same Web application for purposes such as logging.

```
public void doPost(HttpServletRequest req, HttpServletResponse resp)
throws ServletException, IOException
   {
       resp.setContentType("text/html");
       // Other logic
       //PrintWriter pw = resp.getWriter();
       // value of username from the servletcontext set earlier
      userlog("USER :"+ getServletContext()
```

```
                        .getAttribute("com.username").toString());
    // Other logic
}
```

As you can see, using the context attribute is similar to using a global variable. But this isn't a recommended practice when you need global variables. Context should not be used as a data store when it might be used by a single component. The data should be kept as close as possible to the components using it. The context should be used only if a majority of the components need specific data.

TIP

Context could be used for caching lookup values.

ServletRequest Interface

This interface encapsulates all the information associated with a client request including request parameters (form field values and URL parameters), information such as session identifier, and client properties such as address, hostname, and so on. The `service()` method of the `Servlet` interface, which processes all the client requests, takes the `ServletRequest` as its argument. The Web container creates this object. We look at each of the important methods and their use when we discuss `HttpServletRequest`—one of the best-known subinterfaces for implementing HTTP. The servlet request object gives access to the input stream to read binary data from clients, and also provides methods such as `getParameter()` to access character data in the input.

ServletResponse Interface

The servlet container uses this interface to send replies back to the client. This object is also passed as an argument to the service method. This object is created by the Web container and is initially empty. `HttpServletResponse` is the subinterface of `ServletResponse` that's used in `HttpServlets`. We'll look at the methods, along with `HttpServletResponse`, in detail later in the chapter. The response object also gives access to the output stream object and the print writer object, which are used to flush output to the client. The output stream object is for binary data, and the print writer is for character data. If the output contains both binary data and character data, an output stream object should be used.

Other Interfaces in Servlet 2.3

This package contains a host of other interfaces relating to the following features:

- `RequestDispatcher`—Base interfaces for including and forwarding requests to other resources and including their responses.

- Servlet filtering—This feature, introduced in the Servlet 2.3 specification, is used to filter tasks based on the request or the response to/from a resource.
- Context listeners—The Servlet API specification defines set of listener interfaces for servlet context attribute changes and for changes to the servlet context.

The preceding three categories of interfaces complete the interfaces available as part of the `javax.servlet` package. These new interfaces were introduced as part of the expanding servlet functionality. All these interfaces will be dealt in detail when we take a detailed look at request dispatching, filtering, and event handling, respectively.

HTTP Servlet API

So far in this section we've covered the base servlet APIs that comprise the `javax.servlet` package. Let's look at the most popular use of the servlets: HTTP protocol–based HTTP Servlet API. We already saw a simple HTTP servlet example. In this section, we'll look at the APIs that are extended from the `javax.servlet` package specifically designed for the HTTP protocol. The HTTP-based servlet classes are organized into the `javax.servlet.http` package. Figure 14.3 describes the relationship of the `HttpServlet` classes as against the `Servlet` interface and request/response objects. It does not list all the methods in the classes and interfaces, only the important methods.

HttpServlet Class

The base class of all HTTP servlets is the abstract class `HttpServlet`. It extends from the `GenericServlet` class explained earlier in the section. The `HttpServlet` implementer's job is to make sure to implement at least one of the following functions to process the input request:

- `doGet()` for processing `GET` requests
- `doPost()` for handling `POST` requests
- `doDelete()` for handling `DELETE` requests
- `doPut()` for handling `PUT` requests
- `doTrace()` for handling HTTP `TRACE` operations
- `doOptions()` for handling HTTP `OPTIONS` operations

All the supported HTTP methods were listed earlier in Table 14.2. For most practical applications, you'll have to implement only `doGet()` and `doPost()`; you won't have to worry about overriding default implementations for the other methods. The default implementation of `doOptions` automatically determines what HTTP options are supported when a servlet developer overrides a particular service handling method. For example, when a servlet overrides `doPost()`, the supported options are `POST`, `HEAD`, `TRACE`, and `OPTIONS`. Similarly, with `doTrace()`, the default implementation makes sure that a response with all the headers is sent to the trace request.

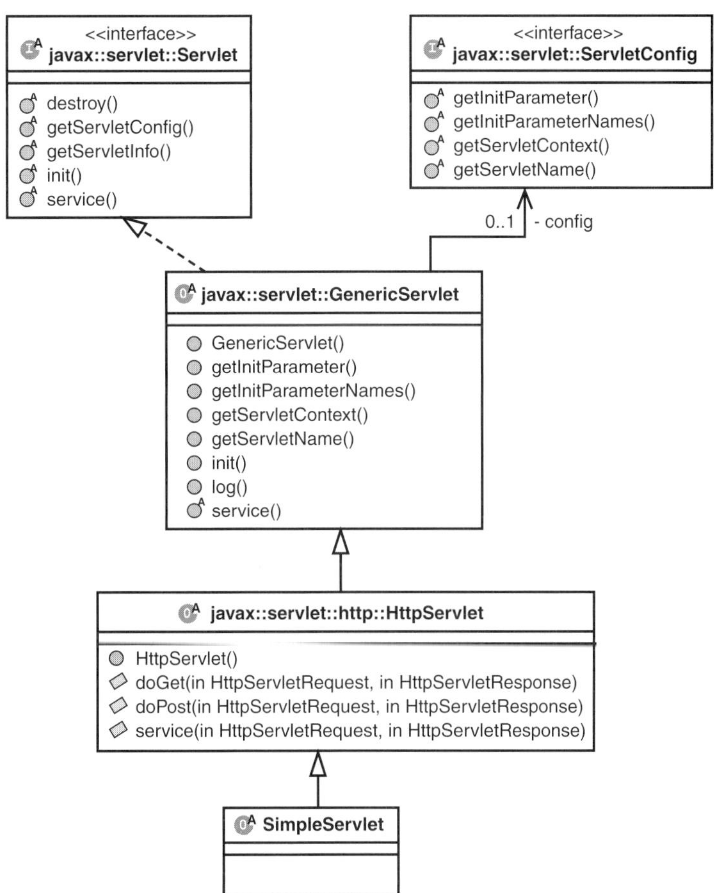

FIGURE 14.3 HttpServlet class relationship.

The `HttpServlet` can also implement life cycle methods such as `init()` and `destroy()` for initializing parameters and cleanup operations, respectively. This abstract class also provides the `getServletInfo()` method that can be used to describe the servlet.

The `service()` method can be implemented for processing all kinds of HTTP requests, including `GET`, `POST`, `DELETE`, and so on, doing so is generally not a good programming practice. We'll look at this aspect when we discuss writing servlets later in the chapter. The default `service()` method redirects the incoming request to the appropriate `do`*`XXX`*`()` method listed in Table 14.1.

Like all servlet types, `HttpServlet` is multithreaded by default. But the developer has to take care of handling static variables and shared resources such as database objects and files. All access to these resources should be synchronized.

This class also provides the utility method `getLastModified()`, which gives the last modified time of the given `HttpServletRequest` object. This can be used for managing an internal cache of a servlet's output. By using this, the container can check whether a requested page has changed, avoiding calling `doGet()` and `doPost()` and reducing server workload. If a page in the cache isn't expired, the browser can use it instead of getting a fresh one from the servlet.

All `doXXX()` and `service()` take `HttpServletRequest` and `HttpServletResponse` objects as arguments.

> **TIP**
>
> As good programming practice, always use `doXXX()` (such as `doGet()` and `doPost()`) to implement the program logic instead of the `service()` method. If you want the `doGet()` and `doPost()` methods to have the same behavior, write `doPost()` with the required behavior and have `doGet()` call `doPost()`.

HttpServletRequest

This interface that encapsulates the request parameters of the client extends `ServletRequest` interface of the `javax.servlet` package explained earlier. The responsibility of creating this object is with the servlet container, in our case, with WebLogic Server. It's passed as an argument to the `service()` and `doXXX()` methods. The methods defined by this interface can be classified into the categories defined in Table 14.5.

TABLE 14.5 HttpServletRequest Important Methods

Category	Method	Description
Authentication	getAuthType	Indicates the authentication scheme used for servlet security. Valid values are BASIC_AUTH, CLIENT_CERT_AUTH, DIGEST_AUTH, FORM_AUTH, or null if no scheme is used.
	getRemoteUser	If previously authenticated, it returns the username; otherwise, it returns null.
	getUserPrincipal	Returns a java.security.Principal object containing the authenticated user information.
	isUserInRole	Returns true if the current user has the specified permission.
Header Information	getHeader	Returns the value of the requested header.
	getHeaders	Returns all header values that are part of the request.
	getIntHeader	Returns the value of the requested header as an integer.

Category	Method	Description
	getDateHeader	Returns the value of the requested header as a Date in long format.
URL Information	getQueryString	Returns the entire string following the ? (or the URL path).
	getRequestURI	Represents part of the URL path that includes the string between the port number value and the query string ?.
	getServletPath	Returns only the servlet name along with the extra path.
	getContextPath	Returns the string representing the context of the request.
Session	getCookies	Returns the cookies embedded in the request.
	getRequestedSessionId	Session ID used by the user.
	isRequestedSessionIdFromCookie	Utility function (self-explanatory).
	isRequestedSessionIdFromURL	Utility function.
	isRequestedSessionIdValid	Utility function.
	getSession	Returns the user session object if present or creates a new one if not. The creation can be controlled with a Boolean argument.

14

Other utility methods, such as `getMethod()`, `getPathInfo()`, `getPathTranslated()`, and inherited methods from the base class, are not explained here. For a full list of the methods available as part of this class, refer to the servlet API documentation at `http://java.sun.com/products/servlet/2.3/javadoc/javax/servlet/http/HttpServletRequest.html`.

We'll see a sample output of the preceding functions when we discuss the simple servlet example in the next section. We'll cover the session and the session-related methods in a separate discussion of implementing sessions in servlets.

Apart from the methods listed earlier, the `HttpServletRequest` interface inherits the methods for attribute handling and parameters encapsulated in the request object. These methods can be grouped into the groups discussed in the following sections.

Using Attributes

Servlets in the same Web application can communicate with each other through attributes. The `ServletRequest` interface provides a set of methods to retrieve and set attribute values to store customized request information. This method is used in conjunction with dispatching requests using `RequestDispatcher`. As explained earlier when we discussed the `ServletContext` interface, methods provided for attribute manipulation are

- `getAttribute()`—Returns the value of the requested attribute identified by a name. Package naming conventions should be adopted in naming attributes.

- `getAttributeNames()`—Returns an enumeration of the attribute names available in the request
- `setAttribute`—Sets the value of a given attribute.
- `removeAttribute`—Removes the attribute from the request.

> **CAUTION**
>
> The Java packages, such as `java.*`, `javax.*`, and `sun.*`, should not be used because these are specialized packages that are part of the JDK.

Some useful attribute keys are `javax.servlet.request.cipher-suite` and `javax.servet.request.key-size`, which are predefined in the request. In an HTTPS request, there's a special attribute `javax.servlet.request.X509Certificate`, which returns an array of the SSL certificates that are associated with the request. The attribute values returned are an array of `java.security.cert.X509Certificate`, which defines the runtime implementation of the X.509 v.3 certificate.

Content Interface

This interface provides a set of functions for reading content-related properties such as reading the content length (`getContentLength()`) and content type (`getContentType()`). If any character encoding is used in the request, `getCharacterEncoding()` returns the name of the encoding; otherwise, it returns null.

Client and Request Properties

If the servlet needs to obtain information about the client or the request, we can use the following functions:

- `getProtocol()`—Returns the name and version of the protocol of the request. For example, `HTTP/1.1`.
- `getRemoteAddr()`—Returns client's IP address.
- `getRemoteHost()`—Returns client machine name if mapped; otherwise, the IP address.
- `getServerName()`—Returns the name of the server processing the request.
- `getServerPort()`—Returns the port number where the server got the request.

Reading Client Input

The `getReader()` and `getInputStream()` return the buffered reader and an input stream, respectively. The reader is used for reading the request as character data, and the input stream is used for reading the request as binary data. But these methods should not be mixed in reading the request.

There are other functions for reading the parameters encapsulated in the request along with the associated values:

- `getParameter()`—Returns the value corresponding to the request parameter (form input fields and URL parameters).
- `getParameterNames()`—Returns an `Enumeration` of parameters.
- `getParameterValues()`—Returns an array of `String` objects representing the values of the parameters.

We already looked at using these functions while developing the first servlet we wrote earlier in the chapter. We'll look at them again when we implement a modified version of the `SimpleServlet` later in the chapter using some of the functions we've discussed.

HttpServletResponse

Similar to the `HttpServletRequest` that extends the `ServletRequest` interface, this interface extends `ServletResponse`, which was explained earlier. `HttpServletReponse` is a special interface for providing HTTP-specific functionality in the servlet reply. It has methods that complement the request interface, such as the following:

- Functions for handling header information such as `addHeader`, `addIntHeader`, `addDateHeader`, `setDateHeader`, `setHeader`, and `setIntHeader`. It also defines a `containsHeader()` function to determine whether or not a particular header exists.
- URL encoding–related functions such as `encodeRedirectURL`, `encodeURL`, and `sendRedirect`. Along with `addCookies`, these functions are covered in detail later in the chapter when we work with sessions (in the section "Handling Sessions").

This interface provides functions for setting error codes and statuses for the response. Before we look at these functions, let's look at some of the common status codes in Table 14.6.

TABLE 14.6 HTTP Servlet Status Codes

Code	Description
SC_OK (200)	Successful request
SC_BAD_REQUEST (400)	Request was syntactically wrong
SC_HTTP_VERSION_NOT_SUPPORTED (505)	Server does not support the HTTP protocol version
SC_INTERNAL_SERVER_ERROR (500)	Internal error in the server while processing the request
SC_NOT_FOUND (404)	Requested resource is not found
SC_UNAUTHORIZED (401)	The request needs HTTP authentication

For a full list of status codes, refer to the Sun Web site at `http://java.sun.com/products/servlet/2.3/javadoc/javax/servlet/http/HttpServletResponse.html`.

Now let's look at the error functions that the `ServletResponse` interface provides:

- `sendError()` comes in two flavors. The first version takes only the status code and the second version takes the status code and a message as an argument. This function is used to send an error response back to the client with one of the status codes defined in Table 14.6.
- `setStatus()` is used to set the status code for the response. The status code is one of the codes defined in Table 14.6.

The super interface of `HttpServletResponse` is `ServletResponse`, which was briefly touched on earlier. Let's look at some of the important methods that `HttpServletResponse` inherits from the super interface.

The `getOutputStream()` and `getWriter()` functions return an output stream and print writer, respectively. The output stream is used when binary data, such as an image or GIF file, is sent back to the client. The print writer is used for sending character data back to the client.

Some of the other included functions are getters for content length and buffer size, along with setters for content length, content type, and buffer size. There are also buffer manipulation functions such as `resetBuffer()` and `flushBuffer()`. *Flushing a buffer* means the response stream is now ready to send. It is said to be *committed*.

We've already looked at using some of these functions in the first servlet we wrote earlier in the chapter. We'll look at some of the response-related functions and the output they create when we get to using the servlet API in the later part of the chapter.

Servlet Exceptions

The exception framework in the Servlet API consists of one basic class: `javax.servlet.ServletException`. This exception is thrown in all request-handling routines, such as `service()`, `doGet()`, `doPost()`, and so on. The `IOException` is also used in these routines in case of an input/output-related exception.

Let's look again at the example of the `GenericServlet` in Listing 14.3. The `service()` method in that example throws `ServletException` and `IOException`. Exceptions can be embedded in other exceptions. For this case, `ServletException` provides a `getRootCause()` method that returns the `Throwable` object that caused the `ServletException`.

UNAVAILABLE EXCEPTION

This exception, which is a subclass of `ServletException`, is used when the servlet becomes unavailable—temporarily or permanently. The exception thrown provides an `isPermanent()` method to identify the type of unavailability. As a servlet container, WebLogic Server is capable of handling both temporary and permanent unavailability in the same fashion. This exception also provides a `getUnavailableSeconds()` method to find out the total downtime.

Servlet Thread Models

Before we look into using some of the functions we've seen as part of the Servlet API, we have to look at the threading model available for servlet developers. As mentioned earlier in the chapter, a servlet that implements the `HttpServlet` or the `Servlet` interface is capable of handling concurrent requests at the same time. A single servlet instance that's created either by the first request or at server startup time spawns multiple threads to handle all these requests through the `doGet()` or the `doPost()` method, based on the request type. In this programming model, the programmer should take care to handle all the shared data in the request processing method via `service()`, `doGet()`, and so forth. This is done by using synchronized blocks and methods. If the programmer forgets to synchronize resources, the system can be left in an invalid state.

The programmer can override this default behavior of the servlet if the servlet implements the `SingleThreadModel` interface. For example, if the `SimpleServlet` discussed earlier implements `SingleThreadModel`, the code snippet looks like the following:

```
public class SimpleServlet extends HttpServlet implements SingleThreadModel
{
          // Servlet Code
}
```

In this model, according to the Sun specification, Web containers must take care of synchronizing the requests to the servlet instance. Because the container processes one request for the servlet loaded in memory, there is no question of sharing data.

Because synchronous access to such a servlet will substantially increase latency, especially if the servlet is used frequently, Web containers have devised ways to make this more efficient by concepts such as servlet pooling and so on. The methodology adopted to synchronize the requests depends on the implementation of the Web container. Some containers queue the requests in the server or, in certain cases, create multiple instances of the `SingleThreadModel` servlet to process simultaneous requests and every request being processed in a single thread.

WebLogic Server provides a servlet-pooling feature for making the `SingleThreadModel` more efficient. WebLogic Server creates an instance pool containing multiple instances of the `SingleThreadModel` servlet based on a configuration parameter. Figure 14.4 shows how to configure the `Servlet Pool Size` parameter.

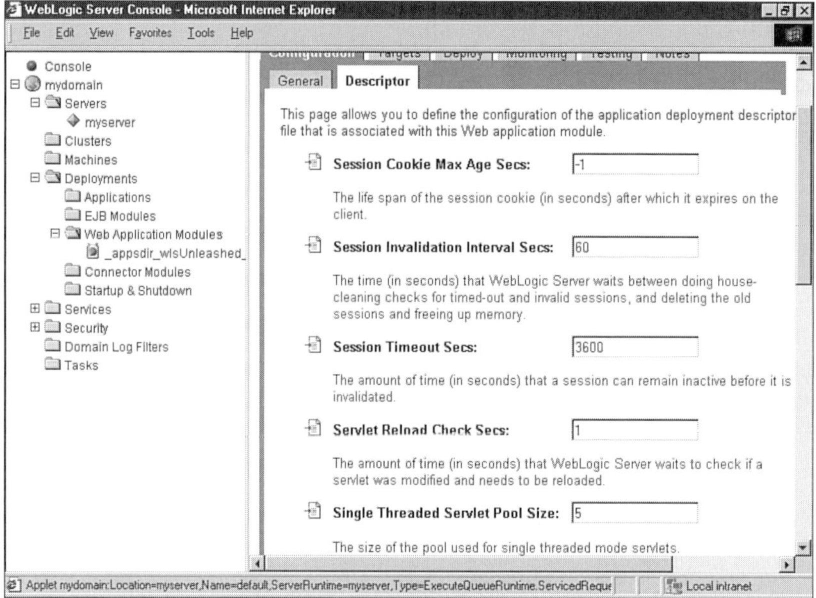

FIGURE 14.4 Servlet pool size configuration.

The default value of this parameter is set to `5` and the pool is created when the first request comes to the servlet. WebLogic Server increments the instances in the pool based on the requests in the server queue.

One important consideration for developers of single-threaded model servlets in WebLogic Server is that you must take care of synchronizing access to shared resources such as database resources in the servlet methods—`service()`, `doGet()`, and `doPost()`—because multiple instances of the same servlet exist that are accessing the shared resources at the same time. The performance impact of synchronization should be considered when designing such a servlet. Because the `SingleThreadModel` offers sluggish performance, or the false impression of thread safety when using multiple instances, it should be discouraged in favor of synchronization blocks/methods.

Using the Servlet API

The most common use of servlets is for handling HTTP requests in Web and application servers. Now we'll look at using the functions we discussed in the last section. We'll also build on the first servlet we created in the chapter.

HTTP Servlet Skeleton

Table 14.1 lists all the methods that are available in an `HttpServlet` interface for handling different types of requests. But the most used are the `doPost()` and the `doGet()` methods, which handle the servlet requests via the `service` method. Listing 14.4 shows a skeleton of a simple HTTP servlet that can handle both `GET` and `POST` requests. In the next section of the chapter, we develop a simple servlet based on this skeleton to convert a given string to its uppercase equivalent.

LISTING 14.4 Simple HTTP Servlet Skeleton

```
import java.io.*;
import javax.servlet.*;
import javax.servlet.http.*;
public class SimpleServlet extends HttpServlet {

       public void init(ServletConfig config)
       {
           // read init parameters from the config
           // initialize common resources like database
       }

       //Request handling methods
       public void doGet(HttpServletRequest request,
                         HttpServletResponse response)
                        throws ServletException, IOException
       {
            // Request Handling Logic
            // Format the output
            PrintWriter out = response.getWriter();
            // Use "out" to send output to web browser
       }

       public void doPost(HttpServletRequest request,
                          HttpServletResponse response)
                          throws ServletException, IOException
       {
            // Request Handling Logic
            // Call the doGet() method to process the POST request
             doGet(request,response);
       }

       public void destroy()
       {
           // clean up operations
       }

}
```

The preceding servlet template introduces some key concepts that are common to all `HttpServlets`. The service processing methods `doGet()` and `doPost()` both take the `HttpServletRequest` and `HttpServletResponse` objects as arguments. The `HttpServletRequest` object is for reading HTTP headers and user input. It provides a host of methods as defined in Table 14.5. The following listing gives a sample output for some of the methods of the `HttpServletRequest` object with respect to the `SimpleServlet`:

```
Request method: GET
Request URI: /wlsUnleashed/SimpleServlet2
Request protocol: HTTP/1.1
Servlet path: /SimpleServlet2
Path info: <none>
Path translated: <none>
Server name: localhost
Server port: 7001
Remote address: 127.0.0.1
Remote host: 127.0.0.1
Scheme: http
Request scheme: http
Requested URL: http://localhost:7001/wlsUnleashed/SimpleServlet2
```

The `HttpServletResponse` object is used for sending the response header, which includes the HTTP status for the request. A typical WebLogic Server HTTP response header looks like this:

```
HTTP/1.1 200 OK
Date: Tue, 06 Apr 2003 21:59:48 GMT
Server: WebLogic WebLogic Server 8.1 Thu Mar 20 23:06:05 PST 2003 246620
Content-Length: 98
Content-Type: text/plain
Connection: Keep-Alive
X-WebLogic-Cluster-List: 1732628108!-1408104675!7001!7002¦195540992!-1408104674!
7001!7002¦533730093!-1408104657!7001!7002¦658650126!-1408104656!7001!7002
X-WebLogic-Cluster-Hash: vnE9rA7Fu4xeOQAoQUfIHPDAXro
Set-Cookie:
JSESSIONID=9QGUOYCxNEOAVJNQPmS0MQs22yW7TslJfiBZps0ZwpqP3EXqQloD!1732628108!
➥-1408104675!7001!7002; path=/
```

The header contains information such as the status of the request, WebLogic version, time of request, content type, and length. The status of the request appears on the first line (`200` indicates success) along with the protocol and version used. Some of the valid statuses were listed earlier in the chapter in Table 14.6. We'll now take a detailed look at the exceptions thrown by the request-handling routines `doGet()` and `doPost()`. Both the `doGet()` function and the `doPost()` function throw `ServletException` and `IOException`, which are explained earlier in the chapter.

Using doGet() and doPost()

It isn't good practice to code the `service()` method as given in the `SimpleServlet` for handling all types of requests; that is, both `GET` requests and `POST` requests. The temptation for such a practice is usually driven by one of the following:

- Simplicity of the function that's implemented, like the `SimpleServlet`
- All the request types—`POST`, `GET`, and so on—have to be handled in the same fashion

But this practice should be avoided for better code organization and for extensibility. Even though their function might be identical, if the `POST` and `GET` requests are coded separately, it keeps open the option of overriding all other functions defined in Table 14.2.

The code in Listing 14.1 can be converted to use the `doPost()` and the `doGet()` methods. Listing 14.5 is the full listing of the modified simple servlet, which contains the `init()` method and the `doGet()` and the `doPost()` methods.

LISTING 14.5 Modified Simple Servlet

```
package wlsunleashed.servlets;

import javax.servlet.*;
import javax.servlet.http.*;
import java.io.*;

public class SimpleServlet extends HttpServlet
{
     private String defaultString="HELLO WORLD";

     public void init(ServletConfig config) throws ServletException
     {
        super.init(config);

        // Check for all initialization parameters
        //Read the INPUT_STRING parameter.

        if ((defaultString= getInitParameter("DEFAULT_STRING")) == null)
            defaultString = "HELLO WORLD";

    }

     // Handles the GET request
     public void doGet(HttpServletRequest req, HttpServletResponse res)
        throws IOException
```

LISTING 14.5 Continued

```
    {

         String convertedString,inputString;

        //read the request parameter INPUT_STRING
       // If the input String is null
       // it returns "hello world" In uppercase

        if ((inputString = req.getParameter("INPUT_STRING"))
            != null) {
            convertedString = inputString.toUpperCase();
        }
        else {
            convertedString =defaultString ;
        }

        // Set the content type first
        res.setContentType("text/html");

        // get the PrintWriter
        PrintWriter out = res.getWriter();

        out.println("<html><head><title>SimpleServlet</title></head>");
        out.println("<body>");
        out.println("<h1>");

        out.println("The input string upper case(d):" + convertedString );
        out.println("</h1></body></html>");

    }

     // Handles the POST request
    // Since the function is too simple and does the same function
    // we will call doGet from doPost
     public void doPost(HttpServletRequest req, HttpServletResponse res)
        throws IOException
    {
        doGet(req,res);
    }
}
```

Because the functionality is not that complex, either the `doGet()` or the `doPost()` can be implemented and the other function can call the implemented function as shown earlier. Because this servlet can handle both HTTP `GET` and `POST` requests, the question arises as to which request type is better. They differ in the way that they transfer parameters to the server. `GET` requests send parameters in a URL string, and `POST` requests send parameters in the request body. `POST` requests are typically used for forms because one of the disadvantages of URL strings is the amount of data that can be passed to the server. The `doGet()` and `doPost()` methods are for convenience only because most Web servers parse the request and group the parameters in collections for the servlet by the time the `doPost()` or the `doGet()` is invoked. But the most obvious advantage is the capability to separate logic to handle different calls to the servlets.

TIP

When you have the same processing logic for both `doGet` and `doPost` methods, you put the processing logic in one and call it from the other one. Also, the processing logic should be implemented in the method that will be used most.

In this section, we covered a basic servlet implementation. Advanced servlet features such as session tracking, dispatching requests to other servlets, JSPs, and cookies, are discussed in detail later. Servlets also provide an elegant mechanism for accessing other J2EE services, including EJBs and XML Web Services, which are explained in detail as well.

Handling Request and Response

Two of the important things we haven't covered so far are the way in which inputs are extracted from the request and the different ways the responses are constructed. The `SimpleServlet` discussed earlier showed one of the most common mechanism for handling the user input and the servlet output.

Extracting User Inputs

We briefly looked at the functions used to retrieve the input from the user during the discussions of the Servlet API and in the `SimpleServlet` example. An HTTP request from the user, usually from the browser, contains information such as the query parameters and session-related parameters such as cookies, encoded URL, and more. The user request also identifies the HTTP request type, which the `service()` method can use to dispatch the request to the corresponding `do`*`XXX`*`()` method. `GET` and `POST` are the most common HTTP request types used. The `GET` method is used when the parameters are embedded directly in a URL, and data is `POST`ed to the server when it is embedded in the body of the request.

Request as Parameters

User parameters are embedded in the `HttpServletRequest` object in the form of key-value pairs. The key-value pairs can be in any order and can be extracted using a variety of ways.

Some of them were listed briefly in the discussion of the Servlet API. We'll look at these functions with respect to the servlet example we saw earlier. The key of the input is "INPUT_STRING" and the value is the string to be converted. The following code snippet reads the key:

```
if ((inputString = req.getParameter("INPUT_STRING")) != null) {
            convertedString = inputString.toUpperCase();
        }
```

If we extend the example to read multiple strings and convert them to uppercase letters, all input strings can be sent with the same key, repeating once for each string sent to the servlet. The `getParameterValues()` function takes a string that represents the key and returns an array of strings that maps to the values for the given key. Similarly, an `Enumeration` of all keys can be retrieved using `getParameterNames()`.

Request in the Body

When the request is embedded in the body of the request, either the parameter functions defined earlier can be used or the data can be read as *raw* data. There are two ways to read binary data sent by the client using the methods provided by the `HttpServletRequest`:

- Using the `getInputStream()` method. If we consider our earlier example—`SimpleServlet`—the code could be modified to read the input as raw data as follows:

  ```
  // Get the input stream and read the data...
  int length = request.getContentLength();
  ServletInputStream in = request.getInputStream();
  if( length != -1 ){
  // read in a fixed number of bytes
  } else {
                  //read until end of file
  }
  ```

- Using the `getReader()` method. This method, which was introduced in Servlet 2.0, provides an alternative to the `getInputStream()` method.

While using the `getInputStream()` function, care should be taken to read no more data than the content length that can be obtained from the `getContentLength()` method. Otherwise, the servlet behavior is unknown. In the case of `getReader()`, the `BufferedReader` returned from the `getReader()` call takes care of the content length and reads the data accordingly.

Creating a Response

Let's now look at different ways to create a response to send back to the client. The `HttpServletResponse` object that's passed as an argument to the service and the `doXXX()` methods provide the methods and the stream to create the output and send it to the client. The response object can be used to set cookies and/or encode URLs for session management along with the client output, which might be HTML content or even simple text. The response created can be grouped into a properties section and a generated user response section. The properties section includes setting predefined headers such as content type, length, encoding, pragma, and so forth.

Specifying Content Type and Length

The type of content is a special header that must be set by the user, and the `HttpServletResponse` interface provides a method for doing so. `setContentType()` has to be set before the output stream or the print writer where the rest of the user response is written. For `SimpleServlet`, where the response is an HTML message, the content type is set to `text/html` as shown in the following code snippet:

```
// Set the content type first
res.setContentType("text/html");
```


Content types are required by the client to determine what kind of data is coming back from the server and to launch the appropriate application to view the content (if needed). For a browser client, the default is usually `text/html`. Some of the most common MIME types are

- `application/pdf`—Acrobat files
- `application/msword`—Word documents
- `application/zip`—Zip file
- `text/css`—Cascading Style Sheet
- `text/plain`—Simple text
- `text/gif`—GIF image
- `text/jpeg`—JPEG image

For a complete official list of registered MIME types, refer to the following site: `http://www.isi.edu/in-notes/iana/assignments/media-types/media-types`. The content type tells the client what application the client has to launch to view the response from the servlet.

Content Headers

During the discussion of the `HttpServletResponse` interface in the API section, we briefly covered the functions that are available for setting the headers in the response. The functions `setHeader()`, `setIntHeader()`, and `setDateHeader()` add new header values to the response. If the header already exists, these functions overwrite the existing value. Because HTTP allows for multiple occurrences of the same header parameter, the `HttpServletResponse` object adds the functions `addHeader()`, `addIntHeader()`, and `addDateHeader()`, which correspond to the previously mentioned set functions. Table 14.7

lists some of the most common header types. No header is mandatory, no header is prohibited, and each header can be interpreted by the browser in any number of ways, but the HTTP specification prescribes a few standard headers with intended browser behavior.

TABLE 14.7 Header Types

Type	Description
Cache-Control	Instructs the client as to whether the document received can be cached. Some valid values are public: Cacheable for all users private: For a single user no-cache: Should not be cached at all max-age=*n*: Document becomes invalid *n* seconds after the document is received by the browser Other valid values are no-store (document is neither cached nor stored), must-revalidate, and proxy-revalidate (validate the document on the server or the proxy).
Expires	max-age header is similar to the Cache-Control header, except this defines a date and time after which the document should be invalidated. This sets an absolute time, and max-age sets a relative time. The setDateHeader() can be used to set the expiry time. If the max-age value is set, it takes precedence over Expires.
Connection	This header is used for managing HTTP connections between the server and client, which may be persistent or non-persistent in nature depending on the value. When the value is keep-alive, the client keeps the connection alive with the server. If close is the value, a new connection is opened for every request. By default, all HTTP 1.1–compliant clients use persistent connections. When using persistent connections, content length should be set using the setContentLength() to indicate the length of the response sent.
Refresh	This parameter tells the browser to automatically refresh the document in *n* seconds. To set this parameter, we can either use the setHeader or setIntHeader function. For example, setIntHeader("Refresh", 20). Additionally, a new URL can also be specified when the refresh is performed. For example, setHeader("Refresh","30;URL=http://www.sams.com"). The refresh tag, an extension supported by both IE and Netscape, is usually set in the HEAD section of the HTML page instead of using this header.
If-Modified-Since	This request-header field is used in a method to conditionally send the output/entity. In other words, the response to a client request will not contain the complete output if the requested entity has not been modified since the time specified in this field.
Last-Modified	This date header indicates the last time the document was modified.
Date	This header sets the date of the request usually in GMT format. The setDateHeader() function can be used for doing this. WebLogic Server sets this date automatically.

> **NOTE**
>
> The `If-Modified-Since` header handles document refreshing efficiently by downloading only when the `Last-Modified` is greater than the `If-Modified-Since`.

The `Cache-Control` header is one of the new headers defined in HTTP 1.1. For detailed description on how the caching is implemented by the HTTP protocol refer to the following links: `http://www.w3.org/Protocols/rfc2616/rfc2616-sec13.html` and `http://www.w3.org/Protocols/rfc2616/rfc2616-sec14.html`. This will give an insight into how caching is implemented by the browsers and the Web servers. For clients that support only HTTP 1.0, use the `Pragma` header for enabling/disabling caching. Servlets should typically include the following code snippet for backward compatibility:

```
// Cache Control
res.setHeader("Cache-Control","no-cache");
res.setHeader("Pragma","no-cache");
```


The `Set-Cookie` tag is a special tag for setting the cookie associated with the response generated. The `Set-Cookie` tag occurs multiple times corresponding to the number of cookies. Alternatively, `HttpServletResponse` provides a special method, `addCookie()`, for adding cookies to the response. We'll look at cookies in more detail when we handle session management.

Output Streams and Writer

The servlet sends the output using a `PrintWriter()` or a `ServletOutputStream()`, depending on the type of data sent back. Both these objects are obtainable from the `HttpServletResponse` object passed as an argument to the `service()` method and `do`*`XXX`*`()` methods. The output objects are obtained using one of the following mechanisms:

```
PrintWriter out = res.getWriter();

ServletOutputStream out = res.getOutputStream();
```

The `PrintWriter` is used when the servlet sends `String` data (such as a plain HTML page) back to the client, and the `ServletOutputStream` is used when sending back byte or ASCII data or a multipart data that includes both forms of data.

> **TIP**
>
> Streams are faster for transferring ASCII back to the client. For example, writing the content of an ASCII file to a `PrintWriter` is slow because it transforms ASCII to String to ASCII again. Instead, get a stream class to read the file and send it to the `ServletOutputStream`.

Unlike the inputs, both `PrintWriter` and `ServletOutputStream` can be used in the same servlet and in the dispatched resources via another servlet or a JSP without generating an `IllegalStateException`. All these outputs are written to the same buffer. The contents are written to the client using the print method as demonstrated in the `SimpleServlet`:

```
out.println("<html><head><title>SimpleServlet</title></head>");
out.println("<body>");
out.println("<h1>");
out.println("The input string upper case(d):" + convertedString );
out.println("</h1></body></html>");
```

After the response is sent, the output streams can be closed if the application wants to close the connection with the client. But WebLogic Server provides the capability to optimize the request-response between a client and server with persistent HTTP connections. To leverage this feature, the servlet should not flush the output or close the stream, and the WebLogic Server should know the length of the response sent to the user. If the servlet flushes the output in the buffer, WebLogic Server cannot determine the length of the response and it cannot use reuse the connection. The content length is automatically determined by the server and added to the header. If all these criteria are met, the connection between the client and the server becomes automatically durable and can then be reused over multiple conversations between the client and the WebLogic Server. There is significant overhead in making connections from the client to the server and the durable connection significantly improves the performance.

The connection does not live forever if there are no requests flowing through it, and the life of the connection can be controlled by the `Duration` property in the WebLogic configuration file. The default value is set to 30 seconds and the maximum is 60 seconds. Figure 14.5 displays the parameters that can be changed related to the durable connection behavior of WebLogic Server.

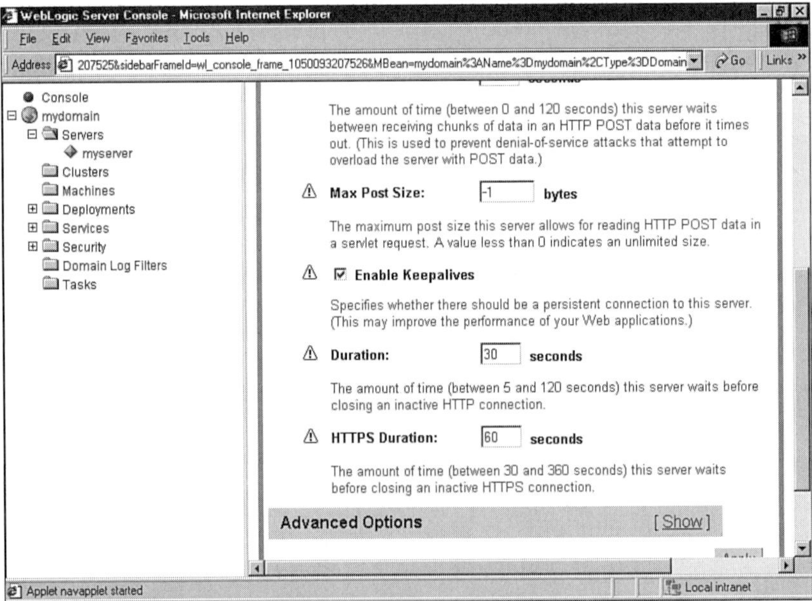

FIGURE 14.5 HTTP connection configuration.

Dispatching to Other Resources

The Servlet specification defines a mechanism for all servlet containers to facilitate the dispatch of requests from one Web component to other Web components such as JSP, servlets, or HTML pages. This can be achieved either directly or indirectly. In the indirect scenario, a Web component such as a servlet returns a page to the browser. This page contains an embedded URL (`META REFRESH` tag) that points to a different Web component. The browser then redirects the client to the other Web component. In a direct dispatch, a servlet might forward the request to another servlet or JSP for further processing, or might include the output of another servlet or JSP in the final output back to the requestor.

The Request Dispatcher

The `RequestDispatcher` interface in the `javax.servlet` package provides a mechanism for forwarding requests to other servlets and including responses from other servlets. The `RequestDispatcher` interface can be created using one of the following ways:

14

- `ServletContext.getRequestDispacher`—Returns the dispatcher for a given path. The object returned acts as a wrapper for the Web component located at the specified path.
- `ServletContext.getNamedDispatcher`—Returns the dispatcher identified by the given name. Servlets and other Web resources can be named using the Web application deployment descriptor (`web.xml`).
- `ServletRequest.getRequestDispatcher`—Returns the dispatcher for a given path.

The difference between the first and the third options is that the specified path is relative to the current context root in the first option and is relative to the current servlet in the third option. When the specified path begins with a `/` in the third option, the path given is from the current context root.

The `RequestDispatcher` interface can either include another Web resource or forward the request to another Web resource using `include()` and `forward()`, respectively. The arguments to these methods are either `ServletRequest` and `ServletResponse` objects (which are passed to the `service()` and `do`*`XXX`*`()` methods) or subclasses of these objects, such as the `HttpServletRequest` and `HttpServletResponse` objects. Alternatively, request and response wrappers with embedded request and response objects, which are explained later, can be used to forward or include using the dispatcher.

Additionally, when the request dispatcher is created using the `getRequestDispatcher()` method, it allows for specifying parameters in the path. In our simple servlet example, requests can be forwarded to a JSP to generate the output for the client as in the following code snippet:

```
String path = "formatter.jsp?INPUT_STRING="+convertedString;
RequestDispatcher rd = ctx.getRequestDispachter(path);
rd.forward(request,response);
```

The parameters specified in the path when creating a request dispatcher override the parameters defined in the request object. In the earlier case, INPUT_STRING in the request object is overridden by the INPUT_STRING defined in the path.

The Include Method

When called on the request dispatcher, the include() method includes the response from another Web component via a servlet. This operation simulates a server-side include when the included resource is static like an HTML page. If the Web component is a servlet or a JSP, the included resource is executed and the output from it is included in the final response of the wrapping servlet to the client. The included servlet or JSP has complete control of the request along with the parameters, but access to the response object is limited. The included resource does not have the privilege to change or add to the header information; namely, it cannot add a cookie, change status, flush the buffer, and the like. The included resource can populate the response by using the ServletOutputStream or Writer that can be obtained from the response object. After that, control is returned to the original component, and it can add even more information to the response if need be.

In our simple servlet, the header information printed before the actual output containing the converted string can be printed using an included JSP or HTML page. Figure 14.6 describes the flow when output from another JSP/servlet is included into the response for a client request. As you can see, the invoked servlet has control over sending the response back to the client.

The Forward Method

The forward() method is used to transfer control from a servlet or JSP to another Web component. This method could be used in functions in which the initial processing is performed by a servlet and the output or some additional processing might be handled by a JSP or another servlet. After the second component is done, control does not go back to the first one. In our simple servlet, the main processing of the uppercase conversion can be done in the servlet and the response can be formatted with the help of JSP using the forward() method. This design provides a big benefit by separating the presentation and the processing logic; that is, it separates HTML code from pure Java code.

```
if (dto.getConfirmationNumber() != null) {
     errorDetected = true;
      req.setAttribute("ErrorMessage",
             "This user has not been confirmed.  Please respond to email sent.")
      ServletContext sc = getServletContext();
      RequestDispatcher rd = sc.getRequestDispatcher("/login.jsp");
      rd.forward(req, res);
}
```

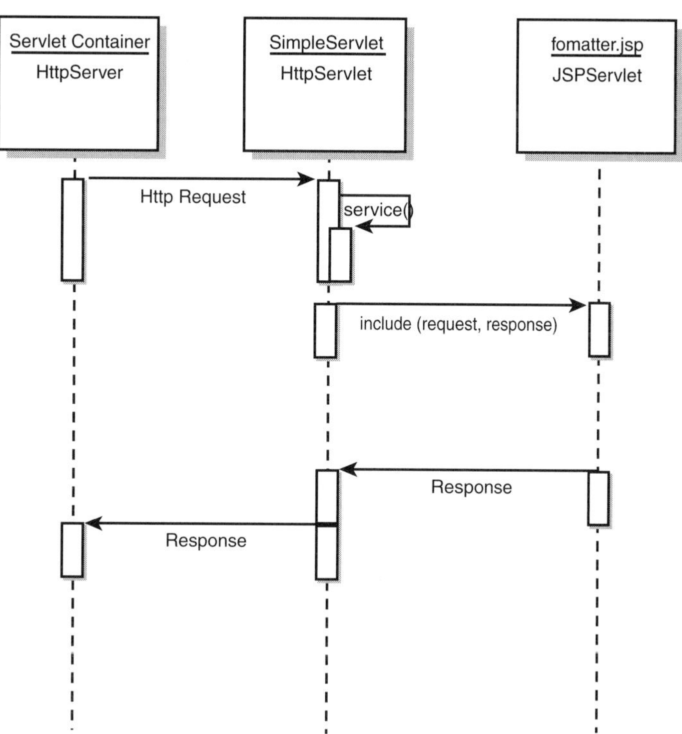

FIGURE 14.6 Include dispatching mechanism.

In the previous Web application login servlet, the `forward()` method is invoked to redirect the user to the login JSP when the user tries to log in with an invalid credential. Figure 14.7 describes the flow when the forward dispatching mechanism is used. In this case, the response is sent directly from the forwarded servlet/JSP to the client.

There are rules governing the use of `forward()` method:

- After forwarding the request, the request URL points to the forwarded page. The original URL is lost after the forward is successful. But if this information is needed, the developer can leverage the set of methods provided by the `ServletRequest` and all other known sub-interfaces for retrieving and setting attribute values. The developer can use it to store customized request information. If the original URL is needed, it has to be stored as a attribute in the request before forwarding.
- No output should be committed to the client before forwarding a request. If the servlet response has been flushed or committed, an `IllegalStateException` is thrown.

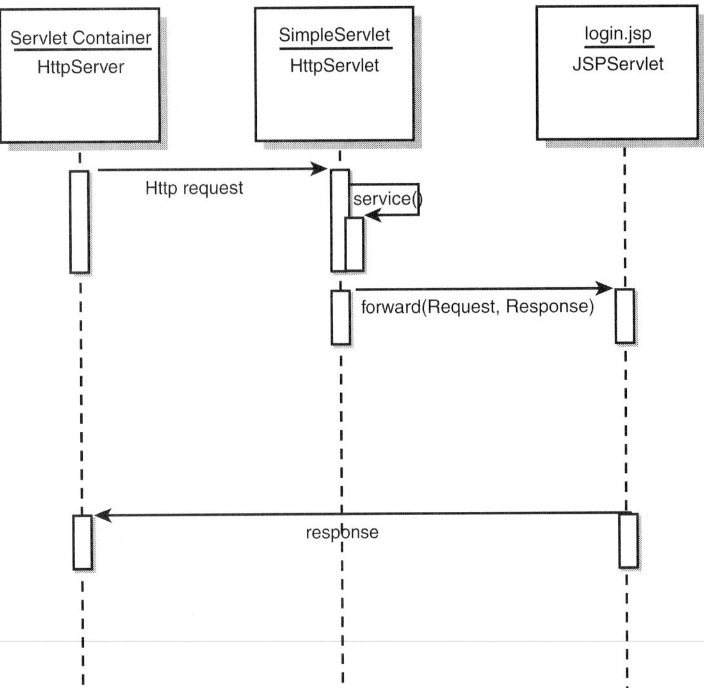

FIGURE 14.7 Forward dispatching mechanism.

- If the response buffer contains data, WebLogic Server clears the content before the request is forwarded.
- Any attempts to retrieve the `Writer` or the `OutputStream` after a request forward in the caller component results in an `IllegalStateException`.

According to the Servlet specification 2.3, authentication is not required for a forwarded request. WebLogic Server provides a way to override this behavior by using the `<check-auth-on-forward/>` element. This element has to be added to the `<container-descriptor>` element of the WebLogic-specific deployment descriptor (`weblogic.xml`) as given here:

```
<container-descriptor>
        <check-auth-on-forward/>
</container-descriptor>
```

Advanced Servlet Programming

We've covered the basic topics of servlet development. The Servlet API covered in earlier sections addresses most of the widely used API, and we also covered how to implement a simple HTTP servlet. We'll now start to discuss some advanced servlet topics with the protocol-independent `GenericServlet` and then move on topics such as servlet sessions, filters, and event listeners.

Generic Servlets

The `javax.servlet` package defines a generic base class, `GenericServlet`, for implementing all servlets irrespective of the underlying transport protocol. Although this servlet form isn't widely used, we'll cover it to complete our discussion of servlet capabilities. `GenericServlet` can be used to implement any servlet that needs to process, in the same manner, requests from different clients that use different protocols to communicate with WebLogic server. `HttpServlet`, which is covered in detail throughout the chapter, is an HTTP-specific servlet that extends from `GenericServlet` and is the most used servlet type.

The `GenericServlet` class that implements the `Servlet` and `ServletConfig` interfaces makes servlet implementation much easier. By these implementations, it takes care of providing simple versions of the life cycle methods `init()` and `destroy()`, and handles the methods from `ServletConfig`. `GenericServlet` handles the request using the `service()` method.

Implementing a Simple Generic Servlet

To implement a generic servlet, the developer has to implement the service method. Let's go over a simple example, which generates the factorial of a given number in Listing 14.6.

LISTING 14.6 Simple Generic Servlet

```
public class FactorialServlet extends GenericServlet {
    public void service(ServletRequest req, ServletResponse res)
        throws ServletException, IOException {
        int number = Integer.parseInt(req.getParameter("NUMBER"));
        res.setContentType("text/html");
        res.writeHeaders();
        ServletOutputStream out = res.getOutputStream();
        String output = "The factorial of " + number +
              "is " + generateFactorial (number);
        out.println(output);
        log(output);
    }

    // This function generates the factorial of a number
    // factorial(n) n! = 1*2*...* (n-1) *n
```

LISTING 14.6 Continued

```
    // returns the factorial
    public long generateFactorial(int number)
    {
            long factorial=1;
            for ( int j=1; j < n; j++ )
            {
                 factorial = factorial*j
            }
            return factorial;
    }
}
```

The FactorialServlet is a simple example of GenericServlet. As you can see, it's similar to the first servlet that we saw in the chapter. The only implemented method is the service() method, which processes the given input number and returns the factorial of that number.

Method Summary

The methods that are available for the servlet extending a GenericServlet class are summarized in Table 14.8.

TABLE 14.8 Generic Servlet Methods

Category	Method	Description
Life Cycle	init() and init(ServletConfig)	Initialization routine that takes no argument or a configuration object that encapsulates initial parameters
	destroy()	Cleanup routine
Configuration Parameters	getInitParameter getInitParameterNames	Functions to read init parameters from the configuration object
Properties	getServletName	Name of the servlet
	getServletInfo	Basic information of the servlet such as author, copyright, and so on
	getServletConfig	Returns the servlet configuration object
	getServletContext	Returns the servlet context; that is, the servlet's runtime environment
Logging	log(Msg) log(Msg,Throwable)	Two flavors of log routines that take a message and a Throwable object as arguments; helps logging messages to application log
Request Handler	service()	Handles client request; takes ServletRequest and ServletResponse as arguments

The log method provided in `GenericServlet` is a rudimentary method that enables servlets to write a simple message to the application log such as the WebLogic Server log. As we said earlier, there are better logging routines in JDK 1.4.

Limitations

Because it is protocol independent, `GenericServlet` comes with a few limitations:

- It does not support cookies.
- `HttpSession` and Session tracking are not supported.
- Redirection is not allowed.

As defined earlier, `GenericServlet` is protocol independent, so it can be used for many protocols, such as FTP, SMTP, and so on. Some of these limitations can be overcome by developing them as part of the servlet, but that makes the developer's job more difficult. The developer has to take care of providing the headers, cookies, session, request types, includes, authentications, and so forth. But these are taken care of for the developer in the case of `Http` servlets that extend the `GenericServlet` and implement the HTTP protocol.

Another limitation is that generic servlets are neither called nor managed automatically. This is as opposed to HTTP servlets, which are called by the server when HTTP messages are received. To make our example generic servlet run, we would have to write some kind of container or server to manage it. All these limitations beg the question: What good are generic servlets?

The answer lies in protocols other than HTTP. For example, some products offer SIP servlet servers or containers. (*SIP* stands for *Session Initiation Protocol*, and is used to set up Internet telephone calls, for example.) A SIP servlet is implemented from a SIP-specific sub interface of the `GenericServlet` interface.

For more information about SIP servlet, see `http://www.jcp.org/en/jsr/detail?id=116`.

Request and Response Streams

For handling binary data in the request and response, the Servlet API defines two classes:

- `javax.servlet.ServletInputStream` (extends `java.io.InputStream`)
- `javax.servlet.ServletOutputStream` (extends `java.io.OutputStream`)

The input stream can be used to read binary data from the user request. As mentioned earlier in the discussion of the `ServletRequest`, the `getInputStream()` function returns the servlet input stream object. This abstract class provides container-implemented `read()` functions. The `read()` functions read *n* bytes at a time and the `readline()` function reads the specified number of characters or stops when the new line is encountered.

The output stream can be used for sending binary data to the user. The output stream can be obtained from the `ServletResponse` object or one of the inherited classes, such as `HttpServletResponse`. The container is responsible for implementing the `write()` methods of the output stream. This class also provides a number of `print()` and `println()` functions for each and every data type.

TIP

For higher performance, streamed output is preferred whenever it's available. For example, in the case of servlets, it can be used for dumping the content of a text file to a Web page.

Request and Response Wrappers

The Servlet API introduced convenient wrapper classes for the `ServletRequest` and `ServletResponse` interfaces and equivalent implementations for the HTTP Servlet API. These classes, which are based on the Decorator pattern, are

- `ServletRequestWrapper` and `HttpServletRequestWrapper`
- `ServletResponseWrapper` and `HttpServletResponseWrapper`

According to Sun Microsystems, "These wrapper classes provide a convenient implementation of the request and response respectively and help users to adapt the request to a servlet and response from a servlet." The wrappers implement the same functions that are defined as part of the corresponding request and response objects. For example, `HttpServletRequestWrapper` stands for `HttpServletRequest`, and `HttpServletResponseWrapper` for `HttpServletResponse`. In other words, you can emulate a request event on the server using `ServletRequestWrapper` and capture the produced output with `ServletResponseWrapper`. Developers can also use these where a servlet might be used outside the container boundaries.

One of the most common uses for employing wrappers is to redirect output to a different output stream. One of the projects that effectively uses this servlet feature is the Apache project JetSpeed. JetSpeed uses wrappers to redirect output to an alternative output stream using the `EcsServletResponse` object. We'll look at an example later in the chapter during our discussion of the servlet filtering. Figure 14.8 describes the wrapper class hierarchy in the Servlet API specification and also includes simple response wrapper.

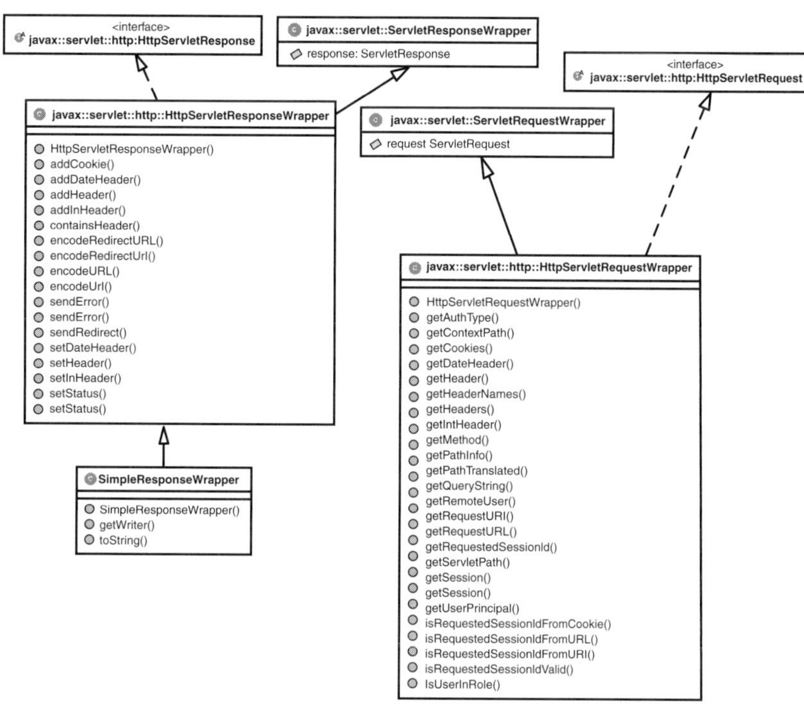

FIGURE 14.8 Class hierarchy—wrappers.

Handling Sessions

Sessions, by the simplest of definitions, enable you to track user's footprints over a Web site composed of many HTML pages or servlets. Sessions are a necessary requirement for all Web applications to be able to track the pages visited by the user and to make a Web site effective and usable. Over the years, many approaches have been adopted to implement sessions in Web applications, but most of them are cumbersome, difficult to implement, and nonstandard. One of the most common approaches was to embed state information as hidden fields in the page or to add it as strings to the URL. Although this approach worked, one main drawback was that the user information was lost when the user navigates out of the Web application to a different site and then comes back to the same site. There was no mechanism for passing information from one session to another.

Sessions and HTTP

By design, HTTP is a stateless protocol and every Web request could potentially open a new connection with the Web Server. In general, Web servers do not maintain state information about the users by default. This is true for a server such as WebLogic Server, even if it can maintain durable connections. In most e-commerce applications like online books, groceries, and electronics, the application has to be aware of the items that a customer has chosen between, a logon and logout in multiple visits. Sessions play a key role in implementing these Web applications. The server must identify the shopping cart of the customer and the things that he added to the cart during his navigation through the many pages of the application.

Sun's Servlet specification defines the `HttpSession` interface, which provides a standard set of approaches for servlet developers and containers such as WebLogic Server alike to map a user's session without tying them to a particular approach. The `HttpSession` object is capable of storing user details on the Web server across multiple requests, and provides a standard way for implementing sessions. It makes the user code more maintainable by hiding the complexities of session management. The `HttpSession` object can also be used to exchange user session details between different servlets. Now we'll have a detailed look at how to use the `HttpSession` object in servlets for session management with WebLogic Server.

Session Tracking Approaches

In this section, let's look at the different approaches available for session management in servlets.

Cookies

Cookies were introduced by Netscape to store user information associated with every Web Server. A *cookie* is defined as a text-only string that is stored temporarily or permanently on the client; that is, the Web browser. The capability to store information in this fashion can be leveraged to store a session identifier. The servlet container is responsible for sending the HTTP cookie to the client in order for the client to use it on every following request, identifying the request as participating in that session. By definition of the Sun Servlet specification, "the name of the session tracking cookie must be `JSESSIONID`." WebLogic Server uses this as the default value when unset, but provides a configuration parameter as part of the `session-descriptor` tag to change the name.

A simple example in which a cookie can be used is in the case of identifying a registered customer. After a user is successfully logged in, customer-related information can be stored in a cookie and sent back to the client. The following code snippet demonstrates the use of cookies to store a customer name:

```
void doPost(HttpSessionRequest req, HttpSessionResponse resp) {
...
String customerName=findCustomerName(accountId);
Cookie sessionCookie = new Cookie("CustomerName", customerName);
resp.addCookie(sessionCookie);
```

After this request is processed, the response contains the cookie `CustomerName`, which is saved in the browser's cache. When the customer returns to the Web application at a later time, this information, which might be used by the processing component, is sent back to the server.

URL-Rewriting

This is a complementary approach to session management, wherein the session ID is embedded into the links of the Web page that's sent back to the client. When the user navigates to these pages using the hyperlinks, the session ID is available to WebLogic Server for extraction as an `HttpSession`. Browsers have the capability to turn off cookies and thereby make session management using cookies impossible. For this reason, this approach should be always implemented so that the server can use this for session management if cookies are disabled. The only major disadvantage of this approach is that when the user comes to the site by clicking a link on an external site or by using a bookmark, the session information is not available at this time for the server.

There are two ways in which URL rewriting can be accomplished. When the servlet returns URLs to the browser, you can use `HttpServletResponse.encodeURL()`. When it redirects them, we have to use `HttpServletResponse.encodeRedirectURL()`. We'll look at both ways with the help of simple examples.

In an online pizza ordering system, you have a servlet with the following line:

```
out.println("<a href=\"/pizzeria/pizzalist\">pizzacatalog<a>");
```

The URL that's sent back to the client can be encoded using `encodeURL` before sending the URL to the output stream.

```
out.println("<a href=\"");
out.println(response.encodeURL ("/pizzaria/pizzalist"));
out.println("\">pizzacatalog</a>");
```

But suppose that you have to redirect the user to a local pizzeria's home page depending on the ZIP code of the customer. The code would look like the following:

```
response.sendRedirect("http://www.pizzeria.com/losangeles/pizzalist");
```

In this case, URL rewriting is accomplished using the `encodeRedirectURL` method. The redirect code will look like the following with URL rewriting enabled:

```
response.sendRedirect(response.encodeRedirectURL
➥("http://www.pizzeria.com/losangeles/pizzalist));
```

On the first request, the URL is encoded even if cookies are turned on. But it will stop encoding URL once it detects that the browser supports cookies. `HttpServletRequest` provides the utility method `isRequestedSessionIdFromCookie()`, which enables servlets to determine whether or not a given session ID was received from a cookie by checking the `Boolean` value returned. This helps the servlet to respond appropriately. Also, when a URL is rewritten along with encoding the parameters, it appends the session ID to the URL with the session ID preceded by a semicolon. For example, the URL

```
"SimpleServlet?INPUT_STRING=Hello World"
```

will be rewritten as

```
"SimpleServlet?INPUT_STRING=Hello+World:JSESSIONID=12343443"
```

Session Configuration

By default, WebLogic Server is enabled for session tracking. You don't need to set any parameters for configuring cookies and URL rewriting. But when some session properties must be modified according to an application specification, WebLogic Server controls the HTTP session configuration, including cookies and URL rewriting, by using the `Session-Descriptor` element tag in the WebLogic-specific deployment descriptor file, `weblogic.xml`. The following XML snippet sets the expiry time (in seconds) of the session ID cookie:

```
<session-descriptor>
  <session-param>
     <param-name>
       CookieMaxAgeSecs
     </param-name>
     <param-value>
      1000000
     </param-value>
  </session-param>
</session-descriptor>
```

Table 14.9 defines some of the valid `session-param` values related to the cookie-based session management in WebLogic Server.

TABLE 14.9 Session Identifier Cookie-Related Session Parameters

Type	Description
CookieName	User-defined name for the session ID cookie. Default value is JSESSIONID.
CookieDomain	Name of the domain for which the cookie is valid. Can only be the server and domain (for example, www.example.org) or the domain (example.org) and nothing else.
CookieMaxAgeSecs	Life of the cookie in seconds. Default is –1, which indicates that the cookies expires when the browser closes (in-memory cookie).
CookiesEnabled	Enables cookies by default, but can be turned off by setting this attribute to false.
CookiePath	Virtual directory where the cookie will be stored and retrieved. This allows multiple JSESSIONID cookies that point to different applications inside the same domain.
CookieComment	Useful tag to add comments to the cookie file.

Secure Sessions

Secure Sockets Layer (SSL) provides an effective mechanism for session management in HTTPS-based request-response. The mechanism allows a servlet engine such as WebLogic Server to identify the client request as being part of a continuing session.

But one important consideration when implementing session is that cookies are not totally secure. You should avoid storing important data in cookies. The only protection that can be offered to cookies is by forcing the browser to send them only if HTTPS is enabled. This can be achieved by using the `setSecure()` method on the `Cookie` class. But this cookie-secure parameter applies only when the cookie's originating server used a secure protocol to set the cookie's value.

Hidden Form Fields

In this approach, a hidden input field is used to store the session information. But this approach is limited in use because it can be used only when every page in a Web application is generated dynamically.

Using the HttpSession Object

The core interface of the session management implementation in servlets is the `HttpSession` interface. Cookies and URL rewriting form the foundation for this high-level interface. For most servers, cookies are the automatic option for propagating the session data to the client and when the browser turns off cookies, URL rewriting is used instead.

Creating the Session Object

The `HttpSession` object is accessible for all servlets through the request object, which is passed as an argument to the `service()` and the `doXXX()` methods. The session can be obtained from the request object as given here:

```
HttpSession session = req.getSession(true);
```

The boolean argument to the `getSession()` method determines whether to create a new session if one does not exist for the specific client. In this earlier code, `getSession` returns the existing session (if one exists) or creates a new one. Alternatively, when the argument is false, `getSession` returns null if the session does not exist.

The `HttpSession` interface provides a rudimentary `isNew()` method that returns true if the server created the session in the `getSession` method, or false if the client sent this session in the request.

NOTE

In authenticated sites, it's advisable to use `getSession(false)` in all servlets. This preserves the existing session and makes sure that no one can enter any part of the site unauthenticated. The exception is your login servlet, where you would use `getSession(true)` if the credentials are good. Even in nonauthenticated sites, making a call to `getSession` at the top of every servlet makes sure that the session isn't lost.

Using the Session Object

The Session object created in the previous step lives in WebLogic Server during the lifetime the session, and is available for the servlet developer to add attributes to and remove attributes from. The collected information is associated with a single client and is available through the HttpSession object on subsequent visits of the client to the Web application.

HttpSession API

The HttpSession interface provides a number of methods for manipulating the client data inside the session object, as well as methods to read the properties of a given session such as the creation time, modified time, and so on. Attributes in the session object are manipulated with the following functions:

- getAttribute()—This function takes a String identifier that identifies the attribute as an argument and returns the corresponding value.
- getAttributeNames()—Returns an enumeration of names of the attributes embedded in the session object. The following code snippet prints the attribute names inside a session object along with the values:

```
HttpSession session = req.getSession(true);
Enumeration ee = session.getAttributeNames();
String attrName,value;
While (ee.hasMoreElements() )
{
       attrName = ee.nextElement();
       value = (String) session.getAttribute(attrName);
       System.out.println("Attribute:"+attrName+"="+str);
}
```

- setAttribute—Sets or overwrites an attribute along with a corresponding value.
- removeAttribute—Removes the attribute from the session object.

The following code snippet extracted from a typical LoginServlet of an e-commerce Web application demonstrates the earlier functions for setting attributes into the user session:

```
HttpSession session = req.getSession(true);
session.setAttribute("CustomerId", dto.getCustomerId());
session.setAttribute("CustomerName", dto.getFirstName() + " " +
➥ dto.getLastName());
if (dto.getIsBuyer().booleanValue())
    session.setAttribute("IsBuyer", "true");
if (dto.getIsSeller().booleanValue())
    session.setAttribute("IsSeller", "true")
```

As mentioned earlier, the HttpSession interface provides a set of useful methods as listed in Table 14.10.

TABLE 14.10 HttpSession Interface

Type	Description
getCreationTime	Returns the creation time in milliseconds.
getLastAccessedTime()	Returns the last accessed time in milliseconds as a Long value.
getId()	Returns the unique identifier for the session. This is the same as the value stored in the JSESSIONID cookie and passed in for URL rewriting.

In an application, where the user-related sensitive data is stored in the session, a logout operation is a must. The HttpSession interface provides a function to invalidate a client session. The invalidate() function, which is called on the user session object, logs the user out. In doing so, it clears all the user-related session data that was collected during the course of the client session, which might have spanned multiple visits to the Web application. The following code snippet is simple example of a logout:

```
HttpSession session = req.getSession(false);
if (session != null) {
      session.invalidate();
}
```

When the same session is referred to after the invalidate call, the servlet container throws an IllegalStateException. This exception can be used to send the user back to the logon screen. The invalidate() call, although it makes the client session invalid, does not remove the user information from the server context. For the purpose of handling sessions across multiple Web applications in the same server, WebLogic Server provides a special set of authentication methods that log out the user from multiple Web applications in the same server context as part of the weblogic.security.servlet.ServletAuthentication object. This object is a WebLogic helper class and is used for implementing form-based authentication. It also helps to simplify the program-based authentication in servlets.

- invalidateAll—Takes the servlet request as an argument and invalidates all the sessions for the current user.
- logout()—Takes the servlet request as the argument and logs out from the current Web app by removing the user authentication data in the session and leaving rest of the session data intact.
- done()—Similar to the logout call.
- killCookie()—Kills the active session identification cookie, leaving the session on the server to time out.

According to the Sun specification, a servlet container such as WebLogic Server should take care of making the HttpSession object unique at the Web application (servlet context) level.

Session Timeouts

Session timeouts play an important role in cleaning up client sessions that stay up for a long time because the client does not come back to invalidate the session.

WebLogic Server provides the following server configuration options for setting the timeout values for sessions. The timeout can be configured using the different configuration elements listed here. These tags are in both Web application deployment descriptors.

- <session-config> <session-timeout> tag (web.xml)
- <session-descriptor> TimeoutSecs parameter (weblogic.xml)

The Web deployment descriptor (web.xml) <session-timeout> element inside the <session-config> element indicates, in number of minutes, the client stays alive. This setting overrides all other timeout settings that can be set elsewhere (for example, the <session-descriptor> timeout parameter) except when it is set to -2. When set to -2, it indicates to the server to use the session-descriptor value instead of the session-timeout value. When set to -1, sessions do not time out and the value set in the <session-descriptor> element is also ignored. The default value is -2. The following XML snippet makes sure that sessions do not time out at all:

```
<session-config>
   <session-timeout>
        -1
   </session-timeout>
</session-config>
```

The session-descriptor element TimeoutSecs session parameter also can be used to set the session timeout values, following the rules explained earlier. The value represented by TimeoutSecs is the number of seconds that WebLogic Server will wait before timing out of a session. The default value is 3600. The following XML snippet sets the timeout to 10000 seconds:

```
<session-descriptor>
  <session-param>
     <param-name>
       TimeoutSecs
     </param-name>
     <param-value>
      10000
     </param-value>
  </session-param>
</session-descriptor>
```

The `HttpSession` API provides the `setMaxInactiveInterval()` function, which overrides the default timeout value set by the servlet container. The `getMaxInactiveInterval()` function call returns the current value of the session timeout. The default value of the session timeout is usually set to `-1`, which indicates that the session never expires.

Session Persistence

WebLogic Server offers a facility to persist sessions in a number of different ways. Session persistence offers quite a few advantages:

- By providing a facility for storing sessions in a permanent store such as a file or a database, session persistence offers increased availability of sessions because they're protected against server crashes.

CAUTION

Even if a session is persisted, it doesn't mean that the session will not be lost. There is a possibility that the server could become unavailable as the session is persisted. The client will see relevant error messages when this situation happens. But the session can be retrieved only by one of the following methods: the user doesn't close his browser (else the cookie could be lost); the server comes up before the session expires; or the client makes a request to the server after it comes back up but before the session expires.

- Enhanced load balancing and optimized performance by enabling caching for sessions in memory, a file, or a database.

Sessions can be persisted in any of the following ways:

- Memory—This is single-server nonreplication persistence in which the session data in stored in the single WebLogic Server instance; therefore, it does not provide failover.
- File—In this mode, sessions are persisted to a file to a directory specified in the server configuration.
- Cookies—This option, which was explained earlier, is limited in the kind of data that can be stored as session data. Cookies only provide a facility to store strings. This is also dependent on the browser's setting for cookies because browsers have the option to turn off cookies. This makes their behavior highly unpredictable and inadequate for most systems. This approach should be avoided.
- Database—In this case, sessions are persisted to a database table using JDBC. This option offers the highest reliability for session persistence, but it comes at a cost of performance overhead.
- In-memory replication—This option can be used in WebLogic clusters.

The session state configuration is managed by the <session-descriptor> element (briefly discussed in the cookies section as well as in the section on session timeouts) along with some of the valid properties in Table 14.8. The main property governing the type of session persistence is PersistentStoreType, which is a session parameter. This property can be set to one of the following values: memory, file, jdbc, cookie, and replicated.

There are associated properties, which are required apart from PersistentStoreType depending on the type of session persistence. Table 14.11 summarizes the list of properties that are part of the session-descriptor element in weblogic.xml.

TABLE 14.11 Session Persistence

Property	Store Type	Description
PersistentStoreDir	file	Specifies the directory where the WebLogic sessions will be stored.
PersistentStorePool	jdbc	Specifies the JDBC connection pool to be used for managing JDBC connections. For a detailed discussion about the JDBC connection pool, refer to "Managing Database Connectivity with JDBC."
JDBConnectionTimeoutSecs	jdbc	Specifies the time in seconds that WebLogic Server waits for a JDBC connection.
PersistentStoreCookieName	cookie	Name of the cookie for cookie-based session persistence. Default is WLCOOKIE.
InvalidationIntervalSecs	60	This value tells WebLogic Server how long it has to wait to do the housecleaning checks for timed-out and invalid sessions and delete them. The range for this element is from 1 second to 1 week (604800 seconds).
SwapIntervalSecs	10	This value indicates the WebLogic Server sleep time between transferring the least recently used sessions from the cache to the persistent store.
CacheSize	1024	Helps to control the number of cached sessions that can be active in memory at a given time.

Some of the additional things that the WebLogic administrator has to remember are listed here:

- When the store type is memory, a session lives only for the duration of the life of the server. That is, when the server goes down, the session state is lost.
- When the store type is file in a WebLogic clustered environment, PersistentStoreDir should point to a shared directory between the servers.
- When the store type is jdbc, the user needs to create wl_servlet_sessions table with read/write permissions for the users of the JDBC connection pool writing the

session. The definition of the `wl_servlet_sessions` table with field names and type can be viewed at the BEA site `http://e-docs.bea.com/wls/docs81/webapp/sessions.html` in the "Using Database for Persistent Storage" subsection.

- Cookie-based session persistence offers a range of benefits. Because the session data is stored in the client, clustering and failover logic are not required. It also makes the life of the server independent of the session persistence; that is, servers can be restarted without losing session data. But cookie-based persistence is suitable only when the sessions contain very little data. There are many limitations to using cookies.

NOTE

At this time, we won't look at the clustering option for session persistence. It's the most efficient option of session persistence for WebLogic clusters, but that discussion is deferred to the chapter on WebLogic clusters (Chapter 36).

A Complete Session Example

We've so far examined, in detail, the `HttpSession` API and how to implement servlets. In this section, we convert the `SimpleServlet` we developed in an earlier section to be session aware. The modified servlet will keep track of the number of times that a client visits the Web site for doing the requested function. Listing 14.7 lists only the modified `doGet()` method with sessions. All the other methods remain the same as defined in Listing 14.5.

LISTING 14.7 Simple Servlet with Sessions

```
// Handles the GET request
    public void doGet(HttpServletRequest req, HttpServletResponse res)
        throws IOException
   {

         String convertedString,inputString;
        //Get the session object
      HttpSession session = req.getSession(true);

        //read the request parameter INPUT_STRING
      // If the input String is null
      // it returns "hello world" In uppercase

         if ((inputString = req.getParameter("INPUT_STRING"))
             != null) {
             convertedString = inputString.toUpperCase();
```

LISTING 14.7 Continued

```
13          }
14          else {
15              convertedString =defaultString ;
16          }
17        // Get the visit count value
18         Long visitCount= (Long) session.getAttribute("visit Count");
19         if (visitCount==null)
20            visitCount = new Long(1);
21         else
22             visitCount = new Long(visitCount.longValue() + 1);
23         session.setAttribute("visit_Count", visitCount);

24          // Set the content type first
25          res.setContentType("text/html");

26          // get the PrintWriter
27          PrintWriter out = res.getWriter();

28          out.println(
➥"<html><head><title>SimpleServlet - Session Enabled</title></head>");
29          out.println("<body>");
30          out.println("<h1>");

31          out.println("The input string upper case(d):" + convertedString );
32          out.println("</h1>");
33          out.println("<br><br>");
34          out.println("Number of Conversions Performed <b>" +
➥ visitCount + "</b> times.<p>");
35          out.println("<h2>Session Data:</h2>
36          out.println("Is this the first time to the site?: " + session.isNew());
37          out.println("<br>Client Identifier: " + session.getId());
38          out.println("<br>First Conversion using the Servlet: " +
➥session.getCreationTime());
39          out.println("<br>Last Conversion Time: " + session.getLastAccessedTime());

40          out.println("</h1></body></html>");
41      }
```

The `session` object is created in line 6. If a session does not exist, `getSession(true)` returns a new session. If it is a returning client, it returns the client's session corresponding to its ID. After creating a new session or retrieving an old session, attributes can be read using getAttribute (line 18) and modified using setAttribute (line 23). The SimpleServlet output is also modified to include the session-related information as demonstrated by lines 28 through 37.

> **TIP**
>
> It's a good practice to create the session at the beginning of the method to make it evident that it participates in a session.

When this servlet is invoked for the first time, you should see output that looks like the following:

```
Number of Conversions Performed 1 times.
Session Data:
Is this the first time to the site?: true
Client Identifier: 2Vg5oH677V1yA9b1fX2vNv76K9Q33hl9Z7SXiIcc2h8azDKQKYJc!
➥-860518150!1050009849936
First Conversion using the Servlet: 1050009849936
Last Conversion Time: 1050009849936
```

The session is not created in subsequent calls, as you can see from the value of First conversion using the Servlet in the following output. All other things have a new value for the second invocation.

```
Number of Conversions Performed 2 times.
Session Data:
Is this the first time to the site?: false
Client Identifier: 2Vg5oH677V1yA9b1fX2vNv76K9Q33hl9Z7SXiIcc2h8azDKQKYJc!
➥-860518150!1050009849936
First Conversion using the Servlet: 1050009849936
Last Conversion Time: 1050009849916
```

Application Events and Listeners

Application events such as session-related events and servlet context–related events were added to Sun's Servlet specifications in version 2.3. These events facilitate notifications when there is a change in the servlet context or in the HttpSession object. The application server is responsible for providing the infrastructure for handling such events with the help of listener classes. The listener classes can be configured using the Web application deployment descriptor, and they respond to the various events that happen during the life of the session object or the servlet context.

The servlet context events are generated during life cycle operations, such as Web application deployment or when it is undeployed, and also during attribute manipulation, including adding, removing, and replacing them. Similarly, HttpSession events are generated during life cycle operations such as activation or passivation of session state as well as during HTTP session attribute maintenance (adding, deleting, and updating an attribute) as shown in Figure 14.9.

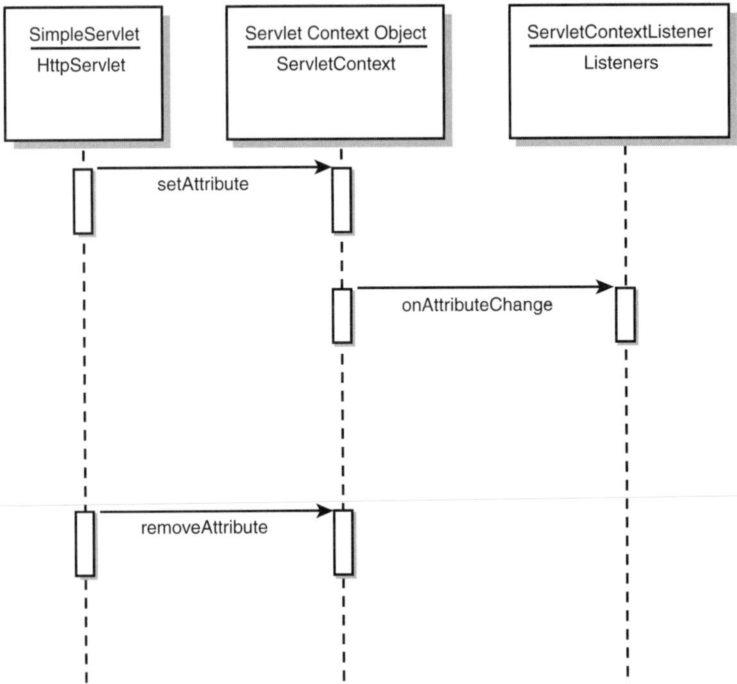

FIGURE 14.9 HttpSession life cycle events.

The life cycle events trigger, especially the servlet context events, could probably be used to initialize or clean up resources such as databases, legacy connections, and so on because the events indicate when the application is deployed or undeployed. On the other hand, HTTP session events can be used to monitor the session state along with its attributes.

Using the Listener API

The Servlet specification defines different sets of interfaces for managing the servlet context–related events and the HTTP session events. The interfaces are defined in the `javax.servlet` and `javax.servlet.http` packages, respectively.

ServletContextListener

The `ServletContextListener` interface manages the life cycle–related events of the servlet context. When a Web application is initialized or created, the `contextInitialized()` method of the listener is invoked and `contextDestroyed()` is called when the application prepares to shut down.

ServletContextAttributesListener
This listener interface is used to implement a listener to handle events when the attributes are `added()`, `deleted()`, or `replaced()` in the servlet context.

HttpSessionListener
The `HttpSessionListener` interface manages the life cycle–related events of the HTTP session state. When the HTTP session is activated or created, the `sessionCreated()` method of the listener is invoked and `sessionDestroyed()` is called when the HTTP session is to be invalidated.

HttpSessionAttributeListener
This listener interface is used to implement a listener to handle events when attributes are `added()`, `deleted()`, or `replaced()` in the HTTP session object. For example:

```
MyAttrListner implements HttpSessionAttributeListener{
// Implmentation methods
}
```


This class reacts to any attribute change that occurs because of either of the following function calls on a session object:

```
Session.setAttribute("object",AnySessionObj);
```

or

```
Session.getAttribute("object");
```

Apart from the interfaces listed here, the Servlet specification also defines `HttpSessionActivationListener` and `HttpSessionBindingListener` for attributes that are bound to a session.

HttpSessionBindingListener
The class implementing this interface is notified with an `HttpBindingEvent` object when an attribute is explicitly bound to a session or unbound from a session. The `HttpBindingEvent` object provides methods to get the attribute name and value that changed. For example:

```
MyBindingObject implements HttpSessionListener{
// Implmentation methods
}
```

In this case, the implementation methods of the class react when it is bound or unbound to a session with one of the following calls on the `session` object:

```
Session.setAttribute("object",MyBindingObject);
```

or

```
Session.removeAttribute("object");
```

At this point, it is good to note the differences between this interface and the `HttpSessionAttributeListener` interface. They seem to do the same thing, but when a class implements `HttpSessionBindingListener`, it works only for binding methods (add/remove). On the other hand, when a class implements `HttpSessionAttributeListener`, it has the capability to react to any attribute change (add/remove/replace).

HttpSessionActivationListener

This interface is for objects that are bound to a session as attributes. The container is responsible for notifying the attributes that implement this interface when a session to which it is bound is activated or passivated. *Passivation* is the process by which sessions are stored in a persistent store for later use in persistent sessions or might be transferred to another server for failover in a WebLogic cluster scenario. *Activation* is the reverse process in which a session is brought back into memory for use with the associated client. EJBs use a similar principle for the different types of Enterprise JavaBeans; this is explained in great detail in the chapter on EJBs. This interface provides the event tracking methods `sessionDidActivate()` and `sessionWillPassivate()` that take an `HttpSessionEvent` object as an argument. The `HttpSessionEvent` represents the changes to the session inside a Web application. This object provides a useful `getSession` method to return the current session.

Configuring Listeners

The listeners are configured in the Web application deployment descriptor `web.xml` using the `<listener>` element. The following XML snippet defines two listeners that implement the `HttpSessionListener` and `HttpSessionAttributeListener` interfaces explained earlier:

```
<web-app>
   <listener>
      <listener-class>servlets.simple.SimpleSessionListener</listener-class>
   </listener>
   <listener>
      <listener-class>servlets.simple.SimpleSessionAttributeListener</listener-
class>
   </listener>

</web-app>
```

WebLogic Server allows multiple listeners for the same event. The listeners are invoked in the order in which they're defined in the `web.xml` file. The only exception to that rule is shutdown events: invocation is in reverse order.

Implementing Simple Http Listeners

In the previous section, we extended the SimpleServlet implementation to include sessions to store the user's footprints along with access history (visit count). Now, in this section, we look at an alternative implementation of tracking counts using the session listener and session attribute listeners.

Simple HTTP Session Listener

Listing 14.8 implements a simple HTTP session listener that, with the help of life cycle events, tracks a client visits to a Web application and prints the output to the WebLogic Server Console. This can be used in conjunction with the session example we saw earlier in the chapter.

LISTING 14.8 Simple HTTP Session Listener

```
package wlsunleashed.servlets;

import javax.servlet.*;
import javax.servlet.http.*;
import java.util.*;
import java.io.*;

/*
*  Simple Session Listener for maintaining the user's footprints
*/

public class SimpleSessionListener implements HttpSessionListener {

  HttpSession session = null;

  // default constructor
  public SimpleSessionListener() {
  }

  // Life cycle event invoked when the session is created
  // Adds a counter to the session to tract the user's visit to the site
  public void sessionCreated(HttpSessionEvent evt){
    session = evt.getSession();
    Long visitCount = new Long(1);
    System.out.println("Session Created");
    session.setAttribute("visit_Count", visitCount);
  }

  // Life cycle event invoked when the session is destroyed
  // Prints the total number of visits to the server by the server
```

14

LISTING 14.8 Continued

```
  public void sessionDestroyed(HttpSessionEvent evt){
    session = evt.getSession();
   System.out.println("Session Destroyed");
    Long visitCount = (Long) session.getAttribute("visit_Count");
    if (visitCount==null)
        visitCount = new Long(1);
    else
        visitCount = new Long(visitCount.longValue() + 1);
    System.out.println("Total Number of Hits="+visitCount.longValue());  }
}
```

Simple HTTP Session Attribute Listener

The session attribute listener can be used with the simple session example that we saw earlier (`SimpleServletWithSession`) to track the exact timing of client visits to the servlet and to print the output to the WebLogic Server Console. Listing 14.9 provides a simple implementation of an attribute listener.

LISTING 14.9 Simple HTTP Session Attribute Listener

```
package wlsunleashed.servlets;

import javax.servlet.*;
import javax.servlet.http.*;
import java.util.*;
import java.io.*;

/*
*  Simple Session Attribute Listener for maintaining the user's
*  access time of the servlet
*/

public class SimpleSessionAttributeListener implements
 HttpSessionAttributeListener {

  public SimpleSessionAttributeListener() {
  }
  /**
   * Invoked when attribute is removed using setAttribute for the first time
   */

   // Tracks the user's access to the servlet using "visit_Count"
   public void attributeAdded(HttpSessionBindingEvent evt) {
```

```
    if ( evt.getName().equals("visit_Count")){
        System.out.print("Session(Attribute Added): " +
➥evt.getSession().getId() );
        System.out.println(" Time accessed:"+ new Date());
    }
  }

  /**
   * Invoked when attribute is removed using removeAttribute
   */
  public void attributeRemoved(HttpSessionBindingEvent evt) {
   System.out.print("Attribute removed: " + evt.getName() +"="+ evt.getValue());
   System.out.println(" in session : " + evt.getSession().getId() );
  }

  /**
   *  // Tracks the user's access to the servlet using "visit_Count"
   */
  public void attributeReplaced(HttpSessionBindingEvent evt) {
   if ( evt.getName().equals("visit_Count")){
        System.out.print("Session(Attribute Replaced): " +
➥ evt.getSession().getId() );
        System.out.println(" Time accessed:"+ new Date());
    }
  }
}
```

Similarly, servlet context listeners (implemented using `ServletContextListener`) and their corresponding attribute listeners can be used both to manipulate resources such as database connections and when servlets use the Web application context to share data or resources between them.

Simple HTTP Listener Configuration

To configure the listeners we've written here, we need to add event listener declarations using the `<listener>` element to the Web application deployment descriptor (`web.xml`). You can define multiple listeners and WebLogic Server will invoke the event listener classes in the order in which they appear in the deployment descriptor.

```
<listener>
    <listener-class>wlsunleashed.servlets.SimpleSessionListener</listener-class>
</listener>
<listener>
    <listener-class>
```

14

```
➥wlsunleashed.servlets.SimpleSessionAttributeListener
➥</listener-class>
</listener>
```

When you invoke the simple session servlet after you configure the attribute listener, the following messages will appear on the WebLogic Console when the attributes change:

```
Session(Attribute Added): 2V298nN1Q7TDWmMFUmpxb3k8ZWmC00joB7ZBMdCPHV3biRQ8DN5W!-
444702951!1050015293694
Time accessed:Thu Apr 10 15:54:53 PDT 2003
Session(Attribute Replaced): 2V298nN1Q7TDWmMFUmpxb3k8ZWmC00joB7ZBMdCPHV3biRQ8DN5
W!-444702951!1050015293694
Time accessed:Thu Apr 10 15:54:54 PDT 2003
```

Filters

The filters concept was introduced in Servlet specification 2.3 to give Web component developers a facility to transform requests and modify the servlet response. Filters are like listeners in that they cannot be invoked directly by a Web client. They are like pre- and post-processors for the request and response, respectively. Filters can modify both the header and content of the request/response. The filter component can work only on an existing request or a response; that is, it cannot create a request or response by itself. This capability provides an advantage for manipulating any associated Web application resource, namely, servlets, JSP, and so on. A single filter can be used to manipulate multiple Web resources' requests and responses.

Figure 14.10 describes the main tasks in a filter and some of the uses of a filter. On an incoming request/response from a Web component such as a servlet, the configured filter extracts the request or response. The filter then applies the rules defined in it on the request/response. The rules applied modify the request/response content, the header information, or both. The rules are applied using a customized version of the request or the response object. As shown in Figure 14.10, filters can integrate with external entities such as databases, files for operations like logging, authentication, caching, and so on. Filters provide the capability to manipulate the request/response before it reaches the Web component/client. Additionally, a given request can be passed through a chain of filters, each implementing a different function such as auditing, logging, encryption, and so forth.

Filters can be used to implement some of the following features:

- Authentication component in Web applications
- Log requests and responses
- Transform XML data using XSLT for presentation
- Implement security features such as encryption
- Cache and audit requests and responses

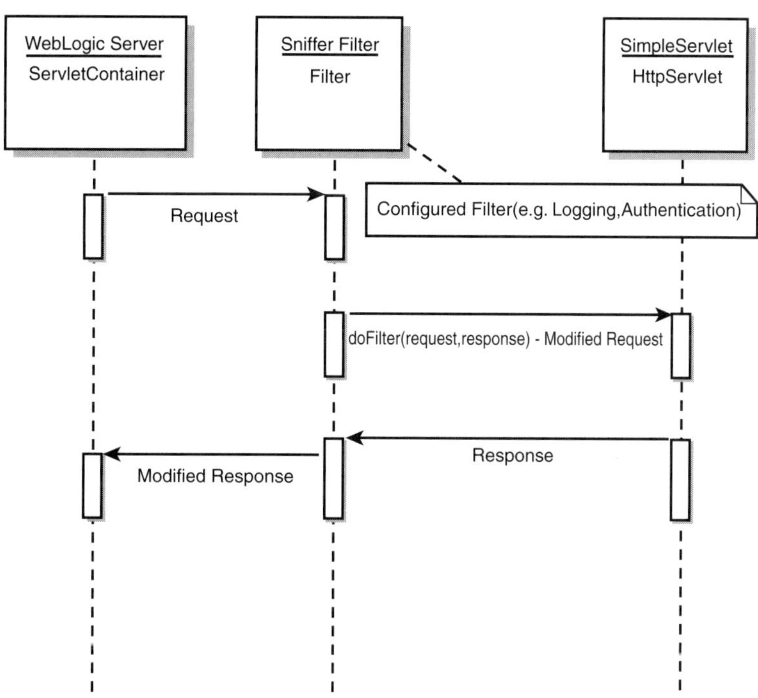

FIGURE 14.10 Filter tasks.

Additionally, the Sun specification suggests that filters can be used for data compression, image conversion, and to trigger external events such as database events.

Filter API

The heart of the filtering concept is the `Filter` interface defined in the `javax.servlet` package. This interface defines the methods for life cycle operations such as initialization and termination as well as for filtering operations. A user-defined filter should implement the following functions:

- `doFilter()`—This method is invoked by the container, implements the filtering logic, and is called every time a client request passes through a filter chain.
- `init()`—An initialization routine that is called by the container before the filter is first used.
- `destroy()`—A cleanup routine that's called by the container before a filter is destroyed.

The `init()` method should be successfully executed before the filter can be used. The `destroy()` method can be used to free up resources such as threads, memory, and so forth and can be used to store any persistent state to a permanent store such as a file or a database. The `finalize` clause is also an alternative for the `destroy` method. But `destroy` and `finalize` should not be heavily relied on because there is no assurance that they will be invoked all the time (for example, in server crashes). So, it is not prudent to rely on this method to persist important information.

The `Filter` API definition includes a configuration interface (`FilterConfig`) and a `FilterChain` interface to link multiple filters for processing the same client request.

FilterConfig Interface

This configuration object is used to pass any user-specified configuration parameters of the filter to the `init()` method. Similar to other configuration objects, such as `ServletConfig`, this interface defines `getInitParameter()` and `getInitParameterNames()` methods for returning the value of a parameter and an enumeration of parameter names, respectively. This interface also provides the utility method `getFilterName()`, which returns the name of the filter as defined in the deployment descriptor. The configuration object also provides a method (`getServletContext()`) to return the current servlet context, thereby giving the filters a handle to the Web application context and their environment settings.

FilterChain

This object is passed as an argument to the `doFilter` method along with the request and response. The `FilterChain` object passes the request and response to the next entity in the chain. If the calling filter is the last filter in the chain, `FilterChain` causes the `service()` method of the servlet to be invoked.

Earlier in this section, we pointed out that filters could be used to perform XSLT transformation on the servlet response before it's presented to the client. Multiple filters could be used to do the transformation depending on the client's capability to present them and some of the filters might not be applied to all client types. A filter chain can be used to configure the set of filters that's to be invoked and the order in which they have to be invoked.

A Simple Filter

Now we'll look at implementing a simple filter that logs the remote host accessing your application. To keep it simple, the filter logs the value to the WebLogic Server Console. Listing 14.10 is a simple sniffer filter implementation.

LISTING 14.10 Simple Filter

```
package wlsunleashed.servlets.;
import java.io.*;
import java.util.*;
import javax.servlet.*;
import javax.servlet.http.*;
```

```
6 public final class SniffFilter implements Filter {
7    private FilterConfig filterConfig = null;

8    public void init(FilterConfig filterConfig) throws ServletException {
9        this.filterConfig = filterConfig;
10    }

11    public void destroy() {
12        this.filterConfig = null;
13    }

14 public void doFilter(ServletRequest request, ServletResponse response,
15      FilterChain chain) throws IOException, ServletException {

16     if (filterConfig == null)
17        return;

18     HttpServletRequest req = (HttpServletRequest)request;

19     Enumeration e = req.getHeaderNames();
20     while(e.hasMoreElements()) {
21       String headerName =(String) e.nextElement();
22       System.out.println(headerName+"="+req.getHeader(headerName));
23    }

24     System.out.println("RemoteHost = "+req.getRemoteHost());

25     chain.doFilter(request, response);
26   }
27 }
```

In line 24 of Listing 14.10, the simple sniffer filter writes the remote hostname accessing this Web application to the console. Because this is the only configured filter in the chain, it calls `chain.doFilter` in line 25, which invokes the servlet instance for which the request was intended.

Simple Filter Configuration

We have to configure the filters using the Web application deployment descriptor (`web.xml`). The following XML snippet provides the configuration of the simple filter discussed earlier:

```
<web-app>
...
```

```
<filter>
    <filter-name>sniffFilter</filter-name>
   <filter-class>wlsunleashed.servlets.SniffFilter</filter-class>
</filter>
<filter-mapping>
    <filter-name>sniffFilter</filter-name>
    <url-pattern>/*</url-pattern>
</filter-mapping>

...
</web-app>
```

The configuration defines the logical name of the filter for the simple filter defined earlier along with the filter mapping that defines the URL pattern for which the filter has been defined.

Parameterized Filters

As we've seen, the `FilterConfig()` interface is used to send initialization parameters, if any, to the filter. The initialization parameters are defined in the `web.xml` file along with the filter element as a sub element. Let's define a default, which will be printed during initialization of the filter.

```
<filter>
    <filter-name>SniffFilter</filter-name>
    <filter-class>wlsunleashed.servlets.SniffFilter</filter-class>
               <init-param>
                     <param-name>welcomeMessage</param-name>
                     <param-value>A Simple Filter Example</param-name>
               </init-param>
</filter>
```

The `welcomeMessage` parameter is accessible to the filter through the `FilterConfig.getInitParameter()` function.

Using Wrappers

One of the most important uses of a filter is the capability to customize a servlet response/request to perform the defined filtering task and to enable overriding of the default behavior of the response. This design enables developers to exercise more control over the responses sent back to the client and to a target Web resource in the filter chain. Filters can be used to add attributes, modify them in a response, and even add attributes to it before it reaches the client.

The filter should modify the response before it's flushed by the processing servlet to the client. The most common approach is to pass a wrapped stream to the processing servlet.

The wrapped stream takes care of preventing the flushing of the response to the original response stream and allows the defined filters to modify the response.

The wrapped or stand-in stream is passed into the servlet using a response wrapper that overrides at least one of two methods—`getOutputStream()` and `getWriter()`—as demonstrated in Listing 14.11.

LISTING 14.11 Simple Response Wrapper

```
package wlsunleashed.servlets;

import javax.servlet.*;
import javax.servlet.http.*;
import java.io.*;

public class SimpleResponseWrapper extends
HttpServletResponseWrapper
{
    private StringWriter output;


    public SimpleResponseWrapper(HttpServletResponse response)
    {
        super(response);
        output = new StringWriter();
    }

    public String toString() {
      return output.toString();
    }

    public PrintWriter getWriter()
    {
        return new PrintWriter(output);
    }
}
```

The general rule for overriding request and response methods is to extend servlet wrapper objects such as `ServletRequestWrapper` and `HttpServletRequestWrapper` for requests, and `ServletResponseWrapper` and `HttpServletResponseWrapper` for responses.

In the simple filter we've defined, we wrap the response in the `SimpleResponseWrapper` to enable modifying the processed response. The wrapped response is passed to the next entity in the filter chain; that is, the servlet instance in our case. The `SimpleServlet` writes the response to the stream that is embedded in the `SimpleResponseWrapper`.

```
PrintWriter out = response.getWriter();
SimpleResponseWrapper wrapper = new SimpleResponseWrapper(
   (HttpServletResponse)response);
chain.doFilter(request, wrapper);
```

When the `chain.doFilter` method returns, the servlet response can be retrieved from the wrapped output stream and customized to our needs. For example, we can add the date time value when the request was completed.

```
StringWriter strWr = new StringWriter();
strWr.write(wrapper.toString().substring(0, wrapper.toString().
➥indexOf("</body>")-1));
      strWr.write("<p>\n<center> <font color='blue'>" +
➥ "Request Processed Time=" +new java.util.Date() +
➥"</font><center>");
strWr.write("\n</body></html>");
response.setContentLength(strWr.toString().length());
out.write(strWr.toString());
out.close();
```

The earlier code snippet modifies the response by adding a date value to the output and sends the output to the client using the print writer obtained from the original response object that was passed to the filter.

Configuring Filter Chains

Earlier, we briefly discussed a simple filter configuration. Let's look at the way that most Web containers (including WebLogic Server) implement filter chains. The container builds a filter chain using the order of filter mappings in the deployment descriptor, which can be determined by the URL pattern or the servlet name. In the simple filter configuration, we used the URL pattern to assign filters to the servlet. As an alternative, filters can be assigned using fully qualified servlet names, as shown here:

```
<web-app>
...
  <filter>
    <filter-name>sniffFilter</filter-name>
    <filter-class>wlsunleashed.servlets.SniffFilter</filter-class>
  </filter>
<filter>
    <filter-name>sniffFilter2</filter-name>
    <filter-class>wlsunleashed.servlets.SniffFilter2</filter-class>
  </filter>
  <filter-mapping>
    <filter-name> sniffFilter</filter-name>
```

```
    <servlet-name>/SimpleServlet/*</servlet-name>
  </filter-mapping>
  <filter-mapping>
    <filter-name> sniffFilter2 </filter-name>
    <servlet-name>/SimpleServlet/*</servlet-name>
  </filter-mapping>

...
</web-app>
```

In this configuration, `sniffFilter` and `sniffFilter2` form the filter chain and are invoked in that order.

WebLogic Server also provides the capability to cache filter chains to improve performance because they don't have to be deciphered for every request.

Servlet Filter Class Reloading

WebLogic Server extends a servlet reloading feature, which has existed for quite some time, to automatically reload associated servlet filters. WebLogic Server checks the timestamp of the filter class prior to applying the filters and compares it to that of the instance in memory. If the version in memory is older than the servlet filter class, WebLogic Server reloads the filters before applying them. This feature comes in handy in development when there are frequent changes to the code. The developer can configure the interval at which the WebLogic Server automatically checks for reloading by using the Server Reload attribute, which is present on the descriptor tab for each Web application configuration, as shown in Figure 14.4.

Best Practices for Implementing Servlets

As we've seen, servlets offer a powerful mechanism for integrating Web servers and enterprise-wide business components. Now let's look at some of the best practices that are adopted in enterprise applications that involve servlets as one of the layers.

- Leverage the MVC pattern—Use servlets as controllers, as described in the MVC pattern. Presentation is typically done using a JSP and the servlet is left to invoke the business component and pass on the necessary data for the presentation layer.
- Use of `SingleThreadModel`—`SingleThreadModel` servlets should be avoided because most of the servlet container implementations have a huge system overhead. Instead use thread synchronization when necessary.
- Use `HttpSessions`—By design, servlets are meant to be stateless component and they use external objects such as `HttpSession` to maintain state information for a user conversation. Application servers serialize inactive sessions and store them on disk because these objects take a lot of memory and the server has to share the allocated

memory efficiently for other resources such as EJBs and JMS resources. Sessions are normally released from memory using the `invalidate()` function or when they time out. So, users have to take care of implementing one of these to make sure that sessions are released when the client is done with the conversation. Also, keep the session object lean and store valuable data in a database instead of storing it as part of session to prevent losing the data in unpredictable server crashes.

- Use the `Init()` method—As explained, the `init()` method is invoked when the servlet instance is created. This is the most convenient method for performing some of the complex logic that must be performed once; for example, JDBC connection pool initialization, EJB home lookup, and so on. The `init()` method is also the best place to initialize the servlet instance variables because this method is threadsafe by default.
- Synchronization in servlets—This should be avoided because large synchronization blocks make a servlet single threaded and thereby decreases the throughput drastically.
- Optimization techniques in the `service()` method—Apart from minimizing the use of synchronization blocks, some of the following optimization techniques can be used as well: setting content-length variables for efficient flushing, using `ServletOutputStream` instead of `PrintWriter`, and using the `print()` method for `println()` and partial data flushing. Along with this, using `StringBuffer` for string concatenation improves performance. Using caching (when appropriate) and pre-generating large Web sites can help, too.
- Using the `destroy` method—The `destroy` method should be used to free up resources such as database connections and initial contexts and to close sockets and files.
- Modularity improvements—All complex logic (for example, EJBs) should be moved to a separate business layer to keep the logic in the servlet simple.
- Shared resources—A servlet being multithreaded should take special care when modifying servlet instance variables because these are shared by multiple resources. Use synchronization and/or transactions.
- Connection pooling—Try to avoid obtaining a connection to the database or a backend legacy application (such as a Tuxedo connection) for every request. Use connection pooling wherever possible and initialize using the `init` method. The developer should take care of releasing connections when the usage is over, such as in the `destroy` method of the servlet. The data source object used in every SQL access should be reused instead of looking up the `javax.sql.DataSource` object. Also in some application servers including WebLogic Server, connections such as JDBC connections can be initialized at server startup time. In those scenarios, it's better to use the server configuration feature to set up the connections rather than doing it

through the `init()` method. For detailed information about WebLogic Server–based JDBC connection pooling, refer to the chapter on JDBC.

- Persistent connections—Avoid using `flush()` in the response because doing so closes the connection between WebLogic Server and the client. WebLogic Server is capable of using persistent connections between the client and the server. The connections are closed by an explicit `flush()` or a keepalive connection parameter in the server configuration file (`config.xml`).
- Understanding the caching options (headers) and their efficient use improves the effectiveness of the servlet.
- A session replication strategy (for example, in-memory or JDBC) should be carefully chosen based on a number of parameters, such as system performance criteria, database availability, and so on.
- Session persistence should not used as a long-term shortage mechanism between long running client conversations because a session might not be alive when the client comes back. The application should instead take care of state persistence in such cases.
- Sessions and cookies—Cookies are usually stored in the client browser for enabling features such as default field values, where the cookie lives in the client browser forever. Sessions should not be used as cookie wrappers and thereby attempt to store long-term client data in a session.
- Automatic servlet reloading—Like most application servers, WebLogic Server provides an auto-reloading feature for servlets, which enables dynamic reloading of servlets at every configured interval to refresh the servlet content. It is a useful feature in development, but should be avoided in a production environment because it tends to degrade performance.

Summary

In enterprise application development, servlets occupy a crucial role in the implementation of the presentation tier and also in forming the bridge between the presentation and the business layer. Although they form a small part of the entire J2EE framework, the Servlet 2.3 API along with the JSP specification provides the backbone for a full-fledged application framework for the presentation layer and for interactions with business components such as EJBs, JMS, and JDBC components, among others.

CHAPTER **15**

Writing WebLogic Server JavaServer Pages

by Malcolm Garland

IN THIS CHAPTER

- Introduction to JSP
- How WebLogic Server Works with Servlets
- When to Use JSPs
- JSP Syntax
- JSP Implicit Objects
- Sample JSP Page
- Configuring and Deploying WebLogic JSP
- JSP Best Practices

This chapter discusses the BEA WebLogic Server 8.1 implementation of JavaSoft's JavaServer Pages (JSP) 1.2, to include JSP utility, syntax, compilation, configuration, and deployment.

Introduction to JSP

JSP is a Sun Microsystems specification that enables you to produce dynamic Web-based applications. WebLogic Server's implementation of the Sun specification employs the Model-View-Controller design pattern (see Chapter 16, "JavaBeans and Model-View-Controller (MVC) Architecture"). This design pattern allows multiple presentation views and varied data update mechanisms with no effect on core application logic. This is accomplished by separating content development from presentation development, which enables Java developers to add JSP code to predeveloped presentation pages (HTML, DHTML, WML, XML) and enables presentation developers to modify Web page appearance without altering dynamic content.

WebLogic Server's implementation of JSP can be coded using either JSP-specific XML-like shorthand tags or actual XML equivalent tags. The application logic with the JSP container (the host for JSP infrastructure) resides on the WebLogic server. The client (usually a Web browser) requests a JSP page (an HTML page with embedded JSP tags), and the JSP page is transitioned into a Java file, which is a servlet class (the compiled JSP page equivalent). This servlet class is executed to service client requests.

NOTE

The JSP page is normally precompiled by the developer, but can be dynamically compiled upon initial client request.

The JSP 1.2 specification is an extension of the JavaSoft Servlet 2.3 specification. For detailed information about these specifications, refer to the JavaSoft documentation site at `http://java.sun.com/products`. WebLogic Server's implementation of JSP 1.2 includes support for defining custom JSP tag extensions among other embellishments to JSP 1.1. Detailed information on WebLogic Server's implementation of JSP can be found at `http://edocs.beasys.com/wls/docs81/jsp`.

The new JSP 2.0 specification is an extension to the JavaSoft Servlet 2.4 specification. JSP 2.0 greatly improves JSP functionality over JSP 1.2 by mandating the use of Java 1.4, adopting a simple expression language (EL) that allows writing scriptless JSP pages, including an EL API, adopting syntax that creates custom actions (packaged within `.tag` files), and adopting a new simple invocation protocol that's used to implement the `.tag` files. BEA WebLogic Server 8.1 does not support JSP 2.0.

How WebLogic Server Works with Servlets

JSP pages are processed using two distinct phases—translation and request processing—as shown in Figure 15.1.

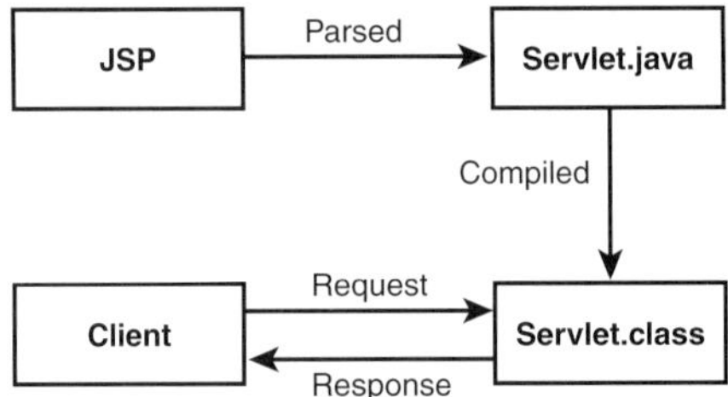

Figure 15.1 JSP processing.

During the translation phase, which happens only during the initial request for the JSP page (assuming no changes), the JSP page is parsed into a Java file and then compiled into a server-side implementation class. This class implements the JavaSoft Servlet 2.3 interface.

NOTE

Translation of the final version of the JSP page is normally the last step of the development process. Within a production environment, all JSP pages should be precompiled to avoid translation phase latency.

The servlet source code resulting from the parsing process is not retained. However, modifying WebLogic JSP configuration parameters, which is discussed within this chapter, will enable automatic retention of this source code.

The WebLogic JSP implementation class that's produced extends the class weblogic.server.jsp.JspBase and implements the interface weblogic.server.jsp.StaleIndicator. This implementation class is made available to WebLogic Server for execution. At this point, the translation phase ends and the request-processing phase begins with the _jspService() method of the implementation class processing client requests.

Let's implement a simple example to see how JSPs are processed on WebLogic Server. Try implementing JSP code that displays counts from 1 to 5, as shown in Listing 15.1.

LISTING 15.1 Counting.jsp

```
<!DOCTYPE HTML PUBLIC "-//W3C//DTD HTML 4.01 Transitional//EN">

<html>
<head>
   <title>Counting</title>
</head>

<h1>This Counts</h1>
<%
   for (int i=1; i<=5; i++) {
%>
   <h2>The Count is: <%=i %> </h2>
<% }
%>

</body>
</html>
```

Notice how Java code is included within HTML code in Listing 15.1, bold lines 9–14. To view this JSP, start your server and deposit the JSP file into your WebLogic domain's applications\DefaultWebApp directory. Then access the page using a browser, as shown in Figure 15.2.

TIP

If you're having problems finding the active default Web application directory, launch the WebLogic Examples Server. Within the server start window, a notice is displayed that contains the URL to access the server's index JSP (this page should launch automatically). Deposit your sample JSP into the corresponding directory (the directory containing the index.jsp file should be ..weblogicHome\samples\server\examples\build\examplesWebApp). If you're still lost, an inspection of the corresponding config.xml file (find <Server DefaultWebApp=".. "—this names the default application) will reveal the absolute path of the default Web application.

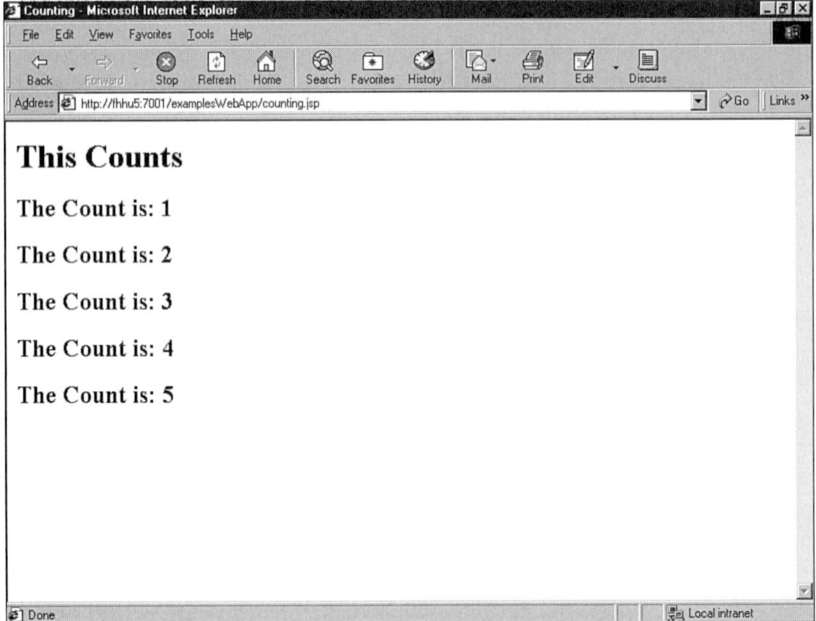

Figure 15.2 Browser view of Counting.jsp.

TIP

The URL displayed in the example is `http://IP(machine_name):port/examplesWebApp/counting.jsp` try also `http://IP(machine_name):port/counting.jsp`.

The `config.xml` server tag's `DefaultWebApp` attribute (that is, `<Server DefaultWebApp="..."</Server>`) controls this behavior. No preface is needed (as with the second option shown earlier) if an application is designated as `DefaultWebApp` within the server tag.

Notice how the Java-implemented logic has been executed and displayed using HTML format. This is an example of the power and utility that the JSP paradigm gives developers. Behind the scenes, you'll also find that the servlet class, `counting.class`, has been created and deposited on your server. The generated Java source file, `__counting.java`, is displayed in Listing 15.2.

LISTING 15.2 _counting.java

```
/* compiled from JSP: /counting.jsp
*
* This code was automatically generated at 8:19:24 AM on Apr 30, 2003
* by weblogic.servlet.jsp.Jsp2Java -- do not edit.
*/

package jsp_servlet;

import java.io.*;
import java.util.*;
import javax.servlet.*;
import javax.servlet.http.*;
import javax.servlet.jsp.*;
import javax.servlet.jsp.tagext.*;

// User imports

// built-in init parameters:
// boolean       _verbose -- wants debugging

// Well-known variables:
// JspWriter out          -- to write to the browser
// HttpServletRequest request  -- the request object.
// HttpServletResponse response  -- the response object.
// PageContext pageContext    -- the page context for this JSP
// HttpSession session      -- the session object for the client (if any)
// ServletContext application   -- The servlet (application) context
// ServletConfig config      -- The ServletConfig for this JSP
// Object page            --
➥the instance of this page's implementation class (i.e., 'this')

/**
* This code was automatically generated at 8:19:24 AM on Apr 30, 2003
* by weblogic.servlet.jsp.Jsp2Java -- do not edit.
*
* Copyright (c) 2003 by BEA Systems, Inc. All Rights Reserved.
*/
public final class __counting
extends
```

15

LISTING 15.2 Continued

```
weblogic.servlet.jsp.JspBase
implements weblogic.servlet.jsp.StaleIndicator
{

 // StaleIndicator interface
 public boolean _isStale() {
  weblogic.servlet.jsp.StaleChecker sci
➥=(weblogic.servlet.jsp.StaleChecker)(getServletConfig().getServletContext());
  java.io.File f = null;
  long lastModWhenBuilt = 0L;
  if (sci.isResourceStale("/counting.jsp", 1051715956000L, "8.1.0.0"))
➥return true;
  return false;
 }

 public static boolean _staticIsStale(weblogic.servlet.jsp.StaleChecker sci) {
  java.io.File f = null;
  long lastModWhenBuilt = 0L;
  if (sci.isResourceStale("/counting.jsp", 1051715956000L, "8.1.0.0"))
➥return true;
  return false;
 }

 private static void _writeText(ServletResponse rsp, JspWriter out,
➥String block, byte[] blockBytes) throws IOException {
  if (!_WL_ENCODED_BYTES_OK || _hasEncodingChanged(rsp)) {
   out.print(block);
  } else {
   ((weblogic.servlet.jsp.ByteWriter)out).write(blockBytes, block);
  }
 }

 private static boolean _hasEncodingChanged(ServletResponse rsp) {
  String encoding = rsp.getCharacterEncoding();
  if ("ISO-8859-1".equals(encoding) || "Cp1252".equals(encoding) ||
➥"ISO8859_1".equals(encoding) || "ASCII".equals(encoding)) {
   return false;
  }
  if (_WL_ORIGINAL_ENCODING.equals(encoding)) {
   return false;
  }
```

LISTING 15.2 Continued

```
  return true;
 }

 private static boolean _WL_ENCODED_BYTES_OK = true;

 private static final String _WL_ORIGINAL_ENCODING = "Cp1252";

 private static byte[] _getBytes(String block) {
  try {
   return block.getBytes(_WL_ORIGINAL_ENCODING);
  } catch (java.io.UnsupportedEncodingException u) {
   _WL_ENCODED_BYTES_OK = false;
  }
  return null;
 }
 private final static String _wl_block0 = "<!DOCTYPE HTML PUBLIC \"
➥-//W3C//DTD HTML 4.01 Transitional//EN\">\r\n\r\n<html>\r\n<head>\r\n
➥<title>Counting</title>\r\n</head>\r\n\r\n<h1>This Counts</h1>\r\n";
 private final static byte[] _wl_block0Bytes = _getBytes(_wl_block0);
 private final static String _wl_block1 = "\r\n    <h2>The Count is: ";
 private final static byte[] _wl_block1Bytes = _getBytes(_wl_block1);
 private final static String _wl_block2 = " </h2>\r\n";
 private final static byte[] _wl_block2Bytes = _getBytes(_wl_block2);
 private final static String _wl_block3 = "\r\n\r\n</body>\r\n</html>\r\n";
 private final static byte[] _wl_block3Bytes = _getBytes(_wl_block3);


 public void _jspService(javax.servlet.http.HttpServletRequest request,
➥javax.servlet.http.HttpServletResponse response) throws java.io.IOException,
➥javax.servlet.ServletException
 {

  // declare and set well-known variables:
  javax.servlet.ServletConfig config = getServletConfig();
  javax.servlet.ServletContext application = config.getServletContext();
  javax.servlet.jsp.tagext.Tag _activeTag = null;
  // variables for Tag extension protocol

  Object page = this;
  javax.servlet.jsp.JspWriter out;
  javax.servlet.jsp.PageContext pageContext =
```

15

LISTING 15.2 Continued

```
  javax.servlet.jsp.JspFactory.getDefaultFactory().getPageContext(this,
➥request, response, null, true, 8192, true);

  out = pageContext.getOut();
  JspWriter _originalOut = out;

  javax.servlet.http.HttpSession session = request.getSession(true);

  try { // error page try block

   _writeText(response, out, _wl_block0, _wl_block0Bytes);
   //[ /counting.jsp; Line: 9]
   for (int i-1; i<=5; i++) { //[ /counting.jsp; Line: 10]
    _writeText(response, out, _wl_block1, _wl_block1Bytes);
    out.print(String.valueOf(i )); //[ /counting.jsp; Line: 12]
    _writeText(response, out, _wl_block2, _wl_block2Bytes);
   } //[ /counting.jsp; Line: 13]
   _writeText(response, out, _wl_block3, _wl_block3Bytes);
  } catch (Throwable __ee) {
   while (out != null && out != _originalOut) out = pageContext.popBody();
   ((weblogic.servlet.jsp.PageContextImpl)pageContext).handlePageException(
➥(Throwable)__ee);
  }

  //before final close brace...
 }
}
```

Comparing the original JSP code in Listing 15.1 to the generated servlet code in Listing 15.2 clearly shows the volume of Java code generated in parsing a single JSP. Note the specific methods implemented within the generated code. Viewing this file is helpful during debug operations. The location of generated files might vary depending on your individual configuration. A file search of your server's root directory will locate the files.

NOTE

The associated Java file is retained only if the JSP parameter `"keepgenerated=true"` is set. JSP configuration parameters and syntax are discussed later in this chapter. You can inspect these parameters by examining the `weblogic.xml` file located in the directory `..\applications\DefaultWebApp\WEB-INF`.

JSP Compiler

The WebLogic Server automatically compiles your JSP pages upon initial client request. However, WebLogic gives you the option of independently compiling JSP pages. This convenience is useful in development and debugging situations.

The WebLogic JSP compiler (`weblogic.jspc`) parses your JSP pages into a `.java` file. This Java file is then compiled to produce the server-side implementation class discussed earlier. The WebLogic JSP compiler is executed as shown here:

```
$ java weblogic.jspc -keepgenerated filename.jsp
```

This line keeps the generated `.java` file for inspection.

> **NOTE**
>
> A compilation warning is issued if the `web.xml` or `weblogic.xml` file isn't present. However, the absence of these files does not prevent successful compilation.

Commonly used JSP compile options are included in Table 15.1. See the BEA documentation site at `http://edocs.beasys.com/wls/docs81/jsp` for detailed JSP compile options.

15

TABLE 15.1 Common JSP Compile Options

Option	Description
-compileAll	Compiles all JSP pages within current directory or directory identified with -webapp option.
-compiler *<compiler-location>*	Specifies compiler to use. Default is javac.
-help	Displays available options.
-k	If compiling multiple JSP pages, continues to compile next JSP page if errors encountered in previous page(s).
-keepgenerated	Keeps generated source code.
-package *<name>*	Sets package name. Default is jsp_servlet.
-webapp *<folder>*	Directory containing an exploded Web application. The compiler will search this directory for tag libraries or Java classes used by the compiling class.

When to Use JSPs

When should you use JSP pages? JSP pages should be used when interactive Web-based content is desired over static content; that is, when content is predicated on user response rather than pre-scripted static text. This dynamic Web-based model is usually accomplished by implementing an n-tier architecture, such as Model-View-Controller, where presentation, application/business logic, and data archiving are layered. Within this layered approach, JSPs should be implemented as the presentation. The JSPs should implement minimal Java code, while providing only a client portal into the application. User requests are serviced by the Controller layer using servlets or other Java objects (such as JavaBeans, Session EJBs, tag libraries, and generic user-defined objects) to implement business and application logic. See Chapter 16 for further details on the MVC design pattern.

Once an n-tier architecture is implemented, JSP pages are useful in situations where presentation development is stable and developed independently or remotely from application logic. In this situation, application development can continue, with updated presentation being shipped to process developers as appropriate. This model is especially effective in situations where presentation is developed in multiple markup formats (other than HTML), such as DHMLT, WML, and XML.

For non-tiered solutions where Web-based applications must run on a variety of platforms, JSP pages should be used to exploit the inherent portability of the Java programming language.

JSP Syntax

JSP syntax can be divided into three classifications: directives, scripting elements, and actions. JSP syntax is modeled on the XML tag model. WebLogic's implementation of JSP 1.2 enables the use of either the standard JSP tags or equivalent XML tags.

Directives

Directives are messages to the WebLogic JSP container, which provides instruction on what to do with the JSP page. Directives are used to control the process of translating the page into a servlet. There are three directives: `page`, `include`, and `taglib`. You may use multiple directives. Their location within the page is irrelevant, except for the `include` directive, which must be at the top of the page. Directives can contain name-value pairs in the form *`attribute`*`="`*`value`*`"`. The syntax is as follows:

WebLogic JSP

```
<%@ directive-type directive-attribute="value" .. %>
```

XML equivalent

```
<jsp:directive-type directive-attribute="value" .. />
```

page Directive

`page` directives instruct WebLogic as to page-dependent properties. Multiple `page` directives are permissible, but name-value pairs must be unique. The syntax for setting `page` directives is as follows:

WebLogic JSP

```
<% page page-directive_attr_list %>
```

XML equivalent

```
<jsp:directive.page page_directive attr_list />
```

Valid page directive attributes are shown in Table 15.2.

TABLE 15.2 page Directive Attributes

<table>
<tr><th>Name-Value Pair</th><th>Description</th></tr>
<tr><td>language="scriptingLanguage"</td><td>Scripting language to use within JSP tags. Only "java" is valid for this entry.</td></tr>
<tr><td>extends="className"</td><td>Designated super class for this JSP page.</td></tr>
<tr><td>import="importPackageList"</td><td>Java packages available to this page.</td></tr>
<tr><td>session="true|false"</td><td>Whether or not page participates in HTTP session.</td></tr>
<tr><td>buffer="none|sizekb"</td><td>Buffering model for initial JspWriter (out).</td></tr>
<tr><td>autoFlush="true|false"</td><td>Whether or not to flush output buffer automatically.</td></tr>
<tr><td>isThreadSafe="true|false"</td><td>Level of thread safety. False supports single thread model.</td></tr>
<tr><td>info="info text"</td><td>String made available to the Servlet.getServletInfo() method.</td></tr>
<tr><td>errorPage="error_url(filename)"</td><td>Designated target destination for exceptions thrown but not caught by implementing page.</td></tr>
<tr><td>isErrorPage="true|false"</td><td>Current page is URL target for exceptions.</td></tr>
<tr><td>contentType="ctinfo"</td><td>Designates character encoding for current JSP page and response. Also designates MIME type for response.</td></tr>
<tr><td>pageEncoding="peinfo"</td><td>Designates character encoding for current JSP page.</td></tr>
</table>

Example

```
<%@ page import="java.util.*, weblogic.db.jdbc.*" %>
```

include Directive

The `include` directive inserts the contents of a designated file into the current JSP page at the location of the `include` tag. This insertion is accomplished at translation (parsing) time, as opposed to the JSP action `include`, which executes at request time. `include` directives are parsed (Java code is included in the translated servlet file); `include` actions are not parsed (code is not included in the translated servlet file). The syntax for the `include` directive is as follows:

WebLogic JSP

```
<%@ include file="relativeURLspec" %>
```

XML equivalent

```
<jsp:directive.include file="relativeURLspec" />
```

Example

```
<%@ include file="login.html" %>
```

taglib Directive

The `taglib` directive identifies a tag library to be used with this JSP page. Use of tag libraries is discussed in Chapter 17, "Using JSP Tag Libraries," and Chapter 18, "Creating JSP Tag Libraries." The syntax is as follows:

WebLogic JSP

```
<%@ taglib uri="tagLibraryURI" prefix="tagPrefix" %>
```

XML equivalent

```
<jsp:directive.taglib uri="tagLibraryURI" prefix="tagPrefix" />
```

`taglib` attributes are detailed in Table 15.3.

TABLE 15.3 taglib Directive Attributes

Attribute	Description
uri	Absolute or relative URI of tag library registered in web.xml.
tagPrefix	Defines prefix string used to identify custom tags; that is, <myPrefix:myTag>. Prefixes starting with jsp, jspx, java, javax, servlet, sun, and sunw are reserved. Prefix must follow XML namespaces specification. WebLogic prefix is wl.

Example

```
<%@ taglib uri="weblogic-tags" prefix="wl" %>
➥(assumes uri registered in web.xml)
```

Scripting Elements

Scripting elements are used for computations within the JSP page. There are three types of scripting elements: declarations, scriptlets, and expressions. We also cover JSP comments under scripting elements.

Declarations

Declarations are used to define page-level (class scope) variables and methods. These variables and methods are available at request time for use by other scripting elements within the page. The declaration must be a syntax-valid statement of the scripting language designated for the page (currently only Java). Declarations do not produce any output on their own. The syntax for declarations is as follows:

WebLogic JSP

```
<%! /* Initialization Java code */ %>
```

XML equivalent

```
<jsp:declaration>
 /* Initialization Java code */
</jsp:declaration>
```

Example

```
<%! int i=0;
  private void start() {
   //..do something..
  }
 %>
```


> **CAUTION**
>
> To guard against corruption due to mismanaged threading, synchronization might be desirable. Setting the `page` directive attribute `isThreadSafe` to false will implement the Java single-thread model, `javax.servlet.SingleThreadModel`.

Expressions

Expressions are designated scripting language (Java) expressions that are executed, coerced into Java strings, and output inline to the JSP page. Expressions must be valid syntax, but do not end in a semicolon (;). Expressions are executed at request time. Expressions are normally used to dereference variables or execute get methods. Expression syntax is as follows:

WebLogic JSP

```
<%= java_expr %>
```

XML equivalent

```
<jsp:expression>
java_expression
</jsp:expression>
```

Examples

```
<%= number %>
```

```
<%= myBean.getName() %>t
```

Scriptlets

Scriptlets will comprise the main body of your embedded code. Scripting elements contain syntax-valid code of the designated page's scripting language (Java), to include declarations and the use of local variables. Multiple lines of code are permissible. You may implement as many scriptlet blocks as desired; however, when translated, the sum of all scriptlet blocks must produce valid syntax. Scriptlet code is executed at request time and may produce output depending on the specifics of the code implemented. If you're implementing intensive or complex logic, you should implement JavaBeans or tag libraries, as opposed to scriptlets, to minimize the amount of Java code in JSP pages, as we discuss later. The syntax for scriptlets is as follows:

WebLogic JSP

```
<%
//..syntax-valid Java code..
%>
```

XML equivalent

```
<jsp:scriplet>
//..syntax-valid Java code..
</jsp:scriplet>
```

Example

```
<html>
<h1>Loop</h1>
<%
  for (int i=1; i<=5; i++) {
%>
   <h2>Loop Number: <%=i %> </h2>
<% }
%>
</html>
```

Comments

JSP comments enable you to include comments that are not viewable to clients executing a browser's View Source option. The comment construct is also useful during development and debugging. Java style comments may also be used within JSP pages. JSP comment syntax is as follows:

```
<%-- comment text --%>
```

Let's implement a JSP using some of the syntax presented so far. The code in Listing 15.3 presents a search view used within the global auction management system (GAMS).

LISTING 15.3 Menu.jsp

```
<!DOCTYPE HTML PUBLIC "-//W3C//DTD HTML 4.01 Transitional//EN">
<%@ page import="com.gams.util.*" %>

<html>
<head>
   <title>GAMS Menu</title>
</head>

<body bgcolor="#C0C0C0">

<%-- Test to determine whether or not user is a seller --%>
<% if (session.getAttribute("CustomerName") != null
➥&& session.getAttribute("IsSeller") != null) { %>
<a href="seller/listItem.jsp" target="main">Sell An Item</a><br><br>
<% } %>

<a href="FindItemsServlet?featured=true" target="main">Browse Featured Items
➥</a><br><br>

Browse By Keyword <form action="FindItemsServlet" target="main"><input type=
➥"text" name="keyword" size="10"><input type="submit"
➥value="Submit"></form>

Browse By Category<br>

<%-- Calculate search key/value pair from category data object --%>
<%
  Hashtable h = new Hashtable();
  h.put("BA1001", "furniture");
  h.put("BA2001", "automotive");
  h.put("BA3001", "jewelry");

  Enumeration enum = h.keys();
```

LISTING 15.3 Continued

```
30   while(enum.hasMoreElements()) {
31     String key = (String)enum.nextElement();
32     String value = (String)h.get(key);
33 %>
34 <a href="FindItemsServlet?catid=<%=key%>" target="main"><%=value%></a><br>
35 <% } %>
36
37 </body>
38 </html>
```

NOTE

The code presented is intended to show examples of JSP syntactic elements. Proper implementation of MVC architecture would implement such logic shown within the Control layer (using an EJB, taglib, JavaBean, or other constructs). Efficient JSP pages should contain little if any implementation logic and no hard-coded data.

Notice the use of `page` directive (import) in line 2, scriptlets in lines 11–14 and 22–35, comments in lines 11 and 22, and expressions in line 34. Also note line 34: The JSP page presents only a client view or portal into the application. The servlet referenced in line 34 receives the client input and processes workflow as needed; that is, the servlet in this case delegates the `find` task to a session EJB, which in turn requests the target data from a relational database. This is an example of the n-tiered MVC work that will be discussed in this chapter and the next. Relating this example to MVC, the JSP provides the client "view," the servlet "controls" the workflow, and the session EJB requests and receives data from a relational database housing the data "model." The client view produced by this JSP is presented in Figure 15.3.

To run this example, place the JSPs in your domain's `applications\DefaultWebApp` directory as discussed earlier. Deposit supporting classes (see Listing 15.3, line 2) in the `WEB-INF\classes` directory (subdirectory of `applications\DefaultWebApp`). Start your server and access the JSPs through your browser as shown at Figure 15.3.

Actions

Actions enable you to manipulate (use, modify, and create) objects, represented as JavaBeans. Actions are implemented using XML syntax only. The JSP 1.2 Specification identifies standard actions that must be implemented. Additional actions may be implemented using the `taglib` directive. There are nine standard actions: `useBean`, `setProperty`, `getProperty`, `include`, `forward`, `param`, `plugin`, `params`, and `fallback`.

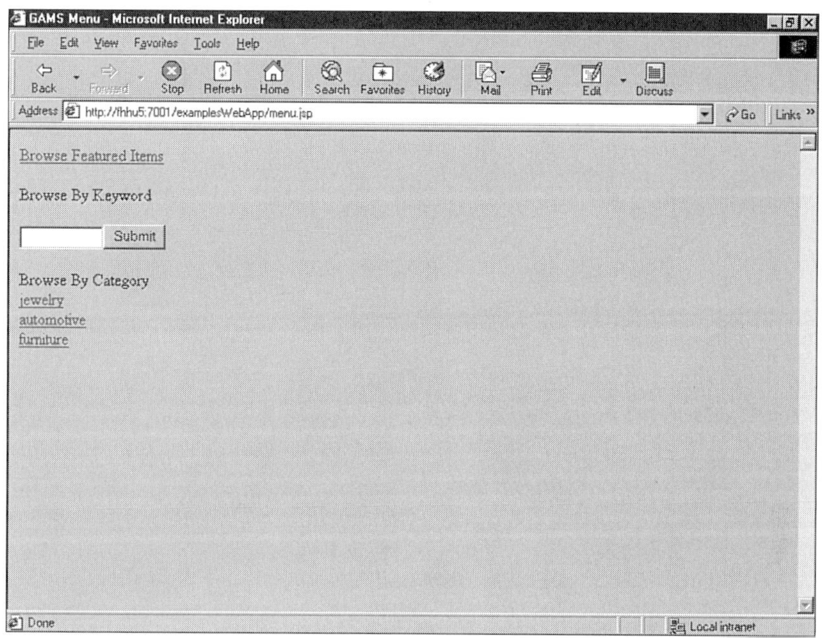

Figure 15.3 Browser view of Menu.jsp.

> **NOTE**
>
> The new JSP 2.0 Specification introduces a new syntax for defining custom actions and a simple invocation protocol for implementing these actions.

useBean

The `useBean` action enables you to instantiate JavaBean objects and to refer to the object later within your code. Initial use of the `useBean` tag attempts to obtain a reference to an existing object. If an object isn't found, an object of the type specified will be instantiated. `useBean` attributes are detailed in Table 15.4. `useBean` scope attributes are detailed in Table 15.5. Refer to Chapter 16 for detailed information on JavaBeans. The useBean syntax is as follows:

```
<jsp:useBean id="name" class="className"
➥scope="page¦request¦session¦application"/>
```

or

```
<jsp:useBean id="name" class="className"
➥scope="page¦request¦session¦application">
```

15

```
body (body may include actions or scriptlets)
</jsp:useBean>
```

Example

```
<jsp:useBean id="account" class="com.globalAuctions.Account" scope="session"/>
<jsp:useBean id="account" class="com.globalAuctions.Account" scope="session">
 <jsp:setProperty name="account" property="AccountNumber" value="NDE4587">
</jsp:useBean>
```

TABLE 15.4 UseBean Attributes

Attribute	Description
id	Name used to identify object instance.
scope	Scope in which object reference is available. Refer to Table 15.5.
class	Fully qualified class name.

TABLE 15.5 UseBean Scope Attributes

Scope	Description
Page	Object stored in PageContext and available only to current page. The object is not available to other pages and is discarded upon completion of page request.
Request	Object stored in current ServletRequest and available to pages included within the current request. Object is discarded upon completion of request.
Session	Object stored in HTTP session and is available to JSP pages used within the current session.
Application	Object stored in Web application and is available to any servlet or JSP pages running within the application.

setProperty

The `setProperty` action defines values of properties within a JavaBean. The bean referenced by the `name` attribute must be defined prior to use. The `setProperty` syntax is as follows:

```
<jsp:setProperty name="beanName" property="property_name" value="value"/>
```

Note that `"value"` may be an expression.

Example

```
<jsp:setProperty name="account" property="AccountNumber" value="NDE4587"/>
```

getProperty

The getProperty action retrieves values of properties from a JavaBean. The values retrieved are coerced to a Java String and printed to output. The name (bean name) attribute must be defined prior to its use. The getProperty syntax is as follows:

```
<jsp:getProperty name="beanName" property="property_name"/>
```

Example

```
<jsp:getProperty name="account" property="AccountNumber"/>
```

include

The include action includes any static or dynamic resource available to the JSP's context into the current page. The action is a de facto redirect; that is, the request or logic flow is redirected to another JSP page and returned. The other page can be a static HTML page, JSP page, or servlet that's available to the context. The include can also pass parameters. Any content produced by the included resource is inserted within the current page at the point of the include tag, where execution continues. (JavaBeans within the including page will have access to any resources defined within the included page.) The included resource may not set any HTTP header resources, such as the setCookie() method.

CAUTION

The URL displayed (included page or the including page?) may be an issue for some developers. That is, which page URL do you want displayed in the user's browser location window? Do you want to audit or track process flow? Do you want the actual processing URL revealed? Is business logic using the display URL? Are there security concerns? and so on. When using the include directive, the including page's URL will be displayed.

Any attempts to set these methods (HTTP header resources) will either be ignored or an exception might be generated. In some situations, use of the forward action in conjunction with decision logic might be desirable over the include action. The include action syntax is as follows:

```
<jsp:include page="relativeURL" flush="true¦false"/>
➥(flush (buffer) is optional, default is false)
```

or

```
<jsp:include page="relativeURL" flush="true¦false">
 <jsp:param .. />
</jsp:include>
```

Examples

```
<jsp:include page="./util/validateAcount.jsp" flush="true"/>

<jsp:include page="./util/validateAcount.jsp" flush="true">
 <jsp:param name="AccountNumber" value="JK45763"/>
</jsp:include>
```

forward

The forward action executes a runtime dispatch of the current request to any static or dynamic resource within the same context as the current page. Execution of the current page terminates within the forwarding page. The forward action may also pass parameters. The request object is modified based on the value of the forward action's page attribute. The forward action's syntax is as follows:

```
<jsp:forward page="relativeURL"/>
```

or

```
<jsp:forward page="relativeURL">
 <jsp:param .. />
</jsp:forward>
```

Examples

```
<jsp:forward page="invalidAccount.jsp"/>

<jsp:forward page="validAccount.jsp"/>
 <jsp:param name="accountNumber" value="<%=account.getAccountNumber()%>"/>
➥ ("account" previously defined)
</jsp:forward>
```

param

The param action tag provides name-value pair information. This tag is used within the include, forward, and params actions. When executing an include or forward action, if the original request object has preexisting parameters, the request will be augmented with the new additional parameters. The new parameters will take precedence. All parameters will be passed. param syntax is as follows:

```
<jsp:param name="name" value="value"/>
```

For an example of param, see the previous example under the forward action.

plugin

The plugin action generates HTML, which enables download of Java plug-in software. This construct enables execution of an applet or JavaBean component. The plugin tag is replaced by either an object or embed tag as appropriate for the designated plug-in. The plugin action also uses embedded params, param, and/or fallback action tags. The plugin action syntax is as follows:

```
<jsp:plugin type="plugin_attribute(s)">
 <jsp:params>
  <jsp:param name="name" value="value"/>
 </jsp:params>
 <jsp:fallback>
  text
 </jsp:fallback>
</jsp:plugin>
```

plugin attributes are detailed in Table 15.6.

TABLE 15.6 Plugin Attributes

Attribute	Description
type	Component type: JavaBean or Applet.
code	Defines the name or absolute pathname of the component with respect to code base.
codebase	Defines base URI for the component. If unspecified, defaults to current URI. Can refer only to subdirectories of current URI.
align	Specifies the position of the component (bottom, top, middle, left, right).
archive	Comma-separated list of URI(s) containing Java classes or other resources supporting component defined by code attribute. Archives using relative pathing are defined with respect to the codebase attribute.
height	Defines the initial height of component display. Defined height does not define height of subsequent windows or other displays created by component.(accepts runtime parameter).
hspace	Specifies amount of space to insert left and right of component.
jreversion	Component required JRE version. Default is 1.2.
name	Refers to contextual name of Java object. Used by other Java objects within the context to reference the named object.
vspace	Specifies amount of space to insert above and below component.
title	Specifies advisory information about component. Information displayed during mouse operations.
width	Defines initial width of component display. Defined width does not define width of windows or other displays created by component. Accepts runtime parameter.
nspluginurl	URL where Netscape version of JRE may be downloaded. Default is implementation defined.
iepluginurl	URL where IE version of JRE may be downloaded. Default is implementation defined.

15

Example:

```
<jsp:plugin type="applet" code="Catalogue.class" codebase="./classes">
 <jsp:params>
  <jsp:param name="auctionNumber" value="AA389"/>
 </jsp:params>
 <jsp:fallback>
  Error Initiating Catalogue Applet
 </jsp:fallback>
</jsp:plugin>
```

params

The `params` action identifies plug-in parameters. The `params` tag is used only as a child of the `plugin` action. Refer to the "plugin" section presented earlier for the `params` tag syntax and an example.

fallback

The `fallback` action designates content display if the plug-in cannot be started. If the plug-in starts but the component cannot be found, a `ClassNotFoundException` will be thrown. The `fallback` tag is only used as a child of the `plugin` action. Refer to the "plugin" section presented earlier for the `fallback` tag syntax and an example.

JSP Implicit Objects

The JSP specification makes 9 built-in objects available to the developer. These objects, provided by the Java API without any additional implementation, provide administrative and utility services to the JSP page. These implicit objects are detailed in Table 15.7.

TABLE 15.7 JSP Configuration Parameters

Object	Class and Description	Scope (Refer to Table 15.5)
request	javax.servlet.http.HttpServletRequest. Triggers service invocation. Usually implemented to reference client information within the request.	Request
response	javax.servlet.http.HttpServletResponse. Response to client request. Encapsulates response data associated with client request. Rarely used in development.	Page
pageContext	Java.servlet.jsp.PageContext. JSP page context. Contains JSP implementation-dependent features, such as optimized JSP writers. Implemented to create other implicit objects.	Page
application	javax.servlet.ServletContext. The Servlet context obtained from servlet configuration object. Usually implemented to track data at application scope.	Application

Object	Class and Description	Scope (Refer to Table 15.5)
out	Javax.servlet.jsp.JspWriter. Writes to output stream. It has methods to write out the primitive data types, Objects, and Strings. Sometimes used as an output object for formatting classes, or for controlling the output buffer.	Page
config	Javax.servlet.ServletConfig. JSP page ServletConfig. May be implemented to access servlet initialization parameters, normally not used in development.	Page
page	Java.lang.Object. De facto "this" reference for the page; generally not used in development.	Page
session	javax.servlet.http.HttpSession. Client session object; HTTP protocol only. Usually implemented to track data session scope data. More information provided later in this chapter.	Session
exception	Java.lang.Throwable. Uncaught throwable which results in error page invocation. May be used in JSP page exception handling.	Page

The session object instances of `HttpSession` (via the `HttpServletRequest`) are the most commonly used implicit object in JSP page development. Weblogic Server supports JSP sessions according to JSP 1.1. Session objects may be used to store small, short-lived objects within the session.

What's a small and short-lived object? You must use your own judgment based upon the performance metrics of your application and the importance of the data. However, large or valuable objects should be stored in a database. This is because JSP sessions are not persisted and there can be a performance bottleneck. For example, you should not store an existing order's line items in a session. They may be lost if the server crashes, and they can take a lot of space, which may slow down the system. However, it's a good idea to store the order in an Entity EJB, and to store the EJB's primary key in the session while it is used.

Objects stored in a session make user-defined or other objects available across several resources; that is, objects stored in one JSP page are available to other JSP pages, servlets, and static HTML pages within the same session. If the session data is a user-defined data type, the class should implement the Java `Serializable` interface. See lines 15 and 22 of Listing 15.3 for an example of session creation and use. The request object is also heavily used in JSP page development. For details on `HttpServletRequest` and `HTTPSession` refer to Chapter 14, "Writing WebLogic Server Servlets," and the JavaSoft documentation site at `http://java.sun.com/products/servlet`.

Sample JSP Page

Let's look at an example using many of the JSP features we discussed. `Display.jsp`, shown in Listing 15.4, displays a JSP that may be used within the GAMS application to display data for an item up for bid. In line 2, we import our supporting classes as before. Note the use of the `include` action in line 3. This facility enables us to insert code contained within the `header.jsp` file (see Listing 15.4) directly into the current JSP. Lines 12–33 implement logic using JSP scriptlets. We'll look at encapsulating program logic into tag libraries in Chapters 17 and 18. Line 7 demonstrates use of the `request` object. This structure allows a page to be implemented by a request originating from a servlet or another JSP page (the item data being passed within the request)—again coding for use within an n-tiered architecture.

LISTING 15.4 DisplayItem.jsp

```
1 <!DOCTYPE HTML PUBLIC "-//W3C//DTD HTML 4.01 Transitional//EN">
2 <%@ page import="com.gams.ejbs.item.*, java.text.*, java.sql.Date" %>
3 <jsp:include page="header.jsp" flush="true"/>
4
5 <html>
6 <head>
7   <title>Global Auctions - Display Item</title>
8 </head>
9
10 <body>
11
12 <%
13   SimpleDateFormat df = new SimpleDateFormat("MMM d, yyyy h:mm a");
14   NumberFormat nf = NumberFormat.getCurrencyInstance();
15
16   //ItemValue iv = (ItemValue)request.getAttribute("itemdata");
17   ItemValue iv = new ItemValue(new Integer(101), "Ming Chair",
➥new Float(550.50), new Date(102, 06, 30));
18
19   float currentBid = iv.getCurrentBid().floatValue();
20   long minimumBid = iv.getMinimumBid();
21
22   float minimalBidAllowed = 0;
23
24   // compute minimal acceptable bid
25   if (currentBid >= minimumBid)
26       minimalBidAllowed = currentBid + .5f;
27   else
28       minimalBidAllowed = minimumBid;
```

LISTING 15.4 Continued

```

  String strCurrentBid = nf.format(currentBid);
  String strMinimalBid = nf.format(minimalBidAllowed);
  String endbiddate = df.format(iv.getEndDateTime());
%>

<table>
<tr><td align="left"><br><br><b>Display Item: </b><%=iv.getItemId()%></td>
➥<td></td></tr>
<tr><td width="200">Title:</td><td><%=iv.getTitle()%></td></tr>
<tr><td>Current Bid:</td><td><%=strCurrentBid%></td></tr>
<tr><td>Auction Ends:</td><td><%=endbiddate%></td></tr>

<% if (session.getAttribute("IsBuyer") == null) { %>
  <tr><td colspan="2" align="left"><b>To bid on this item,
➥please login as a buyer</b></td></tr>

<% } else { %>
  <form action="PlaceBidServlet" method="post" name="bidform"
➥id="bidform" onSubmit="return checkform()">
  <input type="hidden" name="itemid" value="<%=iv.getItemId()%>">
  <input type="hidden" name="itemtitle" value="<%=iv.getTitle()%>">

  <tr><td>Bid Amount:</td><td><input type="text" name="bidamount"
➥size="8"> (Minimum <%=strMinimalBid%>)</td></tr>

  <% if (iv.getQuantityAvailable().intValue() == 1) { %>
  <input type="hidden" name="bidquantity" value="1">
  <% } else { %>
 <tr><td>Bid Quantity:</td><td><input type="text" name="bidquantity"
➥size="5"> (Maximum <%=iv.getQuantityAvailable()%>)</td></tr>
  <% } %>

 <tr><td colspan="2" align="center"><input type="submit"
➥value="Place Bid"></td></tr>
  </form>
<% }%>

</table>

</body>
</html>
```

> **NOTE**
>
> The code presented is intended to show examples of JSP syntactic elements. Proper implementation of MVC architecture would implement such logic shown within the Control layer (using an EJB, taglib, JavaBean, or other constructs). Efficient JSP pages should contain little if any implementation logic and no hard-coded data.

Finally at lines 35–59, the example in Listing 15.4 uses JSP expressions to populate tags within an HTML table.

Let's look at the included file `header.jsp`, shown in Listing 15.5. Note lines 7–9. This is another example of using implicit objects; in this case, the session object. The session object is used to get values that have been put into the session at some point prior to viewing this page—a convenient way to make data available across JSP pages within an application. Note the use of scriptlets to condition references to a logout servlet and a login JSP in lines 9–15.

LISTING 15.5 header.jsp

```
1 <!DOCTYPE HTML PUBLIC "-//W3C//DTD HTML 4.01 Transitional//EN">
2
3 <table>
4 <tr><td>
5 <h1>Welcome To Global Auctions<br></h1>
6
7 <% if (session.getAttribute("CustomerName") != null) { %>
8   Hello <%=session.getAttribute("CustomerName")%>
9   <% if (session.getAttribute("IsSeller") != null) { %>
10        <a href="/seller/displaySellerFees.jsp"
➥target="main">Display Fees</a>    
11    <% } %>
12    <a href="LogoutServlet" target="main">Logout</a>
13 <% } else { %>
14
15 <a href="login.jsp" target="main">Login</a> to Place Your Bid!
16
17 <% } %>
18 </td></tr>
19 </table>
```

Let's look at `login.jsp` as presented at Listing 15.6. Note the use of the request object in lines 10 and 11 to retrieve a request parameter. Also, in line 14 the processing of the actual login logic is delegated to a servlet, keeping with an n-tiered approach of implementing the GAMS application.

LISTING 15.6 login.jsp

```
<!DOCTYPE HTML PUBLIC "-//W3C//DTD HTML 4.01 Transitional//EN">

<html>
<head>
    <title>Login</title>
</head>

<body>

<% if (request.getAttribute("ErrorMessage") != null) { %>
    <b><%=request.getAttribute("ErrorMessage")%></b>
<% } %>

<form action="LoginServlet" method=post>
<table>
<tr><td colspan="2" align="center"><h1>Customer Login</h1></td></tr>
<tr><td width="200"><b>Global Auction Name:</b><br> (ex. AuctionGuy):</td>
➥<td><input type="text" name="gamsAlias" size="10"></td></tr>
<tr><td><b>Password:</b></td><td><input type="password" name="password"
➥size="20"></td></tr>
<tr><td colspan="2" align="center"><input type="submit" value="Login"
➥onClick="top.header.location='header.jsp'"></td></tr>
</table>
</form>

</body>
</html>
```

To run the examples presented, place the JSPs in your domain's `applications\DefaultWebApp` directory. Deposit supporting classes (non-JDK provided imports) in the `WEB-INF\classes` directory (subdirectory of `applications\DefaultWebApp`). Start your server and access the JSPs through your browser as shown in Figures 15.4 and 15.5. JSP configuration is detailed within the next section.

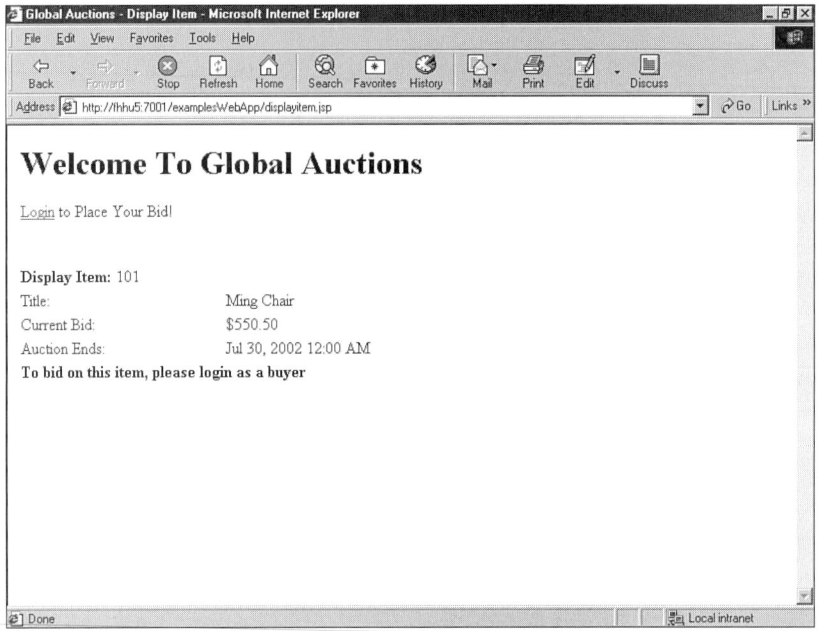

Figure 15.4 Browser view of DisplayItem.jsp (Header.jsp included).

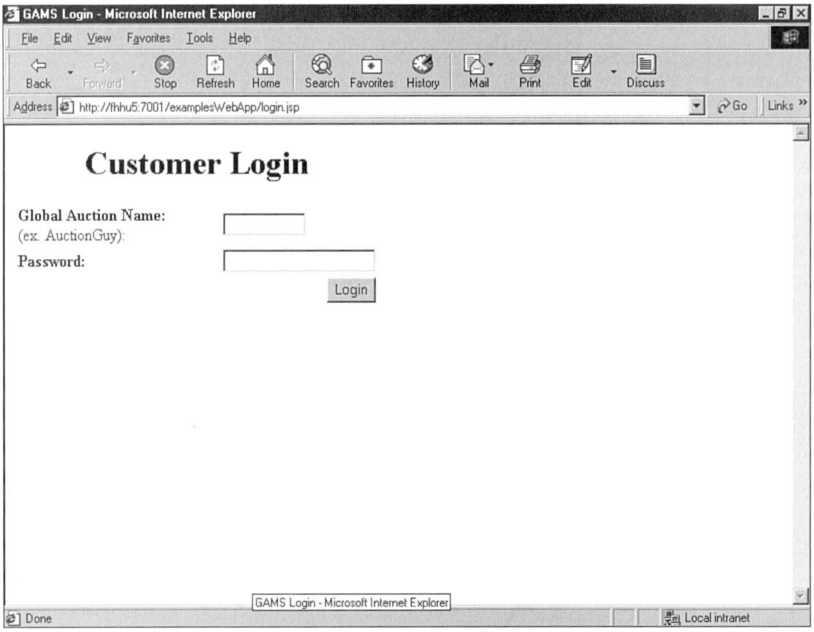

Figure 15.5 Browser view of Login.jsp.

Configuring and Deploying WebLogic JSP

Before JSP pages can be executed within WebLogic Server, the target JSP must be deployed within a Web application, and the Web application's JSP parameters must be configured. The JSP examples used previously relied on the default Web application provided by the WebLogic installation. The following sections detail how to accomplish these tasks within your own user-developed applications.

Configuring WebLogic for JSP

To execute JSP pages within WebLogic Server, you must set the server's JSP configuration parameters. These parameters are defined within your specific application's `weblogic.xml` file. (See Chapter 7, "Deploying Web Applications," for details about the `weblogic.xml` file.)

> **NOTE**
>
> WebLogic JSPs may be configured and executed only within the context of a Web application. The WebLogic Server distribution will includes a default Web application. You can use this default application for development and troubleshooting convenience. However, any JSP developed is assumed to be developed within the context of a greater user-defined Web application. Refer to Chapter 7 for more information.

JSP parameters are value settings that manage the behavior of JSP pages executed on WebLogic Server. These parameters are set using XML tags as such:

```
<jsp-param><param-name>PARAMETER</param-name><param-value>VALUE</param-value>
➥</jsp-param>
```

Commonly used server configuration parameters are detailed in Table 15.8.

> **NOTE**
>
> For more details on JSP configuration parameters, refer to the BEA documentation site at `http://edocs.beasys.com/wls/docs81/webapp/weblogic_xml.html`.

TABLE 15.8 JSP Configuration Parameters

Parameter	Default	Value
CompileCommand	javac. Use this option to implement compilers faster than the generic JDK compiler, such as jikes (IBM), jvc (Microsoft), kopi (DMS), gcj (GCC), or sj (Symantec).	Absolute pathname of Java compiler to use for JSP page compilation.

TABLE 15.8 Continued

Parameter	Default	Value
CompileFlags	None	Passes command-line parameters to compiler.
Compilerclass	None	Java compiler to execute for JSP compilation. If this parameter is set, compileCommand is ignored.
Debug	None	Adds JSP line numbers to generated class files.
Encoding	Platform default	Sets default character set for JSP page. This setting is overridden by JSP page directive setting the contentType attribute.
Keepgenerated	False	Saves the generated Java file.
PackagePrefix	jsp_servlet	Package designated for compiled servlet class resulting from JSP page.
PageCheckSeconds	1	Sets interval at which WebLogic will check for changes to JSP pages. JSP pages are recompiled if changed. Page dependencies are also checked and recompiled if warranted. A setting of 0 checks pages at each request. Use this setting only in development environments. A setting of –1 never checks for changes. This setting is recommended for production environments. Note: This setting can significantly affect performance.
WorkingDir	WebLogic-generated directory	Directory where generated Java files and/or compiled Java classes are placed.

To configure these JSP parameters, modify applicable tags within the `weblogic.xml` file, located in your application's `WEB-INF` directory (refer to Chapter 7). There are two ways of modifying this file, the WebLogic Admin Console and direct text editing.

Configuring JSP Parameters Using WebLogic Builder

To configure JSP parameters for newly developed applications using WebLogic Builder, start the GUI as detailed in Chapter 7. Locate the target application containing your JSPs as shown in Figure 15.6.

Open the target module, and you'll be prompted to create deployment descriptors as shown in Figure 15.7.

Selecting Yes will generate default deployment descriptor XML files, including the `weblogic.xml` file that will host the JSP parameters. To edit JSP parameters, select JSP Settings under the application's archive as shown in Figure 15.8.

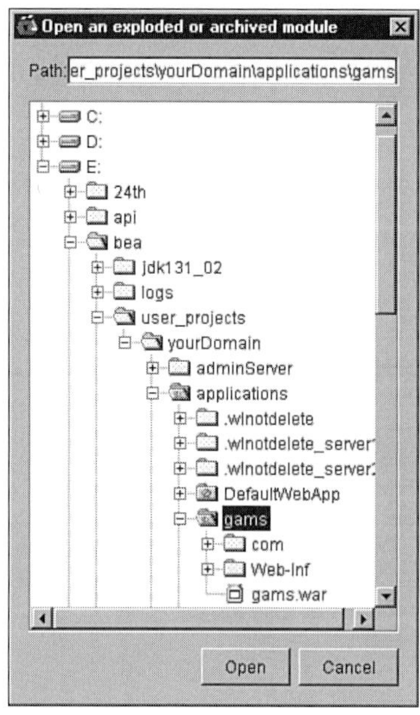

Figure 15.6 Selecting target application.

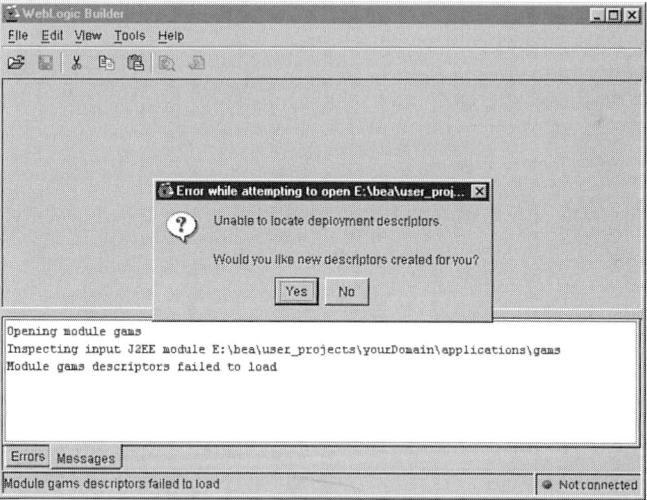

Figure 15.7 Creating deployment descriptors.

Edit the JSP parameter values as needed and save. You may further deploy the application as detailed in Chapter 7.

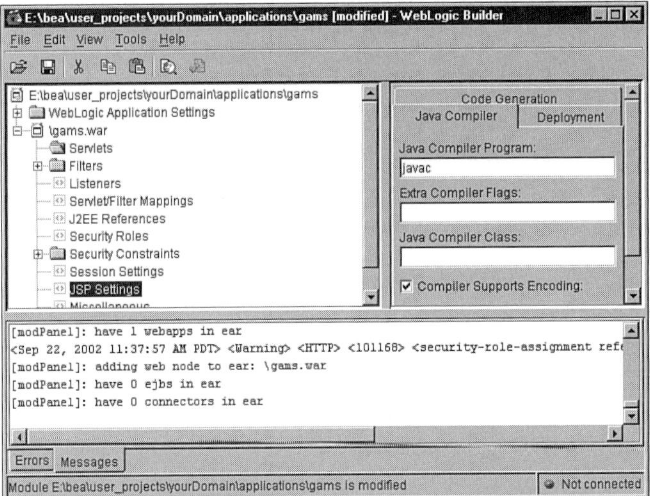

Figure 15.8 Setting JSP parameters.

Configuring JSP Parameters Using the WebLogic Admin Console

> **TIP**
>
> There are various methods in which you may modify configurations parameters. Configuration parameters may be different in development, test, and production environments, but in theory should not be. Development and test environments should mimic the production environment as closely as possible; otherwise, problems might be introduced when migrating applications. Determine the methodology, including the tool employed, that best suits your enterprise.

To set JSP configuration parameters within a preexisting `weblogic.xml` file, start the server and enter your admin server's console at `http://yourURL:port/console`. At the prompt screen, enter your username and password, navigate to the specific Web application, using this sequence: yourDomain→Deployments→Web Application Modules→applicationName, as shown in Figure 15.9.

> **CAUTION**
>
> When configuring JSP parameters using the WebLogic admin console, the `weblogic.xml` file must exist in your application's `WEB-INF` directory prior to starting your WebLogic Server.

> **TIP**
>
> The generic WebLogic installation will install a default application, which includes a default `weblogic.xml`. You can use this default application for JSP development or testing.

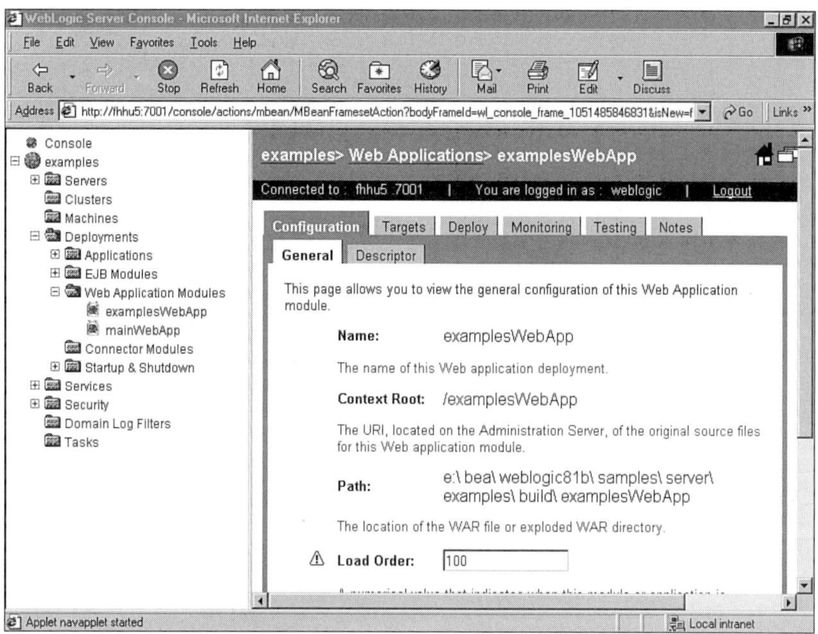

Figure 15.9 Editing a Web app deployment descriptor.

> **TIP**
>
> If encountering errors when persisting JSP configuration parameters using the Admin console, manually edit the application's `weblogic.xml` and restart your server.

Select the Descriptor tab , as shown in Figure 15.10. Modify the JSP parameters as detailed in Table 15.7 earlier in this chapter.

Configuring JSP Parameters via Direct Text Editing

To edit the `weblogic.xml` file (refer to Chapter 7) manually, open it (the file is found within the `WEB-INF` directory under the application's root directory) within a text editor, and modify JSP parameters as detailed in Table 15.7. A sample `weblogic.xml` containing JSP specific parameters is presented in Listing 15.7. Notice how the `pageCheck` parameter is set at lines 8–14 and the `verbose` parameter is set at lines 15–22.

> **CAUTION**
>
> Take special care when editing the `weblogic.xml` or any WebLogic deployment descriptor. Any errant or incorrect additions can crash or otherwise impede server performance. It's prudent to maintain a backup copy of any manually edited XML file.

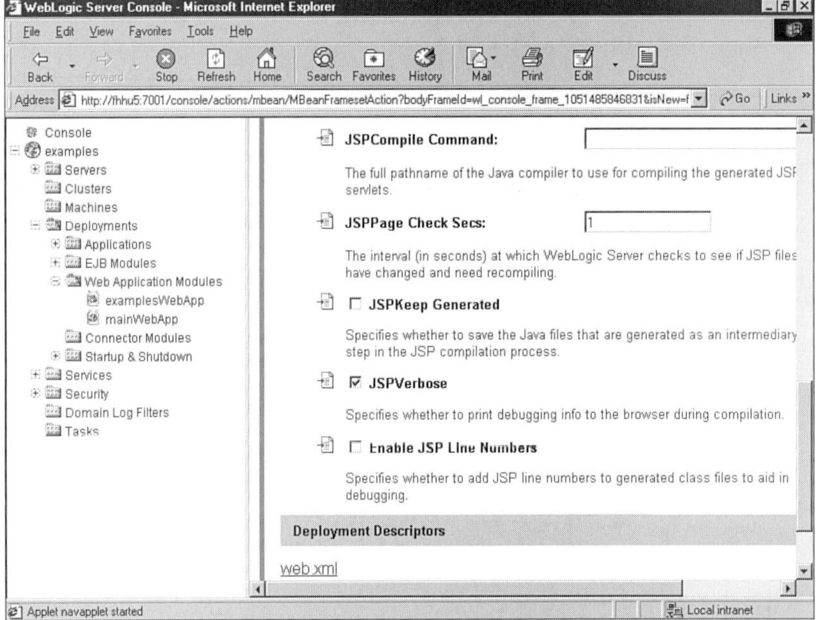

Figure 15.10 Editing the JSP descriptor.

LISTING 15.7 weblogic.xml—JSP-Specific Code

```
<!DOCTYPE weblogic-web-app PUBLIC "-//BEA
Systems, Inc.//DTD Web Application 8.1//EN"
"http://www.bea.com/servers/wls810/dtd/weblogic810-web-jar.dtd">
<weblogic-web-app>
...
 <jsp-descriptor>
  <jsp-param>
   <param-name>
     pageCheckSeconds
    </param-name>
    <param-value>
     1
    </param-value>
   </jsp-param>
   <jsp-param>
    <param-name>
      verbose
    </param-name>
```

LISTING 15.7 Continued

```
    <param-value>
      true
    </param-value>
  </jsp-param>
</jsp-descriptor>
...
</weblogic-web-app>
```

> **TIP**
>
> After you've established a workable set of JSP parameters, copying and pasting the parameters within your application's `weblogic.xml` file is a time-saving strategy. You should establish a set of JSP parameters for development, testing, and production environments. For example, within a production environment, `pageCheckSeconds` should be set to `-1` (no checks), as opposed to the default setting of `1` (check for new version of JSP every second) or the development setting of `0` (check at each request). Within a testing or development environment, you might opt for verbose output, but verbose output might not be desirable for a production environment.

JSP Best Practices

To optimize scalability, maintainability, and deployability, implement a n-tier architecture (Model-View-Controller), separating presentation, application logic, and data archiving.

When implementing complex logic within your presentation layer, use JavaBeans rather than coding intensive scripting blocks. This model promotes code readability and maintainability by organizing application business logic into Java modules. In general, separate Java from your HTML.

Use appropriate `include` options. You should use the `include` directive unless you can justify using the `include` action. If business logic and other Java code are properly abstracted, use of the `include` directive should promote Java code reduction within your JSP page.

To further reduce redundant constructs and improve code readability/maintainability, the use of templates and cascading style sheets should be optimized.

For clarity, use the shorthand JSP tags rather than the more cumbersome XML equivalent tags where possible. However, if you're using XML validation tools, you must use XML equivalent tags.

JSP pages are best implemented within the greater context of an n-tiered layered architecture as provided with the Model-View-Controller design pattern. As discussed in more detail within Chapter 16, JSPs provide the client view or portal into the application. Actual processing of application logic would occur within the Controller or middle-tier layer. The data manipulated as a result of client requests would reside within the Model layer.

Summary

In this chapter, we discussed WebLogic's implementation of JSP 1.2. We've discussed how WebLogic works with JSP servlets to include JSP syntax, coding, and compilation. We further discussed configuration and deployment of JSPs within a WebLogic Server. The next chapter discusses JavaBeans and the MVC architecture.

CHAPTER 16

JavaBeans and Model-View-Controller (MVC) Architecture

IN THIS CHAPTER

- MVC Architecture
- Introduction to JavaBeans
- How to Incorporate JavaBeans into Servlet-JSP Workflow
- MVC Best Practices

by Malcolm W. Garland

This chapter discusses JavaBeans and the MVC design pattern. The J2EE infrastructure implements a three-tiered or layered approach to application implementation. These layers were originally designated as client, middle, and enterprise information systems (EIS). The client tier was conceptualized as the user interface, either a standalone application or a Web browser. The middle tier was visualized as the domain of the business logic where business or application control logic implementations execute. The final tier conceptualized was the EIS—the data store. This architecture conveniently mapped to what had been a long standing design pattern introduced by Xerox: Model-View-Controller. Therefore, to effectively implement J2EE components, developers should possess a basic understanding of the MVC design pattern.

Within this chapter, we also discuss incorporation of JavaBeans into the servlet-JSP workflow. Several MVC best practices are also presented.

MVC Architecture

MVC architecture represents a multi-tiered approach to application implementation. The MVC architecture accomplishes this task by separating application implementation into three distinct layers: presentation, application workflow and business logic, and data store.

The *Model* in MVC represents the data model. Data models are usually implemented as tables within a relational database or Entity EJBs. *View* represents the client presentation components, usually implemented as JSP, servlets, JSP tag libraries, HTML, XML, or WML pages. *Controller* represents implementation of the business logic and application workflow logic responsible for the allocation of resources available to the application. Control logic is usually implemented as servlets, JavaBeans, and Session EJBs.

This layered approached allows decoupling or separation of application functional areas; that is, any changes made within one layer don't necessarily affect implementations within other layers. For example, presentation components may be updated without the need to reimplement any controller logic. Routine updates within the data model don't necessarily affect current presentation components. This paradigm also yields a natural division of labor that enables developers to concentrate on one area of expertise. Presentation can concentrate on presentation issues and no longer be concerned with business logic or data modeling details. Process or control logic developers aren't bogged down with data modeling or presentation details. Database specialists need not concern themselves with workflow or presentation details. This decoupling allows decentralized development with a higher degree of specialization in component implementation.

The J2EE infrastructure implements a MVC design pattern. Let's look at some commonly used design implementations within individual MVC layers.

View Layer Implementations

Java handlers or helper classes are commonly used to implement presentation components. These helper classes and handlers are Java objects such as JavaBeans or JSP tag libraries. These objects are usually implemented within the context of JSP pages, as shown in Figure 16.1.

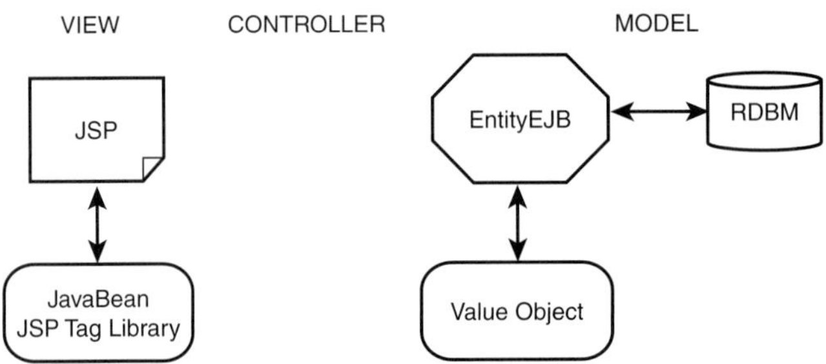

Figure 16.1 View layer, implementing helper classes.

JavaBeans and JSP tag libraries abstract logic (Java code) away from the presentation (HTML, WML, XML) code, supporting the MVC theme of little or no business logic within presentation components. JavaBeans are discussed later in this chapter. JSP tag libraries are discussed in Chapters 17, "Using JSP Tag Libraries," and 18, "Creating JSP Tag Libraries."

Controller Layer Implementations

The implementation of front controllers and dispatchers is a commonly used model within the Controller layer, as shown at Figure 16.2,. Within this paradigm, presentation components—which are usually JSPs, but servlets are often used—issue requests to front controllers. The front controllers then dispatch requests to the applicable business component for processing. These business components are Java objects, which can be Session EJBs, Entity EJBs, JavaBeans, or generic Java objects. The controller receives the responses and redirects the required response to presentation components. Controllers are usually implemented as servlets, as shown in Figure 16.2.

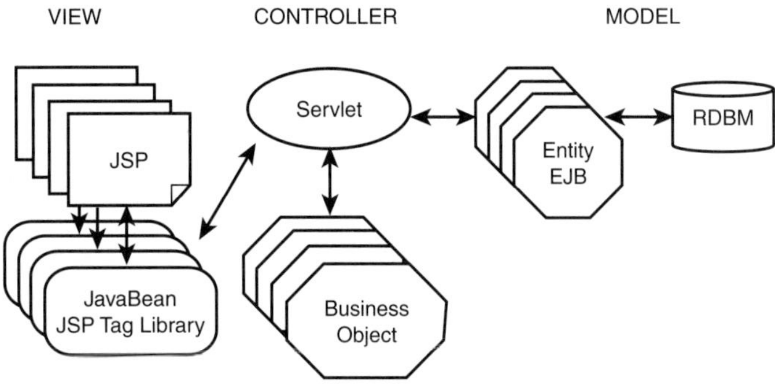

Figure 16.2 Controller layer implementing front controllers.

However, JSP controller implementations are common. The servlet's built-in request/response mechanism (which is shared by JSPs) facilitates this paradigm.

Model Layer Implementations

The Model Layer implementation that supports efficient access to data archives, both relational database and legacy systems, is the value (or transfer) object, as shown in Figure 16.1. Remote method calls are costly in terms of transfer overhead because of serialization and deserialization. The value object, which represents a complete row of a relational database table, reduces this overhead by making one method call, as opposed to the many small method calls usually needed to retrieve EJB attributes (that is, the individual fields within the database table row). Instead of making individual EJB method calls to retrieve individual attributes (database table fields), essentially one EJB method call is made that creates the value object (database table row). The value object is populated locally (that is, on the server side) within the EJB, and then transferred back to the presentation component (the client side), where individual attributes are dereferenced as needed. One remote method call is made versus many remote method calls. Value objects are usually implemented as JavaBeans. For further details about these and other J2EE design patterns, refer to the Sun documentation site at `http://java.sun.com/blueprints/patterns/catalog.html`.

Introduction to JavaBeans

JavaBeans are Java objects developed using specific syntax rules that allow a reusable component architecture. That is, JavaBeans are reusable application components used as either GUI components or, as in our case, JSP helper classes. For more details about JavaBeans and the 1.0 Specification, refer to `http://java.sun.com/products/javabeans/`. JavaBeans generally provide support for

- Introspection—Introspection enables runtime determination of supported events, methods, and properties, so that tools built to the specification can determine how the bean works. Low-level reflection is used to query methods and deduce (using conventional names and type signatures) what properties, events, and public methods are supported. If the developer provides a `BeanInfo` class, that class is used to determine the bean's behavior. A bean `Introspector` class is furnished to provide a standardized methodology of introspecting different beans.

- Customization—Customization, which is applicable to GUI beans, enables developers to customize a bean's appearance and behavior so that application builders built to specification can modify it. Customization is implemented in two ways: GUI property sheets and `Customizer` classes. GUI beans can export a set of properties. These properties can be used to create a GUI property sheet, which lists the properties and provides an editor for each property. This property editor can then be used to update bean properties. `Customizer` classes are AWT components that provide the GUI behavior required to control target beans.

- Events—Events are applicable to GUI beans. They're constructs that convey state change information that can be used to connect beans. Events are conveyed from source `Objects` to target listener `Objects` via method invocations originating from the target listener. Each type of event notification is defined by a unique method. Those methods are grouped within `EventListener` interfaces. Event state objects are used to encapsulate the state associated with a particular event. Custom adapter classes may be used in situations where listeners cannot implement a desired interface.

- Persistence—Saving and restoring object state is also used to support customization in application builders to allow persistence of object state. JavaBeans must support the Java object serialization APIs, which include externalization. If a JavaBean doesn't implement the `hidden state` attribute, third-party tools may be used to restore the state of a serialized JavaBean; otherwise, Java object serialization must be used to save and restore the JavaBean's state.

- Properties—Also known as bean attributes, properties are used to support customization and developer implementation. Properties are the only feature required for non-GUI JavaBean implementations. Further discussion of properties follows.

For use within JSP pages, JavaBeans merely must define properties and implement the accessor methods (getter/setter) associated with those properties. A JavaBean must also implement at least a no-parameter (default) constructor. Properties are discrete attributes of the bean. Attributes may be built-in Java data types or user-defined data types. An attribute must be declared private, and public accessor methods must be defined for each attribute. These methods are of the form `setAttributeName(attribute_data_type)` and `getAttributeName()`. As presented in Chapter 15, "Writing WebLogic Server JavaServer Pages," to implement JavaBeans within a JSP page, you use the `useBean`, `getProperty`, and/or `setProperty` actions. For example, using the `ItemHolderBean` implemented for GAMS to create an item with the following attributes, we can use the following code:

```
<jsp:useBean id="item" class="com.gams.javaBeans.item.ItemHolderBean"
scope="session"/>
<jsp:setProperty name="item" property="itemId" value="3004"/>
<jsp:setProperty name="item" property="title" value="Oriental Rug"/>
<jsp:setProperty name="item" property="currentBid" value="875.00"/>
<jsp:setProperty name="item" property="endDateTime" value="102,10,31"/>
```

To dereference bean attributes, use can use the following code:

```
<jsp:getProperty name="item" property="itemId" value="3004"/>
or
<%=item.getItemId()%>
```


For information about using JavaBeans within JSP pages, refer to the discussion of the `useBean` action in Chapter 15. Listing 16.1 presents a partial code listing for the `ItemHolderBean.java` JavaBean. As you can see, the bean definition for a JSP helper class is pretty straightforward. The bean attributes are defined in lines 8–21. In line 23, the requisite default constructor is defined.

LISTING 16.1 ItemHolderBean.java

```
1 package com.gams.javaBeans.item;
2
3 import java.io.Serializable;
4 import java.sql.Date;
5
6 public class ItemHolderBean implements Serializable
7 {
8   private Integer categoryId;
9   private Float currentBid;
10   private String description;
11   private Date endDateTime;
12   private boolean isFeatured;
```

LISTING 16.1 Continued

```
private Boolean isOpen;
private Integer itemId;
private long minimumBid;
private String pictureFile;
private Integer quantityAvailable;
private Float reservePrice;
private Integer sellerId;
private Date startDateTime;
private String title;

public ItemHolderBean()
{
}
public ItemHolderBean(Integer itId, String title, Float curBid, Date endDate )
{
  itemId = itId;
  title = title;
  currentBid = curBid;
  endDateTime= endDate;
}
public ItemHolderBean(Integer integer, Float float1, String s, Date date, boolean flag, Boolean boolean1, Integer integer1,
    long l, String s1, Integer integer2, Float float2, Integer integer3, Date date1,
    String s2)
{
  categoryId = integer;
  currentBid = float1;
  description = s;
  endDateTime = date;
  isFeatured = flag;
  isOpen = boolean1;
  itemId = integer1;
  minimumBid = l;
  pictureFile = s1;
  quantityAvailable = integer2;
  reservePrice = float2;
  sellerId = integer3;
  startDateTime = date1;
  title = s2;
}
```

LISTING 16.1 Continued

```


public Integer getCategoryId()
{
  return categoryId;
}

public void setCategoryId(Integer integer)
{
  categoryId = integer;
}

public Float getCurrentBid()
{
  return currentBid;
}

public void setCurrentBid(Float float1)
{
  currentBid = float1;
}

public String getDescription()
{
  return description;
}

public void setDescription(String s)
{
  description = s;
}

public Date getEndDateTime()
{
  return endDateTime;
}

public void setEndDateTime(Date date)
{
  endDateTime = date;
}

```

LISTING 16.1 Continued

```
public boolean getIsFeatured()
{
  return isFeatured;
}

public void setIsFeatured(boolean flag)
 {
   isFeatured = flag;
 }

 public Boolean getIsOpen()
 {
   return isOpen;
 }

 public void setIsOpen(Boolean boolean1)
 {
   isOpen = boolean1;
 }

 public Integer getItemId()
 {
   return itemId;
 }

 public void setItemId(Integer integer)
 {
   itemId = integer;
 }

 public long getMinimumBid()
 {
   return minimumBid;
 }

 public void setMinimumBid(long l)
 {
   minimumBid = l;
 }

 public String getPictureFile()
 {
```

LISTING 16.1 Continued

```
    return pictureFile;
  }

  public void setPictureFile(String s)
  {
    pictureFile = s;
  }

  public Integer getQuantityAvailable()
  {
    return quantityAvailable;
  }

  public void setQuantityAvailable(Integer integer)
  {
    quantityAvailable = integer;
  }

  public Float getReservePrice()
  {
    return reservePrice;
  }

  public void setReservePrice(Float float1)
  {
    reservePrice = float1;
  }

  public Integer getSellerId()
  {
    return sellerId;
  }

  public void setSellerId(Integer integer)
  {
    sellerId = integer;
  }

  public Date getStartDateTime()
  {
    return startDateTime;
  }
```

LISTING 16.1 Continued

```
178
179   public void setStartDateTime(Date date)
180   {
181     startDateTime = date;
182   }
183
184   public String getTitle()
185   {
186     return title;
187   }
188
189   public void setTitle(String s)
190   {
191     title = s;
192   }
193 }
194
```

Two constructors (one a 4 parameter and the other a 14 parameter; used to construct `ItemBeanHolder` Java objects) are defined in lines 26–51. The remainder of the code (lines 54–192) defines attribute getter and `setter` methods. Listing 16.2 displays a simple JSP, `viewItemHolderBean.jsp`, which uses the `ItemHolderBean`.

LISTING 16.2 viewItemHolderBean.jsp

```
<!DOCTYPE HTML PUBLIC "-//W3C//DTD HTML 4.01 Transitional//EN">

<html>
<head>
   <title>Global Auctions - View Item Holder Bean</title>
</head>

<body><h1>View Item Holder Bean</h1>
   <jsp:useBean id="item" class="com.gams.javaBeans.item.ItemHolderBean"
➥scope="session"/>
   <jsp:setProperty name="item" property="itemId" value="3003"/>
   <jsp:setProperty name="item" property="title" value="Oriental Rug"/>
   <jsp:setProperty name="item" property="currentBid" value="875.00"/>
<table>
<tr><td>Item Number: </td><td><%=item.getItemId()%></td></tr>
<tr><td>Description: </td><td><%=item.getTitle()%></td></tr>
<tr><td>Current Bid: </td>
```

LISTING 16.2 Continued

```
17   <td><jsp:getProperty name="item" property="currentBid" /></td>
18 </tr>
19 </table>
20 </body>
21 </html>
```

Note the declaration of the JavaBean `item` in line 9. Lines 10–12 implement `<jsp:setProperty>` actions, which set attributes on the `item` bean. Lines 14 and 15 dereference the `item` bean attributes `itemId` and `title` using Java standard method call syntax. Note line 17 where the `<jsp:getProperty>` action is used to dereference attribute `currentBid`. A browser display of `viewItemHolderBean.jsp` is provided in Figure 16.3.

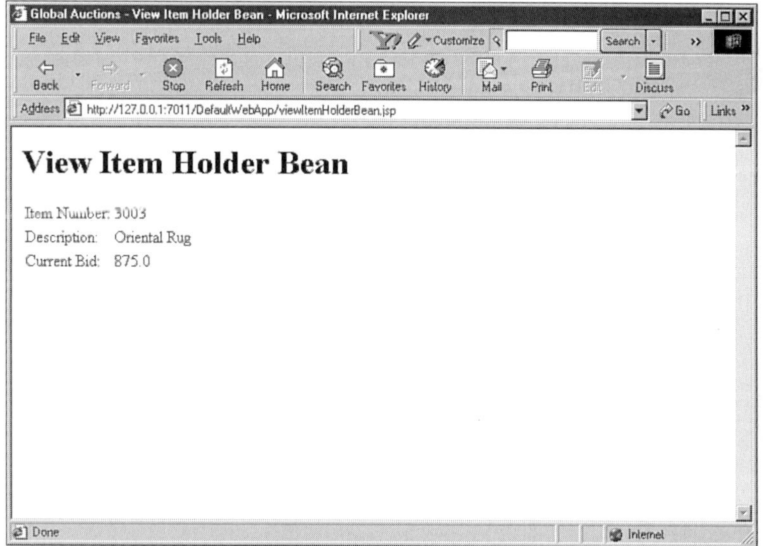

Figure 16.3 Browser display of viewItemHolderBean.java.

How to Incorporate JavaBeans into Servlet-JSP Workflow

JavaBeans are incorporated into the servlet-JSP workflow by implementing a front controller MVC architecture, as shown earlier in Figure 16.2 Within MVC, JSP components, using JavaBeans and JSP tag libraries, generate all requests that generate user presentation. Little or no Java code is contained within JSP pages; instead, Java code is implemented within the supporting JavaBeans and/or JSP tag libraries. Within this model,

JavaBeans provide non–business logic implementations that support JSP presentation. Also in this model, JavaBean implementations may request server-side services, which are processed by servlets functioning within the Controller layer. Servlets control or direct processing of all requests originating from the presentation layer; that is, access to data and forwarding of requests to business units or presentation components as needed. JavaBeans may also be incorporated into the servlet-JSP workflow by implementing logic within the Controller layer. Within this model, the business objects available to Controller layer servlets are implemented to meet JavaBean specifications in addition to their target functional implementations.

MVC Best Practices

MVC best practices are implemented by tried-and-tested J2EE design patterns. These patterns are the result of successful J2EE application implementations. A synopsis of a few of the most successful of these design patterns is presented here.

Presentation Layer Design Patterns

The View Helper design pattern provides a separation of presentation logic from business logic. This separation is accomplished by using view components that implement presentation, while presentation support logic is encapsulated into custom JSP tags or JavaBeans. The view components are usually implemented as JSPs or servlets.

The Composite View design pattern provides a composite presentation view built from subview components. Changes within subview components are propagated to the top-level composite view. The composite view controls the layout of subviews, yielding a consistent look and feel throughout all views. View components are usually implemented as JSPs.

Controller Layer Design Patterns

The Front Controller design pattern provides a central component that controls all application requests. This allows state changes, including views, to be applied uniformly across the application. Additionally, any required code modifications are made in one centralized component. Front controllers are usually implemented as servlets.

The Business Delegate design pattern provides a decoupling of application business logic from using components. This pattern allows complex functionality, such as lookup and remote exception handling, to be accessed using much simpler interfaces. Business delegates are usually implemented as Session EJBs, which further allows a reduction in remote method invocations. The components make one remote call to a Session EJB, which invokes finer-grained services locally (that is, on the server side).

Closely related to the Business Delegate pattern, the Session Fa[cd]ade design pattern provides coarsely grained interfaces to finely grained server-side resources, usually an

Entity EJB. The Entity EJB is essentially wrapped within a Session bean. One remote method call is made to the Session bean, which might invoke several methods on the server-side Entity EJB, thereby reducing remote method calls, while providing for much a simpler client-side interface.

The Intercepting Filter design patterns provides interception and redirection of requests and response where needed. This pattern is applicable in application security and other rule-based access implementations. Implementing interception filters helps manage such complex scenarios by avoiding the necessity of coding access implementations within individual JSPs. One intercepting filter is implemented to handle all access concerns. Interception filters are usually servlets that implement the `Filter` servlet interface.

Model Layer Design Patterns

The Value Object (transfer object) design pattern allows for efficient remote invocations by replacing many finely grained remote method calls with one coarsely grained remote method call. Attributes usually retrieved by the finely grained method invocations are abstracted into one object. One remote method invocation creates and populates the value object locally (server side), and the object is then passed remotely to the client. All attributes are passed in one remote method call (attributes are abstracted within the value [or transfer[object) versus many remote method calls to populate individual attributes. Value Objects may be implemented as JavaBeans.

The Data Access Object design pattern provides encapsulated data store–specific logic, which yields generic client database interfaces across different data stores. The client uses the same interface to access different databases. The determinant logic (meaning the specific database parameters to execute) is handled by the server side.

For further details about these and other J2EE-recommended design patterns, refer to `http://java.sun.com/blueprints/patterns/catalog.html`.

16

GLOBAL AUCTIONS USE OF JAVABEANS MVC

The Global Auctions application implements the MVC architecture. The Front Controller–dispatched design pattern is fully implemented within the Controller layer. Servlets are used to control workflow originating from client requests, through application processing, to final delivery of client response. Servlets, as controllers, are implemented to find items, display items, register customers, service logins, and list auction items. These servlets use as business services, Java objects, and session EJBs, in addition to core WebLogic Server–side resources. For the view, servlets and JSP pages using custom JSP tag libraries and JavaBeans implement user presentation. In addition to the previous servlet use case implementations, JSP pages are also implemented for a bid history display and auction report generation. JavaBeans and JSP tag libraries are used to encapsulate data used for item displays and to provide customer information used by a login servlet. Entity EJBs, embellished with value objects, implement an optimized data model; that is, they provide mappings to a relational database complemented by reduced remote method invocations. As an example of GAMS' implementation of the MVC architecture, the finding items use case is shown in Figure 16.4.

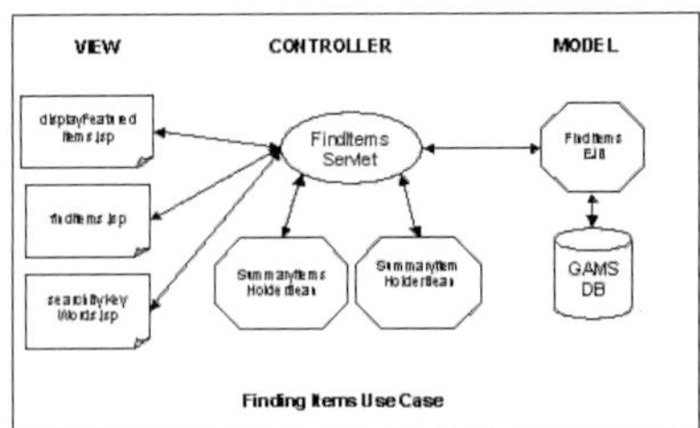

Figure 16.4 Finding items use case.

Summary

In this chapter, we discussed the Model-View-Controller architecture. We saw how this design pattern establishes three separate layers: presentation, control, and model. We discussed common design patterns within each layer, and how JSPs and servlets, augmented with helper classes, can implement nearly Java-free presentation code. We introduced the Front Controller–dispatched design pattern. Finally, we discussed a Model layer implementation using EJBs augmented with value objects. JavaBeans and the role they can play as presentation helper classes or controller business units within an MVC-based architecture were also discussed. In the next chapter, we'll discuss JSP custom tag libraries and how they fit into the MVC architecture.

CHAPTER 17

Using JSP Tag Libraries

by Kunal Mittal

IN THIS CHAPTER

- Use of JSP Tag Libraries
- JSP Tag Library Syntax
- Tag Libraries Shipped with the WebLogic Server
- WebLogic Server EJB to JSP Integration Tool
- Using Tag Libraries—Best Practices
- Additional Resources for JSP Tag Libraries

This chapter discusses how to use JSP tag libraries on the WebLogic server. The JSP tag library construct allows developers to port Java code away from JSP presentation pages by encapsulating Java code within tag implementation classes. Methods of these implementation classes are then called from JSP pages, using XML-like tag syntax. Within this chapter, JSP tag use, tag syntax, and the WebLogic custom tag library are discussed. Additionally, the WebLogic EJB to JSP Integration Tool, tag library resources, and best practices for implementing tag libraries are also addressed.

Use of JSP Tag Libraries

JSP tag libraries are encapsulations of logical constructs, providing for units of reusable functionality. These units of functionality are accessed using custom JSP tags from a JSP page. Consistent with an MVC implementation, JSP tag libraries abstract logic from the JSP presentation layer to the controller layer, thereby reducing Java code within the JSP page. JSP tags are commonly used to implement application-wide functionality that facilitates data presentation such as formatting and processing of output, application wide administrative tasks, defining variables and objects for use within the JSP page, pre- or post-server-side data manipulation, and implementation of server-side processing as required by the application. JSP tag libraries provide for cleaner JSP pages that are more readable, more maintainable, while implementing the MVC architecture. Within this chapter we detail how to use tag libraries in general and specifically how to use the BEA WebLogic provided tag libraries. Tag library creation is addressed within Chapter 18, "Creating JSP Tag Libraries."

JSP Tag Library Syntax

Tag libraries are used within the context of a WebLogic application. To use tags within a tag library, the tag library's `uri` (file location) must first be registered within the application's `web.xml` (application deployment descriptor) file. This file is located in the application's `..\WEB-INF` directory. The tag library's XML syntax is follows:

```
<taglib>
  <taglib-uri>name.tld</taglib-uri>
  <taglib-location>
    /WEB-INF/lib/name-tags.jar
  </taglib-location>
</taglib>
```

To use the library within your JSP page after the tag library's `uri` is set, you must reference the tag library using the `taglib` directive with the syntax that follows:

WebLogic JSP shorthand

```
<%@ taglib uri="name-tags.tld" prefix="yourPrefix" %>
```

XML equivalent

```
<jsp:directive.taglib uri="name-tags.tld" prefix="yourPrefix" />
```

Refer to Table 15.3 in Chapter 15, "Writing WebLogic Server JavaServer Pages," for a complete listing of `taglib` directive attributes. After the tag library is referenced within your JSP page, you can reference tags within the library using JSP syntax as follows:

```
<yourPrefix:tagName attributes>
 optional tag specific body
</yourPrefix:tagName>
```

See Chapter 18 for further examples of using tag libraries.

Tag Libraries Shipped with WebLogic Server

The tag libraries shipped with WebLogic Server are `weblogic-tags.jar` (referred to as WebLogic custom tags) and `weblogic-vtags.jar` (referred to as WebLogic validation tags). These libraries are included within your distribution. They're located within the `BEAHome\WebLogicHome\server\ext` directory. The JARs provided contain implementation classes along with tag library descriptors (TLDs).

WebLogic Custom Tags

The WebLogic custom tags library (`weblogic-tags.jar`) contains classes that assist in the caching and processing of data. The three custom tags are `cache`, `repeat`, and `process`.

The Cache Tag

The cache tag enables work done within the body of the cache tag to be cached. Body content may be cached before or after processing. This construct enables the developer to modify JSP page variables or further process tag body content prior to final output. The cache tag includes attributes for refresh and flush procedures. An example using the cache tag is provided here:

```
<wl:cache name="auctionDbTable" key="accontNumber" scope="session">
<--read account data into cache-->
</wl:cache>
```

The Repeat Tag

The repeat tag allows iteration over several different types of sets (enumerations, iterators, collections, arrays of objects, vectors, result sets, result set metadata, and hash table keys). The repeat tag provides a count attribute to implement simple loops. An example that uses the repeat tag is provided here:

```
<wl:repeat id="currentAuctionItems" set="<%=catalogue.getItems()%>">
➥<--method getItems() returns a String-->
 <%=currentAuctionItems%> <--prints each item-->
</wl:repeat>
```

The Process Tag

The process tag allows query parameter–based processing. This tag enables selective processing based on a name-value-Boolean scheme; that is name, not-name, value, not-value. Here's an example that uses the process tag:

```
<wl:process notname="update"
<!--Only show if there is no update -->
 <form action="post">
  <input type="text" name="accountNumber"/>
  <input type="submit" name="update" value="Update"/>
 </form>
</wl:process>

<wl:process name="Update">
 <!--do the update -->
</wl:process>
```

For detailed information about the specifics of these WebLogic custom tags and their attributes, refer to the BEA documentation site at http://edocs.beasys.com/wls/docs81/jsp/customtags.html.

WebLogic Validation Tags

The WebLogic validation tags library (`weblogic-vtags.jar`) contains classes and a tag library descriptor for three custom tags that, working in unison, implement HTML form user entry validation. The validation schemes issues a warning if required entries are omitted. Additionally, two versions of text comparisons are implemented: text comparison versus a sibling form field (as with password entry confirmations), and text comparison against an existing or regular expression. A framework for custom validation support is also provided. These tags are `summary`, `form`, and `validation`.

The Summary Tag

The WebLogic `summary` tag is the top-level validation tag. The validation tag signals the head and tail of the validation construct. The head `summary` tag defines the name of an error message vector (logs each error message activated), a general error text message, and a redirect page for successful data entry. The error vector and the text message are usually dereferenced using JSP tags. If errors are encountered, the page is redrawn displaying the errant fields. WebLogic `summary` tag syntax is shown here:

```
<prefix:summary name="errorVector" headerText="General Page Error Message"
➥redirectPage="allEntriesValid.jsp">
...form body...> (Note: HTML may be used within form body)
</prefix:summary>
```

The Form Tag

Similar to HMTL forms, the WebLogic `Form` tag defines the physical form. Fields and WebLogic validation tags are defined within the WebLogic `form` tag. One or more forms may be colocated within one set of summary tags. As with HTML forms, the `form` tag defines the `method` and `action` parameters of the form, along with field name-value pairs. WebLogic `form` tag syntax is shown here:

```
<prefix:form method="GET"¦"PUT" action="allEntriesValid.jsp"/>
<--Fields /Field Validations Defined Here-->
<input type="text" name="field" >
...
<input type="submit" value="Button Label">
</prefix:form>
```

The Validation Tag

WebLogic validation tags validates each form field for allowable entries. Validations are implemented via three utility classes: `RequiredFieldValidator` (validates whether a required field is populated), `RegExpValidator` (validates whether a field is equal to a target expression), and `CompareValidator` (validates by comparing one field within the form to another). WebLogic also provides the `CustomizableAdapter` class that allows for user-defined validation. Form fields may have one or more validation tags. WebLogic form validation syntax is shown in the following snippet:

```
<prefix:form method="GET"¦"PUT" action="allEntriesValid.jsp"/>
<--Fields /Field Validations Defined Here-->
<input type="text" name="fieldA" >
<prefix:validator fieldToValidate="fieldA"
validatorClass="weblogicx.jsp.tags.validators.NameValidator"
errorMessage="Field Specific Error Message"
>
<img src="image.gif">Field Specific Error Message
</prefix:validator>
<input type="submit" value="Button Label">
</prefix:form>
```

For detailed information about WebLogic validation tags, including attributes and use, refer to the BEA documentation site at `http://edocs.beasys.com/wls/docs81/jsp/customtags.html`.

Using the WebLogic Server Tag Library

To use the WebLogic Server tag libraries, copy the `weblogic-tags.jar` file to the `WEB-INF/lib` directory of the application containing your JSP pages. Add the tag library's `uri` to your application's `web.xml` file as shown here:

```
<taglib>
  <taglib-uri>weblogic-tags.tld</taglib-uri>
  <taglib-location>
    /WEB-INF/lib/weblogic-tags.jar
  </taglib-location>
</taglib>
```

Finally, you must reference the library within your JSP page as shown:

```
<%@ taglib uri="weblogic-tags.tld" prefix="wl" %>
```

The WebLogic tag Library is now available for use within your JSP page.

Example Using WebLogic Validation Tag Library

Let's work through an example using WebLogic validation tags. In Listing 17.1, `bidSubmission.jsp`, we've implemented a WebLogic JSP validation tag to validate bid requests. Note the custom tag directive in line 2 and the validation declaration in line 4, which includes the redirect success page, `goodBid.jsp`. The JSP takes a HTTP request, which contains a bid item in lines 13–18. Line 22 begins the physical layout of the form with the declarations of the form tag. Lines 25–30 are where we implement our error notice. Notice the HTML tags interspersed throughout the logic.

LISTING 17.1 BidSubmission.jsp

```
<%@ page import="com.gams.ejbs.item.*, java.sql.Date" %>
<%@ taglib uri="weblogicv.tld" prefix="wl" %>

<wl:summary name="errorVector" headerText="<font color=red>Oooops!</font>"
➥redirectpage="goodBid.jsp" >

<html>
<head>
  <title>Global Auctions - Bid Submission</title>
</head>
<body>
<h1>Global Auctions - Bid Submission</h1>

<% ItemValue iv;
 if (null != request.getAttribute("item")) {
   iv = (ItemValue)request.getAttribute("item");
 }
 else {
   iv = new ItemValue(new Integer(101), "Ming Chair", new Float(550.50),
➥new java.sql.Date(102, 06, 30));
 }
 session.setAttribute("item",iv);
%>
 <wl:form method="GET" action="goodBid.jsp" >
 <table>
<%
 if ( errorVector.size() > 0 ) {
   out.println("<tr><td><h2>" + headerText + "</h2></td></tr>");
   out.println("<tr><td><b>Just A Reminder:</b></td></tr>");

   for ( int i = 0; i < errorVector.size(); i++ ) {
     out.println("<tr><td><font color=red>" +
➥(String)errorVector.elementAt(i)+ "</font></td><tr>");
   }
 }
%>
 <tr><td>Item Number:</td><td><%=iv.getItemId()%></td></tr>
 <tr><td>Description:</td><td><%=iv.getTitle()%></td></tr>
 <tr><td>Bid Close Date: </td><td><%=iv.getEndDateTime()%></td></tr>
 <tr><td>Current Bid: </td><td><%=iv.getCurrentBid()%></td></tr>

 <tr><td>Bidder ID: </td><td><input type="text" name="bidderId" ></td></tr>
```

```
40 <wl:validator fieldToValidate="bidderId"
41      validatorClass="weblogicx.jsp.tags.validators.RequiredFieldValidator"
42      errorMessage="Don't Forget Your Bidder ID Number!">
43 <tr><td colspan="2"><font color="red">ID Number is Required!!!</font></td></tr>
44 </wl:validator>
45
46 <tr><td>Bid (per item): </td><td><input type="text" name="bid" ></td></tr>
47 <wl:validator fieldToValidate="bid"
48     validatorClass="weblogicx.jsp.tags.validators.RequiredFieldValidator"
49     errorMessage="How Much Do You Really Want to Bid?">
50 <tr><td colspan="2"><font color="red">Invalid Bid!!!</font></td></tr>
51 </wl:validator>
52 <wl:validator fieldToValidate="bid"
53     validatorClass="com.gams.util.NonZeroValidator"
54     errorMessage="Is That How Much You Really Want To Bid?">
55 <tr><td colspan="2"><font color="red">Invalid Bid!!!</font></td></tr>
56 </wl:validator>
57
58 <tr><td>Quantity(Requested): </td><td><input type="text" name="quantity" >
➥</td></tr>
59 <wl:validator fieldToValidate="quantity"
60     validatorClass="weblogicx.jsp.tags.validators.RequiredFieldValidator"
61     errorMessage="How Many Do You Really Want?">
62 <tr><td colspan="2"><font color="red">Invalid Quantity!!!</font></td></tr>
63 </wl:validator>
64 <wl:validator fieldToValidate="bid"
65     validatorClass="com.gams.util.NonZeroValidator"
66     errorMessage="Is That How Many You Really Want?">
67 <tr><td colspan="2"><font color="red">Invalid Quantiy!!!</font></td></tr>
68 </wl:validator>
69
70 <input type="submit" value="Submit Form">
71
72 </table>
73 </wl:form>
74 </wl:summary>
75 </body>
76 </html>
```

In line 39, note the first field definition, followed by a validation block beginning in line 40. From lines 40–68 form fields are implemented and complemented by validations. Notice the custom validation class in line 65. At line 68, we close the final validation, followed by a form submit button definition in line 70. Note how the button is defined after the last validation, but before the form end tag that occurs in line 73. The validation is closed by the summary end tag in line 74. Listing 17.1 yields the output displayed in Figures 17.1—17.3.

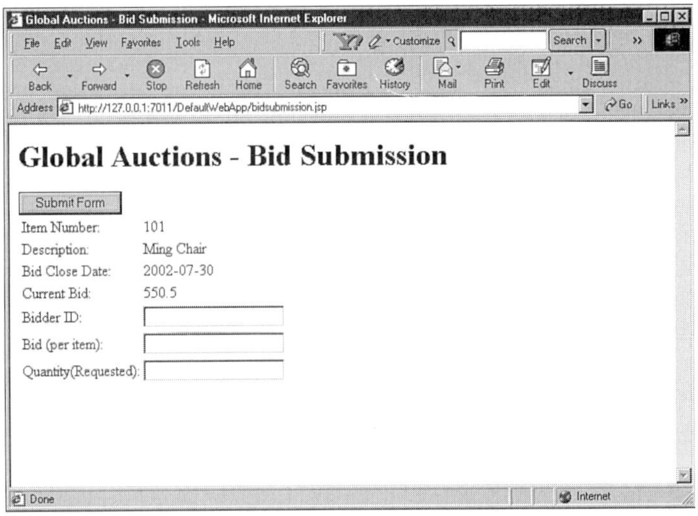

FIGURE 17.1 BidSubmission.jsp, initial state.

The success page, `goodBid.jsp`, is displayed in Figure 17.2.

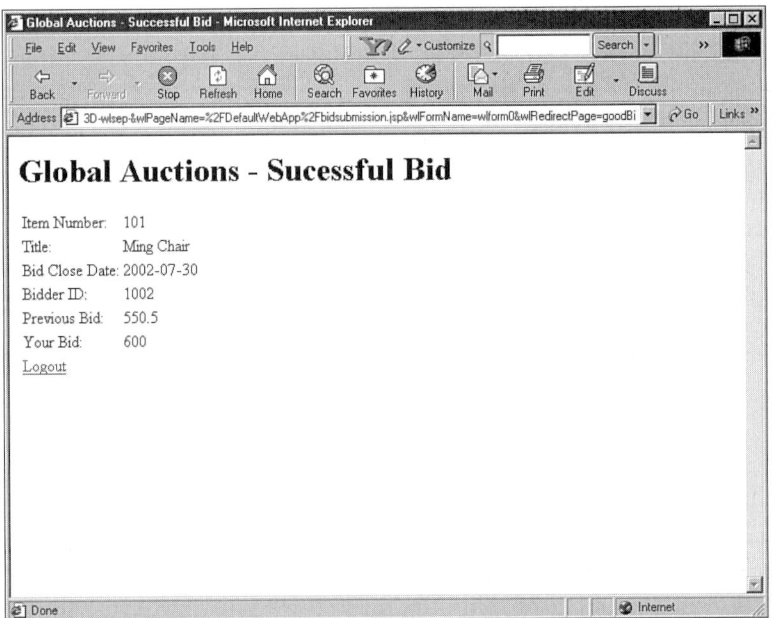

FIGURE 17.2 Successful Bid, GoodBid.jsp.

The validation error notices, also `goodBid.jsp`, is displayed in Figure 17.3.

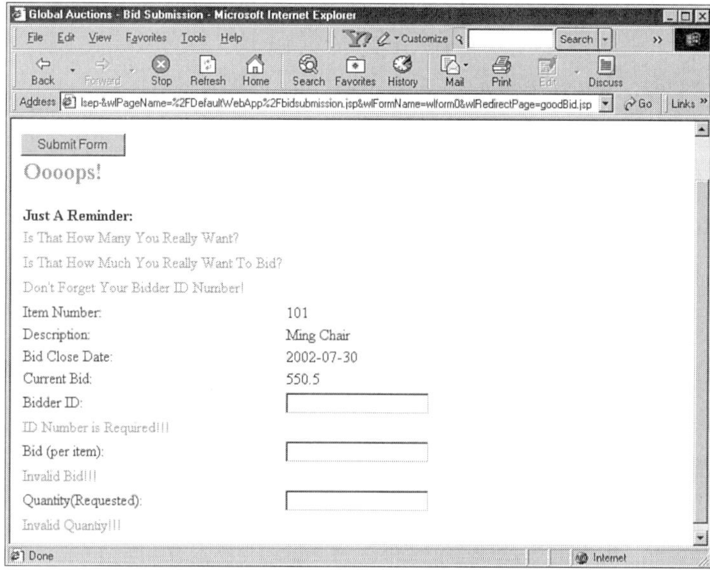

FIGURE 17.3 Unsuccessful Bid, BidSubmission.jsp.

WebLogic Server EJB to JSP Integration Tool

The WebLogic Server EJB to JSP integration tool enables you to execute EJB method calls without implementing an EJB client code within your JSP page. The integration tool generates a JSP tag library associated with each individual EJB. To invoke EJB methods within your JSP page, you need only declare the tag library and implement the applicable JSP tag. For example, you would use our Global Auctions `ItemEJB` like so:

```
<% taglib uri="itemEJB.tld" prefix="itemEJB" %>
➥(assumes uri registered in web.xml)
 //Invoking EJB Create
<itemEJB:home-create itemvalue="<%= iv %>" />
➥(assumes itemValue object--iv created and populated)
```

Compare that to the EJB client implementation shown here:

```
...
ItemHome home;
Hashtable ht = new Hashtable();
ht.put(Context.INITIAL_CONTEXT_FACTORY,
➥"weblogic.jndi.WLInitialContextFactory");
ht.put(Context.PROVIDER_URL, "t3://localhost:7001");
```

```
// lookup ItemHome and store
try {
    InitialContext ic = new InitialContext(ht);
    home = (ItemHome)ic.lookup("ItemHome");
} catch (Exception e) {
    e.printStackTrace();
}
ItemValue iv = new ItemValue();
iv.setItemId(XY4567);
iv.setMinBid(1000);
iv.setDescription("Ming Chair");

Item item = (Item)home.create(iv);
...
```

Notice how much cleaner the implemented of the EJB method calls are. A tag is optionally generated for each EJB method. The tag's attributes are the associated EJB's method parameters. The integration tool supports Stateless and Stateful Session EJBs, and Entity EJBs. For more details about EJBs, see Part V, "Using Enterprise JavaBeans in WebLogic Applications."

Generating EJB to JSP Tag Library

To generate a JSP tag library for an EJB, start the WebLogic EJB to JSP integration tool by executing the `weblogic.servlet.ejb2jsp.gui.Main` application as follows:

```
$ java weblogic.servlet.ejb2jsp.gui.Main
```

When the previous command is executed, the EJB to JSP application window will appear. Set the source directory (the location of the Java files, not the class files corresponding to your EJB) by selecting Preferences from the File menu as shown in Figures 17.4 and 17.5.

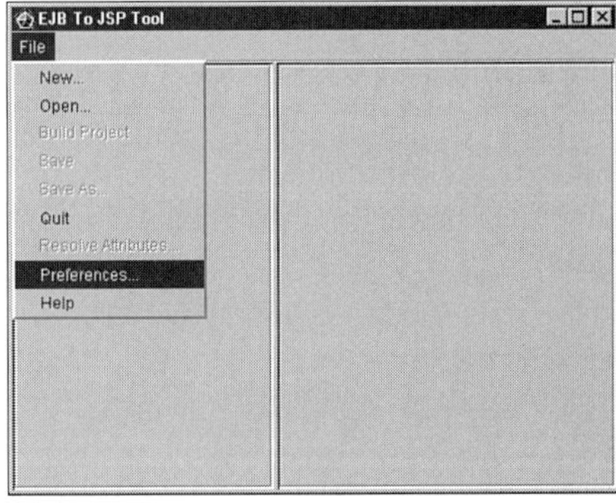

FIGURE 17.4 Selecting preferences.

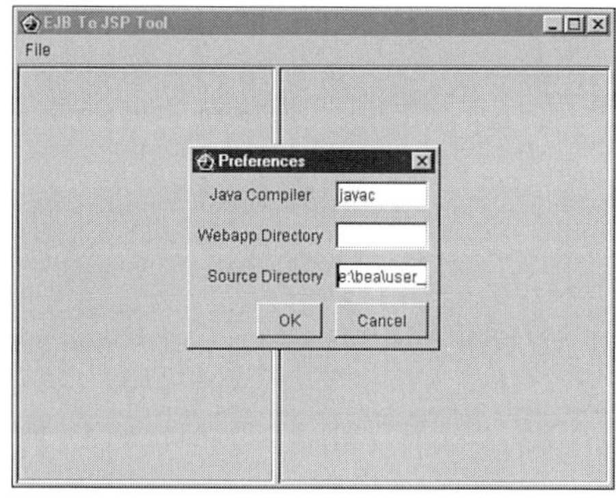

FIGURE 17.5 Setting source directory.

After setting the source directory (select OK to persist selection), select New from the File menu, and then select the target EJB JAR file, as shown in Figures 17.6 and 17.7.

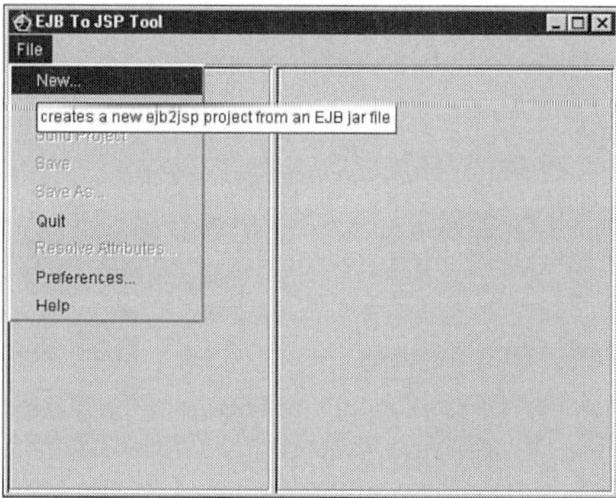

FIGURE 17.6 Selecting new project.

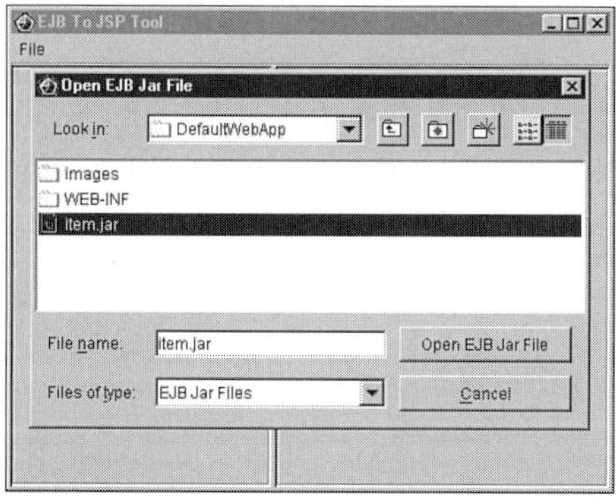

FIGURE 17.7 Selecting EJB JAR file.

After selecting an EJB JAR file, the integration tool creates and displays the project in the left plane of the application window. Highlight Project Build Options under the project's name (the name of the JAR file) and set build options as shown in Figure 17.8.

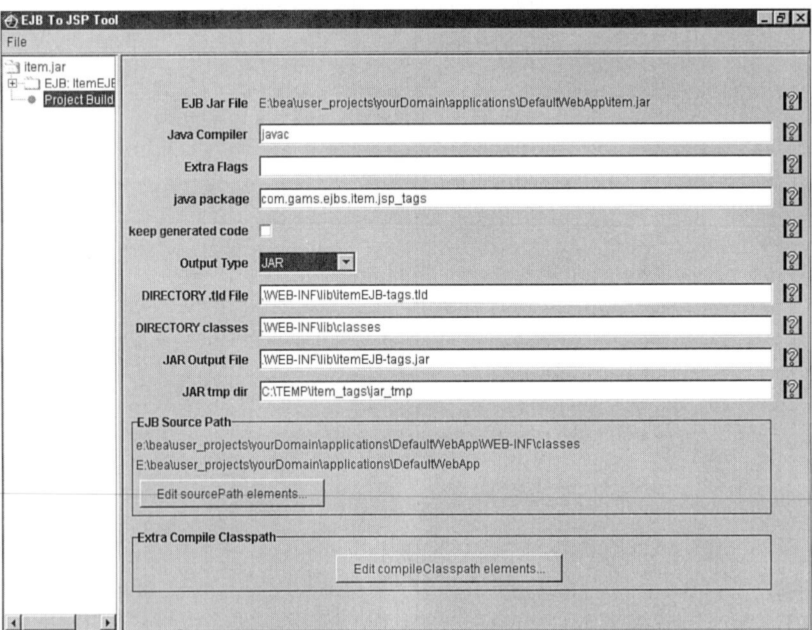

FIGURE 17.8 Setting project build options.

After setting options (relative directory locations and packaging option—JAR file are recommended), build the tag library by selecting Build Project from the File menu, as shown in Figure 17.9.

The tag library will be produced and deposited within the directory selected under build options, as previously discussed.

Using EJB Tags Within a JSP Page

To use the generated EJB tags, register the tag library with your application's `web.xml` as shown here:

```
...
 <taglib>
   <taglib-uri>
    itemEJB.tld
   </taglib-uri>
   <taglib-location>
    /WEB-INF/lib/itemEJB-tags.jar
```

```
    </taglib-location>
  </taglib>
...
```

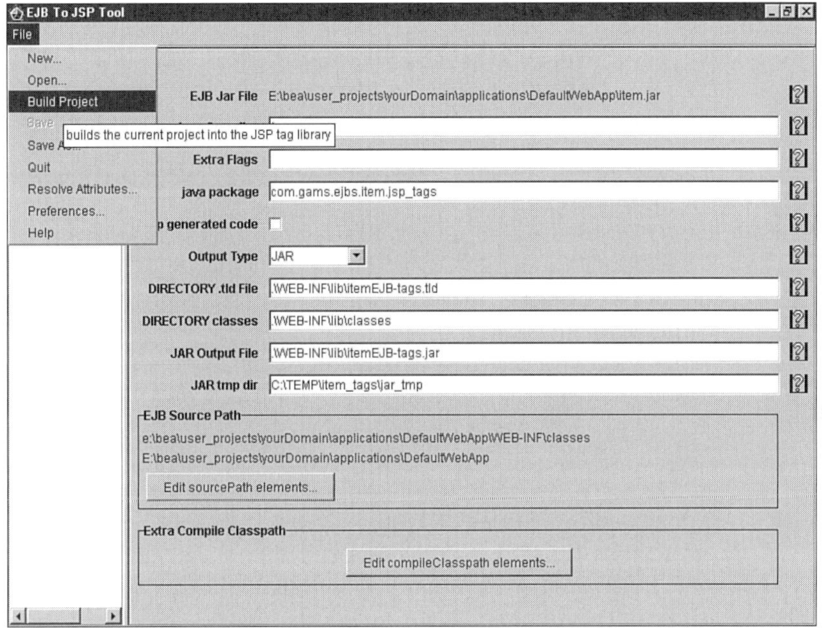

FIGURE 17.9 Building the project.

This ensures that the referenced JAR file is in the given location. You merely declare the tag library and reference the tags within the JSP page, as shown here:

```
<% taglib uri="ItemEJB-tags.tld" prefix="itemEJB" %>
➥(assumes uri is registered within web.xml)
 <b>Create an Item EJB</b></br>//note: method create()
➥returns an item object//
<itemEJB:home-creat itemvalue="<%= iv %>"_return="item"/>
Item Number: <%=item.getItemNumber()%>
Minimum Bid: <%=item.getMinBid()%>
Description: <%=item.getDescription()%>
```

Notice the `_return="it"` construct within the method invocation tag. This construct allows access to the values returned from the associated method; in our example, the `create()` method. This feature is available for EJB methods with non-void return types. If the returned value is a Java primitive data type, the primitive will be returned as the corresponding wrapper class; that is, a `long` will be returned as `java.lang.Long`, and an `int` will be returned as `java.lang.Integer`.

According to the EJB 2.0 Specification, an `EJBHome` interface may contain methods other than `create()` and `find()`. The tags generated for these other home interface methods are prepended with `home-` to avoid confusion.

Method tags generated for Stateful Session and Entity EJBs are required to be within a EJB home interface tag that corresponds to a `find()` or `create()` method. All EJB methods tags within enclosing (single-value) `find()` or `create()` method tags operate on the specific bean instance involved in the `find()` or `create()` method. Our previous example would be modified as shown here:

```
<% taglib uri="ItemEJB-tags.tld" prefix="itemEJB" %>
➥(assumes uri is registered within web.xml)
 <b>Item Information</b></br>//note: method create returns an item object//
<item:home-findByPrimaryKey integer="1001" return="item">
 <itemEJB:setMinimumBid f-"1000"/>
 <itemEJB:setDescription s="Teak Chair" />
 Item Number: <%=item.getItemNumber()%>
 Minimum Bid: <%=item.getMinBid()%>
 Description: <%=item.getDescription()%>
</item:home-create>
```

The `_return` construct will create a page variable referencing the found or created EJB instance. Home tag methods returning a collection of beans will iterate over their body for as many beans as are returned. The `_return` construct refers to the current bean in the iteration. The following code snippet

```
<item:home-findByPrimaryKey _return="item">
 Item Number: <%=item.getItemNumber()%>
 Minimum Bid: <%=item.getMinBid()%>
 Description: <%=item.getDescription()%>
</item:home-findByPrimaryKey>
```

prints a list of all auction items; that is, it iterates through a collection of EJBs.

Default attributes (preset values, such as initial or routine data, sent to your code) can be set using the integration tool as shown in Figure 17.10 (note the Expression field).

If no values are set within the window, all attributes must be provided (passed from the JSP tag attribute).

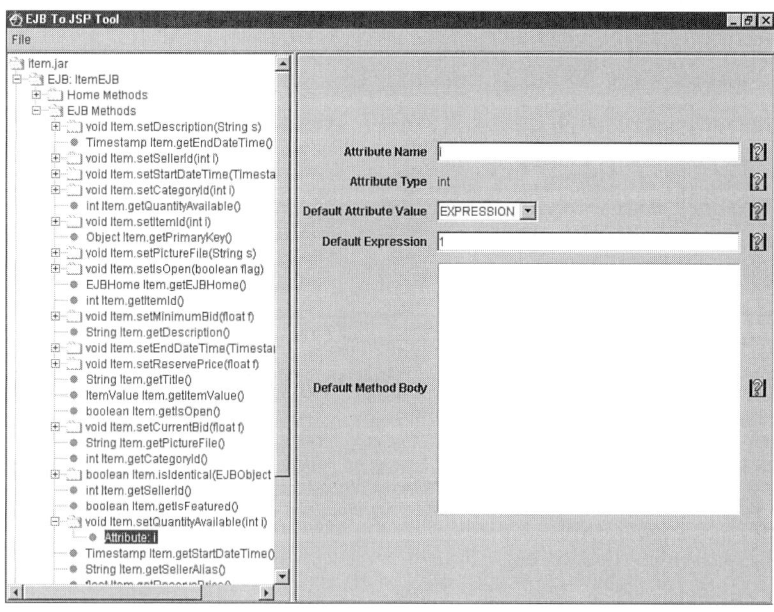

FIGURE 17.10 Setting default attributes.

Using Tag Libraries—Best Practices

Use custom tag libraries in implementing an MVC design pattern. Tag libraries are most effectively used when implementing presentation support behavior specific to JSP pages. Outside of JSP, JSP tags have little or no utility.

Tag libraries should not implement business logic, or common or general behavior. If business logic or common behavior implementations are required, JSP pages via JSP tags should use the services of a business object, such as a JavaBean—again supporting the layer structure of an MVC pattern.

Catalog efficient tag libraries with the goal of building a portfolio of time-saving, efficient, and reusable components. Such a portfolio saves time in routine tasks, especially in the initial stages of a project, by avoiding putting Java code in JSP pages, and by promoting reuse across many JSP pages.

Before implementing your logic, a good search of the previously given tag library resources may yield preexisting functionality that will save you development time.

GLOBAL AUCTIONS USE OF TAG LIBRARIES

The GAMS tag library contains two specialized tags: `SummaryDisplayItem` and `DisplayItem`. `SummaryDisplayItem` facilitates the display of general item information. This tag is used exclusively by the `finditems` JSP page. `DisplayItem` facilitates the display of detailed item information. This tag is used exclusively by the `displayItem` JSP page. These components support the MVC design pattern by abstracting implementation away from presentation into easily useable, self-formatting modules.

Additional Resource for JSP Tag Libraries

As an additional resource, JSP tag libraries may be found at the following Web sites:

- http://java.sun.com/products/jsp/taglibraries.html—JSP Standard Tag Library (JSTL) and tag library tutorials
- http://edocs.beasys.com/wlac/portals/docs/tagscontents.html—Four tag libraries used by the BEA WebLogic portal
- http://Jakarta.apache.org/taglibs—Tag libraries supported by Jakarta taglibs
- http://jsptags.com/tags—Selection of tag libraries
- http://www.jspin.com/home/tags—Selection of tag libraries
- http://www.jdance.com/jsptags.shtm—Listing of tag libraries, tutorials, and articles
- http://java.about.com/cs/jsp/index_2.htm—Listing of tag libraries and tutorials
- http://www.coolservlets.com/jive/docs/taglibs/jivetags.html—Reference documentation for the Jive JSP tag library
- http://www.orionserver.com/tags—Orion's EJB and Util tag libraries
- http://sourceforge.net/projects/jsptags—Selection of tag libraries
- http://www.sosnoski.com/opensrc/taglib—Selection of tag libraries

Summary

In this chapter, we discussed WebLogic's implementation of JSP tag libraries, JSP syntax, and WebLogic's custom and validation tag libraries. We also discussed WebLogic's EJB to JSP integration tool, tag library resources, and some best practices for implementing tag libraries. Hopefully you've grasped how tag libraries can and have helped many developers greatly reduce the Java code within JSP pages. Try comparing the initial examples presented to the final EJB JSP tags. The reduction of Java code and the abstraction of logic out of the presentation layer are dramatic. Consistent development of JSP libraries enables developers to build a portfolio of reusable application components, which saves development time, thus decreasing time to market. As a tool in support of the MVC design pattern, tag libraries play a significant role in abstracting logic away from presentation, while still facilitating code reusability.

In the next chapter, we'll actually create a custom JSP tag library, including implementation of the actual tag code. We'll create and configure the JAR file to include tag library creation, and finally configure and administer of the tag library as a part of your Web application.

CHAPTER 18

Creating JSP Tag Libraries

by Malcolm Garland

IN THIS CHAPTER

This chapter discusses creation of custom tag libraries, when they should be created, their necessary components, commonly used classes and interfaces of the JSP Tag API, and the steps necessary to create the custom tags.

When Should JSP Tag Libraries Be Created?

Supporting MVC design patterns, JSP tag libraries should be created to implement application presentation. The tag libraries should interface business objects such as JavaBeans, EJBs, or other generic Java objects required to implement application functionality. JSP tag libraries in conjunction with business objects should theoretically remove all Java code from presentation implementations. Logic previously implemented using scriptlets in individual JSP pages should be encapsulated within objects, and then interfaced via JSP tag libraries. Using the services of the business objects, the tag libraries process and format data for presentation. This construct provides for presentation units that are available across the current application, and reusable in follow-on development. The presentation code produced using this methodology is cleaner; that is, more readable and maintainable than earlier JSP implementations.

Overview of the Steps Required to Build JSP Tags

Implementing Java classes called *tag handler classes* creates JSP tags. Tag handler classes implement one of two interfaces:

javax.servlet.jsp.tagext.Tag or javax.servlet.jsp.tagext.BodyTag. The Tag interface is implemented for simple JSP tags—those JSP tags without an accompanying tag body. Simple JSP tags are also referred to as *empty body tags*. The BodyTag interface implements tags with an accompanying tag body. Tags can also be implemented by using the abstract class javax.servlet.jsp.tagext.TagSupport or javax.servlet.jsp.tagext.BodyTagSupport. Use of these classes enables the developer to avoid implementing methods that aren't used.

Once the tag handler is implemented, the tag library descriptor (TLD) must be created. The tag library descriptor defines the tag library and provides critical information about the tag, such as the name of the tag handler class and attributes, if any, among other issues. For detailed information about creating the tag library descriptor, refer to http://java.sun.com/j2ee/tutorial and http://edocs.beasys.com/wls/docs81/taglib. After the tag library descriptor is created, use the custom tags to register and deploy the tag library as detailed in the "JSP Tag Library Syntax" section of Chapter 17, "Using JSP Tag Libraries." For example, to create a tag that presents a greeting, we would first implement the TagSupport class as shown in the Greetings.java file in Listing 18.1.

LISTING 18.1 Greetings.java

```
package com.tags;

import java.io.*;
import javax.servlet.jsp.*;
import javax.servlet.jsp.tagext.*;

public class Greetings extends TagSupport
{
  public Greetings() {}

  public int doStartTag() throws JspException {
    try {
         pageContext.getOut().println("<h1>Greetings All</h1>");
    }
    catch (Exception ex) {
         throw new JspException("Greetings Tag:Exception: " +
➥ex.getMessage());
   }
   return SKIP_BODY;
  }
   public int doEndTag() {return EVAL_PAGE;}
}
```

CAUTION

Ensure that you define a package for your class. Tag handlers without package structures might not be found during JSP execution.

Compile the tag support class using your Java compiler. Use the `-d` option to build your package directory (`com.tags` in our example) and then create the TLD as follows:

```
<?xml version="1.0" encoding="ISO-8859-1" ?>
<!DOCTYPE taglib PUBLIC "-//Sun Microsystems, Inc.//DTD JSP Tag Library 1.2//EN"
"http://java.sun.com/dtd/web-jsptaglibrary_1_2.dtd">

<taglib>
 <tlib-version>1.0</tlib-version>
 <jsp-version>1.1</jsp-version>
 <short-name>wl</short-name>
 <uri>http://www.beasys.com/j2ee/tlds/wl-jsptaglibrary_1_0.tld</uri>

 <tag>
  <name>greetings</name>
  <tag-class>com.tags.Greetings</tag-class>
  <bodycontent>empty</bodycontent>
  <description>Displays Greeting</description>
 </tag>

</taglib>
```

Now place the TLD within a `META-INF` subdirectory and JAR the tag class and TLD using the command line as follows:

```
$ jar cvf greetings-tags.jar com META-INF
```

Note that the directory `com\tags` contains your compiled tag support class.

Now deploy the tag library to the `WEB-INF/lib` directory of the target Web application, and register the library within the Web application's `WEB-INF/web.xml` file as shown here:

```
<taglib>
   <taglib-uri>
    greetings.tld
   </taglib-uri>
   <taglib-location>
     /WEB-INF/lib/greetings-tags.jar
   </taglib-location>
</taglib>
```

The tag library is now available for use. To use the tag library, code a JSP by declaring the tag library and using the custom tag as shown here:

```
<%@ taglib uri="greetings.tld" prefix="greet" %>
<!DOCTYPE HTML PUBLIC "-//W3C//DTD HTML 4.01 Transitional//EN">

<html>
<head>
<title>Greetings</title>
</head>
<body>
    <greet:greetings />
</body>
</html>
```

The resulting browser display is shown in Figure 18.1.

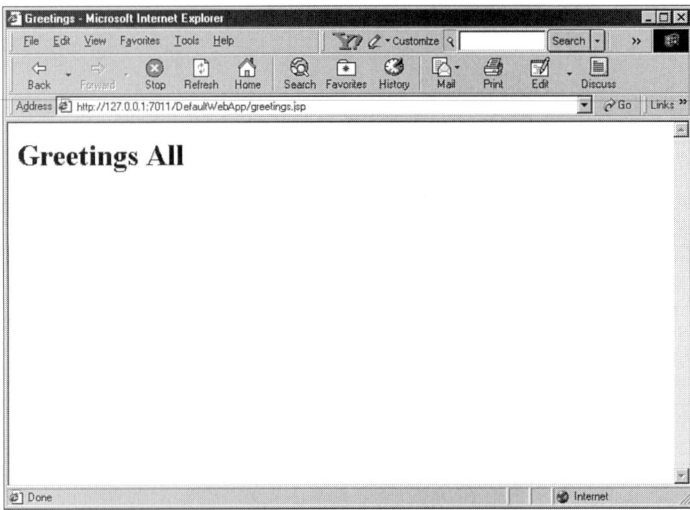

Figure 18.1 Browser view of Greetings.jsp.

Tag Handler Life Cycle

If the container encounters a custom tags during the display of a JSP page, many events take place, beginning with the instantiation of the tag handler as shown in Figure 18.2.

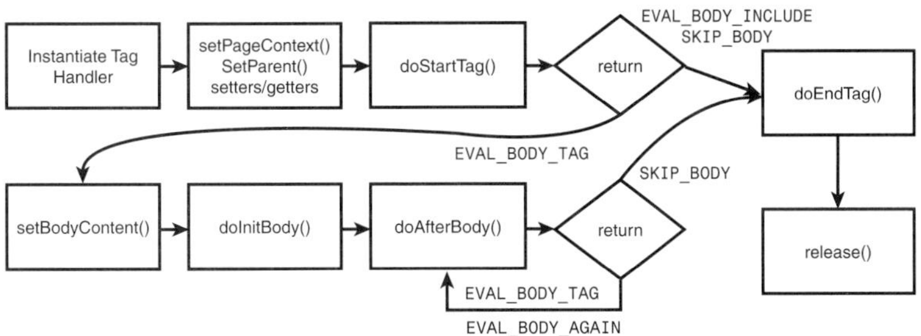

Figure 18.2 Tag handler life cycle.

Execution of the methods implemented within tag handler classes is triggered by these events along the tag handler life cycle. The sequence of method invocation within the tag handler life cycle is as follows:

- Once a JSP tag is encountered, the methods `setPageContext()` and `setParent()` are invoked to set up an environment context for the tag handler. These methods don't have to be implemented if you're using the tag support abstract classes (`TagSupport` and `BodyTagSupport`) for development (as opposed to the tag interfaces).
- Next, the setter methods for tag attributes are invoked. Tag handlers must define setters and getters for all attributes.
- Next, the `doStartTag()` method is invoked. This method is commonly used to initialize any resources for execution of your tag logic. This method should return one of three different values depending on the nature of your tag body, assuming that a tag body is implemented:
  - `Tag.SKIP_BODY` should be returned if you're implementing a simple (empty body) tag. On return of this value, the `doEndTag()` method is invoked.
  - Returning `Tag.EVAL_BODY_INCLUDE` causes evaluation and inclusion of tag body contents. Only classes implementing the `Tag` interface or extending the `TagSupport` class may return this value. On return of this value, the `doEndTag()` method is invoked.
  - `Tag.EVAL_BODY_TAG` causes evaluation of the tag body, followed by invocation of the `doInitBody()` method. Only classes implementing the `BodyTag` Interface or extending the `BodyTagSupport` class may return this value.
- If `EVAL_BODY_TAG` is returned, the `setBodyContent()`method is invoked. This method creates a reference to the `BodyContent` (a JspWriter) buffer, which may be used by the `doAfterBody()` method for processing later in the life cycle. The `BodyContent` buffer contains all output from the tag, including any body content, if any. (At this point, the client does not have access to any output derived from the tag). If the tag is writing output to the JSP page, that output must be written to the parent-scoped

JspWriter (via the `getEnclosingWriter()` method) before the end of the `doEndTag()` method. You don't have to implement the `setBodyContent()` method if you're implementing the `BodyTagSupport` class. This class has the convenience of the `getBodyContent()` method, which provides a reference to `BodyContent`.

- If `EVAL_BODY_TAG` is returned, the `doInitBody()` method is invoked. This method is invoked immediately prior to the body tag being evaluated for the first time. This method is commonly used to prepare scripting variables or place content into the `BodyContent` JspWriter. As discussed earlier, content placed into the `BodyContent` is buffered and isn't available to the JSP page at this point.
- If `EVAL_BODY_TAG` is returned, the `doAfterBody` method is invoked. This method is invoked immediately after the tag body is evaluated and added to the `BodyContent`. This method is commonly used to process work based on the results of the body tag evaluation. To access the evaluated body, use the `getBodyContent()` method if you extended the `BodyTagSupport` class, or use the `setBodyContent()` method if you implemented the `BodyTag` interface (you should have stored a `BodyContent` instance).

NOTE

The JSP 1.2 spec provides a `javax.servlet.jsp.tagext.IterationTag` interface, which enables you to reprocess the tag body if desired. This reprocessing would most likely be driven by a preset condition, much like iteration or loop logic.

The `doAfterBody()` method returns one of two different values depending on the nature of your tag body:

- `Tag.SKIP_BODY` should be returned if no further processing of the tag body is required. Upon return of this value, the `doEndTag()` method is invoked.
- `Tag.EVAL_BODY_TAG (IterationTag.EVAL_BODY_AGAIN)` causes evaluation of the tag body again. The result of the tag body evaluation is appended to the `BodyContent`. The `doAfterBody()` method is invoked again.

To write to the surrounding scope, you can obtain a writer using method `BodyTagSupport.getPreviousOut()` or method `BodyContent.getEnclosingWriter()` as discussed earlier. Both methods return the same JspWriter. Because the `BodyContent` is appended on each iteration through the tag body, you should write to this surrounding scope only when you've decided to return `Tag.SKIP_BODY`.

At this point in the life cycle, the writer in the `pageContext()` is returned to the parent `JspWriter`.

Next, the `doEndTag()` method is invoked. This method is commonly used to perform post–body tag processing, close server-side resources, or to write output to the surrounding scope using the `pageContext.getOut()` method.

The `doEndTag()` method returns one of two different values depending on the nature of your page:

- `Tag.EVAL_PAGE` causes evaluation of the remaining JSP page.
- `Tag.SKIP_PAGE` terminates evaluation of the remaining JSP page.

To conclude the tag handler life cycle, the `release()` method is invoked just before the tag handler instance is made available for garbage collection.

Tag Body Exceptions

The JSP 1.2 spec provides a `javax.servlet.jsp.tagext.TryCatchFinally` interface. This interface enables you to handle exceptions (manage expected programming error conditions) within the tag body using the `doCatch()` and `doFinally()` methods.

Commonly Used JSP Tag Classes and Interfaces

Commonly used interfaces and classes for the definition of JavaServer Pages tag libraries are presented in Tables 18.1 and 18.2. For the complete API, see `http://java.sun.com/products/jsp`.

TABLE 18.1 Commonly Used JSP Tag API Interfaces

Interface	Description
BodyTag	The BodyTag interface extends IterationTag. Used to implement tags with bodies.
IterationTag	The IterationTag interface extends Tag. Used to implement tags with bodies, where iteration is desired.
Tag	Used to implement simple tags; that is, tags with no bodies.
TryCatchFinally	Used to implement exception handling within tag body.

TABLE 18.2 Commonly Used JSP Tag API Classes

Class	Description
BodyContent	Abstraction of tag body content.
BodyTagSupport (see Listing 18.4)	Abstract class for implementing tags with bodies. Used in lieu of the BodyTag interface.
TagExtraInfo (see Listing 18.6)	Abstraction of additional information not contained in tag library descriptor.
TagSupport (see Listings 18.1, 18.2, and 18.7)	Abstract class for implementing simple tags. Use in lieu of the Tag interface.

Creating a Simple Tag

For your first step in creating a simple tag, you must write the tag handler class. Using the helper class, you should extend the abstract class `TagSupport` as shown in Listing 18.2, `SummaryDisplayItem.java`.

LISTING 18.2 SummaryDisplayItem.java

```
package com.gams.ejbs.item;

import java.io.*;
import javax.servlet.jsp.*;
import javax.servlet.jsp.tagext.*;
import java.sql.Date;

public class SummaryDisplayItem extends TagSupport
{
```

Next you must implement setters/getters, and the `doStartTag()` and `doEndTag()` methods as shown here.

```
  ItemValue[] itemArray = null;

  public SummaryDisplayItem()
  {
  }

  public void setItemArray(ItemValue[] iAr)
  {
        itemArray = iAr;
        System.out.println("SummaryDisplayItme:1-ParamConstructor:
        ➥Item array set.....");
  }
  public int doStartTag() throws JspException
  {
       try
       {
          for(int i=0; i<itemArray.length; i++)
          {
             ItemValue iv = itemArray[i];
             Float currentBid = iv.getCurrentBid();
             String strCurrentBid = "";
             if (iv.getCurrentBid() == null)
               {strCurrentBid = "None";}
```

LISTING 18.2 Continued

```
            else
            {
               strCurrentBid = currentBid.toString();
            }
            pageContext.getOut().println("<tr><td>" +
➥iv.getItemId() +"</td><td>" + iv.getTitle() + "</td><td>" +
➥strCurrentBid + "</td><td>" + iv.getEndDateTime() +"</td></tr>");
         }
      return SKIP_BODY;
      }
      catch (IOException ex)
      {
          throw new JspException("Error: IOException while writing
          ➥to client");
      }
   }
}
```

After compiling the tag handler class (use the Java compiler -d option to create your package directory), you must next create or modify an existing tag library descriptor file as shown here:

```
<?xml version="1.0" encoding="ISO-8859-1" ?>
<!DOCTYPE taglib
    PUBLIC "-//Sun Microsystems, Inc.//DTD JSP Tag Library 1.2//EN"
    "http://java.sun.com/dtd/web-jsptaglibrary_1_2.dtd">

<!-- a tab library descriptor -->

<taglib>
 <tlib-version>1.0</tlib-version>
 <jsp-version>1.1</jsp-version>
 <short-name>wl</short-name>
 <uri>http://www.beasys.com/j2ee/tlds/wl-jsptaglibrary_1_0.tld</uri>

 <tag>
  <name>summaryDisplayItem</name>
  <tag-class>com.gams.ejbs.item.SummaryDisplayItem</tag-class>
  <bodycontent>empty</bodycontent>
  <description>Displays Item value Array/with html table tags</description>
  <attribute>
```

18

LISTING 18.2 Continued

```
      <name>itemArray</name>
      <required>true</required>
      <rtexprvalue>true</rtexprvalue>
    </attribute>
  </tag>
</taglib>
```

Name this file `taglib.tld` and save it to the `META-INF` folder. To complete packaging, you should jar the tag library descriptor, tag handler class, and supporting files, if any, into one JAR file. To jar, the tag library descriptor should be placed in directory `META-INF/lib` with the classes deployed within their designated package structure. Your class package structure and the `META-INF` directory should share a common root directory. The following command jars our example:

```
$ jar cv0f itemDisplay-tags.jar com META-INF
```

> **NOTE**
>
> You should notice the `0 jar` command parameter. Some HTML documents do not execute properly if compressed.

Copy the resulting JAR file to the `WEB-INF/lib` directory of your target application. At this point, you must register the JAR file within the application's `web.xml` file as shown here:

```
<taglib>
   <taglib-uri>
    itemDisplay.tld
   </taglib-uri>
   <taglib-location>
    /WEB-INF/lib/itemDisplay-tags.jar
   </taglib-location>
 </taglib>
```

You can use the simple tag within your JSP pages as discussed in Chapter 17. An example of using the simple tag is shown in Listing 18.3 (`FindItems.jsp`).

LISTING 18.3 FindItems.jsp

```
<%@ page import="com.gams.ejbs.item.*, java.sql.Date" %>
<%@ taglib uri="itemDisplay.tld" prefix="item" %>
<!DOCTYPE HTML PUBLIC "-//W3C//DTD HTML 4.01 Transitional//EN">

<html>
<head>
```

LISTING 18.3 Continued

```
<title>Global Auctions - Find Items</title>
</head>
<h1>Global Auctions - Find Items</h1>
<body>
<table width="500">
    <tr><td><b>Item Id</td><td>Title</td><td>Current Bid</td><td>
    ➥Auction Ends</b></td></tr>
<%
   ItemValue iv = new ItemValue(new Integer(101), "Ming Chair",
   ➥new Float(550.50), new Date(102, 06, 30));
   ItemValue iv2 = new ItemValue(new Integer(202), "Ming Horse",
   ➥new Float(1550.50), new Date(102, 06, 30));
   ItemValue[] ivArray = new ItemValue[]{iv, iv2};

   //ItemValue[] ivArray = (ItemValue[])request.getAttribute("itemdata");
   ➥(used if data retrieved from request object)
%>
   <item:summaryDisplayItem itemArray="<%= ivArray %>"/>
</table>
</body>
</html>
```

Viewed through a Web browser, the `findItems.jsp` file yields the displayed in Figure 18.3.

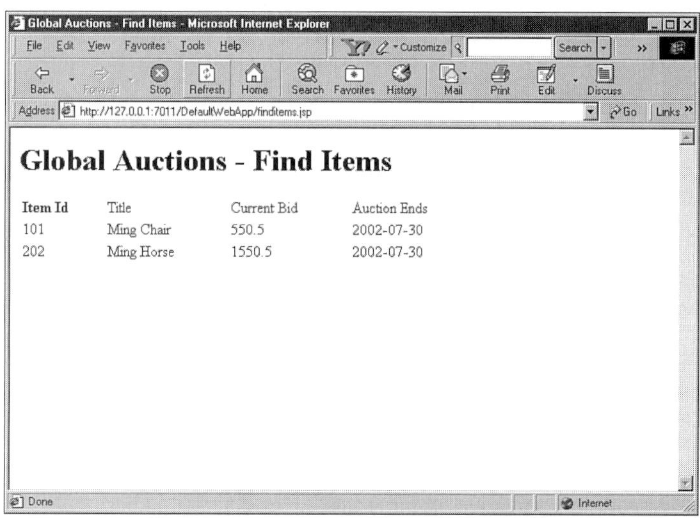

Figure 18.3 Browser view of FindItems.jsp.

18

Creating a Tag with a Body

For your first step in creating a tag with a body, you must write the tag handler class. Using the helper class, you should extend the abstract class `BodyTagSupport` as shown in Listing 18.4 (`DisplayItem.java`).

LISTING 18.4 DisplayItem.java

```
package com.gams.ejbs.item;

import java.io.*;
import javax.servlet.jsp.*;
import javax.servlet.jsp.tagext.*;
import java.sql.Date;

public class DisplayItem extends BodyTagSupport
{
```

Next, you must implement setters/getters, and the methods `doStartTag()`, `doAfterBody()`, and `doEndTag()` as shown here:

```
    private ItemValue item = null;
    private BodyContent bodyContent = null;

  public DisplayItem()
  {
  }

  public void setItem(ItemValue iv)
  {
    item = iv;

  }
  public void setBodyContent(BodyContent bc)
  {
    bodyContent = bc;

  }

  public int doStartTag() throws JspException
  {

        Float currentBid = item.getCurrentBid();
```

LISTING 18.4 Continued

```
        String strCurrentBid = "";
        if (item.getCurrentBid() == null)
         {item.setCurrentBid(new Float(0.0));}
        else
        { strCurrentBid = currentBid.toString(); }

        return EVAL_BODY_TAG;
  }

  public int doAfterBody()
  {
     String strDescription = null;
     if ( null != item.getDescription())
        {strDescription = "Description: " + item.getDescription() +
        ➥bodyContent.getString();}
     else {strDescription = bodyContent.getString();}
     item.setDescription(strDescription);

     return SKIP_BODY;
  }

  public int doEndTag() throws JspException
  {
      try
      {
         pageContext.getOut().println("<tr><td>" + item.getItemId() +
➥"</td><td>" + item.getTitle() + "</td><td>" + item.getCurrentBid() +
➥"</td><td>" + item.getEndDateTime() +"</td><td></tr>");
         pageContext.getOut().println("<tr><td colspan=\"4\">
➥<b>Additional Information: </b>" + item.getDescription() + "</td></tr>");

        return EVAL_PAGE;
      }
      catch (IOException ex)
      {
        throw new JspException("Error:
        ➥IOException while writing to client");
      }
      catch (Exception x)
      {
        throw new JspException("Error:
        ➥Exception while writing to client");
      }
```

18

LISTING 18.4 Continued

```
  }
}
```

Next you must modify the existing (or create a) tag library descriptor file by adding the tag definition code shown here:

```
<tag>
  <name>displayItem</name>
  <tag-class>com.gams.ejbs.item.DisplayItem</tag-class>
  <bodycontent>JSP</bodycontent>
  <description>Displays Item Information/with html table tags</description>
  <attribute>
   <name>item</name>
   <required>true</required>
   <rtexprvalue>true</rtexprvalue>
  </attribute>
</tag>
```

For our example, the tag library descriptor file name is `META-INF/taglib.tld`. To complete packaging, you should jar the tag library descriptor, tag handler class, and supporting files, if any, as previously discussed when creating a simple tag.

Copy the resulting JAR file to the `WEB-INF/lib` directory of your target Web application. At this point, you must register the JAR file within the Web application's `web.xml` file as discussed previously. You can now use the body tag within your JSP pages as discussed at Chapter 17. An example of using the body tag is shown in Listing 18.5.

LISTING 18.5 displayItem.jsp

```
<%@ page import="com.gams.ejbs.item.*, java.sql.Date" %>
<%@ taglib uri="itemDisplay.tld" prefix="item" %>
<!DOCTYPE HTML PUBLIC "-//W3C//DTD HTML 4.01 Transitional//EN">

<html>
<head>
     <title>Global Auctions - Display Item</title>
</head>

<body>
<table width="500">
     <tr><td><b>Item Id</b></td><td><b>Title</b></td><td><b>Current Bid
     ➥</b></td><td><b>Auction Ends</b></td></tr>
<%
```

LISTING 18.5 Continued

```
    ItemValue iv = new ItemValue(new Integer(101), "Ming Chair",
    ➥new Float(550.50), new Date(102, 06, 30));

    //ItemValue iv = (ItemValue)request.getAttribute("item");
%>
    <item:displayItem item="<%= iv %>">
    <!-- Optional Information -->
       This Ming Chair has been certified as authentic.
       ➥Documentation available upon request.
    </item:displayItem>

</table>
</body>
</html>
```

Viewed through a Web browser, file `displayItem.jsp` yields the display at Figure 18.4.

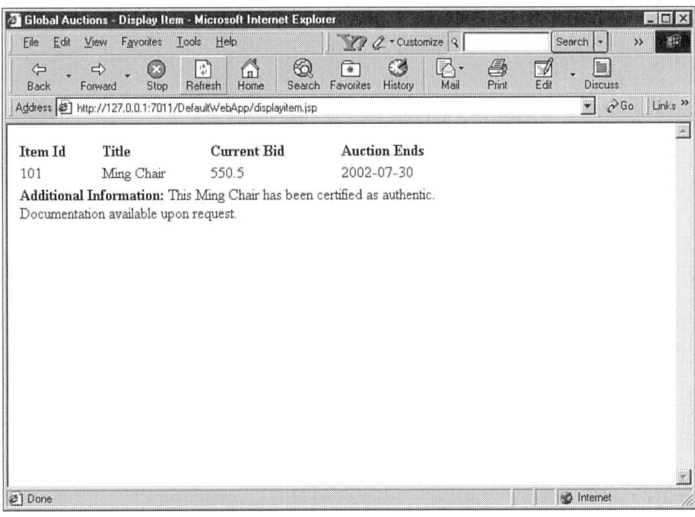

Figure 18.4 Browser view of displayItem.jsp.

Using Custom Tags to Define Scripting Variables

Custom tags may also define scripting variables to use within the JSP page. Scripting variables are used in processing JSP page content, just as variables would be in any Java implementation. The scripting variables can be referenced the same as JavaBeans: by using the `getAttribute()` and `setAttribute()` methods. To create a scripting variable, implement a class that extends the `TagExtraInfo` class as shown in the `GreetingsTei.java` file in Listing 18.6.

LISTING 18.6 GreetingsTei.java

```
package com.tags;

import javax.servlet.jsp.tagext.*;

public class GreetingsTei extends TagExtraInfo
{

  public GreetingsTei() {}

  public VariableInfo[] getVariableInfo(TagData data) {
     return new VariableInfo[] {
           new VariableInfo("bidderId","String",true,
           ➥VariableInfo.AT_BEGIN),
           new VariableInfo("accountStatus","String",true,
           ➥VariableInfo.AT_BEGIN)
    };
  }
}
```

Next implement initialization and variable modification logic within the parent tag handler class, as shown in Listing 18.7, `GreetingsBidder.java`.

LISTING 18.7 GreetingsBidder.java

```
package com.tags;

import java.io.*;
import javax.servlet.http.*;
import javax.servlet.jsp.*;
import javax.servlet.jsp.tagext.*;

public class GreetingsBidder extends TagSupport
{
  public GreetingsBidder() {}

  public int doStartTag() throws JspException  {
      try {
```

LISTING 18.7 Continued

```
         HttpSession session = pageContext.getSession();
         String bidder = "NOT SET";
         String actStat = "NOT SET";

         if (null != session.getAttribute("bidderId")) {bidder =
➥(String)session.getAttribute("bidderId");}

         if (null != session.getAttribute("accountStatus")) {actStat =
         ➥(String)session.getAttribute("accountStatus");}

         pageContext.setAttribute("bidderId", bidder);
         pageContext.setAttribute("accountStatus",actStat);
         pageContext.getOut().println("<h1>Greetings Bidder Number: " +
         ➥pageContext.getAttribute("bidderId") + "</h1>");
         pageContext.getOut().println("<h1>Your Account is " +
         ➥pageContext.getAttribute("accountStatus") + "</h1>");
      }
      catch (Exception ex) {
         throw new JspException("GreetingsBidder Tag:Exception: " +
         ➥ex.getMessage());
      }
      return SKIP_BODY;
   }
   public int doEndTag() {return EVAL_PAGE;}
}
```

Next define the tag handler (if not done previously) and tag extra info class within the TLD as shown here:

```
  <name>greetingsBidder</name>
  <tag-class>com.tags.GreetingsBidder</tag-class>
  <tei-class>com.tags.GreetingsTei</tei-class>
  <bodycontent>empty</bodycontent>
  <description>Displays Bidder Greeting</description>
 </tag>
```

Jar the TLD and subject classes (or add new classes and an updated TLD to an existing tag library JAR file—you can add new tags to existing tag libraries). Register the resultant JAR (if not previously registered) within the target application's `web.xml` as discussed earlier. Finally, you need only code a JSP that uses the scripting variables as shown in Listing 18.8, `GreetingsBidder.jsp`.

LISTING 18.8 GreetingsBidder.jsp

```
<%@ taglib uri="greetings.tld" prefix="greet" %>
<!DOCTYPE HTML PUBLIC "-//W3C//DTD HTML 4.01 Transitional//EN">

<html>
<head>
<title>Bidder Greetings</title>
</head>

<body><table>
<tr><td><greet:greetingsBidder /></td></tr>

    <% session.setAttribute("bidderId","1001");
      session.setAttribute("accountStatus","VALID");
    %>

<tr><td><greet:greetingsBidder /></td></tr>
</body>
```

The browser view produced by `GreetingsBidder.jsp` is presented in Figure 18.5.

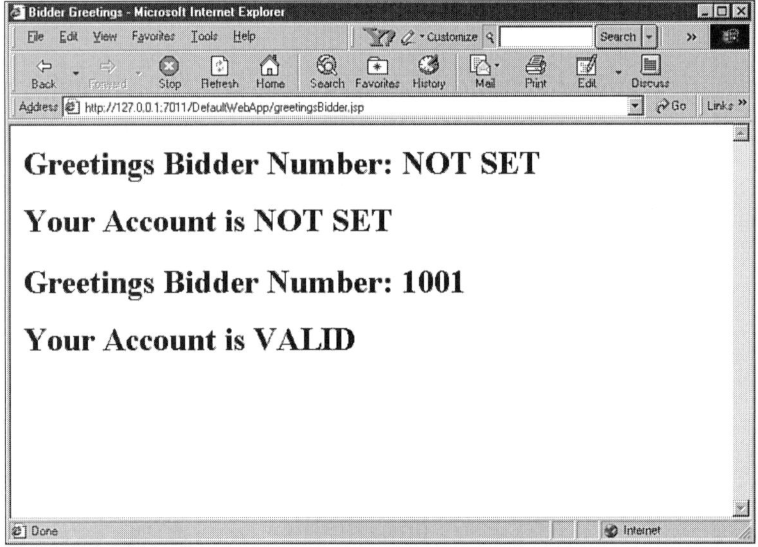

Figure 18.5 Browser view of GreetingsBidder.jsp.

Creating Tag Libraries Best Practices

Use abstract classes rather than interfaces to implement your tags. This strategy facilitates, standardizes, and effectively manages your tag library development.

To ease pending deployments, package your tag libraries and supporting files into JAR files. If you're using tag libraries within deployed libraries, you can never be sure as to the state of your classpath; that is, what files you're actually referencing in support of your tag library. Packaging and then referencing the tag library JAR file validates completeness of the deliverable.

To facilitate version control and file management, package related tag libraries within a common JAR file. Also establish a naming convention for your tag library JAR and the `uri` attribute used to reference the tag library JAR file within the `web.xml` file.

Try to separate tags in two distinct categories: the generic tags that serve as visual components (view) and the application-specific tags that perform the processing (controller). That way the visual components will be useable in other projects.

TAG LIBRARIES CREATED FOR GLOBAL AUCTIONS

There are two tag libraries created for use with the Global Auctions application: `summaryDisplayItem` and `displayItem`. Both were previously presented in examples for simple and body tags.

Summary

In this chapter, we discussed the creation of custom tag libraries—when they should be created and the steps necessary to create them. We reviewed the tag handler life cycle, constructed a simple tag and a simple tag with a tag body. Commonly used classes and interfaces of the Sun JSP Tag API were also presented, along with some JSP tag best practices.

CHAPTER **19**

Working with Struts

by Steve Steffen

IN THIS CHAPTER

- Installing Struts
- Introduction to Struts Architecture
- Configuring Struts
- struts-config.xml File
- Backend Programming Using the Struts Framework
- Front-End Programming Using the Struts Framework
- Struts Sample Application

The Struts framework, created in 2000 as an open source product and released in 2001 under the Apache Software Foundation license, has become the framework of choice for developing JavaServer Pages (JSPs). The Struts framework enables Web applications to decouple the business logic from the presentation layer. That enables programmers to write detailed business logic as Java objects while the JSP pages take care of displaying the actual presentation. The framework implements an MVC (Model-View-Controller) design architecture.

The Struts framework enables flexible and adaptable Web applications to be written on the WebLogic platform. JSP pages are written to contain presentation code, with the business logic contained in the action classes called from the JSPs. The actual mappings to the JSPs and the action classes are contained in an XML file. This enables the programmer to easily change which pages are called and when. Additional pages can be added, or other pages replaced, by simply remapping the XML file.

The Struts framework allows the separation of work among the Web designers, application programmers, and administrators. This enables multiple tasks to be performed at once without requiring Web designers to look at any Java code or Java programmers to look at HTML. Administrators can then modify the order of the pages without having a Java programmer modify a servlet or JSP file.

These benefits are even more obvious when a large site is being maintained. Pages can be exchanged and replaced by simply modifying the XML file, which helps to avoid embarrassing glitches, such as pages being overwritten or information on those pages being lost.

This chapter first tackles how to install Struts on a WebLogic application and then how to define the configuration. Finally, the chapter explains how to write the different parts of a Struts application. This chapter is meant only as an introduction because there isn't enough space here to cover all aspects of Struts. Whole books could be written on the topic.

Installing Struts

To install the binary version of Struts, a few things must be in place. First, make sure that there is an installed version of the Java Development Kit, version 1.2 or later. This shouldn't be a problem because WebLogic ships with a JDK, but it's available for download from Sun if you don't have it. Second, an XML parser that's compatible with the Java API for XML (JAXP) version 1.1 or later is required to parse the various XML files. Again, WebLogic includes an XML parser, but if you want to use another one, Apache offers an open source parser named Xerces that works fine. Just remember to add the associated `.jar` files to the classpath. Third, download the binary version 1.1 or greater of Struts. A source version is also available, but it requires more libraries and must be compiled. This is beyond the scope of this chapter. Table 19.1 shows all the software needed to run Struts.

TABLE 19.1 Software Downloads Required to Use Struts

Software	Download Site
Java2 Development Kit version 1.2 or greater (optional; included with WebLogic)	http://java.sun.com/j2se
Xerces XML parser 1.3.1 (optional; included with WebLogic)	http://xml.apache.org/xerces-j
Struts 1.1 or greater	http://jakarta.apache.org/struts

Now that Struts is downloaded, installation is simple. Unpack the zip file into a temp directory. Then copy the `struts.jar`, `jakarta-oro.jar`, `jdbc2_0-stdext.jar`, and all the `common*.jar` files to the `WEB-INF/lib` directory of the application you want to use Struts with. Then copy all the `struts*.tld` files and all the `*.dtd` files into the `WEB-INF` directory. Now make sure that all the JAR files are in the startup classpath of WebLogic. Table 19.2 shows the directory position of the files.

TABLE 19.2 Struts Application Files Per Directory

Directory	Files
WEB-INF/lib	struts.jar, jdbc2_0-stdext.jar, commons-*.jar
WEB-INF/	struts-*.tld, *.dtd

All the files necessary for Struts are now in the proper place in your Web application. However, before using Struts, certain configuration has to be done.

Introduction to Struts Architecture

The Struts framework depends on the configuration and usage of both XML files and specific classes interacting with each other within a Web application. The main goal of Struts is to separate different aspects of design into logical blocks to free programmers and HTML/Web designers from actual Java code written in JSP files. Struts uses the `struts-config.xml` file, which is configured for each Web app and located in the `/WEB-INF` directory, to hold mappings and directives between pages. This file must have associated entries in `/WEB-INF/web.xml` to be used in the Web app. When application-specific Java code has to run, the `struts-config.xml` file directs the input received from the source file (an HTML, JSP, or servlet page, for example) to an action class. The action class then performs business logic and returns to the `struts-config.xml` file to get the mapping of the next page or object to call depending on what happened in the action class. This handles the display of errors and different pages based on input, or logic within the action class itself.

Forms from input files (most likely HTML or JSP) can be configured to automatically validate themselves via ActionForms. Using Struts custom tag libraries, JSP pages are very clean and free of any Java code. Even error-handling tags are configured to display errors at the page or form level. Figure 19.1 presents a graphical layout of the Struts application flow. Starting with a JSP file, the form is submitted. The action mappings contained within the `struts-config.xml` file are then used to call the ActionForm class to verify the input. If there's an error, the page is recalled and all the Struts error tags display the proper error. If verification is successful, the action mapping designates where to go next. The most common answer is to an action class to process business logic. An action class processes the logic and input from the form and then requests back to the mapping to find the next page to call or refers to the calling page with errors. Also represented on the diagram are Struts-configurable text parameters used with the `<bean:message>` tag. This enables custom text to be replaced easily, and allows for internationalization, which is the capability of Java applications to use other languages and formats in addition to the one the application was written in.

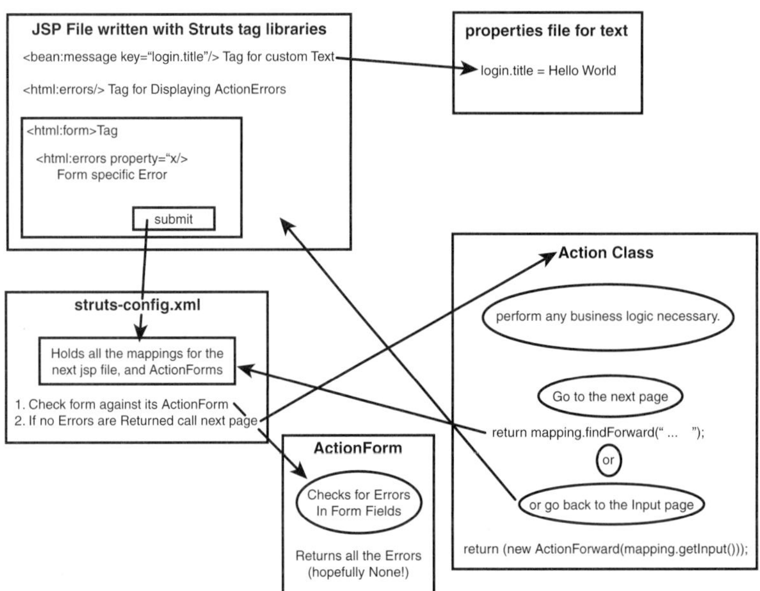

Figure 19.1 Basic Struts application flow.

Configuring Struts

To tie into the power of Struts with your WebLogic Server 8.1 application, the `web.xml` file must be modified with Struts framework information. The `web.xml` file is located in the `WEB-INF` directory and contains information about the Web application. To modify this file, use a simple text editor or an XML editor. The first thing that must be done is to register the action servlet within `web.xml`. Looking at the sample code shown in Listing 19.1, `<servlet> .. </servlet>` tags encapsulate this entire procedure. Line 2 registers the action name to the Struts action class in Line 3. The first parameter value supplied, `application` (in lines 4–7),must refer to a properties file that keeps user-defined text references used with Struts tag libraries within JSPs. The second parameter, `config`, in lines 8–11, refers to the locations of a Struts-specific configuration file that maps how and in what order JSP and servlet pages will be called (this file will be handled in depth later in the chapter). Lines 14–17 map the action servlets to the `.do` extension, which is the default mapping for Struts. This mapping allows Struts actions to be mapped like `.jsp` pages. However, these actions could call many JSP pages based on the `struts-config.xml` file. Finally, lines 18–44 register the Struts-specific tag libraries to WebLogic.

LISTING 19.1 Web.xml

```
<!-- Action Servlet Configuration -->
<servlet>
  <servlet-name>action</servlet-name>
  <servlet-class>org.apache.struts.action.ActionServlet</servlet-class>
  <init-param>
    <param-name>application</param-name>
    <param-value>myApp.properties.ApplicationResources</param-value>
  </init-param>
  <init-param>
    <param-name>config</param-name>
    <param-value>/WEB-INF/struts-config.xml</param-value>
  </init-param>
  </servlet>
<!-- Action Servlet Mapping -->
<servlet-mapping>
  <servlet-name>action</servlet-name>
  <url-pattern>*.do</url-pattern>
</servlet-mapping>
<!-- Application Tag Library Descriptor -->
<taglib>
  <taglib-uri>/WEB-INF/lib/app.tld</taglib-uri>
  <taglib-location>/WEB-INF/lib/app.tld</taglib-location>
</taglib>
<!-- Struts Tag Library Descriptor -->
<taglib>
  <taglib-uri>/WEB-INF/lib/struts.tld</taglib-uri>
  <taglib-location>/WEB-INF/lib/struts.tld</taglib-location>
</taglib>
<!-- Struts Tag Library Descriptors -->
<taglib>
  <taglib-uri>/WEB-INF/lib/struts-bean.tld</taglib-uri>
  <taglib-location>/WEB-INF/lib/struts-bean.tld</taglib-location>
</taglib>
<taglib>
  <taglib-uri>/WEB-INF/lib/struts-form.tld</taglib-uri>
  <taglib-location>/WEB-INF/lib/struts-form.tld</taglib-location>
</taglib>
<taglib>
  <taglib-uri>/WEB-INF/lib/struts-logic.tld</taglib-uri>
  <taglib-location>/WEB-INF/lib/struts-logic.tld</taglib-location>
```

LISTING 19.1 Continued

```
</taglib>
<taglib>
  <taglib-uri>/WEB-INF/lib/struts-template.tld</taglib-uri>
  <taglib-location>/WEB-INF/lib/struts-template.tld</taglib-location>
</taglib>
```

struts-config.xml File

The `struts-config.xml` file resides in the same directory as the `web.xml` file and contains the application flow mappings necessary for correct interaction with Struts. Looking at the sample `struts-config.xml` shown in Listing 19.2, we can quickly see the important features.

LISTING 19.2 struts-config.xml

```
<?xml version="1.0" encoding="ISO-8859-1" ?>
<!DOCTYPE struts-config PUBLIC
        "-//Apache Software Foundation//DTD Struts Configuration 1.1//EN"
        "http://jakarta.apache.org/struts/dtds/struts-config_1_1.dtd">
<struts-config>
<data-sources>
        <data-source key = "myDatabase">
          <set-property property="autoCommit"
                            value="false"/>
           <set-property property="description"
                             value=" Login Validation Database"/>
           <set-property property="driverClass"
                             value="org.postgresql.Driver"/>
           <set-property property="maxCount"
                             value="4"/>
           <set-property property="minCount"
                              value="2"/>
            <set-property property="user"
                             value="myusername"/>
           <set-property property="password"
                             value="mypassword"/>
           <set-property property="url"
                             value="jdbc:postgresql://localhost/myAppDatabase"/>
         </data-source>
       </data-sources>
<!-- ========== Form Bean Definitions =================================== -->
```

LISTING 19.2 Continued

```
<form-beans>
 <!-- Logon form bean -->  <form-bean      name="login"
                 type="myApp.FormBeans.LoginForm"/>
    <!-- Order List -->
 <form-bean      name="orderlist"
                 type="myApp.FormBeans.OrderForm"/>
</form-beans>
<!-- ========== Global Forward Definitions ============================== -->
 <global-forwards>
   <forward   name="login"              path="/login.jsp"/>
 </global-forwards>
<!-- ========== Action Mapping Definitions ============================== -->
 <action-mappings>
<!-- Process a user logon -->
   <action    path="/login"
              type="myApp.action.LoginExec"
              name="login"
              validate = "true"
             scope="session"
             input="/login.jsp">
            <forward name="success"      path="/secondpage.jsp"/>
            <forward name="listorder"    path="/orderlistentry.do"/>
            <forward name="killSession"  path="/SystemError.html"/>
   </action>
<!-- Process a user logoff -->
   <action    path="/logout"
              type="myApp.action.LogoutExec">
     <forward name="success"             path="/logout.jsp"/>
   </action>
<!-- Process an order list -->
   <action path="/orderlistentry"
           type="myApp.action.OrderListExec"
           name="orderlist"
          scope="session"
          input="/orderlistentry.jsp">
     <forward name="success" path="/orderlistdisp.jsp"/>
     <forward name="killSession" path="/SystemError.html"/>
     <forward name="loginAgain" path="/login.jsp"/>
     <forward name="selectSalesArea" path="/salesAreas.jsp"/>
   </action>
 </action-mappings>
</struts-config>
```

The first important actions occur on lines 26–34, where the form beans are registered. *Form beans* are classes used to store actions and values from the JSP page. The parameters are

- `name`, which names the form bean
- The full package and class name of the applications page bean that extends the struts `org.apache.struts.action.ActionForm` class

Sample code is given later in the chapter.

The lines 35–38 deal with global forwards. This registers the name `login` to the `login.jsp` page.

The most important part of the `struts-config.xml` file is the `action-mappings` section. Lines 39–68 give three examples of action mappings used in an application. Struts Optionally allows us to perform data mappings to different databases. This is shown on lines 6–24. This isn't needed; it's just a nice feature for simple applications.

<action-mappings>

Each `<action>` element defines one specific task associated with one action class for each defined mapping. Each associated action performs a task that will forward to one of the `<forward/>` XML tags. The sample code uses three actions: `login`, `logout`, and `orderlistentry`. Each action is associated with a `*.do` extension from the `web.xml` configuration file. So, when calling an action from the Web server, the action always has a `.do` appended. Most action elements define at least

- `path`—The path the application maps to the action. For instance, `http://localhost/myserver/login.do` would call the user login in the example that follows.
- `type`—The full package and class of the action needed.
- `name`—The name of the `<form-bean>` element that's used with the action.

<forward>

The `<forward>` tag tells the Struts framework what page to go to next. The names of these tags are used within the action classes to look up the correct page for an associated action. Most `forward` elements define at least

- `name`—The name of the forward to be performed.
- `path`—The full path to another action, local JSP page, or remote page.

<data-sources>

The `<data-source>` element provides the ability to map multiple databases within the parent element, `<data-sources>`, in one place. An attribute named `key` allows the connections to be distinguished from one another. Within the `<data-source>` element is an element named `<set-property>` that defines

- `property`—The name of the data property
- `value`—The value of the data property

When the `struts-config.xml` file is finished, it will contain the skeleton of the application. Each action will have associated forwards mapping to other actions, JavaServer pages, or servlets.

Back End Programming Using the Struts Framework

The brunt (if not all) of the Java programming when using the Struts guidelines happens in the back end. In this case, *back end* means outside of the presentation layer JSPs or servlets. This section covers the necessary objects required for a basic Struts application to run, starting with the action classes used for the business logic and continuing through the objects and methods used by the action class. This section also covers the ActionForm and its related classes, including error handling.

Action Classes

After the configuration of the `web.xml` and `struts-config.xml` files is complete, attention turns to the actual Java coding of the application. The first step is to write an action class that extends `org.apache.struts.action.Action` and to override the execute method. The execute method is called every time the action class is called. Remember that the action class is mapped to a path within the `<action>` tag in `struts-config.xml`. The following is a skeleton of an action class:

```
import org.apache.struts.action.Action;
import org.apache.struts.action.ActionForward;
import org.apache.struts.action.ActionMapping;
import org.apache.struts.action.ActionForm;
import javax.servlet.*;
import javax.servlet.http.*;

public class LoginExec extends Action {

public ActionForward
       execute(ActionMapping mapping,
               ActionForm form,
```

```
                HttpServletRequest request,
                HttpServletResponse response) throws Exception {
//Code inserted here
}
}//end of LoginExec
```

Four parameters are passed in to the execute method: ActionMapping, ActionForm, HttpServletRequest, and HttpServletResponse. The first two are special classes used by Struts to link the Struts application to the mappings and also to validate that form data is correct. The latter two are the same classes that are passed in during servlet and JSP programming and contain the input (HttpServletRequest) and output (HttpServletResponse) of the servlet. The method returns an ActionForward object that tells the Struts application to redirect or forward the servlet based on actions within the execute method. Let's now explore these Struts classes further.

Using the ActionMapping Class

The ActionMapping class encapsulates the struts-config.xml file for the specific action path called. This link enables the programmer to specify which of the <forward/> tags to use. Using the following example from the struts-config.xml file within the action named login,

```
<forward name="listorder" path="/orderlistentry.do"/>
```

the mapping class can be used to forward to another action called orderlistentry. Using the name parameter in the preceding line, we can call this directly using the findFoward() method:

```
return mapping.findForward("listorder");
```

To return to the original input page, which would be used to display new information such as an error, we can use the getInputForward() method as shown here:

```
return mapping.getInputFoward();
```

The ActionMapping class ties the action mappings to the action servlet and is a crucial part of making Struts work within your Web application.

Using the ActionForm Class

The purpose of the ActionForm class is to validate or change information being sent from the JSP page. An action form class is linked to the action in struts-config.xml in several places. First, it's defined with the <form-bean> tag:

```
<form-bean      name="login"
                type="myApp.FormBeans.LoginForm"/>
```

Then, within the <action> tag, the name parameter links this particular ActionForm to the action class and the scope parameter sets the persistence of the bean:

```
<action
          name="login"
          scope="session"
          >
```

If the properties in the JSP are set up correctly, the action class will contain all the values input by the user.

To write a new ActionForm class, first extend the Struts ActionForm and create the properties you want set. The following is a sample definition of an ActionForm class:

```
package myApp.FormBeans;
import javax.servlet.http.HttpServletRequest;
import org.apache.struts.action.ActionError;
import org.apache.struts.action.ActionErrors;
import org.apache.struts.action.ActionForm;
import org.apache.struts.action.ActionMapping;

public final class LoginForm extends ActionForm {
     // password.
    private String password = null;

     //The customerno.
    private String customerNo = null;
//More Methods
}
```

Then create set and get methods on these properties. The name after the set and get must match those properties in the Struts JSP pages where they are used. For example, if password is used on the JSP page, setPassword(String p) and getPassword() are used:

```
...
public String getPassword() {
       return this.password;
  }
public void setPassword(String p){
            this.password = p;
  }
public String getCustomerNo(){
       return this.customerNo;
  }
```

```
public void setCustomerNo(String c){
        this.customerNo = c;
  }
```

After the properties from the page are set up, the reset() method should be overridden to reset all the data back to its original state. The following code example shows this being done:

```
public void reset(ActionMapping mapping, HttpServletRequest request) {

        this.password = null;
        this.customerNo = null;
}
```

Optionally, the validate method can be overridden to check the input that has been set from the HttpServletRequest. This can be done automatically if the validate attribute inside the <action> parameter within the struts-config.xml file is set to true. If the validation contains errors, the original page will be redisplayed with the errors. This method can return either null or an empty ActionErrors object when there are no errors. In these cases, Struts will forward to the page specified in the action. The default method returns null. The following code shows an example of a validate method:

```
public ActionErrors validate(ActionMapping mapping,
                                       HttpServletRequest request) {
        ActionErrors errors = new ActionErrors();
        if ((customerNo == null) || (customerNo.length() < 1))
          errors.add("customerNo", new ActionError("error.customerno.required"));
        if ((password == null) || (password.length() < 1))
            errors.add("password", new ActionError("error.password.required"));
        return errors;
    }
```

The validate() method is a powerful tool in error validation. The method returns ActionErrors, which is a standard format for all errors in Struts.

Programming Struts Errors

Error handling is one of the most cumbersome and time-consuming activity performed by programmers. The Struts framework provides a standard way of handling errors within the entire application and displaying them to the front-end JSP screen. This is done through the ActionErrors and ActionError classes.

The ActionErrors class keeps all the Struts errors and organizes them based on a key name. This allows Struts to save multiple errors for each key for display later on the JSP page. An ActionErrors.add() method is used to add an error to the application, which is done by passing the add method a String key value and an ActionError. The ActionError class represents one error and the text associated with it. The associated text is usually stored in the resource properties file that's configured in the application parameter of the Struts servlet registration in the web.xml file. This allows for standard Java internationalization. The following is an example of creating an ActionErrors holder and adding a new ActionError to it:

```
ActionErrors errors = new ActionErrors();
        errors.add("result", new ActionError("error.invalid.login"));
```

The preceding example corresponds to this property:

```
error.invalid.login = An invalid username or password was entered.
```

The error message could contain data. It's possible to insert custom text in regions of a text message by adding special placeholders in the actual text of the application properties file. Given the line

```
error.invalid.login = {0} was entered and it is invalid
```

A new ActionError with replacement text would look like this:

```
new ActionError("error.invalid.login", "Garbage");
```

The associated error would then replace the {0} character with the text Garbage.

The ActionError object has constructors with zero and up to four parameters. If you need more than that, or a different object type rather than String is needed, you can use the following constructor to allow unlimited text replacement with objects:

```
ActionError(String key, Object [] params);
```

NOTE

The parameters in the object array of the ActionError constructor do not have to be Strings. They can be the wrapper class of any basic type using the same conventions as the MessageFormat class: http://java.sun.com/j2se/1.4.1/docs/api/java/text/MessageFormat.html.

The following example uses first an Integer value and then a date:

```
ActionError("dateError", new Object[new Integer(2)]
```

Within the action class, after errors are created, they must be saved for display in the forwarding page. This is done by using the `action.saveErrors()` method. This saves the errors to the application and allows the JSP's screens to capture the error.

```
super.saveErrors(request, errors);
```

The error capabilities built into Struts enable programmers to handle errors in a standard way, which saves time when developing without standard error catching.

Database Connectivity

Struts also allows database connections to be stored. Within the action class, a protected field named `servlet` is an `ActionServlet`. The method `findDataSource()` is used to retrieve the data source from the `struts-config.xml` file. The parameter represents the key attribute from the `<datasource>` tag. If you specify `null` for this, the default connection is retrieved. The following sample code opens a connection based on the `myDatabase` entry in `struts-config.xml`:

```
try {
   javax.sql.DataSource dataSource =
     servlet.findDataSource("myDatabase");
   java.sql.Connection myConn =
     dataSource.getConnection();

   //do what you wish with myConnection
 } catch (SQLException sqle) {
   ...
 } finally {

   //always close connection
   try {
     myConn.close();
   } catch (SQLException e) {
   }
 }
```

> **NOTE**
>
> Note that Struts provides data sources, but not pooling, load balancing, or failover of database connections. Refer to Chapter 10, "Managing Database Connectivity Using JDBC," for more information about WebLogic Server data sources.

This section has dealt with the backend programming needed for Struts-based applications. Action classes are written to perform the functionality. Helper classes such as

ActionForm and ActionMapping are used to perform valuable Struts-related activities, such as auto validation and forwarding to the new page or action servlet for display. Errors are stored within the ActionErrors class for later use, and database connections can be stored locally and accessed when needed. All the backend features are then tied into the struts-config.xml file for ease of configuration.

Front-End Programming Using the Struts Framework

To take full advantage of the Struts framework, JSP pages within a WebLogic application have to implement Struts tag libraries that allow them to tie into the back end. Tag libraries, covered in depth in the previous chapters, allow custom HTML tags to be implemented within a JSP page. The Struts tag library creates new tags for virtually every HTML tag. This is done to extend these tags to add Struts-specific properties and to simplify programming JSPs for Web developers who might not have Java skills.

Struts applications usually include at least two tag libraries from Struts:

- struts-html.tld—Contains all the Struts-specific HTML tags
- struts-bean.tld—Contains all the Struts-specific JavaBean tags

These files should be included at the beginning of a Struts JSP page just like any other tag libraries the application might need. Here's an example:

```
<%@ page language="java" %>
<%@ taglib uri="/WEB-INF/lib/struts-bean.tld" prefix="bean" %>
<%@ taglib uri="/WEB-INF/lib/struts-html.tld" prefix="html" %>
```

After these are defined, the JSP can be built using the basic Struts tags. Table 19.3 lists some of the more common Struts tags and their HTML equivalent. The entire list is too large to cover in depth. This chapter concentrates on the HTML <form> tag and getting and setting input fields within with the Struts equivalents.

TABLE 19.3 Common HTML Tags and the Struts Equivalents

HTML Tag	Struts Equivalent	Struts Added Benefit
<html> </html>	<html:html></html:html>	Adds locale support for internationalization
<img>	<html:img>	Adds capability to load from alt text and image from message resources file
<base></base>	<html:base>	Automatically inserts the Web application base
<a> </a>	<html:link></html:link>	Allows the link to be loaded from the request or other bean

> **NOTE**
>
> For a full list of Struts tags and their use, go to `http://jakarta.apache.org/struts/userGuide/dev_html.html`. That page contains the full documentation and examples that are beyond the scope of this book.

Displaying Text in Struts

Struts handles all displayed text within a configurable message resources file. This allows for internationalization with standard Java internationalization settings for `ResourceBundles`. The resource path and name are set up in the `web.xml` file when you register the action servlet. When text must be inserted, a special Struts message tag is available. Refer to the following example:

```
<bean:message key="login.title"/>
```

This line inserts the text associated with the key `"login.title"` into the HTML page. The Struts text insertion method is very simple and straightforward, but highly useful. By default, this tag retrieves the key value from the resource bundle referred to in the `<application>` parameter tag of the `web.xml` file. If another bundle is needed, or if another locale than the default is required, the tag has the `bundle` and `locale` attributes. The following example gets a fully qualified resource bundle for the French locale:

```
<bean:message bundle="myapp.props.newConfigFile" locale="FR" key="login.title"/>
```

Displaying Errors

Struts automatically displays errors if errors are set within the action class or automatic validation with a form bean is active. Within the JSP file, a simple tag is inserted:

```
<html:errors/>
```

The actual HTML that will be inserted at runtime is composed of three items:

- The error header, which is a decoration appearing before the errors. This text is located in a resource bundle under the key mapping `errors.header`.
- The list of errors.
- The footer HTML that's displayed after all the errors; located in `errors.footer`.

> **NOTE**
>
> Nothing is displayed if the error list is empty.

The following code is a typical entry for the `errors.header` and `errors.footer`. Notice the HTML code embedded within.

```
errors.header=<h5><font color="red">Error Occurred</font>
</h5>Please see the following message(s) before proceeding:<ul>
errors.footer=</ul>
```

The error tag also has four properties associated with it for configuration purposes:

- `bundle`—The name of the resource bundle to locate the `errors.header` and `errors.footer` key mappings from.
- `property`—The name of the error key to display only certain errors. If this isn't used, all errors are displayed.
- `locale`—An optional tag for language-specific messages; defaults to Struts value.
- `name`—Name of the request-scope bean where errors have been stored. Defaults to the `Action.ERROR_KEY` constant.

These properties enable you to define certain conditions and position errors where you need them. To display only the errors for a certain key, just specify a property equal to the error key set when the action error was added. For example:

```
<html:errors property="result"/>
```

This is beneficial if you separate errors by field and want to display field error messages for text and data validation.

Using Struts Forms

Forms in Struts were designed to decrease the chance of errors being typed in from the front end. This is accomplished by automatically including input and bean fields within the tags themselves. For instance, using standard HTML, an input field might have a bean associated with a session bean to display information. The code would contain HTML text and some kind of Java call encapsulated in server-side scripting tags. An example of this is displayed here:

```
<input type="text" name="return" value="<%=sessbean.getValue()%>">
```


The Struts tag would be much more readable and it would have the bean associated with the input field through the framework, as shown in the following line:

```
<html:text property="return"/>
```

This is much easier to code and to read later when it needs to be updated.

A Struts form tag is defined similarly to a `<form>` tag in HTML:

```
<html:form action="login.do"
             name="login"
           method="post"
            focus="CUSTOMERNO">
</html:form>
```

The Struts form tags contain attributes of their HTML equivalents, plus other parameters that make cumbersome tasks easier. The following are some extra useful parameters in the `<html:form>` tag:

- `focus`—The field name within the form to focus on when the user first enters the form. JavaScript is generated and inserted in the page to perform the operation.
- `name`—The name of the bean that will be used to populate the input data. This deviates from the HTML use. If the name isn't specified, it is looked up in the action mappings.
- `scope`—The scope of the bean that the page uses. If it isn't specified, it's looked up in the action mappings.
- `type`—The fully qualified Java class name to the form bean used to populate input. If it isn't specified, it's looked up in the action mappings.

Input fields are specified within the Struts form tag, as with HTML. In Struts, there is no input tag as there is in HTML; rather, the actual widget specified by the input `type` parameter is used in the Struts tag format. For example, instead of specifying a check box input field that's checked like this:

```
<input name="coolbox" type="checkbox" <%=(formBean.getCoolbox())?"checked":""%>>
```

The Struts tag looks like this:

```
<html:checkbox property="coolbox"/>
```

Notice the `property` attribute that contains the name of the input field. The `property` attribute is linked to the form bean to set the value at display time. In the form bean, a method named `getCoolbox()` will return a Boolean value: either `true` (display check) or `false` (empty check box).

The `property` value in Struts is contained in all the input tags. This attribute accesses the Struts action form class and gets the associated value from the method. For example,

```
getCar().getCurrentRadioStation()
```

would look like this in the `property` attribute:

```
property="car.currentRadioStation"
```

This works the same way in the bean `property` attribute. This flexibility allows different beans to be reused in applications and hides unnecessary complications.

Listed in Table 19.4 are some of the more common Struts form tags with an example comparing HTML and Struts.

TABLE 19.4 Common HTML Form Input Elements and Struts Example

Function	HTML Tag	Struts Equivalent
Text field	<input type = "text" name = "myname" size = "20">	<html:text property = "myname" size = "20" />
Text area	<input type = "textarea" cols = "50" rows = "4" name = "mytarea" >	<html:textarea property = "mytarea" cols = "50" rows = "4">
Radio button	<input type = "radio" name = "rad1" value = "sel1">	<html:radio property = "rad1" value = "sel1">
Check box	<input type = "checkbox" name = "chk1" value = "sel1">	<html:checkbox property = " chk1" value = " sel1">
Submit Button	<input type = "submit" value = "Submit"> property = "Submit">	<html:submit Submit </html:submit>
Reset button	<input type = "reset">	<html:reset/>
Selection box and options	<select name= "item"> <option value = "i1"> Item 1 </option> </select>	<html:select property ="item"> <html:option value="i1"> Item 1 </html:option> </html:select>

Struts Logic Tags

The Struts application development environment has much more to offer than just simple input and output. The Struts framework also has logic tags for making presentation logic easier. To use these tags within your JSP, add the logic tag library:

```
<%@ taglib uri="/WEB-INF/lib/struts-logic.tld" prefix="logic" %>
```

Now it's possible to check conditions on beans and values, match values, and loop without any Java code. The HTML or code to be run is inserted between the beginning and end tags. The following tags are supported:

- `<logic:equal></logic:equal>`
- `<logic:notEqual></logic:notEqual>`
- `<logic:greaterEqual></logic:greaterEqual>`
- `<logic:lessEqual></logic:lessEqual>`
- `<logic:greaterThan></logic:greaterThan>`
- `<logic:lessThan></logic:lessThan>`

Each of the tags compares the `value` attribute with one of the following:

- `cookie`—Compares with the specified cookie
- `header`—Compares with a header property
- `parameter`—Compares with a request parameter
- `name` and `property`—Compares with a JavaBean specified by the `name` parameter and the property within the JavaBean

The following example shows how a parameter from a request would be compared with the `value` tag:

```
<logic:equal value="Albert Einstein" parameter="Name">
      <b>The Greatest Scientist of all Time!</b>
</logic:equal>
```

Struts includes the substring matching tags, `<logic:match>` and `<logic:notMatch>`. Those tags match on the same attributes as the logic tags, with an additional parameter named `location` that specifies whether it should match either `start` or `end`, as the following example shows:

```
<logic:notMatch value="Einstein" parameter="Name" location="end">
      <b>Welcome Distinguished Guests</b>
</logic:notMatch>
```

The final tag we'll examine is the `<logic:iterate>` tag. This Struts tag is very useful and can very easily display lists of information on dynamic Web pages. The tag is very flexible, and can be used for simple lists or more complex structures. In the following example, we've specified the

- id—The name of the bean that contains the value for each element of the collection.
- scope—The place to look for the attribute. page, request, session, application, or anyscope is allowed. If scope isn't present, the default value is page.
- name—The attribute name that contains the collection to iterate on.
- type—The type of object that's contained in each row of the collection.
- length—The maximum number of iterations.

The following code is taken from the sample application for the Struts application named testStruts.war on the companion CD. No other code is needed to use this tag, but it's looking for a session object named order that contains objects of type myApp.Beans.dataBean. If those criteria are in place, the clean look is evident for looping through fields.

```
<logic:iterate id="mydata"
             name="order"
             type="myApp.Beans.dataBean"
            scope="session" >

  <TR class=bgInner>
    <TD><bean:write name="mydata" property="item"/></TD>
    <TD><bean:write name="mydata" property="qty"/></TD>
    <TD><bean:write name="mydata" property="date"/></TD>
  </TR>
</logic:iterate>
```

Putting It All Together

Listing 19.3 is a Struts JSP page to process an order search and handle any associated errors. This page displays the last five orders from a session bean provided. The message properties are used to get the titles from the application resource file. The <html:form> tag instantiates and uses a form bean and error messages categorized for each input parameter. Listing 19.3 shows the orderlistdisplay.jsp file to clarify the use and layout of a Struts page.

LISTING 19.3 orderlistdisplay.jsp

```
<%@ page language="java" %>
<%@ include file="style.html" %>
<%@ taglib uri="/WEB-INF/struts-bean.tld" prefix="bean" %>
```

LISTING 19.3 Continued

```
<%@ taglib uri="/WEB-INF/struts-html.tld" prefix="html" %>
<%@ taglib uri="/WEB-INF/struts-logic.tld" prefix="logic" %>
<html:html>
<title><bean:message key="orderentry.title"/></title>
<html:base/>
</head>
<BODY>
<TABLE BORDER="0" CELLSPACING="0" CELLPADDING="0" WIDTH=100% HEIGHT="136">

<tr><td class=title2 colspan="2">Struts Example Display Items</td></tr>
  <TR>
    <td class=bg height="75" align="right" valign="top" colspan=2>
         
    </td>
 </TR>

<tr>
  <td colspan="2">
  <table class=tableBorder border="0"
   cellspacing="0" cellpadding="0" width="100%">
    <TR class="bgOuter">
        <TD class=title2 align="left" width="33%">

  <table border="0" cellspacing="1" cellpadding="0" width="100%">
  <TR class=bgInner>
        <TD class=title1 width="50%"><bean:message key="prompt.item"/></TD>
        <TD class=title1 width="25%"><bean:message key="prompt.qty"/></TD>
        <TD class=title1 width="25%"><bean:message key="prompt.date"/></TD>
  </TR>
<logic:iterate id="mydata"
             name="order"
             type="myApp.Beans.dataBean"
            scope="session" >

  <TR class=bgInner>
    <TD><bean:write name="mydata" property="item"/></TD>
    <TD><bean:write name="mydata" property="qty"/></TD>
    <TD><bean:write name="mydata" property="date"/></TD>
  </TR>
</logic:iterate>
</table>
<tr>
```

LISTING 19.3 Continued

```
<td><html:link page="/orderlistentry.jsp">Enter Items</html:link></td>
</tr>
</table>
</td>
</tr>
<tr><td><html:link page="/logout.do">Log Out</html:link></td></tr>
</table>

</body>
</html:html>
```

Notice how clean the code is in Listing 19.3, without any server-side tags that are usually associated with this type of application. The readability is a definite bonus when Web designers need to modify the page for any reason.

NOTE

The Struts framework includes more features and benefits than can be covered here. For more information about configuring and using the Struts framework, log on to `http://jakarta.apache.org/struts/index.html`. That site has more examples and specific documentation about Struts. The following are more Struts references:

- `http://husted.com/struts/`—A site by a Struts developer
- `http://www.jamesholmes.com/struts/console/`—A site for a free Java Struts manager to take a look at
- *Struts Kick Start*, ISBN 0672324725 by Sams Publishing—Everything you need to know and more

Struts Sample Application

The Struts sample application is a fully functional Struts application that enables a user to log in and update a shopping cart. The application is meant as tool to exemplify some of the Struts features talked about in this chapter. The example contains all the libraries needed for Struts in the `WEB-INF/lib` directory. An included batch file builds the application and creates a `testStruts.war` file for deploying on WebLogic. To compile the classes found in the `WEB-INF/classes/*` directories, simply modify the `buildWAR.bat` file to contain the path to `weblogic.jar` and then run it. Use the WebLogic deployment tools to deploy the application either by running the console or running the command-line deployment tool. The login for the application is Customer Number 1234, Password=1234 as shown in Figure 19.2.

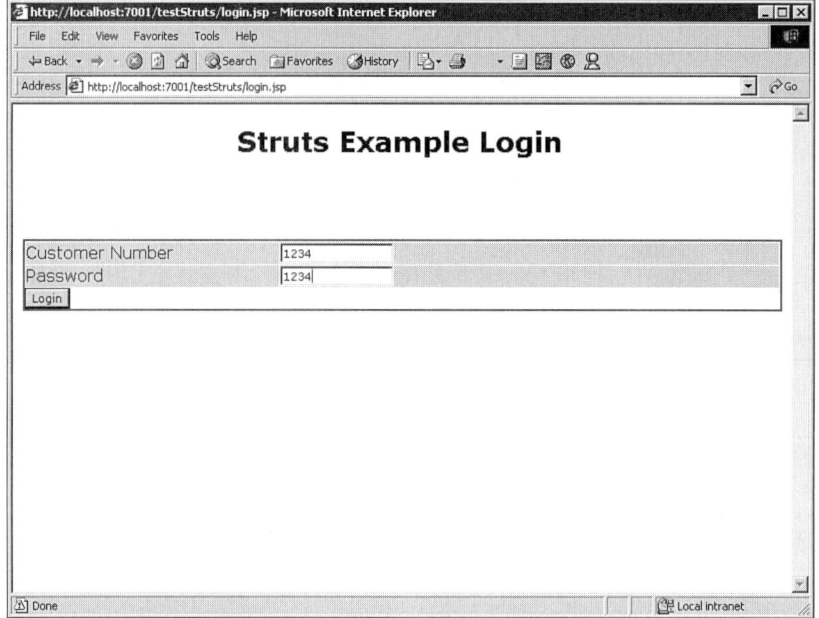

Figure 19.2 Struts sample login page.

Summary

This chapter is meant to be an introduction into the world of Struts. The text covered what Struts is, where to get it, how to install it, and how to use various basic Struts programming elements. The basic design elements of Struts were introduced enough to write a basic Struts application.

Struts methodology will continue to grow in popularity as more Web development teams recognize the need for configurable Web applications with separation of modeling, viewing, and controlling.

PART V

Using Enterprise JavaBeans in WebLogic Applications

IN THIS PART

CHAPTER 20

Enterprise JavaBeans and WebLogic Server

By Saranathan Govindarajan

IN THIS CHAPTER

- EJB Architecture—Overview
- EJB Container
- EJB Implementation
- EJB Deployment Descriptors
- EJB Deployment
- Other EJB Features

Enterprise JavaBeans is considered to be the cornerstone of the entire J2EE framework. In this chapter, we focus on the basics of Enterprise JavaBeans and also look in detail at the EJB configuration options used in the next three chapters. We start with an architecture overview and move on to different types of available Enterprise JavaBeans. In the following section, we look at the runtime environment (EJB container) along with the basic services it provides—namely, security, persistence, transactions, and so on. In the next three chapters, we'll cover the different bean types in detail. We'll use some real-world examples, such as a classic shopping cart, and airline reservation system to explaining some of the concepts.

EJB Architecture—Overview

The Enterprise JavaBeans architecture provides for enabling standard portable solutions to enterprisewide business problems using the Java programming language, thereby leveraging the Write Once, Run Anywhere concept advocated by Java. The standards-based solution enables you to build distributed object-oriented applications by breaking down business rules into components that represent the business model as closely as possible. Component models provide the technology for application developers to build applications based on components driven by their interfaces rather than building new components every time one needs a new function. Let's take a classic business case: the shopping cart example that's used widely in online bookstores, grocery stores, and so forth. Some of the most common components that make up this enterprise application include the customer, shopping cart, and more. These are components that should be readily available in the component market in an easily deployable mode for any application server and can be used to build the complete enterprise application.

ENTERPRISE JAVABEANS DEFINED

Let's look at Sun's definition of Enterprise JavaBeans:

The Enterprise JavaBeans architecture is a component architecture for the development and deployment of component-based distributed business applications. Applications written using the Enterprise JavaBeans architecture is scalable, transactional, and multi-user secure. These applications may be written once, and then deployed on any server platform that supports the Enterprise JavaBeans specification.

Enterprise JavaBeans is based on distributed object technologies, and object middleware usually enables communication between the distributed objects. The object middleware is also responsible for providing the services necessary for transparent access to the different layers of the component irrespective of distributed system complexities (that is, the heterogeneous software/hardware platforms). Distributed component technologies combine the power of middleware technology and the characteristics of components to provide for an interaction between components and they are leveraged well in the EJB implementation.

The architecture also provides services such as transactions, connection management, and location transparency to make it easier for developers to concentrate on the business logic when developing components and leave the management of the infrastructure services to the application server. The architecture also addresses the deployment and life cycle properties of an enterprise bean.

With all these properties, the EJB framework provides an effective solution to most complex business problems; for example, an airline reservation system. These business problems can typically be effectively addressed by breaking them down into different components depending on each component's role within the business solution. For example, in an airline reservation system, the important elements are data components such as customers, tickets, and flights, and the business processes are activities such as making a reservation and so on. The requirements of the business processes and entities are different. The EJB framework addresses this issue very effectively by mapping the business elements into different types of EJBs depending on the mapped business component. We'll look at how these mappings are achieved with the help of the different EJB types when we cover them in the next section.

EJB Types

Enterprise JavaBeans come in three flavors: Session, Entity, and Message-Driven. The EJB types help model the business processes and entities effectively. Apart from this, these beans also differ in what Java technology they use. The underlying Java technology implementing Session and Entity beans is RMI. Different client types can access these objects (servlets or standard Java applications) using distributed object protocols. On the other hand, the Message-Driven bean introduced in EJB 2.0 is based on the Java messaging infrastructure—JMS. Message-Driven beans are asynchronous whereas the other two types respond to synchronous requests. Let's look at each of the EJB types in detail.

Session Beans

Session beans represent business processes. In other words, they represent workflow that describes the steps involved in finishing a business flow or task, such as booking an airline ticket. Session beans usually work with one or more Entity beans or directly with the database itself to implement the workflow. Session beans help to create the interactions between the different entities that make up a business process. In the airline reservation system business case, customer, credit card, and ticket will not make sense without defining the interactions between them, such as customer's reservation, authorization of the credit card, and so on.

Session beans come in two distinct flavors: Stateless and Stateful. The flavor of session bean is based on the type of conversation involved in the business task being executed.

Stateless In the Stateless type of session bean, the conversations between the client and the EJB are limited to one interaction at a time. A Stateless Session bean does not store any state information pertaining to the client that invoked it. This high-performance bean type is used for business processes that finish the defined task in one method invocation. All information required for the execution of the business task is passed to the method. Although passing all necessary information could be construed as a disadvantage, Stateless Session beans offer a host of other advantages:

- Stateless Session beans are less resource-intensive because they don't store information about clients or the previous requests they handled.
- A Stateless Session bean instance is not attached to a single client, thereby enabling multiple clients to share a few instances of the bean (pooling). As soon as a Stateless Session bean completes a request, it's available to process another client request.
- Because the Stateless Session bean is not attached to a particular client, there's no information about the client on the EJB server to store in a temporary store for use at a later time when the same client comes back to process another request. In EJB terms, the Stateless Session bean need not be passivated when the request is complete or activated when a client comes back. This reduces the overhead involved in swapping the bean to another client or pushing it back to the free bean pool. The processes of activation and passivation are explained in detail later in this section.

Although Stateless Session beans do not maintain client state information, they can cache information that can be shared between the clients such as by using a logging file handle or a database connection. But this information does not pertain to a particular client.

In the airline reservation business case, the payment process using credit card is a Stateless Session bean (`ChargeCustomerEJB`). The only task of this EJB is to charge the customer for a successful reservation. After the bean charges a customer for the reservation, it moves to other customers but retains no information from the first client.

All Stateless Session bean instances of a particular type (for example, `ChargeCustomerEJB`) are considered to be the same. Their internal state information does not enable identifying them distinctively by either the client that is accessing them or by the container in which they run. A client does not care which instance of the Stateless Session bean is processing the request because any free instance can do so. This behavior drives the high-performance behavior of beans of this type because they can be pooled, swapped, and reused for multiple clients.

Stateful Stateful Session beans are used to model business processes that span multiple interactions between the client and the EJB server. Every bean instance of this type is associated with a client for the life of the bean instance. In other words, Stateful Session beans can be seen as extensions of the client inside the server. A session bean acts as if it were part of the client inside the server. So, whatever the bean does will be specific to the client that created it. This kind of bean holds client state and is not shared across different client instances. Stateful Session beans store *conversational state*; that is, client identification data that can be used to identify the client between the multiple method calls that define a single business process. This client state information is volatile and is not persisted to a permanent data store as in the case of Entity beans, which are described next.

The specification suggests that once the Stateful Session bean is instantiated, it is associated with the client for its entire life cycle. But to increase performance, most EJB containers (including WebLogic Server) implement a passivation mechanism with Stateful Session beans. The passivation mechanism is explained later in the chapter when we get to EJB life cycle management. In a common business case—the XYZ store sells books online—the customer task (choosing the books he needs), payment option (the customer choosing from the list of options presented to him), and placing the order are good candidates for implementing as a Stateful Session bean. The Stateful Session EJB encapsulates the business logic of assembling the order and placing it on the server, thereby enabling the client to be thin. The bean also stores the conversational state of the client. Table 20.1 lists some of common examples of session beans.

TABLE 20.1 Session Bean Examples

Business Case	Session Bean Type
Credit card verification	Stateless
Shopping cart: online grocery, book store, and so on	Stateful
Online banking: multi-page account management	Stateful
Online airline reservation: travel agent	Stateful
Online sports scoreboard	Stateless
Stock quotes	Stateless

Entity Beans

So far, we've looked at the components that can be used to define application logic: Session beans. These components represented actions; that is, verbs. Session beans help model business processes and also manage workflow. Stateful Session beans provide a framework for storing the client state information that can be used for long-running conversations between the client and the EJB component, which might span multiple method calls. But they cannot be used as persistent data components. The Enterprise JavaBeans specification defines Entity beans for mapping business objects, such as customer and account, into the EJB world. In other words, Entity beans provide a framework for persistent data. They model business processes that are usually expressed as nouns. In the airline reservation business case, credit card, and customer are excellent candidates for modeling as Entity beans because they represent persistent data objects. Let's look at some of characteristics of Entity beans:

- Entity beans have the capability to persist the entity to a permanent storage such as a database.
- Entity beans encapsulate business data such as the customer and credit card. They do not implement any workflow logic—that's done by Session beans.
- Entity beans represent the object form of a database record, thereby providing a convenient and effective mechanism for manipulating the data because these components come with setters and getters (`getLastName()` and `setLastName()` are simpler than the equivalent SQL commands).

When a new Entity bean is created, it actually creates a new record in the persistent store and the bean instance is associated with that record. As the EJB state undergoes state transition, it affects the underlying data record as well. That is, the record is inserted, modified, or removed depending on the operation being performed on the bean instance. The process of keeping the data object, represented by the bean, and the corresponding database record in sync is defined as *persistence*. The type of persistence logic chosen by the bean implementer determines the type of the Entity bean. There are two flavors of Entity beans: bean-managed persistence (BMP) and container-managed persistence (CMP).

Bean-Managed Persistence In this type of Entity bean, the bean implementer has to take care of writing the logic in the Entity bean for all the database operations he wants to perform. All manipulations of the database are manual. The container provides only a basic framework with which it communicates to the bean as to when a database operation such as insert, delete, or update can be performed. From the implementation point of view, BMP involves more effort because the data persistence logic is left to the implementer, unlike CMP, which is discussed next. Although writing the logic for database inserts, updates, and deletes can be construed as a major disadvantage, BMP provides better control in complex database situations, such as heterogeneous data sources in the backend or the use of a complex legacy system where the CMP mechanism isn't adequate for mapping the data objects to Entity beans. Additionally, the implementer has to take care of database changes, such as structure/type changes, because the implemented bean instance is tied to the specific database design.

Container-Managed Persistence In this Entity bean type, the container manages the relationship between the bean instance and the underlying data it represents. The container performs the database manipulations—insertion, deletion, and updating the data records—because it is aware of the relationship of the database fields and the corresponding Entity bean data objects. Container-managed persistence was one of the most key topics that underwent considerable change in the EJB 2.0 specification. One of the major drawbacks in the earlier version was the loosely defined Entity bean relationship. The EJB 2.0 CMP model addresses this requirement very well and now Entity beans can have relationships with other Entity beans, while being fully portable to all EJB containers that implement the EJB 2.0 specification. In addition to bean-to-bean relationships, EJB 2.0 also introduced the Enterprise JavaBeans Query language (EJB-QL), which helps defining the query methods (finder and select) in CMP.

Message-Driven Beans

Message-Driven is a new type of Enterprise JavaBean introduced in EJB 2.0 specification. Although Session and Entity beans are used for synchronous request/response, Message-Driven bean (MDB) is an asynchronous enterprise bean that processes JMS messages from configured topics or queues.

Message-Driven beans are based on the Java Messaging Service (JMS) technology that forms an integral part of the J2EE platform. JMS provides the infrastructure and well-defined APIs for implementing enterprise-messaging applications. Being asynchronous, JMS allows for designing enterprise applications, which do not need a reply immediately. This loosens the links between the client requests and the availability of the application server for processing requests immediately. In the JMS messaging model, a client sends messages asynchronously to a configured destination. The destination determines how the requests are processed. The JMS specification defines two types of messaging models: publish and subscribe (pub/sub) and point to point (ptp).

The pub/sub messaging model is used when the message is to be sent to multiple recipients (for example, stock quotes) and the ptp model is used when the message is to be processed only once (for example, a ticket reservation). The destination type in the pub/sub messaging model is a *topic*, and in the case of the ptp messaging model, it is a *queue*.

In both messaging models, JMS clients send messages to a configured destination. Message-Driven beans pick up the messages asynchronously for processing. It is a common pattern to see an MDB, after processing, put a reply back in a reply destination, and to see that reply picked up by the client that posted the original message. For a detailed description of JMS and about using them, refer to the chapter on JMS (see Chapter 12, "Enterprise Messaging with JMS").

Message-Driven beans are a special type of JMS component that provides a stateless component for processing JMS messages. Being part of the Enterprise JavaBeans framework, the EJB container provides the necessary infrastructure and services such as transactions, security, and concurrency. The container also manages the Message-Driven bean environment and life cycle, including acknowledging messages.

For example, in the online bookstore application, a `ShipmentEJB` could be a Message-Driven bean that processes shipment orders. The orders are sent asynchronously as JMS messages.

EJB Container

Now let's look at the heart of the any enterprise bean implementation: the EJB container. Sun's specification for Enterprise JavaBeans deals with the functions of the container provider in detail, and the defined component model is described in terms of the container's responsibilities with respect to each of the enterprise bean type.

Container Defined

The EJB container provides an operational environment for all the enterprise bean types discussed earlier. It represents the EJB runtime holder that resides within the scope of the EJB server, and is more of a logical entity than a physical resource. In the current specification, the server provider isn't differentiated from the container provider. There's no clear demarcation between the responsibility of the container and the server. The responsibility of the container can be summarized as follows:

- Bean life cycle management manages the creation of the remote objects and home objects for the different bean types.
- Bean resource management involves managing the related resources.
- Provides middleware services such as security, transaction, and concurrency to the deployed beans.

The EJB component model is built on basic interfaces defined by the specification for different bean types. The `EntityBean`, `SessionBean`, and `MessageDrivenBean` are the respective interfaces for the Entity, Session, and Message-Driven beans. Figure 20.1 lists the bean classes for each of the EJB types and the functions they provide. The base interfaces define callback methods that the container invokes during various events such as the creation of new instance, removal of the bean, and so forth. The callback methods for all the bean interfaces enable bean developers to define application-specific logic to manipulate the bean based on its context. It isn't necessary for the bean developer to implement all the callback methods. All the methods are optional and can be left empty (`{ /* do nothing */ }`). We'll look at these interfaces and the related classes later in the chapter when we discuss the EJB implementation.

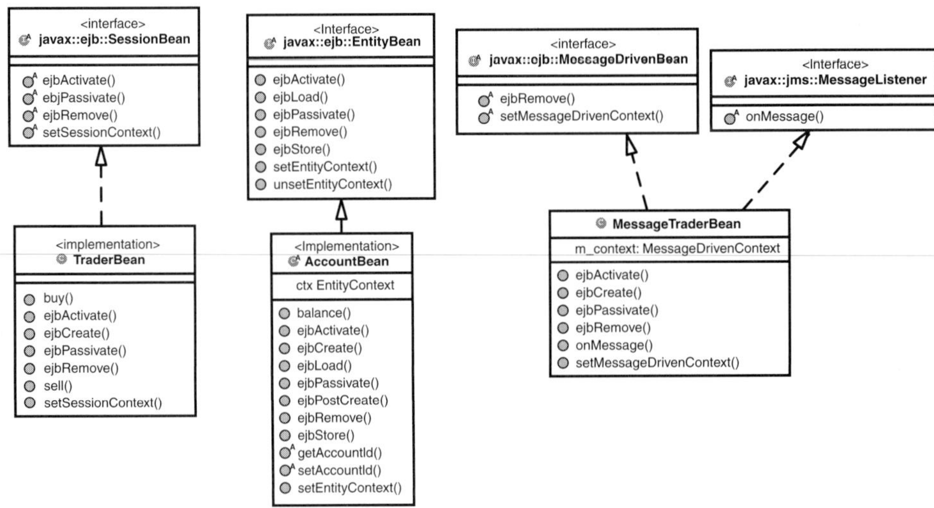

Figure 20.1 EJB interfaces.

Apart from the basic interfaces, the EJB specifications define a context interface: `EJBContext`. This interface gives access to the container's properties, the client information, and the bean's metadata. The EJB specification provides detailed subinterfaces for this context interface for each of the bean types: `EntityContext` for Entity beans, `SessionContext` for Session beans, and `MessageDrivenContext` for Message-Driven beans. Figure 20.2 describes the relationship between the EJB context classes and the bean implementations and also lists the available metadata functions.

The bean container contract also talks about the special JNDI namespace known as the *environment naming context* (ENC). The JNDI ENC forms an important part of the bean container contract. JNDI ENC allows an enterprise bean to interact with other beans and resources, such as JDBC data sources, and also provides access to environment entries (configuration data). We'll take a detailed look at the interfaces and their methods in the next three chapters when we deal with the three bean types in detail.

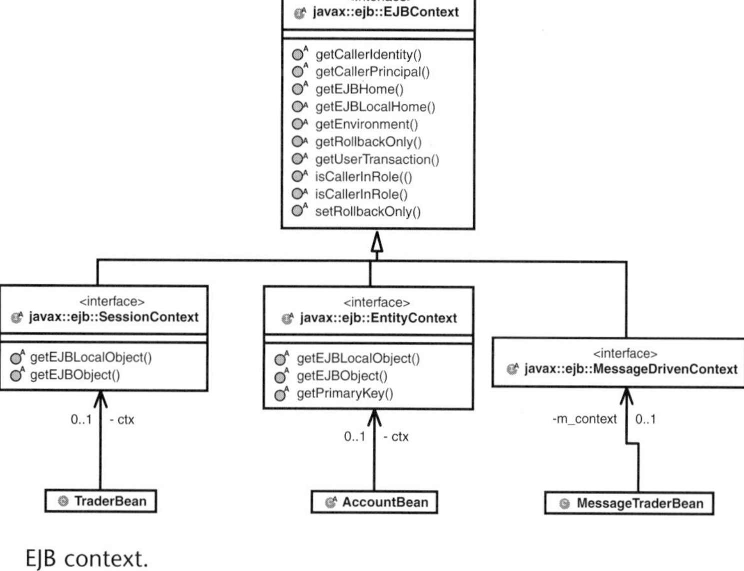

Figure 20.2 EJB context.

Life Cycle Management

So far, we've looked at the different EJB types that cater to different enterprise application requirements and we've also briefly covered about the runtime environment that surrounds Enterprise JavaBeans. Enterprise business applications usually have a high-performance requirement coupled with the fact that there are limited resources at disposal for managing the millions of interactions between the clients and the EJB server. The EJB container has the responsibility for efficiently managing the resources for the EJBs by sharing resources such as threads, TCP socket connections, database resources, and so on. These resources can be increased to a certain extent as the number of clients increase, but doing so reaches a point of diminishing returns at which the resource increase has an adverse effect on the EJB server's performance. Most EJB servers, including WebLogic Server, support instance pooling and activation mechanisms for efficient resource management. The mechanism adopted depends on the bean type. We'll go over each of the mechanisms in this section of the chapter.

Instance Pooling

The concept of instance pooling is not new. It has evolved over years of multitier application framework development. The concept provides an excellent answer for enhanced scalability requirements in enterprisewide business applications. A typical multitier enterprise application might involve many resources, including database connections, file handles, TCP IP socket connections, JMS connections, and other components. In an application server such as WebLogic Server, those resources are used by the various components being served by the container.

As mentioned earlier, the EJB container, which forms an integral part of the application server, transparently provides all resource management functions to the user. Along with this function, it is also responsible for the life cycle operations of the EJBs deployed in the server environment. In other words, the EJB container is responsible for the instantiating the bean instance, invoking the instance on a client request, and removing the bean from memory. But the process of creation of a new bean instance is an expensive operation, and it therefore increases the performance overhead. This could be avoided if there were a mechanism by which the container could process a client request using a bean instance that's already in memory.

Instance pooling allows EJB containers to cache bean instances in memory and use them for servicing client requests as they come, thereby avoiding the cost of creating a bean for every client request. A pool of bean instances can be used to service the client requests, and the number of instances can be fewer than the number of clients. This helps to reduce the resources needed for servicing all client requests. The reuse of EJB components is not limited to any particular bean type and can be used with Stateless Session beans and Message-Driven beans alike. Stateful session beans are not pooled and neither are active Entity beans: They're created as needed. Figure 20.3 describes the life cycle of a Stateless Session bean instance in an instance pool scenario.

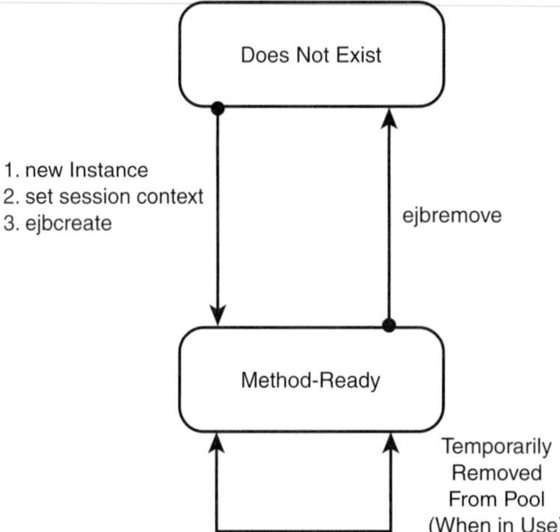

Figure 20.3 Bean instance pool life cycle.

When the bean instance is in a pooled state, it's ready for use to handle a client request because the bean instance has already been instantiated and resides within the container. The pooled instances have no associated identity at this moment. As a response to a client request, a bean instance associated with an identity is linked to a client—this is the ready state of the bean. In this state, the bean instance can respond to client requests. After a client is done with an assigned bean instance, that bean instance is returned to the instance pool and can be used for other client requests.

Instance Swapping

Most EJB vendors leverage the concept of instance pooling in the implementation of Stateless Session beans. Because Stateless Session beans do not store any client state information, a method invocation corresponds to a complete task. The only dependency between method invocations might be the volatile data common to all Stateless instances, such as a log file handler or a database connection. Because all bean instances are equal, it does not matter to the client which bean instance responds to its request. This allows the container to swap bean instances from the pool between client requests. In a real-world scenario, there is a considerable lapse between the client method invocations that enables the EJB container to share the same bean instances between different clients. This allows for efficient use of bean instances and reduces the inactive periods between client requests. It also keeps the number of bean instances considerably less than the number of clients; that is, fewer bean instances are required to service more requests.

WebLogic Server uses the free pool concept to improve the performance of Stateless Session beans and for pooled Entity instances used for home method invocations. The free pool is created from the value set for `initial-beans-in-free-pool` parameter at server startup. This parameter is configured in the WebLogic-based EJB configuration file (`weblogic-ejb-jar.xml`). This configuration file is explained in detail later in the chapter. Because this eliminates the creation of a new instance for the first few requests, the initial response time improves noticeably. The upper limit of the free pool is controlled by both the memory available and the `max-beans-in-free-pool` parameter in `weblogic-ejb-jar.xml`. The WebLogic EJB container swaps the instances from the pool for handling the client requests, as explained earlier. WebLogic Server processes all requests concurrently until all bean instances in the pool are active and the `max-beans-in-free-pool` limit has reached. These parameters are not applicable for Stateful Session beans.

Message-Driven beans, like Stateless Session beans, can leverage the concepts of instance pooling and instance swapping, which allows them to process multiple requests concurrently. Message-Driven beans process messages from a specific destination that's configured at server startup. For example, messages arriving to a destination X can be processed by instances of the particular Message-Driven bean type at the same time. The EJB container takes responsibility for assigning a bean instance for every message. After the message is processed, the bean instance is returned to the free pool to process other messages.

Instance Activation and Passivation

Stateful Session beans, unlike other bean types, maintain client state information between method invocations. A client-bean conversation may span across multiple method calls, and information about the conversation is stored at the bean instance associated with the specific client. The integrity of the conversational state is important for the successful completion of the client task. Stateful Session beans cannot use instance pooling because a bean instance is tied to a client for the life of the bean's service to the client. For efficient resource management, most EJB containers implement the passivation mechanism when dealing with Stateful Session beans. The passivation mechanism is a two-step process: passivation and activation.

In the passivation step, the bean instance is dissociated from the associated EJB object and conversational state is persisted to a secondary storage. The bean has the occasion of cleaning up its state (freeing resources, storing transient data, keeping a handle to retrieve it, and so on) beforehand. Once the bean instance is persisted, the container can use the instance to process another client's request. Because the client executes the methods on the EJB object that communicates with the associated bean instance, the passivation process is totally transparent to the client.

In the activation step, the instance is restored to that state relative to the EJB object. Activation happens when a returning client invokes a method on the passivated EJB object. The container has the responsibility of automatically retrieving the client's conversational state from secondary storage and associating it to the EJB object along with the instance variables assigned to the values equal to the data stored when it was passivated. Other state (resources and transient data) can be retrieved when the container notifies the bean of the activation.

Sun's specification leaves the implementation of the activation mechanism to the vendor. WebLogic Server uses a caching mechanism for implementing the activation mechanism to improve the performance of Stateful Session beans. The cache stores active EJB instances that include the bean instances currently in use as well as the ones that were in use recently. When the EJB instance is present in the cache, it is still associated with the EJB object it was servicing. The cache size is controlled by the `max-beans-in-cache` deployment element of the WebLogic EJB configuration file (`weblogic-ejb-jar.xml`). Along with `idle-timeout-seconds`, the `max-beans-in-cache` parameter gives some control to the WebLogic administrator as to when the EJB container will passivate the bean instance to a secondary storage. If there is no pressure on the resources, WebLogic Server might avoid the passivation even if one of the conditions mentioned here is met. But an administrator can force passivation using the `cache-type` element in the `weblogic-ejb-jar.xml` file that's explained later in the chapter. The `idle-timeout-seconds` element controls the removal of the passivated bean; that is, whether it's permanently removed from the secondary storage. If the EJB deployer does not want the passivated bean to be automatically removed, `idle-timeout-seconds` should be set to `0`.

Finally, the EJB developer has to make sure that WebLogic Server can save all the instance variables relating to the client's conversational state. The container knows how to save

- The primitive data types and serializable classes
- Null-valued nonserializables

- EJB references
- Other EJB-related objects (`SessionContext` objects, JNDI contexts, `UserTransaction` objects, and so on)

All variables that are transient are not serialized. The specification provides the `ejbPassivate()` and `ejbActivate()` callback methods for performing any custom cleanup operations, such as releasing or activating resources (for example, database connections) before the bean instance's passivation or activation. These resources can be restored in `ejbActivate()` if their connection attributes, or handles, are saved in `ejbPassivate()` in serializable variables.

TIP

In theory, passivation is a good idea. In practice, it's a waste of system resources precisely when the system needs those resources the most. But this has to be weighed against the cost at which this service is provided. Because RAM is cheap, a better idea is to make sure that the application has plenty of heap to work with. Also ensure that the cache settings are comfortably set up and thereby make sure that passivation is not needed. The callback method `ejbPassivate()` can be used to convey a message to the administrator suggesting to add more memory or look for memory-hogging process or procedures.

Basic Services

The container is responsible for managing the different bean types that live within its environment from their creation to their eventual eviction. The container provides basic services that include concurrency, transactions, persistence, and security to all the deployed EJBs. The EJB server eliminates the management of these complicated services from EJB developers and enables them to concentrate on the implementation of the business logic.

Transactions

In an enterprise application, tasks are usually completed as units of work. Either all the tasks within a block complete or they are all thrown out. For instance, to execute a funds transfer between two bank accounts, the system should successfully withdraw funds from one account and deposit them into another account. If either of these two operations fails, the system should not make any change permanent to maintain data integrity. In an airline reservation system, the customer should not be charged for the ticket without making sure that she has been allotted a seat.

This behavior is achieved by using transactions in enterprise systems. Transactions are dealt with in detail in Chapter 9, "Processing Transactions with the Java Transaction API." Their use is covered in the chapter context of JDBC (see Chapter 10, "Managing Database Connectivity Using JDBC"), Session beans (refer to Chapter 21, "Working with

Session Beans"), Entity beans (see Chapter 22, "Working with Entity Beans"), and so on. Transaction support is one of the most important features offered by the EJB container. In this section, we take a detailed look at the transaction features that the WebLogic Server container provides for EJBs and how you can control them. Most of these features are common for all the EJB types, so we'll look at them together. Where relevant, we'll look at them separately to distinguish between behaviors in each case.

The container takes care of handling all infrastructure features, such as transactions and security, thus enabling you to concentrate on the business functionality of the bean. If not for these features, you would have to demarcate transactions every time in your code, which is a distraction from the main task for your bean. Beans that make use of this feature of the container are said to have *container-managed* transactions.

Although container management of transactions is a very useful feature, there are some cases in which you might not prefer this behavior. In such cases, you can take complete control of transaction management within the bean. Such beans are said to use *bean-managed* transactions.

Container-Managed Transactions When managing transactions with the container, which is also known as *declarative transaction management*, the transactional behavior of EJBs is controlled by the transaction deployment elements of the deployment descriptors. The container uses these attributes to provide transactional facilities for each method of the bean. Therefore, when any change is required in the transactional behavior, all you have to do is alter the descriptors—you don't have to change the source code. This provides for easier maintainability of your application. Also, the same bean can now be deployed in different applications with different transactional attributes. A WebLogic Server container enables you to control transactional support within a bean at a method level.

Now let's look at the transaction attribute and the predefined values that define transactional behavior. This attribute can take six values in all. They are

- `Never`—When set to `Never`, the container never allows the method to be invoked within the scope of a transaction. If a user transaction is active when the method is invoked, the container throws a `RemoteException` to the remote client or an `EJBException` to the local one. When invoked without an active transaction, the container invokes the method.
- `Not Supported`—This transaction attribute indicates to the container that the bean method does not support transactions. Consequently, the container suspends the client transaction, if any, before passing on the call to the bean method. On completion of the method call, the client transaction resumes.
- `Supports`—This attribute indicates that the bean method supports transactions, but does not require it. Therefore, if the method is invoked within a context of a client transaction, the method is included in the transaction. If the method is invoked

outside of a transaction context, the method also performs outside any transaction context.

- `Required`—Indicates to the container that the method requires a transaction to be present. If invoked within the context of a client transaction, the method is invoked within the same transaction context. If a client invokes this method without its own transaction, the container automatically starts a new transaction and invokes this method within the context of the new transaction. On completion of this method execution, the scope of the new transaction ends.
- `RequiresNew`—When set, this attribute indicates to the container that the method has to be invoked within the context of a new transaction. When a client invokes this method without a transaction, a new transaction is started and the method is invoked. If a client already has an active transaction when it invokes this method, the container temporarily suspends that transaction, begins a new transaction, and invokes this method. On completion of the method, the new transaction is completed and the client transaction is resumed.
- `Mandatory`—Indicates to the container that the method should always be called within a transactional context. If a client invokes this method outside of an active transaction context, the container responds by throwing a `javax.transaction.TransactionRequiredException` exception to the client, without invoking the method. For clients that use local interfaces, the container throws the `javax.ejb.TransactionRequiredLocalException` exception instead.

The transactional attribute behavior described earlier can be tabularized to provide a clearer perspective. For all cases in which the action states that the client transaction was suspended, the transaction is resumed when the method returns control to the container. Wherever new transactions are started, the scope of the new transaction ends when the method returns to the container. This perspective can be seen in Table 20.2.

TABLE 20.2 Transaction Attributes and Container Behavior

Transaction Attribute	Method Invoked Without an Active Client Transaction	Method Invoked Within an Active Client Transaction
Never	Bean method is invoked without a transaction	(remote) RemoteException is thrown or (local) EJBException
NotSupported	Bean method is invoked without a transaction	Client transaction is suspended; bean method is invoked without a client transaction
Supports	Bean method is invoked without a transaction	Bean method is invoked within the scope of the client transaction

20

TABLE 20.2 Continued

Transaction Attribute	Method Invoked Without an Active Client Transaction	Method Invoked Within an Active Client Transaction
Required	New transaction is started; bean method is invoked within the scope of the new transaction	Bean method is invoked within the scope of the client transaction
RequiresNew	New transaction started; bean method is invoked within the scope of the new transaction	Client transaction is suspended; new transaction is started; bean method is invoked within the scope of the new transaction
Mandatory	(remote) TransactionRequiredException or (local) TransactionRequiredLocal Exception thrown.	Bean method is invoked within the scope of the client transaction

In cases where the container begins a transaction for the bean, it monitors your bean method for transactional support. In such cases, the container always commits it, even if there's an application exception, except in these cases:

- If there's a system exception, the transaction is rolled back immediately.
- A bean may also mark the transaction for rollback, regardless of exceptions.

Alternatively, if the client started the transaction, the container doesn't commit or roll back the transaction. The following rules apply in that case:

- If there's a system exception, the transaction is marked for rollback.
- Application exceptions have no direct effect on transactions.
- A bean may also mark the transaction for rollback regardless of exceptions.

As mentioned earlier, transaction attributes can be set at a method level. The attribute used for a method is the most specific attribute that has been defined in the EJB deployment descriptor (`ejb-jar.xml`). We'll look at how transaction attributes are configured when we cover this deployment descriptor later in the chapter.

NOTE

WebLogic Server also enables you to define a custom timeout for transactions started by the container. That way, the container isn't waiting forever for the transaction to finish. You can do this by providing the timeout value in the WebLogic EJB configuration file (`weblogic-ejb-jar.xml`), which is explained later in the chapter. By default, the transaction timeout is set to thirty seconds. Refer to the following link for the BEA documentation on how to configure the `<trans-timeout-seconds>` element: `http://edocs.bea.com/wls/docs81/ejb/reference.html#1072610`.

Bean-Managed Transactions In some occasions, the EJB developer might want to control the transaction management in the bean code and not use container-managed transactions. It is strongly advised that, wherever possible, container-managed transactions should be used rather than bean-managed transactions. This is because container-managed transactions clearly distinguish transactional behavior from business logic, thus enabling EJB developers or deployers to change either without affecting the other. This behavior is managed using the transaction type deployment element in the deployment descriptors.

When this is done, the EJB developer should code the bean implementation to take care of transactions within it using the `java.transaction.UserTransaction` interface. For more information about the `UserTransaction` interface and how to use the Java Transaction Architecture, refer to Chapter 9.

Just a quick note about client-initiated transactions: When a client that is already in an active transaction context invokes a bean-managed transaction, the container first suspends the client's transaction and then invokes the bean implementation. The container does this irrespective of whether the bean implementation starts its own transaction.

Concurrency

As with other primary services, concurrency is interpreted differently for different bean types. This is mainly because of the nature of the bean types. That is, in the context of a Message-Driven bean, concurrency means processing multiple asynchronous messages simultaneously, whereas in the context of Session and Entity beans, concurrency is defined as multiple clients accessing the same bean at the same time.

Session beans do not allow for concurrent access. Stateless Session beans are associated with only one client for the duration of the request being processed. A Stateful Session bean is associated with one client for the duration of the conversation, which could involve multiple interactions between the client and the server. An Entity bean, on the other hand, models real-world objects and has to be accessed concurrently by different clients. For a detailed description of this with respect to Entity beans, see Chapter 22. Concurrency in Message-Driven beans makes these bean types more powerful and enables a high-performance component model.

Clustering

In some critical business applications, system failures even for a little while are not acceptable. Today, most applications are so critical that they're required to be supplemented by multiple copies of the application running in different machines so that even if one copy fails, another copy can take over and complete the task. The process of executing several copies of the same application on more than one machine, with all of them supplementing each other and providing reliable service, is known as *clustering*. Clustering also plays a vital role in improving the scalability of your enterprise. You can increase the capacity of the cluster at any time by adding more copies of your application and/or more hardware into your cluster. For more information on clustering a WebLogic Server deployment, including the benefits it provides for deployed Enterprise JavaBeans, see Chapter 36, "Installing, Configuring and Deploying WebLogic Server Clusters."

Naming

Since EJB specification 1.1, a new concept known as the *environment naming context* has been introduced between the bean and the container. The ENC is a JNDI context, which is specific to each bean, and isn't shared across the server. This ENC defines the environment under which the bean is deployed and is running. The JNDI ENC can be used to access references and environment entries, which contributes to making EJBs portable and flexible. This applies to all bean types. We'll cover some basic examples when we talk about EJB configuration files later in the chapter.

The EJB specification requires the use of JNDI to look up the deployed beans. For a detailed explanation of looking up the beans in the JNDI, refer to Chapter 8, "Naming and Directory Services with JNDI". Enterprise JavaBeans require the EJB developer to use the `PortableRemoteObject.narrow()` method to cast the object returned from the JNDI lookup; that is, cast the remote object references to the appropriate type. We'll look at this function and all the details about the implementation of an EJB in the next three chapters.

Persistence

This primary service offered by the container is mostly linked with Entity beans, although Stateful Session beans need persistence services when a bean instance is passivated. As earlier mentioned, Entity beans, such as customers and gate agents (as in an airline reservation system), need to be stored in a permanent store to satisfy the durability requirements of these entities.

An Entity bean, as defined earlier, provides two kinds of persistence: container-managed and bean-managed persistence. In the case of container-managed persistence, the container takes responsibility for synchronizing the Entity bean's fields to the corresponding database fields. When the persistence is bean-managed, the bean developer has to take care of implementing the logic for synchronizing the data fields in the Entity bean to the corresponding database fields.

The specification provides two callback methods as part of the Entity bean—`ejbStore()` and `ejbLoad()`—for persisting and retrieving durable data, respectively. Figure 20.1 described all the callback methods defined by the Entity bean interface. For container-managed persistence, the specification only imposes the rule on the EJB vendor to support persistence using these methods—the exact mechanism is left to the vendors themselves. The application server uses the `ejbStore()` and `ejbLoad()` methods to write and read data, respectively. These callback methods make sure that all transactional clients use the latest data from the persistent store. WebLogic Server provides several configuration elements in the WebLogic Server–specific EJB configuration files (`weblogic-ejb-jar.xml` and weblogic-cmp-rdbms-jar.xml) that enable you to configure persistence behavior. This is quite useful when for optimizing Entity beans. We'll go into greater detail on persistence in Chapter 22.

Security

Security is a key concern in any enterprise class business application. EJB has a transparent security framework that allows for securing EJB components with no or little code. The EJB specification addresses the authorization using deployment descriptor elements and supports authentication as well via IIOP.

Authentication validates or verifies the user's identity. One common example of authentication is a username/password combination verified against a persistent data store. Although authentication provides a global verification of the user, it's insufficient if a user must be monitored as he navigates through the different components of the system. With EJB 2.0, the security mechanism can be implemented using the standard Java Authentication and Authorization Service (JAAS)—an integral part of the J2EE platform. This mechanism is in addition to IIOP authentication and is more flexible.

Authorization enables EJB deployers to exercise control over the type of permissions that each user has. Authorization can be granular; that is, you can restrict a user's access to particular subsystems, data, and methods. Authorization can be enforced programmatically or declaratively. In the case of programmatic authorization, the security checks are built in the bean's business logic. For declarative security, the container performs the authorization with the help of the deployment descriptor elements defined in the various EJB descriptors.

The main difference between the two authorization mechanisms is that the container takes care of verifying the user's authorization and permissions instead of the bean code. The deployment descriptor provides the method-permission element tag for securing the methods. The container takes care of generating security checks and the associated exceptions if the user identity fails the check.

As with other services described earlier, declarative security makes a bean easier to maintain in terms of security because the roles and security policies can be changed without touching the bean code. But programmatic security plays a key role for complex security implementations in which certain bean instances have to be controlled separately from other instances belonging to the same class that cannot be done using declarative security.

We'll look at some of the elements from the EJB configuration files that are related to security when we discuss them later in this chapter. At that time, we'll cover some of the common tags for all the EJB types. For a complete description of securing WebLogic-based applications including Enterprise JavaBeans, refer to Part VII, "WebLogic Server Security."

EJB Implementation

So far, we've looked at the different types of EJBs as defined by the specification along with the list of services the EJB container offers. Now let's look at what constitutes an enterprise bean. An Enterprise JavaBean is not a single class. An enterprise bean consists of a set of Java files along with a set of XML files that contain the deployment descriptors describing the enterprise bean. For implementing a Session or Entity bean, the EJB developer has to define the component interfaces, the home interface, and a bean class. In the case of Entity beans, the EJB developer could also define a primary key class. Message-Driven beans are different from the Session and Entity bean types in that they require only the bean class and have no need for interfaces.

The Bean Class

All bean types' bean class implements specialized interfaces that extend from the `javax.ejb.EnterpriseBean` interface. Table 20.3 defines the base classes for the different bean types.

TABLE 20.3 Bean Types and Their Base Interfaces

Bean Type	Base Interface for the Bean Class
Session Bean	javax.ejb.SessionBean
Entity Bean	javax.ejb.EntityBean
Message-Driven Bean	javax.ejb.MessageDrivenBean

Figure 20.4 describes the class hierarchy for the bean classes listed in Table 20.2. The Session and Entity bean classes define the bean's business methods and also define the life cycle–related methods; for example, `create`, `remove`, and so on. The bean class should implement all the methods defined in the component interfaces. The bean class doesn't implement the home or component interfaces directly. The method signatures should match exactly with business methods defined in the home and component interfaces, and should have methods corresponding to non-business methods (for example, life cycle methods such as `create`, `remove`, and so forth) in all interfaces. This is because the EJB compiler generates the objects that actually implement the remote home and remote interfaces.

Because the container automatically invokes Message-Driven beans to process JMS requests, these beans implement only the bean class base interface. The home and component interfaces do not apply to Message-Driven beans. A Message-Driven bean implements `javax.jms.MessageListener` apart from `javax.ejb.MessageDrivenBean`. The `MessageListener` interface defines only one method, `onMessage()`, to handle the JMS requests. The container invokes this method automatically. In the future, the specification might address Message-Driven beans handling other kinds of messages.

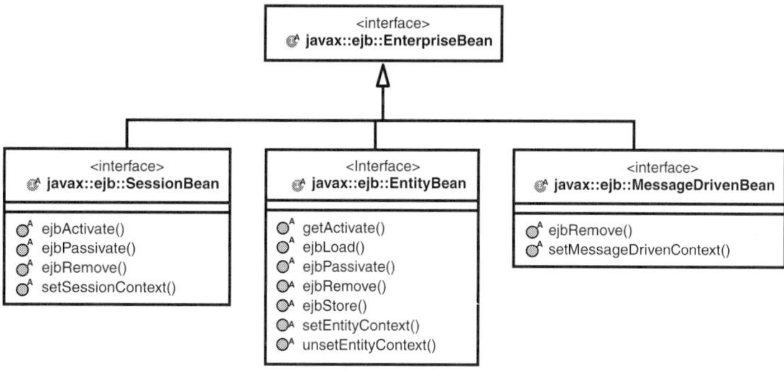

Figure 20.4 Bean class hierarchy.

Remote Interface

The remote interface provides access to the bean's business methods to clients that use the bean. This interface extends from the `javax.ejb.EJBObject` interface, which in turn extends from the `java.rmi.Remote` interface for providing remote connectivity. Figure 20.5 describes the class hierarchy for the remote interface. It contains two sample beans: a Trader Session bean and an Account Entity bean. This interface works with the remote home interface of a bean to provide services to other applications.

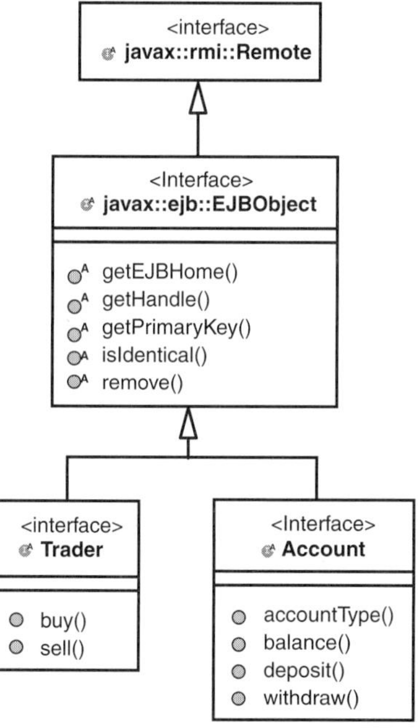

Figure 20.5 Remote interface hierarchy.

EJB Object—javax.ejb.EJBObject

Now let's examine the interface `javax.ejb.EJBObject` from which all bean types' remote interface are extended. This provides the functionality that enables us to use our remote interface over the network using RMI. Apart from this, the `EJBObject` interface provides the client with some very useful methods that describe the bean:

- The `getEJBHome` method on this interface returns a handle to the remote home interface of the bean from which the remote object was obtained. Remote home interfaces are returned as the base type: `javax.ejb.EJBHome`. This interface can then be narrowed to the appropriate type and used. This method is useful when your design moves the remote interface of the bean outside the context in which it has been created. For instance, if you pass the remote interface as a parameter to a method, and the method requires the remote home interface, it can access the remote home interface by invoking this method. This method isn't very useful for the client because the client has the bean's home when it calls a method on that bean, but it provides completeness of EJB's metadata.

- The `getHandle` method returns an object of type `javax.ejb.Handle`. This object is a serializable representation of the remote interface. The client object can serialize this handle and store it for later use. When it again requires access to a remote method, the object can now call the `getEJBObject` method on the handle, as long as the Session bean is still available in the container that generated the handle. If the bean is no longer available, the `getEJBObject` method throws an exception of type `RemoteException`. The only exclusion to this rule is Stateless Session beans because they aren't linked to a single client. This method returns an object that can be cast to the remote interface. When the remote interface has been obtained, the client object can continue to invoke the business methods.

- The `isIdentical` method returns a Boolean indicating whether the `EJBObject` passed as a parameter is identical to the one on which the method is being invoked. Two Stateless Session beans of the same type (that is, their originator home objects come from the same location) are always identical because there is conceptually no difference between the outcomes of an operation on two bean objects of the same type. Therefore, in this one case, this method will always return true. It will also return true when comparing two Entity beans with the same primary key. Note that even when the `isIdentical` method returns true for two objects, the `Object.equal` method might not. This is because, the network-related information that's stored in the `EJBObject` stubs might not match, and the equal method would therefore return false. Using the `isIdentical` method will ignore network-related fields and return the correct result. Additionally, it's good to note that it isn't sufficient that the EJB stub and instance are of the same class—the same home stub must also obtain them. If a single session bean is deployed twice in two different JNDI locations, they will not be identical.

- The `remove` method removes the bean object. For Stateless Session beans, the bean object is not necessarily physically deleted by invoking this method. It might simply be returned to the free pool of bean objects (known as the *method-ready pool*) as illustrated in Figure 20.3. If the client tries to invoke any business method on the remote interface after the `remove` method has been invoked, a `java.rmi.NoSuchObjectException` (a subclass of `RemoteException`) is thrown. For Stateful Session beans, the instance is destroyed. For Entity beans, the data is deleted and the bean instance is moved to the pool or destroyed.
- Note also that the `EJBObject` contains one other method: `getPrimaryKey`. A *primary key* is an object that uniquely identifies an Entity bean among all the available Entity beans. For the sake of this discussion, think of it as mirroring the primary key of the database, although that is not always the case. Thus, primary keys enable the client object to look up data from a persistent store. For more information on primary keys, see Chapter 22. Because Session beans don't have anything to do with persisted data, there is no concept of primary keys for Session beans. Hence, this method is irrelevant for Session beans. The `EJBObject` interface has this method declared in it because the remote interfaces of both Session and Entity beans extend from the interface `EJBObject`. If you try to invoke this method from a session bean, the method throws a `RemoteException`.

Home Interface

The home interface provides applications that want to use the bean access to the bean's life cycle methods. Figure 20.6 illustrates the class hierarchy of the home interface with two examples: `TraderHome` and `AccountHome`. *Life cycle methods* are those used to create new beans, remove existing ones, and find beans based on some criteria. The remote home interface is represented by the interface `javax.ejb.EJBHome`. The bean's remote home interface extends from this interface and provides access to appropriate methods. The `EJBHome` interface, in turn, extends from the `java.rmi.Remote` interface. This interface works along with the remote interface.

Home Object

The remote home interface extends the `EJBHome` interface. This interface provides the remote access functionality to our remote home interface. Apart from this, the `EJBHome` interface also provides the client with some very useful methods that describe the bean.

- The `getHomeHandle` method provided by this interface is very similar to the `getHandle` method of the `EJBObject` interface. This method returns a serializable representation of the remote home object. The object implements the interface `javax.ejb.HomeHandle`. The client can then serialize this form to other clients or for its own future use. When it needs to create another bean instance, it simply re-creates the home object by calling the `getEJBHome` method, which returns the home object that created the handle. This object can then be narrowed to the appropriate remote home object and the bean instances can be created.

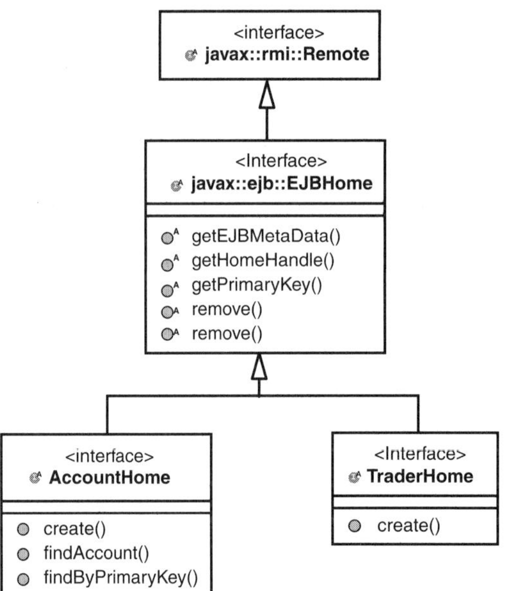

Figure 20.6 Home interface hierarchy.

- The `getEJBMetaData` method returns the metadata that represents the bean. The metadata is returned in an object that implements the `javax.ejb.EJBMetaData` interface. We'll look at the components of the metadata that's returned in this object a little later in the chapter.
- Two versions of the `remove` method are declared in this interface. The first version accepts a `Handle` object as its parameter. The `Handle` object is obtained by invoking the `getHandle` method on the remote object. The effect of invoking this method is the same as invoking the `remove` method on that remote object. When invoked, this method simply releases the Stateless Session bean to the container's free pool and makes it available for other clients. For Stateful Session beans, the bean is destroyed. For Entity beans, the data is deleted and the bean is sent to the pool or destroyed. After this point, if the client tries to use the remote object, a `RemoteException` is thrown. A second version of the `remove` method accepts a primary key as its parameter. As mentioned earlier, primary keys do not mean anything for session beans. Therefore, this method throws a `RemoteException` when invoked.

As mentioned, the `getEJBMetaData` method returns an object of type `EJBMetaData`. This object contains some very important pieces of information that describe the bean. This information is useful for development tools while building applications that use deployed EJBs. Clients that use scripting languages to access the beans can also benefit from this information.

- The `getEJBHome` method returns the remote home object for the bean.
- The `getHomeInterfaceClass` method returns a `Class` that represents the remote home interface of the bean.
- The `getRemoteInterfaceClass` method returns a `Class` that represents the remote interface of the bean.
- The `isSession` method tests whether the bean is a Session bean and returns a `boolean` indicating the result of the test.
- The `isStatelessSession` method tests whether the bean is a Stateless Session bean and returns a `boolean` indicating the same.
- The `getPrimaryKeyClass` method returns the class that represents the primary key for Entity beans. For Session beans, this method should not be invoked because a primary key does not mean anything to a Session bean. If the method is invoked, it throws a `RuntimeException`.

Table 20.4 lists the values returned by the two functions—namely, `isStatelessSession` and `isSession`—related to identifying bean types based on the available session.

TABLE 20.4 Bean Types

Bean Type	isStatelessSession()	isSession()
Stateless Session Bean	true	true
Stateful Session Bean	false	true
Entity Bean	false	false
Message-Driven Bean	Not applicable (no home)	Not applicable (no home)

Local and Local Home Interfaces

If the local home interface of the bean extends from the interface `javax.ejb.EJBLocalHome` instead of the `javax.ejb.EJBHome` interface, other beans residing within the same container can efficiently use the bean. This interface offers similar bean life cycle methods as those offered by the remote home interface. The difference between the two is that when beans are created using this interface, no network connectivity is involved because both the requested and the requestor exist within the same container. This drastically improves performance for such local access. This interface works in conjunction with the local home interface.

The local interface of a bean is similar to the remote interface in that this interface also provides access to the business methods provided by the bean class. This interface works with the local home interface to provide access to the bean instance for other beans within the same container. All method calls made using this interface avoid network protocols, and thus improve performance. The local interface of a bean extends the `javax.ejb.EJBLocalObject` interface.

The same bean may provide both local and remote access, or just any one of them, by including the appropriate set of home and object interfaces in its deployment descriptor. There is a downside to using local interfaces: It reduces the location transparency of the beans. So, if you're sure that the objects will always colocate, give preference to using local interfaces.

TIP

Remote access involves passing parameters by value (copying), whereas local access involves passing them by reference (sharing). If a bean tries to modify its parameters and you switch its access from local to remote (or vice versa), the results are unpredictable. To avoid being trapped, do not modify parameters.

The local component interfaces have been optimized in such a way that any call made using a local interface is made as if it were just another call to any other object on the JVM. This means that with local interfaces, there is no requirement for the parameter objects to be serializable and they are passed by reference to the bean.

The local interface provides similar methods as the `remote` interface. There are a couple of differences between these two interfaces. All other methods provided by the `EJBObject` interface are also provided by the `EJBLocalObject` interface and behave in exactly the same way. We'll list only the differences between the two interfaces here.

- The method `getEJBHome` in the `EJBObject` interface is not available in the `EJBLocalObject` interface. Instead, this interface declares another method, called `getEJBLocalHome`, which returns the local home as an object of type `EJBLocalHome`. This object may then be cast into the appropriate local home and used.
- Unlike the `EJBObject` interface, the `EJBLocalObject` interface does not define a `getHandle` method. Because serialization is not required between collocated objects, this method does not make sense.
- None of the methods throw `RemoteExceptions`.

The `EJBLocalHome` interface, unlike the `EJBHome` interface, has just a single `remove` method that takes a primary key as its parameter. Needless to say, this method cannot be invoked for Session beans. If it is, the method throws a `RemoveException`.

Primary Key

This is a special class that pertains only to Entity bean implementations. It provides an identifier for the database record that the Entity bean represents. This class has to implement `java.io.Serializable`. This class will be used in the finder method (`findByPrimaryKey()` method) of the home interface to locate the specific entity. This is covered in detail in the chapter on Entity beans (see Chapter 22, "Working with Entity Beans").

EJB Exceptions

Because EJBs conform to RMI-IIOP standard, all methods in the remote EJB object and remote home interface have to throw remote exceptions (`java.rmi.RemoteException`). Remote exceptions indicate a network failure or other fatal situations. But the local interfaces and local home are different from the remote counter parts in that they don't throw remote exceptions at all. This is quite obvious because no network functionality is involved when using local interfaces.

EJB separates system-level exceptions from application exceptions. A system-level exception might include fatal situations such as a database failure, a server crash, and so on. The generated implementation classes might handle these errors and provide transparent failover in some cases (such as a server crash) by moving to another bean deployed in the clustered server. All application exceptions are always thrown back to the client. The application exceptions include bean-defined exceptions such as `FinderException` and `CreateException` as well as business exceptions.

EJB Naming Conventions

Let's establish some naming conventions to provide clarity for our discussion of EJBs in the next three chapters. We look at these conventions with the help of one of the real-world examples: an airline reservation system that we use as a business case to explain the session beans in the next chapter. Although we speak about an EJB as a whole, we'll refer to it using its business name with the suffix `EJB`. For example, `AirlineReservationEJB` and `AirlineReservation` EJB. This identifies the EJB as a whole and not the bean class alone. That is, you won't find a file called `AirlineReservationEJB.java`. Instead that name refers to a set of `.java` files. Similarly, when we refer to a Session bean, or just a bean, we're referring to the bean as a whole, which includes all constituents as listed in the previous sections. This goes for Entity beans and Message-Driven beans.

When naming a Bean class, we'll use its business name with the suffix `Bean`; for example, `AirlineReservationBean`. We'll also distinguish between the different types of interfaces by using appropriate suffixes. A remote home interface will be referred to using the business name of the bean along with the suffix `RemoteHome`. For example, the remote home interface for the `AirlineReservation` EJB is called `AirlineReservationRemoteHome`. On the other hand, a local home interface will hold the suffix `LocalHome` to distinguish it from the remote counterpart (for example, `AirlineReservationLocalHome`). A remote interface will be denoted with the business name and the suffix `RemoteObject`, whereas its local object counterpart will have the suffix `Local` appended to the business name. For example, `AirlineReservationRemoteObject` denotes a remote interface for the `AirlineReservation` EJB, whereas `AirlineReservationLocalObject` denotes its local interface.

Note also that when we refer to a *client* in our discussion, we aren't necessarily referring to a user interface unless it is explicitly specified. We're referring to any object that uses the EJB—the client to the bean.

EJB Deployment Descriptors

Before we can attempt to deploy our bean, we have to create a set of deployment descriptors that essentially describe the bean to the container and identify several deployment-time properties. An individual playing the role of a deployer in the application context typically manages these files. The descriptors tell the container how to manage the bean at runtime. Think of the deployment descriptor as a property file that's used by several standalone applications. The advantage of these files is that the code and the runtime properties of an application are clearly demarcated, which enables us to change the runtime properties without rebuilding the application. Deployment descriptors also play a similar role in the world of EJBs.

Some of the information that the descriptors tell the container includes the JNDI name where the bean will be looked up, security, transactional context, and so on. As is obvious from the previous sections, the code did not address any of these properties. An individual who plays the role of a developer in an application context writes the code. This demarcation clearly allows the separation of the two roles. The developer simply assumes that some things, such as transactions and security, will be available when the bean is deployed. The deployer makes these available by editing the deployment descriptors.

There are essentially two deployment descriptors that are needed for deploying a bean into a WebLogic container. A third deployment descriptor is needed for Entity beans. All these are files in the XML format and can be edited using any text editor. Because of this, it's suggested that you familiarize yourselves with the basics of writing an XML file before you continue with this section. This section will address only the format of these XML files as advocated by the specification and WebLogic. For the sake of brevity, this section won't address all possible fields that could be present in the deployment descriptor. You can refer to Sun's and BEA's documentation for a complete list of fields that go into these descriptors as well as the respective DTDs.

These deployment descriptors should be present under a directory called `META-INF/`, which is at the same level as your class files and packages. For instance, the base directory test would contain the packages `com/wlsunleashed/.../*.class` and `META-INF/` as its subdirectories.

The required descriptor files for deploying the different types of beans are as follows:

- The first XML file is called `ejb-jar.xml`, which is part of the EJB 2.0 specification. This file defines several standard parameters that define the bean, such as its home, remote, local home, local object, and bean classes, transaction type supported, whether it's a Stateless or Stateful bean, and so forth. Later in this section, we take a detailed look at some of the attributes of this XML file.

- The second XML file complements the `ejb-jar.xml` file and is called `weblogic-ejb-jar.xml`. This file defines several properties that are specific to the deployment of the bean in WebLogic Server. The properties defined in this file include the JNDI name of the bean, the clustering properties of the bean, the properties affecting the bean's method-ready pool, and more.
- The last of the XML deployment descriptors is the `weblogic-cmp-rdbms-jar.xml`. This is specific to CMP Entity beans and is used to represent Entity beans that are handled by the WebLogic RDBMS CMP persistence type by defining persistence services, such as synchronization of the instance fields with the corresponding fields in the database.

The deployment descriptors can be edited using a text editor or with an XML editor. The descriptor elements can be viewed through the Descriptors tab as shown in Figure 20.7. This is useful for all deployed beans. The XML descriptors can be edited using the WebLogic Builder, which is covered later in the chapter.

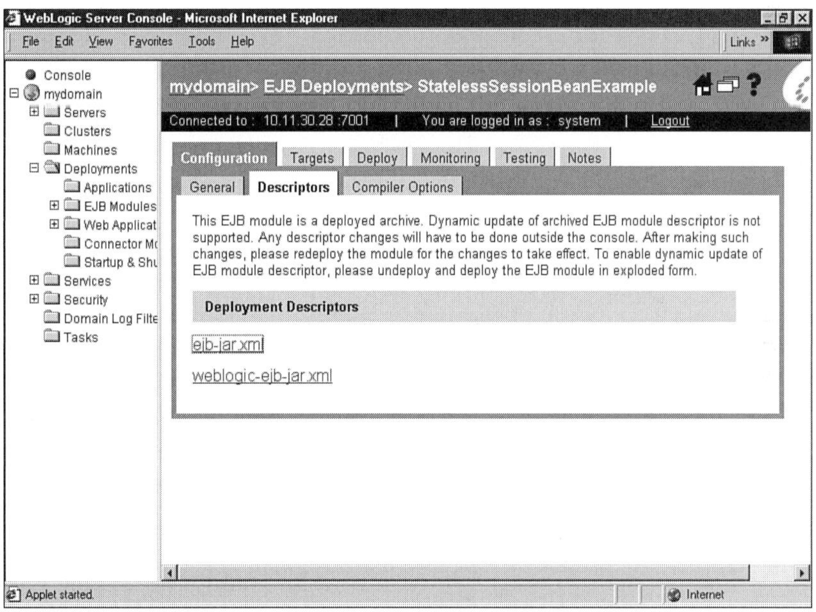

Figure 20.7 WebLogic EJB tuning using the Console.

J2EE Descriptor—ejb-jar.xml

The first deployment descriptor is the `ejb-jar.xml`. This descriptor is part of the Sun Microsystems' EJB specification. This file describes several properties of the bean to the container, which uses it to identify the runtime behavior of the bean. In this section, let's look at some of the properties that are common to most bean types and specific deployment elements and will be covered in detail in the next three chapters. Deployed beans are configured using the deployment elements defined in Table 20.5. The parent element for these elements is the bean type—that is, Session, Entity, or Message-Driven—that's defined under the `enterprise-bean` deployment element.

TABLE 20.5 EJB JAR Deployment Elements

Element Name	Description
ejb-name	Represents the EJB name. This identifies the bean in the container and should be unique. In our naming convention, this should be the bean name with EJB suffix; for example, AirlineReservationEJB.
home	
local-home	Represents the fully qualified name of the EJB's home interface and the local home interface, respectively. Does not apply for Message-Driven beans. For example, AirlineReservationRemoteHome and AirlineReservationLocalHome.
remote	
local	Represents the fully qualified name of the EJB's remote interface and local interface, respectively. Does not apply for Message-Driven beans. For example, AirlineReservationRemoteObject and AirlineReservationLocalObject.
ejb-class	Represents the fully qualified name of the EJB's bean class. For example, AirlineReservationBean.
transaction-type	Defines whether the transaction is container-managed or bean-managed. This does not apply to Entity beans.

The configuration section must contain at least one of the two pairs of home and component interfaces: either the remote interfaces, or the local interfaces, or both. Apart from these elements, the `enterprise-beans` deployment element can also list information about entries that the bean's implementation expects to be present in its environment at runtime, resource references, references to other beans that are used by this bean, security identities, and so on. We'll go over all these optional entries in reasonable detail in the other EJB chapters.

After the EJB deployer has defined all the beans that form the application, the deployer has to express some of the properties that describe the assembly of the beans in this deployment using the `<assembly-descriptor>` deployment element and major element within the `<ejb-jar>` stanza. This stanza describes two key elements of bean deployment: the transaction attributes of the bean's methods and the security. We'll look at these aspects in detail in later sections of this chapter. For a full definition of the deployment elements in the `ejb-jar.xml`, refer to the DTD defined at `http://java.sun.com/dtd/ejb-jar_2_0.dtd`. Listing 20.1 illustrates a simple bean example. This defines a Stateless Session bean: `TraderEJB`. In the `assembly-descriptor` element, we define a method tag that defines the transaction properties of this bean. In this case, all methods have a transaction attribute of `Required` that was explained earlier in the chapter.

LISTING 20.1 ejb-jar.xml

```
<ejb-jar>
 <enterprise-beans>
  <session>
   <ejb-name>TraderEJB</ejb-name>
   <home>wlsunleashed.statelessSession.TraderHome</home>
   <remote>wlsunleashed.statelessSession.Trader</remote>
   <ejb-class>wlsunleashed.statelessSession.TraderBean</ejb-class>
   <session-type>Stateless</session-type>
   <transaction-type>Container</transaction-type>
   <env-entry>
    <env-entry-name></env-entry-name>
    <env-entry-type>java.lang.Double</env-entry-type>
    <env-entry-value>10.0</env-entry-value>
   </env-entry>
  </session>
 </enterprise-beans>
 <assembly-descriptor>
  <container-transaction>
   <method>
    <ejb-name>statelessSession</ejb-name>
    <method-name>*</method-name>
   </method>
   <trans-attribute>Required</trans-attribute>
  </container-transaction>
 </assembly-descriptor>
</ejb-jar>
```

WebLogic-Specific Descriptors

This section describes the WebLogic-specific deployment descriptors that contain elements specific to the WebLogic Server and not identified by the EJB 2.0 specification.

weblogic-ejb-jar.xml

This file contains more properties of the bean's deployment, but only those that are specific to WebLogic Server, including concurrency, caching, and clustering of the beans. This file also maps different resources (JDBC `DataSources`, EJBs, security roles, names, and so on) identified in the `ejb-jar.xml` to actual WebLogic server resources. The DTD governing this XML file can be found at the URL `http://www.bea.com/servers/wls810/dtd/weblogic-ejb-jar.dtd`. At deployment time, the XML parser used by WebLogic Server verifies the XML file against the rules mentioned in the DTD and ensures that the XML follows all the mentioned rules.

20

The `weblogic-ejb-jar.xml` file contains one root-level element called `<weblogic-ejb-jar>`. Within this root element, you may have the following element stanzas:

- Definitely one and possibly more `<weblogic-enterprise-bean>` stanzas that correspond to the `<enterprise-bean>` stanzas of the `ejb-jar.xml` file
- Optional security role assignments to the roles defined in the `ejb-jar.xml` (`<security-role-assignment>`)
- Optional transaction isolation settings on a method level of the bean; this applies only to Entity beans (`<transaction-isolation>`)
- Optional idempotent methods that can be called over and over again producing the same results, without affecting the integrity of the data (`<idempotent-methods>`)

Among these, the most important and mandatory stanza is the `<weblogic-enterprise-bean>` stanza. Here, we look into the contents of this stanza for a Stateless Session bean. Each of these properties identifies several parameters to the WebLogic container that further define the deployment properties of the beans. In this section, you can read about some of the important properties that can be defined for a session bean in a `<weblogic-ejb-jar>` stanza. Several other properties can be defined here. Refer to BEA's documentation for a complete list of possible parameters that can be defined in this XML file.

- The tag `<ejb-name>` identifies the EJB for which the following properties are defined. This name must match that of one bean that is defined in the `ejb-jar.xml` file.
- The `<stateless-session-descriptor>` stanza that identifies several properties for a stateless session bean.
- The `<transaction-descriptor>` stanza that identifies transaction related properties for the bean. More about this tag in the section that discusses transactions later in this chapter.
- The <reference-descriptor> stanza that concretely identifies all the resources that are referenced in the `ejb-jar.xml` file. More on this tag in the section that discusses bean references later in this chapter.
- A `<enable-call-by-reference>` property that tells the container whether it should use call by reference for making local EJB calls. By default, call by reference is disabled. When it's turned on and a client located in the same container as a bean invokes this bean using remote interfaces, WLS automatically optimizes the call, bypassing the RMI communication. The remote object will in effect perform like a local object. By default, parameters are passed by value. This parameter is set either to `True` or `False`. By default, the WebLogic Server container disables call by reference. Enabling call by reference causes any changes that are made to the parameter objects to be visible to the caller. If your bean can handle this, you can explicitly enable call by reference.

- The name under which this bean has to be loaded to be looked up remotely. This can be done by using the `<jndi-name>` tag. Use this tag only if you're using remote interfaces.
- The name under which this bean has to be loaded to be looked up locally. This can be done by using the `<local-jndi-name>` tag. Use this tag only if you are using local interfaces.

For a detailed reference on the parameters in the `weblogic-ejb-jar.xml`, refer to the BEA documentation at `http://edocs.bea.com/wls/docs81/ejb/reference.html`. Listing 20.2 is a simple example of a WebLogic EJB deployment descriptor.

LISTING 20.2 weblogic-ejb-jar.xml

```
<weblogic-ejb-jar>
 <weblogic-enterprise-bean>
  <ejb-name>TraderEJB</ejb-name>
  <jndi-name>wlsunleahesd-TraderHome</jndi-name>
 </weblogic-enterprise-bean>
</weblogic-ejb-jar>
```

weblogic-cmp-rdbms-jar.xml

This XML deployment descriptor file for CMP Entity beans is WebLogic Server–specific. It's used to define entity relationships managed by CMP as well as parameters such as the data source and the table name for the Entity bean. For a full list of deployment elements, along with the syntax, refer to the BEA documentation at `http://edocs.bea.com/wls/docs81/ejb/EJB_reference.html` and the DTD documentation at `http://www.bea.com/servers/wls810/dtd/weblogic-rdbms20-persistence-810.dtd`.

Creating the Deployment Descriptor

As mentioned in the previous sections, the deployment descriptors are simply XML files and can be created using any text editor. But you typically don't start off creating the descriptors from scratch. WebLogic provides some handy-dandy tools that can be used to create a basic set of descriptors for your bean deployment. You can execute the class file `weblogic.ant.taskdefs.ejb20.DDInit` and pass to it the base directory of the classes you want to deploy. This tool scans through the class files and creates the deployment files for you. This tool uses Ant to generate the deployment descriptors. The generated deployment descriptors conform to the EJB 2.0 specification. For more information about using this tool, refer to BEA's documentation at `http://edocs.bea.com/wls/docs81/toolstable/ToolsTable.html`.

Alternatively, deployment descriptors can be created using the WebLogic Builder utility packaged with your WebLogic installation. The next section focuses on using this tool to both create a basic set of deployment descriptors and to deploy your bean into the WebLogic container.

EJB Deployment

The EJB deployment phase follows the EJB development life cycle and generates the deployment descriptors. Deploying a bean into a container is the mechanism by which the container makes the bean ready to process client requests. EJB deployment can be done using one of many ways described here. But before we go into that, let's look at a simple development tool and the directory structure for packaging the EJBs, followed by the different tools used for EJB deployment.

EJBGen

EJBGen is part of the rich set of WebLogic Server utilities that enable faster EJB development. This is an EJB 2.0 code generator. This tool uses the special `JavaDoc` tags that are defined in the bean class to generate the home and remote interfaces along with the deployment descriptors. This greatly helps EJB source maintenance because only the bean class needs to be maintained.

EJBGen is implemented as a doclet and the simplest invocation is as follows

```
javadoc -docletpath <weblogic_library_path>\weblogic.jar -doclet weblogic.tools.
➥ejbgen.EJBGenXXXBean.java
```

where XXXBean.java is the bean class. If EJBGen is used on a bean class that has dependencies with other bean classes, specify the dependent classes in the same command. If `XXXBean.java` is linked to `YYYBean.java` then the above command will be as follows

```
javadoc -docletpath <weblogic_library_path>\weblogic.jar -doclet weblogic.tools.
➥ejbgen.EJBGenXXXBean.java YYYBean.java
```

Let's look at a simple Stateless Session bean example and how we can leverage EJBGen for better code maintenance and development. Let's use the simple Stateless Session bean `TraderBean.java` example provided with the WebLogic Server installation. The related files for this example is present under the `samples/server/examples/src/ejb20/basic/beanManaged` directory contained under the WebLogic Server directory. This bean provides two business methods for buying and selling stocks along with other life-cycle methods defined for the Session bean. In order for the EJBGen to automatically generate the deployment descriptors with the appropriate values, the following snippet with the EJBGen Javadoc tags has to be added to the class-level comment.

```
@ejbgen:session
   ejb-name = statelessSession
    default-transaction = Required
@ejbgen:jndi-name
  remote = ejb20-statelessSession-TraderHome
@ejbgen:ejb-client-jar
   file-name = ejb20_basic_statelessSession_client.jar
@ejbgen:env-entry
  name=WEBL
  type=java.lang.Double
  value=10.0
@ejbgen:env-entry
  name=INTL
  type=java.lang.Double
  value=15.0
@ejbgen:env-entry
  name=tradeLimit
  type=java.lang.Integer
  value=500
```

For the EJBGen to generate the Home and Remote interfaces, the business methods `buy()` and `sell()` add the javadoc tag `@ejbgen:remote-method` to the respective method comment to indicate that these methods have to be exposed as remote methods. After making the changes, on invocation of the following command

```
javadoc -docletpath c:\bea\weblogic81\server\lib\weblogic.jar -doclet
➥weblogic.tools.ejbgen.EJBGenTraderBean.java
```

the deployment descriptors and the Home and Remote interfaces for the TraderBean will be generated. EJBGen also provides a list of options that provides greater control to the user with respect to the generated code.

For a complete list of options and supported tags, refer to `http://e-docs.bea.com/wls/docs81/ejb/EJBGen_reference.html`.

Packaging EJBs

The bean has to be packaged in a particular directory structure so that it can be deployed correctly. The base directory of the bean should contain the classes within the directory tree represented by its package structure. Apart from the classes, the base directory should also contain a `META-INF` directory, which should hold the two deployment descriptor files (`ejb-jar.xml`, `weblogic-ejb-jar.xml` or `weblogic-cmp-rdbms-jar.xml`, if applicable). The base directory becomes the root of the JAR file that's created for deployment.

```
{ejb_base_directory}
---- com/.../*.class
---- META-INF/ejb-jar.xml
---- META-INF/weblogic-ejb-jar.xml
---- META-INF/weblogic-cmp-rdbms-jar.xml
```

In earlier versions of WebLogic Server, there was no tool to compile all related modules within an archive file and make it a deployable unit. The appc compiler performs all the predeployment validation and executes the ejbc compiler on the validated module. The validation performed takes care of specifications compliance of the deployment descriptors. For the convenience of the developer, WebLogic Server also provides an `Ant` task to use the appc compiler. For a complete list of options available for the appc compiler and how to use this tool, refer to `http://edocs.bea.com/wls/docs81/ejb/EJB_tools.html`.

WebLogic Builder Tool

WebLogic provides a very handy tool called WebLogic Builder, which can be used to assemble your bean module and generate and edit the deployment descriptors. You'll also be able to deploy the bean using this tool. If you're using Windows, this program is available from the Start menu, under Programs→BEA WebLogic Platform 8.1→Other Development Tools→WebLogic Builder.

You can also start this from the Command Prompt. First, set your environment by invoking the `setEnv` scripts that you can find in your domain directory. This sets your CLASSPATH to include the relevant JAR files of WebLogic. After you've set the environment, invoke the builder tool by executing the following command:

```
java weblogic.marathon.Main
```

This displays a Swing-based GUI. Alternatively, you can use the prepackaged script `startWLBuilder.sh` (Unix) or `startWLBuilder.cmd` (Windows) that comes with the standard WebLogic Server installation. These files are presented in the `server/bin` directory under the WebLogic root directory.

Open the base directory where your bean classes are stored by clicking on the File→Open menu selection. If you're opening your bean module for the first time and if you don't already have a default set of deployment descriptors, the tool asks whether you want the tool to generate a default set of descriptors for you. Clicking Yes on the pop-up message box generates both the `ejb-jar.xml` and the `weblogic-ejb-jar.xml` for the beans. Following this, the tool opens the bean module and splits up the view into three windows, as shown in Figure 20.8.

The top-left part of the view (left window) lists all the available beans in the module. Under each bean, it lists three parameters: `Tuning`, `Methods`, and `Resources`. The top-right portion of the view (right window) has a tabbed view, which changes based on which subtitle you've clicked on in the left window. The bottom portion of the view is reserved for displaying status messages and errors.

When you have clicked on the topmost entry in the left window that indicates the path of the bean module, the right window enables you to select general options such as roles. We'll discuss roles when dealing with security for session beans. Clicking on the bean name on the left window—`statelessSession`, for example—changes the tabs in the right window. The `statelessSession` is from one of the basic EJB examples packaged within the standard WebLogic Server installation. Now you find three tabs: General, Classes, and Advanced. In the General tab, you can specify the EJB name, the transaction type (Container or Bean), the JNDI name for remote and local lookups, and whether the bean is a Stateful or Stateless Session bean.

In the Classes tab, you can specify the classes that represent the remote home, remote, local home, and local interfaces and the bean class.

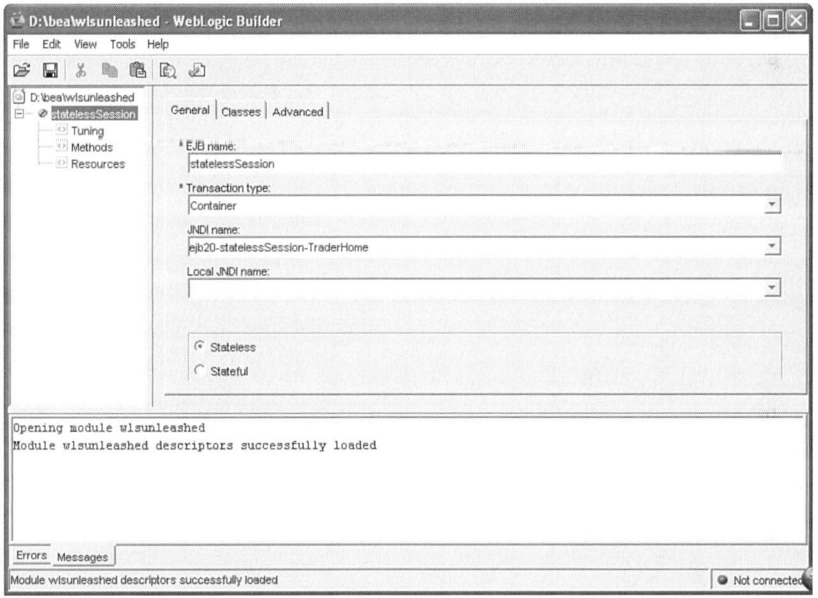

Figure 20.8 WebLogic Builder tool.

With the information given so far, Builder can generate deployment descriptors. When you're done with deployment descriptor generation, you can generate the JAR file that contains your bean modules by clicking the File→Archive menu item, after saving the bean module. This produces a JAR file ready to be compiled by the WebLogic EJB compiler.

After you generate the JAR file, you must validate the deployment descriptors. This can be done by clicking on the Tools→Validate Descriptors menu item. This is an optional step. If you skip it, the server will do it for you when you actually deploy. This is okay for development time, but at production time, it's definitely a good idea to validate the descriptors long before they are deployed. The validation process also generates the RMI stubs and skeletons necessary to make the bean work over the network by invoking the EJBC compiler. During this process, your bean module is checked against several rules that are laid forth by the EJB specification. Correct any reported errors and redo the appropriate steps. At the end of the validation step, the messages window will have the message `ejbc successful`, as shown in Figure 20.9.

You can now deploy the bean by using the Builder tool. For this, you must have WebLogic server running. Click on the menu item Tools→Deploy Module. This first attempts to connect to the running WebLogic Server. It pops up a window that lists the attributes that it can use to connect to the server. Modify these attributes appropriately and click on Connect. After the Builder application connects with the server, you'll see the next window pop up to tell you some information about where the bean is about to be deployed, and also to enable you to specify the name for the bean. This view is presented in Figure 20.10. After you click on Deploy Module, the bean is deployed in the WebLogic Server container. The status bar of the builder tool tells you whether or not the deployment was successful.

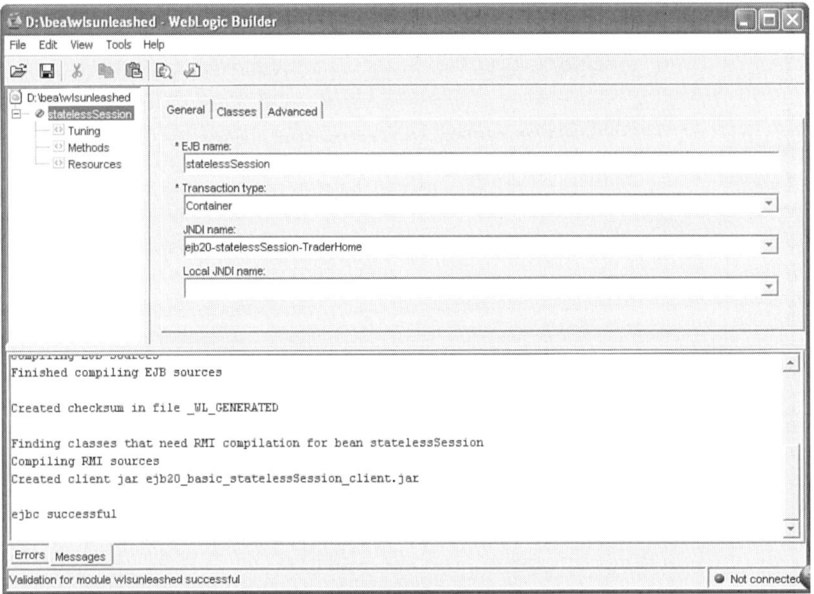

Figure 20.9 EJB Build using the WebLogic Builder tool.

Deploying Using the Console

Alternatively, an EJB can be deployed using the WebLogic Console. This supposes that you've properly packaged your bean beforehand. There is some flexibility between a remote deployment and a local deployment.

Let's look at the local deployment first. Start your WebLogic Server and the WebLogic Console. Navigate to the link Deployments→Applications under your domain in the left-side tree view. Right-clicking this node pops up a menu that provides you with the option to configure a new application. Clicking on this menu item changes the right-side window. Here you'll be able to locate the JAR/EAR file that you originally generated using the Builder tool. If the file isn't present in the list, it can be uploaded to the staging area at this time. See Figure 20.11 for a presentation of this process. Note that you can also select an exploded directory under which the elements of the bean class are located, but let's do it with the uploaded archive file (JAR format) for now.

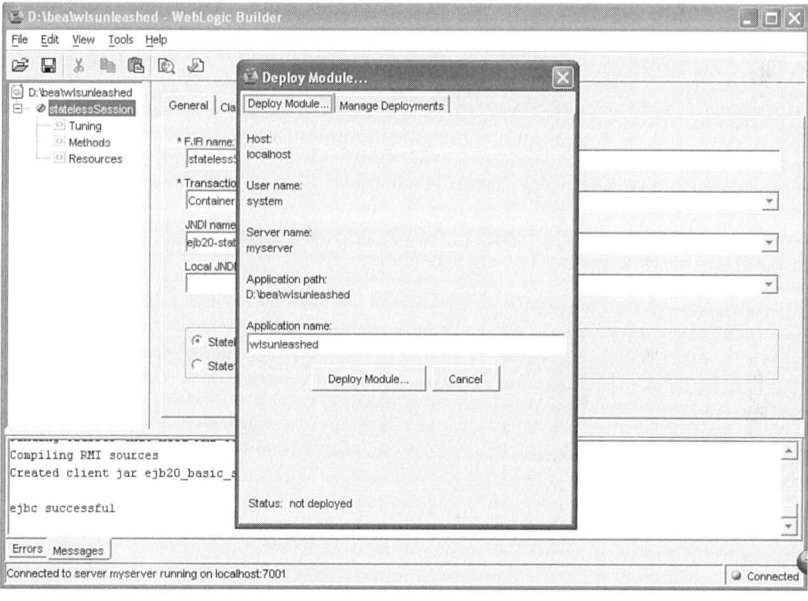

Figure 20.10 Deploying a bean using the WebLogic Builder tool.

When you click on Select next to the JAR/EAR file, the view changes to enable you to specify the targets for the deployment. It also enables you to change the name of the component, if necessary. Choose the server from the Available Servers list and move it to the Target Servers list. This can be seen in Figure 20.12. Because our sample WebLogic Server environment is a single server environment using autodeployment, there's no need to choose a specific target (the administration server is automatically targeted).

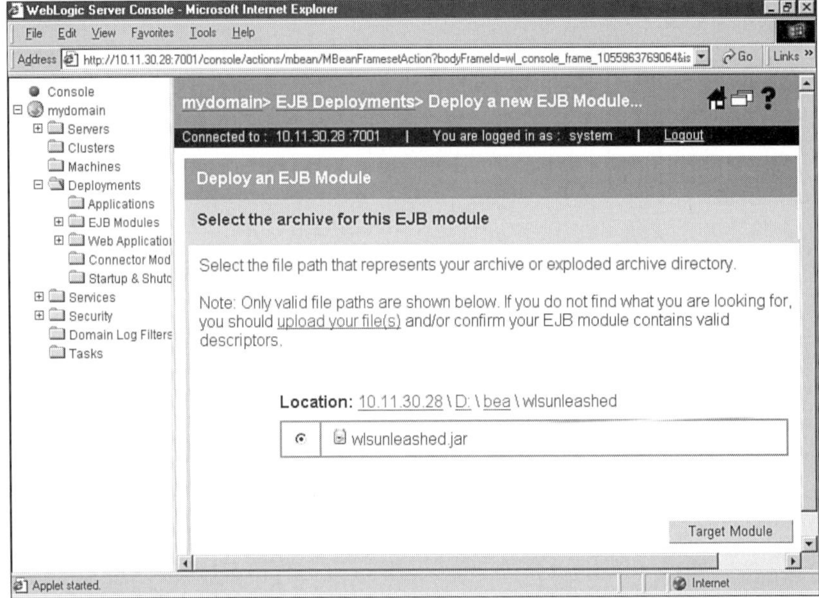

Figure 20.11 Deploying a bean using the WebLogic Console—pick the JAR.

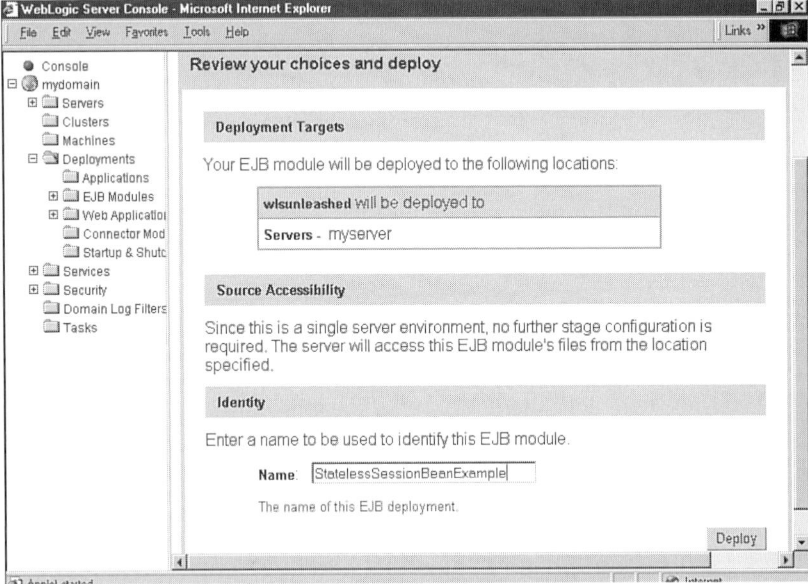

Figure 20.12 Deploying a bean using the WebLogic Console—finishing up.

After this, click on the Deploy button, which displays the deployment status on the screen. The screen is refreshed automatically every 10 seconds. Finally, when the deployment succeeds, the screen will display a view as shown in Figure 20.13.

Alternatively, in a remote deployment using the Console, the deployed application can reside anywhere the user wants. It is uploaded from that directory using the hyperlink and the application is then targeted to the servers, if necessary.

> **TIP**
>
> WebLogic Server collects a lot of information about the deployed EJB and presents it inside the Console in the Tuning tab under the Deployments→EJB Modules menu. The parameters displayed there greatly help in the runtime monitoring of the deployed EJBs and for addressing any performance issues. For a complete list of parameters, refer to `http://edocs.bea.com/wls/docs81/ejb/runtime_monitor.html`.

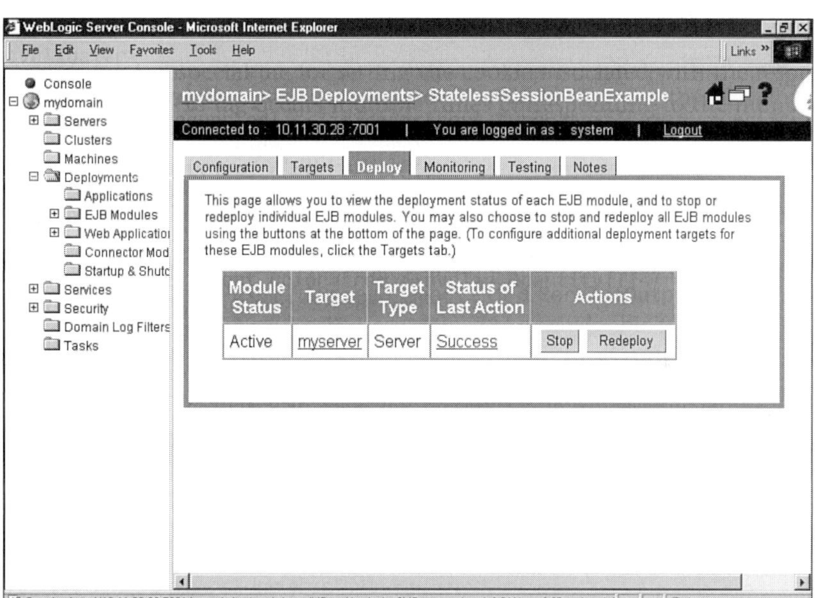

Figure 20.13 Deploying a bean using the WebLogic Console—Done!

Using the weblogic.Deployer Utility

A third way to deploy the bean to the server is by the use of the `weblogic.Deployer` command-line utility. To use this utility to deploy your bean, use the following command line:

```
$ java weblogic.Deployer -adminurl
➥ http://localhost:7001 -name STATELESSSESSION
➥ -user system -targets myserver
➥ -source ./STATELESSSESSION.jar -activate

Enter a password for the user "system":
Operation started, waiting for notifications...
....
#TaskID Action     Status Target     Type  Application   Source
0    Activate    Success myserver    Server STATELESSSESSION
d:\Weblogic_Unleashed\projects\STATELESSSESSION.jar
$
```

Here, the `-adminurl` parameter identifies the URL of the administration server of your application. `-name` is the name of the application, and `-user` identifies the user ID. The `-source` parameter identifies the source archive file or directory from which the files should be deployed into the server. When invoked, the server requests the password for the specified user ID. After you enter the password, the server displays the status of the deployment as shown in the preceding listing.

The Deployer utility takes a lot of parameters. Full documentation of this utility is available on BEA's Web site at `http://edocs.bea.com/wls/docs81/deployment/tools.html`.

TIP

WebLogic Server allows individual EJB classes to be reloaded without the need to redeploy the entire EJB module. This comes in handy during the development phase when changes to the code are frequent. This feature is facilitated with the help of the individual EJB classloader for implementation classes.

Other EJB Features

So far, we've seen the major components that make up Enterprise JavaBeans, including the classes, deployment descriptors, and ways to deploy the beans in a WebLogic EJB container. Now let's briefly look over some of the other features that form an integral part of the EJB specifications.

EJB Security

WebLogic Server provides several security features, which are used by your application in conjunction with the application's security model. The security model is defined by using the appropriate attributes of the deployment descriptors we covered earlier in the chapter. WebLogic Server's security features are based on the concept of security roles. A *security role* represents the function played by a user in the application context. In an airline reservation application, gate agents and ticketing agents could be two of the security roles in the application context.

The EJB deployer can define method permissions (both in the home and the remote interfaces) to security roles. For an airline reservation application example, the business method `reserveSeats` is accessible to ticketing agents, whereas a specialized business method such as `reserveSeatsInLastMinute` would be accessible to gate agents for obvious reasons. If the client's identity is associated with a security role that has permissions on a method, the container allows the method to go through. If not, the container throws a `RemoteException` to the remote client, or an `EJBException` to the local client, without letting the method call go through.

Defining the application security model involves three steps. First, you define security roles. Next, you declare permissions on a method level to each security role. Finally, you associate users or principals to different security roles.

Defining Security Roles

Security roles can be defined by using the `<security-role>` stanza within the `<assembly-descriptor>` block of the `ejb-jar.xml` deployment descriptor. This stanza can contain a description and a role name for the role that you're defining. Listing 20.3 defines two security roles that will be used in an airline reservation application (gate agents and ticketing agents).

LISTING 20.3 Security Role

```
<!-- At the end of the file -->
<assembly-descriptor>
  <security-role>
    <description>
      Users performing this role are the
      Gate agents for the airline.
    </description>
    <role-name>GateAgent</role-name>
  </security-role>
  <security-role>
    <description>
      Users performing this role are the
      Ticketing agents for the airline.
    </description>
    <role-name>TicketingAgent</role-name>
  </security-role>
<assembly-descriptor>
```

The role names have no significance, except that they represent a logical business function that individuals playing this role will perform. Role names can be anything as long as they're descriptive. Note that the <assembly-descriptor> is not associated with any single bean. It's shared across all the beans that are defined in the same deployment descriptor. This gives you the benefit of defining the roles once, and defining method permissions across beans for the same role names.

TIP

WebLogic Server provides its own set of security information that can override the deployment descriptor's roles. For a complete understanding of creating these roles and assignment refer to Part VII of this book, and also look at http://edocs.bea.com/wls/docs81/secwlres/wlres.html.

Declarative Security

Let's look at the last step in the EJB declarative security framework. The first step in defining the declarative security model is to create security roles as seen earlier. The next step is to associate permissions to methods for the different security roles. This is done in the ejb-jar.xml deployment descriptor by using the <method-permission> block. One of these blocks maps the role name with the method to which permission is associated. You can specify the wildcard character (*) in the <method-name> attribute to give permissions to all methods in the bean. You may also define attributes to the methods to provide different permissions to different flavors of the same method. The container always chooses the most specific permission definition for any given method. An existing combination indicates a granted permission. More than one role can be given permission to access the same method. To do this, define multiple <method-permission> blocks.

These blocks appear immediately after the <security-role> blocks within the <assembly-descriptor> stanza. Listing 20.4 defines method permissions for the two methods in our example.

LISTING 20.4 Method Permissions

```
<method-permission>
.   <role-name>GateAgent</role-name>
  <method>
.     <ejb-name>AirlineShoppingCartBean</ejb-name>
.     <method-name>reserveSeatsInLastMinute</method-name>
  </method>
</method-permission>
<method-permission>
  <role-name>TicketingAgent</role-name>
 <method>
.     <ejb-name>AirlineShoppingCartBean</ejb-name>
```

LISTING 20.4 Continued

```
.       <method-name>*</method-name>
.     </method>
  </method-permission>
  <method-permission>
    <unchecked/>
    <method>
      <ejb-name>AirlineShoppingCartBean</ejb-name>
.       <method-name>searchFlights</method-name>
.     </method>
  </method-permission>
```

In this listing, it's quite evident that we provide access rights to `GateAgents` to the `reserveSeatsInLastMinute` method and provide access rights to `TicketingAgents` to all methods. Now take a look at the third method permission stanza (in the bold lines). Here, we define a method permission to the `searchFlights` method, but without a `role-name`. Instead of the `role-name`, we include an empty attribute called `<unchecked>` . This attribute tells the container that any user can execute the method. The container does not perform any security checks for such methods. We just covered the basic version of the `method` element tag. For a detailed description on how `method` tags can be configured and see all the different ways to use them, refer to the `ejb-jar.dtd` at `http://java.sun.com/dtd/ejb-jar_2_0.dtd`.

The next step in declarative security is to associate principals to roles defined earlier. Principals represent actual users and groups that access the system. Assume that John and Jane are gate agents, and Sue and Harry are ticketing agents. So, when John logs in to the system, how does the EJB container know to associate him to the `GateAgents` role? To do this, the container uses the `<security-role-assignment>` block within the `<weblogic-ejb-jar>` stanza in the `weblogic-ejb-jar.xml` deployment descriptor. This block associates different principal names to each role. For our example, we write this block as follows:

```
<security-role-assignment>
  <role-name>GateAgent</role-name>
  <principal-name>John</principal-name>
  <principal-name>Jane</principal-name>
</security-role-assignment>
<security-role-assignment>
  <role-name>TicketingAgent</role-name>
  <principal-name>Sue</principal-name>
  <principal-name>Harry</principal-name>
</security-role-assignment>
```

20

> **NOTE**
>
> WebLogic Server provides its own security realm that can override the deployment descriptor's roles.

Note that these principals should have been defined as principals in the security realm used by WebLogic Server.

> **TIP**
>
> It's considered best practice *not* to associate roles directly to users, but rather to the security realm's groups. That way you don't have to configure in two places (security realm and deployment descriptor) when you create users or administer them. The easiest thing is to associate one role for one group.

Programmatic Security

When we discussed security as one of the basic services offered as part of the EJB framework earlier in the chapter, we mentioned programmatic security. Programmatic security is used when the security of your application depends on the business logic. The WebLogic Server EJB container provides some methods that your bean can call to get information about the caller. These methods can be accessed from the `EJBContext` object in your bean implementation. There are two methods that can come in handy:

- `getCallerPrincipal`—This method returns information about the caller as an object of type `java.security.Principal`. This object contains the name of the principal.
- `isCallerInRole`—When invoked with the name of a role, this method returns a `boolean` indicating whether the caller belongs to that role.

Thus, to provide complex security rules needed by XYZ Airlines, we would not use the default role-based security provided by the container. Instead, we would include the following snippet of code in the `reserveSeats` method:

```
public void reserveSeats() {
  if (!(origin.equals("Los Angeles") &&
     destination.equals("San Francisco"))) {
    // Only certain agents can book these tickets
     if (context.isCallerInRole("ValidAgentForLASector")) {
      // allow booking
    }
    else {
      // Throw EJBException indicating access denied.
     }
  }
```

```
  else {
    // allow booking for all agents
  }
}
```

The role name (in the bold line) is an *alias* to an actual defined role. We check whether the caller is in a role by passing the role alias `ValidAgentForLASector` (this alias must be mapped to a final role in the deployment descriptor). We did not explicitly use `GateAgent`. That's because what we use here is a reference, and we leave it to the deployer to decide which role is considered a `ValidAgentForLASector`. The following XML snippet shows how this link is done using the `role-link` element:

```
<session> <!-- also applies to Entity beans -->
.. <!-- other session tags here -->
<security-role-ref>
  <role-name>GateAgent</role-name>
  <role-link>ValidAgentForLASector</role-link>
</security-role-ref>
</session>
```

Figure 20.14 summarizes the discussion surrounding the WebLogic EJB security features we covered in this section. It illustrates the normal path taken when a user is identified to execute a particular method on the EJB for declarative and programmatic security, respectively.

EJB Environment Entries

The J2EE deployment descriptor `ejb-jar.xml` enables the deployer to define environment entries that can be read at runtime from the bean's environment. The environment entries can be accessed using the JNDI-ENC, as briefly mentioned earlier in the chapter when we talked about the basic services offered by the EJB.

Let's look at the need for environment entries with a help of a simple business case. Consider the following requirement given to us by XYZ Airlines: *At any point in time, each flight should have at least five seats reserved for platinum members who want to fly at the last minute*. Here, it is obvious that the code should not allow any circumstance that will leave fewer than five seats available for any airline. To achieve this, we coded our bean implementation as given here:

```
private static int NUM_RESERVED_SEATS = 5;
...
public void reserveSeats(int flightNumber, int numSeats)
    throws AirlineReservationException {
...
  Properties props = getFlightInfo( flightNumber) ;
```

```
  int numSeatsInDB = Integer.parseInt((String)props.get("NUM_SEATS"));
  if (numSeatsInDB < NUM_RESERVED_SEATS || numSeatsInDB - numSeats
      < NUM_RESERVED_SEATS) {
    throw new AirlineReservationException
      ("Not enough seats.");
  }
...
}
```

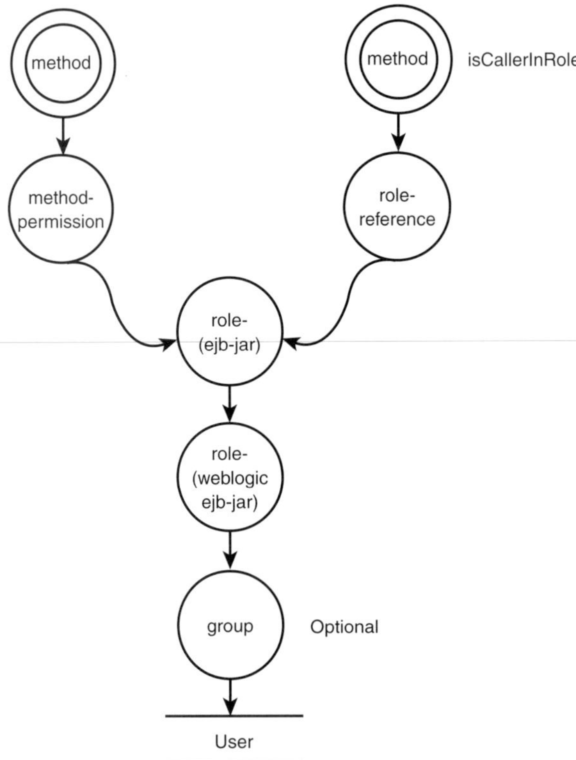

Figure 20.14 EJB security resolution.

This works fine as long as XYZ Airlines does not increase the number of reserved seats to 10 from 5. If they do so, we have no other choice but to change the code of the bean implementation and in so doing make the code error-prone. Environment entries can be defined in the `ejb-jar.xml` file to make the code cleaner by defining properties such as `NUM_RESERVED_SEATS`. These properties can be read from the bean's environment using the JNDI-ENC. These application properties can be stored at deployment time by using a block called `<env-entry>` inside each bean's definition. This element applies to all bean types.

Now let's return to the business case we were looking at and decide how we can use `<env-entry>` to solve our problem. This block contains a description, a name for the environment entry, the type of the entry, and an optional value for the environment entry. The following provides a sample `<env-entry>` block for our airline reservation bean:

```
<session> <!-- also applies to Entity beans and Message-Driven beans -->
.. <!-- other session tags here -->
<env-entry>
  <description>
    The number of seats to be reserved
    for platinum passengers for last minute
    reservations.
  </description>
  <env-entry-name>NumReservedSeats</env-entry-name>
  <env-entry-type>java.lang.Integer</env-entry-type>
  <env-entry-value>5</env-entry-value>
</env-entry>
</session>
```

In this block, we define an environment entry called `NumReservedSeats` and declare it as type `Integer`. We then set this variable to a value of `5`. The `<env-entry-type>` attribute can be set to `String`, or one of the primitive wrapper classes such as `Integer`, `Double`, `Float`, and so on.

The container creates a new environment entry of that type and sets its value to the given value. The variable is loaded into the JNDI ENC context when the bean is deployed. The bean can then retrieve these values form the JNDI tree by looking up the name of the environment entry.

Note that all names are relative to the path `java:comp/env/` in the JNDI tree. Thus, our code looks up the value for the number of reserved seats by using the following code snippet. This can be done in the `ejbCreate` method so that this lookup is done only once.

```
Context context = new InitialContext();
int numReservedSeats = ((Integer) context.lookup(
  "java:comp/env/NumReservedSeats")).intValue();
```

That way, the company can easily change the value of the number of reserved seats in the XML file without having to change the code every time.

TIP

Web applications use environment entries in a similar manner in the `web.xml` deployment descriptor.

EJB and Resource References

References play a key role in removing the hard-wiring that might be done when accessing other EJBs or resources like databases. Such references are declared inside the deployment descriptors that we covered earlier and are used in your bean implementation. One question that's very relevant is why we need references when we can simply define the EJB or resource JNDI name in the bean's environment entries and use that value instead of hard-wiring the JNDI name.

That is certainly possible, but it doesn't leave any room for the container to validate the accuracy of these values. For instance, the container will not be able to tell whether the JNDI name being used is actually tied to the resource that the bean assumes it to be. By using references, the container can perform such validations, as we'll see later on. Moreover, if a resource such as a data source is moved to a new JNDI name, the EJB's code must be modified to reflect the change. Using references, only a deployment descriptor tag will change.

You can define and use three types of references: EJB references (local or remote), resource references, and resource environment references. For a detailed description of how to define these parameters, refer to the DTD defined at `http://java.sun.com/dtd/ejb-jar_2_0.dtd`.

EJB References

An EJB reference ties a name (let us call this the reference name) to the bean to be referenced within the `ejb-jar.xml` deployment descriptor. The reference name need not be the same as the JNDI name of the referenced bean. This reference name is then used within the bean implementation to look up the EJB. Inside the `weblogic-ejb-jar.xml`, this reference name can be mapped to the actual JNDI name of the bean that is being referenced.

You can create two types of EJB references: remote and local references. You can create remote references only if the referenced EJB has a set of remote interfaces. If the referenced EJB has a set of local interfaces, you'll be better off creating a local reference, thus enabling your bean implementation to use the local interfaces of the referenced bean.

The remote reference is created using an `<ejb-ref>` stanza, and the local reference is created using `<ejb-local-ref>` in the `ejb-jar.xml` descriptor. These elements apply for all the bean types and appear under each bean's tag. The following provides a sample remote reference for an `AirlineShoppingCart` EJB:

```
<session> <!-- also applies to Entity beans and Message-Driven beans -->
.. <!-- other session tags here -->
<ejb-ref>
  <ejb-ref-name>ejb/ReservationStatelessEJB</ejb-ref-name>
  <ejb-ref-type>Session</ejb-ref-type>
  <home>com.wlsunleashed.ejb.session.Stateless.
    ➥AirlineReservationRemoteHome</home>
```

```
  <remote>com.wlsunleashed.ejb.session.Stateless.
    ➥AirlineReservationRemoteObject</remote>
</ejb-ref>
</session>
```

The <ejb-local-ref> element contains the same subelements as defined in the <ejb-ref> block used earlier. However, this should be used for colocated beans only.

How does WebLogic Server resolve this name to the JNDI name of the AirlineReservation EJB? It does so by looking for a <reference-descriptor> stanza within the weblogic-ejb-jar.xml deployment descriptor. This stanza sits inside the <weblogic-enterprise-bean> block. It lists all the reference names used in the ejb-jar.xml descriptor and maps them into the appropriate JNDI names. The following lists a typical reference descriptor for the AirlineShoppingCart EJB, which has a corresponding <ejb-ref> defined in the ejb-jar.xml descriptor:

```
<weblogic-enterprise-bean>
...
<reference-descriptor>
  <ejb-reference-description>
    <ejb-ref-name>ejb/ReservationStatelessEJB</ejb-ref-name>
    <jndi-name>RemoteAirlineReservationBean</jndi-name>
  </ejb-reference-description>
</reference-descriptor>
</weblogic-enterprise-bean>
```

When using <ejb-local-ref> in the ejb-jar.xml descriptor, you will use a <ejb-local-reference-description> stanza instead of the <ejb-reference-description> stanza. The contents of both the blocks are exactly the same.

When the bean is deployed into the WebLogic Server container, the container first validates whether the bean that's deployed under the JNDI name matches the description (ejb-ref-type, home/local-home, remote/local interfaces) provided in the ejb-jar.xml descriptor. If this isn't the case, the bean will not be successfully deployed.

Before we move to resource references, let's look at the one of the important optional element; that is, <ejb-link>, which is a subelement of the <ejb-ref> and <ejb-local-ref> elements. This optional element offers an important performance advantage when we refer to another bean residing in the same JAR or EAR file. This element enables WebLogic Server to avoid going to the weblogic-ejb-jar.xml file to resolve the referred EJB's name to the equivalent JNDI name. In other words, the referred EJB can be looked up using the ejb-jar.xml file alone.

The value of the ejb-link element has to be the name of the referred EJB; that is, the value of the <ejb-name> element of the referred EJB. If the referred EJB is in a different ejb-jar.xml file but in the same enterprise application file (EAR), the ejb-link element value should be the name of the referred EJB prefixed with the contained .jar file name and these values should be separated by a hash mark (#); for example, EJB1.jar#bean1. Let's look at an example with the help of the following XML snippet, which defines the Session beans BeanX and BeanY:

```
<session>
...
<ejb-name>BeanX<ejb-name>
...
<ejb-ref>
  <ejb-ref-name>ejb/BeanXEJB</ejb-ref-name>
  <ejb-ref-type>Session</ejb-ref-type>
  <home>com.wls81unleashed.ejb.session.Stateless.BeanXHome</home>
  <remote>com.wls81unleashed.ejb.session.Stateless.BeanXRemote</remote>
  <ejb-link>BeanY</ejb-link>
</ejb-ref>
...
</session>
<session>
...
<ejb-name>BeanY<ejb-name>
...
<ejb-ref>
  <ejb-ref-name>ejb/BeanYEJB</ejb-ref-name>
  <ejb-ref-type>Session</ejb-ref-type>
  <home>com.wls81unleashed.ejb.session.Stateless.BeanYHome</home>
  <remote>com.wls81unleashed.ejb.session.Stateless.BeanYRemote</remote>
</ejb-ref>
...
</session>
```

BeanX refers to BeanY and it can directly look up BeanY using the <ejb-link> element definition. If BeanX was not in the same archive as that BeanY, the <ejb-link> element will include the .jar file as given here:

```
<ejb-link>EJB_Y.jar#BeanY</ejb-link>
```

All reference names (environment entries, EJBs, and resource references) are relative to the path java:comp/env/ within the JNDI ENC context of the bean. Thus, the bean implementation will use the JNDI ENC name "java:/comp/env/ejb/ReservationStatelessEJB" to look up the AirlineReservation Bean. The ejb/ part of the name is optional, but highly desirable because it qualifies the reference as an EJB, as opposed to other resources within the JNDI ENC. While discussing other resources, you'll see that we use appropriate pathnames when accessing each resource to make it clear.

Resource References

Resource references (also known as *resource manager connection factory references* in J2EE terms) are conceptually similar to EJB references except that they refer to the resource factories, such as `DataSource`, JMS connection factories, URLs, and so on. This kind of reference contains a connection factory object (for example, the `DataSource`), not the actual resource itself.

To define a resource reference, include a `<resource-ref>` stanza in the bean's tag in `ejb-jar.xml`. This is applicable for all bean types. This block contains the following parameters:

- `<description>`—An optional description of the resource being referred to.
- `<res-ref-name>`—The reference name of the resource. Note that this is the *suffix* to the JNDI name under which the resource is bound. For example, `jdbc/ds` is accessible through `"java:/comp/env/jdbc/ds"`.
- `<res-type>`—The resource type. The type is specified by the fully qualified class or interface name that is to be implemented by this resource. For example, a `DataSource` resource reference will have a type of `javax.sql.DataSource` as the `<res-type>`.
- `<res-auth>`—This attribute tells the container who will perform authorization when the resource is used in the bean. If it is set to `Container`, the container will automatically perform authentication, depending on the permissions set in the WebLogic Server, before deploying the bean. If it is set to `Application`, the bean is responsible for authenticating itself with the resource.
- `<res-sharing-scope>`—Indicates whether the connections obtained using the resource can be shared. By default, connections are shareable. The values this attribute can take are `Shareable` and `Unshareable`. *Sharable* means other EJBs in this application will be able to look up the resource.

The `<res-ref-name>` specified here is relative to the path `java:comp/env/` of the JNDI ENC of the bean. Although it isn't required, it's cleaner to indicate the subcontext under which a resource falls in the reference name. Table 20.6 provides a suggested list of subcontexts for various resource types.

TABLE 20.6 Naming Resource References in the JNDI-ENC

Resource Type Subcontext	Resource Manager Used (<res-type>)	Suggested Resource
Database connection factory	javax.sql.DataSource	jdbc/
JMS queue connection factory	javax.jms.QueueConnectionFactory	jms/

TABLE 20.6 Continued

Resource Type Subcontext	Resource Manager Used (<res-type>)	Suggested Resource
JMS topic connection factory	javax.jms.TopicConnectionFactory	jms/
JavaMail session factory	javax.mail.Session	mail/
URL connection factory	java.net.URL	url/

As in the case of EJB references, the `<resource-ref>` block uses the `<reference-descriptor>` stanza of the `weblogic-ejb-jar.xml` deployment descriptor to map the reference name to the appropriate JNDI name. The `<reference-descriptor>` block has a `<resource-description>` tag within, one for each resource referred to in the `ejb-jar.xml` descriptor.

Each `<resource-description>` block should have a corresponding `<resource-ref>` block defined in the `ejb-jar.xml` descriptor. A `<resource-description>` block contains a `<res-ref-name>` property that identifies the resource reference based on the given reference name. This stanza also contains the `<jndi-name>` attribute, which links the reference name with the actual JNDI name.

When the bean is deployed, the container verifies whether the resource being referenced is actually of the said type. It also performs necessary authorizations if the `<res-auth>` property is set to `Container`.

Let's look at an example of resource references with a real-life case such as an airline reservation system. The business EJB, such as an `AirlineReservationEJB`, will now have the following block in the `ejb-jar.xml` deployment descriptor under the `<session>` or `<entity>` or `<message-driven>` stanza depending on the bean type:

```
<resource-ref>
  <description>The XYZ DataSource</description>
  <res-ref-name>jdbc/AirlineData</res-ref-name>
  <res-type>javax.sql.DataSource</res-type>
  <res-auth>Container</res-auth>
</resource-ref>
```

We also have a corresponding block in the `weblogic-ejb-jar.xml` deployment descriptor, as shown here:

```
<resource-description>
  <res-ref-name>jdbc/AirlineData</res-ref-name>
  <jndi-name>XYZAirlineDataSource</jndi-name>
</resource-description>
```

Figure 20.15 summarizes the discussion surrounding the EJB and resource references we covered in this section. In this figure, (a) and (b) are the normal path when an EJB or a resource is looked up. But, as we described earlier, `ejb-link` offers a more efficient lookup mechanism for EJBs colocated in the same JAR or EAR file.

One obvious advantage in using references is that you can reconfigure the EJB or resources at any time without going back to change the code. There is a very clear demarcation between what the bean has to know and what it does not. Actual JNDI names under which the EJB or resources are loaded can be abstracted by using EJB and resource references, thus making your bean portable.

Resource Environment References

The resource environment references are another example of environment entries available as part of the `ejb-jar.xml` configuration file. These are used to associate logical names for administered objects that are associated with resources such as JMS destinations, database connections, and so on. The following XML snippet gives an idea of this environment entry:

```
<resource-env-ref>
  <resource-env-ref-name>jms/myQueue<resource-env-ref-name>
  <resource-env-ref-type>javax.jms.Queue<resource-env-ref-type>
</resource-env-ref>
```

The administered objects that are configured using the preceding environment entry are bound in the target WebLogic Server environment using the matching `resource-env-description` element in the `weblogic-ejb-jar.xml` file as given here:

```
<resource-env-description>
  <resource-env-ref-name>jms/myQueue<resource-env-ref-name>
  <jndi-name>wls81unleashed.jms.destn.myQueue<jndi-name>
</resource-env-description>
```

After this configuration is done for these administered objects, they can be used in any J2EE component; that is, any EJB, servlet, and so on. The following code snippet demonstrates how to use this environment entry:

```
InitialContext ic = new InitialContext();
Queue myWLS81Queue =
➥ (Queue)ic.lookup("java:comp/env/jms/myQueue");
```

This environment binds the JMS destination into the consistent `java:comp/env` JNDI tree and in so doing makes the application more portable.

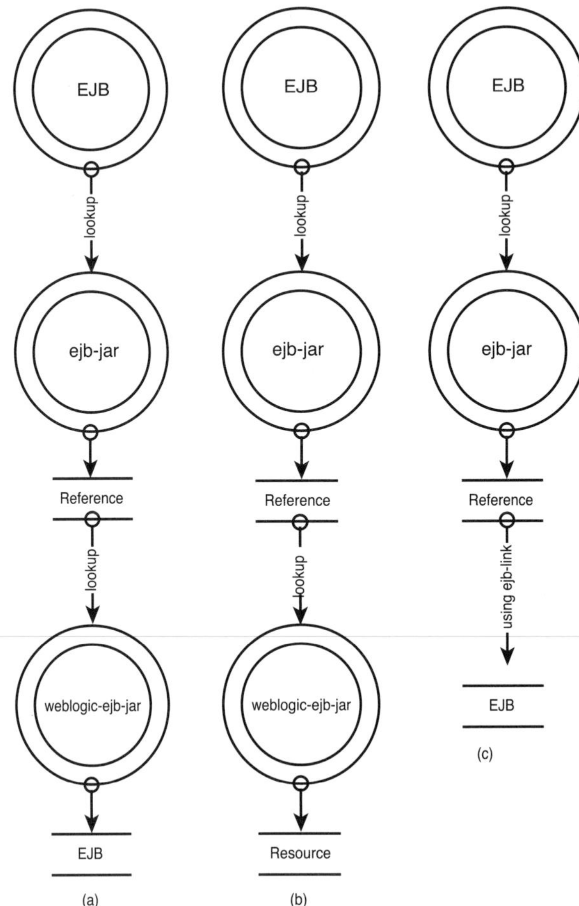

Figure 20.15 Resource References Resolution

EJB-QL

Enterprise JavaBeans Query Language (EJB-QL) was one of the major features presented in EJB 2.0. It was introduced to standardize the behavior of custom finder methods in Entity beans—CMP. Additionally, it addresses the new `select` methods that are actually data queries and are private to one Entity bean. EJB QL is similar to its RDBMS equivalent: SQL. The queries are defined by mapping to the Entity bean schema. Because EJB-QL queries are abstract and independent of the underlying data store, they're portable across data stores and EJB containers. This is covered in detail in Chapter 22, later in the book.

Entity Relationships

Entity relationships formed one of the major features that was missing in the EJB 1.1 specification because Entity beans encapsulate only the persistence fields and had no idea about relationships that exist in the real world. The EJB 2.0 relationship fields address complex relationships between Entity beans, thereby providing a closer mapping of Entity beans to their real-world equivalents. Based on cardinality, there are four major types of relationships: one-to-one, one-to-many, many-to-one, and many-to-many. All these can be unidirectional or bi-directional. The EJB relationships are controlled using the deployment elements in the `ejb-jar.xml` and their related entries in the WebLogic-specific deployment descriptors. For a detailed description of how to manage relationships, see Chapter 22, "Working with Entity Beans."

Summary

We just scraped the top layer of the Enterprise JavaBeans in this chapter. We briefly covered the types of beans, the container, and the services it offers, along with the deployment descriptors that describe the beans. Finally, we covered the different ways to package and deploy Enterprise JavaBeans. We'll cover these topics in detail with respective to each of the bean types in the next three chapters.

CHAPTER 21

Working with Session Beans

by Subramanian H Kovilmadam

IN THIS CHAPTER

- Composition of a Session Bean
- Case Study: XYZ Airlines Online Reservation System
- Working with Stateless Session Beans
- Working with Stateful Session Beans
- Session Beans and WebLogic Server Clustering
- Transactions and Session Beans
- Best Practices

Chapter 20, "Enterprise JavaBeans and WebLogic Server," introduced the various types of Enterprise Beans that you can use in your application. In this chapter, we look at Session Beans in detail. Session EJBs, or Session Beans, manage business processes or workflow that must be performed to achieve the required result. *Workflow* is the sequence of the steps that must be performed to get a job done. In an online booking application, an airline reservation processor may be modeled as a Session Bean, which performs the business function of booking a seat for the customer. Session Beans may use Entity Beans for accessing data to perform their business operations. They may also directly access the database to perform the same tasks.

There are two types of Session Beans, based on their life cycle within the container. They are

- Stateless Session Beans
- Stateful Session Beans

As the name suggests, Stateless Session Beans do not maintain state specific to clients. In other words, the client requests the bean to perform a task, the bean performs the job, returns, and gets ready to process the next request. That isn't to say that a Stateless Session Bean cannot hold any state at all. It can hold state, but any state maintained within a Stateless Session Bean is shared across all clients accessing that bean instance. Stateless Session Beans can and will be shared among different clients. The parameters to the methods themselves may be specific to the client that's calling the method, but the life span of those parameters is complete when the business method completes its processing.

On the other hand, Stateful Session Beans act as extensions of the client inside the application server. Whatever function these beans perform is specific to the client that created the bean. These beans hold client state, and are not shared across different client instances. Note that the state of a Stateful Session Bean is volatile; it isn't persisted, as in an Entity Bean. In other words, if there's a system failure, the state held by a bean instance is gone forever.

This chapter provides a comprehensive study of Session Beans in the context of WebLogic 8.1. We cover EJB Specification Version 2.0, which WebLogic 8.1 is compliant with.

NOTE

For a general overview of EJBs, refer to Chapter 20. Also see Chapter 22, "Working with Entity Beans," and Chapter 23, "Working with Message-Driven Beans," for in-depth studies of those types of EJBs.

This chapter assumes a working knowledge of RMI on the part of the reader. For more information about RMI, refer to Chapter 11, "Creating Distributed Applications with RMI."

Composition of a Session Bean

A Session Bean is composed of three parts: the home interface, the component interface, and the Bean class. The home interfaces list the life cycle methods of the bean, whereas the component interfaces list its business methods. The Bean class, or Bean implementation, is where you code the business logic of the bean's business methods and also define its life cycle methods. All three are required constituents of a Session Bean. If a bean needs to be accessed over the network, you must provide a remote home interface and a remote interface along with the bean implementation. With EJB 1.1, the only way to access an EJB was remotely, and hence a set of remote interfaces was mandatory.

EJB 2.0 introduced a new concept in which Session Beans may be accessed locally by other objects that live within the same EJB container without the overhead of networking calls. This is done by using a set of local home and local interfaces in place of the remote home and remote interfaces. The advantage of using local interfaces is their performance: The bean instance is invoked just like any other object within the JVM, without using RMI. No network overhead is involved.

In this section, we look at these components and the role each of them plays in the usage of the bean. Let's look at the remote interfaces first, followed by the local interfaces.

- The remote home interface—The remote home interface provides applications with access to the bean's life cycle methods over the network. Life cycle methods are used to create new beans, remove existing ones, and find beans based on a given criteria. The remote home interface is represented by the interface `javax.ejb.EJBHome`. The bean's remote home interface should extend from this interface and provide access to appropriate methods. The `EJBHome` interface in turn extends from the `java.io.Remote` interface, thus making it accessible over the network. This interface works in conjunction with the remote interface.
- The remote interface—The remote interface provides access to the bean's business methods. This interface extends from the `javax.ejb.EJBObject` interface, which in turn extends from `java.io.Remote` interface, thus ensuring remote accessibility. This interface works in conjunction with the remote home interface of a bean.
- The local home interface—If the home interface of the bean extends from the interface `javax.ejb.EJBLocalHome` instead of the `javax.ejb.EJBHome` interface, the bean can be efficiently used by other objects residing within the same container. This interface offers bean life cycle methods similar to those of the remote home interface. The difference between the two is that when beans are created using this interface, no network connectivity is involved because both the requested and the requestor exist within the same application, which significantly improves performance. This interface works in conjunction with the local interface. Remember that the specification talks about using local interfaces for objects that lie within the same JVM, but the WebLogic container restricts it further to the same application (that is, JAR, EAR, and so on) This is a direct consequence of the class loader scheme adopted by WebLogic Server, which basically uses objects within the same application only.
- The local interface—The local interface of a bean is similar to the remote interface in that both provide access to the business methods provided by the bean class. This interface works with the local home interface. All method calls made using this interface avoid network protocols and thus improve performance. The local interface of a bean extends `javax.ejb.EJBLocalObject`.
- The bean implementation—The Bean class is the server-side class in which code is written to perform all the business operations and life cycle operations, as listed in its remote home, local home, and remote and local component interfaces. That said, the Bean class does not implement any of these interfaces directly; it merely defines methods that resemble the ones in these interfaces. This is so because the objects that actually implement the home and component interfaces are generated by the EJB compiler. The Bean class should implement the `javax.ejb.SessionBean` interface to identify the bean as a Session Bean. Both Stateless and Stateful Session Beans implement the same interface. This interface in turn extends from `javax.ejb.EnterpriseBean`.

Session Beans should provide a set of local (home and component) interfaces to enable local access to the bean. They also should provide a set of remote (home and component) interfaces to enable remote access. At least one set of interfaces is mandatory, although both can be provided for enabling both remote and local access to a bean.

NOTE

In this chapter, the remote and local interfaces are sometimes referred to as *component interfaces.*

Case Study: XYZ Airlines Online Reservation System

To streamline the discussion on Session Beans, let's work with a simple case study. We're building an online reservation system for XYZ Airlines. The functionality requires us to build a system using which a user can search for flights. Following that, the user reserves one or more seats on a flight that she chooses. We'll code an `AirlineReservation` Stateless Session Bean with two methods in it. To keep this case study simple, let's assume that reserving a seat on a flight translates to reducing the number of available seats in the flight by one.

The company wants to provide a shopping cart–type of interface to the user. The user should be able to buy tickets on as many flights as required and pay for all of them at once in the final step. We'll code an `AirlineShoppingCart` Stateful Session Bean to accomplish this. We won't develop the payment system. All our shopping cart must do is provide the total amount when requested.

Let's work out the database schema that we'll use. To keep it simple, our schema involves only one table: `FlightRecord`. Table 21.1 illustrates the structure of the `FlightRecord` table.

TABLE 21.1 The FlightRecord Table

Column Name	Type	Size
FLIGHT_NO	INTEGER	
AIRLINE	VARCHAR2	100
ORIGIN_AIRPORT	VARCHAR2	100
DESTINATION_AIRPORT	VARCHAR2	100
NUM_SEATS	INTEGER	
TOTAL_COST_PER_SEAT	DOUBLE	

We'll be using PointBase as our database server. The SQL required to create this schema in your PointBase database is provided in the file called `schema.sql`, which is packaged along with this book. Use this SQL file to create the schema in your PointBase database. This file also loads the table with some dummy data for the purpose of our case study. Perform the following tasks prior to proceeding with the rest of this chapter.

Start the PointBase database server and execute the `schema.sql` in the PointBase console, so that the schema is created and the records are populated. When this has been done, start WebLogic Server (leave the database server running). Now create a new JDBC connection pool called `XYZAirlineConnectionPool` using the WebLogic console. Following that, create a new `DataSource` object called `XYZAirlineDataSource`, which uses the previously created connection pool.

NOTE

For more information about any of these tasks and a detailed explanation of how you can perform them, refer to Chapter 10, "Managing Database Connectivity Using JDBC."

Working with Stateless Session Beans

In this section, you learn how to create, deploy, and use a Stateless Session Bean. As discussed earlier, Stateless Session Beans maintain no client-specific conversational state. They perform particular tasks on invocation and return the results to the client. Once that's done, other clients can make requests to the same bean instance. The bean does not distinguish between clients. Neither does it distinguish between first and subsequent calls from the same client. Because of this, a client should not assume that it will get the same instance of the bean every time it performs a request. Stateless Session Beans should typically be used to perform any generic operation that can be performed completely by making a single method call to the bean, and does not depend on client-specific state stored within the bean instance.

Stateless Session Beans are very efficient by construction. In the previous chapter, you read about passivation and activation as techniques the container uses to manage resources effectively. Because these beans don't maintain client specific state, every Stateless Session Bean instance is equivalent to another, and hence does not require passivation or activation. That means these beans do not use too many resources and are lightweight.

The Remote Interface

Clients to the XYZ Reservation System aren't expected to access the `AirlineReservation` EJB directly. They're expected to use the shopping cart bean, which will in turn use this bean to perform the reservation tasks. Therefore, this bean should not provide the capability for remote access; in other words, the bean should not contain a remote interface or remote home interface. All it should provide is a set of local interfaces so that the shopping cart EJB can access the bean services. That having been said, we're still going to create the remote interface and remote home interface for academic reasons.

NOTE

Note that when we refer to a *client* in our discussion, we aren't necessarily referring to a user interface unless explicitly stated. We're referring to any object that uses the EJB—the client to the bean. Also note that in the following discussion, all classes go into the package `com.wlsunleashed.ejb.session.stateless` unless otherwise stated.

In accordance with the naming convention that was laid out in the previous chapter, let's name our remote interface `AirlineReservationRemoteObject.java`.

The `AirlineReservation` EJB provides three pieces of functionality. First, it enables users to search through the airline database for flights that operate between a given set of cities. This function returns an array of flight numbers. The user can then invoke the second method on the bean with a flight number, which returns the flight information as a `Properties` object. The third operation is a reservation method, which books the given number of seats in the given flight.

As mentioned earlier, the remote interface should extend from `javax.ejb.EJBObject` interface. Our remote interface for the `AirlineReservation` EJB will look like the following:

```
import java.rmi.RemoteException;
import java.util.Properties;
import javax.ejb.EJBObject;
public interface AirlineReservationRemoteObject extends EJBObject {
  public int[] getFlightNumbers(String origin, String destination)
    throws RemoteException, AirlineReservationException;
  public Properties getFlightInfo(int flightNumber)
    throws RemoteException, AirlineReservationException;
  public void reserveSeats( int flightNumber, int numSeats)
    throws RemoteException, AirlineReservationException;
}
```

It's obvious from the code that each method in the bean is completely independent of the others. Each operation can be completed by calling exactly one method in the bean. There's no requirement to invoke the methods in any order. All the information needed to perform each operation is passed in as parameters into the methods. Therefore, this bean is an ideal candidate for a Stateless Session Bean.

The parameters and the return types of each of these methods deserve a special mention. Because communication will be over the network using RMI, the data is serialized over the network. For data to be serialized, any non-primitive objects that are passed must be *serializable*; that is, they must implement the tagging interface, `java.io.Serializable`. Null references and primitive types can also be passed as parameters. The same rules hold good for return types as well.

NOTE

Refer to Chapter 20 for a detailed discussion of the methods provided by the parent interface (`javax.ejb.EJBObject`) and their uses. One point to note is that for Stateless Session Beans, the `getPrimaryKey` method is irrelevant. The `EJBObject` interface has this method declared in it because the remote interfaces of both Session and Entity Beans extend from the same interface. If you try to invoke this method from a Session Bean, the method throws a `RuntimeException`.

Understanding Exceptions

All methods in the remote interface throw the exception of type `java.rmi.RemoteException`. The bean implementation usually won't throw this exception from its code. The methods declare this exception in their signatures because the RMI facility can throw this exception when there is any kind of system-level failure while contacting the remote object. By ensuring that all methods in the remote interface throw this exception, the compiler on the client side forces the client to handle `RemoteException`.

The business methods may also throw application exceptions. An *application exception* is any exception thrown by your bean implementation, which indicates an application-level failure (either a violation of a business rule or any other failure that you expect the client to handle). In our case, you can see that our methods throw an exception of type `AirlineReservationException`. Because the application exception class would extend `java.lang.Exception`, which is serializable, exceptions can be thrown over the network for clients to handle.

TIP

Other subsystems that your bean might access could also throw exceptions. For instance, when you attempt an SQL operation, the database driver might throw a `java.sql.SQLException`. It's not a good practice to make your remote interface throw such low-level exceptions to the client. As far as possible, try to handle the exception at the bean level. If you cannot handle it, wrap the exception and throw it as an application exception. This way, you ensure that your bean abstracts the implementation nuances of the subsystems that you use in your bean, while at the same time ensuring that the exception is handled in one way or another.

EJB 2.0 introduced yet another type of exception, called `javax.ejb.EJBException`. This is an unchecked exception (subclass of `java.lang.RuntimeException`), and the compiler won't force your client code to catch this exception type and handle it. These exceptions are usually reserved to report system-level failures that might occur at runtime. For example, if your bean attempts to perform a database operation and the database is down, that can be considered a system exception and reported back using the `EJBException`. This exception can also contain a wrapped exception that can provide more information about the actual condition. This exception object is returned along with the `EJBException`. All other types of exceptions (both in the business logic and in subsystems) should be reported back to the client as application exceptions.

When a runtime exception (such as EJBException) is thrown from a bean, the container first traps this exception. It then discards the bean instance that generated the runtime exception, and replaces it with another bean instance. The exception is then propagated to the client inside a RemoteException for the client to handle it.

The Remote Home Interface

Think of the remote home interface as a factory for the bean. It contains the life cycle methods for the bean. Using the remote home interface, your application can create, find, and remove beans over the network. While developing a bean, you code only the remote home interface, not its implementation.

In accordance with the naming convention that we adopted earlier, we'll name the remote home interface of the bean AirlineReservationRemoteHome. Our remote home interface will consist of a single method to create a bean.

Remote home interfaces extend the javax.ejb.EJBHome interface. The remote home interface of a Stateless Session Bean is required to declare only a single create method that takes no arguments and has no suffixes. This requirement stems because of the life cycle of a stateless Session Bean. The life cycle of this bean is discussed later in this chapter. The create method returns an object that implements the bean's remote interface.

As mentioned earlier, the remote home interface extends from the javax.ejb.EJBHome interface. This interface extends from the java.io.Remote interface, which makes any implementation of the remote home interface eligible for use over the network. The source code for our remote home interface is given in the following snippet:

```
import java.rmi.RemoteException;
import javax.ejb.CreateException;
import javax.ejb.EJBHome;
public interface AirlineReservationRemoteHome extends EJBHome {
  public AirlineReservationRemoteObject create()
    throws RemoteException, CreateException ;
}
```

This remote home interface lists one method for creating a new instance of the bean. The bean instance is returned as an object that implements the remote interface of the bean. Note that the create method throws both java.io.RemoteException and javax.ejb.CreateException. Both exceptions are required to be thrown by this method declaration, so that the client using this bean can handle these exception types. The RemoteException is reported back to the client whenever a system-level failure occurs while accessing the bean, or when the `create` method throws an unchecked exception. When the container wants to let the client know that there was an error while creating the bean, `CreateException` should be used. This exception must be caught and handled by the client.

The Local Interface

The local interface of an EJB is similar to the remote interface in that the local interface also lists all the business operations provided by the bean. These interfaces are used by other co-located clients that exist within the same application as the bean. When used, local interfaces avoid any RMI calls, thus making the calls very efficient. The same bean may provide both local and remote access by including both sets of interfaces, or just any one type of access by including the appropriate set interfaces in its deployment.

The local interface extends from the `javax.ejb.EJBLocalObject` interface. According to the established naming convention, we'll name our local interface `AirlineReservationLocalObject`. The local interface is presented in the following code snippet:

```
import java.util.Properties;
import javax.ejb.EJBLocalObject;
public interface AirlineReservationLocalObject extends EJBLocalObject {
  public int[] getFlightNumbers(String origin, String destination)
    throws AirlineReservationException;
  public Properties getFlightInfo(int flightNumber)
    throws AirlineReservationException;
  public void reserveSeats( int flightNumber, int numSeats)
    throws AirlineReservationException;
}
```

One thing that is strikingly different from the code snippet for a remote interface (refer to the earlier section about the remote interface) is the fact that none of these methods throw `RemoteException`. This is quite obvious because no network is functionality involved in using local interfaces. Your methods can throw application exceptions, which must also extend `java.lang.Exception`. The container and the bean may still throw unchecked exceptions as `EJBException`, which will be reported back to the client.

The local component interfaces have been optimized in such a way that any call made using the local interface is executed as if the bean were just another object on the JVM. That means for local interfaces, there's no requirement for the parameter objects to be serializable, and they are passed by reference to the bean. It also means that you should be very careful to make sure that your application can handle this behavior.

CAUTION

There's a downside to using local interfaces: It reduces the location transparency of the beans. So, if you're sure that the objects will always colocate, you must give preference to using local interfaces; not otherwise.

The Local Home Interface

The local home interface works in conjunction with the local interface. This interface also declares a `create` method to create the bean. The difference between this declaration and the one in its remote counterpart is that the `create` method does not throw `RemoteException`. The `create` method now returns an object that implements the local interface, rather than the remote interface of the bean.

The local home interface extends from the `javax.ejb.EJBLocalHome` interface. The name of the local home interface as specified by our naming convention is `AirlineReservationLocalHome`. The code of the `AirlineReservationLocalHome` interface is presented in the following snippet:

```
import javax.ejb.CreateException;
import javax.ejb.EJBLocalHome;
public interface AirlineReservationLocalHome extends EJBLocalHome {
  public AirlineReservationLocalObject create()
    throws CreateException ;
}
```

The Bean Class

The Bean class contains the implementation of the bean's business functionality. This class does not implement any of the interfaces discussed earlier. Instead, the Bean class defines methods that closely resemble the methods declared in the interfaces. The classes that actually implement the interfaces defined earlier are generated by the container, and the calls are delegated to the bean implementation. The Bean class defines both life cycle methods as well as business methods. Let's first take a look at Listing 21.1, which represents the skeleton of the bean class.

LISTING 21.1 A Bean Class Skeleton

```
import java.rmi.RemoteException;
import java.util.Properties;
import javax.ejb.CreateException;
import javax.ejb.SessionBean;
import javax.ejb.SessionContext;
public class AirlineReservationBean implements SessionBean {
```

LISTING 21.1 Continued

```
  SessionContext context = null;
  public AirlineReservationBean() {
    super();
  }
  public void setSessionContext(SessionContext aContext)
    throws RemoteException {
    System.out.println(" setSessionContext called ");
    context = aContext;
  }
  public void ejbCreate() throws CreateException {
    System.out.println("ejbCreate called");
  }
  public void ejbRemove() {
    System.out.println("ejbRemove called");
  }
  public void ejbActivate() {
    System.out.println("ejbActivate called");
  }
  public void ejbPassivate() {
    System.out.println("ejbPassivate called");
  }
  public int[] getFlightNumbers(String origin, String destination)
    throws AirlineReservationException {
    return null;
  }
  public Properties getFlightInfo(int flightNumber)
    throws AirlineReservationException {
    return null;
  }
  public void reserveSeats(int flightNumber, int numSeats)
    throws AirlineReservationException {
  }
}
```

The business methods haven't been implemented in Listing 21.1, but the code itself is complete enough to be deployed into WebLogic Server. Let's analyze each element of this code.

The EJB specification lays down some strict rules for developers creating the bean implementation. If any rule is violated, the bean cannot be deployed by the container.

First of all, the bean implementation should be declared `public`, and cannot be declared `final` or `abstract`. It should not have constructors other than the default constructor. Any other constructor that's defined will never be used. This is because the container instantiates the Bean class by calling the `Class.newInstance` method, which uses the default constructor. The class must not define a `finalize` method.

The following list details the different methods that have been defined in the Bean class (the ones other than the business methods) and how the container uses them:

- `setSessionContext`—This is the first method invoked by the EJB container on the bean instance, sometime after the bean has been created; that is, after its constructor is invoked. This method passes in an object of type `SessionContext`, which provides several pieces of information to the bean instance about the circumstances under which it's being created and used. The bean can keep a reference to that object for later use.

- `ejbCreate`—This method is invoked by the EJB container on the bean instance after the `setSessionContext` method is invoked, but before any business method has been invoked. This method won't necessarily be called when the client calls the `create` method on the home interface. The container is free to create bean instances whenever it wants, and will call `ejbCreate` on those instances at creation time.

  In the case of Stateless Session Beans, the bean class must define exactly one `ejbCreate` method that doesn't take any parameters and returns nothing. This method corresponds with the `create` method of the remote home and local home interfaces of the bean. This method also must throw application exceptions that are declared in the `create` method of the home interfaces of the bean. This callback method helps your bean instance to perform initialization routines. For example, if your bean requires the use of JDBC resources, they can be looked up in this method.

  The `ejbCreate` method does not add too much value in the case of a Stateless Session Bean. All initialization code can be written in the constructor, giving the exact same results. But as we discussed earlier, you must understand that the only constructor that will be invoked is the default constructor because the bean is created using the `Class.newInstance` method. Note also that if your initialization process requires the session context, you cannot use the constructor for initialization. The advantage of the `ejbCreate` methods become more apparent in Stateful Session Beans and Entity Beans, where you're allowed to overload `ejbCreate` methods and accept different parameters, thus giving different flavors to the bean creation process.

- `ejbRemove`—This method is invoked by the container when the container decides to destroy the bean instance for any reason. This method indicates to the bean that the instance is about to be removed from memory, and provides an opportunity to the bean instance to perform finalization and cleanup procedures. Remember that when a client invokes the `remove` method on the component or the home interface of a

Stateless Session Bean, the bean instance isn't destroyed. It is simply moved to the method-ready pool. It's important to remember that this method isn't invoked when the bean instance is moved back to the method-ready pool; rather, it is invoked only when the bean instance is actually destroyed by the container. However, if the method-ready pool already has enough bean instances, the container may decide to destroy the bean instance, therefore ending up calling the `ejbRemove` method. For more information about method-ready pools, refer to the "Life Cycle of a Stateful Session Bean" section later in this chapter.

- `ejbPassivate` and `ejbActivate`—Chapter 20 introduced you to the concepts of activation and passivation as mechanisms used by the container to conserve resources. Stateless Session Beans do not hold client state, and therefore don't participate in either passivation or activation. These methods are present in the bean class to satisfy the requirements of the inherited interface. These methods don't hold any relevance for Stateless Session Beans. They're never invoked, and do not have to do anything.

Apart from these methods, the Bean class also defines the business methods as declared in the component interfaces. Note that the business methods do not throw `RemoteExceptions`, unlike the component interfaces' methods. The container usually throws these exceptions if it has to.

Developing the AirlineReservation EJB

In the code snippet provided here, the business methods don't have any logic defined. However, it's quite straightforward to code business logic into these methods. The bean implementation that's packaged with this book contains the entire source code `com.wlsunleashed.ejb.session.stateless.AirlineReservationBean`. You can also look up the associated interfaces in the same package.

Any JNDI lookups can be typically performed at initialization time. Therefore, in our bean class, we'll look up the initial context and the `DataSource` object (`javax.sql.DataSource`, used for creating database connections) in the `ejbCreate` method and store it locally in the class. As discussed earlier in this chapter, a Stateless Session Bean instance cannot hold conversational state that's specific to one client, but it can definitely hold state, which will be shared across all clients accessing that bean instance. We'll release all these resources in the `remove` method of the bean instance.

Apart from this, the individual methods function independently of each other. Each method looks up a database connection from the `DataSource` object and uses it to perform its SQL functions. No method depends on any other method to have been (or not to have been) invoked previously. This makes this bean a suitable candidate for the Stateless Session Bean model. Any `SQLException` that might be thrown by the SQL processing is reported to the client as an application exception by wrapping it in the `AirlineReservationException` object. After each method has finished execution, the

Statement and Connection objects are closed by invoking the close methods on these objects. For more information on DataSource and connection pools, refer to Chapter 10.

Deployment Descriptors

Chapter 20 introduced you to deployment descriptors as mechanisms by which you configure your bean deployment in the container. In this section, we don't focus on all the possible parameters that can be set in deployment descriptors, but only on the relevant portions for Stateless Session Beans.

ejb-jar.xml

In this section, we briefly take a look at this descriptor for the Airline Reservation bean. Listing 21.2 presents the ejb-jar.xml file for our bean.

LISTING 21.2 ejb-jar.xml Deployment Descriptor

```
<!DOCTYPE ejb-jar PUBLIC '-//Sun Microsystems, Inc.
➥//DTD Enterprise JavaBeans 2.0
➥//EN' 2.  'http://java.sun.com/dtd/ejb-jar_2_0.dtd'>
<ejb-jar>
 <enterprise-beans>
  <session>
   <ejb-name>AirlineReservationBean</ejb-name>
   <home>com.wls70unleashed.ejb.session.stateless.
➥  AirlineReservationRemoteHome</home>
   <remote>com.wls70unleashed.ejb.session.stateless.
➥  AirlineReservationRemoteObject</remote>
   <local-home>com.wls70unleashed.ejb.session.stateless.
➥  AirlineReservationLocalHome</local-home>
   <local>com.wls70unleashed.ejb.session.stateless.
➥  AirlineReservationLocalObject</local>
   <ejb-class>com.wls70unleashed.ejb.session.stateless.
➥  AirlineReservationBean</ejb-class>
   <session-type>Stateless</session-type>
   <transaction-type>Container</transaction-type>
  </session>
 </enterprise-beans>
 <assembly-descriptor>
  <container-transaction>
   <method>
    <ejb-name>AirlineReservationBean</ejb-name>
    <method-name>*</method-name>
   </method>
   <trans-attribute>Supports</trans-attribute>
  </container-transaction>
```

LISTING 21.2 Continued

```
23.   </assembly-descriptor>
24. </ejb-jar>
```

The first line of this listing identifies the XML document. It specifies to the XML parser that the container will use, that this XML contains a root-element called `<ejb-jar>`, and its DTD can be found in the URL `http://java.sun.com/dtd/ejb-jar_2_0.dtd`. The parser will then validate the contents of this XML file based on the rules laid out by the given DTD. If the parser finds any discrepancy between the XML file and the rules specified, it will report an error and the deployment will not be successful.

This XML file (as in any other XML file) always has one outer element in the document body: `<ejb-jar>`. All other elements of this descriptor lie within the opening and closing `<ejb-jar>` element. From the listing, it's obvious that there are two entries within this stanza: `<enterprise-beans>` (line 3) and `<assembly-descriptor>` (line 15). The only entry that's necessary for deployment is the `<enterprise-beans>` stanza. The `<assembly-descriptor>` stanza is optional, as are the other optional entries that can go within the `<ejb-jar>`.

One EJB deployment descriptor can contain more than one bean. You can also combine different types of beans (Session, Entity, And Message-Driven) within the same EJB deployment. Each bean that's deployed in a bean must have one section within the `<enterprise-beans>` section of the XML. In line 4 of the listing, you find a stanza that begins with the tag `<session>`. This identifies a bean of type `session`. Similarly, you could have other stanzas here—such as `<entity>` and `<message-driven>`—to declare beans of those types.

The `<session>` stanza of the descriptor describes the Session Bean to the container. It must contain the following elements:

- A unique name identifying the bean (`<ejb-name>`).
- The name of the bean's remote interface, if applicable (`<remote>`).
- The name of the bean's remote home interface, if applicable (`<home>`).
- The name of the bean's local interface, if applicable (`<local>`).
- The name of the bean's local home interface, if applicable (`<local-home>`).
- The name of the bean's implementation class (`<ejb-class>`).
- The bean's session management type (`<session-type>`). This indicates to the container whether the bean is stateless or otherwise. The two values it can take are `Stateless` and `Stateful`.
- The bean's transaction management type (`<transaction-type>`). This indicates to the container the type of transaction management that's required for this bean.

The section must contain at least one of the two pairs of home and component interfaces—the remote implementation, the local implementation, or both. The rest of the tags are mandatory. Apart from these tags, this stanza can also list information about entries that the bean's implementation expects to be present in its environment, resource references, references to other beans that are used by this bean, security identities, and more. All these concepts were covered in Chapter 20.

After we've defined all the beans that form our deployment, we can describe some properties that describe the assembly of the beans within this deployment. To do this, we use another element within the `<ejb-jar>` stanza known as the `<assembly-descriptor>`. This stanza describes two key elements of bean deployment: the transaction attributes of the bean's methods and the security. We'll look at these attributes in detail in later sections of this chapter. For now, it's sufficient to understand that the `<assembly-descriptor>` stanza indicated in this listing specifies to the container that all methods in the Airline Reservation bean support user transactions, but none of them requires it. For a detailed study of this section of the descriptor, refer to Chapter 20.

weblogic-ejb-jar.xml

The simple WebLogic Server–specific deployment descriptor used for the Airline Reservation EJB is shown in Listing 21.3.

LISTING 21.3 weblogic-ejb-jar.xml

```
<!DOCTYPE weblogic-ejb-jar PUBLIC '-//BEA Systems, Inc.
➥   //DTD WebLogic 7.0.0 EJB//EN'
➥   'http://www.bea.com/servers/wls700/dtd/
➥   weblogic700-ejb-jar.dtd'>
<weblogic-ejb-jar>
  <weblogic-enterprise-bean>
    <ejb-name>AirlineReservationBean</ejb-name>
     <stateless-session-descriptor>
      <pool>
       <initial-beans-in-free-pool>0</initial-beans-in-free-pool>
      </pool>
      <stateless-clustering>
      </stateless-clustering>
     </stateless-session-descriptor>
     <transaction-descriptor>
     </transaction-descriptor>
     <jndi-name>RemoteAirlineReservationBean</jndi-name>
     <local-jndi-name>LocalAirlineReservationBean</local-jndi-name>
  </weblogic-enterprise-bean>
</weblogic-ejb-jar>
```

Most of the properties that are part of this descriptor were discussed in Chapter 20. We'll look only at the `<stateless-session-descriptor>` stanza (under `<weblogic-ejb-jar>`→`<weblogic-enterprise-bean>`). This stanza can contain two sections: `<stateless-clustering>` and `<pool>`. The `<stateless-clustering>` stanza describes the clustering properties of the Stateless Session Bean. We'll look more about this stanza in the "Clustering a Stateless Session Bean" section later in this chapter. The `<pool>` stanza contains two elements:

- `<max-beans-in-free-pool>`—This parameter identifies to the container the maximum number of bean instances that should be active at any time. As long as the number of instances active in the container is lower than this figure, the container will create new instances of the bean when a request comes in and it cannot find free instances to process the request.
- `<initial-beans-in-free-pool>`—The number of instances that the container will initialize upon server startup. This value will help in tweaking the performance of your bean.

Stateless Session Bean pools will be discussed in the chapter that describes the stateless bean life cycle.

Packaging and Deploying the Bean

Refer to Chapter 20 for a discussion of packaging and deploying the bean. Essentially, you can deploy the bean by itself as described in Chapter 20 or as an enterprise application archive (EAR) file. If you decide to deploy the bean by itself, feel free to do so. For the sake of this chapter, we've provided an Ant script that will enable you to deploy the application as an EAR file.

To use the Ant script, you should have Ant installed in your system. You can download Ant free of cost from `http://ant.apache.org`. This script has been tested with Ant version 1.5. Make sure that you've copied the `optional.jar` into the `lib` directory of your Ant installation to enable access to the optional Ant tasks. Change to the directory under which you'll find the source code for this chapter. You should find some JSP and HTML files and a directory called `airlinedata`, which contains the relevant deployment descriptors along with the source package. Execute Ant by using the following command line. You must provide the base directory of the WebLogic Server installation; for example, `c:\bea\weblogic81`:

```
ant -Dwlhome=c:\bea\weblogic81
```

This line will build the EAR file and place it under the current directory with the name `AirlineReservation.ear`. You can now deploy this file into your WebLogic Server by simply copying the EAR file into the `applications` folder of your domain. Remember to define the appropriate connection pool and data sources before you deploy this EAR file. This Ant task will also create a client JAR file, which must be included in the classpath of standalone clients. This file will be named `AirlineReservationClient.jar`.

Accessing a Stateless Session Bean from a Client

Now that we've deployed our bean into WebLogic Server's container, we're ready to write a client application, which will access the bean, perform a search for the flights, and display the results on screen. In a typical reservation system, this job would be done by a graphical user interface. In our case, we're going to build a text-based interface that enables you to search through the flight information.

Remote Clients to the Bean

Our application, which uses the EJB to search the flight database for flights when given two cities, will be built as a standalone application that will run in its own JVM. Although this requires that WebLogic Server to be up and running, this client won't execute by itself within WebLogic Server's JVM. This type of client is referred to as a remote client.

Invoking a method on the EJB from a remote client involves the following steps:

- Establish an initial context with the server.
- Query the JNDI tree and look up the remote home of the EJB using the name that it's bound under. Note that, by definition, such clients cannot use the local interfaces.
- Create a bean instance by using the life cycle methods of the home interface obtained.
- Call the appropriate method on the bean instance.
- Close the initial context to release resources.

For more information about the steps involving the JNDI tree, refer to Chapter 8, "Naming and Directory Services with JNDI." Listing 21.4 outlines the basic steps to perform an EJB call that have been described in this section.

LISTING 21.4 Simple Client to a Stateless Session Bean

```
try {
   InitialContext ic = null;
   Hashtable props = new Hashtable() ;
   props.put( Context.INITIAL_CONTEXT_FACTORY,
         "weblogic.jndi.WLInitialContextFactory" );
   props.put( Context.PROVIDER_URL,
         "t3://localhost:7001");
   ic = new InitialContext( props ) ;
   Object o = ic.lookup("RemoteAirlineReservationBean");
   AirlineReservationRemoteHome arrho = (AirlineReservationRemoteHome)
     PortableRemoteObject.narrow(o,
       AirlineReservationRemoteHome.class );
```

LISTING 21.4 Continued

```
    AirlineReservationRemoteObject arro = (AirlineReservationRemoteObject)
        arrho.create();
   System.out.println("remote instance created");
   int[] values = arro.getFlightNumbers(origin, destination);
   System.out.println("Flight Numbers between " + origin +
      " and " + destination );
   for (int i = 0; i < values.length; i++) {
      System.out.println(" --> " + values[i] );
   }
   System.out.println ( "-- finished." );
   ic.close();
 }
 catch (Exception ex) {
   ex.printStackTrace();
 }
```

One point of interest in this code listing is highlighted in bold. Notice that the remote home is looked up as merely an `Object`. Following this, we invoke the static `narrow` method on the class `PortableRemoteObject` and cast that into the remote interface. To accommodate remote objects written in languages other than Java, and which don't have any concept of casting between two types, IIOP places the restriction on stubs implementing multiple interfaces. The stub object returned merely implements the interface that is declared to be returned by the remote method. In the case of the `lookup` method, the remote method returns an object of type `Object`; therefore, the stub merely implements the interface specified by this class. To make this stub more usable in our EJB client, Java's RMI IIOP classes provide the `narrow` method in the `PortableRemoteObject` class. When invoked with the stub object obtained from the server along with the interface class, the `narrow` method dynamically casts the object into the right interface and returns an object that can then be cast into the appropriate interface.

This client application can be found in the source folder, under `com/wlsunleashed/ejb/session/stateless/SearchFlightRemoteClient.java`,. To execute this client, make sure that your WebLogic Server is up and running. You also should have deployed the stateless EJB that we built under the remote JNDI name of `AirlineReservationBean`. This will be done automatically if you used the deployment descriptors provided. The client also assumes that the WebLogic Server is running in the `localhost`, listening in port 7001. Invoke this client by passing in the two cities on the command line. Not passing the cities will make the client default to two cities and perform the search. To test this example, you must include the client JAR file generated by the build process in your classpath. The JAR file is named `AirlineReservationClient.jar`, and it contains all the required classes and interfaces for the client side.

Other Components Within the Application Acting as Clients

Other components that live within the same WebLogic application, running inside the same JVM as the EJB, can also access the bean. When we do this, we can actually use the local interfaces and do away with any network overhead while accessing the bean. We'll look at the sample program while working with Stateful Session Beans. For now, it's sufficient to understand that there's not much difference between these clients and the remote clients. One of the few differences is to actually look up the local home from the JNDI tree using the name defined in `<local-jndi-name>` (under `<weblogic-ejb-jar>`→`<weblogic-enterprise-bean>` in the `weblogic-ejb.jar` descriptor) in Listing 21.3. From here on, you can create the local object by invoking the `create` method on the local home. The following steps are involved:

- Obtain the initial context. This time, don't pass any parameters to the `InitialContext`'s constructor. This will make the class create an initial context to the same WebLogic Server instance. For more information about performing JNDI lookups, refer to Chapter 8.
- Look up the local home of the EJB by using the JNDI name under which the local home is bound.
- Create the local object using the life cycle methods of the local home.
- Perform the EJB operations.
- Close the Initial context.

Also note that while using local interfaces with colocated EJBs, you don't need to perform a call to `PortableRemoteObject.narrow` because you are no longer dealing with remote objects. `RemoteExceptions` don't need to be caught either, but `EJBExceptions` may be caught instead.

Life Cycle of a Stateless Session Bean

Figure 21.1 illustrates the life cycle of the Stateless Session Bean within the WebLogic Server container.

Initially, the container does not have any beans. While deploying the bean, you can set up a parameter called `<initial-beans-in-free-pool>` (in `weblogic-ejb.jar`, under `<weblogic-ejb-jar>`→`<weblogic-enterprise-bean>`→`<stateless-session-descriptor>`→`<pool>`), which indicates to the container that you require a certain number of bean instances to be created even before any request arrives to the container. The container creates these instances by first calling the `newInstance` method on the `Class`. The container subsequently invokes the `setSessionContext` and the `ejbCreate` methods on the instances. At this point, the bean instances move to the method-ready pool or the method-ready state.

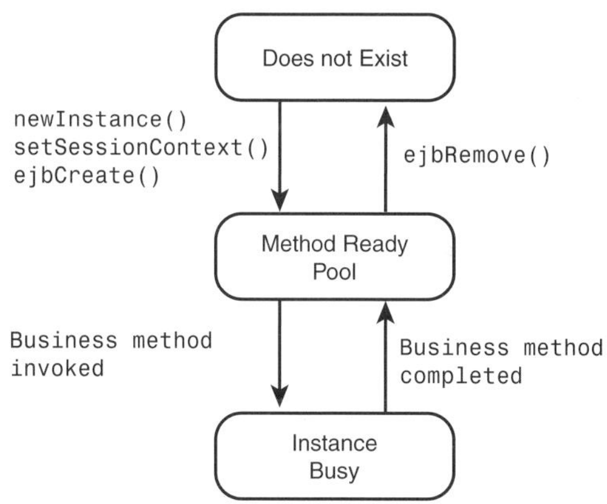

Figure 21.1 Stateless Session Bean Life cycle.

The method-ready pool is a mechanism by which the container pools Stateless Session Bean instances so that they're already created and available when the client invokes a business method on a bean instance. The container creates as many bean instances as specified in the deployment descriptor and populates them into the method-ready pool. When a client request arrives, the container picks up a free bean instance and hands it to the client. Thus, no time is spent creating the bean instance. Also, because initialization code of the bean is usually written in the `ejbCreate` method and that method has also been called already, the bean doesn't spend any time performing initializations. However, if a client request arrives and the container doesn't find any free bean instances, it creates a new instance.

This discussion gives rise to a very important point. We said earlier that a Stateless Session Bean could have only a single `create` method in its home interface—one that doesn't take any parameters. This is because the `create` method invocation on the home interface doesn't necessarily translate into an `ejbCreate` method invocation of the bean instance. For a bean, `ejbCreate` is invoked only once in its lifetime. The home interface's `create` method simply tells the container to provide the client with a bean instance, not necessarily to create one. A second reason is because of the fact that the bean is stateless. Any client-specific initialization you might do in the `ejbCreate` method will not be available when you invoke the business methods.

When a business method is invoked on this bean instance, the container moves the bean instance to a busy state. This bean instance isn't given out to other clients that might request one. The container always returns only idle bean instances to process client requests. After the business method invocation is finished, the instance is returned to the method-ready pool. WebLogic Server provides a mechanism by which you can limit the number of free instances in the free pool. This can be done by setting the parameter `<max-beans-in-free-pool>` (in `weblogic-ejb.jar`, under `<weblogic-ejb-jar>`→`<weblogic-enterprise-bean>`→`<stateless-session-descriptor>`→`<pool>`) to an appropriate value.

When the number of free bean instances exceeds this value, the container starts removing bean instances. Remember that when a client to a Stateless Session Bean invokes the `remove` method on an instance, the container doesn't necessarily remove the bean instance from memory. In fact, this method does nothing. The bean instance returns to the method-ready pool immediately after each method invocation. The container might decide to destroy the bean instance for other reasons, such as the setting of `<max-beans-in-free-pool>`, or other resource crunches. But destruction of a bean instance is never caused directly because a client calls `remove` on the bean.

When bean instances are removed, the `ejbRemove` method is invoked. This provides an opportunity to the bean to release any resources that it might be holding on, and to perform other cleanup tasks. After this method is invoked, the bean instance is de-referenced and made eligible for garbage collection. The bean instance ceases to exist; in other words, it transitions to the "does not exist" state.

Working with Stateful Session Beans

In the previous section, we looked at the different aspects of writing and deploying a Stateless Session Bean. In this section, we look at the Stateful Session Bean. As we go along, you'll see that developing a Stateful Session Bean is very similar to developing its Stateless counterpart. Because of this, you'll find that this section refers you to sections of the Stateless Session Beans discussion wherever relevant. However, you must understand the conceptual differences between these two types of Session Beans.

Unlike its Stateless counterpart, a Stateful Session Bean instance is associated with a client and cannot be shared across different clients. It represents a single client on the application server context. It acts as an extension of the client within the application server, and performs tasks on behalf of a single client. To achieve this, Stateful Session Beans can maintain conversational state, which is specific to a client. Also, Stateful Session Beans aren't pooled as Stateless Session Beans are. The container creates a new instance of a Stateful Session Bean whenever you request one. Having said that, you can use handles to share Stateful Session Beans, but that isn't often done in practice.

For our case study, we must develop a shopping cart bean, which will enable the user to book seats on several flights and pay for them. This is a typical case in which Stateful Session Beans would come in handy. The state that's maintained in the bean will be the total amount that must be charged. Our bean will utilize the Stateless Session Bean that we already developed to perform the actual reservation task.

Similar to Stateless Session Beans, Stateful Session Beans also have the following components:

- The optional remote home interface and a remote interface
- The optional local home interface and a local interface
- The bean implementation

Remember, you have to include a set of remote interfaces, local interfaces, or both in your bean deployment. The following sections describe these components in detail.

The Remote Interface

The first interface we'll create is the remote interface. Unlike the `AirlineReservation` EJB, the `AirlineShoppingCart` EJB requires a set of remote interfaces because the clients of this bean might be accessing it remotely. This interface enables the client to communicate with the Stateful Bean. Using the same naming convention adopted earlier, we'll name our remote interface `AirlineShoppingCartRemoteObject`.

To decide what methods this interface should provide, let's first identify how the client will use the shopping cart bean. As you might remember, the shopping cart bean will behave as an extension to the client.

The client will first instantiate the bean and search for the flights using business methods provided by the bean. It will subsequently use setters in the bean to set the flight number and the number of seats required. Following this, the client will reserve the seats by invoking the `reserveSeats` method on the bean. The client will repeat this set of operations for as many flights the user desires to book seats on. Upon completion, the client will request the bean—the total amount that should be charged to the client.

This gives us all the information we need to create the remote interface. We'll extend this interface from the `javax.ejb.EJBObject` interface. The code snippet follows:

```
import java.rmi.RemoteException;
import java.util.Properties;
import javax.ejb.EJBObject;


public interface AirlineShoppingCartRemoteObject
  extends EJBObject {
  public void setOrigin( String origin )
    throws RemoteException ;
  public void setDestination( String destination )
    throws RemoteException ;
  public void setFlightNumber( int flightNum )
    throws RemoteException ;
  public void setNumSeats( int numSeats )
    throws RemoteException ;
  public int[] searchFlights()
    throws RemoteException, AirlineShoppingCartException;
  public void reserveSeats()
    throws RemoteException, AirlineShoppingCartException;
  public Properties getFlightInfo()
    throws RemoteException, AirlineShoppingCartException;
```

```
  public double getTotalCost()
    throws RemoteException;
}
```

This tells us how the client will invoke the shopping cart bean. As is already obvious, the Stateful Bean does not require that client-specific information be always passed into each business method. It enables us to store client-specific state; therefore, we can have setter methods set the relevant values in the bean before invoking the business methods. Note that, in this case, the client cannot invoke the business methods (namely `searchFlights`, `reserveSeats` or `getFlightInfo`) without invoking the setters. In other words, our business methods do not work on their own; they expect other methods to have been invoked before the business method has been invoked.

Is this the only correct way to code a Stateful Session Bean? Certainly not. This bean was coded this way only to demonstrate this capability. In certain cases, this mechanism offers many advantages. For instance, assume that output from one business method drives the inputs to the next business method invoked by the client. For instance, output from the `getFlightInfo` might drive the input to the `reserveSeats` method. This means that the only information that the client has to provide is the number of seats.

The discussion about serializable objects for parameters and return types also holds true for Stateful Session Beans. Parameters to the methods and return values must be serializable so that they can be sent over the wire. Also, all methods in this interface throw `RemoteException` to satisfy the requirement for RMI communication. You can read more about the types of exceptions that can be thrown by business methods in the "More About Exceptions" section later in this chapter.

The remote interface extends from the `EJBObject` interface. Several methods of the `EJBObject` interface hold similar meanings when invoked in the context of a Stateful Session Bean, as they do with Stateless Session Beans. However, there are a few differences as described in the following list:

- The `isIdentical` method of the `EJBObject` interface checks whether the two beans are identical. For Stateful Session Beans, the rules for such a match are different from those for a Stateless Session Bean (two Stateless Session Bean instances are always identical). The EJB specification states that Stateful Session Beans have a unique identity, which is assigned by the container when the instance is created. By using the `isIdentical` method, the client can determine whether two remote object references refer to the same Session Bean instance.

- When the client invokes the `remove` method on a Stateful Session Bean's remote object, the container immediately removes the bean from the memory. If the client attempts to invoke any business method after removing it, a `RemoteException` is thrown.

The Remote Home Interface

The remote home interface is very similar to the remote home interface of a Stateless Session Bean. The remote home interface is a factory for the remote object, and it extends from the javax.ejb.EJBHome interface. However, unlike a Stateless Session Bean, the remote home interface for a Stateful Session Bean can contain more than one create method. This is because containers do not maintain pools of Stateful Session Beans. These bean instances are created whenever a client invokes the create method on the home instance. Therefore, invoking the create method translates into a corresponding ejbCreate method on the bean class. Because a Stateful Session Bean instance is always associated with a client, the client can choose how the bean instance has to be created, which is unlike a Stateless Session Bean. Each of the create methods returns the remote interface of the bean.

You can even have suffixes for the create methods, thus providing more meaning to the method name. For instance, suppose that we enhance the functionality of our application to support bookings for platinum customers. To differentiate the types of customers, we can either add a Boolean value and invoke the appropriate setter, or alternatively, add another create method called createCartForPlatinumCustomer to make it more obvious.

The remote home interface extends from the javax.ejb.EJBHome interface, just like Stateless Session Beans. For the sake of our shopping cart bean, let's produce two create methods: one that doesn't take any parameters, and a second that takes the origin and destination airports. The second isn't necessary in our case because the bean provides setters, which can be invoked to achieve the same result, but it will help to illustrate the point. The following code snippet illustrates the remote home interface:

```
import javax.ejb.EJBObject;
import java.rmi.RemoteException;
public interface AirlineShoppingCartRemoteHome
    extends EJBObject {
  public AirlineShoppingCartRemoteObject create()
    throws RemoteException, CreateException;
  public AirlineShoppingCartRemoteObject create(
      String origin, String destination )
    throws RemoteException, CreateException;
}
```

As before, our create methods throw exceptions of type RemoteException and CreateException. The bean usually uses the CreateException to indicate to the client that an error occurred while creating the instance. RemoteExceptions are typically used by the underlying RMI implementation to indicate whether any failure occurs while accessing the bean. Note that the create methods are free to throw more application exceptions.

The Local Interface and Local Home Interface

Next, we create a set of local interfaces for the `AirlineShoppingCart` EJB. We don't discuss this in detail, but it's sufficient for you to understand that the concepts for creating local interfaces are very similar to those for creating Stateless Session Beans. However, the methods that go into these interfaces do resemble their remote counterparts for the `AirlineShoppingCart` EJB, which we created in the preceding sections.

As a reminder, local interfaces differ from remote interfaces in the following ways:

- They do not throw `RemoteExceptions`.
- They can have parameters and return types that aren't serializable.
- Parameters are passed by reference; modifying a parameter can affect the caller's context.

The Bean Class

The Bean class provides the bean implementation. The container invokes corresponding business methods on the bean implementation when client requests are made on the RMI stub. This class does not directly implement any of the interfaces that we've already discussed; it simply provides methods that handle both life cycle methods as well as business methods.

Let's first take a look at the skeleton of the Bean class that we'll be writing, as shown in Listing 21.5. We haven't yet coded the logic within the business methods.

LISTING 21.5 Implementation for a Stateful Bean

```
public class AirlineShoppingCartBean implements SessionBean {
  SessionContext context = null;
  public AirlineShoppingCartBean() {
    super();
  }
  public void setSessionContext(SessionContext aContext)
    throws RemoteException {
    System.out.println(" setSessionContext called ");
    context = aContext;
  }
  public void ejbCreate() throws CreateException {
    System.out.println("ejbCreate called");
    // Create the prepared statements
  }
  public void ejbCreate(String origin, String destination)
  throws CreateException {
```

LISTING 21.5 Continued

```
    System.out.println("ejbCreate called");
  }
  public void ejbRemove() {
    System.out.println("ejbRemove called");
  }
  public void ejbActivate() {
    System.out.println("ejbActivate called");
  }
  public void ejbPassivate() {
    System.out.println("ejbPassivate called");
  }
  public Properties getFlightInfo()
    throws RemoteException, AirlineShoppingCartException {
    return null;
  }
  public double getTotalCost() throws RemoteException {
    return 0;
  }
  public void reserveSeats()
    throws AirlineShoppingCartException {
  }
  public int[] searchFlights()
    throws AirlineShoppingCartException {
    return null;
  }
  public void setDestination(String destination) {
  }
  public void setFlightNumber(int flightNum) {
  }
  public void setNumSeats(int numSeats) {
  }
  public void setOrigin(String origin) {
  }
}
```

The rules for coding the Bean class are the same as we discussed for Stateless Session Beans. The different methods that were discussed in that context also hold true in the context of Stateful Session Beans. However, a few concepts are slightly different for Stateful Session Beans. We highlight only those concepts in the following list.

- The remote home (and the local home) interface of a Stateful Session Bean can have more than one `create` method. The Bean class should declare one `ejbCreate` method for every `create` method declared in the home interfaces. Whenever a client invokes a `create` method on the home interface, the container invokes the corresponding `ejbCreate` method on the bean instance. For `create` methods in the home interface that have a suffix, you must define an `ejbCreate` method with the same suffix. For example, for a home interface method called `createCartForPlatinumCustomer`, you must define a corresponding `ejbCreateCartForPlatinumCustomer` method in the Bean class.
- For Stateful Session Beans, you can indicate to the container the number of bean instances that can be present in the cache at a given time. This cache should not be confused with the method-ready pool for Stateless Session Beans. This is just a collection of bean instances that are created by different clients at different points of time. Obviously, some of these bean instances might not be used at all times. When the number of bean instances in the cache reaches the maximum number of bean instances configured, the container frees up resources by passivating some of the bean instances. Passivation involves serializing the bean instance to the file system, thus removing it from memory. Before passivating, the container invokes the `ejbPassivate` method on the bean instance. This gives the bean an opportunity to free up resources that it might be holding up. For more information about passivation and activation, refer to Chapter 20.
- If the client that originally created the bean instance initiates a business method on that bean instance after it's been passivated, the container activates the bean from the file system and invokes the `ejbActivate` method on the bean. This gives the bean an opportunity to perform all the initialization routines.

Of course, apart from these methods, the bean classes should provide implementations for all the business methods defined in the object interfaces. We don't list any code from the business methods here, but you can find the implementation class in the file `com/wlsunleashed/ejb/session/stateful/AirlineShoppingCartBean.java`.

Let's look at a snippet of code from this bean implementation to illustrate the process by which another bean (the `AirlineReservation` bean) present within the same container is invoked. Consider the following snippet of code from the bean implementation:

```
  // The initialization routine called by ejbCreate
private void initialize() throws CreateException {
....
    try {
      Context ctx = new InitialContext();
      reservationHome =
        (AirlineReservationLocalHome) ctx.lookup(
```

```
            "LocalAirlineReservationBean");
    }
    catch (Exception ex) {
      throw new CreateException(ex.getMessage());
    }
....
}

public void reserveSeats() throws AirlineShoppingCartException {
....
    try {
      AirlineReservationLocalObject reservationObject =
        reservationHome.create();
      reservationObject.reserveSeats(flightNumber, numSeats);
      Properties props = getFlightInfo();
      double unitPrice = Double.parseDouble(
        (String)props.get("TOTAL_COST_PER_SEAT"));
      totalCost += unitPrice;
    }
    catch (Exception ex) {
      throw new AirlineShoppingCartException(ex.getMessage());
    }
....
}
```

This code snippet is interesting because of the fact that the shopping cart bean behaves as a client to the `AirlineReservation` EJB that we created earlier.

It's clear from the code that we look up the home object at the time of initialization of the bean. We then use this home instance to create a local object instance in the business method. For a detailed discussion of invoking EJBs, refer to the earlier discussion on Stateless Session Beans.

Deployment Descriptors of a Stateful Session Bean

You have to essentially create the same two deployment descriptors for deploying Stateful Session Beans as you did for Stateless Session Beans. Most of the discussion of deployment descriptors in the earlier sections of this chapter also holds true for Stateful Session Beans. Of course, there are some differences between the deployment descriptors of the two. This section highlights only these differences. To get the complete picture, please ensure that you read this section in conjunction with the section on deployment descriptors for Stateless Session Beans and the introduction provided in Chapter 20.

ejb-jar.xml

The ejb-jar.xml file looks very similar to the one from Stateless Session Beans. The only difference between these two descriptors is the <session-type> tag (under <ejb-jar>→<enterprise-beans>→<session>), which has to be set to Stateful (rather than Stateless) for Stateful Session Beans. Listing 21.6 shows the code of the ejb-jar.xml file, which we use for the AirlineShoppingCart EJB.

LISTING 21.6 ejb-jar.xml for a Stateful Session Bean

```
<!DOCTYPE ejb-jar PUBLIC '-//Sun Microsystems,
➥ Inc.//DTD Enterprise JavaBeans 2.0//EN'
➥ 'http://java.sun.com/dtd/ejb-jar_2_0.dtd'>

<ejb-jar>
 <enterprise-beans>
  <session>
   <ejb-name>AirlineShoppingCartBean</ejb-name>
   <home>
     com.wls70unleashed.ejb.session.stateful.
➥          AirlineShoppingCartRemoteHome
   </home>
   <remote>
     com.wls70unleashed.ejb.session.stateful.
➥          AirlineShoppingCartRemoteObject
   </remote>
   <ejb-class>
     com.wls70unleashed.ejb.session.stateful.
➥          AirlineShoppingCartBean
   </ejb-class>
   <session-type>Stateful</session-type>
   <transaction-type>Container</transaction-type>
   <ejb-local-ref>
    <ejb-ref-name>ejb/ReservationStatelessEJB</ejb-ref-name>
    <ejb-ref-type>Session</ejb-ref-type>
    <local-home>
      com.wls70unleashed.ejb.session.stateless.
➥     AirlineReservationLocalHome
    </local-home>
    <local>
      com.wls70unleashed.ejb.session.stateless.
➥     AirlineReservationLocalObject
    </local>
    <ejb-link>AirlineReservationBean</ejb-link>
```

LISTING 21.6 Continued

```
    </ejb-local-ref>
   </session>
  </enterprise-beans>

  <assembly-descriptor>
  </assembly-descriptor>

</ejb-jar>
```

weblogic-ejb-jar.xml

The second deployment descriptor is the weblogic-ejb-jar.xml file. This descriptor also looks quite similar to that used for Stateless Session Beans. However, in the place of the <stateless-session-descriptor> stanza (under <weblogic-ejb-jar>→<weblogic-enterprise-bean>), this descriptor now contains the stanza <stateful-session-descriptor>. For example:

```
<!DOCTYPE weblogic-ejb-jar PUBLIC '-//BEA Systems,
➥ Inc.//DTD WebLogic 7.0.0 EJB//EN'
➥ 'http://www.bea.com/servers/wls700/dtd/weblogic700-ejb-jar.dtd'>


<weblogic-ejb-jar>
 <weblogic-enterprise-bean>
  <ejb-name>AirlineShoppingCartBean</ejb-name>
  <stateful-session-descriptor>
   <stateful-session-cache>
   </stateful-session-cache>
   <stateful-session-clustering>
   </stateful-session-clustering>
  </stateful-session-descriptor>
  <transaction-descriptor>
  </transaction-descriptor>
  <reference-descriptor>
   <ejb-local-reference-description>
    <ejb-ref-name>ejb/ReservationStatelessEJB</ejb-ref-name>
    <jndi-name>LocalAirlineReservationBean</jndi-name>
   </ejb-local-reference-description>
  </reference-descriptor>
  <jndi-name>AirlineShoppingCartBean</jndi-name>
 </weblogic-enterprise-bean>
</weblogic-ejb-jar>
```

This stanza can contain the following elements:

- An optional stanza, <stateful-session-cache>, which indicates some properties of the Stateful Bean cache within the container.
- An optional <lifecycle> stanza, which defines properties that affect the life cycle of the Stateful Session Bean.
- An optional <persistent-store-dir> to indicate to the container which directory is to be used to store the persisted (passivated) Session Beans.
- A <stateful-session-clustering> stanza that indicates the clustering strategy of the Stateful Session Beans. There's more about this in the section "Clustering a Stateful Session Bean," later in this chapter. This tag is optional.
- The <allow-concurrent-calls> tag can be set to `True` or `False` to indicate to the container whether it should entertain concurrent method invocations. According to the EJB specification, the container throws a `RemoteException` if a second method call arrives to the bean while the instance is already processing a method call. If this parameter is set to `True`, the container blocks the second call and lets it go through after the first call has completed. This tag is optional.

The <stateful-session-clustering> stanza relates to clustering, and you can read more about this stanza in the section "Clustering a Stateful Session Bean" that appears later in this chapter.

<stateful-session-cache> describes the caching strategy of the Stateful Session Bean. A Stateful Session Bean *cache* is a collection of bean instances created by clients at any given time. The container maintains this cache using the parameters defined under this stanza. This stanza contains the following elements

- The optional <max-beans-in-cache> property indicates to the container the maximum number of bean instances that are allowed in memory. The container can passivate bean instances if the number of instances exceeds this value.
- The optional property <idle-timeout-seconds> indicates the number of seconds a bean instance should be idle before it becomes eligible for passivation. This property also indicates the timeout value for passivated beans. If a passivated bean does not receive a request within this time, the bean is evicted.
- The optional <cache-type> property indicates the type of cache to be used for Stateful Session Beans. The value for this property can be either `LRU` (least recently used) or `NRU` (not recently used). When set to `NRU`, the container attempts to passivate instances only when there is pressure on resources and when the number of beans is approaching the value specified for the <max-beans-in-cache> setting. When set to `LRU`, the container passivates bean instances when they reach the <idle-timeout-seconds>, whether or not there is any pressure for resources. The default setting for this parameter is `NRU`.

Deploying a Stateful Session Bean

Creating the deployment descriptors and deploying the bean to WebLogic Server is exactly the same as for Stateless Session Beans. You can refer the sections earlier in this chapter for a detailed discussion on these tasks. The build script packaged with this book also takes care of building the `AirlineShoppingCart` bean. Both the EJBs are built and packaged in the same JAR file. So, if you've already built and deployed the EAR file, you've also deployed the Stateful Bean.

Accessing a Stateful Session Bean from a Client

Let's create a JSP that will access the Stateful Session Bean and enable users to reserve seats on the flights. From the client's perspective, accessing a Stateful Session Bean is no different from accessing a Stateless Session Bean. The client simply uses the business methods published by the object interfaces, just as it did with Stateless Session Beans.

The client to the `AirlineShoppingCart` EJB is comprised of the following files:

- `SearchFlights.html`—Starting point of the client. Enables you to specify two cities between which you need to search for flights.
- `SearchResults.jsp`—Displays the results of the search and enables you to choose one or more flights on which you need seats booked. Also enables you to specify the number of seats and initiate the reserve request.
- `ReserveSeats.jsp`—Performs the reservation for each flight selected and displays the results from the Reservation in a tabular form. Also displays the total cost to be charged to the customer.

NOTE

If you used the Ant script we provided and deployed the EAR file, the Web application containing these files is already part of the EAR file. You can directly access the HTML file by typing `http://localhost:7001/AirlineReservation/SearchFlights.html` in your browser window after deploying the EAR file.

One very interesting side note about the JSP client is that if you look closely at the code, you'll find that the JSP (along with its helper classes) uses the EJB by invoking the local interfaces. As with Stateless Session Beans, other colocated objects can access Stateful Session Beans using local interfaces, if defined. This obviously improves performance by completely avoiding network calls. This works perfectly well if the client is packaged within the same application as the EJB. This is the reason we deploy the application as an EAR file. If you didn't do this, but deployed the EJB independent of the WAR file, the JSP cannot use local interfaces.

Life Cycle of a Stateful Session Bean

Figure 21.2 illustrates the lifecycle of a Stateful Session Bean, within the container.

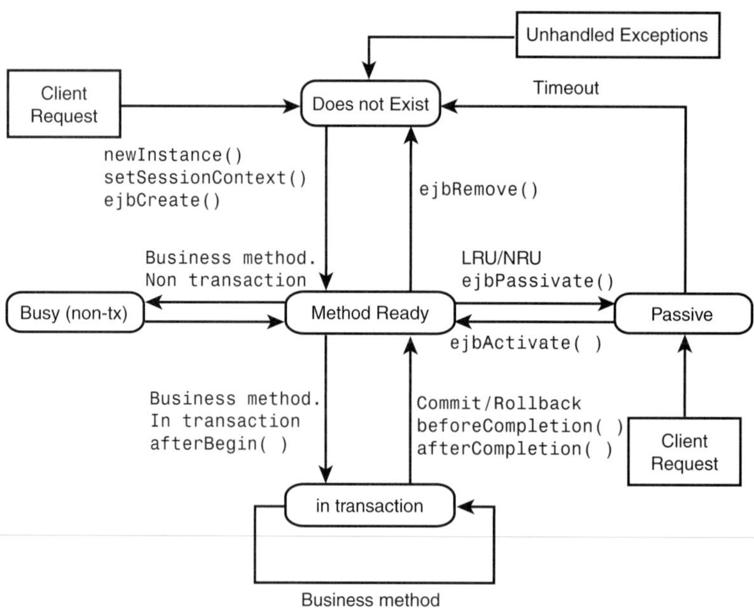

Figure 21.2 Stateful Session Bean Life cycle.

As you can see from the figure, the bean instance may be in three states: Does Not Exist, Method Ready, And Passive. As already mentioned, Stateful Session Beans do not use instance pooling. Therefore, the method ready state of the Stateful Session Bean isn't the same as that of a Stateless Session Bean. Each Stateful Session Bean instance is tied to only one client, and when the client is done with the bean instance, the instance is evicted from memory to save resources.

The bean instance does not initially exist; in other words, it's present in the Does Not Exist state. At this point, when a client tries to create a bean instance by invoking a `create` method on its home interface, the container creates a bean instance by calling the `newInstance` method on the bean class. The container then sets the session context by invoking the `setSessionContext` method. The container invokes the appropriate `ejbCreate` method on the bean instance and allows the bean to initialize itself. The bean is now said to have transitioned to the Method Ready state, and is available for the client to invoke its methods. While in this state, the bean instance can maintain conversational state with the client.

When a business method is invoked outside of a transaction, the bean goes into a busy state. While in this state, the container will not entertain additional client calls. Even if you've set the `<allow-concurrent-calls>` property in `weblogic-ejb-jar.xml` (under `<weblogic-ejb-jar>→<weblogic-enterprise-bean>→<stateful-session-descriptor>`) to `true`, the container will block this call until the first call has completed successfully. After the business method has completed, the bean returns to the Method Ready state.

Stateful Session Beans are, by definition, not transactional components. This means that when a transaction rolls back, it has no effect on the state of the bean instance (that is, the values stored within the bean). However, you can make the bean transactional by making the Stateful Session Bean implement the `javax.ejb.SessionSynchronization` interface. This interface holds three callback methods: `afterBegin`, `beforeCompletion`, and `afterCompletion`. We look at this interface in more detail in the section "Container-Managed Transactions " that appears later in this chapter. For now, it's sufficient to know that the container invokes these methods at appropriate times when a business method is invoked within a transaction.

When a business method is invoked within the boundaries of a transaction, the container first invokes the `afterBegin` callback method. This tells the bean instance that the transaction has begun, and it may perform additional initialization routines during this time. The bean instance goes to an In Transaction state. All business methods that are invoked at this time will return the bean back to the In Transaction state. Once the transaction is committed or rolled back, the instance moves back to the Method Ready state. During this process, two more callback methods, `beforeCompletion` and `afterCompletion`, are invoked in the bean instance.

While performing any business method, both inside and outside a transaction, if the container traps an unhandled exception or a `RuntimeException` is thrown from the bean instance, it evicts the bean and moves it straight to the Does Not Exist state.

When the container needs to free up resources, it may passivate bean instances. At this time, it invokes the `ejbPassivate` method on the bean instance to provide to it with an opportunity to clear up its resources. The EJB specification requires the bean instance to set all variables that aren't serializable to `null`, and to close any open resources in this method. Any field that's declared `transient` will not be serialized. On completion of this method call, the bean instance moves to the Passive state. If a client request comes in for the bean instance while it's in the Passive state, the container activates the bean and invokes the `ejbActivate` method on the instance. At this point, the bean may reinitialize itself. The bean instance then moves back to the Method Ready state.

While in the passive state, the bean instance might timeout before a client request comes in. When this happens, the bean moves back to the Does Not Exist state. This timeout value can be controlled by using the `<idle-timeout-seconds>` tag in the `weblogic-ejb-jar.xml` file, under `<weblogic-ejb-jar>→<weblogic-enterprise-bean>→<stateful-session-descriptor>→<stateful-session-cache>`. Refer to Chapter 20 for a detailed discussion of passivation and activation of beans.

If the client invokes the `remove` method on the bean when it's in the Method Ready state, the container evicts the bean and the bean moves back to Does Not Exist state.

Session Beans and WebLogic Server Clustering

Many business applications are very sensitive to system failures. Companies have to offer 24/7 availability to remain competitive. To minimize system failures, WebLogic enables you to cluster services across multiple server instances. If one server fails, another server can service the request. Thus, clients will seldom realize that there has been a (partial) system failure, and can continue processing transparently.

Cluster provides two advantages to an enterprise:

- Load balancing—Calls are balanced across different cluster instances, thus enhancing performance.
- Failover—Calls that fail due to system failures are retried with other servers in the cluster instance, thus minimizing errors.

You can learn more about WebLogic Server clustering in Chapter 36, "Working with WebLogic Server Clusters." In this section, we look at some clustering strategies that can be adopted with relevance to Session EJBs. We look first at clustering Stateless Session EJBs, followed by an examination of Stateful beans.

Clustering a Stateless Session Bean

As you already know, EJBs use RMI to communicate between the client and the server. The RMI implementation of the home or remote interface on the client side is known as a *stub*. A stub is a network protocol–aware object that communicates with the server to process client requests. When there's more than one instance of the WebLogic Server within the deployment, the stubs that are created are aware of the physical location of the different servers. In other words, these stubs are "replica-aware." They're intelligent enough to reach out to a second server if the first server fails.

Stateless session clustering properties are affected by the `<stateless-clustering>` stanza (under `<weblogic-ejb-jar>`→`<weblogic-enterprise-bean>`→`<stateless-session-descriptor>`) stanza of the `weblogic-ejb-jar.xml` deployment descriptor.

In some cases, you might not want some Stateless Beans to be cluster-aware. You have a choice of making the Stateless Bean methods nonclusterable. The optional parameter `<stateless-bean-is-clusterable>` indicates whether the bean is clusterable. By default, this property is set to `True`. If the bean is clusterable, calls to the stub will be load-balanced across all the cluster participants where the bean has been deployed. The stub also attempts to failover method calls when any server that it's trying to reach is unreachable due to a possible system failure. Needless to say, you can control the load-balancing behavior of the method calls.

Load Balancing Strategy

When we talk of load balancing requests across different server instances, one logical question is in regard to the algorithm used to perform the load-balancing operation. WebLogic Server enables you to configure a load-balancing algorithm for choosing the server to communicate with. This can be done by configuring the optional `<stateless-bean-load-algorithm>` tag (under `<weblogic-ejb-jar>`→`<weblogic-enterprise-bean>`→`<stateless-session-descriptor>`→`<stateless-clustering>`). Valid values for this property are `round-robin`, `random`, and `weight-based`.

WebLogic Server also enables you to write your own load-balancing algorithm by specifying your own class name in the property `<stateless-bean-call-router-class-name>` (under `<weblogic-ejb-jar>`→`<weblogic-enterprise-bean>`→`<stateless-session-descriptor>`→`<stateless-clustering>`). This parameter takes the name of the class that should implement the interface `weblogic.rmi.cluster.CallRouter`. This interface (and hence, your implementation) has a method called `getServerList`. This method accepts the `Method` and an `Object` array as parameters. It returns an array of server names, as defined in the WebLogic Server console. You're free to implement any algorithm to arrive at the list of server names. If your call router class returns a null list of servers, the default load-balancing algorithm is used.

For example, suppose that XYZ Airlines wants to implement clustering in its enterprise. The airline wants all write methods (such as `reserveSeats`) to be routed to a set of dedicated write servers, while sending the searches to a set of dedicated read servers. All other functions can be routed using the default load-balancing algorithm of the server. The following is a sample code of a call-router class:

```
public class AirlineCallRouter implements CallRouter {
private static final String[] writeServers = { "server1", "server3" };
private static final String[] readServers = { "server2", "server4" };

 public String[] getServerList(Method theMethod, Object[] params) {
  if (m.getName().equals("reserveSeats")) {
    return writeServers;
  }
  if (m.getName().equals("searchFlights")) {
    return readServers;
  }
  return null;
 }
}
```

For more information about clustering, see Chapter 36.

Failover Strategy

Consider two of the methods that we coded as part of the `AirlineReservation` EJB: `getFlightNumbers` (which searches for flights based on the origin and destination cities) and `reserveSeats` (which actually performs the reservation). Now assume that the stub attempts to perform one of these methods on `Server-1`. It waits for a while, but eventually receives an error, that isn't a business error (that is, a `RemoteException`). At this point, assume that the stub retries the request on `Server-2`, and that the request goes through successfully. This gives us two scenarios, depending on the stage at which the call to `Server-1` failed:

- The request never reached `Server-1`. It failed even before the bean implementation could receive the request.
- The request made it all the way to the bean implementation, and the call went through successfully. However, some error occurred before the results could be returned back to the client.

In the first case, there's no problem at all. The stub retries the request, receives a successful response, and reports back to the client. However, consider the second case. For the `getFlightNumbers` method, there is again no problem. That's because although the transaction made it all the way to the end, no data was ever changed, and it doesn't hurt to retry the request and get back the same results. It will definitely impact response time, but it doesn't hurt the integrity of the data. However, with the `reserveSeats` method, the reservation went through successfully the first time. Therefore, when the request is retried, the seats will be booked twice! This is obviously a serious condition that should be avoided. WebLogic Server achieves this by making the stub retry requests only for idempotent methods. The Free On-line dictionary of computing defines an idempotent function as

A function f: D -> D is idempotent if f (f (x)) = f (x) for all x in D. I.e. repeated applications have the same effect as one.

Based on this definition of an idempotent function, it's quite obvious that `getFlightNumbers` is idempotent, whereas `reserveSeats` is not.

WebLogic uses the `<stateless-bean-methods-are-idempotent>` parameter in the `weblogic-ejb-jar.xml` deployment descriptor (under `<weblogic-ejb-jar>`→`<weblogic-enterprise-bean>`→`<stateless-session-descriptor>`→`<stateless-clustering>`). If this parameter is set to true, all methods of this stateless bean are considered to be idempotent and can failover. If set to false (which is the default behavior), no methods are considered idempotent, and the stub fails after the first failure. With WebLogic version 8.1, this parameter has been deprecated. Do not use this mechanism; instead, use the one that's discussed next.

In our case, this isn't sufficient because we have one method that's idempotent and one that isn't. To maximize the failover features of our application, we must identify idempotency on a business-method level, rather than in a global level. To do this, we can use the `<idempotent-methods>` stanza under the `<weblogic-ejb-jar>`→`<weblogic-enterprise-bean>` element. Using this stanza, we can list only the methods that are to be treated as idempotent. This element can take a list of methods, defined by the `<method>` stanza. You can look up the structure of a `<method>` tag from its definition in Chapter 20. Thus, when you define idempotent methods, the stub is careful to retry calls only for these methods, and not for every method.

Clustering a Stateful Session Bean

Stateful Session Beans also use replica-aware stubs for supporting clustering within a WebLogic Server clustered deployment. The clustering properties of a Stateful Session Bean are controlled by the stanza `<stateful-session-clustering>` (under `<weblogic-ejb-jar>`→`<weblogic-enterprise-bean>`→`<stateful-session-descriptor>`).

Load Balancing Strategy for Stateful Beans

With Stateless Session Beans, the home interface is considered to be clusterable all the time. The container load balances calls to the home interface. However, with Stateful Session Beans, you have the capacity to override this default behavior. This can be done by setting the parameter `<home-is-clusterable>` (under `<weblogic-ejb-jar>`→`<weblogic-enterprise-bean>`→`<stateful-session-descriptor>`→`<stateful-session-clustering>`) to `False`. If this property is set to `True`, the home methods are not only load balanced, but are also failed over to a second server. The `<home-load-algorithm>` (under `<weblogic-ejb-jar>`→`<weblogic-enterprise-bean>`→`<stateful-session-descriptor>`→`<stateful-session-clustering>`) property determines the load-balancing algorithm to be employed for the home stub. The value to this property can be `round-robin`, `random`, or `weight-based`. You may write your own call router class to define your own load-balancing algorithm by implementing the interface `weblogic.rmi.cluster.CallRouter`. This class should be capable of returning a list of servers that have to be tried for making the call.

At the same time, the remote object's methods are not load-balanced for Stateful Session Beans because only one bean instance is active at a time per client.

Failover Strategy for Stateful Beans

By default, calls to the Stateful Session Bean remote interfaces do not fail over. If a stub receives an exception, it doesn't retry the request. But you can override this behavior by setting the property `<replication-type>` (under `<weblogic-ejb-jar>`→`<weblogic-enterprise-bean>`→`<stateful-session-descriptor>`→`<stateful-session-clustering>`) to `InMemory`. The only other value that this property takes is `None`, which is the default value. So, what is this replication type, and how does it affect failover? The following discussion will help answer this question.

Just like Stateless Session Beans, Stateful beans can also declare idempotent methods by using the `<idempotent-methods>` stanza (under `<weblogic-ejb-jar>`→`<weblogic-enterprise-bean>`) in the `weblogic-ejb-jar.xml` deployment descriptor. Consider the failover mechanism of a Stateless Session Bean for idempotent methods. When a remote object receives an exception, it simply invokes the same method on another instance in a second server. Because all Stateless Session Beans are identical, this works perfectly. However, for Stateful Session Beans, this won't work because Stateful Session Beans are created per client. So, another instance of the Stateful Session Bean won't have the conversational state that was present in the original bean instance to satisfy the request. To handle this issue, a WebLogic Cluster replicates Stateful Session Bean instances to a backup server.

When a server receives a request to create a Stateful Session Bean instance, it creates the instance and identifies a secondary server that will provide failover mechanism for this bean instance. Secondary servers are selected using certain rules as described in Table 21.2.

While creating a WebLogic cluster, you can create machine names using the console and associate WebLogic Server instances to each machine. Different servers that are running on the same physical machine will be associated to the same machine using the console. Servers that aren't associated with any machine names are considered by WebLogic Server to be running in different physical machines.

A *replication group* is a logical grouping of servers that determines which server will be chosen as the secondary server for replicating Stateful Session Beans. While defining servers, you can specify replication Groups for each server. You can also specify the name of the preferred replication group for each server.

When the server to which the request originally arrives attempts to choose a backup secondary server, it ranks the different servers within the WebLogic Server cluster based on two parameters. The ranking table is shown in Table 21.2.

TABLE 21.2 Rules for Deciding the Secondary Replication Server

Does Server Reside on a Different Machine Than The Primary Server?	Does Server Belong to Primary Server's Preferred Replication Group?	Server's Rank
Yes	Yes	1
No	Yes	2
Yes	No	3
No	No	4

The primary server picks as the secondary server the server that has the lowest rank according to this table. The stub that's created is loaded with the information about the primary and the secondary servers and sent to the client.

The entire bean instance isn't replicated across to the secondary server. To conserve resources, only the state information is replicated. All requests from the client continue to go to the primary server (remember, no load-balancing for Stateful Beans). As and when the client makes any changes to the conversational state, the state changes are replicated to the secondary server. For transactional calls, state changes are replicated only after the transaction has committed. For nontransactional calls, state changes are replicated after every call. Figure 21.3 illustrates this process.

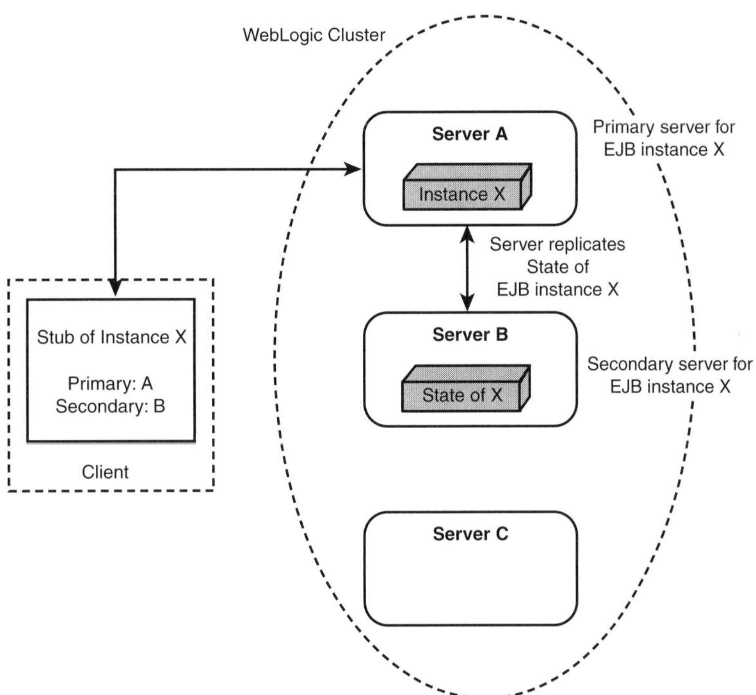

Figure 21.3 Stateful session clustering.

If and when the primary server fails, the stub already has the information needed to contact the secondary server with its request. At this time, the secondary server, which now becomes the primary server, has enough information to re-create the bean instance and the state associated with the client. This server then picks a new secondary server from the available servers list and replicates the state information to the new secondary server. The stub is also updated to reflect the new set of primary and secondary servers on the next method call. This process is illustrated in Figure 21.4.

This way, Stateful Session Beans provide a failover mechanism in a clustered environment. Note, however, that this mechanism has a slight chance of a problem. Imagine that the business method has completed successfully, so the primary server attempts to replicate the state of the bean. If the primary server fails at this stage, before it can successfully complete the replication process, the latest state information never gets to the secondary server. The next request will have to deal with the state as it existed prior to the last call made.

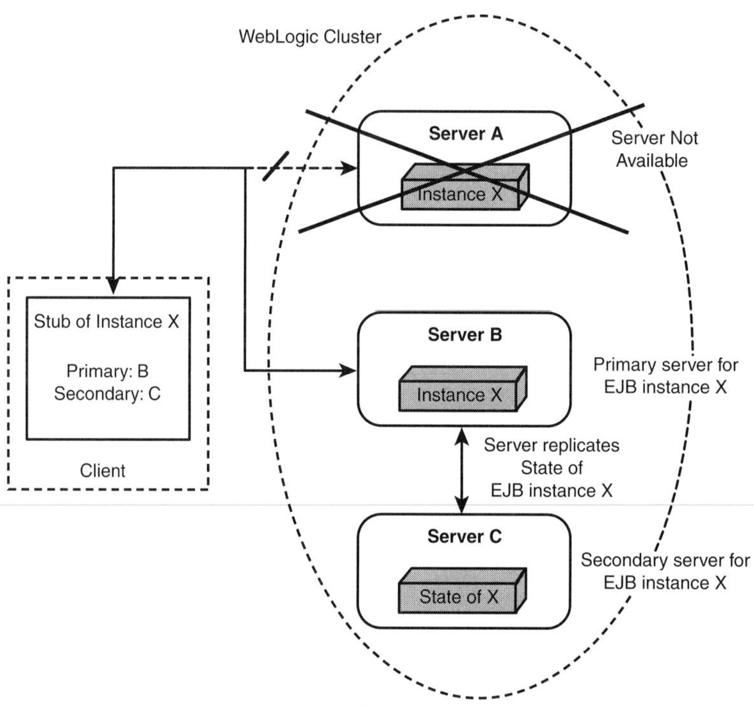

Figure 21.4 Failover scenario for stateful session clustering.

Transactions and Session Beans

Transactions are a mechanism by which your application performs several tasks as a single unit of work. A typical example of transactions would be a banking application executing a funds transfer. This process involves debiting one account and crediting another. If either of these two processes fails, the whole transaction is rolled back. In this chapter, we don't discuss transactions in detail. We look only at different transaction management strategies available to you when you use the WebLogic Server container. You can learn more about transactions in Chapter 9, "Processing Transactions with the Java Transaction API."

There are essentially two types of transaction management for EJBs: container-managed transactions and bean-managed transactions. In this section, we look at these types of transaction management in the context of Session Beans.

Container-Managed Transactions

Container-managed transactions, or CMTs, are a mechanism by which the WebLogic EJB container manages all transactions for you. Your application can focus on the business logic, rather than worrying about nuances of transaction management. CMTs are also often referred to as *declarative transaction management*.

To use declarative transaction management in your bean, simply include the following stanza within the <session> (under <ejb-jar>→<enterprise-beans>) block of your ejb-jar.xml deployment descriptor:

```
<session>
...
  <transaction-type>Container</transaction-type>
</session>
```

After you specify that the container has to manage transactions, you must let the container know which methods require what type of transaction management support. To do this, you introduce a block called <container-transaction> in your ejb-jar.xml (under <ejb-jar>→<assembly-descriptor>). You can provide a default transaction behavior for all methods of your bean by using the wildcard character (*) for the method name. (Refer to Chapter 20 for a more detailed description of the <method> tag.)

Consider the following sample snippet for the AirlineReservation EJB:

```
<assembly-descriptor>
 <container-transaction>
  <method>
    <ejb-name>AirlineReservationBean</ejb-name>
    <method-name>*</method-name>
  </method>
  <trans-attribute>Supports</trans-attribute>
 </container-transaction>
</assembly-descriptor>
```

Here we indicate to the container that all (*) methods of the bean named AirlineReservationBean support transactions. Chapter 20 describes the transaction attributes that can be set for this tag in detail.

We can further refine transactional behavior of some of our methods. For instance, in the following snippet, we tell the container that all methods of this bean support transactions by default, but the reserveSeats method specifically requires a transaction to be present. Thus, the container will start a new transaction if one isn't already present. The container chooses the Required attribute over the Supports attribute because the method defined more specifically indicates the reserveSeats method rather than the generic wildcard method name.

```
<container-transaction>
  <method>
    <ejb-name>AirlineReservationBean</ejb-name>
    <method-name>*</method-name>
  </method>
  <trans-attribute>Supports</trans-attribute>
</container-transaction>
<container-transaction>
  <method>
    <ejb-name>AirlineReservationBean</ejb-name>
    <method-name>reserveSeats</method-name>
  </method>
  <trans-attribute>Required</trans-attribute>
</container-transaction>
```

You can even specify transaction attributes for different flavors of the same method by specifying the `<method-params>` stanza within the method to qualify the method name.

Session Synchronization

One thing you must remember about Stateful Session Beans is that the beans themselves are nontransactional. In other words, if you alter the values stored within the bean during a transaction, those values will not be rolled back if the entire transaction rolls back. Therefore, it becomes necessary for Stateful Session Beans to be aware of transactional activity such as `begin transaction` and `end transaction` so that they can perform additional operations during those times to make the bean transactional.

Session synchronization provides your bean implementation with the capability to make the bean transactional. To achieve this, your bean implementation can optionally implement the `javax.ejb.SessionSynchronization` interface and define three callback methods. The container invokes these methods at appropriate times in the life cycle of the transaction, allowing you to perform such tasks. These methods are

- `afterBegin`—This method is called after the container begins a new transaction. Here you can save the current state of the bean instance into backup variables.
- `beforeCompletion`—This method is invoked just before the container ends (commits or rolls back) the active transaction. At this point, you can verify that the state of the bean instance is sound (validation). If it isn't, you can log this and force a rollback of the transaction.
- `afterCompletion`—This method is invoked after the container has ended (committed or rolled back) the active transaction. The container will also tell you whether the transaction was committed or rolled back by passing in a Boolean value (`true` indicates that the transaction was committed). Here you can restore the bean's state to its earlier state if the transaction was rolled back.

Rolling Back Container-Managed Transactions

We know that the container manages the transaction boundaries for us in the case of declarative transaction management. How does the container know that the transaction has failed and must be rolled back?

The container automatically rolls back the transaction when the bean fails. A bean is considered to fail when it throws a system exception.

Based on this explanation, an application exception isn't considered a failure, and the transaction isn't rolled back. If your bean picks up a condition that indicates the transaction must be rolled back, the bean implementation typically throws an application exception. By definition, application exceptions cannot extend `RuntimeException`. Runtime exceptions are not expected, but business exceptions are.

So, how does your bean instance inform the container that you want this transaction rolled back? To do this, you invoke the `setRollbackOnly` method on the `SessionContext` object. This method tells the container that this transaction must be rolled back, irrespective of the outcomes of other operations that participate in this transaction.

As an example, the following snippet of code indicates to the container that the transaction should never be committed because it violated a business rule:

```
...
If (balance < 200) {
  context.setRollbackOnly();
  throw new BalanceTooLowException();
}
```

Along the same lines, beans that will be part of a transaction can check to see whether other beans have already set the rollback-only option, and avoid processing certain tasks and saving time. This can be done by invoking the `getRollbackOnly` method on the `SessionContext` object, before it does any processing:

```
if (context.getRollbackOnly()) {
  return ;
}
// continue with processing ...
```

Bean-Managed Transactions

Although declarative transaction management can be a very powerful tool, in certain (remote) cases, your application might want more control over transaction management. In such cases, you could use the second type of transaction management known as bean-managed transactions, or BMT for short.

To do this, first set the <transaction-type> attribute (under <ejb-jar>→<enterprise-beans>→<session>) in the ejb-jar.xml to Bean. This ensures that the container won't interfere in transaction management of your bean.

After this is done, you should code your bean implementation to take care of transactions within it. If you want your bean to participate in global transactions, you can use the java.transaction.UserTransaction interface to manage the transactions within your bean. The container provides you with the implementation of the UserTransaction interface in the SessionContext object. As you might remember, the container gives you the SessionContext object by invoking the setSessionContext method of your bean implementation. The following code snippet illustrates the use of UserTransaction in a bean implementation for managing transactions:

```
public void beanMethod() {
  try {
    // context = instanceof SessionContext, set by the
    // setSessionContext method.
    UserTransaction txn = context.getUserTransaction();
    txn.begin();
    // your business logic goes here
    // if all tasks were successful
      txn.commit();
    // else
      txn.rollback();
  }
  catch (Exception ex) {
    // Exception handling logic goes here
  }
}
```

As you can see, we've obtained the UserTransaction object from the session context. Your bean can obtain this object in another way: by looking up the object from the JNDI tree, and looking up the name java:comp/env/UserTransaction. The following code snippet illustrates this process:

```
Context ctx = new InitialContext();
UserTransaction txn = (UserTransaction)
        ctx.lookup("java:comp/env/UserTransaction");
```

This second technique may be used by utility classes invoked by your beans, which don't have access to the session context. Note that this lookup returns null if it's used in the context of container-managed transactions. Note also that getUserTransaction() throws an exception if it's used in the context of container-managed transactions.

NOTE

For more information about the `UserTransaction` interface and how to use the Java transaction architecture, refer to Chapter 9. For more information about JNDI lookups, refer to Chapter 8.

In the case of Stateless Session Beans, transactions that are begun in one method must be ended (committed or rolled back) in the same method. This is because Session Beans aren't tied to a client. If this rule isn't imposed, different clients could potentially invoke the two methods (one that begins the transaction, and one that ends it), which is incorrect.

However, for Stateful Session Beans, you may begin the transaction in one method and end it in a different method. Be very careful while doing this because your bean implementation does not have control over when or if the second method is called by the client. Your bean implementation relies on the client of your bean to invoke the methods in the appropriate order. A preferable alternative to this is to write another bean method that invokes the two methods in the appropriate order, and use container-managed persistence to set the appropriate transaction attribute for this method.

When a bean managed transaction is invoked by a client that's already in an active transaction context, the container first suspends the client's transaction and then invokes the bean implementation. The container does this irrespective of whether the bean implementation starts its own transaction.

Best Practices

In this section, we look at some best practices you can adopt in your bean development to make it more robust.

Default Session Bean Class

While discussing Stateless Session Beans, we said that your bean implementation has to define the `ejbActivate` and `ejbPassivate` methods, in spite of the fact that Stateless Session Beans are never activated or passivated. This arises from the fact that the interface that Session Beans implement is common for both Stateless and Stateful Session Beans. Obviously, this isn't very clean.

Along the same lines, imagine a case of both Stateful and Stateless Session Beans in which the bean implementation has to define all those callback methods. If your bean implementation doesn't need several of those methods, you still have to define these methods to satisfy the requirements of the interface.

One way of overcoming these problems is to create a default Session Bean class that implements the `javax.ejb.SessionBean` interface and provides a default implementation for all these callback methods. Your bean implementation can then extend from this adapter class and override only those methods that you need in your bean implementation. In this way, the bean implementation is clean and doesn't hold unnecessary methods. The downside to this approach is that it affects the inheritance hierarchy of the bean class. Because Java doesn't allow multiple inheritance, you cannot subclass any other business class.

Component Interfaces

It's often tempting to implement the bean's remote or local object in your bean implementation. If you think about it, it seem to make sense because the bean implementation provides concrete implementation for the methods in the remote interface. The EJB specification allows you to do this, but we strongly discourage you from doing so. There are a couple of reasons why you should avoid implementing the remote interface.

The remote interface extends from the interface `javax.ejb.EJBObject`, whereas the local interface extends from the interface `javax.ejb.EJBLocalObject`. These interfaces provide several methods that are meant for the consumption of the client. If you attempt to implement the remote or local interfaces in your bean implementation, the compiler will force you to implement these methods also. These methods simply do not belong in your bean implementation. They belong in the client's stub object that is returned by the container so that the client can invoke those methods to get more information about the bean. If you implement these methods, you're cluttering the bean implementation. Of course, you can hide these methods by using the default implementation we discussed earlier, but simply hiding the methods does not make this a very good practice.

A second reason for discouraging this practice is that a business method of a bean many times accepts a component interface of another bean as a parameter. When the bean method is invoked from within the bean whose component interface is being passed as a parameter, the compiler takes care of not allowing the bean to send a reference to itself by using the Java keyword `this`; using the `this` keyword merely passes the bean class implementation instead of the object stub. The bean is forced to get the object interface from the context and pass that instead. Now imagine if the bean class implements the component interface. This time, using the `this` keyword will fool the compiler into thinking that the object being passed in is the remote stub. Clients should always interact with object interfaces of beans, and not the bean implementation directly. This is the only way in which the container has a say in what's going and can provide services such as transactions and security.

To overcome this, create a business interface that has all the business methods defined in it. The component interface can extend from this business interface and also from `EJBObject`, thus masking as a remote interface. On the other hand, the bean implementation can implement the business interface, therefore implementing only the business methods and not the other methods that it shouldn't implement. This can be seen in Figure 21.5.

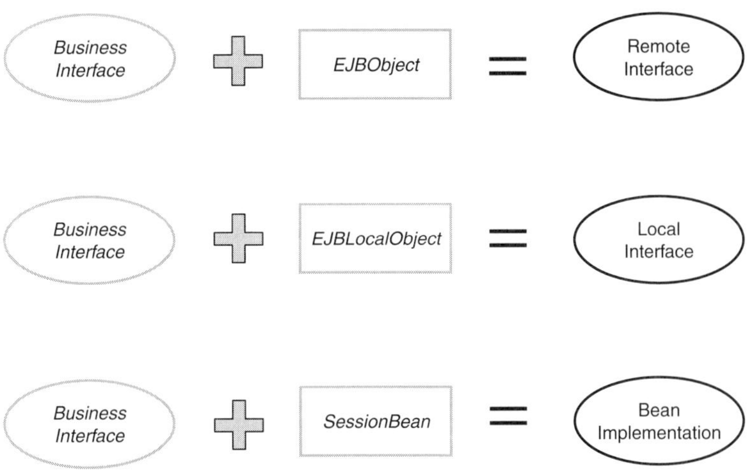

Figure 21.5 Using component interfaces.

Avoiding Stateful Session Bean Chaining

Chaining Stateful Session Beans is making one Stateful Bean dependent on the state of another Stateful Session Bean and so on. Although this is allowed, and can sometimes even be desirable, it can become an issue when a bean down the chain times out or is invalidated because of an uncaught exception. This renders invalid all the state in the beans up the hierarchy, and can result in loss of considerable amount of work. Therefore, try to avoid Stateful Session Bean chaining.

Stateful Session Beans can easily call other Stateless Session Beans because Stateless Session Beans do not hold any conversational state.

Invoking Stateful Session Beans from Stateless Session Beans doesn't make any sense because Stateless Session Beans aren't tied to any single client, whereas Stateful Session Beans are.

Understanding That Session Bean State Is Nontransactional

It's a common misunderstanding that Stateful Session Bean state is transactional. For instance, consider the total cost that's stored within the shopping cart bean. This is built up as and when a new booking is made using this bean instance. At the end, assume that the transaction is rolled back. It's critical to understand that the total cost will not come back to zero by itself. Your bean implementation should write code to ensure that it happens. Session Beans merely pass on their transactional context to the resources that they use. For instance, the data that was originally altered in the database is affected and gets rolled back.

You can simulate transactionality of Session Bean data by implementing the `SessionSynchronization` interface as described earlier in this chapter.

Choosing Transactions Carefully

Transaction granularity should be chosen carefully. Large transactions can lock up system resources, whereas several small ones tend to make the system slow. You must design your transaction granularity in such a way that your application draws a line between these two potential problems. Also, use JTA only when you require global transactions.

Preferring Container-Managed Transactions over Bean-Managed Transactions

You should typically prefer the use of container-managed transactions. The WebLogic Server container provides declarative transaction management, thus abstracting your code from transaction management nuances. You don't have to write explicit code to begin or end transactions. The container does it for you at the scope of each business method. Also, at deployment time you get to tell the container what type of transaction support you desire for each method. This should be the preferred way of getting transaction support from the container.

There can be few cases in which you might have to use bean-managed transactions. For instance, you might have multiple transactions within the same method. The WebLogic Server container demarcates transactions at a method level. A preferred mechanism of tackling this issue is to break this method into multiple methods and let the container handle transactions for each of these methods.

A second reason might be that you may want to span transactions across different method calls in your bean. That is, one method begins a transaction while another method commits or rolls it back. If possible, this practice should be avoided because you're losing control over how and when the other method is invoked. The business method should represent units of work, and only in very rare cases should you need to encompass transactions across units of work. Create a new method that invokes the two methods in sequence. Now use Container Managed Transaction to manage the transaction for this new method.

Third, you might want to control transaction's outcome depending on business logic. This can be avoided simply by letting the container start the transaction, and using `setRollbackOnly()` to force a rollback if the business logic elects to cancel the transaction.

Note that transactions cannot span method calls for Stateless Session Beans. This is because Stateless Session Beans are shared, and there's no way to ensure the order in which these methods will be invoked.

Avoiding Spanning Transactions Across User Think Time

It often seems useful to begin a transaction, and then pass control back to the presentation layer for more information. This is a very bad practice and should be avoided at all costs. The problem with this approach is that the user might take as much time as he wants to respond to the presentation layer. This means either that the resources are locked up until that time or your transaction times out in the meanwhile. Try to break down such operations into multiple transactions. Generally speaking, keep the scope of a transaction strictly within the server context.

Understanding the Implications of the Supports Transaction Attribute

The `Supports` transaction attribute brings your bean into the context of a transaction if the client has an active transaction. If the client does not, your bean does not come under a transaction context. Understand the implications of this behavior. Your bean no longer has control over whether it's being invoked from within a transactional context. If your bean can handle being used without a transaction as well as it can handle being invoked inside of a transaction, there's no problem in using the `Supports` attribute. However, to make it more explicit, consider using `Required`, `RequiresNew`, or `Mandatory` for cases in which you need a transactional context. Similarly, use `Never` or `NotSupported` for cases in which you do not need a transaction at all.

Preferring Stateless over Stateful Beans

Stateful Session Beans are meant to hold a conversational state for a client. Thus, they cannot be shared across clients. Every client creates an instance, uses it, and then eventually removes it. Therefore, the number of Stateful Session Bean instances in your container at any time can grow tremendously, making these beans resource intensive. In a clustered environment, Stateful Session Beans have no load balancing. The calls are always directed to the primary server hosting the bean instance.

On the other hand, Stateless Session Beans are shared and are reused by different clients. Calls to Stateless Session Beans are load balanced across cluster instances. All these factors make stateless Session Beans much more scalable. They use limited resources.

Understand that Stateless Beans can also hold state. The state is just shared across all clients that access them, and isn't specific to a client. So, unless you have to hold client-specific state in the server, give preference to Stateless Beans over Stateful beans.

Avoiding Stateful Session Passivation

The container provides passivation as a service to manage system resources more effectively. But if you think about it, the act of passivation and activation itself has overheads. It obviously takes time to serialize a bean's state to the file system. You must design your application to minimize passivation effects. Of course, the best-case scenario is to keep the client footprint on the container to the minimum. You can effectively use Stateless Session

Beans along with Entity Beans to perform your business tasks. But if you must use a Stateful Session Bean, make sure that the user interface allows for a logout option, which will in turn remove the Stateful Session Bean instance. Memory is cheap nowadays, so it might even make sense to increase the RAM in your server. Keep the heap size and the cache size at optimal values at all times to minimize passivation effects.

Using Appropriate Design Patterns

Design patterns help you design robust and reusable application components. Several core patterns are available for EJB design, which you must consider while designing your EJB applications. Some of the design patterns you can consider are listed in the following sections.

Business Delegate

When your presentation layer invokes EJBs directly, it's exposed to the details of the implementation of the underlying service. This isn't preferable because your presentation layer has to be modified accordingly when the underlying implementation changes. Another problem is that when your client layer invokes services directly, there might not be any caching discipline in your client, and different components of your client might invoke the same service over and over again. This gives rise to lots of network hits, which is undesirable.

To overcome these, you can use the Business Delegate pattern. This reduces the coupling between the presentation layer and the EJB layer and hides the implementation details of the service layer. This layer can also provide caching of data so as to minimize network overheads. You can learn more on this pattern by visiting `http://java.sun.com/blueprints/corej2eepatterns/Patterns/BusinessDelegate.html`.

Session Façade

In an enterprise system, there might be several server-side objects that provide fine-grained functionality. These objects are known as *business objects*. Such objects might include Session Beans, Entity Beans, and even other types of objects that offer business functionality for your client. Business methods typically involve accessing several of these business objects in a particular order to achieve a desired result.

The problem with letting the clients handle the business flow is the duplication of effort between different clients. Also, the clients become tightly coupled with the implementation aspects of the business objects. To avoid this, consider the use of a Session Façade. A Session Façade is typically a Session Bean that manages the flow between the different business objects and provides coarse-grained business functionality for your client systems. All client systems can now access the façade in a uniform manner, and the business logic is centralized. You can read more about this pattern by visiting `http://java.sun.com/blueprints/corej2eepatterns/Patterns/SessionFacade.html`.

21

Service Locator

A Service Locator pattern can be implemented to hide the nuances of creation of EJB objects. Client components reuse the singleton locator object and receive the EJB object without knowing how the object is created. This concept can be extended to use the locator class to create other types of services, such as JMS. You can read more about the Service Locator pattern by following the link `http://java.sun.com/blueprints/corej2eepatterns/Patterns/ServiceLocator.html`.

Avoiding Using Threads

The WebLogic Server container is configured to manage all threads within the JVM. If you create threads from within your Session Beans, the container loses control over the threads created explicitly by your bean implementation and cannot manage the runtime environment of your bean. The container also cannot effectively manage available resources, resulting in slow processing. Remember that when you code to create threads in your bean implementation, the same code will execute in potentially hundreds of bean instances, thus creating hundreds of threads!

Avoiding Using Nonfinal Static Variables

Static variables that are nonfinal are strongly discouraged in the context of EJBs. One reason for this is that the static (nonfinal) model will break in a clustered environment. Data stored in static variables in each server of your cluster might not be the same, which could cause strange behavior. If you have to use static variables, make sure that they're declared `final`.

Summary

Session Beans help to control the workflow of your business application. They can either perform a well-known task and return back to the client, or maintain a conversational state with the client. WebLogic Server container provides several features for security, transaction, and concurrency. You can leave the resource management to the container, and concentrate on coding the business logic of your beans. Session Beans typically work with Entity Beans (which are discussed in the next chapter) to get database access, although Session Beans can directly work with the database, too. Use these concepts effectively while designing your enterprise application and you'll have a robust and scalable application.

CHAPTER **22**

Working with Entity Beans

By Kunal Mittal and Jeff Marin

IN THIS CHAPTER

- What Are Entity Beans?
- What Do Entity Beans Provide?
- Entity Bean Life Cycle
- Entity Bean Classes and Interfaces
- Creating BMP Entity Beans
- Creating CMP Entity Beans
- Relationship Caching in EJBs
- Caching in Entity Beans
- WebLogic Query Language
- Advanced Entity Bean Features
- Tools for Working with EJBs in WebLogic Server 8.1
- EJB Features Deprecated in WebLogic 8.1
- Entity Bean Best Practices

Entity beans are a type of Enterprise JavaBeans used to represent data in some persistent storage; most commonly, a relational database. In this chapter, we learn about the two types of Entity beans—Bean Managed and Container Managed. We also learn about the specific features in WebLogic Server 8.1 that help optimize the performance and management of Entity beans. The chapter concludes with a discussion of some common design issues with Entity beans.

What Are Entity Beans?

Entity beans are representations of information that's persisted in some kind of data store. Although the main focus of a Session bean is to represent business logic, an Entity bean's main objective is to represent persisted business objects. Examples of persisted business objects include orders, order details, customer accounts, and partner information. Although this information is usually stored in a relational database (RDBMS), it can also be stored in many alternative forms, such as a flat file, an object-oriented database, or as XML.

An Entity bean usually represents a row in the database. An Entity bean manages an in-memory copy of the persisted information. This cached version of the information can be used to reduce the number of times that the actual data store must be accessed. When the in-memory version of the data is modified, the Entity bean, in conjunction with the EJB container, updates the underlying data store.

Entity beans shield their clients from understanding the implementation of the underlying data store and the architecture of the persisted information. For instance, clients of an `OrderInfo` Entity bean do not need to know whether the information is stored in a database or in VMS files. They also do not have to understand the underlying data schema. Entity beans offer their clients an object-oriented view of persistent application data. When the underlying data store is an RDBMS, the Entity beans are said to provide an object-relational (O-R) mapping. Entity beans provide a mechanism for representing complex object dependencies or object graphs in an object-oriented format. Figure 22.1 shows a set of relational tables that can be modeled using Entity beans.

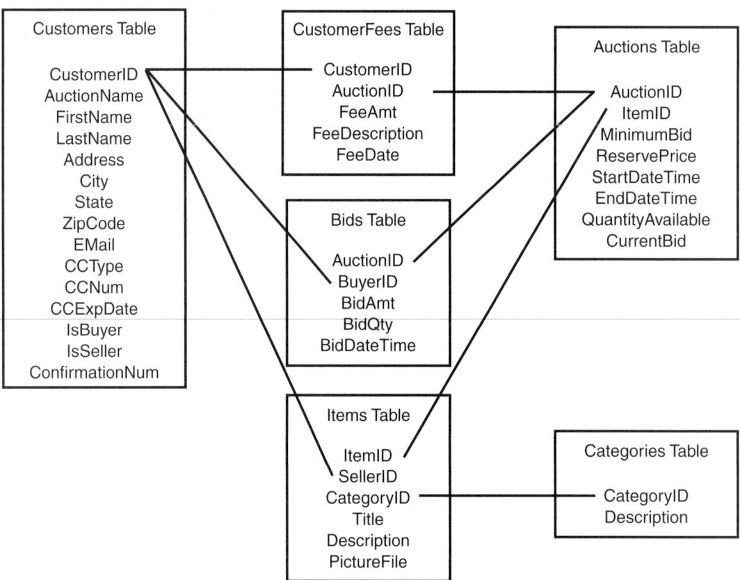

Figure 22.1 The database tables shown in this figure can be modeled using Entity beans.

EJB clients can access EJBs as remote objects. Therefore, when designing and implementing applications that use EJBs remotely, it's important to keep in mind the number of round trips that are required to perform an operation. For example, if the client requests all 100 `Order` Entity beans related to a customer and only one EJB is returned on each round trip, 100 round trips are required to complete this operation. Most likely, the network overhead will be prohibitively expensive and will force a redesign of the application. Making EJB methods coarse-grained (each method performs a lot of functionality) rather than fine-grained (each method performs very little) can have an enormous impact on how many EJB methods are involved in a business operation and, therefore, how much overhead EJB clients will experience.

Container-Managed Persistence and Bean-Managed Persistence

There are two types of Entity beans: Container-Managed Persistence (CMP) and Bean-Managed Persistence (BMP). In CMP, the EJB container is responsible for knowing when and how to insert, update, retrieve, and remove information in the data store. In BMP, the Entity bean itself must provide code for that. The decision of whether to use CMP or BMP is discussed later in this chapter. For now, understand that BMPs can give the developer more flexibility in the design and implementation of Entity beans, but they require a much larger amount of code to accomplish that flexibility. In general, we recommend using CMP wherever possible. However, in certain cases where complex relationships must be managed or some other optimizations have to be performed, BMP might be your only choice.

What Do Entity Beans Provide?

Through the use of the JDBC, I/O, XML, and other APIs, application components such as JSPs and servlets could persist information directly to a data store. However, Entity beans provide a layer of abstraction that can help with the following:

- Reduce dependencies between application components and data store implementation
- Concurrent read and write access to shared data by multiple clients
- Accessible to multiple client types
- Method-level object security
- High scalability
- Behind firewall, extra level of protection for data
- Caching of data with in-memory copy or persistent store

Entity Bean Life Cycle

The EJB container determines when Entity bean objects are created and when they're destroyed. Ultimately, however, client requests determine how the data should be manipulated.

Although the in-memory copy of persisted information is destroyed when the virtual machine is terminated, Entity beans represent persisted information. Because the persisted information can and probably will outlive the JVM that WebLogic Server runs in, we can say that Entity beans outlive WebLogic Server. Figure 22.2 shows the life cycle of an Entity bean.

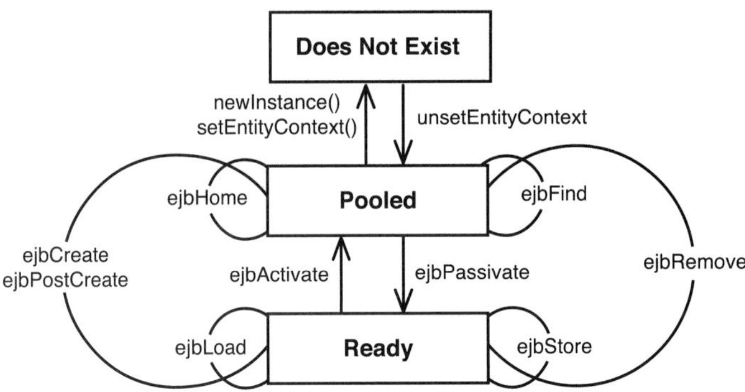

Figure 22.2 The life cycle of an Entity bean.

Entity Bean Classes and Interfaces

As shown in Figure 22.3, there are many parts of an Entity bean. This section takes you through the required parts and the optional ones. It also shows the differences in requirements of BMP Entity beans and CMP Entity beans.

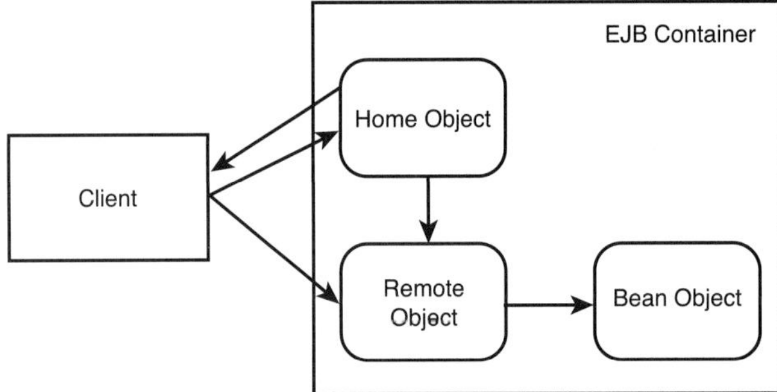

Figure 22.3 The classes and interfaces of an Entity bean.

Primary Keys

Every Entity beans stored in a data store has a primary key associated with it. A *primary key* is a unique identifier that's used to locate existing Entity beans in a data store. A primary key can consist of a single value, such as an integer, or multiple values, such as date of birth and last name. Every Entity bean must have a primary key. As per the EJB specification, the Home interface can implement the `findByPrimaryKey()` method.

Note that not only is a primary key mandatory in an Entity bean, but once it's set in `ejbCreate`, this key's fields cannot change. These limitations are set forth in the EJB specification.

Home Interface

The Home interface of an Entity bean is used to declare methods related to creating new Entity beans, locating existing ones, and for performing a business method that can span across more than one Entity bean.

Creation Methods

An Entity bean can be created in multiple ways with varying amounts and types of information. For example, a Customer Entity bean may be created with merely a customer's Social Security number. If more information is available, we could create one with the customer's Social Security number, name, and phone number. A third option is to create the Customer Entity bean with demographic information such as name, date of birth, and marital status. Creating a new Entity bean equates to a new business object in the data store and a new in-memory copy of that object.

Creation methods must be called with an optional number of types of variables. However, every parameter must be able to be serialized. Each creation method defined in the Home interface is implemented by a corresponding `ejbCreate` and `ejbPostCreate` method with the same parameters in the bean's implementation class. So, if the method `create(int age)` is defined in the `Home` class, the bean class implements this method with an `ejbCreate(int age)` and an `ejbPostCreate(int age)` methods. You can also describe further the create method by adding suffixes. For example, we can have three versions of the create method such as `createByAge(int age)`, `ejbCreateByAge(int age)`, and `ejbPostCreateByAge(int age)`. The return type of the create method is the Remote interface.

Finder Methods

Locating existing Entity beans is accomplished through finder methods. Finder methods can take zero or more parameters to help locate existing Entity beans. For example, a finder method that returns all Entity beans representing orders that have not been paid for could be accomplished without a parameter. A finder method that returns all orders processed within a particular month and year must have the specific month and year passed in as parameters. As a requirement, the Home interface must declare a finder method for locating existing Entity beans using a primary key, named `findByPrimaryKey()`, taking a primary key class object as a parameter and returning a component interface.

The naming convention for finder methods is `findBy`*`XYZ`* where *`XYZ`* is user-specified and refers to the method of locating Entity beans. Each finder method defined in the Home interface will be implemented by a corresponding `ejbFindBy`*`XYZ`* method with the same parameters in the bean's implementation class. So, if the method `findByLastName(String lastName)` is defined in the `Home` class, the bean class will implement this method with an `ejbFindByLastName(String lastName)` method. Finders can return either a single object of a component interface type or a collection of them.

Business Methods

Additionally, the Home interface can contain business methods that do not relate to a particular entity. For example, an Order bean can have a method that closes all orders by marking an Order Completion flag to be true.

Remote Interface

The Remote interface of an Entity bean is used to declare methods that relate to business logic pertaining to a single element of data. Clients of the Entity bean will work with this interface by calling these methods. Because Entity beans represent business objects that have state, many of these methods will be used to store and retrieve the state or attributes of a business object. For example, a Car Entity bean could have `getMake()`, `setMake()`, `getModel()`, `setModel()`, `getColor()`, and `setColor()` as Remote interface methods.

These getter/setter methods work well when an object and its client are in the same JVM, as in the case of JSPs, servlets, and co-located EJBs. However, if the Entity bean client is not in the same JVM, as the case is for standalone Java clients, we want to access multiple attributes simultaneously to reduce the number of round trips between the Entity bean and its clients. One way of doing this is to employ value objects; another is to use a Session bean as a façade to access the Entity beans locally.

Bean Class

The bean class is where the Entity bean methods are implemented. This class implements the `javax.ejb.EntityBean` interface, which defines seven methods that must be implemented. However, in some cases, the actual implementation is an empty method. The EJB container calls each of these methods; the EJB client can't invoke them directly.

- `ejbLoad()` is invoked when the EJB container realizes that the Entity bean needs its states refreshed from the data store. When using BMP, this is where your code is placed to load business object data from a database or other data store and update Entity bean attributes. For CMP, this is just a notification method.
- `ejbRemove()` is invoked when a business object needs to be removed from the data store. When using BMP, this is where your code to remove the business object from a database or other data store is placed. For CMP, this is a notification method.
- `ejbStore()` is invoked when the EJB container realizes that the data store needs to be updated with Entity bean information. When using BMP, this is where your code to update the database or other data store with Entity bean data is placed. For CMP, this is a notification method.
- `setEntityContext(EntityContext)` is invoked when an Entity bean instance is created. The `EntityContext` object provides the Entity bean instance with access to EJB container runtime context information, such as a reference to itself or its primary key. The `EntityContext` object is generally stored in a local variable for further use later.

- `unsetEntityContext()` is invoked when the EJB container will no longer be using this Entity bean instance. It's generally left empty.
- `ejbActivate()` is used to initialize any resources needed by the EJB. By careful not to hold on to resources for the life of the Entity bean that are not required. For example, a database connection can be requested as needed, and should not be tied up for the life of an Entity bean.
- `ejbPassivate()` is used to release resources initialized in `ejbActivate()`. Be sure to release those resources here.

Missing from the `EntityBean` interface are methods to create a new instance of an Entity bean. These are the implementations of the creation methods defined in the Home interface. Because the parameters are application specific, these methods could not be placed in the `EntityBean` interface but are nonetheless required for an Entity bean. Every creation method in the Home interface needs a corresponding `ejbCreate` and `ejbPostCreate` method in the bean class.

- `ejbCreate(`*`parameters`*`)` is invoked when the EJB container needs to create a new instance of an Entity bean and its attributes in the data store. This method is responsible for initializing Entity bean instance attributes and creating a representation in the data store. When using BMP, this is where your code to add the business object to a database or other data store is placed.
- `ejbPostCreate(`*`parameters`*`)` is invoked after its corresponding `ejbCreate` method is called. Further initialization of Entity bean attributes could be placed here. Because `ejbPostCreate` is called after `setEntityContext`, an `EntityContext` is available in this method, but not in `ejbCreate`. Setting up relationships can be done here because the current Entity object is now ready to use. This can be useful for initialization purposes.

Deployment Descriptors

The J2EE specification dictates the use of a deployment descriptor named `ejb-jar.xml` for all EJBs. Entity beans use this XML file to specify runtime behavior, including transactional awareness, primary key information, initial parameters, and security roles for protected methods.

The file `weblogic-ejb-jar.xml` is used to specify WebLogic Server–specific information about one or more Entity beans. This information includes JNDI addresses, persistence, and security information.

Container-Managed Persistence Entity beans must be accompanied by a `weblogic-cmp-rdbms-jar.xml` file. This file contains information about the JDBC data source to use and the associations between Entity bean attributes and RDBMS table fields.

Local Interfaces

Normally, Entity beans are accessed as remote objects as explained in Chapter 20, "Enterprise JavaBeans and WebLogic Server." This makes sense when the client is in a different JVM or container, but if the client is another EJB in the same JVM, there's no reason to reference it as a remote object. Local interfaces allow EJBs to call each other as local objects. This is a much quicker and more efficient way of accessing dependent EJBs. Both the Home and the Remote interface can have local counterparts. The local counterparts are optional, whereas the Home and Remote interfaces themselves are mandatory.

When modeling relationships with Entity beans, dependent business objects can communicate using local interfaces. In fact, for Container-Managed Relationships (CMR), dependent Entity beans must access each other with local interfaces.

Primary Key Class

There are many occasions when the primary key for an Entity bean consists of a single value, such as a string or an integer. Basic data classes (`String`, `Integer`, `Long`, and so on) can then be used as the primary key class. However, a compound primary key consisting of multiple values sometimes will be needed. If this is the case, you have to create a class for the primary key.

Value Object

As mentioned earlier, Remote interface methods usually consist of getter and setter methods for each attribute of a business object. When the Entity bean client is in a different JVM and/or container, calling many of these methods in the context of one business operation adds a lot of network overhead because each method call is remote. *Value objects* are JavaBeans that carry many pieces of information and have getter and setter methods for them. They are just helper classes, like exceptions, objects that are passed as parameters or returned by methods, or any other class that the bean implementation might need. These are generally always used with EJBs, but they aren't required by the EJB specification.

For example, a client can request doctors name, specialty, and contact number information from a Doctor Entity bean. The Doctor Entity bean can create a `DoctorVO` value object and fill it with this information. The client then can extract this information from the `DoctorVO` value object. With one remote method call, the client has actually received three attributes of the Doctor Entity bean. This design pattern is a typical way to optimize access to EJBs.

Creating BMP Entity Beans

The `DoctorEJB` Entity bean represents information about a doctor. Its attributes are an ID, first name, last name, and specialty. The ID will be an `Integer` and it will be the primary key. Because this class is already defined and we're using a single value for the primary key, we don't need a custom primary key class for this Entity bean. In this section, we're going to create an Entity bean with BMP that uses JDBC to access a single table named Doctor in a data store. The database definition for this table is shown in Listing 22.1.

LISTING 22.1 Doctor.ddl

```
CREATE TABLE Doctor (
  ID INTEGER NOT NULL,
  FIRSTNAME VARCHAR(20),
  LASTNAME VARCHAR(20),
  SPECIALTY VARCHAR(20)
);
```

Creating the Home Interface

The Home interface for the `DoctorEJB` Entity bean contains creation methods and finder methods.

Creation Methods

This Entity bean will have one creation method that utilizes a `DoctorVO` value object. Clients wanting to create a `DoctorEJB` instance must create an instance of `DoctorVO` locally, fill it with information, and then pass it to the create method.

```
public Doctor create(DoctorVO doctorVO) throws CreateException, RemoteException;
```

Finder Methods

Clients of this `DoctorEJB` need to locate doctors in four ways: by their ID, by their first and last name, and by their specialty. Because we've decided to use the ID as our primary key, the `findByPrimaryKey` uses the ID as a parameter.

```
public Doctor findByPrimaryKey(Integer primaryKey) throws FinderException,
➥ RemoteException;
public Collection findByName(String firstName, String lastName) throws
➥ FinderException, RemoteException;
public Collection findBySpecialty(String specialty) throws FinderException,
➥  RemoteException;
```

Because primary keys are unique, `findByPrimaryKey` returns zero or one instance of `DoctorEJB`. However, the other `findBy` methods could return multiple `DoctorEJB`s; therefore, their return values are collections of `DoctorEJB` objects. Listing 22.2 shows the complete code for the Home interface.

LISTING 22.2 DoctorHome.java

```
package wls8unleashed.ejb.entity.bmp;
import javax.ejb.CreateException;
import javax.ejb.EJBHome;
import javax.ejb.FinderException;
import java.rmi.RemoteException;
import java.util.Collection;

public interface DoctorHome extends EJBHome {
  public Doctor create(DoctorVO doctorVO) throws CreateException, RemoteException;
  public Doctor findByPrimaryKey(Integer primaryKey) throws FinderException,
➥  RemoteException;
  public Collection findByName(String firstName, String lastName) throws
➥  FinderException,   RemoteException;
  public Collection findBySpecialty(String specialty) throws
➥  FinderException, RemoteException;
}
```

Creating the Value Object

Because our Entity bean's creation method expects a `DoctorVO` object, we should create it here. The client uses this value object to retrieve and modify existing `DoctorEJB`s. This value object is a JavaBean that contains private instance variables to hold the doctor's ID, first and last names, and specialty. It also contains public getter and setter methods to access these attributes. Because we'll be using this object as a parameter in an RMI call, it should be serializable. In addition to getters and setters for all attributes, a handy `toString` method has been included for debugging purposes. Listing 22.3 shows the full code.

LISTING 22.3 DoctorVo.java

```
package wls8unleashed.ejb.entity.bmp;

import java.io.Serializable;

public class DoctorVO  implements Serializable {
        private Integer id;
        private String  firstName;
        private String  lastName;
        private String  specialty;

        public DoctorVO() {
        }
```

LISTING 22.3 Continued

```
    public Integer getId(){
        return id;
    }

    public void setId(Integer id) {
        this.id = id;
    }

    public String getFirstName(){
        return firstName;
    }

    public void setFirstName(String firstName){
        this.firstName = firstName;
    }

    public String getLastName(){
        return lastName;
    }

    public void setLastName(String lastName){
        this.lastName = lastName;
    }

    public String getSpecialty(){
        return specialty;
    }

    public void setSpecialty(String specialty){
        this.specialty = specialty;
    }

    public String toString() {
        StringBuffer result = new StringBuffer("[DoctorVO ");
        result.append(" id: "       + id);
        result.append(" firstName:" + firstName);
        result.append(" lastName:"  + lastName);
        result.append(" specialty:" + specialty);
        result.append("]");
        return result.toString();
    }
}
```

Creating the Remote Interface

The Remote interface is used to declare the business methods of the Entity bean. The Entity bean's clients call these methods. Because we're creating a Web application, our clients will be servlets and JavaServer Pages. In addition to creating getter and setter methods for each attribute of DoctorEJB, we'll also create bulk getter and setter methods that accept a DoctorVO object and return one. In this way, we can store and retrieve the full state of a DoctorEJB with one EJB method call. This is an example of a coarse-grained method and is an excellent way to reduce the network overhead involved in making multiple remote method calls. The full listing for the Remote interface is shown in Listing 22.4.

LISTING 22.4 Doctor.java

```
package wls8unleashed.ejb.entity.bmp;

import java.rmi.RemoteException;
import javax.ejb.EJBObject;

public interface Doctor extends EJBObject {
    public Integer getId() throws RemoteException;
    public String getFirstName() throws RemoteException;
    public void setFirstName(String firstName) throws RemoteException;
    public String getLastName() throws RemoteException;
    public void setLastName(String lastName) throws RemoteException;
    public String getSpecialty() throws RemoteException;
    public void setSpecialty(String specialty) throws RemoteException;
    public DoctorVO getDoctorData() throws RemoteException;
    public void setDoctorData(DoctorVO doctorVO) throws RemoteException;
}to declare the business methods of the Entity bean. The Entity
```

Creating the Bean Class

So far, we've declared methodsto declare the business methods of the Entity bean. The Entity in the Home and Remote interfaces. We now implement those methods in the bean class. Because the class implements the EntityBean interface, let's discuss how the various methods of the interface and the methods of the methods associated to the Home interface will be implemented.

- ejbCreate()—Our ejbCreate method takes a DoctorVO object as a parameter. This method extracts attributes from the DoctorVO object, updates Entity bean instance variables, and performs an SQL INSERT into to the database table.
- ejbPostCreate()—The ejbPostCreate method is empty because we don't need more initialization than what is performed in ejbCreate.

- `ejbLoad()`—This method reads the primary key from the `EntityContext`, performs a `SELECT` into the database using that key, and initializes the Entity bean attributes with the database information.
- `ejbRemove()`—This method reads the primary key from the `EntityContext` and performs a `DELETE` of the table row with this key.
- `ejbStore()`—This method reads the primary key from the `EntityContext` and performs an `UPDATE` of the table row with this key.

Some comments regarding the following code are in order. We create a static final variable called `DATASOURCE` with a value of `java:comp/env/TxDataSource`. That isn't the actual name of the JDBC data source. It's a reference to an external resource that is qualified in the deployment descriptor. The code that performs a JNDI lookup of the data source and grabs an available connection has been consolidated in the `getConnection` method. The code to release the JDBC resources is in the `releaseResources` method. Also note that there is no `setId` method. After an Entity bean has been created, its primary key should never change. Listing 22.5 shows the full code for the bean class.

LISTING 22.5 DoctorEJB.java

```
package wls8unleashed.ejb.entity.bmp;

import javax.ejb.*;

import java.util.*;
import java.sql.*;
import javax.sql.*;
import javax.naming.*;


public class DoctorEJB implements EntityBean {

    private EntityContext ctx;
    private static final String DATASOURCE = "java:comp/env/TxDataSource";

    private Integer id;
    private String firstName;
    private String lastName;
    private String specialty;

    public void setEntityContext(EntityContext ctx) {
        this.ctx = ctx;
    }
```

LISTING 22.5 Continued

```
    public void unsetEntityContext() {
        this.ctx = null;
    }

    public void ejbActivate() {}
    public void ejbPassivate() {}

    public Integer ejbCreate(DoctorVO vo) throws CreateException
    {
        System.out.println("DoctorEJB ejbCreate DoctorVO = " + vo.toString());

        Connection conn = null;
        PreparedStatement ps = null;

        try {
            conn = getConnection();

            id = vo.getId();
            firstName = vo.getFirstName();
            lastName = vo.getLastName();
            specialty = vo.getSpecialty();

            ps = conn.prepareStatement("INSERT INTO Doctor (ID, FIRSTNAME,
               LASTNAME, SPECIALTY) VALUES (?,?,?,?)");
            ps.setInt(1, id.intValue());
            ps.setString(2, firstName);
            ps.setString(3, lastName);
            ps.setString(4, specialty);

            int numrows = ps.executeUpdate();
            if (numrows != 1)
                throw new CreateException("Cannot create Doctor numrows = " + num
                ➥rows);
            ps.close();

            return id;

        } catch (Exception e) {
            throw new CreateException("Cannot create Doctor " + e.getMessage());
        } finally {
            closeResources(ps, conn);
        }
    }
```

LISTING 22.5 Continued

```
    public void ejbPostCreate(DoctorVO vo)
    {
    }

    public void ejbLoad() {

        Integer id = (Integer)ctx.getPrimaryKey();

        try {
            readFromDb(id.intValue());
        } catch (Exception e) {
            throw new EJBException(e);
        }
    }


    public void ejbStore() {
        Connection conn = null;
        PreparedStatement ps = null;

        try {
            conn = getConnection();
            ps = conn.prepareStatement("UPDATE DOCTOR SET FIRSTNAME = ?,
                 LASTNAME = ?, SPECIALTY = ? WHERE ID = ?");

            ps.setString(1, firstName);
            ps.setString(2, lastName);
            ps.setString(3, specialty);

            Integer id = (Integer)ctx.getPrimaryKey();
            ps.setInt(4, id.intValue());

            int numrows = ps.executeUpdate();
            if (numrows != 1)
                throw new EJBException("Cannot update Doctor, id = " +
                ➥id.toString());
        } catch (Exception e) {
            throw new EJBException(e);
        } finally {
            closeResources(ps, conn);
        }
    }
```

LISTING 22.5 Continued

```
    public void ejbRemove() {
        Connection conn = null;
        PreparedStatement ps = null;

        try {
            conn = getConnection();
            ps = conn.prepareStatement("DELETE FROM Doctor WHERE ID = ?");

            Integer id = (Integer)ctx.getPrimaryKey();
            ps.setInt(1, id.intValue());

            int numrows = ps.executeUpdate();
            if (numrows !- 1)
                throw new EJBException("Cannot delete Doctor, id = " +
                ➥id.toString());
        } catch (Exception e) {
            throw new EJBException(e);
        } finally {
            closeResources(ps, conn);
        }
    }


    public Integer ejbFindByPrimaryKey(Integer id) throws FinderException {
        try {
            readFromDb(id.intValue());
            return id;
        } catch(Exception e) {
            throw new FinderException(e.getMessage());
        }

    }

    public Collection ejbFindBySpecialty(String specialty) throws FinderException {
        Connection conn = null;
        PreparedStatement ps = null;

        try {
            conn = getConnection();
            ps = conn.prepareStatement("SELECT id FROM Doctor
                 WHERE UPPER(specialty) LIKE UPPER(?)");
            ps.setString(1, specialty);
```

LISTING 22.5 Continued

```
            Vector doctors = new Vector();
            ResultSet rset = ps.executeQuery();
            while(rset.next()) {
                Integer id = new Integer(rset.getInt(1));
                doctors.addElement(id);
            }
            rset.close();
            return doctors;

        } catch (Exception e) {
            throw new FinderException(e.getMessage());
        } finally {
            closeResources(ps, conn);
        }
    }

    public Collection ejbFindByName(String firstName, String lastName)
            throws FinderException {
        Connection conn = null;
        PreparedStatement ps = null;

        try {
            conn = getConnection();
            ps = conn.prepareStatement("SELECT id FROM Doctor
               WHERE UPPER(firstName) LIKE UPPER(?) AND UPPER(lastName) LIKE
               ➥UPPER(?)");
            ps.setString(1, firstName);
            ps.setString(2, lastName);

            Vector doctors = new Vector();
            ResultSet rset = ps.executeQuery();
            while(rset.next()) {
                Integer id = new Integer(rset.getInt(1));
                doctors.addElement(id);
            }
            rset.close();
            return doctors;

        } catch (Exception e) {
            throw new FinderException(e.getMessage());
        } finally {
```

22

LISTING 22.5 Continued

```
            closeResources(ps, conn);
        }
    }


    private void readFromDb(int id) throws CreateException {

        Connection conn = null;
        PreparedStatement ps = null;

        try {
            conn = getConnection();
            ps = conn.prepareStatement("SELECT ID, FIRSTNAME, LASTNAME,
                 SPECIALTY FROM Doctor WHERE id = ?");
            ps.setInt(1, id);

            ResultSet rset = ps.executeQuery();
            if(!rset.next()) {
                throw new FinderException("Doctor not found, id = " + id);
            } else {
                readFields(rset);
            }

        } catch (Exception e) {
            throw new CreateException(e.getMessage());

        } finally {
            closeResources(ps, conn);
        }
    }


    private void readFields(ResultSet rset) throws SQLException {
        id = new Integer(rset.getInt(1));
        firstName = rset.getString(2);
        lastName = rset.getString(3);
        specialty = rset.getString(4);
    }

    private void closeResources(PreparedStatement ps, Connection conn)
            throws EJBException {
```

LISTING 22.5 Continued

```
        try {
            if (ps != null)
                ps.close();

            if (conn != null)
                conn.close();

        } catch (Exception e) {
            throw new EJBException(e);
        }
    }


    public Integer getId() { return id; }

    public String getFirstName() { return firstName; }
    public void setFirstName(String firstName) {
        this.firstName = firstName;
    }

    public String getLastName() { return lastName; }
    public void setLastName(String lastName) {
        this.lastName= lastName;
    }

    public String getSpecialty() { return specialty; }
    public void setSpecialty(String specialty) {
        this.specialty = specialty;
    }

    public DoctorVO getDoctorData() {
        DoctorVO vo = new DoctorVO();
        vo.setId(getId());
        vo.setFirstName(getFirstName());
        vo.setLastName(getLastName());
        vo.setSpecialty(getSpecialty());
        return vo;
    }

    public void setDoctorData(DoctorVO vo) {
        setFirstName(vo.getFirstName());
```

LISTING 22.5 Continued

```
        setLastName(vo.getLastName());
        setSpecialty(vo.getSpecialty());
    }

    private Connection getConnection() {
        try {
            InitialContext ic = new InitialContext();
            DataSource ds = (DataSource)ic.lookup(DATASOURCE);
            return ds.getConnection();
        } catch (Exception e) {
            throw new EJBException(e.getMessage());
        }
    }
}
```

Creating the Deployment Descriptors

Each Entity bean must be accompanied by either two or three deployment descriptors. In the case of BMP Entity beans, only two deployment descriptors are needed.

The J2EE Deployment Descriptor

All EJBs must have their attributes set in `ejb-jar.xml` and `weblogic-ejb-jar.xml`. This includes the Home and Component interfaces and bean classes. Additionally, BMP Entity beans have their own requirements. In this section, we go over only the most common ones and leave the advanced settings for a later section in this chapter.

- `<persistence-type>`—Can be either `Bean` or `Container`. When using BMP, this value is `Bean`.
- `<prim-key-class>`—The fully qualified name of the primary key class. For this EJB, it is `java.lang.Integer`.
- `<reentrant>`—Specifies whether a thread executing a method on this EJB can enter the bean code more than once. This can occur when bean A calls a method on bean B that then calls a method on bean A. If a bean A is specified as non-reentrant, the EJB container disallows this behavior. If a bean A is specified as reentrant, this behavior is permitted, but a bean client might be able to spawn multiple threads and access the same bean simultaneously from all these threads. This could violate the "single-threaded-ness" of the Entity bean and lead to a potentially dangerous situation. With that in mind, try to avoid using reentrant Entity beans. If you must have this behavior, be very cautious in its use.

- <resource-ref>—As mentioned earlier, the bean class uses a reference to a JDBC data source, not the actual JNDI name. This allows the actual JNDI name to be configurable through deployment descriptors. In `ejb-jar.xml`, we specify the reference; in `weblogic-ejb-jar.xml`, we link the reference to the actual JNDI name.

Listing 22.6 shows the full code of `ejb-jar.xml`.

LISTING 22.6 ejb-jar.xml

```
<?xml version="1.0"?>
<!DOCTYPE ejb-jar PUBLIC '-//Sun Microsystems, Inc.//
DTD Enterprise JavaBeans 2.0//EN' 'http://java.sun.com/dtd/ejb-jar_2_0.dtd'>

<ejb-jar>
  <enterprise-beans>
    <entity>
      <ejb-name>DoctorEJB</ejb-name>
      <home>wls8unleashed.ejb.entity.bmp.DoctorHome</home>
      <remote>wls8unleashed.ejb.entity.bmp.Doctor</remote>
      <ejb-class>wls8unleashed.ejb.entity.bmp.DoctorEJB</ejb-class>
      <persistence-type>Bean</persistence-type>
      <prim-key-class>java.lang.Integer</prim-key-class>
      <reentrant>False</reentrant>
    <resource-ref>
        <res-ref-name>TxDataSource</res-ref-name>
      <res-type>javax.sql.DataSource</res-type>
        <res-auth>Container</res-auth>
    </resource-ref>
    </entity>
  </enterprise-beans>
  <assembly-descriptor>
    <container-transaction>
      <method>
        <ejb-name>DoctorEJB</ejb-name>
        <method-intf>Remote</method-intf>
        <method-name>*</method-name>
      </method>
      <trans-attribute>Required</trans-attribute>
    </container-transaction>
  </assembly-descriptor>
</ejb-jar>
```

The WebLogic Server Deployment Descriptor

`weblogic-ejb-jar.xml` is used for WebLogic Server–specific configuration settings. Later in this chapter, we'll explore advanced settings, but for now we need to be concerned only about linking our data source reference to an actual JNDI name.

The `<reference-descriptor>` tag is used to link our EJB to an external resource. Here we associate the JNDI name `doctorDataSource` with the reference name `TxDataSource`. Listing 22.7 shows the code for `weblogic-ejb-jar.xml`.

LISTING 22.7 WebLogic Deployment Descriptor

```
<?xml version="1.0"?>
<!DOCTYPE weblogic-ejb-jar PUBLIC " -//BEA Systems, Inc.
          //DTD WebLogic 8.1.0 EJB//" "http://www.bea.com/servers/wls810/dtd/
          ➥weblogic-ejb-jar.dtd" >

<weblogic-ejb-jar>
  <weblogic-enterprise-bean>
      <ejb-name>DoctorEJB</ejb-name>
        <reference-descriptor>
        <resource-description>
             <res-ref-name>TxDataSource</res-ref-name>
             <jndi-name>doctorDataSource</jndi-name>
        </resource-description>
    </reference-descriptor>
      <jndi-name>DoctorHome</jndi-name>
  </weblogic-enterprise-bean>
</weblogic-ejb-jar>
```

BMP Comments

The bean class `DoctorEJB.java` contains several lines of code. Imagine having 10 or more BMPs and having to write all this code by hand each time. There are lots of chances to make typographical errors.

If you look at the `ejbCreate` method, you see that the ID for the EJB is extracted from the `DoctorVO` parameter. Who creates this parameter? The client, of course! Then who is responsible for creating the ID for each doctor? The client? If the ID is the primary key and must remain unique, we do not want the client to be in charge of key generation. We need a scalable way of generating keys that are guaranteed to be unique. Because we're using BMP, we must write this code ourselves. It turns out that there are multiple ways of doing this with different levels of complexity and performance.

NOTE

If you're interested in exploring this topic, we recommend that you read Chapter 5, "Primary Key Generation Strategies," of *EJB Design Patterns: Advanced Patterns, Processes, and Idioms* by Floyd Marinescu (ISBN: 0471208310). You can also download a PDF version of this book from TheServerSide at `http://www.theserverside.com/books/EJBDesignPatterns/downloadbook.jsp`.

Creating CMP Entity Beans

In this section, we create a CMP version of the Doctor Entity bean from the last section. This approach illustrates the differences between BMP and CMP from a coding standpoint.

Creating the Home Interface

The Home interface does not change from BMP to CMP. The clients of the Entity bean use the same creation and finder methods from the Home interface.

Creating the Value Object

The same `DoctorVO` class from the BMP example is used with this CMP example. The value object for BMP does not need to be any different that the one used for CMP.

Creating the Remote Interface

Just like the Home interface, EJB clients use the same remote methods, individual getters/setters, and bulk getters/setters.

Creating the Bean Class

This is where the most of the differences between BMP and CMP lie. BMP Entity bean methods provide the persistence mechanism, whereas CMP Entity beans contain only the business logic—the container takes care of effectively managing the data store. (Many of the CMP bean implementation's methods are simply notifications.) This is accomplished by creating an abstract bean class with abstract getter and setter methods for the EJB fields. When the EJB compiler (EJBC) compiles this EJB, a concrete base class with concrete getter and setter methods is generated. This class and its methods contain additional logic to support optimized data store access. Listing 22.8 shows the complete CMP bean class.

LISTING 22.8 The Full Code of the Entity Bean Class

```
package wls8unleashed.ejb.entity.cmp;

import javax.ejb.*;
```

LISTING 22.8 Continued

```
abstract public class DoctorEJB implements EntityBean {

    private EntityContext ctx;

    abstract public Integer getId();
    abstract public void setId(Integer id);

    abstract public String getFirstName();
    abstract public void setFirstName(String firstName);

    abstract public String getLastName();
    abstract public void setLastName(String lastName);

    abstract public String getSpecialty();
    abstract public void setSpecialty(String dob);

    public void setEntityContext(EntityContext ctx) {
        this.ctx = ctx;
    }

    public void unsetEntityContext() {
        this.ctx = null;
    }

    public void ejbActivate() {}
    public void ejbPassivate() {}
    public void ejbLoad() {}
    public void ejbStore() {}
    public void ejbRemove() {}

    public Integer ejbCreate(DoctorVO vo) throws CreateException {
        setId(vo.getId());
        setFirstName(vo.getFirstName());
        setLastName(vo.getLastName());
        setSpecialty(vo.getSpecialty());
        return null;
        }

    public void ejbPostCreate(DoctorVO vo) {
    }
```

LISTING 22.8 Continued

```
        public DoctorVO getDoctorData() {
               DoctorVO vo = new DoctorVO();
        vo.setId(getId());
        vo.setFirstName(getFirstName());
        vo.setLastName(getLastName());
        vo.setSpecialty(getSpecialty());
        return vo;
        }

        public void setDoctorData(DoctorVO vo) {
        setFirstName(vo.getFirstName());
        setLastName(vo.getLastName());
        setSpecialty(vo.getSpecialty());
        }
}
```

The `ejbCreate()` is the only `ejb...()` method that is not simply a notification. It fills the key field and NOT NULL fields with dummy values so that the bean can be created. It does not insert anything into the database. Even though the return type of `ejbCreate()` is always NULL, the `ejbCreate()` method returns the primary key. The container knows how to create the primary key from the bean's key fields.

Creating the Deployment Descriptors

Deployment descriptors are another area in which BMP and CMP Entity beans differ greatly. Although there is much less code and logic in the CMP Entity bean class, much more is present in its deployment descriptors.

The Deployment Descriptors

The `ejb-jar.xml` file needs to change to support CMP persistence. The new version is shown in the following listing. The major change is that we mention the container-managed fields as well as the EJB-QL query codes for the finder methods. Listing 22.9 shows the full code of `ejb-jar.xml`. You can ignore the `<query>` blocks in the code for now. They're related to the EJB query language and are covered later in this chapter.

LISTING 22.9 ejb-jar.xml

```
<?xml version="1.0"?>
<!DOCTYPE ejb-jar PUBLIC '-//Sun Microsystems, Inc.
//DTD Enterprise JavaBeans 2.0//EN' 'http://java.sun.com/dtd/ejb-jar_2_0.dtd'>
<ejb-jar>
```

LISTING 22.9 Continued

```
<enterprise-beans>
  <entity>
    <ejb-name>DoctorEJB</ejb-name>
    <home>wls8unleashed.ejb.entity.cmp.DoctorHome</home>
    <remote>wls8unleashed.ejb.entity.cmp.Doctor</remote>
    <ejb-class>wls8unleashed.ejb.entity.cmp.DoctorEJB</ejb-class>
    <persistence-type>Container</persistence-type>
    <prim-key-class>java.lang.Integer</prim-key-class>
    <reentrant>False</reentrant>
    <cmp-version>2.x</cmp-version>
    <abstract-schema-name>Doctor</abstract-schema-name>
    <cmp-field>
      <field-name>id</field-name>
    </cmp-field>
    <cmp-field>
      <field-name>firstName</field-name>
    </cmp-field>
    <cmp-field>
      <field-name>lastName</field-name>
    </cmp-field>
    <primkey-field>id</primkey-field>
    <query>
      <query-method>
        <method-name>findBySpeciality</method-name>
        <method-params>
          <method-param>String</method-param>
        </method-params>
      </query-method>
      <ejb-ql>
        <![CDATA[SELECT OBJECT(a) FROM Doctor AS a WHERE a.speciality > ?1]]>
      </ejb-ql>
    </query>
  </entity>
</enterprise-beans>
<assembly-descriptor>
  <container-transaction>
    <method>
      <ejb-name>containerManaged</ejb-name>
      <method-name>*</method-name>
```

LISTING 22.9 Continued

```
      </method>
      <trans-attribute>Required</trans-attribute>
    </container-transaction>
  </assembly-descriptor>
  <ejb-client-jar>ejb20_Doctor.jar</ejb-client-jar>
</ejb-jar>
```

The following describes the different parts of this XML file:

- `<entity>`—Each entity bean must be declared in an `<entity>` element.
- `<local-home>`—This element is where you specify the bean's local Home interface.
- `<local>`—This element is where you specify the bean's Local interface.
- `<persistence-type>`—For CMP, this is set to `Container`; for BMP, this is set to `Bean`.
- `<prim-key-class>`—This is where you specify the primary key class.
- `<cmp-version>`—This specifies which EJB CMP version this bean uses. Possible values are `1.x` and `2.x`.
- `<abstract-schema-name>`—This element specifies a name for the bean that can be used in EJB-QL queries. In the example, the Doctor EJB has an abstract schema name of `Doctor`.
- `<cmp-field>`—This element is where persistent entity fields are declared. Field names must begin with a lowercase letter and have corresponding get and set methods within the bean class.
- `<primkey-field>`—This element specifies which field is the bean's primary key field.
- `<query>`—These elements map EJB-QL statements to queries on the bean's Home interface and bean select methods.
- `<query-method>`—This element has two subelements—`<method-name>` and `<method-params>`—which map the query to a method on the bean's Home interface.
- `<ejb-ql>`—This element is where the query's EJB-QL statement is specified. This is discussed later in the chapter.

We mentioned earlier that we need an additional deployment descriptor for CMP. This is a WebLogic-specific deployment descriptor that maps the container-managed fields to the specific columns in the database. Listing 22.10 shows this deployment descriptor.

LISTING 22.10 weblogic-cmp-rdbms.xml

```
<?xml version="1.0"?>
<!DOCTYPE weblogic-rdbms-jar PUBLIC
 '-//BEA Systems, Inc.//DTD WebLogic 8.1.0 EJB RDBMS Persistence//EN'
 'http://www.bea.com/servers/wls810/dtd/weblogic-rdbms20-persistence-810.dtd'>
<weblogic-rdbms-jar>
  <weblogic-rdbms-bean>
    <ejb-name>containerManaged</ejb-name>
    <data-source-name>Doctor</data-source-name>
    <table-map>
      <table-name>Doctor</table-name>
      <field-map>
        <cmp-field>id</cmp-field>
        <dbms-column>id</dbms-column>
      </field-map>
      <field-map>
        <cmp-field>firstName</cmp-field>
        <dbms-column>firstName</dbms-column>
      </field-map>
      <field-map>
        <cmp-field>lastName</cmp-field>
        <dbms-column>firstName</dbms-column>
      </field-map>
      <field-map>
        <cmp-field>speciality</cmp-field>
        <dbms-column>speciality</dbms-column>
      </field-map>
    </table-map>
  </weblogic-rdbms-bean>
  <create-default-dbms-tables>False</create-default-dbms-tables>
</weblogic-rdbms-jar>
```

Let's explore the XML file in more detail.

- `<weblogic-rdbms-bean>`—There is one `<weblogic-rdbms-bean>` element for each CMP bean declared in the EJB deployment descriptor.
- `<ejb-name>`—This must correspond to the `<ejb-name>` of an `<entity>` element in the EJB deployment descriptor.
- `<data-source-name>`—This must be a connection pool set up on the WebLogic Server instance used.
- `<table-map>`—Consists of `<table-name>` and `<field-map>` entries.

- <table-name>—This is the name of the database table to which to persist the bean.
- <field-map>—This element maps an entity field to a column in the table specified in <table-name> through its <cmp-field> and <dbms-column> subelements.
- <create-default-dbms-tables>—Specifies whether the database tables should be created.

We've briefly demonstrated the basics of writing an Entity bean following the EJB specification's BMP and CMP flavors. A new feature with EJBs and in WebLogic is the management of relations within EJBs. Previously, one-many relations and many-many relations had to be modeled either through BMP or through some other mechanism. With EJB 2.*x*, those relations can now be managed through CMP. We discuss this in the next section.

Container-Managed Relations

In this section, we discuss one-to-one, one-to-many, and many-to-many relationship mappings and show you how to support them through the deployment descriptors.

One-to-One Relationships

A one-to-one relationship is one in which for each and every Entity A, there is one and only one Entity B. In our Doctor example, we could assume that each Doctor has one and only one assistant. The following excerpts show how this would be mapped in the ejb-jar.xml and the weblogic-cmp-rdbms.xml files.

Listing 22.11 presents an excerpt from the ejb-jar.xml file showing a one-to-one relationship.

LISTING 22.11 ejb-jar.xml Excerpt

```
<relationships>
   <ejb-relation>
     <ejb-relation-name>Doctor-assistant<ejb-relation-name>
     <ejb-relationship-role>
        <ejb-relationship-role-name>
           Doctor-has-an-Assistant
        </ejb-relationship-role-name>
        <multiplicity>One<multiplicity>
        <relationship-role-source>
           <ejb-name>DoctorBean</ejb-name>
        </relationship-role-source>
        <cmr-field>
          <cmr-field-name>DoctorAssistant</cmr-field-name>
        </cmr-field>
     </ejb-relationship-role>
```

LISTING 22.11 Continued

```
      <ejb-relationship-role>
         <ejb-relationship-role-name>
           Assistant-belongs-to-Doctor
         </ejb-relationship-role-name>
         <mulitiplicity>One</multiplicity>
         <relationship-role-source>
           <ejb-name>AssistantBean</ejb-name>
         </relationship-role-source>
      </ejb-relationship-role>
    <ejb-relation>
</relationships>
```

The <relationships> tag block is placed after the definitions of the enterprise beans in the </enterprise-beans> tag. For each <ejb-relation>, there are two <ejb-relationship-role> tags—one for each side of the relationship. Each one declares the multiplicity of the relationship, the source EJB, and the CMP field of the source EJB that the relationship operates on. The <multiplicity> tag can have the value of One or Many. To represent a 1:1 relationship, both <multiplicity> tags in each <ejb-relationship-role> have to be set to One. For 1:*n* relationships, the entity on the many side of the relationship (Emp, in our case) has its <multiplicity> tag set to Many. For a *n*:*m* relationship, both <multiplicity> tags are set to Many.

Listing 22.12 shows an excerpt from the weblogic-cmp-rdbms.xml.xml showing a one-to-one relationship.

LISTING 22.12 weblogic-cmp-rdbms.xml.xml Excerpt

```
<weblogic-rdbms-relation>
  <relation-name>Doctor-Assistant</relation-name>
    <weblogic-relationship-role>
      <relationship-role-name>Doctor-Has-Assistant</relationship-role-name>
      <relationship-role-map>
        <column-map>
          <foreign-key-column>assistantName</foreign-key-column>
          <key-column> assistantName </key-column>
        </column-map>
      </relationship-role-map>
    </weblogic-relationship-role>
</weblogic-rdbms-relation>
```

It's important to watch out for a few things when working with CMP relationships. Relationships cannot be initialized in ejbCreate(). ejbPostCreate() is used to save the relation fields. The exception to this rule is when a primary key contains a foreign key.

Also, collection relation field getters return non-mutable objects. Trying to change the collection gives exceptions. This is as stipulated in the specification and it wouldn't be fast, anyway. Solution: Don't use collection getters except for read-only. Write new methods to add, remove, modify, and empty the collection.

One-to-Many Relationships

One-to-many relationship means that for an Entity A, there can be one or more Entities of B. In our case, we can model a scenario in which a doctor sees multiple patients. This is a one-to-many relationship between a doctor and patients. The following excerpt shows how this would be mapped in the `ejb-jar.xml` file and the `weblogic-cmp-rdbms.xml` file.

Listing 22.13 presents an excerpt from the `ejb-jar.xml` file showing a one-to-many relationship.

LISTING 22.13 ejb-jar.xml Excerpt

```
<relationships>
   <ejb-relation>
     <ejb-relation-name>Doctor-Patient<ejb-relation-name>
     <ejb-relationship-role>
        <ejb-relationship-role-name>
           Doctor-has-an-Patient
        </ejb-relationship-role-name>
        <multiplicity>One<multiplicity>
        <relationship-role-source>
           <ejb-name>DoctorBean</ejb-name>
        </relationship-role-source>
        <cmr-field>
          <cmr-field-name>doctorPatient</cmr-field-name>
        </cmr-field>
      </ejb-relationship-role>
      <ejb-relationship-role>
         <ejb-relationship-role-name>
           Patient-belongs-to-Doctor
         </ejb-relationship-role-name>
         <mulitiplicity>Many</multiplicity>
         <relationship-role-source>
           <ejb-name>PatientBean</ejb-name>
         </relationship-role-source>
      </ejb-relationship-role>
    <ejb-relation>
</relationships>
```

Listing 22.14 is an excerpt from the `weblogic-cmp-rdbms.xml` file showing a one-to-many relationship.

LISTING 22.14 weblogic-cmp-rdbms Excerpt

```
<weblogic-rdbms-relation>
  <relation-name>Doctor-Patient</relation-name>
    <table-name>doctorPatient</table-name>
    <weblogic-relationship-role>
      <relationship-role-name>Doctor-Have-Patients</relationship-role-name>
      <relationship-role-map>
      <column-map>
        <foreign-key-column>assistantName</foreign-key-column>
        <key-column> assistantName </key-column>
      </column-map>
      </relationship-role-map>
    </weblogic-relationship-role>
    <weblogic-relationship-role>
      <relationship-role-name>Assistant-Belongs-To-Doctor</relationship-role-name>
      <relationship-role-map>
      <column-map>
        <foreign-key-column>doctorName</foreign-key-column>
        <key-column> doctorName </key-column>
      </column-map>
      </relationship-role-map>
    </weblogic-relationship-role>
</weblogic-rdbms-relation>
```

Many-to-Many Relationships

A many-to-many relationship is one where both entities are interrelated. In our example, it's quite typical for a doctor to works at more than one hospital and each hospital has many doctors. This is a typical many-to-many relationship. The following excerpts show how this would be mapped in the `ejb-jar.xml` and `weblogic-cmp-rdbms.xml` files. Listing 22.15 shows an excerpt from the `ejb-jar.xml` showing a many-to-many relationship.

LISTING 22.15 ejb-jar.xml Excerpt

```
<relationships>
   <ejb-relation>
     <ejb-relation-name>Doctor-Hospital<ejb-relation-name>
     <ejb-relationship-role>
        <ejb-relationship-role-name>
           Doctor-have-Hospital
```

LISTING 22.15 Continued

```
        </ejb-relationship-role-name>
        <multiplicity>Many<multiplicity>
        <relationship-role-source>
           <ejb-name>HospitalBean</ejb-name>
        </relationship-role-source>
        <cmr-field>
          <cmr-field-name>doctorHospital</cmr-field-name>
        </cmr-field>
      </ejb-relationship-role>
      <ejb-relationship-role>
         <ejb-relationship-role-name>
           Hospital-have-Doctor
         </ejb-relationship-role-name>
         <mulitiplicity>Many</multiplicity>
         <relationship-role-source>
           <ejb-name>DoctorBean</ejb-name>
         </relationship-role-source>
      </ejb-relationship-role>
    <ejb-relation>
</relationships>
```

Listing 22.16 shows an excerpt from the `weblogic-cmp-rdbms.xml` showing a many-to-many relationship.

LISTING 22.16 weblogic-cmp-rdbms Excerpt

```
<weblogic-rdbms-relation>
  <relation-name>Doctor-Hospital</relation-name>
    <table-name>doctorHospital</table-name>
    <weblogic-relationship-role>
      <relationship-role-name>Doctor-Have-Hospitals</relationship-role-name>
      <relationship-role-map>
      <column-map>
        <foreign-key-column>hospitalName</foreign-key-column>
        <key-column> hospitalName </key-column>
      </column-map>
      </relationship-role-map>
    </weblogic-relationship-role>
    <weblogic-relationship-role>
      <relationship-role-name>Hospitals-Have-Doctors</relationship-role-name>
      <relationship-role-map>
```

LISTING 22.16 Continued

```
      <column-map>
        <foreign-key-column>doctorName</foreign-key-column>
        <key-column> doctorName </key-column>
      </column-map>
      </relationship-role-map>
    </weblogic-relationship-role>
</weblogic-rdbms-relation>
```

There is another concept with respect to relationships in Entity beans: directionality. Relationships can be unidirectional or bidirectional.

Unidirectional Relationships

A unidirectional relationship between Entity A and Entity B is one in which Entity A knows about Entity B, but Entity B has no knowledge of Entity A. That is, Entity A has relation field getters and setters to access Entity B, but Entity B has no relation fields pointing back to Entity A. This type of relationship is implemented by specifying a `cmr-field` deployment descriptor element for the Entity bean from which the relationship originates, and not specifying a `cmr-field` element for the other Entity bean.

Bidirectional Relationships

A bidirectional relationship is one in which Entity A and Entity B are aware of each other. This type of relationship is implemented by specifying a `cmr-field` deployment descriptor element for each of the Entity beans. All examples you saw prior to the last section were bidirectional.

Now that we know how to implement relationships for EJBs in WebLogic, let's now talk about caching. Let's discuss various EJB caching techniques to improve the performance of EJBs in WebLogic.

Relationship Caching in EJBs

Caching of Entity beans and their related Entity beans improves performance by reducing the number of `JOIN` queries that have to be executed. In our earlier example, we had three types of relationships:

- One-to-one—A doctor has an assistant.
- One-to-many—A doctor has multiple patients.
- Many-to-many—A doctor works at multiple hospitals and each hospital has multiple doctors.

The <relationship-caching> tag of weblogic-cmp-rdbms.xml is used to specify caching of these relationships. Listing 22.17 is an excerpt from a weblogic-cmp-rdbms.xml file showing the caching of relationships.

LISTING 22.17 weblogic-cmp-rdbms Excerpt

```
<relationship-caching>
        <caching-name>cacheMoreBeans</caching-name>
        <caching-element>
                <cmr-field>assistantName</cmr-field>
                <group-name>assistants</group-name>
        </caching-element>
        <caching-element
                <cmr-field>patientName</cmr-field>
                <group-name>patients</group-name>
        </caching-element>
        <caching-element>
               <cmr-field>hospitalName</cmr-field>
         <group-name>hospitals</group-name>
        </caching-element>
</relationship-caching>
```

It's important to note that relationship caching is not supported for many-to-many relationships. This is obviously because it can lead to deadlocks.

Caching in Entity Beans

Another aspect of caching is to cache the persistent data between transactions. Caching can be enabled by setting the cache-between-transactions element in the weblogic-ejb-jar.xml to either true or false to enable or disable long-term caching of data, respectively. This feature is available if the concurrency strategy is set to exclusive, readonly, or optimistic.

- Caching Between Transactions with Exclusive Concurrency—This feature is available only when running on a single server. It enables caching when the EJB container has exclusive update access to the data store.
- Caching Between Transactions with ReadOnly Concurrency—The EJB container always performs caching of data between transactions when using readonly concurrency.
- Caching Between Transactions with Optimistic Concurrency—The container uses optimistic checking for conflicts at the end of the transaction. This data is broadcast to the other servers on the cluster and data is cached.

22

An important feature of Entity beans is the capability to do queries. Queries are used to find specific Entity beans and any related Entity beans from the underlying data store. In the next section, we explore the WebLogic-specific extensions to the query mechanism with EJB.

WebLogic Query Language

EJB Query Language (EJB-QL) is a query language that defines finder methods for 2.0 Entity beans with container-managed persistence. The deployment descriptors must define each finder query for Entity beans by using an EJB-QL query string.

NOTE

If you're interested in learning EJB-QL in detail, please visit `http://www.ejb-ql.com`.

In WebLogic, you can use the WebLogic QL to query EJB objects instead of the standard EJB-QL that's defined in the `ejb-jar.xml` file. WebLogic QL is defined in the `weblogic-cmp-rdbms-jar.xml` file. The values for the finder queries in the WebLogic-specific deployment descriptors override the values specified in the standard J2EE deployment descriptors.

The main advantage of using the WebLogic QL is that it's richer in features than the standard EJB-QL. That includes features such as aggregate functions, subqueries, and the Order By clause.

- Aggregate functions—The WebLogic QL enables developers to use `MIN`, `MAX`, `AVG`, `SUM`, and `COUNT`. The aggregate functions behave like SQL functions. They're evaluated over the range of the beans returned by the `WHERE` conditions of the query.
- Subqueries—The relationship between WebLogic QL and subqueries is similar to the relationship between SQL queries and subqueries. Use WebLogic QL subqueries in the `WHERE` clause of the WebLogic QL query. The depth of these subqueries is whatever the database supports.
- Order By clause—The Order By clause specifies a mechanism to order the results of the queries. Sorting is done at the database layer as part of the SQL query.

We've covered all the basic concepts of Entity beans and their usage in the context of WebLogic. Let's now talk about some WebLogic Server 8.1–specific EJB features and enhancements with respect to Entity beans.

Advanced Entity Bean Features

In WebLogic Server 8.1, BEA provides several new features and enhancement to support EJBs in general. In this section, we discuss the ones that apply to Entity beans.

- Automatic database detection—WebLogic Server can query the database to detect which kind of database is being used. If the database detected isn't the same as the database specified in the `database-type` element of the `weblogic-cmp-rdbms-jar.xml` file, preference is given to the type defined in the deployment descriptor.
- Automatic table creation—WebLogic can create the database tables or update them based on the deployment descriptors. This enables developers to manipulate the database structure without having to know how to do so in the context of the database. Developers can choose to disable this feature or specify what operations to support, such as `CreateOnly`, `DropAndCreate`, `DropAndCreateAlways`, and `AlterOrCreate`. You can also specify your own DDLs (database scripts) to create these tables. This is done through the tag `<create-default-dbms-tables>` of `weblogic-cmp-rdbms-jar.xml`.
- Automatic primary key generation—WebLogic supports automatic primary key generation for various databases. It also supports database-specific methods, such as Oracle sequences and the Identity column on Microsoft SQL Server. In addition, WebLogic supports using a specific table defined by the bean developer. This is done using the `<automatic-key-generation>` tag of the `weblogic-cmp-rdbms-jar.xml` file.
- Cascade delete—This feature can be used to delete dependent objects in one-to-one and one-to-many relationships. Cascading delete is not supported for many-many relationships. This can be used two ways:

  •Using the `<cascade-delete>` tag of `ejb-jar.xml`. This deletes the dependent records in memory and explicitly in the database.

  •Using the `<db-cascade-delete>` tag of `weblogic-cmp-rdbms-jar.xml`. This deletes *only* the dependent records in memory; the database has to be configured to delete rows automatically.
- Preventing deadlocks for CMP beans—With the cascading delete feature, deadlocks are more of a problem. This is more common when transactions use concurrent strategies. You can specify a lock order attribute in the deployment descriptor to prevent this problem. Use the `<lock-order>` tag in `weblogic-cmp-rdbms-jar.xml`.
- Granular redeployment of EJBs—You can specify that only the bean class can be redeployed, instead of having to redeploy the entire EJB. However, if the Home or Remote interfaces changes, the entire EJB does have to be redeployed.
- Performance improvements—WebLogic Server provides improved performance for EJB bulk updates, optimistic concurrency, field groups, relationship caching, and EJB redeployment. The Administration Console also allows more fine-grained monitoring and testing of the EJBs.
- Constraining optimistic row checking—You can specify the rows in a table that the EJB container should check when optimistic concurrency is used. Then using the

new `verify-rows` element in `weblogic-cmp-rdbms-jar.xml` enables you to choose between optimistic checking on any row read by a transaction versus only rows updated or deleted by a transaction.

- SQL query order optimization—WebLogic automatically orders the select, update, insert, and delete queries to avoid integrity violations. This would also minimize deadlocks.
- Batch queries—The queries are run in batch mode whenever possible. This helps to improve performance.

In addition to the new features in WebLogic Server 8.1, it's interesting to see the various tools that are provided.

Tools for Working with EJBs in WebLogic Server 8.1

In WebLogic Server 8.1, BEA provides several tools to help create, deploy, and manage EJBs:

- EJBGen—A tool that generates EJB 2.0 code. It takes in EJB class files with JavaDoc comments and then generates the Home and Remote interfaces along with the deployment descriptors. BEA recommends using EJBGen to generate the deployment descriptors because it's a hard task to create them manually.
- DDInit—A command-line tool that looks at a directory containing EJBs and builds the standard J2EE and the WebLogic-specific deployment descriptors.
- Ant tasks to create skeleton deployment descriptors—You can use the Ant tasks shipped with WebLogic to create skeleton deployment descriptors. These will be incomplete because Ant cannot create the desired mappings and configurations.
- WebLogic Builder—A visual tool that enables you to work with the deployment descriptors for your entire enterprise application. It helps you not only with the EJB-specific descriptors, but also enables the management of the entire application deployment process.
- weblogic.Deployer—A command line tool that can deploy your EJBs. This can be run from the command line, a shell script, or included in your Ant scripts.
- Appc—The new EJB compiler that compiles and deploys the EJB to WebLogic Server.
- DDConverter—A command-line tool to upgrade your EJB deployment descriptors from a previous version to the latest version.

In this release of WebLogic, BEA has deprecated several features that have been central to the previous releases of WebLogic. We examine those features in the next section.

EJB Features Deprecated in WebLogic 8.1

Various Entity bean–specific features have been deprecated in this release of WebLogic. These include

- Ejbc—The old ejbc compiler has been replaced by the appc compiler.
- `Sql-select-distinct`—This tag has been deprecated and replaced with support for the `DISTINCT` query as part of the WebLogic Query Language.
- Administration Console editing of deployment descriptors—The EJB deployment descriptors can be viewed from the Administration Console, but must be edited using an text or XML editor. A small subset of elements that relate to tuning and performance can still be edited through the Administration Console.

We've now covered all the important aspects of working with Entity beans in WebLogic. However, no chapter about Entity beans would be complete without an introduction to some design issues in the use of EJBs. The remainder of this chapter addresses some design considerations for the proper use of Entity beans.

Entity Bean Best Practices

- Fine-grained versus coarse-grained Entity beans—Many designers make the mistake of modeling all their entities as EJBs. The decision of what entities to model as EJBs and at what level of granularity is a critical issue to overall system performance.
- Modeling technique—Use the appropriate modeling techniques for your job. Use JDBC, JDO, EJBs, or other data access techniques as appropriate.
- Business logic in Entity beans—Entity beans should encapsulate additional business logic such as marking an account to be closed, determining the type or level of users, or the total for an order. Advanced features of the WebLogic Query Language make this easier. This enforces the MVC architecture.
- Optimize data access—It's important to limit the complexity of joins and other long-running data access operations. We should also minimize data access by retrieving multiple data entries in one query. The use of field groups and relationship caching can be used to help with some of these issues.
- Local interfaces—It's a good idea to use local interfaces when possible to avoid network access. Network access costs time and resources.
- Container-managed transactions—Allowing the container to manage transactions is often a better option than managing them yourself in an EJB. In general, try to use the optimal strategy when deciding when and how to manage transactions. Using the wrong transaction granularity and isolation level can harm performance.

- Session Façade—Never expose Entity beans to anything but Session EJBs. Each call to the EJB container is a transaction. The façade allows a single transaction to access the various methods of the Entity bean through one call to a Session EJB. This façade implementation also provides a loose coupling that allows the Entity bean to swapped out if needed.
- CMP over BMP—In general, use CMP EJBs if you can model your business using them. You get added performance benefits of optimizations from WebLogic's CMP engine (for example, relationship caching) with CMP, which you wouldn't get with BMP.
- Transaction isolation—The use of the appropriate transaction isolation level is important for performance. Chapter 9, "Processing Transactions with the Java Transaction API," explores the isolation levels in detail.
- Indexes for queries—For better database performance, ensure that appropriate indexes have been create for all EJB-QL queries.
- Fast lane reader—The fast lane reader design pattern uses Entity beans for inserts, updates, and deletes to the database. However, for reading data, it uses straight JDBC. This is especially important if you're reading large amounts of data.

Summary

In this chapter, we covered the basics of working with Entity beans in WebLogic Server 8.1. The use of Entity beans can be a blessing or a curse, depending on how, when, and where they're used. We recommended examining your requirements carefully and choosing where you can benefit from the use of Entity beans.

BEA has provided a very significantly improved EJB container with full support for the latest EJB specifications. This chapter has covered all the WebLogic-specific features, enhancements, and tools provided by WebLogic Server 8.1.

CHAPTER 23

Working with Message-Driven Beans

by James Huang

IN THIS CHAPTER

- When to Use Message-Driven Beans
- How to Create Message-Driven Beans
- Sample Message-Driven Bean
- Message-Driven Beans Best Practices

Message-Driven beans are a nice addition in the EJB 2.0 specification; they make JMS and asynchronous interactions much easier to develop in an EJB environment. In this chapter, we discuss when and why to use Message-Driven beans, and explain how to create and use them with a simple example. You can use the sample code as a template and follow the steps to create and use your own Message-Driven beans in your J2EE applications.

When to Use Message-Driven Beans

J2EE, being a standard for distributed computing, makes cross-function business integration very easy. Using JNDI, J2EE applications can easily be found by one another and invoke each other's services, synchronously or asynchronously.

Synchronous interaction is easier and simpler to implement, but is more susceptible to potential failures. Network communication is an obvious source of problems. Different applications might operate in very different environments and at varied paces, and have their own problems that might or might not be visible to the developers of other applications that use them. For instance, a credit card processing application initiates an external service request across the Internet to verify credit card information before starting a transaction, waits for the response, and returns the success or failure status code to the caller. The caller then completes or aborts its own transaction based on the status. This process could easily take up to a few minutes. For an online Web application, users might experience long waits or even timeout problems. Another potential problem is that invocations could block. For instance, if the service agreement with the credit card processing service provider is single-threaded, only one processing can happen at a time. When multiple customers order books at the same time, they will be queued and the wait or time-out situation will be exacerbated.

Asynchronous interaction is more robust and reliable. Network communication poses little loss risk because a well-designed asynchronous framework is supposed to deliver the message sooner or later. Application discrepancy in pace is generally not an issue either (within a certain range, of course). Asynchronous interaction dictates a system design that's very different from its synchronous counterpart. Take the credit card processing case, for example. Suppose that the online store sells e-books. The original system specification would be that users place orders of books, submit credit card information, wait for the transaction to finish, and download the books. With an asynchronous design, instead of completing the whole transaction in a single shot, the system takes the order and credit card information and finishes with a thank-you page. A credit card processing request is placed, which will eventually return the status to the system. After the result has arrived, an email will be sent to the user, telling him to download the purchased books. This is a very common practice.

Asynchronous interactions are realized by messaging systems. The Java Message Service (JMS), a part of the J2EE standard, is a standard API for utilizing enterprise messaging systems. All J2EE-compliant middleware products are required to fully support the JMS specification; WebLogic is no exception. JMS is discussed extensively in Chapter 12, "Enterprise Messaging with JMS."

The EJB 2.0 specification introduces a new type of Enterprise JavaBean: the Message-Driven bean (or MDB, for short). This is a very welcome feature for asynchronous interaction with the J2EE framework. As we know, to receive and process a message, a JMS client has to take a few steps that involve obtaining the initial context, creating a connection and a session, looking for a JMS queue or topic, and waiting to receive a message. Expectedly, a JMS client runs in its own thread. Imagine that you're required to process any number of JMS messages at any time. You would probably do something very similar to what a servlet container would do: create a pool of JMS handlers, each running in its own thread; have a master listener to listen on a particular queue; for each received message, pick a handler from the pool; when the processing is complete, return the handler to the pool. You also need to device a mechanism to specify which JMS server to connect to, which JMS destinations to listen on, and so on. This is exactly what a Message-Driven bean container does. The container takes care of all the chores, such as listening for the incoming messages, security, concurrency, life cycle management, and so forth. The communication details are declared in the standard deployment descriptors. The developers of Message-Driven beans simply focus on the business logic.

How do Message-Driven beans differ from JMS session pools? They are essentially very similar, but MDBs can listen to only one destination, whereas session pools can subscribe to many. MDBs also provide automatic transaction management.

How to Create Message-Driven Beans

Message-Driven beans are very similar to Stateless Session beans in terms of life cycle. There are a few major differences between Message-Driven beans and other types of beans, such as Session beans and Entity beans:

- Message-Driven beans are server-side only components, so unlike other beans, they do not have home or component interfaces.
- Message-Driven beans have one and only one business method, `onMessage()`, that is invoked by the container when a message is received. Other beans may have multiple business methods and their calls are serialized.
- Each deployed Message-Driven bean is associated with the JMS destination specified in the deployment descriptor. Other beans can receive calls from any clients.
- Due to their asynchronous nature, Message-Driven beans do not directly return values nor throw exceptions because the callers simply issue JMS messages and leave. The real caller is the container, which knows nothing about the business and hence is totally ignorant about the result. MDBs can signal the status of the operation by other means, such as sending a response as a distinct JMS message on another destination.

Message-Driven Bean Class

Message-Driven beans are implemented with just one class. The Message-Driven bean class is required to implement two interfaces: `javax.ejb.MessageDrivenBean` and `javax.jms.MessageListener`.

The `javax.ejb.MessageDrivenBean` interface is defined as follows:

```
package javax.ejb;
public interface MessageDrivenBean extends EnterpriseBean
{
 public void setMessageDrivenContect(MessageDrivenContext context)
       throws EJBException;
 public void ejbRemove() throws EJBException;
}
```

Although it isn't in the interface, you must also implement the creation method:

```
public void ejbCreate() throws CreationException;
```

Message-Driven Bean Life Cycle

Message-Driven bean instances can be in one of the two states: does-not-exist or method-ready. A Message-Driven bean instance's life cycle is much like that of a Stateless Session bean:

- The container creates a new instance by calling its class's `newInstance()`, and then calling its `setMessageDrivenContext(context)` and `ejbCreate()` methods, in this order.
- Once created, the bean is in the method-ready pool, ready to process messages sent to its associated JMS destination.
- When the container decides to remove an instance, it calls that instance's `ejbRemove()` method and removes it from the pool. The instance will ultimately be garbage collected.

`setMessageContect(context)` is called by the container to provide the Message-Driven context, which can be saved for later use. The Message-Driven context simply extends `javax.ejb.EJBContext` with no additional methods. The `javax.ejb.EJBContext` interface is defined as follows:

```
package javax.ejb;
public interface EJBContext
{
 // transaction methods
 public javax.transaction.UserTransaction getUserTransaction()
➥throws IllegalStateException;
 public Boolean getRollbackOnly() throws IllegalStateException;
 public void setRollbackOnly() throws IllegalStateException;

 // EJB home methods
 public EJBHome getEJBHome();
 public gEJBLocalHome getEJBLocalHome();

 // security methods
 public java.security.Principal getCallerPrincipal();
 public Boolean isCallerInRole(String roleName);
}
```

The home and security-related methods are not applicable and will throw runtime exceptions if invoked. Message-Driven beans do not have home interfaces, and the JMS messages are received asynchronously, so no sender information is available.

The transaction-related methods are the only ones provided for Message-Driven beans. Message-Driven beans can operate either in container-managed or bean-managed transactions.

Although `getCallerPrincipal()` and `isCallerInRole()` methods cannot be called, you can specify a security identity using `<run-as>`. This would be the identity used when invoking other EJBs, making RMI calls, and any services that accept security identities.

Handling the JMS Message

JMS messages are handled in the only `MessageListener` method:

```
public void onMessage(javax.jms.Message msg);
```

The parameter can be one of the predefined message classes, such as `TextMessage`, `MapMessage`, `ObjectMessage`, and so on, or a custom message class. Note that this method does not throw any exceptions; therefore, you must catch, handle, and log all exceptions.

Setting the Context

Any business logic can be coded in the `onMessage()` method. However, Message-Driven beans are often used as a communication vehicle to dispatch business requests to other beans or services. In all Message-Driven bean methods, you can access JNDI resources either by direct queries or by using `java:comp/env` lookups. It's common to store a local reference to the JNDI Environment Naming Context (ENC) in `setMessageDrivenContext()`:

```
MessageDrivenContext context;
Context jndiContext = null;

public void setMessageDrivenContext(MessageDrivenContext ctxt) {
 context = ctxt;
 jndiContext = new InitialContext();
}
```

Deploying Message-Driven Beans

Message-Driven beans are deployed in the same way as Session beans and Entity beans: by using the deployment descriptor files `ejb-jar.xml` and `weblogic-ejb-jar.xml`. In `ejb-jar.xml`, the `<message-driven>` tag under `<enterprise-beans>` describes the Message-Driven bean. Much as for other types of beans, there can be tags within `<message-driven>`, such as `<ejb-name>`, `<ejb-class>`, and so on. But the tags related to the home and component interfaces are absent. Beyond those, there are these tags specifically for Message-Driven beans: `<message-driven-destination>`, `<message-selector>` and `<acknowledge-mode>`. The following is an example:

```
<ejb-jar>

 <enterprise-beans>

 <message-driven>
   <ejb-name>SnoopQueueMDB</ejb-name>
   <ejb-class>SnoopMDB</ejb-class>
   <transaction-type>Container</transaction-type>
```

```
    <message-driven-destination>
     <destination-type>javax.jms.Queue</destination-type>
    </message-driven-destination>
  </message-driven>

 </enterprise-beans>

</ejb-jar>
```

The <message-driven-destination> must contain a <destination-type> tag. The <message-selector> tag can take a value in JMS message selector syntax, so that this bean will respond to messages that satisfy the condition. This is discouraged for performance reasons because every message will have to check against the expression, which can be expensive. The <acknowledge-mode> tells the container how to acknowledge a JMS message to the sender. The default value is `Auto-acknowledge`; the other valid value is `Dups-ok-acknowledge`.

The `weblogic-ejb-jar.xml` describes the deployed beans in more detail. Its <destination-jndi-name> tag under <message-driven-descriptor> specifies the JNDI name for the JMS target this bean is listening on. The JMS target must exist and match the destination type (`queue` or `topic`) specified in `ejb-jar.xml`; if it does not, the deployment fails.

```
<weblogic-ejb-jar>

  <weblogic-enterprise-bean>
   <ejb-name>SnoopQueueMDB</ejb-name>
   <message-driven-descriptor>
    <pool>
     <max-beans-in-free-pool>10</max-beans-in-free-pool>
     <initial-beans-in-free-pool>2</initial-beans-in-free-pool>
    </pool>
    <destination-jndi-name>weblogic.examples.jms.exampleQueue</destination-jndi-
➥name>
   </message-driven-descriptor>
  </weblogic-enterprise-bean>

</Weblogic-ejb-jar>
```

The <jndi-name> tag is useless because the home interface cannot be retrieved. Configuring the pooling is similar to how it is done for Stateless Session beans.

In WebLogic 8.1, the <dispatch_policy> tag can be used to assign MDBs to a configured execute queue. Previously, that tag applied only to Session and Entity beans.

Sample Message-Driven Bean

Let's do an end-to-end implementation and testing of a Message-Driven bean that will simply print out the information about the received messages. The same class will be deployed as two beans: one will listen on a queue and the other will subscribe to a topic. We'll go through the whole process of creating and deploying the beans, issuing test messages, and monitoring how they behave.

The bean class is straightforward, as shown in Listing 23.1.

LISTING 23.1 SnoopMDB.java

```
import java.util.*;
import javax.ejb.*;
import javax.jms.*;
import javax.naming.*;

public class SnoopMDB implements MessageDrivenBean, MessageListener
{
 private MessageDrivenContext context = null;
 private Context jndiContext = null;

 public void ejbCreate () throws CreateException {}
 public void ejbRemove() {}

 public void setMessageDrivenContext(MessageDrivenContext ctxt)
 {
  context = ctxt;
  try
  {
   jndiContext = new InitialContext();
  }
  catch(NamingException ne)
  {
   throw new EJBExceptin(ne);
  }
 }

 /**
  * The business logic
  */
 public void onMessage(Message msg)
 {
  try
```

```
{
 String text = null;

 System.out.println("===== New Message =====");
 System.out.println("Type:     " + msg.getClass().getName());
 System.out.println("Destination: " + msg.getJMSDestination());
 System.out.println("Message ID: " + msg.getJMSMessageID());

 if ( msg instanceof TextMessage )
 {
  text = ((TextMessage)msg).getText();
 }
 else if ( msg instanceof ObjectMessage )
 {
  text = ((ObjectMessage)msg).getObject().toString();
 }
 else if ( msg instanceof MapMessage )
 {
  StringBuffer sb = new StringBuffer("\n");
  MapMessage mm = (MapMessage)msg;
  Enumeration enum = mm.getMapNames();
  while (enum.hasMoreElements())
  {
   String name = (String)enum.nextElement();
   Object val = mm.getObject(name);
   sb.append("> " + name + " = " + val + '\n');
  }
  text = sb.toString();
 }

 if (text != null)
  System.out.println("Content:    " + text);
}
catch(Throwable t)
{
 System.out.println("?! Failed:  " + t.getMessage());
}
}

}
```

In the code's `onMessage()` method, it prints information about the message and the text content, if available, to `System.out`. The rest of the class is routine. This is just a test bean;

in reality, the type of message is probably predefined or is limited to a few known possibilities. If there are different types of messages to be handled, one option would be to define one MDB for each message type, which would be more efficient and object-oriented. Listing 23.2 shows the EJB deployment descriptor.

LISTING 23.2 ejb-jar.xml

```
<?xml version="1.0"?>
<!DOCTYPE ejb-jar PUBLIC
 "-//Sun Microsystems, Inc.//DTD Enterprise JavaBeans 2.0//EN"
 "http://java.sun.com/j2ee/dtds/ejb-jar_2_0.dtd">

<ejb-jar>

 <enterprise-beans>

 <message-driven>
   <ejb-name>SnoopQueueMDB</ejb-name>
   <ejb-class>SnoopMDB</ejb-class>
   <transaction-type>Container</transaction-type>
   <message-driven-destination>
    <destination-type>javax.jms.Queue</destination-type>
   </message-driven-destination>
   <env-entry>
     <description>This is a bean listening on a queue.</description>
     <env-entry-name>listen_type</env-entry-name>
     <env-entry-type>java.lang.String</env-entry-type>
     <env-entry-value>queue</env-entry-value>
   </env-entry>
  </message-driven>

 <message-driven>
   <ejb-name>SnoopTopicMDB</ejb-name>
   <ejb-class>SnoopMDB</ejb-class>
   <transaction-type>Container</transaction-type>
   <message-driven-destination>
    <destination-type>javax.jms.Topic</destination-type>
   </message-driven-destination>
   <env-entry>
     <description>This is a bean listening on a topic.</description>
     <env-entry-name>listen_type</env-entry-name>
     <env-entry-type>java.lang.String</env-entry-type>
     <env-entry-value>topic</env-entry-value>
```

```
    </env-entry>
  </message-driven>

 </enterprise-beans>

</ejb-jar>
```

In ejb-jar.xml, we defined two Message-Driven beans: SnoopQueueMDB and SnoopTopicMDB. Both beans are implemented by the same Java class, SnoopMDB, but listen for different destination types: javax.jms.Queue and javax.jms.Topic. The vendor-specific deployment descriptor provides further information, as listed in Listings 23.3.

LISTING 23.3 weblogic-ejb-jar.xml

```
<?xml version="1.0"?>
<!DOCTYPE weblogic-ejb-jar
 PUBLIC '-//BEA Systems, Inc.//DTD WebLogic 8.1.0 EJB//EN'
 'http://www.bea.com/servers/wls810/dtd/weblogic-ejb-jar.dtd'>

<weblogic-ejb-jar>

  <weblogic-enterprise-bean>
   <ejb-name>SnoopQueueMDB</ejb-name>
   <message-driven-descriptor>
    <pool>
     <max-beans-in-free-pool>10</max-beans-in-free-pool>
     <initial-beans-in-free-pool>2</initial-beans-in-free-pool>
    </pool>
    <destination-jndi-name>weblogic.examples.jms.exampleQueue</destination-jndi-
➥name>
   </message-driven-descriptor>
   <jndi-name>SnoopQueueMDB</jndi-name>
  </weblogic-enterprise-bean>

  <weblogic-enterprise-bean>
   <ejb-name>SnoopTopicMDB</ejb-name>
   <message-driven-descriptor>
    <pool>
     <max-beans-in-free-pool>10</max-beans-in-free-pool>
     <initial-beans-in-free-pool>2</initial-beans-in-free-pool>
    </pool>
    <destination-jndi-name>weblogic.examples.jms.exampleTopic</destination-jndi-
➥name>
```

```
    </message-driven-descriptor>
    <jndi-name>SnoopTopicMDB</jndi-name>
  </weblogic-enterprise-bean>

</weblogic-ejb-jar>
```

In weblogic-ejb-jar.xml, each bean is designated its respective destination's JNDI names, and we used the JMS example queue and topic in WebLogic 8.1's examples domain.

Let's build and test the beans. Building Message-Driven beans is much simpler than building Entity and Session beans. Simply compile the Java source files, put them (along with deployment descriptor files) under the META-INF/ directory into a single JAR file. We've included the JAR file on the CD at ch23/snoopmdb.jar.

To test run, follow these steps. First, make sure that the JMS destinations are available before deploying the Message-Driven beans. After the beans are deployed, they become listeners of these JMS destinations. You can check and monitor JMS destinations using the WebLogic Console Web application. If all goes well, use a JMS client program to send messages to test.

TIP

If you haven't done it yet, create an instance of the examples domain. You can do this by running the Configuration Wizard. Take note of the administrator username and password because we'll need them shortly.

The examples domain contains a JSM queue and a topic, which are used by our Message-Driven beans. In the WebLogic console, you can check their existence and monitor their status, as shown in Figure 23.1.

Watch for exampleQueue and exampleTopic under Services→JMS→examplesJMSServer→Destinations in the left pane, and check the JNDI name for them in the right. You can click on the Monitor tab in the right pane to monitor their status.

Now deploy the Message-Driven beans by clicking on Deployments in the left pane. Follow the instructions in the right pane to pick our snoopmdb.jar file, and deploy the Message-Driven beans to the examplesServer server. Navigate to Deployments→EJB Modules→snoopmdb in the left pane to verify that the beans are deployed successfully and are running, like that in Figure 23.2.

If so, you should also see that the destinations have listeners attached. Figure 23.3 shows the exampleQueue.

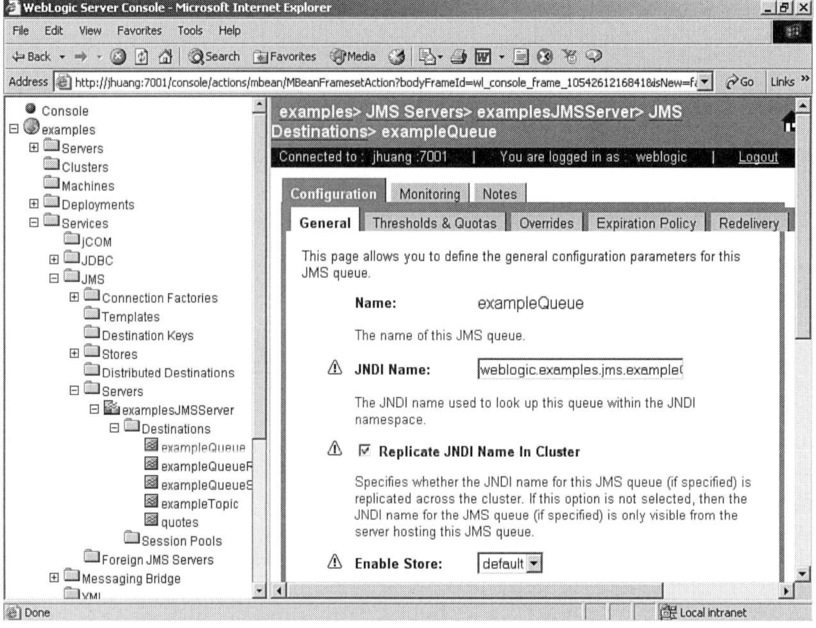

FIGURE 23.1 Checking JMS destinations.

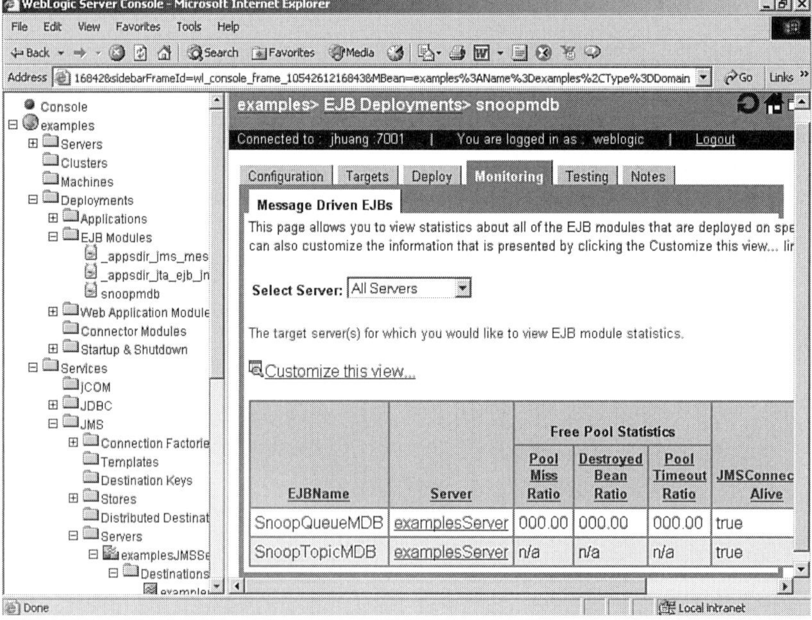

FIGURE 23.2 Checking Message-Driven bean deployment.

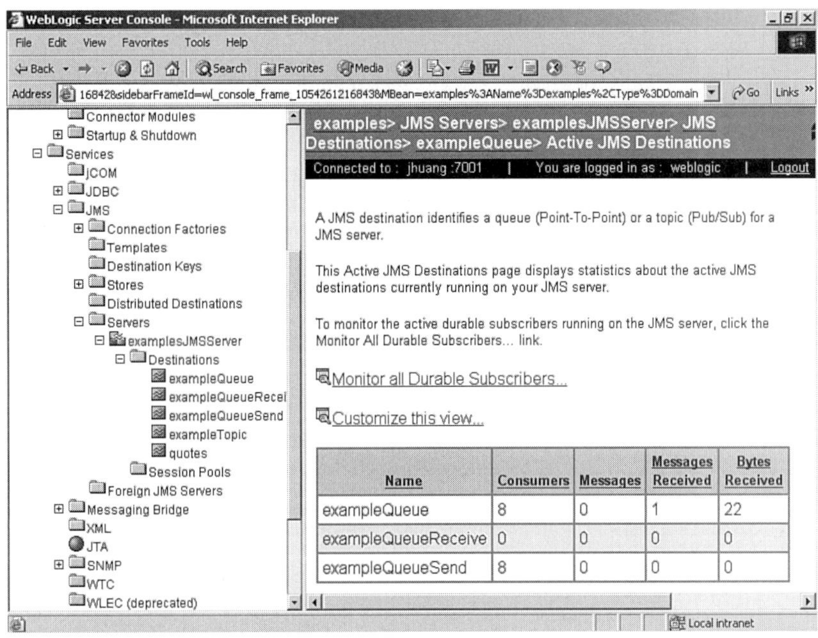

FIGURE 23.3 Monitoring JMS destinations.

Finally, let's send some messages to the destination and see the response from the beans. Listing 23.4 shows a standalone JMS client. The source file and class file can be found on the CD in the `ch23/Test/` directory.

LISTING 23.4 JMSQueueSend.java

```
import java.util.*;
import java.io.*;
import javax.jts.*;
import javax.jms.*;
import javax.naming.*;

public class JMSQueueSend
{
 public static void main(String[] args)
 {
  try
  {
   Properties props = System.getProperties();
```

```
   props.put(Context.INITIAL_CONTEXT_FACTORY,
    "weblogic.jndi.WLInitialContextFactory");
   props.put(Context.PROVIDER_URL, "t3://localhost:7001");
   props.put(Context.SECURITY_PRINCIPAL, "weblogic");
   props.put(Context.SECURITY_CREDENTIALS, "password");
   InitialContext ctx = new InitialContext(props);

   QueueConnectionFactory qconfactory =
    (QueueConnectionFactory)ctx.lookup(
      "javax.jms.QueueConnectionFactory");
   QueueConnection qcon = qconfactory.createQueueConnection();
   QueueSession qsession = qcon.createQueueSession(false,
      Session.AUTO_ACKNOWLEDGE);
   Queue queue = (Queue)ctx.lookup("weblogic.examples.jms.exampleQueue");
   QueueSender qsender = qsession.createQueueSender(queue);
   TextMessage msg = qsession.createTextMessage();
   qcon.start();
   msg.setText("Hello JMS Queue World!");
   qsender.send(msg);
  }
  catch(Throwable t)
  {
   System.out.println("Exception caught: " + t);
  }
 }
} // end of class JMSQueueSend.
```

For the principal and credentials, use the administrator username and password set for this domain. Our Message-Driven beans simply print out the message information and content to `System.out` of the server. Run the client and you'll see this output in the console running your server (see Figure 23.4).

```
Start Server - D:\bea\user_projects\examples\startExamplesServer.cmd
<May 29, 2003 7:19:54 PM PDT> <Notice> <WebLogicServer> <BEA-000355> <Thread "SS
t" listening on port 7002, ip address *.*>
<May 29, 2003 7:19:54 PM PDT> <Notice> <WebLogicServer> <BEA-000365> <Server sta
G>
<May 29, 2003 7:19:54 PM PDT> <Notice> <WebLogicServer> <BEA-000360> <Server sta
>
===== New Message =====
Type:        weblogic.jms.common.TextMessageImpl
Destination: exampleQueue
Message ID:  ID:P<129978.1054261409358.0>
Content:     Hello JMS Queue World!
```

FIGURE 23.4 The Message-Driven bean output.

Message-Driven Beans Best Practices

Just like a Session bean is a façade for the synchronous invocation of business logic, a Message-Driven bean is a façade for asynchronous business logic. Another design pattern is Service Activator. According to the EJB 2.0 specification, Session beans and Entity beans are synchronous, but there are situations in which asynchronous invocations are desirable. Message-Driven beans can naturally serve as service activators. Whenever a client needs an asynchronous service, a JMS message is posted, and the corresponding MDB interprets the request, locates the service, and subsequently invokes it.

In the beginning of this chapter, we used an example to demonstrate the necessity of asynchronous processing use cases. In that example, a fictitious online store accepts credit cards and ships products when payment is received. For a synchronous design, there are two key drawbacks:

- Slow response time—To complete the transaction, we have to sequentially deal with not only internal systems (such as CRM) but also external services (credit card processing). Some of the systems might work at very slow pace, depending on the load, size of database, network connection, and so on.
- Poor reliability and lack of fault tolerance—The success of this transaction depends on that of all the subtransactions, so there are many points of failure.

Asynchronous design fixes both these problems:

- Prompt response time—The user will experience no delay because the ordering process is essentially reduced to information collecting. The transaction is decoupled. How long it takes to complete the transaction becomes irrelevant.
- High reliability, fault tolerance, and scalability—If any one step in the transaction fails abnormally, the system still has the chance to retry until a valid transaction state is reached. Because the back-end processing is decoupled from the user interaction, scaling up the system is extremely easy: Simply adding more Message-Driven beans, either locally or remotely, can deal with increased volume.

When the transaction is finally completed, a notification such as an email will be sent to the user.

Within the message façade, depending on the situation, the business logic can be carried out in different ways. It can use a few Session beans. It can call a single session façade that handles everything. Or it can use one or more other message façades.

Multiple Message-Driven beans can be used so that each point of failure is dealt with by an individual Message-Driven bean. For instance, in our online store example, we need to complete the credit card transaction first, update the CRM system, and send out the email to enable users to download. What if the credit card is charged and money is transferred but the CRM update fails? This CRM update could be repeated until it finally goes through. Thus, we need one queue for the credit card transactions and another for CRM updates. The last Message-Driven bean that listens on the CRM update notification queue can finish the business by sending the email to the customer.

Asynchronous design with a message façade obtains its merits at the expense of benefits of synchronous design, such as strongly typed parameters, return values, and exception propagation. Suppose that the user's credit card has expired or does not have enough funds. A synchronous system can simply throw a `BadCreditCardException` so that the UI can prompt user for a valid one. In an asynchronous system, this process is not straightforward any more because the initiator (the user) might already be offline or off this site. One solution is sending an email that asks the customer to come back to the site and pay with another credit card or another means. Another solution is to have a queue for error messages, which customers can consult through a client application.

Despite the inherent complexity and apparent drawbacks of asynchronous system design, it is very useful and effective for the use cases we just talked about. Message-Driven beans set a standard and make this truly easy for J2EE applications.

Message-Driven beans should follow general guidelines for enterprise beans development, such as using `java:comp/env` resources, and so on.

It's common to use Message-Driven beans to receive messages and dispatch their processing to one or more Session beans, so that such business logic can be shared across synchronous and asynchronous components.

One Message-Driven bean can listen on only one JMS destination; multiple beans can listen on the same destination. A JMS destination can receive any kind of messages. If multiple kinds of beans listen on a same queue, for instance, each processes certain types of messages. Use `<message-selector>` tag to specify this.

Sometimes certain messages must be processed in order. One way to do this is to set the `<max-beans-in-free-pool>` value to `1`, which effectively reduces the message processing to single-thread. If other types of messages can be processed in any order, create separate queues.

Often times there are different ways to fulfill the same set of use cases, especially when Message-Driven beans are involved, so it's wise to compare multiple designs to find the best solution.

Summary

Message-Driven beans make JMS programming much easier. The container provides many infrastructural services so that application developers can focus on the business logic of the asynchronous processing. Asynchronous processing can at times be very useful or even indispensable.

Message-Driven beans are in many ways similar to Stateless Session beans. But unlike Session beans and Entity beans, MDBs are never invoked directly by clients; therefore, they don't need home interfaces and remote objects. For developers, this means that there needs just one source file for a bean, plus appropriate deployment descriptors. The majority of Message-Driven bean development is done in the `onMessage()` method of the `javax.jms.MessageListener` interface, which every MDB class must implement.

The design pattern for Message-Driven beans is, naturally, Service Activator; that is, clients post messages to request services, and MDBs delegate them to appropriate Entity beans or other services.

PART VI

Working with WebLogic Server Applications

IN THIS PART

CHAPTER **24**

Testing and Debugging Applications

By Tom Schwenk

IN THIS CHAPTER

WebLogic has been designed with the capability to support very large, complicated applications that often include hundreds of use cases and can span across many existing applications in an enterprise. Given that, it's no surprise that defects arise in these applications, just as they do in other software products. When building such applications, it's important to take this fact into consideration, and to design them with capabilities for testing, debugging, and real-time logging. This chapter explores some commonly used practices and additional tools for testing and debugging within WebLogic.

In this chapter, you'll learn

- How to design, build, and maintain unit tests for an application to ensure that code modifications do not break existing functionality
- How to instrument code with logging information to monitor the health of a running system and track down problem reports
- How to use an IDE's integrated debugger to step through application code line by line

An Introduction to Software Testing

Testing is an integral part of the software development life cycle. As today's applications become increasingly more sophisticated, proper testing practices are all the more critical. There is an old saying among software developers, "test early, test often," which essentially means that it is easier to test smaller pieces of functionality as they're written than it is to begin testing when the entire application is built. For example, if you were assembling a car, you wouldn't install an engine that you hadn't tested. And if you were building the engine, you wouldn't install spark plugs and fuel injectors if you weren't certain that they worked properly. In software development, such tests of isolated software components are called *unit testing*.

Although unit testing can establish a baseline for determining an application's behavior, unexpected bugs can occur when many components start interacting. Testing the interactions between different components of a system is known as *functional testing*. This type of testing is the most difficult because it requires the application to be driven through all of its possible execution paths, and probed with all of its possible inputs. In some very complex systems, this might be practically impossible to do, so having reliable unit tests available becomes even more important.

When bugs do surface in an application, it's important to be able to locate them quickly. Having a logging system in place allows a record to be kept of what an application has been doing. These logs can provide hints as to what went wrong within an application. However, to really understand what a system is doing, an integrated debugger is required. The integrated debugger allows breakpoints to be set and the application to be paused during execution. You can then step through the code line by line to inspect the values of variables and watch the execution flow.

Finding Problems Early: Unit Testing

Unit testing is one of those essential components of software development that's often not practiced at all or is done in an ad hoc fashion. The idea is that when a system component or unit is written, a set of simple tests is also written to verify that the component works as expected. The tests for all the components in a system should be run on a regular basis, such as after a nightly build, to verify that changes in one part of a system have not broken the expected behavior of another part of the system. Although that seems like a lot of work, and at first glance it might be, thankfully there is a tool called JUnit that speeds the process of writing the tests and automates running them. JUnit is freely available from `http://www.junit.org`.

Installing and Running JUnit

It's relatively simple to get up and running with JUnit. Here are the installation steps:

1. Download the distribution archive from `http://www.junit.org`.

2. Extract the archive onto your system.

3. The extracted `junit.jar` file contains everything you need to build and run JUnit test cases. Put it in your classpath for your builds, and on the command line when you run the tests.
4. (Optional) Ant has some built-in tasks that enable you to run your JUnit test cases directly from Ant. To take advantage of this, place a copy of `junit.jar` in your `%ANT_HOME%\lib` directory.

JUnit runs as a simple command-line Java program. For example,

```
java -cp testCaseClassPath junit.awtui.TestRunner test.case.class.name
```

runs the given test case using JUnit's AWT `TestRunner`. A `TestRunner` is a tool that shows you the progress of the JUnit tests that are running. JUnit comes with three `TestRunners`: `junit.awtui.TestRunner`, `junit.swingui.TestRunner`, and `junit.textui.TestRunner`. The first two `TestRunners` provide a graphical interface to the tool, and the last one is a command-line text interface.

A Simple JUnit Example

Let's take a look at a simple class that we would like to unit test. The class we use in this example is a very simple implementation of a shopping cart, and is shown in Listing 24.1.

LISTING 24.1 Sample Class for Unit Testing (ShoppingCart.java)

```
package wls8unleashed;
import java.io.Serializable;
import java.util.Vector;

public class ShoppingCart implements Serializable {
  private Vector items;
  public ShoppingCart() {
    items = new Vector();
  }

  public void addItem(CartItem item) {
    items.add(item);
  }

  public Vector getItems() {
    return items;
  }

  public int getNumItems() {
    return items.size();
```

LISTING 24.1 Continued

```
  }

  public void emptyCart() {
    items.clear();
  }

  public double getTotalCost() {
    double cost = 0.0;
    for (int i=0; i<items.size(); i++) {
      CartItem item = (CartItem)items.get(i);
      cost += item.getUnitPrice() * item.getQuantity();
    }

    return cost;
  }
}
```

This class relies on another class, `CartItem`, which is shown in Listing 24.2.

LISTING 24.2 CartItem Class Listing (CartItem.java)

```
package wls8unleashed;
import java.io.Serializable;
public class CartItem implements Serializable {
  private double unitPrice;
  private int quantity;
  private String name;

  public CartItem(String itemName, int itemQuant, double price) {
    name = itemName;
    quantity = itemQuant;
    unitPrice = price;
  }

  public String getName() {
    return name;
  }

  public int getQuantity() {
    return quantity;
  }
```

LISTING 24.2 Continued

```
  public double getUnitPrice() {
    return unitPrice;
  }
}
```

To write a proper unit test of the `ShoppingCart` class, we have to write a test case for each method in the class. With JUnit, all test cases are implemented within a class derived from `junit.framework.TestCase`. With that in mind, we'll create a `ShoppingCartTestCase` class as shown in Listing 24.3.

LISTING 24.3 ShoppingCartTestCase Class Listing (ShoppingCartTestCase.java)

```
package wls8unleashed.testing;
import java.util.Vector;
import junit.framework.Assert;
import junit.framework.Test;
import junit.framework.TestCase;
import junit.framework.TestSuite;

public class ShoppingCartTestCase extends TestCase {
  private ShoppingCart cart;
  private CartItem item1;
  private CartItem item2;
  private CartItem item3;

  public ShoppingCartTestCase() {
  }

  protected void setUp() {
    cart = new ShoppingCart();
    item1 = new CartItem("Video Card", 1, 149.99);
    item2 = new CartItem("Monitor", 1, 459.99);
    item3 = new CartItem("Camera", 1, 289.99);
  }

  public void testAddItem() {
    cart.addItem(item1);
    Vector items = cart.getItems();
    CartItem tmpItem = (CartItem)items.get(0);
    Assert.assertEquals(tmpItem.getName(), item1.getName());
    Assert.assertEquals(tmpItem.getQuantity(), item1.getQuantity());
    Assert.assertEquals(tmpItem.getUnitPrice(), item1.getUnitPrice(), 0.0);
  }
```

LISTING 24.3 Continued

```
  public void testNumItems() {
    cart.addItem(item1);
    cart.addItem(item2);
    cart.addItem(item3);
    Assert.assertTrue(cart.getNumItems() == 3);
  }

  public void testTotalCost() {
    cart.addItem(item1);
    cart.addItem(item2);
    cart.addItem(item3);
    Assert.assertEquals(cart.getTotalCost(), 899.97, 0.0);
  }

  public void testEmptyCart() {
    cart.addItem(item1);
    cart.emptyCart();
    Assert.assertTrue(cart.getNumItems() == 0);
  }

  public static Test suite() {
    TestSuite suite = new TestSuite(ShoppingCartTestCase.class);
    return suite;
  }
}
```

Let's take a moment to examine how this test class works. When JUnit runs, it requires the name of a class that has implemented the `static suite()` method. This method is akin to a `main()` method in an ordinary Java program, and serves as the entry point where JUnit begins the testing process.

In our implementation of `suite()`, we create an instance of `junit.framework.TestSuite` and pass in a reference to the `ShoppingCartTestCase` class. When this constructor is used, JUnit automatically finds any `public testXXX()` methods in the given class, and calls each one as its own test case. In this case, we've defined four test methods: `testAddItem()`, `testNumItems()`, `testTotalCost()`, and `testEmptyCart()`. We also defined a `setUp()` method, which JUnit calls before running each test. A `tearDown()` method may also be defined, which can be called after each test.

In the first test case, `testAddItem()`, we're essentially testing to verify that the item we retrieve from the cart is the same as the item we initially added. The method uses the `assertEquals()` method of the `Assert` class to verify that each attribute of the retrieved

CartItem object is equal to that of the original CartItem that was added to the cart. If any of the assertions were false, JUnit would display a message and fail that particular test case.

Unit Testing Inside WebLogic

In the previous example, we demonstrated how to create and run unit tests for existing software components using JUnit. In that situation, the tests were actually run from within the same JVM as JUnit itself. But there are many software components, such as servlets, EJBs, JSPs, and tag libraries, that must be deployed and running inside of WebLogic in order to be tested. So, how do we go about unit testing those types of modules?

There are a couple different answers to that question. The first answer starts at the design phase of the component. It's typically good practice to isolate key logic components in such a way as to make them as free from external dependencies as possible. In addition to promoting testability, such a design promotes greater code reuse.

For example, take our earlier ShoppingCart example. That was a very simple implementation of a core business object. However, within the context of the design of a particular system, the architect might have viewed the shopping cart as being implemented as a stateful session bean. In that situation, we could respond by taking our existing ShoppingCart class, making it implement the javax.ejb.SessionBean interface, and essentially turning it into a session bean.

Another approach would be creating a subclass of ShoppingCart that implements the necessary EJB methods, called ShoppingCartEJBImpl, for example. This would allow the very same ShoppingCart code to be deployed as a session bean or not, without changing or copying any code. And the unit tests that we applied to ShoppingCart would be valid for ShoppingCartEJBImpl as well.

Although designing and implementing your code to be more reusable and more easily testable is always a good thing, it does not completely solve the unit testing problem. There will still be components of the system that must be tested while running inside the WebLogic Server environment. Thankfully, there is another freely available tool called Cactus, which allows JUnit to run tests on any J2EE application server, including WebLogic. Cactus is part of the Jakarta project, and is available at http://jakarta.apache.org/cactus.

Using Cactus to Unit Test Inside WebLogic

Cactus is essentially an extension to JUnit, and leverages many of JUnit's features. What it adds is the capability to run unit tests inside the container. It does so by using a proxy servlet: The proxy servlet instantiates and runs your test case class inside the container. In this way, you can write a test case to check any server-side component, such as a servlet, JSP, JSP custom tag, or EJB, in place. The sequence diagram shown in Figure 24.1 illustrates the flow of execution in a Cactus test case.

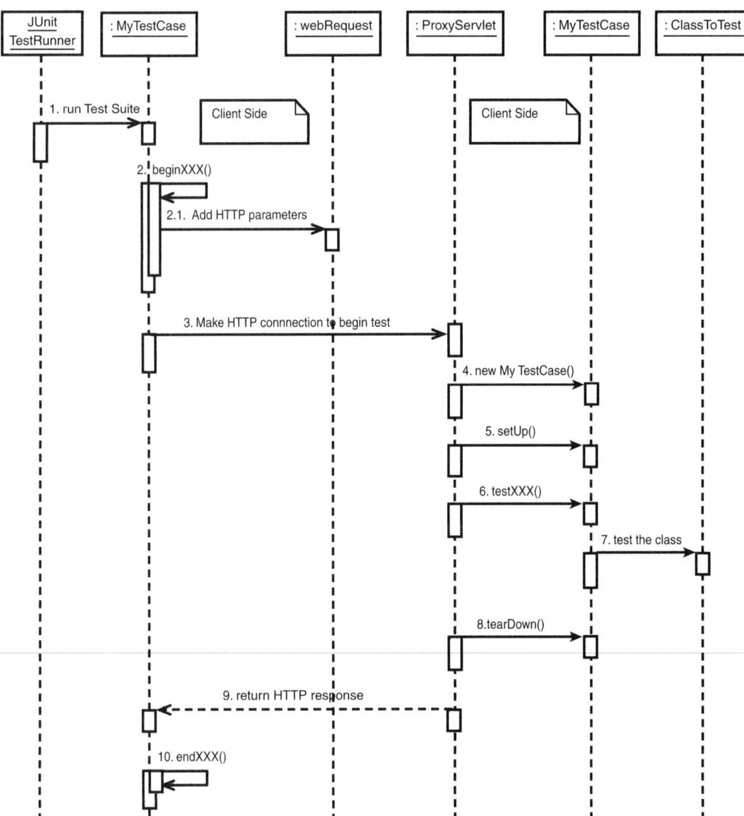

FIGURE 24.1 Cactus unit test sequence diagram.

As Figure 24.1 shows, the process of unit testing with Cactus begins with a JUnit test suite, which is started on the client side. In addition to the `setUp()` and `tearDown()` methods, the test case can implement a `begin`*`XXX`*`()` method and an `end`*`XXX`*`()` method for each `test`*`XXX`*`()` method. The `begin`*`XXX`*`()` and `end`*`XXX`*`()` methods are run on the client side. The `begin`*`XXX`*`()` method can be used to add headers or parameters to the HTTP request that will be sent to the test case. The actual test begins when the HTTP request is sent to the proxy servlet. It instantiates a copy of the test case class on the server side, passes it the information in the request, and calls the `setUp()`, `test`*`XXX`*`()`, and `tearDown()` methods. The response is collected by the proxy servlet and sent back to the client. In the `end`*`XXX`*`()` method, the client can perform validation on the contents of the response.

An Example Using Cactus

To continue our shopping cart example, let's suppose that we have a JSP tag library, which contains a `<cart_items>` tag that is used to display the contents of the shopping cart on the JSP page. To properly unit test the tag library, it must be tested inside the container, with access to all the implicit variables that the container provides, such as `request`, `response`, `pageContext`, and so on.

Listing 24.4 shows how a test case can be written to test a JSP custom tag by invoking the tag directly and calling a test JSP page that uses the tag.

LISTING 24.4 In-Server Unit Test Case (CartItemsTagTestCase.java)

```
package wls8unleashed.testing;
import java.util.Vector;
import junit.framework.*;
import org.apache.cactus.*;
import javax.servlet.jsp.tagext.BodyContent;

public class CartItemsTagTestCase extends JspTestCase {
  private ShoppingCart cart;
  private CartItem item1;
  private CartItem item2;
  private CartItem item3;

  public CartItemsTagTestCase(String name) {
    super(name);
  }

  protected void setUp() {
    cart = new ShoppingCart();
    item1 = new CartItem("Video Card", 1, 149.99);
    item2 = new CartItem("Monitor", 1, 459.99);
    item3 = new CartItem("Camera", 1, 289.99);

    cart.addItem(item1);
    cart.addItem(item2);
    cart.addItem(item3);
    session.setAttribute(ShoppingCart.class.getName(), cart);
  }

  public void testCartItemsTag() throws Exception {
    CartItemsTag tag = new CartItemsTag();
    tag.setPageContext(pageContext);
    int returnCode;
    returnCode = tag.doStartTag();
    assertEquals(tag.EVAL_BODY_BUFFERED, returnCode);
```

LISTING 24.4 Continued

```
    BodyContent bodyContent = pageContext.pushBody();
    tag.setBodyContent(bodyContent);
    tag.doInitBody();
    int count = 0;
    do {
      count++;
      returnCode = tag.doAfterBody();
    } while (returnCode == tag.EVAL_BODY_AGAIN);

    // should have been 3 iterations
    assertEquals(3, count);

    returnCode = tag.doEndTag();
    assertEquals(tag.EVAL_PAGE, returnCode);

    pageContext.popBody();
    tag.release();
  }

  public void testTagOnPage() throws Exception {
    pageContext.forward("/testTag.jsp");
  }

  public void endTagOnPage(WebResponse webResponse) {
    String output = webResponse.getText();
    int index1 = output.indexOf("Video Card 149.99 1");
    assertTrue(index1 > 0);
    int index2 = output.indexOf("Monitor 459.99 1");
    assertTrue(index2 > 0 && index2 > index1);
    int index3 = output.indexOf("Camera 289.99 1");
    assertTrue(index3 > 0 && index3 > index2);
  }

  public static Test suite() {
    return new TestSuite(CartItemsTagTestCase.class);
  }
}
```

Looking at the example, we start our test case by extending `org.apache.cactus.JspTestCase`. This is the class that Cactus provides specifically for testing JSP pages and custom tags. It also provides a `ServletTestCase` for testing servlets and a `FilterTestCase` for testing servlet filters. The `JspTestCase` class makes the JSP implicit objects `request`, `response`, `pageContext`, and `session` available to the test case class. The `setUp()` method of the test case is run on the server before each test method. In this case, we create a `ShoppingCart` object, add a few `CartItem` objects to it, and then add it to the `session`. The tag will be looking for the `ShoppingCart` in the session scope.

In the `testCartItemsTag()` method, we want to call our tag directly. To do so, we need to emulate the tag lifecycle that the tag would undergo if it were being called from a JSP page. Thus, we perform the following operations:

1. Create the tag with the default constructor and pass it the `pageContext` object.
2. Call `doStartTag()` and assert that it returns `EVAL_BODY_BUFFERED`.
3. Create a `bodyContent` object and pass it to the tag. This has to be done because `doStartTag()` returns `EVAL_BODY_BUFFERED`. Also, `doInitBody()` is called on the tag.
4. A loop is created to call `doAfterBody()` as long as it keeps returning `EVAL_BODY_AGAIN`. It should do this once for each item in the cart.
5. The number of iterations is checked against the expected value (`3`).
6. The tag's `doEndTag()` method is called, and cleanup methods are called.

The preceding procedure is a good example of unit testing practice in that it exercises every method in the class that needs to be tested. However, such a practice could become somewhat cumbersome with a large number of custom tags to test. Also, this particular tag creates its own scripting variables that a calling JSP can use to display information. The method just discussed does not have any way to inspect the contents of those variables. To address these concerns, we'll create a simple JSP page that calls the tag and a test case that calls that JSP.

The relevant code from the JSP file is as follows:

```
<test:cart_items>
<%= item_name %> <%= item_unit_price %> <%= item_quantity %>
</test:cart_items>
```

This code simply prints out the item name, unit price, and quantity, separated by spaces.

Referring back to Listing 24.4, the `testTagOnPage()` method simply forwards the request to our test JSP, `testTag.jsp`. The `endTagOnPage()` method is called outside the container, back on the client side, with a `WebResponse` parameter that encapsulates the output generated by the server from the request. The method obtains the output string and asserts that all the expected values are contained in the string, in the proper order. A failure of any of these assertions would cause the unit test to fail.

Installing and Running Cactus

Getting Cactus installed and running correctly is a slightly more involved task than configuring JUnit.

After the Cactus archive file has been downloaded and extracted, there is a `lib\` directory in the extracted directory structure. Within that directory are five JAR files of interest: `aspectjrt.jar`, `cactus.jar`, `commons-httpclient.jar`, `commons-logging.jar`, and `junit.jar`. Note that the actual filenames might have version numbers included with them, which are being omitted for clarity. For example, `aspectjrt.jar` might really be named `aspectjrt-1.0.6.jar`. These files have to be on the compiler's classpath when you build your test cases, and on the JVM's classpath when you launch the test from the client side. These files, minus `commons-httpclient.jar`, also must be available to your application on the server side. With a Web application, placing the JARs into the `WEB-INF\lib` directory of the WAR file takes care of that requirement.

The next step is to configure the proxy servlet within the Web application, which is done by adding an additional servlet and servlet mapping to `web.xml`. In our example, we are testing a JSP custom tag, so we use the `JspRedirector` servlet. Add the following lines to the application's `web.xml` file:

```
<servlet>
  <servlet-name>JspRedirector</servlet-name>
  <jsp-file>/jspRedirector.jsp</jsp-file>
</servlet>
<servlet-mapping>
  <servlet-name>JspRedirector</servlet-name>
  <url-pattern>/JspRedirector</url-pattern>
</servlet-mapping>
```

In addition, the `jspRedirector.jsp` file must be copied from the `web\` directory of the Cactus distribution into the root directory of the Web application.

Finally, the client side must be configured so that it knows how to send messages to the server. That is done by defining the `cactus.contextURL` property in a `cactus.properties` file. The `cactus.properties` file has to be located on the client's classpath. The `cactus.contextURL` property defines the URL where the application to be tested is located. For example, if our application were deployed as `test.war`, the `cactus.properties` file would contain the line:

```
cactus.contextURL=http://localhost:7001/test
```

To run the test, build the application WAR file, deploy it to WebLogic Server, and start the server. Then launch the client from the command line as follows:

```
java -cp %CLASSPATH% junit.textui.TestRunner wls8unleashed.testing.
CartItemsTagTestCase
```

NOTE

Notice that we use `junit.textui.TestRunner` when running Cactus test cases. With the AWT and Swing `TestRunners`, JUnit uses a special classloader that enables it to reload the test case classes without restarting the `TestRunner`. Although this is a convenient feature, it causes some problems with some of the classes Cactus uses internally. Using the text-based `TestRunner` avoids those problems.

Gathering Information with Logging APIs

In the previous section, we discussed the importance of unit testing in application development. Although building and maintain a good suite of unit tests is important for regression testing and quality assurance purposes, a successful run of the test suite cannot possibly be considered a proof that the full system will run flawlessly when deployed to its production environment and opened to its user community. Bugs and unexpected behaviors will always reveal themselves as unanticipated and untested input sequences begin to hit the system. So, when a user reports a bug in the system, what recourse does a programmer have to track down and fix that bug? It is often very helpful to "instrument" server-side code with the help of a logging API, which allows the system to print messages regarding the current state of the system to a log file, a database, or some other destination.

Programmers very often place `System.out.println()` statements within their code as they're developing it so that they can watch the system execute by simply looking at the standard out. Even though this practice is certainly helpful, it's also severely lacking in some of the more useful features that a logging API can provide. For example, when an application is deployed on a cluster of WebLogic servers, it's helpful to aggregate the logs from all the running servers into one place. It's also useful to assign a priority level to the messages to distinguish severe error messages from more routine informational status messages. WebLogic provides its own logging API, which is built on top of the standard `java.util.logging` package that is included with J2SE v1.4. The documentation for this package can be found at `http://java.sun.com/j2se/1.4.2/docs/api`.

WebLogic Logging Services

WebLogic has quite substantial logging capability. It has the capability to log messages on a per-server basis, as well as across an entire domain, which may encompass several physical machines. In addition, the Administration Console provides the capability to manage the log files by specifying maximum file sizes, file rotation schemes, and message filters. These logging mechanisms are used by WebLogic internally to report various system events, but can also be used by application developers through the WebLogic Logging Services. More information about WebLogic Logging Services is available at `http://e-docs.bea.com/wls/docs81/logging/index.html`.

The most straightforward way to use the WebLogic Logging Services within an application is through the `weblogic.logging.NonCatalogLogger` class. The class has a constructor that takes a `String` argument, which is the name that shows up in the log file to identify the particular logger. It also defines the following methods:

- `emergency(String msg)`
- `emergency(String msg, Throwable t)`
- `alert(String msg)`
- `alert(String msg, Throwable t)`
- `critical(String msg)`
- `critical(String msg, Throwable t)`
- `error(String msg)`
- `error(String msg, Throwable t)`
- `warning(String msg)`
- `warning(String msg, Throwable t)`
- `info(String msg)`
- `info(String msg, Throwable t)`
- `debug(String msg)`
- `debug(String msg, Throwable t)`

Each of these methods writes the given message to the log file and marks it with the priority given by the method name. Emergency messages are more severe than alerts, and so on. For the methods that take an additional `Throwable` argument, the stack trace of the `Throwable` is sent to the log file as well.

Listing 24.5 shows a simple servlet class that illustrates the use of the `NonCatalogLogger`.

LISTING 24.5 Servlet with Logging (LogServlet.java)

```
package wls8unleashed.testing;
import weblogic.logging.NonCatalogLogger;
import java.io.PrintWriter;
import java.io.IOException;
import javax.servlet.ServletException;
import javax.servlet.http.HttpServlet;
import javax.servlet.http.HttpServletRequest;
import javax.servlet.http.HttpServletResponse;
```

LISTING 24.5 Continued

```
public class LogServlet extends HttpServlet {
  public void service(HttpServletRequest request,
            HttpServletResponse response)
      throws ServletException, IOException {
    NonCatalogLogger log = new NonCatalogLogger("Logging Demo Servlet");
    log.info("In service() method");
    try {
      PrintWriter out = response.getWriter();
      out.println("This is the Logging Demo Servlet");
    }
    catch (Exception e) {
      log.error("An exception occurred in service()", e);
    }
  }
}
```


In this example, the `NonCatalogLogger` is created with the name Logging Demo Servlet. It sends a message of priority `info` to the log file. If an exception is caught, the servlet sends a message, along with the stack track, as an `error`. After running this servlet, the log file looks like this:

```
###<Jul 21, 2003 11:44:21 AM EDT> <Info> <Logging Demo Servlet> <localhost>
➥<testServer> <ExecuteThread: '10' for queue: 'default'> <WLS Kernel> <>
➥<000000> <In service() method>
```

CAUTION

Be extra certain that logging messages themselves do not cause any errors. All too often, mistakes are made like the following:

```
log.info("Person's name is " + person.getName());
```

If the system is designed in such a way that the `person` object could possibly be `null`, a `NullPointerException` can be thrown trying to log the message. In general, log messages should have the minimal possible effect on the system.

Debugging WebLogic with an Integrated Debugger

When all else fails, there's really nothing better for tracking down problems inside Java code than an integrated debugger. Just about every commercial and freeware IDE available has some sort of debugging capability. These tools enable you to attach a debugger to a running Java process, and by setting breakpoints at certain places in the code, make it possible for you to step through the execution flow line by line and examine the values of variables along the way.

NOTE

WebLogic 8.1 comes with its own IDE, called *WebLogic Workshop*. It contains many advanced debugging features. Workshop is covered in greater detail in Appendix C, "Using WebLogic Workshop 8.1 with WebLogic Server."

Preparing the Application for Debugging

Setting up a WebLogic application for debugging is fairly straightforward. The first thing that has to happen is that the Java code must be compiled with debugging information. This inserts source filenames and line numbers into the compiled `.class` files so that the debugger can step through line by line. This is done by passing in the `-g` flag to `javac` on the command line. For example:

```
javac -g *.java
```

Alternatively, if you were using Ant for doing builds, you would set the `debug` attribute of the `<javac>` task to `true`. For example:

```
<javac srcdir="${src}"
    includes="**/*.java"
    destdir="${build}"
    debug="true"/>
```

After the code has been compiled with debugging information, the next thing to do is to configure WebLogic to accept a connection from a remote debugger. This simply involves adding a few options to the `java` command line in the `startWebLogic` shell script.

The command options required for doing remote debugging in Java are fully documented in the J2SE v1.4 documentation, which is available at `http://java.sun.com/j2se/1.4.2/docs/guide/jpda/conninv.html`. In short, the options needed are `-Xdebug` (which enables debugging for the VM) and `-Xrunjdwp:<sub-options>` (which is what the VM uses to communicate with the external debugger). There are too many possible values for `<sub-options>` to list them all, but here are a few examples of the most common settings:

- `-Xrunjdwp:transport=dt_socket,server=y,address=8101` Opens a socket listener on port 8101 that listens for a connection from a remote debugger. The application starts in a suspended state.

- `-Xrunjdwp:transport=dt_socket,server=y,suspend=n,address=8101` Same as the preceding setting, except the application starts in a running state and is not suspended until the remote debugger has been attached and a breakpoint has been reached.
- `-Xrunjdwp:transport=dt_socket,server=y,address=8101,onuncaught=y, launch=c:\tools\launchide.bat` This delays initialization of the debugging library until an uncaught exception is thrown. When that happens, the VM is suspended and the specified executable is launched to begin debugging the application.

To enable debugging for a WebLogic application, it's necessary to add the appropriate debugging command options to the startup script. For example, if the last line in the startup script `%BEA_HOME%\user_projects\mydomain\startWebLogic.cmd` looks like this:

```
"%JAVA_HOME%\bin\java" %JAVA_VM% %MEM_ARGS% %JAVA_OPTIONS% \
  -Dweblogic.Name=%SERVER_NAME% -Dweblogic.management.username=%WLS_USER% \
  -Dweblogic.management.password=%WLS_PW% \
  -Dweblogic.ProductionModeEnabled=%PRODUCTION_MODE% \
  -Dweblogic.sercurity.policy="%WL_HOME%\server\lib\weblogic.policy" \
  weblogic.Server
```

we would modify the script as follows to enable debugging:

```
set DEBUG_OPTS=-Xdebug -Xrunjdwp:transport=dt_socket,server=y,
➥suspend=n,address=8101
"%JAVA_HOME%\bin\java" %JAVA_VM% %MEM_ARGS% %JAVA_OPTIONS% %DEBUG_OPTS% \
  -Dweblogic.Name=%SERVER_NAME% -Dweblogic.management.username=%WLS_USER% \
  -Dweblogic.management.password=%WLS_PW% \
  -Dweblogic.ProductionModeEnabled=%PRODUCTION_MODE% \
  -Dweblogic.sercurity.policy="%WL_HOME%\server\lib\weblogic.policy" \
  weblogic.Server
```

The last thing to do to be able to debug the application is to configure your IDE for remote debugging. Almost every Java IDE has this capability. In the preceding example, within the debugging properties of the IDE, set remote debugging to `true`, set the remote connection type to `dt_socket`, and set the listen address to `8101`. To debug, first start WebLogic with the startup script, and then click the Debug button in the IDE. You should then be able to set breakpoints, watch variables, and step through the source code as with any Java application.

Debugging JSPs and EJBs

The described debugging method works very well for the application classes with accessible source code. But sometimes it's necessary or just helpful to be able to step into Java code that has been generated by the container. This is often the case when debugging tag libraries, for example. To see the full tag life cycle, it helps to step into the actual JSP code itself. By default, the container removes the `.java` files for classes it generates, but this behavior can be overridden.

In the case of JSP files, this property is set within the `<jsp-descriptor>` element of the `weblogic.xml` deployment descriptor for the application. To keep the generated `.java` files, set the `keepgenerated` property to `true`, as follows:

```
<jsp-descriptor>
  <jsp-param>
   <param-name>
     keepgenerated
   </param-name>
   <param-value>
     true
   </param-value>
  </jsp-param>
  ...
</jsp-descriptor>
```

It's important to note where WebLogic places the generated `.java` files: They go to the same directory where the generated `.class` files go. This directory can be specified by the `workingDir` parameter within the `<jsp-descriptor>` element of `weblogic.xml`; otherwise, they go into `WEB-INF\classes`. This is important because your IDE has to know where the source code for those modules resides, so that it can find the appropriate source for the code it's debugging.

A similar process can be followed for generating source code for the stubs, skeletons, and other supporting classes for EJBs. Although there should not typically be any bugs within the generated classes themselves, it's often helpful to be able to step through those classes to see a more complete picture of the system. When building EJBs, simply specify the `-keepgenerated` flag to the `weblogic.appc` tool on the command line. For example:

```
java weblogic.appc -keepgenerated <other options> ejbApp.jar
```

Best Practices

In this section, we list some practical considerations to keep in mind when testing and debugging applications.

Unit Testing Best Practices

Now that we've seen examples of some of the more popular unit testing tools out there, here are a few tips that enable these tools to yield their maximum benefit:

- Write unit tests early. Some people even say that the test cases for a class should be written before the class itself. When a component of a system is designed, the desired behavior of the component is encoded into a series of unit tests. The implementation of the component is complete when all the tests run successfully.
- When writing the tests first isn't possible, extra care should be taken to prevent writing tests that simply make the existing code pass. The test cases should be derived from requirements documents and sound logic, not from an existing implementation. The author of a test case should be concerned only with the interface to an implementation, not the inner workings of that implementation.
- Run tests often. This is typically something that can be run, at the very least, during an automatic nightly build. That way, any changes to the system that have broken existing functionality are detected right away.

Logging Best Practices

Having a powerful logging API at your disposal certainly makes it easier to generate and collect information about a system, but really that is only half of the solution. The real trick is to use the logging facilities to their fullest advantage. This essentially means finding the balance between logging enough relevant information to be helpful when tracking down problems, but not so much information that the system becomes overwhelmed with log files. Here are some points to consider when putting logging messages into your system:

- Choose the right priority for the message. Try to come up with a convention for what constitutes an error, warning, info, debug, or other type of message, and stick to it. Messages such as `emergency` or `critical` should be used very sparingly, if at all. Treat debug messages as information that's useful for trying to locate a specific problem, but that could go away at any time if the need no longer exists. Treat info messages as key status messages that report the current state of the system.
- Identify each message. With server applications, many users can be using the system at one time. In such cases, it's very helpful to extract a single user's session from the myriad log messages being generated. This can be done by placing a session ID or some application-specific user information into every message that's generated. This makes it much easier to track down the problems reported by a specific user, and to follow a single execution path through the system.
- Think about what information would be useful when responding to a bug report from a user. That can be difficult because it isn't easy to know what information you'll need to know to track down some problem that you don't even know exists. Simple messages such as `Entering method` *`XXX`* and `Leaving method` *`XXX`* typically don't provide a great deal of information, but instead just clutter up the logs. Generate log messages based on conditionals and include the values of key variables.

- Make logging as inexpensive as possible from a processing standpoint. This ties in with not placing logging statements all over the code as a shotgun approach to logging. Including too many log statements slows down the system and makes the code less readable. Also consider the cost of generating the log itself. Try to limit the number of string concatenations done in a single statement. When printing out variables, try to print out local `String` variables whenever possible. Use the `StringBuffer` class as an alternative when you have to do a lot of concatenation.

Debugging Best Practices

Finally, here are a few tips that will help make debugging applications go smoother:

- Choose the right breakpoints. Ideally, you want the breakpoints as close to the error as possible to avoid hitting the breakpoint too often or needing to single-step through many lines of code. If an exception is thrown, work backward from there.
- Consider conditional breakpoints. These breakpoints are triggered only when a given expression becomes true. This comes in handy for breaking inside loops with many iterations when you are interested in the iterations near the end. Conditional breakpoints can slow down the debugging process because they require additional overhead, so use them sparingly.
- Use remote debugging to debug applications in different hardware environments. Although Java is a cross-platform language, sometimes there will be cases in which a bug will be seen in the production environment that cannot be reproduced in the development environment. With remote debugging, you can attach to that Java process on a remote machine and step through the code as if it were running locally. Obviously, this should never be done on a machine that is currently live to the public!

Summary

Testing and debugging are key elements of the software development process. Unit testing provides the ability to find functional mistakes early in the development process, and to detect when code changes break existing functionality. Using logging APIs, it's possible to gain greater insight into the behavior of a running system and manage it accordingly. For truly in-depth understanding of an application, nothing beats integrated debugging, in which the application can be paused and stepped through line by line.

CHAPTER 25

Optimizing WebLogic Server Applications

By Jeff Marin, Tom Schwenk, and Mark Artiges

IN THIS CHAPTER

Applications that have been *unit tested* have shown that they can perform their expected functionality in a controlled environment. In many cases, this simulates a single user running the application where all dependent resources, such as database connections and memory, are readily available. Although this is an important step in the development of WebLogic applications, unit testing, by itself, is not sufficient to confidently deploy an application in a live setting. To increase your chances for successful deployment, you must attempt to simulate the actual environment of your running application. This includes accurately modeling users in terms of behavior and numbers.

Defining Different Types of Performance Tests

Throughout this chapter, we use a few terms that are related to optimizing WebLogic applications. These terms are often mistakenly used interchangeably, but in fact they refer to distinct tasks. To eliminate any ambiguity, we define these terms here:

- *Performance testing* is the act of measuring how long specific functionality within an application takes to execute. The information gathered from this test indicates which parts of an application are slower and faster than others.

- *Load testing* is the act of monitoring application behavior as a large number of simulated users are simultaneously accessing an application. The information gathered from this test shows how the application performs under user load. This includes actual performance times and potential software bugs.
- *Stress testing* involves simulating user load and denying the application resources that it is dependent on, including network bandwidth, RAM, and database connections. This test shows how the developers have handled low-resource conditions or whether they have handled them at all. Applications that do not have access to required resources should behave in a graceful, predictable manner and should not lose and/or damage critical information.

Together, these three types of tests produce information that unit testing was not designed for. These are flaws in application design and implementation that produce errors and/or performance issues when executing in a simulated live environment. Sometimes, it is not defects that affect performance; it is just that we have not taken advantage of the various performance tunings available to us.

Preparing for Performance and Load Testing

The idea behind testing is to execute your application in a setting that closely simulates the actual environment it will be running in. This means the following:

- Reproduce the production application environment—This includes hardware and external resources such as your database environment
- Attempt to accurately simulate actual user behavior—This includes determining the types of users who will be accessing the application and how they will be using it
- Attempt to accurately simulate the number of actual users—This includes determining the maximum number of users per user type that will simultaneously be accessing the application
- Stress testing—Monitor application behavior as dependent resources such as database connections and memory are denied

It is a good idea to think about the performance of the system right from the beginning—in the design phase. In fact, it is important to collect as much information as possible about the expected usage load of the system, and what expectations exist with regard to performance-related metrics such as response times before design begins. Having this information will be critical for making design decisions, and will facilitate the design of the performance and load tests.

Simulating User Behavior and Working with Business People

An important part of testing is to simulate user behavior. Software development does not occur in a vacuum. Applications are created to automate tasks and to enable employees and customers. Individuals outside of the software development department are usually responsible for the initial conception of new projects. They are integral in determining functional specifications because they have intimate knowledge of how users will access the application. Therefore, they should be very involved in determining performance goals and simulating user behavior. Although it is tempting for software developers to predict user behavior, this responsibility falls more squarely on the shoulders of the business people who have been involved with the application from its inception.

Determining When to Performance Test

Performance testing our application can uncover potential problems at various stages of development. The earlier that problems are uncovered is directly related to the amount of time and resources that must be spent to correct them, as depicted in Figure 25.1. This means that performance testing should occur

- During Design—As an application is designed, architects and developers have many technologies and architectures available to them to meet functional specifications. Each technology and architecture carries associated performance costs. It is important to balance performance with architectural issues, such as code reusability and flexibility enabled by necessary levels of abstraction and encapsulation.
- During implementation—As application code is tied together to perform larger tasks, performance testing should take place. It is possible that various code combinations will cause performance to suffer. Testing at this phase can pinpoint those areas if they exist.
- Before deployment—After the complete application has been assembled, performance testing should be carried out using the actual production environment with simulated user load.

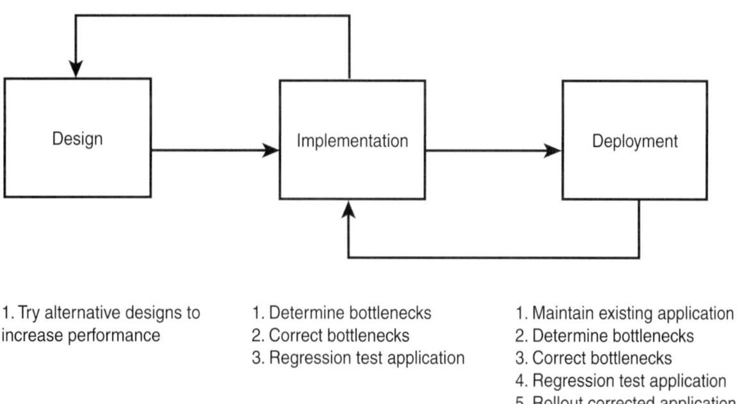

FIGURE 25.1 Finding problems early minimizes the time and resources that are spent to correct them.

The Validity of Benchmarks

Although numerous benchmarks have shown how WebLogic applications run under different hardware and software configurations, the applications being executed are very specific and are different from your application. Even though it is tempting to compare these applications to yours and intuitively determine how your application will perform, there is no substitute for your own performance testing. Because there are multitudes of factors that affect performance, such as hardware (including CPU and RAM) and software (including operating system and settings), you owe it to your users and yourself to performance test during design and implementation, but before you deploy your application in a live setting.

However, benchmarks can be useful when determining the running environment of your WebLogic applications. The most useful benchmark is ECperf. ECperf consists of representatives from many application server vendors such as BEA, IBM, and Sun Microsystems. Together, they have developed a specification and a toolkit for measuring the performance of J2EE application servers. More information about ECperf can be found at `http://www2.theserverside.com/ecperf/index.jsp`.

How to Performance Test

It is very important to have a well-defined methodology when performance testing your applications. That methodology should include precise goals that have to be met. Without goals and a methodology to achieve them, performance testing could potentially never end. For example, if your goal is to make the application run as fast as possible, when will you know that you have achieved that goal? Your team might spend months to make your application perform 1% better. In most situations, that amount of time and resources would not warrant the outcome. In this section, we discuss how to quantitatively measure performance, establish reasonable performance goals, and identify performance issues within the system.

Measuring Performance

It is important for everyone involved in performance testing to have the same definition of measuring performance. This includes business people, quality assurance people, project managers, and software developers. Performance is usually tied to the type of application. Most applications fall under one of the following types:

- Interactive applications—These applications are used by people and involve a user interface. Users enter data, submit requests, and wait for a response. The performance of the application is based on how long users must wait for a response. This is referred to as *response time* and is measured in seconds or smaller units, such as milliseconds. Average response time (ART) is calculated by adding the total response times for an operation and dividing it by the number of times the operation is executed.

- Backend Applications—These applications perform batch processing of a large number of tasks or transactions. It is very important that everyone agrees on what a transaction is in the context of the application. The performance of these applications is based on how many transactions can be performed in a specific amount of time. This is referred to as *transactions per unit of time*. The unit of time is typically a second, hence the acronym *TPS* or *transactions per second*.

Defining Goals

The performance goals for an application are distinctly tied to the type of application and user load. For example, a performance goal could be that with 500 simultaneous users, the maximum response time of our WebLogic application should be no more than 5 seconds, except for user registration, which can take up to 9 seconds.

Benchmarking

After we have defined our goals, we execute our WebLogic application using a simulated number of users and we measure its performance. Load testing tools come in many shapes, sizes, and prices from open source to commercial versions that run in the thousands of dollars. LoadRunner for BEA WebLogic from Mercury Interactive and OptiBench Enterprise from Performant are load testing tools that work with WebLogic Server. More information about LoadRunner is available at `http://www-heva.mercuryinteractive.com/products/loadrunner/`. Visit `http://www.performant.com/solutions/` for more information about OptiBench.

25

Using a load testing tool, we run functionality within the application multiple times and use an average response time or transactions per second to make our readings more accurate.

Profiling

After benchmarking your WebLogic application and discovering performance issues, the next step determining what is causing the problems. Although the sources of the problem can vary, we have a variety of tools at our disposal to narrow the possibilities. To find our bottlenecks, we use tools to monitor network usage, CPU utilization, memory allocation, database execution plans, and other profiling tools. We now take a closer look at using these tools to profile the various system components.

Profiling WebLogic Server

The Administration Console can be used to monitor memory usage and garbage collection activity at the server level. Garbage collection activity is detected by noticing large drops in the current memory usage. The Administration Console can also be used to monitor the throughput and the activity of the default execute queue. JDBC connection pools can be monitored from the Administration Console as well.

Profiling the Database

Every major RDBMS includes monitoring software to display the number of connections to the database and the SQL statements that are executing. Developers can ask the database for an execute plan of how a SQL statement will be run. They can then tune the SQL and the database to optimize performance.

Profiling Network Traffic

With the abundance of cheap, fast, reliable networking hardware available these days, the network itself is rarely a source of resource contention in enterprise applications. Still, it is important to have some quantitative understanding of the network bandwidth an application requires so that the appropriate hardware can be acquired. To this end, there are several network sniffing applications available that can inspect all the traffic on a TCP network. One such tool, Ethereal, is available at `http://www.ethereal.com`.

Ethereal enables you to see all the network traffic coming and going through a network interface. You can filter this data by port, destination, and protocol to give you a better picture of your network utilization. For example, capturing all the data moving across port 7001 of your WebLogic server machine will enable you to see how many bytes per request your application is receiving and sending.

Application Code

To see how our WebLogic application is behaving, we use a Java profiler. Although the HotSpot JVM itself offers several options for monitoring heap allocation and CPU usage, they are not very helpful when trying to profile only your WebLogic application and not WebLogic Server itself. However, there are many commercial profiling tools, such as JProbe and OptimizeIt, to track the resources (such as memory and CPU usage) that your WebLogic application is using, as well as the specific Java code that is potentially using these resources inefficiently. Both of these products will help reveal hotspots in the application that are caused by using excessive CPU cycles or by allocating too much memory. Information about JProbe is available at `http://www.sitraka.com/software/jprobe/` and information about OptimizeIt is available from `http://www.borland.com/optimizeit/`.

Interpreting Results

After the WebLogic application has been analyzed from several viewpoints, the results have to be interpreted and the solutions must be implemented.

Although the process of optimizing WebLogic applications can seem daunting at times, you will typically find that performance problems are associated with a lack of resources. The problem can sometimes be solved by re-architecting the application or by performance tuning. Other times, there is no alternative to adding more resources. The following are common places to look for a performance problem due to lack of resources:

- CPU—While conducting load tests, there will be times when the application is not meeting performance requirements and the CPU of the WebLogic Server machine is at or near 100%. The causes of these can either be the WebLogic application itself or garbage collection. Later in this chapter, we will discuss how to monitor garbage collection.

- I/O—There are times when the performance of a WebLogic application suffers due to its inability to interact quickly with the database or the network.
- Database—In many cases, WebLogic applications will be bottlenecked by the RDBMS. Sometimes this is due to bad application architecture in which too many round trips to the database are occurring. In other cases, the database itself should be tuned, such as by adding indexes.
- Network—Although it is a rare case because networks are quite fast these days, they can become saturated with traffic to a point where client requests take too long to reach WebLogic Server and then to return to the client.

Areas to Tune

The performance of a WebLogic application is highly dependent on the environment it is running within. As Figure 25.2 depicts, this environment includes both hardware and software components. Each of these components has an effect on the performance of WebLogic applications. Performance, load, and stress testing can help determine the components that need to be configured or replaced to increase the performance of WebLogic applications.

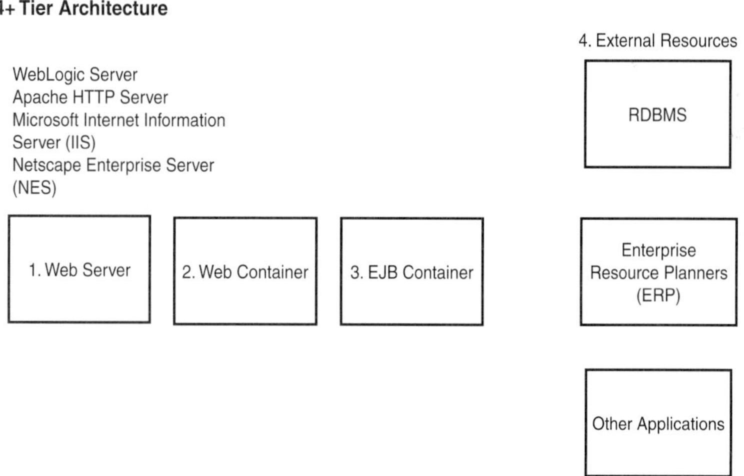

FIGURE 25.2 The environment of WebLogic applications is a complex composition of hardware and software components.

The performance of a WebLogic application is highly dependent on the makeup of the machine (or machines, if you're using a cluster) it is executing on. As shown in Figure 25.3, WebLogic applications depend on multiple layers of hardware and software that can be modified to increase performance.

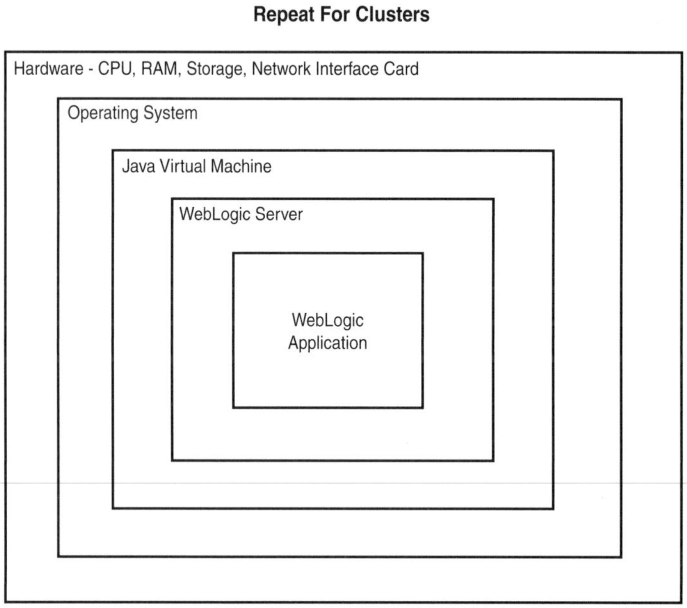

Repeat For Clusters

Hardware - CPU, RAM, Storage, Network Interface Card

Operating System

Java Virtual Machine

WebLogic Server

WebLogic Application

FIGURE 25.3 WebLogic applications are dependent upon software and hardware.

Operating System

Although WebLogic Server is written in Java (except for some native libraries to increase performance) and can theoretically run on any Java Virtual Machine, BEA has certified only specific hardware platforms, operating systems, and JVMs for use with WebLogic 8.1. The BEA WebLogic Server certifications page can be found at `http://e-docs.bea.com/wls/certifications/index.html`. It includes only configurations that have passed thorough testing by BEA. For many configurations, BEA lists known problems and tips to improve performance. For example, WebLogic Server running under Solaris can be hampered by a lack of available file descriptors. Also, there are certain Solaris TCP tuning parameters that can improve performance.

CPU and RAM

For every hardware platform and operating system, BEA recommends a minimum CPU type and speed and a minimum amount of RAM. In production, however, the CPU and

RAM required depend on your WebLogic application and your acceptable performance levels.

In many cases, CPU availability or RAM availability binds the performance of WebLogic applications. In Windows, the available memory and bandwidth can be determined from the Task Manager as shown in Figure 25.4. Under Unix, the `top` command displays memory usage, CPU utilization, and disk access on a process-by-process basis.

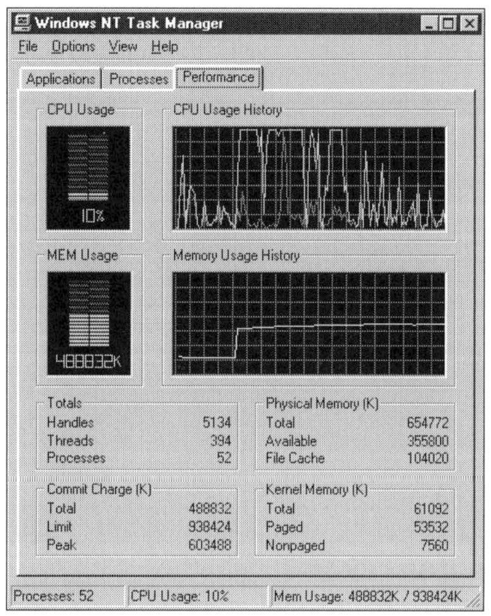

FIGURE 25.4 The Task Manager shows total CPU and memory utilization as well as on a process-by-process basis.

Network Performance

The performance of your network can have a large effect on the performance of WebLogic applications. Internal and external clients depend on available bandwidth to connect with WebLogic applications. Additionally, these applications will need to connect with external resources, such as an RDBMS. If you are using WebLogic Server clustering, these instances will require network bandwidth for internal communication.

Work with your network administrator to identify network bottlenecks and to procure the network monitoring software available for your operating system. That software will help pinpoint when the performance of your WebLogic application is being diminished by your network.

The network media, network interface cards and their drivers, switches, hubs, and routers being utilized all have an effect on the network speed. In many cases, one or more network components will become a bottleneck and affect the entire performance of the network.

Choice of Java Virtual Machine

Many BEA-certified configurations of WebLogic Server offer a choice of multiple JVMs. This includes the Sun JDK 1.4 HotSpot JVM and BEA JRockit Virtual Machine. If you have a choice of JVMs for your configuration, it is prudent to performance test using multiple JVMs.

BEA JRockit is included in the WebLogic 8.1 products. It is a highly optimized JVM with many features that make it ideal for WebLogic Server, including scalability, multiple garbage collection options, high performance, and a management console for the JVM itself. More information about BEA JRockit can be found at `http://www.bea.com/products/weblogic/jrockit/index.shtml`.

Java Virtual Machine Options

Every JVM includes options that can affect performance—the most prevalent of which are the heap and garbage collection parameters. We will examine each of these options in detail.

The JVM Heap

The *heap size* is the amount of memory that the JVM has to work with. WebLogic server code and WebLogic application code create instances of Java classes that are held in this memory. By default, WebLogic Server executes with an initial heap size of 32MB and a maximum of 200MB, as set in the `startWLS.cmd` and `startWLS.sh` batch files found in the *WL_HOME*`\weblogic81\server\bin` directory.

The JVM allocates more memory for its heap until it reaches the maximum amount allowed. Setting the initial and maximum sizes to be equal relieves the JVM of having to decide when to increase the heap size and reduces the time spent on garbage collection. This can increase performance of the JVM. When the heap has run out of free memory, an attempt to allocate additional memory will result in a `java.lang.OutOfMemoryError`. (See Table 25.1, which shows the syntax for setting the initial and maximum heap sizes.)

The larger the heap, the better WebLogic Server will perform. However, if the heap becomes larger than available memory, your operating system will swap pages of information to disk. This will severely affect performance. You should set the initial and maximum heap to be 80%–85% of available RAM. It is recommended to run WebLogic Server on a separate machine than the database and other applications. If this is the case, allocate 80%–85% of the total RAM of the machine. If not, calculate how much RAM is available after the other applications' needs and allocate 80%–85% of it to WebLogic Server. The Administration Console contains performance graphs that include the current JVM heap size and its current usage, as shown in Figure 25.5. Garbage collection can be manually forced from this page as well.

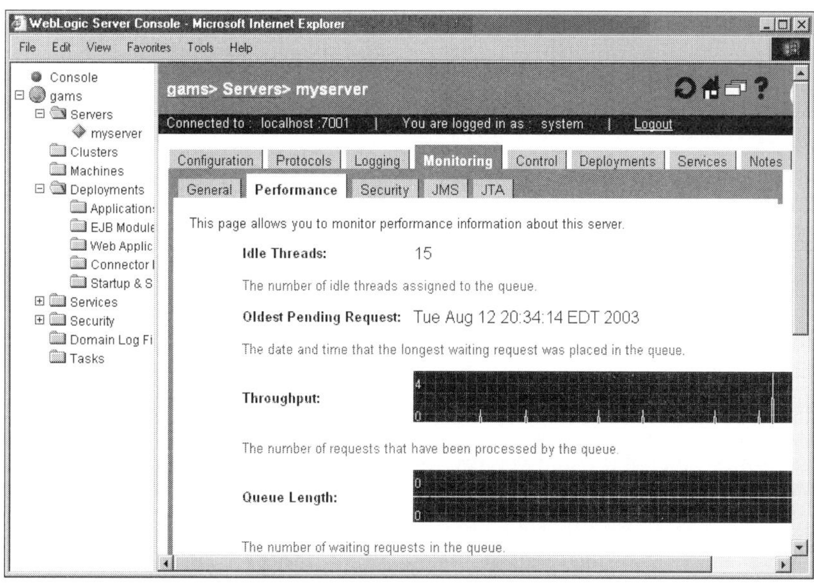

FIGURE 25.5 The Administration Console provides performance graphs to monitor the JVM heap and the execute queue length.

Garbage Collection

A separate thread within the JVM manages garbage collection. Every so often, it looks through the heap and releases unused Java objects in a manner dependent on the garbage collection algorithm being used. Unless you are using an incremental garbage collector, all other threads within the JVM come to a halt when this occurs. Obviously, this is quite disruptive and has a severe effect on the performance of WebLogic applications. Reducing the amount of time spent in garbage collection can have a dramatic increase in WebLogic application performance. We want to limit how often garbage collection occurs and how long it takes to complete each time it occurs.

Conventional garbage collection examines every object in the heap to determine which objects are no longer being used. This can take a while, especially when many objects are on the heap. The Sun JDK 1.4 HotSpot JVM offers a generational garbage collector that takes advantage of the fact that most Java objects on the heap have very short lives. It allocates new objects in Eden in a contiguous manner in memory, which is faster to access. As shown in Figure 25.6, when garbage collection occurs, it removes dead objects from Eden and moves the few surviving objects to Survivor Space 1 or to Survivor Space 2 on the next garbage collection. On subsequent garbage collections, surviving objects are moved to the old object area of the heap. The HotSpot JVM also contains an incremental garbage collector that runs more often, but has less to do each time. This eliminates the long, user-detectable pauses associated with traditional garbage collection. Information on tuning garbage collection can be found at `http://java.sun.com/docs/hotspot/gc/index.html`.

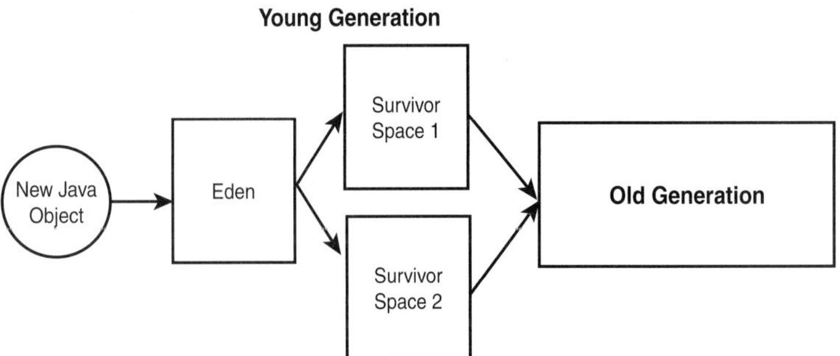

FIGURE 25.6 The HotSpot JVM allocates new objects in Eden and copies them to Survivor Space 1 or 2, whichever is available.

Table 25.1 iterates some of the more commonly used tuning options for the Sun HotSpot JVM.

TABLE 25.1 Some Sun JDK HotSpot Tuning Options

Command-Line Option	Description
-hotspot	Run in client mode, this option provides quicker start times and a reduced memory footprint; ideal for client or GUI based applications.
-server	Run in server mode to provide long-running server applications with the fastest possible operating speeds. Check whether Server JVM is supported on your platform.
-verbose:gc	Display detailed information when garbage collection occurs. Use for profiling and turn off in production. Redirect output to a log file.
-Xms*n*	Initial heap size where n is the size in bytes. Use k or K for kilobytes, m or M for megabytes, and g or G for gigabytes. Default is 2MB.
-Xmx*n*	Maximum heap size in bytes. Same syntax as -Xms. Default is 64MB.
-Xincgc	Enables incremental garbage collector. Runs run smaller, more frequent collections to avoid the longer, heavier, full garbage collections.

Java VM settings should be changed at the WebLogic domain level by modifying the `startWebLogic.cmd` or `startWebLogic.sh` file in the domain directory as shown in Listing 25.1.

LISTING 25.1 Excerpt from startWebLogic.cmd in the Domain Directory

```
@rem Set JAVA_VM to the java virtual machine you want to run. For instance:
@rem set JAVA_VM=-server
set JAVA_VM=

@rem Set MEM_ARGS to the memory args you want to pass to java. For instance:
@rem set MEM_ARGS=-Xms32m -Xmx200m
set MEM_ARGS=
```

More information about the Sun HotSpot JVM is available at `http://java.sun.com/docs/hotspot/index.html`. Information there includes JVM command-line options, how to tune garbage collection, and how Java threads are matched to operating system threads.

Threading

Another important JVM option is determining the optimal threading model. JVMs have the capability to map Java threads to native threads on a one-to-one basis or a many-to-one basis. Having the capability to map multiple Java threads to one native thread can potentially increase throughput in your application. For more information about threading models under Sun HotSpot JVM, please refer to `http://java.sun.com/docs/hotspot/threads/threads.html`. For information about threading models under the WebLogic JRockit JVM, please refer to `http://edocs.bea.com/wljrockit/docs81/tuning/index.html`.

WebLogic Server Tuning

WebLogic Server can handle a large number of simultaneous clients through the use of threads and queues. As shown in Figure 25.7, a client request comes in on a port being serviced by WebLogic Server. An available socket thread then reads the request and places it on the execute queue. When an execute thread becomes available, it reads the request and performs the desired action within the WebLogic application. WebLogic Server includes options to change the behavior of these threads and queues.

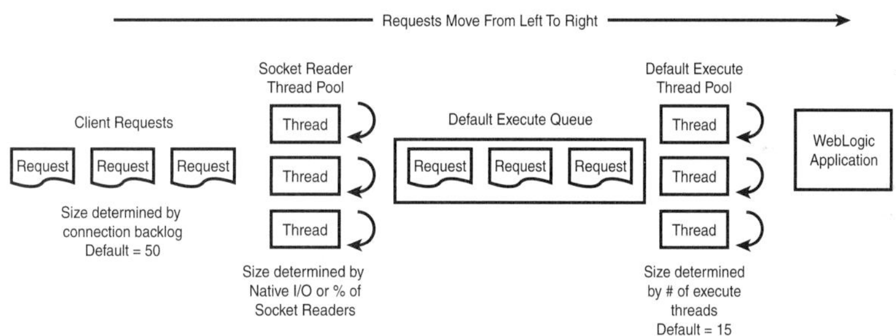

FIGURE 25.7 Client requests must be handled by a socket reader thread and an execute thread before reaching the WebLogic application.

WebLogic Server Performance Packs

WebLogic Server performance packs allow WebLogic to use native platform-optimized sockets rather than Java socket readers, which improves performance tremendously. The BEA WebLogic Server certifications list details which platforms have performance packs available. If you are using a performance pack, make sure that it is enabled in the `config.xml` file with the statement: `NativeIOEnabled=true`. The default `config.xml` that ships with WebLogic Server contains this statement. This value can also be set on the Tuning tab in the Server Configuration page in the Administration Console. As shown in Figure 25.8, make sure that the Enable Native IO check box is enabled to use the performance pack.

If you are not using a performance pack, a percentage of execute threads must be allocated to act as socket readers. The default is 33%, but the percentage can be set between 1% and 99%. When setting this value, it is important to balance the number of socket reader threads and execute queue threads so that client requests are accepted and are executed efficiently. This value can be modified in the Administration Console, as shown in Figure 25.8.

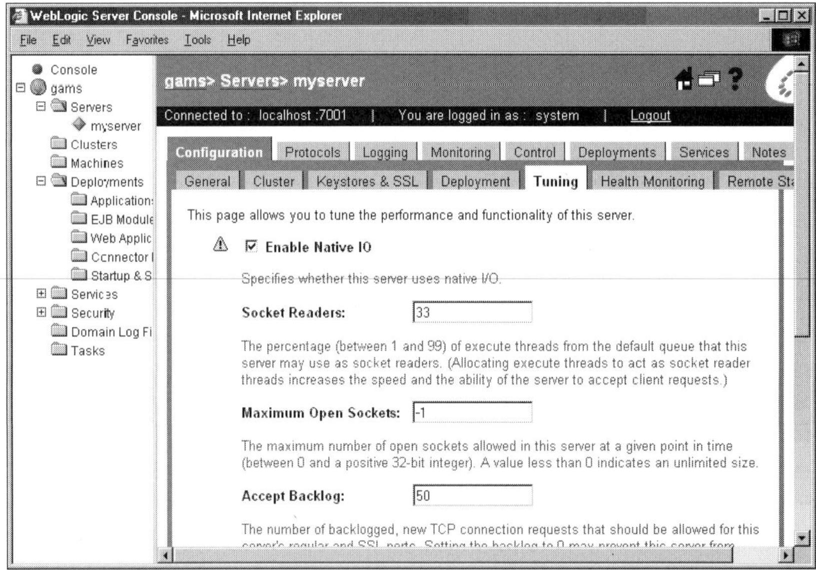

FIGURE 25.8 The Administration Console can be used to modify the percentage of execute threads to use as socket readers.

The Default Queues and Execute Threads

By default, WebLogic Server starts with one default execute queue serviced by 15 execute threads. When all of these threads are busy, client requests will remain in the execute queue. In some circumstances, adding more execute threads increases performance of WebLogic applications. However, because each CPU within a machine can execute only one thread at a time, having too many threads can actually decrease performance because of thrashing. Thrashing occurs when more time is spent switching between threads and maintaining the thread pool than actually servicing client requests.

If the execute queue is filling up with requests and the CPU of the machine running WebLogic Server has not reached 100%, the execute thread count should be increased. This situation can occur when execute threads are waiting on external resources such as database requests or network bandwidth. The number of requests waiting on the execute queue and oldest pending request can be monitored from the Administration Console as shown in Figure 25.5.

The optimal number of execute threads depends on many factors, including hardware platform, operating system, choice of JVM, and the WebLogic applications that are executing. It is prudent to experiment with the number of execute threads when CPU utilization is less than 100%. Another thing to keep in mind is that the maximum number of simultaneous JDBC connections from WebLogic is the number of execute threads minus one. That means if there are fewer execute threads than JDBC connections in a JDBC connection pool, all the connections could never be used simultaneously. Chances are that this is not the behavior you are looking for.

The number of execute threads can be changed on a server-to-server basis from the Administration Console, as shown in Figure 25.9. To get to the page, click the server name in the left panel and then click the Monitoring and General tabs in the right panel. Click on the Monitor All Active Queues link. This will display all of that server's execute queues. In addition to the default queue, WebLogic Server also creates dedicated queues for distributed garbage collection and for communication with the Administrative Console using HTML and RMI. From the Configuration tab, click on the default queue. This will display the current activity of the execute threads. Click on the Configure Execute Queue link and then click on the default link. After you change the thread count, you will need to restart WebLogic Server.

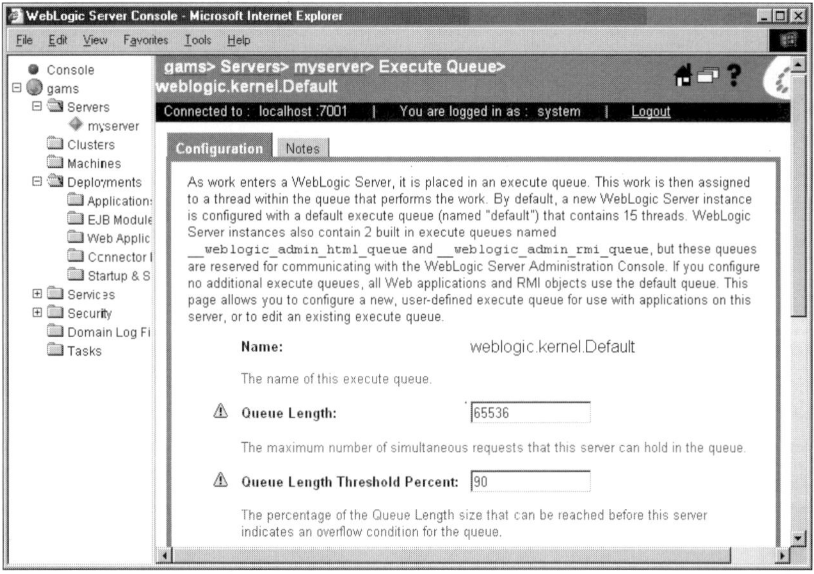

FIGURE 25.9 The number of execute threads can be modified from the Administration Console.

Handling Overflow Conditions

Determining the optimal number of execute threads is an important step in tuning WebLogic applications under normal conditions. WebLogic Server also allows thread counts to change when applications are running under peak conditions in order to accommodate additional client requests. An error message is logged when a threshold is crossed. This threshold is a percentage of the total number of threads in use or not available to handle client requests because they are considered stuck. The overflow condition can then be used to create additional threads, if desired.

As shown in Figure 25.9 and explained in Table 25.2, several parameters can be modified in association with thread count. Keep in mind that additional threads will remain in use even when peak usage for the application has ended. If the thread count was optimized previously under normal conditions, the extra threads will decrease performance over time. For this reason, the parameters in Table 25.2 should not be used for tuning; they are merely a mechanism for dealing with abnormal conditions. Instead, check the log for overflow errors and adjust the actual thread count as a substitute for relying on the threads increase parameter as tuning parameter.

TABLE 25.2 WebLogic Server Thread Count for Overflow Conditions

Thread Tuning Parameter	Description
Queue Length Default = 65536	The number of simultaneous client requests that the queue can hold. WebLogic Server doubles the length of the queue if outstanding requests reach this value.
Queue Length Threshold Percent Default = 90	Percentage of queue that needs to be full to trigger an overflow condition. Overflow conditions are logged.
Threads Increase Default = 0	The number of threads added to the queue when an overflow condition occurs.
Threads Minimum Default = 5	The smallest number of threads that can be assigned to the execute queue.
Threads Maximum Default = 400	The largest number of threads that can be assigned to the execute queue.

Additional Execute Queues

The default execute queue and its associated threads are general purpose and will service all client requests directed toward the Web and EJB containers. Your WebLogic application might contain certain servlets, JSPs, and EJB that are deemed to be much more critical than the rest of the application. This could be functionality that will be utilized by senior management, such as the generation of profit and loss reports. If this is the case, you can create a specific queue to service the application components that implement the critical functionality. The execute threads that service this queue will not have to compete with threads that service the default queue and the performance of critical functionality will be more insulated from the rest of the WebLogic application.

Conversely, general application functionality can be assigned to a special queue to limit the effect of regular or perhaps nonpaying customers. For example, imagine a WebLogic application that represents an online brokerage where any guest can check stock prices, but only paying customers can buy and sell securities. If too many people are checking stock prices, it could negatively affect the paying customers' experience. We can set up a special queue for browsing stock prices and limit the number of threads associated with it. In this way, our guests will experience delays before our paying customers will.

New execute queue are created from the administration console on a server-by-server basis. Click on the server name in the left pane and then the Monitoring and General tabs in the right pane. Click on the Monitor all Active Queues link, click the Configure Execute Queue link, and then click the Configure a New Execute Queue link. You will now see a page similar to the one shown in Figure 25.9. Enter queue information and click the Create button. You will need to restart WebLogic Server for this new execute queue to be created.

Assigning servlets and JSPs to the execute queue is accomplished by entering the queue name as the value of the `wl-dispatch-policy` parameter in `web.xml`, as shown in Listing 25.2.

25

LISTING 25.2 Excerpt from web.xml

```
<servlet>
 <servlet-name>SpecialServlet</servlet-name>
 <jsp-file>/gams/showFeeReport.jsp</jsp-file>
 <init-param>
 <param-name>wl-dispatch-policy</param-name>
 <param-value>SpecialQueue</param-value>
 </init-param>
</servlet>
```

Assigning EJBs and RMI objects to an execute queue is accomplished by using the `-dispatchPolicy` option with the RMIC or EJBC compilers.

Backlog Connections

As shown in Figure 25.7, client requests must wait for a socket reader thread before being placed on an execute queue. By default, the maximum number of waiting client requests allowed is 50. When the number of waiting requests reaches that amount, WebLogic Server will refuse new connections. To accommodate more client requests, the client request backlog can be increased. This value can be changed from the Tuning tab, as was shown in Figure 25.8. Keep in mind that this will consume more memory within WebLogic Server.

Automatically Detect Low Memory Conditions

In addition to the JVM performing garbage collection, WebLogic Server can be set to detect low memory situations and force garbage collection on a server-by-server basis as shown in Figure 25.10 and explained in Table 25.3.

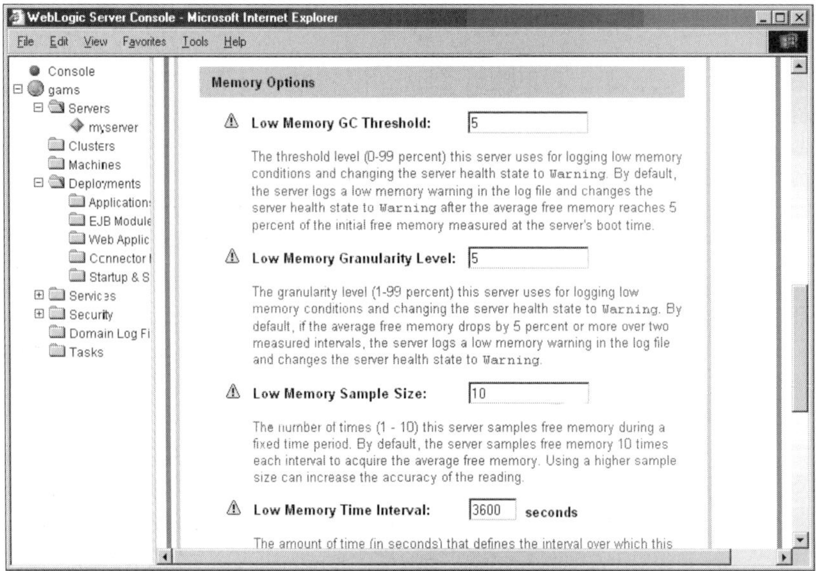

FIGURE 25.10 WebLogic Server memory configuration options can be viewed and modified with the Administration Console.

TABLE 25.3 WebLogic Server Memory Configuration Options

Memory Configuration Option	Description
Low Memory GC Threshold Default = 5%	The percentage of initial free memory that forces garbage collection. For example, 10% means that when free memory is less than 10% of initial free memory, garbage collection will be forced.
Low Memory Granularity Level Default = 5%	The percentage of average free memory between intervals that triggers log file entry and changes server health state to Warning.
Low Memory Sample Size Default = 10	The number of times per interval to check for low memory conditions.
Low Memory Time Interval Default = 3600	The number of seconds in an interval.

Detecting Stuck Threads

WebLogic Server can detect when threads have not completed their assigned task within a certain amount of time. These threads are marked as stuck and a log entry is created. As explained in Table 25.4, there are two parameters associated with stuck threads.

When all threads in the default queue are considered stuck, WebLogic Server can no longer service client requests. Periodically check the log file for stuck threads and correct the architecture of your application to prevent them from reoccurring. You might want to reduce the detection of stuck threads from the default of 10 minutes to a value more suitable to your application. In this way, problems can be detected and corrected sooner.

TABLE 25.4 Stuck Thread Parameters

Stuck Thread Parameter	Description
Stuck Thread Max Time Default = 600	The number of seconds that must pass before a thread that has not completed its assigned work is marked as stuck.
Stuck Thread Timer Interval Default = 600	How often to check for stuck threads.

Choosing a Faster Java Compiler

By default, WebLogic Server uses the standard `javac` Java compiler found within your `JAVA_HOME` directory to compile JSP Servlet files. This will typically be Sun's JDK or BEA's JRockit, depending on how your application is configured. Other compilers such as SJ or Jikes might compile significantly faster; you'll need to try them out to see which yields the best performance. From the Administration Console's General Configuration tab, you can set the JSP servlet compiler. This is shown in Figure 25.11. Be sure to add the required JAR files in the Append to Classpath parameter.

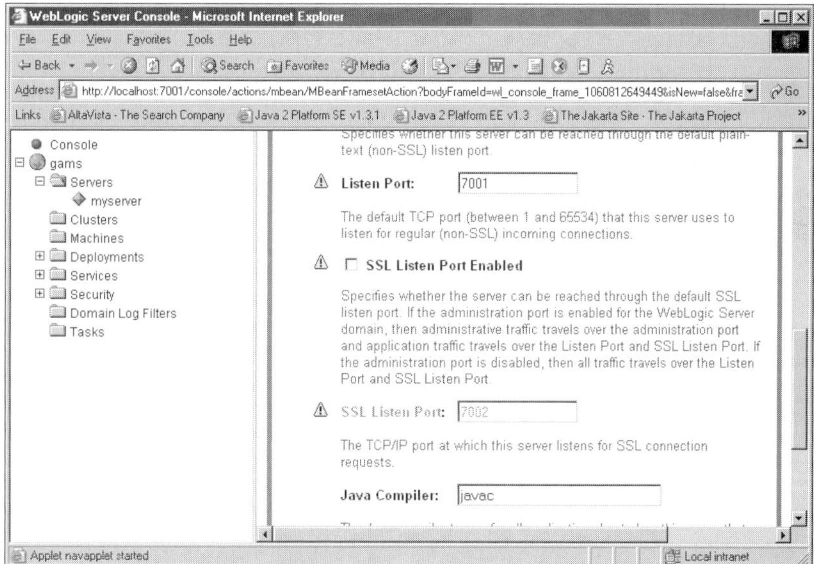

FIGURE 25.11 WebLogic Server can use a different compiler for JSP servlet files to improve performance.

The JSP servlet compiler can also be specified in a WebLogic application's `weblogic.xml` file. Use the `-compileCommand` and `-precompile` parameters to specify the compiler and whether to precompile the JSP servlet file when WebLogic Server is started.

The `weblogic.ejbc` utility, which generates EJB container classes, uses the standard Java compiler as well. When executing this utility, use the `-compiler` parameter to use a different compiler.

Using Production Mode

During development, auto-deployment allows developers to copy whole applications or individual J2EE components to the WebLogic Server domain directory. WebLogic Server will automatically detect and execute these new applications and components. However, auto-deployment consumes resources because WebLogic Server must continually check auto-deployment directories for changes. Make sure that WebLogic Server is started in production mode when your applications are running live. By default, WebLogic Server runs in development mode. To have it run in production mode, add `-Dweblogic.ProductionModeEnabled=true` to the batch file or command line that starts WebLogic Server.

Log File Sizes

WebLogic Server supports multiple types of log files. When using WebLogic Server as a Web server, the HTTP log tracks every HTTP GET and POST request made to a WebLogic Server domain. This log file can be analyzed and important statistics, such as number of visitors and page views per day, can be extracted from it. By default, this HTTP log will grow in size indefinitely. As the file gets larger, more resources are required to update it. As shown in Figure 25.12, the size of the HTTP log file can be restricted by creating a new log file on a chronological basis (called *rotation*) or when the log file reaches a certain size. If you are using an external Web server, be sure to set HTTP log rotation parameters suitably.

Although the WebLogic Server domain log takes a long time to become large and unwieldy, by default, there is no rotation set on it and it will grow indefinitely as well. In the Administration Console, click on the domain name in the left panel, and then click on the Logging and Server tabs in the right panel. Set the rotation parameters as shown in Figure 25.13. The server domain log should be set to rotate.

Using WebLogic Server Clustering

When you have exhausted all the resources of a single instance of WebLogic Server and have tuned the JVM, the operating system, and your application, the only way to improve performance is to cluster two of more instances of WebLogic Server. This situation occurs when the CPU of your single instance is at or near 100% and adding execute threads does not improve performance.

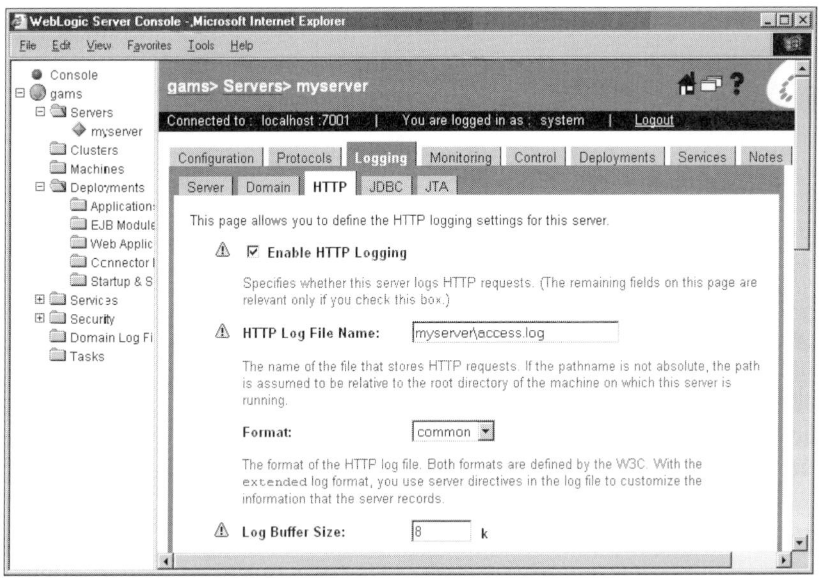

FIGURE 25.12 WebLogic Server offers many settings to reduce the size of HTTP log files.

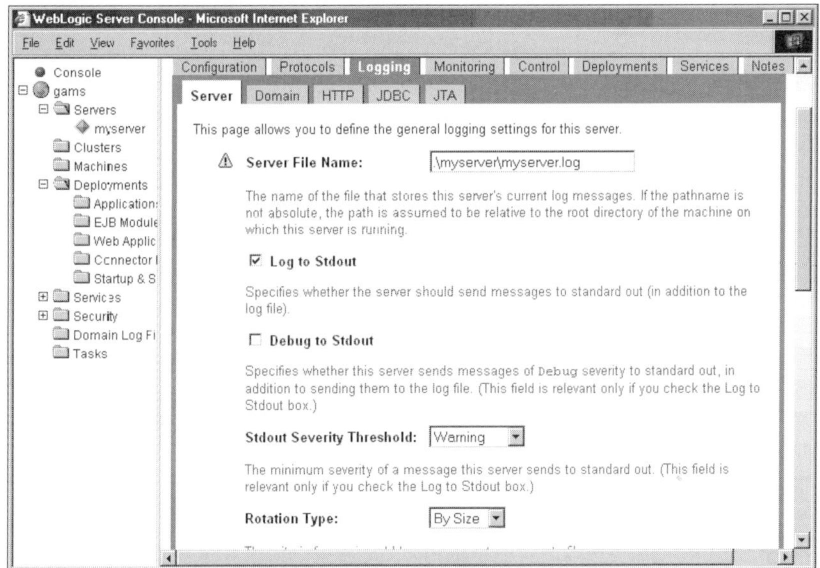

FIGURE 25.13 WebLogic Server offers many settings to reduce the size of domain log files.

WebLogic Server can work with a dedicated load balancer or a supported Web server can be retrofitted with a WebLogic Server supplied plug-in that acts as a load balancer. WebLogic Server 8.1 supplies load-balancing plug-ins for Netscape Enterprise Server, Apache Server, and Microsoft Internet Information Server. It also includes in own `HttpClusterServlet` when using a WebLogic instance to act as a load balancer.

Almost all J2EE components can be load balanced in a cluster, including HTTP sessions, EJBs and RMI objects, JMS destinations, and JDBC connection pools. For more information about setting up and using WebLogic Server clusters, please see Chapter 36, "Installing, Configuring, and Deploying WebLogic Server Clusters."

Database and SQL Tuning

For a vast majority of WebLogic applications, database access is a critical piece of functionality and potentially a good source for performance tuning. For example, there can be issues with the number of database accesses that an application is making, which might encourage an application developer to cache in memory values that don't change frequently, instead of retrieving them each time. Or there could be an issue with how long a particular query is taking to return, which might be improved by adding indexes or using temporary tables on the database. There are several other factors concerning the general performance of the database itself as well as WebLogic's communication with the database, which we will now examine more closely.

Connection Pools

Compared to actually executing an SQL statement, establishing a connection to the database is a very slow operation. Connection pools allow WebLogic Server to be in charge of establishing connections to the RDBMS and distributing those connections to WebLogic Server applications as they are needed. Additionally, connection pools can be set up to automatically grow and shrink depending on application needs. Increasing the initial number of connections in the pool will make WebLogic Server slower to start, but applications will not have to wait when requesting a database connection. Ideally, the best performance will be achieved when the number of connections in the pool is equal to the number of connections needed by WebLogic applications.

Caching Prepared Statements

Each JDBC connection pool can potentially cache SQL prepared statements. When a WebLogic application calls a prepared statement that is in the cache, the database does not have to parse the SQL. This reduces the load on the database and leaves more CPU cycles for other tasks. By default, the number of prepared statements the cache can hold is set to 0. Change this number, benchmark your application, and observe how it affects performance. If your application uses prepared statements, chances are that you will see an improvement. There are some restrictions on how this cache can be used. Please see `http://e-docs.bea.com/wls/docs81/jdbc/performance.html` for more information.

JDBC Driver Type

The type of JDBC driver will affect performance. Database connections using Type 1 drivers must incur the cost of going through an ODBC driver as well, whereas Type 4 drivers tend to perform the best because communication with the database is direct and there is no need to go through ODBC or a native interface.

Database Schema Design

In many cases, our WebLogic applications must use an existing database schema and attempt to get the best performance from it. In other cases, we have the opportunity to design the schema with our WebLogic application in mind. If this is the case, make sure that you design with performance in mind. Although using normal form in database design represents a popular mindset, you must also consider the performance costs of the database schema you ultimately decide to use.

Using Correct Indexes

SQL statements are executed by the database in a variety of ways each with an associated performance cost. For example, when a `SELECT` statement is executed and the `WHERE` clause is based on columns for which there are no indexes, the database must perform a full table scan. This means that every row in a database table must be examined to determine whether it meets the `WHERE` clause criteria. If the table has many rows, performance will suffer and your RDBMS will be working harder than it needs to. Creating additional indexes on these columns will improve performance on these queries and throughput of the database as a whole.

25

Using Stored Procedures

Although using stored procedures ties your code to a particular version of SQL and, ultimately, to a database vendor, they can potentially improve the performance of your SQL related code. However, by putting business logic in the database in addition to the middle tier, you are potentially making your application harder to maintain. You need to find the correct balance among performance, maintainability, and portability that meets both performance requirements and company policies towards software design. An interesting note is that Oracle9*i* allows stored procedures to be created in Java, thus gaining performance and keeping business logic in Java.

Reducing the Number of Round Trips

If your WebLogic application performs more round trips to the database, performance will suffer. In some cases, it might be possible to cache database updates until a later time and then perform all of them with one trip to the database. This practically removes the overhead associated with network communications (assuming that your database is running on a separate machine). Also, if it is possible to execute all of these updates in a single transaction, the database will be able to process them faster than using separate transactions for each update because of the underlying database locks associated with transactions.

Caching Data in the Middle Tier

If information from the database is static or changes infrequently, consider caching it at the middle tier to avoid extra trips to the database. This can be achieved with read-only Entity EJBs or by binding your custom data class to the JNDI tree.

Smart SQL

Using SQL smartly simply means that performance should be a priority when designing the SQL statements in your application. There is usually more than one way of implementing desired functionality. Some issues to consider are whether or not to use correlated sub-queries and temporary tables to improve performance. Because there is no right answer for every situation, the best way to know which techniques run faster is by benchmarking. Another thing to consider is moving older, less frequently used information into historical tables to reduce the load on the database when this information is not needed.

Enterprise JavaBean Tuning

One of the most common enemies of good performance in WebLogic applications is incorrect usage of EJBs. When used correctly, EJBs can help make applications much easier to build and maintain. But when applied incorrectly, they can create additional performance overhead that can slow down a system tremendously. We will discuss some common approaches to avoiding this pitfall.

Using a Session Façade Pattern

Direct method calls to EJBs from servlets, JSPs, and thick clients involve the overhead of network communications that can be hundreds of times more costly than a local method call. In an effort to improve performance, do not have these clients access entity EJBs directly; rather, use a Stateless Session EJB as a mediator to an Entity EJB. The Stateless Session EJB can then access the Entity EJB using a local interface that acts like a local method call and does not incur any network communications overhead. This design pattern also increases maintainability by providing a layer of abstraction and makes it easier to handle changes in the Entity bean's methods.

Using Coarse-Grained Methods and Value Objects

Create a value object that can hold every attribute of an Entity EJB. A *value object* is a JavaBean with get and set methods. Then, create an Entity EJB coarse-grained method that will accept this value object. In this way, a client can set all the Entity EJB attributes with one method call. Similarly, create a coarse-grained method that will return a value object so that a client can query all the Entity EJB attributes with one method call.

Tuning Deployment Descriptor Parameters

WebLogic Server supports several EJB tuning parameters that can be defined in the deployment descriptor, `weblogic-ejb-jar.xml`. One such parameter, `entity-cache`, an application-level cache of Entity beans. This pool of beans can speed access to various data by eliminating database round-trips. It has several parameters that can be tuned, including the maximum size of the cache and timeout values for refreshing the cache. Try different values for these options depending on your application.

One parameter of the `entity-cache` element that deserves further discussion is `concurrency-strategy`. This property defines how WebLogic handles concurrent access to an Entity bean held in the cache. This value may be one of `"Exclusive"`, `"Database"`, `"ReadOnly"`, or `"Optimistic"`. `"Exclusive"` and `"Database"` guarantee that only one transaction at a time will be able to write to an entity bean, and in so doing incur the largest performance overhead. If static data is being read as an Entity bean, it should be marked as `"ReadOnly"`, which is much faster because the object never needs to be updated in the cache after it's been read in. If the value is set to `"Optimistic"`, the EJB container makes sure that any data being updated by the transaction has not changed since the transaction started. It does this by comparing fields in the Entity EJB and the database. If something has changed, the EJB container rolls back the transaction. The theory is that if two objects have a reference to a bean, the container optimistically assumes that only one of them will actually be modifying it at a given time. By reducing the amount of time that database locks are held, performance can be increased.

25

Another area where performance can be tuned is with transaction isolation levels. The `isolation-level` element of the `transaction-isolation` element is used to declare the isolation level of an entity or session bean on a per-method basis. This value can be one of `"TransactionSerializable"`, `"TransactionReadCommitted"`, `"TransactionReadUncommitted"`, and `"TransactionRepeatableRead"`. If you are willing to make a trade-off between data consistency and performance, consider using `"TransactionReadUncommitted"`. This value, sometimes referred to as a *dirty read*, allows the transaction to see updated by uncommitted data from other transactions. Because it doesn't have to lock access to that data during another transaction's update, performance can be increased.

The transaction granularity is also something that should be considered for performance reasons. For example, if several Entity beans are to be updated within one Session bean method, it should typically be created as one transaction for all, as opposed to an individual transaction for each. This is primarily to reduce the overhead of acquiring transaction contexts. But it usually makes sense from an application standpoint as well, where you'd want either all or none of your changes in a given method to be committed to preserve data integrity.

Performance Testing EJBs

Bean-test from Empirix is able to work with WebLogic Server and can simulate client load, perform stress testing, and pinpoint performance issues in EJBs. Go to `http://www.empirix.com` for more information about Bean-test.

A Performance Testing and Tuning Example

In this section, we will discuss performance testing and tuning techniques in the context of a real-world application. Our example will be focused on an application called The Global Auction Management System (GAMS). GAMS is a WebLogic application representing an online auction where

- Guests can browse for items by category, keyword, and whether or not it is a featured item. They can also view the existing bids for an item.
- Guests can register so that they can place items for sale and bid on items as well.
- Sellers can list items for sale. They are charged a listing fee and a selling fee.
- Buyers can bid on items until an auction ends. At auction's end, the buyer with the highest bid is awarded the item.
- The GAMS accounting department can run reports on listing and selling fees.

In the following sections, we will demonstrate the performance testing of the GAMS application with a tool called Grinder.

The Grinder Load-Testing Tool

Grinder is an open source load-testing tool written in Java that is easy to use and provides extremely useful feedback for benchmarking WebLogic applications. Grinder has many very useful features, and you should refer to `http://sourceforge.net/projects/grinder` for the latest release of Grinder and the most up to date information. The book titled *J2EE Performance Testing with BEA WebLogic Server* by Peter Zadrozny, Philip Aston, and Ted Osborne also contains some useful information about Grinder.

The Grinder Architecture

Grinder consists of worker processes that execute test scripts that simulate user behavior. The worker processes can run alone or they can report their performance back to the Grinder console. As shown in Figure 25.14, the console is in charge of stopping and starting one of more worker processes.

The Grinder console dialog is shown in Figure 25.15. It is used display performance statistics collected by one or more Grinder clients. The performance information collected can then be saved to disk to compare with other performance information.

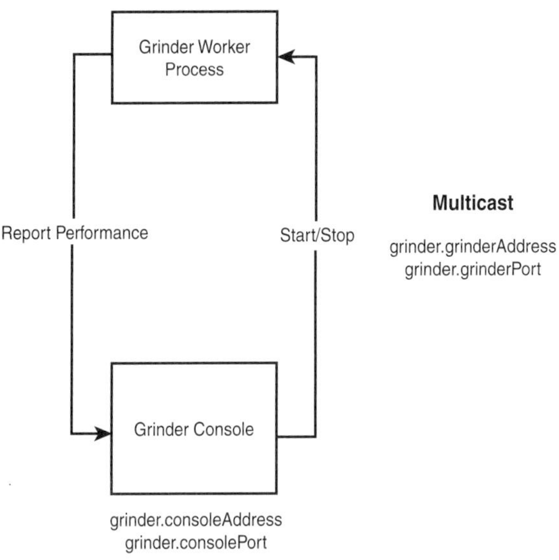

FIGURE 25.14 The Grinder console controls Grinder worker processes using IP multicast. The workers report their performance to the console.

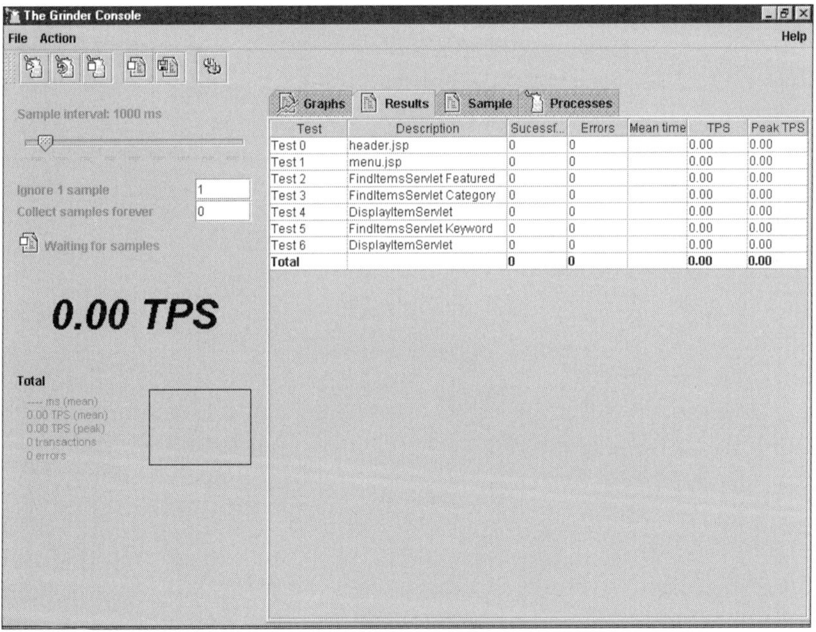

Test	Description	Sucessf...	Errors	Mean time	TPS	Peak TPS
Test 0	header.jsp	0	0		0.00	0.00
Test 1	menu.jsp	0	0		0.00	0.00
Test 2	FindItemsServlet Featured	0	0		0.00	0.00
Test 3	FindItemsServlet Category	0	0		0.00	0.00
Test 4	DisplayItemServlet	0	0		0.00	0.00
Test 5	FindItemsServlet Keyword	0	0		0.00	0.00
Test 6	DisplayItemServlet	0	0		0.00	0.00
Total		**0**	**0**		**0.00**	**0.00**

FIGURE 25.15 The Grinder console provides graphical and numeric displays of performance statistics.

Grinder clients are able to execute Grinder property files. These files consist of parameters related to communicating with the console, how many users to simulate, simulated client requests, and the number of times to cycle through the client requests. Client requests can come in many forms and Grinder plug-ins are used to execute these requests. The most common plug-in is the HTTP plug-in, and the most common request is connecting with a URL in the application to be load tested. The HTTP plug-in contains many features, including cookie support, and the ability to use HTTP authentication and to use data files when posting to a URL. This plug-in can also check URL responses and determine whether they were successful. To enable this, you need to define a string that will be contained within a successful URL response.

The sample Grinder properties file shown in Listing 25.3 instructs Grinder to performance-test connecting with `www.yahoo.com` and `www.monster.com`. It will create three Grinder worker processes, each one running in its own JVM. Each JVM will then spawn 10 threads. This will, in effect, simulate 30 simultaneous clients. In this case, it will cycle through the two URLs a total of 10 times and then it will stop. If we want the Grinder worker process to run until it is explicitly stopped by the console, we can set the number of cycles to 0.

LISTING 25.3 A Sample Grinder Properties File

```
grinder.processes=3
grinder.threads=10
grinder.cycles=10
grinder.jvm.arguments=-Xint

grinder.consoleAddress=localhost
grinder.consolePort=6372
grinder.grinderAddress=228.1.1.1
grinder.grinderPort=1234

grinder.plugin=net.grinder.plugin.http.HttpPlugin
grinder.test0.parameter.url=http://www.yahoo.com
grinder.test1.parameter.url=http://www.monster.com
```

Grinder worker processes will create log files containing valuable information such as connection times and error information. Each thread within a Grinder worker process will create a data log file that contains response times and the number of connection errors that occurred. Each thread will also create an error log file that contains error details if one or more errors occurred on this thread.

Another possible entry in a Grinder properties file is the JVM options. When we use Grinder to load-test our applications, we want the performance of Grinder to remain constant so that we can detect performance changes within our WebLogic application. As shown in Listing 25.3, we pass the `-Xint` argument to the JVM. This argument turns off code optimization within the JVM of the worker process and stabilizes its performance.

GAMS Benchmarking Environment

As shown in Figure 25.16, the environment used to benchmark GAMS consists of three machines connected by a 100 Mbps Ethernet switch. We have separate machines for WebLogic Server and the Oracle 8.1.7 database. Additionally, we use a separate machine to run the Grinder console and the Grinder worker processes.

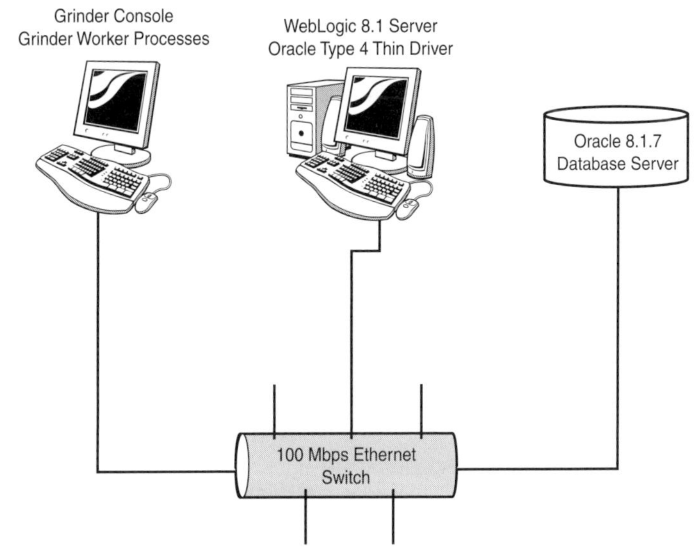

FIGURE 25.16 The Grinder console and its client(s) should be on separate machines from WebLogic Server and the RDBMS so that performance statistics are not skewed.

Specifying Performance Goals for GAMS

To begin testing, we first must define requirements for the performance of the system. The performance goals for GAMS are as follows:

- Guests should not have to wait more than 3 seconds for an item search.
- Guests that register should not have to wait more than 5 seconds when registering.
- Sellers should not have to wait more than 5 seconds to list an item without a picture. If they are listing an item with a picture less than or equal to 50KB in size, they should not have to wait more than 10 seconds.
- Buyers should get immediate response after bidding and should see their bid posted asynchronously within 15 seconds.
- The GAMS accounting department should be able to run a report within 15 seconds.

The preceding response times should hold with up to 100 simultaneous users. Because our benchmarking environment is a 100Mbs LAN, we are not taking into account the transmission time that an Internet client would experience nor are we measuring the render time that a browser needs to display the HTML responses.

Understanding User Behavior

After speaking with our business people, we are told that at any given time, 75% of our user population will be guests, 5% will be registering, 10% will be sellers, and 10% will be buyers. Of course, a single person will probably be all three at some point, but these percentages are just a ballpark estimate for simulation purposes. We are also told that a member of the GAMS accounting department could run a report at any time.

Creating User Scripts

For each user type, we generate a test script. That is, a set of Web pages that each type of user will typically visit.

- Guest `User`—Visit home page, do a category search, display an item, do a keyword search, display an item
- Registering user—Register
- Seller—Log in, list an item, list another item, log out
- Buyer—Log in, bid on item, log out
- GAMS accounting—Log in, run report, log out

Because we are using Grinder, each one of these user scripts is actually a Grinder properties file. Grinder properties files can be created by hand, but doing so is a tiresome and error-prone task. The TCPSniffer tool that comes with Grinder can automatically create properties files. TCPSniffer tracks a user's HTTP requests through a Web browser and can record them to a Grinder properties file. It also records the amount of time between requests. We used TCPSniffer to create the user scripts for the four types of users explained earlier. Listing 25.4 is an excerpt from the guest user script.

LISTING 25.4 An Excerpt from guest.properties

```
grinder.test100.parameter.url=http://localhost:7001/header.jsp
grinder.test100.sleepTime=2684
grinder.test100.description=header.jsp

grinder.test101.parameter.url=http://localhost:7001/menu.jsp
grinder.test101.sleepTime=0
grinder.test101.description=menu.jsp
```

```
grinder.test102.parameter.url=http://localhost:7001/FindItemsServlet?featured=true
grinder.test102.sleepTime=40
grinder.test102.description=FindItemsServlet Featured

grinder.test103.parameter.url=http://localhost:7001/FindItemsServlet?catid=5
grinder.test103.sleepTime=2564
grinder.test103.description=FindItemsServlet Category

grinder.test104.parameter.url=http://localhost:7001/DisplayItemServlet?itemid=65
grinder.test104.sleepTime=3385
grinder.test104.description=DisplayItemServlet

grinder.test105.parameter.url=http://localhost:7001/FindItemsServlet?keyword=e
grinder.test105.sleepTime=4006
grinder.test105.description=FindItemsServlet Keyword

grinder.test106.parameter.url=http://localhost:7001/DisplayItemServlet?itemid=67
grinder.test106.sleepTime=3284
grinder.test106.description=DisplayItemServlet
```


The first three URLs, due to the use of frames, represent the GAMS home page. This is followed by a search for all items in category number 5 (Computers), display item 65, search for all items with the letter *e* in the title, and display item 67. Notice the sleep time (measured in milliseconds). TCPSniffer added this line and it represents the amount of time the Grinder worker process will wait before requesting the next URL. This simulates the amount of time that a user would need to read the Web page currently in front of him before moving to the next one.

Initializing Our Environment

To better simulate real-life usage of GAMS, we should have some actual data already in the database. This involves having some registered users, items, and bids.

We start with three users. Every item and every bid will belong to one of these three users.

We decided to pre-fill the ITEM tables with 100 items having item IDs of 1 to 100, spread out evenly over six categories, with half the items being featured items. The titles of the items will consist of their category name followed by a number 1–100. The description will be the title name plus the word *description*.

We made the end date of these items to be 7 days away so that their auctions would not end while we were testing. We also created five random bids per item to more closely simulate actual data. We disabled all email messages being sent so that we would not overflow the email server.

We also set the GAMS Connection Pool initially with five connections and a maximum of five connections. The JVM heap is initialized at 128MB with a maximum of 128MB.

Selecting a JVM

One of the first steps to benchmarking is selecting the JVM that gives you the best performance. Because we are running WebLogic Server 8.1 on Windows NT, we can use Sun's JDK 1.4.1 or BEA's JRockit, both of which are included with WebLogic. You should load-test your WebLogic application against each certified JVM and select the JVM that offers optimal performance. For the rest of this example, we will assume the use of Sun's JDK.

Testing Strategy

We have five types of users represented by five Grinder properties files. We ultimately want to test performance with all types of simulated users running at the same time, but doing so right away will make it more difficult to solve performance issues. Instead, we will run each script by itself, solve performance issues, and then run the scripts simultaneously.

When running each script by itself, we would like to uncover performance issues quickly. Therefore, for this part of our performance tuning, when we run the individual Grinder properties files, we will make all the user's think times equal to zero. This will represent a worst-case situation in which users are inundating our application with requests. Running the scripts in this manner will cause our performance issues to show up sooner so that we can resolve them more quickly.

Initial Benchmarking

Our initial benchmarking of GAMS will load-test with 10 simulated guests to get an idea of performance with a small number of users as shown in Listing 25.5.

LISTING 25.5 Simulating 10 Users

```
grinder.processes=1
grinder.threads=10
grinder.cycles=0
```

Using Random Client Parameters

Looking back at Listing 25.4, you can see that every time this user script is run, it will query for the same item category and the same item IDs. We need a way to randomize this information. The Grinder HTTP plug-in supports this through the use of string beans. A String bean is a user-defined Java class that works with the Grinder HTTP plug-in to create strings in any way you see fit.

In our `guest.properties` file, we will change the URLs for requests 3, 4, 6, and 7 as shown in Listing 25.6. Where the hardcoded values were, we now have function names wrapped in < and >.

LISTING 25.6 Hardcoded Values Have Been Replaced

```
grinder.test103.parameter.url=http://localhost:7001/FindItemsServlet?
➥catid=<getCatID>
grinder.test104.parameter.url=http://localhost:7001/DisplayItemServlet?
➥itemid=<getItemID>
grinder.test106.parameter.url=http://localhost:7001/FindItemsServlet?
➥keyword=<getKeyword>
grinder.test107.parameter.url=http://localhost:7001/DisplayItemServlet?
➥itemid=<getItemID>
```

As shown in Listing 25.7, we have created a simple Java class called `GuestStringBean` with the public methods `getCatID`, `getItemID`, and `getKeyword`. The Grinder client will call these methods in creating the request URL.

LISTING 25.7 The GuestStringBean Class

```
package com.gams.performance;

public class GuestStringBean {
 private int NUMCATEGORIES = 6;
 private int NUMITEMS = 100;
 private String vowels[] = {"a", "e", "i", "o", "u" };

 // return a random number between 1 and NUMCATEGORIES
 public String getCatID() {
 int catid = (int)(Math.random() * NUMCATEGORIES) + 1;
 return new Integer(catid).toString();
 }

 // return a random number between 1 and NUMITEMS
 public String getItemID() {
 int catid = (int)(Math.random() * NUMITEMS) + 1;
 return new Integer(catid).toString();
 }

 // return a random vowel
 public String getKeyword() {
 int letternum = (int)(Math.random() * vowels.length);
 return vowels[letternum];
 }
}
```

25

The `GuestStringBean` class needs to be compiled and added to the `classpath`. It can then be added to `guest.properties` like this:

```
grinder.plugin.parameter.stringBean=com.gams.performance.GuestStringBean
```

Installing and Configuring Grinder and Test Application

To set up Grinder on your machine, follow the following steps:

1. Unzip the distribution `.zip` file to a location on your hard drive. We'll refer to this as `GRINDER_DIR`.
2. Add `GRINDER_DIR\lib\grinder.jar` to your `classpath`.
3. Compile the `GuestStringBean` and `RegisteringUserStringBean` classes.
4. Place the path to the compiled classes in your `classpath`.

Starting the Console

Start the Grinder console by opening a command prompt and entering **`java net.grinder.Console`**. Then open another command prompt and enter **`java net.grinder.Grinder guest.properties`**. By default, the Grinder client will execute the `grinder.properties` file unless we specify a different properties file. The Grinder client will output its command-line parameters and then state that it is waiting for the console to start it, as shown in Figure 25.17.

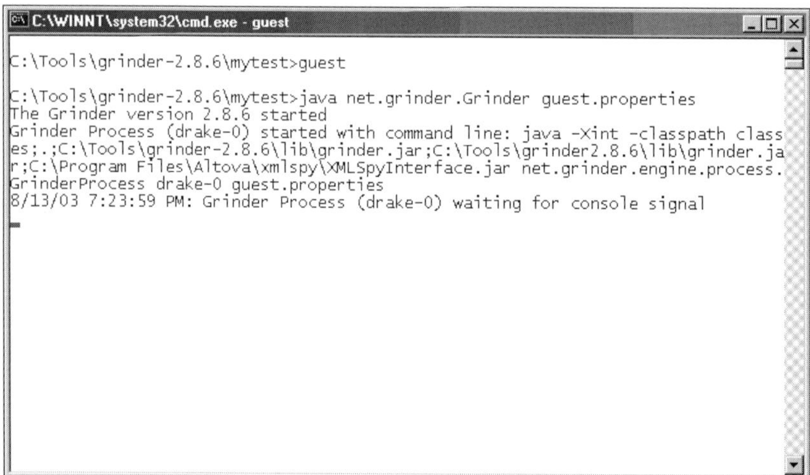

FIGURE 25.17 The Grinder client is waiting to be started from the console.

Go back to the Grinder console and click on the Graphs tab. You will see seven test areas for each of the seven URL requests in the `guests.properties` test script as shown in

Figure 25.18. If you look at the Results and Samples tabs, you will see seven rows of information. Click on the Processes tab and you will see that one process with 10 threads is in a ready state.

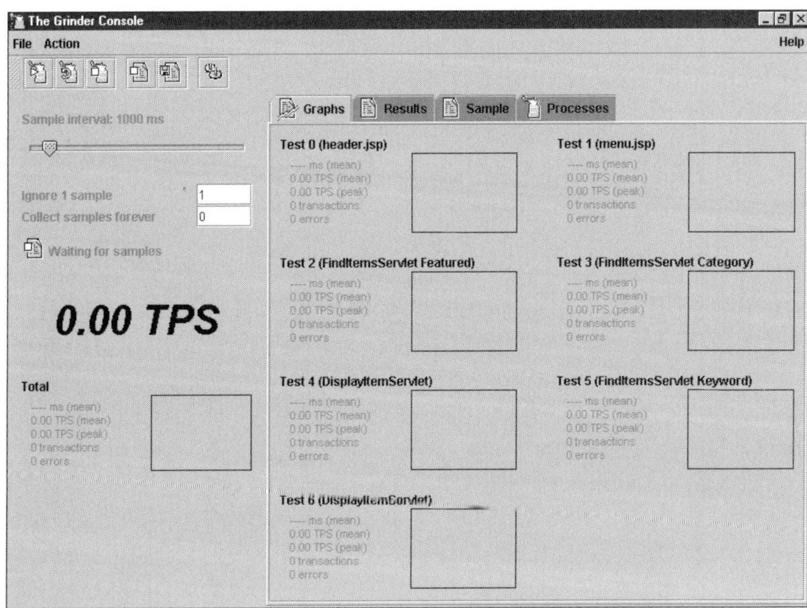

FIGURE 25.18 The Grinder console is ready to collect performance data from the Grinder clients.

Before starting our Grinder client, make sure the Sample Interval setting is set to 1000ms. This means that worker processes will report their performance to the console once a second. Also, the line `grinder.reportToConsole.interval=1000` has been added to `guest.properties` to reduce the CPU usage of the Grinder worker process.

Starting Our Grinder Clients Threads

We now go to the menu of the console and choose Start Processes or click the leftmost button in the toolbar. Each of the client threads will now execute the `guests.properties` test script and you can monitor their performance. Click on the Results tab to see performance information on each URL. We noticed our initial mean times were very high and they tended to go down over time.

We waited until we had collected 100 samples of performance information and then stopped collecting information by going to the Action menu and choosing Stop Collection. Next, we stopped our worker processes by choosing Stop Processes from the Action menu. Looking at the Results tab reveals the performance statistics in Table 25.5.

TABLE 25.5 10 Users, 0 Sleep Times, 30 Samples

Description	Rounded Mean Time
header.jsp	234
menu.jsp	151
Featured Search	318
Category Search	150
Display Item	225
Keyword Search	165
Display Item	148
Total	199 (Avg)

The Grinder worker process has created two log files, `out_nameofmachine-0.log` and `data_nameofmachine-0.log`. The latter file contains the actual response times per URL, per thread, and per cycle, as shown in Listing 25.8.

LISTING 25.8 Excerpt from data_XXX-0.log

```
Thread, Cycle, Test, Transaction time, Errors
1, 0, 100, 2994, 0
9, 0, 100, 2994, 0
7, 0, 100, 2994, 0
```

Because this file is comma delimited, we can import it into spreadsheet software such as Microsoft Excel. After importing the data into Excel, we can sort it by cycle number, thread number, and test number. Then we can create a pivot table as shown in Figure 25.19. From it we can see that the average response times for all tests in cycle 0 is 1465ms. This number then drops to 168 in cycle 1 and then 142 in cycle 2. These first three cycles take longer than other cycles because WebLogic Server takes a little time to get to optimal performance. One of the reasons for that is because WebLogic Server must convert JSP files to servlet Java files and then compile them the first time they are accessed.

We would like the Grinder console to disregard response times from the first three cycles. On the console GUI, we can set the Ignore X Samples parameter. In our last benchmarking, we took 30 samples and ended up running through around 30 cycles of our URLs, so we almost have a one-to-one correspondence between the number of samples and number of cycles. Therefore, if we ignore the first three samples, we should end up ignoring the first three cycles of performance data. Because we are taking 30 samples, we can afford not to use performance from more than three cycles. We want to make very sure that we are not incurring the initial startup times for our application, so we decide to set the `ignore` parameter in the Grinder console to 5, restart WebLogic Server, and rerun our load-test.

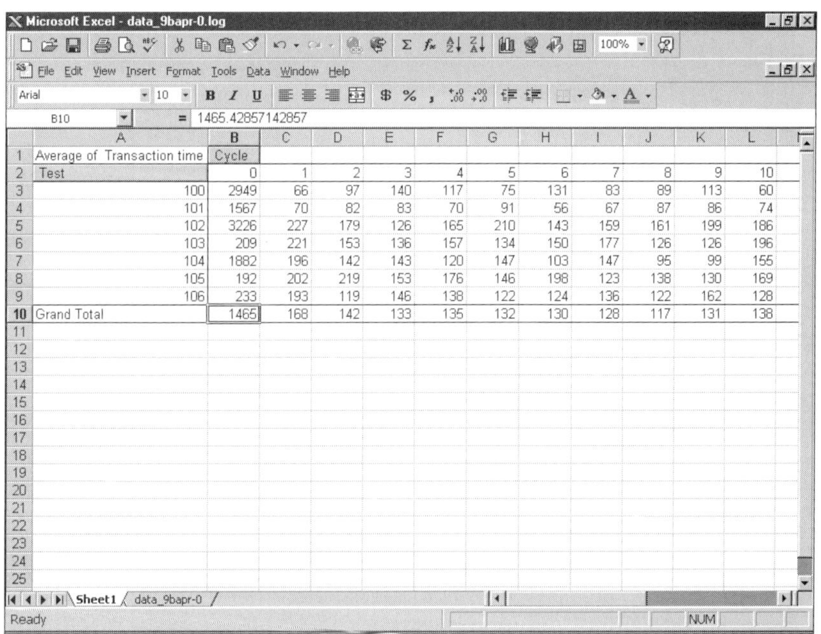

Average of Transaction time	Cycle										
Test	0	1	2	3	4	5	6	7	8	9	10
100	2949	66	97	140	117	75	131	83	89	113	60
101	1567	70	82	83	70	91	56	67	87	86	74
102	3226	227	179	126	165	210	143	159	161	199	186
103	209	221	153	136	157	134	150	177	126	126	196
104	1882	196	142	143	120	147	103	147	95	99	155
105	192	202	219	153	176	146	198	123	138	130	169
106	233	193	119	146	138	122	124	136	122	162	128
Grand Total	1465	168	142	133	135	132	130	128	117	131	138

FIGURE 25.19 Excel's pivot table enables us to view our average response times per cycle per test.

As you can see in Table 25.6, without the initial performance numbers factored in, our mean times have gone down. Not only have they gone down, but they now are more intuitive. Clearly, the requests that involve the database take considerably longer than the ones that do not (`header.jsp` and `menu.jsp`).

TABLE 25.6 10 Users, 0 Sleep Times, 30 Samples, Ignore First 5 Samples

Description	Rounded Mean Time
header.jsp	76
menu.jsp	65
Featured Search	302
Category Search	144
Display Item	208
Keyword Search	174
Display Item	126
Total	157 (Avg)

Increasing the Number Of Users

Now let's double the number of users and see how the application responds. The results, shown in Table 25.7, display the mean times with 10 and 20 users side by side. We can see that the AART (Average Average Response Time) has more than doubled from 157 to 324 and each of the individual mean times have doubled as well.

TABLE 25.7 10 and 20 Users, 0 Sleep Times, 30 Samples, Ignore First 5 Samples

Description	Mean Time 10 Users	Mean Time 20 Users
header.jsp	76	133
menu.jsp	65	244
Featured Search	302	604
Category Search	144	301
Display Item	208	392
Keyword Search	174	311
Display Item	126	268
Total	157 (Avg)	324 (Avg)

When we increased the number of users to 30, we were refused a connection to `header.jsp` three times. To solve this problem, we changed the `AcceptBacklog` parameter from the default value of 50 to 200 and reran the load-test at 30 users. This produced the performance data in Table 25.8. We now started tracking total transactions per second. This represents the throughput of our application and WebLogic Server. At 30 users, we have a total TPS of 55.1.

TABLE 25.8 30 Users, 0 Sleep Times, 30 Samples, Ignore First 5 Samples

Description	Mean Time 30 Users	Mean Time 30 Users (AcceptBacklog="200")
header.jsp	296 (3 errors)	243
menu.jsp	336	344
Featured Search	912	793
Category Search	480	452
Display Item	558	547
Keyword Search	465	436
Display Item	355	398
Total	490 (Avg)	461 (Avg)
Total TPS	52.8	55.1

We then ran tests at 40, 80, and 120 users, as shown in Table 25.9. When we reached 120 users, Featured Search was almost at our maximum acceptable response time (MART) of 3 seconds. Because of this, we felt that by the time we reached 140 users, we would be at more than 3 seconds. As we progressed from 40 to 140 users, our total throughput fell from 53.0 to 48.2. We were serving more clients, but we were getting less actual work done per second.

TABLE 25.9 40, 80, 120, 140 Users; 0 Sleep Times; 30 Samples; Ignore First 5 Samples

Description	Mean Time 40 Users	Mean Time 80 Users	Mean Time 120 Users	Mean Time 140 Users
header.jsp	369	478	930	1740
menu.jsp	233	605	761	1730
Featured Search	981	1690	2880	3410
Category Search	688	1340	2520	2770
Display Item	815	1740	2750	3110
Keyword Search	597	1190	2150	2590
Display Item	492	1090	1980	2580
Total (Avg)	606	1170	1940	2590
Total TPS	53.0	53.2	49.8	48.2

Tuning the Database

It was noticed that the Category Search and the Keyword Search were taking the longest amounts of time. Both of these searches relied on finder methods within the Item Entity EJB. Oracle 8.1.7 includes Oracle DBA Studio, which can be used to monitor database connections and to study Oracle's execution plans for SQL statements. The SQL associated with the Featured Search, the Category Search, and the Keyword Search did not use an index and required full table scans of the ITEM table. With only 100 items, we were seeing a drop in performance. Because more items would be added to the table when the application was live, we knew these performance problems would only get worse. It was time to create indexes as shown in Listing 25.9.

LISTING 25.9 Three Indexes Added to the ITEM Table

```
CREATE INDEX IDX_ITEM_CATEGORY ON ITEM(CATEGORYID);
CREATE INDEX IDX_ITEM_TITLE ON ITEM(TITLE);
CREATE INDEX IDX_ITEM_ISFEATURED ON ITEM(ISFEATURED);
```

We then reran the load-test at 140 users. Unfortunately, we did not see any performance gain in the three searches. Then we noticed that all three finder methods create SQL prepared statements. JDBC connection pools, by default, do not cache these statements, but caching can be explicitly turned on. We created a cache that could hold up to 20 prepared statements. When a prepared statement is already in the cache, the SQL does not have to be re-parsed and performance is improved. As you can see in the third column of Table 25.10, adding the cache reduced the time of our searches considerably.

25

TABLE 25.10 140 Users, 0 Sleep Times, 30 Samples, Ignore First 5 Samples, Indexes Created

Description	Mean Time 140 Users Added Indexes	Mean Time 140 Users Added PreparedStatementCacheSize="20"
header.jsp	1950	810
menu.jsp	1340	664
Featured Search	3500	3160
Category Search	2870	2800
Display Item	3040	2580
Keyword Search	2570	2220
Display Item	2790	2060
Total	2620 (Avg)	1990
Total TPS	48.0	55.6
CPU Usage	> 90%	> 90%
RDBMS CPU Usage	~ 18%	~ 13%

At this point, we tried many options to improve performance. We tried both decreasing and increasing the number of execute threads, but performance went down in both cases. The same was true for the maximum number of connections in the JDBC connection pool. We also used the WebLogic Server Administration Console and noticed that there was plenty of memory available in the Java heap.

Looking at Architecture

Having exhausted the possibilities for tuning WebLogic Server, we investigated how to fine-tune our application. We were already taking advantage of the performancegains of the façade pattern and coarse-grained value objects.

Using Straight JDBC Code

We were curious to see whether using straight JDBC code for our Category Search could improve performance over using the Item Entity EJB finder method. We created a method called `getItemsInCategory2()` in `GAMSFacadeBean` that mimicked the functionality of `getItemsInCategory()` but instead of using the `ItemBean` EJB, it used direct JDBC calls. We then changed `FindItemsServlet` to call `getItemsInCategory2()` instead of `getItemsInCategory()`. We reran our load-test at 140 users and observed the mean time of the Category Search. Unfortunately, this had virtually no effect on performance because this JDBC code was not able to take advantage of the entity cache.

Using Optimistic Locking

We noticed that the only attribute that could change within an Item EJB was its current bid. We could change `ProcessBidBean` to make a direct JDBC update and then change `ItemBean` to read-only EJB. We would then explore the most optimal read-timeout value that was also satisfactory for our users. In this way, we could avoid calling unnecessary `ejbLoad()` from our `ItemBean`. We decided to pursue this option if extra tuning was necessary, but because we were already below the required response times, we decided not to pursue this experiment.

Registering Users

Now it was time to simulate guests that are trying to register so that they can buy and sell items on GAMS. We created a `registeringuser.properties` file as shown in Listing 25.10.

LISTING 25.10 Excerpt from the registeringuser.properties File

```
grinder.plugin=net.grinder.plugin.http.HttpPlugin
grinder.plugin.parameter.stringBean=com.gams.performance.RegisteringUserStringBean

grinder.test200.parameter.url=http://localhost:7001/registertemp.jsp
grinder.test200.description=RegisterUser
grinder.test200.parameter.ok=Welcome
grinder.test200.parameter.post=registeruser.dat
grinder.test200.parameter.header.Content-Type=application/x-www-form-urlencoded
```

When we call `registertemp.jsp` to create a new customer, we post the contents of the `registeruser.dat` file as shown in Listing 25.11. This file was created by TCPSniffer and then modified by us. Notice the `<getGamsAlias>` and `<getEmailAddress>` parameters. The `createNewCustomer()` in the `GAMSFacadeBean` will check for duplicate aliases and email addresses; therefore, we need to create unique values for these fields.

LISTING 25.11 registeruser.dat File

```
firstname=joe&lastname=shmoe&gamsalias=<getGamsAlias>&password=aaaaaaa
➥&password2=aaaaaaaa&emailaddress=<getEmailAddress>
➥&address=123+main+st&city=mycity&state=ny&zipcode=12345
➥&cctype=Amex&ccnum=3623723623&ccexpdate=12%2F02
```

Also notice the line `grinder.test0.parameter.ok=Welcome`. So far, we have been testing for success only by whether we were able to connect with a URL. When called successfully, `registertemp.jsp` will respond with the message `Welcome new user`. The line `grinder.test0.parameter.ok=Welcome` instructs Grinder to look for the word *Welcome* in the response. If Grinder doesn't see *Welcome*, it assumes that the test ran with an error.

For this to work correctly, we must be able to generate unique GAMS aliases and email addresses. We could have `getGamsAlias` and `getEmailAddress` generate some random characters, and most of the time we would probably get lucky, but we would like a more reliable method. Grinder allows for advanced String beans that actually implement the `StringBean` interface. The methods `initialize`, `doTest`, `endCycle`, and `beginCycle` are called by Grinder as well as `getGamsAlias` and `getEmailAddress`. The `initialize` method is passed a `PluginThreadContext`. From this object, we can find out what our process and thread numbers are and use them to generate unique aliases and email addresses. We create a class called `RegisteringUserStringBean` that implements the `StringBean` interface as shown in Listing 25.12.

25

LISTING 25.12 RegisteringUserStringBean.java File

```
package com.gams.performance;

import net.grinder.plugin.http.StringBean;
import net.grinder.plugininterface.PluginThreadContext;
import net.grinder.common.Test;

public class RegisteringUserStringBean implements StringBean {
 private PluginThreadContext context;
 private String processIDString;
 private int count = 0;

 public void initialize(PluginThreadContext context) {
 this.context = context;
 String idString = context.getGrinderID();
 int split = idString.lastIndexOf("-");
 processIDString = idString.substring(split+1);
 }

 // return alias based on value of count
 public String getGamsAlias() {
 count++;
 return "sampleuser" + processIDString + "A" +
   context.getThreadID() + "A" + count;
 }

 // return email based on value of count
 public String getEmailAddress() {
 count++;
 return processIDString + "A" + context.getThreadID() +
   "A" + count + "@abc.com";
 }

 public boolean doTest(Test test) { return false; }
 public void endCycle() { }
 public void beginCycle() { }
}
```

First we executed `registeringuser.properties` with 10 simultaneous users for 30 samples (30 seconds) and ignored the first 5 samples. This created 358 new users with a mean time of 979ms. Then we erased these test users from WebLogic Server security and from the CUSTOMER table in the database. We created a class called `com.gams.util`.

RemoveTestUsers to do just that. We then executed with 50 simultaneous users and got a mean time of 2790ms with throughput of 17.8 TPS. Because this type of user represented a small percentage of the total users, we were happy with this performance. Also, at this performance level, we can potentially register almost 18 new customers a second. This equates to over 1.5 million new customers a day.

Simulating Sellers

To simulate sellers, we created three data files: login.dat, listitem1.dat, and listitem2.dat. These files were created by TCPSniffer and then modified by us. These files are used with seller.properties as shown in Listing 25.13. The file login.dat will hold the username and the password of one of our pre-registered customers. We post this file to j_security_check to use J2EE Web application security. Then we call ListItemServlet twice: once with listitem1.data and once with listitem2.data. Then we call logout.jsp. listitem2.data includes 19KB of picture information.

LISTING 25.13 seller.properties File

```
grinder.processes=1
grinder.threads=1
grinder.cycles=1

grinder.jvm.arguments=-Xint

grinder.receiveConsoleSignals=true
grinder.reportToConsole=true
grinder.logDirectory=c:\\grinderlogs

grinder.plugin=net.grinder.plugin.http.HttpPlugin
grinder.plugin.parameter.useCookies=true

grinder.test300.parameter.url=http://localhost:7001/j_security_check
grinder.test300.description=Login
grinder.test300.parameter.post=login.dat

grinder.test301.parameter.url=http://localhost:7001/ListItemServlet
grinder.test301.description=ListItem1
grinder.test301.parameter.header.Content-Type=multipart/form-data;
➥boundary=---------------------------7d2d1165296
grinder.test301.parameter.post=listitem1.dat
grinder.test301.parameter.ok=listed

grinder.test302.parameter.url=http://localhost:7001/ListItemServlet
grinder.test302.description=ListItem2
```

25

LISTING 25.13 Continued

```
grinder.test302.parameter.header.Content-Type=multipart/form-data;
➥boundary=---------------------------7d2d1180122
grinder.test302.parameter.post=listitem2.dat
grinder.test302.parameter.ok=listed

grinder.test303.parameter.url=http://localhost:7001/logout.jsp
grinder.test303.description=Logout
```

Executing `seller.properties` with 10 and 100 users for 30 samples and ignoring the first 5 samples elicits the mean times shown in Table 25.11. These times are well within our performance requirements.

TABLE 25.11 Mean Times for seller.properties

Description	10 Users	100 Users
Login	222	1960
ListItem1	339	2500
ListItem2	639	4890
Logout	124	2530
Total	328 (Avg)	3000 (Avg)
Total TPS	26.1	29.6

Buyers

As shown in Listing 25.14, we use a similar approach to simulating buyers as we used when simulating sellers. The login and logout process is the same. In this case, we call `PlaceBidServlet` posting the contents of `placebid1.dat`. This file was created by TCPSniffer.

LISTING 25.14 buyer.properties File

```
grinder.test401.parameter.url=http://localhost:7001/j_security_check
grinder.test401.description=j_security_check
grinder.test401.parameter.header.Content-Type=application/x-www-form-urlencoded
grinder.test401.parameter.post=login.dat
grinder.test401.description=Login

grinder.test402.parameter.url=http://localhost:7001/PlaceBidServlet
grinder.test402.parameter.header.Content-Type=application/x-www-form-urlencoded
grinder.test402.parameter.post=placebid1.dat
grinder.test402.description=Place Bid

grinder.test403.parameter.url=http://localhost:7001/logout.jsp
grinder.test403.description=Logout
```

Executing buyers.properties with 10 and 100 users for 30 samples and ignoring the first 5 samples elicits the mean times shown in Table 25.12. These times are well within our performance requirements.

TABLE 25.12 Mean Times for buyer.properties

Description	10 Users	100 Users
Login	218	1480
Place Bid	196	1130
Logout	27.4	1100
Total	147 (Avg)	1240 (Avg)
Total TPS	57.8	73.0

GAMS Accounting Fee Report

At any point in time, a member of the GAMS accounting department may log in and run the Display Fee Report. This report lists the 50 most recent selling and listing fees charged by GAMS. To simulate these users, we created the test script shown in Listing 25.15. We post the file acctlogin.dat to j_security_check. This file contains the username and password of the GAMS accounting person.

LISTING 25.15 accounting.properties File

```
grinder.test500.sleepTime=1000
grinder.test500.parameter.url=http://localhost:7001/j_security_check
grinder.test500.description=AccountingLogin
grinder.test500.parameter.post=acctlogin.dat

grinder.test501.sleepTime=1000
grinder.test501.parameter.url=http://localhost:7001/accounting/displayFeeReport.jsp
grinder.test501.description=DisplayFeeReport
grinder.test501.parameter.ok=Display

grinder.test502.sleepTime=1000
grinder.test502.parameter.url=http://localhost:7001/logout.jsp
grinder.test502.description=AccountingLogout
```

Running accounting.properties with 10 and 100 users for 30 samples and ignoring the first 5 samples produces the mean times shown in Table 25.13. because there would be only one accounting person on GAMS at a time, this was an academic exercise.

TABLE 25.13 Mean times for accounting.properties

Description	10 Users	100 Users
Accounting Login	220	3980
Display Fee Report	9650	15400
Accounting Logout	11	Did not run
Total	2510 (Avg)	5560 (Avg)
Total TPS	2.8	2.76

Running All Tests Together

Finally, we need to run all of these test scripts at the same time to simulate all user types accessing simultaneously. If we want to simulate 100 users and we use our initial user type percentages, we should create 75 guests, 5 registering users, 10 sellers, and 10 buyers. With 100 users, we are well within the Maximum Acceptable Response Rates (MART) we discussed earlier, as shown in Table 25.14. With 200 users, most of the tests are within the MART, except for `header.jsp` and Display Item, which does not get called.

TABLE 25.14 Mean Times for All Scripts

Description	100 Users	200 Users
header.jsp	445	7480
menu.jsp	491	248
Featured Search	1210	2960
Category Search	640	1650
Display Item	145	756
Keyword Search	627	561
Display Item	302	?
Register User	821	1010
Login	420	1760
ListItem1	487	1010
ListItem2	1520	1580
Logout	434	604
Login	881	1110
Place Bid	340	511
Logout	175	381
Accounting Login	1260	2460
Display Fee Report	860	1080
Accounting Logout	356	383
Total	602 (Avg)	1780 (Avg)
Total TPS	40.2	43.6

Best Practices

After thoroughly covering the more rigorous aspects of performance testing and tuning with WebLogic, it is time to look at some best practices, or rules of thumb, to keep in mind as you design and develop applications.

General Considerations

In general, make sure that you have the most recent versions of software and service packs for all parts of the system: database, JVM, OS, drivers, and so on. Sometimes software updates contain bug fixes that improve performance, or contain new optimizations (Not to mention fixes for security.) Also remember that, from the onset, high-level architecture design should always be mindful of performance. Changes to this level late in the development cycle often are not feasible. Low-level optimizations, on the other hand, should be reserved until later in the cycle—preferably until the last minute. Optimization at this level earlier in the cycle is less than fruitful because 80% of the execution time of an application is often consumed by 20% of its software.

Plan for Performance Testing

The idea behind testing is to execute your application in a setting that closely simulates the actual environment it will be running in. This means

- Reproduce the production application environment—This includes hardware and external resources such as your database environment.
- Attempt to accurately simulate actual user behavior—This includes determining the types of users that will be accessing the application and how they will use it.
- Attempt to accurately simulate the number of actual users—This includes determining the maximum number of users per user type that will simultaneously be accessing the application.
- Stress testing—Monitor application behavior as dependent resources such as database connections and memory are denied.

JRockit 8.1 Memory Management

On startup, the JRockit JVM is configurable, enabling you to mange memory allocations more effectively. Here are a number of parameters that you should pay special attention to:

- `-Xmx` is the maximum heap size for the JVM. You will want to set this to the largest size possible. Doing so will reduce the amount of memory allocations required during times of high CPU usage. The chosen amount should be something less than the total amount of memory available on the machine. (The default value is 75% of available memory.) Be sure to consider the memory requirements of any additional applications running on the machine, however. The downside of specifying too large a heap size is that you may inadvertently cause excessive page faults, which can lead to a potential thrashing condition on the system. When an operating system runs low on memory, it must momentarily page any information it does not have room for to disk. When the paged information becomes needed, a page fault occurs and a read to disk is required to retrieve the missing information. Thrashing typically occurs when the operating system winds up spending an inordinate amount of time servicing page faults, and not enough time doing meaningful work. This will dramatically degrade the performance of your application.

- `-Xms` is the initial heap size. Set this to the same size as the maximum heap size.
- `-Xns` sets the size of the young generation (nursery). Set this higher if your application makes use of a large number of temporary objects.

EJB Tuning

The overhead associated with the creation and destruction of beans is expensive. To help alleviate this cost, WebLogic maintains a pool of pre-allocated beans to be served up to clients. There are a number of parameters that can be specified during the deployment process, which can have beneficial effects on performance. Practicing good design techniques will enhance performance as well.

EJB Pool Size

By default, WebLogic sets the maximum number of EJBs available in the free pool to an unlimited amount. The number of instances created is restricted only by the amount of memory you have allocated in the JVM settings we spoke of earlier. This should work fine for most applications and should not be changed. What you are seeking here is an optimal use of memory. If the number is lowered, it might result in increased object creation; if set higher more memory will be used.

Initial Beans in Free Pool

By default, WebLogic will not allocate any beans in the free pool at startup. It is a good practice to initialize some beans so that initial response times are not hindered by bean creation. You should set this number to the anticipated number of clients initially accessing the system under load.

Cache EJBHome Object References

When a client wants to access an EJB, it must first get an EJB `Home` object reference via the JNDI tree. It is good practice to create a cache of EJBHome objects that can be reused so as to alleviate the redundant process of JNDI lookups.

Release Resources

Just before a bean is removed from the pool, the EJB container will call the `ejbRemove()` method. Be sure to make use of this opportunity to release any resources that might have an effect on performance. For example, you might have acquired a `Home` object reference to another Session or Entity bean or a data source reference.

Session Façade

Network overhead is incurred every time you remotely access an Entity bean. Wrapping Entity beans within a Session bean reduces the number of network calls required by a client. For example, if a client wanted to access an online account, they might need to retrieve an `AccountEntityBean`, `AddressEntityBean`, `BillingHistoryEntityBean`, and so on. Each bean access requires its own network call. If you were to wrap these calls in an `AccountManager` Session bean, which in turn was responsible for processing the calls to the required Entity beans on the client's behalf, the transaction could be handled in one call. The Session bean will access the Entity beans locally, thus eliminating the remote calls and improving performance.

General Java Coding Tips

Given that WebLogic Server applications are written in Java, they can take full advantage of best coding practices as found in the language. Some specific examples of the kinds of optimization that can be gained by effective coding techniques are discussed in the following sections.

Recycle Java Objects

If you are constantly creating and discarding Java objects, you might get performance gains by creating an object factory that hands out instances of objects. When the instances are no longer needed, they are returned to the factory that can then issue them to another client. Although there is some overhead to maintaining the factory, the reduction in object creation can still improve performance. Use a Java profiler to spot frequent object creation in your code and use object factories where appropriate.

Cache Reusable Things

While your applications are executing, they will create things that can be reused later. This could be strings, database information, RMI method call results, and so on. Cache this information—you avoid the repeated overhead of having to re-create it each time. If you are running out of memory to store this information, go buy more memory. It is very cheap these days!

Use the Correct Java Collection

The Java Collections Framework includes many data structures that meet the requirements of many data scenarios. It is important to not only use the right Collection interface that gives you correct results, but also to use the one that gives you the best performance. Before choosing to use a collection, make sure that you understand the performance implications of choosing it. For example, a `TreeMap` enables you to iterate through a set in an ordered manner, whereas a `HashMap` allows for quicker key lookups.

TIP

You can find additional Java coding tips at `http://www.javaperformancetuning.com/tips/rawtips.shtml`. This page contains thousands of optimization tips for Java.

Summary

This chapter focused on optimization of WebLogic applications. Performance is an issue that should be dealt with at the design, implementation, and deployment phases. Developers should not wait until months have been spent coding to decide that the performance of their code should be tested. There are open source performance tools that even those on the tightest budgets can afford.

Before you attempt to load-balance and optimize your completed applications, make sure that everyone involved with the application—including business development, sales, customer service, and so on—is using the same metrics to quantify performance (for example, average response time) and that they all agree on the same quantities of acceptable performance (for example, MART should be 3 seconds or less).

When this has occurred, a performance and tuning strategy needs to be worked out before any load testing or tuning occurs. If you don't have the whole picture worked out beforehand, chances are that you will be repeating load tests and tuning sessions unnecessarily.

After a strategy has been decided upon, play with the application to get a sense of how it responds and where it might have performance issues. Then create some load-balancing tests that simulate actual users. Benchmark the application with these tests and use the tools that are at your disposal to correct performance problems that show themselves.

PART VII

WebLogic Server Security

IN THIS PART

CHAPTER 26

Web Applications and Security

By Steve Steffen and Jeff Marin

IN THIS CHAPTER

- Overview of Security Issues for Web Applications
- Trends That Are Affecting Security
- Areas of Vulnerability
- Attacks
- Technologies to Address Security Risks
- Best Practices to Address Security Risks

Every day, computers around the world are hacked into and used for malicious purposes. Living in a media-driven society, we expect to hear reports of these incidents on the news and read about them in newspapers. However, these events are rarely reported due to embarrassment and damage to the reputation of the company or government agency that these computers are under the control of. Therefore, it's up to us in the software development food chain to proactively research and stay current on trends in security and security break-ins.

In addition to risks involved with closed systems, Web applications running on a private intranet or the public Internet are dependent on the underlying security of the hardware and software they're executing on. This chapter discusses the security risks that our Web application–dependent hardware and software are exposed to. It discusses current trends in security, such as the proliferation of viruses and the difficulties in securing complex IT infrastructures and applications. The chapter finishes with a list of practical ways to prevent your Web applications and their dependent hardware and software from being subverted from their intended usage.

Overview of Security Issues for Web Applications

Whether you plan on providing e-commerce or just enabling your employees, providing access to services through the Internet offers many competitive advantages over alternative methods. The lower costs of performing transactions, coupled with the opportunity of customizing the user interface depending on customer preferences and buying habits, are too great for businesses to ignore.

However, by exposing internal applications to the Internet, businesses are taking on many risks not normally associated with standalone applications. Companies not familiar with these risks will introduce security late into their development cycle, if at all. According to the CERT Coordination Center (`http://www.cert.org`), a center of Internet security expertise, the number of security incidents and vulnerabilities is not only rising every year, it's going up exponentially. If you're conducting or plan to conduct business over the Internet, these statistics should alarm you and prompt you to have an overall security policy in place as soon as possible.

The simplicity of the Internet is both a curse and a blessing. It allows customers around the world to connect to a Web site by simply typing a URL in their browser. They don't have to worry about how their requests get to us. The Internet infrastructure routes traffic to its intended destination using standard protocols such as HTTP. All our customers need to do is have a connection to the Internet and an Internet browser. However, this also gives access to our Web site to people who aren't interested in using our services or buying from us. That is, with an Internet connection, people all over the world can attempt to break into our Web site using standard Internet protocols. It's this openness of the Internet that makes it both easy to use and easy to exploit.

Additionally, it's prudent either to have full-time security personnel on your staff or bring in the resources of an outside firm to perform a security evaluation and make recommendations. Securing corporate data should be the first priority of any software development endeavor because the costs of ill-gotten access are prohibitively large. In many cases, the value of corporate data is a large percentage of the total value of a business.

Security and accessibility tend to be opposite goals at first. The most secure data resides on a machine in a protected location, with no access by anybody and without any connection to the Internet or any other networks. In this situation, there's no accessibility by users—legitimate or otherwise. The idea behind setting a security policy is to keep data secure from people who have no right to view and/or alter it without making access from legitimate users prohibitively difficult or time-consuming. Keeping data both secure and accessible is no easy matter considering that tools for hacking are easily available on the Internet and new viruses are constantly being created.

This section introduces you to some of the ways that crackers can affect normal Internet business flow. After examining exposure to risk, we offer solutions to reduce the opportunities for crackers to change the way you do business on the Internet. This section isn't meant to be a primer on securing your infrastructure, but it raises points that should be researched and implemented when extending your IT landscape toward the Internet.

Trends That Are Affecting Security

Over the past decade, the computer software and the IT community at large have experienced patterns in events that threaten the security of computers worldwide. This section discusses some of these trends; later sections talk about how to deal with these threats.

The Power of Crackers

In addition to legitimate Web application users, there are those who either casually or regularly attempt to illegally access computers and their data using a variety of methods. For the purposes of this discussion, we'll refer to these people as *crackers*. This chapter discusses how the numbers of crackers have grown and how their tools have become much more powerful. Combine this with a proliferation of viruses and the complexity of securing Web applications, and you can see why computer security experts have become very concerned about the state of security on the Internet and overall.

Years ago, crackers were considered highly skilled people who understood the internal structure of hardware platforms, operating systems, and applications. With this knowledge, they were able to uncover weaknesses in design and exploit them. They were able to share these ideas by congregating regionally. As the use of LANs and WANs became more popular, crackers were able to unleash their viruses and their counterpart worms on their unsuspecting victims.

Turning the clock ahead to present times shows that their efforts have substantially increased. First, just like every other special interest group, crackers are using the Internet itself to publish weaknesses in operating systems and computer applications. Although there are mail lists to let system administrators know about these weaknesses, crackers generally subscribe to them as well and may therefore know about them before or at the same time that legitimate users are informed. Second, crackers are now building tools for novice crackers to use. In doing so, they're increasing the legions of people who have the capability to disrupt and sabotage companies' IT investments.

Crackers now have tools that enable them to find vulnerable victims on the Internet and attack those victims after they're found. These tools have the capability to work with each other to attack hosts in combination as well. Stopping the use of these tools has been a cat-and-mouse game. As detection software is created, cracker tools become more automated and sophisticated, and can figure out ways to attack hosts without being stopped and without being detected. These tools have become smarter and can alter their behavior either randomly or based on certain circumstances.

The Sophistication of Today's Systems

The number of different software packages, operating systems, and hardware platforms that are running within a company's infrastructure continues to increase each year. With each new component come security risks. Many software manufacturers have spent most of their efforts in providing new and better functionality with security being put on the back burner.

Software packages such as database servers, application servers, and email servers are all written by people and, subsequently, are prone to application bugs and security oversights. Although it's common practice for software vendors to release patches for their products when these bugs are discovered, it might be too late for a system that's already been compromised. Also, due to the fact that a company is supporting so many different software packages and hardware platforms, system administrators might not have the time or the insight to apply patches when they're initially released. As crackers increasingly find more security vulnerabilities, more patches are released, and the possibility of a system administrator overlooking one goes up.

Companies looking to reduce their risk tend to purchase software that has been in use for some time and whose stability has been tested. Many times, companies purchase software that has widespread use such as the Apache Web server or Microsoft's Internet Information Server. As the popularity of these applications grows, they unfortunately become a very lucrative target for people to break into because by doing so many computer systems can be compromised.

The Proliferation of Viruses

Although there seems to be no universal definition of a computer virus, in general, a virus is executable code that, when run, produces a side effect unbeknownst to the person running the code. Sometimes this behavior does not cause any damage to the system running it, whereas other times the effects can be devastating.

New viruses are coming out on a daily basis. Due to the availability of information available on the Internet, system vulnerabilities are widely published and tools for creating viruses are easily obtained—there seems to be no end to this trend.

Viruses attack vulnerabilities in operating systems and software applications. Many viruses have exploited the macro languages that accompany applications such as Microsoft Word and Excel. The power of these languages makes them an easy target for crackers. By adding a self-running macro to a Word or Excel document, a cracker can cause great harm on a system. Thankfully, those applications can be configured to disallow self-running macros to execute.

Most viruses share some or all of the characteristics described in the following sections.

Reproduce Themselves

Some viruses have a means of reproducing themselves by attaching themselves to other files on a machine. Those files are then infected with the same virus and continue to reproduce themselves. Some viruses attempt to reproduce by emailing themselves either to one email address at a time or to everyone contained in an email address book. However, viruses that use this method must be opened and executed by the person reading the email. To ensure the probability of this occurrence, viruses in many cases disguise themselves as legitimate files (such as Microsoft Word documents) that have self-running code, which executes when the document is viewed.

Cause System Damage

These viruses intentionally cause damage to the systems they run on. Examples of this include deleting or altering files, collecting and distributing confidential information, degrading performance, and changing the security settings on the machine itself.

Communicate with Virus Creator

These viruses don't cause any system damage and their existence is therefore kept secret. Their intent is to quietly communicate with the virus creator, who can then use these viruses to perform other tasks such as view confidential information and perform attacks on other machines.

Disable Security Settings

These viruses usually install themselves on a host computer and then listen for incoming connections on specific ports. A cracker can contact the virus on these ports and direct it to perform some malicious activity.

Payload and Trigger

The *payload* is the destructive action that a virus performs and the *trigger* is an event that must occur before the virus delivers the payload. Triggers can be based on a date or system activity.

Virus Hoax

This isn't a virus but merely a rumor about a fictional virus. The intent of the rumor is to cause general panic. The best way to confirm the presence of a new virus is by contacting an authority on the subject such as Symantec or McAfee, both makers of antivirus software.

Trojan Horse

This is an application that claims to be something else and is used to unsuspectingly collect sensitive information. An example could be an electronic postcard that someone emails you. When this code is run, the postcard is displayed as expected. However, this code is also collecting confidential information from your system and sending it to a cracker.

Worm

This is a virus that puts a priority on reproducing itself to other machines. The worm's author can achieve this by having the worm perform a mass emailing of itself to everyone in an address book. It then creates a situation that fools the email recipients into running the worm. An example of this was the Anna Kournikova virus. A recipient received an email from someone he knew with a subject line of `Hi: Check This Out`. The email had an attachment named `AnnaKournikova.jpg.vbs`. At first glance, this would look like an innocent JPG file and because the email was from someone the recipient knew, most people just double-clicked on the attachment to view it. However, they ended up executing the virus on their machine, and the virus then emailed itself to everyone in their address book.

The Power of Worms

Like a virus, a worm is code that can either be malignant (such as reformatting a hard drive) or passive (such as changing icons on a PC desktop). In both cases, worms have the additional attribute of self-propagating. An example of this is emailing themselves to everyone in your address book or everyone on your instant messaging buddy list. Because of this, worms can infect a large number of systems in a short amount of time. The Code Red worm was able to infect more than 250,000 systems in only 9 hours. Moreover, worms can be used as denial of service tools.

Other Cracker Techniques

In addition to viruses mentioned earlier, crackers employ numerous techniques to illegally access networks and computers and the information they contain. This includes getting login information either by stealing it, guessing it, or using password-cracking software. Crackers take advantage of bugs in software and operating systems and exploit them to get access and security rights to information that they shouldn't have.

Areas of Vulnerability

Web applications require an infrastructure to run on including a connection to the Internet—this includes both hardware and software. An example of this is shown in Figure 26.1. To get to a Web application, an end user points a browser at your Web site by typing in a domain name such as `www.sams.com`. A DNS server converts this domain into an IP address and forwards the end user's request to this IP address. The request has to pass through a varying number of routers depending on how direct a route exists between the end user's machine and your Web site. After going through a number of routers, the request arrives at your Web server. However, rather than letting the Web server be connected directly to the public Internet, a firewall is used to limit the types of requests that can pass into the Web server. Machines on the other side of this firewall are said to be in the DMZ or demilitarized zone—an area in the infrastructure that has been made more secure through the use of the firewall.

Each of these components must be secure in order for the Web application to run as intended. This section discusses some of the vulnerable points in this infrastructure and how they can be attacked.

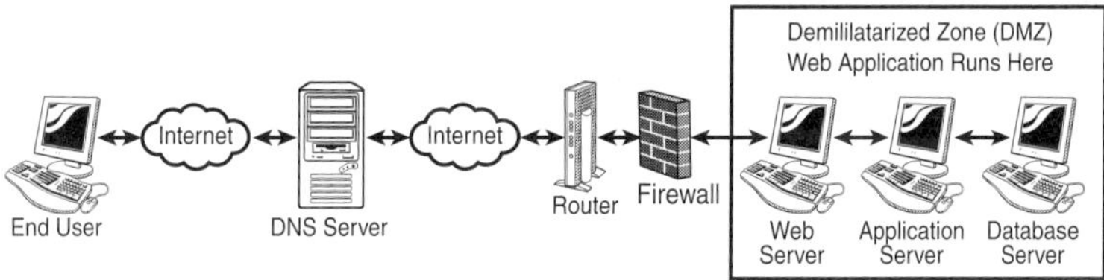

Figure 26.1 A sample IT infrastructure connected to the Internet.

DNS Servers

Domain Name Service (DNS) is the distributed, hierarchical, global directory on the Internet that translates a name (for example, `www.sams.com`) to an IP address (for example, `165.193.123.117`). If this ISP directory structure is tampered with, traffic meant for a Web site can be directed to a Web site under control of a cracker. Also, if a large-scale denial of service attack is launched on multiple DNS servers high in the hierarchy, whole top-level domains (such as `.com` and `.edu`) could become inaccessible. DNS servers usually reside at a company's ISP and are not under their direct control. However, you should make sure that your ISP has DNS running on secure servers because if they're tampered with, there's a chance your Web traffic will be affected.

Routers

Routers direct traffic from network to network. They're essential to messages getting to their destinations. Routers are designed to communicate with each other for the purposes of delivering messages. They use routing tables to establish the best paths between routers. If a cracker can change these routing tables, he can redirect traffic away from its intended destination. This will make the destination host unavailable to clients. For all intents and purposes, this is the same as shutting down this host.

Most routers allow remote management. This enables network administrators to monitor and restart routers without having to be physically present. However, this also introduces the possibility of giving unauthorized personnel access. Remote access to routers should be monitored and restricted as well as possible. Routers also support many services such as Telnet and SNMP. If these services aren't needed, they should be turned off.

Hosts and Applications

Machines that run Web servers, application servers, databases, and other IT resources are vulnerable to attacks due to the almost infinite number of combinations of hardware platforms, operating systems, and software that they're composed of. Because of their public nature, Web servers must additionally have their IP address directly accessible from the Internet. This makes them a very popular target for crackers. To keep these hosts secure, system administrators must keep a look out for security warnings and subsequent patches from hardware, operating system, and software vendors.

Transactions in the Field

Transactions that are delivered over the Internet in plain text expose themselves to being intercepted and altered. To keep sensitive information private, encrypt it with an algorithm whose strength matches the sensitivity of the information it's protecting. The stronger the algorithm, the more overhead is introduced in encrypting and decrypting communication.

Attacks

When crackers attempt to break into or disable systems, their behavior can be categorized as a certain type of attack. This section discusses different ways that a network (such as the Internet) can be used to attack systems, attacks that can come from inside your infrastructure, and how crackers can divert your legitimate Internet traffic.

Network Attacks

Denial of Service (DoS) attacks drain a Web host of a scarce resource. This could be a resource such as open TCP connections or the amount of memory allocated to receiving client requests. After this resource has been overly used, it isn't available to service real client requests.

Buffer overflows occur when a network address receives more data than the program supporting that address can hold.

Programs that service network addresses (Web servers, FTP servers, email servers, and so forth) have been written to work with multiple diverse clients simultaneously. These programs need to store information in memory in data buffers. When these data buffers are full, they can no longer service client requests. By filling these buffers with bogus client requests, crackers can deny access to legitimate users.

In the SYN flood attack, a source host starts a TCP conversation using an invalid IP address. The destination host sends out an ACK to that IP address and cannot start the conversation until it receives a reply. The destination keeps an entry of this soon-to-be-started conversation in a connection queue. Because the IP address isn't valid, the reply never comes and the conversation stays in the connection queue for a certain period of time. If many requests to start TCP connections to invalid IP addresses occur in a short period of time, the connection queue will be full. When this occurs, other services based on TCP, such as email, FTP, and serving of Web pages, will be denied to genuine users.

The Internet Protocol (IP) requires that packets that are too large for a router to handle must be split into multiple smaller packets. These packets are then reassembled at a destination host using packet-offset values that indicate how reassembly should occur. In a teardrop attack, the attacker changes the offset values in these packets and confuses the destination host. This in itself would only mean that the packet wasn't sent correctly.

However, in some cases, if the destination host hasn't been configured to handle this situation, the change causes the machine to crash.

Spoofing is the process of forging someone else's Internet identity or IP address. For instance, when a cracker can spoof an email server, he can then send thousands of email messages that appear to be coming from that server. In a Smurf attack, an IP address is spoofed and then used as the reply address in an ICMP echo call (ping). If enough of these pings occur simultaneously, the innocent spoofed program running at this IP address will be overwhelmed with traffic and cannot effectively handle any real client requests.

There are many other popular attacks such as the fraggle attack, mail-bomb attack, ping of death, trinoo attack, tribe flood network, stacheldraht, and ICMP ping flood. Be sure that your hardware/software solution and/or your ISPs have taken the necessary steps to thwart the efforts of those attempting to bring down your Internet presence using attacks such as these. As we'll see in later chapters, WebLogic Server has such configurable settings to protect against some of these attacks.

Distributed Network Attacks

Perhaps one of the most frightening attacks and the one hardest to fight is the Distributed Denial of Service (DDoS) attack. In this type pf attack, an attacker has employed the use of many unsuspecting, innocent systems to send traffic to a host. As Figure 26.2 points out, these multiple sites overwhelm the target Web host and just as in a standard DoS attack, cut off its capability to serve legitimate clients.

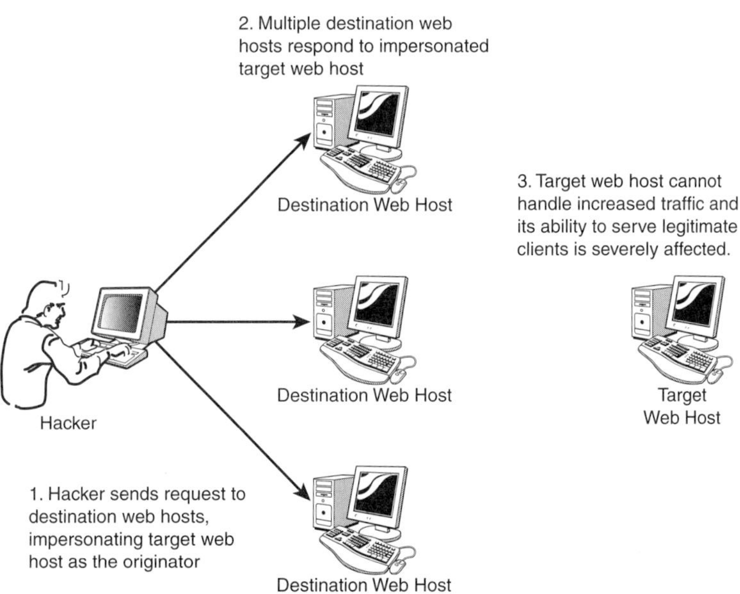

Figure 26.2 A cracker can impersonate Web hosts and get them to unsuspectingly perform a distributed denial of service attack.

Enterprise Attacks

If an attacker chooses, he can try to get into your system by getting you to run a virus program or a worm. These can be delivered as email attachments or downloaded from Web sites. Once run, these viruses can do many things. Some email out sensitive files, whereas others just display a message from the cracker who created the virus. Some viruses will attempt to collect sensitive information such as usernames and passwords. A cracker can then communicate with the virus at a later date and collect this information.

Packet Sniffers

A *packet sniffer* is a piece of software that communicates with a network interface card and asks it for all packets of information it receives. Sniffers have a rightful place in the toolkit of network administrators, but in the hands of a cracker, they can be used to view sensitive information such as usernames and passwords, especially when information isn't encrypted. To protect against these types of attacks, companies can use antisniffer tools. These tools can detect whether a packet sniffer is being used. After it's detected, a packet sniffer can be found and disabled.

Man-in-the-Middle Attacks

This type of attack redirects Internet traffic and enables a cracker to eavesdrop on a conversation, as depicted in Figure 26.3. The cracker can then use this information for personal gain. For instance, when Joe wants to connect to his online bank, `www.mybank.com`, he types the URL in his browser. A cracker routes this request to another IP address by corrupting a DNS server (as discussed earlier) or by corrupting the host table on Joe's PC. The host table will contain an entry for `www.mybank.com` with the IP address of the cracker's host. This host table can be corrupted by getting Joe to run an EXE file on his PC.

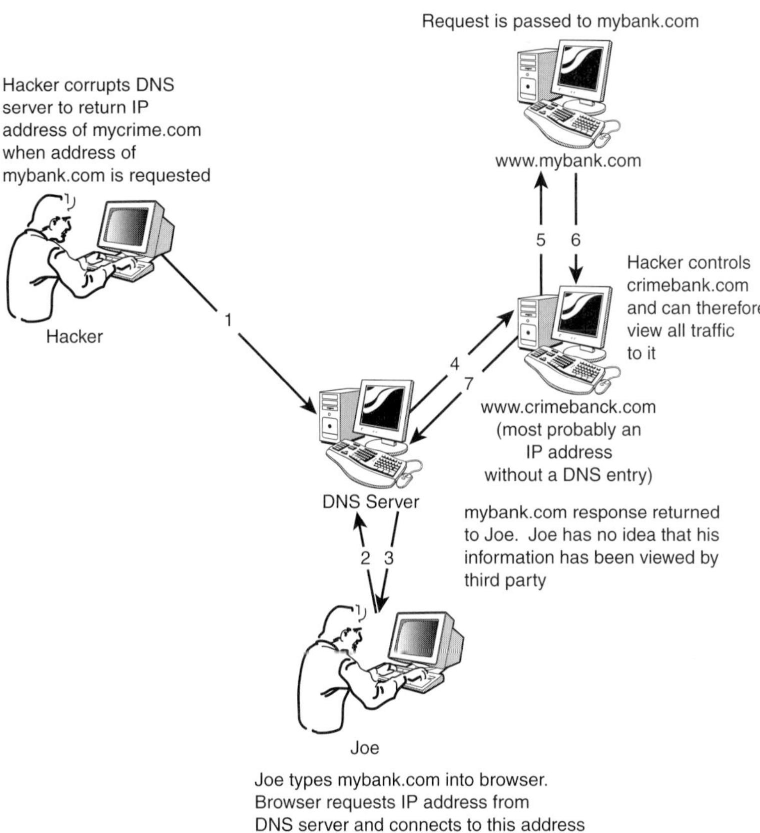
Request is passed to mybank.com
Hacker corrupts DNS server to return IP address of mycrime.com when address of mybank.com is requested
www.mybank.com
5
6
Hacker controls crimebank.com and can therefore view all traffic to it
1
Hacker
4
7
www.crimebanck.com (most probably an IP address without a DNS entry)
DNS Server
mybank.com response returned to Joe. Joe has no idea that his information has been viewed by third party
2
3
Joe
Joe types mybank.com into browser. Browser requests IP address from DNS server and connects to this address

Figure 26.3 A cracker can redirect traffic to his IP address and then view information being sent to the original address.

Technologies to Address Security Risks

Although there are many ways of breaking into computer infrastructures, numerous technologies can be employed to reduce the security risks. This section discusses some of them, and the next section discusses best practices.

Encryption

By its nature, TCP is not a secure protocol. In TCP, all information is delivered in clear text. Therefore, if someone can intercept TCP packets, she'll be able to read the information contained in them. When this information is public in nature, for example, catalog information at a department store, this is perfectly okay. However, to securely transmit private, sensitive information on the very public Internet, this information must be encrypted.

Encrypting information involves putting the original information through an algorithm that converts it to an unreadable format. An encryption key is used to determine how the algorithm will exactly encrypt the data. This enables many organizations to use the same algorithms in their own unique ways. This is just like having two homeowners who use the same lock manufacturer, but each has a unique key to open the lock.

After the information has been encrypted, it can be sent to its recipients. For the recipients to read the information, they must apply a decryption algorithm using a decryption key. Of course, the information sender must be very careful about who has this decryption key. If it falls into the wrong hands, people who should not be able to read data will be able to.

There are two standard ways of encrypting and decrypting. When the number of recipients is small and well known, symmetric cryptography can be used. In this case, the same key is used to encrypt and decrypt messages. Both the sender and receivers of messages must possess this key and the sender distributes it in a secure manner.

When the number of recipients is large or changes considerably over time, public key cryptography is the preferred method. One key is used to encrypt messages (a public key) and another is used to decrypt them (a private key). This is referred to as *asymmetric* encryption. Only intended recipients should possess the private key. When sending messages on a public network (for example, the Internet), someone might be able to see an encrypted message, either legitimately or not, but only those who possess the private key can decrypt it.

Although asymmetric encryption is very useful for the Internet, it turns out that the algorithms are more than a thousand times slower than symmetric cryptography. For this reason, many corporations use a combination of both methods to secure different types of information.

Encrypting information is one of the best ways to protect yourself against packet sniffers and man-in-the-middle attacks. Keeping decryption keys out of the hands of someone who could use them against you is equally important.

Encryption can be done in one of two places:

- A the application level using encryption software; for example, PGP (`www.pgp.com`)
- At the network level using encrypted communication protocols, for example, HTTPS

Authentication, Data Integrity, Nonrepudiation, and Digital Signatures

Signatures are used for identity authentication and digital signatures have the same purpose in cyberspace. Before sending out a message, the sender puts it through an algorithm that produces a hash value. Each message produces a unique hash value. This hash value is then encrypted with the sender's private key and attached to the original message. Because only the sender has this private key, receivers can be sure of the source of the message. This provides authentication just as a hand-written signature does.

The encrypted hash value serves as the message's digital signature. A message receiver decrypts the message using the sender's public key and puts it though the same hashing algorithm. If the hash value is the same as the original, the receiver can be sure that the message has not been altered in transit. This provides data integrity and nonrepudiation. Nonrepudiation is important in that it ensures that the sender of a message cannot claim that he isn't the originator of that message. For example, a bank account holder sends a transfer transaction using an encrypting message. He later attempts to dispute this transaction with the bank. The bank states that the message was encrypted with the account holder's private key and therefore he originated the transaction. Additionally, digital signatures are continuing to become a de facto standard on the Internet and the legal bindings associated with them are moving towards those associated with written signatures.

The information inside of a digital certificate includes the name and other personal information of the party for which the certificate was issued, the name of the CA that issued the certificate, the public key, and the start and end date of the certificate lifetime. Certificates are only valid for a period of time and CAs can revoke certificates.

Digital signatures are used in digital certificates. A *digital certificate* is a file that contains security information about one's identity, including your name and contact information, expiry date, a public key, and an encrypted digital signature (thumbprint) produced by a trusted organization. The latter is the proof that the certificate is valid and has not been altered. The key in a digital certificate can be used for encrypting messages and digital signatures. When both the client and the server use digital certificates, both parties get the benefit of authentication, data integrity, and nonrepudiation. An example of this is shown in Figure 26.4.

Certificate Authorities

Certificate authorities (CAs) are trusted entities that issue digital certificates and keep a copy of them in a very secure manner. CAs generally have strict security policy in place using mechanisms such as smart cards and biometrics (such as retina scans and fingerprinting) to track the whereabouts of their employees.

Individuals and corporations apply with certificate authorities to request digital certificates. The CAs verify applicant credentials to ensure that they are who they say they are and this involves checking public records for businesses. When the CA is certain of the applicant's credentials, it issues the digital certificate. This is sent to the applicant and a copy is placed in a public certificate directory. As depicted in Figure 26.5, Internet Explorer contains a certificate manager that stores certificate information including the CA that issued it.

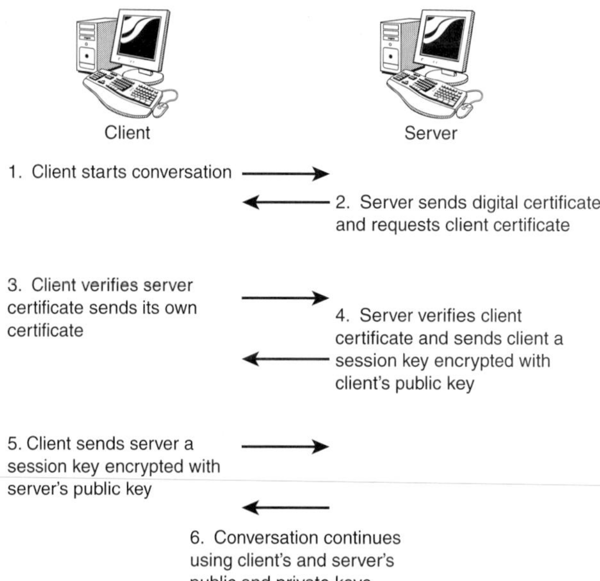

Figure 26.4 Both clients and servers can use digital certificates for mutual security benefits.

Secure Sockets Layer

SSL is a protocol that works with digital certificates to provide authentication for a Web server and optionally for a Web client. It also encrypts data sent so that only authorized parties can read it. Additionally, it ensures that messages sent are not altered in transit. SSL can work with TCP/IP-based protocols by using SSL tunneling. *SSL tunneling* means that SSL records are placed or tunneled within TCP/IP records. Hypertext Transfer Protocol with SSL (HTTPS) allows a Web browser and a Web server to communicate using SSL.

Public Key Infrastructure

When digital certificates and cryptography are used in combination to provide authentication, data integrity, and nonrepudiation, the resulting landscape is referred to as Public Key Infrastructure (PKI). Using PKI, businesses and individuals can confidently exchange information and enact business transactions over the public Internet and be confident that their messages provide authorization, and are private and unalterable.

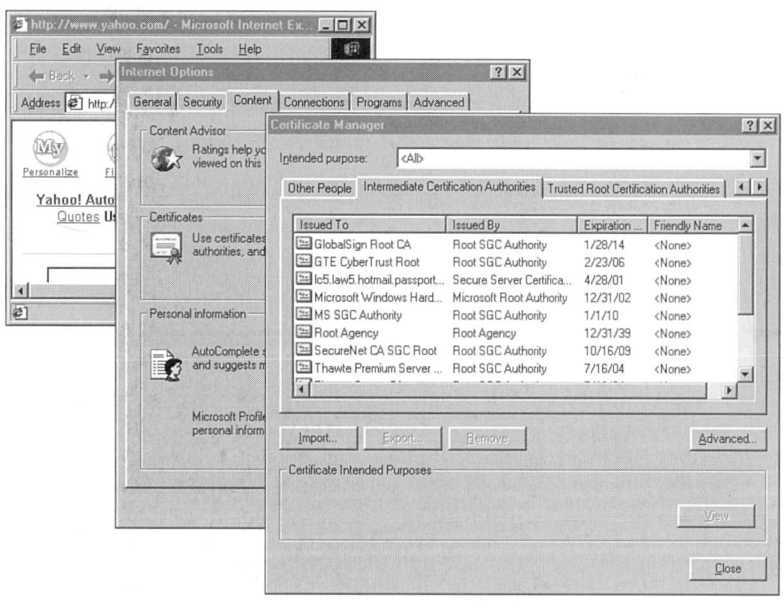

Figure 26.5 Internet Explorer includes a certificate manager that keeps track of CAs and client certificates.

Antivirus Software

Once installed on a machine, antivirus software scans that machine's files looking for viruses. This software can be run manually or can be set up to run on a regularly scheduled basis. Antivirus software keeps an internal database of what viruses look like and how to find them. For example, at the time of this writing, Symantec's Norton AntiVirus, a leading antivirus application for Windows, has database entries for more than 61,000 viruses! It's important to keep this internal database current. As shown in Figure 26.6, antivirus software can also keep track of the last time new virus definitions were loaded, when your machine was last scanned for viruses, and how many viruses have been found.

Antivirus software should be installed on each computer in your organization. The software also should be updated regularly as new viruses are detected. Thankfully, most antivirus software has a means of automating its updates. Once a cracker has a program running on your computer, he can use it for his own purposes. A virus can initiate communication back to the attacker to exchange information. Therefore, it's important to have personal firewall software running that will detect this communication, disallow it, and expose the virus that's running.

Virus hoaxes are created to cause computer users to panic. Fortunately, there are many places on the Internet to verify whether a virus is real or fictitious. Symantec and McAfee, both vendors of antivirus software, have created the following Web pages for this purpose:

`http://www.symantec.com/avcenter/hoax.html` and `http://vil.mcafee.com/hoax.asp`. The best way to avoid being duped by virus hoaxes is to keep your antivirus software and its virus definitions current.

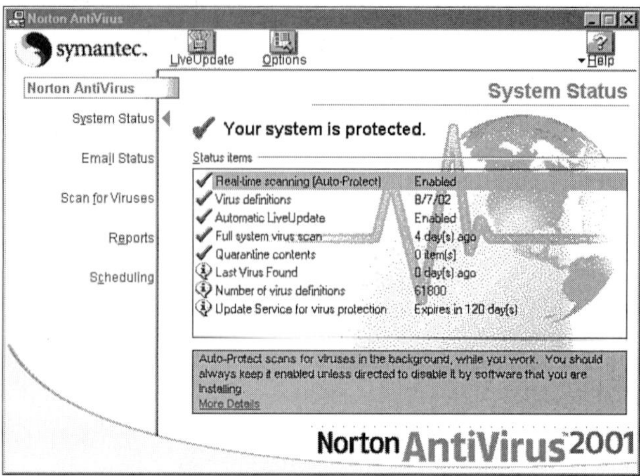

Figure 26.6 Antivirus software such as Norton AntiVirus keeps a database of virus definitions and scans for them in emails and on drives.

Personal Firewall Software

When a machine is connected to the Internet, it's fairly easy for software on that machine to communicate through the Internet. Sometimes this is intended, as in an Internet browser. The best way to monitor which applications are allowed to use the Internet is by installing personal firewall software. This software monitors all applications attempting to use the Internet and enables you to maintain strict control over what applications can access the Internet and what protocols they can use. An example of this is in Figure 26.7.

Firewalls

Firewalls are either hardware- or software-based and are used to restrict communications between two different areas of a network. They're typically placed between the public Internet and a company's private network. If used correctly, firewalls severely reduce the threat of being hacked. However, many protocols such as Firewall-Friendly FTP and SOAP are marketed as firewall friendly and are intended to go through firewalls undisturbed. If there are security issues with these protocols, an attacker will be able to exploit them without having to worry about getting past a firewall.

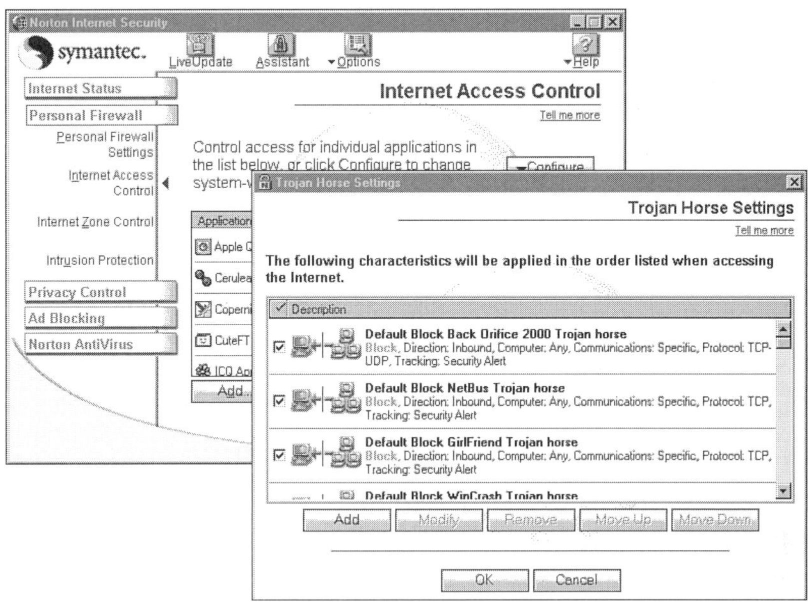

Figure 26.7 Personal firewall software such as Norton Internet Security permits only certain software to communicate with the Internet. It's especially useful in stopping Trojan horses.

Depending on the resources available, a corporation might want to add additional firewalls to gain increases in security. One such method is to put a stateful firewall between each tier in the infrastructure. Stateful firewalls keep track of client requests and can pair up requests and responses. This can help prevent rogue code running on the Web or application server from initiating a request. Each stateful firewall is configured to allow only incoming requests (or responses to incoming requests) on a specific protocol. The decision to use multiple firewalls is a balancing act of security versus performance versus cost. If the information in a database and/or the functionality of the application server is critical, you should consider placing these components behind multiple firewalls, as depicted in Figure 26.8. However, the extra firewalls can dramatically raise the cost of the system and decrease its performance.

Antisniffer Tools

As mentioned earlier, packet sniffers are a tool for eavesdropping on communications sent over computer networks. Because a packet sniffer simply makes copies of information without changing the original, it can be difficult to detect one running on your network. Ethernet networks work by broadcasting packets of information to every machine on a network. Each of these machines has a network interface card (NIC) listening for these packets. When a NIC sees a packet not intended for the IP address it's assigned to, it just ignores that packet. However, a packet sniffer consists of a network interface card listening for messages that aren't intended for it. This is also referred to as operating in promiscuous mode. Antisniffers are tools that can detect when network interface cards are operating in promiscuous mode.

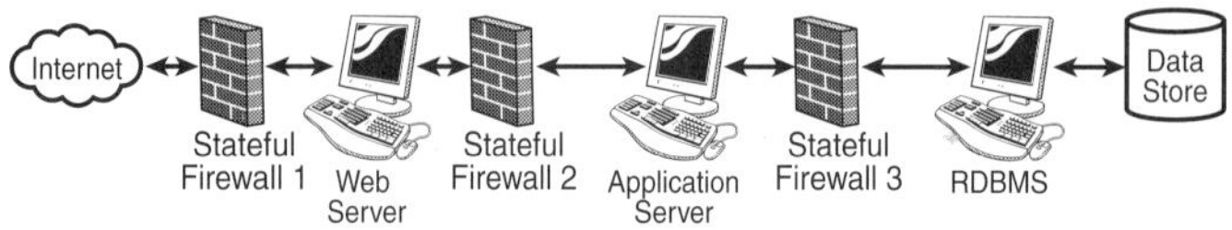

Figure 26.8 Stateful firewall 1 allows only incoming TCP requests (or responses to these requests) to reach the Web server. Firewalls 1 and 2 provide similar protection to the application server and the RDBMS.

Best Practices to Address Security Risks

Technologies by themselves have never solved any problems. People must know where, when, and how to use them in the context of solving their security needs. This section offers suggestions on how to minimize the security risks that your company faces when performing transactions on the Internet.

Have a Companywide Security Policy

This type of policy ensures that anyone with access to a workstation and/or server follows company guidelines. When people have an understanding of the implications of not following these guidelines, they're more likely to follow them. Examples of a security policy include always having antivirus software running, not executing applications sent through email, and always running personal firewall software.

A company's security policy should include how Internet browser security is configured. Internet browsers generally have many settings related to security. For example, as depicted in Figure 26.9, Internet Explorer allows certain URLs to be trusted and to allow a more lax security policy when a user visits those Web sites.

Of course, any policy that isn't followed will have no significant effects on the business processes of a company. Identified members of a company's IT department should assist users in following this policy and others should be given the authority to enforce that the policy is followed.

Keep Machines Physically Secure

It's important to keep the machines in your IT infrastructure physically secure. This obviously includes Web servers, database servers, and application servers, but it also includes desktop systems and laptops. If a cracker has physical access to a machine, it will be very easy for him to mess with it. This includes installing cracking software and disabling antivirus software.

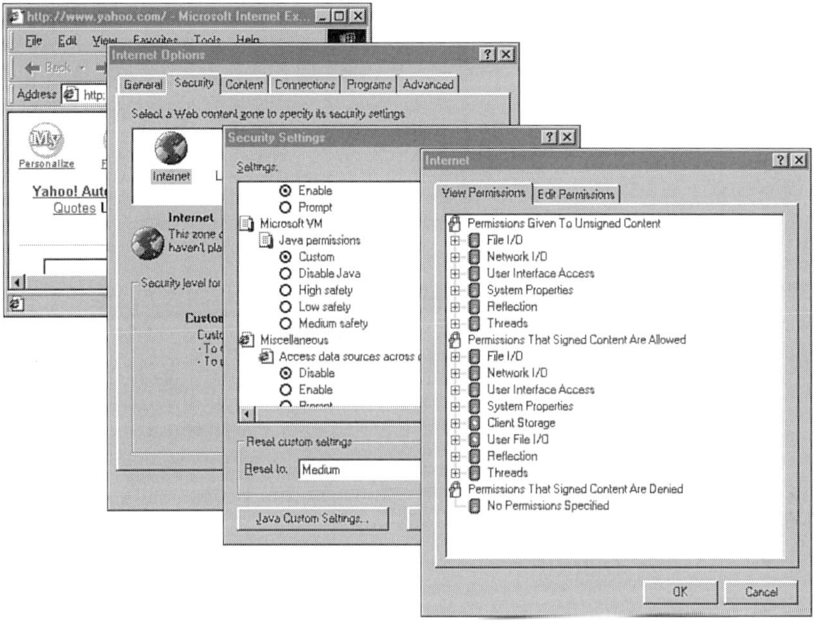

Figure 26.9 The security settings in Internet Explorer give an administrator much granularity to work with. Here we see how the security settings of the Java Virtual Machine within Internet Explorer can be configured.

Keep Up with Security Fixes

As mentioned earlier, signing up with a security update newsletter ensures that you have access to the latest security exploits and corresponding fixes as they are discovered and patched. It's important to acquire and apply security fixes as soon as possible because crackers have access to the same information and can exploit new security vulnerabilities before you've had a chance to patch them up.

Mailing lists for security vulnerabilities are available from many places, two of them being `http://www.ntbugtraq.com/` and `http://www.securityfocus.com/`. BEA also puts out security advisories that are available at `http://dev2dev.bea.com/resourcelibrary/advisories.jsp?highlight=advisoriesnotifications`. A subscription service to these advisories is also available.

Use Complex Passwords and Keep Them Secure

The easiest way for a cracker to break into your system is by getting hold of an existing password or by guessing one. Your company's security policy should include guidelines on acceptable passwords and where passwords should be stored. Generally, passwords should not be written down. It isn't that difficult for a user to remember a single password. If users are expected to remember multiple passwords, they can use software that encrypts and stores passwords on their hard drives. Access to all these passwords is then available by remembering just one password.

The idea of a complex password is one that isn't easily guessed. Using longer passwords (eight or more characters), avoiding single words, and using lowercase and uppercase letters, punctuation marks, and special symbols make the task of guessing a password made much more difficult. Another technique of keeping a network more secure is by making passwords expire. If a user's password gets into the wrong hands, it becomes obsolete when the user is forced to choose a new one.

Encrypt Communications and Use Certificates

Although encrypting and decrypting information will put more overhead on your IT infrastructure, both you and your customers will have the confidence that goes along with knowing that your business transactions are private and unalterable. This improved confidence will result in increased usage and, ultimately, higher profitability.

Simplify Your Infrastructure

As your infrastructure grows, it becomes much more difficult to manage and secure. As connections to partner networks are added, the security of your network becomes the lowest common denominator of the security of your partners networks. Some users will want wireless access that opens up a can of worms concerning security. The bottom line is to provide access to information while maintaining security. If your security policy is too rigid, some users might feel justified in going around it and doing things such as setting up an unauthorized FTP server. Finding the right balance isn't easy but educating your users is a way of making this task a bit easier.

Look at Log Files and Event Logs!

No matter how tightly security is controlled, there always remains the possibility that someone will find a way around it. Operating systems, Web servers, application servers, and database servers all have the capability to monitor system status and client requests through the use of log files. Log file tracking must usually be configured and turned before log files will be generated. Log files track client requests by many characteristics, such as time, source IP address, and port. Because the size of these log files tends to be quite large, looking at the raw data in them is usually not very helpful. However, these are software packages that take the raw data and look for patterns that indicate the gathering of information and possible system break-ins by crackers. However, creating log real-time log files will have an affect on the performance of the machine that is creating them. If this results in unacceptable performance, a choice between security and performance must be made. At that point, be prudent in determining the tiers in your architecture where log files are critical. If this means increasing your hardware capabilities, it's a small price to pay considering the extra security and hopefully peace of mind that come with keeping log files.

Summary

As depicted in this chapter, you can see that although the Internet offers significant advantages over alternatives methods when it comes to providing access to information and services, there are many issues that must be considered and dealt with. Security isn't a topic that should be taken likely. Letting anyone have access to a cash register in a retail business is asking for trouble. Similarly, not having a proper security policy in place both internally and in regard to your Internet landscape is something that will eventually come back to bite you.

The tools available to crackers today make it relatively easy to find weak links in your infrastructure and to maximize the exploitation of such. Luckily, the tools to fight these would-be attackers have become stronger as well. Unfortunately, these tools cannot research, purchase, install, and configure themselves. A companywide initiative must take place for these events to happen.

In the next chapter, we'll talk about specific security issues concerning WebLogic and Java. We'll see how WebLogic implements the J2EE specification for security and extends it with functionality to provide superior security services.

CHAPTER 27

How WebLogic Server Implements Security

by Jeff Marin and Paul J. Perrone

IN THIS CHAPTER

As the use of Java code at the enterprise level is ushered in with increased industry penetration of J2EE, the security features of the middleware become all the more important. It is no longer sufficient just to be able to support multiple security protocols. Rather, the application server must be adaptable to new security technologies and be manageable under conditions involving complex security requirements. Routine tasks should be relatively easy to perform and support for backward compatibility should be out of the box. WLS 8.1 delivers on all of these expectations and more. By far, it boasts the most powerful security model of any J2EE application server on the planet.

Being a J2EE 1.3–compliant application server, WebLogic Server implements the J2EE security specification. Being a Java application itself, WebLogic Server runs in a JVM with J2SE security. In this chapter, we take a brief look at the security models within J2SE and J2EE and then plunge into the extensive security features offered with WebLogic Server 8.1.

The J2SE Security Model

Java bytecode running within a JVM can potentially perform malicious acts. Because of this, all code must run under the auspices of a security manager—which every JVM includes. The security manager provides highly granular control over what code can and cannot do. Although most applications run under the default security manager, the J2SE specification allows for customized security managers to be implemented and executed within the JVM.

Security managers must be told how to control access to restricted resources. This is accomplished with a security policy file. When the JVM is started, command-line options allow the use of a custom security manager and policy file. If no policy file is specified, the default policy file that is shipped with the Java runtime is utilized.

A *policy file* consists of one of more grant entries. Each *grant entry* consists of source code/permission pairs. The source code can be specified using an URL representing the path of the classes, with or without wildcards. The permissions are specified by a list of access rights to restricted resources that the source code is granted. The J2SE specification includes provisions for code to be signed or encrypted using keys found in digital certificates. Grant entries can also provide access to restricted resources based on the name of the code signer. Both methods of granting permissions are intended to give only trusted and known classes access to restricted resources.

Both J2SE and J2EE come with a utility called keytool. This utility is used to create digital certificates. These certificates can be used in a development environment. However, for a production environment, a Certificate Authority such as VeriSign or Entrust should be used to digitally sign the certificate and put it in a public directory. The J2EE version of keytool adds a Java cryptographic extension provider that implements RSA algorithms and thus allows RSA-signed certificates to be imported. The next chapter will take you through the process of generating a digital certificate, having it signed by a CA, importing it into WebLogic Server, and using it with the SSL protocol.

BEA WebLogic Server uses a customized policy file named `weblogic.policy` that is located in `[WEBLOGIC_HOME]\weblogic81\server\lib`. This file sets permissions for WebLogic Server itself and for the applications running within it. Using this file unmodified is usually acceptable, but when running third-party software, you might want to restrict resources available to that software. This can be accomplished by modifying the `weblogic.policy` file. More information can be found at `http://e-docs.bea.com/wls/docs81/secmanage/index.html`.

J2EE Security Model

The security model within J2EE is a continuation of the J2SE security model. In the J2SE model, one of the primary focuses of the security policy is based on where the code is located or who has signed the code with a digital certificate. In the J2EE model, the focus is on who is executing the code or, rather, who is remotely invoking the server-side code. This paradigm shift makes sense because J2EE code runs within a container located in the application server, which is in a secure location and controlled by IT personnel. The application deployer and administrator will decide what application code to deploy on this server. Potentially every user of the application will have access to this code and usually this is not within the security expectations of the application. The concern here is thus not so much untrusted code, but rather untrusted users.

Users

A *user* is considered any entity that is accessing a J2EE application. Sometimes a user is an actual person and other times it is a client application or another application server. A user must be identified through some credentials. This is confidential information that they should be in possession of, such as a username and password or a digital certificate. When attempting to sign on to a J2EE application, the user presents the credentials and the J2EE application server or the application code then matches the information with a pre-registered user. From this point forward, application code is now designated as running under that user's control.

It is important to understand that a J2EE user is not the same thing as a user in another context. J2EE users are separate entities than users defined in operating systems, databases, EIS instances, mainframes, and other applications. In typical enterprise applications, J2EE users must be mapped to users in other systems and this mapping can be specified in different ways.

Groups

J2EE groups represent an efficient way of categorizing sets of J2EE users with similar characteristics, such as working in the same department or location, having the same job title, or reporting to the same manager. As the number of users grows, specifying security policies on an individual basis becomes prohibitively time-consuming and error-prone. Security policies assigned at a group level allow large numbers of user security policies to be set simultaneously, reducing the amount of work required by an application administrator. Creating the correct grouping structure for your users is an important step in setting and maintaining user level security.

Roles

J2EE roles represent a type of functionality that one or more users or groups have in common. Some examples are the ability to change budget information, the ability to return merchandise, and the ability to change an organization's chart of employees. When developers create code that will be restricted, they assign roles to that code. Only users and groups that are assigned to that role should be able to execute this code. When the code is deployed, these roles will then be associated with actual users and groups. By associating the code with roles instead of actual users, the developer creates a level of abstraction that allows the group to be portable across multiple environments, departments, and even companies.

For example, suppose that a servlet has been created for changing the organization chart of a company. Because this code should not be executed by just anybody, it is considered a restricted resource and assigned to the role of `OrgChartModifier`. This servlet is packaged as third-party software and sold to other companies. When those companies deploy the servlet, they associate actual users and groups that have the ability to change the organization chart with the role of `OrgChartModifier`. This is depicted in Figure 27.1.

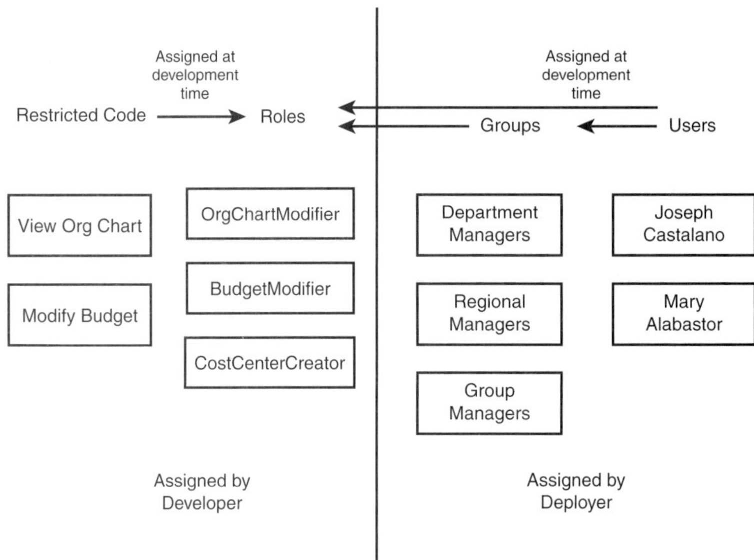

FIGURE 27.1 Assigning restricted code to roles and associating roles with users and groups allows code to be portable in its support for security.

Restricted Resources

By default, every resource within a J2EE application can be executed or accessed by any user. The Web container and the EJB container will allow anybody to access a JSP or HTML file, execute a method on a servlet or an EJB. If the EIS tier is set up to connect with an EIS instance using a specific authentication policy, access to that instance will be granted to every user. Although this might not sound completely unreasonable in a controlled environment such as a small department within a company, it is a recipe for chaos on the public Internet.

Most Web applications have a combination of restricted and public resources. Anonymous application clients are allowed to perform certain unrestricted actions, such as browsing a catalog, requesting product information, and possibly creating an anonymous shopping cart. However, within the course of their visit, many Web sites will ask the user to identity herself. This will occur when the user is requesting a controlled resource. Examples of this are checking out a shopping cart and accessing member or subscription holder information. If a user does not have the proper authorization to access a requested resource, he might be notified as shown in Figure 27.2.

Declarative security through deployment descriptors allows developers and deployers to protect access to EJB methods, access to Web application components (servlets, JSPs, HTML pages, and so on), and access to EIS instances (for example, SAP and PeopleSoft).

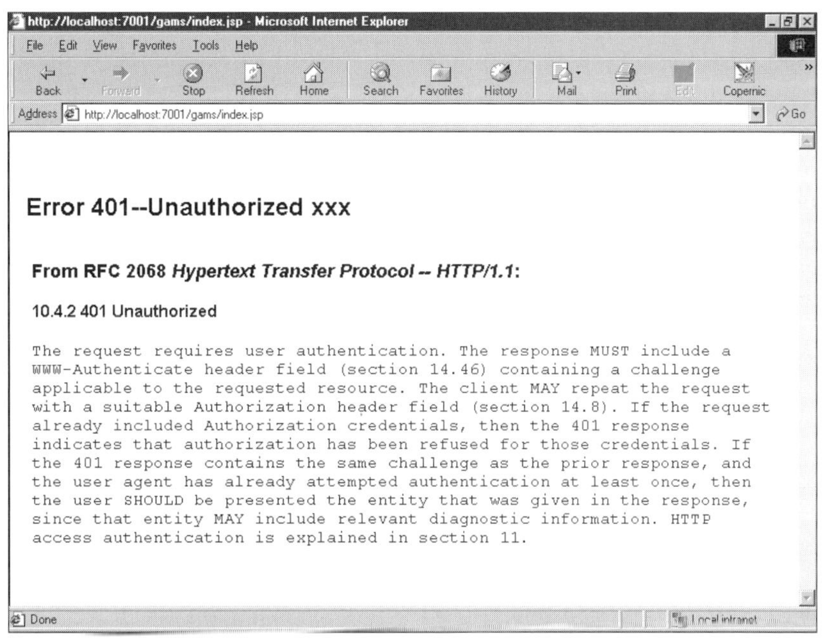

FIGURE 27.2 An unauthorized or unauthenticated user will be rejected when trying to access a restricted resource.

The Web Application Deployment Descriptor

Every Web application running in a J2EE application server must be associated with a `web.xml` file. This XML file has an accompanying DTD that can be found at `http://java.sun.com/dtd/web-app_2_3.dtd`. The `web.xml` file offers a vendor-neutral method for specifying many attributes about a Web application, including authentication method, name of application welcome page, and security constraints. Web applications running on BEA WebLogic Server can also specify additional information in accompanying WebLogic-specific deployment descriptors. Although these files can potentially hold a lot of information, this chapter and the following one will describe with a few of their attributes that relate to security.

Authentication

The act of asking clients to identify themselves is referred to as *authentication*. This involves asking the client to present some secret information of which only it is in possession. The most common form of this is a username and a password. However, this information can take other forms, such as digital certificates, smart cards, and biometric-based methods such as fingerprinting, voice recognition, and fingerprinting. Authentication of Web users is performed differently from non-Web users. Authentication of non-Web users is discussed later in this chapter in the section titled "Java Authentication and Authorization Service."

The J2EE specification states that an application server must be able to authenticate its Web users in three ways. Consequently, in addition to other techniques, WebLogic Server can authenticate users in the following ways as well:

- HTTP basic authentication—This type of authentication uses the browser's built-in identification dialog. This provides developers with a quick and dirty method of asking users to identify themselves. It requires no additional code, but the look of the dialog cannot be changed. After the user enters his information and presses the submit button, his username and password are Base64-encoded and sent to the server. An example of this is shown in Figure 27.3. Unfortunately, Base64 encoding is not the same as encryption. This means that the user's information is essentially sent in the clear and can be viewed by packet sniffers.

FIGURE 27.3 Web browsers have the built-in capability to display a dialog that requests a username and a password.

  A variation of basic authentication is digest authentication. Digest authentication does not transmit user names and passwords in clear text. Rather, it uses a message digest. A *message digest* is a fixed-length encoding of some information that uses an algorithm for encryption. The default algorithm is MD5. MD5 produces a 128-bit hash of the original data and is high speed. WebLogic Server supports the MD5 and Secure Hash Algorithm (SHA) message digest algorithms. SHA is more secure and produces 160-bit hashes but is slower than MD5.

- Form-based authentication—Form-based authentication allows a Web page to collect identification information from a user. This requires more work because the Web page has to be created. However, the user is presented with a more visually appealing user interface. An example of this is shown in Figure 27.4. As in HTTP basic authentication, this information will be sent to the server without being encrypted.

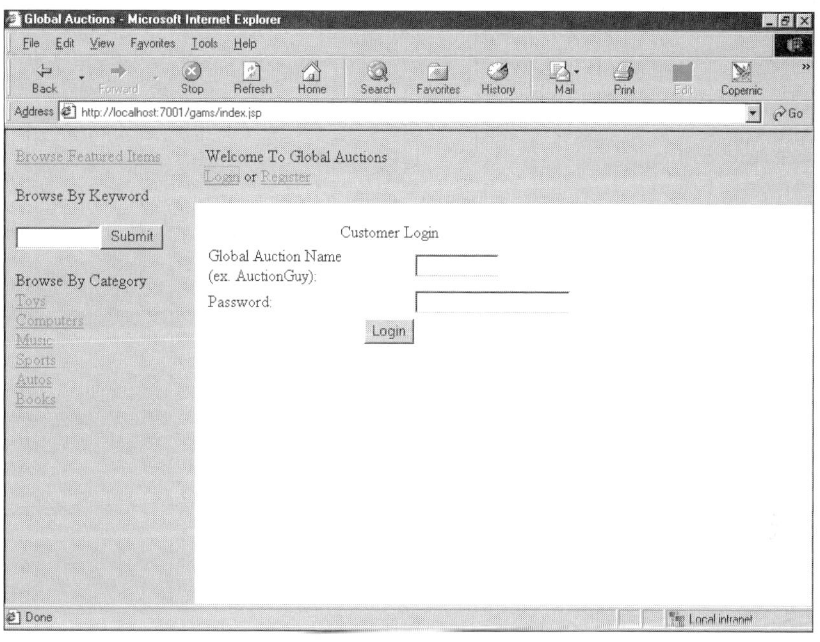

FIGURE 27.4 Form-based authentication allows the login process to be customized with a look and feel similar to the rest of the Web site.

- Client certificate authentication—This type of authentication involves encryption by default and uses a server and optionally a client digital certificate to negotiate encryption keys. After this negotiation takes place, the rest of the user session takes place using SSL over HTTP (HTTPS). A server-side certificate is used to encrypt the communication, and a client-side certificate is used to authenticate the user. When using only a server-side certificate, the user still needs to be authenticated.

> **NOTE**
>
> SSL can be employed for all types of authentication mentioned here, allowing the information to be encrypted before being sent to the server. The theory of SSL is discussed in Chapter 26, "Web Applications and Security." Chapter 28, "Working with WebLogic Server Security Features," discusses how to set up SSL in WebLogic Server.

How Is the Authentication Method Specified?

Within the `web.xml` file, the XML element named `<login-config>` is used to specify the basic authentication method to be used by a Web application. Within this element are other elements named `<auth-method>`, `<form-login-page>`, `<form-error-page>`, and `<realm-name>`. Listings 27.1, 27.2, and 27.3 illustrate how to establish the authentication method for Web users of Web applications.

LISTING 27.1 Example of Using http-basic Authentication

```
<login-config>
 <auth-method>BASIC</auth-method>
 <realm-name>myrealm</realm-name>
</login-config>
```

LISTING 27.2 Example of Using Form-Based Authentication; Notice That Both the Login Page and a Login Error Page Must Be Stated

```
<login-config>
 <auth-method>FORM</auth-method>
 <form-login-config>
  <form-login-page>/login.jsp</form-login-page>
  <form-error-page>/loginerror.html</form-error-page>
 </form-login-config>
</login-config>
```

LISTING 27.3 Example of Using Client Certificate Authentication

```
<login-config>
 <auth-method>CLIENT-CERT</auth-method>
</login-config>
```

The Administration Console or WebLogic Builder tool can be used to change these settings, which are reflected inside a Web application's `web.xml` file. To accomplish this using WebLogic Builder, open a Web application using the File menu Open option as illustrated in Figure 27.5.

This will open a new window allowing various ways to configure your Web application. Click on the Web application name in the left panel and then take note of the Login tab in the right panel, as shown in Figure 27.6.

After clicking on the Login tab in the right panel, you will be presented with a screen to input your login configuration for the Web application as shown in Figure 27.7.

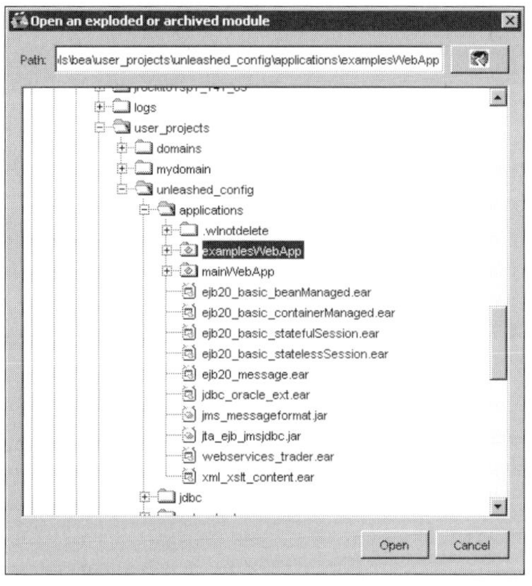

FIGURE 27.5 Opening a Web application using the WebLogic Builder tool.

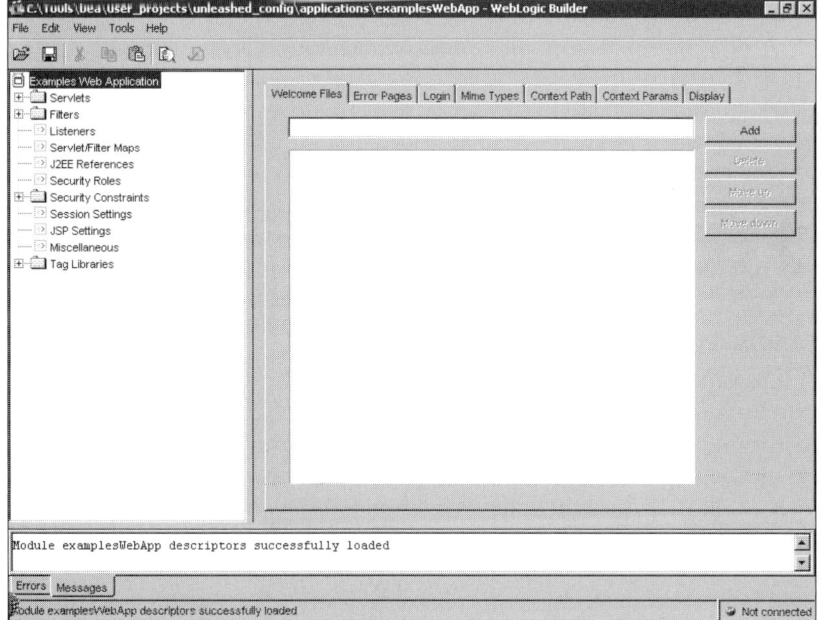

FIGURE 27.6 To change the login method of a Web application, click on the Web application's name in the left panel.

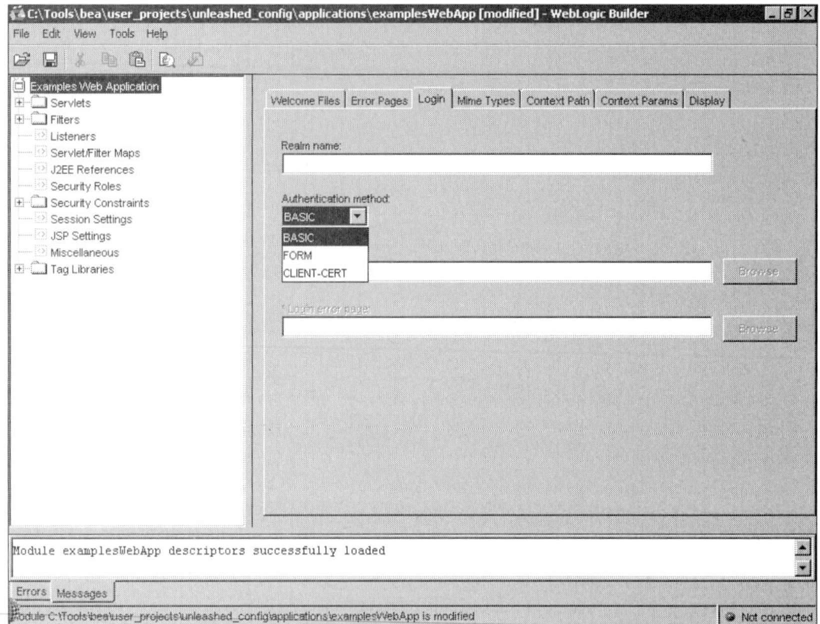

FIGURE 27.7 This screen enables you to select which login configuration to use for this Web application.

After setting the login configuration, or anything else in `web.xml` or WebLogic Server–specific `weblogic.xml` deployment descriptors, you must save these changes back to the XML files. Simply click the File menu's Save option as shown in Figure 27.8. You can also archive your changes back to a WAR file by clicking on the File menu's Archive option, which is also shown in Figure 27.8.

How Is Security Specified?

J2EE applications can delineate restricted resources and those users who have access to them in two ways: declarative security and programmatic security. However, within a single application, both methods of security delineation can be employed. This section discusses both declarative and programmatic security. It discusses how each method works, when to use each, and their advantages and disadvantages.

Declarative Security

The standard method of declaring who can access restricted resources is accomplished through XML-based deployment descriptors created by J2EE application developers. When developers create their respective EJBs, servlets, JSPs, Java classes, and other resources that are part of applications, the developers must indicate where access will be restricted. The application deployer then takes these descriptors and modifies them to work within the WebLogic Server runtime environment.

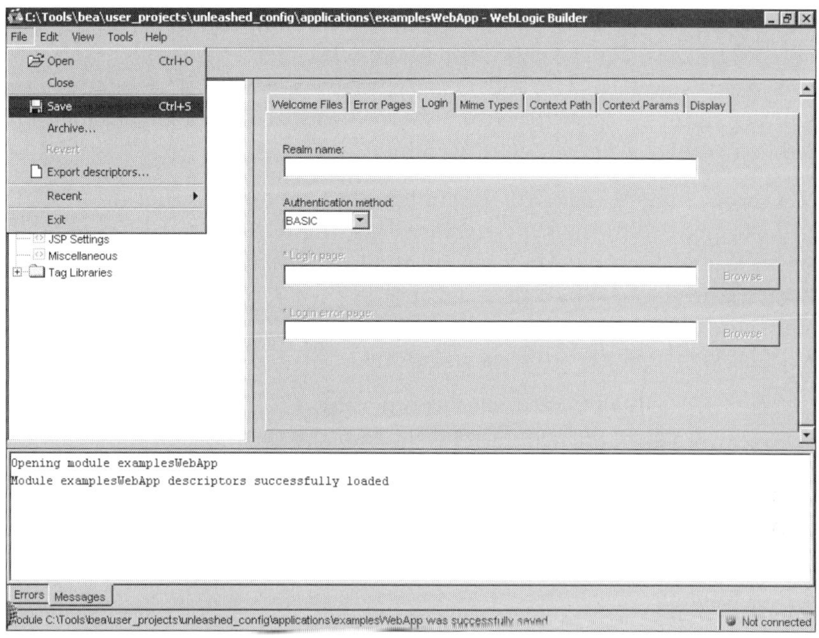

FIGURE 27.8 You must persist your changes back to the XML deployment descriptors and WAR file.

When declarative security is employed, the J2EE container is required to enforce this security. If the client is attempting to access a restricted resource or to execute a restricted method of an EJB, the container must first verify that the client has been authenticated and then make sure that they are in one of the roles that has been authorized access to that EJB's method.

The advantages of using declarative security are that security restrictions to existing code can be modified in XML-based deployment descriptors without changing and recompiling application code. This is significant because changes in application code are more likely to produce unexpected insecure side effects than are changes to deployment descriptors. Declarative security is much easier to deal with in the modification and maintenance of Web applications.

J2EE Web Components

Security constraints are set up on a Web application–level basis, as specified in the `web.xml` and `weblogic.xml` deployment descriptor files. Within `web.xml`, restricted resources such as servlets, JSPs, and HTML pages are referenced by specific URLs or URL patterns, the HTTP method that is used to access them, and the user roles that are allowed access.

Within the web.xml file, security constraints are specified within the XML element named <security-constraint>. Within this element are other elements named <web-resource-collection>, <auth-constraint>, and <user-data-constraint>. The weblogic.xml deployment descriptor file is used to link user roles as specified in web.xml with principals as specified in a WebLogic Server security realm.

Listing 27.4 shows a sample web.xml file containing a set of URLs that have been marked as restricted. As specified in the <url-pattern> tag, these URLs are all located in or below the /pages/managers directory. The manager and systemadmin roles have been defined to be allowed access to these URLs if they use an HTTP Get method. Notice that these roles must be defined within a <security-role> tag. In weblogic.xml, these roles will be associated with actual WebLogic Server users and groups.

The <transport-guarantee> tag specifies whether these resources will be protected with encryption. Possible values are NONE, INTEGRAL, and CONFIDENTIAL. NONE means that these resources can be accessed using the standard HTTP protocol. INTEGRAL indicates that a request to these URLs should be sent in a way that it could not be changed in transit. CONFIDENTIAL indicates that the request should be encrypted. The use of INTEGRAL and CONFIDENTIAL usually indicates that the HTTPS protocol (SSL over HTTP) will be required to access these resources.

LISTING 27.4 A Sample web.xml File with Security Constraints

```
<?xml version="1.0" encoding="UTF-8"?>
<!DOCTYPE web-app PUBLIC '-//Sun Microsystems, Inc.//DTD Web Application 2.3//EN'
 'http://java.sun.com/dtd/web-app_2_3.dtd'>
<web-app>
<security-constraint>
 <web-resource-collection>
  <web-resource-name>ManagerResources</web-resource-name>
  <description>
   Only managers are allowed access to these resources.
  </description>
  <url-pattern>/pages/managers/*</url-pattern>
  <http-method>GET</http-method>
 </web-resource-collection>
 <auth-constraint>
  <description>
   The following roles have access to these pages
  </description>
  <role-name>manager</role-name>
  <role-name>systemadmin</role-name>
 </auth-constraint>
 <user-data-constraint>
```

```
    <description>
     This is how the user data must be transmitted
    </description>
    <transport-guarantee>NONE</transport-guarantee>
  </user-data-constraint>
</security-constraint>

<security-role>
  <role-name>manager</role-name>
  <role-name>systemadmin</role-name>
</security-role>

</web-app>
```

In addition to manually changing the `web.xml` file, you can use the Administration Console or WebLogic Builder tool. When using the WebLogic Builder tool, select the Web application you are interested in, as illustrated in Figure 27.5. You must also link roles defined in `web.xml` to users and groups (principals) defined in WebLogic Server. This is done is `weblogic.xml`. An example of this is shown in Listing 27.5.

LISTING 27.5 A sample weblogic.xml File That Assigns the Roles of manager and systemadmin to Users and Groups Within WebLogic Server

```
<!DOCTYPE weblogic-web-app
 PUBLIC "-//BEA Systems, Inc.//DTD Web Application 8.1//EN"
 "http://www.bea.com/servers/wls810/dtd/weblogic810-web-jar.dtd">

<weblogic-web-app>

 <security-role-assignment>
  <role-name>manager</role-name>
  <principal-name>johnq</principal-name>
  <principal-name>managergroup</principal-name>
 </security-role-assignment>

 <security-role-assignment>
  <role-name>systemadmin</role-name>
  <principal-name>carlw</principal-name>
  <principal-name>jaimem</principal-name>
  <principal-name>systemadmingroup</principal-name>
 </security-role-assignment>
</weblogic-web-app>
```

Modification of security roles may also be performed through the Administration Console or WebLogic Builder tool. While editing a Web application through the WebLogic Builder tool, click on the Security Roles option in the left panel, as shown in Figure 27.9.

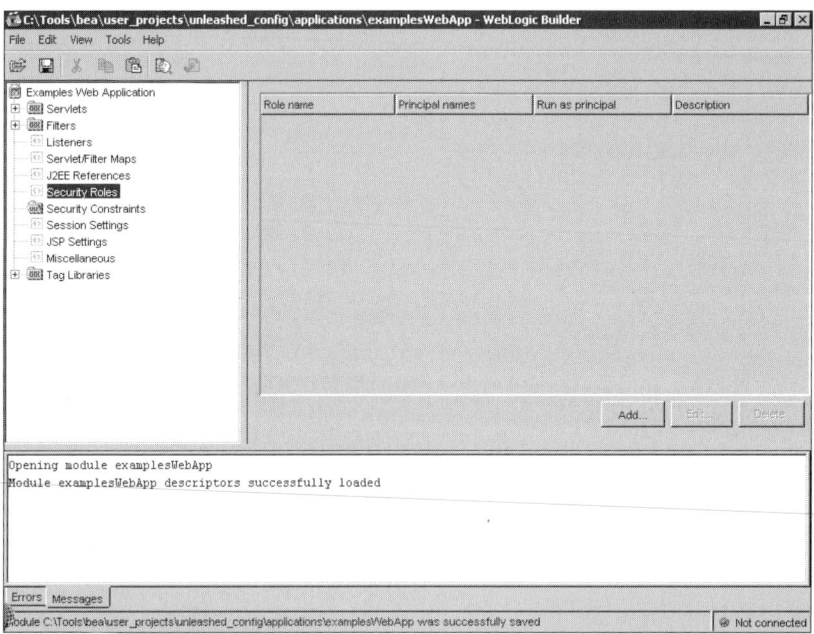

FIGURE 27.9 Clicking on the Security Roles option will enable you to modify security role information from within WebLogic Builder.

By clicking on the Add button in the right panel shown in Figure 27.9, a window will pop up and enable you to then add new roles and add principals to those roles, as illustrated in Figure 27.10.

Enterprise JavaBeans

EJBs are deployed in EJB JAR files, separate from the WAR files that hold Web container components. They are also executed in their own container environment. EJBs can potentially be accessed from components in many different Web applications. The security constraints of EJBs are specified on a bean-by-bean basis.

According to the J2EE specification, every deployed EJB must have an associated `ejb-jar.xml` file. This file is used to specify many attributes about the EJB, including security constraints. The DTD for this file is located at `http://java.sun.com/dtd/ejb-jar_2_0.dtd`.

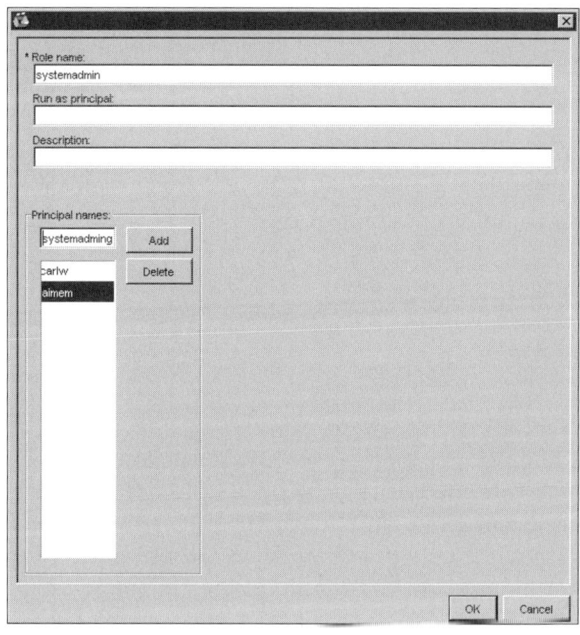

FIGURE 27.10 You can create new roles and add principals to those roles using WebLogic Builder.

Within the `ejb-jar.xml` file, you use the XML element named `<method-permission>` to restrict execution rights of an interface method to one or more specific user roles. WebLogic also uses a `weblogic-ejb-jar.xml` file to specify WebLogic Server–specific EJB information. In the context of security, client authentication information for EJBs accessed using IIOP can be specified.

Listing 27.6 contains part of an `ejb-jar.xml` file that sets the security restrictions for an EJB. In this example, the security role named `manager` is allowed to access any method of the `WithdrawFunds` EJB.

LISTING 27.6 A Sample ejb-jar.xml File Snippet with Security Constraints

```
<security-role>
 <role-name>manager</role-name>
</security-role>
<method-permission>
 <role-name>manager</role-name>
 <method>
  <ejb-name>WithdrawFunds</ejb-name>
  <method-name>*</method-name>
 </method>
</method-permission>
```

Just as `weblogic.xml` is used to associate security roles in `web.xml` with users and/or groups in WebLogic Server, `weblogic-ejb-jar.xml` is used in combination with `ejb-jar.xml`. An example of this is shown in Listing 27.7.

LISTING 27.7 A Sample weblogic-ejb-jar.xml Snippet to Associate ejb-jar.xml Security Roles with WebLogic Server Users and/or Groups

```
<security-role-assignment>
 <role-name>manager</role-name>
 <principal-name>johnq</principal-name>
 <principal-name>managergroup</principal-name>
</security-role-assignment>
```

Information in `ejb-jar.xml` and `weblogic-ejb-jar.xml` files for deployed EJBs can also be modified with the Administration Console and WebLogic Builder tool. You first load an EJB JAR or J2EE EAR file into the WebLogic Builder. In Figure 27.11, we have opened a J2EE EAR file that is associated with an EJB JAR file. After opening the J2EE EAR file properties in the WebLogic Builder tool and selecting an EJB JAR file, we can add roles to the deployment descriptor for the EJB JAR file as illustrated in Figure 27.11.

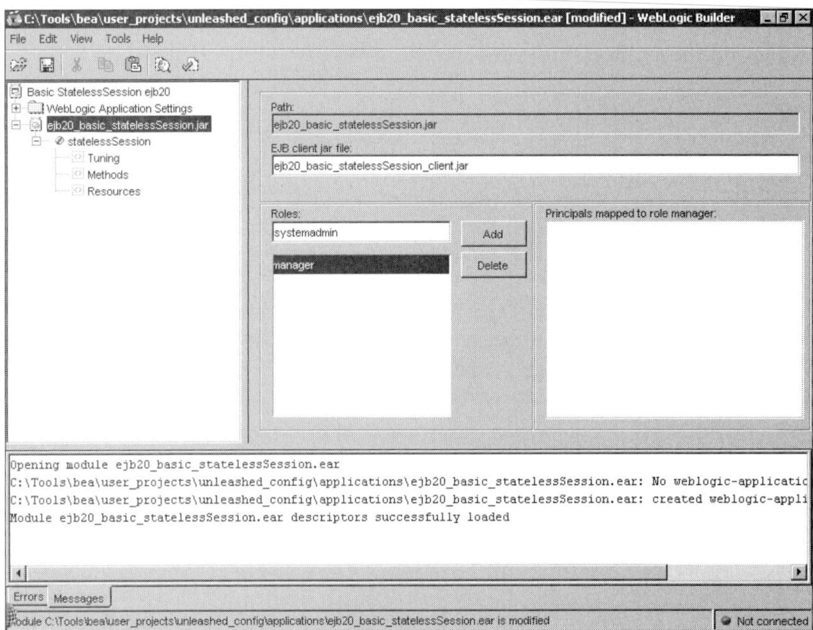

FIGURE 27.11 Open an EJB in WebLogic Builder so that you can add security roles to the EJB JAR deployment descriptor file.

After selecting an EJB within an EJB JAR file, select the Methods option in the left-side panel for that EJB, as illustrated in Figure 27.12. Then select the Permissions tab in the right-side panel also as illustrated in Figure 27.12. It is here that you can set security properties for an EJB.

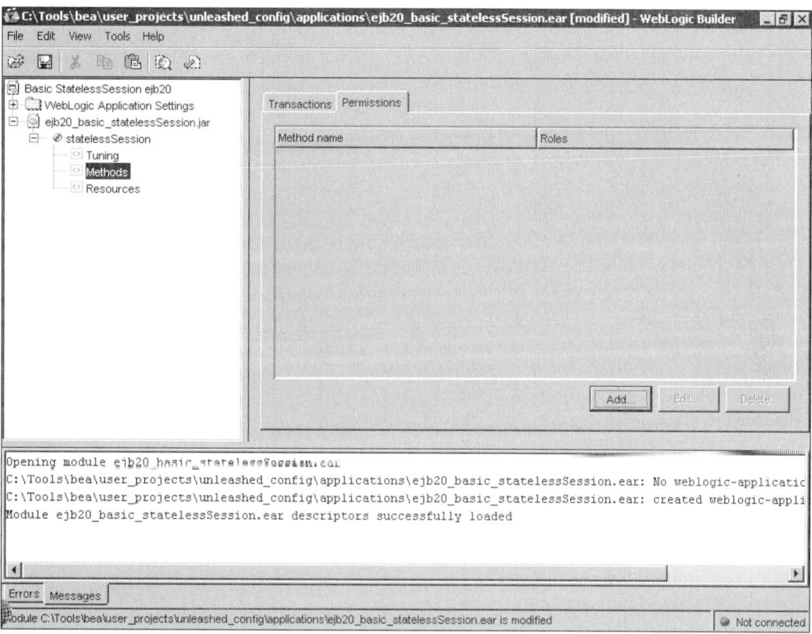

FIGURE 27.12 Select the Permissions tab in the right-side panel when modifying the deployment properties for an EJB's methods.

After selecting the Add button in the right-side panel as shown in Figure 27.12, a window will pop up as shown in Figure 27.13. It is within this window that you specify which roles have access to which methods on the particular EJB.

EIS Tier

Declarative security to EIS instances is set with deployment descriptors that are packaged with resource adapters. According to the J2EE specification, every deployed resource adapter must have an associated `ra.xml` file. Within this file is an XML element named `<authentication-mechanism>`. This element denotes how clients will authenticate themselves and is specific to the EIS instance. Possible mechanisms include username and password, digital certificates, and Kerberos ticketing. Other elements such as `<credential-interface>` and `<security-permission>` are used to declare EIS security. An example of this is in Listing 27.8.

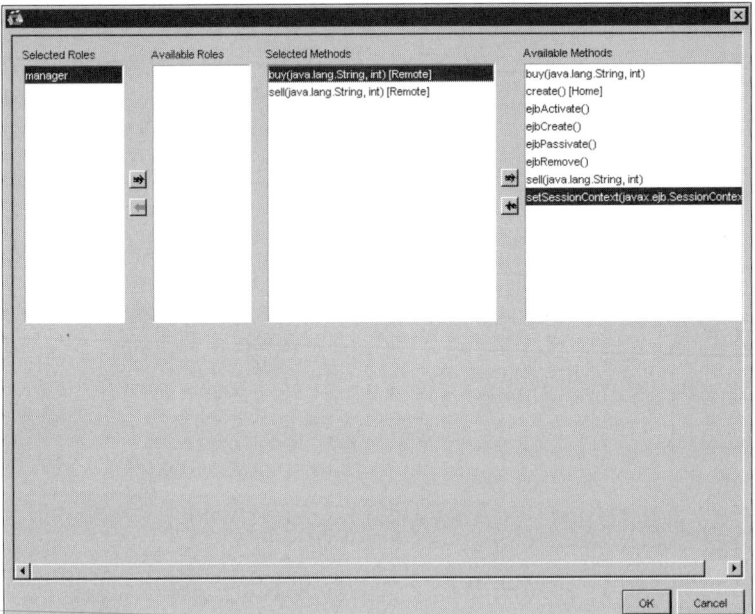

FIGURE 27.13 This window enables you to define which EJB methods are accessible by particular roles.

LISTING 27.8 A Code Snippet from ra.xml That Illustrates How to Specify Authentication Using Passwords

```
<authentication-mechanism>
 <authentication-mechanism-type>BasicPassword</authentication-mechanism-type>
 <credential-interface>javax.resource.security.PasswordCredential</credential-
➥interface>
</authentication-mechanism>
```

Programmatic Security

Using declarative security can be too restrictive for some situations. For example, security requirements of an application might involve roles that are dynamic. One case of this would be giving frequent, high-spending customers first access to new products. If these products are viewed and purchased using specific servlets and JSPs, the components should be restricted to only those customers. Unfortunately, the criteria used to judge who these customers are can change over time (for example, the criteria of more than 50K annual purchases might change to 100K). Also, as customer activity changes, the membership of this group changes as well (for example, Joe's SuperStore places a 37K order and it is now in this group). Declarative security is not flexible enough to accommodate this type of security.

With this flexibility comes the price of having to modify, recompile, and redeploy code whenever the business rules concerning application security policies changes. However, as we will see later in this chapter, WebLogic also has some built-in mechanisms for dynamic security policies that do not require changes to application code.

When programmatic security is employed, the hosting container will not attempt to enforce security because it has no idea what your security requirements are. This job is left up to the application component code.

J2EE Web Components

Programmatic security is available for servlets and JavaServer Pages. Both have access to a `HttpServletRequest` object when accessed in the context of a client request. The `HttpServletRequest` object contains these methods relating to users, roles, and principals.

- `getRemoteUser()`—Returns the login name of the client making this request or null if the client has not been authenticated
- `getUserPrincipal()`—Returns a `java.security.Principal` with the name of the client making this request or null if the client has not been authenticated
- `isUserInRole()`—Returns a `boolean` indicating whether the user is a member of a specified role

Using these methods and associated business logic, it is possible to come up with a dynamic security mechanism that meets your design requirements.

Enterprise JavaBeans

Programmatic security is also available for EJBs through the use of the `EJBContext` object. This object has two methods related to users, roles, and principals that act like the `HttpServletRequest` methods in the previous section:

- `getUserPrincipal()`
- `isCallerInRole()`

When used in combination with business logic, dynamic security can be customized to meet just about any design specification.

EIS Tier

Whether an EIS instance is being accessed by a servlet, JSP, or EJB, the user, role, and principal information will be available to the calling code. This code will then be responsible for taking this information and logging in to the EIS instance. The calling code will include EIS instance signon code and the EIS tier container will not be responsible for creating connections to EIS instances. The EIS resource adapter will accept client credentials and attempt sign on.

How Security Works in WebLogic Server

The security model in WebLogic Server 8.1 has changed considerably from previous versions. As in other areas of the J2EE specification, WebLogic Server meets the security requirements of J2EE and then extends them in many directions to offer developers and administrators many additional features to make their jobs easier. The J2EE security specification does not specify any security-specific tools or user interfaces from compliant application servers. In fact, this is a key area for differentiation and WebLogic Server has taken full advantage of it. As illustrated in Figure 27.14, WebLogic Server security builds on security offered through J2SE and J2EE (including JAAS).

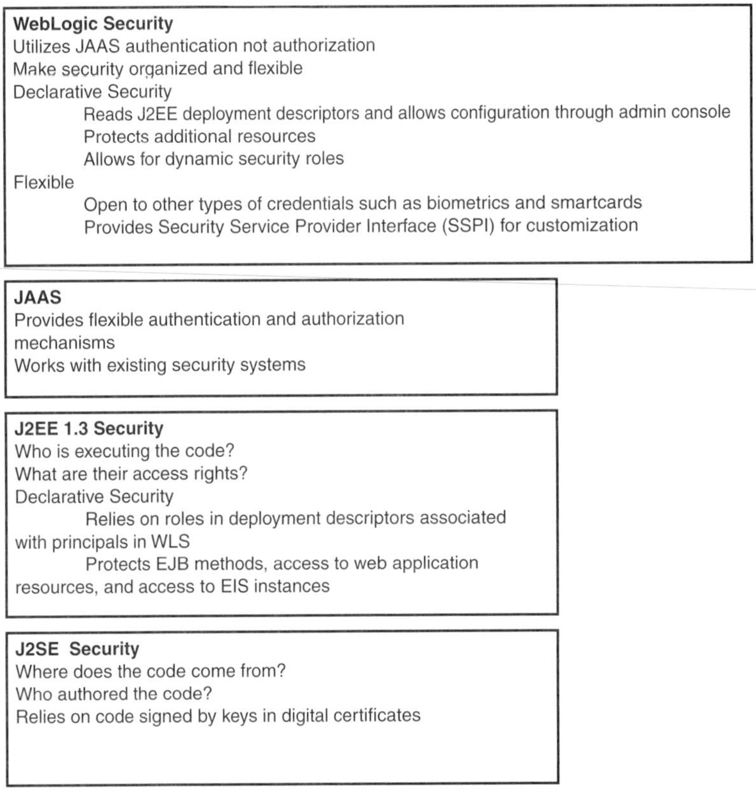

WebLogic Security
Utilizes JAAS authentication not authorization
Make security organized and flexible
Declarative Security
 Reads J2EE deployment descriptors and allows configuration through admin console
 Protects additional resources
 Allows for dynamic security roles
Flexible
 Open to other types of credentials such as biometrics and smartcards
 Provides Security Service Provider Interface (SSPI) for customization

JAAS
Provides flexible authentication and authorization mechanisms
Works with existing security systems

J2EE 1.3 Security
Who is executing the code?
What are their access rights?
Declarative Security
 Relies on roles in deployment descriptors associated with principals in WLS
 Protects EJB methods, access to web application resources, and access to EIS instances

J2SE Security
Where does the code come from?
Who authored the code?
Relies on code signed by keys in digital certificates

FIGURE 27.14 WebLogic Server relies on the underlying security of J2SE, J2EE, and JAAS.

The WebLogic Server security model is based on a modular design that exposes a set of Security Service Provider Interfaces (SSPIs) for authentication, authorization, auditing, and other security features. This allows third-party vendors to create security software that will seamlessly integrate with WebLogic Server. By integrating with WebLogic Server, third-party software is configurable from the WebLogic Server administration console.

Goals of WebLogic Server Security Framework

To secure WebLogic applications running inside of the WebLogic Server container environment, the WebLogic Server security framework set out to accomplish the following goals:

- Security as a service—Security is now viewed as a service available to application components. Application components call upon WebLogic Server security for features such as authentication and authorization. Due to its modular nature, WebLogic Server allows third-party software vendors to integrate their security solutions seamlessly. The configuration of this software is from the same administrator console used for configuring other aspects of WebLogic Server. As new security technologies become available, existing applications can take advantage of them. For example, if authorization by fingerprinting is used in the future, WebLogic Server can utilize a third-party software vendor's authorization module. Then application code will utilize this module with little or no changes to the application code.
- Separation between security code and application code—Developers are encouraged and have more reasons to not put security-related code inside of application code. One reason for this is that WebLogic Server security policies allow decisions concerning security to be based on business logic, reducing the need for security-related code. Keeping this separation is important because it allows the security features of an application to change independent of application code changes.
- Ship more functionality out of the box—In the past, developers were responsible for implementing some security-related with code. WebLogic Server now supplies more security functionality out of the box. For instance, auditing is now a feature of WebLogic Server, configurable from the Administrator Console.
- Unified security model—With WebLogic Server 8.1, all security configurations can be set from the Administrator Console. In the past, security was configured in many different ways.

Java Authentication and Authorization Service

While the J2SE security model has been specific about how security should be implemented, the J2EE specification has left many aspects ambiguous. This has caused application server vendors to implement security models that are extremely proprietary, thus compromising one of Java's key principals of write once, run anywhere. The Java Authentication and Authorization Service (JAAS) specification puts a stake in the ground and gives application server vendors more direction on how to implement security. This spec comes with a set of classes and interfaces for authenticating users based on flexible credentials and for authorizing users access to restricted resources. JAAS version 1.0 is an optional package of the Java 2 SDK version 1.3.x, but it is a standard package in version 1.4.

JAAS implements a Java version of the Pluggable Authentication Model (PAM) framework. Originally developed in the Unix world, PAM allows for a flexible authentication and authorization system that can evolve separately from the rest of a security framework and from applications that rely on this framework. As new authentication technologies such as biometrics, Kerberos ticketing, and smart cards become available, security providers can provide software that connects their new hardware to JAAS.

The JAAS API defines a `LoginModule` abstraction that connects authentication hardware and software to the rest of the IT infrastructure. This is similar to the concept of using hardware drivers to connect computer hardware to an operating system. The JAAS API also defines a `LoginContext` abstraction that calls on one or more `LoginModule` abstractions to authenticate a user, as illustrated in Figure 27.15.

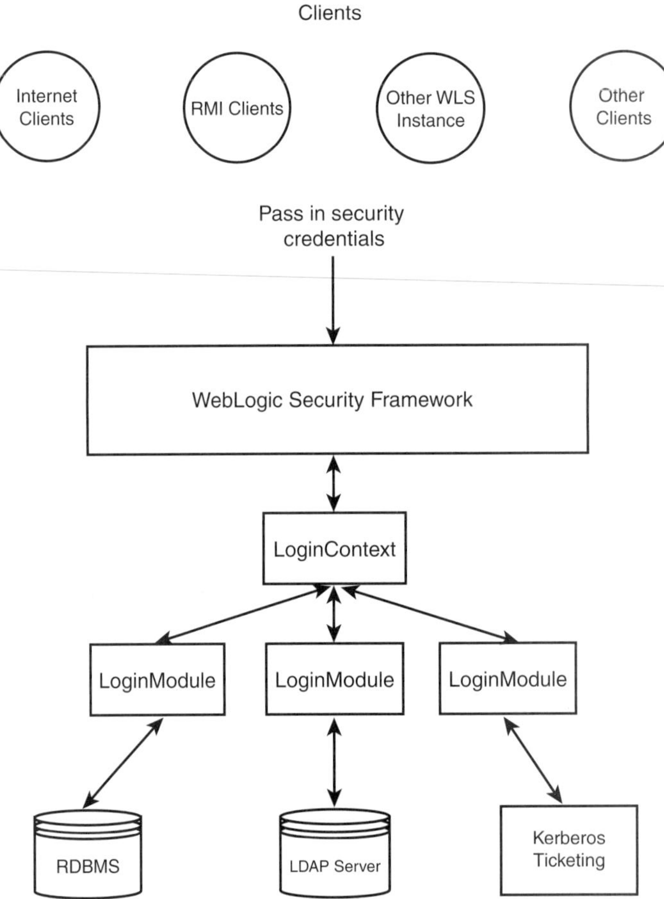

FIGURE 27.15 WebLogic Server uses JAAS for a flexible authentication model. Out-of-the-box and customized LoginModule abstractions are used to connect the WebLogic Server security framework to different data sources and security mechanisms for authentication purposes.

WebLogic Server implements the JAAS version 1.0 specification and uses it for authentication purposes only. The JAAS specification for authorization states that a policy file should be used to indicate who is allowed access to restricted resources. However, WebLogic Server uses security realms and roles to determine user access. Your need to learn JAAS at the API level is based on your security requirements. Out of the box, WebLogic Server ships with JAAS authentication modules to handle username/password combinations, digital certificates, and many external LDAP servers. If your applications require additional methods of authentication, you'll either need to obtain custom `LoginModule` implementations or write your own. In the next chapter, we'll discuss JAAS development.

Subjects and Principals

JAAS defines new terms for dealing with authentication. The definition of the term *principal* is an identity assigned to an authenticated user of an application or computing resource such as a socket or a file. The definition of the term *subject* is a container for authentication information including a set of principals. In the JAAS API, there are classes to represent subjects and principals.

When a client is being authenticated, a `LoginContext` will create a new `Subject` object. The `LoginContext` then passes the empty `Subject` object to one or more `LoginModule` objects. As each `LoginModule` authenticates the client using its own respective method, they will create `Principal` objects. The `LoginModule` objects will then populate the `Subject` object with these `Principal` objects. For example, a single authenticating user may invoke multiple `LoginModule` objects that generate principals based on the user's name and their Social Security number.

After a client has been authenticated, the client application will receive a `Subject` object filled with associated `Principal` objects. When the client application attempts to perform restricted operations on a remote system, it will pass its `Subject` object with the request. The remote system, in our case WebLogic Server, will determine whether any of the embedded principals have the correct access rights to perform this task.

WebLogic Server Security Realms

At the top of the WebLogic Server security model hierarchy is the security realm. As depicted in Figure 27.16, a security realm integrates all information associated with security, including users, groups, authenticators, and authorization information. A realm includes a set of security providers that each performs specific security-related functions. Every WebLogic Server domain must have at least one active security realm. There can be multiple realms, but only one can be active at a time.

WebLogic Server is configured out of the box with a default realm called `myrealm`. This can be seen in the Administration Console as shown in Figure 27.17. Inside of this realm, WebLogic Server ships with its own default implementations of each of these security providers. If your security needs are not met by the WebLogic Server implementations, you are free to purchase other implementations from third-party vendors or to write your own. A single security realm can integrate security providers that come with WebLogic Server, are created for custom purposes, and are purchased from third-party security software vendors.

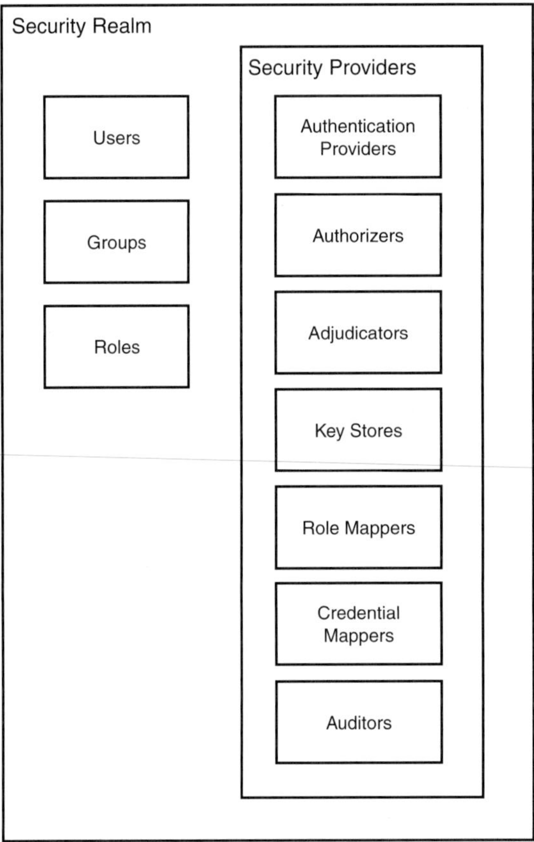

FIGURE 27.16 Realms provide an integrated structure to all the security information and functionality within an application.

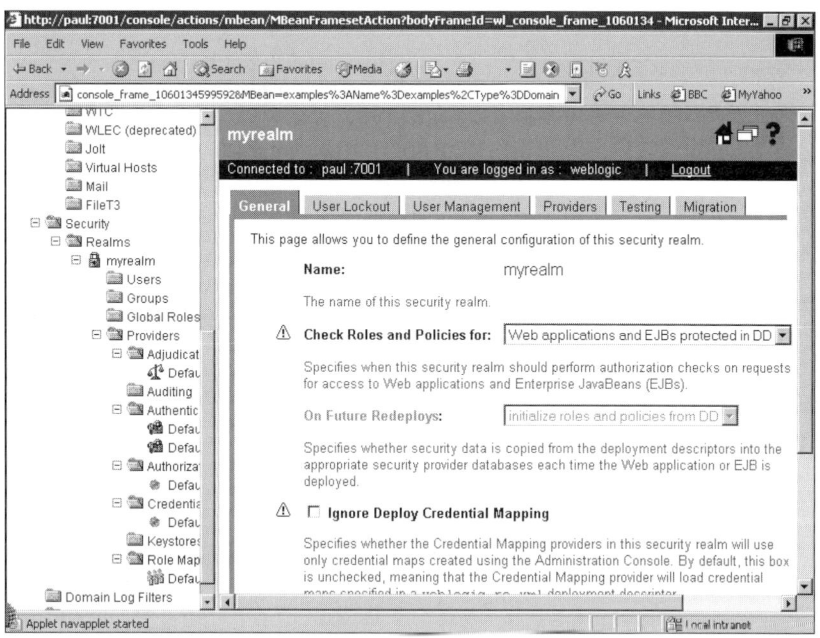

FIGURE 27.17 The default security realm called myrealm contains WebLogic Server–supplied security providers.

Every WebLogic Server domain must have at least one security realm with which it is associated. If a domain is created and it is associated with the `myrealm` realm and then this realm is removed, you will not be able to start WebLogic Server in this domain.

Security Roles

Security roles are used to group together users that share access rights to restricted resources. Security roles are similar to groups in the sense that they are both collections of users. However, whereas the membership of a group is fairly static and modifiable only by an administrator, rules are used to define the membership of a role. This makes the membership of roles dynamic. WebLogic Server enhances static security roles represented in J2EE deployment descriptors with dynamic ones set through the Administrator Console. Security roles replace the access control lists (ACLs) used in previous versions of WebLogic Server.

The WebLogic Server security framework enhances J2EE security and enables most resources to be protected. These include resources from the JDBC, JNDI, JMS, EJB, Web application, and administration subsystems.

Security Providers

As mentioned earlier, a single security realm within WebLogic Server consists of security providers that are each assigned a specific set of responsibilities in regard to maintaining the security of Web applications. In this section, we discuss each type of security provider and what it is responsible for.

Authentication Providers

Authentication providers are responsible for taking client credentials and matching them with a registered WebLogic Server user. These credentials can come in many shapes and sizes. Examples include username and password, digital certificates, and fingerprints.

Authentication providers are responsible for invoking JAAS `LoginModule` objects that will determine valid `Principal` objects based on supplied client authentication credentials. The authentication provider will return a populated JAAS `Subject` object back to a remote client after a successful login. Because remote clients hold and can possible modify `Subject` objects, principal validators are used to ensure that the embedded `Principal` objects have not been tampered with. The WebLogic principal validation provider signs and validates WebLogic Server principals, users, and groups. If you need to work with principals from another application, such as SAP, you might need to create a custom principal validator.

When remote clients attempt to authenticate with WebLogic Server using a token, it is referred to as *perimeter authorization*. These tokens are client credentials such as digital certificates. Identity asserters are responsible for accepting tokens that are generated outside of WebLogic Server and associating them with a WebLogic Server username. Then they pass the token back to WebLogic Server where they are authenticated. Although identity asserters can handle many types of tokens, they can handle only one at a time, and the type that is configured as active. To handle multiple types of tokens, there must be multiple identity asserters.

The WebLogic authentication provider (named `DefaultAuthenticator`) uses an embedded LDAP server to store user and group information. The provider authenticates users by matching their usernames and passwords with the information in the embedded LDAP server. This provider allows for a configurable minimum password length with default of `8`.

The WebLogic identity assertion provider (named `DefaultIdentityAsserter`) can accept tokens for X.509 digital certificates and Common Secure Interoperability (CSIv2) identities. CSIv2 is a standard for securing operations made over RMI-IIOP. If you need to handle other types of tokens, such as Kerberos or SAML, you will need to create or purchase a custom `IdentityAsserter`.

Authorizers

Authorization providers are responsible for determining when an authenticated user has access to a restricted resource. This is performed at runtime by comparing security policies with the identity of the authenticated user. When asked whether a user can access a restricted resource, an authorizer can vote `PERMIT`, `DENY`, or `ABSTAIN`. The adjudicator will use this information to make a final decision on access.

The WebLogic Server authorization provider (named `DefaultAuthorizer`) can read in security policies declared in deployment descriptors. After these policies are stored in WebLogic Server, they can be modified from the Administration Console. However, these changes are not written back to the original deployment descriptor. They are, however, stored in the embedded LDAP server. The consequence of this is that if the application component is deployed again, the security policy in the deployment descriptor will overwrite information in the LDAP server.

Adjudicators

When configuring an application with complex security policies, it is possible that multiple security policies could be in place to protect a restricted resource.

Imagine a bank where an `Account` EJB with a deposit method is marked as restricted. A security policy with one authorization provider is set up based on the time of the day. It must be between 9 a.m. and 6 p.m. for the deposit method to be available. Another security policy set up with a different authorization provider is also set for this method based on the `CanDeposit` role. Let's say that both bank tellers and managers are included in this role. When a bank teller tries to make a deposit at 6:02 p.m. because the bank had to stay open for a very wealthy client, should access be allowed? This scenario is illustrated in Figure 27.18. The job of an adjudicator is to decide whether to give access to a restricted resource when different authorization providers return different access rights.

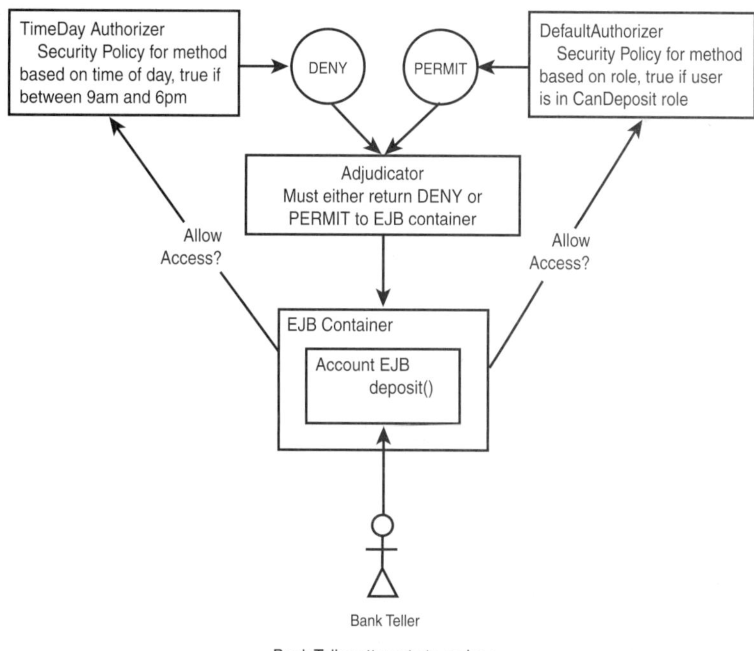

FIGURE 27.18 Adjudicators get the final say when authorizers can't agree on whether to grant access.

27

The WebLogic Server–supplied adjudicator provider (named `DefaultAdjudicator`) provides a very simple mechanism to make this decision. If the `RequireUnanimousPermit` attribute is set, all authorization providers must respond with a `PERMIT` vote in order to allow the user access. If the attribute is disabled, `ABSTAIN` votes will be ignored. If you are using multiple authorizers and you need a more complex decision-making process to decide on access, you will need to develop or purchase a custom adjudicator.

Keystore Providers

Keystore providers allow the private keys of users to be stored in a password-protected database. This provides an extra level of protection for this sensitive information. Applications that use SSL with keys and certificates must use have a default realm with a defined keystore provider.

The WebLogic Server keystore provider stores keys and certificates generated with the J2SE keytool. This provider stores both users' private keys and trusted CA certificates. The keytool utility or the WebLogic Server ImportPrivateKey utility can be used to add private keys to this providers' private key file.

Role Mapping Providers

Role mapping providers allow the WebLogic Server security framework to use complex business logic that determines at runtime if a user is in a particular role. The WebLogic Server security framework allows roles to be created based on rules concerning username, group membership, and time of day. The business logic contained in a role mapping provider can use rules that are much more complex and are application specific. Role mapping providers give role information to authorizers to help them determine whether a user should have access to a restricted resource.

The WebLogic Server role mapping provider (named `DefaultRoleMapper`) contains an attribute named `RoleDeploymentEnabled`. When set, this provider will use roles that have been set in Web application and EJB deployment descriptors (in `weblogic.xml` and `weblogic-ejb-jar.xml` files). This provider uses the roles in deployment descriptors and WebLogic Server security roles set in the Administrator Console. If your organization already has a role mapping implementation in place, you need to create a custom role mapping provider that will utilize that system.

Credential Mapping Provider

Credential mapping providers provides a means of determining credential information to authenticate a user on an external systems based on whomever is the current user. These external systems include databases and EIS instances.

The WebLogic Server credential mapping provider (named `DefaultCredentialMapper`) contains an attribute named `CredentialMappingDeploymentEnabled`. When set, this provider will read credential mapping information from deployment descriptors (in `weblogic-ra.xml`) in resource adapters when they are deployed. This provider maps WebLogic Server users and groups to usernames and passwords in external systems. If you want to map to other credentials, such as Kerberos tickets, you will need a custom credential mapping provider.

Auditing Providers

Auditing providers provide a way to collect, store, and distribute information supplied by other security providers (most notably, authentication and authorization providers). If they have been configured to do so, other security providers will pass auditing providers `AuditEvent` objects representing actions auditing such as login and logout. Auditing providers will then read the information in these `AuditEvent` objects and store them in their own designated mechanisms, examples of which are LDAP and RDBMS. Typical auditing events are authentication on name and password or tokens, and user account locking and unlocking. Auditing providers store this information for the purposes of nonrepudiation.

The WebLogic auditing provider stores audit information in a file named `DefaultAuditRecorder.log` located in your WebLogic application domain's root directory (for example, `[WEBLOGIC_HOME]\user_projects\domains\mydomain`). This provider stores the audit events in Table 27.1. This provider can store events based on its current severity level. These levels are `NONE`, `INFORMATION`, `WARNING`, `ERROR`, `SUCCESS` and `FAILURE`. If you want to output to another file or another medium, such as a database, you will need a custom auditing provider.

TABLE 27.1 WebLogic Auditing Provider Events

Audit Event	Description
AUTHENTICATE	Username/password authentication occurred
ASSERTIDENTITY	Perimeter (token-based) authentication occurred
USERLOCKED	User account locked for too many invalid login attempts
USERUNLOCKED	User account has been cleared
USERLOCKOUTEXPIRED	User account lock has expired

27

Rules About Security Providers and Realms

Due to the way security providers work with the WebLogic Server security framework, there are rules concerning which providers are required and which can occur more than once in a security realm. These are described in Table 27.2.

TABLE 27.2 Security Provider Rules

Security Provider	Required?	Multiple Allowed?
Authentication	Yes	Yes
Identity Assertion	No	Yes
Principal Validation	Yes	Yes
Authorization	Yes	Yes
Adjudication	Yes (only if there are multiple authorization providers)	No
Role Mapping	Yes	Yes
Auditing	No	Yes
Credential Mapping	No	Yes

Migration from WebLogic Server 6.x

Because the security framework in WebLogic Server since version 7.0 and later has been completely overhauled from previous versions, existing security solutions must be updated to work with versions 7.0 and 8.1. This includes existing security realms and any custom security code. This section provides a brief overview of this topic. More information can be found at `http://e-docs.bea.com/wls/docs81/upgrade/upgrade6xto81.html#security`.

Compatibility Realm

In providing an overhauled security framework, BEA has tried not to alienate existing users by providing a security compatibility mode. If you boot WebLogic Server 8.1 using a WebLogic Server 6.x `config.xml` file, two security realms will be created: the `myrealm` realm as described earlier and the compatibility realm. The compatibility realm, along with Realm adapter authentication providers, will allow access to existing users, groups, and access control lists (ACLs). This realm is deprecated and should be used as an interim method while you reconfigure your application to work with 8.1 security.

Realm Adapter Authentication Provider

The realm adapter authentication provider is a special type of authentication provider that enables you to continue to use users and groups stored in a Windows NT, Unix, RDBMS, or custom WebLogic Server 6.x security realm. It provides limited capability to 6.x security realms. Refer to WebLogic Server documentation to make sure that your applications will work with the limited feature set offered by such backward compatibility.

Summary

In this chapter we covered security, starting with the J2SE model based on where code comes from and how code can be trusted with digital certificates. Then we discussed the J2EE security model for authentication as well as access control that defines roles and access rights to restricted resources. We continued with an overview of JAAS and the Pluggable Authorization Model (PAM). We then talked about the WebLogic Server security framework and the features within it, including security realms and providers.

In the next chapter, we will discuss and demonstrate additional steps necessary for implementing security in WebLogic Server applications. We will discuss how to create WebLogic Server users, groups, roles, and security policies, and how LDAP is used. You will be introduced to the JAAS APIs and how to provide security for non-Web users. We will also discuss how to use digital certificates and SSL. All this and more…so, if you're ready to get started, turn the page!

CHAPTER 28

Securing WebLogic Server and WebLogic Server Applications

by Jeff Marin and Steve Steffen

IN THIS CHAPTER

- Protecting WebLogic Server Applications
- Securing Java Clients
- Introduction to JAAS
- Creating a Custom Security Provider
- Using Secure Sockets Layer
- Establishing Trust Between Domains
- Securing Best Practices

In this chapter, we discuss how to secure applications that run on WebLogic Server and how to secure WebLogic Server itself. WebLogic Server applications can potentially have many resources that must be restricted to authorized users. The J2EE specification allows EJB methods, EIS instances, and Web components to be restricted. WebLogic Server extends this by allowing just about every other resource to be restricted as well. This includes resources related to JMS, JNDI, JDBC, Web services, COM objects, and the administrator console.

Protecting WebLogic Server applications without protecting WebLogic Server itself is a futile task. There's no point in creating users, groups, and roles and then trying to protect them with security policies if hackers can just bypass the whole security framework and tap into our sensitive data and business logic. Therefore, in this chapter, we discuss the mechanisms that WebLogic Server supplies to deter hackers from disrupting our applications and bringing down WebLogic Server itself.

Protecting WebLogic Server Applications

In this section, we start with how to secure applications using the default WebLogic Server security providers. We see how these providers work with the J2EE security model and demonstrate how to manage and configure these providers.

Selecting a Realm

To start off, we will use the default realm named myrealm. This realm is configured with WebLogic Server–supplied security providers. When a new domain is created, myrealm is the only realm in that domain and it's the default realm for the new domain as well, as shown in Figure 28.1. Applications running in this domain use myrealm for their security unless another realm is created and set as the default.

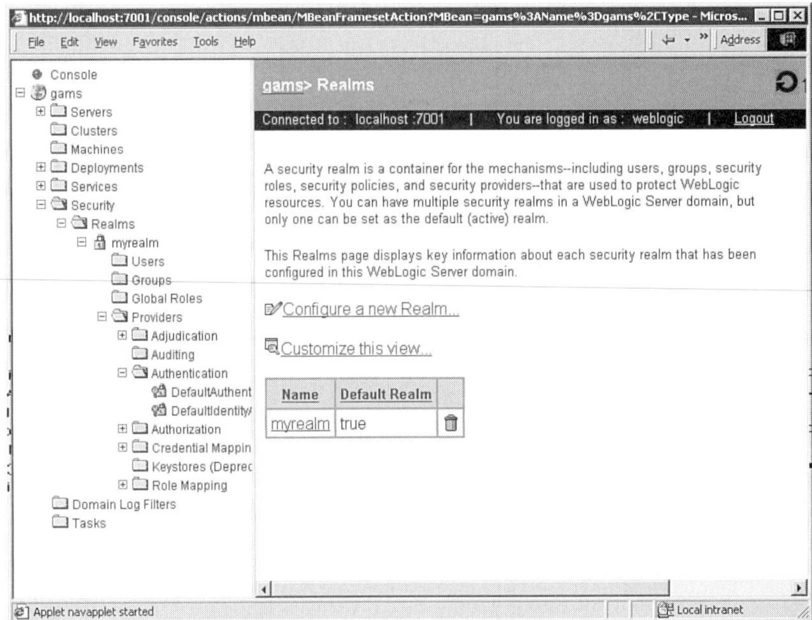

Figure 28.1 A domain starts with myrealm as the default realm.

Defining Users and Group

The way users, groups, roles, and security policies are configured in this section is particular to the WebLogic default security providers. When using a different provider, please refer to that provider's manual.

The first step in securing applications is to define WebLogic Server users and groups. To define user and groups in a realm, it must have a configured authentication provider. Our default realm starts off configured with the WebLogic authentication provider named DefaultAuthenticator, as shown in Figure 28.2. This provider enables us to set the minimum password required for users.

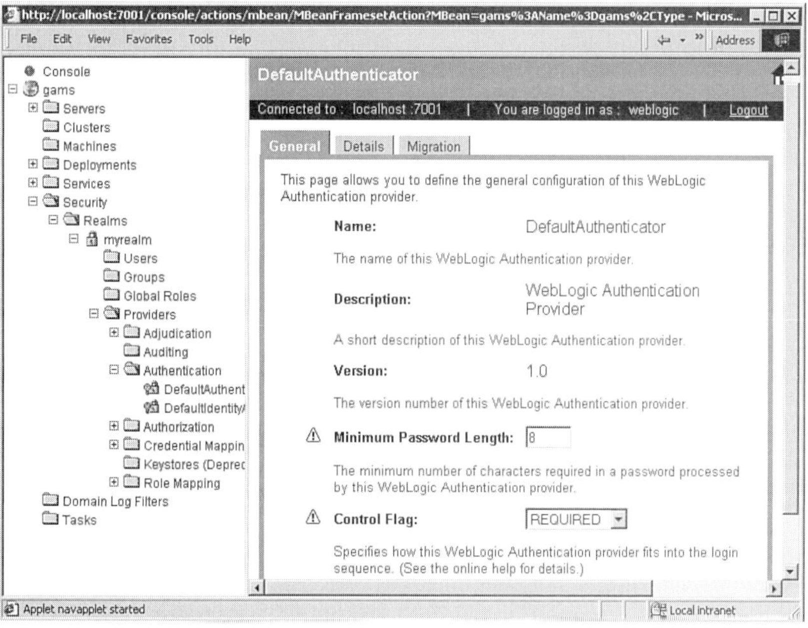

Figure 28.2 DefaultAuthenticator is the preconfigured authentication provider for myrealm.

This provider uses an embedded LDAP server to store user and group information. Together with the WebLogic authorization provider, DefaultAuthenticator introduced in WebLogic 7.x replaces the File realm that was available in WebLogic Server 6.x.

Defining Users

If you already have users and groups defined externally, you won't want to enter them by hand. Please refer to the sections later in this chapter concerning configuring other authentication providers, specifically the section "Using External LDAP Servers." If you're migrating from an older version of WebLogic Server, refer to the section "Migrating Security from Previous WebLogic Server Versions." Also note that if you're migrating, there's no predefined user named `guest` in WebLogic Server.

To display registered WebLogic Server users, open the Console and click on the Users tab in the left panel. The right panel will display the current users. Although you haven't created any users yet, you'll see a default user is already present. This is the administrator user that boots up WebLogic Server in this domain—it was set up when the domain was created. This user must be part of the Administrators group in order for it to be able to boot WebLogic Server.

New users are created by clicking the Users tab in the left panel and then clicking on the Configure a New User link in the right panel. This will display the Create User form shown in Figure 28.3. Enter the user information and click the Apply button. The username must be unique for the realm. Be sure to enter at least the minimum number of characters for the password.

CAUTION

Also make certain that the passwords match. After a user has been created, the username cannot be changed but the password can. A description is optional.

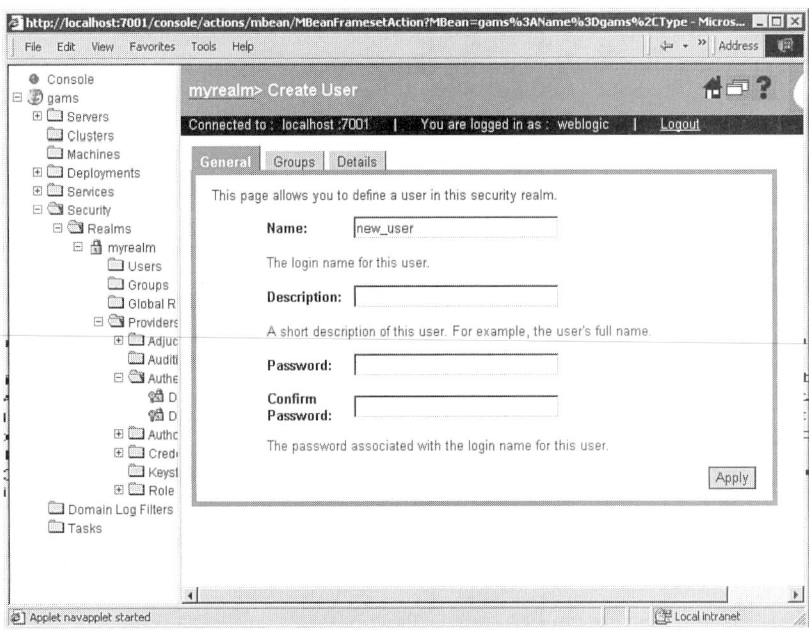

Figure 28.3 Create new users by entering their WebLogic Server name and password.

Users can be added to a group by selecting the user and then clicking on the Groups tag in the right panel. This will display the Groups form as shown in Figure 28.4. To add a user to one or more groups, select the groups in the Possible Groups column and click the highlighted right arrow. To remove a user from one or more groups, select those groups from the Current Groups list and click the highlighted left arrow.

When there are many users, you can display only users whose names meet a filter condition. Type a username in the Filter By: text box and click the Filter button. Only that user will be displayed. You can use the asterisk (*) only as a wildcard character, as shown in Figure 28.5.

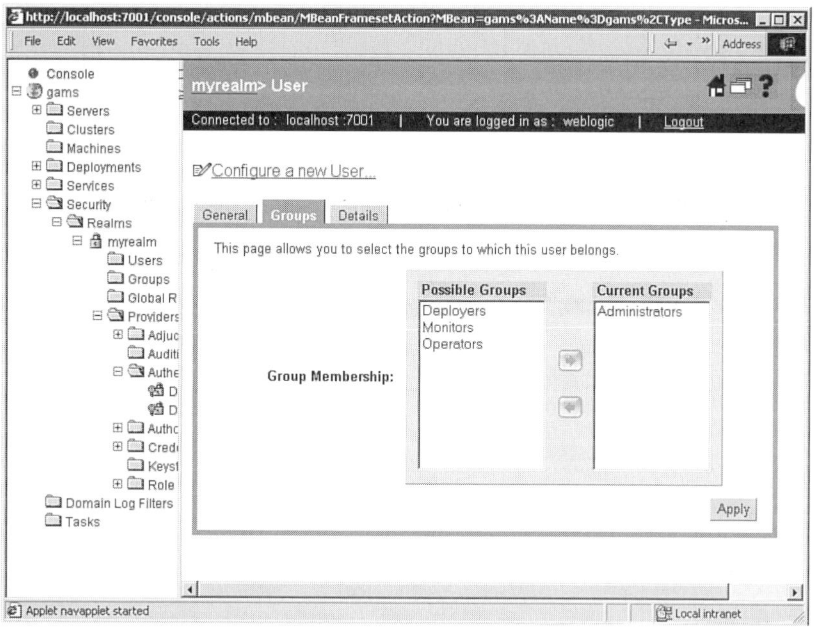

Figure 28.4 Users can be members of one or more groups.

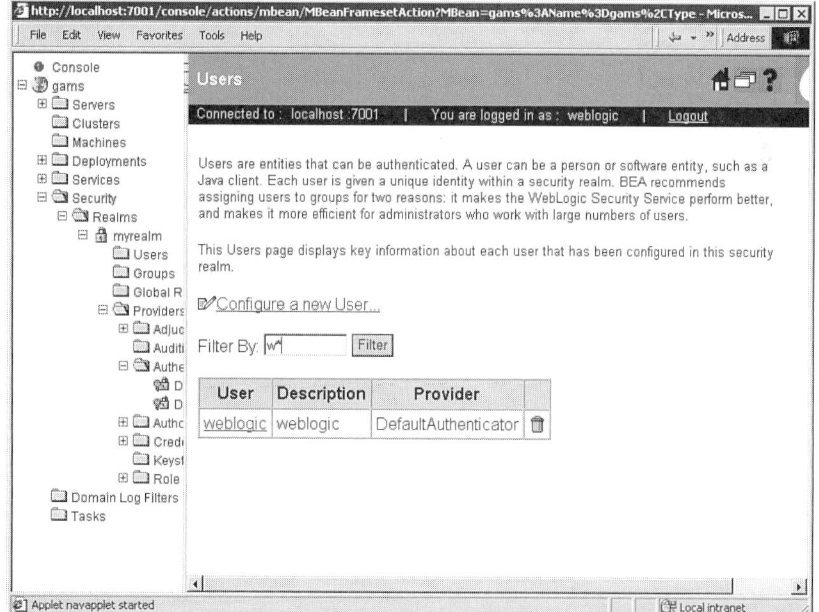

Figure 28.5 Large numbers of users can be filtered.

A user can be deleted by clicking on the trashcan icon next to his name, as shown in Figure 28.6. Before the user is deleted, you'll have a chance to confirm this action.

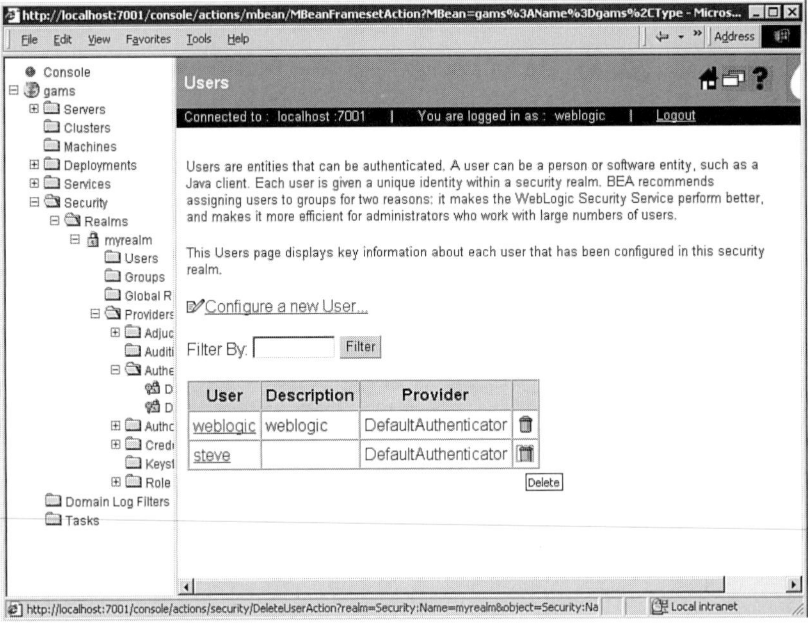

Figure 28.6 Users are deleted by clicking the trashcan icon.

Defining Groups

Groups allow collections of users to be categorized according to some common characteristics such as job title, department, and physical location. The choice of groupings should be based on security requirements of applications that will use this realm. When assigning security roles and policies to groups to determine resource access, every member of the group will be assigned the same role and policy. This makes assigning security to large numbers of users a manageable task. You're strongly encouraged to use groups and to choose correct groupings according to your application's security needs. Groups can contain other groups in a hierarchical fashion.

To display registered WebLogic Server groups, click the Groups tab in the left panel—the right panel will display the current groups. WebLogic Server starts with a number of default groups as shown in Table 28.1.

TABLE 28.1 Default WebLogic Server Groups

Group Name	Description
Administrators	These users can view and change all resource attributes and start and stop WebLogic Server. By default, this group includes the user who started WebLogic Server in this domain.
Operators	These users can view all resource attributes and can start and stop WebLogic Server. This group is initially empty.
Deployers	These users can view all resource attributes and deploy applications and EJBs. This group is initially empty.
Monitors	These users can view and modify all resource attributes and perform unrestricted operations. This group is initially empty.

To crate a new group, click on the Groups tab in the left panel and then click on the Configure a New Group link in the right panel. This displays the Create Group form shown in Figure 28.7. Enter a group name and (optionally) a description, and click the Apply button. Group names must be unique within a realm.

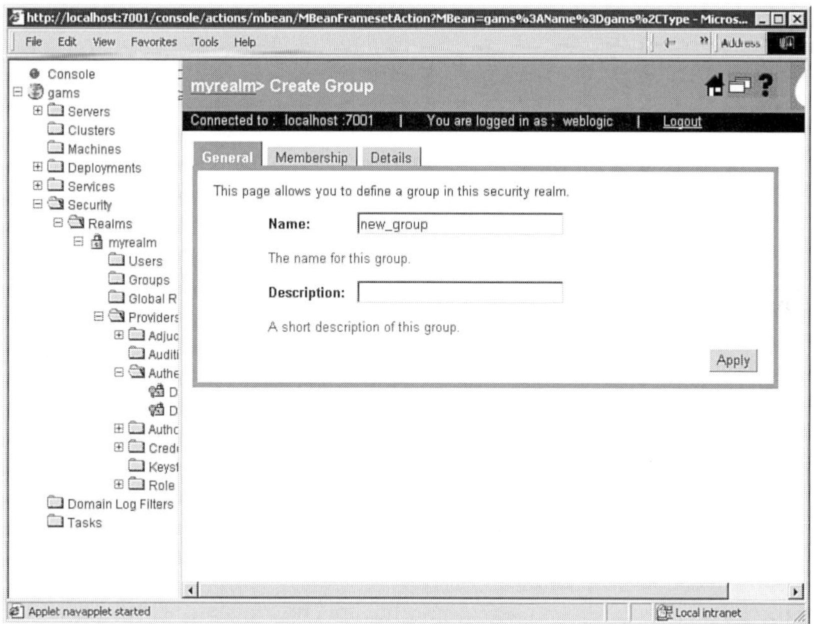

Figure 28.7 Create a new group by entering its name.

28

After a group has been created, it can be included in other groups. Groups can be added to other groups by selecting the group and then clicking on the Membership tag in the right panel. This displays the Membership form shown in Figure 28.8. To add a group to one or more groups, select one or more groups in the Possible Groups column and click the highlighted right arrow. To remove a group from one of more groups, select the group from the Current Groups list and click the highlighted left arrow. Creating a group hierarchy allows for easier management of security policies, but only if the hierarchy lends itself to the security requirements of the application the users will be accessing.

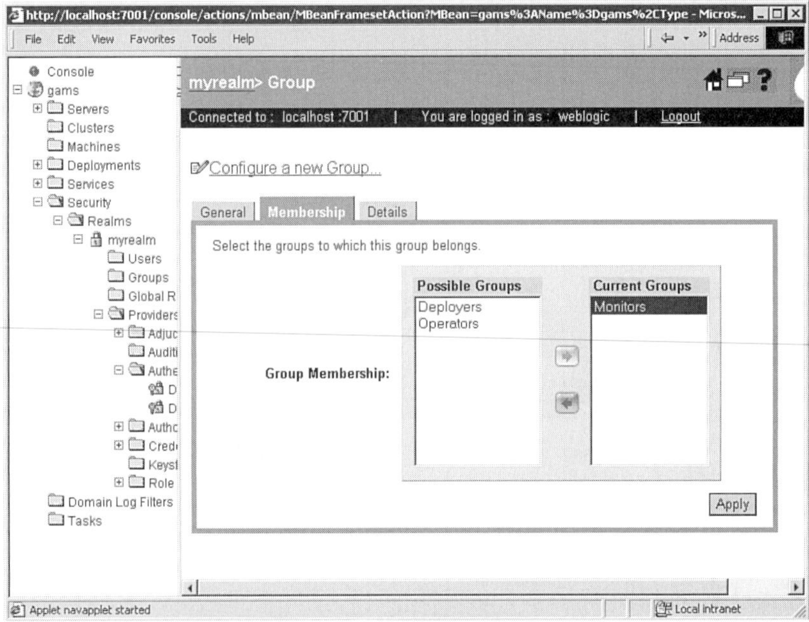

Figure 28.8 Groups can be members of other groups.

When there are many groups, you can display only groups whose names meet a filter condition. Type the group name in the Filter By: text box and click the Filter button. Only that group will be displayed. You can also use the asterisk (*) as a wildcard character as shown in Figure 28.9.

A group can be deleted by clicking on the trashcan icon next to its name, as shown in Figure 28.10. Before the group is deleted, you have a chance to confirm this action.

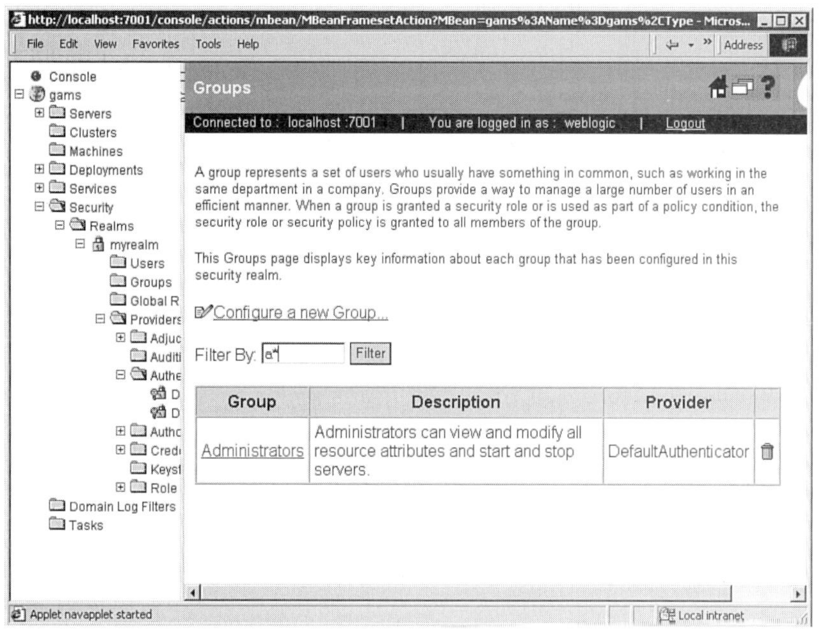

Figure 28.9 Large number of groups can be filtered down.

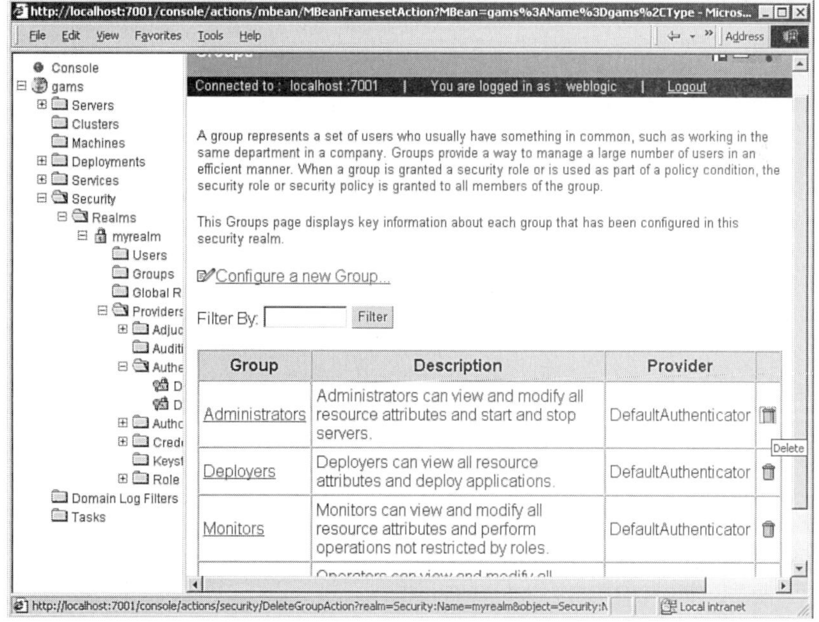

Figure 28.10 Groups are deleted by clicking the trashcan icon.

Granting Global Roles

A *role* represents a collection of users who share permissions to access restricted resources. Although WebLogic Server groups are static collections whose membership is defined by system administrators, the membership of a role is determined dynamically based on information such as username, group membership, or time of the day. Roles can be assigned to both WebLogic Server users and groups. Security policies are then assigned to roles to determine access to restricted resources. For efficient management, it's recommended to assign roles to groups rather than individual users. WebLogic Server has two different types of roles:

- Global roles—These are roles that span many different resources. We'll later see how global roles can be used to grant permissions to access your applications' components. WebLogic Server ships with a number of default roles, as depicted in Table 28.2. These roles have been granted to WebLogic Server groups by default. Although you can create as many roles as necessary for WebLogic Server applications, only the roles in Table 28.2 can view or change WebLogic Server configuration information.

TABLE 28.2 Default WebLogic Server Global Roles

Role Name	Permissions Granted
Admin	View and modify server configuration. Deploy most resources. Start and stop WebLogic Server. Includes members from Administrators group.
Deployer	View nonencrypted server configuration attributes and deploy most resources. Includes members from Deployers group.
Operator	View nonencrypted server configuration attributes. Start, stop, and resume WebLogic Server. Includes members from Operators group.
Monitor	View nonencrypted server configuration attributes. Includes members from Monitors group.
Anonymous	All users are granted this role.

- Scoped Roles—A role that's associated with a specific resource such as access to a JMS connection factory or a JDBC connection pool.

Creating Global Roles

In the administrator console, click on the Globals Roles tab in the left panel and the Configure a New Global Role link in the right panel. Enter the name of a role and click the Apply button. Names of global roles must be unique.

The *role statement* for a role is a set of conditions that determines membership for that role. To set the role statement for a role, select the role and then click the Conditions tab in the right panel. A role statement is composed of one or more role conditions. Each role condition can be based on username, group membership, and time of the day. Although a role can be based on individual username, it's a much better practice to base it on group membership.

> **NOTE**
>
> Global roles take precedence over local roles specified in the `weblogic.xml` and `weblogic-ejb-jar.xml` files.

To add a role condition to the role statement, select the role condition in the right panel and click the Add button. A window will open to enable you to further specify the condition.

If you base the new condition on group membership, you can select one or more groups, as shown in Figure 28.11. Type the name of each group and click the Add button. These groups must be defined with the new authentication provider of the realm.

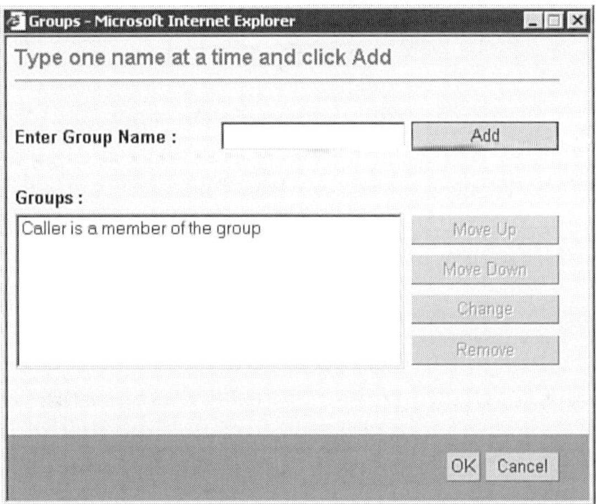

Figure 28.11 Adding a role condition based on group membership.

If more than one group is added, you can decide whether a user needs to be in all the groups or at least one of them, as shown in Figure 28.12. Select the word *or* in the Groups list and click the Change button; doing so changes the word *or* to the word *and*.

The connecting word between group names can be one of the following:

- And—Implies that the user must be a member of every group
- Or—Implies that a user must be a member of at least one group

For more complex conditions, *or*s and *and*s can be mixed together. If this is done, WebLogic Server evaluates the expression from top to bottom. More restrictive statements should be toward the bottom. Selecting a statement and then clicking the Move Up or the Move Down button changes the order of that statement.

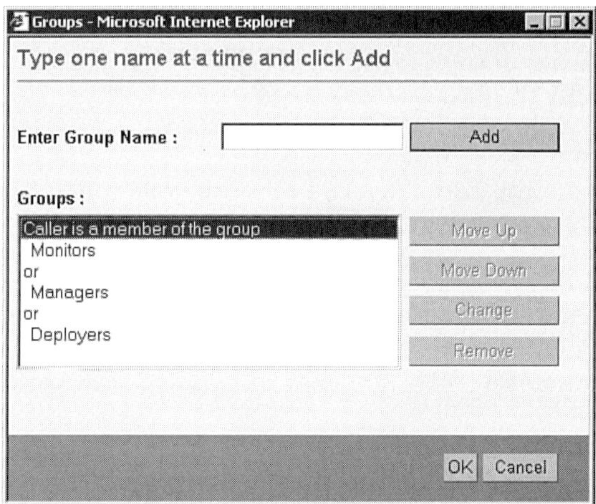

Figure 28.12 Creating a complex group membership condition.

Adding a new condition based on username is essentially the same process as adding a condition based on group membership. A new condition based on time enables you to set the starting and ending times that users are granted this role.

Combining Conditions

As was the case with complex group conditions, a role statement can consist of many individual conditions that are connected with *and*s and *or*s, as shown in Figure 28.13. Each *and* can be changed to an *or* and vice versa. Click on the line that starts with this word and press the Change button. When creating complex role statements, more restrictive conditions should come later because WebLogic will evaluate these conditions from top to bottom and left to right.

Role information is stored with that user and group information. In the case of the WebLogic authentication and authorization providers, this information is stored in an embedded LDAP server.

Granting Scoped Roles

Scoped roles apply to only a single resource, such as a branch of the server JNDI tree. To grant a scoped role to a resource, highlight the resource in the administrator console, press the right mouse button, and select the Define Scoped Role link, and then click on the Configure a New Scoped Role link. The Create Role form will then be displayed as shown in Figure 28.14. Enter the name of the role and click the Apply button. Then create a role statement in the same way you created a global role. Scoped roles can be applied to many resources, including the JNDI tree, EJB methods, Web services, and Web application components.

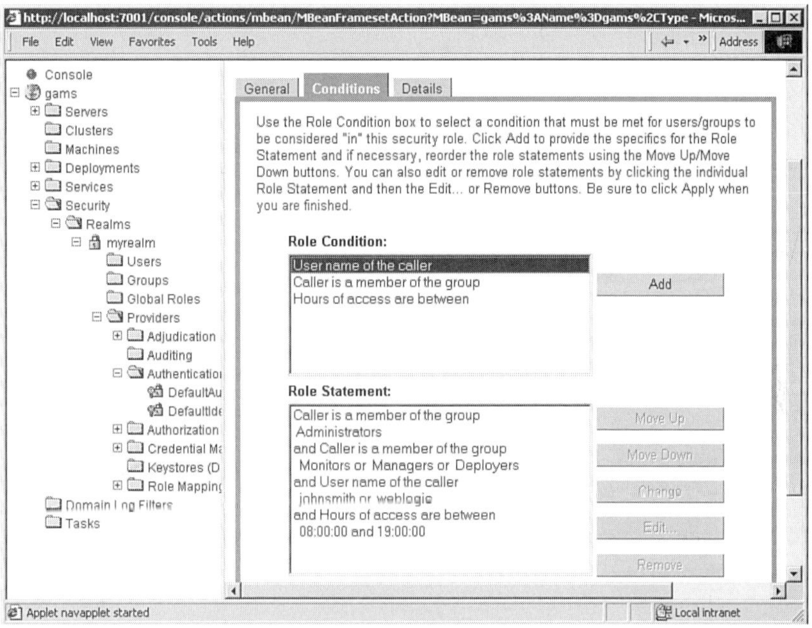

Figure 28.13 A role statement can end up being complex.

Creating Security Policies

After an application client has been successfully authenticated, the process of determining access levels for restricted resources is referred to as *authorization*. WebLogic Server uses security policies to answer the question of "Who has access?" Instead of using the access control lists (ACLs) employed in previous versions, WebLogic Server now utilizes security policies. Security policies specify access rights for a user, group, or role with a specific resource or type of resource. Out of the box, security policies can also be based on the time of the day. Because the WebLogic Server security framework is very flexible, custom security policies could be based on virtually any data and business logic.

Security policies are used to answer the question of who has access to a restricted resource. A security policy enables us to define a link between a WebLogic Server resource and a user, group, role, or time constraint. Policies can be associated with a type of resource or an individual resource. If assigned to a type, new instances of that type will inherit the same security policy.

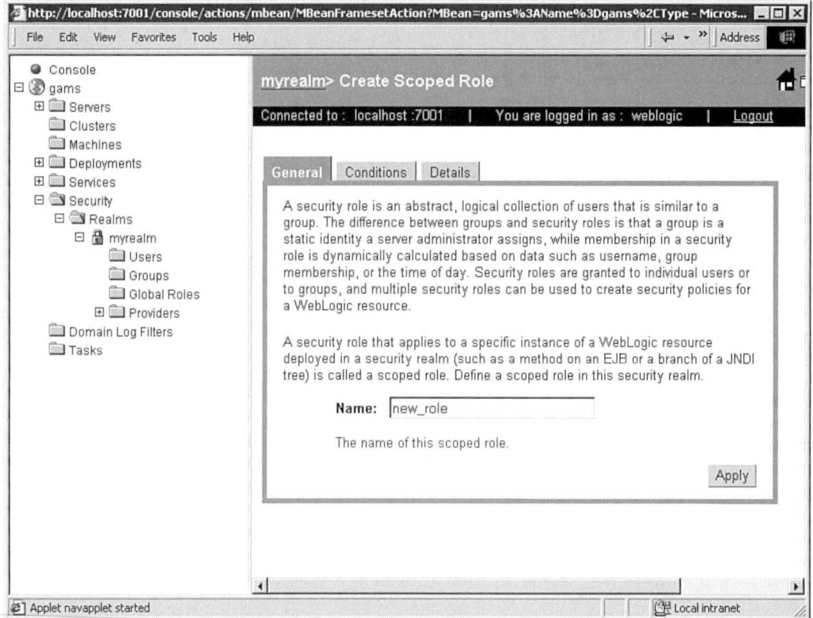

Figure 28.14 Create scoped roles by selecting a resource and pressing the right mouse button.

WebLogic Server comes with predefined security policies for its resources, as shown in Table 28.3. The policies are based on groups and roles. Although policies can be based on individual users, basing them on roles and groups is highly recommended for efficient management.

TABLE 28.3 Default WebLogic Server Security Policies

WebLogic Server Resource	Security Policy
Administrative	Admin, Deployer, Operator, and Monitor roles
COM	jCOMRole role
EIS	Everyone group
EJB	Everyone group
JMS	Everyone group
JDBC	Everyone group
JNDI	Everyone group
Mbean	Everyone group
Server	Admin, Operator roles
Web Service	Everyone group

Creating a security policy is like creating a scoped role. First highlight the resource you're interested in. This can be either an individual resource such as a specific EJB or a type of resource such as all EJB deployments. Press the right mouse button and select the Define Security Policy link. Figure 28.15 shows what the security policy screen looks like.

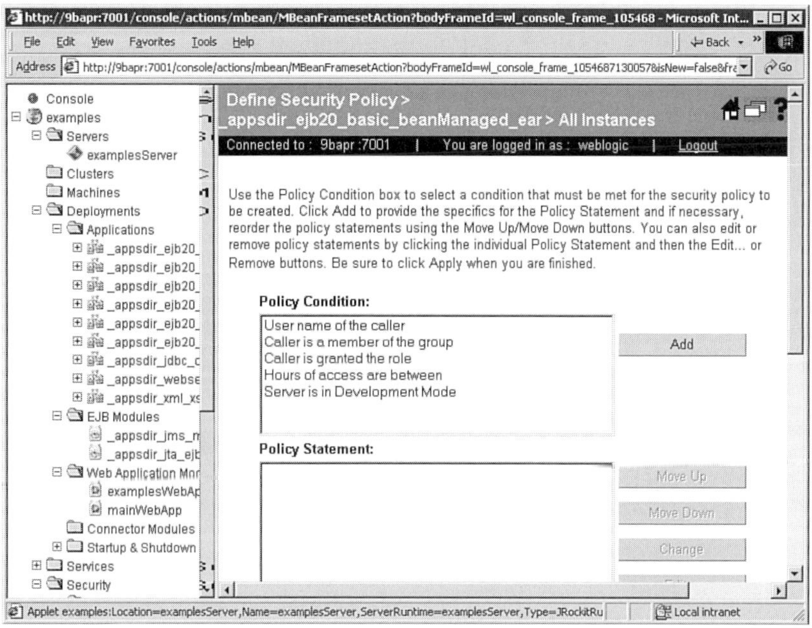

Figure 28.15 Create a security policy by selecting a resource and pressing the right mouse button.

Now create the policy statement based on policy conditions. The instructions for doing this are the same as for roles, with the exception that security policies can be based on username, group membership, role membership, and time of the day. Security policies can be applied to many resources, including the JNDI tree, EJB methods, Web services, and Web application components. Security policies specified in J2EE deployment descriptors can be viewed and modified in the admin console.

The Lightweight Directory Access Protocol

The Lightweight Directory Access Protocol (LDAP) is a universal mechanism for storing virtually any type of information, including information required for ACLs. LDAP provides for a hierarchy of information. Examples of this are that users can be grouped by department, and ZIP Codes can be grouped by county and then by state. There is virtually no limit to the levels of information that can be stored in LDAP. Many software vendors have adopted LDAP for storing user and group information in their products.

Configuring the Embedded LDAP Server

The WebLogic authentication, authorization, role mapping, and credential mapping providers use an embedded LDAP server to store user, group, role, and security policies. Information from these providers is stored in the admin server and replicated to all managed servers in the domain. At the present time, this LDAP server can only be used internally by WebLogic Server. In the future, BEA might open up the LDAP subsystem that would allow applications to store their information there as well.

To change attributes for the embedded LDAP server, click the domain name in the left panel of the admin console. Click on the View Domain Wide Security Settings link at the bottom of the screen, and then click the Embedded LDAP tab. You will then see the Embedded LDAP configuration form, as shown in Figure 28.16. From here, you can change backup, cache, and cluster information.

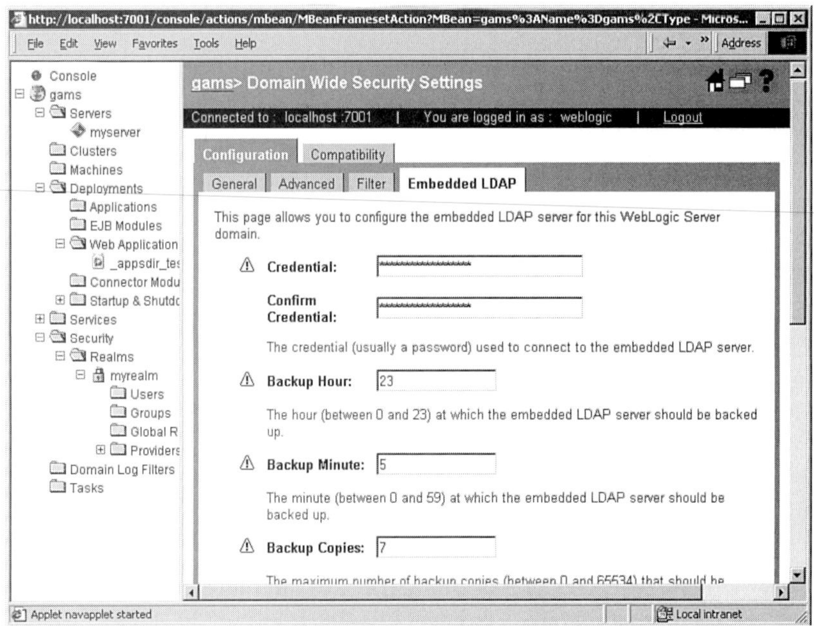

Figure 28.16 Configuring embedded LDAP server settings.

Using External LDAP Servers

In addition to the default authentication provider, WebLogic Server comes with several other authentication providers that can use Novell's LDAP server, Sun's iPlanet LDAP server, Microsoft's Active Directory LDAP server, and the Open LDAP server. Each of these security providers requires configuration information including the following:

- Host and port of the LDAP server
- WebLogic Server principal and password used to connect to LDAP server
- How users and groups are stored and where they're stored in the LDAP server

To use an external LDAP server, click on the Authentication tab, found under Providers in the appropriate realm in the left pane of the administration console, and select the appropriate LDAP vendor you want to connect with. You then have an opportunity to enter configuration information. An example of this is shown in Figure 28.17.

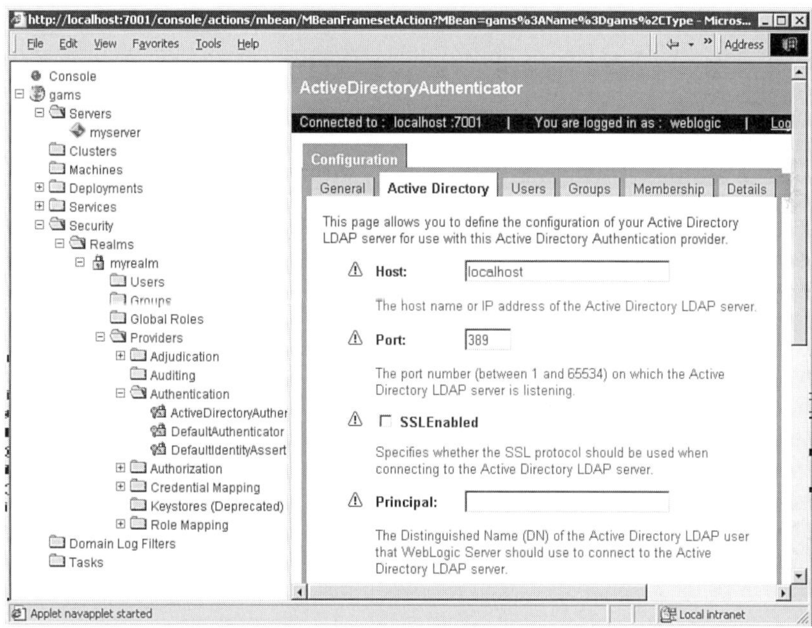

Figure 28.17 External LDAP servers can be accessed from WebLogic Server.

Migrating Security from Previous WebLogic Server Versions

In the current version of WebLogic Server, the File, Caching, LDAP, Windows NT, Unix, RDBMS, and custom security realms have been deprecated. WebLogic Server now ships with compatibility security to enable you to continue to use your 6.x security realms. The only security realm available in compatibility security is the Compatible realm. The Compatible realm comes with realm adapter providers that allow 6.x security realms to be used. It's important to remember that the realm adapter providers have been deprecated and should not be relied upon for future security. They should be used only until your applications have been upgraded to work with the latest version.

NOTE

Information about using compatibility security can be found at `http://e-docs.bea.com/wls/docs81/secmanage/security6.html`. For more information about migration issues, please refer to Appendix C, "Migration from Previous Versions."

Customizing the Default Realm

So far, we've been using the default realm, myrealm, with all the default WebLogic Server security providers. However, there are many cases in which this configuration will not be sufficient:

- Custom security provider—There are times when the WebLogic security providers won't do. This could involve tapping into an existing security mechanism, such as an external role mapper, or building a more complex provider, such as an advanced adjudicator. For instance, if you already have or want to store user and group information in a database, you need a custom security provider.
- Additional security providers—Your application's security requirements might necessitate additional security providers. For instance, you might want to authenticate against an external LDAP server in addition to the WebLogic Server–embedded LDAP server.
- Migration from a previous WebLogic Server version—When you're ready to upgrade from the Compatible realm, you might need to customize the default security realm. When migrating from the Compatible realm, creating a brand-new realm for testing purposes is recommended. In that realm, you can configure security providers and populate it with security data (user, groups, roles, and security providers). When the new realm is thoroughly tested, set it as the default realm.

Choosing a Default Realm

Every WebLogic Server domain can have one or more security realms. However, only one can be the default realm. To set a realm as the default, click on the domain name in the left panel of the admin console. Click on the View Domain-wide Security Settings link on the bottom right and then click on the General tab underneath. This will display the General Security form shown in Figure 28.18. Select the default realm and click the Apply button.

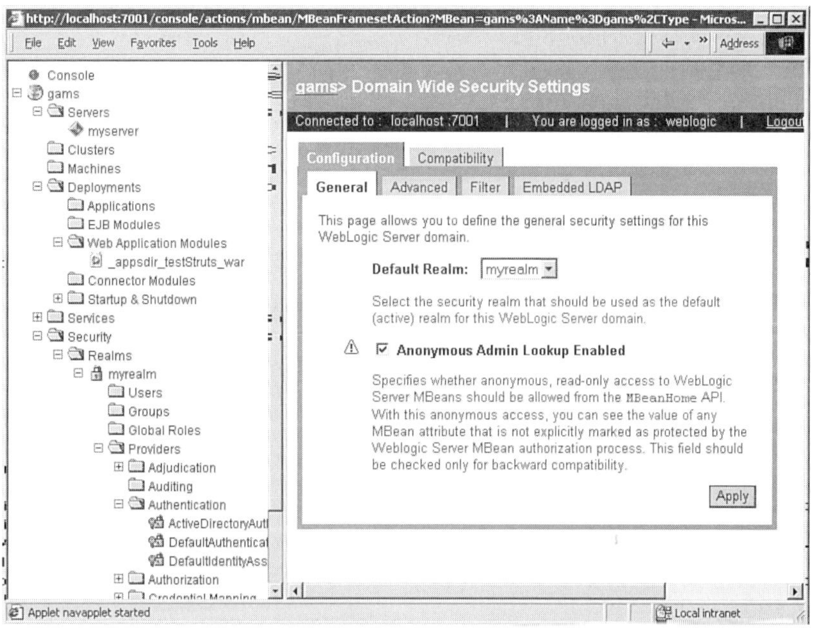

Figure 28.18 Setting a default security realm.

Securing Java Clients

Unlike Web clients using Internet browsers, application clients require a different strategy for implementing security. In the past, application clients of WebLogic Server used JNDI for authentication. Although JAAS is a standard extension to security in J2EE 1.3, it's the preferred method of application client authentication in WebLogic Server. Security implementations based on JNDI works under WebLogic Server, but some methods in the `weblogic.jndi.Environment` class based on JNDI authentication have been deprecated. This is why BEA recommends using JAAS for all username and password authentication. For two-way SSL authentication, JNDI is used because JAAS does not handle this.

WebLogic Server, being J2EE 1.3–compliant, supports Java Authentication and Authorization Service (JAAS) version 1.0. WebLogic Server supports JAAS authentication on the server, and JAAS authentication and authorization on application clients. To authenticate application clients, using JAAS is preferred over JNDI, but this chapter will cover both ways starting with the JNDI authentication.

JNDI Authentication

JNDI uses the security models already in place in the Java platform; it does not implement its own. That being said, there are several environment variables that can be used within

JNDI. For a simple authentication within JNDI with WebLogic Server, your must create a `Hashtable` object and include the following key mapping fields, which are contained within the `javax.naming.Context` object:

- `Context.INITIAL_CONTEXT_FACTORY`—Defines the fully qualified context factory to use to create an initial context
- `Context.PROVIDER_URL`—Defines configuration for the service provider to use; in this case, WebLogic
- `Context.SECURITY_PRINCIPAL`—Holds the principal for authenticating the caller to the service
- `Context.SECURITY_CREDENTIALS`—Holds the credentials for authenticating the caller to the service

After setting these parameters, create a new `initialContext` with the variables and then perform the lookup on the resource. If it does not authenticate, an exception is thrown. Listing 28.1 gives an example of using JNDI authentication to get an object.

LISTING 28.1 A JNDI Call to WebLogic

```
Context con = null;
try{
Hashtable environment = new Hashtable();
      environment.put(Context.INITIAL_CONTEXT_FACTORY,
                          "weblogic.jndi.WLInitialContextFactory");
      environment.put(Context.PROVIDER_URL, "t3s://weblogic:7002");
            environment.put(Context.SECURITY_PRINCIPAL, "user");
environment.put(Context.SECURITY_CREDENTIALS, "password");
con = new InitialContext(environment);
Object myEJB = (Object) con.lookup("myEJB");
}catch(NamingSecurityException e){
}finally{
if (context != null)
con.close();
}
```

Listing 28.1 is an example of a one-way SSL authentication with JNDI. If a private key and a chain of X.509 certificates are needed as an extra measure of security, two-way SSL authentication is required. To find more information about two-way SSL authentication, BEA has information on edocs at `http://edocs.bea.com/wls/docs81/security/SSL_client.html`.

Introduction to JAAS

As discussed in the last chapter, JAAS introduces the following classes: `Subject`, `Principal`, `LoginContext`, and `LoginModule`. We'll now see how to uses these classes and others to authenticate WebLogic Server application clients.

JAAS Login Configuration File

According to J2SE specifications, to keep JAAS login implementations separate from application code, a login configuration file is used at runtime to determine which `LoginModules` should be used for client authentication. A login configuration file contains one or entries of the following form:

```
<entry name> {
<LoginModule> <flag> <LoginModule options>;
<LoginModule> <flag> <LoginModule options>;
    . . .
    };
```

The entry name, used in application code, is associated with one or more `LoginModules` at runtime. An example of this is

```
Sample {
weblogic.security.auth.login.UsernamePasswordLoginModule required debug=false;
};
```

You can specify the location and name of the JAAS login configuration file using either the command line or the Java security properties file:

- Command line—Set the system property when starting the JVM like the following example:

  ```
  Djava.security.auth.login.config==file:D:/jaas.conf
  ```

- Java security properties file—One or more configuration files can be specified with the following format:

  ```
  login.config.url.XXX=file:D:/jaas.conf
  ```

  where XXX starts at 1 followed by 2, and so on. The Java security properties file is located in the `JAVA_HOME\jre\lib` directory and is called `java.security`.

Callback Handlers

JAAS employs a flexible model for gathering client credentials whether they are username and password pairs or another form. Callback handlers are sent to `LoginContexts` and

LoginModules. These are functions that call into the application client itself. For instance, if the username isn't supplied, a LoginModule will call an appropriate callback and the application client can decide how to respond. It might present the end user with a window or collect the information from a swiped smart card. Callbacks do not impose any restrictions on how application clients can gather their client credentials.

Applications implement the CallbackHandler interface found in the javax.security.auth.callback package. This interface contains a single method:

```
public void handle(Callback[] callbacks)
throws IOException, UnsupportedCallbackException
```

When a LoginModule needs client credentials, it invokes the CallbackHandler and passes it information in the form of an array of callbacks. Each of the following classes implements the Callback interface specified in the javax.security.auth.callback package:

- NameCallback—Used to request username
- URLCallback—Used to request URL
- PasswordCallback—Used to request password
- TextInputCallback—Used to request generic text information
- TextOutputCallback—Used to provide information, warnings, or error messages

How a callback handler responds to these callbacks is completely application specific. Listing 28.2 is an example of a CallbackHandler that uses the JOptionPane Swing class to display a dialog box to supply a missing username, password, or URL.

LISTING 28.2 A CallbackHandler That Displays Swing Dialog Boxes to Request Missing Information

```
import java.io.*;
import javax.security.auth.callback.Callback;
import javax.security.auth.callback.CallbackHandler;
import javax.security.auth.callback.UnsupportedCallbackException;
import javax.security.auth.callback.TextOutputCallback;
import javax.security.auth.callback.PasswordCallback;
import javax.security.auth.callback.TextInputCallback;
import javax.security.auth.callback.NameCallback;
import weblogic.security.auth.callback.URLCallback;

import javax.swing.*;
class SwingCallbackHandler implements CallbackHandler
{
private String username = null;
```

LISTING 28.2 Continued

```
private String password = null;
private String url = null;

public SwingCallbackHandler() { }
public SwingCallbackHandler(String pUsername, String pPassword, String pUrl)
  {
username = pUsername;
password = pPassword;
url = pUrl;
  }

public void handle(Callback[] callbacks)
throws IOException, UnsupportedCallbackException
  {
for(int i = 0; i < callbacks.length; i++)
    {
if(callbacks[i] instanceof TextOutputCallback)
      {
// Display the message according to the specified type
TextOutputCallback toc = (TextOutputCallback)callbacks[i];
switch(toc.getMessageType())
        {
case TextOutputCallback.INFORMATION:
System.out.println(toc.getMessage());
break;
case TextOutputCallback.ERROR:
System.out.println("ERROR: " + toc.getMessage());
break;
case TextOutputCallback.WARNING:
System.out.println("WARNING: " + toc.getMessage());
break;
default:
throw new IOException("Unsupported message type: "
          toc.getMessageType());
        }
      }
else if(callbacks[i] instanceof NameCallback)
      {
// Display dialog box for name if not present
NameCallback nc = (NameCallback)callbacks[i];
if (username == null || username.length() == 0) {
```

28

LISTING 28.2 Continued

```
String s = JOptionPane.showInputDialog("Please enter your name");
if (s == null)
s = "";
nc.setName(s);

        }
else {
nc.setName(username);
        }
      }
else if(callbacks[i] instanceof URLCallback)
      {
// Display dialog box for url if not present
URLCallback uc = (URLCallback)callbacks[i];
if (url == null || url.length() == 0) {
String s = JOptionPane.showInputDialog("Please enter URL");
if (s == null)
s = "";
uc.setURL(s);
        }
else {
uc.setURL(url);
        }
      }
else if(callbacks[i] instanceof PasswordCallback)
      {
PasswordCallback pc = (PasswordCallback)callbacks[i];
// Display dialog box for password if not present
if (password == null || password.length() == 0) {
// Note: JAAS specifies that the
// password is a char[] rather than a String
String s = JOptionPane.showInputDialog("Please enter password");
if (s == null)
s = "";
int passLen = s.length();
char[] passwordArray = new char[passLen];
for(int passIdx = 0; passIdx < passLen; passIdx++)
passwordArray[passIdx] = s.charAt(passIdx);
pc.setPassword(passwordArray);
        }
else {
```

LISTING 28.2 Continued

```
pc.setPassword(password.toCharArray());
        }
      }
else
      {
throw new UnsupportedCallbackException(callbacks[i],
"Unrecognized Callback");
      }
    }
  }
}
```

As you can see, the constructor for `SimpleCallbackHandler` takes a username, password, and a URL. It responds to the following callbacks: `TextOutputCallback`, `NameCallback`, `URLCallback`, `PasswordCallback`, and `TextInputCallback`. In the case of `NameCallback`, `URLCallback`, `PasswordCallback`, and `TextInputCallback`, if information isn't present, `SimpleCallbackHandler` prompts the end user at the command line, reads the user's input, and calls the appropriate method in the callback. In the case of `TextOutputCallback`, it logs the information.

Instantiating LoginContext

To start things off, application clients will instantiate a new instance of `LoginContext`. The `LoginContext` class, found in the `javax.security.auth.login` package, has four different signatures for its constructor. In this version, we're passing an index into the JAAS login configuration file and a callback handler. The index was discussed in the "JAAS Login Configuration File" section. This code should be wrapped in a `try/catch` block in case the entry name isn't found in the JAAS login configuration file or if other errors occur.

```
try {
loginContext = new LoginContext("UserPswd",
new MyCallbackHandler(username, password));
} catch(SecurityException se) {
// respond to exception
} catch(LoginException le) {
// respond to exception
}
```

UsernamePasswordLoginModule

WebLogic Server ships with a `LoginModule` suitable for application clients called `UsernamePasswordLoginModule`. It's included with an application client and executes on

28

the client. It requires three parameters: username, password, and the URL of the WebLogic Server instance to perform authentication against. To use `UsernamePasswordLoginModule` in your application clients, place a reference to it in the JAAS login configuration file.

Calling the login() Method

After a successful instantiation, the `login()` method should be called. This method should also be in a `try/catch` block because it can throw a `LoginException` derived exception.

```
try {
loginContext.login();
} catch(FailedLoginException le) {
// respond to exception
} catch(AccountExpiredException ae) {
// respond to exception
} catch(CredentialExpiredException ce) {
// respond to exception
} catch(Exception e) {
// respond to exception
}
```

After a successful login, we can request a populated `Subject` object from the `LoginContext`.

```
Subject subject = loginContext.getSubject();
```

PrivilegedAction and PrivilegedExceptionAction

`PrivilegedAction` is an interface found in the `java.security` package and is used to execute code that requires user authentication and authorization. To run privileged code, create a class that implements the `PrivilegedAction` interface. This interface only has one method:

```
public Object run()
```

The return object is application dependent and represents the results of the privileged code. If the privileged code might throw an exception, implement the `PrivilegedExceptionAction` interface instead. This interface only has one method:

```
public Object run() throws Exception
```

Listing 28.3 is an example of a `PrivilegedAction`.

LISTING 28.3 A PrivilegedAction That Calls on the EJB Methods

```
import java.security.PrivilegedAction;
import java.util.Hashtable;

import javax.rmi.PortableRemoteObject;
import javax.naming.*;

import examples.ejb20.basic.beanManaged.AccountHome;
import examples.ejb20.basic.beanManaged.Account;

import java.util.*;
public class JaasAction implements PrivilegedAction
{
private static final String JNDI_NAME = "ejb20-beanManaged-AccountHome";
private String url;
public JaasAction(String url)
  {
this.url = url;
  }

public Object run()
  {
try {
// look up AccountHome
Hashtable ht = new Hashtable();
ht.put(Context.INITIAL_CONTEXT_FACTORY,
"weblogic.jndi.WLInitialContextFactory");
ht.put(Context.PROVIDER_URL, "t3://localhost:7001");
InitialContext ic = new InitialContext(ht);
Object obj = ic.lookup(JNDI_NAME);
AccountHome home =
(AccountHome)PortableRemoteObject.narrow(obj, AccountHome.class);
// create new Account
Account account = home.create("123456", 10000);
// find and display all Account with balances > $1500
Collection coll = home.findBigAccounts(1500);
Iterator iter = coll.iterator();
while(iter.hasNext()) {
Account temp = (Account)iter.next();
System.out.println(temp.getPrimaryKey() + ":" + temp.balance());
        }
```

LISTING 28.3 Continued

```
// remove Account just created
account.remove();

} catch(Exception e) {
e.printStackTrace();
    }

return null;
  }
}
```

Executing the Code

We can now instantiate the class that implements `PrivilegedAction` or `PrivilegedExceptionAction` class and invoke its run method. However, we must associate the run method with the `Subject` object we've extracted from our `LoginContext`. The `Security` class, found in the `weblogic.security` package, contains a mechanism for this. The `Security` class contains two methods for this purpose: one for `PrivilegedAction` and one for `PrivilegedExceptionAction`.

```
public static Object runAs(javax.security.auth.Subject user,
java.security.PrivilegedAction action)
throws java.lang.IllegalArgumentException
public static Object runAs(javax.security.auth.Subject user,
java.security.PrivilegedExceptionAction action)
throws java.security.PrivilegedActionException,java.lang.IllegalArgumentException
```

The next two lines of code demonstrate how to instantiate the `PrivilegedAction` class and execute its run method:

```
MyPrivilegedAction myAction = new MyPrivilegedAction();
Security.runAs(subject, myAction);
```

An alternative is to use an anonymous inner class as shown here:

```
Security.runAs(subject, new PrivilegedAction() {
public Object run() {
// run privileged code
  }
);
```

Creating a Custom Security Provider

There are times when application needs demand the use of a customer security provider. As each security provider was described in the previous chapter, a mention was made of situations that require a custom security provider. The first step is deciding which type of custom provider you need.

The `weblogic.security.spi` package contains classes for custom security providers to implement and extend. There's an interface here for every kind of provider in the WebLogic Server security framework, including `AdjudicatorProvider`, `AuthenticationProvider`, and `AuthorizationProviders`. All these interfaces extend the `SecurityProvider` interface. The methods of these interfaces are callback methods that WLS invokes in precise situations of the security framework's life cycle. In other words, WLS interacts with the security provider classes by calling the interface methods after specific events occur.

Your custom security provider must implement one of these interfaces. Additionally, some utility classes must be written to extend the classes or implement the interfaces `IdentityAsserter`, `PrincipalValidator`, and `LoginModule`.

BEA offers a collection of sample custom security providers available at the code direct section of its dev2dev site at `http://dev2dev.bea.com/codelibrary/code/security_prov81.jsp` These examples are meant to be a starting point and should not be used in production environments. Look for WebLogic Server 8.1: Sample Security Providers and download the `SampleSecurityProviders81.zip` file. When unzipped, this file contains a `readme.pdf` file with instructions on how to understand, build, and run the customer security providers.

Unzip this file so that the `sample_security_providers` directory is under your `bea_home` directory. For example, if WebLogic Server is installed at `c:\bea`, the new directory should be `c:\bea\sample_security_providers`.

In this section, we look at the issues involved in creating a custom authentication provider. The sample custom authentication provider uses a `Properties` object to store user and group information and stores the object in a file. This is an example of a custom security provider database. There is also a customer login module that works with this provider.

28

To create a custom authentication provider, we must create a class that implements `AuthenticationProvider`. Because `AuthenticationProvider` extends `SecurityProvider`, that interface must be implemented as well.

Implementing SecurityProvider

The `SecurityProvider` interface has three methods that need to be implemented. Here are the methods and the events that might trigger them:

```
public void initialize(ProviderMBean providerMBean,
SecurityServices securityServices)
```

The preceding line allows the security provider to initialize itself—it's called when WLS starts. The `initialize` method takes two parameters:

- `providerMBean` is a managed bean (MBean) and has configuration data that allows our customer provider to be managed in WebLogic Server. An MBean is a Java class that represents a Java Management eXtensions (JMX) manageable resource. The WebLogic Server admin console uses MBeans to configure WebLogic Server resources. Therefore, to control our security provider with the admin console, we must interface with WebLogic Server using this MBean. This MBean will be created later in this section with the WebLogic Server WebLogicMBeanMaker utility.
- `securityServices` is an object that allows our custom provider to obtain and use an auditor provider.

```
public String getDescription()
```

The preceding line returns a brief description of the custom security provider. This shows up in the console when listing the security providers.

```
public void shutdown()
```

The preceding line shuts down the custom security provider. This is invoked when WLS shuts down.

Implementing AuthenticationProvider

```
public AppConfigurationEntry getAssertionModuleConfiguration()
```

This method is called to get an identity assertion provider's `LoginModule`. The returned `AppConfigurationEntry` contains information about the associated `LoginModule` including its class name. This method is called by the associated MBean.

```
public IdentityAsserter getIdentityAsserter()
```

This line indicates which `IdentityAsserter` is associated with this authentication provider (or null if we aren't supporting mapping tokens to usernames). The returned class has the callbacks that are invoked when a user's name is to be verified during authentication.

```
public AppConfigurationEntry getLoginModuleConfiguration()
```

This indicates which `LoginModule` is associated with this authentication provider. `AppConfigurationEntry` is a JAAS class that holds the `LoginModule`'s class name, control flag, and configuration map. This interface is utilized by the MBean.

```
public PrincipalValidator getPrincipalValidator()
```

The preceding line indicates which `PrincipalValidator` is associated with this authentication provider. The `PrincipalValidator` class is used to verify that `Principals` placed in a `Subject` have not been tampered with since the `Subject` was filled with `Principals`.

SampleAuthenticationProviderImpl

The `SampleAuthenticationProviderImpl` class implements the `AuthenticationProvider` interface. This class enables the authentication provider to initialize, start, and stop. This class is a sample of what you would code when implementing the `AuthenticationProvider` interface. The following are some excerpts from `SampleAuthenticationProviderImpl.java`:

```
public void initialize(ProviderMBean mbean, SecurityServices services)
  {
System.out.println("SampleAuthenticationProviderImpl.initialize");
// Cast the mbean from a generic ProviderMBean to a SampleAuthenticatorMBean.
SampleAuthenticatorMBean myMBean = (SampleAuthenticatorMBean)mbean;
// Set the description to the sample authenticator's
// mbean's description and version
description = myMBean.getDescription() + "\n" + myMBean.getVersion();

// Instantiate the helper that manages this provider's user and group definitions
database = new SampleAuthenticatorDatabase(myMBean);
// Extract the JAAS control flag from the sample authenticator's mbean.
// This flag controls how the sample authenticator's login module is used
// by the JAAS login, both for authentication and for identity assertion.
String flag = myMBean.getControlFlag();
if (flag.equalsIgnoreCase("REQUIRED")) {
controlFlag = LoginModuleControlFlag.REQUIRED;
} else if (flag.equalsIgnoreCase("OPTIONAL")) {
controlFlag = LoginModuleControlFlag.OPTIONAL;
} else if (flag.equalsIgnoreCase("REQUISITE")) {
controlFlag = LoginModuleControlFlag.REQUISITE;
} else if (flag.equalsIgnoreCase("SUFFICIENT")) {
controlFlag = LoginModuleControlFlag.SUFFICIENT;
} else {
throw new IllegalArgumentException("invalid flag value" + flag);
    }
  }
```

The implementation details of your custom security provider might be completely different from this one. In our example, when the provider is initialized, it reads its description from the MBean. This description will be set in the admin console when a system administrator configures this provider in the security realm. Then it initializes its internal database of usernames and groups. Another class, `SampleAuthenticatorDatabase`, is responsible for initializing a `Properties` object by either reading a preconfigured properties file (if this provider has already been utilized in this realm) or by creating one from scratch. Look at `SampleAuthenticatorDatabase.java` for more information about this class.

The last step any custom security provider should perform in its `initialize()` method is to analyze and store the configuration information. In our example, this means the `getControlFlag()` method is called on the MBean. The system administrator determines the value of this flag when the provider is configured and it's used by the WebLogic Server security framework to determine whether authentication from this provider is required for a user to be authenticated. This JAAS control flag is important when multiple authentication providers have been configured.

```
public PrincipalValidator getPrincipalValidator()
  {
return new PrincipalValidatorImpl();
  }
```

This provider works with WebLogic Server users and groups, so we can use the default `PrincipalValidator`. This default implementation class is named `PrincipalValidatorImpl`. It's common to reuse any WLS security classes to fill in the holes of your custom security provider implementation.

```
public AppConfigurationEntry getLoginModuleConfiguration()
  {
// Don't pass in any special options.
// By default, the sample authenticator's login module
// will authenticate (by checking that the passwords match).
HashMap options = new HashMap();
return getConfiguration(options);
  }

private AppConfigurationEntry getConfiguration(HashMap options)
  {
// add the "database helper" object to the options so that the
// login module can access the user and group definitions
options.put("database", database);
// make sure to specify the sample authenticator's login module
// and to use the control flag from the sample authenticator's mbean.
return new
AppConfigurationEntry(
```

```
"examples.security.providers.authentication.SampleLoginModuleImpl",
controlFlag,
options
      );
  }
```

The `getLoginModuleConfiguration()` method calls the private `getConfiguration()` method. Together, these two methods create an `AppConfigurationEntry` object and populate it with the class name of the associated login module (`SampleLoginModuleImpl`), the JAAS control flag, and a `HashMap` to hold the provider database. The associated `LoginModule` will use this database. The `AppConfigurationEntry` class is part of the JAAS API and is in the `javax.security.auth.login` package.

Implementing LoginModule

Every authentication provider must have one associated `LoginModule`, and `SampleAuthenticationProviderImpl` is no exception. The `LoginModule` interface is from the JAAS specifications and is included in the `javax.security.auth.spi` package. The `LoginModule` is responsible for determining whether client credentials are sufficient and then filling a supplied `Subject` object with a `Principal` object that meets authentication requirements.

The `LoginModule` interface is composed of the following methods:

```
public void initialize(
Subject         subject,
CallbackHandler callbackHandler,
      Map             sharedState,
      Map             options
    )
```

A `LoginContext` calls this method, passing in a Subject that will be populated with `Principals`, a `CallbackHandler` for communicating with the end user for client credentials, a `sharedState` for communication with other `LoginModules`, and options to configure this `LoginModule`.

```
public boolean login() throws LoginException
```

This is phase one of the login process. A `LoginContext` will call this method and the `LoginModule` performs a lookup on its internal store of users and groups. It might invoke callback handlers passed in the `initialize()` method if client credential information is needed. The `LoginModule` will attempt to authenticate and will store the `Principals` objects internally.

```
public boolean commit() throws LoginException
```

This is phase two of the login process. If the calling LoginContext's overall authentication succeeded, it calls this method. This is where the Subject object is populated with the authenticated Principals from the login() method.

```
public boolean abort() throws LoginException
```

This is also phase two of the login process. If the calling LoginContext's overall authentication does not succeed, it calls this method. The LoginModule should clean up any private state established in the login() method.

```
public boolean logout() throws LoginException
```

This is called by LoginContext to log out a Subject. The LoginModule could remove Principals and Credentials from the Subject object.

SampleLoginModuleImpl

SampleLoginModuleImpl implements the LoginModule interface. Here are some excerpts from SampleLoginModuleImpl.java.

From the initialize method:

```
// Get the object that manages the user and group definitions
database = (SampleAuthenticatorDatabase)options.get("database");
```

SampleLoginModuleImpl gets access to the internal database of its associated authentication provider, SampleAuthenticationProviderImpl.

From the login method:

```
// Verify that the user exists. The login fails if not.
if (!database.userExists(userName)) {
throwFailedLoginException("Authentication Failed: " +
"User " + userName + " doesn't exist.");
}
```

The database is now used to verify the username exists. Also from the login method:

```
// since the login succeeded, add the user and its groups to the
// list of principals we want to add to the subject.
principalsForSubject.add(new WLSUserImpl(userName));
addGroupsForSubject(userName);
```

An internal vector called principalsForSubject is populated with WLSUsersImpl and WLSGroupImpl objects. These represent the Principals for this user.

From the commit method:

```
subject.getPrincipals().addAll(principalsForSubject);
```

The `Subject` object is populated with `Principals` from the `principalsForSubject` vector.

MBean Definition Files and WebLogic MBeanMaker

Each custom security provider needs to have an associated MBean definition file (MDF). The MDF states the name, display name, package, class, persistence policy, and custom attributes of the custom security provider.

The WebLogic MBeanMaker tool takes an MDF file as input and outputs an MBean interface file, an MBean implementation file, and an MBean information file. All these files are necessary for the creation of MBeans.

> **NOTE**
>
> More information about MDF files and MBeanMaker is available at `http://e-docs.bea.com/wls/docs81/dvspisec/design.html`.

Building the Custom Security Providers

The custom providers are accompanied by an Ant build script. Open a command prompt, go to the `WL_HOME\server\bin` directory, and run the `setWLSEnv.cmd` script to set up your environmental variables. Then go to the `beahome\ sample_security_providers` directory and type **`ant`**. The `ant` command will run the `build.xml` script. This script invokes MBeanMaker, creates a JAR file named `wlSampleSecurityProviders.jar`, and copies the JAR file to the `WL_HOME\server\lib\mbeantypes` directory. Once this JAR file is in this directory, the providers are available to use in a security realm.

Running the Custom Security Providers

Create a new WebLogic Server domain with the Configuration Wizard. From the Windows Start Menu, select Programs, BEA WebLogic Platform 8.1, Configuration Wizard. Select a WebLogic Server domain and change the default name from mydomain to sampledomain. Proceed through the wizard pages and accept system defaults for all information except the setting for the Create System User Name and Password page. On that page, set the username to *sampleuser* and the password to *samplepassword*. The sample providers rely on this information to work unmodified.

Boot WebLogic Server in this domain. Open the admin console with your Internet browser. Log in using `sampleuser` and `samplepassword`. Create a new security realm named SampleRealm. This realm will have no providers in it. Configure the following providers as depicted in Table 28.4.

TABLE 28.4 Default WebLogic Server Groups

Provider Type	Provider Name
Adjudicator	Default Adjudicator
Auditor	Sample Auditor
Authentication	Sample Authentication
Identity Asserter (under Authentication Provider)	Sample Identity Asserter
Authorizers	Sample Authorizer
Credential Mapper	Default Credential Mapper
Key Store	Default Key Store
Role Mapper	Sample Role Mapper

We're now going to set the realm as the default realm for this domain. Click on the sampledomain node in the left panel, and click on the View Domain-wide Security Settings link in the right panel. Set the default realm to be SampleRealm and click the Apply button.

Now let's shut down WebLogic Server from the admin console. Expand the Servers node in the left panel and click on the myserver node. Click on control in the right panel and then click on the Shutdown This Server link.

Boot WebLogic Server in the sampledomain domain and look at the WebLogic Server command prompt. Each of the custom security providers will output initialization to this window. The output should include the following:

```
SampleLoginModuleImpl.initialize
SampleLoginModuleImpl.login
        userName        = sampleuser
        passwordHave    = samplepassword
        groupName       = Administrators
SampleLoginModule.commit
```

This output reveals that `SampleLoginModuleImpl` is being called with our login parameters, *`sampleuser`* and *`samplepassword`*. The custom providers also come with a client to test perimeter authentication. Please refer to the `readme.pdf` that accompanies the BEA sample code from the dev2dev site.

Where to Go from Here

This chapter has just covered the basics of creating custom security providers. The sample providers are just meant to introduce developers to the concept of creating customer providers. There are many issues to consider when creating a custom security provider, such as custom attributes and methods, admin console enhancements, and best practices. Please visit `http://e-docs.bea.com/wls/docs81/dvspisec/index.html` for much more information about this topic.

Using Secure Sockets Layer

WebLogic Server can be configured to work with the Secure Sockets Layer (SSL) protocol. SSL is the Internet standard for secure communication and provides end-to-end encryption of transmitted data.

There are two pages in the administrator console that configure SSL support. To get to these pages, expand the Servers node in the left panel and click on one of the servers executing your domain. In the right panel, click on the Configurations tab. The two SSL pages can be reached by clicking on the General or Keystores & SSL tab. The General page allows SSL to be enabled and the SSL port to be set, as shown in Figure 28.19. Enabling SSL requires an SSL port to be chosen. Enabling or disabling requires WebLogic Server to be restarted. Simply enabling SSL will encrypt client connections. This will provide data integrity and make communications confidential. However, it will not allow the server or the client to authenticate itself.

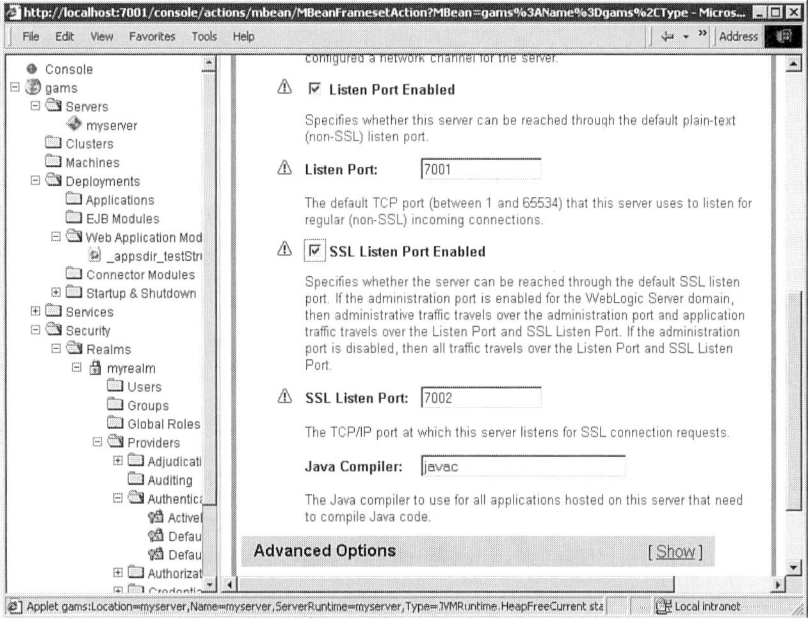

Figure 28.19 The General page allows us to enable and disable SSL and to select the SSL port.

For the server to be able to authenticate itself to clients, it must have a private key and a digital certificate.

Generating Digital Certificates

To use SSL within WebLogic Server, you need a digital certificate. The sample certificates that come with WebLogic Server can be used in a development environment, but for production purposes, you must create your own. There are several ways of doing this as the following sections point out.

CertGen Tool

The CertGen tool can be used to generate certificates and private keys to be used for testing, not for production. The CertGen tool is found in `weblogic.jar` and is started with the following syntax:

```
java utils.CertGen password certfile keyfile
```

This command will generate certificate files named `certfile` and private key files named `keyfile`. The private key's password will be the one entered. Before executing this tool, copy the files `CertGenCA.der` and `CertGenCAKey.der` from the `WL_HOME/server/lib` directory to the directory you are running the tool in.

Certificate Request Generator Servlet

To use SSL in a production environment, you must request and get a certificate and private key from a trusted certificate authority (CA). Examples of CA are Entrust (`www.entrust.com`) and VeriSign (`www.verisign.com`). CAs expect requests to come in a format called a certificate signature request (CSR). WebLogic Server 7.x came with a servlet that collects information from you and generates a private key file (`.der` extension), a CSR in binary format (`.dem` file), and in ASCII format (`.pem` file). WebLogic 8.1 still comes with the Web application `certificate.war` that contains the certificate signature request servlet. However, this Web application has been deprecated as of 8.1 and BEA recommends using the keytool utility mentioned in the next section.

keytool Utility

Another option for generating private keys and certificates is the keytool utility that comes with the JDK. This utility stores private keys and certificates in a keystore. By default, this file is named `.keystore` and its location is determined by the value of the `user.home` environmental variable. To generate keys and certificates, use the following syntax:

```
keytool -genkey -alias myalias -keypass mypassword
```

This will generate a key pair—a public and private key—and wrap the public key into a X.509 v1 self-signed certificate. The alias *`myalias`* will be used to refer to this key pair when using keytool in the future. The password *`mypassword`* will be used to protect the private key.

keytool has many options for generating, importing, and managing private keys and digital certificates. For more information, please go to the following URL: `http://java.sun.com/j2se/1.3/docs/tooldocs/win32/keytool.html`.

SSL for Server Authentication

To have WebLogic Server authenticate itself to clients, WebLogic Server must be able to find its private key and digital certificate. You will either refer to them by their filenames or by their alias in a keystore. This information will be entered into the SSL page in the administrator console. To get to this page, expand the Servers node in the left panel and click on the name of the server to configure. Click on the Configuration tab in the right panel and then click on the Keystores & SSL tab. You'll see the SSL form shown in Figure 28.20.

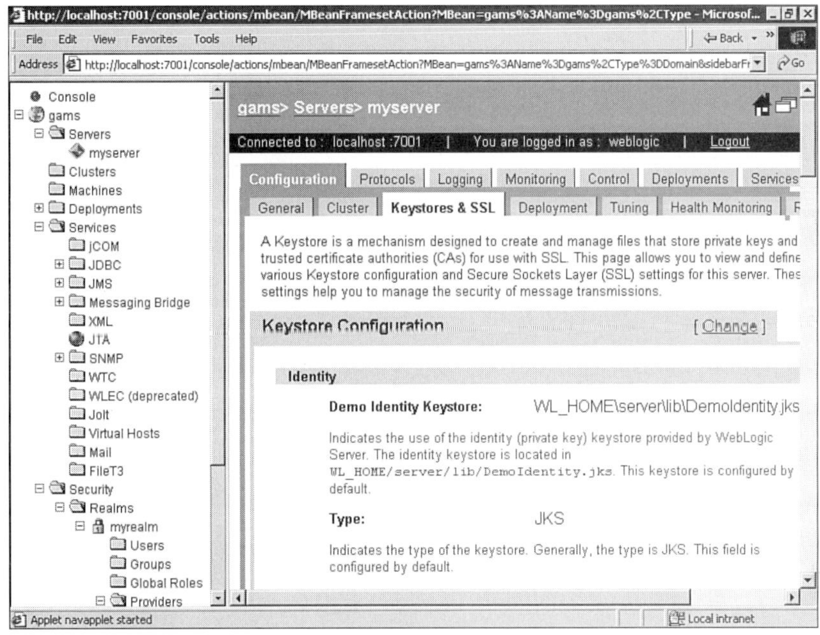

Figure 28.20 The SSL page contains information specific to certificates and private keys used by the server.

When using a keystore:

1. Make sure that the WebLogic keystore provider has been configured properly as explained earlier.
2. Enter the same alias into the Server Private Key Alias field that you used when you configured the keystore.
3. Enter the same password into Server Private Key Passphrase field that you used when you configured the keystore.

When using filenames:

1. Enter the name and location of the certificate file into Server Certificate File Name field.
2. Enter the name and location of the key file into Server Key File Name field.

In either case, click the Apply button and reboot WebLogic Server.

SSL for Mutual Authentication

To request clients for digital certificates, you must have SSL enabled and also set the Two Way Client Cert Behavior: drop down in the advanced options in the Keystores & SSL page in the administrator console.

If set, the Client Certificate Enforced attribute requires a client to present a certificate. If the client cannot present a certificate, WebLogic Server ends the SSL connection.

If set, the Client Certificate Requested But Not Enforced attribute request a client to present a certificate. If the client cannot present a certificate, WebLogic Server continues the SSL connection. In this case, the connection is encrypted, but the client is not authenticated.

Establishing Trust Between Domains

In previous versions of WebLogic Server (before 7.x), principals could be shared and trusted between domains by making the system passwords in those domains to be the same. Version 8.1 provides more security by adding a Credential attribute for each domain. In order for domains to trust each other, they must have the same Credential attribute. A simple string is used to set the attribute. To make this string more secure, use numbers and uppercase and lowercase letters.

To set the Credential attribute for a domain, click on the domain in the left panel of the administrator console. Click on the View Domain-wide Security Settings link in the right panel and then click on the Advanced node. Make sure that the Enable Generated Credential is unchecked, enter a string that represents the Credential attribute for this domain, and confirm it. Click the Apply button and reboot WebLogic Server. Perform these steps for each domain you want to have in a trust relationship.

Securing Best Practices

The section discusses WebLogic Server technologies and business practices to increase security of Web applications, WebLogic Server, and the hardware that supports your servers.

Setting User Lockout

With every realm, WebLogic Server provides attributes for protecting user account against dictionary attacks. Dictionary attacks occur when hackers attempt to log in as a user by guessing a password using every word in a dictionary. The user lockout attributes define incorrect logins and what behavior causes accounts to be locked.

These attributes are initially set to the highest level of protection. To change these settings, click on the realm name in the admin console and then click on the User Lockout tab in the right panel. This will display the Security Passwords form as shown in Figure 28.21. The most pertinent attributes are

- Lockout Enabled—If checked, user accounts are capable of being locked from access.
- Lockout Threshold—The maximum number of consecutive invalid login attempts before the account is locked. Default is 5.
- Lockout Duration—When locked, how many minutes the account is locked for.
- Lockout Reset Duration—The number of minutes in which consecutive invalid login attempts must occur for account to be locked.

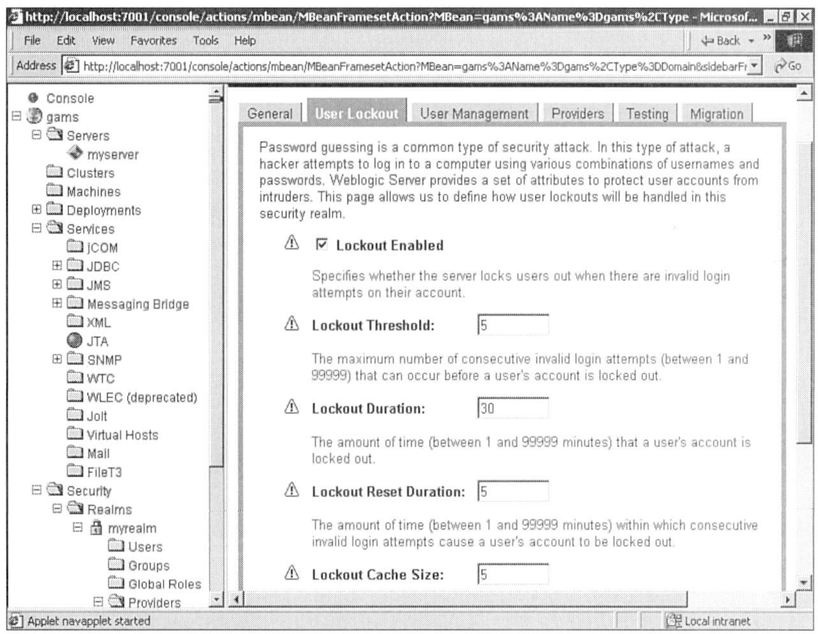

Figure 28.21 Setting user lockout increases protection against dictionary attacks.

After a user account has been locked, it can be unlocked. To do this in the admin console, click on the appropriate server on the left pane and then on the Monitoring tab in the right pane. Click on the Security tab and list the user that is locked. The Security details form will be displayed as shown in Figure 28.22. Click the Unlock button and that user will again be able to log in.

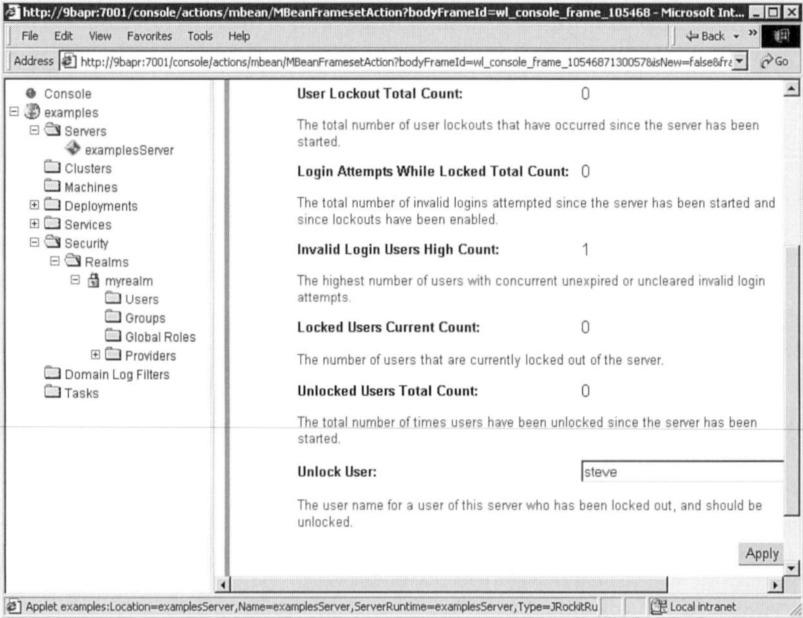

Figure 28.22 Unlocking a user account.

Connection Filtering

Connection filters allow WebLogic Server to accept or reject client connections based on their origin and the protocol used. This provides an extra level of security against unauthorized access and denial of service (DoS) attacks. Unfortunately, to implement this feature, you must obtain Java code that implements the `ConnectionFilter` and the `ConnectionFilterRulesListener` interfaces. WebLogic Server comes with examples for this in the `examples.security.net` package. For more information about using connection filters, please refer to `http://e-docs.bea.com/wls/docs81/security/con_filtr.html`.

BEA Dev2Dev Advisories and Notifications

From time to time, BEA releases patches for WebLogic Server that address security-related issues. You can sign up to be notified when new patches are released by entering your information at http://contact2.bea.com/bea/www/advisories/login.jsp. To view recent notifications, go to http://dev2dev.bea.com/resourcelibrary/advisories.jsp?highlight=advisoriesnotifications.

Securing the WebLogic Server Machine and File Systems

There's no point in configuring the WebLogic Server security framework without securing the actual machines that are running WebLogic Server. Hiring a security expert to ensure there are no weaknesses that would enable a hacker to access these machines through either operating system or applications loopholes is recommended.

You should create an OS-level user that will be the only user able to execute WebLogic Server and be able to view and modify WebLogic Server directories and files. Avoid sharing these files and directories with user accounts on other machines. This decreases the chances of creating security loopholes for hackers.

Machines executing WebLogic Server should be kept in a secured environment where unauthorized users will not have physical contact with the machine or its network connections.

Do not install development tools on a production machine so as to give hackers a chance to execute utilities such as Java and EJB compilers. In short, keep the number of applications and utilities on a production machine to a bare minimum.

Protecting Network Connections

Connections between the Internet, a Web server, WebLogic Server, databases, and EIS instances should be protected with firewalls. These firewalls should allow only protocols that clients should be using. For instance, a Web server should allow only HTTP and HTTPS connections and disallow any other protocols. Additionally, stateful firewalls can ensure that communications originating from your facility are in response to a client request and not from rogue code that's communicating with the hacker who placed it in your infrastructure. Of course, having this many firewalls does add cost and reduces performance of your infrastructure. What's needed is a balanced approach among security, cost, and performance. At the very least, a DMZ (demilitarized zone) should be created between the Internet and your IT infrastructure through the use of a single firewall.

Preventing Denial of Service Attacks

A denial of service (DoS) attack prevents legitimate users access to WebLogic Server applications and resources. Hackers usually accomplish this type of attack by sending WebLogic Server an enormous number of requests that can either be slow to respond to, are incomplete, or are very large. WebLogic Server can be configured to reduce the opportunities hackers have to cause DoS attacks.

To configure these options, expand the Servers node in the left panel of the administrator console and click on the server name. Click on the Protocols tab. This will display the Connection Protocols form shown in Figure 28.23.

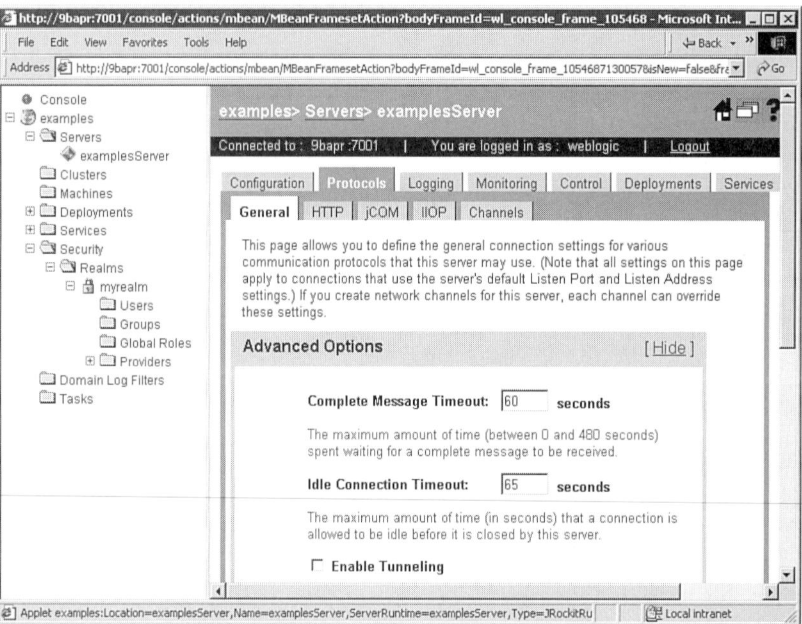

Figure 28.23 Each protocol's attributes can be set from this page. Careful configuration can reduce hackers' attempts at DoS attacks.

For each of the T3, HTTP, IIOP, and COM protocols, a system administrator can set up a channel that restricts the maximum message size allowed and how long to wait before a complete message is delivered. Reducing the maximum message size restricts the amount of memory that WebLogic Server allocates. Reducing the message timeout guards against messages that never complete and take up WebLogic Server resources. Channels are a new feature of WebLogic Server 8.1 to allow more than one network interface card (NIC) to disperse traffic and to listen for requests on multiple ports. Each WebLogic Server can have multiple channels configured, but it must have a unique combination of protocol, listen address, and port.

Additional attributes specific to HTTP can be set in the Connections HTTP form shown in Figure 28.24. To configure these options, expand the Servers node in the left panel of the administrator console and click on the server name. Click on the Protocols tab in the right panel and then click on the HTTP tab.

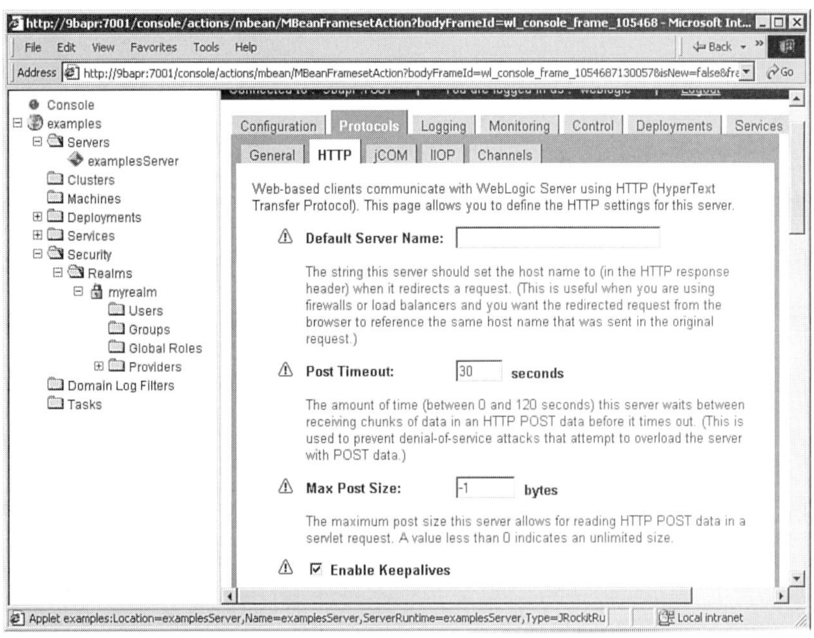

Figure 28.24 This form is used to set HTTP-specific attributes including some related to preventing DoS attacks.

The Post Timeout Secs setting determines how many seconds to wait between reading HTTP `POST` data. Some DoS attacks attempt to overload the server with HTTP `POST` data. Making this value higher gives WebLogic Server more time to digest the information and not overload its resources. The Max Post Time setting determines how long to wait for an HTTP POST operation to complete before timing it out. Some hackers send many incomplete HTTP `POST` requests, which can lock up the server—reducing this number frees up resources for other client requests. Max Post Size determines the largest chunk amount of HTTP `POST` data that WebLogic Server will accept. Hackers might try to overload the server with huge requests. Reducing this number reduces opportunities for WebLogic Server to be overloaded.

Turning On Auditing

When auditing is turned on, auditing events such as invalid logins are logged. Checking this log will show patterns of hacker activity. Setting up an audit provider turns on auditing. In the admin console, expand your default security realm, expand the Providers node, and click on the Auditing node. In the right panel, click on the Configure a new Default Auditor link. This enables you to use the WebLogic-supplied auditing security provider. You will then see the form for creating a new default auditing provider as shown in Figure 28.25.

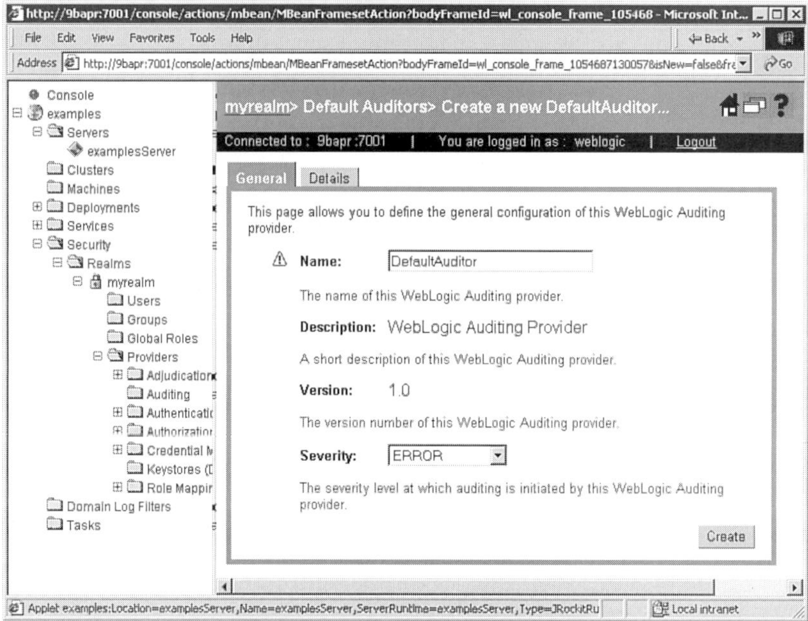

Figure 28.25 This form enables you to choose the severity level of audit events to log.

Set the severity level you're interested in and click the Create button. You must then restart WebLogic Server for auditing to take place. Once auditing is turned on, the auditor will create and fill a log file at `WL_HOME\`*`yourdomain`*`\DefaultAuditRecorder.log`.

Additional Security Recommendations

For additional security recommendations, refer to the "Best Practices to Address Security Risks" section of Chapter 26, "Web Applications and Security," and at `http://e-docs.bea.com/wls/docs81/lockdown/practices.html`.

Summary

Security is a very large topic and although we have covered a lot of material in Chapters 26, 27, and 28, there are many more circumstances and issues related to security that can show up as your application needs become more complex. Please consult with a security expert, the BEA newsgroups dealing with security, BEA customer support, and WebLogic Server security documentation for answers to these complex security questions.

PART VIII

WebLogic Server Enterprise Application Integration

IN THIS PART

CHAPTER 29

WebLogic Server and XML Technologies

by Subramanian H Kovilmadam

IN THIS CHAPTER

- Introduction to XML
- Defining an XML Document
- XML Parsers
- WebLogic Server XML Streaming API
- Other Useful XML Features
- Extensible Stylesheet Language
- Best Practices for Working with XML

Today's enterprise applications seldom function in isolation. Different systems communicate with each other and pass data between each other to perform business functions. For example, consider a reservation system that books airline tickets. The system is functionally aware of the process for booking airline tickets, but it knows nothing about the process involved in charging the customer's credit card for the tickets booked. So, it communicates with the bank's application to charge the amount to the credit card. The bank application does what it does best: charge the card. We have several independent systems working with each other for an enterprise to function. That having been said, there's no way to guarantee that the different applications will use similar definitions for their data structures. For that matter, we can't even guarantee that different applications are written using the same programming language. So, how do these systems communicate with each other? In other words, is there a standard mechanism for data transfer between different heterogeneous systems in the enterprise?

A typical solution for the problem at hand is that the technical designers of both the reservation and the payment systems assemble in a conference room and discuss what data elements should be sent to the banking system to enable a credit card payment. Assume that the bank requires that the credit card number, type, and expiration date, along with the amount, for making a payment. If the payment goes through successfully, the bank returns a message along with an authorization number. If the payment fails, the bank returns a text message indicating the reason why the card failed.

After the data elements have been identified, the next thing that must be ironed out is the format in which the data will be sent.

In this chapter, we look at some of the basic XML technologies available to the developer. We touch on XML DTDs and schemas and look at various parsing techniques. We also learn how to transform an XML document into another XML document, or even an HTML document, by using transformation.

Introduction to XML

This chapter isn't meant to provide a comprehensive study of XML (Extensible Markup Language). However, we'll look at the basic components of an XML document, which will aid our study of the usage of XML in the context of WebLogic Server. If you're already familiar with the structure of an XML document, you may skip this section and move along to the next section of this chapter.

The Standard Generalized Markup Language (SGML), defined in the ISO standard 8879:1986, outlines the process for data interchange between different subsystems that makes it structured and consistent. You should be familiar with one type of an SGML document: an HTML document. HTML is a subset of SGML. As you might already know, an HTML document is nothing but a structured representation of data in such a way that a browser that understands HTML can display the data by using the data formats specified in the HTML document. The browser uses these format requirements in conjunction with the user's preferences to display the data. Thus, an HTML document ensures that the formats are always adhered to, irrespective of which browser or application uses the document. How the formats are rendered may depend on the settings of the browser.

HTML is presentation oriented. It does not concern itself with interpreting the data that's represented; all it knows is how the data looks to the user. Thus, if you have your application reading an HTML document, it'll be very difficult to make your application understand the document's content. This is where XML fits in. Like HTML, XML also derives from SGML and can be considered a subset of SGML. However, unlike HTML, XML is not about data presentation. XML does not address the format of the data; instead, it enables you to describe the structure and meaning of your data.

XML is a foundation for many different standards and protocols. Notably,

- Web Services technologies
- J2EE and WebLogic deployment descriptors
- Ant

As its name suggests, XML is extensible. You can use an XML document to describe data using elements that you define for your application. Any other application that has to use this data needs to be aware of the elements that it has to look for in the document. When the application understands the tags and how to parse them, it can easily access the data being sent. Because of these reasons, XML has become the de facto standard for data transfer over the Internet.

For instance, in our example, Listing 29.1 could be a sample XML file that the airline sends to the bank for billing the credit card.

LISTING 29.1 A Payment XML Document

```
1. <?xml version="1.0"?>
2. <!DOCTYPE paymentInfo SYSTEM "paymentinfo.dtd">
3. <paymentInfo>
4.  <creditCard number="1234123412341234" type="MC" expiration="03/2005"/>
5.  <amount>354.99</amount>
6. </paymentInfo>
```

It's very evident from this listing that unlike an HTML document, an XML document does not have any predefined tags, although the structure of the XML document is quite similar to an HTML document in that it has elements and attributes. You're free to decide on and use elements that best describe your data. For instance, here we have defined an element called `creditCard`, which has three attributes: `number`, `type`, and `expiration`. We also have an `amount` element, which indicates the total amount to be charged. Both these tags are wrapped inside a root element called `paymentInfo`. As long as the bank is aware of the format, the billing application can easily use the data that is being passed in by the airline.

An XML document consists of two parts: the header and the content.

The XML Header

The XML header describes the XML file. As you can see in line 1 of Listing 29.1, we tell the user that the contents are formed based on the version 1.0 specification of XML. The header can also contain other attributes such as the encoding and an indication of whether the document can stand alone or requires other documents to make it complete.

In line 2, the header contains the `DOCTYPE` definition of the document. The airline and the bank have mutually agreed on a set of tags that they'll use to communicate. But how does the bank ensure that the requests adhere to the agreed structure? The bank system uses a dictionary that's based on the mutually agreed structure. This dictionary is known as a *document type definition* or *DTD* document. The `DOCTYPE` is a mechanism by which the XML indicates to the parser which DTD it conforms to. Based on this definition, the parser validates whether the XML follows all the rules laid out using the DTD. In line 2 of this example, we indicate to the parser that the XML uses a DTD called paymentinfo.dtd (which resides in the file system) by using the keyword SYSTEM. Using the SYSTEM keyword makes the parser look for the DTD either in the relative or absolute file system or in the URL, based on the data that's provided.

XML documents may also use DTDs that lie in some public domain. To do this, they use the keyword PUBLIC instead of SYSTEM. If you look at the ejb-jar.xml file, which describes an EJB deployment, you'll notice that the DOCTYPE is given as follows:

```
<!DOCTYPE ejb-jar PUBLIC '-//Sun Microsystems, Inc.
   //DTD Enterprise JavaBeans 2.0//EN' >
```

Here we indicate to the parser that it needs to pick up the DTD mentioned in the PUBLIC domain under the name Sun Microsystems, Inc.//DTD Enterprise JavaBeans 2.0//EN.

You can combine both the SYSTEM and PUBLIC keywords to specify to the parser that it must look for the PUBLIC ID first, as shown in the following header. If the parser cannot resolve the PUBLIC ID, it can then use the SYSTEM URL to specify the DTD. However, the SYSTEM keyword is omitted when combining the two.

```
<!DOCTYPE ejb-jar PUBLIC '-//Sun Microsystems, Inc.
   //DTD Enterprise JavaBeans 2.0//EN'
  'http://java.sun.com/dtd/ejb-jar_2_0.dtd'>
```

Apart from these, you may also see other tags in the header that describe processing instructions (or PIs) of the XML. These header elements typically consist of a target followed by the data. The data is normally represented as key-value pairs, although that isn't a requirement.

Remember that although the header provides more meaning to your XML document, it isn't required for the XML to be complete. All these tags are optional. If your XML document includes a DOCTYPE declaration and the parser validates it, the document is considered to be valid. If the document doesn't contain a DOCTYPE, the parser won't validate it. In such a case, your XML document will be considered well formed if it follows the rules laid out by the W3C about the structure of XML documents. Not using a DOCTYPE obviously prevents the parser from validating the document, and improves performance at the expense of checking for the validity of the document. Needless to say, valid XML documents should also be well formed.

The XML Content

As mentioned earlier, the XML content is pretty much open for definition by the application in question. It does have to be well formed; that is, it must conform to some basic rules that are laid out by the W3C. The W3C document can be accessed online at http://www.w3.org/xml. This section aims at defining some of the pieces of the puzzle that make up your XML content.

Elements

An element in an XML document describes a piece of data. Consider lines 4 and 5 in Listing 29.1. We define two elements, one being a creditCard and the other being an amount. At a first glance, these two might look different, but they really aren't that different. Each element describes a particular piece of the data.

Elements are made up using arbitrary element names, which are enclosed in angled brackets (< and >). Names must begin with a letter or an underscore. Names can be of any length, and can contain letters, numbers, underscores, hyphens, and periods. Names cannot contain embedded spaces. Element names are case sensitive. You can typically use the same naming conventions that you follow for naming Java variables to create XML element names. Understand that element names can be as descriptive as you choose, but making them unnecessarily long can cause confusion while reading the XML file.

All open elements must be closed. Elements are closed by using an ending tag, which consists of a forward slash (/) followed by the name of the element that's being closed; for example, </amount>. Between an opening and closing element tags, you may have any number of sub-elements and raw text.

XML tags cannot be nested, but HTML tags can be. HTML does not require the document to be well formed, whereas XML does.

Now consider the difference between lines 4 and 5 in Listing 29.1. Line 4 describes a credit card element and looks like the following:

```
4.    <creditCard number="1234123412341234" type="MC" expiration="03/2005"/>
```

This is a well-formed element. However, it doesn't have a closing tag of </creditCard>. Or does it? In the case of an HTML document, for many tags you must explicitly define the closing tag for an empty tag such as this. But in the case of an XML document, you can use a shortcut to close the tag, thus reducing the clutter in your document. The shortcut is the use of a /> characters to close your element. This is the same as defining the creditCard tag with its attributes, closing the tag with the angle bracket, and subsequently including a </creditCard> tag. Thus, in this case, we define an element called creditCard, define some attributes to it, and close it all within the same tag. This concept can be extended to define empty tags, which act like Booleans in your XML document. For instance, if the airline were to tell the bank that the bank needs only to authorize the amount and not actually make the charge, it could add a new element, <authorizeOnly/>, in its XML document. These are known as *empty tags*. Of course, in an XML document, there are several ways in which a particular piece of data can be represented. For instance, the <authorizeOnly/> tag means the same as a <operation type="authorize"/> element.

The root element is the top-level element that does not include the header information. There can be only one root element in your XML document in order to make it a well-formed XML. For instance, in our examples, the <paymentInfo> element forms the root element. For all practical purposes, the root element is like any other element in the XML document. It is just special because it describes the data that's represented by the document.

Attributes

Consider line 4 in Listing 29.1. From this line, it's obvious that an element can contain not only data between the start and end tags, but it can also contain attributes. Attributes define an element. Attributes are defined as key-value pairs within the starting tag of an element. Thus, in our credit card example, the attributes of the credit card are its number, type, and expiration date. Naming attributes follow the same rules as naming elements. The value of the attribute is enclosed within a set of either single or double quotes. Typically, it is standard practice to use double quotes for specifying values. Thus, you can define an element called `<paymentInfo>` as follows, which practically replaces the entire XML document described earlier:

```
<paymentInfo cardNum="xxx" type="xx" expDate="xx/xxxx">
  200.00
</paymentInfo>
```

Here you list the credit card data as attributes and the amount as the value of the element. Another form of representing the same data is the following:

```
<paymentInfo>
  <creditCard>
    <number>xxxx</number>
    <type>xx</type>
    <expDate>xx/xxxx</expDate>
  </creditCard>
  <amount>200.00</amount>
</paymentInfo>
```

So, which is the correct way of representing this XML? Well, there are no correct or incorrect ways. These are all different representations. What determines whether a data is to be represented as a value or an attribute of an element? Again, there is no hard-and-fast rule to determine this. One general rule of thumb is that if a data can have multiple values or is very long, that data is generally better off defined as an element rather than an attribute of an element. Also, data that's defined using attributes can be described in the DTD. In other words, the DTD can tell to the parser the possible valid values that can go into an attribute. Thus, if your data requires that kind of validation, you should choose to use an attribute rather than an element. Finally, the order of the data might be important, or data could be repeated. In such cases, using elements instead of attributes allows repetition of tags and validation of the order of the data . Attributes cannot be repeated nor can their order validated.

Entity References

Sometimes it becomes important that you use characters that are usually considered special characters in your XML data. For instance, you already know that an XML file is built using tags that are wrapped in angle brackets. So, how would you use an angle bracket within your data? For instance, if you want to represent the mathematical condition `x < y` as an XML `condition` element, how would you do it? The first thing that comes to mind is to represent it as follows:

```
<condition>x < y</condition>
```

It doesn't take more than a few seconds to realize that this does not make this document a well-formed XML document. That leaves us with the question how we represent the less than symbol in XML. To represent such data, you use entity references. An *entity reference* is a special symbol that represents different data within an XML document. Thus, when a parser parses out your document and encounters an entity reference, it knows to replace it with the correct data that's represented by that entity reference. Entity references are of the format `&[reference-name];`, where the *[reference-name]* part of the reference is replaced with the appropriate entity name. These symbols are the same ones that are used in HTML and URLs. The valid entity references are listed in Table 29.1.

TABLE 29.1 XML Entity References

Data Represented	Data	Entity Reference Used
Less than bracket	<	<
Greater than bracket	>	>
Ampersand	&	&
Double quote	"	"
Apostrophe	'	'

Thus, you can represent the mathematical condition as

```
<condition>x &lt; y</condition>
```

A parser that parses this element will know to replace the `<` with a < symbol.

CDATA Section

Sometimes, certain data that's represented by your XML document may be so complex that it's better for the parser not to attempt to parse it, and to simply feed it to the application. An example of this would be a snippet of code that is embedded within your XML document. Your code will probably make use of so many special characters that if you use entity references for each of them, you're bound to mess up the XML document. One way of avoiding this is by wrapping your data within a `CDATA` block. By doing so, you're instructing the parser not to attempt to parse the data, but simply to return it to the application. These data elements don't contain any entity references. They are considered to be raw text. Thus, a condition block that uses CDATA looks like this:

```
<condition>
  <![CDATA[
    x < y ;
  ]]>
</condition>
```

Comments

You can include comments within an XML document by beginning them with the string <!-- and ending them with -->. The following is a valid comment within an XML document:

```
<!-- This document represents a mathematical condition -->
```

Namespaces

A namespace qualifies a name. Conceptually, namespaces in XML are very simple, but can cause a great deal of heartburn in understanding if you don't work with an example. Consider the simple XML file shown in Listing 29.2, which describes how a book inventory has to be displayed on the screen. It has embedded HTML code to provide formatting.

LISTING 29.2 XML with Two Types of Data Embedded

```
<html>
  <head><title>Book Inventory</title></head>
  <body>
    <bookInventory>
      <table>
        <tr>
         <td>Title</td><td>Published by</td>
        </tr>
        <tr>
          <td>
            <title>
             WebLogic Server Unleashed
           </title>
          </td>
          <td>
            <publisher>SAMS Publications</publisher>
          </td>
        </tr>
      </table>
```

LISTING 29.2 Continued

```
20.        </bookInventory>
21.    </body>
22. </html>
```

Here we're creating an HTML table that contains information about some books. All is well when we look at it, but consider an application parsing through this XML document. It has to deal with a whole lot of HTML code, when all it's looking for is the data about the books. Look at lines 2 and 11. In line 2, we display the title of the HTML page, and in line 11, we have the title of the book. Both the tags are defined as `title`. Although this is correct, it can get very tricky for an application that's parsing through this XML document.

To work around this, XML namespaces were introduced. An XML namespace is essentially a qualifier to a name. Instead of saying `title`, you would now qualify the title to either the presentation logic or to the data. The XML 1.0 specification used URIs for qualifying tag names. Namespace qualifier URIs are written within curly braces just before the tag/attribute names. Thus, the `title` tag that specifies the title of the page may be written as

```
<{http://www.w3.org/html}title>
  Book Inventory
</{http://www.w3.org/html}title>
```

However this is bound to make the XML unreadable. To overcome this problem, XML also provides a shorthand mechanism to specify namespaces. To specify a shorthand, use the reserved `xmlns` tag. For example, here we create a `presentation` namespace that points to the HTML namespace, and then use it to qualify all HTML tags in our XML file.

```
<presentation:html xmlns:presentation=" http://www.w3.org/html ">
  <presentation:head><presentation:title>
    Book Inventory
  </presentation:title></presentation:head>
...
```

Here we specify a shorthand called `presentation` by defining the attribute `xmlns:presentation` to the `html` tag. We point this shorthand to the URI that qualifies HTML. When we specify a tag or an attribute that is of type `html`, we simply add the prefix `presentation:` to the tag name; for example, `presentation:title`. Note that children of all levels within the `html` tag will have access to this shorthand.

If you try typing in the URI that we specified into a Web browser's address bar, there's a very good chance that your browser will take you nowhere. This is because the XML specification does not require that the URI specified be valid or even that it exists. All the specification requires is a unique URI that can then be used by applications to access the data.

Given all this, the complete XML document with namespaces defined for `html` and the data would look as follows:

```
<presentation:html xmlns:data="http://www.xyzcompany.com/books"
    xmlns:presentation="http://www.w3.org/HTML/1998/html4">
  <presentation:head><presentation:title>
   Book Inventory
  </presentation:title></presentation:head>
  <presentation:body>
   <data:bookInventory>
     <presentation:table>
      <presentation:tr align="center">
        <presentation:td>Title</presentation:td>
        <presentation:td>Published by</presentation:td>
      </presentation:tr>
      <presentation:tr align="left">
        <presentation:td><data:title>WebLogic Server 7.0 Unleashed
           </data:title></presentation:td>
        <presentation:td>
          <data:publisher>SAMS</data:publisher>
        </presentation:td>
      </presentation:tr>
     </presentation:table>
   </data:bookInventory>
  </presentation:body>
</presentation:html>
```

You can also specify a default namespace by not having any prefix to the `xmlns` attribute. Any tag or attribute that isn't prefixed by a namespace tag will be associated with the default namespace.

Defining an XML Document

XML documents can be defined using other documents. The definition document serves as a dictionary for the XML document. The advantage of using such definition documents is that, when used in conjunction with the XML document, you can be sure that the XML document follows certain basic rules as laid out in the dictionary. This reduces the chance of processing errors in your application. Such documents also serve as a handshake between two different systems that communicate with each other using XML documents.

An XML dictionary can be described using two types of definition documents: document type definitions (DTDs) and XML schemas. In this section, we look at both methods of dictionary definition.

Document Type Definition

As we briefly touched on earlier, a DTD is like a dictionary for the XML document. It describes the valid structure of an XML document. DTDs make XML documents more usable because the parser can validate the document before the application receives the data. DTDs offer a very flexible way of describing what elements must be present in an XML document, what the valid values for their attributes are, and so forth. Although this chapter briefly introduces the concept of DTDs, it isn't intended to be a comprehensive discussion of DTDs. We only introduce some concepts that will help you write basic DTDs for your XML. If you're already familiar with writing DTDs for XML documents, you may skip this section and proceed to the next.

Let's consider the sample XML document in Listing 29.3, which describes an email document.

LISTING 29.3 An XML Document That Describes an Email

```
1. <email>
2.   <from name="John Doe" id="johndoe@xyzcompany.com"/>
3.   <to name="Jane Doe" id="janedoe@xyzcompany.com"/>
4.   <to name="SomeOther Doe" id="someotherdoe@xyzcompany.com"/>
4.   <cc name="YetAnother Doe" id="yetanotherdoe@xyzcompany.com"/>
5.   <subject>Hello!</subject>
6.   <options>
7.     <read_receipt/>
8.     <priority type="Normal"/>
9.   </options>
10.   <body>
11.     Hello, how are you doing.
12.   </body>
13. </email>
```

Elements

All keywords within your DTD begin with the <! symbol. The elements of your XML document are denoted by using the `ELEMENT` keyword. The DTD has one such line for each element of your XML. The `ELEMENT` keyword is followed by the name of the element, which is then followed by the content model of the element. The *content model* describes the data that can be contained within this element. The content model is defined by using opening and closing parentheses that enclose the contents. An element can contain one of two types of content: other elements or textual data. If an element contains other elements, the content model lists the names of the contained elements. For instance, the `element` tag that describes the `<options>` element in lines 6 through 9 will be as follows:

```
<!ELEMENT options (request_receipt, priority)>
```

When an element is defined like this, the parser ensures that the contained subelements must appear once, and only once, within the parent element. Now look at the element <email> in the XML document. There can be several <to> elements within the <email> element, each describing a single To address. Also, the email can have one or more <cc> tags that indicate carbon copy recipients, but they have to be optional. To define such rules, you append a recurrence modifier to the element name in question. A recurrence modifier indicates several properties of the element as shown in Table 29.2.

TABLE 29.2 DTD Recurrence Modifiers

Modifier	Example	Implies
?	options?	Can appear once, but may be absent (0..1)
+	to+	Must appear at least once, but can optionally be repeated n number of times (1..n)
*	cc*	Can appear any number of times, and may be absent (0..n)

Thus, the element <email> will be defined as follows to indicate that it must contain at least one <to> element, but optional <cc> elements:

```
<!ELEMENT email (from, to+, cc*, subject, options?, body)>
```

If an element contains data, the content model has the word #PCDATA within the parentheses. For instance, the element <subject> is defined as follows within the DTD:

```
<!ELEMENT subject (#PCDATA)>
```

Empty elements are defined using the EMPTY keyword instead of the content model. For instance, the <read_receipt/> element indicates that the sender has requested a read receipt from the recipients. This can be defined using the following DTD entry:

```
<!ELEMENT read_receipt EMPTY>
```

Attribute List

Consider the following line of the XML document from Listing 29.3:

```
4.     <to name="Jane Doe" id="janedoe@xyzcompany.com"/>
```

Here we define attributes to the <to> element. There are two attributes: name and id. To define the attributes of an element, use the ATTLIST keyword. This indicates the element name and properties of all the attributes that belong to that element. For each attribute, there is one segment that contains the attribute name, the attribute type, and a flag that indicates whether the attribute is required. For instance, the following illustrates a DTD entry for the <to> element:

```
<!ATTLIST to
  name CDATA #REQUIRED
  id CDATA #REQUIRED
>
```

Here we indicate that name and id are of type CDATA (text) and that both are required. Now consider the priority element in the XML file. Priority has to be restricted to Normal, High, or Urgent. It cannot take any other values. You can do this by setting up constraints on the attribute instead of the CDATA keyword, as follows:

```
<!ATTLIST priority
  type ( Normal ¦ High ¦ Urgent ) #REQUIRED
>
```

Putting all the pieces together, we come up with the full email DTD:

```
<!ELEMENT email (from,to+,cc*,subject,options,body)>
<!ELEMENT from EMPTY>
<!ATTLIST from name CDATA #REQUIRED
     id CDATA #REQUIRED>
<!ELEMENT to EMPTY>
<!ATTLIST to name CDATA #REQUIRED
     id CDATA #REQUIRED>
<!ELEMENT cc EMPTY>
<!ATTLIST cc name CDATA #REQUIRED
     id CDATA #REQUIRED>
<!ELEMENT subject (#PCDATA)>
<!ELEMENT options (read_receipt, priority)>
<!ELEMENT read_receipt EMPTY>
<!ELEMENT priority EMPTY>
<!ATTLIST priority type CDATA #REQUIRED>
<!ELEMENT body (#PCDATA)>
```

XML Schema

You can also describe an XML document using an XML schema instead of a DTD. An XML schema is a specification recommended by the World Wide Web Consortium (W3C; http://www.w3c.org). An XML schema is a much more powerful and flexible mechanism of defining XMLs than a DTD. Although a DTD can validate the structure of an XML document, a schema can additionally validate data types and data. It's possible to define data elements and the actual data (such as list of values or data patterns) that they can take. Even though a DTD has its own format, an XML schema is itself an XML document. A schema uses (and supports the use of) the concept of namespaces extensively, so it is important that you understand namespaces well before you proceed.

Using a schema, you can define

- The elements of an XML document and their attributes
- Their content or lack thereof

- Their attributes
- Ordering, hierarchy, and number of elements
- Data types of the content or attributes, and default values

Because an XML schema is itself an XML document, the schema has its own XML schema definition, which can be accessed by visiting the URL http://www.w3c.org/2001/XMLSchema.xsd. This schema document defines several core data types, which you can then extend to create your own custom data types. Those data types can then be referenced within your schema just like basic data types. In this section, we look briefly at creating XML schemas to define your XML documents. This section is not meant to be an exhaustive discussion of the features of XML schemas.

XML schemas are also extendable. In other words, you could write a common schema definition library and then write other definitions that extend from this common library. Let's now look briefly at the components of an XML schema definition document.

The schema Element

Refer to Listing 29.3 for a simple XML document that represents an email. In the previous section, we wrote a DTD to define this XML. In this section, we'll write a schema to define the same XML. Because a schema is also an XML document, it should be both well formed and valid. The root element of an XML schema is always a `schema` element in the XSD namespace.

```
<?xml version="1.0"?>
<xs:schema xmlns:xsd="http://www.w3.org/2001/XMLSchema"
targetNamespace="http://www.mycompany.com/schemas"
xmlns="http://www.mycompany.com/schemas">
```

Here we define the prefix `xs` to point to the namespace for any XML schema. Any element that belongs to this namespace should be prefixed with `xs:`. For example, we define the root element as `xs:schema` because the XML document represents an XML schema. We can also define other namespaces that we'll be using in our schema. In the preceding snippet, we define that any element defined with the `xs` prefix points to the namespace `"http://www.w3.org/2001/XMLSchema"`. Along with this, we also define that the target namespace for the schema that we're creating is `http://www.mycompany.com/schemas/email`.

As a reminder, the URL specified need not physically exist. It is only a referring URL that identifies the namespace and makes it unique. By including the tag `xmlns="..."` in this line, we indicate that any element that has not been qualified by a prefix belongs to the default namespace, which also happens to be the target namespace for the schema.

Simple Elements

The body of the schema is built by defining elements. Each element is associated with a data type. As indicated earlier, the schema definition already defines basic data types. You may then define your own data types that are either built as extensions of these basic data types or as a collection of other elements. This scheme promotes reusability of data types within the schema and even across schemas. A simple element is an element in an XML file, which has a body, but does not encompass other elements. Nor do simple elements have attributes. For example, in the email XML, the `<body>` element is a simple element. It is defined using the schema tag `element`. The syntax for defining a simple element is

```
<xs:element name="body" type="xs:string"/>
```

In the preceding line, we define the body tag of our XML and indicate that it can contain data of type `string`. This data type is a built-in data type defined by the XML Schema definition. You can use other data types while defining elements. Some of the most commonly used data types are `xs:string`, `xs:decimal`, `xs:integer`, `xs:boolean`, `xs:date` and `xs:time`.

While defining a simple element, you can also define a default value by including the `default` attribute to the element tag. This attribute indicates the value that is set to the element being declared if no other value is specified. You can alternatively define fixed elements that take a particular value and nothing else.

Attributes

You can define an attribute for an element in your XML by using the `attribute` tag. For example, the `priority` tag in our email XML has an attribute called `type`. This can be defined by using the `attribute` tag as follows:

```
<xs:attribute name="type" type="xs:string"/>
```

This indicates that the `type` attribute is of type `xs:string`. Other than `xs:string`, attributes may also use any of the data types discussed earlier. Attributes may be defined as fixed by using the `fixed` attribute of the `attribute` tag. For example:

```
<xs:attribute name="..." type="xs:string" fixed="value"/>
```

You may also provide a default value by using the `default` attribute. Here's an example:

```
<xs:attribute name="..." type="xs:string" default="defaultValue/>
```

Attributes may be defined as required or optional by using the `use` attribute of this tag. This attribute takes one of two values: `required` or `optional`. For example, in the case of the `type` attribute, we expect it to be present in all cases; therefore, we add the `use` attribute as follows:

```
<xs:attribute name="type" type="xs:string" use="required"/>
```

In the earlier email example , we can see that we have at least one user-defined data type that can be reused; namely, the `emailAddress` data type. The other elements are not reusable within the schema, (and we assume in other schemas), and hence need not be defined as explicit data types.

Restrictions

By defining an attribute of a particular type, the schema ensures that no XML document passes validation with data that does not correspond to the defined type. For example, if you have an attribute defined as type `xs:integer` and pass in a string value, the XML document will fail validation. This is known as a *restriction*. You can define several restrictions on the data by using the `xs:restriction` tag. We look at a few examples in the remainder of this section.

Consider the type attribute of the email document. Assume that we would like to place a restriction on this attribute to ensure that the type is always one of `Low`, `Normal`, or `High`. To do this, we create a simple data type, which is an extension of the basic `string` data type, but has an additional restriction on it. Thus, we modify the definition of the `type` attribute as follows:

```
<xs:attribute name="type" use="required">
  <xs:simpleType>
   <xs:restriction base="xs:string">
    <xs:enumeration value="Low"/>
    <xs:enumeration value="Medium"/>
    <xs:enumeration value="High"/>
   </xs:restriction>
  </xs:simpleType>
</xs:attribute>
```

Here we define a new type and use it within the `type` attribute. However, this new type cannot be reused by other elements or attributes. If we want to use this type in other elements, we'll have to define it outside the `attribute` tag and give it a name. We can then specify the type of the `type` attribute to the name indicated. The following listing describes how this is done:

```
<xs:simpleType name="priorityDataType">
  <xs:restriction base="xs:string">
   <xs:enumeration value="Low"/>
   <xs:enumeration value="Medium"/>
   <xs:enumeration value="High"/>
  </xs:restriction>
</xs:simpleType>
<xs:attribute name="type" type="priorityDataType" use="required"/>
```

You may also place restrictions based on patterns by using the `xs:pattern` tag within the `restriction` tag. This tag takes any standard regular expression to define valid patterns. For example, to specify that an element can take only lowercase letters and should have at least one character, you can define a restriction as

```
<xs:restriction base="xs:string">
  <xs:pattern value="[a-z]+"/>
</xs:restriction>
```

You can also define a restriction on the number of characters that an element (or attribute) can have by using the `xs:length` tag. Here's an example:

```
<xs:restriction base="xs:string">
  <xs:length value="2" />
</xs:restriction>
```

Complex Elements

Complex elements have other embedded elements and/or attributes. In the email document, it's easy to see that there are several complex elements. A complex element is defined using a syntax that's similar to that of a simple element, but is defined with the type set as a complex data type. As you saw earlier, this can be done either explicitly by using the `type` attribute (and thus creating reusable complex data types), or by embedding the definition of the complex data type within the element tag.

Let's define an `emailAddressType` data type that represents the following elements:

```
<from name="John Doe" id="johndoe@xyzcompany.com"/>
<to name="Jane Doe" id="janedoe@xyzcompany.com"/>
<cc name="YetAnother Doe" id="yetanotherdoe@xyzcompany.com"/>

<xs:complexType name="emailAddressType">
 <xs:attribute name="name" type="xs:string" use="required"/>
 <xs:attribute name="id" type="xs:string" use="required"/>
</xs:complexType>
<xs:element name="from" type="emailAddressType" />
<xs:element name="to" type="emailAddressType" />
<xs:element name="cc" type="emailAddressType" />
```

29

As you can see, we defined one complex data type and reused it across three different elements. Now let's define the complex type for the `options` tag of our XML. This has two child elements: a `read_receipt`, which is an empty element, and a `priority` tag:

```
<options>
 <read_receipt/>
 <priority type="Normal"/>
</options>
```

```
<xs:simpleType name="priorityDataType">
  <xs:restriction base="xs:string">
   <xs:enumeration value="Low"/>
   <xs:enumeration value="Medium"/>
   <xs:enumeration value="High"/>
  </xs:restriction>
</xs:simpleType>
<xs:element name="options" >
  <xs:complexType>
   <xs:sequence>
    <xs:element name="read_receipt">
      <xs:complexType/>
    </xs:element>
    <xs:element name="priority">
      <xs:complexType>
       <xs:attribute name="type"
          type="priorityDataType" use="required"/>
      </xs:complexType>
    </xs:element>
   </xs:sequence>
  </xs:complexType>
</xs:element>
```

As you can see in this example, we've created nested complex types to define the options tag of our XML. The `options` tag is defined to have a sequence, which contains the `read_receipt` tag followed by the `priority` tag. The `read_receipt` tag is defined as empty, whereas the `priority` tag is defined to be a complex type that has one attribute. If the `options` tag were to have an attribute, it would be defined after the `xs:sequence` block.

You can also define complex data types that extend from other complex data types. To do this, you use the `xs:extension` tag. After extending from a base data type, you can add more elements and attributes to the new data type. For example, the following code would create a new subtype of the `options` type, which would add the `expirationDate` attribute:

```
<xs:complexType name="expiratingOptions">
 <xs:complexContent>
  <xs:extension base="options" insert="prepend">
   <xs:attribute name="expirationDate" type="xs:date"/>
  </xs:extension>
 </xs:complexContent>
</xs:complexType>
```

Indicators

Indicators control how elements are used within an XML document. The `xs:all` indicator represents that the contained elements may occur in any order, but only once. For example, the following complex type indicates that the person's name should have a first name and last name, but not necessarily in any order:

```
<xs:complexType name="personsName">
  <xs:all>
   <xs:element name="firstname" type="xs:string"/>
   <xs:element name="lastname" type="xs:string"/>
  </xs:all>
</xs:complexType>
```

The `choice` indicator, on the other hand, indicates that either one child element, or the other, can occur. For example, the following block defines the payment information to be from either a checking account or a credit card:

```
<xs:element name="paymentDetails">
 <xs:complexType>
  <xs:choice>
   <xs:element name="checkingAccountNumber" type="xs:string"/>
   <xs:element name="creditCardNumber" type="xs:string"/>
  </xs:choice>
 </xs:complexType>
</xs:element>
```

The sequence indicator, which should be familiar to you, indicates that the child elements appear in the given sequence. The `minOccurs` and `maxOccurs` indicators indicate the minimum and maximum number of times a given element can occur. For example, if your document has to provide for a minimum of one and a maximum of three addresses per person, your schema would look like this:

```
<xs:element name="address" type="addressType" minOccurs="1" maxOccurs="3"/>
```

However, in the case of the email, there is no way to tell how many to addresses your email should have. In such cases, the `maxOccurs` indicator should be set to a special value of `unbounded` to indicate that there could be any number of the particular element in your document.

Using all of these elements, we can now put together the XML schema for the email XML document. The schema is given in the examples in the file `email.xsd`. Listing 29.4 shows this file.

LISTING 29.4 XSD Document for the Email XML

```
<?xml version="1.0" encoding="UTF-8"?>
<xs:schema xmlns:xs="http://www.w3.org/2001/XMLSchema"
  elementFormDefault="qualified"
  attributeFormDefault="unqualified">
<xs:element name="email">
 <xs:complexType>
  <xs:sequence>
   <xs:element name="from" type="emailAddressType"
       minOccurs="1" maxOccurs="1"/>
   <xs:element name="to" type="emailAddressType"
       minOccurs="1" maxOccurs="unbounded"/>
   <xs:element name="cc" type="emailAddressType"
       minOccurs="0" maxOccurs="unbounded"/>
   <xs:element name="subject" type="xs:string"
       minOccurs="1" maxOccurs="1"/>
   <xs:element name="options">
     <xs:complexType>
       <xs:sequence>
        <xs:element name="read_receipt">
          <xs:complexType/>
        </xs:element>
        <xs:element name="priority">
          <xs:complexType>
            <xs:attribute name="type"
                 type="priorityDataType"
                 use="required"/>
          </xs:complexType>
        </xs:element>
       </xs:sequence>
     </xs:complexType>
    </xs:element>
    <xs:element name="body" >
     <xs:simpleType>
       <xs:restriction base="xs:string">
         <xs:pattern value="[a-zA-Z0-9 ]+"/>
       </xs:restriction>
     </xs:simpleType>
    </xs:element>
  </xs:sequence>
 </xs:complexType>
</xs:element>
<xs:complexType name="emailAddressType">
```

LISTING 29.4 Continued

```
  <xs:attribute name="name" type="xs:string" use="required"/>
  <xs:attribute name="id" type="xs:string" use="required"/>
</xs:complexType>
<xs:simpleType name="priorityDataType">
  <xs:restriction base="xs:string">
   <xs:enumeration value="Low"/>
   <xs:enumeration value="Normal"/>
   <xs:enumeration value="High"/>
  </xs:restriction>
</xs:simpleType>
</xs:schema>
```

NOTE

For more information about XML schemas, consult

- `http://www.w3.org/TR/xmlschema-0`
- `http://www.w3.org/TR/xmlschema-1`
- `http://www.w3.org/TR/xmlschema-2`

XML Parsers

We've now written our first XML document, which describes an email. The next thing we need to do is to actually process the document and display it on the screen. The screen should display all the components of an email as described in the XML document. We've seen that the XML document is quite easy to read with the naked eye because it provides a definite structure to your data. But how do you make a software application read your XML document? To do so, you must use some tool that will parse through the file and give access to the contents of the document in a convenient format, which can then be handled using other applications. You'll find a variety of such tools in the market. They're known as *XML parsers*.

Parsers are of two types:

- Validating parsers make sure that the XML document is validated against a specified DTD or XML schema. Thus, a document that has been successfully parsed by a validating parser is considered well formed and valid.
- Nonvalidating parsers don't require the XML document to be validated. They do require that the XML document be well formed, but not necessarily valid. Such parsers provide increased performance, but don't guarantee valid data.

You need to have an XML parser in your classpath in order to work with the examples for this chapter. You can easily get a parser from the Internet. Several free parsers are available. The choice of which parser you want to use depends on two factors: the conformity of the parser to the XML specification and the speed of parsing.

NOTE

Some of the sites where you can find free XML parsers on the Internet are

- Apache Xerces: `http://xml.apache.org/xerces2-j`
- Sun Microsystems' Crimson: `http://xml.apache.org/crimson`
- IBM XML4J: `http://alphaworks.ibm.com/tech/xml4j`

WebLogic Server comes bundled with the Apache Xerces parser. Thus, you don't need to download the parser separately for the sake of the examples given in this chapter. For the rest of this chapter, we'll assume that you're using the bundled Xerces parser.

The next step is to use the APIs associated with XML parsers to parse your XML document. There are several APIs that you can use to parse XML documents. Two of the most common XML parsing APIs are SAX and DOM. In the following sections, we'll learn how to use these APIs to parse and use your XML documents. Let's use the email XML document for parsing (see Listing 29.5).

LISTING 29.5 The Email XML Document

```
<?xml version="1.0"?>
<!DOCTYPE email SYSTEM 'EMail.dtd'><email>
  <from name="John Doe" id="johndoe@xyzcompany.com"/>
  <to name="Jane Doe" id="janedoe@xyzcompany.com"/>
  <to name="SomeOther Doe" id="someotherdoe@xyzcompany.com"/>
  <cc name="YetAnother Doe" id="yetanotherdoe@xyzcompany.com"/>
  <subject>Hello!</subject>
  <options>
    <read_receipt/>
    <priority type="Normal"/>
  </options>
   <body>
    Hello how are you doing.
   </body>
</email>
```

SAX

SAX stands for *Simple API for XML*. It began as a Java-only API, but you can currently find SAX-based parsers for other languages. Different parsers implement the common SAX interfaces; any application written using this API is guaranteed to work with different parsers as long as the application and the parsers conform to the specifications of the interface. The Apache Xerces parser that's bundled with WebLogic Server supports SAX version 2.0.

SAX parsers generate events based on your XML document. Your application will provide handlers to handle the events generated by the SAX parser. Examples of events include start and end of an element, and so on. This section is intended to provide an introduction to the SAX API.

You can parse your XML documents with a SAX parser by using a SAX reader. A SAX reader is any class that implements the interface `org.xml.sax.XMLReader`. This class is provided by the implementation of the SAX parser. The class we'll use that implements this interface is `weblogic.apache.xerces.parsers.SAXParser`. This class and other interfaces that we'll use are available in the `weblogic.jar` library of your WebLogic installation. Be sure to include this file in your classpath to execute any examples given in this chapter.

The following sections describe the various steps involved in parsing an XML document using the SAX API.

Instantiate the Reader

The first step in using a SAX parser is instantiating the SAX reader. This is done by using a reader factory class, `org.xml.sax.helpers.XMLReaderFactory`. This factory is capable of generating different SAX readers for you, based on certain parameters. You can invoke the `createXMLReader` method on this factory and pass to it the name of the class you want to instantiate. Alternatively, you may also specify this name in the environment variable `org.xml.sax.driver` and not pass any parameters to the `createXMLReader` method.

```
XMLReader aReader = XMLReaderFactory.createXMLReader
➥    ("weblogic.apache.xerces.parsers.SAXParser");
```

Parsing the Document

After you've instantiated an `XMLReader` instance, you can pass the XML document into the reader and request it to parse the document by invoking the `parse` method on the reader. The document can be passed in as an instance of `org.xml.sax.InputSource`. This object encapsulates several useful pieces of information about the represented document. You may create an `InputSource` object either by passing to it an URI that identifies the document or by passing a IDs `java.io.InputStream` or `java.io.Reader` object that resolves to the XML document. The difference between these mechanisms is that when invoked with a URI, any relative system specified with respect to the XML document are resolved automatically. If invoked using the `InputStream` or the `Reader` objects, you must explicitly set

29

the system ID by using an appropriate setter. For example, the following block of code parses the email document:

```
InputSource inputSource = new InputSource("d:/temp/email.xml");
aReader.parse(inputSource);
```

When the parse method is invoked, it initiates the parsing of the XML document. At this time, your application can receive events generated by the parser and handle them appropriately. The parse method throws an exception of type org.xml.sax.SAXException if it encounters any error while parsing. For example, if your XML document isn't well formed, the parser generates this exception. The event handler (that you code) can also optionally generate this exception to indicate errors. Your application must catch this exception and handle it.

Content Handler

In the previous section, we saw that the parse method of the XML reader object generates events. Your application can trap these events and handle them by using a content handler. A content handler is a class that implements the interface org.xml.sax.ContentHandler. This interface specifies several callback methods, which will be invoked by the parser at appropriate times. You code into these callback methods to handle the events appropriately. In this section, we look at the different methods that must be implemented by your content handler implementation. Note that several of the callback methods throw an exception of type SAXException. You can report any problems with the XML from your callback methods as a SAXException. The client will catch this exception and handle it. The following list describes the different callback methods in the handler class:

- While parsing an XML document, the parser creates a document locator object. This object gives you information about the parsing process at any point in time; for example, which line of the document is currently being parsed. The parser provides you with a handle of this locator class by invoking the setDocumentLocator method on the content handler. It's normally a good practice to store the locator object locally because it will be useful while logging, reporting errors, and so on. The locator object is specified by the interface org.xml.sax.Locator.

  ```
  void setDocumentLocator( Locator locator );
  ```

- The parser informs your application when parsing actually begins. This is done by invoking the startDocument method. You can put initialization code in this method. The startDocument method is the first method to be invoked in the parsing life cycle after the setDocumentLocator method.

  ```
  void startDocument() throws SAXException;
  ```

- The endDocument method is invoked at the end of the parsing process. This is the last method invoked in the parsing process. You can put cleanup code here.

```
void endDocument() throws SAXException;
```

- Any processing instructions in the document header are passed on to the content handler by invoking the processingInstruction method. The parser provides this method with the target and its data. One example of a processing instruction is the tag used to link an XML with its style sheet:

```
<?xml-stylesheet type="text/xsl" href="./GenericRootNodeTemplate.xsl"?>

void processingInstruction(String target, String data) throws SAXException
```

- The startPrefixMapping callback method is invoked when a namespace is declared in an element. This method is always invoked before the element callback is invoked for that element. The startPrefixMapping method is passed the prefix of the namespace and the URI it maps to. For more information about namespaces, refer to the "Namespaces" section earlier in the chapter. For example, in a definition such as <presentation:html xmlns:presentation=" http://www.w3.org/html ">, the prefix is passed in as presentation, whereas the URI is passed in as http://www.w3.org/html. This should let your handler know what to do with events that are generated with that prefix. Remember that the namespace is valid for all sub-elements within this element.

```
void startPrefixMapping(String prefix, String URI) throws SAXException;
```

- The endPrefixMapping method is invoked just after the element that has declared a namespace has been closed. This method is invoked with the prefix of the namespace that has ended because the element to which it is associated has been closed. This method is invoked after the element callback method has been invoked for that element.

```
void endPrefixMapping(String prefix) throws SAXException;
```

- The startElement method is one of the element callback methods of the content handler. The element callback methods collectively provide your content handler with access to the actual data represented by the document. This method is invoked with the name of the element in three different forms: the URI of the namespace to which it is associated, the local name of the element, and the Q name or the complete name, which includes the namespace prefix, if any. In addition to the names, the method also provides your handler with access to the attributes of the element, all wrapped in an org.xml.sax.Attributes object. You can iterate through the contents of this object and access each of the attributes.

```
void startElement(String namespaceURI, String localName, String qName,
➥Attributes attributes) throws SAXException;
```

- The endElement element callback method is invoked when the element is closed. This method is also provided with the three types of names: the namespace URI, the local name, and the Q name of the element. Note that when an element has subelements within it, the parser will invoke the startElement for the parent element, followed by the start and end element callback methods for the subelements, prior to invoking the end element callback method for the parent element. (Remember, no nested elements in XML!) In other words, the parser invokes the callback methods in the same order in which it encounters elements and data within the XML document.

```
void endElement(String namespaceURI, String localName, String qName)
➥throws SAXException;
```

- Elements in an XML document can consist of additional elements, textual data, or a combination of the two. The characters element callback method is invoked to provide access to the textual data associated with the element. Note that all the data within an element may not be passed into this method in one invocation. Depending on the implementation of the parser, the method can be called back one or many times. In either case, the parser passes to your content handler a character array containing the text and the starting and ending indexes. You would typically concatenate the data passed into this method and finally use it in the endElement method. For this same reason, it's a mistake to assume that the start parameter is always going to be zero. The data that's returned can start from a nonzero index. This is so because the parser may reuse arrays to return the data to the content handler. It can do it without errors as far as it reports the starting and ending indexes of the character array. A typical implementation of this method is

```
contentString += new String( chars, start, end);
```

  Here's the method's signature:

```
void characters(char[] chars, int start, int end) throws SAXException;
```

- Sometimes there is whitespace between two elements when you aren't expecting it to be there. For instance, consider the XML snippet `<email>  <from>`. Here we have a couple of spaces between the two elements, although they aren't really meant to be part of the data. They're there just to provide a visual format to the XML. When the XML document references a DTD or XML schema, the parser knows that whitespace isn't expected because the DTD will indicate this. In such cases, the parser will report whitespace in the method ignorableWhitespace and pass the same parameters as for the characters method. Note that when your XML does not refer to a DTD or XML schema, there's no way for the parser to know whether whitespace is ignorable or intentional; thus, all whitespace is passed into your handler in the `characters` method. In other words, the `ignorableWhitespace` method should never be called when your XML does not refer to a DTD or XML schema.

```
void ignorableWhitespace(char[] chars, int start, int end) throws SAXExcep-
tion;
```

- XML enables you to refer to user-defined entities in your document. You can then define these entities from within the DTD or XML Schema. When the XML is parsed by a nonvalidating parser, there's no way for the parser to substitute the entity references. In such cases, the parser skips those entities. But before it skips them, it lets your content handler know that it's skipping it by invoking the `skippedEntity` method.

```
void skippedEntity(String entityName) throws SAXException;
```

Initialization code can either be put in the constructor, or the `setDocumentLocator` or `startDocument` methods. If you put initialization code in the constructor, it will be called only once when the class is instantiated, before any kind of processing is done. If you put it in the `startDocument` method, the parser has already started parsing your document. If your application can handle it, you should choose to put your initialization code in this method. If you absolutely must perform initialization routines prior to the parsing, `setDocumentLocator` might be a good place. It's a good idea to avoid overloading the `setDocumentLocator` method, because, as the name suggests, it is meant to be a mutator method. Overloading it with initialization code might not be a good idea.

Similarly, finalization code may be put either in the `endDocument` or the `finalize` methods. The `finalize` method is called only once: upon garbage collection of the parser object. This method might not always be called, however (see `http://java.sun.com/j2se/1.4.2/docs/api/java/lang/Object.html#finalize()`), so be careful what you put in there. In most cases, `endDocument` should work perfectly well.

Now that we've defined a content handler, how do we tell the parser which content handler to use? We do this by invoking the `setContentHandler` method on the `XMLReader` prior to invoking the `parse` method. Thus, the complete listing that parses the document would look as follows:

```
XMLReader aReader = XMLReaderFactory.createXMLReader(DEFAULT_PARSER);
aReader.setContentHandler( new EMailContentHandler() );
InputSource inputSource = new InputSource(xmlFile);
aReader.parse(inputSource);
```

Let's briefly look at how this handler has been constructed and how it works. Look at the source code listing for the email handler:

```
package com.wlsunleashed.xml.sax;
import com.wlsunleashed.xml.sax.email.EMail;
import com.wlsunleashed.xml.sax.email.EMailAddress;
import com.wlsunleashed.xml.sax.email.EMailOptions;

import org.xml.sax.Attributes;
import org.xml.sax.ContentHandler;
import org.xml.sax.Locator;
import org.xml.sax.SAXException;

public class EMailContentHandler implements ContentHandler {
  /** The e-mail object */
  private EMail eMail = null;

  /** Provides information about the parsing process. */
  private Locator documentLocator = null;

  /** A temporary string buffer to hold the contents of elements */
  private StringBuffer contentString = null;

  public void setDocumentLocator(Locator locator) {
    documentLocator = locator;
  }

  public EMail getEMail() {
    return eMail;
  }

  public void characters(char[] chars, int start, int end)
          throws SAXException {
    contentString.append(chars, start, end);
  }

  public void endDocument()
           throws SAXException {
    System.out.println("Processing has ended!");
  }

  public void endElement(String namespaceURI, String localName, String qName)
          throws SAXException {
    if (localName.equals("subject")) {
      eMail.setSubject(contentString.toString());
      contentString = new StringBuffer();
```

```
    return;
  }

  if (localName.equals("body")) {
    eMail.setBody(contentString.toString());
    contentString = new StringBuffer();

    return;
  }
}

public void endPrefixMapping(String prefix)
           throws SAXException {
}

public void ignorableWhitespace(char[] chars, int start, int end)
             throws SAXException {
  System.out.println("ignorableWhiteSpace "
            + documentLocator.getLineNumber() + " - "
            + documentLocator.getColumnNumber() + " - " + start
            + " - " + end);
}

public void processingInstruction(String target, String data)
              throws SAXException {
}

public void skippedEntity(String entityName)
          throws SAXException {
}

public void startDocument()
          throws SAXException {
  System.out.println("Processing begins .. ");
  eMail = new EMail();
}


public void startElement(String namespaceURI, String localName,
             String qName, Attributes attributes)
         throws SAXException {
  if (localName.equals("from")) {
    eMail.setFromAddress(
```

```
        new EMailAddress(attributes.getValue(0),
                 attributes.getValue(1)));

    return;
  }

  if (localName.equals("to")) {
    eMail.addToAddress(
        new EMailAddress(attributes.getValue(0),
                 attributes.getValue(1)));

    return;
  }

  if (localName.equals("cc")) {
    eMail.addCcAddress(
        new EMailAddress(attributes.getValue(0),
                 attributes.getValue(1)));

    return;
  }

  if (localName.equals("options")) {
    eMail.setOptions(new EMailOptions());

    return;
  }

  if (localName.equals("read_receipt")) {
    eMail.getOptions().setReadReceipt(true);

    return;
  }

  if (localName.equals("priority")) {
    eMail.getOptions().setImportance(attributes.getValue(0));

    return;
  }

  if (localName.equals("subject") || localName.equals("body")) {
    contentString = new StringBuffer();
```

```
            return;
        }
    }

    public void startPrefixMapping(String prefix, String URI)
                throws SAXException {
    }
}
```

We have an Email object along with an accessor method for it. After completing the parsing, the requesting class can get a hold of this Email object by using the accessor method. This object is built up using the contents of the email XML file. In the setDocumentLocator method, we first accept the document locator instance and store it locally. This will be useful to get document-related information later on, if we implement detailed error reporting, and so forth.

We initialize the local variables in the startDocument method. And in the startElement method, we begin filling in the contents of the Email object whenever we receive an event. The event type is identified using the local name of the event tag. Any attributes of that tag is obtained from the Attributes object. In this simple implementation, we take the order of attributes for granted and hard-code the indexes.

TIP

In practice, you should define constants to define these indexes. Better still, if you cannot guarantee the order of attributes, you should write code to scan for the name of the attribute before processing it.

Note the special processing for the subject and the body tags. The startElement method does nothing for these two tags. It simply initializes a local variable called contentString. This string is populated using the characters method, as shown in the code. Finally, when the endElement method is invoked, it populates the Email object with the contents of the contentString variable.

The handler is very stateful in nature. It must always be aware of the location of the tag with respect to the whole XML document. This is because the same tag name may be used in different sections of the same document, and may provide different meanings. Therefore, the handler should always be aware of the state under which the particular tag is being processed.

Complete source code that parses the email XML is provided on the CD at the end of the book, in the folder for this chapter. You can execute the class com.wlsunleashed.xml.sax.EMailClient and pass the Email.xml file to it. This class displays the contents of the Email XML document in a simple Swing-based client. Play around with this example a little bit; try changing the XML document and see how that affects the output.

Error Handler

You can specify a custom error handler that will be called whenever an error occurs during the parsing process. This will enable you to handle errors in an appropriate way and either allow processing to proceed or stop processing completely. A class that has to act as an error handler should implement the `org.xml.sax.ErrorHandler` interface. This interface specifies three methods: `error`, `fatalError`, and `warning`. Each of these methods takes a `SAXParseException` as a parameter, and can throw a `SAXException`.

The `SAXParseException` object contains the line number on which the error occurred, the URI of the document that caused the error, and details about the exception, including the message and a stack trace. The error handler can handle these messages in an appropriate way. Warnings are reported using the `warning` callback method, whereas nonfatal errors are reported using the `error` method. The default behavior is to continue parsing the document after this method has finished processing. But if the method implementation decides to stop processing, it can throw a `SAXException` from either of these methods and the parser will stop processing the document. On the other hand, when a fatal error occurs, the parser invokes the `fatalError` method and will then stop processing as specified by the XML specification. Validation errors are typically reported as nonfatal errors, whereas an XML document that is not well formed results in a fatal error.

Refer to the file `com/wlsunleashed/xml/sax/EMailErrorHandler.java`, that is included in the CD for a sample implementation of the `ErrorHandler` interface. In this example, we print out all warnings, errors and fatal errors, but intercept warnings. For errors and fatal errors, we throw a new `SAXException` object, which essentially halts processing. The source is listed here:

```
public class EMailErrorHandler implements ErrorHandler {

  public void warning(SAXParseException warn) throws SAXException {
        // We shall print out all warnings and ignore them
        printException(warn);
  }

  public void error(SAXParseException error) throws SAXException {
    // print out the error & exit
    printException(error);
    throw new SAXException(error);
  }

  public void fatalError(SAXParseException error) throws SAXException {
        // print out the error & exit
```

```
        printException(error);
        throw new SAXException(error);

  }

  private void printException(SAXParseException exception) {
    System.out.println("Error occurred while parsing the XML document");
    System.out.println("Line # = " + exception.getLineNumber());
    System.out.println("Column # = " + exception.getColumnNumber());
    System.out.println(exception.getMessage());
    System.out.println("Stack Trace");
    exception.getCause().printStackTrace();
  }
}
```

Other SAX 2.0 Features

In addition to the features of the SAX API discussed here, SAX 2.0 also supports some additional features. You can use SAX 2.0 methods to get and set feature flags and property values in XML readers. The feature flags and property values affect the way the XML reader behaves while parsing your XML, such as during validation. You can read more about the advanced features of SAX 2.0 by visiting the official SAX Web site at `http://www.saxproject.org`. There are also two more types of handlers that you can define, one for resolving entities—if you want the flexibility of overriding the default entity resolution process—and another for handling callbacks when advanced DTD features such as notations and unparsed entities are encountered by the parser.

We aren't going to discuss these features in this chapter for the sake of brevity.

Default Handler

After discussing all these handler methods, we now know that the specification enables us to define a bunch of callback methods. That's very flexible, but can be quite painful if all you need are a couple of these methods and not all of them. In such cases, your handler can extend the `org.xml.sax.helpers.DefaultHandler` class. This class provides default implementations for all the methods in all the four handler interfaces. Your handler class may then override only the methods that you require for your application, thus keeping your code clean.

XML Parsing Using DOM

Another common XML parsing API is the DOM API. DOM stands for Document Object Model. DOM is a standard that was developed by the World Wide Web Consortium (W3C) (unlike SAX, which evolved based on discussions on mailing lists). DOM was not designed for Java alone, and you can easily find DOM-based parsers for any language. But, of course, we'll be dealing with a DOM parser for Java here. In this section, you get a basic overview of the DOM specification. It isn't intended to be a comprehensive discussion on the features of DOM. You can very easily find books that discuss DOM in detail. A good place to learn basic DOM is the URL `http://www.w3schools.com/dom`.

A DOM parser converts an XML document into an object model, which can then be accessed using standard APIs by your application—hence the name *Document Object Model*. As mentioned earlier, DOM is intended to be cross platform; therefore, it's very easy to find parsers written in several languages that subscribe to the DOM way of handling XML. DOM standardizes concepts into levels rather than versions. The latest level of DOM specification is Level 3. WebLogic Server ships with a Xerces DOM parser that is based on the DOM Level 2 core specification, with some Level 3 features.

The Basics of DOM

SAX gives you a piecemeal representation of the XML document. It makes the data available to your application one piece at a time. DOM, on the other hand, does not do that. After parsing the document, DOM provides all the data as a tree of objects to your application at one go. All the data is loaded in memory in the object model, and your application receives a reference node of this model. You can then navigate through this model using the API to get to the actual data. Remember that the DOM specification does not outline the methods involved specifically, rather it simply focuses on the model of the document.

The object model consists of the XML data represented in a tree format. The tree is built using components called *nodes*, represented by the interface `org.w3c.dom.Node`. All the objects of the tree implement this interface. The root node of the DOM tree is known as the `Document` node, and is represented by using the object `org.w3c.dom.Document`. Other objects such as `Element`, `Attr`, `Text`, and so on make up the entire DOM object model. An example DOM structure is represented in Figure 29.1.

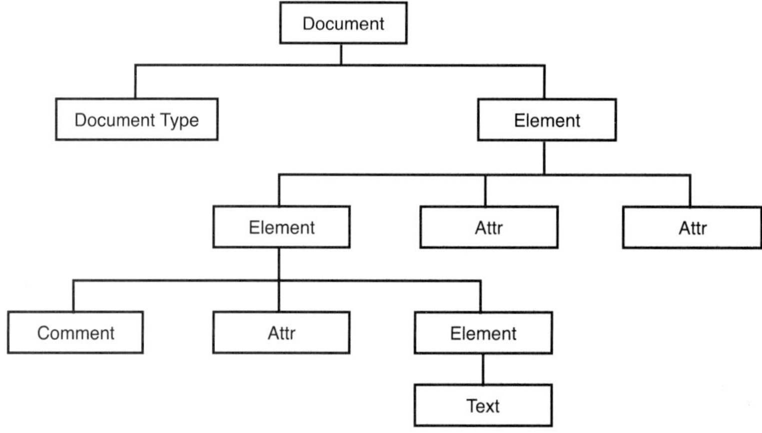

FIGURE 29.1 The DOM structure representation.

As you can see from the figure, the tree model is very strictly followed in a DOM representation. For example, the `Text` node is a child, rather than an attribute, of the `Element` node. This is to maintain the strict tree structure of the model. All the nodes implement the same `Node` interface, so you can use the basic navigation methods present in this interface on any type of node without worrying about what type it is. Navigation methods include methods such as `getParent`, `getChildren`, and so forth. One important point is that a method such as `getChildren` does not return a Java collection. It returns custom collections such as `NodeList` and `NamedNodeMap`, which are essentially part of the DOM classes.

Parsing an XML File

Parsing an XML document using DOM is quite straightforward: instantiate the parser and parse the document. You can then query the parser to get a handle to the in-memory `Document` object that was created while parsing the document. The following code snippet parses an XML document:

```
DOMParser aParser = new DOMParser();
aParser.parse(xmlFile);
Document doc = aParser.getDocument();
```

When you actually code this and try to compile this code, your compiler will complain about catching two exceptions. The first is `java.io.IOException`, which will be thrown if there are any I/O errors while accessing the XML document. That is perfectly understandable, but the second exception that your compiler will complain about is `SAXException`! Now this is definitely strange behavior! As strange as it might seem at first, remember that although the DOM model gives you a complete tree representation of your XML document, it does not specify how the parser should construct the tree. The tree can surely be constructed using an underlying SAX parser and then handed over to you. Because there's no specified standard describing how this should be done, it is quite common for DOM parsers to use SAX to construct the model.

Processing the Document Tree

The `getDocument` method returns a `Document` object, which is essentially the handle to the object model for your application. You might also find parsers that will return the `Document` object directly from the `parse` method without you having to explicitly invoke the `getDocument` method.

As mentioned earlier, all the objects implement the `Node` interface. The node interface contains all the relevant methods that enable you to navigate the tree and get to the data. The first step in identifying the data is to identify the type of the node you're dealing with. You can do this by invoking the `getNodeType` method on the `Node` interface. This returns an integer value that corresponds to the different node types, as indicated in Table 29.3. All these integer values are defined as constants in the `Node` interface.

TABLE 29.3 DOM Node Types

Node Type (Constants Defined in the Node Interface)	Node
DOCUMENT_NODE	The document handle
ELEMENT_NODE	An element in the XML
TEXT_NODE	A text element (contents of an element)
CDATA_SECTION_NODE	CDATA element
COMMENT_NODE	A comment
PROCESSING_INSTRUCTION_NODE	A processing instruction
ENTITY_REFERENCE_NODE	Entity reference
DOCUMENT_TYPE_NODE	The DOCTYPE of the document

After you've identified the node type, you can access the data contained in the node by invoking the appropriate methods on the object. For example, the `getNodeName` method returns the name of the element. The `getChildNodes` returns a list of child nodes to this node (class NodeList). The `getAttributes` method returns a list of attributes for an element node (class `NamedNodeMap`). Each attribute implements the `Node` interface again, and the `getNodeName` returns the attribute name. The `getNodeValue` method returns the value of the attribute.

In some cases, you can cast the object to an appropriate type to get more specific data. For example, for processing instructions, you can cast the `Node` to a `ProcessingInstruction` interface, and access the target and the data by invoking the `getTarget` and `getValue` methods, respectively, although the same information can be obtained in a less-intuitive way by using the `getNodeName` and `getNodeValue` methods. Similarly, you may cast a document type node into a `DocumentType` object, and access the public and system IDs by invoking the `getPublicId` and `getSystemId` methods.

You can look at a working example of using a DOM parser by compiling and executing the class `com.wlsunleashed.xml.dom.XMLTreeViewer`. This class creates a DOM tree out of any given XML file and displays a tree view on a frame. Although the code is interspersed with Swing calls to draw the tree, the use of the DOM classes should be quite clear from looking at the example.

Modifying the DOM Tree

We now know how to access a DOM tree constructed using a DOM parser. It's equally easy to change the contents of a DOM tree. You might remember that with SAX, you can only read the data—it isn't possible to change it. But DOM is mutable, and this gives you a very good reason for using DOM rather than SAX when you need this flexibility. DOM can be used to hold and manipulate, both in memory and in XML files, the data of an application.

You can create a new document by using the `createDocument` method on the `Document` instance. Similarly, the `createDocType` method can be used for creating a `DocType` element.

Also, there are similar methods such as `createElement`, `createTextNode`, and `createCDATASection` to create the appropriate nodes. Nodes may be appended as children to other nodes by using the `appendChild` node on the `Node` interface. If you want to use namespaces in your elements, you would use the `createElementNS` method rather than the `createElement` method on the `Document` object.

NOTE

You might wonder why the `createElement` method has not been simply overloaded instead of using a method with a specific name. Remember that the DOM specification is not specific for Java. In order to cater to other languages that might not have the flexibility of method overloading, the specification provides for different method names.

To modify an existing DOM tree, you can use methods such as `removeChild` and `appendChild` on the `Node` interface to replace nodes. The `Element` object also has setter methods that may be used to change attributes of the elements. Similar to elements, you can set namespace-specific attributes by using the appropriate methods.

You can learn more about these features by visiting the Web site at `http://www.devguru.com/Technologies/xmldom/quickref/xmldom_intro.html`.

Java API for XML Processing

Now that we've seen some basic XML parsing using SAX and DOM, let's look at an abstraction layer over these parsers created by Sun, known as the *Java API for XML processing*, or *JAXP* for short. This abstraction enables you to use parsers in a vendor-neutral way, and also handle some difficult tasks with DOM and SAX with ease. One confusing aspect of JAXP is that Sun's Crimson XML parser is bundled along with the JAXP classes. Having said that, JAXP itself does not include any parsing capabilities. You can access Sun's parser, as well as any other parser such as Xerces, by using JAXP. It cannot parse XML documents without an underlying DOM, SAX, or an other kind of parser. It only provides an easier way to access the parsing capabilities of DOM and SAX parsers.

WebLogic Server provides JAXP version 1.1, which supports both DOM level 2 and SAX 2.0 via Xerces 2.1.

JAXP and SAX

To understand why JAXP is so useful, look at the following snippet of code that we used earlier on to work with XML parsers:

```
import org.xml.sax.InputSource;
import org.xml.sax.SAXException;
import org.xml.sax.XMLReader;
import org.xml.sax.helpers.XMLReaderFactory;
...
```

```
String DEFAULT_PARSER = "weblogic.apache.xerces.parsers.SAXParser";
XMLReader aReader = XMLReaderFactory.createXMLReader(DEFAULT_PARSER);
aReader.setContentHandler( new EMailContentHandler() );
InputSource inputSource = new InputSource(xmlFile);
aReader.parse(inputSource);
```

Obviously, we're tying this code with the WebLogic Xerces implementation of the SAX parser, and that is clearly hard-coded in the code. This means that if you want to start using a different implementation of the SAX parser, you must modify your code to do it. JAXP provides you with a clean and flexible way of avoiding this by letting you use a parser in your code, and picking the parser using system properties. All the JAXP interfaces and classes can be found in the `javax.xml.parsers` package. Any class or interface that we refer to in this section belongs to this package unless otherwise stated.

JAXP provides you with a `SAXParserFactory` object, which you can use to create the underlying SAX parser. This object uses some system variables to figure out which parser must be created. The `newSAXParser` method in this object returns a `SAXParser` object, which can then be used for parsing the document. Remember that the underlying vendor-specific parser does the actual parsing. JAXP only provides a vendor-neutral abstraction to the parsers.

```
import javax.xml.parsers.SAXParserFactory
...
SAXParserFactory factory = SAXParserFactory.newInstance();
factory.setValidating(true);
SAXParser parser = factory.newSAXParser();
...
```

How does the factory know which parser to instantiate? It looks into the environment of your application for a property known as `javax.xml.parsers.SAXParserFactory`. This property is expected to indicate the class to be instantiated. This class and its associated classes and interfaces should be present in your application's classpath. If the factory can find the class, it instantiates it and enables you use it.

Note that we set the properties of the parser that we will use in the factory. For instance, we set the property that will make the factory return a validating parser by using the `setValidating` method of the factory. You can also set other properties (such as `setNameSpaceAware`) to further define the attributes of your parser. The factory may throw two different types of exceptions. It throws the `FactoryConfigurationError` when the parser specified cannot be loaded for any reason. It throws the `ParserConfigurationException` when you request a feature that isn't supported by the underlying implementation of the parser.

After you have the SAXParser object, you can parse your document by passing it into the parse method. The SAXParser object that wraps the actual parser can also tell you whether the parser is a validating parser and whether it is namespace-aware by invoking the appropriate methods. Before you parse, of course, you want to set the content handler that handles the SAX events. You can do this by passing in your handlers using an appropriate flavor of the parse method. You can also obtain the underlying parser directly by invoking the getXMLReader method on the SAXParser object. After you get this object, you can set the different handlers directly to it as we've already discussed.

You can also set other vendor-specific properties by using the setProperty method on the SAXParser object. This method takes a name and a value. The name is usually a URI that identifies the property. A typical example of a feature name is http://xml.org/sax/features/validation, which indicates whether the parser supports validation. Similarly, you can also retrieve values stored in properties by using the getProperty method. These methods throw the SAXNotRecognizedException if the property isn't recognized and SAXNotSupportedException if the property isn't supported by the underlying parser.

JAXP and DOM

Using JAXP with DOM is quite similar to using it with SAX. Instead of a SAX parser factory, we use a document builder factory. The newDocumentBuilder method of this object (the DocumentBuildFactory) returns a document builder (DocumentBuilder) object, which can help you parse the document. As with SAX, you set document builder properties, such as validating and namespace-aware, into the factory before getting the DocumentBuilder object. These methods also throw the same exceptions that the SAX version did. The only noticeable differences between the SAX and DOM versions are simply the types of factory and parser objects that you use. The rest of the code is identical.

Like SAX, the DocumentBuilderFactory uses an environment variable called javax.xml.parsers.DocumentBuilderFactory to identify the class to be instantiated for your application.

The DocumentBuilder class enables you to parse the document and get a org.w3c.dom.Document object by using the parse methods. There are different flavors of the parse method that you can use depending on your input source. A sample invocation is given here:

```
DocumentBuilderFactory dbf = DocumentBuilderFactory.newInstance();
DocumentBuilder db = dfb.newDocumentBuilder();
Document doc = db.parse(inputSource);
```

We haven't provided any examples that use JAXP, but as you can see from the discussion, using JAXP is quite straightforward. Take it as an exercise to change the email client and the XML tree viewer that we discussed while talking about SAX and DOM to use JAXP.

WebLogic Server XML Streaming API

You can also parse XML documents using WebLogic Server's implementation known as the *Streaming API*. This API is based on SAX, but gives you more control than SAX while parsing your document. This API enables you to be proactive rather than reactive. In other words, you request events from the parser and process them, rather than waiting for events from the parser as you do with SAX. For this reason, this kind of parsing is known as *pull parsing*. You can parse not only XML documents using the Streaming API, but also DOM trees and SAX events.

Parsing an XML Document

You can parse any XML source by using the Streaming API. Parsing an XML document typically involves the following steps.

Creating an XML Input Stream

The WebLogic Server XML Streaming API classes and interfaces can be found in the package `weblogic.xml.stream`. All classes and interfaces referenced in this section belong to this package unless otherwise stated. This package contains a factory, which provides you with the starting point for the XML streaming process. This factory, the `XMLInputStreamFactory`, will create an XML input stream from the input stream passed in. To do this, you invoke the `newInputStream` method, which returns an object of type `XMLInputStream` to you. The following code snippet demonstrates the process of creating the input stream:

```
XMLInputStreamFactory factory = XMLInputStreamFactory.newInstance();
XMLInputStream inputStream = factory.newInputStream(
    new FileInputStream("c:\temp\doc.xml"));
```

The preceding example is the easiest way of creating an XML input stream. The factory enables you to complicate it further by filtering the XML events that the stream returns. There are several ways of filtering the events. You can filter it by type, by name of the element, by namespace, or by a combination of namespace and type. You can also create custom filters if you require enhanced filtering capabilities.

To filter the events that are generated from the stream, create a filter and pass it on to the `newInputStream` method. You can create different filters as discussed in Table 29.4. We haven't discussed `XMLEvents` yet, but for this discussion, it's enough to know that an `XMLEvent` is simply a wrapper for an event that is generated by the parser. Events may be seen as being similar to SAX events such as start element, end element, and so forth.

TABLE 29.4 XML Events Filters

Filter Type	Description
TypeFilter	Filters based on the type of events; for instance, start element, end element, and so forth. We'll discuss element types in detail in just a second. For example, you can create a type filter by using the following construct: `new TypeFilter(XMLEvent.START_ELEMENT ¦ XMLEvent.END_ELEMENT )`
NameFilter	Filters events based on element names. For example, `new NameFilter("subject")`.
NameSpaceFilter	Filters based on namespaces. This enables you to receive elements that are part of a particular namespace only. For example, `new NameSpaceFilter("http://www.emailnamespace.com")`.
NameSpaceTypeFilter	Enables you to filter based on namespace and type. For example, `new NameSpaceTypeFilter("http://www.emailnamespace.com", XMLEvent.START_ELEMENT ¦ XMLEvent.END_ELEMENT)` will return start and end element events that belong to the given namespace.

As mentioned earlier, you can also create a custom filter if your application requires enhanced filtering. A custom filter is your own class that implements the `ElementFilter` interface. This interface defines an `accept` method that takes an `XMLEvent` as its parameter and returns a `boolean` indicating whether it is an acceptable event. Based on the return from this method, the event is either passed to you or dropped. Just as in regular filters, you create an instance of the custom filter and pass it to the `newInputStream` method to enable custom filtering of events.

With an input stream, you can process events only once. In other words, once an event has been served, you cannot get it back. But if your application requires that flexibility, you should use a buffered input stream rather than a regular input stream. Using the `newBufferedInputStream` method of the factory can create a buffered input stream. This method returns a `BufferedXMLInputStream` object. You can also specify filters while creating a buffered input stream. After you've created the buffered input stream, you can mark a position by invoking the `mark` method. You can subsequently go back to that position by invoking the `reset` method.

You can read more, including an example on filtering and `BufferedInputStream`, by visiting the URL `http://edocs.bea.com/wls/docs81/xml/xml_stream.html#1092257`.

29

Navigating Through the Stream

You can process the stream by using some methods present in the `XMLInputStream` object. You can consider this stream object as an enumeration of XML events. This object has a `hasNext` method that returns a `boolean` indicating whether the stream has more events. If it has more events, you can access the next event by invoking the `next` method on the stream. The `next` method returns an `XMLEvent` object, which can then be processed by your application. Remember that the hasNext and the next methods have already applied any filtering rules that you've requested on the events, so you'll receive only filtered events.

```
while (inputStream.hasNext()) {
  XMLEvent anEvent = inputStream.next();
  processEvent(anEvent);
}
```

You can also invoke methods in the XMLInputStream object to skip elements. When you invoke the skip method, the input stream is positioned to the next event in the stream. You can pass an integer into the skip method to skip more than one event. You can also skip until you reach a particular element by passing in the element name into the skip method. You can invoke the skipElement method to skip an element along with its sub-elements. You can invoke the peek method to take a peek at the forthcoming element without actually reading it out of the stream.

You can also get a sub-stream out of the input stream by invoking the getSubStream method. This method returns an XMLInputStream object, which essentially contains a copy of the next element, along with its sub-elements, as an input stream. The position on the parent input stream is not changed. What you get is a copy. If you want to skip this element in the parent input stream, you should explicitly invoke the skipElement method.

When you're done parsing the stream, close it by invoking the close method.

Processing an Event

To process an event, you must identify the type of the event that's being processed. Consider this as equivalent to the different node types that we handled when we discussed DOM. You can get an event type by invoking the getType method on an XMLEvent object. The event may be of different types, as indicated in Table 29.5. For each type of event, your application will receive a distinct event object from the stream that subclasses the XMLEvent class. You can see the actual subclass that will be returned in Table 29.5.

TABLE 29.5 XML Event Types

Event Type	Description	Represented by Subclass of XMLEvent
CHANGE_PREFIX_MAPPING	Indicates that the prefix mapping has been changed from one namespace to another	ChangePrefixMapping
CHARACTER_DATA	Indicates that the event has the body of the element	CharacterData
COMMENT	Indicates a comment	Comment
END_DOCUMENT	Indicates the end of a document	EndDocument

TABLE 29.5 Continued

Event Type	Description	Represented by Subclass of XMLEvent
END_ELEMENT	Indicates the end of an element	EndElement
END_PREFIX_MAPPING	Signals the end of a prefix mapping scope	EndPrefixMapping
ENTITY_REFERENCE	Represents an entity reference	EntityReference
PROCESSING_INSTRUCTION	Indicates a processing instruction	ProcessingInstruction
SPACE	Indicates that the event contains whitespace	Space
START_DOCUMENT	Indicates the start of an XML document	StartDocument
START_ELEMENT	Indicates the start of the element	StartElement
START_PREFIX_MAPPING	Indicates the beginning of the prefix mapping scope	StartPrefixMapping

Thus, you would typically have a `switch case` statement in your application's `processEvent` method to enable you to process different event types. In the following code snippet, we demonstrate the use of such a `switch case` statement.

```
switch(theEvent.getType()) {
  case XMLEvent.START_ELEMENT:
    // process a start element
    break;
  case XMLEvent.END_ELEMENT:
    // process an end element event
    break;
  ...
}
```

To access the data within the events, you can convert the events into the appropriate interfaces as indicated in Table 29.5. After you cast the object, you can then access methods present within the interface to get to the data. For instance, the `StartDocument` interface provides you with access to the system and public IDs; the `StartElement` interface can be used to access the attributes of the element, the namespace information, and so forth.

NOTE

A more efficient way of performing this task is to create overloaded methods that perform various tasks based on the parameter passed in. For instance, we could create several `processEvent` methods and have multiple flavors of it based on the type of parameter passed in; for example, `processEvent(StartDocument doc)`, `processEvent(StartElement element)`, and so on. We could then allow the object-oriented method overloading to take charge of invoking the right method.

We don't discuss all the methods that you can access through each interface. You can look that up in the BEA API documentation for this package by accessing the URL `http://edocs.bea.com/wls/docs81/xml/xml_stream.html#1092257`.

The XMLEvent interface includes a getName method that returns an object of type XMLName. This interface enables you access to the local name, the namespace URI, and the qualified name of the element name.

A simple XML stream-based processing is listed in the following code. In this example, we print out the name of the root node and its system ID. This is followed by a listing of all elements in the XML, along with their attributes, if any. The events in the stream are read using a while loop in the process method. Each event is then passed to the processEvent method as discussed earlier.

```
public class ProcessXML {
  /** The XML file to be processed */
  private String fileName = null;

  public ProcessXML(String file) {
    fileName = file;
  }

  private void process()
         throws FileNotFoundException, XMLStreamException {
    XMLInputStreamFactory factory =
         XMLInputStreamFactory.newInstance();
    TypeFilter aFilter =
          new TypeFilter(XMLEvent.START_DOCUMENT
             ¦ XMLEvent.START_ELEMENT);

    XMLInputStream inputStream =
          factory.newInputStream(
              new FileInputStream(fileName),
                       aFilter);

    while (inputStream.hasNext()) {
      XMLEvent anEvent = inputStream.next();
      processEvent(anEvent);
    }
  }

  /**
   * Method processEvent.
   *
   * @param anEvent
   */
  private void processEvent(XMLEvent anEvent) {
    switch (anEvent.getType()) {
```

```
    case XMLEvent.START_DOCUMENT:

      StartDocument startDoc = (StartDocument) anEvent;
      System.out.println(" In Start Doc: ");
      System.out.println("  -- Name = " +
             startDoc.getName());
      System.out.println("  -- System Id = " +
             startDoc.getSystemId());

      break;

    case XMLEvent.START_ELEMENT:

      StartElement startElem = (StartElement) anEvent;
      System.out.println(" In Start Element: ");
      System.out.println(" -- name = " + startElem.getName());

      AttributeIterator attrs = startElem.getAttributes();

      while (attrs.hasNext()) {
        Attribute anAttr = attrs.next();
        System.out.println(" -- Attr name = " +
                     anAttr.getName());
        System.out.println(" -- -- Attr value = " +
                     anAttr.getValue());
      }

      break;

    default:
      System.out.println(
          "If you see this message, the "
              + " filter has been changed");
      break;
    }
  }
}
```

Look up the example `com.wlsunleashed.xml.stream.ProcessXML` on the CD, in the folder for this chapter. You can see a typical usage of the XML Streaming API to process an XML document. This example simply parses the XML document and prints its contents on the screen. Invoke it with any XML document as its parameter.

Generating New XML Documents

The Streaming API can be used not only to parse existing XML documents, but also to create new documents. While creating new documents, you can also append existing XML documents in the new ones.

Opening an Output Stream

To create a new XML document, you first create an output stream instead of the input stream that we created while reading a document. Creating an output stream is achieved by using a factory. The class for this factory is `XMLOutputStreamFactory`. It has a `newOutputStream` method that returns a new output stream based on the writer that you pass as an input. The writer can be constructed out of a flat file or any other output stream. The following code snippet creates a new output stream to be used for creating XML documents:

```
XMLOutputStreamFactory factory = XMLOutputStreamFactory.newInstance();
XMLOutputStream outputStream = factory.newOutputStream(
        new PrintWriter(System.out, true) );
```

The output stream can also be constructed out of a `Document` object, in which case it constructs the DOM tree based on the data passed in. All these methods throw an exception of type `XMLStreamException`, which indicates that there was an error in trying to create the output stream.

The output stream object (`XMLOutputStream`) consists of `add` methods that you can use to add attributes, text value, `XMLEvents`, and the contents of an `XMLInputStream` object. When you're done with the output stream, you close it by invoking the `close` method.

Writing the XML Elements

You first create elements of different types before you add them onto the output stream. Elements can be created by using the `ElementFactory` class. This class has a list of `create` methods, which will let you create elements of different types. For example, you will find a method `createStartElement`, which creates a start element based on the attributes. Similarly, you'll see a `createAttribute` method, which creates an attribute of an element. Use the appropriate `create` method to create an element and add it to the output stream to write the XML.

For example, consider the following XML document:

```
<email>
  <to name="John Doe" id="john@doe.com" />
  <subject>This is a Test</subject>
</email>
```

To write this simple XML document, you would use the following code snippet (assume that the output stream has already been created):

```
outputStream.add( ElementFactory.createStartElement("email") );
outputStream.add(ElementFactory.createStartElement("to") );
outputStream.add(ElementFactory.createAttribute("name", "John Doe"));
outputStream.add(ElementFactory.createAttribute("id", "john@doe.com"));

outputStream.add(ElementFactory.createEndElement("to") );
outputStream.add(ElementFactory.createStartElement("subject") );
outputStream.add(ElementFactory.createCharacterData("This is a test"));
outputStream.add(ElementFactory.createEndElement("subject") );
outputStream.add(ElementFactory.createEndElement("email") );
```

Adding Another XML Document

You can also embed an existing XML document inside the XML that you're creating by creating an input stream and adding it to the output stream. For example, the following code snippet does this. Assume that we've already created an input stream object and an output stream object prior to this code snippet.

```
outputStream.add( inputStream ) ;
```

This code automatically adds the entire XML event stream present in the input stream into the output stream, thus including it in thc output XML document.

Included with this book is a sample code that writes a simple XML document onto the screen. You can execute it by invoking the class `com.wlsunleashed.xml.stream.WriteXML`. You can pass another XML document as a parameter into this XML; in that case, the passed-in document will be included in the output.

Other Useful XML Features

WebLogic Server provides several features that you can use for developing XML-based applications. We already looked at one of the key features provided by WebLogic Server: the Streaming API. Apart from that, there are also some other features that can be quite useful. In this section, we briefly look at some of those features.

WebLogic Fast Parser

In addition to the Apache Xerces parser that's packaged with WebLogic Server, another parser implementation is included in the package: the WebLogic Fast Parser. This is a high-performance, SAX-based parser that's intended to be used for small- to medium-sized XML documents. Note that this parser does not support DOM. You can use Fast Parser by using the parser class `weblogic.xml.babel.jaxp.SAXParserFactoryImpl`. Visit the URL `http://edocs.bea.com/wls/docs81/xml/xml_apps.html#1084718` for more information.

WebLogic Server XML Registry

WebLogic Server provides a good abstraction for configuring several XML parameters using the administration console. For instance, you can configure the parser that you want your application to use instead of the default WebLogic Server parser by using the XML registry. This mechanism enables you to separate the code from the configuration of the parameters in your application. Each server can have a maximum of one registry associated with it. If no registry is associated with a server, the default values are used.

You can perform two types of configurations using the XML registry:

- Configure parsers and transformers
- Configure external entities

While configuring parsers and transformers, you have the flexibility to decide on the parser or transformer at deployment time, and avoid any hard-coding in your application. You can also define multiple parsers/transformers for different XML types. Understand that the parsers defined in the registry will be used only if your code uses JAXP. If you directly use the underlying parser, the registry entries will not be used.

CAUTION

To use the WebLogic Server XML registry, your application must use JAXP.

You can also configure the registry to resolve the external entities used in XML documents. These entities are referenced using a public or a system ID. You can make the server cache these entities locally to avoid the overhead of network access every time an entity is referenced. The external repository from which the entity is retrieved must support a HTTP protocol (such as a URI). You can also configure the server to expire the local cache at regular intervals so that the latest version of the referenced entity is always available for your application.

Your code does not explicitly refer to any of these parameters defined in the registry. When you invoke the parser using JAXP, WebLogic Server automatically looks up the registry and uses the appropriate parser. Similarly, when your XML document references the entity, the server knows to look up the registry for local entity caching rules.

Configuring a Parser in the Registry

To configure a parser in a registry, you must first create a new registry. Open the WebLogic Server console, and navigate to the link mydomain→services→XML. Right-clicking this link pops up a menu that has a `Configure a new XML Registry` option. Clicking this menu item will provide you with a form to create a new registry. Specify the name of the registry, along with the qualified class names of the document builder factory, the SAX parser factory, and the transformer factory (for transforming XML documents) in the appropriate boxes. These specify new default factories to use in JAXP, instead of the ones used by WebLogic Server. You can leave one or more of these boxes empty (other than the name, of course), which tells the server that the default value should be assumed for that type. For instance, if you want the server to use the default transformer factory, simply leave that box blank. The fifth parameter is the When to Cache property, which can take three possible values:

- `cache-on-reference`—This value indicates that the external entities should be cached when they're first referenced.
- `cache-on-initialization`—This value indicates that the external entities should be cached on server initialization.
- `cache-never`—Indicates that external entities should never be cached.

Note that the When to Cache property on this screen provides the default caching mechanism for this XML registry. You can further refine this behavior by explicitly setting appropriate caching strategies for certain entities. Any entity that does not define an explicit caching strategy will use the strategy defined on this screen. The creation process is shown in Figure 29.2.

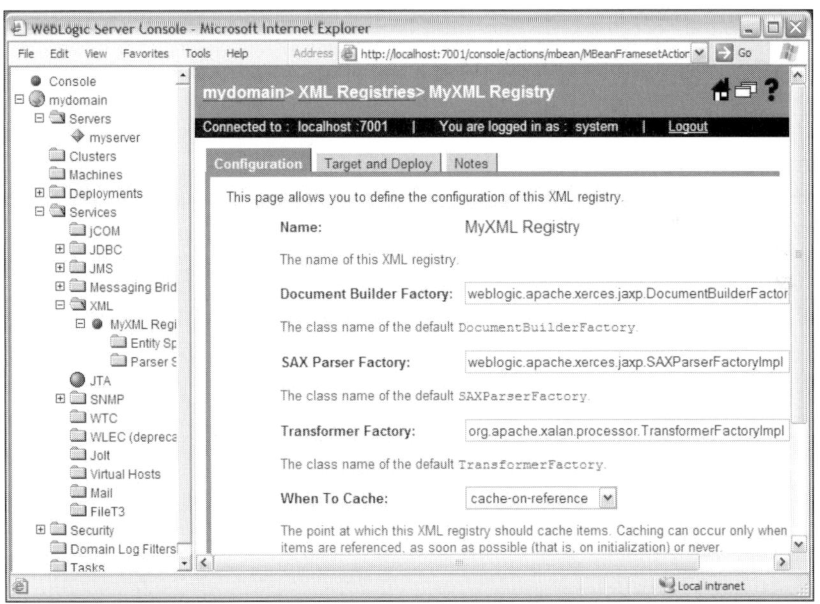

FIGURE 29.2 Creating a new XML registry.

After you've entered all the values, clicking the Create button will create the registry for you. After creating the registry, don't forget to switch to the Target and Deploy tab and select the servers (or clusters) on which you would like your registry to be targeted and deployed.

Configuring Parsers for Individual Document Types

After you've configured a registry, you can define different parsers for parsing individual document types. Document types are recognized by using the public ID, system ID, or the root element name of the document.

> **CAUTION**
>
> WebLogic Server searches only the first 1000 bytes of your XML document for known document types. If your `DOCTYPE` declaration doesn't fall within this limit, the server will use the default parser.

To configure parsers for individual documents, you must first create an XML registry. To learn how to create an XML registry, look at the previous section. Remember that this step is optional, and if you don't specify individual settings for each XML type, the default settings from your XML registry are used.

When you've created the XML registry, navigate to that entry in the tree view. Exploding this element will show two more elements: Entity Spec Entries and Parser Select Entries. Right-click the Parser Select Entries option and click on the Configure a New XMLParserSelectRegistryEntry option. This will display a form on the right side of the console, where you can specify the public ID, system ID, and root element tag, followed by the document builder factory and SAX parser factory. Make sure that you enter either the public or the system IDs, and the fully qualified root element tag in this form. You will also find another field called Parser Class Name, which you can ignore. That field is provided only for backward compatibility.

When you've added all this information, click the Create button to create the registry entry. Configuring individual parsers for different documents is shown in Figure 29.3.

The parser can be retrieved by using a simple JAXP code snippet without knowing anything about which factory is being instantiated. For example, in the following code snippet, we instantiate the factory and get a new parser from it. WebLogic Server automatically hands out an instance of the SAX Parser Factory that we configure in the registry for the particular XML type.

```
import javax.xml.parsers.SAXParserFactory
...
SAXParserFactory factory = SAXParserFactory.newInstance();
factory.setValidating(true);
SAXParser parser = factory.newSAXParser();
...
```

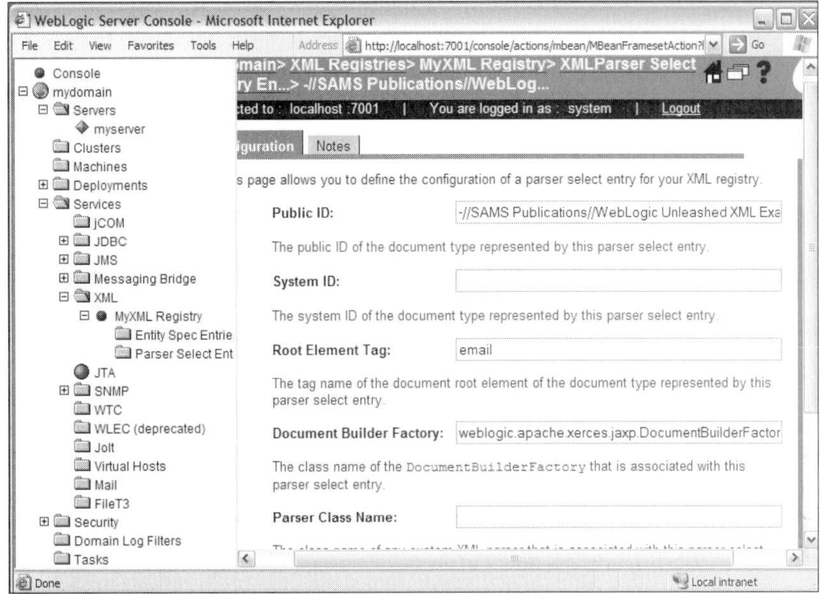

FIGURE 29.3 Configuring the parsers for different documents.

Configuring External Entity References

XMLs often refer to external entities. For example, consider the EJB deployment descriptors. The `DOCTYPE` entry of the file `ejb-jar.xml` refers to the external entity that provides the DTD for the XML file. This entry is provided in the following code snippet:

```
<!DOCTYPE web-app PUBLIC
    "-//Sun Microsystems, Inc.//DTD Web Application 2.3//EN"
    "http://java.sun.com/dtd/web-app_2_3.dtd">
```

As you can see, we're referring to a DTD that resides on a Sun Microsystems Web site. The parser will obviously have to access this entity to parse the XML and validate it, which it will do over the network. If the parser has to do this network access every time it parses any XML that refers to this entity, it could be quite performance intensive. You can reduce this overhead by configuring the server to cache the entity locally, and refresh the local cache at regular intervals. You can configure the server to cache the entity either at server startup or at the time the entity is first referenced.

To configure entity references, you must first create an XML registry. Remember that this step is optional. If you don't perform this step, the server will use the default setting that you specified while creating the registry.

After you create an XML registry as described earlier, you can expand the created node on the tree in the WebLogic Server console. This will reveal a node named Entity Spec Entries. Right-clicking this node will reveal an option to create a new entity spec entry. Click on this option. Doing so will populate the right window of the console with a form to create the entry, as shown in Figure 29.4. You can now enter the public ID, system ID, the entity URI from which the entity can be accessed, an option indicating when the server should cache the entity, and a cache timeout interval.

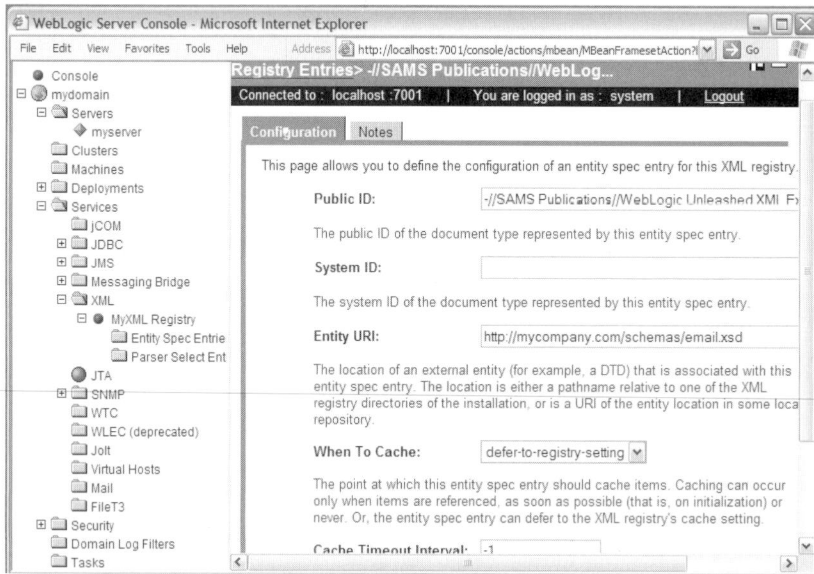

FIGURE 29.4 Configuring the external entities.

In the choice for server caching strategy, there is an option to defer to registry setting. If you select this, the server will use the default caching strategy chosen when you created the XML registry.

By default, the server uses a value of 500KB for the cache memory size, 5MB for the cache disk size, and 120 seconds for the cache timeout interval. You can change these default values of the cache, per server, by clicking on the server under the Servers node in the tree. On the server configuration, click on Services tab, and the XML submenu. There you can configure the server to use the registry that you previously created if you have not deployed the registry already on this server. You can also specify the memory size (in KB) and the disk size (in MB), along with the default cache timeout interval. The process of configuring the cache defaults is shown in Figure 29.5.

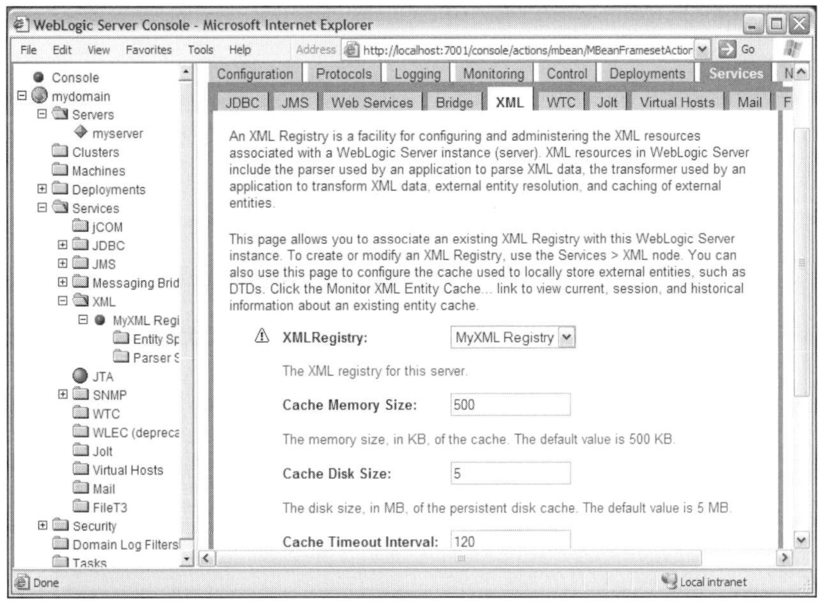

FIGURE 29.5 Configuring the server cache.

XPath Pattern Matching

XPath is a W3C standard that allows you to find parts of an XML document, which forms an important part of creating XSLT (XSL-based transformation) rules. It resembles traditional file system paths and identifies various parts of an XML document. For example, look at the following XML shown in Listing 29.6.

LISTING 29.6 The Book List XML

```
<booklist>
    <book name="Adventures of Tintin Vol. 1">
        <publisher>Little Brown &amp; Co </publisher>
        <isbn>0316359408</isbn>
        <price>14.00</price>
    </book>
    <book name="The Ultimate Simpsons in a Big Ol&apos; Box">
        <publisher>Harperperennial Library</publisher>
        <isbn>0060516305</isbn>
        <price>35.00</price>
    </book>
    <book name="Bart Simpson&apos;s Guide to Life">
        <publisher>Perennial Press</publisher>
```

LISTING 29.6 Continued

```
        <isbn>006096975X</isbn>
        <price>15.00</price>
    </book>
    <book name="Harry Potter and the Order of the Phoenix">
        <publisher>Scholastic</publisher>
        <isbn>043935806X</isbn>
        <price>18.00</price>
    </book>
</booklist>
```

The XPath representation of the root element (`booklist`) is

```
/booklist
```

while the XPath representation of the publisher element is

```
/booklist/book/publisher
```

Depending upon the context, you may also define relative paths. Relative paths do not begin with the root slash (/), whereas all absolute paths do. XPath expressions can also contain conditions. For instance, to extract all books that are priced at more than $15.00, you would use the following XPath expression:

```
/booklist/book[price > 15]
```

You can also use conditionals on attributes. An attribute is used in a similar way as an element, with the ampersand (@) symbol before its name. For example, to select the book titled *Bart Simpson's Guide to Life*, use the following XPath expression:

```
/booklist/book[@name = "Bart Simpson&apos;s Guide to Life"]
```

XPath also provides useful functions to perform several tasks in your XML. For example, you can get a count of the given tags by using the `count()` function. For example, `count(/booklist/book)` returns a count of books in the booklist. We have access to several string manipulation functions (such as `concat`, `contains`, and so on) as well as other node set functions (such as `last`, `local-name`, and the like). To learn more about XPath, refer to the Web site at `http://www.w3schools.com/xpath`.

WebLogic enables you to use XPath to perform pattern matching within an XML file. An XML document can be represented as a DOM tree, an `XMLNode`, or an `XMLInputStream`. You can use the following classes depending on the representation of your XML document, to perform XPath pattern matching. To discuss the various types of XPath classes, we use the email XML file shown in Listing 29.7.

LISTING 29.7 The Email XML

```
<email>
  <from name="John Doe" id="johndoe@xyzcompany.com"/>
  <to name="Jane Doe" id="janedoe@xyzcompany.com"/>
  <to name="SomeOther Doe" id="someotherdoe@xyzcompany.com"/>
  <cc name="YetAnother Doe" id="yetanotherdoe@xyzcompany.com"/>
  <subject z="a" t="b" c="c">Hello!</subject>
  <options>
    <read_receipt/>
    <priority type="Normal"/>
  </options>
  <body><![CDATA[Hello]]></body>
</email>
```

If your document is represented as a DOM tree, you can use the DOMXPath class. We'll use this class to count the number of people to which this email is being sent. To do this, we'll first parse the document using a DOM parser and get the Document object. You can read more about this step in earlier sections of this chapter. Following this, we'll create a DOMXPath object, passing to it the XPath query that we want to execute. In this case, we want to query the number of to addresses:

```
DOMXPath numRecipientsXPath = new DOMXPath("count(email/to)");
```

The next step is to run this query on the Document object created earlier. You can do this by invoking one of the evaluateAs*XXX* methods present in this object. Because we're dealing with a count, we expect to receive from the query a number represented as a double in the DOMXPath object. Thus, the following code snippet provides us with the count:

```
double numRecipients =
   numRecipientsXPath.evaluateAsNumber(theDocument);
```

Depending on your XPath query, the output may be a type of data other than a double. Instead of a double, you can get back a boolean (use evaluateAsBoolean) or a String (use evaluateAsString) from your query. Your query can also return a set of nodes (Set of org.w3c.dom.Node), in which case you'll invoke the evaluateAsNodeset method on the object. This method returns a set (java.util.Set) that contains objects of type org.w3c.dom.Node.

The example com.wlsunleashed.xml.xpath.DOMRepresentation illustrates a simple XPath query. Invoke this example using the fully qualified path to the email.xml file, which is also provided. The following code is a function from this sample, which indicates how certain nodes are obtained from the XML and printed out:

```
private void listRecipients()
          throws XPathException {
  DOMXPath recipientsXPath = new DOMXPath("email/to");
  Set recipients = recipientsXPath.evaluateAsNodeset(document);
  Iterator iter = recipients.iterator();
  System.out.println("This email is being addressed to");

  while (iter.hasNext()) {
    Node aNode = (Node) iter.next();
    System.out.println("* "
          + aNode.getAttributes().getNamedItem("name")
            .getNodeValue());
  }

  recipientsXPath = new DOMXPath("email/cc");
  recipients = recipientsXPath.evaluateAsNodeset(document);
  iter = recipients.iterator();
  System.out.println("This email is being copied to");

  while (iter.hasNext()) {
    Node aNode = (Node) iter.next();
    System.out.println("* "
         + aNode.getAttributes().getNamedItem("name")
             .getNodeValue());
  }
```

StreamXPath

The `StreamXPath` class is used to perform XPath matches on an `XMLInputStream` object. Although conceptually similar to `DOMXPath`, its use is a little different, as you'll see in this section. To use this class, you must first create the object, passing in the query to be performed. In our example, we're simply going to list all the To addresses in the `email.xml` file. In the following snippet, we instantiate a `StreamXPath` object, whose root is set at the particular node (to):

```
StreamXPath recipientsXPath = new StreamXPath("email/to");
```

The next step is to create a factory of type `XPathStreamFactory` and register the XPath object as a listener. Remember that because WebLogic XML Streaming is SAX-based, the processing isn't as straightforward as using a DOM tree. To register the XPath object as a listener, you must instantiate an object that implements the `XPathStreamObserver` interface. In our example, we create an inline class that processes the events received. This interface contains three methods:

- `observe(XMLEvent)`—This method is invoked every time an *XMLEvent* is received, but one that isn't an attribute or a namespace.
- `observeAttribute(StartElement, Attribute)`—This method is invoked when an attribute is encountered.
- `observeNamespace(StartElement, Attribute)`—This method is invoked when an namespace is encountered.

Thus, in our example, we use the following code snippet:

```
XPathStreamFactory factory = new XPathStreamFactory();
factory.install(recipientsXPath,
    new XPathStreamObserver() {
     public void observe(XMLEvent event) {
      System.out.println(
       "Observing Event " + event.getName());
       processEvent(event);
     }
     public void observeAttribute(StartElement e, Attribute a) {
      System.out.println(
        "Observing Attribute " + a.getName() +
        " on element " + e.getName());
     }
     public void observeNamespace(StartElement e, Attribute a) {
      System.out.println(
        "Observing Namespace " + a.getName() +
        " on element " + e.getName());
     }
   });
```

As you can see from this code, we simply print out the message received. The `processEvent` method prints out additional information about each event received.

The final step is to actually trigger processing. To do this, we'll first create an `XMLInputStream` by using an instance of the `XMLInputStreamFactory` class. For more information about this, read the "WebLogic Server XML Streaming API" section earlier in this chapter. We would normally have processed the stream that we received, but because we need to perform pattern matching, we'll create a new stream by passing this stream into the `XPathFactory` instance. You can now process the events from this stream. This will also generate events and send them to the XPath object when there are matches based on the query. This is demonstrated in the following code snippet:

```
XMLInputStreamFactory streamFactory =
           XMLInputStreamFactory.newInstance();
```

```
XMLInputStream inputStream = streamFactory.newInputStream(
              new FileInputStream(fileName));
XMLInputStream searchStream = factory.createStream(inputStream);
while (searchStream.hasNext()) {
   XMLEvent anEvent = searchStream.next();
}
```

As you can see from the `while` loop, we don't perform any processing with the events generated, but simply parse through the stream. The processing occurs in the `StreamXPath` object on events that match the given search criteria.

The complete source code is provided in `com.wlsunleashed.xml.xpath.StreamRepresentation.java`. Invoke this file, and pass in the complete path to the `Email.xml` file, which is also provided.

XML Editor

BEA offers a tool for editing XML documents. Obviously, you can edit XML documents with any editor such as vi or WordPad. But this editor provides some XML-specific features, such as validation of the XML document, and so on. You can download the XML Editor from the BEA dev2dev Web site by accessing the link `http://dev2dev.bea.com/resourcelibrary/utilitiestools/xml.jsp`.

The XML Editor is a pure Java XML editor, which lets you both create and edit XML files. The editor displays XML files in both a hierarchical tree form as well as a text form. It validates the document using either DTDs or XML Schemas, or simply parses them without validation. The editor supports Unicode. You can use drag-and-drop features using the tree display. The editor provides you with features that will let you insert items into the XML as mentioned in the DTD. The usage of the XML Editor is demonstrated in Figure 29.6.

XMLBeans

XMLBeans is a new way of parsing and working with XML documents . It enables you to work with Java objects to access the contents of the XML rather than use the traditional parser approach. The Java objects are generated on the basis of the schema that describes the XML document, so it's mandatory that you have a schema that defines your XML document. After they're generated, the objects can be accessed very intuitively. For example, imagine accessing your XML document by making calls such as `emailDocument.getToAddressList()`. To learn more about XMLBeans, refer to the BEA Web site at `http://dev2dev.bea.com/technologies/xmlbeans/overview.jsp`.

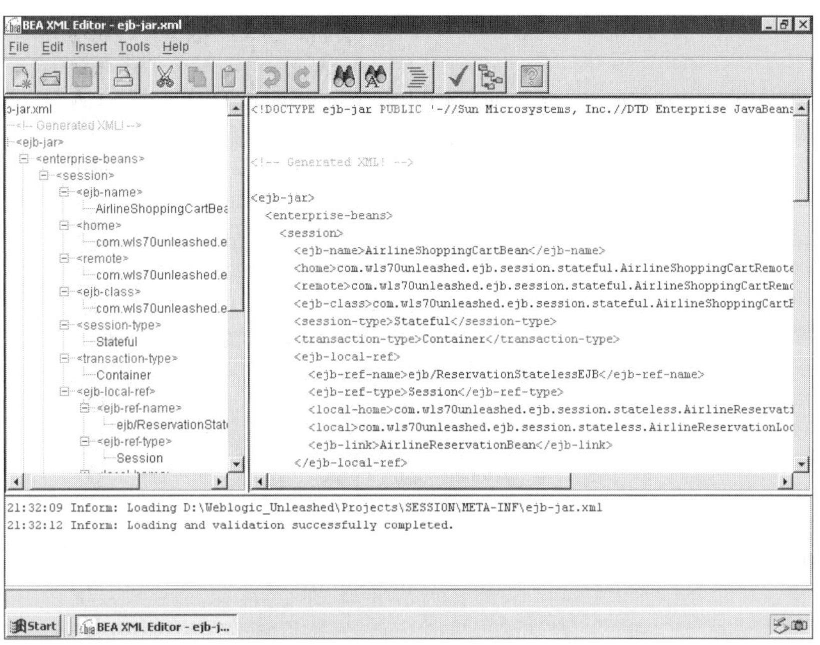

FIGURE 29.6 Using the BEA XML Editor.

Extensible Stylesheet Language

In the HTML world, a CSS file is a style sheet that describes how browsers should interpret the HTML file in a standard manner. It is in this file that you describe the display properties of different HTML tags; for example, a table. This provides a level of separation between the formats of the HTML document and its contents. However, by definition, HTML does not provide the kind of separation that XML does. So, how do we specify the display formats for an XML file? We use Extensible Stylesheet Language, or XSL. XSL is a W3C standard and you can learn more about it by visiting the Web site at `http://www.w3.org/Style/XSL`.

XSL consists of the following components:

- XSLT—A language to transform the XML to its desired output. The desired output may be another XML document or any other format such as HTML.
- XPath—A language for defining the contents of the XML document.

XSL Style Sheet

To better understand XSL, we'll work with an example. Consider the XML document shown in Listing 29.8, which describes a list of books, each book's publisher, its year of publication, and its price. This document lists four books. You can find the schema that describes this document on the CD, under the name booklist.xsd. The corresponding XML file is named booklist.xml.

LISTING 29.8 Booklist.xml

```
<?xml version="1.0" encoding="UTF-8"?>
<booklist>
 <book name="Adventures of Tintin Vol. 1">
  <publisher>Little Brown &amp; Co </publisher>
  <isbn>0316359408</isbn>
  <price>14.00</price>
 </book>
 <book name="The Ultimate Simpsons in a Big Ol&apos; Box">
  <publisher>Harperperennial Library</publisher>
  <isbn>0060516305</isbn>
  <price>35.00</price>
 </book>
 <book name="Bart Simpson&apos;s Guide to Life">
  <publisher>Perennial Press</publisher>
  <isbn>006096975X</isbn>
  <price>15.00</price>
 </book>
 <book name="Harry Potter and the Order of the Phoenix">
  <publisher>Scholastic</publisher>
  <isbn>043935806X</isbn>
  <price>18.00</price>
 </book>
</booklist>
```

To assign a style sheet for an XML file, you can use the following special XML header, after the XML definition header:

```
<?xml-stylesheet type="text/xsl"
  href="./GenericRootNodeTemplate.xsl"?>
```

Let's first write a style sheet that displays this XML file in the browser as a table with the name and the price as columns in a table. To do this, we write the style sheet document. The style sheet document is another XML document (and hence begins with the XML declaration) that conforms to the schema described at the URL http://www.w3.org/1999/XSL/Transform. The root node of the style sheet file is either a stylesheet tag or a transform tag. Thus, the following identifies the beginning of a style sheet document:

```
<?xml version="1.0" encoding="UTF-8"?>
<xsl:stylesheet version="1.0"
  xmlns:xsl=" http://www.w3.org/1999/XSL/Transform">
```

XSL works based on templates. You specify a template and provide the rule under which that template is matched. When matched, the set of tasks indicated under the template is executed. For example, to match the root node of your XML document, you would match for the / tag. So, the following style sheet prints out the phrase `Found a Root Node` in an HTML document whenever any XML root node is matched:

```
<?xml version="1.0" encoding="UTF-8"?>
<xsl:stylesheet version="1.0"
   xmlns:xsl="http://www.w3.org/1999/XSL/Transform">
 <xsl:template match="/">
  <html>
   <head>
    <title>Matched</title>
   </head>
   <body>
    Found a Root Node.
   </body>
  </html>
 </xsl:template>
</xsl:stylesheet>
```

In this example, we look for a root node match and print out the HTML code directly. One thing to keep in mind while writing XSL documents is that, unlike HTML documents, XSL documents do not tolerate HTML code that is not well formed. This is because the XSL document itself is an XML and the HTML code that you write forms part of this XML document. Because any XML document should be well formed, the HTML code inside it is also expected to be well formed.

Now that we've written our first XSL style sheet, let's add a little meat into it. We access the values of the source XML document by using the `xsl:value-of` tag. This tag is used to access the value from the source XML and write it into the destination stream (which could be an XML or HTML file). We specify the `select` criterion for the `value-of` element. The `select` criterion can be any valid XPath string (we'll look at XPath in a minute). So, in the `booklist.xml` document, we can access the ISBN number of the book by using the following `value-of` tag:

```
<xsl:value-of select="/booklist/book/isbn"/>
```

If we were to include this tag instead of displaying `Found a Root Node` in the style sheet, we could actually see the ISBN number of the first book in the XML document.

```
<?xml version="1.0" encoding="UTF-8"?>
<xsl:stylesheet version="1.0"
   xmlns:xsl="http://www.w3.org/1999/XSL/Transform">
 <xsl:template match="/">
  <html>
   <head>
    <title>Matched</title>
   </head>
   <body>
    <xsl:value-of select="/booklist/book/isbn"/>
   </body>
  </html>
 </xsl:template>
</xsl:stylesheet>
```

Because we have more than one book in our list of books, we want to display information about all the books, not just the first one in the list. Hence, there is an obvious need for some kind of a looping mechanism. This is achieved by using the `xsl:for-each` tag. This tag also takes a `select` criterion (XPath string) and loops through all the entries that are returned by the XPath query. Thus, in our case, we loop through a list of books that are found in the `booklist` element and display the ISBN number and the price of each book, in a table on the screen.

```
<?xml version="1.0" encoding="UTF-8"?>
<xsl:stylesheet version="1.0" xmlns:xsl="http://www.w3.org/1999/XSL/Transform">
 <xsl:template match="/">
  <html>
   <head>
    <title>Book List</title>
   </head>
   <body>
    <table border="1">
     <tr>
      <th>ISBN</th>
      <th>Price</th>
     </tr>
     <xsl:for-each select="/booklist/book">
       <tr>
        <td><xsl:value-of select="isbn"/></td>
        <td><xsl:value-of select="price"/></td>
       </tr>
     </xsl:for-each>
     </table>
```

```
    </body>
  </html>
 </xsl:template>
</xsl:stylesheet>
```

Within the root template, we first output the header code for the HTML document. We follow that with the code that defines the table and its header. Then we loop for each node that matches the pattern `/booklist/book`. Each match corresponds to one book in the booklist XML document. For each matched node, we write its ISBN number and the price to one row in the table. Finally, we close the `table`, `body`, and `html` tags. Remember that the document must be well formed, even though HTML is usually very lenient.

Another interesting aspect of the preceding code is the following code snippet:

```
<td><xsl:value-of select="isbn"/></td>
```

Note that we specify only `isbn` in the `select` criterion, and not the whole path of the tag. This is because the XPath query is smart enough to look for this specified criteria within the `select` criterion mentioned in the `for-each` loop. You can still provide the entire path, which would also be correct. You can access other nodes that lie outside the boundaries of the `/booklist/book` node by providing an absolute path. Think of it as a file system, and you're under a particular directory.

There is a second way to perform the looping action, this time without using the `for-each` tag. This approach uses the template concept more extensively.

In the previous code snippets, we declared the templates with the match specified as `/`. As mentioned earlier, this template is always matched when the root node of the XML document is encountered. We can further define templates that match other sub-nodes of your XML document. For example, we could create a template that matches the `book` node, which can then be applied for every `book` tag encountered. Note that the transformer does not apply the template for you. You have to request the templates to be applied on the source document.

```
<?xml version="1.0" encoding="UTF-8"?>
<xsl:stylesheet version="1.0" xmlns:xsl="http://www.w3.org/1999/XSL/Transform">
 <xsl:template match="/">
  <html>
   <head>
    <title>Book List</title>
   </head>
   <body>
    <table border="1">
     <tr>
      <th>ISBN</th>
```

29

```
      <th>Price</th>
     </tr>
     <xsl:apply-templates select="/booklist/book"/>
     </table>
    </body>
  </html>
 </xsl:template>
 <xsl:template match="book">
  <tr>
   <td><xsl:value-of select="isbn"/></td>
   <td><xsl:value-of select="price"/></td>
  </tr>
 </xsl:template>
</xsl:stylesheet>
```

Here we define a template that matches a `book` tag. When matched, it simply writes out one row of the table. This template is applied within the template for the root node by the following line:

```
<xsl:apply-templates select="/booklist/book"/>
```

This is the line that indicates to the transformer that templates should be applied on all tags that matches the given `select` tag. The transformer then takes care of invoking the appropriate template for each book element before executing following statements within the root template. This is useful not only for looping, but also for controlling the order in which the child nodes are processed within the XML document. For instance, you could write a style sheet that prints all the ISBN numbers and titles, and then prints all prices in a second table.

XSL also enables you to test for conditionals within your style sheet. For instance, if you wanted to print out only those books that are less than $17.00, you could use the `xsl:if` condition:

```
<xsl:template match="book">
 <xsl:if test="price &lt; 17">
  <tr>
   <td><xsl:value-of select="isbn"/></td>
   <td><xsl:value-of select="price"/></td>
  </tr>
 </xsl:if>
</xsl:template>
```

If you want implement an `if-then-else` block instead, you would use the `xsl:choose` tag. That tag has following format:

```
<xsl:choose>
 <xsl:when test="price &lt; 17">
  . Do something in this case
 </xsl:when>
 <xsl:otherwise>
  . Do something else in this case
 </xsl:otherwise>
</xsl:choose>
```

Thus, the complete XSL style sheet document that displays the booklist as a HTML document is given in Listing 29.9.

LISTING 29.9 Booklist.xsl

```
<?xml version="1.0" encoding="UTF-8"?>
<xsl:stylesheet version="1.0"
  xmlns:xsl="http://www.w3.org/1999/XSL/Transform">
<xsl:template match="/">
 <html>
  <head>
    <title>Book List</title>
  </head>
    <body>
      <table border="1">
       <tr>
        <th>ISBN</th>
        <th>Name</th>
        <th>Price</th>
       </tr>
       <xsl:apply-templates select="/booklist/book"/>
      </table>
     </body>
  </html>
</xsl:template>

<xsl:template match="book">
  <xsl:if test="price &lt; 17">
   <tr>
     <td><xsl:value-of select="isbn"/></td>
     <td><xsl:value-of select="@name"/></td>
     <td><xsl:value-of select="price"/></td>
   </tr>
  </xsl:if>
</xsl:template>
</xsl:stylesheet>
```

29

After you've created and linked the XML file and corresponding XSL file, many browsers can transform the XML into the format defined in your XSL. You can also use JAXP transformers to transform the XML document on the server side.

Transforming the XML File

The XML file can be transformed by using the style sheet on either the client side or on the server side. On the client side, a recent popular browser should be compliant with the standards laid out by XSL. By including the `stylesheet` tag in the XML document and pointing it out to the XSL document, you can simply open the XML document on your browser and the document will be transformed automatically. Open the `booklist.xml` document provided in the CD and see how the document is displayed. Remember, you need Internet Explorer with a version greater than or equal to 6 to do this because this is the first version of IE that is fully compliant with the standard. This mechanism is useful if you do not want to burden your back-end server with transformation overhead. The JSP can simply return an XML document with the appropriate style sheet linked, and the browser can take care of the transformation.

XML documents can also be transformed on the server side. To do this, you can use JAXP. We've already learned how to parse an XML document using JAXP. In this section, we look at how to *transform* using JAXP. The `javax.xml.transform` package provides all the requisite classes for transforming your XML document.

To use JAXP, you should parse the XML document first by using either SAX, DOM, or stream. The parser output should then used by the transformer to perform the transformation. First, you use the `javax.xml.transform.TransformerFactory` class to create a new transformer instance. That class provides an instance of the transformer object, which then performs the transformation.

```
TransformerFactory tf =
  TransformerFactory.newInstance();
// Create the transformer for the given stylesheet
Transformer transformer =
  tf.newTransformer(new StreamSource(stylesheet));
```

Finally, you transform the XML document by providing the source and destination streams into the transform method of the transformer. This method uses the already-set style sheet to perform the transformation and writes the output into the destination stream. Remember that the destination stream could very well be the output buffer of a servlet or JSP, thus sending the transformed output back to the client.

```
// Transform the XML document giving the source and
// destination streams
transformer.transform(new StreamSource(source),
  new StreamResult(System.out));
```

Execute the `com.wlsunleashed.xml.transform.XMLTransform` class (packaged on the CD) and pass to it an XML document and its corresponding XSL style sheet.

Best Practices for Working with XML

In this section, we see some of the best practices we can adopt while working with XML.

Custom Validation

Sometimes, XML validation may be overkill. The parser usually performs several types of validations, and if you don't want all those happening, you can write custom code, in your SAX handler or while traversing your DOM hierarchy, to perform the required validations and turn the parser validation off. This will improve the performance of your XML application.

Using External Entity Resolution

It's faster to access entities from the local machine than over the network. Because of this, use external entity resolution to cache the entities locally. This is also bound to improve performance.

Using JAXP

JAXP is an open standard for parsing XML documents. Although it uses DOM or SAX underneath, using JAXP is preferable to using a the underlying parser directly. This provides you with the flexibility of changing the parser if necessary. Also remember that to take advantage of certain features of WebLogic Server (such as the XML registry), you should use JAXP.

Schemas Versus DTDs

In terms of validation of an XML document, XML schemas are much more powerful than DTDs. Schemas enable you to validate both the structure and the data elements of an XML. Therefore, it's a good idea to code your XML to a schema, rather than a DTD.

Considering the Type of Parser

It's important to choose the parser well. If your application does not require a DOM tree, you should not use DOM. DOM consumes a lot more memory and is performance intensive. SAX, on the other hand, is event based, so it provides better performance.

XML Design

Designing an XML efficiently is an important aspect of ensuring good performance for your application. It's important to keep the XML format simple and well formatted. There are several design patterns available for designing a good XML document. You can refer to the Web site at `http://www.XMLPatterns.com` for a discussion of some of these patterns.

Summary

XML is an industry standard in communicating data between heterogeneous systems. At the same time, XML can be overkill in some cases and using it might degrade the performance of your overall application. Therefore, before you architect your system to use XML, consider why you need XML and whether any other alternatives (such as Java objects, databases) would work for you.

CHAPTER 30

WebLogic Server and Web Services

by Jeff Marin and Kunal Mittal

IN THIS CHAPTER

Although many attempts have been made in the past to integrate applications that run on different hardware platforms, execute in different operating systems, and are written in a variety of computer languages, none has become the universal glue that its originators have envisioned. Those attempts include CORBA, COM, EDI, and IIOP.

With the advent of the Internet and universal worldwide connectivity based on standards such as TCP/IP and HTTP, the idea of universal integration technology has been revisited. Machines connected to the Internet can easily communicate using network-level protocols such as HTTP and FTP, but for applications to speak, a higher-level language is required. That higher-level language is XML (and its various dialects).

This chapter focuses on the various aspects of Web Services and how WebLogic Server provides tools and support for their construction and orchestration. We'll talk about various source code–level tools, such as ANT tasks, as well as the WebLogic Workshop UI tool that helps developers build Web Services.

What Are Web Services?

Simply put, Web Services allow applications that are running on any hardware platform, in any operating system, and written in any computer language, to invoke application logic and to exchange information with each other. This is possible because these applications have been configured to send and receive messages in a consistent format, such as XML. Web Services know how to construct XML that represents a service request of another application and how to construct XML that represents their internal data. In addition, Web Services can parse XML requests coming from other applications and invoke their underlying functionality in response to these requests.

Web Services provide the capability for systems to be loosely coupled and easily interoperate with other software systems, without having to go through weeks or months of integration efforts. Systems can discover each other dynamically through search type functionality (UDDI, discussed later) and negotiate their interactions automatically (WSDL, discussed later). The messages exchanged by the systems are XML-based messages with some wrapper information (SOAP, discussed later).

What Are Web Services Used For?

Web Services are designed to allow applications of all kinds to communicate despite their many differences in design and runtime environments. Web Services have an added feature in that larger Web Services can be built from smaller ones. If one Web Service returns tomorrow's weather given a ZIP Code and another Web Service returns fashion tips based on the weather, a third Web Service could then call the other two and provide fashion tips when given a ZIP Code. It could also provide value by searching for the best prices for its fashion recommendations—perhaps by invoking another Web Service. Each of these Web Services might invoke code running on a mainframe, a Unix machine, or a Windows machine. It really doesn't matter what the runtime environment is as long as each Web Service knows how to communicate using XML dialects.

NOTE

Although the idea behind Web Services is not a complex concept, in practice, it could revolutionize how computer applications are built for the foreseeable future. The ease with which applications from different departments, companies, and countries can invoke each others' services will have an enormous affect on how various groups of technologists collaborate on software development. The possibilities of creating new applications from existing building blocks that are available from all over the world are limitless.

Support for Web Services in WebLogic

BEA has recognized the potential of Web Services. Many of the new features found in WebLogic Server 8.1 revolve around support of Web Services. These new features include support for asynchronous transactions, generation and orchestration of Web Services, and tools to ease the development of Web Services. The following is a detailed list of features:

- Security and data encryption—WebLogic Server 8.1 enables you to configure data security for Web Services. This is done using digital signatures and encryption.
- SOAP support—WebLogic Server supports SOAP messaging. It allows an application running on one server to exchange messages or execute Web Services on another server. WebLogic can ensure that this interaction happens. However, it's important to remember that this reliable SOAP layer is specific to the WebLogic environment. JMS can be used to store SOAP messages. This helps in asynchronous processing of the messages, as well as providing a level of scalability and fault tolerance. WebLogic Server provides support for using SOAP 1.2 as the message format. WebLogic Server also supports the SOAP with Attachments API for Java (SAAJ) 1.1.

ASYNCHRONOUS PROCESSING

Asynchronous processing is a concept that is becoming increasingly popular in the world of transactions and is especially important for Web Services. Let's get straight to an example so that we can understand this better.

Assume that you're applying for a home loan. You go to one of the many Internet sites that enable you to apply for such a loan. The site promises to get you multiple quotes from leading lenders. You have the ability to apply for the loan and then to receive an email from the site to inform you that you've received some quotes. You don't have to wait online to receive the quotes. This is important because the process of issuing a quote based on your loan application generally needs a manual review of your application, which cannot always be done in real-time.

This is an example of an asynchronous process or transaction. In the Web Services world, a Web Service might trigger multiple Web Services, and then go and do something else. When the Web Service that is triggered responds, the originating Web Service must process the result from this Web Service and decide what to do next. This is the basic idea behind an asynchronous Web Service.

You can refer to the Workshop documentation for more details on asynchronous Web Services. Go to the Workshop docs at `http://edocs.bea.com/workshop/docs81/doc/en/core/index.html` and click on Designing Asynchronous Interfaces in the left navigation bar in your browser.

- Web Services—WebLogic has support for long-running, asynchronous Web Services. This means that a Web Service issues a callback to indicate to the client that it has completed. The client need not wait for this callback. When the client receives the callback, it can continue processing. These Web Services can be RPC-based or document-based.
- Conversational Web Services—Web Service client state information can be persisted on the server and maintained across several method invocations. This reduces the amount of data that needs to be passed back and forth between the client and server.

- Object serialization—XMLBeans and other technologies provide the capability to manipulate value objects using Java code or XML. Behind the scenes, WebLogic maintains both the value object in java, as well as an XML representation of this value object.
- Web Services execution—WebLogic Server supports the execution of Web Services over HTTP and JMS.
- J2EE and Web Services—Web Services utilize the benefits of the underlying WebLogic Server and J2EE architecture, including security, scalability, and reliability. J2EE components such as stateless session EJBs and JMS components can be used to implement Web Services.
- Ant tasks for Web Services—Several Ant tasks are part of WebLogic Server to aid in creating, packaging, and deploying Web Services.
- UDDI support—WebLogic Server comes with a full UDDI registry and explorer that can be used to publish private and public registries for Web Services. This enables Web Service developers or providers to register their Web Services and potential consumers to find these Web services, much like a search engine.
- WebLogic Workshop—This is a unified development environment for developing, testing, and deploying applications on WebLogic Server.
- JWS extension support—This set of Javadoc tags allows a Web Service to be created with a single file and builds a complete Web application to support the Web Service. BEA has submitted this to the Java Community Process for adoption as a standard.
- WebLogic Server Administration Console integration—The existing Administration Console can be used to deploy and monitor Web Services.
- Testing Web Services—WebLogic Workshop creates a home page for Web Services created with it. These pages provide all the details of the Web Services, as well as the capability to test the Web Services and to see the various steps as they execute.

Web Service Technologies

Web Services rely on several pluggable technologies to seamlessly provide functionality to their clients and to invoke other Web Services. Understanding these technologies is important to Web Service developers. That means you can use any number of technologies, or other technologies that are not discussed in this chapter, and you'd use only those technologies you need. (However, it is generally recognized that SOAP is the base technology for Web Services.) None of the Web Services technologies use special tools; everything is text-based. This is a big difference from CORBA, in which you have to use special software and the whole flock of features and libraries. This section discusses these technologies.

Simple Object Access Protocol

Simple Object Access Protocol (SOAP) is employed for exchanging information using XML as a base language. For more information about XML, please refer to Chapter 29, "WebLogic Server and XML Technologies." SOAP was originally co-authored by Microsoft, DevelopMentor and UserLand Software. Other companies such as IBM and Lotus have worked on later versions of SOAP. A SOAP message is defined to have three parts, as shown in Figure 30.1. The different parts of a SOAP message are

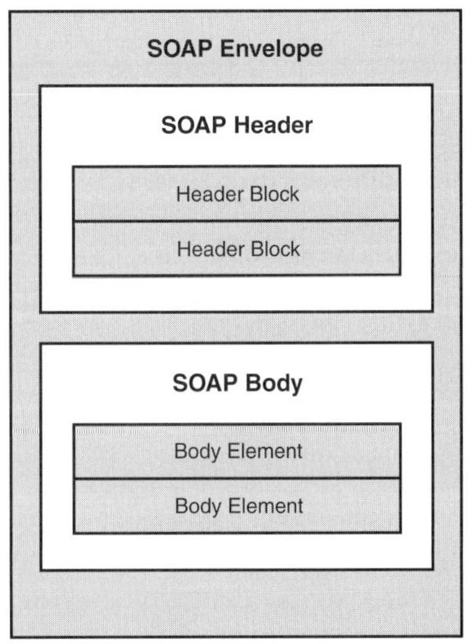

FIGURE 30.1 Structure of a SOAP message.

- SOAP envelope—A container for the SOAP header and body. It also defines the processing rules for the SOAP message.
- SOAP header—An optional component of a SOAP message. It contains security and transaction management type details.
- SOAP body—This component contains the data or the actual contents of the message. The SOAP body can contain any sort of messages. However, it generally contains data related to an operation to execute on a Web Service and the parameters to pass to that operation.

Listing 30.1 shows an example of a SOAP message. You can see the SOAP header and body with some dummy information.

LISTING 30.1 A Sample SOAP Message

```
<SOAP-ENV:Envelope xmlns:SOAP-ENV="http://schemas.xmlsoap.org/soap/envelope/"
 SOAP-ENV:encodingStyle="http://schemas.xmlsoap.org/soap/encoding/">
 <SOAP-ENV:Body>
  <m:GetWeather xmlns:m="Some-URI">
   <zipcode>07726</zipcode>
  </m:GetWeather>
 </SOAP-ENV:Body>
</SOAP-ENV:Envelope>
```

SOAP isn't tied to any specific protocol, but it is usually discussed in relation to HTTP. If HTTP is used to send and receive SOAP messages, they can pass through firewalls that are usually configured to allow port 80 (HTTP) requests. This is important because it allows applications to communicate without requiring port security to be loosened. However, it also means that Web Services must be carefully written to guard against SOAP messages that can misuse Web Services or otherwise harm its runtime environment, whether intentionally or not. Although security has not been a focal point of SOAP, WebLogic Server provides its own security services for Web Services that will be discussed later in this chapter. More information about SOAP can be found at `http://www.w3.org/TR/SOAP/`.

SOAP messages come in two types: RPC-oriented (Remote Procedure Call) and document-oriented. RPC-oriented SOAP messages contain the names of specific Web Service operations and their input and output parameters. Document-oriented SOAP messages contain only data. A Web Service operation receives this message and then applies its business logic, depending on the contents of the XML. RPC-oriented SOAP messages are more typical and Web Service operations expecting document-oriented SOAP messages must be explicitly configured this way.

WebLogic Server 8.1 provides an implementation of SOAP 1.1, SOAP 1.2, and SOAP with Attachments API for Java (SAAJ) specifications. SOAP messages can become large and complicated, but as we'll see, WebLogic Server automates the creating and processing of SOAP messages most of the time. Web Service developers are then left with more time to write business logic and can let WebLogic Server take care of the underlying plumbing.

Web Service Definition Language

Web Service Definition Language (WSDL) is an XML-based specification for defining attributes about Web Services, including the operations it supports, the input and output parameters of those operations, and the URL that the Web Service is connected to. WSDL files are usually quite verbose and complex. Thankfully, under most circumstances, the tools in WebLogic Server generate the WSDL file for us.

WebLogic Server 8.1 supports WSDL 1.1. More information about WSDL can be found at `http://www.w3.org/TR/wsdl`.

Universal Description, Discovery and Integration

Universal Description, Discovery and Integration (UDDI) is a specification that standardizes how to register Web Services in a registry and how to find other Web Services. Public registries allow organizations to advertise the Web Services they offer. WebLogic Server 8.1 supports UDDI 2.0 and comes with its own UDDI registry. Additionally, it comes with a UDDI directory explorer to search private and public UDDI registries and a UDDI client API to programmatically search through these registries. More information about UDDI is available at `http://www.uddi.org`.

WebLogic Server Web Services Architecture

All the preceding technologies can play a role in Web Services, as shown in Figure 30.2. The request-response cycle for Web Services can be summarized as follows:

1. A Web Service client sends a SOAP message to a Web Service.
2. The Web Service processes the message and invokes an operation within it.
3. This operation might require the services of J2EE components such as EJBs and JDBC data sources.
4. This operation might require the services of other Web Services. In this case, the Web Service will become the client of these other Web Services.
5. The operation finishes processing and returns a SOAP message to the original client.

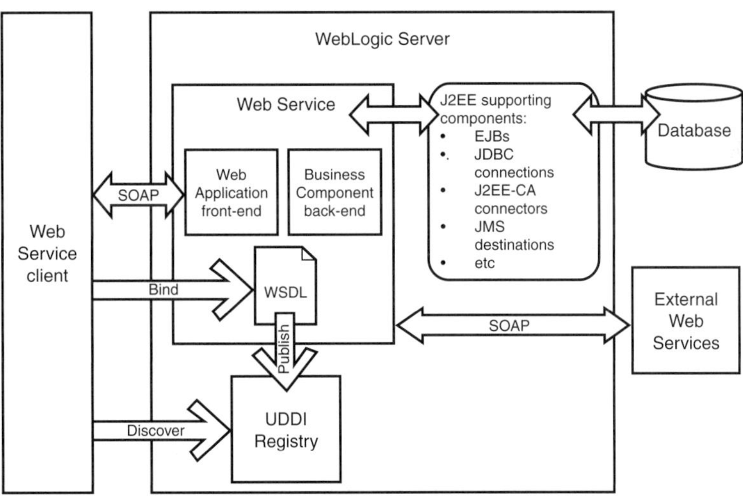

FIGURE 30.2 How the Web Service technologies fit together.

Also shown in the diagram is the WSDL file that describes the Web Service. Web Service clients that want to connect to the Web Service can consume this file. This file can also be published to a UDDI registry where interested parties can discover it.

Tools for Creating Web Services in WebLogic

WebLogic Server 8.1 provides two separate tools for creating Web Services—each tool is aimed at a different type of developer.

Applications developers are defined as programmers who do most of their coding at the business-logic level and are not as interested in packaging and deployment issues. They would like to solve business problems effectively and quickly. Applications developers are expected to have thorough domain knowledge of the industry they work in. Their equivalents in the Microsoft world are Visual Basic programmers. They would use a tool such as WebLogic Workshop to create and deploy Web Services.

Enterprise developers are concerned with business problems, but are more interested in the architecture of applications, how components collaborate, and how to get the most out of the underlying plumbing. Enterprise developers are expected to have a thorough understanding of J2EE concepts and its various APIs. Their equivalents in the Microsoft world are Visual C++ programmers. These developers like to get their hands dirty with code. They would write some of the Web Services code by hand or use a source code–level tool. WebLogic provides several Ant tasks to generate some or most of the code and to help with the deployment of Web Services.

The WebLogic Workshop Tool

Application developers will appreciate the benefits that WebLogic Server offers. WebLogic Workshop is an IDE for creating, debugging, and deploying J2EE applications, including Web Services. WebLogic Workshop enables application developers to write business logic and not worry about the plumbing that makes Web Services work. These Web Services can utilize existing J2EE components, such as JDBC data sources and Enterprise JavaBeans, and can invoke other Web Services as well. The ability to concentrate on business logic enables application developers to build and debug complex Web Services efficiently and quickly.

Java Code and Ant Tasks

Enterprise developers will appreciate the flexibility in coding Web Services by hand and then using BEA-supplied Ant tasks to automate many tasks, such as creating Web Service deployment descriptors, creating Web Service client code, and creating serialization classes.

Ant is a build tool written in Java that can automate many tasks performed by Java developers, such as compiling, packaging, and deploying components and applications. Ant is very flexible and can be extended in many ways through custom Ant tasks. WebLogic Server 8.1 includes Ant right out of the box and provides BEA-specific Ant tasks to benefit

WebLogic Server developers. For more information about Ant, please visit `http://ant.apache.org/`.

By catering to these two types of developers, WebLogic Server enables developers to collaborate more effectively in the design, implementation, and deployment of Web Services. Enterprise developers can potentially create J2EE components, such as Enterprise JavaBeans, that application developers can create Web Services from using WebLogic Workshop. In this way, both types of developers can work in an environment where they are most likely to succeed.

Creating Web Services with Java Code

In this section, we build a complete working Web Service using Java code and Ant tasks. We go through the steps involved in designing, implementing, deploying, and testing this Web Service.

Choosing and Implementing a Backend Component

Although there are many decisions to be made in designing a Web Service, the most important one is choosing a J2EE backend component. Although not required for a Web Service, a common purpose of Web Services is to allow clients to connect with existing J2EE components. WebLogic Server allows three types of backend components to be wrapped in a Web Service. After you've chosen which type of component to utilize, you must implement the component if it has not already been created.

Stateless Session Bean

A Web Service is wrapped around a method of a Stateless Session Bean when the focus of the Web Service is to perform self-contained operations, where each operation is accomplished in a single step. This is what is called a *stateless* component because no state is kept on behalf of the client. Examples of stateless operations are

- Computing mortgage rates based on credit and home data
- Querying for weather conditions for a given ZIP Code
- Requesting the current price of a stock

The two components that we talk about next are also stateless. However, a Web Service implemented as a Stateless Session EJB enables you to leverage the capabilities of Stateless Session Beans, such as scalability, life cycle, security, and transaction management.

Java Class

Web Services that are wrapped around methods of Java classes are also stateless. However, unlike Stateless Session Beans, WebLogic Server creates only one instance of the Java class. That one instance is required to service all client requests, which is not a scalable solution.

On the flip side, one argument for using a Java class to implement Web Services is the simplicity involved. Writing, deploying, debugging and testing a Stateless Session EJB implementation of a Web Service is more time-consuming than using a vanilla Java class. Another advantage of using a Java class is that you do not require an EJB container to run the Web Service. A Web Service implemented using a Java class could run on WebLogic Server Express (which is not an EJB container).

JMS Listeners

Web Services can also act as listeners for JMS queues and topics. For more information about JMS, please refer to Chapter 12, "Enterprise Messaging with JMS." A Web Service is wrapped around a JMS listener when the Web Service needs to be asynchronous. You might need this in the following cases:

- Processing a delayed event, such as an order
- Working on a loan application

Other Web Service Features

In addition to the topics discussed so far, Web Services built with Java can also have the following attributes:

- Asynchronous—Long-running Web Service operations can invoke a callback on the Web Service client. See `http://e-docs.bea.com/wls/docs81/webserv/design.html#1052549` for more information.
- Stateful Web Services—Web Services can persist client state using JDBC and/or Entity EJBs. See `http://e-docs.bea.com/wls/docs81/webserv/design.html#1058330` for more information.

Packaging Web Services

A Web Service in WebLogic Server is deployed as a Web application in a WAR file that is wrapped in an EAR file, as shown in Figure 30.3. The WAR file contains backend components such as a Web service client JAR file, Java class files, EJB JAR files, and deployment descriptors.

The easiest way to generate this packaging is to use the Ant `servicegen` task. These are the steps to using `servicegen`:

1. Create a staging directory to build your Web Service.
2. Compile and package Web Service backend components into this staging directory. For Stateless Session Beans, copy the JAR to this directory. For Java classes, copy the class file here in the proper directory reflecting its package.

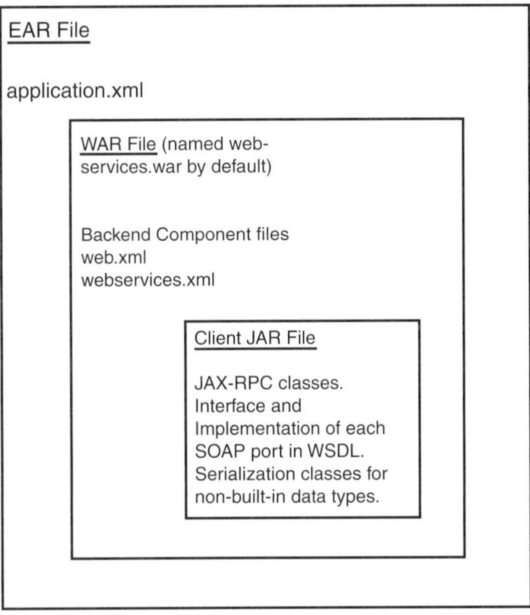

FIGURE 30.3 Web Services are WAR files packaged inside an EAR file.

3. Create a `build.xml` Ant script in the staging directory.
4. Open a command prompt and execute the `setWLSEnv.cmd` file from the *`WL_HOME`*`\server\bin` directory. You should now be able to execute the Ant tool.
5. Make sure that the `webservices.jar` file that is located in `%BEA_HOME%\weblogic81\server\lib` is in your classpath.
6. Type **`ant`** at the command prompt to execute the contents of `build.xml`.

Building a Web Service with a Java Class Back End

Now we're going to build a Web Service from scratch based on a Java class. The Java class we're going to use is shown in Listing 30.2. It has one public method, called `getGreeting()`, that takes a `String` and returns a `String`. This method will become an operation in our Web Service.

LISTING 30.2 A Sample Java Class to Be Used as a Web Service

```
import java.util.Date;

public class JavaWebService {
 public JavaWebService() {
```

LISTING 30.2 Continued

```
 }
 public String getGreeting(String name) {
  return "Hello, " + name + " the local time is " + new Date();
 }
}
```

When using a Java class to build a Web Service, the Java class must follow certain rules:

- Must have a no-argument constructor.
- Public methods will be translated into Web Service operations.
- Must not start any threads because all code runs within WebLogic Server.
- Must be thread-safe because WebLogic Server creates only one instance of this class and shares it among all Web Service client requests.

Creating the build.xml Ant Script

Creating Ant scripts is not a simple thing, but it does get easier over time. Listing 30.3 illustrates an Ant script that invokes the `servicegen` task.

LISTING 30.3 An Ant Script to Create a Web Service from a Java Class

```
<project name="buildWebservice" default="ear">
 <target name="ear">
  <servicegen
    destEar="testWebService.ear"
    contextURI="WebServices" >
   <classpath>
     <pathelement path="${java.class.path}" />
     <pathelement path="." />
   </classpath>
   <service
    javaClassComponents="JavaWebService"
     targetNamespace="http://www.getgamma.com/webservices/javaclass"
     serviceName="TestWS"
     serviceURI="/TestWS"
     generateTypes="True"
     expandMethods="True"
     style="rpc" >
     <client
      packageName="com.wls8unleashed.webservices.javaclass"
     />
```

LISTING 30.3 Continued

```
    </service>
   </servicegen>
 </target>
</project>
```

We assume that you compile your Java classes using some script or by hand. This script file does the following:

- Look at `JavaWebService.class` and convert all public methods (`getGreeting`) into a Web Service operation
- Create a deployment descriptor called `web-services.xml` with information from `build.xml` and `JavaWebService.class`
- Create a Web Service client JAR file that contains a proxy to call the Web Service from a Java client
- Create a file called `web-services.war` that contains the front-end Web application
- Create a file called `testWebService.ear` that contains all the preceding files

In Listing 30.3, lines 6–9 add the current directory to the classpath so that the Java components in the staging directory will be found. The build script contains elements that will determine the URL of the Web Service. The URL that is used to invoke a Web Service has the following form:

```
protocol://host:port/contextURI/serviceURI
```

- `protocol` defaults to HTTP but can be set to HTTPS
- `host` is the machine that WebLogic Server is running on
- `port` is the port that WebLogic Server is listening on
- `contextURI` is set in the `servicegen` Ant task in `build.xml`
- `serviceURI` is set in the `servicegen` Ant task in `build.xml`

So, given a host of `www.mydomain.com` and a port of 7001, the URL of the Web Service in Listing 30.2 is `http://www.mydomain.com:7001/WebServices/TestWS`.

In depth information about the `servicegen` Ant task can be found at `http://e-docs.bea.com/wls/docs81/webserv/anttasks.html#1063540`.

30

Executing the build.xml Ant Script

To create the `testWebService.ear` file in the staging directory, do the following:

1. Copy the `JavaWebService.class` to the staging directory and create the `build.xml` file in the same directory.
2. Copy the `setWLSEnv.cmd` from a user-defined WebLogic Server domain to the staging directory.
3. Execute the `setWLSEnv.cmd` script to set environmental variables to work with WebLogic tools. Remember, you need to ensure that the `webservices.jar` file is in the classpath.
4. Now execute `build.xml` by typing **`ant`** on the command line. The Ant command will execute a script called `build.xml` in the current directory by default. You can specify another script by using the `-buildfile` option.

If everything goes correctly, you will have created the `testWebService.ear` file in the staging directory.

Deploying the Web Services As an Exploded Directory

While you're developing your Web Service, it's much easier to debug if you deploy it as an exploded directory rather than as an EAR file. If you're using `servicegen`, change the `destEar` attribute to a name without an extension. `servicegen` will use this as a directory name rather than an EAR file. You can extract the files out of `web-services.war` (including `web-services.xml`) and place them in the WebLogic Server directory structure as a Web application. You can then modify the backend Java class (the business logic, not the interface) and the Web Service will pick up the changes. If the interface has to be changed, you must re-create the `web-services.xml` file.

Deploying the Web Service As an EAR File

Web Service EAR files are deployed just like other EAR files. Start WebLogic Server, if it is not already started, and open the Administrator Console. Expand the Deployments node in the left panel and then click on the Applications node. Click on the Deploy a New Application link in the right panel. This is shown in Figure 30.4. Locate the Web Services EAR file that you want to deploy and then click Deploy.

The next screen attempts to deploy the EAR file to your selected servers. If all goes well, you'll see a message indicating that the embedded `web-services.war` file was deployed correctly, as shown in Figure 30.5.

After the Web Service has been successfully deployed, you'll see it listed under the Web Service Components node and the Applications node, as shown in Figure 30.6.

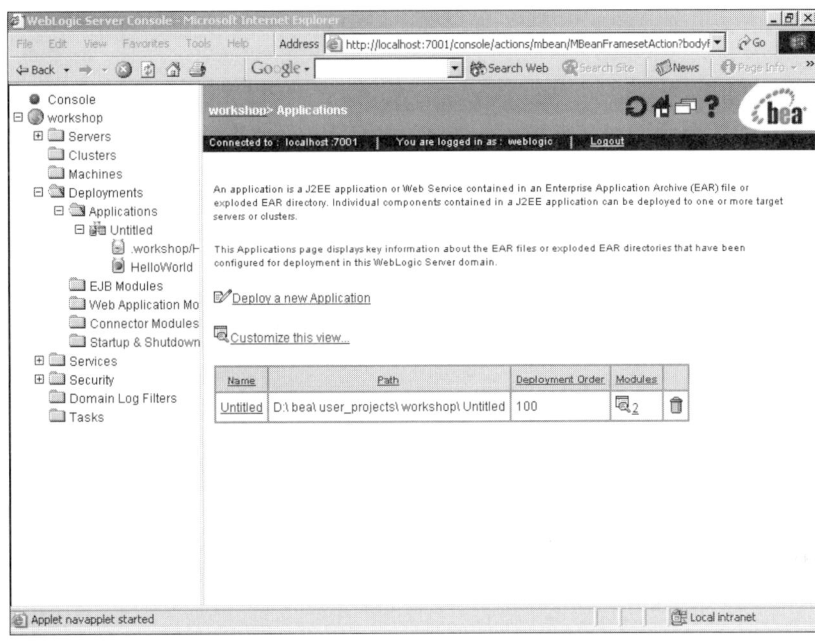

FIGURE 30.4 Select the Web servers you want to deploy the Web Service on.

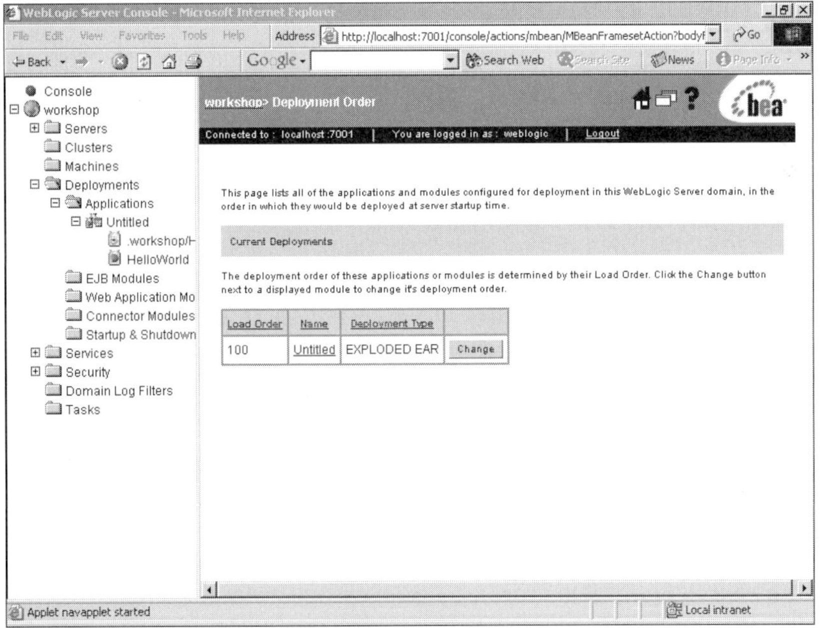

FIGURE 30.5 A successful deployment of the Web Service.

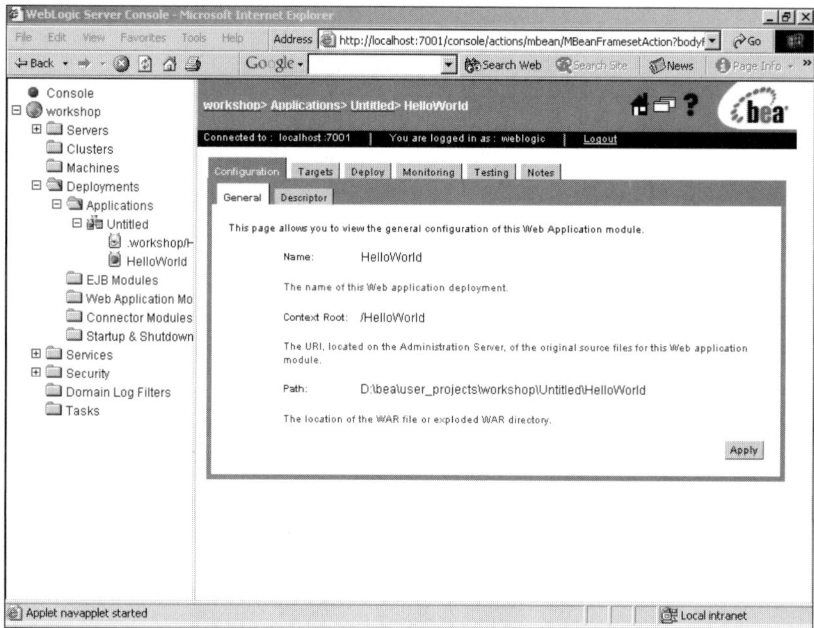

FIGURE 30.6 Deployed Web Services show up under the Applications node.

The Web Service Home Page

Every Web Service deployed under WebLogic Server has a home page. The URL for a Web Service home page is `protocol://host:port/contextURI/serviceURI`. The home page enables us to do the following:

- Test the operations of the Web Service
- Download the Web Service client JAR file
- View and download the WSDL for the Web Service

Click the Testing tab to see the link to the home page for the Web Service. This is shown in Figure 30.7.

Notice that the input parameter from the SOAP request was converted into a Java `String` object and sent into the `JavaWebServices getGreeting()` method. The `JavaWebServices getGreeting()` then output a string that was placed in the SOAP response message. This conversion from XML to Java and back again was taken care of for us by WebLogic Server.

Viewing a WSDL Go back to the Web Service home page and click the Service Description link. This will display the WSDL for the Web Service, as shown in Listing 30.4. Notice that the WSDL is quite verbose and was generated for us by WebLogic Server.

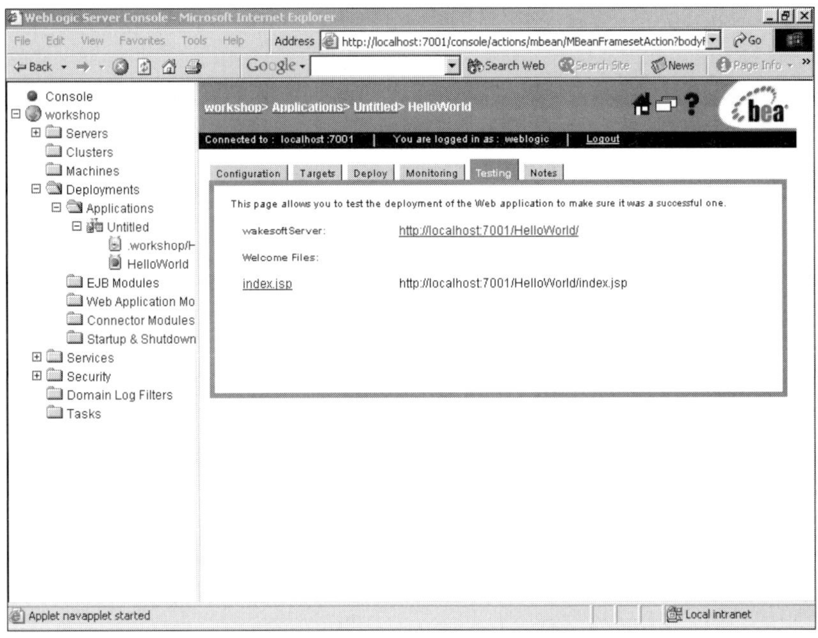

FIGURE 30.7 The Web Service home page enables us to test the deployed Web Service.

LISTING 30.4 The Generated WSDL File for Our Simple Web Service Is Quite Verbose

```
<?xml version="1.0" encoding="utf-8"?>

<definitions xmlns:s="http://www.w3.org/2001/XMLSchema"
  xmlns:http="http://schemas.xmlsoap.org/wsdl/http/"
  xmlns:soap="http://schemas.xmlsoap.org/wsdl/soap/"
  xmlns:soapenc="http://schemas.xmlsoap.org/soap/encoding/"
  xmlns:tns="http://www.getgamma.com/webservices/javaclass"
  xmlns:mime="http://schemas.xmlsoap.org/wsdl/mime/"
  targetNamespace="http://www.getgamma.com/webservices/javaclass"
  xmlns="http://schemas.xmlsoap.org/wsdl/">
 <message name="getGreeting" >
  <part name="string" xmlns:partns="http://www.w3.org/2001/XMLSchema"
    type="partns:string" />
 </message>
 <message name="getGreetingResponse" >
  <part name="result" xmlns:partns="http://www.w3.org/2001/XMLSchema"
    type="partns:string" />
 </message>
```

LISTING 30.4 Continued

```
 <portType name="TestWSPort" >
  <operation name="getGreeting" >
   <input message="tns:getGreeting" />
   <output message="tns:getGreetingResponse" />
  </operation>
 </portType>
 <binding name="TestWSPortSoapBinding" type="tns:TestWSPort" >
 <soap:binding style="rpc" transport="http://schemas.xmlsoap.org/soap/http" />
  <operation name="getGreeting" >
   <soap:operation soapAction="" style="rpc" />
   <input>
    <soap:body use="encoded"
      namespace="http://www.getgamma.com/webservices/javaclass"
     encodingStyle="http://schemas.xmlsoap.org/soap/encoding/" />
   </input>
   <output>
    <soap:body use="encoded"
       namespace="http://www.getgamma.com/webservices/javaclass"
      encodingStyle="http://schemas.xmlsoap.org/soap/encoding/" />
   </output>
  </operation>
 </binding>
 <service name="TestWS" >
  <documentation>todo: add your documentation here</documentation>
  <port name="TestWSPort"
   binding="tns:TestWSPortSoapBinding">
   <soap:address location="http://localhost:7001/WebServices/TestWS"/>
  </port>
 </service>
</definitions>
```

Although a full explanation of WSDL is beyond the scope of this book, understanding the basics will serve us well as our Web Services grow more complex and we are forced to modify WSDL files by hand. The following is a list of major sections with WSDL files:

- `definitions`—Defines namespaces for the rest of the document, including SOAP, WSDL, and the namespace for this Web Service. A namespace is a way of referencing XML elements from multiple sources without having their names conflict with each other. For example, line 5 associates the prefix `tns` with elements from our Web Service, and line 18 refers to the `getGreetingResponse` XML element defined within this WSDL file. Line 10 refers to `partns:string`, which is the XML element named string in the partns namespace. Line 10 also associates the prefix partns with the URI http://www.w3.org/2001/XMLSchema. It will be used to prefix tags from the W3C XML Schema definition. You can learn more about XML namespaces at http://www.w3.org/TR/1999/REC-xml-names-19990114/Overview.html. Alternatively, doing a Google search for *xml namespaces* should lead you to several good resources on this topic.

- message—Defines the SOAP messages used with the Web Service. Each message can be composed of one or more parts, each representing a parameter with a specific data type. There are two messages in this WSDL file—getGreeting and getGreetingResponse—and each is composed of a single parameter that is a String.
- types—Indicates any custom data types used by the Web Service. Although WSDL attempts to define a data type specification, it defaults to the W3C XML Schema specification. This specification defines many commonly used data types, such as string, integer, float, time, and date. If you're using a data type that isn't supported, such as an array of strings, you have to include a types section in the WSDL file that clearly indicates the composition of the user-defined data type.
- soap:binding—Defines what type of SOAP messages are used with this Web Service. This can have one of two values:
  - Document—The body and response of SOAP messages will simply consist of an XML document indicating the Web Service operation and its parameters. An analogy for a Document Web Service is sending an email. You do not need to wait for the person to receive and read the email. You can move on to do other things.
  - RPC—The body and response of SOAP messages will include XML wrappers around the Web Service operation and its parameters. RPC Web Services are more of the request-response style. For example, if you're calling someone who does not have a voicemail, you expect the person to respond. This is a good analogy of a RPC Web Service.

NOTE

A good article that compares document-style Web Services versus RPC-style Web Services is http://www.devx.com/enterprise/Article/10397/0/page/3

The method of calling the Web Service is also defined. The statement transport= http://schemas.xmlsoap.org/soap/http indicates that SOAP over HTTP will be used.

- `portType`—Combines message elements to form one-way or round-trip operations. Within this element, you'll find the defined operations for the Web Service. In this case, there is one operation named `getGreeting` that accepts a `getGreeting` message and returns a `getGreetingResponse` message.
- `service`—Contains documentation on the Web Service and the URL for invoking it.

A Web Service Test Client Web Services running in WebLogic Server can be invoked from many types of clients, including Microsoft .NET, Cape Clear, Apache SOAP, Microsoft SOAP Toolkit, and Java (via JAXM and JAX-RPC). There are many companies involved in Web Services. For a good overview of the industry, visit `http://www.webservices.org/`.

JAX-RPC is a specification for building Web Service clients written in Java and includes several classes that we'll use in this section. Java clients can call Web Services in one of two ways:

- *Static* clients use the Web Service–specific client JAR file and the strongly typed Java interface of that Web Service.
- *Dynamic* clients retrieve a WSDL file from the service at runtime and use this to identify Web Service operations and the parameters they take. This is similar to using Java reflection to interrogate and invoke methods.

INTRODUCTION TO JAX-RPC API

JAX-RPC is a specification for Java clients that want to access Web Services. The JAX-RPC API allows Java clients to connect to Web Services without having to worry about the underlying protocols. In fact, Web Services created with WebLogic Server tools take care of most of the effort in converting XML to and from Java classes and parameters. Web Services are invoked as if they were local objects, and the JAX-RPC implementation classes take care the complexities of serialization of parameters and communication with the remote Web Service. The architecture is shown in Figure 30.8.

The JAX-RPC specification defines a set of APIs in many packages. The classes and interfaces focused on the client programming model are found in the `javax.xml.rpc` package. Table 30.1 lists the most commonly used classes and interfaces from that package.

TABLE 30.1 JAX-RPC Interfaces and Classes

Interface or Class	Description
Service	Main point of communication to a Web Service
ServiceFactory	A factory class for creating Service instances; used with dynamic clients
Stub	A local object that represents the remote Web Service
Call	Used with dynamic clients to invoke a Web Service operation
JAXRPCException	Exception related to the JAX-RPC runtime mechanisms

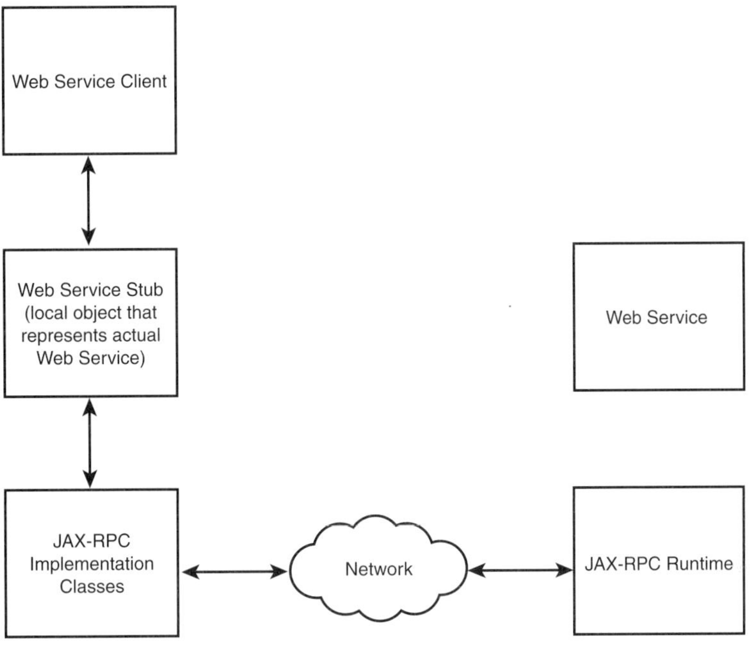

FIGURE 30.8 How JAX-RPC links clients to Web Services.

Writing a Static Web Service Client

In this section, we write a static client to our Web Service using the client JAR files. Before we attempt to invoke our Web Service, we must set the following system properties:

- `javax.xml.soap.MessageFactory`—The name of class used as a factory for creating `SOAPMessage` objects
- `javax.xml.rpc.ServiceFactory`—The name of class used as a factory for the creation of instances of the type `javax.xml.rpc.Service`

In both cases, WebLogic Server supplies classes for these two purposes and they are included in the `webserviceclient.jar` and associated files. The `main()` method in Listing 30.5 illustrates this. When we compile and execute this code, we need `TestWS_client.jar` and `webserviceclient.jar` in our `CLASSPATH`.

LISTING 30.5 A Static Java Client for the TestWS Web Service

```
package com.wls8unleashed.webservices.javaclass;

public class WebServiceClient {
  public static void main(String[] args) {
```

LISTING 30.5 Continued

```
    // Setup the global JAXM message factory
    System.setProperty("javax.xml.soap.MessageFactory",
      "weblogic.webservice.core.soap.MessageFactoryImpl");
    // Setup the global JAX-RPC service factory
    System.setProperty( "javax.xml.rpc.ServiceFactory",
      "weblogic.webservice.core.rpc.ServiceFactoryImpl");

    // Parse the argument list
    WebServiceClient client = new WebServiceClient();
    String wsdl = (args.length > 0? args[0] : null);
    client.callWS(wsdl);
  }

  public void callWS(String wsdlURI) {
    try {
      TestWSPort testWS = null;
      if (wsdlURI == null) {
        testWS = new TestWS_Impl().getTestWSPort();
      } else {
        testWS = new TestWS_Impl(wsdlURI).getTestWSPort();
      }

      String str = testWS.getGreeting("Jessie Marin");
      System.out.println(str);

    } catch (Exception e) {
      e.printStackTrace();
    }

  }
}
```

The `callWS` method instantiates a `TestWS_Impl` object either using a WSDL file or without using one. We then use this object to get an instance of `TestWSPort`. `TestWSPort` is the local stub that enables us to invoke Web Service operations as demonstrated with the code `testWS.getGreeting("Jessie Marin")`.

Writing a Dynamic Web Service Client

If the Web Service you're invoking is not written in Java or you do not have access to the client JAR file, you can invoke the Web Service by simply utilizing its WSDL as shown in Listing 30.6. We use a Java client to invoke a Web Service. The Web Service itself might or might not be implemented in Java. However, for the client, you still need the WebLogic JAX-RPC implementation JAR file in your CLASSPATH.

LISTING 30.6 A Dynamic Java Client for the TestWS Web Service

```
import java.net.URL;
import javax.xml.rpc.ServiceFactory;
import javax.xml.rpc.Service;
import javax.xml.rpc.Call;
import javax.xml.rpc.ParameterMode;
import javax.xml.namespace.QName;

public class DynamicWebServiceClient {
  public static void main(String[] args) {
    // Setup the global JAXM message factory
    System.setProperty("javax.xml.soap.MessageFactory",
      "weblogic.webservice.core.soap.MessageFactoryImpl");
    // Setup the global JAX-RPC service factory
    System.setProperty( "javax.xml.rpc.ServiceFactory",
      "weblogic.webservice.core.rpc.ServiceFactoryImpl");

    try {
      // create service factory
      ServiceFactory factory = ServiceFactory.newInstance();

      // define qnames
      String targetNamespace = "http://www.getgamma.com/webservices/javaclass";

      // create service
      QName serviceName = new QName(targetNamespace, "TestWS");
      URL wsdlLocation = new URL("http://localhost:7001/WebServices/TestWS?WSDL");
      Service service = factory.createService(wsdlLocation, serviceName);

      // create call
      QName portName = new QName(targetNamespace, "TestWSPort");
      QName operationName = new QName(targetNamespace, "getGreeting");
      Call call = service.createCall(portName, operationName);

      // invoke the remote web service
      String result = (String) call.invoke(new Object[] {"Jessie Marin"});

      System.out.println(result);
    } catch (Exception e) {
```

LISTING 30.6 Continued

```
            e.printStackTrace();
        }
    }
}
```

This code utilizes `ServiceFactory` to generate a new instance of `Service` that is tied to the `TestWS` Web Service by associating it with the WSDL. In this code, we have attributes from the WSDL file, such as the target namespace, Web Service name, port name, and operation name.

NOTE

To retrieve the WSDL for a Web Service, you can end the URL with `?WSDL`.

Example: `http://localhost:7001/WebServices/TestWS?WSDL`

NOTE

In this section, we introduced the JAX-RPC API. For more information on this, please refer to `http://java.sun.com/xml/jaxrpc/`.

Exception Handling with JAX-RPC

The JAX-RPC specification includes a `SOAPFaultException` exception to be thrown from the Java backend component of a Web Service. If these components throw another exception, WebLogic Server attempts to map it to a SOAP fault as closely as possible, but using `SOAPFaultException` ensures that clients receive the most useful exception information. The `SOAPFaultException` class contains very detailed information concerning the nature of the exception.

For a complete example using JAX-RPC, please refer to `http://java.sun.com/webservices/docs/ea1/tutorial/doc/JAXRPC.html`.

The Web Service–Specific Client JAR File

To build a static Web Service client in Java, you need the client JAR file for that Web Service. The client JAR can be downloaded from the Web Service home page, if the Web Service originator created one. If you cannot access the JAR file, you can create one from the Web Service WSDL file that you can also download from the Web Service home page. The Ant task `clientgen` creates a client JAR from a WSDL file or a Web Service EAR file. Please visit `http://e-docs.bea.com/wls/docs81/webserv/anttasks.html#1080160` for more information about `clientgen`.

The client JAR file contains implementations of the classes and interfaces in Table 30.1 in the JAX_RPC sidebar. The client JAR for the previous example is named `TestWS_client.jar`. The contents include the following:

- `TestWS_Impl`—Implements the JAX-RPC service interface. Web Service clients instantiate this class.
- `TestWSPort`—A local interface that represents the Web Service. It contains one method: `getGreeting`.

In general, `servicegen` creates the following files:

- Client JAR file—*`WebServiceName`*`_client.jar`
- Service interface—*`WebServiceName`*`_Impl.java`
- Stub interface—*`WebServiceName`*`Port.java`

The WebLogic Server Client JAR Files

In addition to the specific client JAR file, you also need a WebLogic Server JAR file. These files are available at `WL_HOME\server\lib`. You will use one of the following files, depending on the situation:

- `webserviceclient.jar`—Contains the runtime implementation of the JAX-RPC APIs
- `webserviceclient+ssl.jar`—JAX-RPC APIs with implementation of SSL
- `webserviceclient+ssl_pj.jar`—JAX-RPC APIs with implementation of SSL for the CDC profile of the Java 2 Micro Edition (J2ME)

DOWNLOADING THE WEB SERVICE CLIENT JAR FILE

To download this client JAR file, go to the Web Service home page. The Click here link downloads the client JAR file when you click it. By default, the name of this file is *`WebServiceName`*`_client.jar`. In our case, the name of the client JAR file is `TestWS_client.jar`.

Creating a Web Service with a Stateless Session Bean Back End

The process of creating a Web Service from a Stateless Session Bean is pretty straightforward. Implement the bean and create its JAR file. Listing 30.7 contains the code for the `DoctorInfoBean`. Running the EJBGen tool against it will create the EJB support classes and the EJB JAR file.

LISTING 30.7 Stateless Session Bean Using EJBGen

```
package com.wls8unleashed.webservices;

// This is an EJBGen-annotated class

import java.rmi.RemoteException;
import java.util.*;
import javax.ejb.*;
import javax.naming.*;
import javax.rmi.PortableRemoteObject;

/**
 *
 * @ejbgen:session
 *   ejb-name = DoctorInfoEJB
 *   default-transaction = Required
 *
 * @ejbgen:jndi-name
 * remote = com.wls8unleashed.webservices.DoctorInfoHome
 *
 * @ejbgen:ejb-client-jar
 *   file-name = DoctorInfo_client.jar
 */
public class DoctorInfoBean implements SessionBean {

 private SessionContext ctx;

 /**
 * @ejbgen:remote-method
 */
 public String getGreeting(String name) {
   return "Hello, " + name + " the local time is " + new java.util.Date();
 }

 public void setSessionContext(SessionContext c) {
  ctx = c;
 }

 public void ejbCreate() {}
 public void ejbActivate() {}
 public void ejbPassivate() {}
 public void ejbRemove() {}
}
```

Place the JAR file in a staging directory and create an Ant script that contains the `servicegen` task, as shown in Listing 30.8. Here you can see that the EJB JAR file is listed.

LISTING 30.8 Ant Build Script for Creating a Web Service with a Stateless Session Bean

```
<project name="buildWebservice" default="ear">
 <target name="ear">
  <servicegen
    destEar="DoctorInfoWS.ear"
    contextURI="MedicalServices" >
   <classpath>
     <pathelement path="${java.class.path}" />
     <pathelement path="." />
   </classpath>

   <service
     ejbJar="DoctorInfo.jar"
     targetNamespace="http://www.getgamma.com/webservices/ejb"
     serviceName="DoctorInfoWS"
     serviceURI="/DoctorInfoWS"
     generateTypes="True"
     expandMethods="True"
     style="rpc" >
     <client
      packageName="com.wls8unleashed.webservices.ejb"
     />
   </service>
  </servicegen>
 </target>
</project>
```

When you run the script file, the `DoctorInfoWS.ear` will be created. Deploy this file and the embedded `DoctorInfo` EJB will be deployed as well. The Web Service home page is located at `http://`*`host`*`:`*`port`*`/MedicalServices/DoctorInfoWS`.

Working with Nonsimple Data Types

In the `TestWS` Web Service, `getGreeting` accepts a `String` as input and returns a `String` as output. `String` is a commonly used data type and is considered a built-in data type. However, Web Services deployed in the real world have more complex data type requirements. WebLogic Server defines three types of Web Service operation parameters:

- Built-in data types are automatically converted between Java and XML by WebLogic Server. This includes the following Java data types: `int`, `short`, `long`, `float`, `double`, byte, boolean, char, java.lang.Integer, java.lang.Short, java.lang.Long, java.lang.Float, java.lang.Double, java.lang.Byte, java.lang.Boolean, java.lang.Character, java.lang.String, java.math.BigInteger, java.math.BigDecimal, java.lang.String, java.util.Calendar, java.util.Date, and byte[].

- Supported data types that are not built in require special components (such as a serializer class) to be used as Web Service parameters. However, the servicegen and autotype Ant tasks can generate these components automatically. This includes the following Java data types: an array of any built-in Java data type, JavaBean whose properties are any built-in Java data type, java.util.List, java.util.ArrayList, java.util.LinkedList, java.util.Vector, and java.lang.Object (in some cases).
- Not supported and not built-in data types require special components to be used as Web Service parameters. These components must be generated manually.

Creating an Operation with a Supported Data Type

Let's create a Web Service that returns six numbers suitable for playing lotto, except that the same number can show up more than once. Our Web Service returns these numbers as a vector, as shown in Listing 30.9.

LISTING 30.9 Web Service Returning a Vector

```
import java.util.Date;
import java.util.Vector;

public class LottoWebService {
  public LottoWebService () {
  }


  public Vector getLottoNumbers() {
    Vector vec = new Vector();
    for(int i=0; i<6; i++) {
      Integer lottoNumber = new Integer((int)(Math.random()*60)+1);
      vec.add(lottoNumber);
    }
    return vec;
  }
}
```

If we run the build.xml that contains the Ant servicegen task, we will generate a new testWebService.ear file. Just as before, there will be a TestWS_client.jar in the web-services.war within the EAR file. There will now be two extra classes: VectorHolder and VectorCodec. These files will be used to convert between the Java data type Vector and XML.

We can now create a static Java client that calls the getLottoNumbers operation as shown in Listing 30.10. The JAX-RPC runtime handles all the code required to convert between the Vector data type and XML. In this case, it has converted the Vector to an array of Objects.

LISTING 30.10 Web Service Client Calling getLottoNumbers

```
public void callWS(String wsdlURI) {
  try {
    TestWSPort testWS = null;
    if (wsdlURI == null) {
      testWS = new TestWS_Impl().getTestWSPort();
    } else {
      testWS = new TestWS_Impl(wsdlURI).getTestWSPort();
    }

    System.out.print("Lotto numbers are: ");


    Object[] nums = testWS.getLottoNumbers();
    for(int i=0; i<nums.length; i++) {
      Integer lottoNumber = (Integer)nums[i];
      System.out.print(lottoNumber.toString()+" ");
    }
    System.out.println(" Good Luck!");


  } catch (Exception e) {
    e.printStackTrace();
  }

}
```

Working with User-Defined Data Types

Creating a Web Service with a user-defined data type requires the following information:

- A Java class to represent the user-defined data type
- An XML schema to describe the Java class

- A serialization class to convert between the Java class and XML
- The data mapping information for the Java class

In some cases, this information can be automatically generated with the autotype Ant task. For example, suppose that we want to return a variable of type DoctorInfo from a Web Service operation, as shown in Listing 30.11. This class must implement Serializable and must contain a no-argument constructor.

LISTING 30.11 A User-Defined Java Class to Be Returned from a Web Service Operation

```
package com.wls8unleashed.webservices.autotype;

import java.io.Serializable;

public class DoctorInfo implements Serializable {
  public int id;
  public String firstName;
  public String lastName;
  public float officeVisitCharge;

  public DoctorInfo() {
  }

  public DoctorInfo(int id, String firstName, String lastName,
   float officeVisitCharge) {
    this.id = id;
    this.firstName = firstName;
    this.lastName = lastName;
    this.officeVisitCharge = officeVisitCharge;
  }
}
```

To generate the required information, create an Ant build script that calls the autotype Ant task. An example of this is shown in Listing 30.12.

LISTING 30.12 Ant Build Script for Invoking the autotype Ant Task

```
<project name="createAutotype" default="createautotype">
 <target name="createautotype">

  <autotype javatypes="com.wls8unleashed.webservices.autotype.DoctorInfo"
       targetNamespace="http://www.getgamma.com/autotyper"
       packageName="com.wls8unleashed.webservices.autotype"
```

LISTING 30.12 Continued

```
       destDir="d:\tempautotype" >

   <classpath>
     <pathelement path="${java.class.path}" />
     <pathelement path="." />
   </classpath>
  </autotype>
 </target>
</project>
```

This script instructs `autotype` to create the data typing components for the `DoctorInfo` class in the `com.wls8unleashed.webservices.autotype` package. It will place these components in the `d:\tempautotype` directory. The following components will be generated:

- A XML schema and mapping file called `types.xml` that describes the `DoctorInfo` class and how to map from the Java class to XML
- The files `DoctorInfoHolder.java` and `DoctorInfoCodec.java`, which are used as serialization classes

For a list of supported data types and other information about `autotype`, please visit `http://e-docs.bea.com/wls/docs81/webserv/assemble.html#1060696`.

Creating a Web Service with a User-Defined Data Type

We're now going to create a Web Service based on the Java class file in Listing 30.13. In previous releases of WebLogic Server, we used the `servicegen` Ant task to create the entire Web Service, including the EAR file, its internal WAR file, and the Web Service deployment descriptor, `web-services.xml`. Now that we have a user-defined data type, we have to perform some of this by hand.

LISTING 30.13 Java Class Used as Web Service

```
package com.wls8unleashed.webservices.autotype;

import java.util.Hashtable;


public class DoctorWebService {
        Hashtable doctorHash = null;

  public DoctorWebService() {
    doctorHash = new Hashtable();
```

LISTING 30.13 Continued

```
    DoctorInfo di = new DoctorInfo(1, "Troy", "Chin", 89.25f);
    doctorHash.put(new Integer(1), di);
    di = new DoctorInfo(2, "Rina", "Caprario", 95.72f);
    doctorHash.put(new Integer(2), di);
  }

  public DoctorInfo getDoctorInfo(int doctorID) {
    Object key = new Integer(doctorID);
    DoctorInfo di = (DoctorInfo)doctorHash.get(key);
    return di;
  }
}
```

We need to generate a `web-services.xml` deployment descriptor for our Web Service. WebLogic comes with an Ant task called `source2wsdd` that can create a `web-services.xml` file from a Java class. Because we're using a Java class back end for our Web Service, we can use `source2wsdd` as shown in Listing 30.14.

LISTING 30.14 Script File to Invoke source2wsdd

```
<project name="createWSDD" default="WSDD">
 <target name="WSDD">

  <source2wsdd
   javaSource="DoctorWebService.java"
   typesInfo="d:\tempautotype\types.xml"
   ddFile="web-services.xml"
   serviceURI="/DoctorAutoTypeService">

   <classpath>
     <pathelement path="${java.class.path}" />
     <pathelement path="." />
   </classpath>

  </source2wsdd>
 </target>
</project>
```

Listing 30.14 uses the XML schema information for `DoctorInfo` that's contained in `types.xml`, which was generated by `autotype`. When this script is executed, it will create a `web-services.xml` file that contains our XML schema information.

More information about source2wsdd can be found at http://e-docs.bea.com/wls/docs81/webserv/assemble.html#1056639.

Assembling the Web Service

At this point, you have all the elements of the Web Service:

- Deployment descriptor—web-service.xml, which was created with source2wsdd
- User-defined data type components—XML schema (now in web-services.xml) and codec classes created with autotype
- Java backend component—Some Java component that implements the business logic for the Web Service

You can assemble these by hand into a deployable EAR file, or you can use the wspackage Ant task. A build script that uses wspackage is shown in Listing 30.15.

LISTING 30.15 Script File to Invoke wspackage

```
<project name="createWSDD" default="WSDD">
 <target name="WSDD">

  <wspackage
   output="DoctorWebService.ear"
   contextURI="DoctorWebService"
   codecDir="d:\tempautotype"
   webAppClasses="com.wls8unleashed.webservices.autotype.DoctorWebService"
   ddFile="web-services.xml">

   <classpath>
     <pathelement path="${java.class.path}" />
     <pathelement path="." />
   </classpath>

  </wspackage>
 </target>
</project>
```

In Listing 30.15, we specify the location of web-services.xml, the Java backend class for the Web Service, where the codecs (serialization classes) are stored, and the contextURI of the Web Service. After this script has been executed, you'll have a DoctorWebService.ear file that can then be deployed. After the EAR file has been deployed, the Web Service home page will be located at http://host:port/DoctorWebService/DoctorAutoTypeService.

TIP

We've used Ant tasks to automate generation of the `web-services.xml` file, XML schema and data mapping, and serialization classes. If you need to perform these tasks manually, please visit the following URL for more information: `http://e-docs.bea.com/wls/docs81/webserv/customdata.html`.

Working with SOAP Message Handlers

WebLogic Server offers a way of intercepting incoming and outgoing SOAP messages with a SOAP message handler. SOAP message handlers can be run on either the Web Service client or in WebLogic Server with the actual Web Service. Message handlers can be used for many purposes, such as encryption and decryption. A Web Service client can run a handler that encrypts SOAP messages, and the server can run a handler that decrypts the message before it reaches the Web Service. In this way, SOAP messages are not sent in the clear over the Internet.

Message handlers can be grouped together to form chains. These message handlers can then work together to perform various modifications and inspections of the SOAP messages. Each handler has a `handleRequest()` method and a `handleResponse()` method, as shown in Figure 30.9. Every Web Service can have message handlers, and a Web Service can be created with only message handlers. For more information about SOAP message handlers, please visit `http://e-docs.bea.com/wls/docs81/webserv/interceptors.html`.

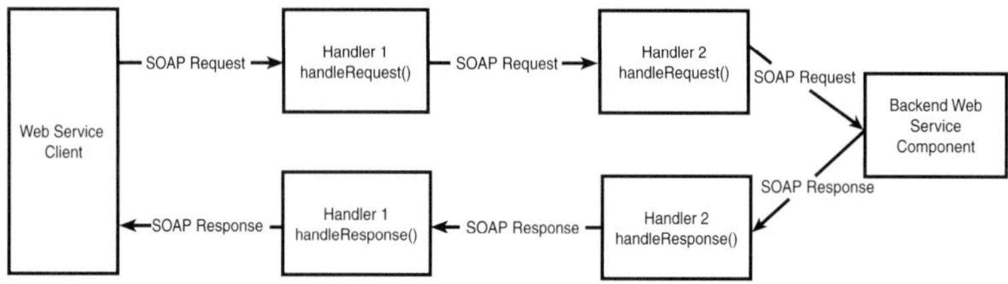

FIGURE 30.9 Message handlers can be chained together.

Securing Web Services

There are many ways to secure Web Services running on WebLogic Server. Because Web Services run as standard Web applications, they can be secured in the same way. These are the ways in which Web Services can be secured:

- Assign a security policy or role to the Web Service from the Administration Console.
- Secure the Web Service URL by modifying `web.xml` and `weblogic.xml` in the Web Service WAR file.

- Secure the backend Stateless Session Bean by modifying `ejb-jar.xml` and `weblogic-ejb-jar.xml`.
- Use the HTTPS protocol for the Web Service by modifying `web-services.xml`. You must also turn on SSL in WebLogic Server. For more information about using SSL with Web Services, please visit `http://e-docs.bea.com/wls/docs81/webserv/security.html`.

Working with the UDDI Directory Explorer

WebLogic Server comes with a UDDI directory explorer, as shown in Figure 30.10, that can be invoked at the following URL: `http://host:port/uddiexplorer`. The UDDI directory explorer can be used to search public and private UDDI registries. It can also be used to configure the WebLogic-supplied UDDI registry and publish Web Services to it.

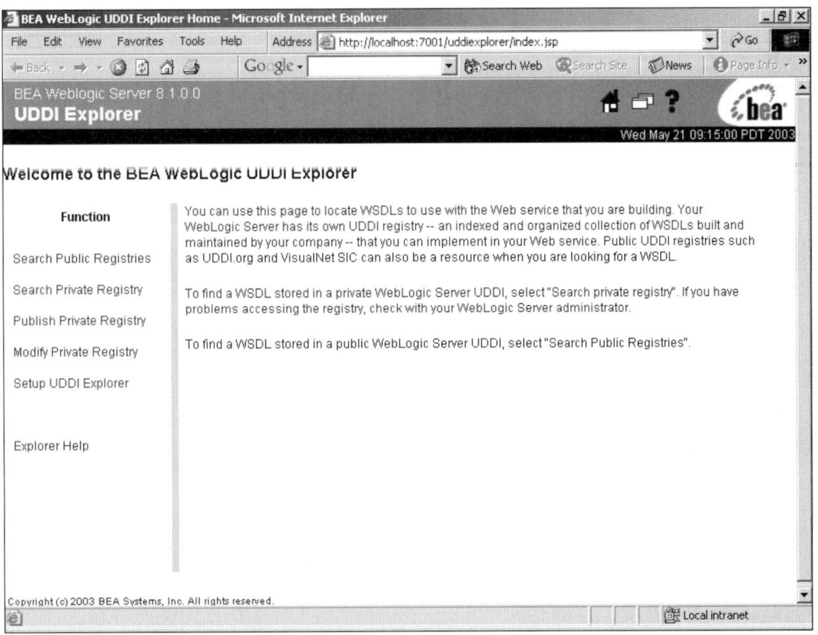

FIGURE 30.10 The UDDI explorer provides access to public and private UDDI registries.

Creating Web Services with WebLogic Workshop

WebLogic Workshop offers a compelling alternative to creating Web Services with pure Java code. WebLogic Workshop has a very user-friendly GUI that makes creating Web Services and all the tasks associated with it as painless as possible. WebLogic Workshop enables application developers to write code that deals with business logic and to utilize existing J2EE components, such as JDBC data sources, EJBs, and JMS destinations. Application developers also can call other Web Services quite easily.

> **NOTE**
>
> It is important to note that with the 8.1 release, WebLogic Workshop has matured from being purely a Web Services tool to a tool that allows complete J2EE application development. Workshop is now the single UI/IDE for the BEA WebLogic Platform. To learn more about Workshop's features, refer to `http://dev2dev.bea.com/articles/Sjogreen_02.jsp`.

WebLogic Workshop Architecture

WebLogic Workshop relies on the runtime framework of WebLogic Server 8.1. Web Services written in WebLogic Workshop are represented by Java files with a JWS extension. These files have a special meaning to WebLogic Server 8.1, as shown in Figure 30.11.

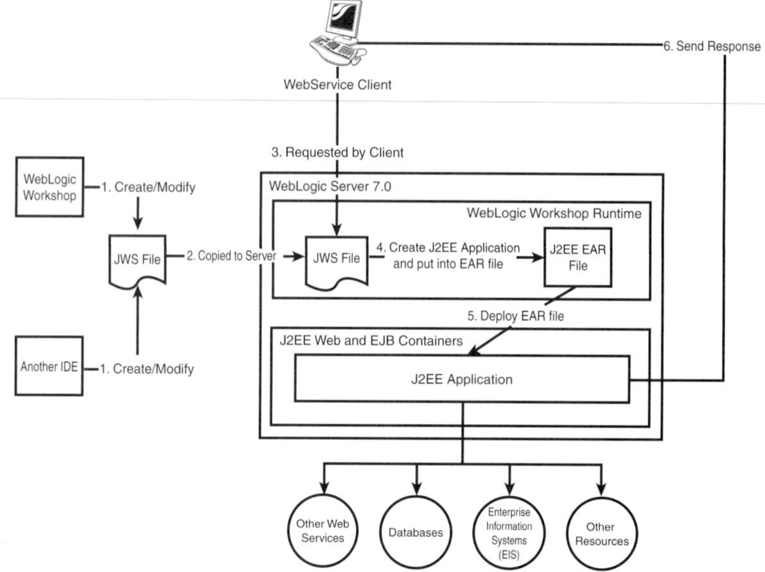

FIGURE 30.11 JWS files are generated with WebLogic Workshop and converted to a J2EE application when requested by a client.

Although WebLogic Workshop is an excellent IDE for creating and modifying JWS files, any IDE can be used. After the JWS file has been created and copied to WebLogic Server, a client request will invoke the WebLogic Workshop runtime framework to create an entire

J2EE application from the JWS file. The client request will then be handed off to this application, which will respond to the client request.

JWS Files and JSR 181

Although the J2EE specification offers an enormous amount of functionality across many technologies, it can be quite difficult to use due to the sheer number of APIs available. Although enterprise developers appreciate the flexibility and power offered by J2EE, the Java community has recognized that an easier method of creating J2EE applications would help developers and increase the usability and popularity of J2EE.

Java Specification Request (JSR) 181, titled *Web Services Metadata for the Java Platform*, attempts to do just that. This JSR defines a set of Javadoc-style comments that can be added to standard Java source files. The goal of this JSR is to develop a simpler model for creating Web Services that can be used for Rapid Application Design. This JSR is sponsored by representatives from BEA, IBM, Cisco, Oracle, SAP AG, Sun Microsystems and others. It is based on the JSR 175, regarding code metadata. However, at the time of this writing, WebLogic Server and Apache AXIS are the only J2EE Application Servers to support JWS files. More information about JSR 181 can be found at `http://www.jcp.org/jsr/detail/181.jsp`.

JWS files are regular Java source files with metadata added in the form of Javadoc-style comments. These comments specify information such as

- The methods (and parameters) of Web Services
- The Web Service URL and supported protocols and document types
- The conversational state of a Web Service invocation
- The WSDL file of an external Web Service

Listing 30.16 shows a sample JWS file named `HelloWorld.jws`. The name of the class, the name of the file, and the name of the corresponding Web Service are all the same: `HelloWorld`.

LISTING 30.16 A Sample JWS File

```
public class HelloWorld {
  /* @jws:operation */
  public String getGreeting() {
    return "Hello, World!";
  }
}
```

Only one operation is defined: `getGreeting()`. The comment immediately preceding `getGreeting()`, `@jws:operation`, informs the code generation engine that this isn't an internal class method, but is a Web Service operation. Copying this file to a Workshop-enabled WebLogic Server domain and then requesting it from a Web Service client will generate the supporting code for the Web Service based on this JWS file.

The WebLogic Workshop GUI

To see WebLogic Workshop in action, from the Start menu, choose BEA WebLogic Platform 8.1→WebLogic Workshop→WebLogic Workshop. When WebLogic Workshop starts for the first time, it will look like Figure 30.12.

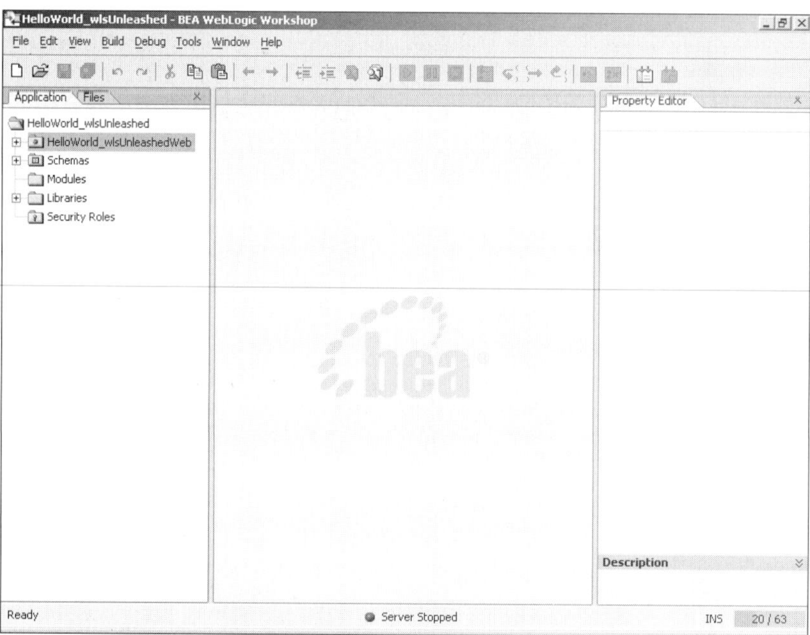

FIGURE 30.12 The beautiful WebLogic Workshop GUI.

The GUI is broken up into several areas, or *panes*. The following list describes each pane:

- Application tree—Represents all projects in the current application and all components (such as Web Services) in each project. WebLogic Workshop ships with many examples right out of the box, as shown in Figure 30.12.
- Palettes—Displays all operations and controls available or used in the current Web Service.

- Property Editor—Displays and allows modification of the currently selected operation, control, or Web Service.
- Description—Displays information about the currently selected operation, control, or Web Service.
- Tasks—Displays possible actions that you might want to take on the currently selected operation, control, or Web Service.
- Design View—The center part of the GUI. This area hosts the graphical representation of the Web Service.

The Design View represents the Web Service client on the left, the Web Service in the middle, and the associated database, EJB, and other controls on the right.

The Source View displays the actual source code of the JWS file for the Web Service, as shown in Figure 30.13. WebLogic Workshop always keeps the information displayed by these two views in sync. If a property is changed in the Design View, switching to the Source View will reveal that the property has changed there as well, and vice versa.

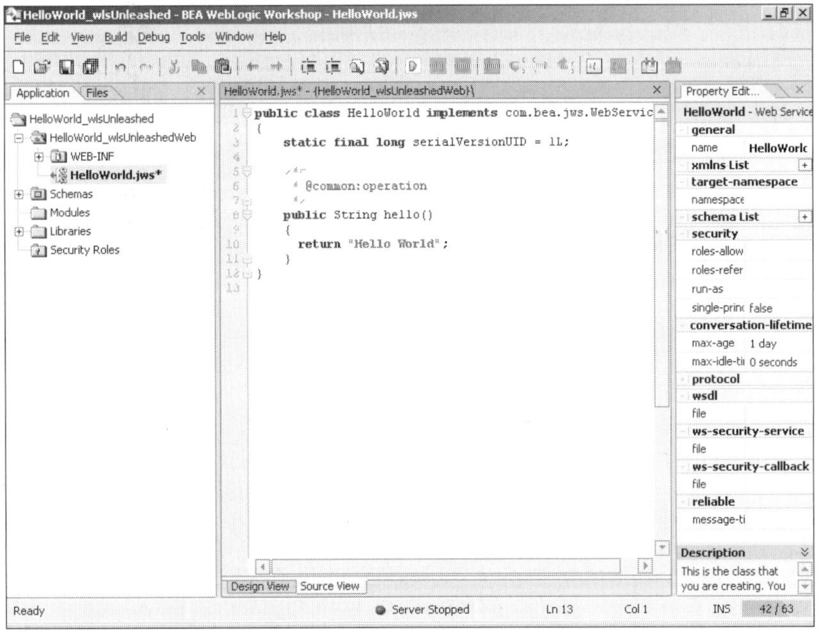

FIGURE 30.13 The Source View.

Creating a Web Service in WebLogic Workshop

The simplest way to create a new Web Service is to add one to the default sample application that WebLogic Workshop starts in. After starting WebLogic Workshop, from the File menu, choose New and then Web Service. The Create New File window will appear. Choose Web Service and type **`greetings.jws`** for the filename. After you click the OK button, you are placed in the Design View. Now we'll add a method named `greetings` to our Web Service.

Adding a Method

Notice that you see the Web Service client interface on the left side of the Design View. We're going to add an operation for it to this interface. Right-click on Design view and choose Add Method. You'll now see a new method added with the default name of `newMethod1`. The name will be selected. Type in a new name of `sayHello` and press the Enter key. Your Design View should look like Figure 30.14.

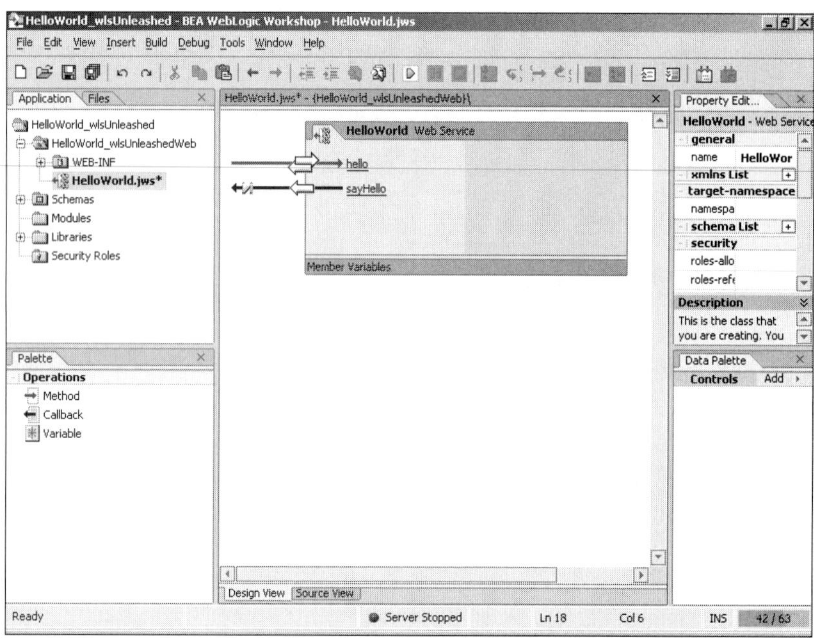

FIGURE 30.14 The Design View with a new method.

We now need to write the code that will become the business logic of this method. Click on the method name (`sayHello`) in the canvas. You will be placed in Source View. `sayHello` currently returns a void and accepts no parameters. We're going to change `sayHello` to return a `String` and to take a `String` parameter called `name`. `sayHello` will use the passed-in `name` to return its `String`. Change `sayHello` so that it matches the method shown in Figure 30.15.

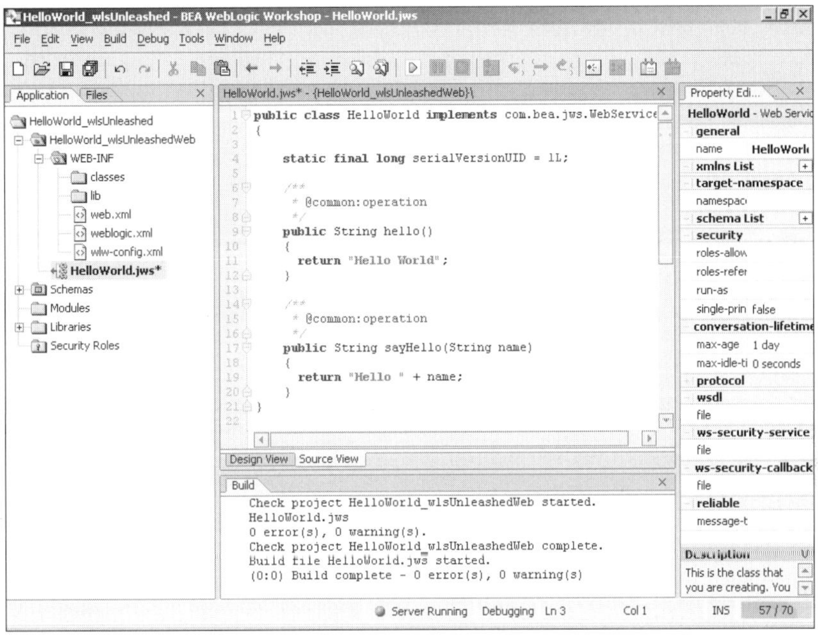

FIGURE 30.15 The sayHello method has been changed.

Running Our Web Service

Now that we've defined a method with a little business logic, we can invoke our Web Service. At the top of the WebLogic Workshop GUI is a toolbar containing a blue arrow. This button is for debugging; click it. You should see a window explaining that WebLogic Server is not running. The red light and the `Server Stopped` message in the status bar can also confirm this. Click the OK button to start WebLogic Server.

WebLogic Server will execute in the Workshop samples domain. This is a domain that ships with WebLogic Server and WebLogic Workshop, and is found in the `WL_HOME\weblogic81\samples\workshop` directory. This domain is a WebLogic Workshop domain and contains special files that are not normally found in a standard domain.

After WebLogic Server starts, a special browser window will open as well. If the browser window does not open, you might have to tell WebLogic Workshop where your Internet browser's executable file is located. Select Tools menu→Preferences. The Preferences window will display. Select the Browser category and then change the value in the Browser Path field.

The browser window will display the Web Service's Test View, as shown in Figure 30.16. This is the home page for Web Services created with JWS files. There are four tabs at the top of the Test View that will display different Web pages when clicked.

The Overview page allows access to the WSDL files and client JARs, as shown in Figure 30.16. There is also a link here to convert this Web Service to a WebLogic Workshop control so that it can be invoked from other WebLogic Workshop Web Services.

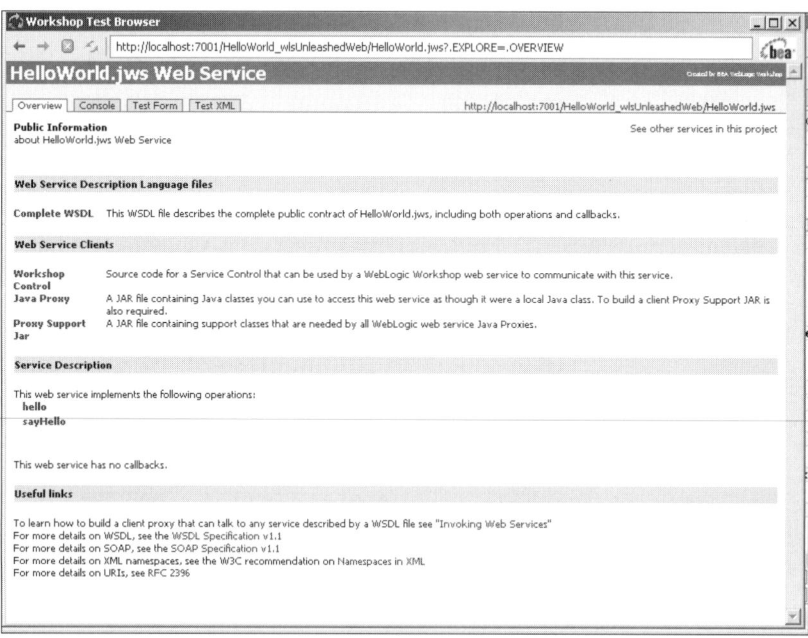

FIGURE 30.16 The overview page provides access to the WSDL and client JAR files.

The WebLogic Workshop runtime framework will log SOAP messages associated with our Web Services. We can use those logged messages to verify that our Web Services are executing correctly. The console page enables us to set the configuration of this logging mechanism. Workshop Web Services are implemented using various resources, such as EJBs and JMS queues. You see this as a link in Figure 30.17.

The Test Form page allows Web Service operations to be executed, as shown in Figure 30.18. An input field is present for each input parameter. You can enter values for these parameters and click the accompanying execute button, named after the Web Service operation.

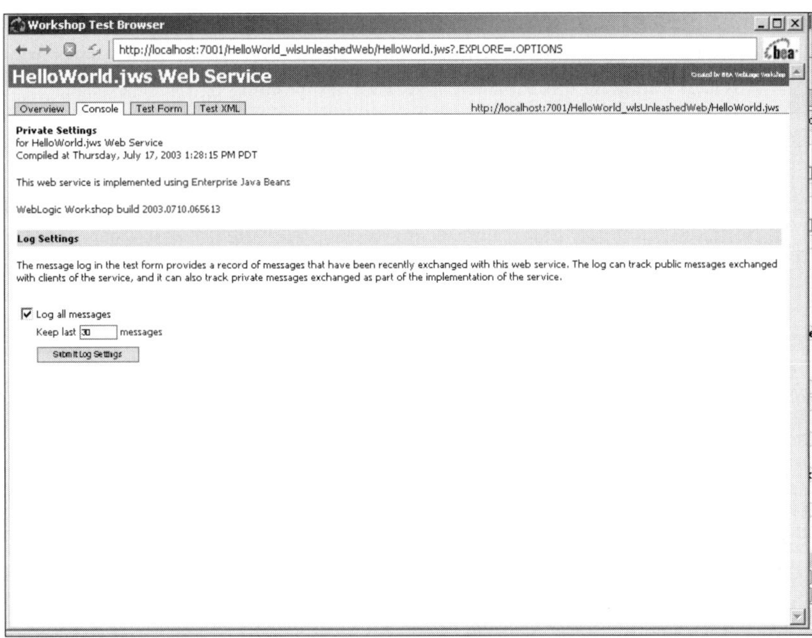

FIGURE 30.17 The console page provides access to log and conversation information.

FIGURE 30.18 The Test Form page enables us to verify Web Service operations.

The operation results will be displayed as shown in Figure 30.19. Web Service operations that call on other resources will have multiple entries in the message log for each external resource invocation. Clicking the Refresh link will show each of these entries.

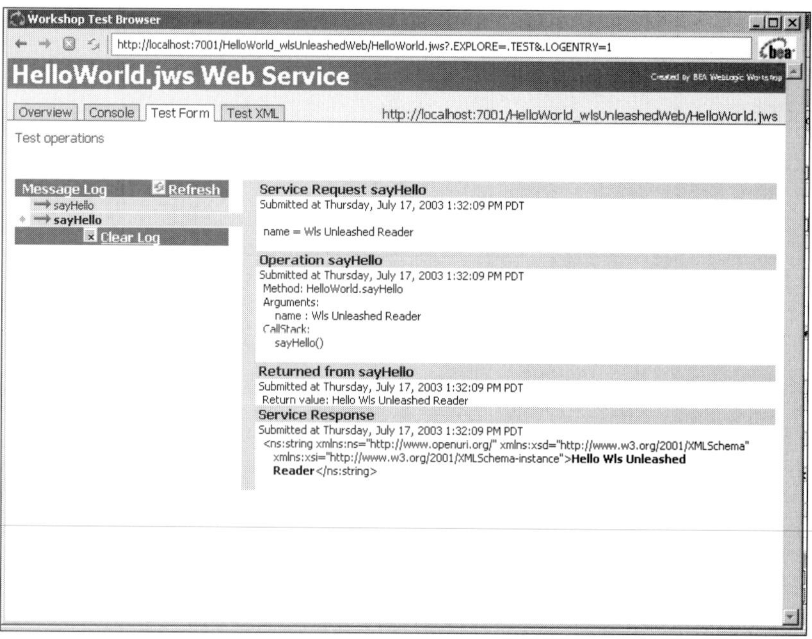

FIGURE 30.19 The Test Form page displays the operation results.

The Test XML page works similar to the Test Form page, except that it displays the full SOAP request and response messages, as shown in Figures 30.20 and 30.21. For each operation input parameter, substitute the parameter name with an actual value. Then click the button named after the Web Service operation.

Modifying Our Web Service

While you're running the test, you're free to change both the business logic and the input and output parameters of Web Service operations. Switch to WebLogic Workshop and change the `sayHello` method to match Listing 30.17. Then click the Save button or choose File, Save.

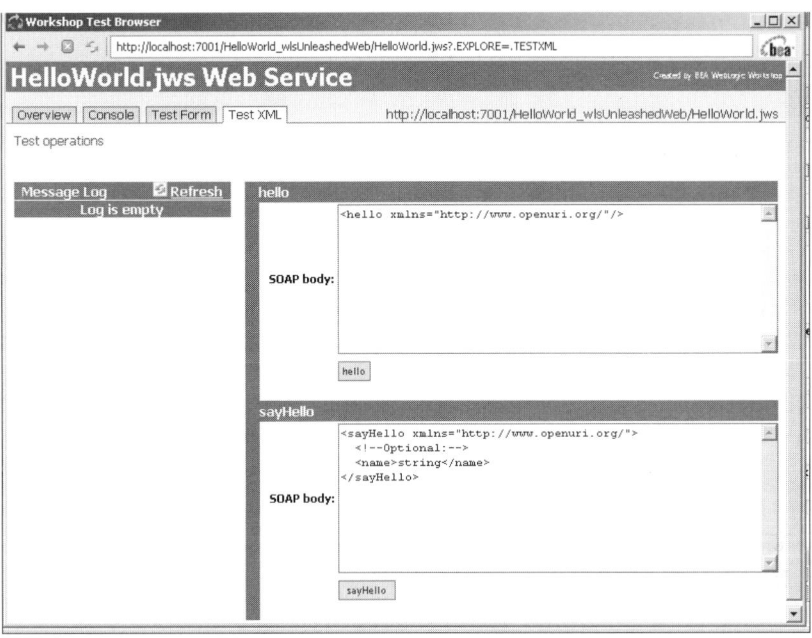

FIGURE 30.20 The Test XML page enables us to modify the SOAP request XML.

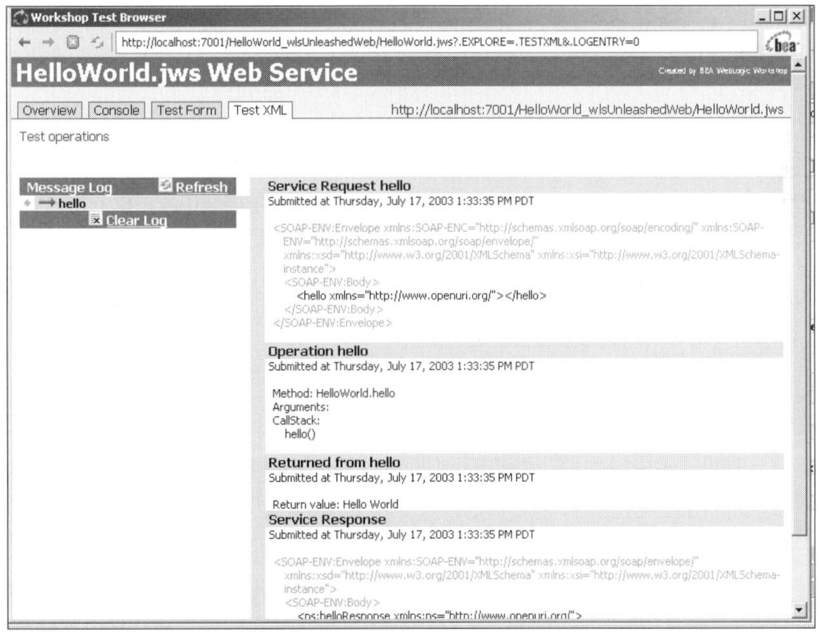

FIGURE 30.21 The Test XML page enables us to inspect the SOAP request and response messages.

LISTING 30.17 sayHello Now Takes Two Parameters

```
public String sayHello(String name, int age)
{
  return "Hello " + name + " greetings from WebLogic Workshop.\n" +
      "You are " + age + " years old.";
}
```

Return to the test view and click on the Test Form tab. Click on the Test Operations link at the top of the page. WebLogic Server will now regenerate our Web Service. When it finishes, you'll see two input fields where you can enter a name and an age. Enter values in these fields and click the sayHello button. The results of the new business logic will be displayed. You can certainly appreciate how easy WebLogic Workshop and its runtime framework make creating and debugging Web Services.

When you finish testing the Web Service, either close the browser window containing the test view or switch to WebLogic Workshop and select Debug, Stop. You can shut down WebLogic Server by right-clicking on the Server Running message at the bottom on the GUI and choosing Stop WebLogic Server. (WebLogic Server can be started from this menu as well.)

Creating a WebLogic Workshop Domain

So far, we've been working in the WebLogic Workshop samples domain. Now let's create our own domain to work in. The easiest way to create a new WebLogic Workshop domain is by using the Configuration Wizard (which is started from the Start menu). We need to create a basic WebLogic Workshop domain. For more information about how to create a domain, please see Appendix A, "Quick Reference for Creating New Domains for WebLogic Development."

Listing 30.18 shows the basic settings you need to use when creating the new Workshop domain using the Configuration Wizard as described in Appendix A.

LISTING 30.18 Settings for MyWorkshopDomain

```
Domain Name:     MyWorkshopDomain
Server Type:     Single Server (Standalone Server)
Domain Template Name: WebLogic Workshop
Server Name:     myServer
Install Directory:  d:\bea\user_projects\domains\MyWorkshopDomain
Listen Address:    localhost and primary IP address
Listen Port:     7001
SSL Listen Port:   7002
Windows Start Menu:  yes
User Name:      weblogic
Password:       *******
```

Setting Up Our Environment

In addition to creating a WebLogic domain, we're also going to create a database, a JDBC connection pool, and a JDBC data source for this domain. We're going to use the PointBase engine that ships with WebLogic Server. We'll also create a database for our use.

1. First, start the PointBase engine. This can be done by running the `startPointBase.cmd` file in the `BEA_HOME\weblogic81\common\bin` directory. You'll probably want to create a desktop icon if you plan to run this command often.
2. Then you need to start the PointBase Console. From the Start menu, choose BEA WebLogic Platform 8.1→Examples→WebLogic Server 8.1→Server Tour and Examples→PointBase Console.
3. When the PointBase Console starts, enter the information shown in Figure 30.22. The default username and password are `PBPUBLIC` (uppercase).
4. Make sure that Create New Database or Overwrite Existing Database is checked.

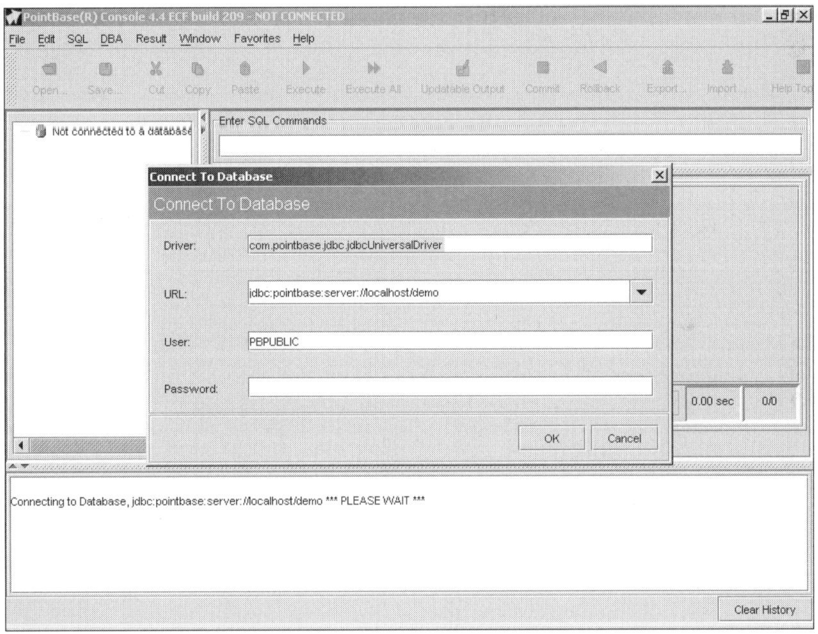

FIGURE 30.22 Enter this information to create the books database.

This will create a new database called books in the `WL_HOME\weblogic81\common\eval\pointbase\databases\` directory. Let's now copy the SQL found in the `bookddl.txt` file on the accompanying CD, and enter it into the PointBase console, as shown in Figure 30.23. Then execute the SQL by pressing F5 or selecting SQL→Execute All. This will create a Book table and load it with three books. You can now close the PointBase Console, but keep the PointBase engine running.

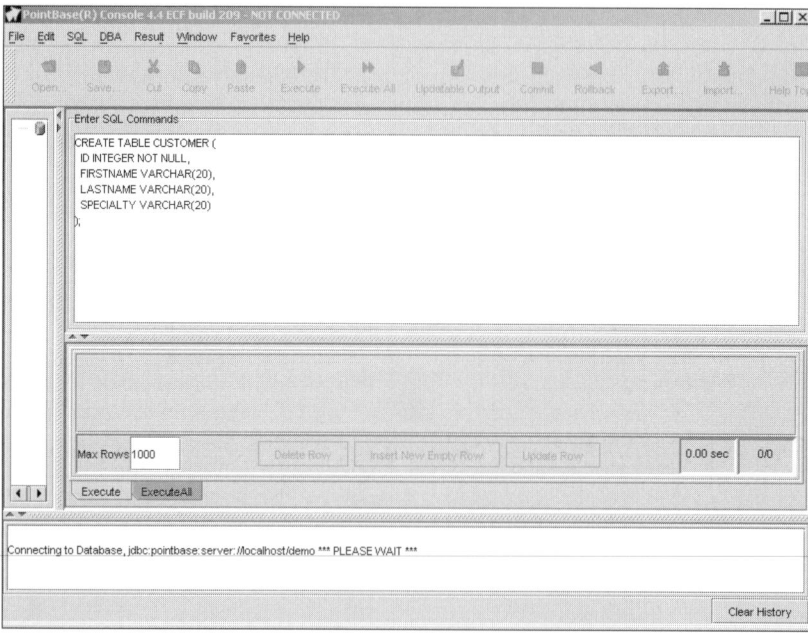

FIGURE 30.23 Place the SQL in the PointBase Console and execute it.

Now we need to create a JDBC connection pool and data source. Start WebLogic in the `MyWorkshopDomain` domain. There should be a menu item on the Start menu for this under BEA WebLogic Platform 8.1→User Projects. After WebLogic Server has started, open the console and create a JDBC connection pool with the information in Listing 30.19. Also set the pool to support local transactions. For more information about creating JDBC connection pools and data sources, please refer to Chapter 10, "Managing Database Connectivity Using JDBC."

You could also do this through the Configuration Wizard. If you choose to do it this way, please see Appendix A.

LISTING 30.19 Attributes for the Books Connection Pool

```
Name: Books Connection Pool
URL: jdbc:pointbase:server://localhost/servicesdb
Driver Classname: com.pointbase.jdbc.jdbcUniversalDriver
Properties (Line 1): user=PBPUBLIC
Properties (Line 2): password=PBPUBLIC
```

Now create a Tx data source with the information in Listing 30.20. For both the connection pool and the data source, make sure that you target `myServer`.

LISTING 30.20 Attributes for the Books Data Source

```
Name: Books Data Source
JNDI Name: BooksDS
Pool Name: Books Connection Pool
```

Configuring WebLogic Workshop for Our Domain

Out of the box, WebLogic Workshop is configured to work with its sample domain. To change this, choose Tools, Application Properties. The Preferences window will open. Click on the WebLogic Server tab. You'll see the current values for connecting to WebLogic Server.

To point WebLogic Workshop to `MyWorkshopDomain`, change the Server Home directory setting to `WL_HOME\user_projects\domains\MyWOrkshopDomain` or wherever the parent directory of `MyWorkshopDomain` is located. Set the other settings to match Figure 30.24. You're now ready to create a new application.

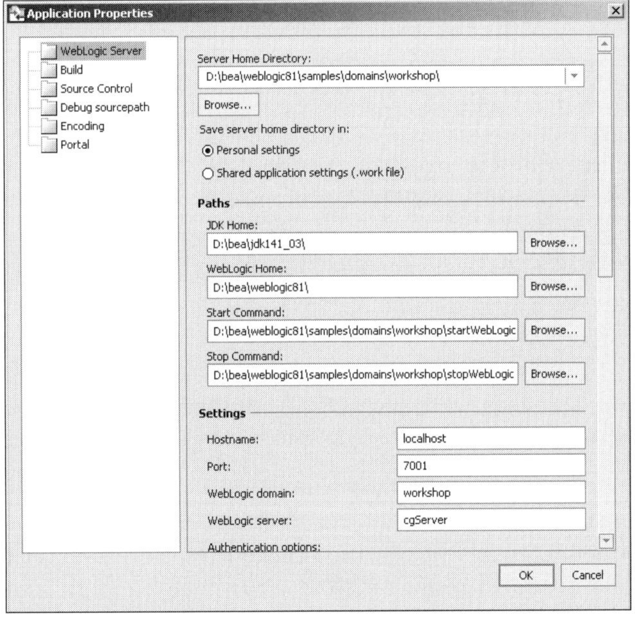

FIGURE 30.24 Application properties.

Creating a New WebLogic Workshop Application

Now that we've configured WebLogic Workshop to work with our new domain. To create a new application, do:

1. First, close the current application by choosing File, Close Application.
2. Then create a new application by choosing File, New Application and entering **`MyApplication`** for the application name.
3. Select the new domain `MyWorkshopDomain`, and then click on Create.
4. We now have a new application, but we also need a project. Select File→New→Project. Select the Web Service Project, enter **`MyWebServices`** for the project name, and click the Create button. This will create a Web application named `MyWebServices` in `MyWorkshopDomain`. This also will be the base `contextURI` for the Web Services created in this project.
5. The Create New File window will appear. Let's go ahead and create a new Web Service. Select Web Service and enter **`BookInfo`**.

Working with WebLogic Workshop Controls

WebLogic Workshop introduces the concept of Web Service controls. Controls allow access to external resources, such as databases and EJBs, and take care of most of the implementation details. In this way, we can access those resources without needing intimate knowledge of J2EE, such as JDBC, JMS, and EJB APIs. WebLogic Workshop currently ships with dozens of controls, including the following:

- Database control—Used to access an existing JDBC data source.
- Web Service control—Used to access an external Web Service.
- EJB control—Used to access an existing EJB.
- JMS control—Used to access an existing JMS destination.
- Timer control—Used to invoke an action on a regular scheduled basis.
- J2CA Adapter control—Used to access Enterprise Information Systems (EIS) using JCA adapters. You must have WebLogic Integration installed to utilize this control.

Working with the Database Control

The BookInfo Web Service will have a method called `getBookForSubject` that returns all books in the previously created Books data source that match a given subject. First, let's add a database control.

1. Open the Design View, and in the Data Palette, click on the Add drop-down field and choose Database Control.

2. Add the information for the fields shown in Figure 30.25. Name the control bookDB. Enter **`BookDatabaseControl`** as the JCX file.

3. Clicking the Browse button brings up a window with all defined JDBC data sources in WebLogic Server (if it is running). If WebLogic Server is not currently running, a window is displayed that asks if you would like WebLogic Server to start running.

4. After you've entered the values, click the Create button.

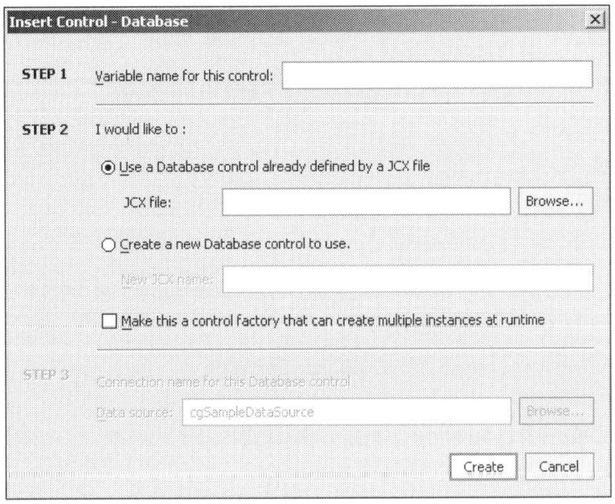

FIGURE 30.25 Enter the database control information.

You've just created a `bookDB` database control, as shown in the Design View. You've also created a new class, called `BookDatabaseControl`, and a variable called `bookDB` of that type. Click on the Source View tab to confirm this. Also notice that the Project Tree now includes the `BookDatabaseControl.jcx` file. This file holds the control's available operations. This control also can be used with other Web Services. You can double-click on the filename to edit the control's source code. You can also edit the control's properties with the Properties Editor in the Design View. The database control will return book information to us. We would like to have this information available in a Java class called `Book`.

Creating the Inner Book Class

One step toward accomplishing this is by creating an inner class called `Book`. This class must extend `Serializable` and have a no-argument constructor. The members' names are important and must match the database fields. Enter the code as shown in Figure 30.26.

Adding the getBooksForSubject Method

Now that we have defined the `Book` class, we can create a method on `bookDB` that returns a set of books that match our criteria. From the Design View, right-click on the `bookDB` control and choose Add Method from the menu. Call the method `getBooksForSubject` and press Enter. The arrow to the right of the `getBooksForSubject` method represents the

SQL query of the method. Right-click on the arrow and choose Edit SQL. Enter the information as shown in Figure 30.27.

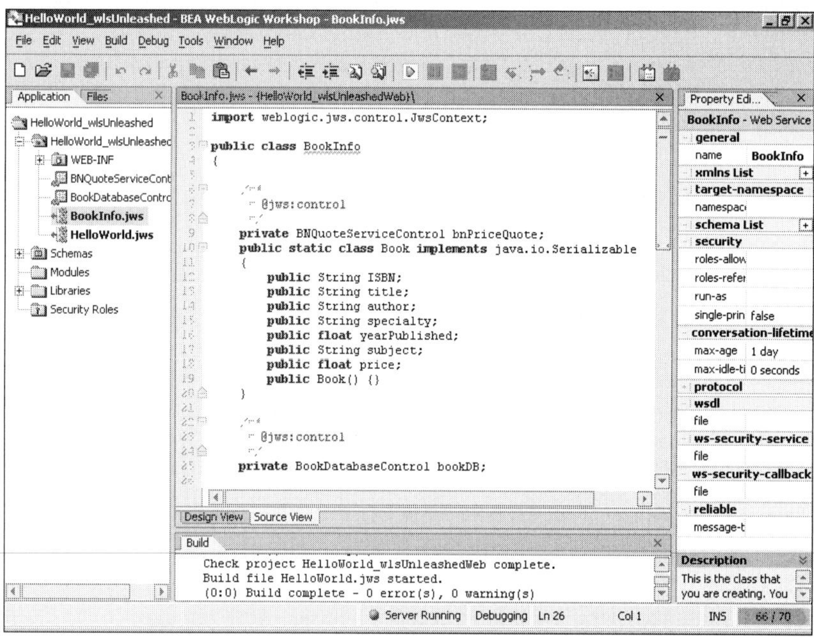

FIGURE 30.26 Inner Book class.

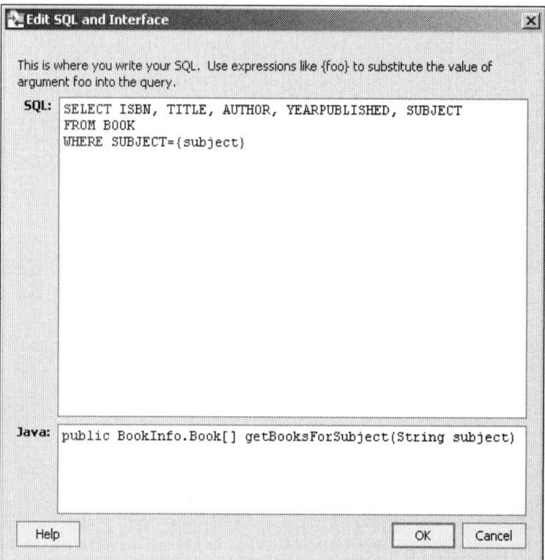

FIGURE 30.27 Enter this information for the SQL and the Java fields.

The method signature has been changed to accept a parameter named `subject` and to return an array of `BookInfo.Books`. Because `Book` is an inner class, we refer to it in this way. The WebLogic Workshop runtime will match column names in the `Book` table with field names in the `Book` class by default. A custom XML mapper can be used to alter this behavior.

The SQL will return books where the `SUBJECT` column is equal to the `subject` parameter. Notice that the `WHERE` clause contains `{subject}`. The curly braces specify that the subject parameter value will be placed in the `WHERE` clause when constructing the SQL to send to the data source. This gives us a dynamic way of generating SQL.

Connecting to the Database Control

We now need to add a Web Service operation that will invoke the `getBooksForSubject` database method. Go back to the `BookInfo` document. From the Design View, right-click and choose Add Method. Name this method `showBooks`. Click on the showBooks link and you will be transferred to Source View with the cursor in the `showBooks` method. Change the `showBooks` method to match the code in Listing 30.21. Here we accept a subject and return an array of `Book` objects. We pass the subject on to the `bookDB` control and then return the array of books.

LISTING 30.21 The New Look of showBooks()

```
/**
 * @jws:operation
 */
public BookInfo.Book[] showBooks(String subject)
{
  return bookDB.getBooksForSubject(subject);
}
```

Save the project and test it by selecting Debug, Start. This will bring up the Test View. Go to the Test Form page and test the `showBooks` method. Enter a subject with the value **`INSPIRATIONAL`**, **`BUSINESS`**, or **`FANTASY`** to retrieve an actual book. You will notice that the price is always zero.

Working with the Service Control

Another very useful control is the service control. This control allows our Web Service to invoke another Web Service. Notice that our `Book` class contains a price field, but that we do not have a price column in the database. Instead, we're going to use a Web Service to get the current book price from Barnes & Noble (see `http://www.barnesandnoble.com`). One way to do this is to utilize an existing Web Service found in a UDDI registry.

XMethods is a UDDI registry found at `http://www.xmethods.com`. It contains a plethora of active Web Services that can be used. One of these is the Barnes and Noble Price Quote.

The WSDL for this Web Service is located at `http://www.xmethods.com/sd/2001/BNQuoteService.wsdl`.

In the Design View of WebLogic Workshop, right-click and select Add Control→Add Web Service. Enter the values for the fields in Figure 30.28. Name the control `bnPriceQuote`. Notice that the preceding WSDL URL is entered into the File or URL field. Click the Create button.

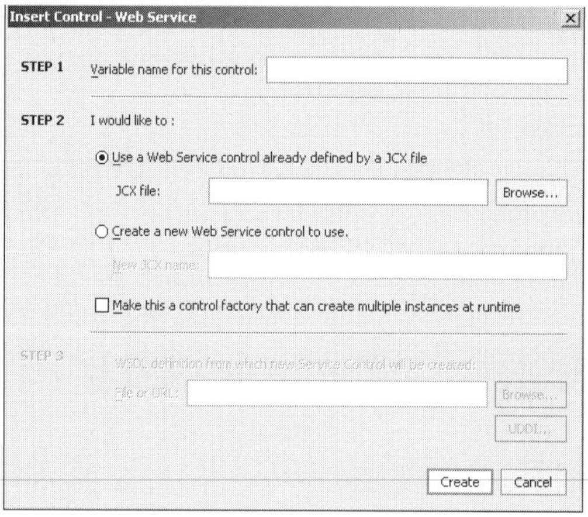

FIGURE 30.28 Enter this information for the Web Service.

You'll now see the `bnPriceQuote` service control on the Design View with a `getPrice` method on the left of it. The WebLogic Workshop runtime retrieved the WSDL file, made a local copy, parsed it, and created a method for every operation found in it. Click on `getPrice` and the document structure will display information about this method. Select `bnPriceQuote` and you should see `getPrice(java.lang.String isbn)`. This indicates that the method expects an ISBN number for the book whose price we are looking for.

Let's call the `getPrice` method from our Web Service operation. Click on the showBooks link and edit the `showBooks` method to match Listing 30.22. After we get our list of books from the database control, we go through each one and get the price from the Barnes and Noble Price Quote service. We place this information back in the `book` object. Now, when you test this Web Service, you'll see actual price information from the Barnes & Noble book catalog. In practice, if we were dealing with many books, we would like to get price information in a bulk method rather than one by one. This design is useful for learning about service controls, but it should not be used in production where many Web Service requests would be generated and the performance of the operation would suffer.

LISTING 30.22 Change showBooks to Utilize the Barnes & Noble Price Information

```
public BookInfo.Book[] showBooks(String subject)
{
  BookInfo.Book[] books = bookDB.getBooksForSubject(subject);

  for(int ii=0; ii<books.length; ii++) {
   Book book = books[ii];
   float price = bnPriceQuote.getPrice(book.ISBN);
   book.price = price;
  }

  return books;
}
```

Using the Debugger

WebLogic Workshop has a built-in debugger and gives the developer the ability to set breakpoints, inspect variables, and change source code on the fly.

1. To set a breakpoint, go to Source View, and click on the left margin of a line of executable code.
2. Then click the little green arrow on the toolbar or select Debug, Start.
3. The Test View will display as normal. Enter parameter values in the Test Form page and press the button named for the method being tested.

   When the WebLogic Workshop runtime reaches your breakpoint, the WebLogic Workshop window will display and the operation will be suspended at the breakpoint, as shown in Figure 30.29.

You can now inspect and modify variables in the debugging windows at the bottom of the screen. The Debug menu shows the options for continuing execution, and stepping into, over, and out of lines of code. Being able to inspect and modify server-side source code and its variables is very powerful and should make the Web Service development process less painful.

Other WebLogic Workshop Features

In addition to the capabilities discussed in this chapter, WebLogic Workshop and the runtime framework offers additional features. Following is a list of some of these:

- Conversational Web Services—The capability to persist client state over a certain number of Web Service operations. This information is held in Entity EJBs that are created and maintained by the WebLogic runtime without any coding required.

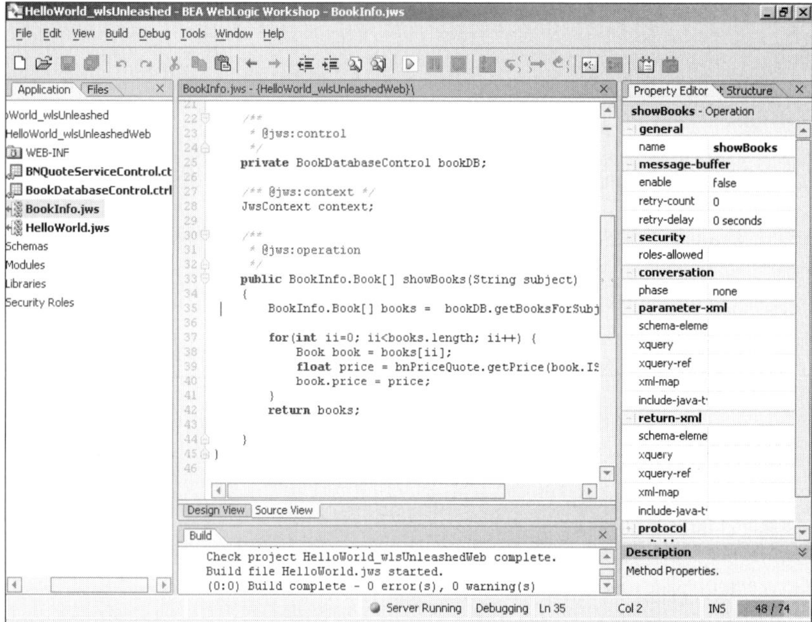

FIGURE 30.29 Invoking a Web Service from Workshop.

- Buffer operations—The capability to save client requests in a JMS message queue to safeguard against server failures and to accelerate processing. These queues are created and maintained by the WebLogic runtime without any coding required.
- Asynchronous operations—The capability to issue a callback to a Web Service client when an operation has completed, rather than immediately, which can be very useful for long-running operations and for event notifications.
- Custom control creation—Third-party software vendors can create their own controls to plug into their GUI and runtime framework. You can also create your own controls.
- Custom XML mapping—The ability to make complex XML data types correspond to Java class attributes, using JavaScript code to manipulate the conversion of Java to and from XML.

For more information about WebLogic Workshop, please visit `http://e-docs.bea.com/workshop/docs81/index.html`.

Web Services Best Practices

This section offers some practical tips on technologies and processes to utilize when designing, implementing, and deploying Web Services.

> **TIP**
>
> You can read several other best practices for Web Services at `http://www-106.ibm.com/developerworks/views/webservices/articles.jsp?sort_order=desc&expand=&sort_by=Date&show_abstract=true&view_by=Search&search_by=Best+practices`.
>
> A good book on design patterns for Web Services is the new Paul Monday book: *Web Services Patterns: Java Edition* (ISBN: 1590590848).

Debugging Flag

If your Web Services are generating errors, it's quite useful to inspect the SOAP request and response messages for them. In many cases, this will lead you to the cause of the problem. The WebLogic Server Web Service architecture has the capability to print SOAP request and response messages to a command prompt. This can be performed at the server and/or the client. Add the flag `-Dweblogic.webservice.verbose=true` to the startup script for your client application (when using the WebLogic Server –generated proxy) or WebLogic Server. Be aware that this should be done only in the development phase of your project because of the loss in performance that results from the overhead involved in printing these debugging messages.

Ensure Interoperability

A client of a Web Service should be able to effectively access and communicate with that Web Service regardless of the language it was written in and no matter what hardware and operating system it is running on. To ensure this, keep up to date with Web Service technologies such as SOAP and WSDL, and avoid proprietary vendor extensions that do not follow these standards. The purpose of the Web Services Interoperability Organization is to track the interoperability of different Web Service implementations. Please visit its Web site at `http://www.ws-i.org/`. The SOAPBuilders Interoperability Lab, found at `http://www.xmethods.com/ilab/`, provides interoperability testing for different SOAP implementations.

Code for Failure

When your Web Service relies on other Web Services for processing, there is a probability that the external Web Service will not work as expected in the future. Be sure that you use `try/catch` blocks and appropriate business logic to recover gracefully from these errors.

Reduce the Amount of Network Overhead

Although your Web Service can call many other Web Services, which can then in turn call a multitude of others, the amount of network overhead involved can be prohibitively large for clients waiting for a response—especially synchronous clients. Try to reduce network overhead by executing business processes locally whenever possible.

Become More Familiar with Web Service Technologies

There are many technologies that Web Services are dependent on, such as SOAP, XML schemas, WSDL, UDDI and more. Become familiar with them as well as the WebLogic technologies, such as the `web-services.xml` file, the WebLogic Ant tasks, and the WebLogic Workshop runtime framework. For a complete list of Web Services technologies supported in WebLogic Server, please refer to `http://dev2dev.bea.com/technologies/webservices/standards.jsp`.

Summary

Although still in their infancy, Web Services are poised to revolutionize the way software is written in the future. Web Services' potential for ubiquitous access makes an extremely compelling argument for lowered transaction and software development costs.

WebLogic Server 8.1 offers tremendous support in building, implementing, debugging, deploying, and securing Web Services. By building on the J2EE infrastructure, Web Services running in WebLogic Server enjoy extensive scalability, reliability, and security.

In this chapter, we discussed these features and demonstrated how a simple Web Services can be written, deployed, and tested using WebLogic Workshop.

Application developers can enjoy the ease of use with WebLogic Workshop and the runtime framework, whereas enterprise developers can take pleasure in the power of WebLogic Server's Ant tasks and the flexibility of creating Web Services by hand.

In the next chapter, we will discuss the Java Connector Architecture that allows applications running in WebLogic Server to communicate with and leverage the functionality found in Enterprise Information Systems (EIS).

CHAPTER 31

Legacy Integration with the J2EE Architecture

By Steve Steffen and Mark Artiges

IN THIS CHAPTER

- The J2EE Connector Architecture and the J2EE Platform
- WebLogic's Java Connector Architecture Defined
- J2EE Connector Architecture and the Enterprise
- Working with Java Connector Architecture Components
- Security Concerns
- Transaction Management
- Configuring WebLogic J2EE CA
- Writing Resource Adapters
- Packaging and Deployment Issues
- J2EE Connector Architecture Example

As companies embrace the concept of e-business, one of the most challenging tasks they face is reconciling the new business model with the existing legacy systems that they already have in place. Existing enterprise information systems (EISs) must become Web-aware and accessible for any true enterprise-based e-business initiative to have a real chance at being a success. The compelling possibility of real-time collaboration with partners and suppliers that B2B (business to business) e-commerce solutions brings to the table promises to contribute to a company's bottom line. In today's competitive marketplace, where customers crave immediacy along with exceptional service, such integration efforts are not merely nice to have but represent a real necessity. The challenge is providing this synergy across the heterogeneous platforms that typically exist. Failing this, companies run the real risk of falling behind their competition.

A company whose entire business information system is provided by a single vendor would be an oddity. The norm is an in-house assortment of best-of-breed enabling technologies that have evolved over time. Integrating them has always been a sore point. These legacy systems, collectively known as EISs, must be linked to application servers that stand between them, the Internet, and their customers.

Adding to the problem is the fact that when most application servers connect to EIS systems, they do so in a proprietary manner. A huge amount of effort—not to mention cost—is required to develop customized access mechanisms to each of these systems. That is precisely the problem the J2EE Connector Architecture addresses and what this chapter is about. The J2EE Connector Architecture is a specification, contained within the J2EE 1.3 platform, which defines a standard architecture for integrating heterogeneous EISs.

In this chapter, we'll explore this new Sun Microsystems—provided technology and the advantages it affords. We'll look at the overall architecture and its place within Sun's J2EE platform. We'll go over its role as an EAI (enterprise application integration) tool and how it makes possible seamless connectivity in the enterprise.

The J2EE Connector Architecture is a standard heavily based on the notion of a contract existing between a calling party and a receiver. There are system-level contracts, connection management contracts, transaction management contracts, security management contracts, and so on. Each of the contracts will be defined and understood as it exists in relation to the others.

As always, there are security concerns when integrating between systems. We'll learn about the extensive mechanisms that the J2EE Connector Architecture provides in this area as well.

The core of the J2EE Connector Architecture standard is realized in the implementation of what is known as a *resource adapter*. These software-adapter drivers are where much of the specification is implemented. We'll finish the chapter by spending an ample amount of time on the design, implementation, and deployment of these adapters.

The J2EE Connector Architecture and the J2EE Platform

The J2EE Connector Architecture is a specification contained within a much broader specification, known as Sun Microsystems' J2EE platform. It's important to understand exactly where the J2EE Connector Architecture fits within this larger scheme, especially in the area of component containers. J2EE specifies the use of containers to house elements. Client applications, servlets, JavaServer Pages (JSPs), Enterprise JavaBeans (EJBs), and resource adapters are all held in containers. The containers provide deployment and runtime support to the components residing within them. J2EE provides different kinds of containers depending on the type of support that the elements within them require. There are *Web containers* that host JSPs, servlets, and static HTML pages, *EJB containers* for EJBs, and *application client containers* that host standalone application clients. With the advent of the Java Connector Architecture, J2EE-compliant application servers have extended their support to include resource adapters that are hosted in *connector containers*. The containers themselves run in the context of an application server that provides additional transaction support. They can be monitored and administered through WebLogic Server's Administration Console.

The Java Connector Architecture, being a Sun Microsystems–proposed solution from its inception, was designed to draw heavily on the supporting infrastructure of the J2EE platform. It is built on top of and is intended to complement the J2EE specification—not to compete with it. The Java Connector Architecture fills a void that had heretofore been unaddressed by Sun. Issues related to integration with existing EIS systems were a notable omission from the original J2EE specification. The Java Connector Architecture remedies this by building on the component model and transaction and security infrastructures as they currently exist in the J2EE platform. From the beginning, BEA has sat on the expert group responsible for the Java Community Process associated with the development of this standard along with Sun, IBM, iPlanet, Netscape, Oracle, Motorola, and a few others. WebLogic's own implementation of the J2EE Connector Architecture standard represents a pure Java solution to the problem of EIS integration.

So far, there seems to be a wide acceptance for this technology. It has been adopted by many infrastructure vendors as a core part of their platforms and in some cases as their main solution for tying together Web-based and legacy systems. Some of the vendors incorporating the Java Connector Architecture into their product lines include BEA, iPlanet, SilverStream, IBM WebSphere, Oracle, Allaire, Borland, and HP.

WebLogic's Java Connector Architecture Defined

The J2EE Connector Architecture establishes a standard universal mechanism for connecting the J2EE platform to heterogeneous EISs. (see Figure 31.1). It relies on a series of interrelated contracts to establish connectivity between a J2EE-compliant application server and a legacy enterprise management system.

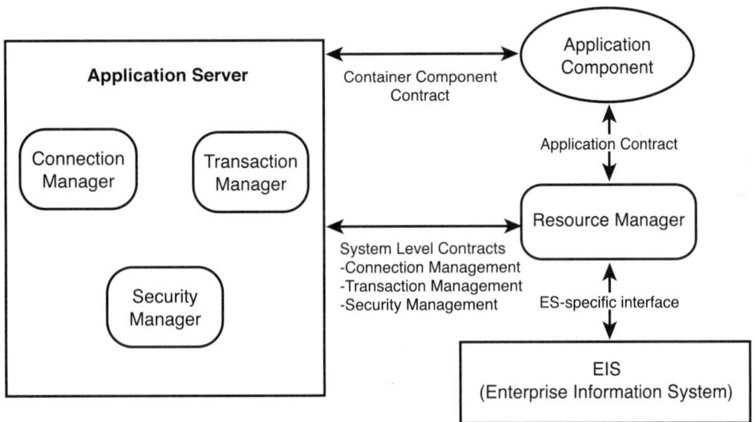

FIGURE 31.1 The Java Connector Architecture.

WebLogic's implementation of the J2EE Connector Architecture standard provides a pure Java solution to the problem of connectivity between WebLogic's application server and an EIS. By using the J2EE Connector Architecture's uniform API, EIS vendors no longer have to continually customize their products to accommodate the inherent idiosyncrasies found in each J2EE application server on the market. After a connectivity solution has been developed for one application server, it should in theory work on any other application server that supports the standard. For example, a J2EE Connector Architecture resource adapter developed to enable access to an ERP (enterprise resource planning) application in conjunction with WebLogic should be able to plug into a WebSphere J2EE-compliant application server without modification. Portability across heterogeneous application server environments is thus ensured.

By conforming to the J2EE Connector Architecture standard, BEA WebLogic does not require added custom code to extend its support connectivity to different EISs. No matter what the targeted system, the API to access it is neutral. The Connector Architecture enables an EIS vendor to provide a standard resource adapter for its EIS. The resource adapter plugs into WebLogic Server and provides the underlying infrastructure for the integration between an EIS and WebLogic Server. By supporting the Connector Architecture, BEA WebLogic Server is assured of connectivity to multiple EISs. In turn, EIS vendors need provide only a single standard Connector Architecture–compliant resource adapter that has the capability to plug into BEA WebLogic Server.

NOTE

BEA WebLogic Server 8.1 is completely compliant with the J2EE Java Connector Architecture specification along with J2EE 1.3, and is backward compatible with J2EE 1.2 as well.

J2EE Connector Architecture and the Enterprise

Connecting disparate EIS systems throughout the enterprise is a lofty goal indeed. It's fraught with the kind of complex problems that can always be found in the integration of incompatible interfaces. The J2EE Connector Architecture attempts to untangle this web through mechanisms of standardization.

What Is an EIS?

Just exactly what is an EIS system? When we speak of EIS systems, we're usually talking about the core applications that a business runs on. They often have a long-standing history with a company and represent a significant part of the IT budget. Over time, a great deal of effort is spent in their customization and fine-tuning in order to tailor them to a particular organization's needs. A significant investment has been made in their implementation and deployment and in the personnel required to maintain them with the hope that they will provide a competitive advantage in the marketplace. More often than not, they've become so entrenched that the thought of replacing them just isn't a viable option. Known projects of rewriting EIS systems have cost millions, shipped late, or never ship at all because the deployment phase was too complex. Another argument against rewriting an EIS is, "Why fix it if it's not broken?" Claims that EIS system doesn't integrate well or uses an older technology are not heavy enough in the scale to warrant rewriting large amounts of well-functioning code.

Some types of systems that could be classified as EIS systems are Oracle ERP (Enterprise Resource Planning) Financials, IBM CICS and IBM IMS applications, SAP R/3, PeopleSoft, J.D. Edwards, CRM (Customer Relationship Management), and Supply Chain Management to name a few.

Although each of these applications is full-featured and offers extensive services and advantages in its own right, they tend to be isolated. The application exists as an island in and of itself. Integration options with other platforms are not readily available; when they are available, they invariably come in a proprietary fashion. External applications wanting to connect to these EIS systems must endure a complex, labor-intensive effort in the manual creation of customized adapters.

Implications for Enterprise Application Integrators

Seizing on yet another opportunity to add value, some system integrators have specialized in an area known as EAI (enterprise application integration). These vendors provide tools to simplify the process of application integration, albeit still in a vendor-specific fashion. Each offers its own proprietary adapters built to work with its own products, which allow for synchronous and asynchronous communication between EISs. With each of these products, data must be translated between the native formats found across systems. This data mapping represents the most time-consuming aspect of system integration because complex business objects must be painstakingly mapped between applications. EAI vendors provide visual tools to aid developers in this process. Their products typically supply message brokers, which enable point-to-point and publish/subscribe messaging. Messaging is often the core mechanism used to provide connectivity between heterogeneous systems.

The J2EE Connector Architecture in no way conflicts with the work being done by EAI vendors. From the onset of the formation of the standard, the intent has always been to aid EAI initiatives, not to supplant them. In the "Working with Java Connector Architecture Components" section of this chapter, we learn about the Common Client Interface (CCI), which defines a standard low-level client API for accessing EIS resource adapters. The goal of this API has always been to provide a least common denominator, base-level API that is available to all EAI vendors in the hope of finally achieving some base level of standard interoperability between them. EAI vendors are expected to build out the API, but a great deal of work is still left to be done. They're looked upon to deliver on a more full-featured interface for application developers who desire quick and easy access to EIS resources. EAI vendors will continue to add value to the proposition in areas such as data mapping, message brokering, workflow, and user interface integration.

Business-to-Business e-Marketplaces

Companies are increasingly looking for better ways to integrate their information systems to more effectively collaborate with suppliers and partners over the Web. Early out-of-the box B2B (business-to-business) initiatives were quick to market but lacked the real-time access to legacy systems that true complex e-business solutions demand. Opening up access to the information repositories of a company allows for real-time availability of goods and services. This makes Internet-based B2B propositions very compelling for companies because they open up new opportunities that simply have not existed before.

For example, a widget supplier (see Figure 31.2) can dial up over the Internet through a common browser (which one could argue is already as ubiquitous as the telephone) and, with proper authentication, in seconds tie directly into a company's mainframe data. The client can communicate via universally recognized protocols of XML over HTTP to access a WebLogic application server–hosted JSP. In turn, the JSP calls an Enterprise JavaBean through a middle-tier servlet, caching information garnered from an EIS system exposed though a standard resource adapter. This loosely coupled configuration achieves the connectivity sought after, while respecting the lines of demarcation that typically exists between systems. Adopting such an e-market approach breathes new life into aging legacy systems. The significant investment already made in this area can be leveraged substantially.

Deployment costs in establishing relationships with new suppliers are next to nothing. Orders are fulfilled in real-time. This has huge implications for just-in-time manufacturing, inventory control, and the overall cost of doing business.

The ramifications of seizing on this technology are tempting because after a company's information systems become accessible across any geographic boundary, the company's reach in effect becomes global.

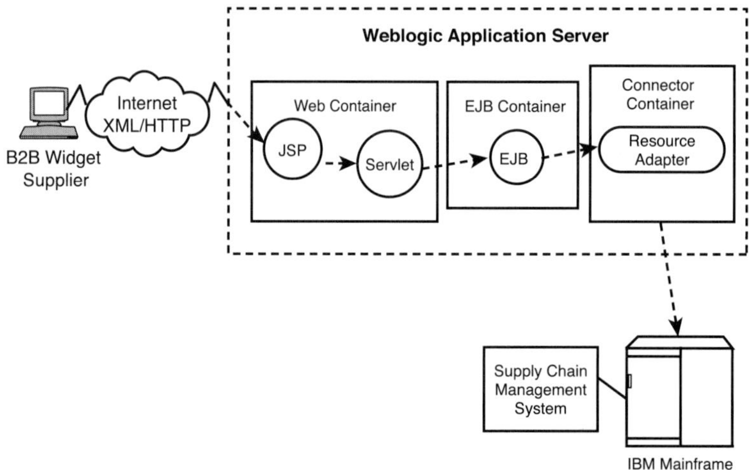

FIGURE 31.2 B2B e-commerce connectivity.

Challenges Facing the J2EE Connector Architecture

So far, this all sounds too good to be true. However, it's important to keep in mind that the J2EE Connector Architecture is by no means a mature standard at this point. And although it does have considerable momentum behind it and promises to be a unifying force, the one drawback that does exist can be found in the fact that the J2EE Connector Architecture is still a standard provided by a single vendor. As with all emerging standards, only time will tell how complete its ultimate acceptance will become.

Full-featured enterprise information systems offer an enormous amount of functionality and services to companies. The degree of feature availability they contain is directly proportional to the complexity of their overall system design. Internally, these systems can be quite complex. Behind the scenes, performance and high availability are achieved through custom optimization and proprietary designs. The programming models used vary widely across different EISs and elements of transaction and security management are particularly unique.

All this makes integration efforts all the more difficult. It's critical that proven application development tools be continually upgraded and enhanced beyond the base standard that the J2EE Connector Architecture offers to ease the tasks associated with enterprise system integration.

It is a given that for any API to effectively mask lower level EIS connection mechanisms from view, a certain amount of overhead must be incurred. However, Web applications demand speed and must be able to scale to a large number of concurrent users, all vying for the same resources managed by the EIS system. Any undue latency at the application level will not sit well with customers.

Working with Java Connector Architecture Components

The Java Connector Architecture is comprised of a number of components. Let's take a look at each of them here.

Resource Adapters

The central component of the Java Connector Architecture is the resource adapter or driver. It serves as the main point of contact between a WebLogic application server the EIS systems and client applications. It plays a pivotal role in providing the system-level software driver used by WebLogic to access an EIS. The driver itself lives within the address space of the WebLogic application server. The system-level contracts, connection management contract, transaction management contract, and security management contract are all implemented by the resource adapter. The application contract is fulfilled by the Common Client Interface between the application component and the resource adapter. There is also a system contract, fulfilled by the system-level programming interface, between the resource adapter and the application server. This includes the management of connections, security, and transactions.

A uniform resource adapter is a huge benefit for EIS vendors because they now need only to write to a single API that supports one standard resource adapter. The adapter can then be plugged into any J2EE-compliant application server. Vendors no longer need to customize their product to be supported by different J2EE servers.

The benefit for J2EE application vendors is that only one method of communication is required for all EISs. The complexity of the integration problem is thus exponentially simplified. The application API known as the System-level Programming Interface (SPI) includes support for connection management, transaction management, and security.

The benefit for application programs is that they can use the same resource adapter. This part of the J2EE Connector Architecture is known as the Common Client Interface. You might have one or more EISs that you want to use as the back end for your application. CCI enables you to seamlessly combine as many as you like into a single application that uses JSPs, servlets, and EJBs to communicate with them. A third part of the Connector Architecture is a standard deployment and packaging procedure for resource adapters.

System-Level Contracts

For an EIS resource adapter to conform with the Java Connector Architecture standard, it must adhere to the rules defined in the specification. Rules regarding connectivity between the application server and an EIS are set forth in the form of system-level contracts. The system-level contracts are

- Connection management contract
- Transaction management contract
- Security contract

The contracts define methods and procedures of communication between an application server and an EIS. Each contract commits the application server vendor and the EIS vendor providing the resource adapter to abide by the guidelines set forth in the connector specification portion of the J2EE Connector Architecture proposal. The guidelines themselves elaborate on the responsibilities that each side must address in order to maintain a uniform interface.

Connection Management

The connection management contract dictates that the resource adapter must take ownership of creating physical connections to the EIS. The application server is responsible for maintaining a managed pool of connections to the resources that the resource adapter exposes. Client applications establish connections via the pools provided by the application server to available resource adapter instances. An application server registers itself as a listener with the resource adapter to monitor events during the life of a connection. This is required for the application server to dynamically manage the connection pool.

Transaction Management

A transaction management contract exists between a transaction manager and an EIS. It is used by an application server to access the transaction manager. The transaction manager can then be used to manage transactions across multiple resource managers.

Security Management

A security management contract is defined to provide secure access to an EIS and to ensure a secure application environment. It guards against unauthorized access and security breaches that threaten the safety of the EIS as well as the information resources it manages and the clients that access them.

In this case as in others, the J2EE Connector Architecture fulfills its security management obligations by drawing on the larger J2EE standard of which it is a part. Authentication and authorization procedures are derived from JAAS (Java Authentication and Authorization Service). JAAS services are called on to enforce legitimate EIS access through JAAS references incorporated directly into the connection management interfaces.

Common Client Interface

The Common Client Interface (CCI) defines a standard low-level client API for accessing an EIS resource adapter. The API is primarily intended for use by EAI tools to provide a standard method of EIS access that they can conform to. The initial goal of the specification was for use by EIS vendors. It is intended that these vendors build on the base standard to provide a more full-featured interface for application developers. Because it serves as a standard across different EISs, it can be used as a means to span transactions across them.

CCI leverages the J2EE JavaBean architecture and Java Collection framework. It uses these components in the creation, management, and execution of connections with an EIS. The CCI itself has no EIS-specific implementations and thus can be used unchanged across any EIS that conforms to the J2EE Connector Architecture standard.

The CCI calls for a remote function call interface method of function execution to be used with an EIS. Its primary concerns are in dealing with the calling of remote EIS functions and interpreting their results. Data types bear the most glaring dissimilarity across EIS systems and account for the lion's share of development time during integration efforts. The CCI makes no EIS-specific distinctions on data types and marshals data types in a neutral fashion across disparate EISs. However, it can tie into EIS repositories containing metadata on local EIS data types and pass that information on to higher-level APIs to interpolate.

In addition, the Java Connector Architecture also defines a standard SPI (service provider interface) that permits access to a transactional resource manager from the transaction, security, and connection management facilities of the application server.

BEA-Supplied J2EE-CA Adapter Client Example

WebLogic 8.1 ships with a Java Connector Architecture example that's installed at `bea\weblogic81\samples\server\examples\src\examples\jconnector\simple`. Let's take a look at the key piece of Java code contained in this example, which is used to access the resource adapter:

```
private Connection getConnection() throws SQLException
{
  InitialContext initCtx = null;
  try {
    initCtx = new InitialContext();
    DataSource ds = (javax.sql.DataSource)
    initCtx.lookup("java:comp/env/eis/BlackBoxNoTx");
    return ds.getConnection();
  } catch(NamingException ne)
```

The example uses a resource adapter that is accessed via an EJB using JDBC in conjunction with the Black Box resource adapter from the Sun reference implementation. As you can see, a simple JDBC `getConnection` method wraps the adapter call that is made available via the JDBC connection pool configuration on the application server. This represents a seamless method of integrating with EIS resources.

Commercially Available J2EE-CA Adapters

A number of J2EE-CA adapters are currently available in the marketplace and are being used to great effect. Here's a brief list of some of the key vendors in the industry and the types of connectors they provide. In-depth information on individual solutions can be found at the following individual vendor Web site links:

- RAI provides resource adapters for SAP, Siebel, and PeopleSoft. `http://www.resourceadapters.com/php/_Products.php`
- Attunity Connect for BEA WebLogic offers certified adapters for legacy and mainframe systems. `http://www.attunity.com/data_integration/j2ee_adapter.htm`
- insevo provides a wide varity of connectors, including J.D. Edwards, Oracle, and SAP. `http://www.insevo.com/ibm.cfm`
- iWay supports more than 250 EISs, including Ariba, Lawson, and Clarify. `http://www.iwaysoftware.com/products/ibmproducts.html`
- LIBRADOS has adapters for Oracle Ebusiness, SAP R3, CICS, and MQSeries. `http://www.librados.com/products.php`

Security Concerns

The security contract ensures secure access to an EIS from application components. The contract itself incorporates the Java Authentication and Authorization Service into the connection management interfaces used by the resource adapter.

Security-Related Terms

Before going over the mechanisms of authentication available with WebLogic, we first need to define a number of security-related terms that are used extensively in the security contract. Authentication mechanisms make use of the following elements:

- Principals
- Credentials
- Subjects

Principal

A *principal* gives an entity an identity for the purposes of secure authentication in the enterprise. The methods and vehicles providing authentication can vary throughout the enterprise, but the principal itself can remain the same. An *initiating principal* is a security principal used by a client application interacting with a particular EIS. Through a generic credential interface, the embedded credentials of a principal can be retrieved and then used to authenticate the principal. For example, the resource adapter uses the credentials passed to it from the application server during the process of authentication. Security attributes are associated with a security principal. They provide information about the authentication and authorization mechanisms containing permissions and credentials.

Credential

A *credential* is provided by a subject and contains a reference to the security-related information used to authenticate a principal. Credentials are acquired during the authentication process or through what is called a *principal delegation*, where a principal grants another principal rights to use its credential. A Password credential class is used to wrap the username and password to be passed from the app server to the resource adapter. It has the get and set assessor methods to retrieve the username and password as well as `getManagedConnectionFactory` and `setManagedConnectionFactory` methods to specify the connection factory instance for which a username and password have been set up by the application server.

Subject

WebLogic Server bundles up security information into what is known as a *subject*. The subject contains the complete set of information required to describe an entity. It includes embedded principal and credential data that is passed by the WebLogic Server to the resource adapter for the purposes of authentication and authorization.

Before users are granted access to WebLogic Server–protected resources, they must provide a valid form of identification. Information identifying a particular user is passed to WebLogic Server in the form of a credential. Credentials may contain either a username and password or a digital certificate, which in turn are processed by one of the two types of authentication mechanisms supported by WebLogic Server.

Password Credential Mapping Mechanisms

The J2EE Connector Specification, Version 1.0 Final Release defines two types of credentials that resource adapters can use during the process of authentication:

- Generic credentials
- Password credentials

When using generic credentials, the `GenericCredential` interface defines how to access the security credentials of a principal. Through this interface, the resource adapter is able to retrieve the credentials passed from the application server.

When using password credentials, the `PasswordCredential` class is used to encapsulate a username and password, which is passed from the application server to the resource adapter. The class provides get methods for retrieving the values of the username and password. It also provides a `getManagedConnectionFactory` and a `setManagedConnectionFactory` that can be used to get or set the managed connection factory instance that WebLogic sets up for the username and password.

The security policy used by a resource adapter in accordance with the specification can be provided by the WebLogic Server runtime environment housing the resource adapter or within the resource adapter itself. In the latter scenario, WebLogic Server provides a standard method for deployed resource adapters to plug their own authorization and authentication mechanism into WebLogic's own storage mechanism.

WebLogic Authentication Mechanisms

Applications typically have to authenticate with an EIS before they can successfully connect and access the resources of the EIS. The J2EE Connector Architecture defines two types of authentication mechanisms for this purpose: password authentication and certificate authentication.

Password Authentication

With password authentication, the principal identification information of username and password are sent to WebLogic Server in clear text format. If so desired, this information can be encrypted through SSL or HTTPS protocol.

Certificate Authentication

With certificate authentication, an SSL or HTTPS client requests connections to WebLogic Server by presenting a digital certificate. In return, WebLogic Server presents its own digital certificate to the client. The client then verifies it and an SSL connection is established. The CertAuthenticator class is used to determine which WebLogic Server user owns the certificate. It does so by examining the provided digital certificate and then using this information to authenticate the user from the WebLogic Server security realm.

A mechanism known as mutual authentication is available as well. With mutual authentication, WebLogic Server requires authentication for itself and from the requesting client. Through this mechanism, access can be restricted to trusted clients who present a digital certificate issued by a trusted certificate authority.

Sign-on Mechanisms

WebLogic's implementation of the Java Connector Architecture supports both authentication schemes defined in the specification. They are

- Container-managed sign-on
- Application-managed sign-on

When a J2EE component is deployed, a reference element describing the type of authentication requested by the component lies within its deployment descriptor. Specifically, the resource-ref element declares the resources used by the component and the res-auth sub-element defines the chosen authentication method: container managed or application managed. WebLogic defaults to container-managed sign-on in the event it cannot determine the security mechanism chosen.

Container-Managed Sign-on

J2EE components often take advantage of different security providers and operate in different protection domains than the EIS systems they access. Under such conditions, the J2EE container in which the client resides can be configured to manage the authentication process on behalf of the client. This form of authentication is known as *container-managed resource manager sign-on*.

In the case of container-managed sign-on, the container provides security information to the resource adapter in the form of a resource principal, which is provided to the resource adapter wrapped as a JAAS subject. A *resource principal* is a security principal that references a security context in a session with an EIS. All sign-on information is handled by the container on behalf of the component. Here is a sample credential mapping:

```
<security-principal-map>
        -<map-entry>
                <initiating-principal>rauser</initiating-principal>
                <initiating-principal>unleashedclient</initiating-principal>
                -<resource-principal>
                      <resource-username>scott</resource-username>
                        <resource-password>tiger</resource-password>
                </resource-principal>
        </map-entry>
```

Application-Managed Sign-on

Under different circumstances, it might be important for a component to manage the process of authentication more directly. The Java Connector Architecture provides application-managed resource manager sign-on in these cases. In this scenario, the client application itself is able to manipulate the authentication details of the sign-on process. The WebLogic application server passes connection requests directly to the resource adapter in their unaltered state. The resource adapter then handles the call using the client-provided authentication information for sign-on to the EIS. In this scenario, security information is passed through the `getConnection` method of the connection factory encapsulated in a `ConnectionRequestInfo` object. A typical example of such an object is

```
public class customConnectionRequestInfo implements ConnectionRequestInfo {
  private String username;
  private String password;
  ...
}
```

Note that `ConnectionRequestInfo` is an empty interface used to pass the object references around the connector's framework.

Transaction Management

The capability to handle transactions is a key component in the J2EE Connector Architecture. Transaction management allows different operations to be performed independently, but the transactions are either all committed or all rolled back, keeping the integrity of the transaction intact. Database operations have incorporated this feature for many years, but the capability to allow transactions with EIS systems is a significant step in building applications that incorporate multiple systems. Unfortunately, not every resource adapter will support full two-phase commit protocol transactions. Each resource adapter specifies the level of transaction support available.

Transaction Support

WebLogic 8.1 incorporates three different transaction support levels based on the J2EE-CA 1.0 specification. In the section "Configuring Resource Adapters" later in this chapter, you'll see where to define these in the `ra.xml` file.

- None—No transaction support exists.
- Local support—Local support allows the resource adapter to manage its own transactions. This support level does not allow participation in two-phase commit protocol and is not compatible with any JTA/JTS transactions.
- XA support—XA support includes local support and is able to manage the transaction external to the resource adapter. This means that the resource adapter supports either one- or two-phase commit protocol and can take place in larger JTA/JTS transactions that require data integrity.

No Transaction Support

If a resource adapter does not support transactions, it cannot use any connections to the EIS in a transaction. If an application uses a resource adapter that doesn't support transactions and it needs to use a connection in a transaction, it has to interact through another resource manager that does contain transaction support.

Local Transaction Support

Local transactions are limited to the container. They can be managed locally by the resource adapter or by the container. However, they cannot take part in any two-phase transactions, including JTA/JTS. When an application component such as an EJB wants to connect to the EIS system, the application server starts a local transaction. When the component closes the connection, the application server performs a commit on the local transaction followed by a cleanup of the EIS connection. Local transactions use one-phase commit protocols or the interpretation of them based on the EIS implementation. To use local transactions when connecting to a resource adapter, simply get your transaction from a JNDI lookup, begin the transaction, and then either commit or roll it back. Here's an example:

```
Connection connection = null;
InitialContext initialcontext = new InitialContext();
ConnectionFactory connectionfactory =
            initialcontext.lookup("java:comp/YourConnectionFactory");
UserTransaction userTransaction =
(UserTransaction) initialcontext.lookup("java:comp/UserTransaction");
// start userTransaction
userTransaction.begin();
connection = connectionfactory.getConnection();
// do some work
// commit transaction
userTransaction.commit();
```

XA Transaction Support

XA transactions are managed externally to the resource adapter. If XA transactions are supported, the resource adapter must support both one- and two-phase commit protocols (one-phase commits are used for optimization purposes). When an application component makes a request to an EIS system, the application server lists the connection to the EIS system within the transaction manager. The entire transaction is maintained for the duration until it is committed or rolled back. If the connection is closed by the application component, the application server then unlists the EIS connection from the transaction and cleans up the underlying EIS connection. The resource adapter contains any of the proprietary needs of the EIS system and adheres to the J2EE Connector Architecture specification for XA transactions to implement the two-phase commit protocol.

If two-phase commits are allowed, the resource adapter and underlying resource manager must be JTA/JTS compliant and correctly implement the `XAResource` interface.

If the entire operation is contained within one resource manager, the application server can optimize the transaction by using a local transaction instead of a JTA/JTS transaction for performance reasons. To implement a XA transaction, the resource adapter must be XA transaction compliant. The code for demarcating the XA transaction looks exactly like that of the local transaction except for one detail: Two resource adapters are being called within one transaction instead of one. The transaction manager takes care of rolling back both transactions if they fail. In fact, the programmer does not even have access to the XA transaction objects. They're completely contained within the resource adapter. This includes any exceptions that are thrown along the way.

```
Connection connection1 = null;
Connection connection2 = null;
InitialContext initialcontext = new InitialContext();
ConnectionFactory connectionfactory1 =
 initialcontext.lookup("java:comp/YourConnectionFactory1");
 ConnectionFactory connectionfactory2 =
 initialcontext.lookup("java:comp/YourConnectionFactory2");
UserTransaction userTransaction =
(UserTransaction) initialcontext.lookup("java:comp/UserTransaction");
 // start userTransaction
 userTransaction.begin();
 connection1 = connectionfactory1.getConnection();
 connection2 = connectionfactory2.getConnection();
// do some work
// commit transaction
 userTransaction.commit();
```

Configuring WebLogic J2EE-CA

Configuring and deploying a resource adapter in WebLogic is a straightforward process. The end result is a special Java archive file called a *resource adapter archive* (`*.rar`), or RAR file for short. Each RAR file has all the classes needed for the resource adapter plus the configuration XML files `ra.xml` and the WebLogic-specific `weblogic-ra.xml`.

Resource Adapter Developer Tools

BEA makes several tools available for configuration and deployment of the J2EE-CA. Minimally, you need at least a text editor to modify or create the `ra.xml` and `weblogic-ra.xml` files. Although when you actually deploy the RAR file within WebLogic 8.1, it creates a `weblogic-ra.xml` file and puts that file in the RAR automatically. If you deploy the resource adapter expanded—meaning not in a RAR file but just a simple directory structure—you can edit the weblogic-ra.xml file from the console. After editing, simply click Apply at the bottom right of the screen, and the changes are updated and the resource adapter is redeployed.

When creating or modifying the ra.xml file, an XML editing tool is beneficial. WebLogic provides a XML editor: WebLogic Builder, which is included with WebLogic 8.1.

Configuring Resource Adapters

Resource adapters are meant to be configured and optimized for your intended application. Earlier in the chapter, the ra.xml and weblogic-ra.xml files were discussed. These two files hold the entire configuration for the resource adapter. When editing the configuration files, a few conventions must be followed. First, each tag has a corresponding end tag. Second, case should be followed not only in the name of the tag itself, but also in its value if needed. Finally, to use the default value of an optional element, omit the tags altogether or specify an empty value within the tags.

The file mandated to hold all the J2EE Adapter Architecture–specified configuration is called ra.xml. The DTD can be found at http://java.sun.com/dtd/connector_1_0.dtd.

Required Tags

The main element in a ra.xml file is the <connector></connector> element. All other elements are contained within these tags. For the connector to validate against the DTD, it must contain these five elements:

- <vendor-name>—This contains the name of the vendor supplying the resource adapter.
- <spec-version>—This contains the version of the J2EE Connector Architecture specification being used.
- <eis-type>—This contains the description information used to identify the EIS system that the resource adapter is connecting to.
- <version>—This contains the version of the resource adapter provided by the vendor.
- <resourceadapter>—This contains the all the information on the specific resource adapter, including fully qualified names of the classes or interfaces required as part of the J2EE Connector Architecture specification.

Optional Tags

Optionally, four other tags can be specified within the connector tags: display-name, description, icon, and license. The display-name and description tags are text tags that are for display in resource adapter tools. The icon tag specifies icons that can be displayed with the resource adapter. The license tag tells the user whether a license is required to be distributed with the resource adapter.

The resourceadapter Tag

The `resourceadapter` tag and associated subtags are most important in the configuration of the resource adapter. This tag specifies what classes the resource adapter uses for each of the required interfaces in the J2EE Connector Architecture specification, plus other required parameters. The following list describes the required tags:

- `<managedconnectionfactory-class>`—Contains the class that implements `javax.resource.spi.ManagedConnectionFactory` interface.
- `<connectionfactory-interface>`—Contains the `ConnectionFactory` interface that is supported by the resource adapter.
- `<connectionfactory-impl-class>`—Contains the class that implements the `<connectionfactory-interface>`.
- `<connection-interface>`—Contains the connection interface used by the adapter.
- `<connection-impl-class>`—Contains the class that implements the `<connection-interface>`.
- `<transaction-support>`—Contains the level of transaction support. Only three values are allowed: `NoTransaction`, `LocalTransaction`, and `XATransaction`.
- `<reauthentication-support>`—Contains either `true` or `false`, depending on whether the resource adapter allows re-authentication of a managed connection.

Optional tags that are included in the specification are as follows:

- `<config-property>`—Configuration properties that are loaded for the `ManagedConnectionFactory` class
- `<authentication-mechanism>`—Can optionally contain an authentication mechanism supported by the resource adapter
- `<security-permission>`—Specifies the security permission specified by the resource adapter

To learn more about the intricacies of the `ra.xml` file, information is available from Sun as part of the J2EE-CA specification located at `http://java.sun.com/j2ee/connector/download.html`.

WebLogic-Specific Configuration

The J2EE Connector Architecture forbids any extra configuration within the `ra.xml` file. To allow application server vendors the opportunity to fine-tune resource adapters, connector vendors must use an external configuration medium that can contain application server–specific information. WebLogic puts this information in the `weblogic-ra.xml` file. If the `weblogic-ra.xml` file does not exist, it is automatically generated when the resource adapter is deployed. The DTD can be found at `http://www.bea.com/servers/wls810/dtd/weblogic810-ra.dtd`.

The weblogic-ra.xml file has a root node labeled <weblogic-connection-factory-dd> and several configuration parameters, but only two that are required. The two required parameters are as follows:

- <connection-factory-name>—Defines the logical name of the specific resource adapter.
- <jndi-name>—Defines the JNDI name that points to the ConnectionFactory object used by the connector. WebLogic Server automatically creates a factory and binds it to this JNDI name at deployment time.

The optional parameters should be configured to optimize the needs of the intended application. The following is a list and a brief description of each parameter:

- <description>—A text description of or information about the deployed resource adapter.
- <ra-link-ref>—A mapping value that associates multiple connection factories with one deployed resource adapter.
- <native-libdir>—If native libraries are present for the deployment of a resource adapter, this tag specifies the directory that they should be placed in. It is required if there are native libraries.
- <pool-params>—This tag has several subtags that configure the connection pool handled by WebLogic. If this tag and the associated subtags are not present, WebLogic enters default values for them. If you deploy the resource adapter exploded in directory format, most of the properties are editable from the WebLogic console under the Deployments/Connector Modules on the left side tree, and Configuration/Descriptor on the right side. If the resource adapter was deployed as a .rar file, only links to view the ra.xml and weblogic-ra.xml files are present in the console. Please refer to the console help and the DTD for the weblogic-ra.xml mentioned earlier for a description of each parameter.
- <logging-enabled>—This value specifies whether logging is turned on or off for the ManagedConnectionFactory or ManagedConnection class. The value can be true or false. If true, the output is sent to the value of the <log-filename> value.
- <log-filename>—The full path to the file where the ManagedConnectionFactory or ManagedConnection class will send its logging output if the <logging-enabled> value is true.
- <map-config-property>—This element corresponds to the <config-entry> tag in the ra.xml file. Any property placed here will be available inside the ManagedConnectionFactory and override any property of the same name set in the ra.xml file.

The following excerpt from a weblogic-ra.xml file shows some of the optional configuration properties in use. These properties enable logging, specify the name logging file, and map a property from the ra.xml file to a new value based on the <config-property-value> in the weblogic-ra.xml file.

```
<weblogic-connection-factory-dd>
<connection-factory-name>eis/jcaconn</connection-factory-name>
<jndi-name>eis/jcaconn</jndi-name>
<logging-enabled>true</logging-enabled>
<log-filename>jcaoutput.log</log-filename>
<map-config-property>
<config-property-name>ConnectionURL</config-property-name>
<config-property-value>jdbc:pointbase://localhost/demo</config-property-value>
</map-config-property>
</weblogic-connection-factory-dd>
```

Writing Resource Adapters

Writing resource adapters is a lot of work. It's not an easy task and should be done by EIS vendors and third-party providers. If you have to actually compile the classes needed for a resource adapter, the Java software for J2EE version 1.3 or greater is required. All the required classes are also included in the weblogic.jar found in the <weblogic_root>\server\lib directory. Sun has a tool that integrates into Sun ONE Studio to facilitate writing resource adapters. This tool is not free, but it could save significant time, especially if more than one adapter is being written. A trial version is downloadable from Sun at http://wwws.sun.com/software/download/index.html.

As previously covered in this chapter, resource adapters are separated into three main areas: connection management, security management, and transaction management. When writing a resource adapter, certain interfaces must be present and correctly implemented for the resource adapter to work in application servers. The implemented interfaces work together with the ra.xml file to provide the three management areas of a resource adapter. In fact, each of these interfaces and some of the objects that they return have to correspond exactly to the entries in the ra.xml file under the <resourceadapter> tag.

NOTE

This section is intended to give an overview of the minimum interfaces needed to write a resource adapter per the J2EE Connector Architecture 1.0 specification. It is meant as an informational illustration to understand resource architecture better, but is not intended as the sole reference for writing resource adapters. For a thorough examination of the subject, see *Java Connector Architecture: Building Enterprise Adaptors* by Atul Apte from Sams Publishing, ISBN 0672323109.

Interfaces Needed for the Connection

The ManagedConnectionFactory interface retrieves the connection from the EIS system. The main purpose of this interface is to provide a single point to manage EIS-specific ManagedConnection factory instances. This interface includes pooling support in the form of ManagedConnection instance management. Also, the security contract is supported through the createManagedConnection method. This object is identified to the application server with the <managedconnectionfactory-class> tag in the ra.xml file. The Object type returned by the createConnectionFactory methods has to implement the interface written in the <connectionfactory-interface> entry. The actual class returned must correspond to the <connectionfactory-impl-class> tag. Figure 31.3 shows the relationships between the classes in the resource adapter and the ra.xml file.

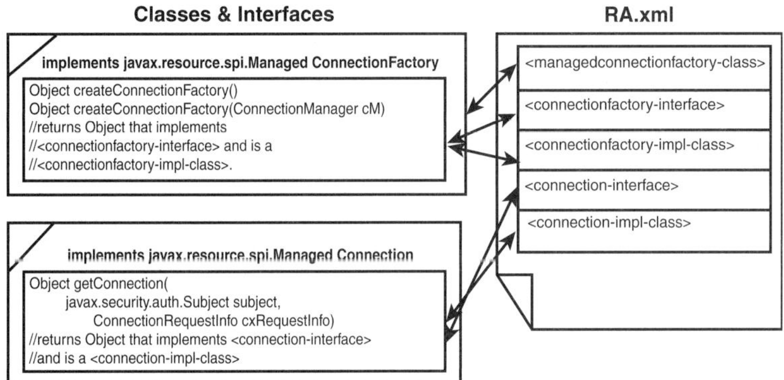

FIGURE 31.3 Relationships between the classes in the resource adapter and the ra.xml configuration file.

The following is the interface for ManagedConnectionFactory:

```
public interface javax.resource.spi.ManagedConnectionFactory
extends java.io.Serializable {
public Object createConnectionFactory(
       ConnectionManager connectionManager) throws ResourceException;
public Object createConnectionFactory() throws ResourceException;
public ManagedConnection createManagedConnection(javax.security.auth.Subject sub-
ject,
ConnectionRequestInfo cxRequestInfo)
throws ResourceException;
public ManagedConnection matchManagedConnections(java.util.Set connectionSet,
javax.security.auth.Subject subject,
ConnectionRequestInfo cxRequestInfo) throws ResourceException;
public boolean equals(Object other);
public int hashCode();
}
```

The ManagedConnection interface provides access to many functions within a resource adapter. The main function of the implemented class is to retrieve the LocalTransaction interface and the XAResource interface for use in transactions. This is also where the ConnectionEventListener is set to notify the application server of transaction events. Using this interface, log writers can be retrieved for writing output to the log files, and they can be substituted with custom writers. The Object returned by the getConnection method must implement the same interface as entered in the <connection-interface> tag in the ra.xml file. The actual class returned must match the <connection-impl-class> tag. The following code is the interface specification. To see this mapping graphically, refer to Figure 31.3 that was shown earlier.

```
public interface javax.resource.spi.ManagedConnection {
public Object getConnection(javax.security.auth.Subject subject,
                            ConnectionRequestInfo cxRequestInfo)
throws ResourceException;
public void destroy() throws ResourceException;
public void cleanup() throws ResourceException;
public void addConnectionEventListener(ConnectionEventListener listener);
public void removeConnectionEventListener(ConnectionEventListener listener);
public ManagedConnectionMetaData getMetaData() throws ResourceException;
public void associateConnection(java.lang.Object connection) throws ResourceException;
public LocalTransaction getLocalTransaction() throws ResourceException;
public XAResource getXAResource() throws ResourceException;
public java.io.PrintWriter getLogWriter() throws ResourceException;
public void setLogWriter(java.io.PrintWriter out) throws ResourceException;
}
```

The ManagedConnectionMetaData interface is just a utility class that's used to get information about the resource adapter. The implemented class needs to get information from the ManagedConnection interface about the underlying connection to the EIS system. This is needed specifically for the getUserName() method, which returns the current user. Notice that the specification leaves open how you retrieve this information. The following is the mandatory interface:

```
public interface javax.resource.spi.ManagedConnectionMetaData {
public String getEISProductName() throws ResourceException;
public String getEISProductVersion() throws ResourceException;
public int getMaxConnections() throws ResourceException;
public String getUserName() throws ResourceException;
}
```

The ConnectionManager interface is how the resource adapter supplies the application server with the connection request. The implemented class must be serializable and is called by the resource adapter's ManagedConnectionFactory class. The following is the interface and its lone method:

```
Public interface javax.resource.spi.ConnectionManager extends java.io.Serializable {
public java.lang.Object allocateConnection(ManagedConnectionFactory mcf,
ConnectionRequestInfo cxRequestInfo) throws ResourceException;
}
```

Transaction Management Contracts

Transaction management contracts between the resource adapter and the application server exist to maintain a standard set of protocols and interfaces. This allows different resource adapters to use the standard transaction support and deploy on any application server that adheres to the J2EE Connector Architecture specification.

Both local and XA transaction support have different contract obligations. If the transaction supports a local transaction, the resource adapter is required to support the `LocalTransaction` interface, and WebLogic or other application servers in turn support the `ConnectionEventListener` interface.

- `LocalTransaction`—Resource adapter–defined begin, commit, and rollback methods for local transaction management. It is then required to notify the application server's `ConnectionEventListener` of the action if the transaction is not container managed.

  ```
  public interface javax.resource.spi.LocalTransaction {
  public void begin() throws ResourceException;
  public void commit() throws ResourceException;
  public void rollback() throws ResourceException;
  }
  ```

- `ConnectionEventListener`—Application server's defined listeners for the associated `LocalTransaction` interface:

  ```
  public interface javax.resource.spi.ConnectionEventListener {
  // Local Transaction Management related events
  public void localTransactionStarted(ConnectionEvent event);
  public void localTransactionCommitted(ConnectionEvent event);
  public void localTransactionRolledback(ConnectionEvent event);
  }
  ```

With these two contracts in place, transaction management with local support works without a hitch. Because the application server knows of all the events happening in the local transaction, it can clean up any transactions with other components.

XA-compliant contracts are more complex. The specification gives the vendors of EIS systems the choice of being XA compliant, or not, to allow gradual migration to J2EE Connector Architecture. The interface for XA-compliant transactions is the `XAResource` interface. The following code is the interface for the `XAResource`:

```
public interface javax.transaction.xa.XAResource {
public void commit(Xid xid, boolean onePhase) throws XAException;
public void end(Xid xid, int flags) throws XAException;
public void forget(Xid xid) throws XAException;
public int prepare(Xid xid) throws XAException;
public Xid[] recover(int flag) throws XAException;
public void rollback(Xid xid) throws XAException;
public void start(Xid xid, int flags) throws XAException;
}
```

This interface follows the JTA/XA and JTS specifications. A vendor is not required to support two-phase commits within the resource adapter/resource manager. It is required only to handle the one-phase commit when `XAResource.commit(XID, true);` is called. This makes it imperative for programmers using vendor-specific connectors to read the documentation of each connector being used before setting up any transaction strategy for a specified system if JTA/XA or JTS is being used. Remember that if only one resource manager is being used, the server optimizes the transaction and uses a one-phase commit local transaction. Distributed transactions requiring two-phase commits need a fully JTA/XA or JTS compatible resource adapter. Consequently, this leaves out several of the most popular EIS systems, such as SAP, because they don't support two-phase commits.

With the connection interfaces in place, we can turn our attention to transaction management. Transaction management is configured by the `<transaction-support>` tag in `ra.xml`. Transaction management is not required by a resource adapter because `NoTransaction` can be used for this tag. If the connector supports local transactions as discussed in the previous section, the `LocalTransaction` interface must be present. If the transaction level supports XA transactions, both the `LocalTransaction` and the `XAResource` interfaces must be implemented and returned by the `ManagedConnection` implementation. If a transaction level is not supported or not correctly identified, a `ResourceException` is thrown when the adapter is deployed.

The `XAResource` interface is needed if the transaction level is set to `XATransaction`. This interface provides the capability to participate in JTA/XA and JTS transactions.

Error Resolution

The exception handling in a resource adapter is handled in most cases by throwing a `javax.resource.ResourceException`. This class extends `java.lang.Exception` and adds three key methods for retrieving, setting, and getting errors from EIS systems. These methods are listed here with a description:

- `getErrorCode()`—This method returns a `String` of the specific vendor error code.
- `getLinkedException()`—This method returns a `java.lang.Exception` linked to a lower-level problem. If there is none, null is returned.

- `setLinkedException(java.lang.Exception e)`—This method sets a `java.lang.Exception` to retrieve via the `getLinkedException()` to find the lower-level problem.

Putting It All Together

So far in this section, the link between the `ra.xml` file and the actual interfaces and classes have been shown. The deployment procedure and the client code to connect to the resource adapter have not been shown.

There are two types of applications:

- Managed applications—The client code relies on the server to access the resource adapter; for example, a J2EE application (Web, EJB, EAR applications).
- Non-managed applications—The client calls the resource adapter classes directly.

Managed Applications

Figure 31.4 diagrams how a managed application interacts with WebLogic Server, the resource adapter, and the EIS system.

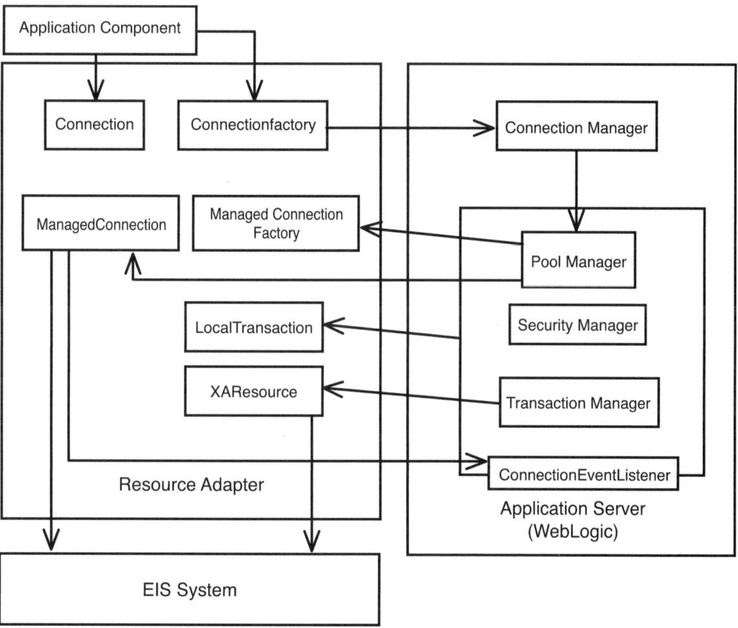

FIGURE 31.4 Managed connection architecture.

WebLogic Console Resource Connector Access

When a resource adapter is deployed, it has an entry in the WebLogic JNDI lookup. This name corresponds to the <jndi-name> inside the weblogic-ra.xml file. When an application uses this resource adapter (deployed using a managed application approach), there must be an entry in the deployment descriptor similar to this:

```
<resource-ref>
  <res-ref-name>eis/GAMSJCA_RA </res-ref-name>
  <res-type>javax.sql.DataSource</res-type>
  <res-auth>Application</res-auth>
</resource-ref>
```

The <res-ref-name> tag of the deployment descriptor of the application and the <jndi-name> tag from the weblogic-ra.xml file should match exactly. When the calling component looks up the JNDI reference, the server calls the class referenced in the ra.xml file under <managedconnectionfactory-class>, which is required to implement ManagedConnectionFactory. The application server then calls the createConnectionFactory method, which returns the interface specified in the <connectionfactory-interface> tag. The following sample code looks up the JNDI interface and maps the return value to the correct value. We assume that the ra.xml file setting for the return interface is javax.sql.DataSource.

```
InitialContext initCtx = null;
  try {
      initCtx = new InitialContext();
      DataSource ds = (javax.sql.DataSource) initCtx.lookup("GAMSJCA_RA");
  }catch(Exception e){
}
```

The next step is to obtain the connection from the datasource:

```
InitialContext initCtx = null;
Connection con = null;
  try {
      initCtx = new InitialContext();
      DataSource ds =
      (javax.sql.DataSource)
      initCtx.lookup("java:comp/env/eis/GAMSJCA_RA");
con = ds.getConnection();

  }catch(Exception e){}
```

The previous case is a JDBC example. If J2EE-CA implements the optional Common Client Interface (CCI), the code would look very similar, with only different implementing classes:

```
InitialContext initCtx = null;
javax.resource.cci.Connection con = null;
 try{
    initCtx = new InitialContext();
    javax.resource.cci.ConnectionFactory cf =
    (javax.resource.cci.ConnectionFactory)
    initCtx.lookup("java:comp/env/eis/GAMSJCA_RA");
    con = cf.getConnection();
 }catch(Exception e){}
```

After you get the connection, perform whatever duties you have to do, such as retrieving, updating, or inserting data into an EIS, and then close the connection like this:

```
con.close();
```

This is just an example of a connection. Let's look at doing something useful with an adapter. Listing 31.1 shows an excerpt from the `ConnectJCASAPBean.java` file in the SAP sample included on the CD that comes with this book. This is a good example of CCI code because we get the connection, create an interaction object to interact with the EIS system, create a mapped record to get the input fields and structures, and use the `ResultSet` object to insert and retrieve tables for the call to SAP.

LISTING 31.1 SAP Connection, Population of Function, and Call

```
Interaction interaction = connection.createInteraction();

              // create Mapped record for BAPI
              MappedRecord in = connectionfactory.getRecordFactory().
              ➥createMappedRecord
                ("BAPI_MATERIAL_GETLIST");
        // Input
           in.put("MAXROWS", String.valueOf(maxrows));
        // Create Result set for Input Parameters
        ResultSet matnrSelection = (ResultSet)in.get("MATNRSELECTION");
        matnrSelection.moveToInsertRow();
        matnrSelection.updateString("SIGN", "I");
        matnrSelection.updateString("OPTION", "CP");
        matnrSelection.updateString("MATNR_LOW", searchtext);
        matnrSelection.insertRow();
       // get MappedRecord for output
       MappedRecord out = (MappedRecord) interaction.execute(null, in);
              // extract results
              ResultSet matnrList = (ResultSet) out.get("MATNRLIST");
              vec = toVector(matnrList);
              interaction.close();
```

Unmanaged Application

Figure 31.5 shows how an unmanaged application interacts with WebLogic Server, the resource adapter, and the EIS system.

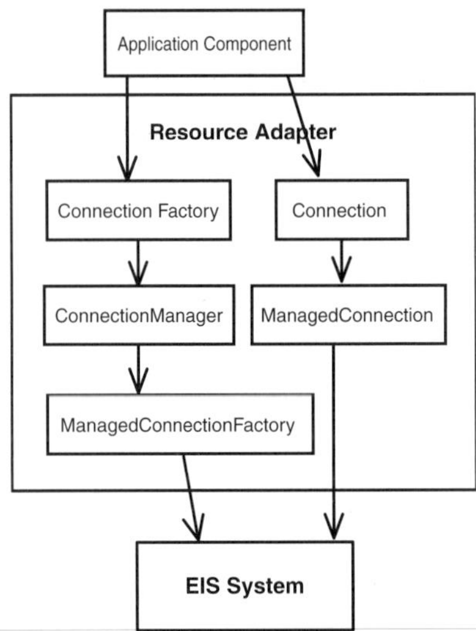

FIGURE 31.5 Unmanaged connection architecture.

An application does not have to be managed by a server. The J2EE architecture also allows direct access to the resource adapter. In such a case, the code to implement a transaction using CCI would look much like this:

```
javax.resource.cci.ManagedConnectionFactory mcf = null;
javax.resource.cci.ConnectionFactory cxf = null;
javax.resource.cci.Connection connection = null;

try {
  mcf = new ECIManagedConnectionFactory();
   cxf = (javax.resource.cci.ConnectionFactory) mcf.createConnectionFactory();
   connection = cxf.getConnection();
...//do work
}catch(Exception e){
}
connection.close();
```

As you see, the main difference is the creation and instantiation of the `ManagedConnectionFactory` class. Everything else remains constant. Of course, you give up any container-managed features, such as credential mapping, transaction management, and so on. Most of the time, and particularly when using WebLogic, you'll take advantage of managed applications. If you need to call an EIS within a standalone application and don't want WebLogic to manage anything for you, you can still use the resource adapter this way.

Packaging and Deployment Issues

Packaging and deploying resource adapters in WebLogic is a straightforward process.

Packaging Resource Adapters

To package a resource adapter into a `.rar` file, gather the classes or library files that contain the classes conforming to the J2EE Connector Architecture specification. Place those files in the root directory of the `.rar` file. Also place within the root directory any native libraries (Windows `.dlls` or Unix `.so` files) needed for the EIS system.

Next, create a directory called `META-INF` in the root directory and place the `ra.xml` and `weblogic-ra.xml` files there. Refer to the "Configuring WebLogic J2EE-CA" section for help in creating these files. Then add any other required resources, such as images, readme files, or HTML help files, into or off of the root directory. The directory should look similar to this example, which shows an SAP RAR staging directory:

```
META-INF/
          ra.xml
          weblogic-ra.xml
sapjra.jar
sapjco.jar
sapjcorfc.dll
librfc32.dll
```

When these files are in place, create a RAR file in the root directory using the Java `jar` utility as shown in the following example:

```
jar -cf <myresourceadapter>.rar *
```

After the RAR file has been created, it's ready to be deployed within WebLogic Server.

Deploying Resource Adapters

A resource adapter can be deployed either as a standalone connector or as part of an Enterprise Archive (EAR) file. If the resource adapter is deployed as a standalone connector, any application can access it. If it's deployed within an EAR file, only that application can access it.

EAR File Deployment

To deploy a resource adapter within an EAR file, place the RAR file within the EAR, just as you would place it in a Web archive (WAR) file or a JAR file. After the file is in the directory, the `application.xml` file must be modified to include the `<connector>` tag.

`<connector>` is a new tag included in the J2EE 1.3 specification. If your `application.xml` file has a link to an older DTD, it will not work. Simply modify the older DTD declaration to a newer one found in the new specifications. The following is the sample entry in the `application.xml` file and includes the earliest DTD that will still work:

```
<?xml version="1.0" encoding="UTF-8"?>
<!DOCTYPE application PUBLIC '-//Sun Microsystems, Inc.//DTD
J2EE Application 1.3//EN'
'http://java.sun.com/dtd/application_1_3.dtd'>
<application>
....
<module>
<connector>myresourceadapter.rar</connector>
</module>
....
</application>
```

When the file has been included in the EAR and the `application.xml` file has been updated, deploy the EAR file. The resource adapter will be available to only this application.

RAR File Deployment

It's also possible to deploy a RAR file so that all applications can access it. This is possible in a couple different ways. The first way is through the WebLogic console. The WebLogic console is found at `http://`*`url`*`:`*`port`*`/console`, where *`url`* is the location of WebLogic Server and *`port`* is the port that WebLogic is configured for. The console login screen will display, and after entering the username and password, you should see the WebLogic Server home page.

On the left side of the screen, you should see the domains configured for this server. Inside the domain link is a node called Deployments, and under this link is another node called Connector Modules. If you click on Connector Modules, the right side of the screen will display all the current connectors, with a link labeled Deploy a New Connector Module. Clicking on this link starts a wizard to deploy or upload a connector module.

The first step is to point to the `.rar` file or the directory under which the `META-INF/ra.xml` and associated files are located. When the files have been located, click on the Target Module button. The next screen enables you to change the name to identify the connector module. After everything is correct, simply click Deploy to deploy the resource adapter. The adapter is now listed in the navigation tree on the right side of the screen, as shown in Figure 31.6.

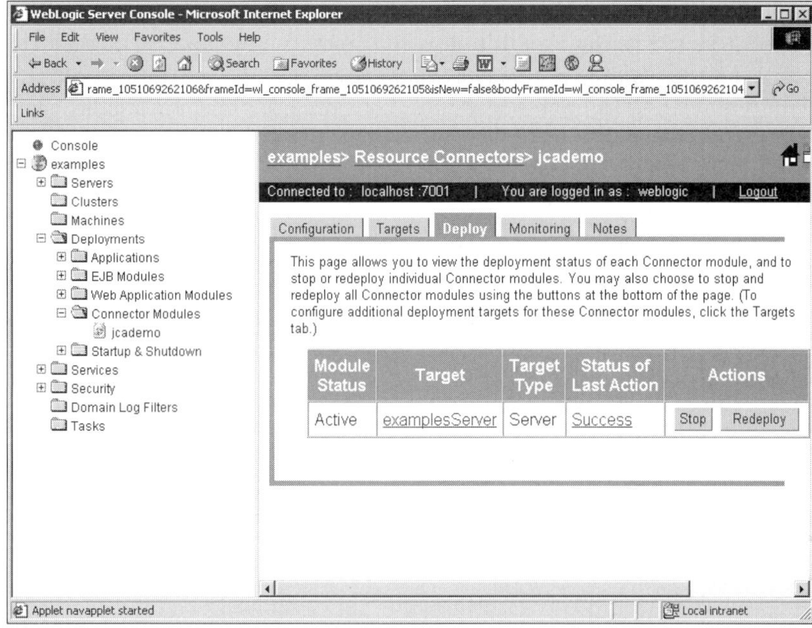

FIGURE 31.6 WebLogic Console resource connector deployment.

WebLogic also comes with a command-line utility called `weblogic.Deployer`. This tool enables you to deploy, redeploy, remove, and deactivate a connector. The following is a simple command to deploy a RAR file on a local instance of WebLogic Server:

```
java weblogic.Deployer -username weblogic -password weblogic
➥-deploy myresourceadapter.rar
```

Note that the preceding line assumes a default WebLogic installation on `http://localhost:7001`. If your implementation is different, please adjust the tool appropriately by reading the instructions.

For more information about `weblogic.Deployer`, look at this site: `http://e-docs.bea.com/wls/docs81/deployment/tools.html`.

J2EE Connector Architecture Example

The first J2EE Connector Architecture example found under the JDBC directory on the CD uses a simple sample resource adapter from Sun Microsystems to connect to a database. The second example uses the resource adapter from SAP to connect to an SAP system and retrieve materials.

Both examples contain two JSP files, one for input and one for output, which are included in a Web application that uses an EJB to talk to the J2EE-CA adapter. The first example inserts records and sends the contents out to a screen for display. The second example enables you to query SAP for materials (if you have an SAP system available, that is). The associated instructions enable you to become familiar with deploying a resource adapter in WebLogic. You can also familiarize yourself with the configuration and look at the sample code used to connect to resource adapters.

The following is a JDBC example. You might be wondering, "Aren't there JDBC drivers for doing this?" Yes, there are, and this adapter is a demonstration of how to write one. We're using this kind of adapter because you probably don't have an EIS server running on your development computer, and it would be impossible for you to really learn about J2EE-CA without deploying one.

Setting Up the JDBC Example

To compile and run the example, a database is required. We'll use the PointBase `EXAMPLES.BANDS` database for our example. PointBase comes with WebLogic Server 8.1, but it has to be started. The command to start PointBase is

```
<weblogic home dir>\common\eval\pointbase\tools\startPointBase.cmd
```

This command should be placed in your startup script for WebLogic Server.

After the database has been installed, download the source directory into the temporary directory of your choice. In the source directory are three directories and two XML files: `application.xml and build.xml`. Each directory contains a separate component, as listed here:

- `EJB`—This directory contains all the files required to build the EJB that calls the resource adapter. It is called by the JSPs in the Web application.
- `jca`—This directory contains the J2EE-CA adapter that we'll use to connect to the PointBase database.
- `root`—This directory contains the Web application.
- `application.xml`—The file for deployment of the `.ear` file.

The `build.xml` file is an Ant script that builds and packages the entire application. This file needs the location of the `weblogic.jar` file to compile the EJB. This is set up in the `weblogicjar` property at the beginning of the file. Also, make sure the `bin` directory of your JDK is in your `PATH` for compilation.

To deploy the application, start the WebLogic console. The default location is `http://localhost:7001/console`. Go to the correct server on the domain and deploy the application EAR file as shown in Figure 31.7.

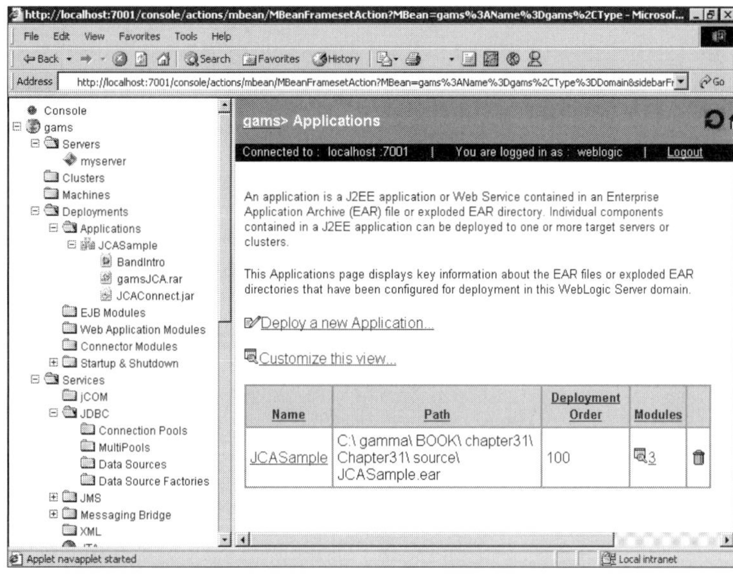

FIGURE 31.7 WebLogic console application deployment.

After the application has been deployed, create a credential mapping for the J2EE-CA to log in to the database. This is done by simply right-clicking on the gamsJCA.rar tree node on the left interface. Choose the last selection labeled Define Credential Mappings as shown in Figure 31.8.

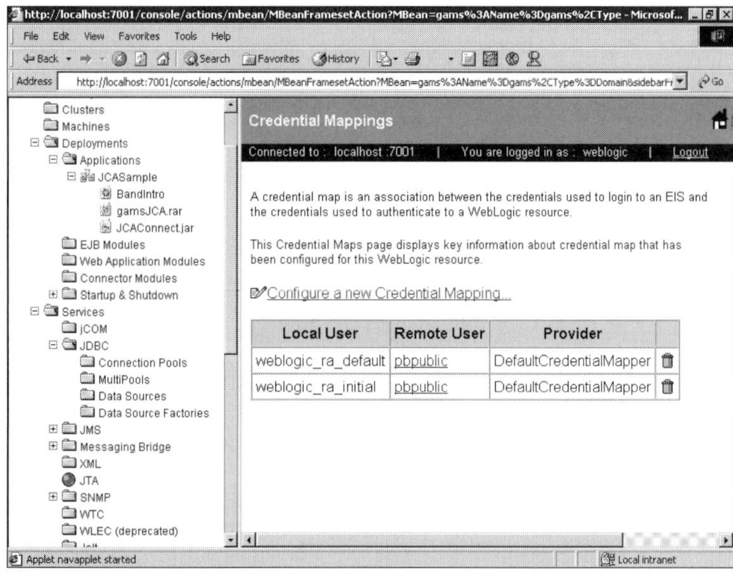

FIGURE 31.8 WebLogic resource adapter credential mapping screen.

Once you're inside, define a default credential mapping for the local user (`weblogic_ra_default`) and the remote user (`pbpublic` with the password `pbpublic`). After these have been defined, you can run the application to insert bands into a database and display all the bands in that database as shown in Figures 31.9 (the input screen) and 31.10 (the output screen).

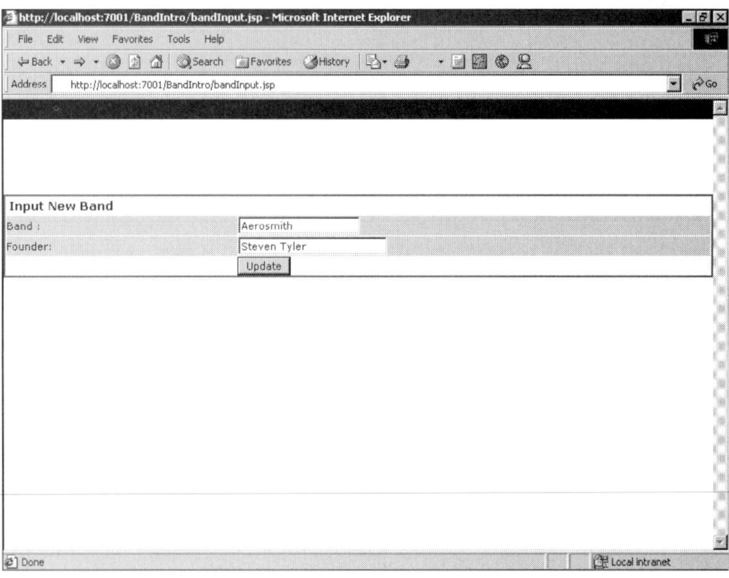

FIGURE 31.9 Band input screen.

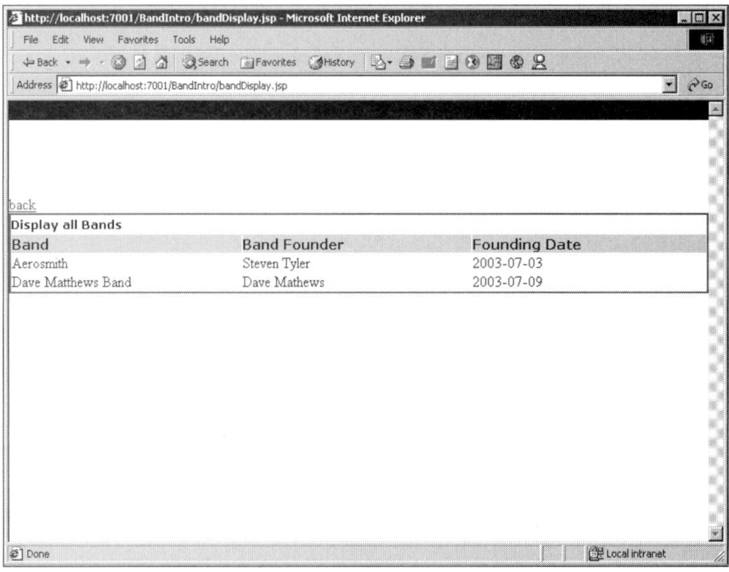

FIGURE 31.10 Band output screen.

Setting Up the SAP Example

The second example requires SAP system access and the ability to obtain the SAP resource adapter and the SAP Java Connector (JCo) version 2.0 or greater. The resource adapter and Java Connector are free for all of SAP's partners and customers. They are available from a secured SAP site at `http://service.sap.com/connectors`. After obtaining the resource adapter, it must be configured for use with WebLogic and your SAP system. The following steps must be followed:

1. Un-jar the `sapjra.rar` file into a temporary staging directory.

2. Modify the `ra.xml` file located in the `META-INF` directory with the appropriate login configuration. The login configuration settings are contained in the `<config-property>` tags. Each has a name type and a value associated with it. If you don't have this information, ask a basis person at your company to help you. The values must be filled out with your SAP system information as follows:

    - `SAPClient`—The number of the SAP client that you're connecting to
    - `UserName`—The background SAP username needed for the connection
    - `Password`—The password of the background SAP username
    - Language—The language you're connecting with; for example, `EN`
    - `ServerName`—The name or the IP address of the SAP server
    - `PortNumber`—The system number of your SAP system; for example, `00`

3. Follow the directions to install JCo on your system. Then move the `sapjco.jar` file into the staging directory root with the `sapjra.jar` file. For help, see Chapter 32, "Using SAP's Java Connector with WebLogic Server."

4. Create a `.rar` file by issuing the following command with the Java `jar` utility:

    ```
    jar -cf saprar.rar *
    ```

5. After the `.rar` file has been created, import it into WebLogic using the console. To do this, simply log in to the console and click on Connector Modules, which is listed under the Deployments tab on the left side of the screen. Figure 31.11 shows what this should like.

6. Copy the contents of the SAP directory on the CD to a staging directory on your hard drive.

7. Move the `sapjca.jar` file from the staging directory you set up for the `.rar` file into the SAP staging directory you just created.

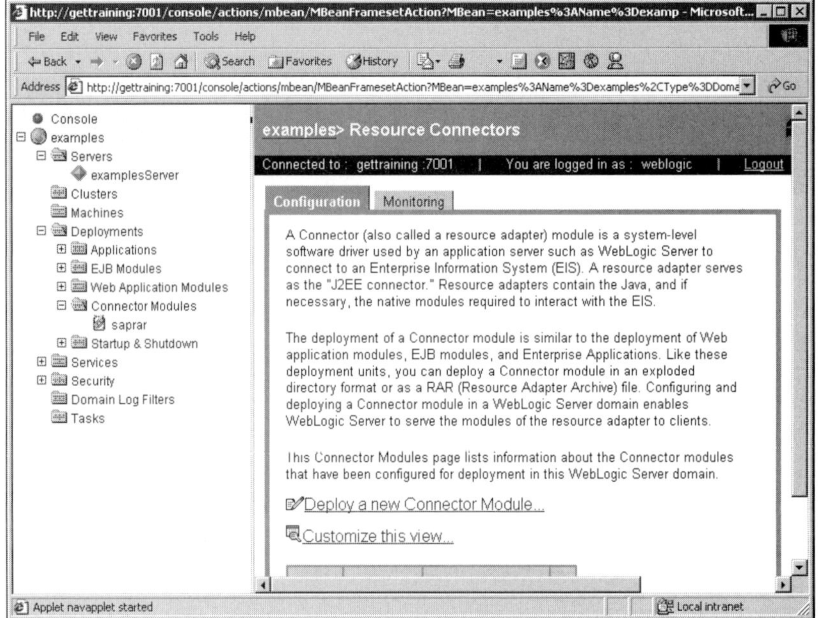

FIGURE 31.11 Deploying a standalone connector.

8. Build the application `.ear` file for the SAP application. The SAP directory on the CD contains an Ant script called `build.xml` for this task. You must configure two properties for this script:

   - `weblogicjar`—Corresponds to the location of the `weblogic.jar` file
   - `sapjcajar`—Corresponds to the location of the `sapjca.jar` file contained in the staging directory you set up

   The build script will build an application file called `JCASAPSample.ear` that will be contained in the staging directory (this is a temporary directory created by the Ant script).

9. Deploy this application using the WebLogic console and then run the application to query materials by entering in this address in your Web browser: `http:localhost:7001/SAPMaterials`. Doing so brings up a screen that looks like Figure 31.12.

   On this screen, enter any search criterion for materials in your SAP system, or enter `*` to get a full list. (The list will be truncated to 100 materials for performance reasons.) After you click the search button, a screen similar to the one shown in Figure 31.13 is displayed.

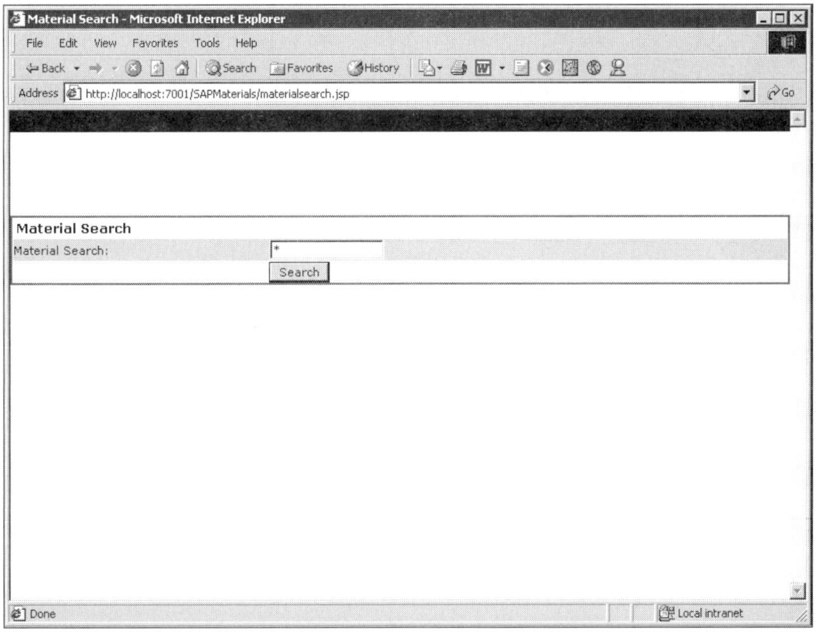

Material Search - Microsoft Internet Explorer
File Edit View Favorites Tools Help
Address http://localhost:7001/SAPMaterials/materialsearch.jsp

Material Search
Material Search: *
Search

Done Local intranet

FIGURE 31.12 Sample SAP application search screen.

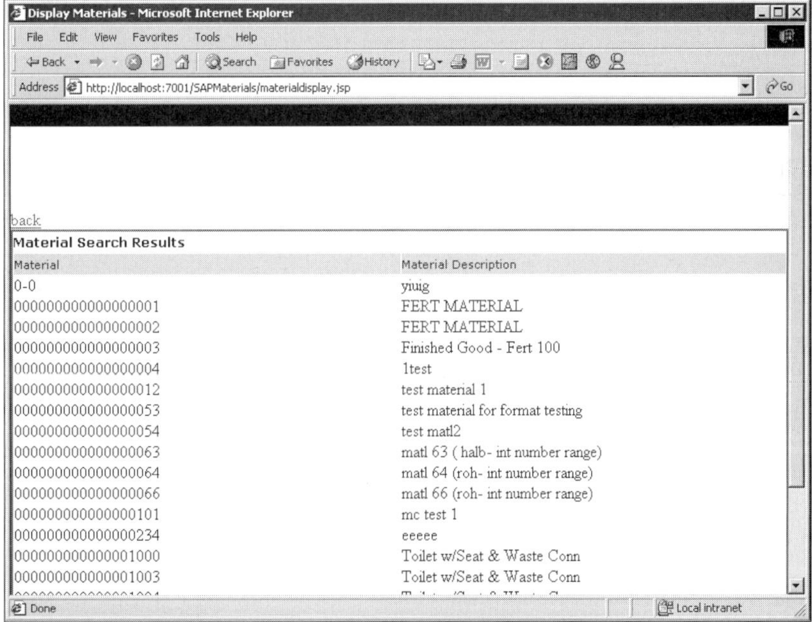

FIGURE 31.13 Sample SAP application display screen.

Summary

The J2EE Connector Architecture promises to make life easier for Java programmers who need to connect to EIS systems. But until vendors and third-party software companies support the entire J2EE specification and release corresponding resource adapters that work with these systems, the J2EE Connector Architecture is lacking support for widespread adoption. Just as important as functionality is the adoption of the Common Client Interface that standardizes the client code written against the resource adapter. With that said, the J2EE Connector Architecture is still a big leap toward making proprietary connector APIs a thing of the past.

CHAPTER **32**

Using SAP's Java Connector with WebLogic Server

By Steve Steffen

IN THIS CHAPTER

- What Is JCo?
- Installing JCo
- SAP System Setup
- Client Programming in JCo
- Calling an SAP Function
- Exception Handling in JCo
- Server Programming in JCo
- Useful BAPIs and RFCs

Started in 1972 by former IBM employees, Systems, Applications, and Products in Data Processing (SAP) is a world leader in enterprise resource planning software used to run large corporations. SAP's main product, R/3, runs on several platforms and runs different kinds of applications such as financial, sales and distribution, production planning, and human resources. All these applications work together in one system.

SAP is primarily written in its own proprietary language named Advanced Business Application Programming (ABAP/4), a fourth-generation language similar to COBOL. Using ABAP and configuration settings, SAP systems can be uniquely tailored to each individual customer. SAP is not a database; it sits on top of the customer's database of choice. The strength of an SAP system lies in its capability to adapt and meet the needs of the customer. When SAP realized it needed to harness the power of Java and the Internet, it created JCo.

This chapter covers the aspects of connecting, sending data to, and retrieving data from SAP. You learn how to use JCo to call an SAP system. Additionally, you learn how to create a program that listens for and accepts calls from an SAP system.

What Is JCo?

SAP, recognizing the power of Java, first released Java connections with a CORBA environment that worked with already-released connection technology for C and Visual Basic programming. This initial product was buggy and incredibly frustrating to work with. In late 2000, SAP announced JCo, a JNI-based solution that enabled Java programmers to work with the same technologies they're used to. JCo worked much better than the CORBA version, which required the IDL interfaces to be regenerated every time the interface changed within SAP, whether or not it was used in the Java application. JCo enables Java programs to call SAP remote function call–enabled functions; conversely, JCo also enables SAP to call Java programs. JCo works with any SAP system after 3.1H and is available for many platforms, including Windows and Linux.

NOTE

SAP JCo should not be mistaken for the J2EE-CA resource adapter for SAP. The first has a proprietary interface that is widely used. The second is in beta form and was not recommended for production environments at the time of this book's release. The resource adapter for SAP is covered in Chapter 31, "Legacy Integration with the J2EE Connector Architecture," as an example of a current J2EE Connector Architecture. The resource adapter has a standard interface, but came out much later, so it's not as common. In the future this could change.

Remote Function Call

Any realtime communication by SAP systems to the outside world is done through remote function calls (RFCs). There are three kinds of RFCs: synchronous, transactional, and queued. A Java program normally attaches to a synchronous RFC.

ABAP can be used to write different kinds of programs in SAP. One kind of program is a function module. A function module that's RFC-enabled can be called from an external source. SAP has delivered several thousand RFC-enabled function modules, including business application programmer interfaces (BAPIs) that encapsulate the SAP internal business process and enable external systems to interface to it. BAPIs are technically constructed the same as RFC-enabled function modules, but are grouped together in the SAP business object repository (BOR) and have some additional features for organizational purposes. As far as a Java programmer is concerned, when connecting to SAP through JCo, a BAPI and an RFC-enabled function module are the same. BAPIs and RFC-enabled functions can have two different states:

- Released—The function module has been released for customer use, and SAP promises not to make major changes to the function.
- Not Released—The function module is not ready for production-level applications, and SAP reserves the right to make changes as necessary.

It's not uncommon to use unreleased RFC-enabled functions. Just beware of problems that can arise when SAP administrators apply support Hot Packs that fix bugs and provide extended functionality between releases. When that happens, a system that worked one minute can be broken the next.

CAUTION

In fact, even released functions can sometimes be changed and require updates on the Java side. This happens infrequently, but when it does, problems can arise in external systems. If this occurs, be sure to contact an SAP Basis person to find out what the Hot Pack changed.

SAP Data Handling

RFC-enabled function modules use three different types of data:

- Import parameters—Parameters that are being sent into the function module before processing
- Export parameters—Parameters that are being sent back to the calling program after processing
- Table parameters—This type can be sent in and received back

Import and export parameters can be a field or a complex structure. A *field* is the smallest abstraction of data for JCo, whereas a *structure* is a set of ordered fields that is equivalent to a row in a table. A *table* is a structure with multiple rows.

Each import and table parameter can be specified as either optional or mandatory within the function module configuration. Export parameters are always optional.

SAP Data Dictionary

One of the best features of SAP is the separation of data from the actual database native data types. The separation takes place in the SAP data dictionary. Each field value in a parameter is based on either a native SAP data type or a data element in the data dictionary. Each element is dependent on either a built-in data type or a domain. A domain stores information such as the SAP native data type, length, number of decimals, output length, conversion routine, and check table.

The conversion routine and check tables are specific to SAP. Conversion routines convert data from the internal format SAP stores to an external format for displaying the data. Unfortunately, this isn't handled automatically within RFC calls. Programmers have to convert data on the inbound to make sense within SAP. For instance, the `DOC_TYPE` field is used in the SAP order type field within `BAPI_SALESORDER_SIMULATE` in the `ORDER_HEADER_IN` structure.

A standard SAP order type is `OR`. Most people would incorrectly assume that populating it with `OR` would cause a standard order to be created. Actually, an error will be thrown because the internal type `TA` is assigned to `OR`, and a conversion routine converts it from `OR` to `TA` when it's displayed within SAP. Several conversions might take place, depending on the domain.

Help values are the possible entries for a field. They're very helpful in SAP because most fields are based on codes that must be correctly entered. Help values could be useful when programming outside of SAP, but these values are normally restricted for users in a Web application because such users don't understand all the SAP codes.

There are BAPIs in SAP that convert values in and out of SAP and get the help values for specific fields. These are mentioned later in this chapter in the "Useful BAPIs and RFCs" section.

Installing JCo

JCo is a free tool provided by SAP to its customers and partners. It currently runs on Microsoft Windows NT 4.0 with Service Pack 4 or later, Windows 2000, Linux Kernel 2.2.14 or later, Sun Solaris 2.8 or later, IBM AIX 4.3 or later, HP-UX 11.0 or later, and Compaq Tru64 5.0 or later. The only way to get a copy of JCo is to be a partner or customer and have a valid ID for the SAP service site named SAPnet.

Downloading JCo

The software can be downloaded on the Internet at `http://service.sap.com/connectors`. This site requires a login with an active ID and password. If you work for a company that has SAP, you must apply for an OSS ID or ask someone to login and download the software for you. JCo must be the correct version for the operating system environment it will run in.

JCo 1.1

After receiving the zipped file from JCo, unzip it into a temp directory. To install on a Microsoft Windows machine, JCo needs three `.dll` files put in the `windows/system32` directory and the `jco.jar` file in the classpath of your Java compiler and runtime environment of WebLogic Server. Table 32.1 shows the location for the 1.1 version of JCo.

TABLE 32.1 Location of JCo Files for 1.1 Installation

Files	Location
jco.jar	Must be in the compile time and runtime classpaths.
jRFC11.dll	SAP DLL needed to run JCo on JDK 1.1. Place in the <*windows root*>/system32 directory.
jRFC12.dll	SAP DLL needed to run JCo on JDK 1.2 or later. Place in the <*windows root*>/system32 directory.

TABLE 32.1 Continued

Files	Location
Librfc32.dll	SAP DLL containing the RFC runtime library 4.6D or higher.
msvp60.dll	Windows DLL; make sure that you have this version or newer in the <*windows root*>/system32 directory.

JCo 2.0

JCo 2.0 requires Java runtime libraries 1.2 or greater. Installation is a bit different because the files have changed. The `jco.jar` file has been replaced with `sapjco.jar`. The `jRFC12.dll` file has been replaced with `sapjcorfc.dll`. The required `librfc32.dll` file must support the runtime library 6.20 or greater. Table 32.2 shows the location for the 2.0 installation of JCo.

CAUTION

If you've previously installed the 1.x version of JCo, remove the `.dlls` from your system because they cause conflicts with JCo 2.x.

TABLE 32.2 Location of JCo Files for 2.0 Installation

Files	Location
sapjco.jar	Must be in the compile time and runtime classpaths.
sapjcorfc.dll	SAP DLL needed to run JCo on JDK 1.2 or higher. Place in the <*windows root*>/system32 directory or keep in the same directory and add the directory to the path statement.
librfc32.dll	SAP DLL containing the RFC runtime library 6.20 or higher.

SAP System Setup

Certain things in the SAP system must be set up for access to JCo. The first order of business is a valid username and password that the Java program needs to connect to SAP. The username has to have certain authentications in SAP. The authorization objects needed are S_RFC, ACTVT:16, and FUGR. Table 32.3 contains all the function groups needed, based on the SAP system release that's running.

TABLE 32.3 SAP Function Group Access Needed for JCo

SAP Release	Function Groups
3.1H and greater	RFC1, SG00, SRFC, SUNI, SYST
4.0A and greater	RFC1, SDIF, SG00, SRFC, SUNI, SYST, SYSU
4.6A and greater	RFC1, SDIF, SG00, SRFC, SYST, SYSU
4.6D and greater	RFC1, SDIFRUNTIME, SG00, SRFC, SUNI, SYST

If the preceding settings are unfamiliar to you, don't fret. An SAP basis administrator for your system will set up the system correctly if she has this information.

Client Programming in JCo

When client programming within JCo, a Java program that calls an SAP system requires the programmer to know the correct procedures for connecting to SAP. As an introduction to this section, I've listed the classes that will be used in the following sections to create a client program:

- `JCO`—This class provides many static helper functions for connecting to SAP.
- `JCO.Client`—A connection to SAP, either a single connection or a pool, is supported.
- `JCO.Repository`—A storage location for RFM data that's dependent on the client connection or pool.
- `JCO.Function`—An encapsulation of the function that's being called.
- `JCO.Field`—This class is used to represent one field.
- `JCO.Structure`—This class represents an entire structure.
- `JCO.Table`—Represents a table in SAP.
- `JCO.ParameterList`—This class contains all the imports, exports, or tables contained in the function.

CAUTION

When using WebLogic 8.x and *any* SAP connector or adapter that uses JCo, including the BEA SAP Adapter the SAP J2EE-CA, or the JRockit runtime environment, will throw a `java.lang.StackOverFlowException` when performing the SAP call. This also occurred in WebLogic 7.x and there is currently no fix. You must use the JRE 1.2 or above from Sun. This might change in the future.

Import Statements

When the `jco.jar` or `sapjco.jar` file is in the classpath, the programmer should include the following `import` statement in the class:

```
import com.sap.mw.jco.*;
```

This statement gives access to all the JCo classes and avoids the need to fully qualify the class name.

SAP Connection

The first task in connecting to SAP is to create a client:

```
JCO.Client client = null;
```

The client is responsible for connecting and executing the SAP call. To create a client, we must use some of the helper methods in the `JCO` class. The following is an example of the `JCO.createClient` method.

```
client = JCO.createClient("500",     //Client
             "myUser",    //User ID
             "myPass",    //Password
             "EN",      //Language
             "192.168.1.2" //Application Server
             "00");
```

The `createClient()` method in JCO is a static method that is used to create an SAP client. This particular method is overloaded eight times in JCO and can be used with several different options, including reading from a `java.util.Properties` object.

> **NOTE**
>
> Some SAP systems require you to specify an SAP router string to connect to your SAP application server. The format looks like this:
>
> `/H/<sap router>/H/<application server>`
>
> To find out whether your system requires this, ask your basis administrator.

After the client has been created, we can do something useful with it. The `JCO.Client` class has three methods that are used to connect execute and disconnect from SAP.

To open a connection to SAP, the client calls its `connect()` method. The method throws a `JCO.Exception` if the connection cannot be established, so it should always be enclosed in a `try catch` statement:

```
try{
  client.connect(); //connect to SAP
}catch(JCO.Exception ex){
    ex.printStackTrace();
}
```

This call uses the parameters used to create the client object to open the connection. Conversely, to close an open connection, use the `disconnect()` method:

```
client.disconnect(); //disconnect from SAP
```

The `execute()` method is used to do work within the program. This method can be called in a number of different ways. The `execute()` method is overloaded 13 times and is very flexible. This method is covered in the "Calling an SAP Function" section of this chapter.

Pooling SAP Connections

In most cases, when connecting a Web application to SAP, the connection contains only one login to SAP. The underneath connection enables the Java program to call SAP functions, and the programmer builds in the login and password authentication. It makes sense to pool the connections to SAP and not to reopen the connections each time a call to the SAP system is needed. In that case, we must pool the properties. JCo natively supports pooling, but you must understand how to do it—it isn't handled for you.

The first thing to do is to create a `JCO.Pool` object:

```
private static final String POOL_NAME = "MyPool";
...
JCO.Pool pool = JCO.getClientPoolManager().getPool(POOL_NAME);
```

This method takes a `String` as an argument that represents the unique pool name. Now we check whether the pool is null.

If it's null, we create a new client. Instead of using the `JCO.createClient` method, use `JCO.addClientPool`. This method is similar, but also has parameters for the pool name and the number of active connections that a pool can contain before it refuses to create another client. The `JCO.getClient()` method accepts a pool name, and optionally, a Boolean refresh flag to refresh the connection. The following code shows an example of creating and retrieving a client from a pool.

NOTE

This refresh flag is important on older 3.1 versions of SAP because the R/3 system cannot refresh the connection; it has to disconnect and reconnect, which is a huge performance hit. On new R3 systems, this is done automatically in JCo when the client is returned to the pool.

```
if(pool == null){
    JCO.addClientPool(POOL_NAME,    // Pool Name
             10,       // Number of Connections
             "500",      // Client
             "myUser",    // User Name
             "myPass",    // Password
             "EN",      // Language
             "192.168.1.2", // Server Name or IP
             "00");      // System No
        }
```

```
try{
client = JCO.getClient(POOL_NAME);
}catch(JCO.Exception e){
    if(e.JCO_ERROR_RESOURCE == e.getGroup())
       System.out.println("Pool is Full");
    else
       e.printStackTrace();
}
```


The pool will try to get a connection. If that connection is busy, another one will be created. If the number of connections exceeds the maximum that's specified in the client pool, an exception is thrown. To connect to different SAP systems in the same file, just specify a different pool name. A separate pool will then be created.

After the pool is created and we make a call to SAP, we must use the `JCO.releaseClient` method to release the client object back to the pool:

```
JCO.releaseClient(client);
```

CAUTION

In a multithreaded environment, be careful using the `JCO.Client` object. This object, if retrieved from one thread, should never be used or accessed in another.

Loading Parameters from a Properties File

Another way of using the `JCO.addClientPool` and `JCO.createClient` methods is to use load them from a properties file. The following is a sample of such a properties file. The complete list of properties supported is contained in the JavaDocs under the `JCO.createClient(Properties p)` method. The JavaDocs can be found in the JCo home directory under `docs\jco\com\sap\mw\jco\JCO.html`.

```
jco.client.client = 500
jco.client.user  = myUser
jco.client.passwd = myPass
jco.client.lang  = EN
jco.client.sysnr = 00
jco.client.ashost = 192.168.1.2
...
```

The `JCO.addClientPool` and `JCO.createClient` methods support loading the attributes from a `java.util.Properties` object. To read the properties from a file into the `Properties` object, a `resourceBundle` can be used. The following is a method that loads the file and returns the `Properties` object or null if the bundle is not found:

```
private Properties loadProperties(String propertiesFile){
ResourceBundle myResourceBundle = null;
try{
myResourceBundle = ResourceBundle.getBundle(propertiesFile);
}catch(MissingResourceException e){
    e.printStackTrace();
    return null;
}
Properties myProperties = new Properties();
Enumeration e = myResourceBundle.getKeys();
String tempString = "";
while(e.hasMoreElements()){
   tempString = (String)e.nextElement();
   myProperties.setProperty(tempString,
        myResourceBundle.getString(tempString));
}
return myProperties;
}
```

The code for creating the client then becomes easier to maintain because a change to the SAP server parameters does not require the programmer to recompile:

```
...
Properties mySAPProp = loadProperties("myApp.properties.saplogin");
client = JCO.createClient(mySAPProp);
...
```

Calling an SAP Function

Until this point, this chapter has dealt with establishing and discontinuing connections from SAP. The next step is to call the functions of and retrieve data from SAP.

The first step is to create a `JCO.Repository` object. This object calls SAP and dynamically retrieves all the metadata for each function called. The other alternative, which is hard-coding the function's interface, is not a good idea because the interfaces can change as SAP systems are upgraded and support packs are installed.

Calling one of three different constructors creates the repository. Each constructor has two different parameters. The first parameter is `java.lang.String`, which is used to name the repository. The second parameter is `JCO.Client`, a pool name, or an array of pool names. The following code uses a predefined pool name:

```
JCO.Repository myRepository = new JCO.Repository("JCOrep", POOL_NAME);
```

After the repository is created, it's used to get an `IFunctionTemplate`, which in turn returns a `JCO.Function` object with its `getFunction()` method. In the following example, the `BAPI_MATERIAL_GETLIST` BAPI is retrieved:

```
JCO.Function myFunc = mrep.getFunctionTemplate(
          "BAPI_MATERIAL_GETLIST").getFunction();
```


The `JCO.Function` now contains information regarding its import, export, and table parameters as well as all the information necessary to complete a call to SAP.

The actual call is performed within the `JCO.Client` object's `execute()` method:

```
client.execute(myFunc);
```

This BAPI will return all the BAPIs on the current system and pertinent information about them. To use the data, the programmer must know how to access the import, export, and table data.

Java and SAP Type Conversion

SAP and Java have very different concepts of data types. JCo has conversions for each of the SAP data types, a `getString()` method that returns the data type as a string, and a `getValue()` method that returns an object of the correct type. JCo tries to convert the type passed in to the associated ABAP type. If this isn't possible, a runtime exception is thrown. There are associated set and get methods for each Java type. The JavaDocs for `JCO.Record` contain a very helpful conversion table that explains how JCo converts each ABAP type into a Java type when a method is called. Table 32.4 lists the SAP types, the associated Java objects, and the access method used to retrieve the data.

TABLE 32.4 JCo Conversion Table

ABAP Type	JCo Type	Java Type	JCo get Method
C-Character	JCO.TYPE_CHAR	String	getString()
N-Numeric	JCO.TYPE_NUM	String	getString()
g-String	JCO.TYPE_STRING	String	getString()
b-1 byte int	JCO.TYPE_INT1	Int	getInt()
s-2 byte int	JCO.TYPE_INT2	Int	getInt()
I-4 byte int	JCO.TYPE_INT	Int	getInt()
P-Binary Coded Decimal	JCO.TYPE_BCD	BigDecimal	getBigDecimal()
X-raw data	JCO.TYPE_BYTE	byte[]	getByteArray()
y-raw data (variable)	JCO.TYPE_BYTE	byte[]	getByteArray()
F-Float	JCO.TYPE_FLOAT	Double	getDouble()
D-Date	JCO.TYPE_DATE	Date	getDate()
T-Time	JCO.TYPE_TIME	Date	getDate()

When putting data into fields and tables for a call to SAP, the `setValue()` method is overloaded for use with all the JCo data types besides `JCO.TYPE_DATE` and `JCO.TYPE_TIME`. SAP expects the date in the format YYYYMMDD, but allows the dates 00000000 and 99999999 that break the `java.lang.Date` format. On the outbound, JCo changes 00000000 to null and 99999999 to 12/31/9999, but on the input, it's not correct to do this conversion. Instead, use the `setValue()` method to set a `String` object. Time conversions have a similar problem: Outbound values work as the Java `date` object, but the programmer must set inbound values by using a `String` value.

JCo has introspection objects for conversion from SAP to Java. Every object that can access field-level data has a `getType()` method that gives the JCo type for the field. The following program snippet shows the conversion and gives an example of retrieving the data for every SAP data type. Of course, you can use the `getString()` method for every field if the program needs to display only the unformatted data as a string as on a Web site.

```
JCO.Table matnrlist = jfun.getTableParameterList().getTable("MATNRLIST");


    for(int rows =0; rows < matnrlist.getNumRows();
            rows++,matnrlist.nextRow()){
       for(int cols = 0; cols < matnrlist.getNumColumns(); cols++){
           switch(matnrlist.getType(cols)){
           case JCO.TYPE_INT1:
           case JCO.TYPE_INT2:
           case JCO.TYPE_INT:
              int jcoint = matnrlist.getInt(cols);
              break;
           case JCO.TYPE_CHAR:
           case JCO.TYPE_NUM:
           case JCO.TYPE_STRING:
              String jcostring = matnrlist.getString(cols);
              break;
           case JCO.TYPE_BCD:
              BigDecimal jcobcd = matnrlist.getBigDecimal(cols);
              break;
           case JCO.TYPE_DATE:
              java.util.Date jcodate = matnrlist.getDate(cols);
              break;
           case JCO.TYPE_TIME:
              java.util.Date jcotime = matnrlist.getTime(cols);
              break;
           case JCO.TYPE_FLOAT:
              double jcofloat = matnrlist.getDouble(cols);
              break;
           case JCO.TYPE_BYTE:
           case JCO.TYPE_XSTRING:
              byte[] jcobyte = matnrlist.getByteArray(cols);
```

```
            break;
        default:
            System.out.print("Incompatible Type");
        }

    }//end of cols
}//end of rows
```


Setting and Getting Data

JCo has helper classes for dealing with import, export, and table parameters. These classes encapsulate structures, tables, and fields. The `JCO.Function` object has associated methods to create the data structures needed to work with fields. The `getImportParameterList()`, `getExportParameterList()`, and `getTableParameterList()` methods return a `JCO.ParameterList` object that contains references to all the associated objects. The `JCO.ParameterList` object contains methods to get the individual object that needs to be populated. The methods take the name or the index of the parameter. Table 32.5 contains a list of these methods and what they return.

TABLE 32.5 JCO.ParameterList Functions

Object Returned	Method Name	Description
JCO.Field	getField(String)	
	getField(int)	Returns the field object for individual field parameters
JCO.Structure	getStructure(String)	
	getStructure(int)	Returns the structure object for import and export structures
JCO.Table	getTable(String)	
	getTable(int)	Returns the table object for tables
java.lang.Object	getValue(String)	
	getValue(int)	Returns the object for the given parameter

On simple scalar fields, it isn't necessary to convert to the `JCO.Field` object. The `setValue()` method has this capability. `setValue()` has two arguments: The first is the value and the second is the field name.

```
myFunc.getImportParameterList().setValue("10","MAXROWS");
```

The `MAXROWS` field is now set to a value of `10`. Remember that JCo has the capability to convert different types into the correct type for the field. If the data is incompatible with the type, JCo throws an exception.

To set a structure value, first get the structure from the input parameter list:

```
JCO.Structure matnrselection =
       jfun.getImportParameterList().getStructure("MATNRSELECTION");
```

This next step is to set the field with the setValue() method:

```
matnrselection.setValue("I","SIGN");
```

For scalar fields and structures, it's very easy to retrieve data. The previous section discussed JCo types and the necessary access modifiers to retrieve them. The getString() method works for all types because JCo converts the values to java.lang.String. To access a single field, the call looks almost the same except that the getExportParameterList() function is used:

```
int output = jfun.getExportParameterList().getInt("SOMEFIELD");
```

Working with structures is the same, except that we must get a JCO.Structure first and then get the value by passing in either the field name or the column index:

```
JCO.Structure return = jfun.getExportParameterList().getStructure("RETURN");
String num = return.getString("NUMBER");
```

Although single fields and structures are important, most work with remote-enabled function modules is done through tables.

Working with Tables

So far, this chapter has dealt with single fields and structures. Last, but certainly not least, we'll discuss working with tables. Although single fields and structures are specified as either import or export, table values are passed both in and out of SAP. Tables also contain multiple rows that must be traversed, created, and deleted. Before dealing with setting and getting the data, the first step is to retrieve the JCO.Table object from the function:

```
JCO.Table matnrselection jfun.getTableParameterList("MATNRSELECTION");
```

The next step seems backward to most people. Instead of filling a row with data and then appending it to a table, JCo does it in the opposite order. First, create the row with the appendRow() method, and then set the value of the individual fields within the row:

```
matnrselection.appendRow();
matnrselection.setValue("I","SIGN");
matnrselection.setValue("CP", "OPTION");
matnrselection.setValue("FERT-100","MATNR_LOW");
```

Internally in the JCO.Table object, when the appendRow() method is called, a row is created and the row pointer is set to the newly created row. For performance reasons, JCo allows multiple rows to be created at once with the appendRows(int *rows*) method that has the number of rows to be created as an argument. The row pointer is set to the first row that was created. JCo allows the manipulation of the row pointer through the following methods:

- `nextRow()`—Sets the row pointer to the next row
- `previousRow()`—Sets the row pointer to the previous row
- `firstRow()`—Sets the row pointer to the first row
- `lastRow()`—Sets the row pointer to the last row
- `getNumRows()`—Returns the number of rows
- `getRow()`—Gets the position of the row pointer
- `insertRow(int` *`row`*`)`—Creates a row and sets the row pointer to the row specified
- `deleteRow(int` *`row`*`)`—Deletes the row at the specified position
- `deleteAllRows()`—Deletes all rows in the table
- `setRow(int` *`row`*`)`—Sets the row pointer to the one specified

Now that the methods in `JCO.Table` are defined, let's manipulate them in a demo program. The `BAPI_MATERIAL_GETLIST` function will return a queried list of materials. This function uses `MATNRSELECTION` to send in the material query; we can use this just for an example and print out the result (see Listing 32.1). This is an excerpt from the `JcoTableFun.java` example that you can find in the `/examples` directory on the companion CD. In lines 1 and 2, the function is retrieved from SAP. Lines 3 and 4 get the table `MATNRSELECTION` and assign it to the variable `matnrselection`. Line 5 appends a row; line 6 sets the value of the `MATNR_LOW` field to the value `"Row1"`. Line 7 creates three more rows. Line 8 sets the value of the second row. Line 9 moves to the next row. Line 10 sets the data in the third row. Line 11 sets the current row to the second row (remember that the row numbers start at 0). Line 12 deletes the current row. Line 13 goes to the last row. Line 14 sets the value of the last row to `"LastRow"`. Line 15 inserts a row in the third position. Line 16 inserts the value `"New 3rd Row"` into the third row. Line 17 moves to the first row. Lines 18–22 print out the data in the `MATNR_LOW` field of the `MATNRSELECTION` table we just populated.

LISTING 32.1 Example of Manipulating Tables

```
1 JCO.Function jfun =
2 mrep.getFunctionTemplate("BAPI_MATERIAL_GETLIST").getFunction();
3    JCO.Table matnrselection =
4 jfun.getTableParameterList().getTable("MATNRSELECTION");
5       matnrselection.appendRow();
6       matnrselection.setValue("Row1","MATNR_LOW"); //set at first position
7       matnrselection.appendRows(3);
8       matnrselection.setValue("Row2","MATNR_LOW");//set at position 2
9       matnrselection.nextRow(); //move to the 3rd row
```

LISTING 32.1 Continued

```
    matnrselection.setValue("Row3","MATNR_LOW");//set at position 3
    matnrselection.setRow(1); //go to the second row
    matnrselection.deleteRow();//delete the current 2nd row
    matnrselection.lastRow();//go to last row
    matnrselection.setValue("LastRow","MATNR_LOW");//set at last row
    matnrselection.insertRow(2);//insert a row in the 3rd position
    matnrselection.setValue("New 3rd Row","MATNR_LOW");//set new 3rd row
    matnrselection.firstRow();//move to first row
  for(int rows = 0; rows <    matnrselection.getNumRows(); rows++){
    System.out.print("Row = " + matnrselection.getRow() + " ");
    System.out.println("Value = " + matnrselection.getString("MATNR_LOW"));
    matnrselection.nextRow();
     }
```

When the preceding sample from Listing 32.1 and `JcoTableFun.java` is compiled and run, the second row is deleted, the new third row is inserted, and there are exactly four rows:

```
Row = 0 Value = Row1
Row = 1 Value = Row3
Row = 2 Value = New 3rd Row
Row = 3 Value = LastRow
```

The data within the rows is retrieved using the same functions discussed when using a structure. All the `get` methods covered in the data type conversion section also apply to a table row. Remember, the internal row pointer must point to the row where the data you need access to is stored.

Transactions in SAP

When building applications using multiple systems, the concept of transactions is very important. For instance, if an application needs to create a sales order within SAP and update a second database for a separate material management system, the complete logical unit of work would state that if the call to SAP succeeds but the database call fails, the application would roll back the SAP transaction to keep the data in sync. Most SAP BAPIs and RFCs do not implicitly support transactional type processing, specifically using two-phase commits. Some of the newer BAPIs support one-phase commits, but with one caveat: The programmer must write the code for the commit or rollback. Any function that supports this model must have special BAPIs called while holding the same connection to SAP. The two special-case BAPIs are

- `BAPI_TRANSACTION_COMMIT`—Commits the work done by the transaction-enabled BAPI
- `BAPI_TRANSACTION_ROLLBACK`—Rolls back the work done by the transaction-enabled BAPI

This would be a nice feature on all inbound SAP calls. Unfortunately, that isn't the case. In fact, without reading the documentation on the function, there's no way to tell whether a function needs a commit or even if the operation is supported.

One frequently used BAPI that needs an external commit is BAPI_SALESORDER_CREATEFROMDAT2. Let's look at a sample call using this BAPI within a transaction as shown in Listing 32.2. The most important part of using the transaction BAPI is calling it with same connection without closing it. Listing 32.2 gives an example of using a transaction in with SAP.

LISTING 32.2 Transactional Processing in JCo

```
JCO.Function bapi_sales_create =
   mrep.getFunctionTemplate("BAPI_SALESORDER_CREATEFROMDAT2").getFunction();
JCO.Function commit       =
   mrep.getFunctionTemplate("BAPI_TRANSACTION_COMMIT").getFunction();
JCO.Function rollback     =
   mrep.getFunctionTemplate("BAPI_TRANSACTION_ROLLBACK").getFunction();
try{
client.connect();
client.execute(bapi_sales_create);

if(!"".equals(bapi_sales_create.getExportParameterList()
    .getString("SALESDOCUMENT")))
    client.execute(commit);
else
    client.execute(rollback);
}catch(Exception e){
    e.printStackTrace();
}
JCO.releaseClient(client);
...
```

This example is very simple and commits only when a valid document number is returned from the created sales order. The steps are the same even as the transaction processing needs grow:

- Create or retrieve a client
- Call the RFC or BAPI that supports external database commits
- Call BAPI_TRANSACTION_COMMIT or BAPI_TRANSACTION_ROLLBACK either to commit or remove the work based on a business decision
- Release the client back to the pool or disconnect

NOTE

This is a perfect place to use the EJB `SessionSynchronization` interface. The `Commit` function could be executed in the `beforeCompletion()` method, and could force a rollback if it fails.

Filtering SAP Data

Certain SAP functions can have hundreds of parameters. Storing all that data on the client side can have a serious impact on performance. JCo enables the programmer to filter out the import, export, and table parameters that aren't needed. This does not mean that they aren't transferred from SAP. The client receives all the data, but JCo just ignores the data that was set as inactive. The `setActive()` method is used to filter the parameters that aren't needed at runtime. The `JCO.ParameterList` object contains the `setActive()` method. Here's an example of filtering out a table that isn't needed:

```
bapi_sales_create.getTableParameterList().setActive(false, "ORDER_CFGS_INST");
```

JCo does not support the filtering of individual fields in a structure or table.

Exception Handling in JCo

Exception handling is a very important part of writing software. This intensifies when connecting to many heterogeneous systems. JCo error handling enables programmers to encapsulate SAP errors and correctly warn users of problems.

JCo throws only runtime exceptions, which means a `try-catch` block isn't needed around JCo calls (that is, the compiler won't complain if the method doesn't use `throws`). However, when programmers write JCo programs, this might not be beneficial because they may inadvertently miss error handling and crash the runtime environment. In some cases this is fine, such as in standalone, run-once programs. But when programming Web sites, this isn't acceptable. The end user wants to be informed if there is a problem and directed in what she can do about it (even if it's a fatal system error). When programming JCo in Web environments, always catch and process or display as many errors as possible. JCo has three different types of exceptions:

- `JCO.Exception`—The base exception thrown by JCo and the parent of the other two exceptions.
- `JCO.ConversionException`—A JCo exception thrown when an incompatible value is entered into a field and cannot be converted.
- `JCO.AbapException`—A JCo exception thrown from the function being called within SAP.

JCo Exception

The base class of all JCo exceptions is JCO.Exception. This object classifies errors into several different error groups that can be retrieved with the getGroup() method. Check the Java documentation on JCO.Exception for more information. This is found in from the JCo home directory in docs\jco\com\sap\mw\jco\JCO.Exception.html.

The class uses two methods: getKey(), which returns the error key, and toString(), which returns a description of the error. Sometimes this message isn't very pretty, as in the case of network errors.

The following code checks for the resource that's unavailable in a connection pool and prints out a better error message:

```
try{
  client = JCO.getClient(POOL_NAME);
}catch(JCO.Exception e){
    if(e.JCO_ERROR_RESOURCE == e.getGroup())
     System.out.println("Pool is Full, create a larger one");
    else{
     System.out.println("Group   = " + e.getGroup());
     System.out.println("key     = " + e.getKey());
     System.out.println("Message = " + e.toString());
     System.exit(1);
    }
}
```

Conversion Exceptions

The "Java and SAP Type Conversion" section earlier in this chapter describes how JCo tries to convert values from set and get methods into the proper format. If this format is unacceptable and cannot be converted, a conversion exception is thrown. When working with input from a Web application and passing it to SAP, it's a good idea to catch these conversion exceptions and gracefully display errors back to the screen for invalid data. The following code checks for a conversion exception on an input parameter and saves the error for later processing:

```
try{
  ordersched.setValue(myQty,"REQ_QTY");
}catch(JCO.ConversionException ce){
    System.out.print("Error Key = " + ce.getKey());
    System.out.print("Error Text = " + ce.toString());
    Error = ce.toString(); //display back to front end
}
```

ABAP Exceptions

SAP has different ways of handling exceptions thrown in remote-enabled functions. BAPIs traditionally have a return structure that holds any error message or runtime exception thrown within the ABAP code. The return table usually has a similar type and can be programmatically accessed on the Java side and use the Java error handling. This definitely isn't the case 100% of the time. Some BAPIs and most RFCs have a different method for handling errors that throw ABAP exceptions.

The first segment of code lists a return table that contains errors from a BAPI. The `TYPE` field contains a one-character field representation that uses `E` to specify an error. This code loops and prints out all the errors and warnings. The following code is an example of retrieving errors.

```
client.execute(bapi_sales_create);
JCO.Table bapireturn =
  bapi_sales_create.getTableParameterList().getTable("RETURN");
if(bapireturn.getNumRows()>0){
    for(int num_err = 0; num_err < bapireturn.getNumRows();num_err++){
     if("E".equals(bapireturn.getString("TYPE"))){
       //an error
       System.out.println("Error: " + bapireturn.getString("MESSAGE"));
     }
     else{
       // a warning
        System.out.println("Warning: " + bapireturn.getString("MESSAGE"));
      }
    }
}
```

The second type of error handling found most often in RFCs is exceptions that are thrown and listed in the RFC. These errors are thrown during the execute method. When `JCO.AbapException` is thrown, the `getKey()` method returns the exception that was thrown.

The following sample code looks for an error message thrown by `RFC_READ_TABLE`, which is a useful function for getting table data from SAP:

```
try{
 client.execute(bapi_sales_create);
}catch(JCO.AbapException ae){
 if("SOME_ERROR".equalsIgnoreCase(ae.getKey()))
   System.out.println("Table is not Found");
}
```

Each of the previous examples is explored further in a sample program on the companion CD in `examples/JCoTestExceptions.java` for this chapter.

Sample Web Application for JCo

Instead of setting up a complex framework for the SAP connection, this sample uses JCo in only a JSP and a JavaBean. In a Web environment, the SAP connection is usually done within some sort of business object (an Action class in Struts or an EJB, for instance).

The example contains two JSPs and a JavaBean. The first JSP is a selection page, and the second contains the JCo call and lists the output. The JavaBean contains references to the `MATNRSELECTION` table, which has a common SAP structure known as a *select-option*. This is how ABAP handles searching. The structure has four different fields:

- The `SIGN` field can accept either `I` or `E`, meaning an inclusive or exclusive search, respectively. An inclusive search returns what was specified in the other fields. An exclusive search returns everything except what was specified in the query.
- The OPTION tab specifies the operation to perform. The `OPTION` field uses a two-digit code. In the following example, we use `CP` (standing for *contains pattern*), which enables us to use the `*` wildcard character. More documentation of this and other function modules this can be found in SAP under the transaction BAPI.
- `MATNR_LOW` and `MATNR_HIGH`, which contain the search values.

All the source for the application is contained with the compiled classes on the CD. They're located on the companion CD in the `/webClient` directory for this chapter. The JSPs are listed here, and the SAP connection JavaBean is in `WEB-INF/classes/myApp/beans/MaterialSearch.java`. To deploy the Web example, you must

- Download and install the JCo software from SAP (free for partners and customers).
- Copy the Web application directory named `webClient` from the `ch32` directory on the companion CD to any temporary directory on your hard drive.
- Add `jco.jar` or `sapjco.jar` from the JCo install directory to the Web application's `WEB-INF/lib` folder, and the content of `.../SAP/WEB-INF/classes` to the Web application's `WEB-INF/classes` folder.
- The properties file must be configured with your SAP information. The location of the file is `WEB-INF/classes/myApp/properties/saplogin.properties`.
- Add a new application to the WebLogic domain, starting by picking the `webClient` directory from the temp location on your hard drive.
- Run the application by entering the following URL in a Web browser:

  `http://[weblogic server web address]:[port]/webClient`

When the application is correctly installed and the URL is typed in, you'll see the screen shown in Figure 32.1.

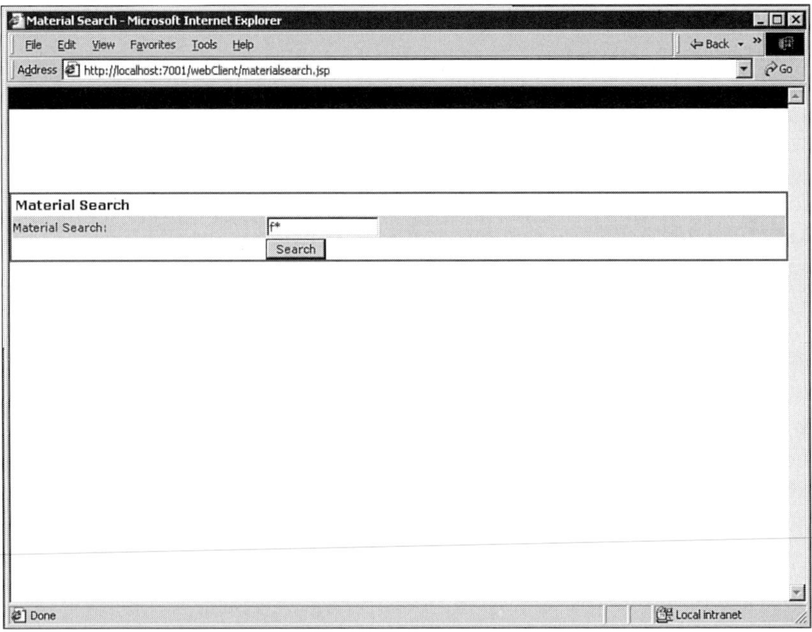

Figure 32.1 webClient application start screen.

At this screen, type in material or a search criterion with an * to return a list of materials from SAP. The search length is limited to 100 items for performance and time reasons.

Server Programming in JCo

JCo provides the capability not only for the Java side to call SAP, but also the other way around, so that SAP can call Java. This would be very useful in cases in which immediate notification is necessary. For instance, when a special condition is applied in SAP, email must be sent to all Web-based customers residing on an external database. In this section, we discuss how to set up a JCo server and listen for incoming calls. The code for this section is located in the `/server` directory on the companion CD. A complete working version plus sources is included.

Creating a JCo Server

A JCo server must be configured internally in SAP. An SAP system cannot just call an external program without having the skeleton of the import, export, and table parameters defined within the system. Instead of creating our own custom RFC for this example, let's use an RFC that has already been defined: `RFC_CUSTOMER_GET`. This function can be accessed through SAP transaction SE37. It contains two optional input parameters and one table parameter. Figure 32.2 is a screenshot of the table dictionary object needed for our function. This information must be created within our server as a repository.

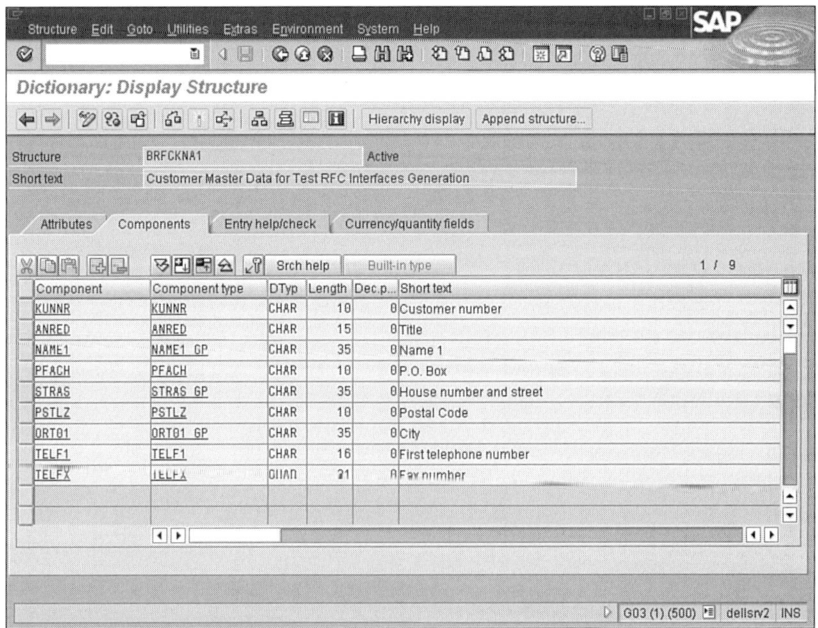

Figure 32.2 SAP data dictionary screen.

Earlier in this chapter, we discussed how JCo automatically creates the repository object and populates it with the correct metadata. However, when implementing the JCo server, we have to define our own repository. This information should be defined as static and usually can be an inner class. In our example, I've defined a wrapper class with two internal classes:

- `Repository`—Contains a new repository object that extends the basic repository and implements `IRepository`
- `Server`—Extends a `JCO.Server` object and handles all the requests for our program

The wrapper class implements `JCO.ServerExceptionListener` to handle any exceptions that might be thrown. It also contains a simple `main()` method that calls the `runServer()` method to start the server. The following code shows how this works:

```
public class JCoServer implements JCO.ServerExceptionListener{

    protected static IRepository repository; //define my Repository
    JCO.Server server = null;         //define my Server
...
public static void main(String[] argv)
  {
    JCO.setTraceLevel(0);
    JCoServer myserver = new JCoServer();
    myserver.runServer();
  }
```

Creating a Repository

Next we define the inner class for our repository. This class is defined as static because we don't need to instantiate the data more than once. We need this class because we're defining our own repository for the server, and cannot use `JCO.Repository`, which is specifically used in client programs.

```
//Create a static repository to hold all metadata for our functions.
  static public class Repository extends
     JCO.BasicRepository implements com.sap.mw.jco.IRepository {


    public Repository(String repname)
    {
      super(repname);
    }
  }
```

With the inner class `Repository` defined, we must now create the data for the repository. For performance reasons, we use a static block within the wrapper class. This code will be run only once: when the class is instantiated. The important JCo class needed to add the metadata is `JCO.MetaData`. This class has an overloaded `addInfo()` method that's used to add different types of metadata. In our case, we need to define two types of metadata:

- Function interface data—Metadata that defines the import, export, and table parameters for the function
- Structure definition data—Metadata that defines the underlying structure of the import, export, and table parameters

The addInfo() method for adding our function interface data contains these arguments:

- name—Name of the field
- type—JCo data type
- length—Length of the parameter used if the parameter is a scalar
- offset—Field offset in the JCo buffer used if a parameter is a scalar
- decimals—Number of decimals a field contains; used with JCO.TYPE_BCD and JCO.TYPE_FLOAT
- flags—Specifies whether the parameter is an import (JCO.IMPORT_PARAMETER), an export (JCO.EXPORT_PARAMETER), an optional (JCO.OPTIONAL_PARAMETER), an inactive (JCO.INACTIVE_PARAMETER), or a table (insert int value 0) parameter
- structure_metadata—Takes an object, but for structures and tables, populate with the name of the underlying structure in SAP

When creating data for the structure, we do not need the flags or the table metadata. So, the addInfo() method has an overloaded method without these parameters added.

The final step is storing the JCO.MetaData objects in the repository. The repository object has two methods for this:

- addFunctionInterfaceToCache()—Adds the function metadata to the repository
- addStructureDefinitionToCache()—Adds the structure metadata to the repository

Now that we know what each function does, let's look at the code. Listing 32.3 is the static block within our wrapper class used to define our repository data.

LISTING 32.3 Defining the JCo Repository

```
//for performance reasons, define a singleton for repository
  static {
    repository = new Repository("serverRepository");

    JCO.MetaData functionMetaData = new JCO.MetaData("RFC_CUSTOMER_GET");
    functionMetaData.addInfo("KUNNR",
           JCO.TYPE_CHAR,  10, 0, 0, JCO.IMPORT_PARAMETER , null);
    functionMetaData.addInfo("NAME1",
           JCO.TYPE_CHAR,  35, 0, 0, JCO.IMPORT_PARAMETER, null);
    functionMetaData.addInfo("CUSTOMER_T",
           JCO.TYPE_TABLE, 0, 0, 0, 0,  "BRFCKNA1");
```

LISTING 32.3 Continued

```
    repository.addFunctionInterfaceToCache(functionMetaData);

    JCO.MetaData structureMetaData = new JCO.MetaData("BRFCKNA1");
    structureMetaData.addInfo("KUNNR", JCO.TYPE_CHAR, 10, 0, 0);
    structureMetaData.addInfo("ANRED", JCO.TYPE_CHAR,  15, 10, 0);
    structureMetaData.addInfo("NAME1",  JCO.TYPE_CHAR,  35, 25, 0);
    structureMetaData.addInfo("PFACH",  JCO.TYPE_CHAR,  10, 60, 0);
    structureMetaData.addInfo("STRAS",  JCO.TYPE_CHAR,  35, 70, 0);
    structureMetaData.addInfo("PSTLZ",  JCO.TYPE_CHAR,  10, 105, 0);
    structureMetaData.addInfo("ORT01",  JCO.TYPE_CHAR,  35, 115, 0);
    structureMetaData.addInfo("TELF1", JCO.TYPE_CHAR,  16, 150, 0);
    structureMetaData.addInfo("TELFX",  JCO.TYPE_CHAR,  31, 166, 0);

    repository.addStructureDefinitionToCache(structureMetaData);
  }
```

Notice how the offset length has to be specified in the structure metadata and not in the parameters. The offset is very important; if it's incorrect, the values will be populated incorrectly.

With the repository created and stored, we're ready to create the `JCO.Server` objects and ultimately receive messages from SAP.

Creating the JCO.Server Objects

The `JCO.Server` object must be extended to do anything useful with SAP. In our example, we create an inner class for extending the JCo server and create a constructor. The constructor takes a very specific set of arguments. The list of arguments in our example is as follows:

- Gateway host—The SAP gateway server name or IP address
- Gateway service number—The service number; usually `sapgw00`
- Program ID—The program ID that must match the program ID specified in the RFC
- Repository—The function `Repository` object

> **TIP**
>
> If you aren't familiar with these terms, contact your SAP basis administrator to help you set them up.

```
//Create a server to take requests from SAP
 static public class Server extends JCO.Server {

    public Server(String gwhost, String gwserv,
           String progid, IRepository repository)
    {
      super(gwhost,gwserv,progid,repository);
    }
...
}
```

32

Now that we have the basic object taken care of, let's look at the `handleRequest()` method that must be overridden (it's empty `{ }` by default). The `handleRequest()` method is called every time the SAP system contacts JCo. The lone argument passed is a `JCO.Function` object. At this point, the programmer is free to do whatever he wants. I suggest checking for each function your application supports, and then minimally writing a separate method for each function. To keep the example readable, our sample application only contains one function and populates a table if the customer is correctly matched. Let's examine the code shown in Listing 32.4.

LISTING 32.4 Handling a Request from SAP

```
// The default method handles nothing. override for all functions that are needed
    protected void handleRequest(JCO.Function function)
{

  System.out.println("function " + function.getName() + " called from SAP");

  if (function.getName().equals("RFC_CUSTOMER_GET")) {
    JCO.Table tables =
    function.getTableParameterList().getTable("CUSTOMER_T");
    System.out.println(
    function.getImportParameterList().getString("KUNNR"));
  if("1234567890".equals(function.getImportParameterList().getString("KUNNR"))){
    tables.appendRow();
    tables.setValue("1234567890", "KUNNR");
    tables.setValue("Michael Jordan", "NAME1");
    tables.setValue("91607", "PSTLZ");
    tables.setValue("USA", "STRAS");
    tables.setValue("CALIFORNIA", "ORT01");
    tables.setValue("818-555-5555", "TELF1");
   }
```

LISTING 32.4 Continued

```
    else{
     throw new JCO.AbapException(
         "NO_RECORD_FOUND","No Current Record could be found!!!");
    }
  }
}//handleRequest
```

The code in Listing 32.4 could be separated into a separate method, but for this short example, there's no need to do so. Using the same methods we learned about on the client side, we first check the customer number KUNNR. If it matches the required value, we return a row of data to SAP. If it doesn't match, we throw an ABAP exception.

TIP

The first argument in the exception thrown has to match one of the exceptions in the RFC interface within SAP. If it doesn't, a short dump will occur in SAP. You can verify this by looking at transaction SE37, entering the program name, and clicking on the Exceptions tab.

SAP RFC Setup (SM59)

Without setting up the RFC destination within SAP, programs cannot call your Java application. There are some very specific instructions for setting up the RFC destination to work with your program. First, it must be a TCP/IP connection type. Second, the activation type must be Registration and the program ID must match the program ID given when the Java server was started. This is the link that registers your server to the SAP RFC. To set up an RFC, either you or a SAP basis person must log on to SAP and go to transaction SM59. Figure 32.3 shows the screen.

Running the Server Application

To run the server application, simply follow these steps:

1. Copy the `/server` directory from the companion CD to your computer's hard drive.
2. Set the correct path to your `jco.jar` or `sapjco.jar` in the `startserver.bat` file located in the `/server` directory.
3. Make sure that `java.exe` is in your classpath.

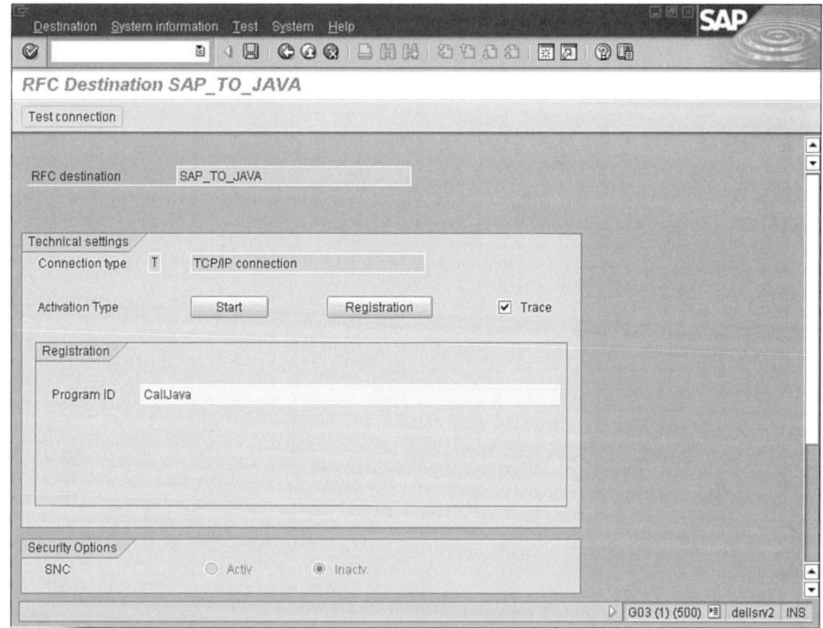

Figure 32.3 SAP RFC setup screen.

4. Start the JCO server by clicking on the `startserver.bat` file.
5. Make sure that the RFC settings are correct as specified in the "SAP RFC Setup (SM59)" section earlier in this chapter.
6. Go to transaction SE37 in SAP.
7. Enter **`RFC_CUSTOMER_GET`** and press the F8 key to go to the Test Function Module screen.
8. Fill in the RFC target sys: value with the correct RFC destination name from SM59.
9. Populate the KUNNR value with `1234567890` to return address information or any other value to return a `NO_RECORD_FOUND` exception.

Figure 32.4 shows the testing screen in SE37.

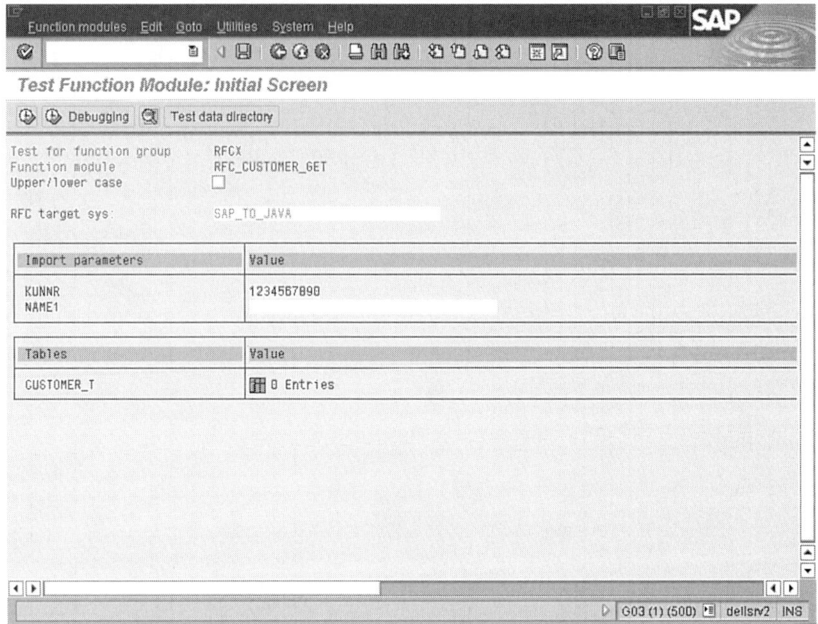

Figure 32.4 Testing the Java server from inside SAP.

Useful BAPIs and RFCs

Working with SAP can be a hunt-and-peck typing mission, especially if you're not familiar with the system. Here are a few RFCs and BAPIS that prove to be very useful:

- `BAPI_MONITOR_GETLIST`—Returns a list of all available BAPIs, including release dates, versions, and status.
- `BAPI_SALESORDER_SIMULATE`—Used to simulate an order in SAP.
- `BAPI_SALESORDER_CREATEFROMDAT2`—Used to create sales orders within SAP. Supports two-phase commits.
- `BAPI_SALESORDER_GETLIST`—Returns a list of sales orders for a customer.
- `BAPI_CUSTOMER_CHECKPASSWORD`—Used to check the password of an Internet user.
- `BAPI_CUSTOMER_EXISTS`—Verifies that the user exists in the system.
- `BAPI_MATERIAL_GETLIST`—Returns a list of materials out of SAP.
- `BAPI_MATERIAL_AVAILABILITY`—Returns the availability of materials.
- `DDIF_FIELDINFO_GET`—Returns useful metadata on fields and tables within SAP.

- RFC_READ_TABLE—Returns data from a table specified by the user and a where clause.
- RFC_FUNCTION_SEARCH—Searches for RFCs and BAPIs within SAP.
- RFC_GET_FUNCTION_INTERFACE—Returns the interface for the RFC or BAPI.
- BAPI_TRANSACTION_COMMIT—commits work done by BAPIs that support external database commits
- BAPI_TRANSACTION_ROLLBACK—Rolls back work done by BAPIs that support database rollbacks.
- BAPI_HELPVALUES_GET—Returns help values for fields and parameters.
- BAPI_FIELDHELP_GETDOCU—Returns the documentation for the BAPI fields and parameters.
- BAPI_CONVERSION_INT2EXT—Converts data from internal format to external format.
- BAPI_CONVERSION_EXT2INT—Converts data from external format to internal format.

For a more complete listing of SAP BAPIs and their function, check out http://www.zoption.com/eziobapi.htm. This site breaks each BAPI into its correct area and is searchable for each version of SAP.

Summary

In this chapter, we covered most of the aspects of programming in JCo. More resources can be found inside SAPnet at http://service.sap.com. This site requires a valid customer or partner user ID.

We saw that JCo provides an easy-to-use API to connect to SAP. It has proven itself stable and production worthy. This API is proprietary, however. SAP released a J2EE-CA compatible connector early in 2003 in a beta version. This connector was covered in Chapter 31. Other companies, including BEA, have SAP connectors. Some of these companies are also already J2EE-CA compliant. The basis of all these J2EE-CA–compliant connectors is JCo. JCo will continue to be used as the backbone of SAP-Java connectivity even after J2EE-CA matures less in the Web arena and more in standalone applications.

CHAPTER **33**

WebLogic Server's jCOM Java/COM Bridge

By Mark Artiges

IN THIS CHAPTER

- Understanding jCOM
- How jCOM Works
- Determining Whether jCOM Is a Good Fit for Your Application
- Deciding on the Right jCOM Environment Setup
- Zero Client Installs
- Choosing Among DCOM, Native In Process, and Native Out of Process Modes
- Early and Late Binding Models
- Securing Your Java Objects Against Unauthorized Access
- Working with jCOM Tools
- The Bank Account Example—Java Client Accessing a COM Component
- The Inventory Item Example—COM Client Accessing an EJB
- Event Handling
- Dealing with the Data Types

To date, a significant investment has been made by companies in the development and deployment of middleware component frameworks adept at serving up business logic to the enterprise. Sun Microsystems and Microsoft—chief among vendors providing such infrastructures—both offer extensive yet dissimilar solutions whose approach is inherently divergent if not wholly incompatible.

As these distributed object paradigms proliferate over the Internet, a transparent mechanism to integrate such differing techniques would be deemed nothing short of God-sent for most companies. jCOM is one of BEA's answers to this dilemma. It provides us with a formidable weapon in our arsenal to furnish a stable yet seamless mechanism for Microsoft COM and Java objects to interoperate with one another.

In the first part of this chapter, we define in detail what jCOM is and does, and discuss where it fits in with the other platform integration tools at our disposal. Under what circumstances does jCOM make sense? What are its advantages and disadvantages? When would another tool possibly be more appropriate?

We then look at the modes and methods of deploying jCOM and environmental issues, such as server setup and securing access to our objects. You'll learn how to use the WebLogic-provided jCOM tools that lie at the heart of jCOM. Those powerful tools do much of the work for us by automating configuration tasks and in the automatic generation of facilitating classes.

As always, the best way to know a thing is through experience, so the thrust of the information is presented in the context of individual examples. We go through a step-by-step example that depicts a Java client accessing a COM component, and then we turn around and go in the opposite direction with an example that shows a COM client accessing an Enterprise JavaBean.

Finally, we touch on the way that jCOM facilitates the event-driven aspects of COM and Java-based languages and the primitive data type mappings that occur between them.

Understanding jCOM

WebLogic jCOM is an implementation of what is termed a *Java/COM bridge*, which can simply be defined as a software bridging mechanism for facilitating quick and easy access from Java applications to Microsoft COM/DCOM components. In turn, Microsoft COM applications can access Java-based objects through this mechanism as well. Beyond the relative simplicity of its implementation, the most appealing aspect of this approach is its transparency. To the Java programmer, a COM object looks the same as any other Java object. To the COM developer, remote Java objects appear as though they were native COM components. As found in these objects, data types are masked from view through dynamic type mappings done by the jCOM runtime engine. Remote object data types are dynamically translated into the primitive types found within the calling program's own idiom: COM data types appear like Java primitive types to the Java developer, whereas Java data types look like COM data types to the COM developer.

This transparency can help to satisfy the needs many companies have when struggling to reconcile the divergent approaches to distributed object technologies found in the Sun and Microsoft camps—camps that more often compete than cooperate.

jCOM helps to bridge the gap, as it were, that typically exists between Sun Java shops looking to maintain a Java-centric (and thus platform independent) environment and their Microsoft counterparts looking to leverage the use and reuse of the multitude of COM components that exist out there.

Currently, the BEA WebLogic jCOM source is entirely based on Intrinsyc Software's J-Integra product that was obtained through a licensing agreement between the two companies. The code base was originally developed by Linar, which Intrinsyc acquired in January of 2001. J-Integra entertains the largest install base of any pure Java/COM bridge out there and is fast becoming an industry standard. So far, integration efforts with WebLogic Server have been limited to installation and conformity issues. But going forward, BEA plans to increase the level of integration with J-Integra, improving scalability and manageability.

How jCOM Works

jCOM is said to work *bi-directionally*, which simply means that it allows communication in either direction between Java and COM components. Java objects can call COM components and, in turn, COM components can call Java objects. Of course, there exist two very disparate underlying architectures responsible for the wire-level communication that supports these distributed component frameworks.

At runtime, jCOM internally sets up a dual-protocol stack environment that accommodates support for each of these underlying infrastructures independent of one another (see Figure 33.1). For COM components, there is an implementation of COM/DCOM over DCE remote procedure calls; for Java objects, there is an implementation of RMI (Remote Method Invocation) over Java Remote Method IIOP (Internet Inter-ORB) protocol. Calls intended to cross between these stacks are handled through an internal translation that effectively masks the lower-level protocols from view. To an EJB, a call from a COM client looks as if it came from a Java client; to a COM component, a call from a Java client appears as if it came from an ordinary COM client.

jCOM provides tools that you can use to auto-generate the higher-level COM/DCOM proxies and RMI stubs that clients use to marshal their calls between these infrastructures. Optionally, jCOM can be set up in a native mode fashion, utilizing native operating system dynamic link libraries to alleviate the network overhead of DCOM and thereby dramatically improving performance.

Let's look at a Java object calling a COM object:

```
import com.weblogicunleashed.account.*;
clsAccount account = new clsAccount();
double accountBalance = getAccountBalance("John Doe");
```

Figure 33.1 illustrates the standard flow of events that takes place when a Java object wants to access a COM component. The Java object first initiates its call to the jCOM-generated proxy object for that particular COM component. The proxy then communicates with the jCOM runtime engine, which in turn sends its messages via COM/DCOM as encapsulated remote procedure calls over TCP/IP to the COM component sitting in the Windows environment. At the lowest levels, jCOM uses standard Java networking classes on the server to make the call.

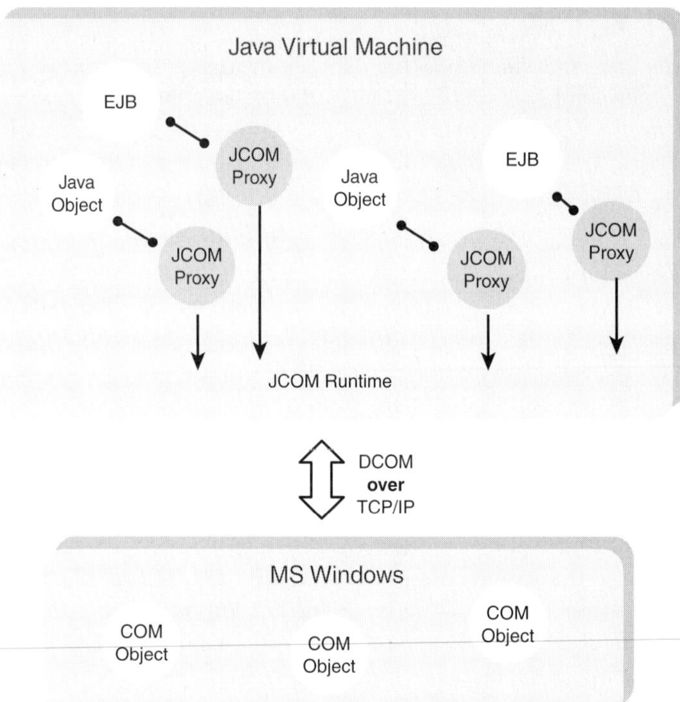

FIGURE 33.1 jCOM runtime environment.

Determining Whether jCOM Is a Good Fit for Your Application

Tying Microsoft and Java platforms together is no small feat by any means. The jCOM runtime engine as bundled with BEA WebLogic Server 8.1 comes as a welcome addition to a platform already rich in connectivity options. When dealing with COM/Java interoperability issues, it should fit nicely into the integration requirements of many applications. It isn't the only option you have at your disposal, though.

Other forms of middleware exist to assist you in your efforts to glue things together. Web Services come quickly to mind, as does the J2EE Connector Architecture (J2EE-CA), which can play a role. Initiatives coming out of .NET could be drawn upon, too. It's beyond the scope of this chapter to go into any of these alternatives in too much detail but they do bear mentioning—especially in the context of determining whether a solution makes sense in relation to all the other things that might be going on in the enterprise. For additional information about Web Services, refer to Chapter 30, "WebLogic Server and Web Services." For J2EE-CA, see Chapter 31, "Legacy Integration with the J2EE Connector Architecture."

It's also worth noting that the J-Integra product as shipped from Intrinsyc has a plug-in available called the J2EE-CA/COM Bridge, which does its bridging via the J2EE Connector Architecture. Using the J2EE Connector Architecture paradigm, you could write your own resource adapters for your EJBs and have them serviced by the J2EE-CA/COM Bridge plug-in sitting on top of the J-Integra runtime engine. The J2EE Connector Architecture promises to add value by not compromising the portability of EJBs across platforms. For example, if you have a mixed application server environment (possibly with WebSphere or Oracle application servers) used in conjunction with WebLogic and need to port EJBs across these platforms, a closer look into a J2EE Connector Architecture–enabled solution might be in order.

Then there is the whole Web Services phenomenon to consider. The rapid adoption of Web Services, based on least common denominator protocols such as XML and HTTP, is quickly becoming as pervasive as the Internet itself. Web Services are implemented via SOAP (Simple Object Access Protocol). This protocol is formulated by Microsoft and is an integral part of its latest product strategy, including the new technologies to supersede COM. So, that makes it all the easier to access Microsoft Web Services–enabled COM legacy applications in this manner. In a nutshell, XML ties together data where DCOM ties objects. If your application is an enterprisewide one or is geographically dispersed, Web Services will make deploying and maintaining the application much easier. However, Web Services will probably be slower than DCOM, given the marshaling of objects to verbose XML on one end, transferring large chunks of data on the network, and having to interpret them through an XML parser on the other. Although Microsoft is clearly behind Web Services and the use of SOAP to expose normal COM calls over the network, it in no way sees SOAP as a general replacement for DCOM. COM components with complex data types may require the creation of wrapper objects and custom mappers to expose these objects. Many DCOM features such as life-management and passing objects by reference, and some COM data types, don't map to the current SOAP specification and by Microsoft's admission probably never will.

Intrinsyc also has a product called Ja.NET that allows clients for Enterprise JavaBeans using .NET-supported languages. Integration with ASP.NET and EJBs is available as well. It is supported under BEA WebLogic Server and can be used if you have .NET-specific dependencies in your application.

Deciding on the Right jCOM Environment Setup

The focus of a well-planned distributed object enterprise implementation should concentrate on the overall needs of an individual application. Such needs can vary widely depending on the nature of the business problem at hand. Some things you might want to take into consideration include the following: Is this application more likely to be I/O intensive or CPU intensive? Will there be considerable database activity? Are there any required processor-intensive tasks such as financial calculations, estimates, planning forecasts, and so on? Do you think it will need to scale and grow as data volume increases and business needs change? As a distributed design, are there any geographical or security issues to take into account? Where do you think the potential bottlenecks are most likely to occur? In the end, what will be the TCO (total cost of ownership) of the intended solution?

Through its strategic partnering with the J-Integra product, jCOM has a proven track record in delivering battle-tested solutions that address such application demands. The product has been designed to be flexible in its configuration and implementation so as to be somewhat customizable to a particular application's requirements.

With that said, to have jCOM perform as you expect, you must familiarize yourself with a number of configuration and setup options.

Whatever your application entails, you'll be using jCOM as the middleware to bridge communication between the COM and Java objects it uses. The configuration decisions you'll make will revolve around the physical location of objects, where they reside within an operating system, and the protocols used to communicate between them.

You'll decide on issues such as whether to use a zero client install. You'll choose among DCOM, native out of process, and native in process modes and whether to bind your objects with early or late binding.

Don't worry about what all of these terms mean right now. We go over them in detail when we look at the advantages and disadvantages found in each approach. By the end of this chapter, you'll not only be able to make an informed decision on how to make jCOM best fit your application, but you'll also be well on your way to seeing it implemented after having a chance to work with some of the provided examples.

Zero Client Installs

A zero client installation (as J-Integra calls it) is available with jCOM. This refers to an environment setup where COM clients can access Java objects without any WebLogic-specific code required on the client machine. It's the least intrusive of any option in terms of impact to the client, but it does require the location of the WebLogic Server to be hard-coded into the client code where the call initiates from.

When COM clients make calls to jCOM-exposed Java objects, they need some means of determining exactly where the Java objects they're calling are located. In COM, components are referenced by a human-readable string called a *moniker* or through the use of a machine-readable unique identifier called a *class ID*. For example, in Visual Basic, `GetObject("prodServer:com.acme.widgetclass")` is an example of a moniker reference. jCOM maps monikers and class IDs to Java classes, which run in a specific JVM identified by a JVM ID. The `prodServer` in the moniker reference is the JVM ID used to identify the particular Java virtual machine being called.

With jCOM, COM clients can identify a WebLogic Server in two different ways. One way, which we delve into in more detail later, is to use the jCOM-provided regjvm tool to place an entry in the client machine's registry. The other is the zero client form we're discussing here, where the server location is hardcoded into the client. Zero client installs leave it up to the internal COM client code to locate the WebLogic Server by referring to an object reference moniker for the server.

There are two methods of obtaining the object reference moniker for the WebLogic Server you're going to call. By default, WebLogic Server comes preloaded with a servlet that you can access to display the object reference moniker for that particular server. Start WebLogic and point your browser to `http://localhost:7001/bea_wls_internal/com` (change the server address and port number if required). What you'll see is an encoded string containing the IP address of the WebLogic Server and the port number it's listening on. You simply cut and paste this string into the client code. Please note that this servlet is installed only with the examples server.

Alternatively, you can run the `com.bea.jcom.GetJvmMoniker` Java class directly to access this information. Specify the full name or TCP/IP address of the WebLogic Server machine and port number as parameters in the form

```
java com.bea.jcom.GetJvmMoniker localhost 7001
```

The text displayed is also automatically copied to the clipboard for you to paste into your code. The moniker you receive through either of these methods remains valid as long as the host and port number of the server remain unchanged. In Visual Basic, you would place the object reference moniker into your code like this:

- `Set jvm = GetObject("objref:TUVPVwEAAAAABAIAAAAAAMAMQBdAAAAAAAKAP//AAAAAAAAA......")`
- `Set vector = jvm.get("java.util.Vector")`

An EJB should be accessed through JNDI like this:

- `Set jvm = GetObject("objref:TUVPVwEAAAAABAIAAAAAAMAMQBdAAAAAAAKAP//AAAAAAAAA......")`
- `Set mobjHome = jvm.get("prodServer:jndi:MyEJBHome")`

The upside to a zero client installation is that it affords you the least amount of overhead at deployment time. This could be advantageous if you have a large number of clients to install and you're fairly certain that the server IP and port number will remain constant. If either of these does change, you must remember to obtain a new moniker from the server and reinsert it into the code on all the client machines. Early binding, which we'll learn about shortly, is not supported at all on a zero client which might or might not be a desirable thing.

Choosing Among DCOM, Native In Process, and Native Out of Process Modes

You can choose from three different setup modes with jCOM. Each relates to the physical configuration of your objects and the means of interprocess communication used between them. The modes are DCOM mode, native out of process mode, and native in process mode. Each mode addresses particular needs and has distinct advantages and disadvantages over the other.

DCOM Mode

The first option, DCOM mode, provides the most versatility and is required when the COM client and Java objects will be located on different physical machines (see Figure 33.2). DCOM is a wire-level protocol that was originated by Microsoft to allow distributed COM objects to communicate over the network.

Although DCOM can run over many protocols, it runs on top of TCP/IP when used in conjunction with jCOM. DCOM mode uses a pure Java implementation, so there no native COM code (no DLLs) is required on the Java server side. Therefore, the operating system can be Unix or any other environment with an installed JVM. This can be a clear advantage, but it comes at the expense of performance. Each call between applications incurs a network delay. The delay exists even when objects reside on the same machine.

Native Out of Process Mode

Native out of process mode is available when you're running the client and server on the same machine. As shown in Figure 33.3, in this mode, all interprocess communication occurs via COM.

Native In Process Mode

Native in process mode is essentially the same as native out of process mode except for the fact that everything is run within the process memory space of the client application (see Figure 3.4). In this scenario, everything you need to bridge between your COM client application—JVM, Java objects, and jCOM runtime—are contained in the process address space of the COM client application.

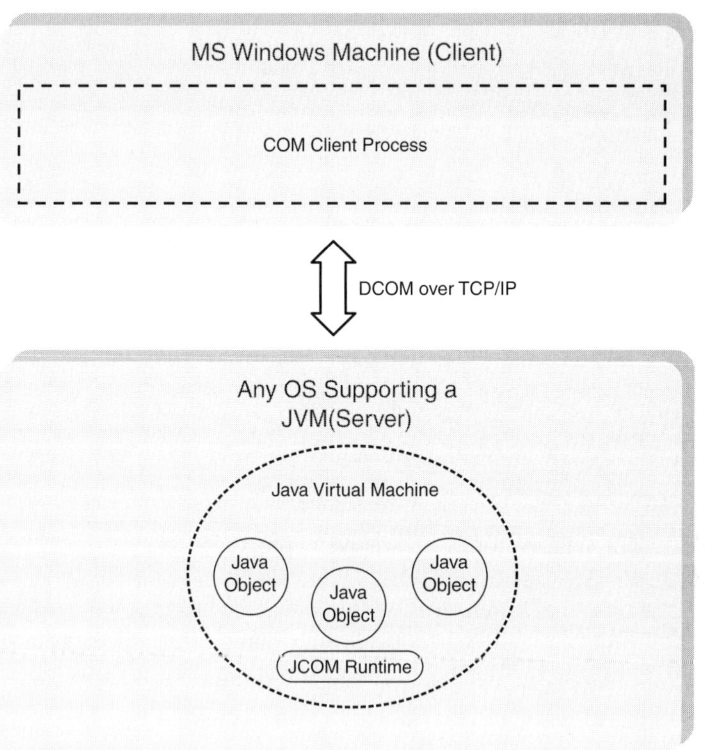

FIGURE 33.2 Accessing Java objects in DCOM mode.

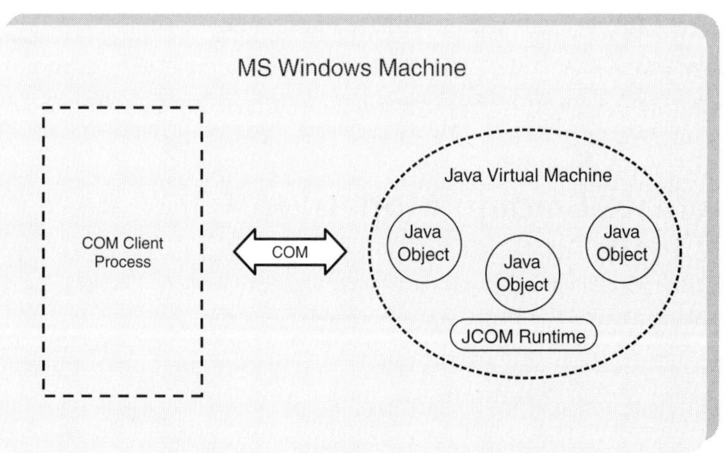

FIGURE 33.3 Accessing Java objects in native out of process mode.

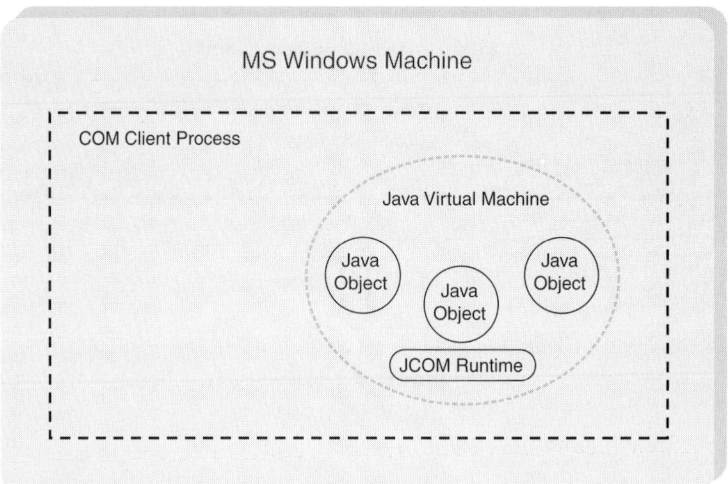

FIGURE 33.4 Accessing Java objects in native in process mode.

It's important to note that when running under each of the native modes, WebLogic Server must be installed on the server machine where both the COM and Java objects will reside. A separate license for WebLogic Server is not required for this purpose, however.

As the name implies, native modes use native calls. Whether between COM clients and WebLogic, or Java objects and COM applications, the call is a native one and is therefore compiled and optimized by the operating system, which results in improved performance. Native modes also take advantage of WebLogic's T3/IIOP protocols when communicating between the COM client and WebLogic Server. This helps to speed things up as well because fewer overall network calls are required to perform individual programming steps. You also gain access to WebLogic's failover and load balancing features in native mode. Because native libraries are currently available only for Microsoft Windows environments, WebLogic Server must run on a Windows machine to work in native mode.

Early and Late Binding Models

When you use jCOM to enable a COM client to access your Java objects, it is jCOM's job to make sure that your Java objects look exactly like any other COM component to that client. Remember: One of the main goals here is transparency.

To that end, you'll choose between an early- or late-bound method of object binding directly in support of COM's early and late binding models.

From a COM perspective, when a client program initiates a call to a COM component, the methods and properties of the component referred to by the calling program must be verified to see whether they actually exist and have been specified correctly. This process is known as *binding*. The verification itself can occur in one of two ways. One approach uses what is called *early binding*: At compile time, an object's properties and methods are exposed through a virtual method table (VTBL). In *late binding*, information about the object being called is available only at runtime through the `IDispatch` interface.

The choice to use early or late binding is predicated on the particular needs of the individual application and the overall environment in which that application resides. With that in mind, we'll next look at each of these modes of object awareness in greater detail while keeping our focus on the advantages and disadvantages found in each. A summary of our findings is listed in Table 33.1.

TABLE 33.1 Early Versus Late Binding Summary

Early Binding	Late Binding
Complex to implement (must create type libraries and wrapper objects for type verification)	Easy to implement (no type library or wrapper object creation required)
Faster (no type checking required at runtime)	Slower (type checking required on each call).
Inflexible (static implementation requires code modifications to type libraries and wrappers when underlying component changes)	Flexible (dynamic implementation allows components to change on the fly)
More reliable (compile-time syntax checking catches errors up front)	Less reliable (error prone because type checking is not available until runtime)
Easier to program with clear code (type library access to defined object elements)	No programming access to object elements

Early Binding

Probably the most compelling reason to opt for the early binding mode of serving up your Java objects is the age-old need for speed. Early binding is without a doubt faster and here's why: With this mode, all the binding procedures are over with before your program is even run. Because syntax and data types are detectable, they can be verified beforehand along with object references, which can be resolved and compiled. With the quality control aspects out of the way, we render code devoid of the inherent overhead associated with the binding process. This dramatically reduces the time required to access property values of an object.

Now, for jCOM to support an early binding model, it requires some extra effort on your part to make sure that the information required for type checking is available at compile time in the form of type libraries. Wrappers for the server objects must be generated as well, making it—for some—an even more complex proposition. The client requires a type library, and wrappers are required on the server. If the client and server are running on separate machines, the type library and wrappers must be generated on the same machine and then copied to the systems where they're required.

Although more complex, early binding winds up being more reliable in the long run. The syntax and type checking done at compile time cause programming mistakes to show up earlier. In this way, simple errors such as type mismatches can be caught and dealt with earlier in the process. The calling program's code itself becomes clearer because object variable declarations can specifically match the types of objects being called. The objects being used by a procedure are then more clearly represented by the variables that refer to those objects.

From a pure programming standpoint, the static nature of early binding allows some IDEs to show the Java objects for which you have generated type libraries. Through the type library, a developer can readily check out what properties and methods are available for a particular object while coding simply by looking them up in an object browser.

The downside to statically mapping object elements is that if any changes are made to the underlying component, corresponding changes must be made to the type libraries and wrappers associated with that component as well. This might result in less flexible code that can't adapt to shifting interfaces.

Late Binding

Late binding has the main advantage of being a somewhat plug-and-play proposition. You'll definitely be able to get up and running faster, but at the expense of a significant performance hit.

The reason for this degradation, as you might recall, is found in the extensive overhead incurred when performing the object verifications we spoke of earlier.

Because the `IDispatch` interface is a dynamic mapping between objects, it forces objects to describe themselves at runtime, much in the same way that reflection does in Java. Here the compiler takes for granted that all references made to the called object are in good order. It is at runtime that errors become evident. They can then be trapped and handled accordingly, but this necessitates that a constant interrogation take place to verify the validity of each individual call. Calling programs must dynamically locate remote objects and verify the methods and attributes of those objects for each invocation. You can just imagine the overhead this begins to incur.

The `IDispatch` interface requires that calls going between clients and servers marshal their arguments into a consistent form understandable by both. Types must map correctly between objects. This translation, which is done in real-time, not only slows things down but also can limit the data types that can be passed using this technique.

Overall, the dynamic type mapping found in late binding tends to be a more flexible solution because changes in the underlying components don't require the regeneration of any wrappers or type libraries. However, without compile-time syntax checking, more runtime failures are likely to occur because they will not have been caught up front by the compiler.

Securing Your Java Objects Against Unauthorized Access

As of WebLogic 8.1, jCOM security is now completely handled by WebLogic Server's security mechanism of roles and permissions. All configuration is done through the WebLogic Administrator Console. You must grant access rights to your Java objects in order for them to be exposed to COM clients. The best way to familiarize yourself on how to do this is through the inventory item example found in this chapter. It steps you through the process of granting access rights to individual classes in your application. In that example, you use the Administrator Console under the WebLogicServer/Services/JCOM category to control access to these individual classes (see Figure 33.5). Detailed information about granting and revoking access to individual classes can be found at `http://e-docs.bea.com/wls/docs81/ConsoleHelp/security_7xa.html`.

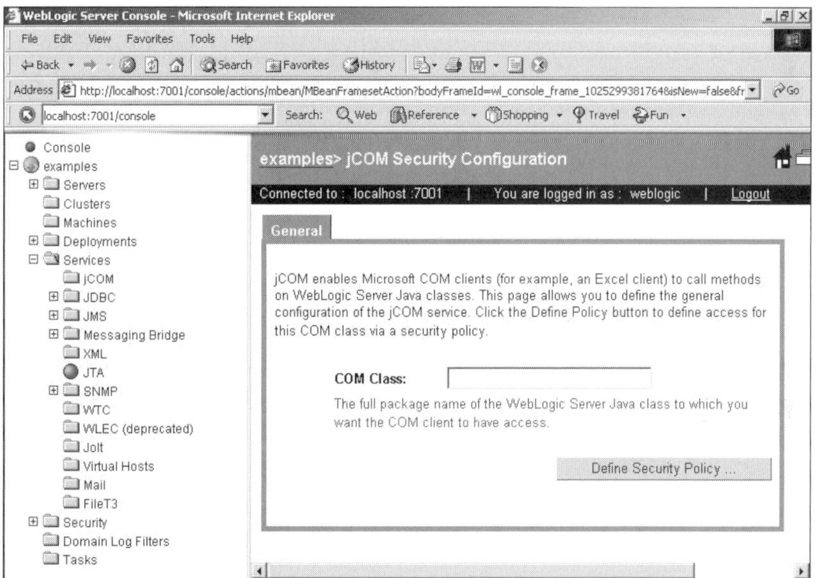

FIGURE 33.5 Admin Console WebLogicServer/Services/JCOM COM security control screen.

jCOM does not currently enforce any security restrictions on callbacks. Therefore, if you pass a Java object reference to a COM object, that COM object has full access to the object.

NOTE

Additional J-Integra classes are shipped with WebLogic in the `weblogic.jar` (which contains all the jCOM runtime), which can be used to discover the identity of COM clients calling your Java code. When a COM client invokes methods in your Java object via jCOM, you can call

- `com.linar.jintegra.AuthInfo.getCallerDomain()` which will, if it can be ascertained, return the NT domain of the COM client that initiated the current call.
- `com.linar.jintegra.AuthInfo.getCallerUser()` will return, if it can be ascertained, the NT username of the COM client that initiated the current call.

Working with jCOM Tools

Beyond some initial configuration done on WebLogic Server, most of the actual work you'll do will involve the jCOM-provided tool programs. These programs lie at the heart of jCOM and are used to generate and deploy all the elements you'll need to expose individual objects between platforms.

We'll go over four programs (some come with both a GUI and command-line version) in detail.

- com2java
- java2cOM
- regjvm
- regtlb

NOTE

The examples section of this chapter contains working examples of each of these tools.

Connecting to COM with com2java

This tool is used to generate the individual Java proxy code modules that you'll need to access COM components. Think of it as making "COM available 2 Java"; that is, making COM components available to Java clients.

All COM objects have type libraries associated with them in one form or another which, among other things, define the interfaces and classes contained within the component. The location of the associated type library for a particular component might not always be that easy to find, however. That's because type libraries (the file extension `.tlb` or `.olb` denotes a type library) might be embedded within other files such as DLLs or, as in the case of Visual Basic, in the executable itself.

After you locate the type library that defines the COM component you want to expose, you'll want to feed this into com2Java to generate the Java classes you need from the other end. The tool will scan the library looking for any enumerations, COM interfaces, and COM classes it can find.

Let's take a look at the classes you will see coming out of this tool.

For every enumeration found, a Java interface will be generated containing constant declarations for items in the enumeration.

For each COM class found, a corresponding Java class will be generated with the same name as the COM class. These are the classes that your client programs will typically invoke.

COM has a type of interface called an automation interface that we're interested in. It allows an object to publish a list of properties and functions at runtime. This is the `IDispatch` interface we spoke of earlier and it is used with late binding. When using early binding, the properties and methods of an object are made available at compile time via the VTBL.

The tool will generate a Java interface and a Java class for each interface found in the type library. The name of the generated Java interface will be the same as the COM interface. The name of the Java class will be the same as the COM interface with `Proxy` appended to the end of it. For example, if you have a COM interface named `WindowsHelper`, the Java interface will also be `WindowsHelper`, and the implementation class (which implements this interface) will be named `WindowsHelperProxy`. As you might expect, the generated Java interface will map the COM interface into a Java recognizable format with a subsequent Java proxy class generated that will be used to access COM objects that implement the interface.

We earlier described com2java as making "COM available 2 Java"; well, there's actually more to it. In addition, the generated Java class can also be used by COM components to access methods in Java objects that implement this interface. Use of com2java in this way represents a special use of the tool. Why is it called com2java? It is a simple way for us to remember the main purpose of the tool, especially in relation to its alter ego, java2com, which we will talk about next.

There is a GUI version (see Figure 33.6) as well as a command-line version of this utility. They can be found in the `\bea\weblogic81\server\bin` directory as `com2java.exe` and `com2javacmd.exe`, respectively. To examine a working example of this tool, see the bank account example found later in this chapter.

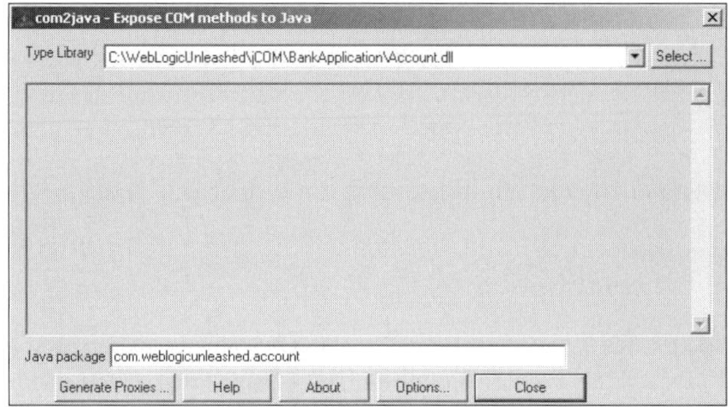

FIGURE 33.6 Exposing COM objects via the com2java tool.

Connecting to Java with java2com

This tool is used to generate the elements required to expose Java objects to COM clients. Think of it as making "Java available 2 COM"; that is making Java objects available to COM clients.

java2com uses Java's reflection API to analyze the Java classes you intended to make available to COM clients. It creates a COM IDL (Interface Definition Language) file, which is compiled by the Microsoft MIDL compiler to create a type library for the COM client and additional wrapper classes used by jCOM to facilitate early binding (`vtable`) access to Java objects. It does this analysis recursively, working its way through each of the classes and interfaces used in parameters or fields of every class until all the Java classes and interfaces accessible in this manner have been analyzed.

If you need to automate the process, you can use the command-line version of java2com to run the tool from within a batch file or possibly an Ant build script, as we'll do in the inventory item example. If so, you'll create a `java2com.xml` file (containing information about the classes you want to process), which you'll specify as a parameter on the command line. The GUI version is depicted in Figure 33.7.

> **NOTE**
>
> To run this utility, go to a command prompt and run `\bea\weblogic81\server\bin\setWLSEnv.cmd` to set up the environment. Then run `\bea\weblogic81\server\bin\java2com.bat` to invoke the tool. You'll have a chance to use this tool in the Inventory Item example found later in this chapter.

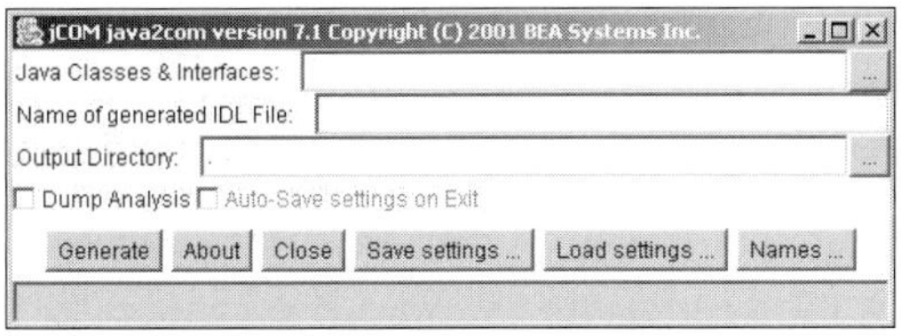

jCOM java2com version 7.1 Copyright (C) 2001 BEA Systems Inc.
Java Classes & Interfaces:
Name of generated IDL File:
Output Directory:
Dump Analysis Auto-Save settings on Exit
Generate About Close Save settings ... Load settings ... Names ...

FIGURE 33.7 Exposing Java objects via the java2com tool.

NOTE

A potential conflict arises when the server hosting the Java object and the client making calls to it are on different machines. Wrapper files that come out of java2com are compiled and go on the server. The IDL file that comes out of java2com is compiled by the MIDL compiler to create a type library and goes on the client. Depending on where you run the java2com tool, you'll have to redistribute these files to the correct location. Wrappers to a location on the server are made accessible via the classpath of the WebLogic Server, and the type library to the client must be registered in the client machine's registry through the regtbl tool.

On each invocation of the java2com tool, a unique identification stamp is embedded into all the files it creates. The stamp serves to link the files together and is required for communication between them to be successful at runtime. You can not run the java2com tool to produce wrapper files and then later run it again to create an IDL file. Whether it is done on the client or the server is not important; what is important is that it is done at the same time. Of course, the consequences of this are that if you make any changes to the Java object you're exposing, you'll have to regenerate all the wrappers and the type library from scratch and redistribute them to their proper locations.

JVM Registration via the regjvm Tool

When COM clients make calls to jCOM exposed Java objects, they need some means of determining exactly where the Java objects they're calling are located. The way they do this is by looking up the required information in the Registry. You use the regjvm tool to place an entry in the client machine's Registry that references the Java virtual machine where the Java objects you're exposing will reside. The regjvm tool can be used to create and manage all such JVM references on a machine.

In the "Deciding on the Right jCOM Environment Setup" section of this chapter, we learned about the three different setup modes for jCOM: DCOM, native in process, and native out of process. We discussed the distinct advantages and disadvantages they have in relation to one another and the inherent tradeoffs found in each. When you've made the decision on what mode best fits your application, you use the regjvm tool to manage this configuration on the client machine.

There is a GUI and command-line version of this utility and both can be found in the `\bea\weblogic81\server\bin` directory as `regjvm.exe` and `regjvmcmd.exe`, respectively. You can invoke the GUI tool simply by clicking on it in Windows Explorer. For the command-line version, start a command shell and then invoke `\bea\weblogic\81\server\bin\setWLSEnv.cmd` to set up the environment correctly. You then can run the command-line version of this utility with the following syntax:

```
- regjvmcmd.exe serverName IPAddress[PortNumber]
```

where *serverName* is the WebLogic Server name, *IPAddress* is the IP address of the machine, and *PortNumber* is the port the server is listening on.

> **NOTE**
>
> When you use the regjvmcmd tool to enter a new JVM with a name that already exists in the Registry, such as when you want to change the hostname or port of the machine where the JVM resides, the regjvmcmd tool will not overwrite the original entry. If this is the case, you'll have to unregister the old JVM reference first and then reregister it with the new hostname and port changes. You can do this through the GUI tool or at the command line. The command line syntax is
>
> `regjvmcmd.exe /unregister serverName`

The GUI version of this tool also can be used to accomplish the same results, as depicted in Figure 33.8.

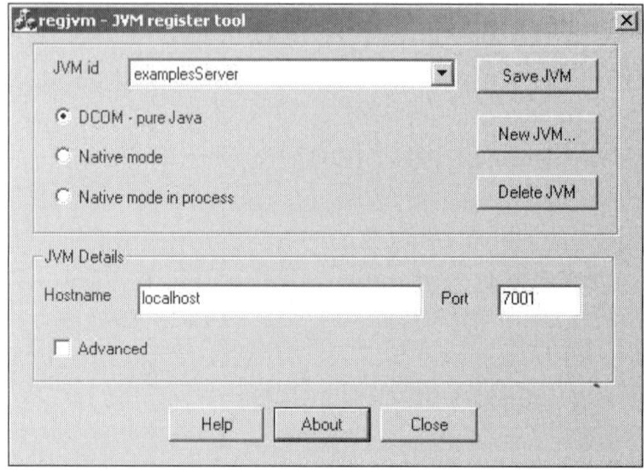

FIGURE 33.8 Registering the JVM via the regjvm tool.

regtlb

This tool comes into use when a COM client calls a Java object through the early binding method. As you recall, early binding is when the COM client has access at compile time to the elements of the Java server object by way of scanning a local type library that you've created for the Java server object being called. This type library is produced by the java2com tool, which creates an IDL file that is in turn compiled by the Microsoft MIDL compiler. The resulting type library must be registered in the client machine's Registry so as to be available to the COM client making the call. This is where the regtlb tool comes in. You use it to register the associated type library for the Java server object in the client machine's Registry and link it to the JVM where the object will reside. The jCOM runtime engine will also use this information for linking type library defined object calls to the appropriate wrapper classes on the server.

There is only a command-line version of this utility, and it can be found in the `%WEBLOGIC_HOME%\server\bin` directory as `regtlb.exe`. Figure 33.9 shows an example of `regtlb`. The syntax of the command is

```
regtlb.exe typeLibrary.tlb aRegisteredJVM
regtlb.exe /unregisterall
```

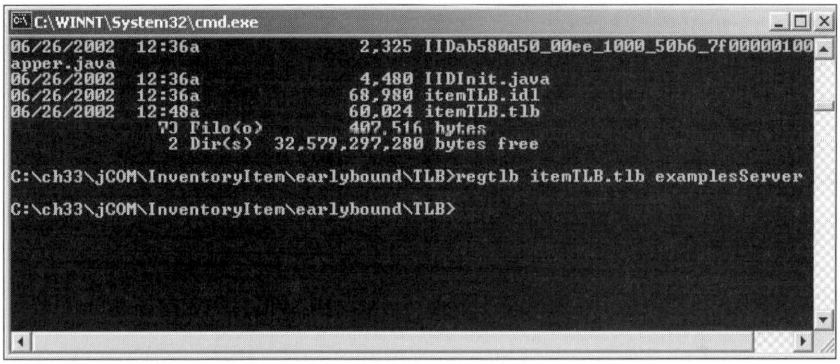

```
C:\WINNT\System32\cmd.exe
06/26/2002  12:36a               2,325 IIDab580d50_00ee_1000_50b6_7f00000100
apper.java
06/26/2002  12:36a               4,480 IIDInit.java
06/26/2002  12:36a              68,980 itemTLB.idl
06/26/2002  12:48a              60,024 itemTLB.tlb
              73 File(s)        407,516 bytes
               2 Dir(s)  32,579,297,280 bytes free

C:\ch33\jCOM\InventoryItem\earlybound\TLB>regtlb itemTLB.tlb examplesServer

C:\ch33\jCOM\InventoryItem\earlybound\TLB>
```

FIGURE 33.9 Registering type libraries with regtlb.

You can use `regtlb /unregisterall` to have the regtlb tool unregister any previously registered type library versions. A demonstration of the use of this tool is provided in the inventory item early binding example later in this chapter.

NOTE

If the type library you're using was not created by a java2com-generated IDL file, you'll be prompted to give the name of the Java class that is to be instantiated for each COM class. When the type library is created via the java2com tool, regtlb can automatically determine the Java class name that corresponds to each COM class in the type library. The COM class descriptions in the type library will be of the form `Java class java.util.Observable`.

Additional information about individual parameters found in the jCOM tools can be found in the BEA WebLogic Server Programming jCOM Manual available at `http://e-docs.bea.com/wls/docs81/jcom/index.html`.

The Bank Account Example—Java Client Accessing a COM Component

WebLogic Server 8.1 ships with a number of examples that help guide you through the development of various WebLogic Server–related technologies. Three of these examples pertain to jCOM specifically and can be found in the `\bea\weblogic81\samples\server\examples\src\examples\jcom` directory. You'll find that all the provided WebLogic jCOM examples, depict a bank account interface application with COM-based front ends accessing an EJB-housed back end on WebLogic Server. What is not provided, however, is an example going in the opposite direction, showing a Java front end accessing a COM-based back end. We'll remedy that here.

In our example, we'll take a similar bank account interface application and serve it up with a Java JSP front end accessing business logic residing in a COM component on the server. This example assumes that you have the WebLogic examples server loaded on your machine. If not, you can still use the example, but you'll have to deploy it into your own WebLogic configuration. The sample code can be found on the accompanying CD-ROM at the back of the book.

Creating the JSP Front End

First, we'll create the JSP front end for the bank account application. To do this, simply copy the `BankAccount.jsp` source from the ch33`\jCOM\BankApplication` directory on the accompanying CD-ROM and place it in the `%WEBLOGIC_HOME%\samples\server\examples\build\examplesWebApp` directory.

`BankAccount.jsp` contains the presentation and business layer logic for our application. Take a look at Listing 33.1. The first thing you'll notice is that from a Java perspective, there doesn't seem to be any discernable way of telling that the COM component (`clsAccount`) we're calling is anything other than a regular Java class—and that's exactly what we want. All the underlying proxy mechanisms used to access this component are hidden from view. You typically want to break out the business logic from the `BankAccount.jsp` and place it the middle tier as a servlet, but we've included it here for the sake of expediency.

LISTING 33.1 BankAccount.jsp

```
<%! private clsAccount account; %>
<% // Create an Account COM Component and keep a handle to it in the session.
account = (clsAccount)session.getAttribute("objAccount");
if ( account == null )
 account = new clsAccount();
// Keep track of all the user messages during the session.
Vector messages = (Vector)session.getAttribute("messages");
if ( messages == null )
```

LISTING 33.1 Continued

```
 messages = new Vector();
// Get form variables.
String accountName = request.getParameter("accountName");
boolean NEW_ACCOUNT = true;
if (accountName == null)
 accountName = "";
else
 NEW_ACCOUNT = accountExists(accountName);
```


Creating the Account COM Back-End Component

Second, we'll create the back-end account COM component. This example assumes that WebLogic Server and the COM component will live on the same Windows machine. Create a directory called `C:\ch33\jCOM\BankApplication` to keep the component in.

The account com component for this example was created with Visual Basic. You can copy the associated dynamic link library (`Account.dll`) for this component from the `ch33\jCOM\BankApplication` example directory on the CD and place it in the `c:\ch33\jCOM\BankApplication` directory, or you can perform the following steps with Visual Basic to re-create the component by hand. I highly recommended the latter so that later on you can experiment with your own changes to this component and test the corresponding results.

Creating the Account COM Back-End Component by Hand

Using Visual Basic, follow these steps to create the account COM back-end component by hand:

1. Start Visual Basic and create a new Active X DLL project.
2. Change the project name to Account and the class name to `clsAccount`.
3. Cut and paste the code from the `clsAccount.txt` file (on the CD) to the `clsAccount` class.
4. Click File, Save Project As and save your project in the C:`\ch33\jCOM\BankApplication` directory.
5. On the File menu, click `Make Account.dll` to create the dynamic link library for this component.

Installing the COM Component on the Server

Now we'll perform the tasks required to successfully install the COM component on the server. This is the COM component that will be exposed via jCOM and made available to our Java objects.

Registering the Component

Whether you created the component by hand or simply copied it from the CD-ROM, you'll still have to register it on the Windows machine. You do so with the following command:

```
C:\ch33\jCOM\BankApplication> regsvr32 Account.dll /s
```

If you need to unregister the component later, the command is

```
regsvr32 /u /sAccount.dll
```

Setting Up Component Services

This supposes that you're using Windows XP. It could be different depending on which version of Windows you're using. If you're using Windows XP, you can follow these steps to set up component services on your machine:

Steps to setup component services on your machine:

1. On the Control Panel under Administrative Tools, open Component Services.
2. Expand the items Component Services, Computers, My Computer. Select COM+ Applications and use the menu selection Action, New, Application to create an empty server application called jCOM.
3. In Component Services, right-click on the jCOM application that you just created and select Properties. On the Security tab, select Perform Access Checks Only at the Process Level and set the Authentication Level for Calls as Connect.
4. Next, open the jCOM directory under Components and then open the Components directory. Drag and drop the `Account.dll` you created from the `C:\ch33\jCOM\BankApplication` into the `Components` directory.

NOTE

If you get an automation exception such as `AutomationException: 0x80040154 - Class not registered at com.linar.jintegra.bp.b(Unknown Source)` when running the example, it's because the Component Services step was not performed correctly.

If you get an automation exception such as `AutomationException: 0x80070005 - General access denied error in 'Invoke' at com.linar.jintegra.Rpc.a(Unknown Source)`, it's because the security step was not completed properly.

So far, we've created a JSP front end and a COM component back end for our application. If you program in Java, Visual Basic, or both, at this point you might be saying to yourself, "But there's nothing special going on here." This is pretty standard fare so far. There's nothing out of the ordinary in the JSP or the COM code that would spark any interest and, of course, this is all by design.

com2java Proxy File Generation

The last step before server setup is to create the jCOM middleware that we'll use to glue these tiers together. Perform the following steps to create these elements:

1. Go to the `%WEBLOGIC_HOME%\server\bin` directory and run `com2java.exe`.
2. Select `c:\ch33\jCOM\BankApplication\Account.dll` as the type library to scan.
3. For the package name, use `com.weblogicunleashed.account`.
4. Click Generate Proxies and select a temporary directory of your choosing to place the generated proxy files in.

com2java has created four proxy files for us to be used at the API level to access the Account COM component. They are `_clsAccount.java`, `_clsAccountProxy.java`, `clsAccount.java`, and `JintegraInit.java`, respectively. We'll compile these classes and place them on WebLogic Server in a directory where they will be available to our application.

All the jCOM-related classes needed for compilation can be found in the `\bea\weblogic81\server\lib\weblogic.jar` file. Make sure that you reference this JAR archive correctly in your class path when compiling.

On WebLogic Server, create the directory structure `\bea\weblogic81\samples\server\examples\build\examplesWebApp\WEB-INF\classes\com\weblogicunleashed\account` and place all four compiled classes there to make them available to our application.

WebLogic Server Setup

jCOM comes installed with WebLogic Server 8.1 but must be enabled through the Administration Console. We'll now enable COM calls for our application:

1. Bring up the Administration Console.
2. On the left pane, click Servers and then examplesServer.
3. On the right pane, click the Protocols tab and then the jCOM tab.
4. Check the Enable COM check box.
5. Click Apply.
6. Restart the server for these settings to take effect.

Running the Bank Account Interface Application

Point your browser to `http://localhost:7001/examplesWebApp/BankAccount.jsp`, and you should see the bank account interface as depicted in Figure 33.10.

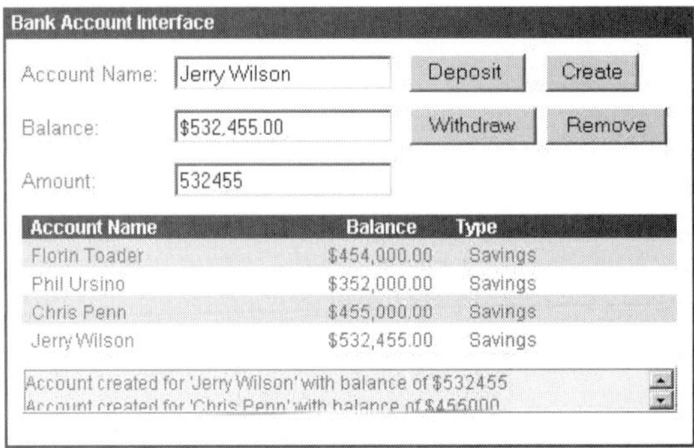

FIGURE 33.10 Bank account application.

Within the application, requests are handled by the JSP page, which makes calls to the Account COM component via the `clsAccount` object. Again, to keep things simple, all data is persisted within the COM object for the duration of a particular session. Ordinarily, the back-end component would cache information to a database as its EJB counterpart does in the WebLogic Server–provided examples.

If you created the COM component by hand, as suggested earlier, you might be tempted to make some minor changes to it and then immediately try to rerun the example. If you do, you'll see the following error pop up on the WebLogic Server Console:

```
java.lang.RuntimeException: Attempt to invoke a non-dispatch method on an
object that only supports IDispatch (if this is a VB component, have you
rebuilt it and forgotten to re-run com2java?)
```

This is because the com2java-generated proxy classes specifically make reference to a particular compilation of the COM object. If you set binary compatibility in Visual Basic and the interface for your class does not change you can make minor code changes without the need to re-run com2java. But be aware that if you do not set binary compatibility then any time you make changes to the COM component, or even if you just remake the DLL, you will have to rerun the com2java utility to ensure correct code synchronization.

The Inventory Item Example—COM Client Accessing an EJB

In the inventory item example, we'll expose an Inventory Item EJB and access it through a Visual Basic COM client. The Item EJB can be found in the `c:\ch33\jCOM\InventoryItem\earlybound` directory. Make sure that it's deployed and available on WebLogic Server. We will access this bean in a late bound and then an early-bound fashion.

The main difference between the early-bound and late-bound examples is that for early bound access, an additional task is required: creating and deploying a type library and wrapper classes for the bean.

The example presumes that you have both WebLogic and the COM client on a Microsoft Windows machine. You'll need Visual Basic 6.0 and the Microsoft MIDL compiler available on your machine as well. The Microsoft MIDL compiler comes bundled with the Microsoft Platform SDK and can be found on Microsoft's Web site. The code files for this example can be found on the accompanying CD-ROM at the back of the book.

First, copy the `InventoryItem` sample directory from the `ch33\jCOM\InventoryItem` directory on the accompanying CD-ROM and place it on your machine at `C:\ch33\jCOM\InventoryItem\`.

Next, we'll set up everything that's required on WebLogic Server to expose the Inventory Item EJB.

WebLogic Server Setup

There are a few things that we will need to do in order to set up the WebLogic Server correctly for this example. This will be done through the WebLogic Server's administrator's console.

First, make sure that the Inventory Item EJB is deployed and is targeted to the examples server.

To enable COM calls on WebLogic Server, do the following:

1. Bring up the Administration Console.
2. On the left pane, click Servers and then examples server.
3. On the right pane, click the Protocols tab and then the jCOM tab.
4. Check the Enable COM check box.
5. Click Apply.
6. Restart the server for these settings to take effect.

Next, we'll need to administer the security settings on WebLogic Server to allow access to our objects. Additional jCOM-specific security settings are required because the COM client will be accessing our objects remotely.

1. Bring up the Administration Console.
2. On the left pane, click Services and then jCOM.
3. On the right pane, enter: `java.util.*`.
4. Click Define Policy.
5. If the Policy Condition lists `Caller is a Member of the group everyone`, skip to step 7. If not, you must create the policy condition now. In the Policy Statement box, select Caller Is a Member of the Group and click the Add button.
6. In Enter Group Name, enter **`everyone`** and click the Add button.
7. Next, grant access to all the classes in the Item package containing the EJB. Go back to the Services/jCOM tab and on the right-side pane, enter **`com.jcom.inventoryitem.*`**.
8. In the Policy Statement box, select Caller Is a Member of the Group and click the Add button.
9. In Enter Group Name, enter **`everyone`** and click the Add button.
10. Next, grant access to the `JCOMHelper` class used in early binding. Go back to the Services/JCOM tab and on the right-side pane, enter **`JCOMHelper`**.
11. In the Policy Statement box, select Caller Is a Member of the Group and click the Add button.
12. In Enter Group Name, enter **`everyone`** and click the Add button.

NOTE

You can find more in-depth information about granting and revoking access to classes in the BEA electronic documents found at: `http://e-docs.bea.com/wls/docs81/secintro/index.html`.

Next, register the Java virtual machine where the COM client can find the EJB with the following command:

```
regjvmcmd.exe examplesServer localhost[7001]
```

Change the server name and port number where applicable.

For more details on regjvmcmd, refer to "Working with jCOM Tools," earlier in this chapter.

Everything we've done thus far is required for both early and late binding. Now we get to the specific differences between the late and early approaches.

The Inventory Item Visual Basic Client Accessed with Late Binding

This example demonstrates the capability for a Visual Basic client program to access an Enterprise JavaBean using the late binding method. Step-by-step instructions are provided.

Creating the VB Client

Open the VB project `InventoryItemLateBound.vbp` located in the `c:\ch33jCOM\InventoryItem\LateBound` directory you created from the files located on the accompanying CD at the back of the book.

Open the form code and the first thing you'll notice is the manner in which a handle to the Item bean is obtained. It is similar to any other VB object creation:

```
'Bind the EJB ItemHome object via JNDI
  Set mobjHome = CreateObject("examplesServer:jndi:
➥jcom-inventoryitem-itemHome")
```

Here you reference the server where the bean resides and the JNDI name it was deployed with.

As you can see in Listing 33.2, coding occurs as usual with Visual Basic, but because we do not have access to a type library for the item bean, everything must be referenced as an object. Here you can clearly see the tradeoff you're making. Late binding will get you up and running quickly, but you program somewhat in the dark.

LISTING 33.2 Visual Basic Bank Account Client Code Listing

```
Private Sub ListItem()
Dim objItem As Object
Dim title As String
'Handle errors
On Error GoTo ErrOut
Set objItem = mobjHome.Create()
title = objItem.getItem()
MsgBox ("EJB Accessed:: " + title)
Exit Sub
```

Run the code by pressing F5. As depicted in Figure 33.11, you should see a message box that displays the results of your EJB method call.

The Inventory Item Visual Basic Client Accessed with Early Binding

Early binding requires the creation of a type library that is registered in the client machine's Registry and associated wrapper classes that are compiled and placed in the classpath of WebLogic Server. This can be a somewhat labor-intensive task, so I highly recommend the use of a build tool such as Ant to expedite the process. If you haven't worked with Ant before, now is as good a time as any to start. In the `C:\ch33\jCOM\InventoryItem\earlybound` directory, you'll find the Ant build script `build.xml` as well as everything else you need to accomplish early binding. As we go through this process, open each of the files and inspect them. The goal here is for you to later be able to copy and alter these files to suit your own implementations.

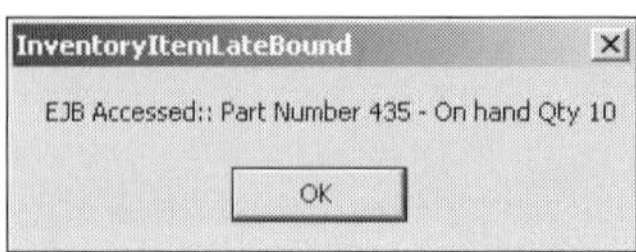

FIGURE 33.11 Inventory Item Visual Basic client.

Follow these steps to invoke the Inventory Item Visual Basic client with early binding:

1. The Ant tool reads from the `build.xml` file, which calls in properties from the `inventoryitem.properties` file. Open the `inventoryitem.properties` file and make any changes necessary referring to the location of your particular WebLogic Server installation. Make sure that the `SERVER_NAME` points to the WebLogic Server name where the `Item.ejb` has been deployed. The default is `examplesServer`.
2. Next, run `cmd.exe` and open up a command window. Traverse to the `C:\ch33\jCOM\InventoryItem\earlybound` directory. Set up the environment by running `setInventoryItemEnv.cmd`. Remember to do this first—before running any of the following command-line programs.
3. Initialize the build script with the command **`ant init`**.
4. Compile the `jCOMHelper` class, which contains a method to narrow an object obtained from WebLogic Server to a local object. The compiled class is placed in the build directory and in the `item_earlybound.jar` file. In a moment, we'll add all of the wrapper classes we need to this JAR file and then place it in the classpath of WebLogic Server. The command to run is **`ant compile.helper`**.
5. Next, we generate the Java wrappers and IDL file with the java2com tool. java2com recursively goes through the classes you provide (separated by a space) and generates an IDL file that will be compiled into a type library in a subsequent step. At the same time, it creates all the associated wrapper classes you need for WebLogic Server. For more detailed information about java2com, see "Working with jCOM Tools" in this chapter. Bring up the java2com GUI tool with the Ant command **`ant java2com`** (see Figure 33.12). Now make the following entries into the java2com tool:

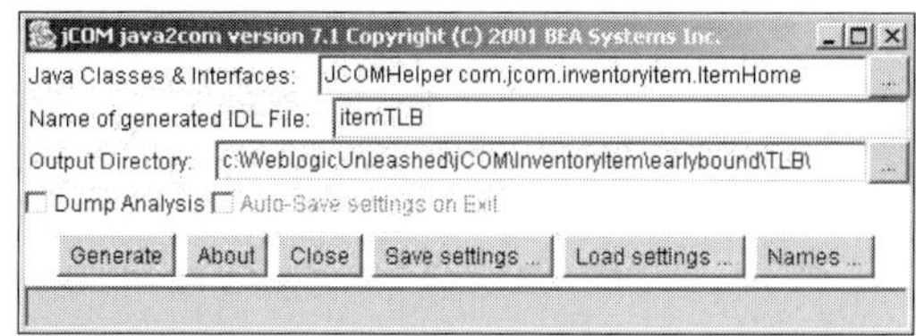

FIGURE 33.12 Early binding via the java2com tool.

- Java Classes & Interfaces: **`JCOMHelper com.jcom.inventoryitem..ItemHome`**
- Name of Generated IDL File: **`itemTLB`**
- Output Directory: **`C:\ch33\jCOM\InventoryItem\earlybound\TLB\`**
- Now click on Names so that we can eliminate a few classes before we generate the files as shown in Figure 33.13. We need to do this because by default the java2com tool omits certain classes that, if present at compile time, will generate errors. Select `*.toString`->"" and click Remove Selected. Select `class java.lang.Class`->"" and click Remove selected. After you have done this, click Close and then Generate.

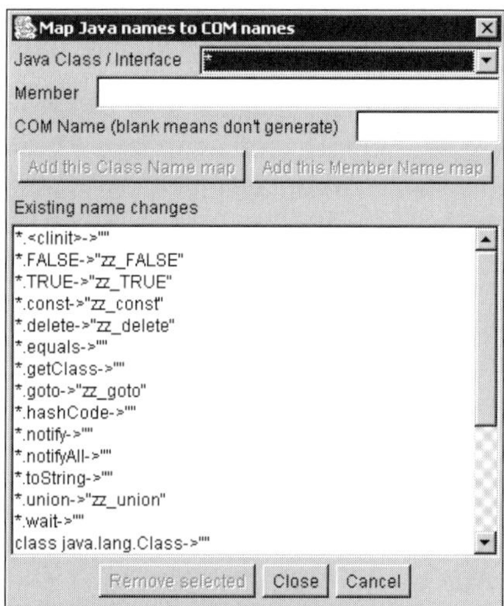

FIGURE 33.13 Map Java names to COM names.

In the `TLB` directory, you'll find the IDL file and all the corresponding Java wrapper source files for the Item bean. Be aware that the generation of an IDL file and wrapper classes for a bean must be done through a single invocation of the java2com tool. This is because the files bear stamped identifiers used to link them together at run time. If you need to, you can move and compile these files on different machines later but initially they must be generated together.

6. We now need to compile all the wrapper classes, jar them, and place them in the class path of WebLogic Server. To compile the classes, use the Ant command: **`ant compile.wrappers`**.

   All the compiled wrappers can now be found in the build directory and have been archived in the `item_earlybound.jar` file. You must place the `item_earlybound.jar` file and the `itemClient.jar` found in the `c:\\jCOM\InventoryItem\earlybound` directory in the classpath explicitly. Having them in an EAR file is not sufficient. In the `startWebLogic.cmd` for your domain (`mydomain` is the default), insert

   ```
   set CLASSPATH=C:\ch33\jCOM\InventoryItem\earlybound\
   item_earlybound.jar;C:\ch33\jCOM\InventoryItem\earlybound\item_Client.jar
   ```

7. Next we compile the generated IDL file into a type library. To do this, you must have installed the MIDL compiler we spoke about earlier. In your command window, traverse to the directory where the MIDL compiler is installed and run the `SetEnv.Bat` so that the MIDL can be found. Go back to the early-bound example directory and run the Ant build tool to compile the type library:

   ```
   ant compile.idl
   ```

   Without the build tool, the syntax would be

   ```
   midl itemTLB.idl
   ```

8. The resulting type library (`itemTLB.tlb`) must be accessible to the Visual Basic client. We accomplish this by placing it in the registry of the client machine with the regtlb tool. The Ant build script will invoke regtlb through the `ant` command:

   ```
   ant reg.tlb
   ```

   Without the build tool, the syntax is

   `regtlb /unregsterall` (to unregister all existing type libraries)

   ```
   regtlb itemTLB.tlb examplesServer
   ```

Creating the VB Client

Open up the VB project `InventoryItemLateBound.vbp` located in the `c:\ch33\\jCOM\InventoryItem\earlybound` directory you created from the files located on the accompanying CD at the back of the book.

From the Projects menu, select References. Make sure that the itemTLB is available for the project as in Figure 33.14.

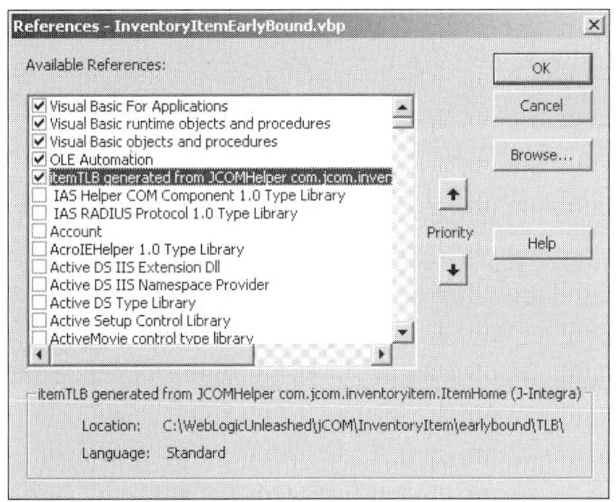

FIGURE 33.14 Visual Basic references.

Open up the form code. Look through the code and notice the differences between this and the late-bound version. The distinction here being that you can now see the methods signatures and attributes of the Item bean as you interact with it. The nomenclature of the code is clearer because we no longer have to refer to everything simply as object.

Run the code by pressing F5, and you should see the same results as shown in the early-bound version you saw earlier.

Event Handling

Both COM and Java technologies support the notion of an *event*—something occurring dynamically at run time that a listening thread can take action on. It should come as no surprise that the mechanisms each uses to accomplish this are sufficiently incompatible. Here we'll again look to jCOM to come to the rescue and provide a transparent way of conversing between the two.

A COM class defines an event through the use of a interface—more specifically, a source interface. COM classes that implement the interface use it to subscribe to the events defined therein.

Java events are defined by an interface derived from `java.util.EventListener`. Java event handlers are used to respond to events. You register the events you want to have handled with a specific event handler.

Although perhaps an oversimplification, for our purposes what is important to know is that jCOM allows COM objects to subscribe to Java events as though they were COM events. In turn, Java objects can subscribe to COM events using standard Java mechanisms.

The com2java tool is used to hide COM event implementations from view. It does this by reading the associated type library and rendering Java equivalents for each source interface it finds. When com2java finds an interface, at a minimum, there must be one COM class that uses the interface as a source interface. It then adds two methods to the generated Java class. It inserts a standard Java `addAppEventsListener` and `removeAppEventsListener` method in a manner familiar to Java programmers when subscribing to events in Java. A corresponding `java.util.EventListener` interface is then generated for the class.

It is a requirement of the Java event-driven model that each method in an interface have a single parameter that is an instance of a class derived from the `java.util.EventObject` class. To comply with this, java2com generates an additional class for each method in an event interface to hold the parameters.

The last Java convention that java2com must contend with is the use of an adapter class. In Java, the adapter class provides empty default implementations for each method in the interface. This enables a class to be created from the interface without having to implement all the methods in the interface, which with some interfaces can become quite lengthy. java2com therefore generates an adapter class for each event interface it finds.

For COM clients accessing event-driven Java objects, the java2com tool generates source interfaces for all Java events found in a Java class. These will be made available to the COM client through the generated type library, which can be used to subscribe to events in the standard COM way. Event-driven programs are thus supported.

Dealing with the Data Types

After jCOM is configured and up and running, you'll find that the only real day-to-day programming task you'll encounter is in dealing with the data types that you send and receive from the server objects you've exposed. From a Java or COM client perspective, you'll need to reconcile between individual idiosyncrasies in the primitive data type mappings that jCOM provides.

Overall, jCOM should be given credit for providing a workable solution to a difficult problem and doing a very good job of mapping primitive and complex data types across platforms into a form familiar to programmers on either side. But as with all integration efforts, you shouldn't expect perfection. For example, a COM `VariantEnumeration` type is mapped to a `java.lang.Enumeration` in Java. COM enumerations have no equivalent to the `hasMoreElements()` method, so you'll have to work around this by using the `nextElement` method until you get a `NoSuchElementException`.

As an alternative, under the Server/ServerName/Connections/jCOM tab on the WebLogic Server Console, you can check Prefetch Enums. In the background, jCOM will pre-fetch the next element so that `hasMoreElements()` will work correctly.

See Table 33.2 for a sample of how types are mapped between COM and Java. I refer you to the J-Integra Web site documentation where you will find very useful detailed listings of all the latest type mappings: `http://www.intrinsyc.com/support/j-integra/doc/`. In Contents, look under Reference/Type Mapping.

TABLE 33.2 Late Binding Type Mapping and Coercion Early Versus Late Binding Summary

Visual Basic Variant Type	Java Primitive Type
VARIANT BOOL	java.lang.Boolean
unsigned char	java.lang.Byte
double	java.lang.Double
float	java.lang.Float
long	java.lang.Integer
short	java.lang.Short
Decimal	java.math.BigDecimal
DATE	java.util.Date
BSTR	java.lang.String

Summary

As we've seen, under certain conditions a tool such as jCOM can come in pretty handy. Although perhaps not *detente*, it does make it possible for Microsoft and Java applications to live in peaceful coexistence. Let's face it: A huge investment has been laid out in each of these technologies. On either side, you'll find an ample supply of people passionate in their convictions about the inherent merits of a particular solution—a solution eagerly embraced by an all-too-firm commitment on the part of the advocates of each. Given the status quo, a closer merging of these heterogeneous paradigms doesn't seem likely anytime soon.

It is in this context that jCOM starts to make sense. Again, the most intriguing aspect here being transparency. Underlying object architectures can be effectively isolated, and thus completely hidden from view. This makes our life so much easier as programmers. The mundane chore (not to mention the training costs) of staying versed in the myriad of trivial syntactical permutations between languages can all but be eliminated. For Java programmers, the mantra of a pure Java, write-once-run-anywhere solution can be adhered to; COM developers can keep pumping out those COM components and IS managers can leverage benefits found in both worlds.

So, if you're looking for a stable yet seamless mechanism of communication between your Java and Microsoft objects, keep jCOM in mind—it might well turn out to be the method of choice.

CHAPTER 34

CORBA and Tuxedo Integration

by Saranathan Govindarajan

IN THIS CHAPTER

- WebLogic Tuxedo Connector
- RMI over IIOP

WebLogic Server provides a robust enterprise connector that extends the Tuxedo domain services and Tuxedo CORBA objects to the Java world. Tuxedo has been providing a highly scalable and reliable environment in which to develop business services for a long time. Many mission-critical applications currently running in the Tuxedo environment have been developed over the last few decades. WebLogic Tuxedo Connector (WTC) helps in seamlessly integrating these Tuxedo applications in the WebLogic Server environment. The consistent API interface eases the development, deployment, and management of applications that leverage the Tuxedo transaction services and CORBA objects in real-time without having to learn the underlying CORBA API implementation and Tuxedo ATMI.

The main focus of this chapter is a look at WTC and how it can be used to integrate Tuxedo-based services and CORBA objects with the WebLogic Server environment. We will look in great detail at how to implement a simple WTC client for a Tuxedo application that's packaged with the Tuxedo product. We'll also see how we can integrate Tuxedo queues with JMS. We also cover WebLogic RMI-IIOP, which allows heterogeneous clients talk to WebLogic Server using the standards-based IIOP protocol. The most important use of this technology is the capability to integrate disparate clients, namely CORBA/IDL clients, to different WebLogic Server–based components such as EJBs. This chapter does not talk about implementing a Tuxedo service or a CORBA object. For more information about how to program in the Tuxedo application domain, refer to `http://edocs.bea.com/tuxedo/tux80/`.

WebLogic Tuxedo Connector

WebLogic Tuxedo Connector provides bi-directional interoperability between Tuxedo application servers and WebLogic Server applications. The interoperability is enabled by the Java Application-To-Transaction-Monitor Interface (JATMI), which is modeled on the Tuxedo ATMI.

WTC has the following core functionalities built in:

- Bi-directional interoperability—Tuxedo services/CORBA objects can be invoked from EJBs and vice versa
- Outbound transaction propagation from WebLogic applications into Tuxedo domains
- Seamless integration of WebLogic services into legacy applications using the e-Link adapters
- Bi-directional domain and ACL security propagation
- Messaging integration between Tuxedo /Q and JMS
- Capability to maintain a pool of connections from WebLogic into Tuxedo
- Capability to include Tuxedo services as part of the WebLogic Integrator (WLI) work-flow processes
- XML-based configuration file

Figure 34.1 shows the integration components involved in WTC-based WebLogic Server–Tuxedo integration.

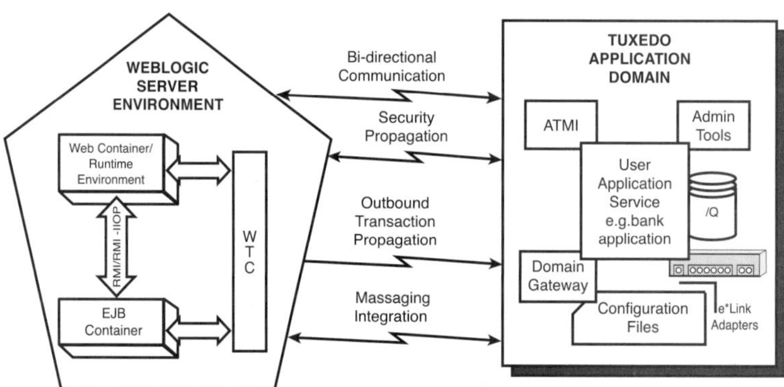

Figure 34.1 WTC and Tuxedo integration components.

Additionally, domain-level failover and fallback, which have been at the core of the Tuxedo application domain, have also been incorporated in the WTC implementation. This facilitates easier administration along with the simple XML-based configuration file.

WTC and JOLT

One of main questions asked by many people familiar with developing Tuxedo application is how WTC compares with an existing product: Jolt. BEA Jolt, similar to WTC, is a Java-based interface to Tuxedo domains that helps in exposing Tuxedo services to the Java world. The functionality of Jolt and WTC might sound very similar, but there are some differences in what they offer. WTC complements the functionality of Jolt and should not be construed as a replacement for it. Jolt is the only option for accessing Tuxedo application services when the client is a generic Java client or the services accessing the Tuxedo services are running on a non–WebLogic Server solution. Both Jolt and WTC can be used when accessing Tuxedo domains from a WebLogic Server environment. Jolt connection pools can be configured and managed when used in conjunction with WebLogic Server. Let's look at the main differences between Jolt and WTC:

- WTC APIs are based on Tuxedo ATMIs that are completely different from the Jolt APIs.
- WTC provides an integrated transaction mechanism encompassing both Tuxedo services and WebLogic services.
- WTC manages connectivity between Tuxedo and WebLogic application using Tuxedo /T domains. Jolt manages connectivity into a Tuxedo application with the help of server listeners configured at a particular port and handlers that manage the distribution of requests to the appropriate Tuxedo servers.
- WTC `tBridge` provides for closer integration between Tuxedo /Q and JMS advanced messaging services, whereas Jolt provides no support for accessing /Q.
- WTC does not support double-byte character sets or international character sets, but Jolt does.
- WTC does not support Tuxedo 6.5 running on VMS, AS/400, and OS/390 platforms.

JATMI Programming

Now let's get to building applications using WTC. As mentioned earlier, the JATMI provides the interface between WebLogic and Tuxedo applications. The building blocks of programming using JATMI are

- ATMI primitives
- Typed buffers

The JATMI primitives are very similar to the Tuxedo ATMI primitive calls and are simple Java-based APIs. These APIs enable the communication between WebLogic Server and Tuxedo as well as provide APIs to manage transactions and manipulate proprietary typed buffers. We'll look at the available APIs later in the chapter when we get to implementing WTC-based Tuxedo clients.

The JATMI typed buffers are the WTC equivalent of the Tuxedo ATMI typed buffers and are used for transporting data to the service calls. Table 34.1 summarizes the typed buffers of WTC and Tuxedo.

TABLE 34.1 Communication Buffers

JATMI	Tuxedo	Description
TypedString	STRING	Character array terminated by NULL
TypedCArray	CARRAY	Byte array
TypedFML	FML	Well-defined data type including occurrence, length, and identifier
TypedFML32	FML32	Similar to FML, but provides bigger buffers
TypedXML	XML	XML-based message buffer
TypedView	View	View description file-based buffer
TypedView32	View32	Similar to View with bigger buffers

We'll now move to developing clients based on the JATMI programming basics we've covered so far. Many different client types can be created, depending on the communication type used with the Tuxedo Server.

> **NOTE**
>
> As mentioned earlier, it's assumed that you have some basic working knowledge of Tuxedo: developing, configuring and maintaining a simple Tuxedo domain. For learning how to do those things, refer to `http://edocs.bea.com/tuxedo/tux81/interm/atmiprog.htm`. When fully installed, Tuxedo software comes with a basic set of examples covering the different features of the software. One of the sample applications is a simple bank application: bankapp. This C-based application is an ATMI application and the services defined as part of the application are basic account-related operations. The functions performed are opening and closing accounts, inquiring on balances, and withdrawing, depositing, and transferring funds from one account to another. For a full tutorial of how to use bankapp, refer to `http://edocs.bea.com/tuxedo/tux81/tutor/tutba.htm`.

Let's now discuss the process of building a simple JATMI client for accessing the INQUIRY Tuxedo service that's part of the bank application described earlier. INQUIRY Tuxedo service returns the account balance for a given account number.

Basic Configuration

Let's start by creating a connection between the WebLogic Server and the Tuxedo domain running our sample Tuxedo application (bankapp). The connection creation mechanism is different from regular Tuxedo clients that use the ATMI function `tpinit()` to connect to the Tuxedo domain. With WTC, the connection is created at startup using a `WTCServer` MBean. The `WTCServer` MBean uses the configuration parameter defined by the user as part of the startup and creates the connections to the remote domain.

> **NOTE**
>
> All WTC configuration parameters are defined in the `config.xml` file.

WTC configuration can be performed using the WebLogic console. Figure 34.2 describes how to define the `WTCServer` base configuration. As the figure indicates, we create a `WTCServer` with `MyWTCService` as the name; this has to be attached to a target WebLogic Server.

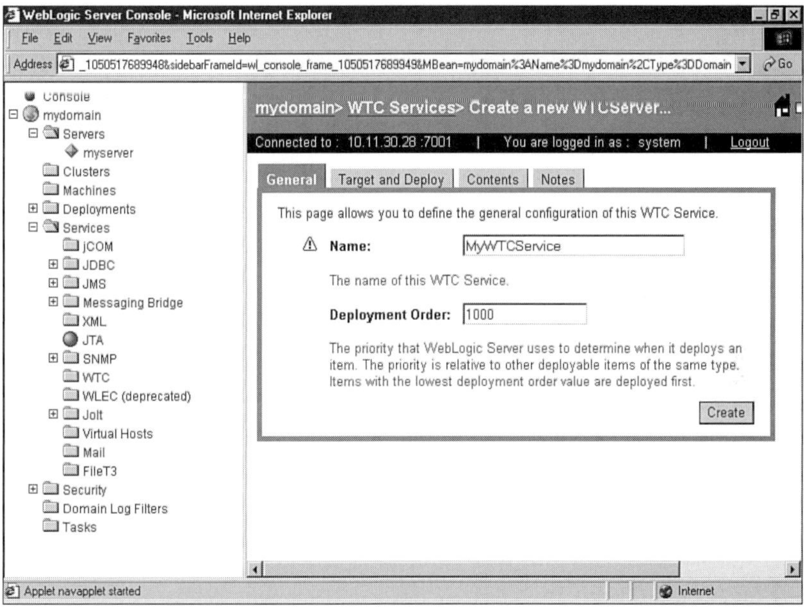

Figure 34.2 Define a WTC server.

After defining the WTC server within the WebLogic environment, we must name the local access point (port) that's used for communicating with the back-end Tuxedo server. Figure 34.3 describes how to define the local Tuxedo access point.

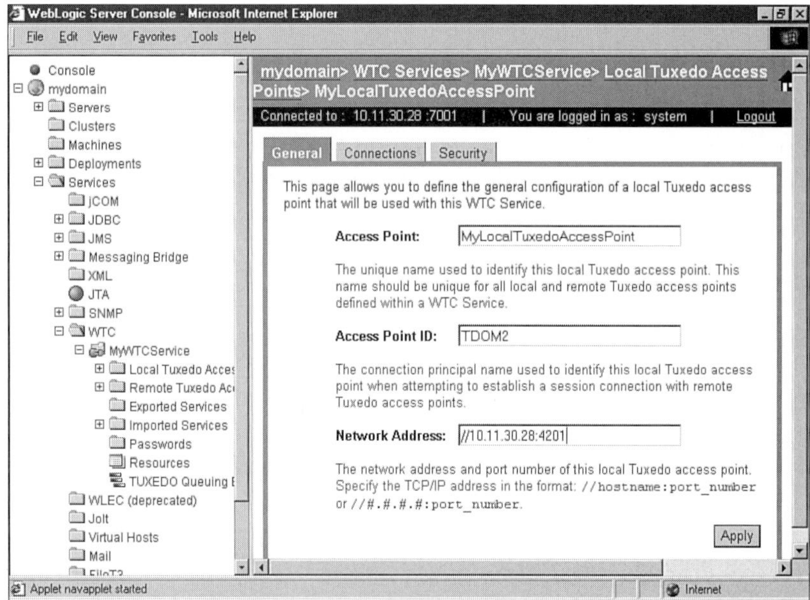

Figure 34.3 Local Tuxedo access point.

Finally, we must configure the port number in the remote Tuxedo domain that is listening to the WebLogic Server–based requests. Figure 34.4 describes how to define the remote Tuxedo access point.

At the end of this process, the `config.xml` file would be updated with the `WTCServer` MBean configuration and be ready for opening up Tuxedo services such as balance inquiry in our sample bank application. The next step in the process is to import the services from the remote Tuxedo domain. Because we aren't exposing services in the WebLogic Server to the Tuxedo world, there's no need for any services to be exported. Figure 34.5 shows how to import a remote Tuxedo service. We're importing the INQUIRY Tuxedo service that's advertised as part of the sample bank application.

The following XML snippet gives you an idea of the `WTCServer` MBean configuration after executing the aforementioned steps:

```
<WTCServer Name="MyWTCService" Targets="myserver">
  <WTCLocalTuxDom AccessPoint="MyLocalTuxedoAccessPoint"
    AccessPointId="TDOM2" ConnectionPolicy="ON_STARTUP"
    Interoperate="Yes" NWAddr="//[WLS-SERVER_IPADDR]"
    Name="WTCLocalTuxDom-1050527739007"/>
  <WTCRemoteTuxDom AccessPoint="MyRemoteTuxedoAccessPoint"
    AccessPointId="TDOM1" ConnectionPolicy="ON_STARTUP"
    LocalAccessPoint="MyLocalTuxedoAccessPoint"
```

```
    NWAddr="//172.18.26.24:4201"
    Name="WTCRemoteTuxDom-1050527826102"/>
  <WTCImport LocalAccessPoint="MyLocalTuxedoAccessPoint"
    Name="WTCImport-1050527894290"
    RemoteAccessPointList="MyRemoteTuxedoAccessPoint"
    RemoteName="INQUIRY" ResourceName="INQUIRY"/>
</WTCServer>
```

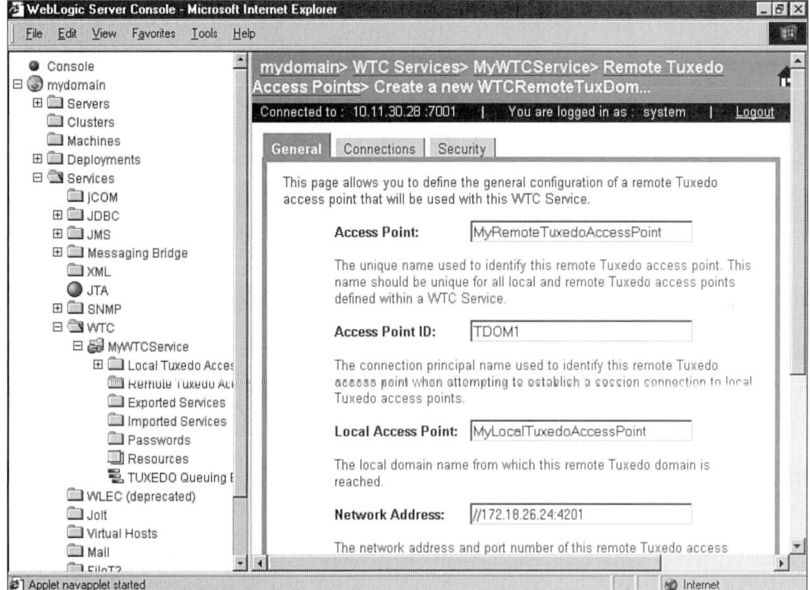

Figure 34.4 Remote Tuxedo access point.

> **NOTE**
>
> The `Interoperate` attribute in `WTCLocalTuxDom` helps to integrate WTC services with Tuxedo services defined in an earlier version of Tuxedo (6.5).

As you can see from the configuration file snippet, we've defined the following parameters:

- Remote domain parameters, including the network address and connection policy
- Local domain parameters
- Imported remote services and exported remote services

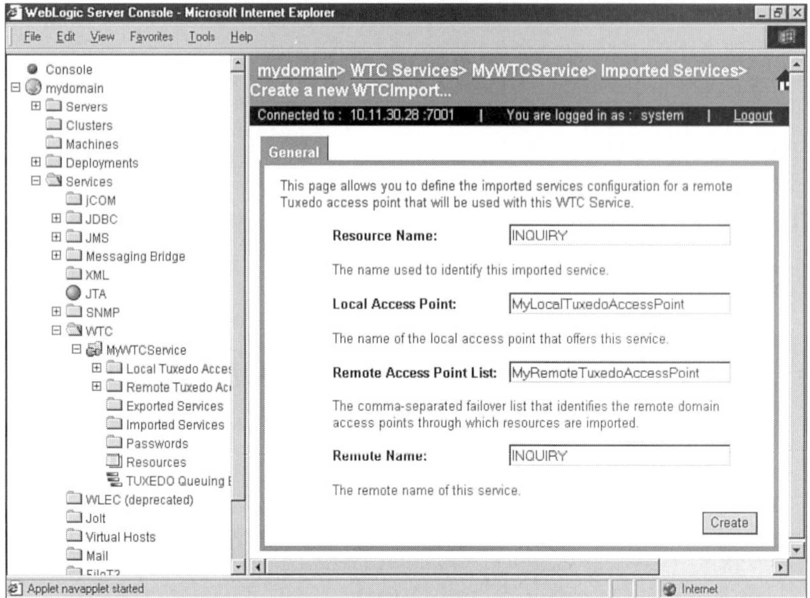

Figure 34.5 Importing services.

The Connection policy parameter set up as part of the `WTCRemoteTuxDom` / `WTCLocalTuxDom` MBean determines the conditions under which the local domain connects to the remote domain. Valid values for the parameter are

- `ON_DEMAND`—A connection is attempted only when requested by either of the domain services—either a client request or an administrative request. This is the default setting.
- `ON_STARTUP`—A domain gateway attempts to establish a connection with its remote domain access points at gateway server initialization time.
- `INCOMING_ONLY`—A domain gateway does not attempt an initial connection to remote domain access points at startup and remote services are initially suspended. When the domain gateway of the local domain access point receives an incoming connection, a connection is made and services are advertised if successful.

The `interoperate` attribute inside `WTCLocalTuxDom` is a special attribute that enables a local Tuxedo access point to interoperate with remote Tuxedo domains that run on versions earlier than 6.5. The earlier configuration sets up a simple connection between WebLogic Server and a remote Tuxedo domain. Other parameters within each of the MBean configurations can be added for increased security, encryption, and so on. WebLogic Tuxedo Connector configuration is managed by the set of MBeans defined in Table 34.2.

TABLE 34.2 WTC Configuration MBeans

MBean	Description
WTCServer	The parent WTC MBean used for setting the interoperability attributes required for WTC–Tuxedo domain connectivity.
WTCLocalTuxDom	Defines the properties of the local domain.
WTCRemoteTuxDom	Defines the properties of the remote domain.
WTCExport	Provides information about the services available in the local domain. This is an optional bean configuration. If unspecified, all services are advertised to the external domains.
WTCImport	Provides information about services imported and available on remote domains.
WTCPassword	Provides information for interdomain authentication through access points of type TDOMAIN.
WTCResources	Defines the FML and VIEW field tables and application passwords for the domain.
WTCtBridgeGlobal	Provides global configuration information and advanced messaging between WebLogic Server and Tuxedo.
WTCtBridgeRedirect	Provides the source, target, direction, and transport of a message.

For detailed information about the list of attributes for the MBeans we've used and the ones listed in Table 34.2, refer to `http://edocs.bea.com/wls/docs81/config_xml/index.html`.

The Tuxedo system administrator has to make some changes depending on the setup of the remote Tuxedo system. As you can see from the earlier configuration, WTC requires a remote /T domain to be configured as part of the Tuxedo application. Refer to the BEA Tuxedo domains guide at `http://edocs.bea.com/tuxedo/tux81/interm/admin.htm#dom` for more information about Tuxedo domains (/T domains). If the existing Tuxedo application does not have a domain set up (like our bank application), a new domain must be configured to correspond to the remote access point in the `WTCServer` MBean. If the existing Tuxedo application already has domains set up, the Tuxedo administrator has to make sure that a domain configuration matches the remote access point defined as part of the `WTCServer` MBean. The changes to the Tuxedo domain can be summarized as follows:

- Add the required group definitions for the domain administration server and the gateway domain servers in the Tuxedo configuration file (that is, the UBB file):

```
*GROUPS
DMADMGRP  LMID=SITE1 GRPNO=100
DMGRP  LMID=SITE1 GRPNO=200
```

- Add the domain administrative server and gateway domain servers to the list of servers available as part of the Tuxedo application:

```
      *SERVERS
DMADM     SRVGRP=DMADMGRP SRVID=200
GWADM     SRVGRP=DMGRP   SRVID=220
GWTDOMAIN  SRVGRP=DMGRP   SRVID=240
```

- The last step is to configure the Tuxedo domain configuration that has been already set up as the remote access point in the WebLogic Server environment:

```
#
*DM_LOCAL_DOMAINS
#
TDOM1 GWGRP=DMGRP
TYPE=TDOMAIN
DOMAINID="TDOM1"
BLOCKTIME=10
MAXDATALEN=56
MAXRDOM=89
DMTLOGDEV="[LOGDIR]/bankApp_dm"
AUDITLOG="[LOGDIR]/bankApp_aud"
DMTLOGNAME="DMTLOG_BANKAPP"
CONNECTION_POLICY="ON_STARTUP"
#
*DM_REMOTE_DOMAINS
#
#
TDOM2    TYPE=TDOMAIN
  DOMAINID="TDOM2"
#
#
*DM_TDOMAIN
#
TDOM1 NWADDR="//175.18.26.24:5966"
    NWDEVICE="/dev/tcp"
TDOM2 NWADDR="//47.11.30.28:5966"
    NWDEVICE="/dev/tcp"
#
*DM_LOCAL_SERVICES
     INQUIRY LDOM="TDOM1"
```

Establishing a Connection

Now we've set up the Tuxedo connections. Let's get down to writing some client code. The Tuxedo connections established as part of the startup process are registered in the JNDI under the name `tuxedo.services.TuxedoConnection`. A `TuxedoConnection` object can be obtained using the `getTuxedoConnection()` method of `TuxedoConnectionFactory`, which gives the live Tuxedo connection to the client:

```
try {
  ctx = new InitialContext();
  tcf = (TuxedoConnectionFactory)
      ctx.lookup("tuxedo.services.TuxedoConnection");
}catch (NamingException ne) {
  // Could not get the Tuxedo object, throw (Service Not Available) TPENOENT
  throw new TPException(TPException.TPENOENT, "Could not get
  ➥TuxedoConnectionFactory :"
  + ne);
}
myTux = tcf.getTuxedoConnection();
```


Before we get to use this Tuxedo connection, let's take a step back and learn about one of the important features of BEA Tuxedo: the Field Manipulation Language (FML). Table 34.1 listed the message buffers that are available as part of the Tuxedo system. FML-based buffers (FML and FML32) represent the most used Tuxedo buffers for data exchange between the client and the Tuxedo service. Let's look at programming FML buffers; we'll use them to implementing the bankapp client using WTC.

Field Manipulation Language Programming

FML is a well-defined set of buffer management functions for efficient transfer of data between Tuxedo components. FML contains attribute-value pairs called *fields*. The attribute is a field identifier and the value represents the corresponding content. Additionally, FML facilitates multiple occurrences of an attribute-value pair. In other words, FML can be considered as a three-dimensional hash table, where the third dimension is the occurrence of a field. FML provides named access to the fields used in the communication between the processes involved in the Tuxedo domain.

FML—Size Does Matter FML comes in two sizes. The original version of the buffer (FML16) is based on a 16-bit value for the length of the fields. It also limits the number of fields that can be defined to 8191 unique fields. The individual field lengths can be up to 64K bytes and a total buffer size of 64KB. FML32 allows for about 30 million fields and field and buffer lengths of about 2 billion bytes.

FML in WTC FML in WTC is a limited implementation of the full FML capability. Table 34.3 summarizes the field types and the associated object types supported by FML.

TABLE 34.3 FML Field Types and Objects

Field Types	Object Equivalent
FLD_SHORT	Short
FLD_LONG	Long
FLD_CHAR	Character
FLD_FLOAT	Float
FLD_DOUBLE	Double
FLD_STRING	String
FLD_CARRAY	byte[]
FLD_FML32	TypedFML32
FLD_PTR	TypedBuffer

`FLD_VIEW32`, `FLD_INT`, and `FLD_DECIMAL` are not yet supported.

The FML fields used in the buffer should be defined in a field table. Listing 34.1 lists a section of the bank application field table that's defined as part of the bank application Tuxedo example.

LISTING 34.1 Bank Application Field Tables (bankflds)

```
#FML
# Fields for database bankdb
# name              number type  flags  comments
ACCOUNT_ID            110   long  -     -
ACCT_TYPE            112   char  -     -
ADDRESS             109   string -     -
AMOUNT              117   float  -     -
BALANCE             105   float  -     -
TELLER_ID            116   long  -     -
#
# non database fields
SBALANCE             201   string -    dollar format
SAMOUNT             202   string -    dollar format
#END
```

The field table defined in Listing 34.1 has to be converted into a Java class before implementing the corresponding WTC—Tuxedo client. WTC provides utility classes—`mkfldclass` and `mkfldclass32`—as part of the `webLogic.wtc.jatmi` package. The utility produces a Java class that implements the `FldTbl` interface. The following command is used to generate the Java class:

```
java weblogic.wtc.jatmi.mkfldclass wlsunleashed.wtc bankflds
```

The second argument to the command is the package name for the generated field table class and third argument is the field table's filename. Listing 34.2 shows parts of the generated Java file. As you can see, the field names defined in Listing 34.1 are converted to Java final native types that can be referenced in the WTC Tuxedo client code.

LISTING 34.2 Generated Java Equivalent of bankflds

```
package wlsunleashed.wtc;

import java.io.*;
import java.lang.*;
import java.util.*;
import weblogic.wtc.jatmi.*;

public final class bankflds
    implements weblogic.wtc.jatmi.FldTbl
{
    Hashtable nametofieldHashTable;
    Hashtable fieldtonameHashTable;

    /** number: 110 type: long */
    public final static int ACCOUNT_ID = 8302;
    /** number: 112 type: char */
    public final static int ACCT_TYPE = 16496;
    /** number: 109 type: string */
    public final static int ADDRESS = 41069;
...
...
   public String Fldid_to_name(int fldid)
    {
        if ( fieldtonameHashTable == null ) {
            fieldtonameHashTable = new Hashtable();
            fieldtonameHashTable.put(new Integer(ACCOUNT_ID),
            ➥"ACCOUNT_ID");
...
...
...
   }
   public int name_to_Fldid(String name)
    {
        if ( nametofieldHashTable == null ) {
            nametofieldHashTable = new Hashtable();
```

LISTING 34.2 Continued

```
            nametofieldHashTable.put("ACCOUNT_ID",
            ➥new Integer(ACCOUNT_ID));
            nametofieldHashTable.put("ACCT_TYPE",
            ➥new Integer(ACCT_TYPE));
            nametofieldHashTable.put("ADDRESS",
            ➥new Integer(ADDRESS));
...
...
...
    }

}
```

After `bankflds.java` is compiled, the resulting class must be added to the classpath of the application. The `WTCResources` MBean has to be updated at this point to include the generated class file. Figure 34.6 shows how to add this resource to the configuration.

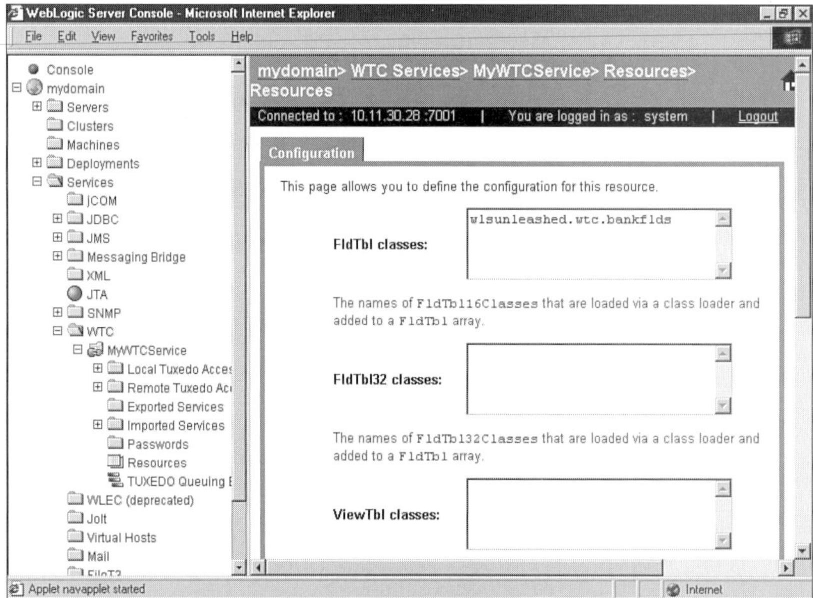

Figure 34.6 Configuring WTC resource files.

The following XML snippet shows the configuration of the `WTCResources` MBean after adding our FML field table class file:

```
<WTCResources FldTbl16Classes="wlsunleashed.wtc.bankflds"
      Name="WTCResources-1050529865843"/>
```

The bankflds class implements weblogic.wtc.jatmi.FldTbl—this is a common interface that can be used by both FML16 and FML32 buffers. Using a common interface simplifies the applications implementing it and provides the capability to easily switch between the buffers if needed.

Let's move to manipulating the FML buffers. The weblogic.wtc.jatmi.FML is the main FML interface used by both FML16 and FML32 buffers. The main functions defined by this interface are needed for populating, deleting, and extracting fields from a FML buffer. They are Fchg, Fdel, and Fget, respectively.

- Fchg adds the given object to the FML buffer whose ID is contained in the key to the fielded buffer. The key includes the occurrence of the field.
- Fdel deletes the particular occurrence from the fielded buffer.
- Fget retrieves a copy of the object stored in the FML buffer of the given field ID and the occurrence.

The interface also provides functions for retrieving the field number, field types, and names. Subinterfaces to this FML interface correspond to the size of the FML buffer: TypedFML and TypedFML32. These interfaces add more functionality to the FML interfaces pertaining to buffer manipulation, including Fadd. Fadd is also used to add fields to the buffer. As you can see, all the described functions are exactly mapped to a corresponding Tuxedo function. For more information about the FML and subinterfaces, refer to http://edocs.bea.com/wls/docs81/javadocs/weblogic/wtc/jatmi/package-tree.html. Now let's move on to using some of the functions in the bank application WTC client.

Input Typed Buffers

The inputs to service requests are packed into the message buffers defined in Table 34.1. The INQUIRY Tuxedo service requires the inputs (namely the account number) to be sent in an FML buffer. The first step in using a typed buffer is to create it. This is a common step with every typed buffer. Let's look at two types of typed buffer creation.

If the typed buffer being used is TypedString, the creation of the buffer is simple:

```
myData = new TypedString(myInputString);
```

In the case of our client, we need to create a FML16 buffer as follows:

```
TypedFML myData = new TypedFML(new bankflds());
```

An instance of the field table class we created earlier has to be passed to the TypedFML constructor. At this time, the buffer is ready to populated. The input to the INQUIRY service is the account number of the customer, which returns the balance along with the account number. The following code snippet populates the input FML buffer with the account number:

```
try {
  myData.Fchg(bankflds.ACCOUNT_ID,0, new Integer(getId()));
} catch (Ferror fe) {
  log("An error occurred putting data into the FML buffer. The error is "
    + fe);
 }
```

The arguments to the `Fchg` function are the field name (as defined by the field table class), field repetition (occurrence), and field value. Each FML field can be repeated multiple times in the same FML buffer. Now let's discuss how to use the created buffer and invoke a Tuxedo service to perform the requested function.

Invoking Tuxedo Services

WebLogic Tuxedo Connector supports the following communication mechanisms with a remote Tuxedo domain:

- Request-response communication
- Conversational communication
- Queue-based communication (`enqueue` and `dequeue`)

Request-Response Communication In the request-response mode, a software module acting as a client sends requests to a server and waits for a response. The response can be returned either synchronously or asynchronously. JATMI provides APIs for both asynchronous and synchronous request-response models.

The JATMI call `tpcall` is used for synchronous request-response mode. The INQUIRY service call sends the account balance request and waits for the response without proceeding to other tasks. Listing 34.3 describes how the service call is made and the exceptions it must handle. The return value (`myRtn`) to the service call is also a typed buffer, which is explained later in the chapter. The exceptions generated are also explained later in the chapter.

LISTING 34.3 Service Invocation

```
try {
   myRtn = myTux.tpcall("INQUIRY", myData, 0);
} catch (TPReplyException tre) {
  log("tpcall threw TPReplyExcption " + tre);
  throw tre;
} catch (TPException te) {
```

LISTING 34.3 Continued

```
  log("tpcall threw TPException " + te);
  throw te;
} catch (Exception ee) {
  log("tpcall threw exception: " + ee);
  throw new TPException(TPException.TPESYSTEM, "Exception: " + ee);
}
```

Alternatively, the service call could have been made asynchronously. In this case, the client need not wait for the response to come back and can proceed to other tasks. The client can come back later and fetch the response using a call descriptor. The call descriptor is returned as part of the service invocation. The JATMI calls that are used in an asynchronous mode are

- `tpacall`—Invokes the Tuxedo services asynchronously
- `tpgetreply`—Retrieves replies of previously made asynchronous calls
- `tpcancel`—Cancels a previously issued asynchronous call (nontransactional) identified by a call descriptor

Conversational Communication In conversational communication, a half-duplex communication channel is kept open between the WTC and the Tuxedo domain conversational server. The initiator is the process that controls the message send; the subordinate process can only receive messages. The initiator and the subordinate hold state information related to the state of the conversation. A logical connection stays alive until a termination event takes place. A single conversation can involve any number of messages between the initiator and the subordinate. Figure 34.7 describes the steps involved in a conversational service invocation from WTC into the Tuxedo domain. Establishment of the connection between the servers is similar to the mechanism described for request-response mode.

The lists of JATMI calls, which are used in a conversational mode, are

- `tpsend`—Sends messages to the conversational server
- `tprecv`—Receives messages on an open communication channel
- `tpdiscon`—Generates the event to disconnect the conversation

These functions are exposed to the WTC conversational client using the `weblogic.wtc.jatmi.TPServiceInformation` class, which implements a `weblogic.wtc.jatmi.Conversation` interface.

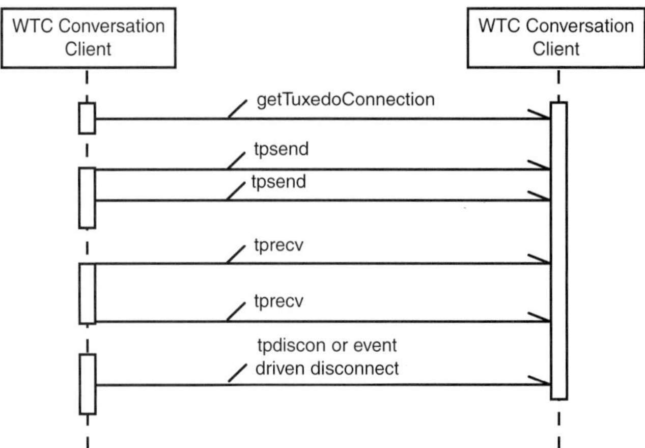

Figure 34.7 WTC in a conversational communication.

Queue-Based Communication In addition to the preceding types of calls, messages can also be sent asynchronously to the Tuxedo service with the use of Tuxedo /Q. The `weblogic.wtc.jatmi.EnqueueRequest` class provides the same functionality as that of its Tuxedo equivalent, `tpenqueue()`. It places requests on the configured Tuxedo queue for processing by the requested Tuxedo service. Similarly, `weblogic.wtc.jatmi.DequeueReply` processes replies from Tuxedo for a previously queued request. It performs the same function as the Tuxedo equivalent (`tpdequeue`). This exactly extends the /Q interfaces to the WebLogic Server environment.

Exceptions Framework

The WebLogic Tuxedo Connector handles exceptions using the following classes.

Ferror This exception is thrown when manipulating the FML buffer; such as when adding, deleting, and changing elements to the buffer.

TPException This exception represents all `TPException` failures. All exceptions of this type are generated by the core WTC calls, such as `tpcall`, `tpacall`, `tpenqueue`, `tpdequeue`, and so on. This exception class provides methods that give the details about the system failure. It also provides `getReplyRtn` method to give the data that's associated with the system failure.

TPReplyException This exception is used when throwing an exception from the Tuxedo service interface. The error object should indicate the Tuxedo error code: `TPESVCERR` or `TPESVCFAIL`. It also provides a `ReplyRtn` object, which can contain user data to be returned in the failure case and the `tpurcode` to be returned.

Output Processing

Output from service requests is packed into the message buffers defined in Table 34.1. The INQUIRY Tuxedo service returns the outputs (account balance) in an FML buffer. The following code snippet explains how to extract the information from the returned buffer. The FML buffer interface provides the `Fget()` function to extract the values from the buffer.

```
myDataBack = (TypedFML) myRtn.getReplyBuffer();
try {
  balance = (String) myDataBack.Fget(bankflds.SBALANCE, 0);
} catch (Ferror fe) {
 log("An error occurred getting data from the FML32 buffer.
 ➥The error is "+ fe);
}
```


After the service calls are completed over the initiated connection, the connection should be released using the `tpterm()` call as demonstrated here:

```
myTux.tpterm(); // Closing the association with Tuxedo
```

Complete Example of a WTC Client

So far, we've seen the pieces of WTC client. Now let's put all those pieces together. Listing 34.4 is a complete example of a WTC client. This code can be used inside any of the J2EE components (for example, EJBs and servlets) to invoke a Tuxedo service.

LISTING 34.4 WTC Client

```
public String getBalance() throws TPException, TPReplyException {
   String balance = "";
   Context ctx;
   TuxedoConnectionFactory tcf;
   TuxedoConnection myTux;
   TypedFML myData;
   TypedFML myDataBack;
   Reply myRtn;
   int status;

   try {
     ctx = getInitialContext();
     tcf = (TuxedoConnectionFactory) ctx.lookup(
        "tuxedo.services.TuxedoConnection");
   } catch (NamingException ne) {
     // Could not get the tuxedo object, throw TPENOENT
     throw new TPException(TPException.TPENOENT,
```

LISTING 34.4 Continued

```
        "Could not get TuxedoConnectionFactory : " + ne);
    }
    myTux = tcf.getTuxedoConnection();
    myData = new TypedFML(new bankflds());
    try {
       myData.Fchg(bankflds.ACCOUNT_ID,0, new Integer(getId()));
    } catch (Ferror fe) {
       log("An error occurred putting data into the FML32 buffer.
       The error is " + fe);
    }
    try {
      myRtn = myTux.tpcall("INQUIRY", myData, 0);
    } catch (TPReplyException tre) {
      log("tpcall threw TPReplyExcption " + tre);
      throw tre;
    } catch (TPException te) {
      log("tpcall threw TPException " + te);
      throw te;
    } catch (Exception ee) {
      log("tpcall threw exception: " + ee);
      throw new TPException(TPException.TPESYSTEM, "Exception: " + ee);
    }

    log("INQUIRY tpcall successful!");

    myDataBack = (TypedFML) myRtn.getReplyBuffer();

    try {
      balance = (String) myDataBack.Fget(bankflds.SBALANCE, 0);
    } catch (Ferror fe) {
      log("An error occurred getting data from the FML32 buffer.
        The error is " + fe);
    }
    myTux.tpterm(); // Closing the association with Tuxedo

    return balance;
}
```

WTC Service EJB

We've already talked about invoking a remote Tuxedo service from a WebLogic Server–based J2EE component. JATMI also provides the infrastructure needed to implement a service EJB that can be invoked from a remote Tuxedo domain. Let's examine the steps involved in implementing a simple service EJB that can be invoked from a remote Tuxedo domain.

Implementing a Service EJB

The first step in the implementation of the service EJB is to identify the service and the input data. We also need to identify the special flags associated with the service execution. The `weblogic.wtc.jatmi.TPServiceInformation` class provides all this information using the functions defined in Table 34.4.

TABLE 34.4 TPServiceInformation Functions

Service Information Functions	Description
getServiceData	Returns a TypedBuffer that can be type-cast to the appropriate buffer as defined in Table 34.1
getServiceName	Returns the name of the service
getServiceFlags	Returns the flags associated with this service

This class also provides the methods to implement the conversational server. All buffers defined in Table 34.1 can be used to pass the data from the Tuxedo client to the server.

Listing 34.5 displays the main function associated with the Hello World service EJB. As you can see in the first line, the argument to the service method is an instance of `TPServiceInformation` class. This instance is used in the function body to obtain the service input and metadata information such as the service name. Also, the return value for this function is an object that implements `weblogic.wtc.jatmi.Reply`. The input argument type—`TPServiceInformation`—is a subclass of `weblogic.wtc.jatmi.TuxedoReply` that implements the `Reply` interface. So, the same buffer can be used to send the output back to the calling Tuxedo domain.

LISTING 34.5 Hello World Service EJB

```
public Reply service(TPServiceInformation mydata) throws TPException {
   TypedString data;
   String name;
   TypedString greeting;

   data = (TypedString) mydata.getServiceData();
   greeting = "Hello World" + data.toString().toLowerCase();
   data = new TypedString(greeting);

   mydata.setReplyBuffer(return_data);
   return (mydata);
}
```

JATMI Transactions

WebLogic Tuxedo Connector supports outbound transactions propagation from WebLogic into the Tuxedo domain. WTC uses the Java Transaction API (JTA) to manage transactions.

Transactions can be defined with the WTC client classes or the Tuxedo services. A transaction encompasses a starting point, a set of program statements, and an end point. A call to the `begin()` method in the initiator begins the transaction. A transaction is terminated by a call to either `commit()` or `setRollbackOnly()`. The terminating calls must be invoked by the initiator. All services invoked between `begin()` and the terminating calls form part of the transaction. The `setTransactionTimeout()` function call is used to ensure that service requests are replied to within a specified reasonable time or are terminated abnormally if the reply isn't sent within the specified time. On a successful return from `commit()`, all changes performed during the transaction are persisted permanently to a data store. The call to `setRollbackOnly()` is used to return to the initial state without committing any changes performed during the transaction.

The transaction began in WebLogic and is propagated to the Tuxedo domain using the `TuxedoConnection` object obtained after initiating the transaction with a JTA call `begin()`.

TPNOTRAN Flag

Tuxedo service routines called within the transaction boundary defined by begin and commit/rollback are part of the current transaction. If a particular Tuxedo call must be excluded from a transaction, the corresponding `tpcall` or `tpacall` can be called with the `flags` parameter set to `TPNOTRAN`. In this case, all operations performed by the called service are excluded from the current transaction and are not affected by the outcome of the current transaction.

Tuxedo Transaction Primitives and JTA

As we saw in Chapter 9, "Processing Transactions with the Java Transaction API," JTA manages the transactions with the following three main interfaces:

- `Transaction`—This interface is used to enlist resources, synchronize registration, and perform transaction completion and status query operations.
- `TransactionManager`—This interface is used by the application server to communicate to the transaction manager for transaction boundary demarcation on behalf of the application.
- `UserTransaction`—This interface, which is a subset of the `TransactionManager` interface, offers more control to restrict access to the transaction object.

All JTA transaction primitives have equivalent Tuxedo primitives for outward propagation of transactions. Table 34.5 compares the two sets of primitives.

TABLE 34.5 JTA Versus Tuxedo

JTA	Tuxedo
begin()	tpbegin()
commit()	tpcommit()
abort()	tpabort()

Additionally, transaction time in JTA can be using `setTransactionTimeout()`, whereas the `tpbegin` call takes the timeout value as an argument. Tuxedo also provides a `tpgetlev` call to determine whether a particular routine is in a transaction that's managed by `getStatus()` in JTA.

WTC and JMS

WTC provides a bi-directional JMS interface for the J2EE components of WebLogic Server to communicate with the Tuxedo domain. This is accomplished using the `tBridge` component of the WTC. The components involved in this specific integration are WebLogic JMS and Tuxedo /Q. For more information about setting up Tuxedo /Q, refer to `http://edocs.bea.com/tuxedo/tux81/qgd/qadm.htm`. JMS messages can be text messages, byte messages, or XML-based message streams. The messages are transferred to the Tuxedo environment to be executed by a Tuxedo service or targeted to a /Q environment.

34

The `tBridge` section of the `WTCServer` configuration element in the `config.xml` file manages the connectivity of the `tBridge` component into the Tuxedo environment. No additional application programming is involved in establishing the connection and forwarding the requests. The `tBridge` connector does not support the `ObjectMessage`, `MapMessage`, and `StreamMessage` types.

tBridge Configuration

The `tBridge` component establishes a one-way data connection between instances of a JMS queue and a Tuxedo /Q or a JMS queue and a Tuxedo service. A `WTCtBridgeRedirect` MBean represents this connection.

The `WTCtBridgeGlobal` and `WTCtBridgeRedirect` MBeans of a `WTCServer` MBean are configured and deployed to a target server to establish the connectivity between the domains. The connections established are of the following types:

- `JmsQ2TuxQ`
- `TuxQ2JmsQ`
- JmsQ2TuxS

JMSQ2TuxQ This configuration reads messages from a given JMS queue and forwards them to the specified Tuxedo /Q. The following XML code snippet configures the `JMSQ2TuxQ`:

```
<WTCtBridgeRedirect
   Direction="JmsQ2TuxQ"
   Name="jms0"
   ReplyQ="JMSRPLYQ"
   SourceName="wlsunleashed.jms.jms2TuxQueue"
   TargetAccessPoint="TDOM2"
   TargetName="BANKQUEUE"
   TargetQspace="QSPACE"
   TranslateFML="NO"/>
```

The `tBridge` provides simple translation between XML and FML32 to provide connectivity to existing Tuxedo systems. This simple translation is controlled by the `TranslateFML` element. The valid values for this element are `NO` and `FLAT`. The `BytesMessage` from JMS is automatically converted to a `TypedCARRAY`, and `TranslateFML` set to `NO` converts the `TextMessage` to `TypedString`. When `TranslateFML` is set to `FLAT`, the `TextMessage` from JMS is converted to a `TypedFML32` buffer.

TuxQ2JMSQ The following configuration reads messages from a given Tuxedo queue and forwards the messages to the specified JMS queue. The following XML snippet configures `TuxQ2JMSQ`:

```
<WTCtBridgeRedirect
  Direction="TuxQ2JmsQ"
   Name="tux0"
   SourceAccessPoint="TDOM2"
   SourceName="BANKQUEUE"
   SourceQspace="QSPACE"
   TargetName="wlsunleashed.jms.Tux2JmsQueue"
   TranslateFML="NO"/>
```

All message types defined in Table 34.1 are supported in this message-forwarding mechanism except the `VIEW` message type. `TypedString`, `TypedFML`, `TypedFML32`, and `TypedXML` are converted to `TextMessage` when they're to be processed by the receiving JMS queue. The `TranslateFML` attribute controls the data translation when required using the built-in `tBridge` converter. When set to `FLAT`, data is converted from FML to XML by the `tBridge`. The message buffer is converted using the field-by-field values without knowledge of the message hierarchy.

JMSQ2TuxS This configuration reads from a given JMS queue, synchronously calls the specified Tuxedo service, and places the reply back onto a specified JMS queue. The following XML configuration snippet configures `JMSQ2TuxS`:

```
<WTCtBridgeRedirect
   Direction="JmsQ2TuxS"
   Name="tux0"
```

```
ReplyQ="WebLogic.jms.Tux2JmsQueue"
SourceName="wlsunleashed.jms.Jms2TuxQueue"
TargetAccessPoint="TDOM2"
TargetName="AUTH_CC"
TranslateFML="FLAT"/>
```

The supported JMS message types are BytesMessage and TextMessage, which are converted to TypedCARRAY and TypedString or TypedFML32, respectively. The TextMessage from JMS is converted to a String buffer or a FML buffer based on the TranslateFML parameter defined in the configuration. In the preceding case, the message in XML format is converted to a corresponding FML32 buffer and placed in the Tuxedo domain queue to be processed by the AUTH_CC Tuxedo service. The reply is then translated from FML32 to XML and placed in wlsunleashed.jms.Tux2JmsQueue.

WTC Security

Remote Tuxedo domains can be controlled to access the services defined and advertised in the WLS domain using the access control lists (ACLs). There are distinct elements in the WTCServer MBean that controls the inbound requests into WTC and outbound requests into the remote Tuxedo domains. The AclPolicy element controls the inbound policy from a remote Tuxedo domain and the CredentialPolicy element defines the outbound policy. The valid values for AclPolicy and CredentialPolicy are

- LOCAL—When AclPolicy is set to LOCAL, local service access does not depend on the value of the credential policy. When the remote Tuxedo domain's credential policy is set to LOCAL, the result depends on the user credentials of the caller.
- GLOBAL—When AclPolicy is set to GLOBAL, local service access depends on the value of the credential policy. When the remote domain credential policy is set to GLOBAL, then the request has the credentials of the caller.

These parameters can be configured using the WebLogic Console as shown in Figure 34.8.

Similarly, the security parameter in the WTCLocalTuxDom is used to authenticate incoming connections from remote domains and outgoing connections requested by local domains. The valid values for this parameter are

- NONE—Incoming connections from the remote domain are not authenticated.
- Application Password—Incoming connections from remote domains are authenticated using the application password defined in the WTCPassword MBean.
- Domain Password—In this case, connections between the local and remote domains are authenticated using password pairs defined in the WTCPassword MBean.

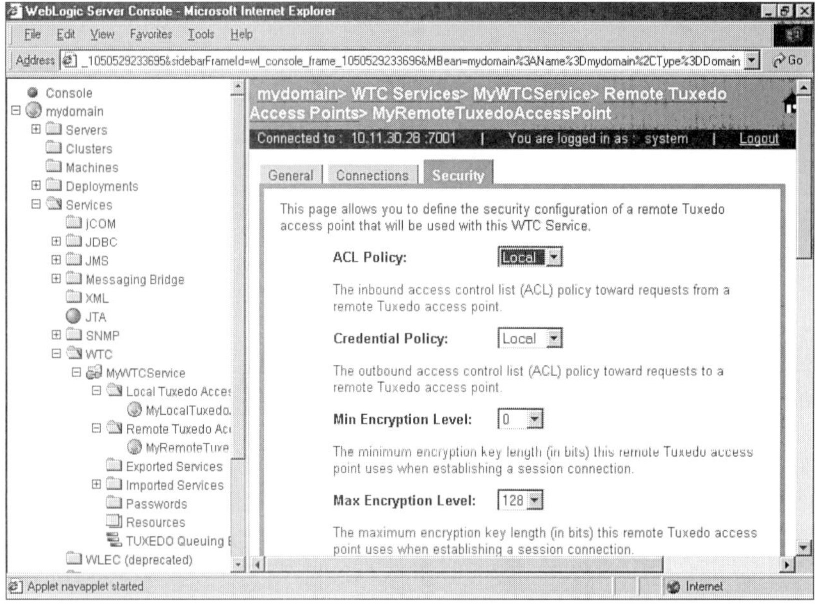

Figure 34.8 Remote Tuxedo domain security configuration.

These parameters also can be configured using the WebLogic Console, as shown in Figure 34.9.

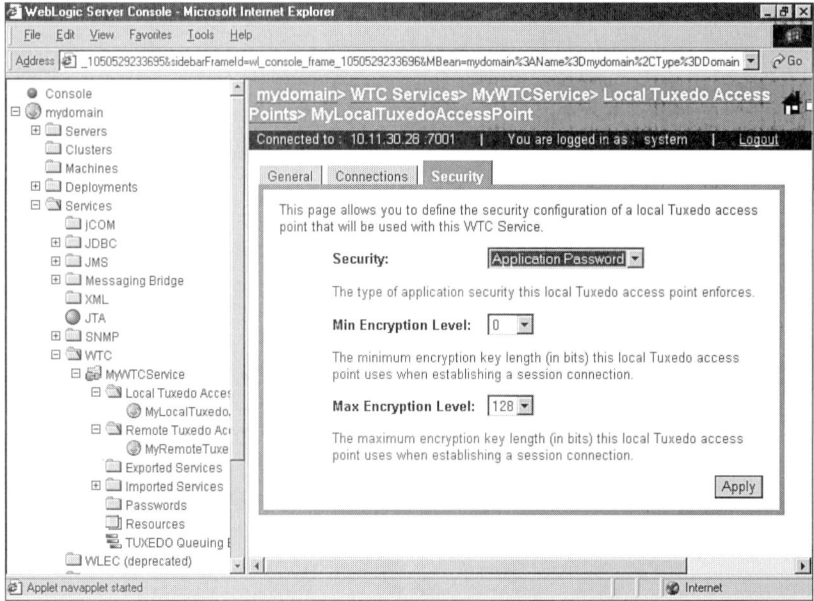

Figure 34.9 Local Tuxedo access point security configuration.

NOTE

The security parameter of the WTC domain and the remote Tuxedo domain should match for a successful connection.

WTC and WebLogic Clusters

There are certain limitations with WTC when working with WebLogic clusters. All the servers in the cluster must have a configured WebLogic Tuxedo Connector. The WTC binding is not automatically propagated across the servers in the cluster. Additionally, all instances should have the same services advertised using the `WTCImport` MBean. The J2EE components using the WTC should also be deployed on all the servers of the cluster. Inbound RMI/IIOP and outbound CORBA are not supported in clusters.

Additionally, WTC allows for an unlimited number of backup domains for a given WTC service. It provides a domain-level failover mechanism that transfers to alternative remote domains when a primary remote domain fails. It also provides failback to the primary remote domain when it's restored.

WTC and Workflow Processes

WTC provides the essential infrastructure for integrating the business flows defined using the WebLogic Process Integrator (WLI) to use the services defined in a remote Tuxedo domain. The integration components are provided by the `tBridge` interface.

WLI uses the JATMI to invoke the remote Tuxedo services. eLink adapter services can be invoked from WLI-defined business components. The buffers used to transfer messages for the business call are based on `FML32`. WLI exception handlers can be defined separately to process exceptions.

Synchronous Integration

The messages from WLI to the remote Tuxedo domain can be sent synchronously or asynchronously. The messages from WLI are pushed to the JMS queue, which uses the `tBridge` interface to invoke the target Tuxedo service. The message is converted to/from XML/FML using the built-in translator. The response is picked up by the business operation from the response queue.

Asynchronous Integration

WLI and Tuxedo /Q provide the infrastructure for asynchronous message integration. Asynchronous integration is bi-directional. There is a 1:1 relationship between JMS queue and /Q. WLI writes the message to the JMS queue, which invokes the target /Q based on the message. The reverse integration is achieved by the requests from the Tuxedo /Q to the corresponding JMS queue. The workflow defined in WLI waits for the message on the JMS queue.

Now, we'll move to the CORBA integration mechanisms available in a WebLogic Server environment. The first half of the discussion covers WebLogic RMI over IIOP, which is the enabling technology for CORBA integration.

RMI over IIOP

Java Remote Method Invocation (RMI) technology run over Internet Inter-ORB Protocol (IIOP) extends Common Object Request Broker Architecture (CORBA) services and distributed computing capabilities to the Java 2 environment.

RMI over IIOP Dissected

RMI is the Java standard for distributed computing. In simpler terms, RMI enables networked applications to obtain a reference to an object that resides elsewhere in the network, and to invoke methods on that object as though it resides on the local virtual machine.

CORBA, which is defined by the OMG (Object Management Group), is a well-known distributed-object programming model that supports a number of languages such as C++ and Smalltalk.

IIOP is a communication protocol that works well over heterogeneous networks via the Internet. Because IIOP is a TCP/IP-based proxy, CORBA is one of the many architectures that use it as a communication protocol. The IIOP protocol connects CORBA products from different vendors, ensuring interoperability among them.

RMI-IIOP is essentially a marriage of RMI and CORBA. By extending RMI to work over IIOP, the possibilities become endless. In a homogeneous, Java-to-Java environment, RMI-IIOP opens the communication to use the standardized IIOP protocol. But the greatest benefit that can be leveraged from the marriage is that it allows for easier application and platform integration between the components written in C, Smalltalk, and Java components. The components interact using the Interface Definition Language (IDL). Using RMI over IIOP, objects can be passed both by reference and by value over IIOP.

WebLogic RMI-IIOP

The WebLogic Server 8.1 RMI-IIOP implementation has the following features:

- IIOP-enabled communication in a homogeneous Java-to-Java environment—RMI clients can use the IIOP protocol to invoke objects running in WebLogic Server. The release of Java 1.3 JDK facilitates this capability.
- CORBA integration—CORBA/IDL clients written in C++ or Smalltalk can be seamlessly integrated into the services in WebLogic. The Object By Value specification from the Object Management Group defines an enabling technology for exporting the Java object model into the CORBA/IDL programming model. This facilitated the

exchange of complex data types between the two models. WebLogic Server can support Object By Value with any CORBA ORB that correctly implements the specification.

- Heterogeneous clients can be connected to WebLogic Server EJBs.
- Object Transaction Services 1.2 (OTS 1.2) support, which enables transactions in RMI-IIOP.
- Hot code generation for `iiop` stubs.
- A WebLogic IIOP client is fully clusterable.
- CSIv2 (Common Secure Interoperability, version 2) provides security features such as client authentication, delegation, and privilege functionality.
- Full support for the COS-Naming API.
- Bi-directional interoperability between WebLogic Server and Tuxedo clients—This integration is described in detail in the earlier section on the WebLogic Tuxedo Connector.

Figure 34.10 indicates how WebLogic Server acts as a client and as a server for other ORB/RMI clients.

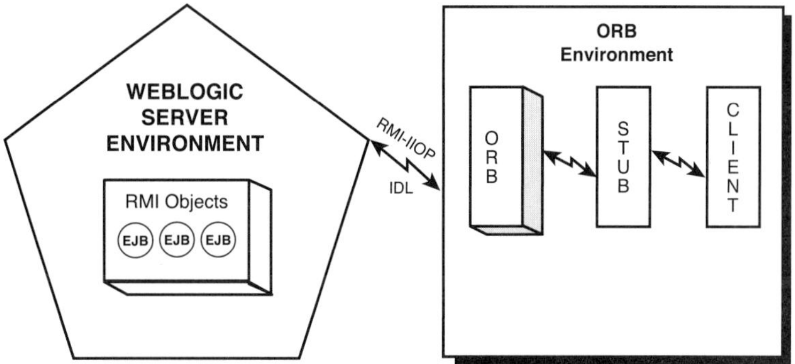

Figure 34.10 WebLogic—CORBA integration.

With WebLogic RMI over IIOP, remote interfaces can be written in the Java programming language and implemented using Java technology and the Java RMI APIs. Those interfaces can be implemented in any other language that's supported by an OMG mapping and a vendor-supplied ORB for that language. Additionally, clients can be written in other languages using the IDL derived from the remote Java technology–based interfaces.

Programming Models: IDL Versus RMI

RMI/IIOP can be used with IDL clients and RMI clients. Both models share the following characteristics:

- Interoperable environment between heterogeneous systems
- Use of ORB and IIOP as the transport protocol for distributed applications

The client program can use only one of the interfaces. That is, it can use either IDL or RMI, but not both.

RMI/IIOP with RMI Java Clients

This programming model combines the power of RMI with the underlying transport mechanism as IIOP. Pure WebLogic RMI clients that use t3 as the communication protocol need to distribute the WebLogic classes to the client layers. IIOP is an industry standard; this aids in easier migration as compared to t3, which is a proprietary standard of BEA.

RMI/IIOP with CORBA/IDL Clients

In this programming model, non-Java clients and Java objects can seamlessly interoperate in the same environment using RMI/IIOP as the transport mechanism. IDL interfaces can be generated from the Java code, which can integrate with the WebLogic Server. The model involves an ORB and a compiler that creates an IDL interface.

RMI/IIOP with a Tuxedo Domain

The WebLogic to Tuxedo Connector described earlier uses RMI/IIOP as the underlying transport mechanism to integrate Tuxedo domain applications with the WebLogic Server. WTC also enables Tuxedo to invoke WebLogic Server EJBs and other applications in response to a service request.

RMI/IIOP with EJB

Enterprise JavaBeans use RMI over IIOP for their distributed object model. EJB interoperability in heterogeneous server environments is achieved when EJBs are implemented using the RMI over IIOP protocol. Coupling EJBs with CORBA with RMI/IIOP provides the following advantages:

- Enterprise beans in one EJB server can access enterprise beans in another EJB server.
- A non-Java platform CORBA client can access any enterprise bean object.
- A Java client using an ORB from one vendor can access EJBs residing on another J2EE-compliant EJB server.

The mapping information needed for the CORBA/IDL clients can be generated from the EJB interfaces using the WebLogic utility `weblogic.ejbc`. The IDL files it generates represent the CORBA definition of the EJB interface.

WTC and CORBA Interoperability

WTC enables objects deployed in WebLogic Server to invoke CORBA objects deployed in a Tuxedo domain. The CORBA Java outbound API defines the following procedures for the interoperability of WebLogic Server objects into Tuxedo CORBA objects:

- Instantiate the WTC ORB in the bean.

  ```
  props.put("org.omg.CORBA.ORBClass","weblogic.wtc.corba.ORB");
  ORB orb = (ORB)c.lookup("java:comp/ORB");
  ```

- Obtain object references. The CosNaming service is used to get a reference to an object in the remote Tuxedo CORBA domain.

  ```
  org.omg.CORBA.Object greetingfactory_oref =
  ➥orb.string_to_object("corbaname:tgiop:helloWorld#Greeting_factory");
  ```

  where

  `helloWorld` is the domain ID of the Tuxedo domain specified in the Tuxedo UBB.

  `Greeting_factory` is the name that the object reference was bound to in the Tuxedo CORBA CosNaming server.

- Invoke the target method.

In Listing 34.6, the code provides an example of invoking a simple WTC ORB using the concepts described earlier.

LISTING 34.6 Simple WTC ORB Invocation

```
throws RemoteException
{
   System.out.println("Welcome " + aName);

   try {
    // Initialize the ORB.
     String [] greets
     Properties Prop;
     Prop = new java.util.Properties();
     Prop.put("org.omg.CORBA.ORBClass","webLogic.wtc.corba.ORB");

     ORB orb = (ORB)c.lookup("java:comp/ORB");
    // Get the Greeting factory.
    org.omg.CORBA.Object greeting_fact_oref =
    orb.string_to_object("corbaname:tgiop:helloWorldp#Greeting_factory");
```

34

LISTING 34.6 Continued

```
    //Narrow the Greeting factory.
    GreetingFactory greeting_factory_ref =
    GreetingFactoryHelper.narrow(greeting_fact_oref);

    // Find the simple object.
    Greeting greet = greeting_factory_ref.find_greeting();

    // find salutation
    String salutation = GreetingFactoryHelper.findSaluation(aName);
    // Format a Greeting
    org.omg.CORBA.StringHolder wish=
     new org.omg.CORBA.StringHolder("Hello "+salutation+" "+ aName);

    return wish.value;
   }
   catch (Exception e) {
    throw new RemoteException("Unable to invoke TUXEDO CORBA server: " +e);
   }
}
```

Additionally, Tuxedo CORBA objects can invoke EJB services deployed in WebLogic Server. The CosNaming service has bound WebLogic Server's name service, which the client can use to locate the required service.

Limitations

There are some inherent limitations to using RMI-IIOP on both the client and server. Some of the limitations are

- Because the RMI server object and the IDL client have different type systems, it could potentially cause name conflicts and classpath problems. The client classes and server-side classes should be separate.
- Incorrect marshalling of unchecked exceptions.
- Value types as defined in the CORBA specification have to be used for passing objects by value. Value type implementations are bound by the platform they're defined on.
- Java types that have their own serialization logic (that is, have `writeObject()` defined in them) are mapped to custom value types in IDL. Custom code has to be written for unmarshalling such objects on the client.

Summary

CORBA and Tuxedo integration enabled by RMI/IIOP and WTC provides WebLogic Server–based applications to participate fully in the world of n-tier enterprise distributed systems. Together with Java, CORBA/Tuxedo technologies provide businesses with a way to extend their heterogeneous enterprise systems, complete with legacy data, to include widespread client access over the Web.

PART IX

Administering WebLogic Applications

IN THIS PART

CHAPTER **35**

Managing Applications with the Administration Console

By Bernard Ciconte

IN THIS CHAPTER

- WebLogic Server Administration
- Connecting to the Administration Console
- Overview of the Administration Console User Interface
- Configuring the Console
- Configuring the Application Server Domain
- Managing Network Resources
- Deploying Applications and Modules
- Configuring WebLogic and J2EE Services
- Administering Security Realms
- Configuring Domain Log Filters
- Monitoring Administrative Tasks

BEA WebLogic Server provides a variety of technologies to host J2EE applications and the supporting subsystems. The WebLogic Administration Console provides the very important feature of organizing the configuration and control of the system resources into a common graphical user interface (GUI). All aspects of the WebLogic Server system administration are made available through a standard Web browser, such as Microsoft Internet Explorer or Netscape Navigator. This includes configuration of the WebLogic Server domain itself and the services provided by WebLogic Server, as well as the configuration and deployment of your J2EE components and applications.

In this chapter, you learn how to use the WebLogic Administration Console effectively. You're provided with a description of every WebLogic Server management function and how to configure and control each function through the Administration Console. When applicable, best practice tips and cautions are clearly identified for a particular topic. References to online help also give you an easy-to-follow, step-by-step guide for configuring a given resource. The sections in this chapter are organized to map directly to the order in which the resources and services are presented in the Administration Console. This correlation provides a quick reference between the information in this chapter and using the WebLogic Administration Console.

WebLogic Server Administration

The WebLogic Administration Console provides an easy-to-use interface to perform system administration of WebLogic Server. The underlying architecture of the Administration Console is the Java Management Extension (JMX) API. System administration uses Java objects called MBeans that provide attributes and operations to control and store the parameters for various management functions. The Administration Console presents an organized hierarchy of MBeans to configure system resources. The root node of the resource tree is the domain. The domain contains subnodes for all aspects of WebLogic Server administration. Each node defines properties to customize the configuration of the particular resource or service. Common administration tasks that are performed using the WebLogic Administration Console are

- Configure, start, and stop WebLogic Servers
- Deploy applications, Web applications, and EJBs
- Configure WebLogic and J2EE services
- Configure security realms
- Monitor system performance

All aspects of WebLogic Server administration can be performed with the Administration Console.

> **NOTE**
>
> The BEA WebLogic Server also provides command-line tools to perform server administration.

The user interface for the Administration Console enables you to navigate to the console pages for system resources. When a resource is selected, the console page for that resource is displayed, enabling you to modify attributes or run operations controlled by that resource. The following sections in this chapter show you how to connect to the Administration Console and manage system resources.

BEA WebLogic provides extensive online documentation for WebLogic Server 8.1. The home page for WebLogic Server 8.1 documentation includes links in the System Administration categories for

- Administration Console Online Help
- Extending the Administration Console

NOTE

Refer to the online documentation from BEA WebLogic at `http://e-docs.bea.com/wls/docs81` for additional information about the WebLogic Administration Console.

Connecting to the Administration Console

The WebLogic Administration Console is a J2EE application that uses JSP. The user interface is therefore accessed through a Web browser, such as Microsoft Internet Explorer or Netscape Navigator. To access the Console, connect to the system that is hosting the WebLogic administration server. The URL is specified using either standard HTTP or secure HTTPS, depending on whether the Secure Sockets Layer (SSL) has been enabled on the WebLogic Server. The hostname portion of the URL can be specified using one of the following specifications:

- Hostname of system running the WebLogic administration server.
- IP address of the system running the WebLogic administration server.
- `localhost` if the Web browser is being run on the same system as the WebLogic administration server.
- 127.0.0.1 is the well-known IP address for `localhost`.

The default port for standard HTTP is 7001. The default port for secure HTTPS is 7002. Following the port number is the console context path. The default context path for the Administration Console is `"console"`. Some sample URL addresses to access the WebLogic Console are

- `http://localhost:7001/console`
- `https://localhost:7002/console`
- `http://wls:7001/console`

Figure 35.1 shows the first screen presented by the WebLogic Console: the login screen. The Username and Password fields are the administrative username and password for the WebLogic Server domain that is being accessed.

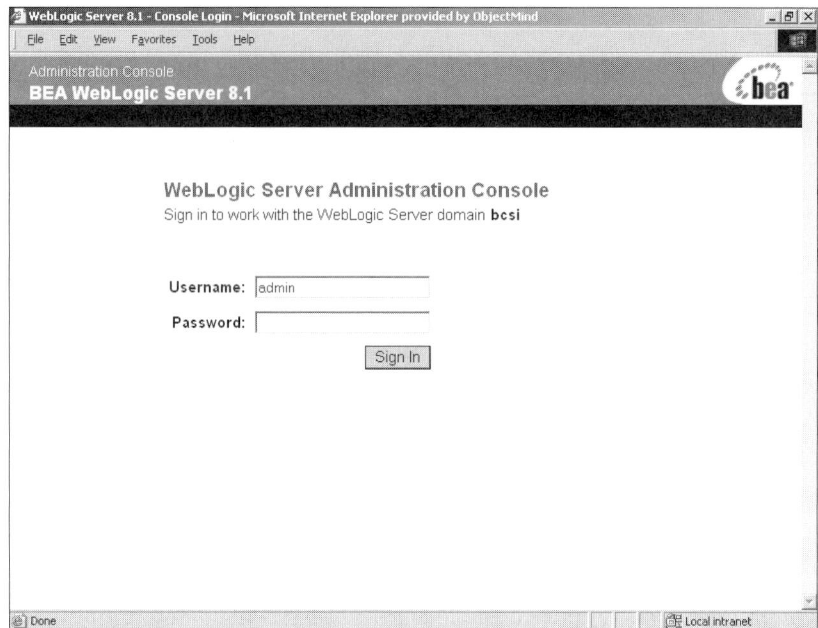

FIGURE 35.1 The first page displayed by the Administration Console is the login screen.

Overview of the Administration Console User Interface

The purpose of this section is to describe the layout of the Administration Console. A detailed description of significant fields on each console page is provided in the remaining sections of this chapter following this overview.

The Administration Console user interface contains two panes. The left pane displays the navigation tree that enables you to navigate through a hierarchical tree of system resources. The right pane displays the console page for the selected resource. Figure 35.2 shows the BEA WebLogic Server home page. The home page is displayed after successfully logging on to the Administration Console.

The navigation tree shown in the left pane contains a hierarchy of elements called *nodes*. Each node has an icon and a name. The icon gives a quick visual representation of the node type. A small plus or minus symbol to the left of the icon indicates that the node contains a list of sub-nodes beneath it. This structure organizes the resources into a hierarchy with the domain being the root of the navigation tree. Selecting a node by left-clicking its name in the navigation tree opens the MBean for that node and displays the console page on the right pane. Selecting the plus symbol or the icon displays the sub-nodes for that entry in the navigation tree. Right-clicking a node in the navigation tree displays a pop-up menu that contains the options to open, open in a new window, and a list of node-specific configuration choices.

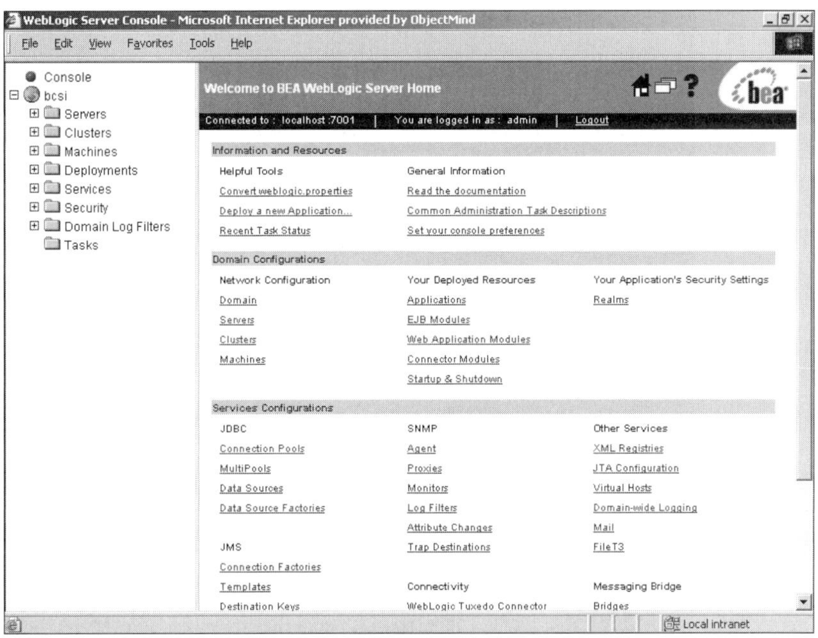

FIGURE 35.2 The home page provides direct links to all aspects of WebLogic Server administration.

The right pane is used to display the console page for the selected node in the navigation tree. The top portion of the console page is a banner. The right side of the banner contains icons to

- Return to the console home page for the active domain
- Open this page in a new window
- Display help for this panel

Below the banner is the hostname and login account information. This line also contains a Logout from the Administration Console link. The remainder of the right pane is the console page for the selected node. Every console page can be displayed with or without help text. The default configuration for the Administration Console is to display help text. This feature is described in more detail in the section "Configuring the Console," later in this chapter. The help text is a valuable feature of the WebLogic Administration Console and provides documentation for each feature and attribute in the context of its use. Figure 35.3 shows the console page for the domain. It is opened by left-clicking on the domain name (bcsi, in this example) in the navigation tree.

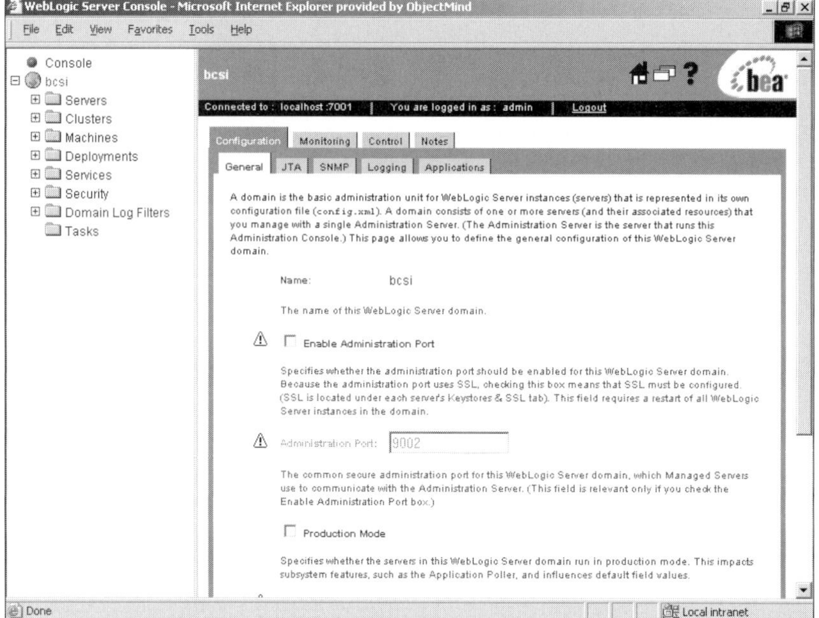

FIGURE 35.3 The domain console page provides access to configure and monitor the resources represented by the domain.

NOTE

This symbol indicates that the resource is not dynamically configurable. A change to this type of resource requires restarting the WebLogic server for the change to take effect.

Every console page has a question mark icon in its banner to display help text for that panel. Figure 35.4 shows the Administration Console help screen for the domain. The console help screen provides valuable information about the current console page.

- An overview of the selected console page
- Corresponding tasks documented in online e-docs
- Related topics documented in online e-docs
- A table fully describing all the attributes on the console page

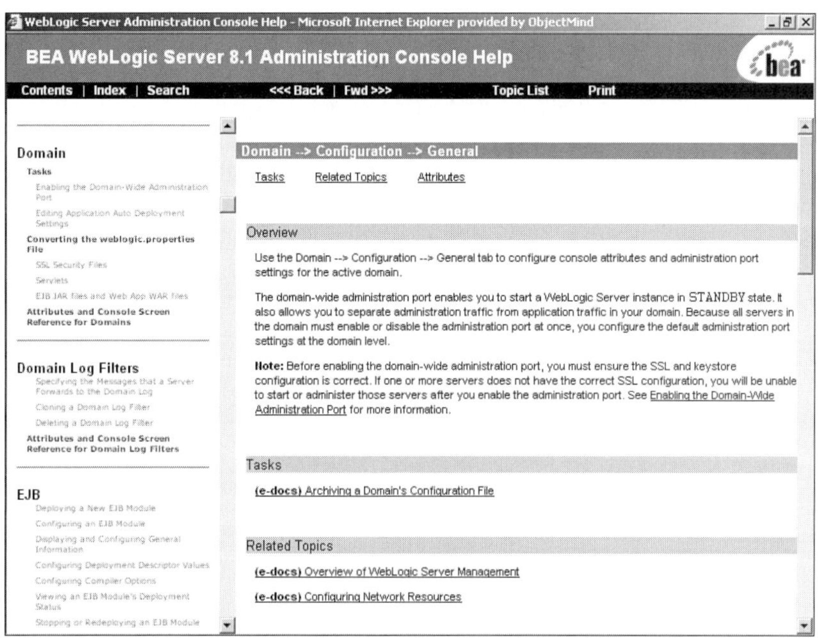

FIGURE 35.4 The Administration Console's help screen provides a complete description of the current console page.

As noted in the opening paragraph, the remainder of this chapter follows the same order as the navigation tree on the Administration Console. Each section provides an overview of the console page with a description of the attributes and operations controlled by that console page. Each console page is specific to the node selected in the navigation tree. There is a common format for console pages. When a console page is used to provide settings for a list of attributes, the attributes are organized on tabbed panels. The tab label indicates the settings that are configured by that tab panel.

Configuring the Console

The first entry in the navigation tree is Console. Clicking on the Console node opens the console configuration page. Figure 35.5 shows the page to configure the WebLogic Administration Console. This is the same page that's displayed when you click the Set Your Console Preferences link on the WebLogic administration server home page. The page contains two tabs: the Preferences tab and the Versions tab. The Console Preferences page allows customization of the attributes that control the display of the Administration Console.

35

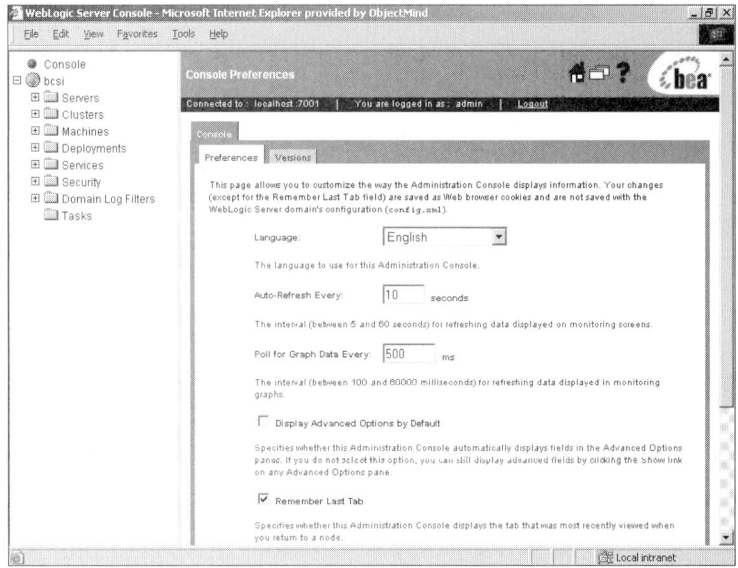

FIGURE 35.5 The Console Preferences page enables you to customize how the Administration Console displays information.

When the Display Help Text attribute is disabled, help text is not displayed on any configuration page. Figure 35.6 shows the Console Preferences page with the help text disabled.

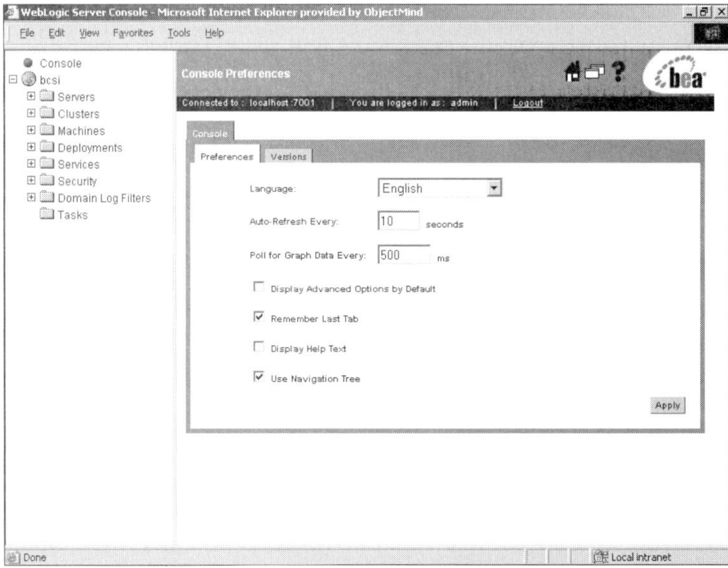

FIGURE 35.6 Administration Console pages are displayed without help text if Display Help Text is disabled.

The Console Preferences page for the Versions tab is shown in Figure 35.7. This page enables you to view the WebLogic Server version information.

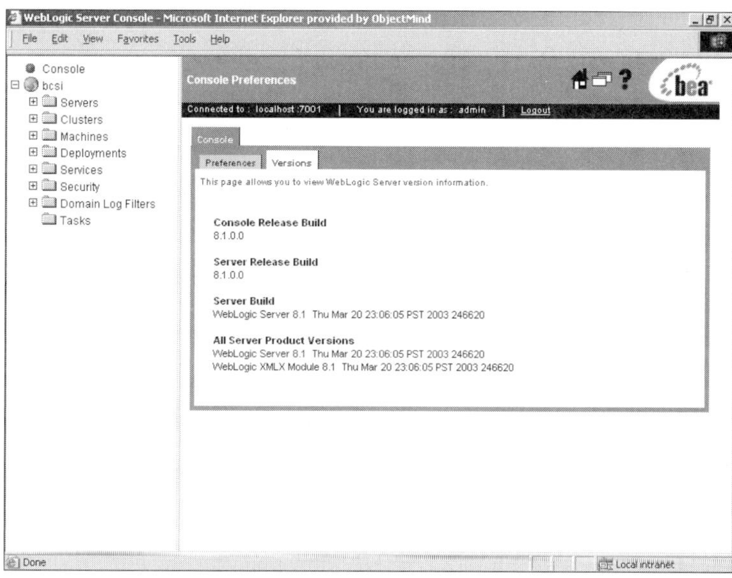

FIGURE 35.7 The WebLogic Server version information is displayed on the Console Preferences page under the Versions tab.

Configuring the Application Server Domain

WebLogic Server defines the domain as the basic administration unit. A domain contains one or more servers that are managed from a single administration server that hosts the Administration Console. The domain defines configurable attributes that are viewed and modified with the Administration Console and stored in the file `*BEA_WebLogic_Root*\user_projects\*domain_name*\config.xml`. The configuration properties for the domain are organized on five tabs:

- General
- JTA
- SNMP
- Logging
- Applications

Whether you have one system running a single instance of WebLogic Server or a cluster of machines running many servers, it is controlled by a common domain. The scale of your system affects the choices made for domain configuration. The default values work well for the majority of installations, but following the tuning tips from the online documentation to match your application needs will greatly enhance performance.

TIP

Refer to the BEA WebLogic online documentation, `http://e-docs.bea.com/wls/docs81/perform/`, for tips on tuning your WebLogic Server domain.

In addition to the configuration properties, the console page for the domain enables you to monitor the servers and control the run state of the servers in the domain. Figure 35.8 shows the display when monitoring servers is selected. The Customize This View link enables you to control which columns are displayed in the table for each server.

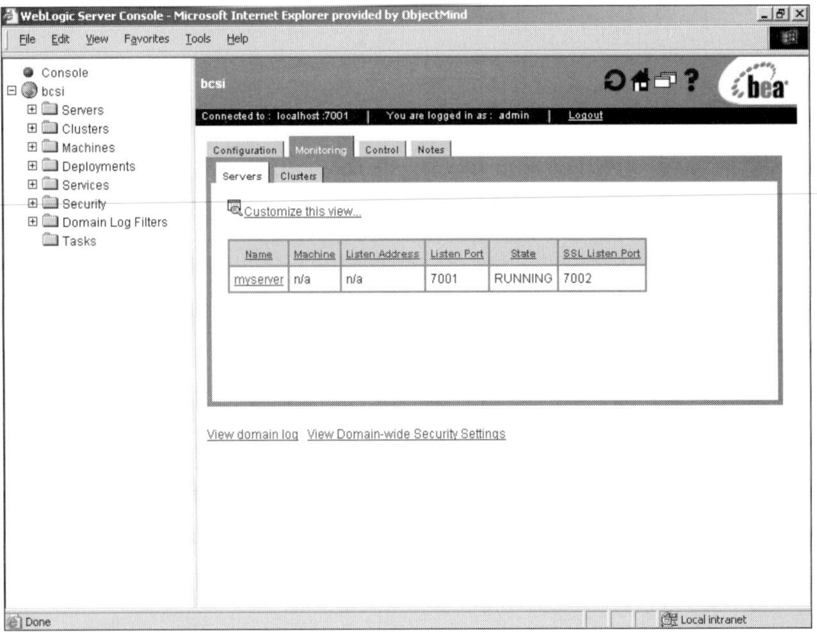

FIGURE 35.8 The Administration Console enables you to monitor the run state for all the servers defined in the domain.

The Control tab on the domain console page enables you to set the state for all servers in the domain or to control servers individually. Figure 35.9 shows the WebLogic Server domain console page for the Control tab.

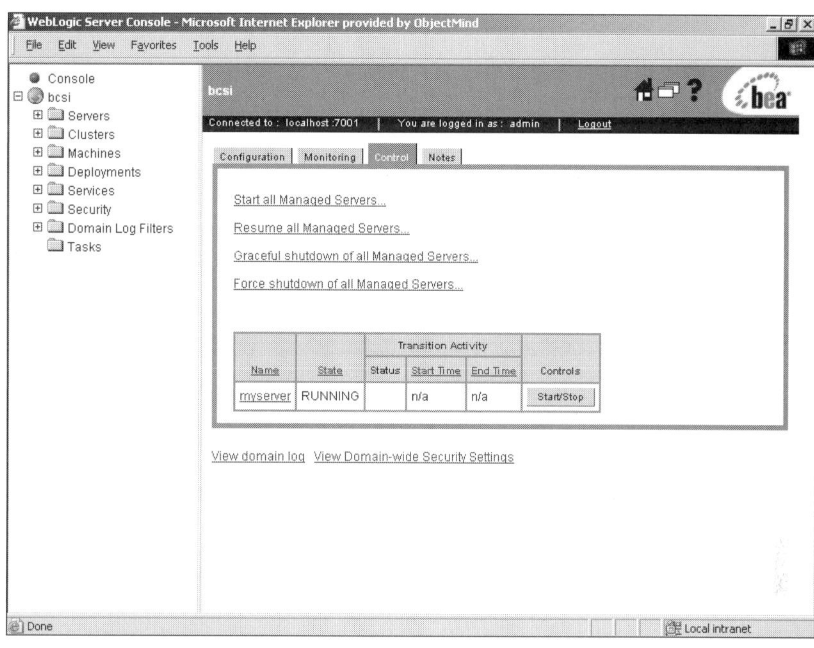

FIGURE 35.9 The run state for the servers in the domain are controlled as a group or individually from the Administration Console.

The following sections provide a description of the five tabs under Domain Configuration.

General Configuration for the Domain

Clicking on the domain name opens the console page for the domain. Figure 35.10 shows the console page for the general configuration attributes of the domain. This is the same console page that was shown previously in Figure 35.3. Now it is being shown with the advanced options and without help text. Displaying help text is a console option that was introduced earlier in this chapter.

The BEA WebLogic Server home page contains a link for Common Administration Task Descriptions. One of the common system administration tasks performed with the Administration Console is to enable the domainwide administration port. By default, the administration port is disabled for the domain. The administration port enables you to start servers in the STANDBY state, and to separate administration traffic from application traffic. Being a domainwide configuration option, it is used by all servers in the domain. The administration port uses SSL; therefore, SSL must be configured before enabling the administration port. The configuration page for each server contains a Keystores and SSL tab for configuring SSL on that server. Refer to the "Configuring a Server" section later in this chapter for more information about configuring the Secure Socket Layer on WebLogic Server.

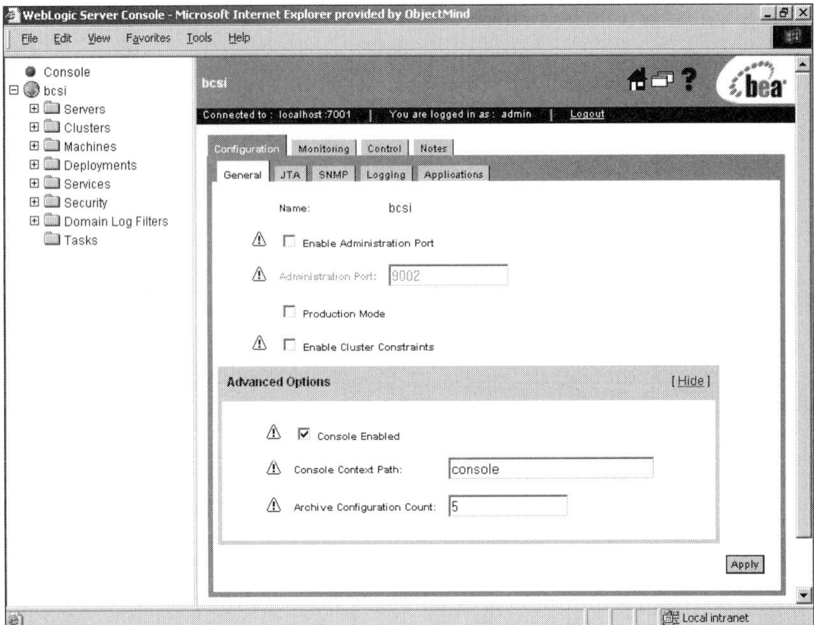

FIGURE 35.10 WebLogic Server provides general configuration attributes over the domain.

JTA Configuration for the Domain

The Java Transaction API (JTA) provides Java applications and J2EE Entity Beans with transaction management over database updates. Doing so guarantees that transactional database changes are completed as a group or not at all to achieve the ACID (atomicity, consistency, isolation, and durability) properties of a high-performance transaction. The WebLogic Server domain configuration for JTA enables you to set specifications for error detection during the transaction. The criteria for JTA error detection include timeouts and maximum limits for iteration cycles and number of simultaneous transactions. The domainwide JTA configuration is used by the transaction managers on each server in the domain. In addition, each server individually defines monitoring and logging configuration parameters for JTA. Refer to the "Configuring a Server" section later in this chapter for more information about the logging and monitoring attributes for a server.

SNMP Configuration for the Domain

Simple Network Management Protocol (SNMP) is the dominant standard for network management. SNMP provides a framework to define information and a protocol to exchange that information between SNMP agents on the network. A WebLogic administration server has the capability to respond to requests from SNMP managers and to send SNMP trap notifications to SNMP managers using the WebLogic SNMP service. The

WebLogic domain configuration for SNMP defines whether the SNMP service is enabled on the administration server. If the SNMP service is enabled, the remainder of the SNMP configuration attributes specify the configuration of the SNMP service.

Logging Configuration for the Domain

The WebLogic logging service collects messages from the multiple WebLogic Server instances running in the domain into a single domainwide message log. Each WebLogic Server instance defines a configuration for its domain log filter. See the "Configuring Domain Log Filters" section later in this chapter for more information. The domainwide message provides the system administrator with a single reference point to monitor all messages forwarded from the WebLogic Server instances in the domain. This is a very convenient feature of the WebLogic Server domain. The configuration for domainwide logging specifies the domain filename and criteria for controlling the amount of disk space used by the log files.

Applications Configuration for the Domain

The Application Manager is responsible for deploying and managing applications in the WebLogic Server domain. The Auto Update Interval attribute on this console page is used by the Application Manager for performing auto-deployments.

NOTE

Refer to the BEA WebLogic Server online documentation at

`http://e-docs.bea.com/wls/docs81/deployment/concepts.html`

for more information about auto-deployment.

Managing Network Resources

The network configuration for a WebLogic Server domain is specified by

- Servers
- Clusters
- Machines

These are the first three subnodes below the domain in the navigation tree. The following sections provide information for specifying the network configuration for the WebLogic Server.

Configuring a Server

A configured instance of WebLogic Server is the definition of a server. Each server runs in its own Java Virtual Machine (JVM), using its own configuration. The WebLogic Server domain must have one server that acts as the administration server. The Administration Console is hosted on the administration server. A typical production environment also has one or more managed servers, which are instances of WebLogic Servers used to host enterprise applications.

Creating, configuring, and monitoring servers is one of the most important and common tasks performed with the Administration Console. The server is the engine that executes your Web applications and services and, therefore, proper configuration is key to providing a high-performance, reliable platform. Adding and Removing Servers in an Existing Domain is one of the links on the Common System Administration Tasks help page. This page can be accessed directly from the Administration Console home page. A complete step-by-step guide is provided for all aspects of creating, configuring, and removing managed servers.

As shown in Figure 35.11, the Servers console page displays a table of key information about each server that has been configured in the current WebLogic Server domain. The page also contains links to Configure a New Server and Customize This View.

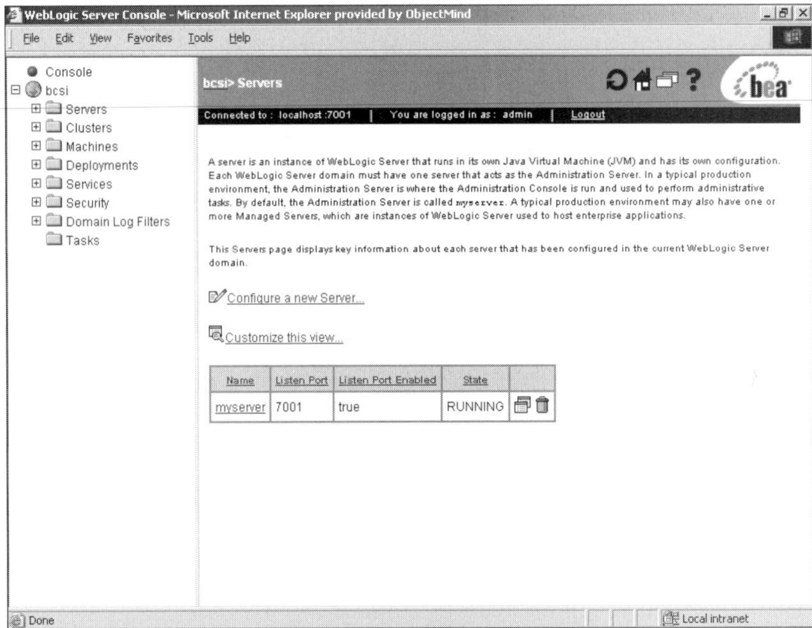

FIGURE 35.11 The Servers page displays key information about each server that has been configured in the current WebLogic Server domain.

Clicking on the Configure a New Server link opens the console page to create a WebLogic Server instance. The configuration for a WebLogic Server is organized under seven tabs:

- General
- Cluster
- Keystores & SSL
- Deployment
- Tuning
- Health Monitoring
- Remote Start

The choices for configuring a new server very much depend on how the server will be used. For example, WebLogic provides a Java application called Node Manager that enables you to control the managed servers in a cluster. Certain configuration attributes of the server must be specified to make the managed server accessible to Node Manager. The parameters that are required for Node Manager are defined later in this section.

> **NOTE**
>
> Refer to the BEA WebLogic Server online documentation at
>
> `http://e-docs.bea.com/wls/docs81/adminguide/nodemgr.html`
>
> for an overview of Node Manager.

In addition, the servers in a cluster communicate with each other through the multicast of cluster events. If you want the new server to listen for cluster multicast events, you must configure the cluster before configuring the server. See Chapter 36, "Installing, Configuring, and Deploying WebLogic Server Clusters," for further information about clusters.

The General tab under Configuration contains the form to create a new WebLogic Server. After creating a new server, the other tabs on the console page for the server become enabled. The new server will run on a host computer, and optionally be a member of a cluster. The server configuration attributes Machine and Cluster provide this information. The choices for the Machine attribute are (none) or a list of configured machines. The server needs to be assigned to a machine if you want to use Node Manager to start the server; otherwise, the default value (none) can be used. If you're using Node Manager, you must configure the Machine attribute before configuring the server.

By default, a server is accessed through the IP address or hostname of the computer that is hosting the server. As always, if the request is from the same computer as the server, `localhost` can be used as the hostname. The configuration for the Listen Address enables you to restrict the valid listen addresses for the server. By specifying `localhost` explicitly as the Listen Address, only processes residing on the same machine as the server can to connect to the server. For this configuration, the client must explicitly specify `localhost` as the hostname to connect to the server. If you specify an IP address or DNS name, attempts to connect using `localhost` will fail.

NOTE

The Listen Address value is ignored if a network channel is configured for this WebLogic Server. See the "Configuring Server Protocols" section later in this chapter for further information about network channels.

After the new server has been created, its entry appears in the table of configured WebLogic Servers, as shown in Figure 35.11 earlier in this chapter. Clicking on the server name in the table opens the configuration for that server. The general configuration tab will now contain a link to show the advanced options for that server in addition to the general configuration options shown previously. The advanced options enable you to specify options for the Java compiler, RMI compiler, and EJB compiler when one of these compilers is used by this server. The additional advanced options include the startup mode for the server, which can be specified as either RUNNING or STANDBY. The significance of the Startup Mode setting is specified in the console help text.

The Cluster tab is enabled for each configured WebLogic Server. The configuration of the cluster enables you to define how this server will behave when it is part of a cluster. After creating the cluster, you must configure servers to be a member of the cluster.

The Keystores & SSL tab contains the console page for specifying the keystores and SSL configurations. A *keystore* is a mechanism designed to create and manage files that store private keys and trusted certificate authorities (CAs) for use with SSL. The console page allows you to view and change the various keystore configuration and Secure Sockets Layer (SSL) settings for this server. These settings help you to manage the security of message transmissions. Figure 35.12 shows the Keystore Configuration portion of the Keystores & SSL console page. Figure 35.13 shows the SSL Configuration portion of the same page. With the exception of the keystore passphrase, the format of this console page requires you to click on the Change link before it allows you to set any other values for the configuration.

The Deployment configuration page for a WebLogic Server enables you to define the default staging mode for this server. This allows you to control whether application files are uploaded to the administration server or copied to a managed server during deployment. The directory path for staging or uploading is also specified in this configuration.

The Tuning configuration page enables you to provide settings to tune the performance of this server. There are many e-docs to help you specify the tuning configuration that bests suits your system requirements.

TIP

Check the Administration Console help on the Tuning console page for a direct link to the e-docs "BEA WebLogic Server Performance and Tuning Guide."

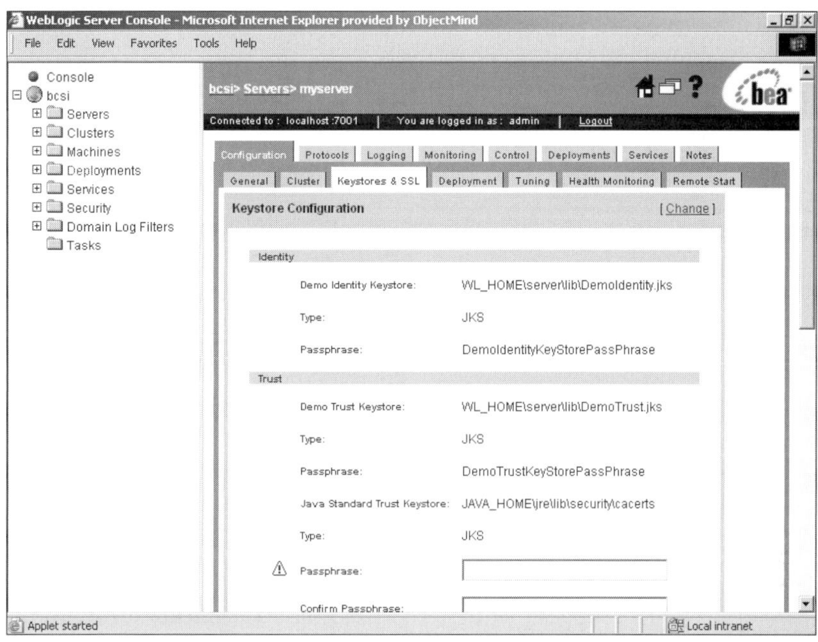

FIGURE 35.12 The keystore is used for storage of private keys and trusted certificate authorities.

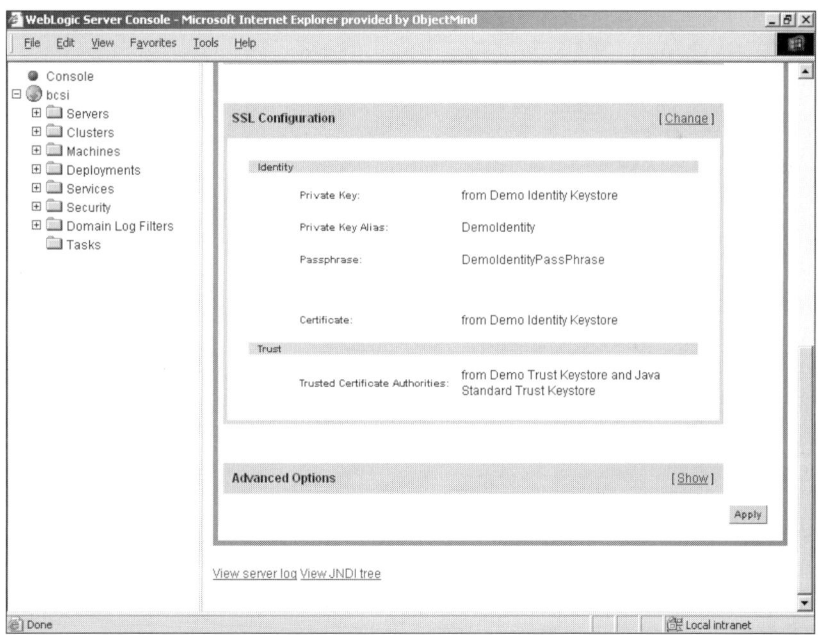

FIGURE 35.13 The SSL configuration page enables you to view and specify settings for the Secure Sockets Layer used by this server.

The advanced options for Tuning are divided into Memory Options and Managed Server Independence. The Memory Options enable you to control this server's automatic detection and correction of low memory conditions. The Managed Server Independence settings enable you to control the availability of the managed server in the absence of the administration server.

> **NOTE**
>
> On the Tuning advanced options page, the Low Memory Time Interval setting is not used if the JRockit VM is used because the memory samples are collected immediately after a VM-scheduled garbage collection.

The health monitoring capability for a server is used to improve the reliability and availability of the servers in a WebLogic Server domain. The configuration for health monitoring primarily enables you to give permission to the Node Manager to restart or shut down servers that fail their self-health monitoring criteria.

Finally, the Remote Start tab enables you to specify the settings that the Node Manager uses to start this server on a remote machine. The Node Manager is a standalone Java program provided by WebLogic Server that you can use to start, restart, monitor, and shut down managed servers.

> **NOTE**
>
> The directories specified in the Remote Start configuration page are paths on the machine running Node Manager.

Configuring Server Protocols

The Protocols tab on a server's console page enables you to define connection settings for various communication protocols. As shown in Figure 35.14, the five tabs for configuring protocols are

- General
- HTTP
- jCOM
- IIOP
- Channels

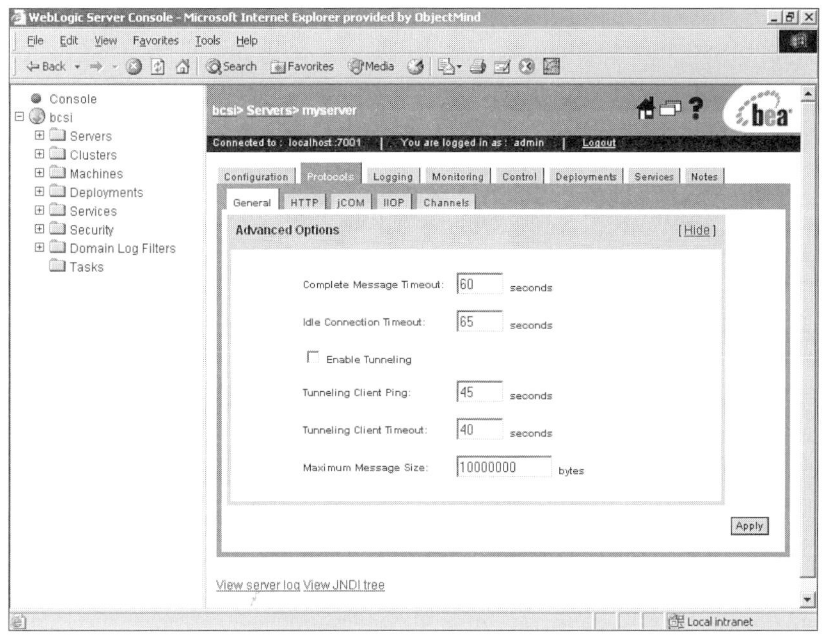

FIGURE 35.14 The various protocols used by the server share general connection settings.

Notice that all general protocol settings are listed as Advanced Options. The general configuration for server protocols specifies default values that can be overridden by the network channel. The timeout settings enable you to specify criteria for error detection for connections and messages on the network channel. The maximum message size helps prevent denial-of-service attacks by specifying the maximum amount of memory that the server can allocate for the message. The protocol configuration also enables you to enable tunneling. If you use the T3, T3S, HTTP, HTTPS, IIOP, or IIOPS protocols, you must enable tunneling.

Web-based clients communicate with the WebLogic Server using HTTP (Hypertext Transfer Protocol). The HTTP settings control the communication between Web-based clients and WebLogic Server. The HTTP protocol settings for a WebLogic Server improve performance of the Web-based clients and help prevent denial-of-service attacks when set properly. The Default Server Name should be set to the hostname of your default HTTP Web server. The Post Timeout setting prevents the server from being overloaded with POST data that might have been caused as a denial-of-service attack. The Max Post Size enables you to limit the amount of HTTP Post data in a servlet request. The default Max Post Size is `-1`, which indicates an unlimited number of bytes. It is recommended to set the Enable Keepalives option to possibly improve performance of your Web applications. When keepalives are enabled, the Duration field specifies the number of seconds to maintain the HTTP Keepalive before timing out the request. Similarly, HTTPS Duration specifies the number of seconds for the secure HTTPS Keepalive timer.

TIP

Set the HTTP Default Name Server when you're using firewalls or load balancers and you want the request from the browser to reference the same host that was sent in the original request.

The HTTP protocol also includes advanced options. The help text for many of these options includes a tip in parentheses of when that option might be necessary for your Web applications.

CAUTION

The Accept Context Path in Get Real Path attribute is a compatibility switch that will be deprecated in future releases of WebLogic Server.

The jCOM protocol enables you to use COM (Component Object Model) objects from Java applications. COM is the underlying software architecture that performs client/server-based interprocess communication for Microsoft Windows applications. One of the most common implementations based on COM is ActiveX, which provides a Microsoft-language-neutral interface that allows Visual C++ and Visual Basic applications to invoke methods on a Dynamic Loaded Library (DLL) in an ActiveX server. All jCOM settings are contingent on jCOM being enabled. The Administration Console help for jCOM provides a direct link to the e-docs for "Programming WebLogic jCOM." The console help also includes a step-by-step guide for "Enabling and Configuring jCOM."

The IIOP protocol enables you to use CORBA (Common Object Request Broker Architecture) objects from Java applications. All IIOP settings are contingent on IIOP being enabled and are listed as Advanced Options. The Administration Console help for IIOP provides a direct link to the e-docs for "Programming WebLogic RMI over IIOP." The console help also includes a step-by-step guide for "Enabling and Configuring the IIOP Protocol."

As noted previously, you configure a network channel to be used in place of the listen address for a server. A network channel enables you to listen for requests on multiple ports, as well as separate network traffic by physical NIC cards. The Administration Console help for network channels provides direct links to the e-docs for "Understanding Network Channels" and "Configuring Network Channels." The Administration Console help also includes a Tasks link to the step-by-step guide for "Configuring a Custom Network Channel for a Non-Clustered Server."

Configuring Server Logging

The Logging tab on a server's console page enables you to define logging settings for various WebLogic Server resources and communication protocols. As shown in Figure 35.15, the five tabs for configuring logging are

- Server
- Domain
- HTTP
- JDBC
- JTA

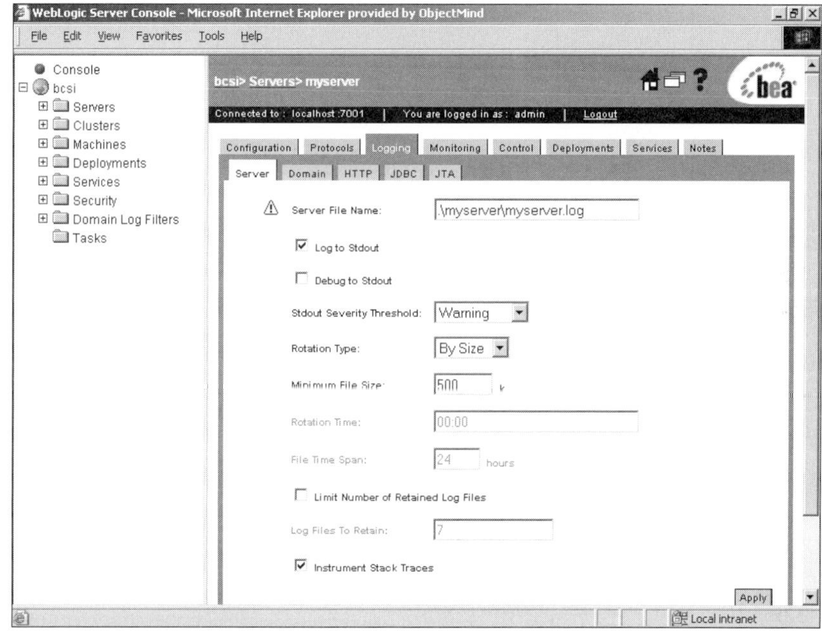

FIGURE 35.15 The Server tab provides individual logging configuration for various server resources and communication protocols.

The Server tab enables you to define the general logging settings for this server. The Domain tab enables you to specify whether this server logs to the WebLogic Server domain log file. To configure a domain log filter, refer to the "Configuring Domain Log Filters" section later in this chapter. The HTTP and JDBC tabs enable you to enable and disable logging for the particular protocol. HTTP logging is enabled by default, and JDBC logging is disabled by default. The JTA tab enables you to specify the path prefix for the JTA transaction log files.

Monitoring Servers

The Monitoring tab for a server enables you to monitor general information about the server. The five tabs provided on the Monitoring page are

- General
- Performance
- Security
- JMS
- JTA

The General tab enables you to monitor general information about the selected server. Figure 35.16 shows the general monitoring console page with the Advanced Options. This page contains three links to enable you to

- Monitor All Active Queues
- Monitor All Connections
- Monitor All Active Sockets

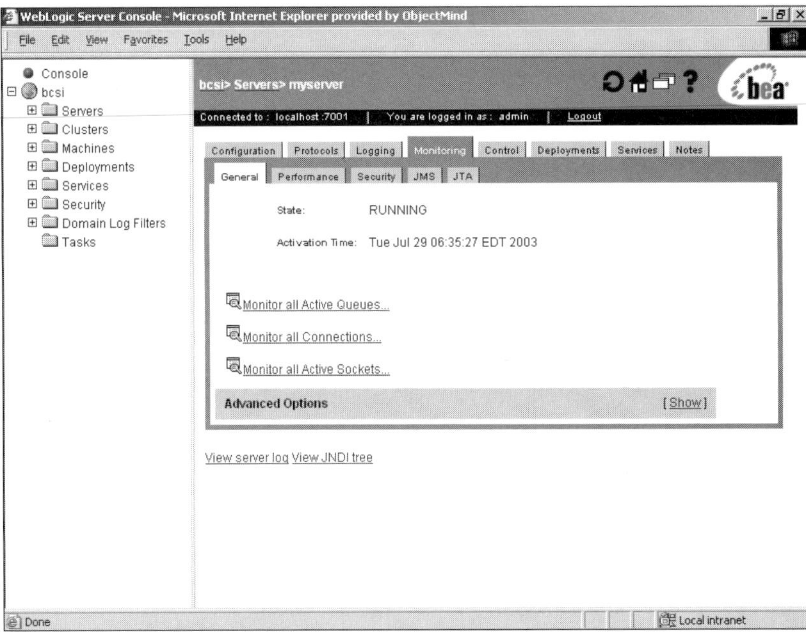

FIGURE 35.16 The General Monitoring console page for a server enables you to view and monitor general information about the selected server.

The Performance tab enables you to monitor performance information about the selected server. As shown in Figure 35.17, the Performance Monitoring page shows three graphs that are dynamically updated to show throughput, queue length, and memory usage for the selected server. This page also provides a button to enable you to force garbage collection on the server that is being monitored. There is also a link to modify graphing preferences. This is simply a direct link to the Console Preferences page shown in Figure 35.5 earlier in this chapter.

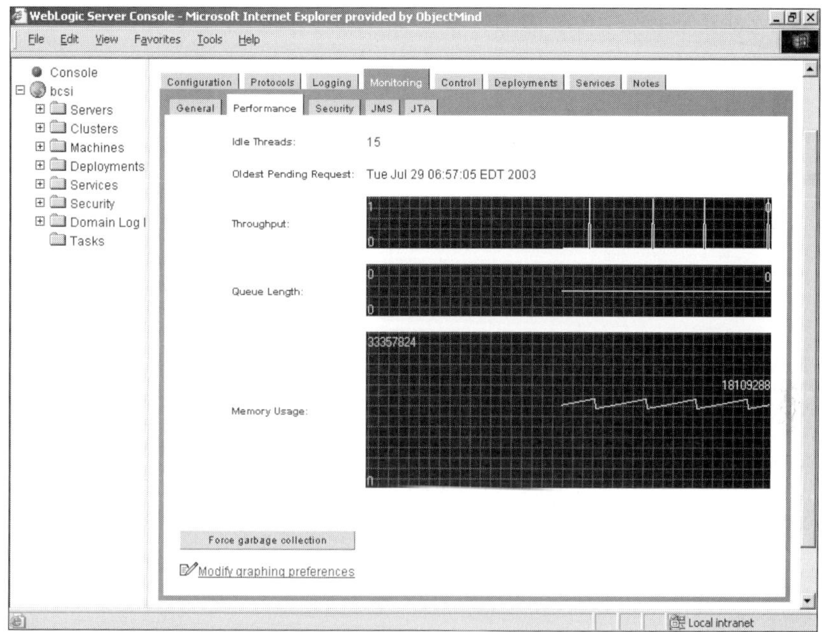

FIGURE 35.17 The Performance Monitoring console page for a server enables you to monitor the performance information about the selected server.

The Security tab enables you to monitor security information about the selected server, as well as unlock a user on that server. Figure 35.18 shows the console page for monitoring security information on a server.

The JMS tab enables you to monitor JMS information about the selected server. Figure 35.19 shows the JMS Monitoring console page. This page contains three links to enable you to

- Monitor All Active JMS Connections
- Monitor All Active JMS Servers
- Monitor All Pooled JMS Connections

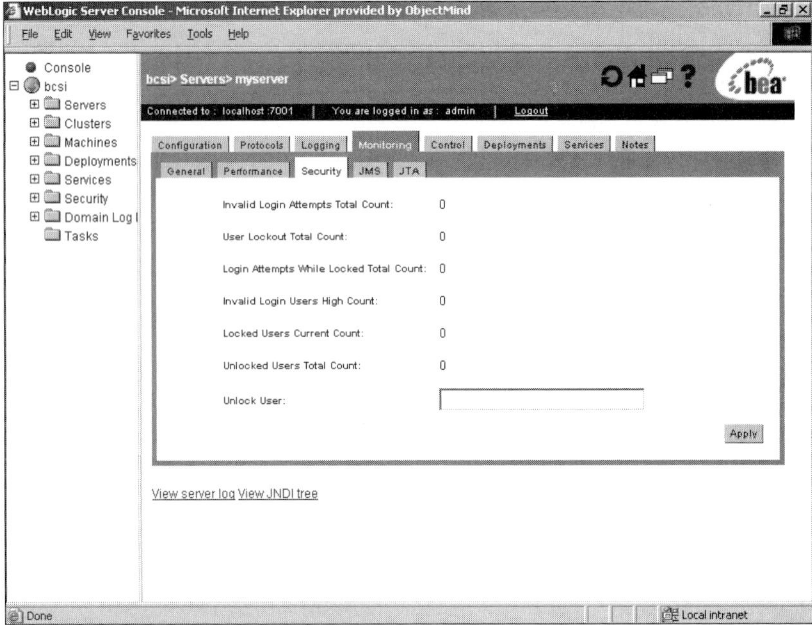

FIGURE 35.18 The Security Monitoring console page for a server enables you to monitor the security information about the selected server as well as unlock a user.

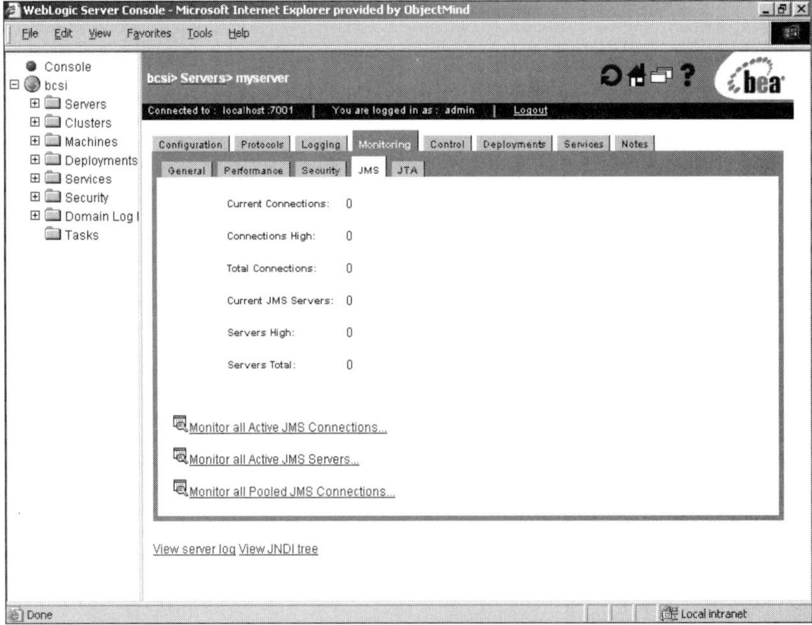

FIGURE 35.19 The JMS Monitoring console page for a server enables you to monitor JMS information about the selected server.

The JTA tab enables you to monitor statistics about transactions coordinated by the selected server. Figure 35.20 shows the JTA Monitoring console page.

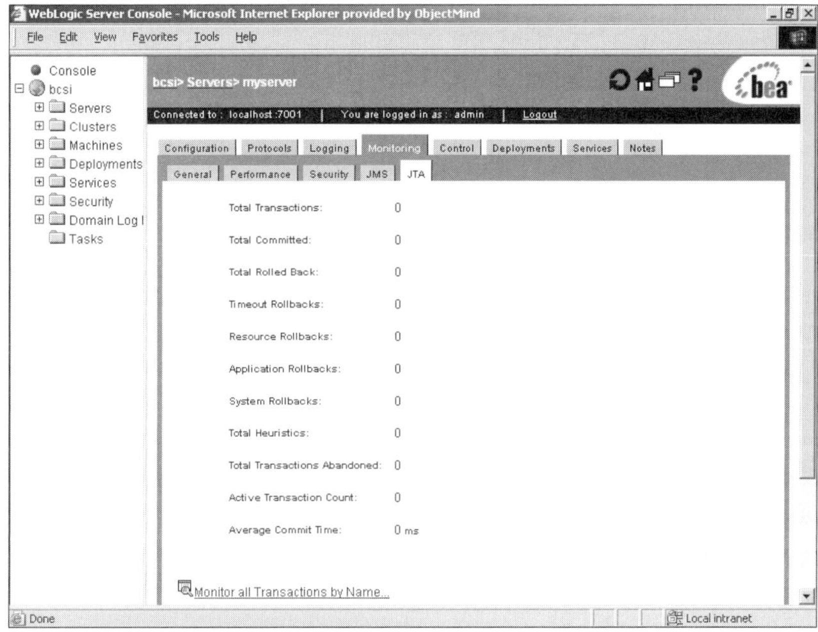

FIGURE 35.20 The JTA Monitoring console page for a server enables you to view statistics about transactions coordinated by the selected server.

Controlling Servers

The Control tab for a server enables you to change the state of the current server. You can also view the current status of the server. The six tabs provided under the Control tab are

- Start/Stop
- Remote Start Output
- JMS Migration Config.
- JMS Migrate
- JTA Migration Config.
- JTA Migrate

The Start/Stop tab enables you to change the state of the selected server. Figure 35.21 shows the Start/Stop Control console page.

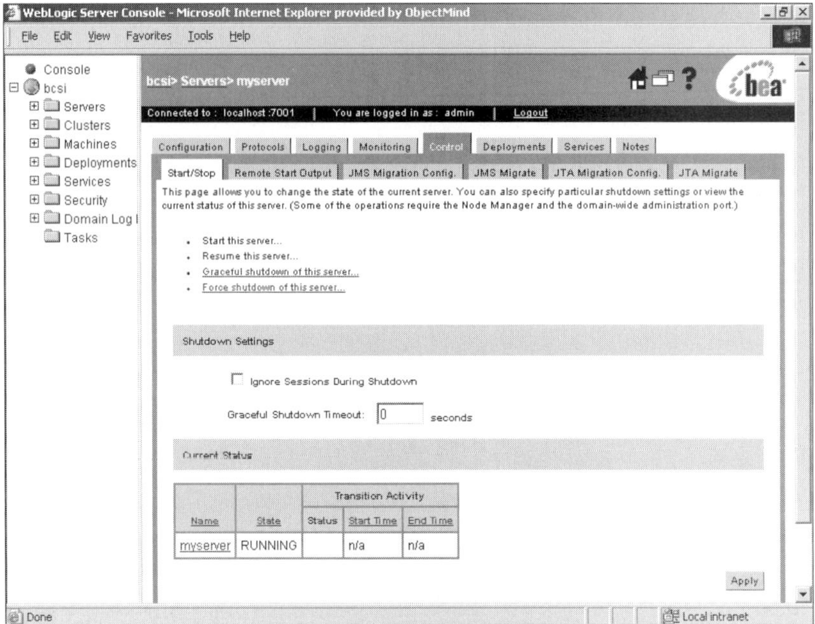

FIGURE 35.21 The Start/Stop Control console page enables you to change the state of the server, specify shutdown settings, and view the current status.

The Remote Start Output tab enables you to view the standard out and standard error output from the selected server and the output from the Node Manager. Figure 35.22 shows the Remote Start Output console page.

In addition, the Control tab for a server also includes four tabs to enable you to configure and perform a migration for a JMS server or JTA Transaction Recovery Service from a failed server to another server in the cluster. The server must be a member of a cluster in order to migrate the JMS or JTA service to another server in the same cluster. The capability to administer failover through migration is key to the high availability and reliability of the WebLogic Server cluster. The Administration Console help for both JMS Migration Config and JTA Migration Config provide direct links to the common related topics on e-docs:

- Migrating a Pinned Service to a Target Server Instance
- Migrating When the Currently Active Host Is Unavailable

By default, you can migrate the JMS server or JTA server to any other server in the cluster. The JMS Migration Config and JTA Migration Config enable you to specify a list of chosen target servers to limit the servers that can be the target for the migration.

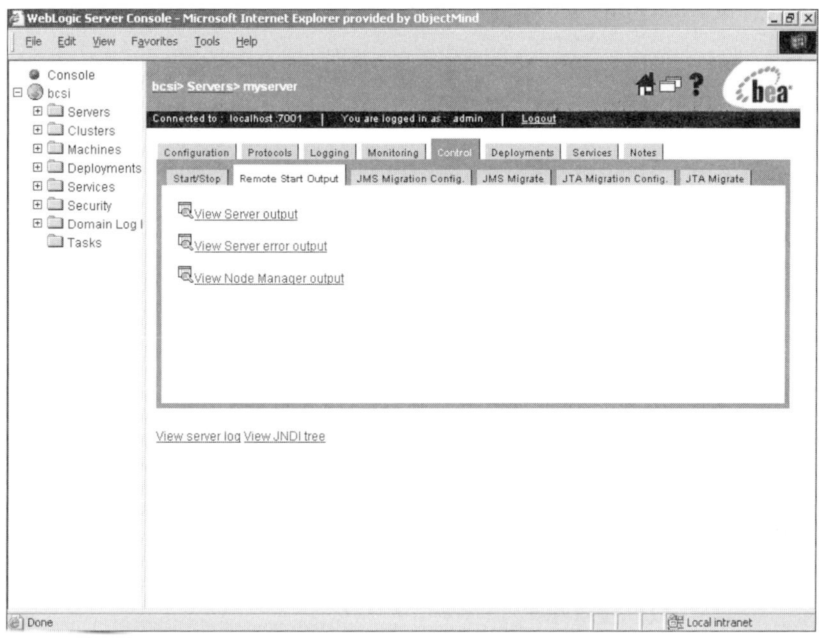

FIGURE 35.22 The Remote Start Output console page enables you to view the standard out and standard error output from the selected server, as well as Node Manager output.

CAUTION

If you configure a list of chosen target servers, you must add the current server to the chosen server list or you will not be able to migrate back.

The JMS Migrate tab and JTA Migrate tab enable you to specify the attributes for the respective migration. The Cluster attribute is the name of the cluster that the server is a member of. The Current Server attribute is the name of the server that currently owns the respective service. Finally, the Destination Server attribute is the server that the respective service will be migrated to. The Destination Server is selected from a list of chosen target servers.

Viewing Deployments on a WebLogic Server

The Deployments tab on the server console page enables you to view key information about the deployments that have been made on the selected server. The tabs under Deployments are organized in the same manner as the subnodes in the navigation tree.

- Applications
- EJB Modules

- Web Modules
- Connector
- Startup/Shutdown

The console page for these tabs displays key information about the deployment. See the section "Deploying Applications and Modules" later in this chapter for information on how to configure an application or module for deployment.

Viewing Services on a WebLogic Server

The Services tab on the server console page enables you to view key information about the J2EE and WebLogic objects that have been deployed as services on the selected server. The tabs under Services are organized as follows:

- JDBC
- JMS
- Web Services
- Bridge
- XML
- WTC
- Jolt
- Virtual Hosts
- Mail
- File T3

The console page for each tab displays key information about the service. See the section "Configuring WebLogic and J2EE Services" later in this chapter for information about how to configure a service for deployment.

Configuring Clusters

One server in a cluster must be designated as the administration server while the other servers are managed servers. Figure 35.23 shows the Clusters console page, which enables you to view the key fields for configured clusters as well as to create a new cluster.

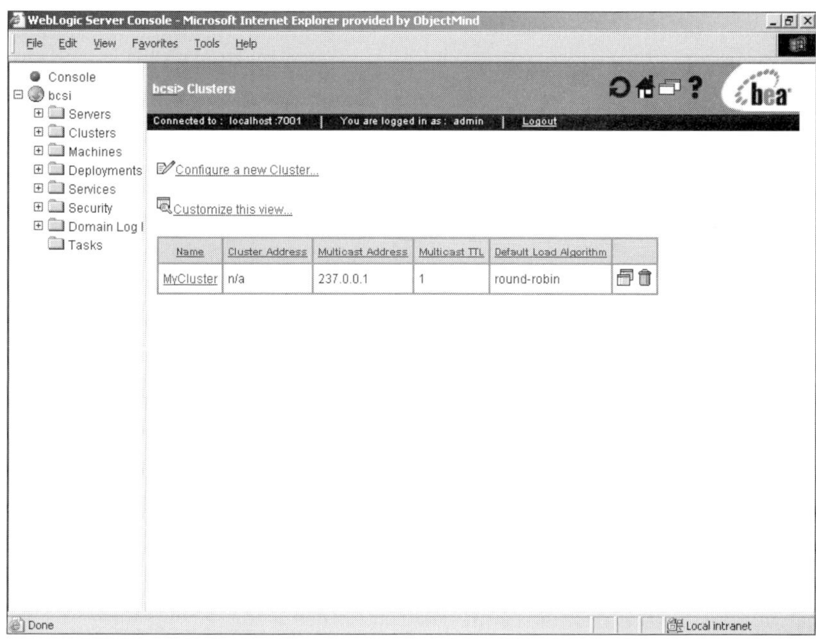

FIGURE 35.23 A cluster appears to the clients as a single WebLogic Server instance to provide increased scalability and reliability.

Clicking on the name of a configured cluster or clicking the Configure a New Cluster link opens the console page for the cluster. The configuration for a cluster is organized on three tabs:

- General
- Multicast
- Servers

General Configuration for a Cluster

The general configuration console page is used to create the first instance of the cluster. After the cluster has been created, the remaining configuration tabs become enabled. The general configuration specifies the clusterwide configuration parameters, including the cluster address and default load algorithm. The cluster address identifies the managed servers in the cluster and is used by Entity and Stateless EJBs to construct the hostname portion of URLs. The cluster address may be specified as a comma-separated list of the hostnames or IP addresses. However, in a production environment, it is recommended to specify a DNS hostname that maps to the addresses of the managed servers in the cluster. The Administration Console help for clusters contains a Tasks link to a step-by-step guide for “Configuring a Cluster.” The console help also provides direct links to the related e-docs topics “Cluster Address” and “Load Balancing Algorithms for RMI Objects and EJBs.” Both of the e-docs related topics are in “Using WebLogic Server Clusters.”

Multicast Configuration for a Cluster

IP multicast is a simple broadcast technology that is used by the servers in the cluster to communicate service availability and heartbeat messages to each other. The servers subscribe to a given IP address and port number to listen for these messages. A multicast address is an IP address in the range from 224.0.0.0 to 239.255.255.255. The configuration for the cluster multicast enables you to specify the multicast address and port number along with additional configuration attributes.

Servers Configuration for a Cluster

The Servers configuration enables you to add servers to the cluster from a list of configured servers. The servers that are added as cluster members listen for cluster multicast events. Figure 35.24 shows the Servers Configuration console page.

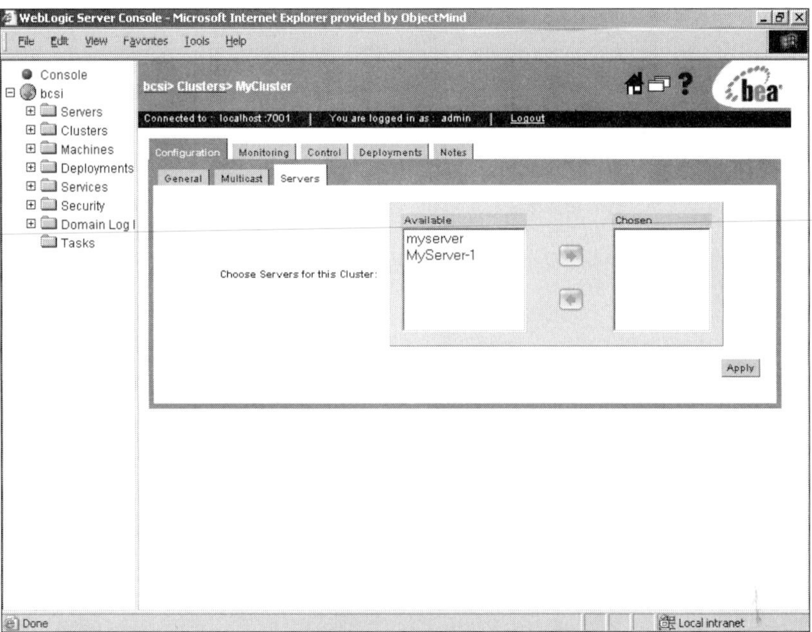

FIGURE 35.24 The servers that are chosen as cluster members listen for cluster multicast events.

Configuring Machines

A *machine* identifies the physical system that hosts one or more WebLogic Server instances. The machine must also run Node Manager to enable you to control managed servers on that machine from a remote machine. Figure 35.25 shows the Machines console page, which enables you to view the key fields for configured machines as well as to create a new machine.

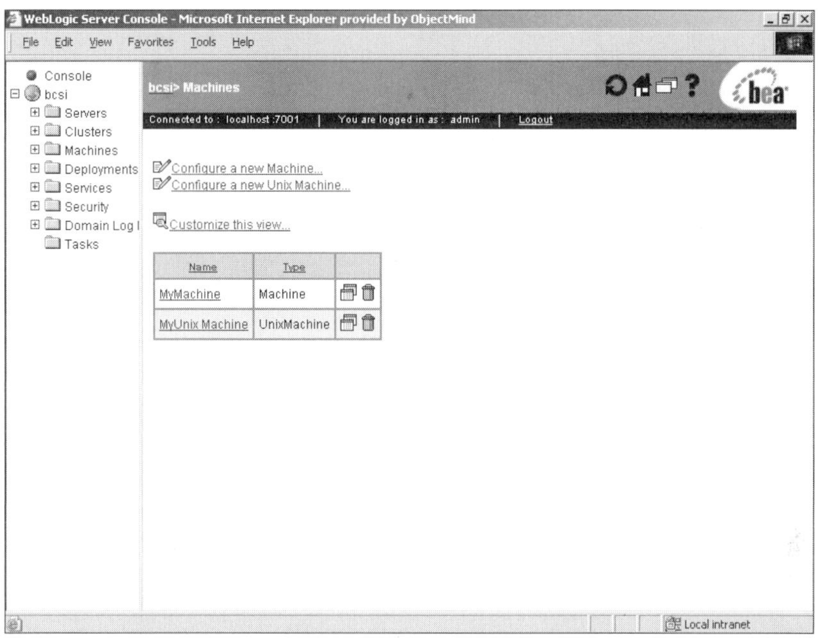

FIGURE 35.25 A machine is the logical representation of a computer that hosts one or more WebLogic Server instances.

The console page for a machine is opened by clicking on the name of a configured machine or by clicking the Configure a New Machine or Configure a New Unix Machine link. The configuration for a machine is organized on three tabs:

- General
- Node Manager
- Servers

The general configuration for a machine that hosts a WebLogic Server is dependent on whether it is running a Unix-based operating system, such as Sun Solaris, or a non-Unix operating system, such as Microsoft Windows.

The Node Manager tab enables you to configure the listen address and listen port for Node Manager. As mentioned previously, Node Manager enables you to control managed servers from a remote machine, and is required if you want to use the Administration Console to control managed servers.

The Servers Configuration page for a machine enables you to select the servers that run on the machine from a list of configured servers. Figure 35.26 shows the console page for configuring servers for a machine.

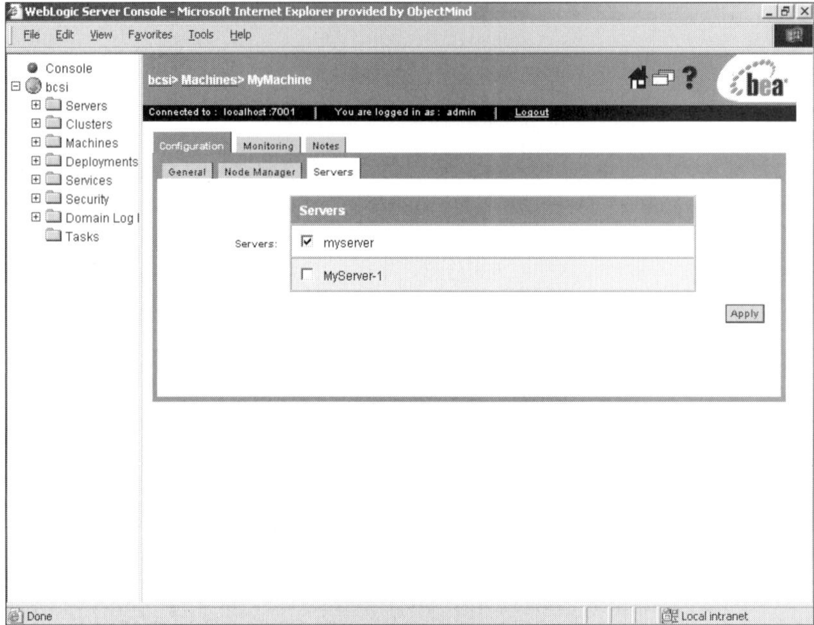

FIGURE 35.26 The Servers Configuration page enables you to select which WebLogic Server instances run on this machine.

The Administration Console help for Machines contains Task links for Configuring a Machine, Cloning a Machine, Deleting a Machine, and Assign a WebLogic Server Instance to a Machine. The console help also provides direct links to the related topic in the e-docs "Configure a Machine to Use Node Manager."

Deploying Applications and Modules

The purpose of WebLogic Server is to host Java 2 Enterprise applications and modules. A J2EE application is deployed in an Enterprise Archive File (EAR). An EJB module is deployed in a Java Archive File (JAR), and a Web application module is deployed in a Web Archive File (WAR). The WebLogic Administration Console provides an easy-to-use interface for the deployment of

- Applications
- EJB modules
- Web application modules
- Connector modules
- Startup and shutdown classes

The first step in deploying either an application or module is to select the archive or exploded archive directory that contains the components and valid descriptors being deployed. Figure 35.27 shows the console page for deploying an application. The page enables you to navigate through the file system to select the archive that is being deployed.

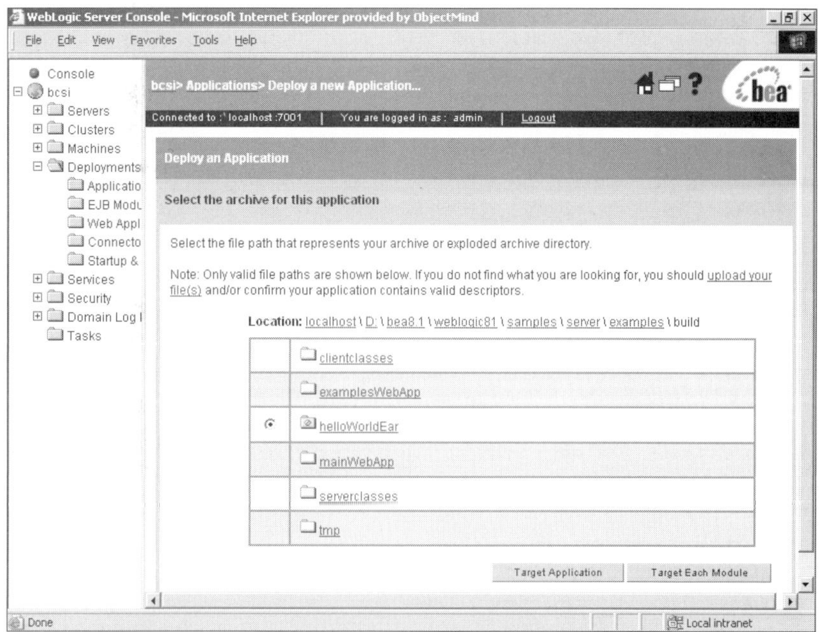

FIGURE 35.27 The Servers Configuration page enables you to select which WebLogic Server instances run on this machine.

After selecting the archive, click the Target Application button to select the servers and/or clusters on which you would like to deploy the application or module. Figure 35.28 shows the console path for selecting targets for an application that is being deployed.

After checking the servers and/or clusters targeted for deployment, click the Continue button. The final step of deployment enables you to review your choices and deploy the application or module. Figure 35.29 shows the console page to deploy an application.

When you click the Deploy button, you'll receive status information indicating the progress of the deployment. You might receive an error if the deployment is unsuccessful.

NOTE

For further information on deploying Web applications, see Chapter 7, "Deploying Web Applications."

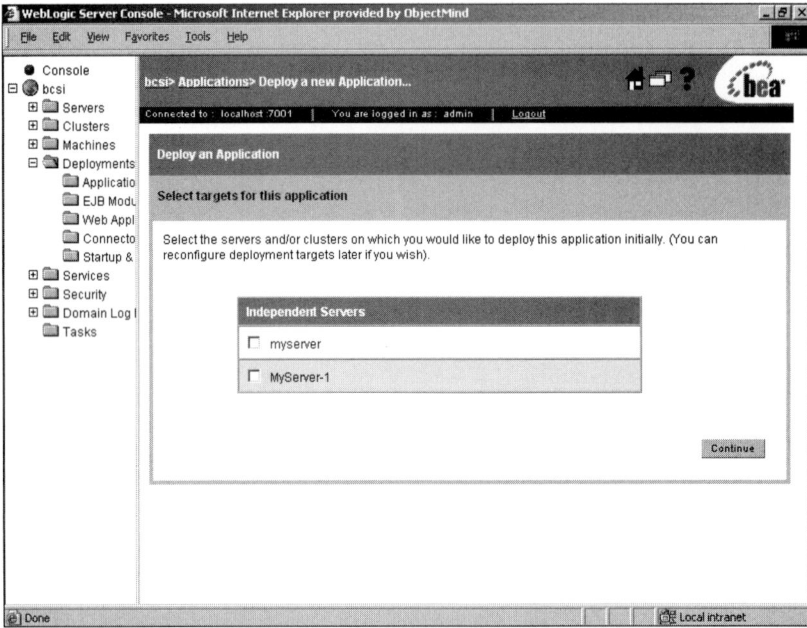

FIGURE 35.28 The second step of deployment is to select the servers and/or clusters on which you would like to deploy.

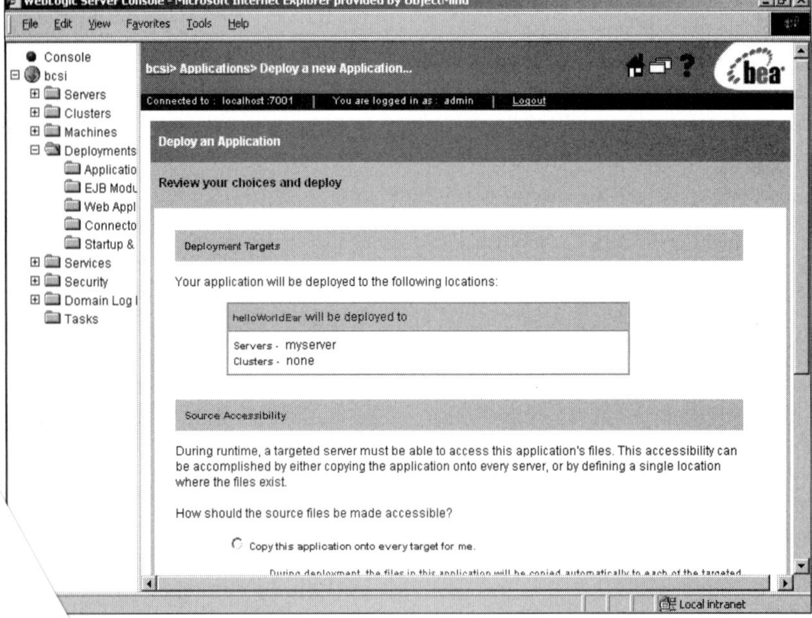

The final step of deployment is to review your choices and deploy the applica-

Configuring WebLogic and J2EE Services

The Services node in the navigation tree contains subnodes for each of the WebLogic and J2EE services provided by WebLogic Server. Each service may control multiple resources that are individually configured and monitored. The services available on WebLogic Server 8.1 are

- jCOM
- JDBC
- JMS
- Messaging Bridge
- XML
- JTA
- SNMP
- WTC
- WLEC (deprecated)
- Jolt
- Virtual Hosts
- Mail
- FileT3 (deprecated)

Each of the WebLogic and J2EE services is individually created and configured from the WebLogic Administration Console. Many of the services must be deployed on WebLogic Server after being created. The initial console page for each service enables you to create a new instance of the service. After a service instance has been created, the Target and Deploy tab on the console page becomes enabled for a service that requires deployment. Figure 35.30 shows an example of the Deploy and Target console page for a JDBC MultiPool.

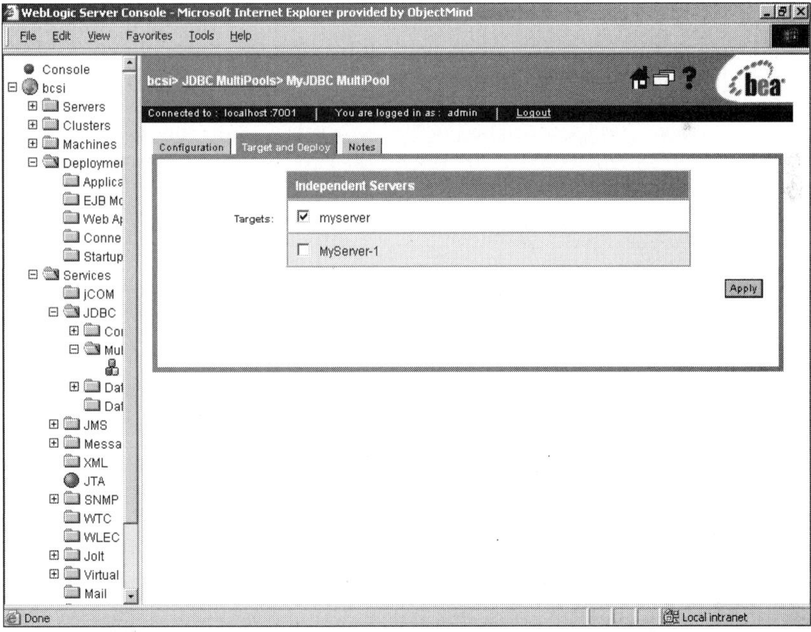

FIGURE 35.30 The Target and Deploy tab enables you to select the servers or clusters on which you would like to deploy a service resource.

The following resources include a Target and Deploy tab on their console page:

- JDBC MultiPool
- JMS Connection Factories
- JMS Foreign JMSServer
- Messaging Bridge
- XML Registry
- WTC Service
- Jolt Connection Pool
- Virtual Host
- Mail Session

In addition to the resources listed, the JDBC Connection Pool and JDBC DataSource combine creating and deploying on a target server or cluster as the final step in creating the new instance. Also, the Domain Log Filters configuration includes a Targets tab that enables you to specify the servers on which you would like to use the domain log filter. The form to target servers for the domain log filter has the same format. However, in this case, you are not deploying the filter; you are requesting the server to use the filter.

The following sections provide a brief description for each of the services, as well as instructions for configuring and monitoring the resources used by that service.

NOTE

The WLEC service was deprecated in BEA WebLogic Server 7.0. Users should migrate WLEC to the WebLogic Tuxedo Connector (WTC). This chapter does not provide a description for WLEC. Refer to the description for the WTC service.

CAUTION

The FileT3 service was deprecated in BEA WebLogic Server 7.0. Users should stop using the FileT3 service.

iguring the jCOM Service

M service enables Microsoft COM clients, such as Microsoft Excel, to call methods
asses deployed on WebLogic Server. The console page for jCOM configuration
efine Security Policy button to define access for the COM class via a security
35.31 shows the console page for defining a security policy.

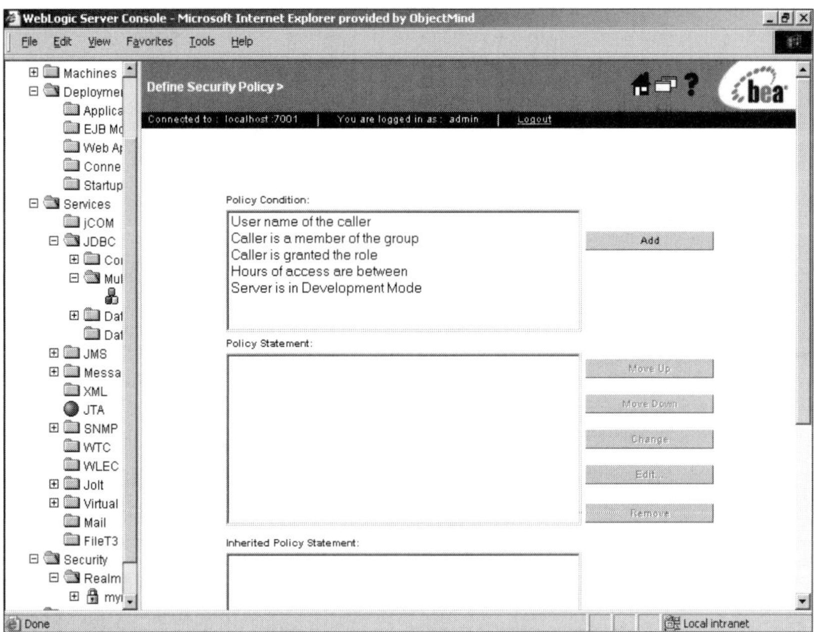

FIGURE 35.31 The jCOM security policy enables you to select policy conditions that are specific to your policy statement.

To create the policy statement, select a condition from the Policy Condition list that must be met, and then click the Add button. A pop-up window will display specific to the selected condition. The additional information for the specific policy condition is entered on the pop-up window. Figure 35.32 shows the pop-up window for the User Name of the Caller Is policy condition. To configure the policy, type a username in the text field, and then click the Add button. Repeat this for as many usernames as necessary. When all the usernames have been added, click the OK button to store the policy condition.

Configuring the JDBC Service

The JDBC service contains the resources used by Java Database Connectivity. The resources for JDBC are

- Connection pools
- MultiPools
- Data sources
- Data source factories

The initial console page for each of the JDBC services provides a link to configure a new instance for the selected service type. The following sections provide instruction for configuring the JDBC resources.

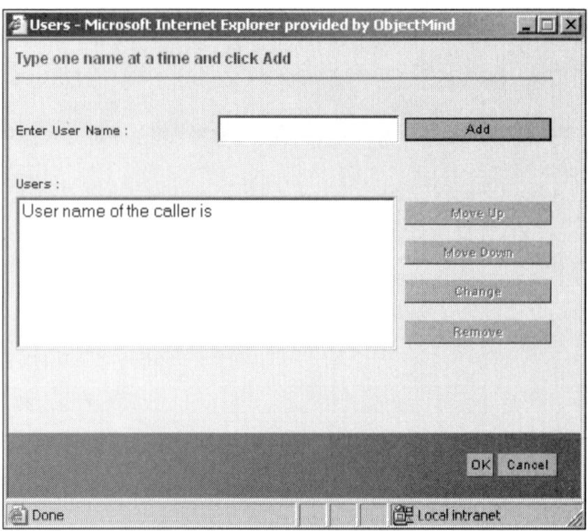

FIGURE 35.32 The specific information is entered on a pop-up window after the Add button for the policy condition has been clicked.

Configure a JDBC Connection Pool

A JDBC connection pool manages the connections between your applications and the database. The JDBC connection pool encapsulates the JDBC driver. The configuration for a JDBC connection pool requires you to select the database type and database driver that are associated with the new connection pool. A JDBC data source links an entry in the JNDI tree to a JDBC connection pool. The application looks up a JDBC data source to gain access to the connection pool. A connection pool is a very efficient way to manage the open connections between applications and the database. During the startup of WebLogic Server, the configured connection pools are registered and immediately create JDBC connections. The applications borrow connections from the connection pool, use them, and return them to the connection pool by closing the JDBC connection.

Figure 35.33 shows the console page that is displayed after clicking the Configure a New JDBC Connection Pool link. The first step is to choose a database by selecting the database type and database driver. The default database type is PointBase and the default database driver is PointBase's Driver (Type 4XA) Versions:4.X.

After selecting the database type and driver for the installed database, click the Continue button at the bottom right of the console page. The next step is to define the connection properties, as shown in Figure 35.34.

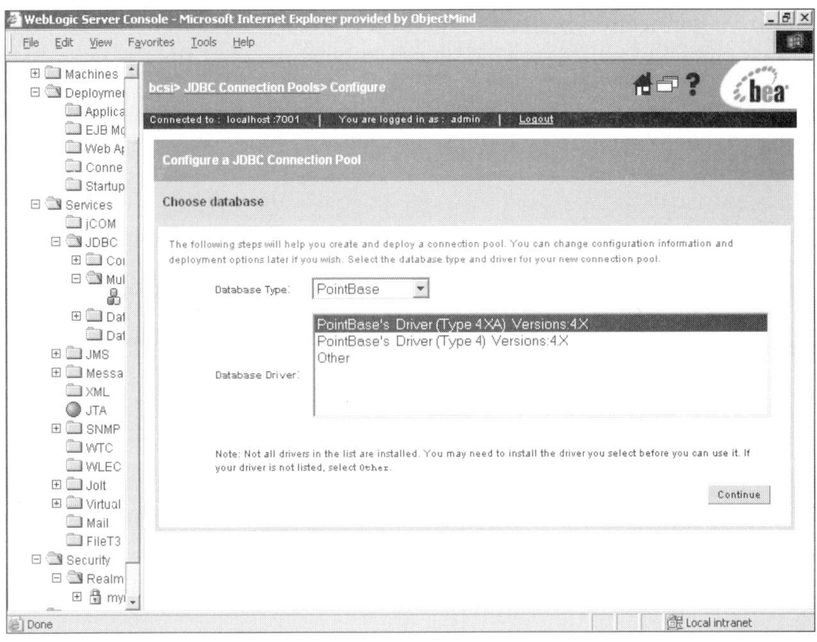

FIGURE 35.33 The first step to configure a JDBC connection pool is to select the database type and driver.

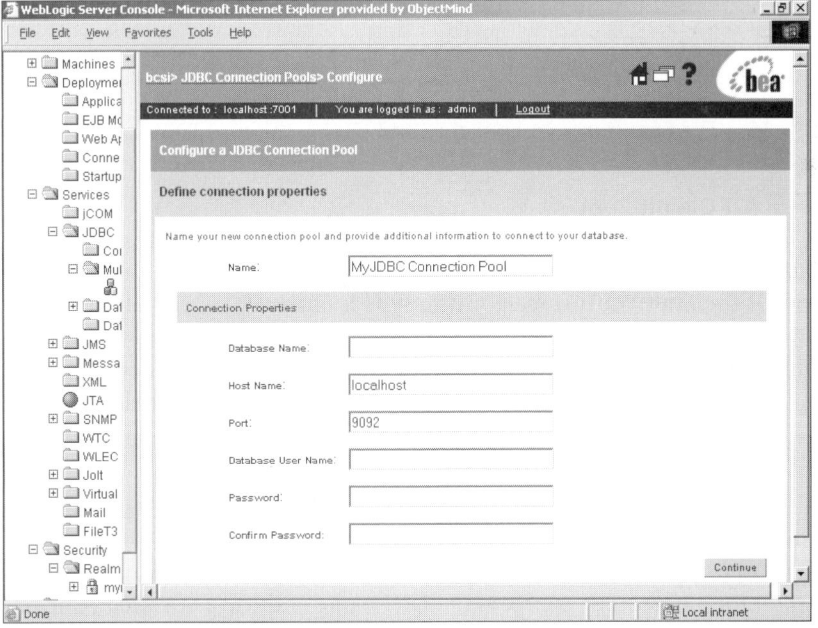

FIGURE 35.34 The second step is to configure the connection properties for the JDBC Connection Pool.

The third step for connection pool configuration is to test the driver configuration. This console page includes a Test Driver Configuration button to test the database connection.

The fourth and final step is to create and deploy the connection pool on the targeted WebLogic Server. Figure 35.35 shows the Create and Deploy page for a system that has only one WebLogic Server.

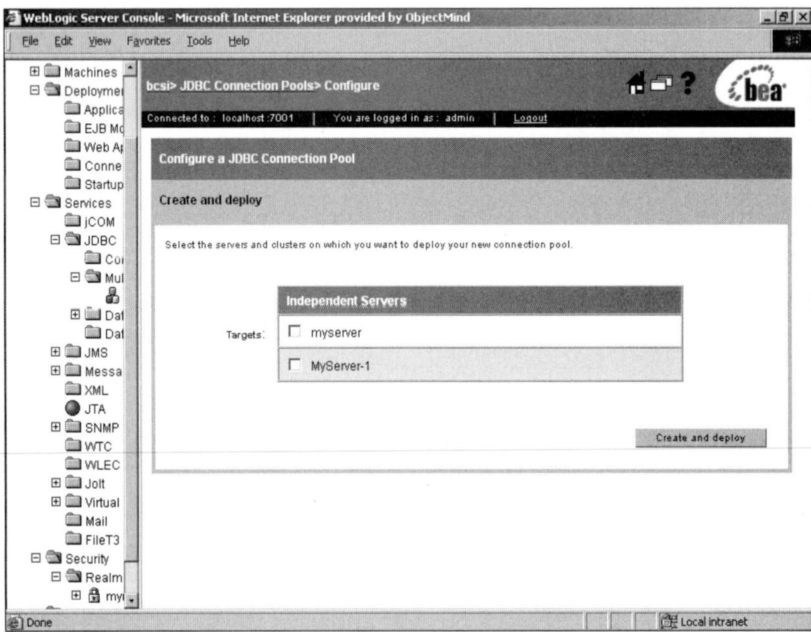

FIGURE 35.35 The final step is to configure and deploy the new JDBC connection pool.

Configure a JDBC MultiPool

A JDBC MultiPool is a pool of connection pools that are configured for load balancing or high availability. The required configuration to create a MultiPool is the name and algorithm type for the MultiPool. The algorithm type is either High-Availability or Load-Balancing. After the MultiPool has been created, the Pools tab becomes enabled. The Pools Configuration page enables you to select from a list of available connections pools to include as part of the MultiPool. Figure 35.36 shows the console page for the Pools tab.

The configured MultiPool must be targeted for deployment before it can be used, as shown earlier in this chapter in Figure 35.30.

Configure a JDBC Data Source

A JDBC data source provides a link between a JNDI tree and a connection pool. The configuration for a JDBC data source is its JNDI name and the associated connection pool. The final step in creating a new JDBC connection pool is to target and deploy on a server.

The JDBC connection pool must be associated with a connection pool and deployed on a server before it can be used. The application looks up the JDBC data source name using JNDI to retrieve a data source object. The connection request made on the data source is supplied by the associated connection pool.

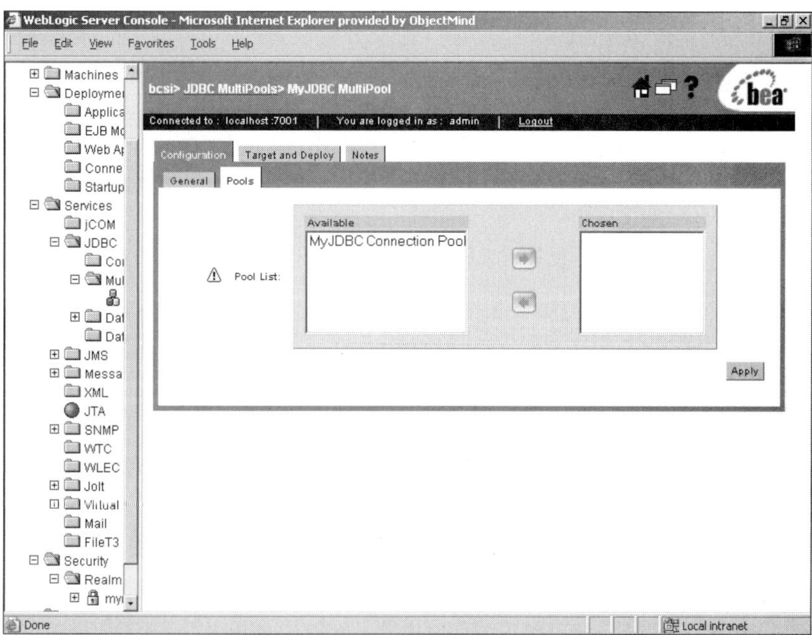

FIGURE 35.36 After the MultiPool has been created, you must add connection pools from the available pool list to be members of the new MultiPool.

Configure a JDBC Data Source Factory

An enterprise application deployed on WebLogic Server might provide a supplemental deployment descriptor named `weblogic-application.xml`, which is used to configure application scoping. Within the deployment descriptor, you can configure JDBC connection pools and associated data sources that are created when the application is deployed. Data sources and connection pools created in this manner are known as *application-scoped data sources* and *application-scoped connection pools*.

A JDBC data source factory provides the default connection pool values for an application-scoped connection pool. An enterprise application that creates application-scoped connection pools requires that a data source factory be created before it can be deployed. The Administration Console help for JDBC data source factories contains a Tasks link for "Creating and Configuring a JDBC Data Source Factory." The console help also provides direct links to the related topics "Application-Scoped JDBC Data Sources and Connection Pools" and the e-docs "Resource Factories" in Programming WebLogic EJB.

Configuring the JMS Service

The JMS service contains the resources used by the Java Messaging Service. The resources for JMS are

- Connection factories
- Templates
- Destination keys
- Stores
- Distributed destinations
- Servers
- Foreign JMS servers

The initial console page for each of the JMS services provides a link to configure a new instance for the selected service type. The following sections provide instruction for configuring the JMS resources.

JMS Thresholds and Quotas

The threshold and quotas enable you to define the maximum messages/byte quotas, the upper and lower message/byte thresholds, the maximum allowable message size, and whether message and/or byte paging is enabled for the JMS resource. The Threshold & Quotas tab is located on the configuration page and is enabled after the JMS resource has been created. The following JMS resources allow configuration for Thresholds & Quotas:

- JMS templates
- JMS distributed topics
- JMS distributed queues
- JMS servers

Configure a JMS Connection Factory

Connection factories are objects that enable JMS clients to create JMS connections. A connection factory is thread-safe; it allows multiple threads to access the JMS connections simultaneously. After you've defined a JMS server, you can configure multiple connection factories to create connections with attributes predefined by that connection factory. The configuration for a JMS connection factory is organized on three tabs:

- General
- Transactions
- Flow Control

The general configuration is where you specify the name and JNDI name for the connection factory, as well as configure the attributes that control the delivery of messages by JMS connections created by this factory. After the JMS connection factory has been created, it must be targeted and deployed on a server before it can be used. The Administration Console help for the JMS connection factory provides a step-by-step guide titled "Configuring a JMS Factory." The related topics in e-docs are "WebLogic JMS Fundamentals," "Managing WebLogic JMS," and "Developing a WebLogic JMS Application."

Configure JMS Templates

The JMS template attributes are inherited by the JMS destinations that use them, with the exception of the Name attribute, which is used by only the JMS template. The General Configuration page for a JMS template enables you to specify its name and choose from existing JMS destination keys to inherit from the JMS template. Figure 35.37 shows the configuration console page for a JMS template.

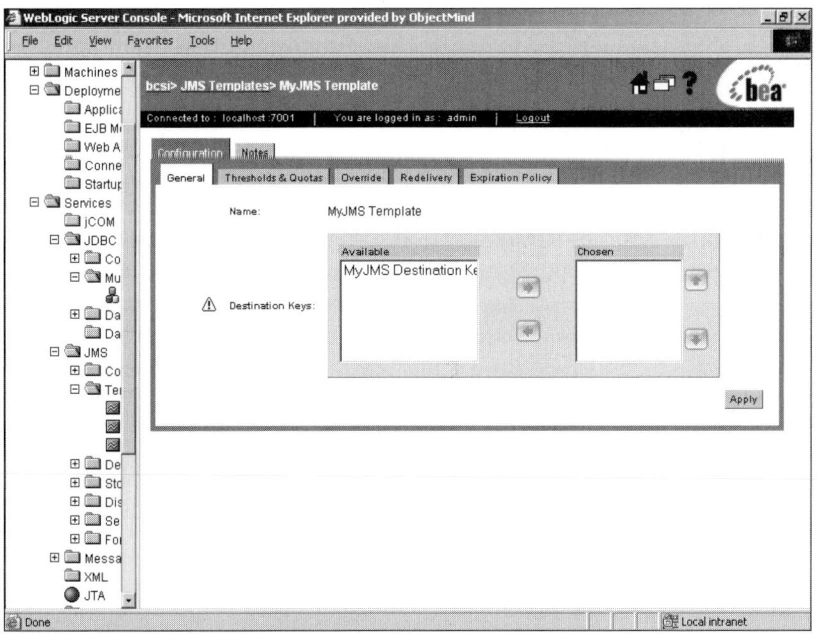

FIGURE 35.37 The JMS template attributes are inherited by the JMS destinations that are chosen.

The General Configuration page is used to create a JMS template. After the template has been created, the Override, Redelivery, and Expiration Policy tabs become enabled.

The last tab on the JMS template configuration page is Expiration Policy. The expiration policy applies to expired messages found on a JMS destination. The choices are (none),

Discard, Log, and Redirect. The (none) and Discard settings have the same effect: The expired message is removed from the system without being logged. The Log setting specifies that a log message be written to the server log file when the expired message is removed. The Redirect option indicates that the message is moved to the error destination defined for the topic. When the expiration policy is set to Log, the Expiration Logging Policy setting enables you to specify what information about the message is logged. See the online help for detailed information about the valid logging policy details.

Configure JMS Destination Keys

You create JMS destination keys to define the sort order for messages that arrive on a specific JMS destination. The JMS queues and JMS topics that you create use the JMS destination key to order the messages that arrive at that destination. The Administration Console help for the JMS destination key provides a step-by-step guide for "Configuring a JMS Destination Key." The related topics in e-docs are the same as those specified for "Configuring a JMS Connection Factory."

Configure JMS Stores

A *JMS store* is a physical repository for storing persistent message data and durable subscribers. A JMS store can also be used for paging messages to disk when memory has been exhausted. A store is created either as a JMS JDBC store or a JMS file store. A JMS JDBC store is associated with the JDBC connection pool that provides the database connection. A JMS file store is associated with an existing directory on the file system. A file store enables you to specify the synchronous write policy that defines how the store will write data to the disk. The Administration Console help for JMS JDBC Store contains a task link for Creating a JMS JDBC Store. The Administration Console help for JMS File Store contains a task link for Creating a JMS File Store. Each task link provides a step-by-step guide for creating the respective JMS store. A direct link for the related topic on e-docs, "WebLogic JMS Fundamentals," is provided on the Administration Console help for either type of JMS store.

> **CAUTION**
>
> The Direct-Write policy for a JMS File Store might not be transactionally safe on some Windows systems.

Configure JMS Distributed Destinations

JMS distributed destinations enable you to configure multiple physical JMS destinations as members of a single distributed destination that can be served by multiple WebLogic Server instances in a cluster. You can add multiple JMS topics to a distributed topic, and add multiple JMS queues to a distributed queue. See the section "Configure JMS Servers" later in this chapter for information on configuring physical JMS topics and JMS queues.

The console page for the Members tab enables you to configure a new distributed topic member for a distributed topic and configure a new distributed queue member for a distributed queue. The member configuration for a distributed queue is used to map a distributed queue member name to a physical JMS queue. The member configuration for a distributed topic is used to map a distributed topic member name to a physical JMS topic.

Configure JMS Servers

A JMS server manages connections and message requests on behalf of JMS clients. A JMS server contains the configuration for one or more JMS destinations, which are JMS queues or JMS topics. A JMS queue provides point-to-point communication. A JMS topic acts as a publish/subscribe repository for messages. After the JMS server has been created, the Configure Destinations link is added to the bottom of the general configuration console page for the JMS server. This link enables you to create and configure physical JMS queues and JMS topics. The JMS server also supports session pools that enable an application to process messages concurrently. JMS session pools are rarely used because they are not a required part of the J2EE specification and do not support JTA user transactions. The JMS session pools are superceded by message-driven beans (MDBs).

NOTE

For further information about MDBs, see Chapter 23, "Working with Message-Driven Beans."

The Administration Console help for JMS destinations provides a step-by-step guides named "Creating a JMS Topic" and "Creating a JMS Queue."

Configure Foreign JMS Servers

A foreign JMS server maps foreign JMS connection factories and foreign JMS destinations into the local WebLogic JNDI tree. This allows foreign JMS connection factories and destinations to appear in the WebLogic JNDI tree as local JMS objects. The configuration for the foreign JMS server specifies the information that allows WebLogic Server to reach the remote JNDI provider. After the foreign JMS server has been created, the Configure Foreign JMSConnectionFactories and Configure Foreign JMSDestinations links are added to the bottom of the configuration console page for the foreign JMS server. These links enable you to specify the mapping between the local JNDI name and the remote JNDI name for the JMS connection factory or JMS destination, respectively. The Administration Console contains a Tasks link named Creating a Foreign JMS Server. The Administration Console help also provides a direct link to the related topic in e-docs: "Using Foreign JMS Providers with WebLogic Server."

Configuring the Messaging Bridge Service

Each WebLogic messaging bridge consists of two destinations that are being bridged. Messages are received from the source destination and forwarded to the target destination. For each source and target destination being bridged, whether it is a WebLogic JMS implementation or a third-party JMS product, you must configure a JMS bridge destination instance. The Messaging Bridge service contains subnodes in the navigation tree that enable you to configure the messaging bridge and the bridge destinations.

- Bridges
- JMS bridge destinations
- General bridge destinations

The initial console page for each of the Messaging Bridge resources provides a link to configure a new instance of the selected resource type. The following sections provide instruction for configuring the Messaging Bridge resources.

Configure a Messaging Bridge

A *messaging bridge* transfers messages between two message providers. The console page for configuring bridges includes three tabs under the Configuration tab:

- General
- Connection Retry
- Transactions

The General Configuration page is used to create the bridge. Two significant attributes of the messaging bridge configuration are the Source Bridge Destination and the Target Bridge Destination. A messaging bridge cannot be created unless those values are specified. The source and target bridge destinations define the JMS destinations that are being bridged. The bridge sends messages to the target destination that it read from the source destination. The values for the source and target are chosen from a list of the JMS bridge destinations that have been created. After the messaging bridge has been created, the Connection Retry and Transactions tabs become enabled. The messaging bridge must be targeted for deployment on a server before it can be used. The Administration Console help contains a Configuring a Messaging Bridge Instance link that leads you to a step-by-step guide.

Configuring JMS Bridge Destinations

The JMS bridge destination is used by the WebLogic messaging bridge to connect to a JMS messaging product. The configuration for the JMS bridge destination specifies the name of the bridge destination within the domain and the configuration for the resource adapter used to communicate with the specified destination. The attributes referencing the adapter include its JNDI name, the adapter's CLASSPATH, and the properties to pass to the adapter. The default resource adapter JNDI name is `eis.jms.WLSConnectionFactoryJNDIXA`. The resource adapter must be deployed as a connector module.

NOTE

For more information about JMS connections see Chapter 12, "Enterprise Messaging with JMS."

Configuring General Bridge Destinations

The general bridge destination is used by the WebLogic messaging bridge to connect to a non-JMS messaging product. A custom adapter must be provided by the third-party vendor to access non-JMS source or target destinations. The Administration Console help for general bridge destinations provides Configuring General Bridge Destinations and Configuring a Messaging Bridge Instance links. The related topic link on the console help page is "Simple Access to Remote or Foreign JMS Providers."

Configuring the XML Service

The XML Registry enables you to configure the XML resources used by WebLogic Server. The Administration Console help for XML registries provides a brief overview of the XML registry for WebLogic Server, as well as related task links for "Configuring a Parser or Transformer Other Than the Built-In," "Configuring a Parser for a Particular Document Type," and "Configuring External Entity Resolution." The related topic on e-docs that the Administration Console help provides a direct link to is "Administering WebLogic Server XML."

The attributes for configuring an XML registry specify the class names for the document builder factory, SAX parser factory, and transformer factory. The default parsers are from the Apache Xerces project and the default transformer is from the Apache Xalan project, which are the industry standard Java classes for XML. In addition to the Java class names for the XML factories, the name of the XML registry is specified and the choice for when to cache is selected as cache-on-reference, cache-at-initialization, or cache-never. The default is cache-on-reference.

Configuring the JTA Service

The JTA service node in the navigation tree is a direct link to the domain configuration tab for JTA. Refer to the "JTA Configuration for the Domain" section earlier in this chapter for information about configuring the JTA service.

Configuring the SNMP Service

The Simple Network Management (SNMP) service is defined by the following six resources, as shown on the Administration Console home page in Figure 35.2 earlier in this chapter:

- Agent
- Proxies
- Monitors

- Log filters
- Attribute changes
- Trap destinations

The SNMP service node in the navigation tree is a direct link to the domain configuration tab for the SNMP agent. Refer to the “SNMP Configuration for the Domain” section earlier in this chapter for information for configuring the SNMP agent. The navigation tree and the Administration Console home page provide links to the console pages for the SNMP resources. The initial console page for each of the SNMP resources provides a link to configure a new instance of the selected resource type. The following sections provide instruction about configuring the SNMP resources.

Configure SNMP Proxies

WebLogic Server uses an SNMP master agent that acts as a proxy for other SNMP agents. The SNMP proxy is configured with a root object identifier (OID). If the SNMP agent receives a request containing OIDs that fall below this root in the OID tree, WebLogic Server forwards the request to the SNMP proxy. The Administration Console help for SNMP proxies includes a link to the step-by-step guide named “Configure an SNMP Proxy.” The console help also provides direct links to the e-docs “WebLogic SNMP Management Guide” and “WebLogic SNMP MIB Reference.”

Configure SNMP Monitors

The WebLogic SNMP agent enables you to configure Java Management Extension (JMX) monitors. The JMX monitors poll WebLogic resources at a specified interval to check for the occurrence of conditions or the crossing of thresholds. The three monitors that you can create for WebLogic SNMP are

- Gauge monitor
- String monitor
- Counter monitor

The monitor is configured with an MBean type, which is effectively the WebLogic Server subsystem that is being monitored. When the monitor detects that a chosen attribute is beyond a threshold for a gauge or counter monitor, or fails a string comparison for a string monitor, an SNMP trap is generated. The configuration page for each of the SNMP monitors provides the same list of the Monitored MBean Type, which is a very extensive list. Figure 35.38 shows a portion of the available selections.

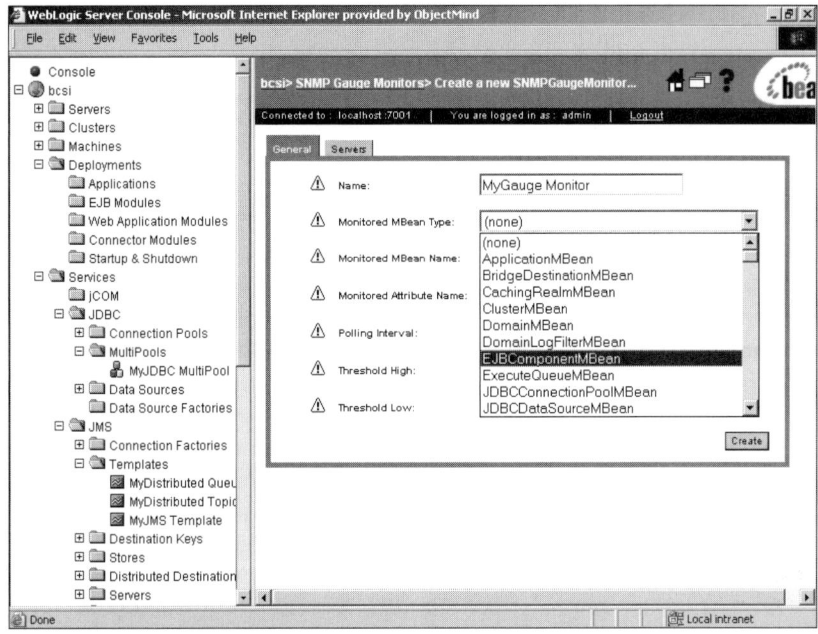

FIGURE 35.38 The Monitored MBean Type for an SNMP monitor enables you to select the WebLogic Server subsystem to monitor.

Configure SNMP Log Filters

The subsystems and modules deployed on a WebLogic Server instance generate log messages to communicate status information. The log messages are broadcast as JMX notifications. A WebLogic SNMP agent uses log filters to specify the criteria for which log messages it wants to receive. The configuration for an SNMP log filter specifies the minimum severity level for messages that will be selected, as well as lists of subsystem names, user IDs, and messages IDs that it is interested in selecting. The severity level is specified from the ordered list:

- Info
- Warning
- Error
- Notice
- Critical
- Alert
- Emergency

All messages at the specified level or a higher level are selected by the SNMP agent using this log filter.

The selection criteria can also be specified as a message substring that must be matched in the message text. The messages that are selected by the SNMP agent generate an SNMP log notification trap. The Administration Console help provides a link to the step-by-step guide, "Configure a Notification Log Filter." The related topics from e-docs are "WebLogic SNMP MIB Reference" and "WebLogic SNMP Management Guide."

Configure SNMP Attribute Change Traps

The SNMP Attribute Change trap enables you to configure the SNMP agent to send a trap immediately after an attribute has been changed. This is in contrast to the SNMP monitors introduced earlier in this chapter that generate traps by polling for changes. The configuration for an SNMP Attribute Change trap enables you to specify the attribute MBean type, the name of a specific instance of an attribute MBean, or an attribute name that is registered in the WebLogic Server MIB. The configuration also enables you to choose on which servers to enable trap generation. The Administration Console help for this page includes a direct link to the e-docs named "WebLogic SNMP MIB Reference." That reference is used to select the configured attribute name for this Attribute Change trap. The console help also provides a link to the step-by-step guide, "Configuring an Attribute Change."

Configure SNMP Trap Destinations

SNMP trap destinations specify the community name used by the SNMP agent. The community name provides the credentials for sending trap notifications to the target SNMP manager. The Administration Console help provides a link to the step-by-step guide, "Creating a Trap Destination."

Configuring the WTC Service

The WebLogic Tuxedo Connector (WTC) provides bi-directional integration between WebLogic applications and Tuxedo. It allows WTC clients to access Tuxedo services and allows Tuxedo clients to invoke WebLogic Server applications. The general configuration for WTC is simply the name of the WTC service. After the WTC service has been created, it must be deployed on WebLogic Server instances. The Contents tab on the WTC console page enables you to configure the following:

- Local Tuxedo access point
- Remote Tuxedo access point
- Exported service
- Imported service
- Passwords
- Resources

- Tuxedo queuing bridge
- Redirections

Each of the preceding items is listed as a tab for the contents of the WebLogic Tuxedo Connector. There is a separate Administration Console help for each of the configurable items to guide you through the configuration process.

Configuring the WLEC Service

The WebLogic Enterprise Connectivity (WLEC) has been deprecated by the WebLogic Tuxedo Connector. Refer to the section "Configuring the WTC Service" earlier in this chapter for configuring WTC.

Configuring the Jolt Service

Jolt is a Java-based client API that manages requests to the WebLogic Tuxedo Services through a Jolt Service Listener (JSL) running on the Tuxedo server. The Jolt client class library can be used by servlets running in WebLogic Server to provide the interface to the BEA Tuxedo services. The configuration for Jolt is maintained by a Jolt connection pool. A Jolt connection pool stores the primary addresses and failover addresses that are used to establish a connection to the Tuxedo domain. Jolt provides connection failure handling by using two lists of JSL addresses for each connection pool. The primary addresses are used to establish a connection between this Jolt connection pool and the Tuxedo domain. The failover addresses are used if a connection defined in the Primary Addresses field cannot be established. The addresses are specified in the standard URL format of `//hostname:port`. Multiple addresses are separated by semicolons.

Like the Addresses tab, the User tab becomes enabled after a Jolt connection pool has been created. Each network connection is authenticated through a security identity that is established as a security context in WebLogic Server using the values specified as the User configuration for the Jolt connection pool.

NOTE

The Jolt user role and application password are required only when the security level in the Tuxedo domain is `USER_AUTH_ACL` or `MANDATORY_ACL`.

TIP

Check the Administration Console help for a direct link to the e-docs for "BEA Jolt."

35

Configuring the Virtual Hosts Service

Virtual hosting enables you to specify which hosts will be served by the Web applications on this server. At least one hostname must be entered in the Virtual Host Names list to create a virtual host. After the virtual host has been created, the Logging tab becomes enabled.

> **NOTE**
>
> The remaining fields on the Logging console page are relevant only if Logging Enabled is checked.

Like the Logging tab, the HTTP tab also becomes enabled after a virtual host has been created. The virtual host must be targeted and deployed on WebLogic Server instances before it can be used.

Configuring the Mail Service

WebLogic Server includes the JavaMail API version 1.1.3 reference implementation from Sun Microsystems. The JavaMail API enables you to add email capabilities to your WebLogic Server applications.

> **NOTE**
>
> JavaMail is the client-side API to provide email capabilities from your WebLogic Server applications to an existing mail server.

Your WebLogic Server modules and applications access JavaMail through JNDI. The mail session object bound in the JNDI tree provides the configured session properties to the Web application. The configuration for the mail session is therefore its JNDI name and a list of properties. The mail session must be targeted for deployment on WebLogic Server instances before it can be used.

Administering Security Realms

A *security realm* is a container for the mechanisms that are used to protect WebLogic resources. Your WebLogic Server is installed with a default security realm, named `myrealm`. The default security realm simplifies the configuration and management of security by providing pre-configured

- WebLogic authentication
- Identity assertion
- Authorization
- Adjudication

- Role mapping
- Credential mapping

If the default security realm meets your security requirements, you need only to define

- Groups
- Users
- Global Roles

To configure groups, users, and global roles for the default security realm, expand Security and Realms in the navigation tree and click on myrealm. The User Management tab on this console page enables you to manage the three items in the preceding list. The Administration Console help provides a detailed overview for managing your WebLogic security realm. The table of contents panel on the left side of the console help provides direct links to the step-by-step guides for the administrative tasks of configuring the security realm.

WebLogic Server enables you to create a new security realm if the default security realm does not suit your security requirements. The security realm configuration page enables you to combine WebLogic and custom security providers in the configuration of the new security realm. The new security realm must then be set as the default security realm for your domain. To create a new security realm, click on the Realms node in the navigation tree. The Realms console page provides the Configure a New Realm link.

Configuring Domain Log Filters

The WebLogic Server maintains a single domainwide log file, as described in the section "Logging Configuration for the Domain," earlier in this chapter. The domain log filter specifies which messages a WebLogic Server instance sends to the domain log. The message must pass all criteria in the filter to be logged. The configuration for the domain log filter specifies the minimum severity level of the message for the server to forward it to the domain log. The configuration also enables you to filter log messages based on the user ID for which the associated messages are sent. By default, messages are not filtered by user ID; therefore, messages from all user IDs are forwarded to the domain log. The domain log filter may also specify specific subsystems that the server will forward to the domain log. By default, messages are not filtered by subsystem; therefore, messages from all subsystems are forwarded to the domain log.

Monitoring Administrative Tasks

Some administrative tasks, such as deployments, service migrations, and attempts to start and stop managed servers, take varying amounts of time to complete. The Tasks console page enables you to monitor the completion status of all tasks that are in progress: It displays a table containing tasks in progress and completed tasks that have not yet been purged. If tasks are available, you can click on the task's description to get more information about the task. Doing so displays a form that enables you to select the Status tab and Details tab for the selected task. The Status tab displays more detailed information about the task. The Details tab enables you to view the exceptions and stack traces of the task if it failed to complete. The Tasks console page also includes a Purge Tasks button to enables you to clear completed tasks from the tasks list.

Summary

The Administration Console provides the WebLogic Server administrator with a comprehensive tool to monitor and configure all aspects of WebLogic Server. The integrated help text provides a quick reference for every field on the configuration pages, and the console help provides an overview and direct links to the tasks and related topics for the current page. The easily accessible help features and overall design of the Administration Console make it an easy-to-use, yet very powerful tool. The navigation tree clearly shows the extensive variety of services provided by WebLogic Server to meet all of your J2EE Web application needs.

CHAPTER 36

Installing, Configuring, and Deploying WebLogic Server Clusters

by Kunal Mittal and Joe McGuire

IN THIS CHAPTER

- Introduction to WebLogic Server Clustering
- Creating and Configuring the Physical Cluster Environment
- Clustering Applications and Components
- Failover Support for Clustered Services
- Cluster Best Practices

This chapter covers the installation of WebLogic Server clusters, and the deployment and configuration of applications and services in the clustered environment.

Introduction to WebLogic Server Clustering

Undoubtedly the two most important attributes of robust distributed applications are their capacity to scale and their availability. Effective application services must be able to meet the ever-increasing demands on application and Web servers through the addition of more servers to handle the load. Applications and services must be available 24 hours a day / 7 days a week, and increased loads or system failures should appear transparent to the end user.

WebLogic achieves scalability and high availability through the implementation of clusters. A *cluster*, loosely defined, is an environment where services are shared across two or more servers in a domain. Scalability is achieved through load balancing across these servers, and high availability is achieved by the failover capability of other servers to pick up the client processing in the event of a server's overload or failure.

For the developer, most components are built to the same specification whether or not they are to be deployed in clustered environments. There might be, however, considerations with servlets and JSPs, and EJB and RMI components. If your servlets and JSPs are going to use HTTP session state replication, you must remember to make your Web components serializable. If your EJBs are going to use replica-aware stubs, you must make changes to the deployment descriptor and recompile. For RMI component replication, you must generate the replica-aware stubs with the WebLogic RMI compiler.

Clustering, however, is not at all transparent to the WebLogic administrator. It is the job of the administrator to install and configure the servers participating in a cluster, and to deploy and configure applications onto that environment.

There are many different ways to configure a physical cluster, as defined by your needs and available resources. You will also find that configuring a cluster is as much an art form as it is a science. The following is a list of components and services that you can deploy and configure in a cluster:

- HTTP session—Replication provided for failover of the client's session in servlets and JSPs.
- EJB components and RMI objects—Replication provided through replica-aware stubs distributed among multiple application servers.
- JMS service—Scalability achieved through distributed JMS destinations and connection factories (a new feature since version 7; however, no failover support is yet provided).
- JNDI service—Replication provided through a clusterwide JNDI tree.
- JDBC data sources—Load balancing achieved via clustered connection pools.

This chapter breaks down clustering into two sections:

- The first section covers setting up your physical clustering environment.
- The second section covers clustering services for your applications and components.

Creating and Configuring the Physical Cluster Environment

Clusters can be set up in a variety of ways. In the basic model, there is an administration server with two or more managed servers. The server instances can be on the same or different physical workstations, but the rule of thumb is generally to put one server instance per CPU.

To illustrate the concepts in installing and configuring a physical cluster, we will create a very basic example consisting of an administration server with two managed servers, all on the same physical workstation. Now, in any kind of testing or production development, you would want to have these distributed on different CPUs or workstations. However, the assumption is made that as a student you are most likely working on a single workstation environment—hence this simple topology. The installation is shown in Figure 36.1.

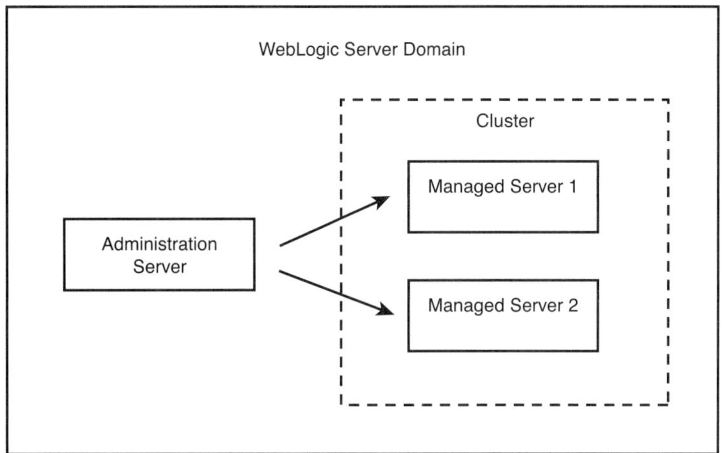

FIGURE 36.1 Our simple clustered environment.

Creating the Cluster Domain

The first step is to make sure that you have a clustering license. The BEA license file is an XML file with a `.bea` extension. It contains separate license elements and keys for different server functions. Open the `license.bea` file in the `\bea` root directory in a text or XML editor. If you see an XML element entry for `Cluster` with a valid signature and expiration date, you're all set. Otherwise, contact your BEA vendor for a clustering license.

The next step is to create the cluster environment. WebLogic 8.1's new Configuration Wizard makes creating a cluster easier than it ever was before. Your domain, administration server, managed servers, and cluster are installed and configured through the GUI. For a complete walkthrough on how to use the Configuration Wizard, please refer to Appendix A, "Quick Reference for Creating New Domains for WebLogic Development." In this chapter, we expand on the clustering options available through the Configuration Wizard.

To start the Configuration Wizard from the Start menu, click on Programs→BEA WebLogic Platform 8.1→Configuration Wizard.

As you are going through the Configuration Wizard as explained in Appendix A, at step 6 you'll see a screen asking whether you want to configure your cluster. This screen is shown in Figure 36.2.

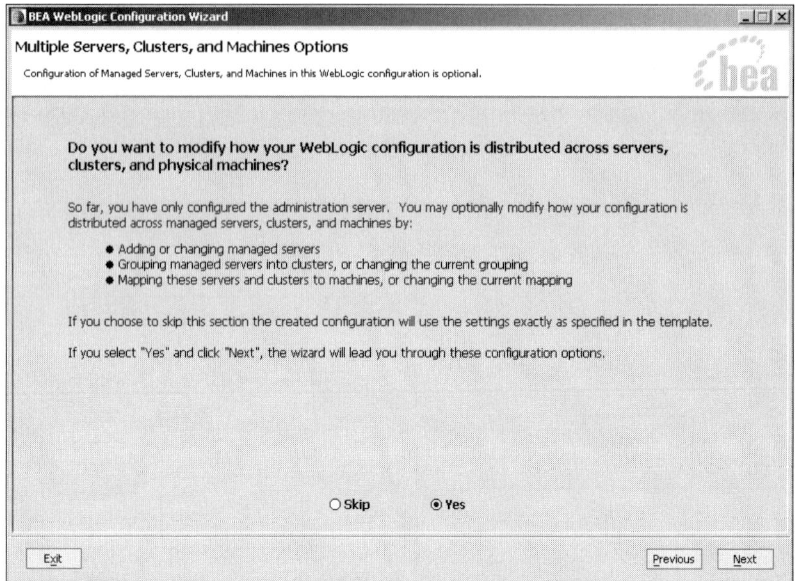

FIGURE 36.2 Choose whether to set up clusters.

The Configuration Wizard then shows you a screen in which you can set up your managed servers, as shown in Figure 36.3. When you're finished, click Next to continue.

- Name—This corresponds to the unique name of the managed server in the domain.
- Listen Address—This corresponds to the IP address of the machine hosting the managed server. In both of our managed servers, this will be the same because we're using one workstation. However, if these were hosted on different workstations, we would use the appropriate IP of each. Our illustrative example uses the default local IP 127.0.0.1 or simply `localhost`.

  Because IP addresses must be pre-configured, all of your managed server instances must have fixed IP addresses!

> **NOTE**
>
> The capability to share one IP address among managed servers running on the same machine (provided that each has a different listen port) has been a feature of WebLogic Server starting from the 7.x release. In earlier versions, you had to have a different IP address for each server instance.

TIP

If you cannot use fixed IP addresses, you can use DNS names. On a Windows machine, you can set up local DNS names by adding entries to `%WINDOWS_HOME%\system32\drivers\etc\hosts`. On a production machine, using fixed IP addresses is recommended.

- Listen Port—You can set up a cluster either by having multiple IP addresses, one for each server, or by having the server listen on different ports, as shown in Figure 36.3.
- SSL Listen Port—For servers with the same IP, the SSL ports must also be different.
- SSL Enabled—To allow or disallow a server for processing SSL requests.

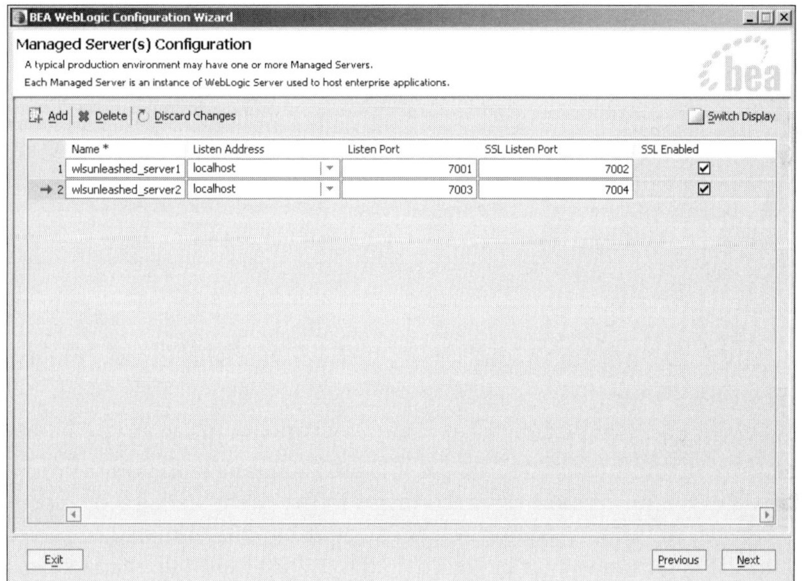

FIGURE 36.3 Set up managed servers.

The next window asks you to set up the cluster. Create a cluster as shown in Figure 36.4. When finished, click Next to continue.

- Name—This corresponds to the unique name of the cluster.
- MultiCast Address—Enter a multicast address for the cluster. This address must begin with 237.xxx. xxx.xxx, 238.xxx.xxx.xxx, or 239.xxx.xxx.xxx.
- Multicast Port—Enter a numeric value for the multicast port. The range of values is 1 to 65535.

36

- Cluster Address—This is either the DNS name or a comma-separated list of IP:ports for each managed server, as shown in Figure 36.4.

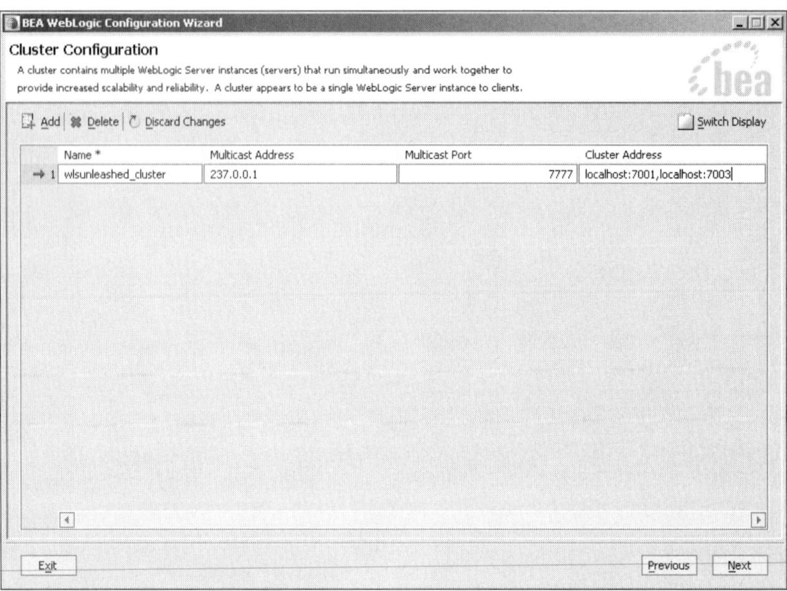

FIGURE 36.4 Create a cluster.

The next step is to assign the managed servers to the cluster. This is very straightforward, as shown in Figure 36.5.

The next step is to set up the host machine. We typically use the machine that has the Node Manager as the host machine because it is used to manage the rest of the WebLogic Server cluster. The administration server connects to the Node Manager on this host. Via the Node Manager, the administration server can start individual managed servers in the cluster. Fill in the details as shown in Figure 36.6 to set up the Node Manager and then click Next.

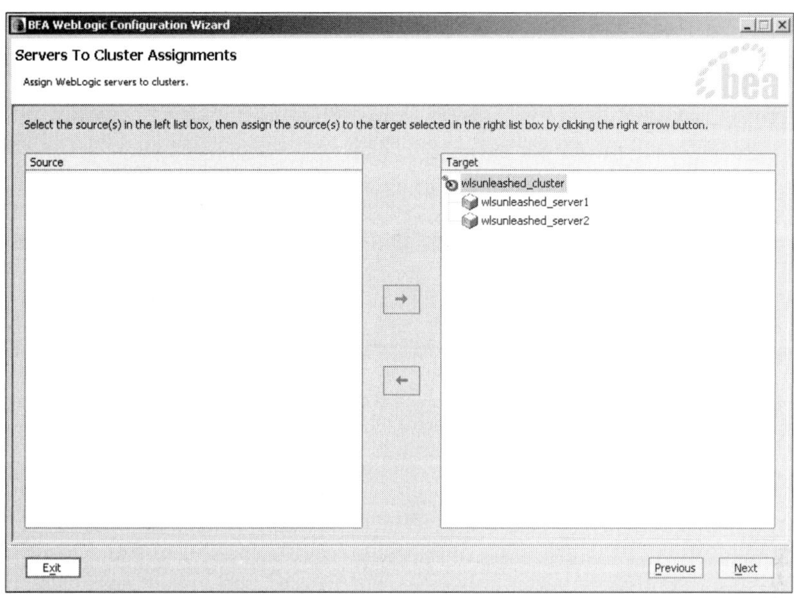

FIGURE 36.5 Assign managed servers to the cluster.

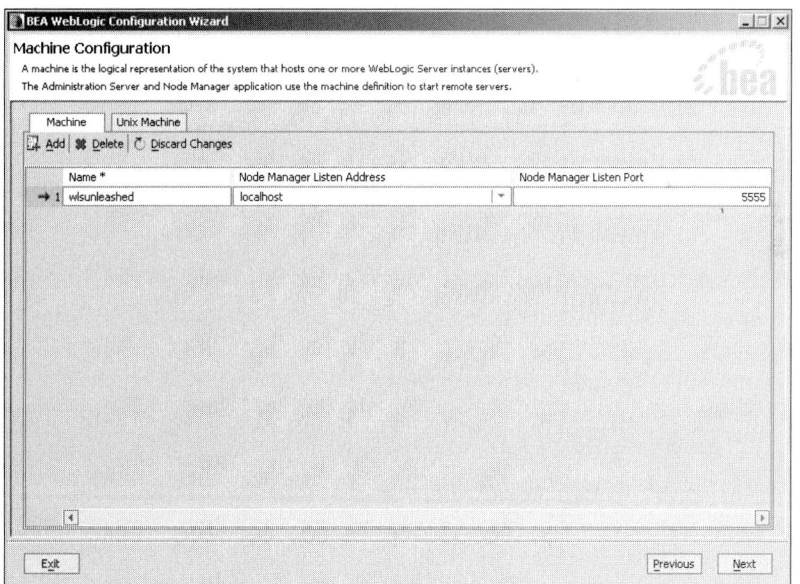

FIGURE 36.6 Set up the machine configuration.

The next step is to assign the clusters and servers to the machine configuration from the previous screen as shown in Figure 36.7.

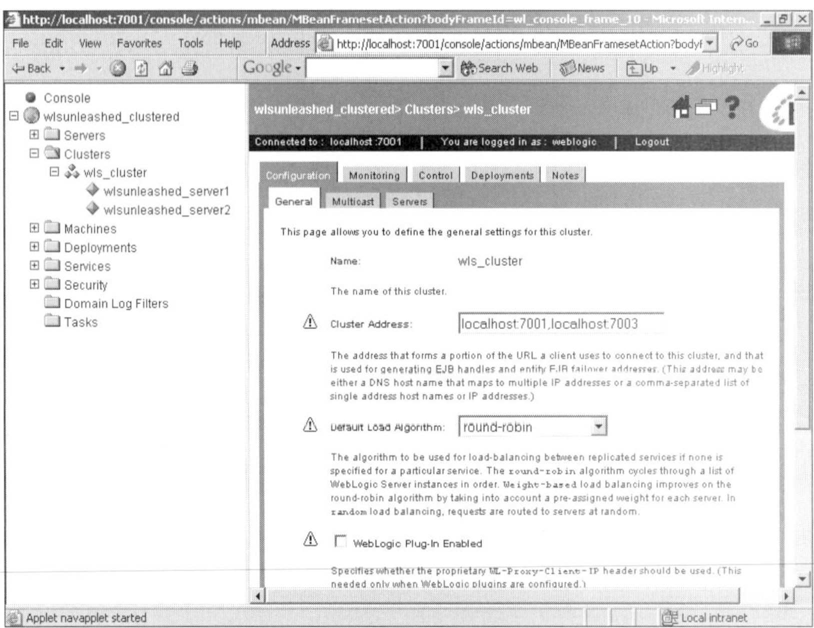

FIGURE 36.7 Assign servers to a machine.

Follow the steps as shown in Appendix A (after step 7 and onward to page 1317), to complete the creation of your clustered domain. For purposes of our example, we named the domain `wlsunleashed_clustered`.

Starting the Administration and Managed Servers in a Cluster

Now let's start up the administration server for our new `wlsunleashed_clustered` domain. You can either click on the link created in the Windows Program Manager at Start→Programs→BEA WebLogic Platform 8.1→User Projects→wlsunleashed_clustered→ Start Server, or you can run the `startWebLogic.cmd` file created in the `%BEA_HOME%\user_projects\wlsunleashed_clustered` directory.

After the `wlsunleashed_clustered` domain has started for WebLogic Server, log in to the Administration Console. Expand the Clusters category on the left, and click on the cluster to see the details of your cluster as shown in Figure 36.7.

You can start the managed servers using the Control tab of the cluster as shown in Figure 36.8. You can start all the managed servers or choose to start them individually.

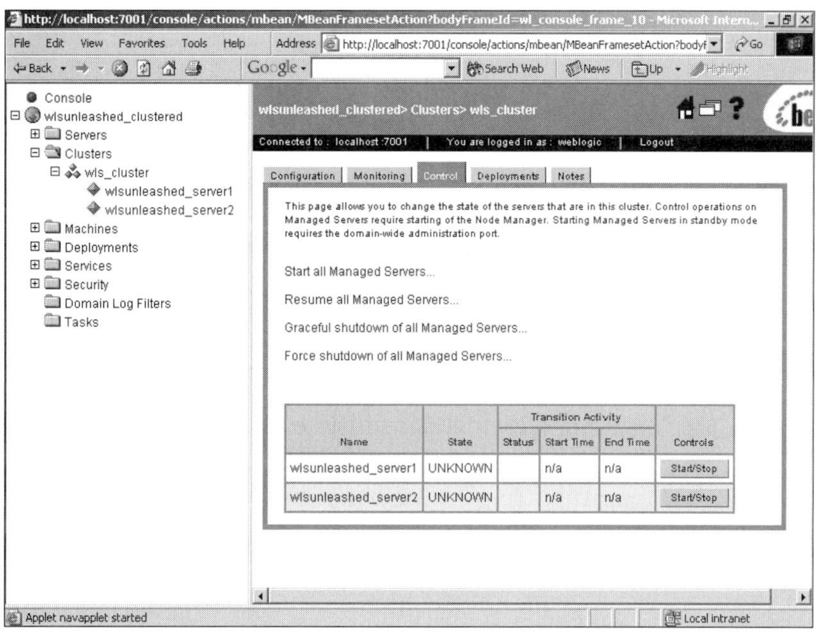

FIGURE 36.8 Start the managed servers.

To control the managed servers individually, click on a server and go to the Control tab as shown in Figure 36.9. You can use the links there to start, stop, or resume that managed server.

You should probably spend some time browsing the various tabs of the cluster configuration to become familiar with the types of changes that you can make through the administration console. These are pretty straightforward configuration options and enable you to modify the cluster options you used when you first set up your cluster in the Configuration Wizard.

You can start the managed servers from the Administration Console or using the `startManagedWeblogic` command-line script.

Using an HTTP Proxy to Access the Cluster

Now we have in place our domain with its administration server and clustered managed servers. In our example, where all servers have the same IP address but different ports, client access would be easy because all Web applications would resolve to the same IP address. But what about a real-world deployment, where the managed servers are running on different IP addresses? How would an application know which IP address to resolve to? The answer is to have your clients access your clustered applications via an HTTP proxy server.

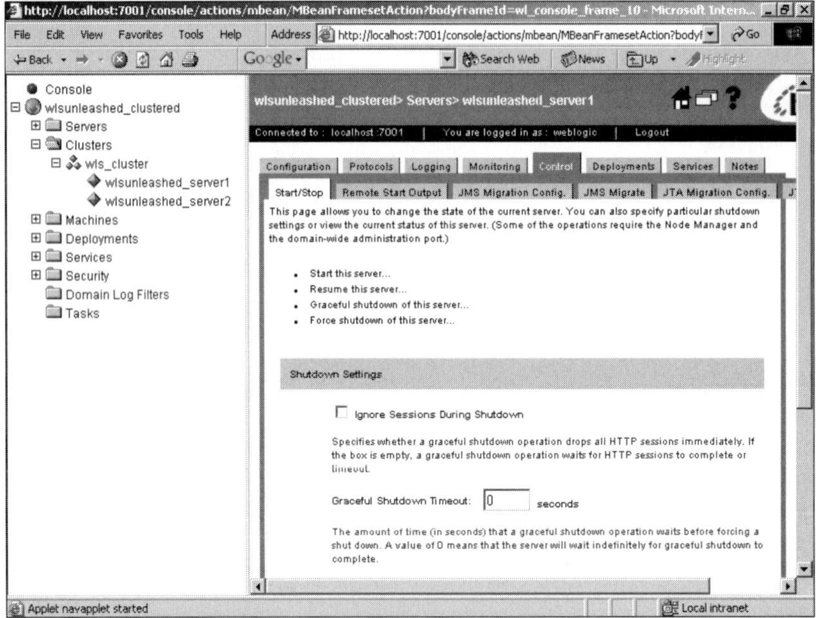

FIGURE 36.9 Control managed servers individually.

There are two ways to implement a proxy server:

- Use an instance of WebLogic Server and the `HttpClusterServlet`
- Use a third-party proxy server, such as Apache Microsoft IIS or Netscape iPlanet, with the WebLogic proxy plug-in

For our example, we will use the `HttpClusterServlet` on our administrative server in our domain. Using the administrative server for a proxy is okay for development, but in a production environment, you might want to go to an independent instance to work as a proxy. The `HttpClusterServlet` class is included in the `weblogic.jar` file, so it's already in the classpath. You need to deploy the `HttpClusterServlet` just as you would any other servlet (as shown in Chapter 7, "Deploying Web Applications"). The final step is to set a flag to enable the proxies to this servlet. This check box option is on the General tab of the cluster configuration page as shown in Figure 36.10.

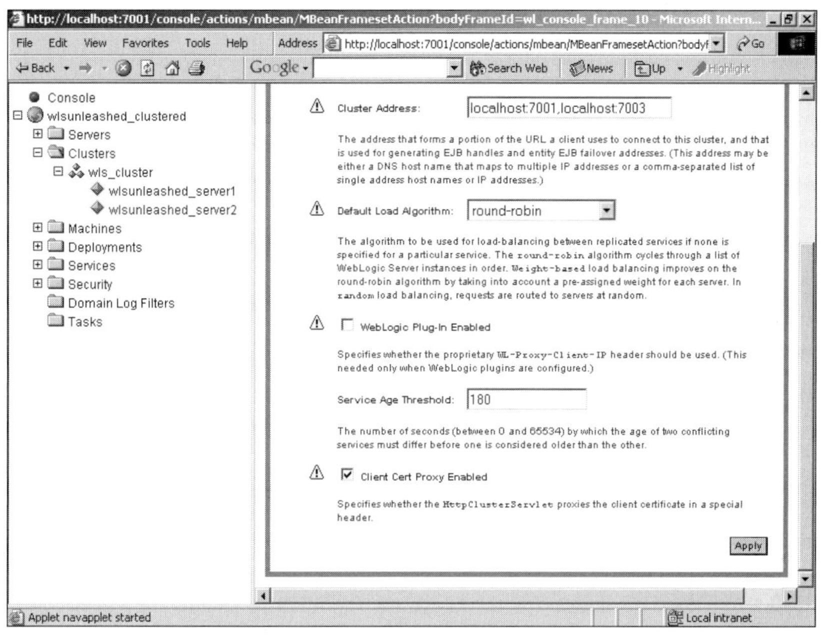

FIGURE 36.10 Enabling proxies.

USING THE HTTPCLUSTERSERVLET

`HttpClusterServlet` is a special pre-defined servlet as part of the WebLogic Server that can be used to proxy the requests to a cluster. `HttpClusterServlet` is set up the same way as other servlets. The following XML snippet explains how to configure a basic `HttpClusterServlet` in the `web.xml` file. The `defaultServers` in the `init-param` element tag define the list of servers in the WebLogic cluster.

```
<web-app>


<servlet>
<servlet-name>HttpClusterServlet</servlet-name>
<servlet-class>weblogic.servlet.internal.HttpClusterServlet</servlet-class>


   <init-param>
   <param-name>defaultServers</param-name>
   <param-value>wlsunleashed_server1:7001|wlsunleashed_server2:7003
   </param-value>
   </init-param>
</servlet>
```

```
<servlet-mapping>
<servlet-name>HttpClusterServlet</servlet-name>
<url-pattern>/</url-pattern>
</servlet-mapping>

<servlet-mapping>
<servlet-name>HttpClusterServlet</servlet-name>
<url-pattern>*.jsp</url-pattern>
</servlet-mapping>

</web-app>
```

The `<init-param>` tag can also be used to define the load algorithm to use as well as to enable debugging. The servlet mapping in the preceding XML snippet redirects all JSP servlet requests to the WebLogic cluster. Similar mappings need to be added for `.htm` and `.html` files if the HttpClusterServlet has to serve those files back to the client. The requests are directed to the cluster based on the load algorithm. This servlet forms a bridge between the client and the cluster passing the HTTP requests to one of the servers in the cluster and, on the return, passes the servlet output (for example, an HTML page) back to the client.

By default, WebLogic Server uses cookies for storing session identifiers on the client. If the Web browser does not support cookies, URL rewriting can be used to store session identifiers.

`HttpClusterServlet` also facilitates failover to secondary servers in case the primary server goes down. This servlet takes care of forwarding the next request from the client to the secondary server. WebLogic Server promotes the secondary server to the new primary and selects a new secondary server for replicating session state. All this information is updated on the client's session as well for future interactions.

`HttpClusterServlet` is at the heart of the WebLogic-specific implementation of in-memory session replication infrastructure using proxies. The classes are defined in the `weblogic.servlet.proxy` package. As mentioned earlier, this servlet is similar to other HTTP servlets because the base class to this class, `GenericProxyServlet`, is derived from the `HttpServlet` class. This package also provides the following utility classes:

- `HttpClusterServlet.Server`—Represents each backend server and its properties
- `HttpClusterServlet.RequestInfo`—Utility object to store details about each request, including primary server, list of servers available, content and content length, and so on
- `HttpClusterServlet.ServerList`—List of servers in the cluster

Clustering Applications and Components

Now that we have our clustered environment installed and configured, we can get to the business of applying load balancing and providing failover for our applications and components.

In a clustered environment, we can achieve failover protection and load balancing of our components and services, specifically

- Servlet and JSP failover provided by HTTP Session replication
- EJB and RMI object replication provided by replica-aware stubs distributed among multiple application servers
- JMS service scalability achieved through distributed JMS destinations and connection factories (no failover support)
- JDBC data sources load balancing achieved via clustered connection pools
- JNDI service failover provided by replication through the cluster-wide JNDI tree

In this section, we will first take a look at the various available types of load balancing, and then we'll look at each of the failover and/or replication services provided to each in a WebLogic Server cluster.

Load Balancing Algorithms

There are several algorithms that an object can use for load balancing. HTTP session state utilizes only round-robin, whereas RMI and EJB objects may use any of the algorithms:

- Round-robin—This algorithm is similar to the old token-ring concept. Each request is routed to the next WebLogic Server as we cycle through each server in the cluster. If HTTP session state clustering is enabled, this is the only load balancing algorithm available to the proxy. In general, round-robin is the recommended algorithm to use, especially if all the servers are similar (CPU, memory, other load factors, and so forth).
- Weight-based—The weight-based algorithm improves on the round-robin algorithm by taking into account a pre-assigned weight for each server. We assign a weight between 1 to 100 through the Administration Console. The proportion of the load that the server will bear is in proportion to the other servers in the cluster. For instance, if there are two servers in a cluster and one is designated at 100, and the other 75, the first server will do 25% more work than the second. When deciding on weight, take into consideration the CPU performance of each server and the number of pinned objects. (*Pinned* objects are unclustered objects that reside on that server.)
- Random—This algorithm chooses the next replica by generating a random number and then pointing to the corresponding server. It is recommended only where each server has similar processing power and each is hosting identical services. Note that there might be a small processing cost to generate a random number on every request, and a slight probability that the load will not be even over a small number of runs.

- Round-robin-affinity—This algorithm is a slight modification to the round-robin algorithm and adds server affinity between external Java clients and server instances. *Server affinity* simply means that the number of opened sockets is minimized; existing sockets are preferred over opening new ones. Failover also tries to use existing connections.
- Weight-based-affinity—This algorithm is a slight modification to the weight-based algorithm and adds server affinity between external Java clients and server instances.
- Random-affinity—This algorithm is a slight modification to the random algorithm and adds server affinity between external Java clients and server instances.

The Clusterwide JNDI Tree

Before we get into any discussion of how objects are persisted in a cluster, we should mention how objects are addressed in a cluster. A WebLogic Server cluster provides a clusterwide JNDI tree that is replicated across all the servers participating in the cluster. Although the tree is replicated on multiple servers, it appears as a single tree to a client.

The clusterwide JNDI tree is used to access both replicated and pinned objects. *Pinned objects* are those components that are hosted on a server that participates in a cluster, but is itself not replicated in the cluster. Because of this, if the server that hosts a pinned object goes down, the object will no longer be accessible to other servers in the cluster. For replicated objects, clients look up the object on the clusterwide JNDI tree and obtain its replica-aware stub (more on replica-aware stubs later in the chapter). The stub contains the list of server instances that hosting the object and based on its load-balancing algorithm connects the client to it.

HTTP Session State Replication

Imagine, if you will, a Web application that provides online auto insurance. A customer is connected to the Web server hosting the application, filling out forms and continuing through a number of pages. The information gathered from this user is stored in an HTTP session object on the application server. Now imagine that as the user nears the completion of the forms, there is a server failure. What will happen to the user's information? Is his data lost for good? Must he start over and re-enter all of it? If so, will he become frustrated and give up, or worse, go to a competitor's Web site? Not if his session was replicated across other servers in a clustered domain!

Web applications using servlets and JSPs achieve failover through replication of their HTTP session across the multiple servers in the cluster. Any server failure will appear transparent to the end user because his application will move to a backup server, grab the replicated session, and continue as though nothing had happened.

HTTP sessions may be persisted in one of five different ways:

- None (in-memory on a single server)
- In a file
- In a JDBC-compliant database
- In client-side cookies
- In memory replicated across a cluster

It is the memory-based replication across a cluster that is of interest to us, and we will cover that in detail, but before we go into the details, we'll go over the other four approaches to persistence and explain the pros and cons of each.

None (Local Memory Session Persistence)

Memory-based persistence on a single server really provides no persistence at all. The HTTP session information is stored only in that server's active memory. Performance is terrific, but the obvious drawback is that if the server should go down or run out of memory, the session information will be lost.

To set memory-based persistence, you modify the WebLogic-specific deployment descriptor `weblogic.xml`. Under the `<session-descriptor>` element, set the `PersistentStoreType` property to `memory`, as in the following:


```
<session-descriptor>
 <session-param>
  <param-name>
   PersistentStoreType
  </param-name>
  <param-value>
   memory
  </param-value>
 </session-param>
</session-descriptor>
```

File-Based Session Persistence

In file-based session persistence, HTTP session information is written out to a file on the local workstation. Performance is not as good as in-memory persistence because it is writing session information to the disk, but you get good reliability.

File-Based persistence is configured in the WebLogic-specific deployment descriptor `weblogic.xml`. Under the `<session-descriptor>` element, set the `PersistentStoreType` property to `file` and define a persistent store directory for file output in the `PersistentStoreDir` property. The default directory is under the `/WEB-INF` directory of the

Web application, although you can define any directory you want to with a relative or absolute path. The <session-descriptor> for file-based memory persistence might resemble the following:

```
<session-descriptor>
 <session-param>
  <param-name>
   PersistentStoreDir
  </param-name>
  <param-value>
   session_db
  </param-value>
  <param-name>
   PersistentStoreType
  </param-name>
  <param-value>
   file
  </param-value>
 </session-param>
</session-descriptor>
```

CAUTION

You must create the file output directory (/session_db in our example) manually under the /WEB-INF directory of your Web application because WebLogic will not do it for you!

File-based persistence can also be made clusterable by sharing the output directory among the other servers in the cluster.

JDBC-Based Session Persistence

In JDBC-based session persistence, the HTTP session information is written to a JDBC-compliant database through a configured connection pool. Like file-based persistence, performance is a little less than in-memory persistence because it is writing to a database, but there is greater data integrity by having the session information in the database.

To set JDBC-based memory persistence, you again modify the WebLogic-specific deployment descriptor weblogic.xml. Under the <session-descriptor> element, set the PersistentStoreType property to jdbc and name the persistent store pool you are using for data output in the PersistentStorePool property (this example uses MyConnectionPool), as in the following example:

```
<session-descriptor>
 <session-param>
  <param-name>
```

```
    PersistentStorePool
   </param-name>
   <param-value>
    MyConnectionPool
   </param-value>
   <param-name>
    PersistentStoreType
   </param-name>
   <param-value>
    jdbc
   </param-value>
  </session-param>
</session-descriptor>
```

Cookie-Based Session Persistence

In cookie-based session persistence, the session information is written out to a cookie file on the client's workstation. It offers no performance gain over server-side file-based persistence, but keeping the data on the client-side prevents data from filling up storage space on the server. The obvious drawback is that cookies must be enabled on the client's browser. This might work for an intranet application where you know the configuration of the browser, but might not work well on the World Wide Web.

To configure cookie-based session persistence, you again modify the WebLogic-specific deployment descriptor `weblogic.xml`. Under the `<session-descriptor>` element, set the `PersistentStoreType` property to `cookie` and, optionally, name the cookie you are using for data output in the `PersistentStoreCookieName` property (this example uses `SessionCookie`), as in the following example:

```
<session-descriptor>
  <session-param>
   <param-name>
    PersistentStoreCookieName
   </param-name>
   <param-value>
    SessionCookie
   </param-value>
   <param-name>
    PersistentStoreType
   </param-name>
   <param-value>
    cookie
   </param-value>
  </session-param>
</session-descriptor>
```

CAUTION

Only `String` attributes may be stored in a cookie. Attempting to persist any other data object will throw an `IllegalArgument` exception!

In-Memory Session Replication Across a Cluster

Now we turn our attention to the most robust and fastest option for HTTP session replication: persistence across managed servers in a cluster. To whichever server the client first connects, a primary session state is created and stored in that server's memory. A replica session state is then created and stored in the memory of a second server instance in the cluster. Through a process called *in-memory replication*, the two sessions are kept concurrent. If the host server fails, the primary session fails over to the secondary session and the client proceeds unaware of the change.

The following paragraphs will show you how to use in-memory session replication in a cluster to make your Web component sessions persistent.

First, your Web components must be serializable, so you must make all of your Web components implement the `java.io.Serializable` interface.

Next, you must set up WebLogic Server to access the cluster via a proxy. There are three ways to doing this:

- Access all Web applications through the `HttpClusterServlet` on an instance of WebLogic Server
- Access all Web applications through a third-party proxy server, such as Apache, Microsoft IIS, or iPlanet, with the WebLogic Proxy plug-in
- Use a hardware load-balancing solution, such as the Alteon load balancer.

If you are using the `HttpClusterServlet`, you can configure the load-balancing algorithm from within the Administration Console, as defined earlier in the chapter. If you are using a third-party plug-in or a hardware solution, you can use the load-balancing tools provided with these servers.

Finally, we configure the application to use in-memory session replication across a cluster. In a text or XML editor, open the WebLogic-specific deployment descriptor `weblogic.xml`. Under the `<session-descriptor>` element, set the `PersistentStoreType` property to `replicated`, as in the following example:

```
<session-descriptor>
 <session-param>
  <param-name>
   PersistentStoreType
  </param-name>
```

```
    <param-value>
      replicated
    </param-value>
  </session-param>
</session-descriptor>
```

EJB and RMI Components via Replica-Aware Stubs

In a clustered environment, EJB and RMI objects are replicated and hosted on each server. When a client wants to access one of these objects, how does it know on which server to connect? The answer lies in the replica-aware stub.

Unlike a single-server environment, when a client connects to a clustered component, it is really connecting to its replica-aware stub. The replica-aware stub holds the logic to redirect the client to an EJB or RMI object on one of the servers in the cluster, based on some load-balancing algorithm. If the stub is unable to connect to one of the servers, it redirects to another and repeats the call.

Let's first take a look at how to create replica-aware stubs for our objects, and then how to configure WebLogic Server to use them in a cluster.

Compiling RMI Objects to Support Clustering

For an RMI object to support clustering, we have to compile it to create the necessary replica-aware stubs. This is done with the WebLogic RMI compiler tool, `weblogic.rmic`. The following example shows a command to create replica-aware stubs for an RMI object, `MyRMIObject`:

```
java weblogic.rmic -clusterable packagename.MyRMIObject
```

You might want to also declare additional parameters in your object, such as declaring that it is idempotent:

```
java weblogic.rmic -clusterable -methodsAreIdempotent packagename.MyRMIObject
```

When we declare an object idempotent, we are stating that if the object's method is called repeatedly, the outcome will be the same as if the method had been called only once. For instance, you would want an object that withdraws money from an account to do so only once, even if the method were called a number of times during a network or server failure.

Using `-methodsAreIdempotent` allows the RMI stubs to fail over and use load balancing. If you skip this option (if at least one method in the interface is not idempotent, you should not use it), the stub will not fail over, but will still use load balancing.

We might also want to implement the `CallRouter` interface as a way of ascribing a load-balancing algorithm to the object:

```
java weblogic.rmic -clusterable -callRouter packagename.MyRMIObject
```

36

The CallRouter interface is described in the WebLogic Cluster API. It is invoked by the clusterable stub each time a remote method is called. The interface allows the router to determine the server to which the call should be routed programmatically.

For more information on using the weblogic.rmic compiler tool, consult the BEA documentation at http://edocs.bea.com/wls/docs81/rmi/rmi_program.html.

Compiling EJB Objects to Support Clustering

The weblogic.appc compiler utility is used to create remote stubs for EJBs to be deployed in a cluster. Unlike the compilation for RMI components, replica-aware stubs will be automatically created if they are described in the EJB's deployment descriptor. Additional parameters, such as idempotence or the use of a CallRouter, may also be described in the deployment descriptor. When weblogic.appc is run on the component, these attributes are read from the weblogic-ejb-jar.xml file and automatically generated by the compiler.

For more information about using the weblogic.appc compiler tool, consult the BEA documentation at http://e-docs.bea.com/wls/docs81/ejb/implementing.html#1125457.

Clustering JDBC Connections

Although WebLogic Server does not supply specific failover capabilities for JDBC connections, it does not mean that clustering for JDBC objects is not entirely unsupported. Through the use of connection pools and multipools, we can achieve some load-balancing functionality. The steps are as follows:

1. First, we will need two or more database instances that are replicated and synchronized. (Replication is not provided by WebLogic Server and must be configured separately.) Create a connection pool to each.
2. Next add the connection pools to the cluster.
3. Now create a multipool and add the connection pools to the multipool.
4. Then add the multipool to the cluster.
5. Next, create a DataSource object and assign the name of the multipool to the Pool Name attribute.
6. Add the DataSource object to the cluster.
7. Configure the multipool for load balancing (the default is round-robin).

Now we have a load-balancing multipool configured. When a connection is requested, the data source accesses the connection pool from the multipool list in a round-robin order, instead of always calling the first connection pool in the list.

The load-balancing multipool also offers some failover support, but only prior to the start of a transaction. If the WebLogic Server instance that is already hosting the JDBC connection fails, any transaction in progress will roll back and the application will need to reconnect to the data source and start again. What multipools can do, however, is redirect us to the next connection pool in the list if the one it first tries to access is down.

HTTP Sessions and Clusters

HTTP sessions can be configured to replicate to other servers in the cluster, thereby offering failover for servlet session states. When a servlet session is initiated using the `HttpSession.getSession()` call, the session is created on the server to which the client connected. This is the primary session state and it is also replicated to a secondary server in the same WebLogic cluster. The secondary replica is kept up to date for any unforeseen failures and can be used if the primary server of the client fails. The secondary server is chosen by WebLogic Server and, by default, it tries to create the replica in a server that is not in the same physical machine as that of the primary server. Alternatively, cluster groups can be created and can be used to control the creation of secondary replicas in the server or server group you want.

To leverage in-memory replication of session state, servlets have to be accessed using either a Web server farm running WebLogic proxy plug-ins or a load director. In the first alternative, the proxy maintains information about the servers in the WebLogic cluster that hosts the Web application, and takes care of forwarding the requests to these instances using a round-robin strategy along with failover logic to identify the secondary replica in case the primary server fails.

Clustering WebLogic JMS

Earlier releases of WebLogic provided no clustering capabilities for JMS. Starting with WebLogic Server 7.0, there is failover support for JMS by enabling you to create and distribute your queue and topic messages across multiple destinations. If one server instance fails, traffic is diverted to the remaining destinations.

Configuration of a new distributed destination is done within the Administration Console. The following example will walk you through the creation of a topic:

1. Start WebLogic Server for the clustered domain, and open the Administration Console.
2. In the left panel, under Services, click on the JMS icon.
3. Click on the Distributed Destinations icon to display the links to create either a topic destination or a queue destination in the right panel, as shown in Figure 36.11.

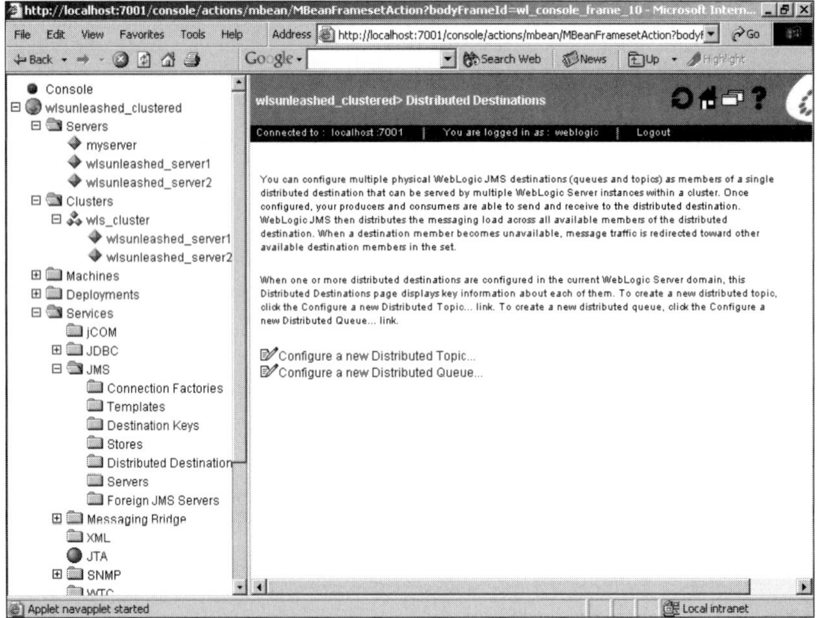

FIGURE 36.11 Create a new distributed topic or queue.

4. Click on the link Configure a New Distributed Queue. The JMS Distributed Queue configuration page is shown in the right panel. We will use the values for Name and JNDI Name as shown in Figure 36.12. The choices for the Load Balancing Policy are either Round-Robin or Random. For our example, we will use Round-Robin.

5. By clicking the Auto Deploy tab, we can define to which WebLogic Server instances we want the queue members to be automatically created. If we want to use existing queue members, we can click on the Members tab to create distributed queue members for them. Let's define a destination to create members automatically by clicking on the Auto Deploy tab, as shown in Figure 36.13.

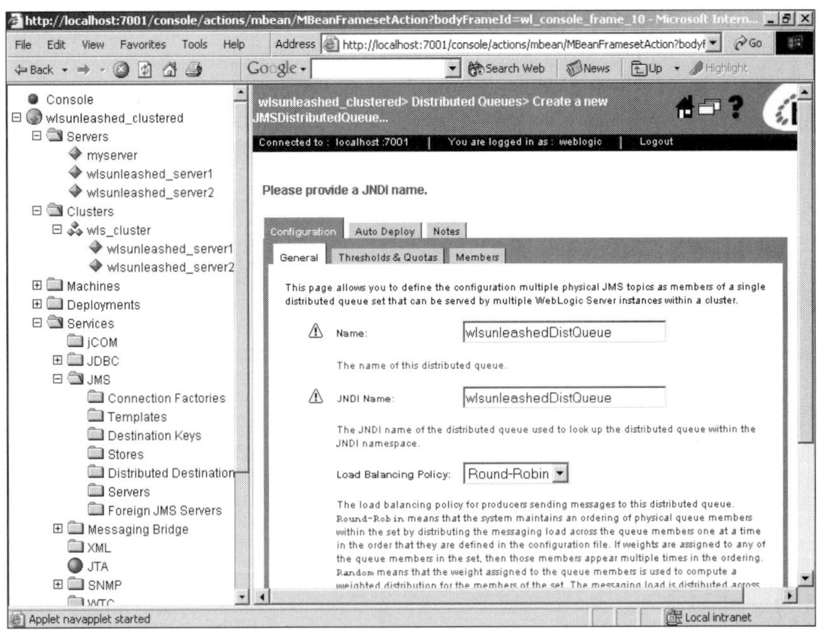

FIGURE 36.12 Configure a new distributed queue.

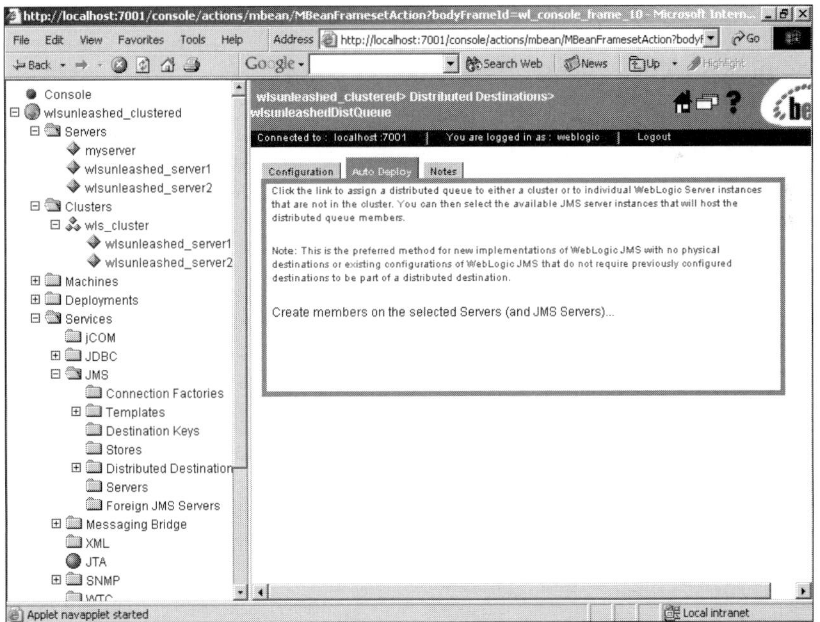

FIGURE 36.13 Creating distributed queue members automatically.

6. Click on the Create Members on the Selected Servers (and JMS Servers) link. From the list, select the cluster you want to target your topic. In our example, we'll select the cluster `wls_cluster` as shown in Figure 36.14. Click Next to continue.

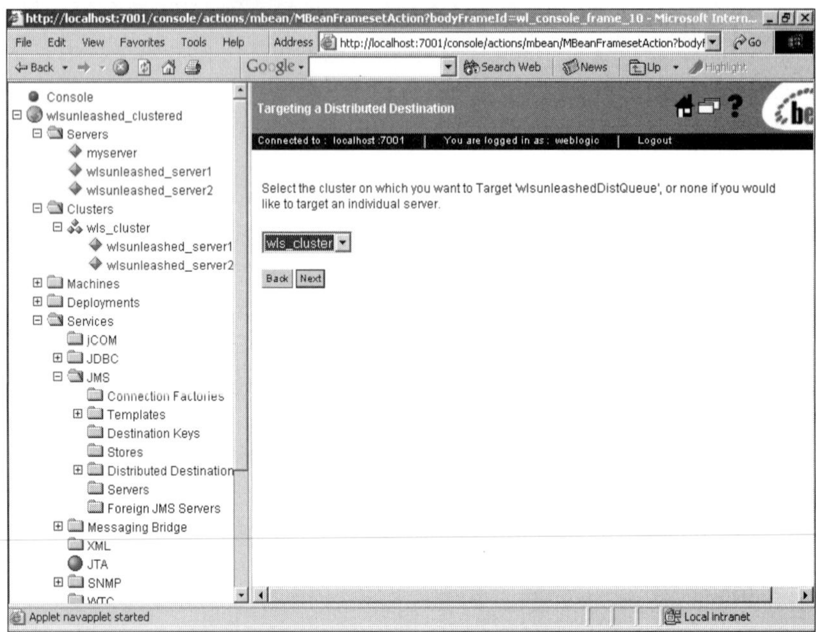

FIGURE 36.14 Select the cluster for your distributed target.

7. Next, select the servers on which you want to create your members, as shown in Figure 36.15. Click Next to continue.

8. Next, select the JMS servers on which you want to create your members, as shown in Figure 36.16.

9. Click Next to continue, and then click Apply when you're asked to commit your changes. Repeat the steps to create additional topic or queue members.

The creation of distributed topics destinations is similar to what we have just shown for queues. Consult the BEA documentation for more details: `http://e-docs.bea.com/wls/docs81/jms/implement.html#1260801`.

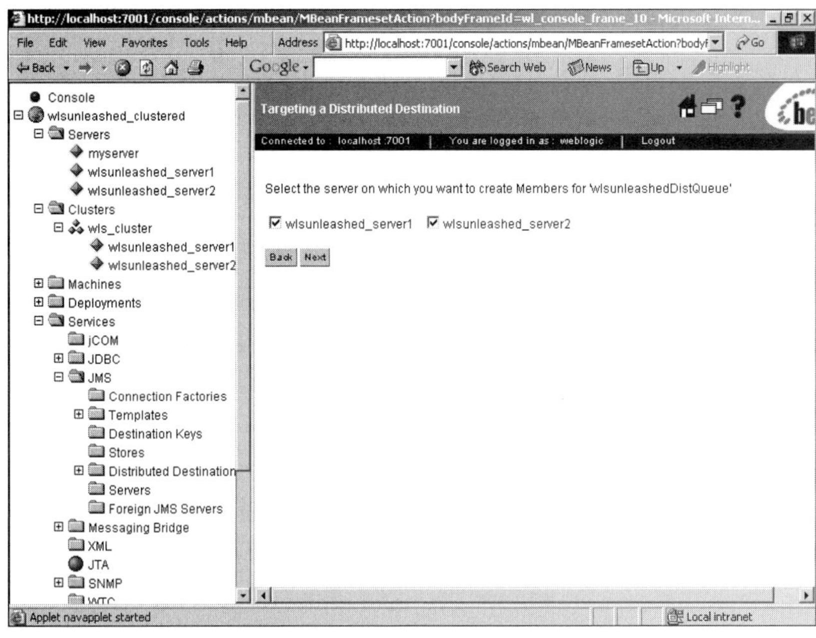

FIGURE 36.15 Select the servers on which you want to create your members.

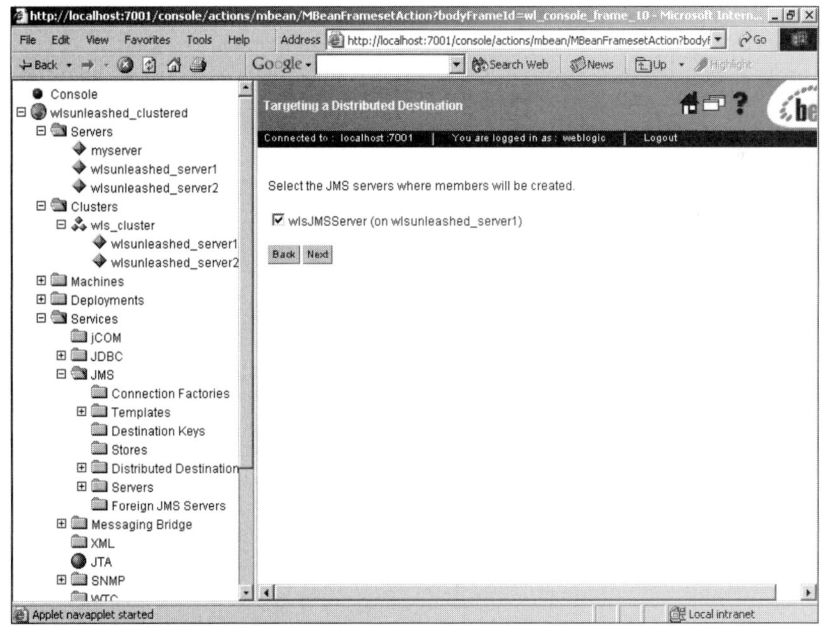

FIGURE 36.16 Select the JMS server on which you want to create your members.

Failover Support for Clustered Services

There are two mechanisms through which WebLogic can detect server failures in a cluster:

- Monitoring IP socket connections to a peer server
- Sending and receiving heartbeat messages

Failure Detection Using IP Sockets Between Peer Server Instances

When a server connects to one of its peers in a cluster through an IP socket, WebLogic Server monitors errors on that socket. Should there be an unexpected closure, the peer server is marked as failed and all of its associated services are removed from the clusterwide JNDI naming tree.

Failure Detection Using Regular Server Heartbeat Messages

If the clustered server instances are not using open sockets for peer-to-peer communication, failed servers can still be detected via the heartbeat. All server members in a cluster can use multicast to broadcast and receive heartbeat messages between other servers in the cluster. The default regular intervals are set at 10 seconds. If there are three consecutive missed heartbeats (30 seconds), the peer server is marked as failed and all of its associated services are removed from the clusterwide JNDI naming tree.

Cluster Best Practices

The law of diminishing returns applies to clustering. Each new server added to the cluster means that the original servers must synchronize their HTTP sessions and replicate their stubs on one more server. The replication messages being exchanged can build up pretty quickly to the point where I/O traffic begins to impede performance. You might find that it is better to have, say, four clusters with two nodes apiece, than to have two clusters with four nodes. In this section, well talk about several options when working with clusters and how to best optimize the way that an application is deployed on a cluster.

Single-Tier Clustering Architecture

A simple way to set up a cluster is to have the entire application deployed on each server instance. BEA calls this the *combined tier architecture*. The benefits of this architecture are

- Easy to set up—Deploying the entire application on each server is easy and can be easily automated as part of a deploy process.
- Easy to administer—Because the entire application is on each machine, you do not need to set up a separate bank of Web servers or worry about configuring proxy plug-ins.

- Load balancing—You need only one load balancer in front of your application servers.
- Security—Placing a firewall in front of your load balancer enables you to set up security with minimal firewall policies and administration.
- Performance—A cluster of this type is optimal when the presentation tier (JSPs, HTML, and so on) is lightweight, and accesses objects such as EJBs, JDBC, and so forth.

The major drawback of this sort of clustering architecture is that you add the load of processing HTML content and other presentation content on the more expensive application server. You can get better load balancing and performance by separating the servlet and HTML content onto the Web tier.

This architecture also prevents load balancing between method calls to clustered EJBs. This is generally a good idea: The container tries to use the local object's instance of making remote calls. However, if the load on one server becomes uneven, it can eventually become more efficient to take the network hit of using a remote object, rather than processing the methods using the local object.

Multitier Clustering Architecture

The concept here is to split the static HTTP content and servlets on one cluster and use another cluster for the EJBs. The advantages of this concept are

- Load balancing for method calls to clustered EJBs.
- You can have two load balancers, one for each cluster.
- Overall, this improves the availability of the system.
- You can use WebLogic Express or Tomcat to serve servlets.
- Security—You can have separate security for each cluster to further protect access to your objects by untrusted clients.

Proxy Clustering Architecture

This is probably the most commonly used architecture that we have seen. Here, we split the static content onto a Web server such as the Apache Web Server, but leave the JSPs, servlets, EJBs, and so forth on the application server. We need to configure a proxy plug-in between the Web server and the application server.

We can also combine the multitier architecture with the proxy architecture to have an MVC-like deployment architecture. In this case, the static content is on a cluster of Web servers, followed by a cluster of servlet containers that host the JSPs and servlets. Lastly, there is a cluster of application servers that run the EJBs and so on.

For more information about various clustering architectures and details on how to work with proxies, please refer to the WebLogic Server documentation at `http://edocs.bea.com/wls/docs81/cluster/planning.html#1118661`.

Summary

Creating and configuring a cluster might at first seem a daunting task, but it is well worth the effort. Clustering is an essential ingredient to building robust distributed applications, and as I have stated, it is as much an art as it is a science. You will benefit from experimenting with different configurations to find the one that best suits your individual environment and configuration.

CHAPTER **37**

Configuring Management Applications with JMX Services

by Joe McGuire and Gurpreet Singh Bhasin

IN THIS CHAPTER

- What Is JMX and Why Would You Want It?
- A Basic MBean Example
- How WebLogic Uses JMX
- JMX Notification Model and Monitors

Distributed enterprise computing environments are comprised of many different physical and virtual resources, such as the network, the servers, as well as the application components running in the environment. Success is dependent on all of these resources working together at their most efficient capacity. A major strength of distributed computing environments is their capability to scale; however, as the number of resources increases, so does the number of possible points of failure.

To avert failure, system administrators require a means to manage and monitor these resources. Those who have been doing so usually employ a variety of different protocols and services, such as SNMP (Simple Network Management Protocol), to monitor and manage their physical devices. They might also use a variety of off-the-shelf or custom-built applications and services to monitor and manage applications and systems.

This has meant that developers and system administrators have had to become proficient in a number of different protocols and systems tools that normally have a steep learning curve and/or high price tag. Fortunately, the J2EE specification provides an easy and inexpensive Java-based solution that can be applied to every resource in a distributed environment—both hardware and software.

In this chapter, we explore the Java Management Extensions (JMX) API, how it's used by WebLogic Server, and how you can use it for your own resources.

What Is JMX and Why Would You Want It?

JMX provides both the architecture and the services needed to actively administer, monitor, and manage resources. The WebLogic 8.1 distribution supports JMX version 1.0. Although it's a relatively new API, JMX is quite robust and through the use of JMX management components can be used to monitor and manage most any resource. JMX can even map to any existing management protocol, such as SNMP or HTTP.

What JMX Can Do for You

JMX allows for the administration of all resources in your environment. This is basically done by encapsulating a component in a JMX wrapper object and exposing its attributes and/or methods in a JMX server environment.

JMX provides administration services for both hardware and software components. Let's look at the services JMX provides in a little more detail:

- Hardware monitoring and management—The entire physical infrastructure can be monitored for health, performance, and failure. Such devices may include, but are not limited to, network switches, hubs and routers, Web and application servers, databases, load balancers, modems, and filers. Your JMX components can provide management logic, so that if the load on a server should become too great, you can move some of the load to a backup server. You can also configure event notifications via email or pager.
- Software monitoring and management—As with hardware, your software components can also be monitored for health, performance, and failure. Manageable resources may be EJBs, servlets, Java classes, log files, and databases. JMX components can provide you a variety of management functionality such as logging events, dynamically changing the number of connections available to a connection pool, starting and stopping applications, gathering statistics about transactions, reporting Web page hits, and triggering notifications via email or pager.

Through the use of critical event triggers, JMX can provide the capability to avert failure *before* it happens. You can program failover logic so that the applications handle themselves, send out pages, or write out data to files for human intervention.

JMX also provides you with the flexibility and control to expose as little or as much of the resource as needed. For instance, you can choose to expose the ability to start and stop a

Web server, but not to change configuration settings, or perhaps to expose a single method in an application that sends out a log file of transaction statistics.

WebLogic Server employs JMX for all of its management and monitoring functions. As we cover later in the chapter, the Administration Console and the `weblogic.Admin` utility use them exclusively.

The Structure of JMX

A Java management system requires a number of basic components configured in adherence to the JMX architecture. To understand the structure of a JMX system, it is first necessary to identify and define a few of these components:

- Managed resource—This is any resource that can be managed or monitored in some way. It might be a physical device, such as a switch or Web server, or it might be an application component or a connection pool.
- MBean—A managed resource is encapsulated into a managed bean, or MBean. Stated another way, an MBean is a Java wrapper class that contains the resource to be managed.
- MBean server—MBeans themselves require management, and this is done through an MBean server. The MBean server provides a registry for looking up MBeans.
- JMX agent—An MBean server requires a container in which to reside—that is provided by the JMX agent. The JMX agent manages the MBean server, creates MBean relationships, loads classes, and provides monitoring services.
- Management application—The management application is used to communicate with a JMX agent. This is the application through which you can interact with your managed resources. It might be a Web application such as WebLogic's Administration Console, a standalone application, or perhaps a command-line utility such as `weblogic.Admin`.

Now let's take a look at how these components work together in a JMX system.

Suppose that we have an Entity EJB running on an application server that we would like to manage in some way. We would first encapsulate our managed resource (the EJB) into a Java wrapper object (an MBean), and deploy it into WebLogic Server (the JMX agent).

The MBean must be managed by an MBean server, so we'll create an MBean server and configure it through the Administration Console. It's the job of the MBean server to manage a group of MBeans. JMX Agent runs in the WebLogic Server container and manages the MBean servers.

Finally, we create a management application that communicates through the JMX agent to manage and monitor the resource via its associated MBean. The JMX agent provides protocol adapters and connectors that allow communication between the management application and the protocols. The management interface of an MBean is exposed, without exposing a reference to the object itself, through a process called *instrumentation*.

Now that we've defined the players in a JMX system and given a high-level scenario of the management process, let's take a look at the architecture of a JMX system. The architecture of a JMX system is divided into three layers, as shown in Figure 37.1:

1. Distributed layer—This is the outermost layer from the managed resources. It's here that management applications communicate with the JMX agent through the appropriate protocol.
2. Agent layer—This is the middle layer that contains the MBean server and JMX agent. It's here that such services as monitoring, dynamic MBean loading, timer, and MBean relationships are provided.
3. Instrumentation layer—This layer contains the MBeans and is the layer closest to the resources being managed. This is where instrumentation takes place (exposing the management interface of a resource's MBean, thereby enabling manipulation of that resource).

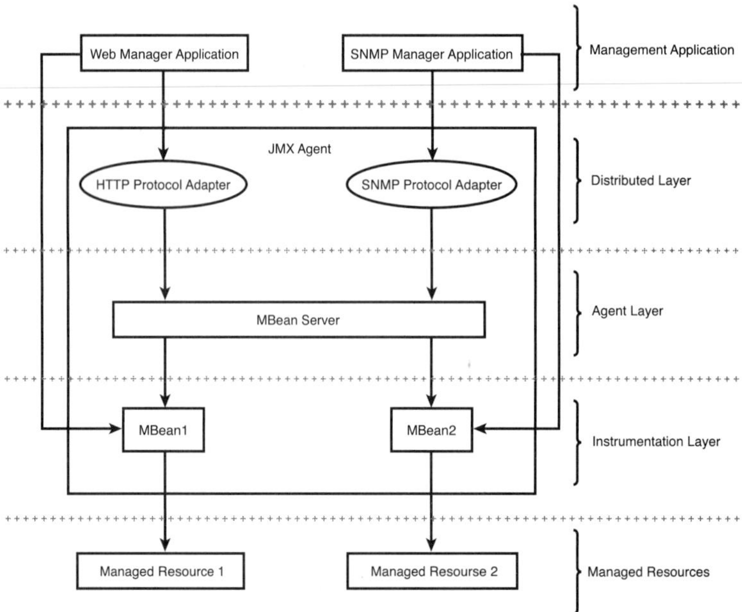

Figure 37.1 JMX architecture.

MBean Templates

There are four basic models, or templates, on which MBeans are built:

- Standard—Standard MBeans implement their own interface. The developer creates an MBean interface and the MBean class provides an implementation for its methods.
- Dynamic—Dynamic MBeans implement the `javax.management.DynamicMean` interface. This interface provides the capability for modifying resource attributes at runtime.
- Open—An Open MBean is really a Dynamic MBean, but one that uses a small set of universal Java types, or basic data types, which expose their functionality. They provide the capability for exposing and managing resources discovered at runtime.
- Model—Model MBeans are also a type of Dynamic MBean. They provide a generic template for managed resources, so users can expose info without creating new MBean classes.

It's important that you don't confuse the four MBean templates with the three functional MBean types defined by BEA: Runtime, Configuration, and Administrative MBeans. These will be covered in the next section.

A Basic MBean Example

To better understand how WebLogic uses JMX, it will be helpful to first develop our own simple Standard MBean example and see how it works. The main steps for creating a Standard MBean are as follows:

1. Write the standard MBean interface.
2. Write a class that implements the standard MBean interface. (If you want to turn some of your existing classes into MBeans, you would write a Standard MBean interface for the class and then have your class implement it.)
3. Create a JMX agent to register the MBean and manage it.

Let's go over the steps in greater detail with the use of an example. Suppose that we have a climate control application, and we also have a simple class whose only purpose is to set and get the temperature as an integer value.

The first thing we'll do is to write our MBean interface `ThermostatMBean.java`. We'll use the standard MBean template, and in it we'll define methods to set the temperature, return the temperature, and display the temperature, as in Listing 37.1.

LISTING 37.1 ThermostatMBean.java

```
public interface ThermostatMBean {

  // set the MBean's temperature value
  public void setTemp(int temp);

  // return the MBean's temperature value
  public int getTemp();

  // display the MBean's temperature value
  public void printTemp();

}
```

Next, we'll write the `Thermostat` class that provides the implementation for the MBean interface. When we speak of an MBean, we're referring to the class that implements the MBean interface. Remember that MBeans conform to the JavaBean specification, and like all JavaBeans, they should implement `java.io.Serializable`, and contain private attributes and public getter and setter methods for accessing and changing those attributes.

Our `Thermostat` class therefore implements `ThermostatMBean` and `Serializable`, and defines just one attribute, the temperature, as an integer value. We'll create two constructors: one that takes no object and defines the default temperature value at 0, and a second that takes an integer and sets the initial temperature value to that integer. Finally, we provide an implementation for the setter (`setTemp(int temp)`), getter (`getTemp()`), and display (`printTemp()`) methods in our MBean interface. The completed `Thermostat` class is shown in Listing 37.2.

LISTING 37.2 Thermostat.java

```
public class Thermostat implements ThermostatMBean, java.io.Serializable {

  // declare an integer variable for the temperature
  private int temp;

  // first constructor
  public Thermostat() {
    this.temp = 0;
  }

  // second constructor
```

LISTING 37.2 Continued

```
  public Thermostat(int temp) {
    this.temp = temp;
  }

  // set the MBean's temperature value
  public void setTemp(int temp) {
    this.temp = temp;
  }

  // return the MBean's temperature value
  public int getTemp() {
    return temp;
  }

  // print the MBean's temperature value
  public void printTemp() {
    System.out.println( "The temperature is " + temp + " degrees." );
  }

}
```

The resource we want to manage is the temperature given by the integer attribute. Now that we have our MBean, we must somehow make it available for management. To do that, we require a JMX agent.

Recall from our JMX architecture diagram that the Agent layer provides management services. The next class we create will be our JMX agent. The agent class will create an MBean server instance to contain the MBean, and will register a new instance of our `Thermostat` MBean.

Before we write the class, we must also think of how the users are going to interface with the MBean. Again, recall the architectural diagram's Distributed layer. The Distributed layer contains the protocols necessary to interact with the MBean, such as HTTP or SNMP.

We'll use a Web interface, so we want to use an HTML adaptor. But how? WebLogic's Administration Console contains the HTTP protocols in its own HTML adaptor for interacting with its MBeans but, unfortunately, it doesn't provide an implementation for our custom-made MBeans. We could spend a lot of time developing our own HTML adaptor, but that would be beyond the scope of this book.

Luckily, Sun provides a free HTML adaptor in its `com.sun.jdmk.comm` package as part of its JMX Instrumentation and Agent Reference Implementation. Note that this package is contained in the Sun JMX Reference Implementation, and is *not* part of the standard JMX

API. It contains supporting extension classes for JMX. It also contains an HTML server and protocol adaptors necessary for us to view and manage our MBean via a browser interface. To download the Reference Implementation support classes, go to the Sun Web site at

```
http://java.sun.com/products/JavaManagement/download.html
```

From the link, download the binary code in the zip file `JMX-1_1-ri.zip`. After downloading, expand the file and add the `.jar` file to your system's `CLASSPATH` statement, such as in the following script:

```
Set CLASSPATH=%CLASSPATH%;C:\jmx_1.1_ri_bin\lib\jmxri.jar;
C:\jmx_1.1_ri_bin\lib\jmxtools.jar;
```

Now we can write our JMX agent class, which also contains the HTML adaptor through which we can manage the resource in our MBean. We create a class `ThermostatAgent`, which imports the `javax.management` and `com.sun.jdmk.comm` packages:

```
import javax.management.*;
import com.sun.jdmk.comm.*;
```

Next, we create a class variable for the MBean server:

```
private MBeanServer mbs = null ;
```

Then we create the constructor, which creates the MBean server and HTML adaptor, registers and identifies the MBean, and registers and starts the HTML adaptor:

```
public ThermostatAgent() {
```

In the next line, we create the MBean server by calling the `createMBeanServer()` method of the `MBeanServerFactory` class and passing it a `String` value for the name of this agent's domain, `ThermostatAgent`. By specifying a JMX agent domain name, the JMX server is able to manage groups of MBeans belonging to that domain:

```
mbs = MBeanServerFactory.createMBeanServer("ThermostatAgent");
```

We next create the HTML adaptor:

```
HtmlAdaptorServer adaptor = new HtmlAdaptorServer();
```

Remember, we're using the Sun HTML adaptor implementation that provides not only the protocols to communicate with our MBean, but also a Web server to host the Web interface. Next, we create the `Thermostat` MBean instance:

```
Thermostat tstat = new Thermostat();
```

When registering MBeans, the MBean server needs a unique reference to every MBean it manages. We provide this by creating an instance of the `javax.management.ObjectName` class for every MBean that will be registered with that MBean server. In our example, we need two: one for the HTML adaptor (remember, it's an MBean itself) and one for our custom MBean `Thermostat`:

```
ObjectName adaptorName = null;
ObjectName thermostatName = null;
```

The MBean registrations and HTML adaptor start are done in a `try/catch` block:

```
try {
```

In the next line, we instantiate the `ObjectName` object. The MBean object name consists of two parts: the domain name and the key/value list. When we instantiated our MBean server, we defined the name of our JMX domain to be `ThermostatAgent`. The domain name really can be anything because it's used only to provide context for the JMX agent when other agents exist. This isn't related to the WebLogic Server domain entity. The second part of the object name is the key/value list. The key/value list is a mechanism to differentiate MBeans within an MBean server. It's therefore important that the key/value pairs be unique. For our example, we will define the key `name` and give it the value `thermostat1`, as in the following:

```
thermostatName = new ObjectName("ThermostatAgent:name=thermostat1");
```

We don't need to define our `adaptorName` object name because it defaults to the name of the class, `HtmlAdaptorServer`. Next, we can register our MBeans with the MBean server:

```
mbs.registerMBean(tstat, thermostatName) ;
mbs.registerMBean(adaptor, adaptorName);
```

We next set the port for the HTTP server provided in the Sun HTML adaptor. The default port is `8082`:

```
adaptor.setPort(8082);
```

Finally, we can start our HTML adaptor:

```
    adaptor.start();
  }
  catch(Exception e) {
    e.printStackTrace();
  }
}
```

Now let's create our `main()` method. The `main()` method creates a new MBean agent by calling the `ThermostatAgent()` constructor:

```
public static void main(String[] args) {
  ThermostatAgent tagent = new ThermostatAgent();
  System.out.println("ThermostatAgent is running");
}
```

The complete code for our JMX agent, `ThermostatAgent.java`, is given in Listing 37.3.

LISTING 37.3 ThermostatAgent.java

```
import javax.management.*;
import com.sun.jdmk.comm.*;

public class ThermostatAgent {

  // declare an MBean server class variable
  private MBeanServer mbs = null;

  // constructor
  public ThermostatAgent() {

    // instantiate the MBean server instance and its
        //domain "ThermostatAgent"
    mbs = MBeanServerFactory.createMBeanServer("ThermostatAgent");

    // create the HTTP protocol adaptor MBean
    HtmlAdaptorServer adaptor = new HtmlAdaptorServer();

    // create an instance of the Thermostat MBean
    Thermostat tstat = new Thermostat();

    // create the object names for both the adaptor MBean
        // and Thermostat MBean
    ObjectName adaptorName = null;
    ObjectName thermostatName = null;

    try {
      // instantiate the ObjectName instance for Thermostat MBean
      thermostatName = new ObjectName
              ("ThermostatAgent:name=thermostat1");

      // register the Thermostat MBean with the MBean server
```

LISTING 37.3 Continued

```
      mbs.registerMBean(tstat, thermostatName) ;

      // register the adaptor MBean with the MBean server
      mbs.registerMBean(adaptor, adaptorName);

      // set the adaptor's port (default = 8082)
      adaptor.setPort(8082);

      // start the Web server
      adaptor.start();
    }
    catch(Exception e) {
      e.printStackTrace();
    }
  }

  // main method calls the constructor
  public static void main(String[] args) {
    ThermostatAgent tagent = new ThermostatAgent();
    System.out.println("ThermostatAgent is running");
  }
}
```

To test our MBean, we can start the JMX agent in a command prompt window with

```
C:\>java ThermostatAgent
```

When the JMX agent is started, the Web server also starts. If you coded the example, you should see the `ThermostatAgent is running` message, as shown in Figure 37.2.

Now that the Web server and JMX agent are running, we can open up a browser window and interact with the JMX server. The URL is *`host:port`*, where *`host`* is the server name and *`port`* is the port number (default = `8082`). In our example, we use the hostname `localhost` and the default port `http://localhost:8082`, as shown in Figure 37.3.

The default page for our HTML adaptor is the Agent View. The Agent View shows the name of the domain the agent is registered on and also shows all MBeans registered within that domain. In our example, there are three MBeans: the Java management implementation `JImplementation`, the `HtmlAdaptorServer` (default name value `HtmlAdaptorServer`), and our own `Thermostat` (which we gave the unique name value `thermostat1`). The Filter by Object Name field enables you to filter the MBean list.

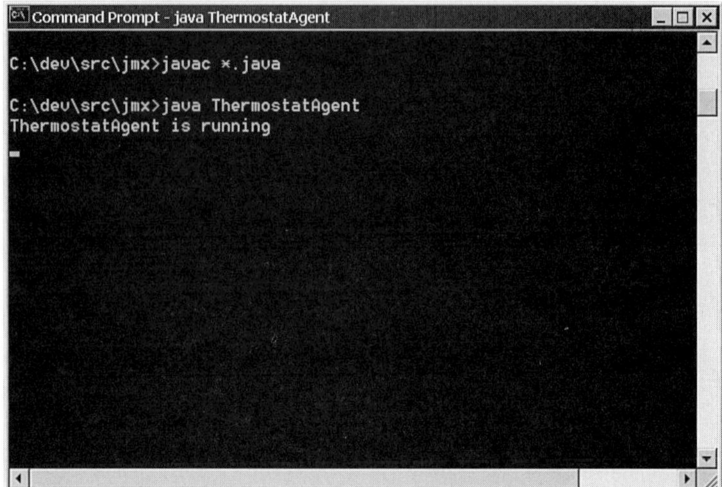

Figure 37.2 ThermostatAgent and HTTP Web server running.

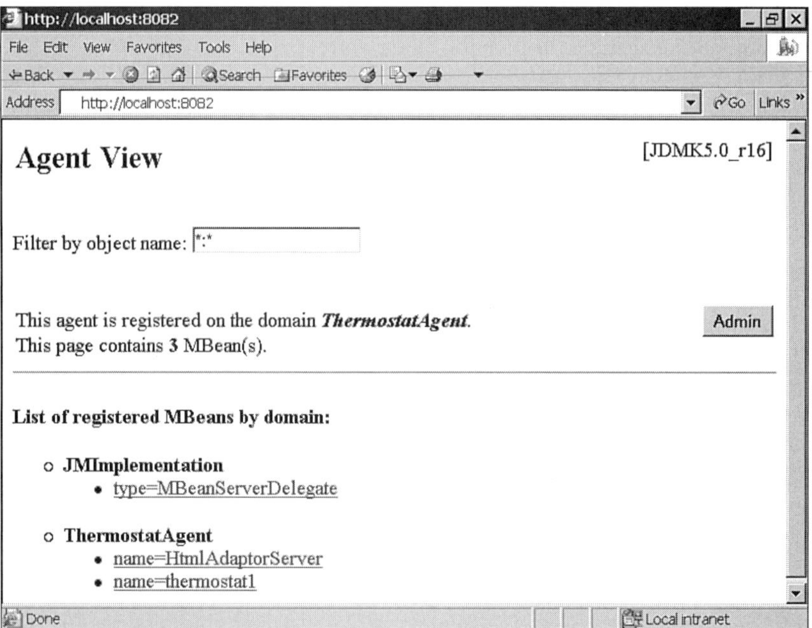

Figure 37.3 Agent View page.

From the Agent View, you can get to the MBean View pages by clicking on the name of the MBean and the Admin View page by clicking on the Admin button.

Let's take a look at the MBean View pages first. Under the `JMImplementation` domain, click on the `MBeanServerDelegate` MBean link. This will bring you to the MBean View page for `MBeanServerDelegate`. The MBean View page displays information such as the MBean's class name, its attributes, and its operations. The list of `MBeanServerDelegate`'s attributes is shown in Figure 37.4.

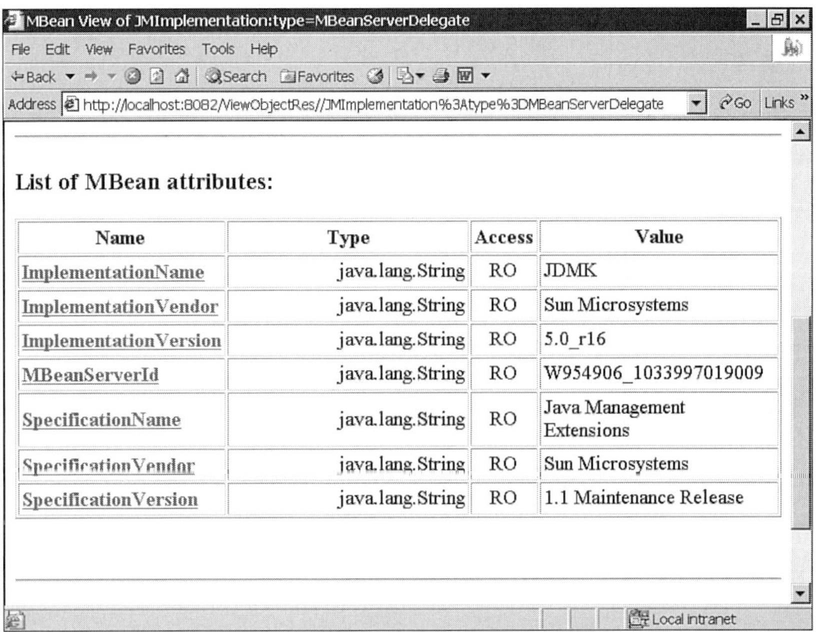

Figure 37.4 MBean attributes for MBeanServerDelegate.

The `Name` column refers to the attribute name, `Type` shows its object type, `Access` refers to read-write capability, and finally the `Value` column shows the present attribute value. Notice in the `MBeanServerDelegate` MBean that the access is read only (`RO`). This tells us that each attribute has exposed only its getter method. A write (`RW`) value would tell us that the setter method is also exposed, enabling us to change the value.

Now let's look at the MBean View page for the `HtmlAdaptorServer` MBean. From the Agent View page, click on the link for `HtmlAdaptorServer` under the `ThermostatAgent` domain. The list of `HtmlAdaptorServer`'s attributes is shown in Figure 37.5.

Notice that some of the attributes, such as `Port`, have write capability. Recall our `adaptor.setPort(8082)` method. Because we have write access to the `Port` attribute, we could change the port number on the fly from within our MBean View page.

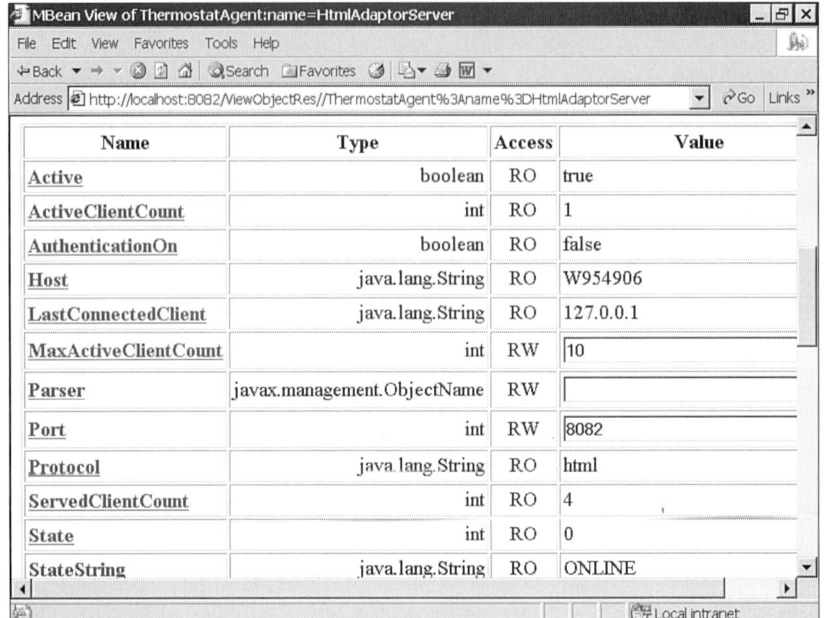

Figure 37.5 MBean attributes for the HtmlAdaptorServer MBean.

Next, let's look at the MBean View page for our `Thermostat` MBean. From the Agent View page, click on the `thermostat1` link under the `ThermostatAgent` domain. As shown in Figure 37.6, there's only one attribute, `temp`, for our temperature.

There is also one operation, `printTemp`, which we defined in our `printTemp()` method. The HTML adaptor Web page conveniently places the operation in a command button. Notice that we can change the value of the `temp` attribute to some integer, click `Apply`, and the change is committed. We can prove this by changing the default temp value of `0` to `37` and then clicking the `printTemp` operation. The `printTemp()` method is called and a confirmation page is displayed, as shown in Figure 37.7.

Proof that the value has changed can be seen in the output written to the command window, as in Figure 37.8.

We now see the statement `The temperature is 37 degrees`. You can continue to change the `temp` attribute within the HTML adaptor Web page and see the results in the command window. If you put in a noninteger value, an `InvalidAttributeValueException` error is thrown.

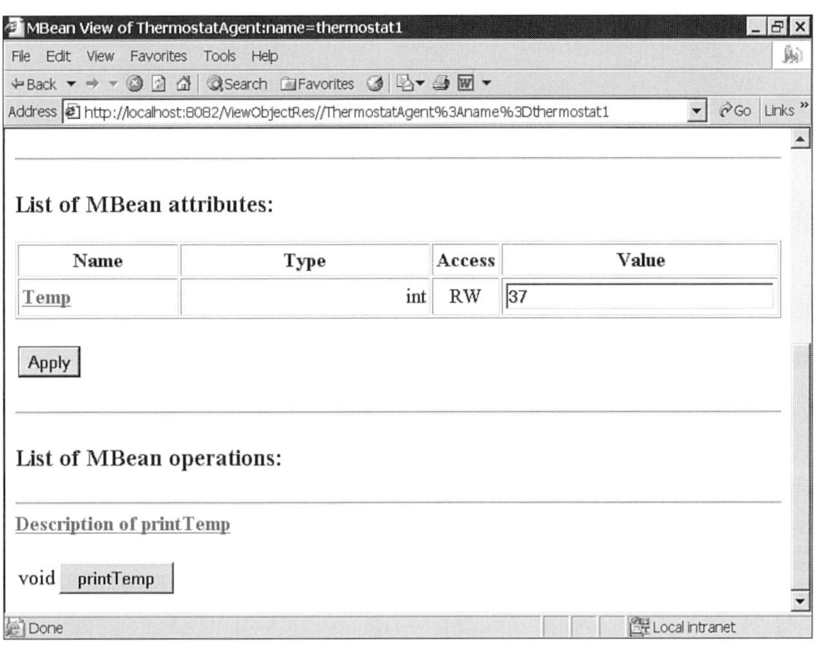

Figure 37.6 MBean attributes for the Thermostat MBean.

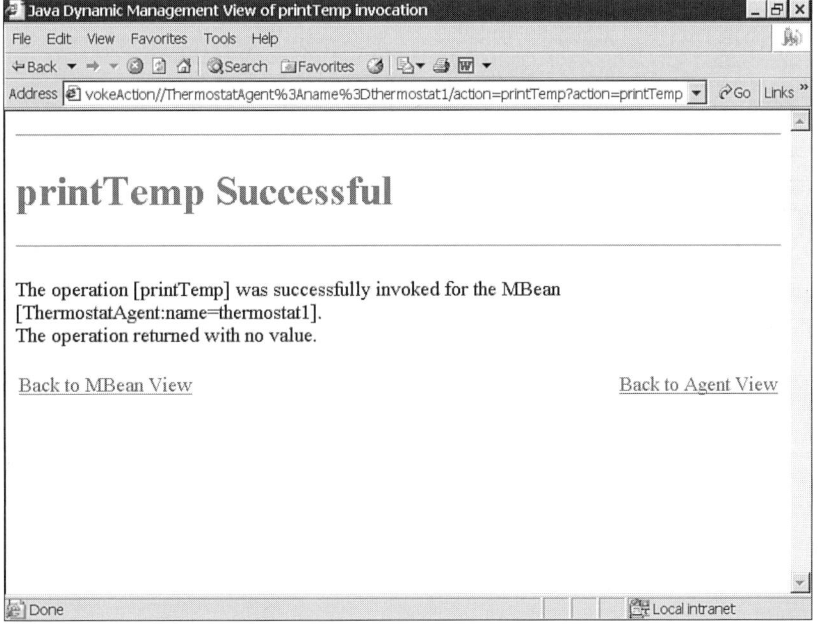

Figure 37.7 Operation Success page.

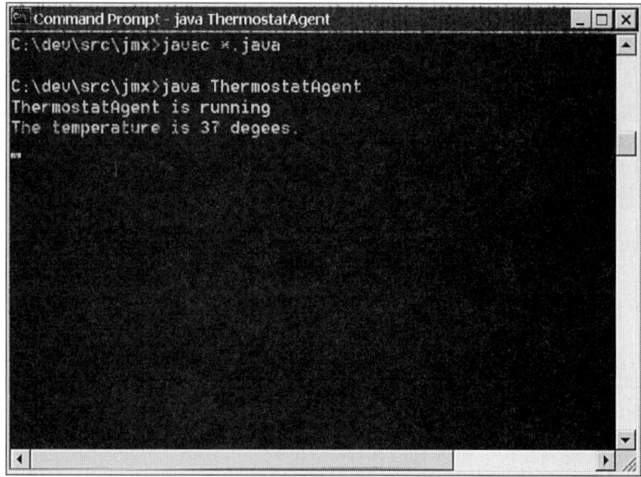

Figure 37.8 Command window confirmation.

The final page is the Admin View. From this page, you can create or unregister MBeans on the fly to the JMX agent without having to write any code. The domain name is given, and by adding the name and value as *name=value*, and specifying the Java class and class loader, you can create or unregister in the action field, as shown in Figure 37.9.

http://localhost:8082/Admin/Main/?
File Edit View Favorites Tools Help
Address http://localhost:8082/Admin/Main/?

Agent Administration [JDMK5.0_r16]

Back to Agent View

Specify the object name and java class of the MBean to add, delete or view the constructors of:
(Optionally provide a class loader name for loading the specified class.)

Domain: ThermostatAgent
Keys:
Java Class:
Class Loader:
Action: Create
Send Request Reset

Local intranet

Figure 37.9 Agent Administration View page.

Registering Custom MBeans in the WebLogic MBean Server

WebLogic has its own built-in adaptors (both HTTP and SNMP) and MBean server that you can use to manage both your own custom MBeans and WebLogic's MBeans.

In the following example, we walk through registering our `Thermostat` MBean in the WebLogic MBean server. To do this, we create a client class that registers and manages our `Thermostat` MBean in the WebLogic Server MBean server. The client will be called by a main method, and may optionally take a single `String` argument representing an integer value to set the `temp` attribute.

In a text editor, create the client class `ThermostatClient.java`.

Import the necessary classes:

```
import weblogic.management.MBeanHome;
import weblogic.management.Helper;
import weblogic.management.RemoteMBeanServer;
import javax.management.*;
```

Next, our class declaration:

```
public class ThermostatClient {
```

Now we'll declare a main function. Recall that our `Thermostat` MBean has two constructors: one empty and one that takes an integer. In our `ThermostatClient` class, we can pass to our main method either a `String` representing an integer value for the temperature or nothing. A `String` parameter will set and return the `Thermostat` MBean's `temp` attribute to that value. Passing in no parameter will return either the `Thermostat` MBean's default `temp` value (which we defined in our code as `0`) or the current attribute value if the MBean is already registered:

```
public static void main(String[] args) {
```

We now need to create an instance of the domain's administration server's `MBeanHome`. We'll do this through the use of the `weblogic.management.Helper` class. WebLogic Server provides the `Helper` class as a utility to obtain the server or administration `MBeanHome`. The `getMBean()` method in `Helper` takes the `String` values for username, password, and WebLogic Server URL, and the name of the target server in the domain. Our example uses the default username and password of `weblogic` and `weblogic`, the server's URL `t3://localhost:7001`, and the name of the target server, which we'll define as managed server `myserver`:

NOTE

The JMX specification defines standards for management objects. However, it does not provide a standard for accessing those objects. The server vendor defines how to access a particular `MBeanServer`. For example, WebLogic uses the `Helper` class for the server.

What does this do to your MBeans? They're still portable across any other J2EE server. So, you can potentially reuse them. However, the access mechanism changes on a new server.

```
MBeanHome mbh = Helper.getMBeanHome("weblogic", "weblogic",
"t3://localhost:7001", "myserver");
```

Next we use our instance of the `MBeanHome` to obtain an instance of the MBean server running in WebLogic Server. `weblogic.management.RemoteMBeanServer` implements the `javax.management.MBeanServer` class, adding the `getMBeanServer()` method:

```
RemoteMBeanServer mbs = mbh.getMBeanServer();
```

We can then call on the many methods contained in the `javax.management.MBeanServer` parent class to manage the MBean.

Now create an instance of our `Thermostat` MBean:

```
Thermostat tstat = new Thermostat();
```

Then create the object name for the `Thermostat` MBean:

```
ObjectName thermostatName = null;
```

Now, in a `try/catch` block, we perform the steps to register our MBean with the WebLogic MBean server. We first instantiate our `ObjectName`:

```
try {
  thermostatName = new ObjectName("ThermostatAgent:name=thermostat1");
```

Within the first `try/catch` block, we use another `try/catch` block to register the MBean. This will catch a `javax.management.InstanceAlreadyExistsException` error. When the MBean is registered for the first time, no parameter is sent to the `Thermostat` MBean class's constructor. The empty constructor is called and the MBean's temp attribute is set to its default value of `0`:

```
Try {
  mbs.registerMBean(tstat, thermostatName);
}
catch(InstanceAlreadyExistsException ie) {
  System.out.println("MBean ("+thermostatName+") is already registered.");
}
```

Now our `Thermostat` MBean is registered on the WebLogic MBean server. The next lines of code check whether any `String` value was passed into the main method of our `ThermostatClient` class, and if so, change the `temp` attribute of the `Thermostat` MBean. This is done in another `try/catch` block to catch an `ArrayIndexOutOfBoundsException` error. If there is a passed-in parameter, the code will parse it for its `Integer` value. Remember, MBeans are managed through the MBean server. To change a runtime attribute value, we use the `setAttribute` method of the MBean server instance, passing it in the `ObjectName` value of the MBean, and an instance of the `Attribute` class.

The `Attribute` class is an object that contains the `String` value for the name of the attribute you want to modify along with the new value to which you want it changed. The parameters sent to the `Attribute`'s constructor are important, and the source of some confusion. Let's look at the first parameter for `Attribute`'s constructor, the `String` name of the attribute we want to manage in our MBean class.

In our example, we want to manage the attribute for the temperature. The `String` name we want to pass to the constructor is `Temp`. Recall that in our MBean we defined the private attribute with a lowercase letter *t*, as in `temp`. However, the name we're passing comes from the `String` value parsed from the public method, `setTemp`, *not* the attribute name of the lowercase `temp`! It's from `setTemp` that we therefore need the uppercase `Temp`.

Now let's take a look at the second parameter that we pass to `Attribute`'s constructor. This is the `Object` value that we want to change the MBean attribute. The key here is *Object value*. `Attribute`'s constructor takes an instance of the super class `Object`, but not primitives, such as `int`. That's no problem if you're dealing with an `Object`, like a `String` value. But the `temp` attribute in our MBean is the primitive `int`. Therefore, we must first convert the `String` argument passed into the client's main method into the `Object` class `Integer` instead of an `int`. We then pass the `Integer` value to `Attribute`'s constructor. When passed to the MBean's constructor or `setTemp()` method, the `Integer` value will downcast appropriately to `int`.

Now that we've defined our `Attribute` object, we can modify our MBean via the MBean server's `setAttribute` method:

```
try {
  if(args[0]!=null) {
    Integer i = new Integer(args[0]);
    Attribute att = new Attribute("Temp", i);
    mbs.setAttribute(thermostatName, att);
  }
}
catch(ArrayIndexOutOfBoundsException ae) {
}
```

If no argument is passed to the client's main method, the attribute will not be modified.

Next we print out the current value of our `Thermostat` MBean's temperature value by invoking the `getAttribute()` method on the MBean server. The `getAttribute()` method takes two parameters: the ObjectName value `thermostatName`, and the `String` name of the attribute we want to get, `Temp`:

```
      System.out.println("Temperature =
➥("+thermostatName+") from MBeanServer = "+ mbs.getAttribute
(thermostatName, "Temp"));
catch(Exception e) {
  e.printStackTrace();
}
```

The `getAttribute()` method, which `RemoteMBeanServer` inherits from `MBeanServer`, returns an object of type `Object`.

To unregister the MBean from the MBean server, we call the `unregisterMBean` method on the MBean server instance, passing the `ObjectName` as the parameter, such as:

```
mbs.unregisterMBean(thermostatName);
```

You might want to comment out the `unregisterMBean` method while you're testing. The finished `ThermostatClient` class is given in Listing 37.4.

LISTING 37.4 ThermostatClient.java

```
import weblogic.management.MBeanHome;
import weblogic.management.Helper;
import weblogic.management.RemoteMBeanServer;
import javax.management.*;

public class ThermostatClient {

  public static void main(String[] args) {

    MBeanHome mbh = Helper.getMBeanHome("weblogic",
➥"weblogic", "t3://localhost:7001", "myserver");
    RemoteMBeanServer mbs = mbh.getMBeanServer();

    Thermostat tstat = new Thermostat();

    ObjectName thermostatName = null;

    try {
      thermostatName = new ObjectName("ThermostatDomain
                       :Name=thermostat1");
```

LISTING 37.4 Continued

```
      try {
        mbs.registerMBean(tstat, thermostatName);
      }
      catch(InstanceAlreadyExistsException ie) {
        System.out.println("MBean ("+thermostatName+") is already
➥registered.");
      }

      try {
        if(args[0]!=null) {
          Integer i = new Integer(args[0]);
          Attribute att = new Attribute("Temp", i);
          mbs.setAttribute(thermostatName, att);
              }
      }
      catch(ArrayIndexOutOfBoundsException ae) {
      }

      System.out.println("Temperature = ("+thermostatName+")
➥from MBeanServer = " + mbs.getAttribute(thermostatName, "Temp"));

      //mbs.unregisterMBean(thermostatName);
    }
    catch(Exception e)
    {
      e.printStackTrace();
    }

  }

}
```

Now let's test the ThermostatClient application in a running instance of WebLogic Server. The following steps register the `Thermostat` MBean on the WebLogic's MBean server instance, and enable us to test our client application:

1. First, be sure that you've added our custom `Thermostat` classes in the WebLogic Server startup classpath.
2. Now start your WebLogic Server.
3. Open a new command window, and run the `ThermostatClient` application.

We have defined the usage as `java ThermostatClient [integer]`

```
C:\dev\src\jmx>java ThermostatClient
```

When `ThermostatClient` is first registered, it sets the `Thermostat` MBean's initial value to `0`. If a value was passed to the client's main method, the `setAttribute` method is run on the MBean server instance, and the attribute is then assigned that value. In Figure 37.10, we see the result when no initial value was passed in (`0`).

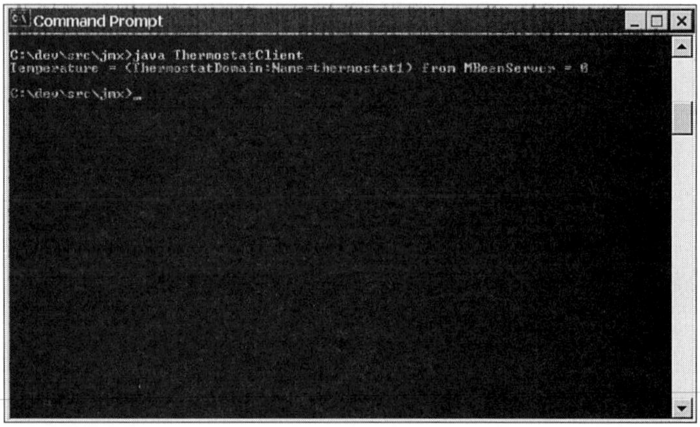

```
C:\dev\src\jmx>java ThermostatClient
Temperature = (ThermostatDomain:Name=thermostat1) from MBeanServer = 0

C:\dev\src\jmx>
```

Figure 37.10 Initial Thermostat MBean report.

If you've commented out the `unregisterMBean` method, the MBean remains registered on the MBean server. We can run the ThermostatClient application again, this time passing in a new temperature value to change it to. The application will report that the MBean is already registered, change the `Thermostat` MBean's temperature attribute to the new value, and then report the attribute's new value, as shown in Figure 37.11.

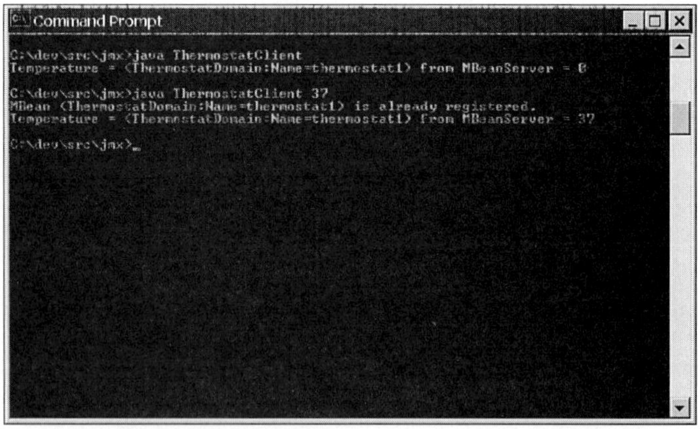

```
C:\dev\src\jmx>java ThermostatClient
Temperature = (ThermostatDomain:Name=thermostat1) from MBeanServer = 0

C:\dev\src\jmx>java ThermostatClient 37
MBean (ThermostatDomain:Name=thermostat1) is already registered.
Temperature = (ThermostatDomain:Name=thermostat1) from MBeanServer = 37

C:\dev\src\jmx>
```

Figure 37.11 Subsequent Thermostat MBean report.

We've now seen how to create our own custom MBeans, register them in the WebLogic Server MBean server, and run a client that interacts with the MBean via the MBean server. In the next section, we look at how WebLogic Server uses JMX objects to manage its own resources, and how we can access WebLogic Server's own MBeans to use them in our own monitoring applications.

How WebLogic Uses JMX

Every subsystem and component that comprises WebLogic Server is a resource and, as such, can be managed. Whether it's a mail session, a JMS server, or a connection pool, WebLogic Server uses a JMX object to manage it. Take a look in the Administration Console and click behind one of the question mark icons that appear next to every field and component. A pop-up box is displayed that shows not only what the item is, but also its associated MBean. Similarly, the `weblogic.Admin` utility also calls upon MBeans to manage resources.

WebLogic Server MBeans

To manage and monitor its resources, WebLogic Server defines and utilizes numerous types of MBeans:

- Configuration MBeans—These are simply MBeans used for managing resources. Attributes are exposed through getter (read) and setter (write) methods. In addition, operations may be called by exposing the appropriate methods.
- Runtime MBeans—These are MBeans that return real-time data about the resources being managed in a running domain. They are typically read-only.

Configuration MBeans

Configuration MBeans are used to manage resources in a domain. WebLogic Server employs two different kinds of configuration MBeans to enhance performance as well as manage changes between an administrative and managed server.

In a typical scenario of one administration server with one or more managed servers, the administration server employs its own configuration MBeans, or *Administrative* MBeans, to manage its resources. These MBeans are then replicated to each managed server in the domain. The MBean replicas hosted on the managed servers are *Local Configuration* MBeans.

It's important to distinguish between the two beans. Changes to the Administration MBean properties are domainwide and persisted in the `config.xml` file. Changes made to Local Configuration MBeans are temporary, and apply only to the current session. Both Administrative and Local Configuration MBeans may be viewed or modified via the `weblogic.Admin` utility, or by calling the MBean's getter or setter methods; however, only Administrative MBeans may be viewed or changed with the Administration Console. To change a Local Configuration MBean value, you can use the `weblogic.Server` options in the managed server's startup script.

Runtime MBeans

Runtime MBeans are used to return the performance data of resources in a running domain. Runtime MBeans on the administration server are not replicated to other domain members, and each server in the domain has its own set of Runtime MBeans. It's also important to note that Runtime MBeans pertain only to the current state, and therefore are not persisted. Runtime MBeans may be viewed or changed in the `weblogic.Admin` utility, the Administration Console, or programmatically via the JMX API.

The WebLogic JMX Extensions

WebLogic provides hundreds of MBeans that manage all of its resources, and these MBeans all extend WebLogic's own set of JMX extensions. These MBeans map roughly to the objects available in the WLS console. The WebLogic Server set of management extensions, `weblogic.management`, extends the `javax.management` API. When used to manage resources in WebLogic, they add a great deal of functionality to the Sun API; however, because WebLogic's management extensions are hidden, you cannot use them in your own custom MBeans. The WebLogic extensions enable you to persist changes to the `config.xml` file, or to receive remote MBean notification events on an application running in a different JVM than the WebLogic Server JVM.

Accessing WebLogic Server MBeans

Now that we've seen some of the different kinds of MBeans defined in WebLogic Server, let's look at how we can access and manage resources with those MBeans. To get an idea of the many different WebLogic MBeans available to you, refer to the `weblogic.management.WebLogicMBean` interface in the WebLogic Server API. Its subinterfaces are MBeans that contain the many resources you can manage.

NOTE

The following URL provides more API information about WebLogic MBeans:

`http://e-docs.bea.com/wls/docs81/javadocs/index.html`

Just remember that the MBeans are under the `Weblogic.management` package.

For our example, we'll do something simple, such as retrieve the administration server's state and the host and port it's listening on. To do so, we make use of the `weblogic.management.runtime.ServerRuntimeMBean`. The `ServerRuntimeMBean`'s `getState()` method returns a `String` value for the state of the server. Its `getAdminServerHost()` method returns a `String` value for the name of the host it's listening on, and its `getAdminServerListenPort()` returns an `int` value for the listening port.

In a text editor, create and save a file `WLSMBeanClient.java`.

First, import the necessary file packages:

```
import weblogic.management.MBeanHome;
import weblogic.management.Helper;
import weblogic.management.runtime.ServerRuntimeMBean;
import javax.management.*;
```

We then need to determine which interface is best to access our MBean. If your application is accessing only WebLogic Server MBeans, you have the choice to use the WebLogic `MBeanHome` interface or the standard JMX compliant `MBeanServer` interface. An application that manages any custom MBeans, or may be used in a container other than WebLogic Server, needs to use the `javax.management.MBeanServer` interface. Because our application is accessing only a WebLogic Server MBean, we'll use the more convenient `weblogic.management.MBeanHome` class.

Each server in a WebLogic Server domain contains its own instance of `MBeanHome`. The `MBeanHome` on an administration server, however, has access to all the MBeans on all server instances in the domain. If we need to access an Administration MBean or MBeans distributed on more than one WebLogic Server instance, we would use the Administration `MBeanHome`. If your MBean manages a resource on only one managed server instance, you have the choice to use the local server `MBeanHome`. The local `MBeanHome` connects you directly to the MBean on the managed server instance, and thus is a little more efficient than routing through the administration server.

In our example, we're accessing an MBean running on the administration server, so we'll use the Administration `MBeanHome` interface. There are two ways in which we can retrieve the `MBeanHome` interface. We can either use the standard JNDI lookup or a utility class provided by WebLogic, the `weblogic.management.Helper` class. We'll take the easy approach and use the `Helper` class. The `Helper` class defines two methods: `getAdminMBeanHome()` to get an administration MBeanHome instance and `getMBeanHome()` to get a local `MBeanHome` instance.

For our example, we'll define a main method and create an instance of our Administration MBean home where `weblogic` is the admin username, `weblogic` is the password, and `t3://localhost:7001` is the URL:

```
public static void main(String[] args) {
  try {

    MBeanHome mbh = Helper.getAdminMBeanHome("weblogic", "weblogic",
➥"t3://localhost:7001");
```

Now that we have an instance of our `MBeanHome`, we can create an instance of the `ServerRuntimeMBean` MBean from it. The `getRuntimeMBean()` method takes two `String` parameters: The first is the name of the server instance the MBean is resident on and the second is the WebLogic MBean's type.

A quick note on MBean types: Knowing and declaring the type are essential to creating instances of WebLogic Server MBeans. However, it isn't always clear what type the MBean you want actually is. The MBean type is normally derived from the MBean class, less the MBean suffix. Thus, type ServerRuntime is derived from the class name ServerRuntimeMBean. Had we been looking to access a ServletRuntimeMBean, its type would be ServletRuntime, and so forth. This is not, however, a hard-and-fast rule. Configuration MBeans, for instance, often add a -Config suffix to the MBean root name. So, the type of ServerMBean (a configuration MBean) would be ServerConfig.

For our client example, we'll pass in to the getRuntimeMBean() method the default name myserver for the domain's administration server. The second parameter to pass is the type of MBean it's creating, which in our example will be the ServerRuntime type:

```
ServerRuntimeMBean wlmb = (ServerRuntimeMBean)mbh.getRuntimeMBean
➥("myserver", "ServerRuntime");
```

Now we can call methods on the ServerRuntimeMBean MBean, such as getState(), getAdminServerHost(), and getAdminServerListenPort():

```
System.out.println("The admin server's current state is " + wlmb.getState() + ".");
System.out.println("The admin server is listening for connections on " +
➥wlmb.getAdminServerHost() + ":" + wlmb.getAdminServerListenPort() + ".");
```

You can then end the try/catch block and the main method. The complete WLSMBeanClient.java class is given in Listing 37.5.

LISTING 37.5 WLSMBeanClient.java

```
import weblogic.management.MBeanHome;
import weblogic.management.Helper;
import weblogic.management.runtime.ServerRuntimeMBean;
import javax.management.*;

public class WLSMBeanClient.java {

  public static void main(String[] args) {
    try {
      MBeanHome mbh = Helper.getAdminMBeanHome("weblogic", "weblogic",
➥"t3://localhost:7001");
      ServerRuntimeMBean wlmb = (ServerRuntimeMBean)mbh.getRuntimeMBean
➥("myserver", "ServerRuntime");
      System.out.println("The admin server's current state is " +
➥ wlmb.getState() + ".");
      System.out.println("The admin server is listening for connections on "
➥+wlmb.getAdminServerHost() + ":" + wlmb.getAdminServerListenPort() + ".");
```

LISTING 37.5 Continued

```
    }     catch(Exception e)
    {
      e.printStackTrace();
    }
  }
}
```

Now let's test the client application in a running instance of WebLogic Server. Start your WebLogic Server. Then open a new command window, and run the `WLSMBeanClient` application:

```
C:\dev\src\jmx>java WLSMBeanClient
```

The application will create an instance of the administration server's MBeanHome and an instance of its `ServerRuntimeMBean` from which you can manage its resources. In Figure 37.12, we see the output of our client application, showing the state of the administration server and the address and port it's listening on.

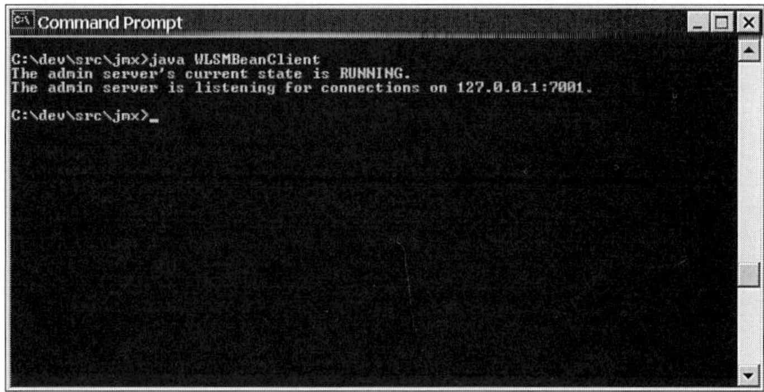

Figure 37.12 Calling methods on the ServerRuntimeMBean.

JMX Notification Model and Monitors

We have thus far described the JMX architecture, built our own custom MBeans, accessed WebLogic MBeans, and learned how to manage those MBeans in an MBean server. Now we'll add the last major component to our discussion of JMX and WebLogic Server: JMX MBean notifications.

The JMX notification model is built on the Java event model. Client applications are registered as notification listeners with MBeans that are event broadcasters through the implementation of certain interfaces. Triggered by events, the broadcasting MBean sends a notification object to all registered listeners. An additional class, the notification filter, can be used to filter events based on certain parameters.

The JMX specification restricts all registered listeners to be running within the same JVM as the MBean broadcaster. The WebLogic extensions expand on the JMX specification through the use of its `RemoteNotificationListener` class, which can receive event objects from outside the JVM.

The Notification Broadcaster

To illustrate, we'll create a simple example using a notification broadcaster, a notification object, and a registered notification listener. We will return to our `Thermostat` MBean example. Because it's the job of the MBean to send its own notifications, we'll make our `Thermostat` MBean a notification broadcaster.

All WebLogic MBeans are already notification broadcasters because they implement the `javax.management.NotificationBroadcaster` interface. However, if you want to make your own custom MBean a notification broadcaster, you have two ways to do so. The first is to implement the `NotificationBroadcaster` interface as WebLogic MBeans do. The other is to make it extend the `NotificationBroadcasterSupport` class. This class already implements the `NotificationBroadcaster` interface, but also includes a convenient `sendNotification()` method.

So, returning to our `Thermostat` MBean, we'll make it extend the `NotificationBroadcasterSupport` class. It will still implement its MBean interface and `Serializable`:

```
public class Thermostat extends NotificationBroadcasterSupport
    implements ThermostatMBean, java.io.Serializable {
```

The only other part the `Thermostat` MBean that must change is the `setTemp()` method. We want a notification to be generated any time the `setTemp()` method is called. The notification will be sent to any registered listeners (which we'll define in the next step). In our `setTemp()` method, we'll create a new `Notification` object.

There are a few constructors for creating a notification. In our example, the `Notification`'s constructor takes five parameters: A `String` representing the type of the notification (we'll define ours as `Thermostat.test`), the notification object source (our MBean class), a number representing the notification's sequence in the MBean (`-1` because we don't need to keep track of sequence), the current time stamp given in milliseconds, and finally a `String` representing the message (ours will include the changed temperature value). Finally, we'll call the `sendNotification()` method of the `NotificationBroadcasterSupport` class, passing it our notification:

```
public void setTemp(int temp) {
  this.temp = temp;
  String message = "The temp has been changed to " + temp + ".";
  Notification notification = new Notification(
    "Thermostat.test",
    this,
    -1,
    System.currentTimeMillis(),
    message);
  sendNotification(notification);
}
```

NOTE

The `sendNotification()` method of the `NotificationBroadcasterSupport` class will block until it receives a handback object from each registered listener indicating that all notifications were received. (Handbacks are discussed in the next section.)

That's all the modification needed to make our `Thermostat` MBean a notification broadcaster. The complete revised `Thermostat` MBean is shown in Listing 37.6.

LISTING 37.6 Thermostat.java

```
import javax.management.NotificationBroadcasterSupport;
import javax.management.Notification;

public class Thermostat extends NotificationBroadcasterSupport
    implements ThermostatMBean, java.io.Serializable {

  // declare an integer variable for the temperature
  private int temp;

  // first constructor
  public Thermostat() {
    this.temp = 0;
  }

  // second constructor
  public Thermostat(int temp) {
    this.temp = temp;
  }
```

LISTING 37.6 Continued

```
  // set the MBean's temperature value
  public void setTemp(int temp) {
    this.temp = temp;
    String message = "The temp has been changed to " + temp + ".";
    Notification notification = new Notification(
      "Thermostat.test",
      this,
      -1,
      System.currentTimeMillis(),
      message);
    sendNotification(notification);
  }

  // return the MBean's temperature value
  public int getTemp() {
    return temp;
  }

  // print the MBean's temperature value
  public void printTemp() {
    System.out.println( "The temperature is " + temp + " degrees." );
  }
}
```

The Notification Listener

Next we'll create the notification listener class. The listener class will register itself as a listener to the notification broadcaster. It receives two parameters in its `handleNotification()` method: a Notification object and an Object that represents the handback. The handback is sent back to the notification broadcaster from the listener (the broadcaster will block until its handback is returned). For our notification listener, we'll modify our `ThermostatClient` class.

Usually, you wouldn't have your listener in the same class that registers the MBean (for WebLogic MBeans, the MBean is usually already registered), but for the sake of simplicity our client will do both. Because the `addNotificationListener()` method takes a parameter that is the instance of the listener object itself (in this case, our client class), we must rearrange our `ThermostatClient` to have a main method that calls a constructor, and have the MBean registration and notification listener added in the body of the constructor. First, let's import the necessary packages:

```
import weblogic.management.MBeanHome;
import weblogic.management.Helper;
import weblogic.management.RemoteMBeanServer;
import weblogic.management.RemoteNotificationListener;
import javax.management.*;
```

In the Sun JMX specification, broadcasters can send notifications only to listeners in the same JVM. The WebLogic extensions, however, make it possible for listeners to receive remote notifications from outside its JVM. This is done by the `weblogic.management.RemoteNotificationListener` interface, which implements the `NotificationListener` interface:

```
public class ThermostatClient implements RemoteNotificationListener {
```

The `RemoteNotificationListener` is very useful for us because we're registering an MBean to run in the WebLogic Server JVM, but our listener is running in a separate JVM in its own command window.

Next we'll define our main method. The main method might or might not receive a passed-in `String` representing an integer to change the `temp` attribute. If it receives a value, it calls the constructor with it. If not, it calls the constructor with an empty `String`:

```
public static void main(String[] args) {
  try {
    // call the constructor with a value
    ThermostatClient tc = new ThermostatClient(args[0]);
  }
  catch(ArrayIndexOutOfBoundsException ae) {
    // call the constructor with an empty String
    ThermostatClient tc = new ThermostatClient("");
  }
}
```

Now our constructor statement that receives a `String`:

```
public ThermostatClient(String input) {
```

The first thing we do in the constructor is create an instance of the `MBeanHome` with the help of the `Helper` object where `weblogic` is the default username, `weblogic` is the password, `t3://localhost:7001` is the server's URL, and `myserver` is the name of the target server in the domain:

```
MBeanHome mbh = Helper.getMBeanHome("weblogic", "weblogic",
➥"t3://localhost:7001", "myserver");
```

37

Next, use the MBeanHome instance to create an instance of the RemoteMBeanServer:

```
RemoteMBeanServer mbs = mbh.getMBeanServer();
```

The following two lines create an instance of the MBean and create an empty ObjectName to reference it:

```
Thermostat tstat = new Thermostat();
ObjectName thermostatName = null;
```

In a try/catch block, we now instantiate the ObjectName:

```
try {
  thermostatName = new ObjectName("ThermostatDomain:Name=thermostat1");
```

Within that try/catch block, we register the MBean with the MBean server. We do this in its own try/catch block to catch an InstanceAlreadyExistsException:

```
try {
  mbs.registerMBean(tstat, thermostatName);
}
catch(InstanceAlreadyExistsException ie) {
  System.out.println("MBean ("+thermostatName+") is already registered.");
}
```

Now we add the notification listener to the MBean. The listener may be added by either the MBean directly or by the MBean server instance through the use of the addNotificationListener() method (which is contained in both the MBeanServer interface and the NotificationBroadcasterSupport class that the MBean extends). We'll add the listener by way of the MBean server because communication with an MBean is preferably done through the MBean server.

The MBeanServer's addNotificationListener() method takes four parameters: the ObjectName of the MBean, the listener object, the notification filter object (optional), and the handback object.

A notification filter is an object that implements the NotificationFilter class and does just what it says. Notifications are sent to the filter and those meeting certain criteria are passed to the listener. For our simple discussion, we won't use any filters, so we'll leave this null. The *handback* object is the context that's sent to the listener when a notification is emitted. In the current example, we aren't passing the context to the listener, but in other cases, we might send an object to the listener containing some data depending on the notification.

```
mbs.addNotificationListener(thermostatName, this, null, null);
```

The next block of code is the conditional statement that looks to see whether a new temperature attribute was passed into the main method. If so, it converts the `String` to an `Integer`, creates an `Attribute` object, and sends it to the MBean server to change the MBean's attribute. The `setAttribute()` method takes two parameters: the `ObjectName`, and the `Attribute`:

```
if(input != "") {
  Integer i = new Integer(input);
  Attribute att = new Attribute("Temp", i);
  mbs.setAttribute(thermostatName, att);
}
```

We can then get the new attribute from the MBean server via the `getAttribute()` method:

```
System.out.println("Temperature = ("+thermostatName+") from MBeanServer =
➥"+ mbs.getAttribute(thermostatName, "Temp"));
```

If you want your code to unregister the MBean (convenient for testing purposes), you would use the following:

```
mbs.unregisterMBean(thermostatName);
```

For this example, however, we'll keep it commented out.

Close the `try/catch` blocks, and our constructor is complete:

```
  }
  catch(Exception e) {
    e.printStackTrace();
  }
}
```


The final piece of our notification listener is to provide an implementation for the `RemoteNotificationListener`'s `handleNotification()` method. The `handleNotification()` method takes two parameters, which are received from the notification broadcaster: the notification and the handback object. We can then call methods on the notification:

```
  public void handleNotification(Notification n, Object handback) {
    System.out.println("Notification type: " + n.getType());
    System.out.println("Notification message: " + n.getMessage());
  }
}
```

The handleNotification() can be used for other tasks as well. Instead of just printing on the console, this method could be used to send an email through JavaMail if the temperature exceeded a certain tolerance level.

That's all there is to our notification listener class. The complete code is in Listing 37.7.

LISTING 37.7 ThermostatClient.java

```
import weblogic.management.MBeanHome;
import weblogic.management.Helper;
import weblogic.management.RemoteMBeanServer;
import weblogic.management.RemoteNotificationListener;
import javax.management.*;

public class ThermostatClient implements RemoteNotificationListener {

  public static void main(String[] args) {
    try {
      // call the constructor with a value
      ThermostatClient tc = new ThermostatClient(args[0]);
    }
    catch(ArrayIndexOutOfBoundsException ae) {
      // call the constructor with an empty String
      ThermostatClient tc = new ThermostatClient("");
    }
  }
  public ThermostatClient(String input) {

    // create the MBeanHome with the Helper class
    MBeanHome mbh = Helper.getMBeanHome("weblogic",
➥"weblogic", "t3://localhost:7001", "myserver");

    // create the RemoteMBeanServer with the MBeanHome
    RemoteMBeanServer mbs = mbh.getMBeanServer();

    // create an instance of the Thermostat MBean
    Thermostat tstat = new Thermostat();

    // create an empty ObjectName
    ObjectName thermostatName = null;

    try {
      // instantiate the Object name
```

LISTING 37.7 Continued

```
      thermostatName = new ObjectName
➥("ThermostatDomain:Name=thermostat1");

      try {
        // register the MBean with the RemoteMBeanServer
        mbs.registerMBean(tstat, thermostatName);
      }
      catch(InstanceAlreadyExistsException ie) {
        // alert if MBean already registered
        System.out.println("MBean ("+thermostatName+") is
➥already registered.");
      }
      mbs.addNotificationListener(thermostatName, this, null, null);
      if(input != "") {
        Integer i = new Integer(input);
        Attribute att = new Attribute("Temp", i);
        mbs.setAttribute(thermostatName, att);
      }
      System.out.println("Temperature = ("+thermostatName+")
➥from MBeanServer - "
➥+ mbs.getAttribute(thermostatName, "Temp"));
      //mbs.unregisterMBean(thermostatName);
    }
    catch(Exception e) {
      e.printStackTrace();
    }
  }

  public void handleNotification(Notification n, Object handback) {
    System.out.println("Notification type: " + n.getType());
    System.out.println("Notification message: " + n.getMessage());
  }
}
```

To test the ThermostatClient as a notification listener, start your instance of WebLogic Server. In a separate command window, set your environment classpath and run the ThermostatClient application. In Figure 37.13, I've first registered the MBean and set no initial value (`0`). I then ran it again, passing in `67`. The application changes the attribute to `67` and sends a notification to the client that has registered as a listener. The `handleNotification()` method then prints the notification's type and message:

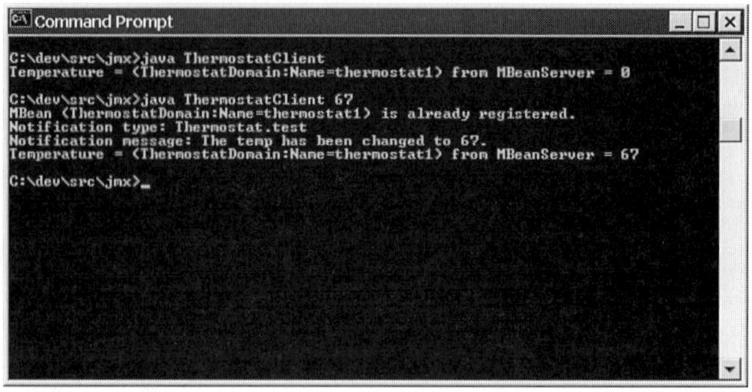

```
C:\dev\src\jmx>java ThermostatClient
Temperature = (ThermostatDomain:Name=thermostat1) from MBeanServer = 0

C:\dev\src\jmx>java ThermostatClient 67
MBean (ThermostatDomain:Name=thermostat1) is already registered.
Notification type: Thermostat.test
Notification message: The temp has been changed to 67.
Temperature = (ThermostatDomain:Name=thermostat1) from MBeanServer = 67

C:\dev\src\jmx>_
```

Figure 37.13 ThermostatClient results as notification listener.

Although this is a simple example, the notification model adds communication to your MBeans. Notifications can alert you when thresholds are met or attributes are changed, and can trigger other actions based on those notifications. A pager can be set off if the number of connection pools reaches a certain level, or perhaps the number can be dynamically increased. A log file can be written to whenever a certain Web page or application is accessed. Together, MBeans and notifications give you much more control to your environment.

Summary

The JMX API and WebLogic's JMX extensions provide a powerful platform with which to manage and monitor resources. Together they provide the system administrator a configurable set of tools for managing and monitoring of resources in a WebLogic domain. We've seen how to create our own MBeans and access WebLogic MBeans, and manage them through an interface or programmatically through the API. We've also seen how to make our MBeans communicate with us through the notification model. Although JMX is a relatively new API, it will become a powerful tool that you'll undoubtedly turn to more and more to better manage your environment.

CHAPTER 38

Administration via the Command-Line Interface

by Joseph McGuire and Gurpreet Singh Bhasin

IN THIS CHAPTER

- Administration Commands
- Command Examples and Scripts
- Using the Command Interface Commands to Build Scripts
- Using Ant with the Command-Line Interface
- Best Practices for Command-Line Interface Administration

In addition to the browser-based Administration Console, WebLogic Server also provides a command-line interface for WebLogic administration. The command-line interface is a good alternative for those who want to use command scripts, do not have access to a Web browser, or just prefer the command-line interface to the graphical user interface. In this chapter, we list the commands and discuss some examples of using them. We also list best practices for using commands and how they can help in administering WebLogic Server. We hope the examples in this chapter help you appreciate the power and ease of using the command-line interface for controlling WebLogic Server.

The material in this chapter guides the reader towards making use of the powerful command line commands that Weblogic Server 8.1 provides.

Administration Commands

Accessing the command-line interface is easy. Use the following to employ the command-line interface for administering WebLogic Server 8.1.

1. Start WebLogic Server.
2. Open a new command-prompt window.
3. Set the environment by navigating to and running the `setWLSEnv.cmd` file. This is usually located at `C:\bea\weblogic81\server\bin`, where `C:\bea` is the default installation directory (although yours might be different).

Note that my installation directory is `F:\bea\weblogic81`; therefore, the command on my machine lies on the path `F:\bea\weblogic81\server\bin`.

In this chapter, we work with the F: drive as the root directory. Your typical installation would be in the C: or D: drive. For running the scripts, you just replace the F: with C: (or D:).

To avoid confusion, please note that this is not the only installation directory in WebLogic 8.1. If you chose to install samples while installing WebLogic Server, another directory where you have a WebLogic environment-setting script is

```
C:\bea\weblogic81\samples\domains\examples
```

You might also have projects in the `C:\bea\user_projects` directory.

For the purpose of this chapter, we discuss the environment commands in reference to the directory `C:\bea\weblogic81\server\bin`. However, you could try them with any other directory.

4. Run the WebLogic Server administration command (`weblogic.Admin`) from within the command-prompt window.

Syntax

The syntax for using WebLogic Server administration commands is always in the following form:

```
java weblogic.Admin [-url URL] -username username -password password COMMAND
arguments
```

Where

- *`URL`* is the listening address of the WebLogic Server. The server could either be an administration server or a managed server.

  The format is `[`*`protocol`*`://]`*`hostname`*`:`*`port`*. The protocol is optional and the default is `t3:`. The default URL is `t3://localhost:7001`.

- *`username`* is the name of user running the command. The username should have the privileges to run the command. These privileges are assigned by the administrator. This parameter is mandatory.

- *`password`* is the password associated with the username specified in the *`-username`* argument. This parameter is mandatory.

NOTE

Commands are *not* case-sensitive.

A NOTE ON PROTOCOL SUPPORT WHILE USING THE COMMAND-LINE INTERFACE

The `url` argument of the command-line interface supports t3, HTTP, t3s, HTTPS, and IIOP protocols. The default protocol used for a nonsecured port is t3. For example, the command `java.Admin -url localhost:7001` is interpreted as `java.Admin -url t3://localhost:7001`.

For a port that is secured by Secure Sockets Layer (SSL), you can use only the t3s or HTTPS protocol.

WebLogic Server commands can be categorized in the following categories:

- Server life cycle commands
- Server state commands
- JDBC connection pool commands
- MBean management commands
- Batch command
- Cluster commands

The syntax for using commands is as follows:

```
java [-Dweblogic.security.SSL.ignoreHostnameVerifcation=true]
     [-Dweblogic.security.TrustKeyStore=DemoTrust]
     weblogic.Admin [ [-url ¦ -adminurl] [protocol://]listen-address:port]
     -username username -password password
     COMMAND-NAME arguments
```

where

- *`username`* is the name of user running the command. The username should have the privileges to run the command.
- *`password`* is the password associated with the username specified in the *`-username`* argument.
- *`COMMAND_NAME`* is the command to be run.
- *`arguments`* are parameters required for the command. Some commands have optional or no parameters.

To avoid replicating what is in the documentation for WebLogic Server 8.1, we briefly mention what each command does. We also discuss scripts where such commands can be used. For an exhaustive listing, please refer to the following link:

`http://e-docs.bea.com/wls/docs81/admin_ref/index.html`

Server Life Cycle Commands

The commands in this category are

- `START`—This command starts a managed WebLogic Server in the RUNNING mode using a node manager.
- `STARTINSTANDBY`—This command starts a managed WebLogic Server in the STANDBY mode using a node manager. This command is now deprecated.
- `SHUTDOWN`—This command is used to gracefully shut down an instance of WebLogic Server.
- `CANCELSHUTDOWN`—This command is used to cancel the `SHUTDOWN` command on a WebLogic Server. It is deprecated.
- `FORCESHUTDOWN`—This command is used to terminate a WebLogic Server without waiting for active sessions to complete (that is, it kills the process).
- `LOCK`—This command is used to prevent nonprivileged logins on a WebLogic Server. This command can be run by the administrator only. It is deprecated.
- `UNLOCK`—This command is used to unlock a WebLogic Server to allow nonprivileged logins. It is deprecated.
- `DISCOVERMANAGEDSERVER`—This command is used to re-establish control by the administrative server over the managed servers. It is useful in case the administration server goes down and when it is brought up again it is unable to maintain a connection to the managed servers in the domain.
- `RESUME`—This command changes the state of a WebLogic Server from STANDBY to RUNNING.

Server State Commands

The commands in this category are as follows:

- `HELP`—This command is used to provide usage information about other Java `weblogic.Admin` commands on the console.
- `VERSION`—This command gives the version of WebLogic Server.
- `PING`—This command is used to verify whether a WebLogic Server is running and accepting client requests.
- `GETSTATE`—This command returns the state of a WebLogic Server.
- `LIST`—This command lists the various objects on node in the JNDI tree.
- `CONNECT`—This command gives the roundtrip time to a WebLogic Server and the time the connection is maintained.

- LICENSES—Used to list the license information for the given server.
- SERVERLOG—This command displays the contents of the current log file for the given server.
- THREAD_DUMP—This command provides a detailed list of threads currently executing on WebLogic Server.

JDBC Connection Pool Commands

The commands in this category are as follows:

- EXISTS_POOL—Checks for the existence of a specific JDBC connection pool.
- TEST_POOL—This command gets a connection from a JDBC connection pool and releases it.
- CREATE_POOL—This command is used to create a JDBC connection pool.
- RESET_POOL—This command is used to close and reopen all connections in a JDBC connection pool.
- ENABLE_POOL—Enables a JDBC connection pool after it has been disabled. Deprecated; use RESUME_POOL instead.
- DISABLE_POOL—Temporarily prevents clients from accessing a connection pool. Deprecated; use SUSPEND_POOL instead.
- SUSPEND_POOL—Same as DISABLE_POOL.
- RESUME_POOL—Same as ENABLE_POOL.
- SHUTDOWN_POOL—Closes all connections in a JDBC pool. Afterward, the connection pool is undeployed from all target servers.
- DELETE_POOL—Removes the connection pool from all target servers. Afterward, the connection pool is removed from the configuration.
- DESTROY_POOL—Same as DELETE_POOL. Deprecated.

MBean Management Commands

The commands in this category are as follows:

- CREATE—Creates an instance of an administration MBean or local configuration MBean. BEA recommends that this command not be used to create local configuration MBeans.
- GET—Displays MBean attributes as name-value pairs and JMX object names.
- SET—Sets a specified attribute for a configuration MBean.

- INVOKE—Invokes a management operation on one or more MBeans.
- QUERY—This command is used to query an MBean with a given WebLogicObjectName pattern.
- DELETE—Deletes a given MBean.

Batch Command

There is only batch command for WebLogic Server 8.1: BATCHUPDATE. This command executes a sequence of weblogic.Admin commands that are specified in a text file.

Cluster Commands

The commands in this category are as follows:

- CLUSTERSTATE—Returns cluster information about a WebLogic cluster.
- STARTCLUSTER—Starts all servers in a cluster which have been configured to use a node manager.
- STOPCLUSTER—Initiates forceful shutdown of all servers in a cluster.
- VALIDATECLUSTERCONFIG—Validates cluster related elements in the config.xml file for the domain and reports errors that occur.
- MIGRATE—Migrates a JMS service or a JTA transaction recovery service to a targeted server within a server cluster.

Command Examples and Scripts

For the remainder of the chapter, we illustrate how to use some commands and scripts to make it easier to administer WebLogic.

NOTE

All command examples (except where noted) in this chapter run against WebLogic Server configured in the directory F:\bea\weblogic81\server\bin. Your installation directly might be different. Most users typically install WebLogic Server in the C:\ partition, so they have the WebLogic Server directory as C:\bea\weblogic81\server\bin.

The common requirement for running all commands is that the WebLogic server must be up and running.

HELP

I find HELP to be one of the most useful commands. If you forget a command or the category the command is in, do the following:

1. Start a new command console.
2. Set the WebLogic classpath by running `setWLSEnv.cmd`.
3. Just type **`java weblogic.Admin`**.

The command window will now show the various ways you can invoke the `HELP` command. The good thing is you don't have to remember even the `HELP` command (see Figure 38.1).

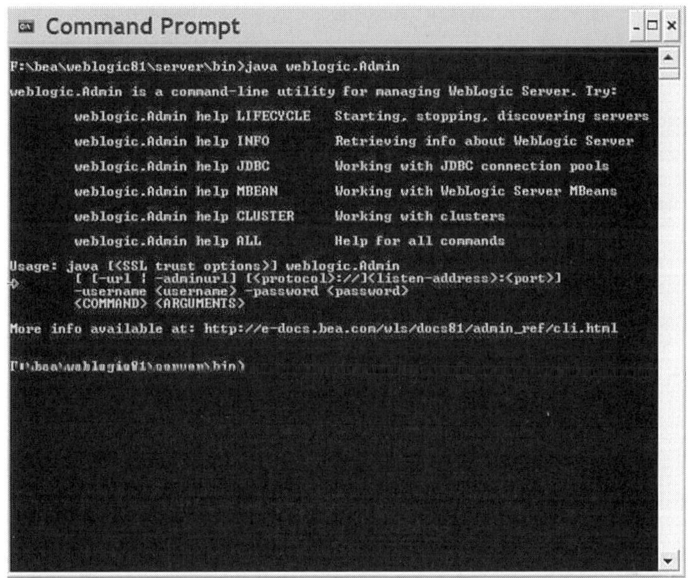

FIGURE 38.1 Running *java weblogic.Admin* without any parameters.

PING

`PING` is an extremely useful command. It is used to determine whether a given instance of WebLogic Server is up and running. It can detect the running servers and gives an error message in case of a failure of WebLogic administration server. If the administration server is not running, the Web-based console will not run and you cannot determine from the console (because the console doesn't run) whether the various managed servers in the domain are running. Figure 38.2 shows various ways you can run this command.

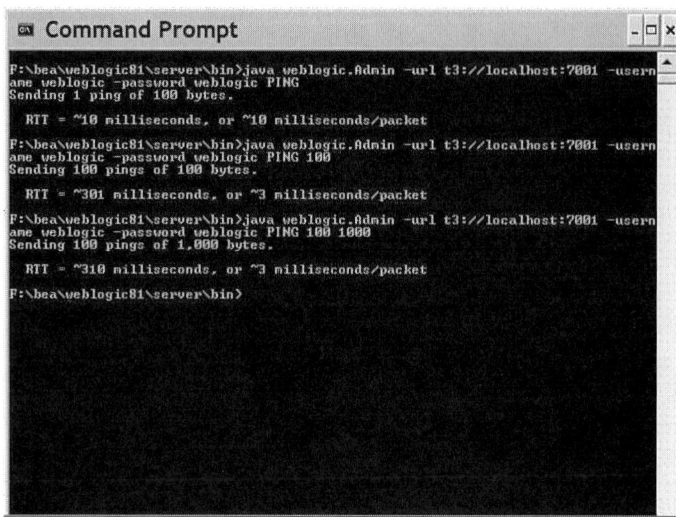

FIGURE 38.2 *PING* command issued to the administration server.

LIST

The `LIST` command is used to view the bindings of a node in the JNDI naming tree.

Because the default configuration of WebLogic Server does not have many objects in the JNDI tree, we run the `LIST` command against a sample server. This is installed in `C:\bea\user_projects\medrec`.

1. Start the MedRec server with the command **`startMedRecServer.cmd`**.
2. In a separate command window, set the classpath with the `setWLSenv.cmd`.
3. Now run the following command:

   ```
   java weblogic.Admin -url t3://localhost:7001 -username
   weblogic -password weblogic LIST
   ```

The data returned from the `LIST` command will resemble the output in Figure 38.3, showing the contents of the `examples` program that's installed by default in WebLogic Server 8.1.

THREAD_DUMP

This command provides a list of the threads currently running on a Weblogic Server instance.

In a new command window, run the following command:

```
java weblogic.Admin -url t3://localhost:7001 -username weblogic -password weblogic
THREAD_DUMP
```

FIGURE 38.3 *LIST* command issued to the administration server.

Note that the `THREAD_DUMP` command prints the thread dump in the window running WebLogic Server and not in the window where the command was issued (see Figure 38.4).

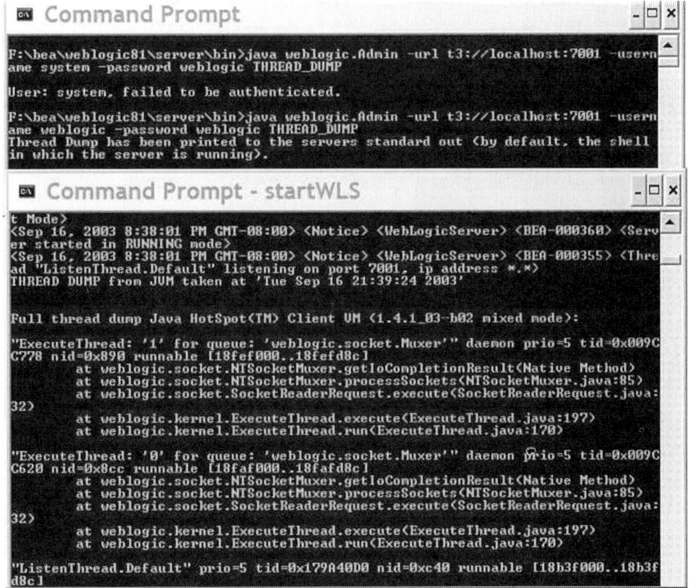

FIGURE 38.4 *THREAD_DUMP* command issued to WebLogic Server.

Using the Command Interface Commands to Build Scripts

Setting the environment and typing out the administration commands can be a test of your patience and typing skills. Luckily, we can set our environment and run our administration commands from a single command (`.cmd`) file or script. Scripts add greater management and administration efficiency, which we'll illustrate in an example.

For all the script examples, follow these common steps:

1. Start the Launch Medical Records example application by navigating to All Programs→BEA WebLogic Platform 8.1→Examples→WebLogic Server MedRec→Launch Medical Records.
2. Open a command window and navigate to `/bea/weblogic81`.

   On my machine, the full path is `F:\bea\weblogic81`. A typical path might be `C:\bea\weblogic81` or `D:\bea\weblogic81`.

> **CAUTION**
>
> The following example presupposes that you're running Windows. On Unix variants, your scripts will end in `.sh` and have different syntax.

3. In a text editor, create a new text file and save it as `getVersion.cmd`.
4. Next, we set an environment variable for the WebLogic `HOME`:

   ```
   @rem set environment variable for WebLogic Home
   set WL_HOME=F:\bea\weblogic81
   ```

5. The following line calls the `setWLSEnv.cmd` file that sets our environment:

   ```
   @rem set the environment
   call %WL_HOME%\server\bin\setWLSEnv.cmd
   ```

6. Finally, we can run the administration command. In this example, it will display the version of WebLogic Server software that the target server (denoted in the `-url` attribute) is running:

   ```
   @rem Run the Administration Command
   java weblogic.Admin -url t3://localhost:7001 -username %1 -password %2 VERSION
   ```

   Here `%1` and `%2` are parameters for the username and password, respectively.

7. Save the file as `getVersion.cmd` and save it in the location `F:\bea\weblogic81`. The content of the `getVersion.cmd` file is contained in Listing 38.1.

NOTE

We have not hard-coded the username and password in the file. This is a very important practice. The authors have seen various production environments in which the username and password were hard-coded in the scripts, thereby compromising security of the system. We strongly recommend that you use parameterized scripts as a security measure.

LISTING 38.1 getVersion.cmd

```
echo off
@rem set environment variable for WebLogic Home
set WL_HOME=F:\bea\weblogic81
@rem set the environment
call %WL_HOME%\server\bin\setWLSEnv.cmd
@rem Run the Administration Command
java weblogic.Admin -url t3://localhost:7001 -username %1 -password %2 VERSION
```

To run the script, navigate to the command file from the window and run the command as `getVersion.cmd` *`user pwd`* where *`user`* is the password for your WebLogic Server and *pwd* is the password.

The output returned in the command window will resemble the following:

```
WebLogic Server 8.1 Thu Mar 20 23:06:05 PST 2003 246620
WebLogic XMLX Module 8.1 Thu Mar 20 23:06:05 PST 2003 246620
```

NOTE

Your exact output will depend on which version of WebLogic Server software you're running and the variation of the date.

Listing 38.2 shows another very useful script. This script detects whether a given instance of WebLogic Server is running. You might wonder why you can't just check it under the Admin Console GUI through a browser. Well, if the administration server is down for whatever reason, the console will not run.

Open a new text file and copy the following text in a file called `isServerUp.cmd`.

LISTING 38.2 isServerUp.cmd

```
@echo off
@rem set environment variable for WebLogic Home
set WL_HOME=f:\bea\weblogic81
@rem set the environment
```

```
call %WL_HOME%\server\bin\setWLSEnv.cmd
@rem Run the Administration Command
echo off
java weblogic.Admin -url t3://localhost:7001 -username %1 -password %2 CONNECT
echo off
if %ERRORLEVEL% == 1 (
echo Server is DOWN.
) else (
echo Server is UP.
)
```

You can run this command as

```
isServerUp.cmd user pwd
```

where *user* is the password for WebLogic Server and *pwd* is the password.

TIP

If you do manage multiple administration servers or multiple managed servers, you might want to parameterize even the server address.

Listing 38.3 presents another script that retrieves the server log file. Please note that the `SERVERLOG` file gets only the 500 latest entries of the current log file on the server. It does not get any archived log files.

LISTING 38.3 getLog.cmd

```
@echo off
@rem set environment variable for WebLogic Home
set WL_HOME=f:\bea\weblogic81
@rem set the environment
call %WL_HOME%\server\bin\setWLSEnv.cmd
@rem Run the Administration Command
echo off
java weblogic.Admin -url t3://localhost:7001 -username %1 -password %2 SERVERLOG >
➥%3
@rem echo off
echo ERRORLEVEL =  %ERRORLEVEL%
if %ERRORLEVEL%== 0 (
echo Logs retrieval SUCCESSFUL.
) else (
echo echo Logs retrieval FAILED.
del %3.
)
```

You can run this command as

```
getLog.cmd user pwd
```

where *user* is the password for your WebLogic Server and *pwd* is the password.

Another important place where the command-line scripts are useful is managing JDBC connection pools. In the course of an application, there might be a need to suspend and then resume a JDBC connection pool. You could do this by either running the `java weblogic.Admin` commands for the JDBC pool or by enclosing these commands in a script as shown in Listing 38.4.

LISTING 38.4 bouncePool.cmd

```
@echo off
@rem set environment variable for WebLogic Home
set WL_HOME=F:\bea\weblogic81
@rem set the environment
call %WL_HOME%\server\bin\setWLSEnv.cmd
@rem Run the Administration Command
echo off
java weblogic.Admin -url t3://localhost:7001 -username %1 -password %2 SUSPEND_POOL
➥-poolName %3
pause
java weblogic.Admin -url t3://localhost:7001 -username %1 -password %2 RESUME_POOL
➥-poolName %3
```

You can run this command as

```
bouncePool.cmd user pwd poolname
```

where *user* is the password for your WebLogic Server, *pwd* is the password, and *poolname* is the connection pool.

This command suspends a JDBC connection pool and then resumes it after the user presses the Enter key. `%1` and `%2` are the values for the username and the password, and `%3` is the name of the JDBC connection pool to be suspended (and resumed).

38

NOTE

The BEA documentation incorrectly mentions that `SUSPEND_POOL` can take an optional `true` or `false` argument to determine whether to preserve the current connection pool or to destroy and re-create it. WebLogic Server SP 1 *does not* support this parameter at the time of writing this book. This is a known issue and has the BEA change request number CR100625. BEA plans to fix this bug in a future release. In the meantime, you could still use the `SUSPEND_POOL` command which defaults to the `false` behavior.

The `SHUTDOWN_POOL` command also does not take the Boolean parameters and BEA plans to fix that in the next release.

Using Ant with the Command-Line Interface

The version of Ant that ships with WebLogic Sever 8.1 has built-in tasks specific to WebLogic Server. The `wlserver` Ant task enables you to start, reboot, shut down, and connect to an existing WebLogic Server instance or create a new one. The `wlconfig` Ant task enables you to change the configuration of a WebLogic Server domain. The sample Ant script build file shows how to create and delete a connection pool in the MedRec domain that is installed when you install WebLogic Server with examples. Listing 38.5 shows a script that calls an Ant task file.

LISTING 38.5 runAntTask.cmd

```
@echo off
@rem set environment variable for WebLogic Home
set WL_HOME=f:\bea\weblogic81
@rem set the environment
call %WL_HOME%\server\bin\setWLSEnv.cmd
@rem Run the Administration Command
echo off
ant -Dusername=weblogic -Dpassword=weblogic
```

The Ant task in the preceding script calls the build file as shown in Listing 38.6.

LISTING 38.6 build.xml

```
<project name="jdbcPoolDEMO" default="delete-pool">
<target name="create-pool">
<wlconfig url="t3://localhost:7001" username="${username}" password="${password}">
<query domain="medrec" type="Server" name="MedRecServer" property="medrecserver"/>
<create type="JDBCConnectionPool" name="demoPool" property="medrecpool">
<set attribute="CapacityIncrement" value="1"/>
<set attribute="DriverName" value="com.pointbase.jdbc.jdbcUniversalDriver"/>
<set attribute="InitialCapacity" value="4"/>
<set attribute="MaxCapacity" value="15"/>
<set attribute="Password" value="MedRec"/>
<set attribute="Properties" value="user=MedRec"/>
<set attribute="RefreshMinutes" value="0"/>
<set attribute="ShrinkPeriodMinutes" value="10"/>
<set attribute="ShrinkingEnabled" value="true"/>
<set attribute="TestConnectionsOnRelease" value="false"/>
<set attribute="TestConnectionsOnReserve" value="false"/>
<set attribute="URL" value="jdbc:pointbase:server://localhost:9092/demo"/>
<set attribute="Targets" value="${medrecserver}"/>
</create>
```

```
<query domain="medrec" type="JDBCConnectionPool" property="poolName"/>
</wlconfig>
<echo> Pool created=${poolName}</echo>
</target>
<target name="delete-pool" depends="create-pool">
<wlconfig url="t3://localhost:7001" username="${username}" password="${password}">
<delete mbean="${poolName}">
</delete>
</wlconfig>
</target>
</project>
```

This Ant project first creates a JDBC connection pool by the name `demoPool` in the medrec domain and then deletes the pool.

You can run this command as

```
runAntTask.cmd user pwd
```

where *user* is the password for your WebLogic Server and *pwd* is the password. You can also call the Ant task directly.

Best Practices for Command-Line Interface Administration

All `weblogic.Admin` commands return a value of `0` in case of success and `1` in case of failure. The return value can be checked in DOS scripts with the variable `ERRORLEVEL`.

Here is an example of such usage:

```
java weblogic.Admin -url t3://localhost:7001 -username %1 -password %2 CONNECT
if ERRORLEVEL 1 echo Server is down
```

38

Using scripts and a command-line interface greatly simplifies Weblogic Server administration. When you want to stop a managed server, it is much more efficient to open a link from the Program Manager to your `stopWLS.cmd` file than to open up a browser, navigate through the interface, and stop the server.

Command scripts make the commands much more manageable and efficient. One such script that you'll want to create right away is one that gracefully shuts down WebLogic Server. Using Ctrl+C is essentially a `FORCESHUTDOWN` and, as previously stated, can cause unexpected results such as rollbacks and session loss. The contents for `stopWLS.cmd` are presented in Listing 38.7.

LISTING 38.7 stopWLS.cmd

```
echo on
@rem set environment variable for WebLogic Home
set WL_HOME=F:\bea\weblogic81
@rem set the environment
call %WL_HOME%\server\bin\setWLSEnv.cmd
@rem Run the Administration Command
java weblogic.Admin -url t3://localhost:7001 -username %1 -password %2 SHUTDOWN
```

To save yourself the step of having to open a command-window, create a shortcut for the `stopWLS.cmd` file and place it in your Program Manager group for WebLogic 8.1, alongside your `startWebLogic.cmd` link. Now whenever you want to gracefully shut down your WebLogic Server, you can do it with the click of a single icon.

Try using Ant tasks, which are portable across different operating systems. However, some system administrators are more comfortable in shell scripts or command scripts in which they do not need to have knowledge of Java and Ant.

CAUTION

Usernames and passwords should not be stored in the scripts.

Summary

Being a good WebLogic administrator means knowing the administrative commands and the command-line interface. It's a good idea to create a library of scripts for the commands that you use most often. Although the WebLogic Administrative Console provides the features you would need to control WebLogic Server, scripts have their own role and are sometimes easier to use.

PART X

Appendices

IN THIS PART

APPENDIX A

Quick Reference for Creating New Domains for WebLogic Development

by Kunal Mittal and Joe McGuire

IN THIS APPENDIX

- Creating a New WebLogic Server Domain
- Deploying an HTML Page
- Deploying a JSP
- Deploying a Servlet

You can use this appendix as a quick reference for completing the simple task of creating a new domain and deploying HTML pages, JavaServer Pages (JSPs), and servlets.

In previous versions of WebLogic Server, a default deployment structure was built during installation. The `mydomain` domain was automatically created, and a default Web application (aptly named DefaultWebApp) was installed under `mydomain`. Although completely configurable, many users retained and utilized that default domain installation for their deployments.

WebLogic Server 8.1 asks you to be a little more original. Other than the `examples` and `MedRec` domains, no custom domains or Web applications are installed during the default installation. The custom installation asks whether you want to create a new domain. If you choose the default installation, you'll have to build your own application structure—one that is best suited to you and your environment.

Creating a New WebLogic Server Domain

In this section, we outline the steps to create a new domain, thereby creating an environment to host your Web and enterprise components.

Like most people, the first thing you probably did after installing WebLogic 8.1 was to start it up to see how it works. You probably did this by starting either the MedRec application (which includes the Getting Started application) or the `examples` server. In case you've been looking for them, they're tucked away under the `%BEA_HOME%\weblogic81\samples\server` directory of your WebLogic 8 installation. That isn't a very convenient location for your own applications.

In the following steps, we'll create a new domain and default Web application directory.

Domain Creation with the Configuration Wizard

WebLogic Server 8.1 improves on previous versions by making domain creation and management easier than ever. To create a domain in WebLogic 7, you had to go through the Administration Console of a domain that was set up at installation by default, such as the `mydomain` or `MedRec` domain. This merely created a new domain directory with a bare-bones `config.xml` file. You still had to copy the `SerializedSystemIni.dat`, `fileRealm.properties`, `setEnv.cmd`, and `startWebLogic.cmd` files into your new domain directory from an existing domain directory, and then edit those command files with the new domain parameters. WebLogic Server 8.1 introduced a new utility, the Configuration Wizard, which made domain creation simple and efficient. You could still create domains through the Administration Console, but I'm sure that after you use the Configuration Wizard, you wouldn't want to create domains in any other way.

WebLogic Server 8.1 ships with a drastically improved version of the Configuration Wizard. It includes many new options for not only creating your domain, but also for customizing your server settings, such as JDBC pools, JMS queues, managed servers, and so on. We'll explore each of these options in greater detail in this appendix.

The Configuration Wizard contains templates that help you to create new domains or to extend existing domains by adding managed servers. The Configuration Wizard runs in both a GUI mode and a Console mode, but for expediency's sake, we'll look at the GUI mode for our example:

1. Start the Configuration Wizard utility. For Windows, navigate from the Start button:

   Start→Programs→BEA WebLogic Platform 8.1→Configuration Wizard

   For Unix users, open a command-line shell and navigate to the `\common\bin` subdirectory of the WebLogic Server installation and run the `dmwiz.sh` script.

2. The Configuration Wizard GUI application starts and displays a form to choose a template and name for your new domain, as shown in Figure A.1.

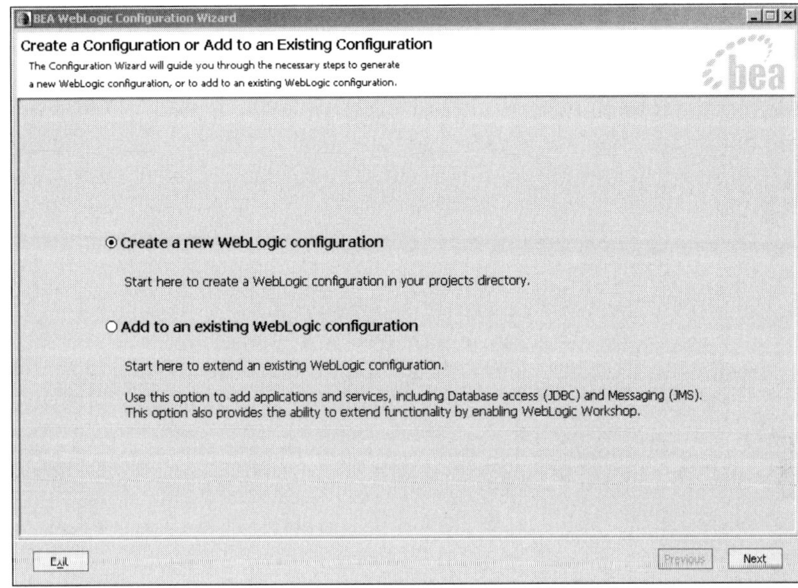

FIGURE A.1 The first form of the Configuration Wizard asks you to create a new domain or add to an existing domain.

3. Select Create a New WebLogic Configuration and click on Next to go to the next screen.

   The next form enables you to choose what type of domain you want to create. Select the Basic WebLogic Server Domain as shown in Figure A.2 and click on Next.

4. You now see a screen shown in Figure A.3 below that shows you an Express option and a Custom option. The Express option is a subset of the Custom option. We'll walk through the Custom Configuration option.

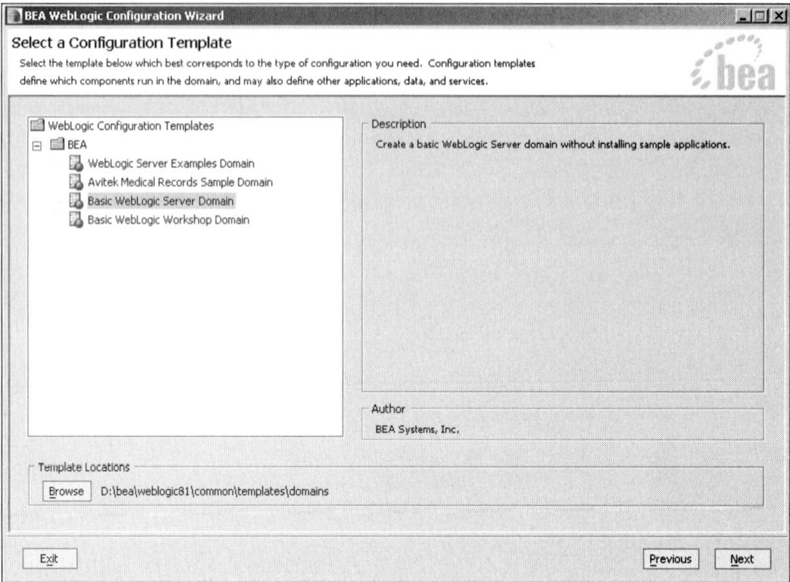

FIGURE A.2 Choose a domain configuration.

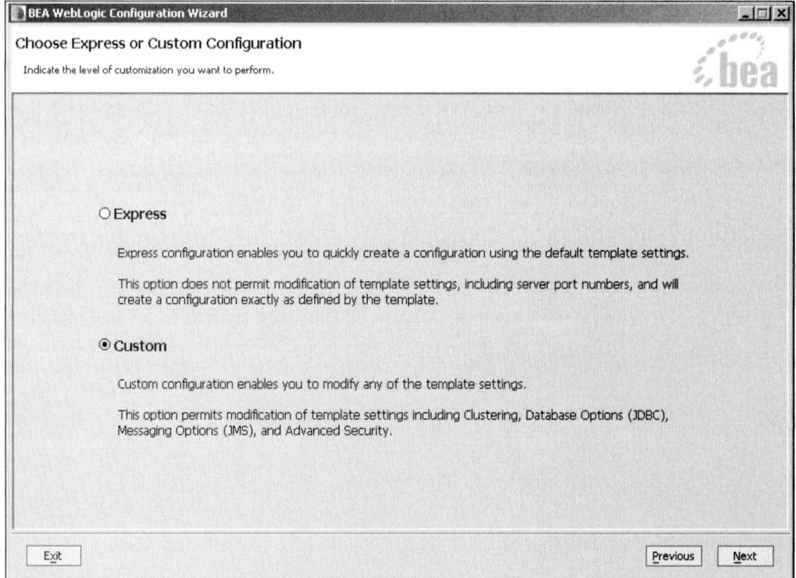

FIGURE A.3 Express or customized configuration.

5. On the next screen as shown in Figure A.4, you define the name and ports for your WebLogic Server instance. We'll leave these as the default settings.

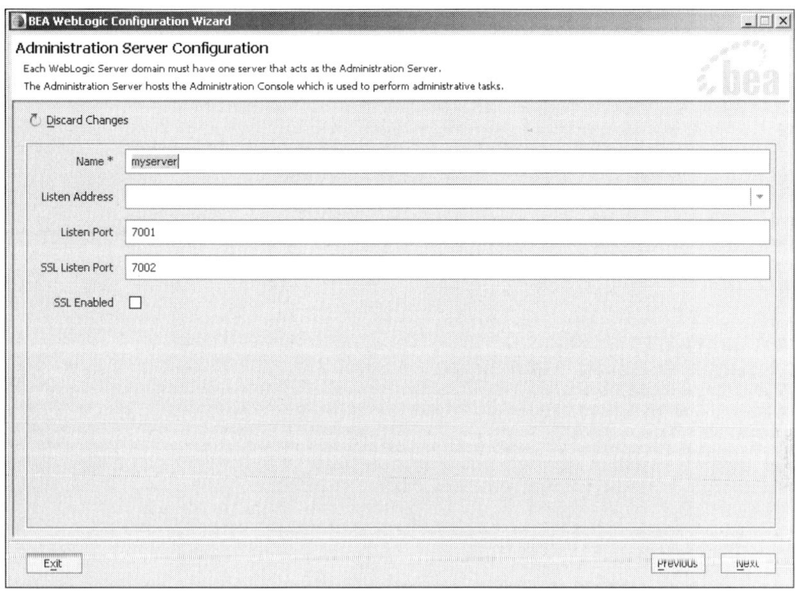

FIGURE A.4 Administration server configuration.

6. You're now presented with an option to configure multiple servers, define your cluster, and so on. This is shown in Figure A.5. For now, just select Skip and move on by clicking Next. If you want to set up a cluster, refer to page 1219.

7. The screen shown in Figure A.6 asks whether you want to configure your JDBC components. We'll walk through this, so select Yes and click Next.

A

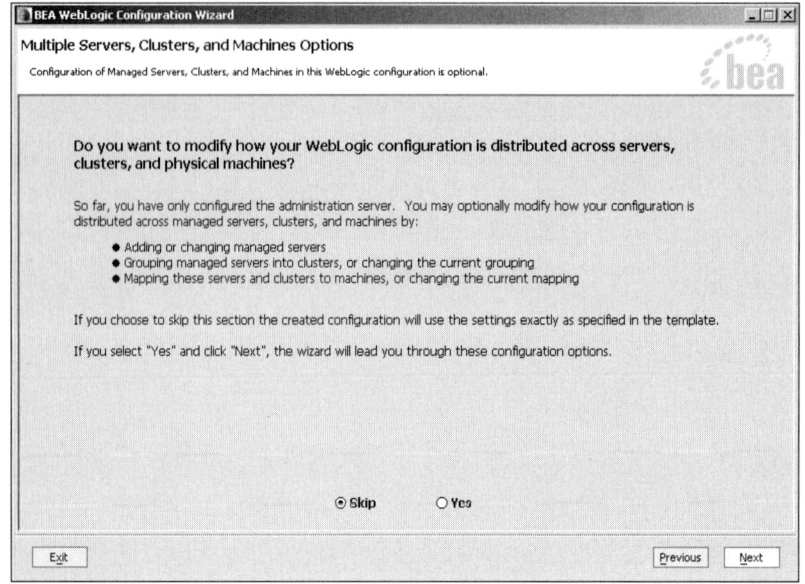

FIGURE A.5 Server and cluster choices.

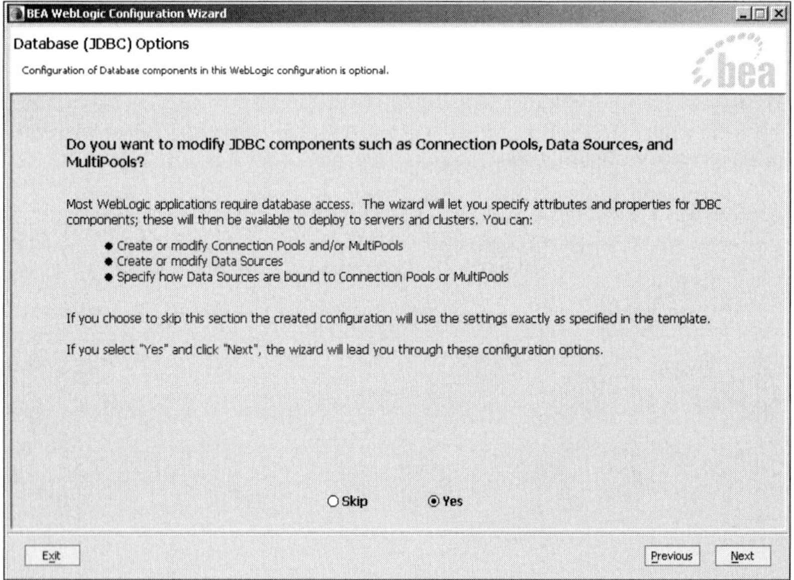

FIGURE A.6 JDBC options.

8. Click Add to add a new JDBC connection pool and specify its properties. An example is shown in Figure A.7. There are drop-down menus to help you with the driver settings and URL. Click Next.

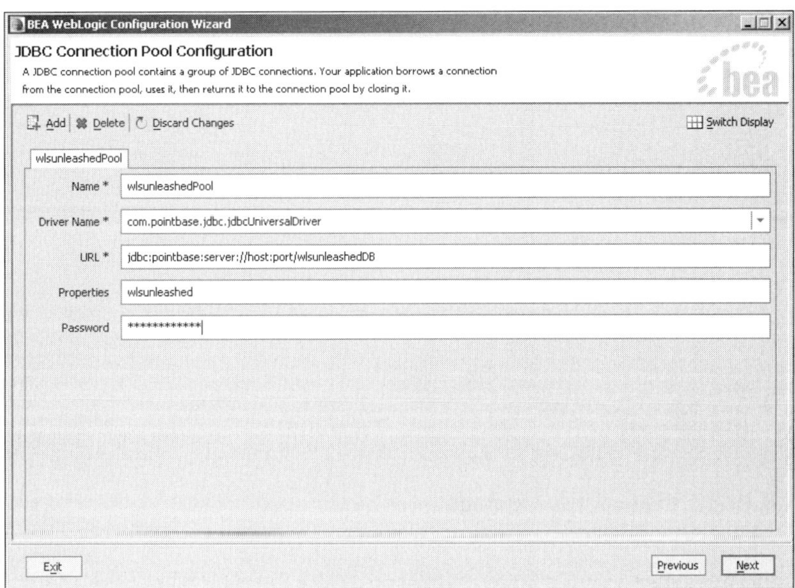

FIGURE A.7 JDBC connection pool settings.

9. The next screen as shown in Figure A.8 enables you to set up multipools. We'll ignore this for now. Click Next.

10. This screen, as shown in Figure A.9, is where you can set up data sources and transaction data sources. The settings are straightforward with drop-down lists to help you. For now, let's leave this alone. Click Next.

A

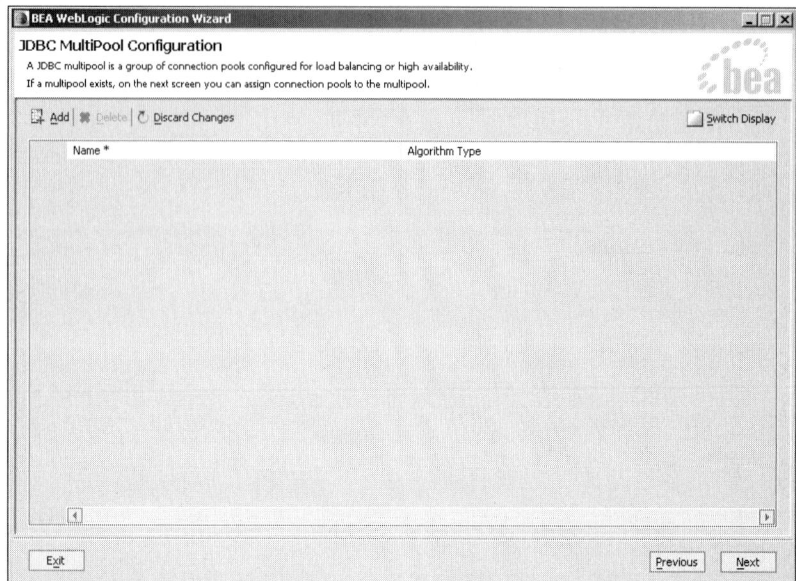

FIGURE A.8 JDBC multipool configuration.

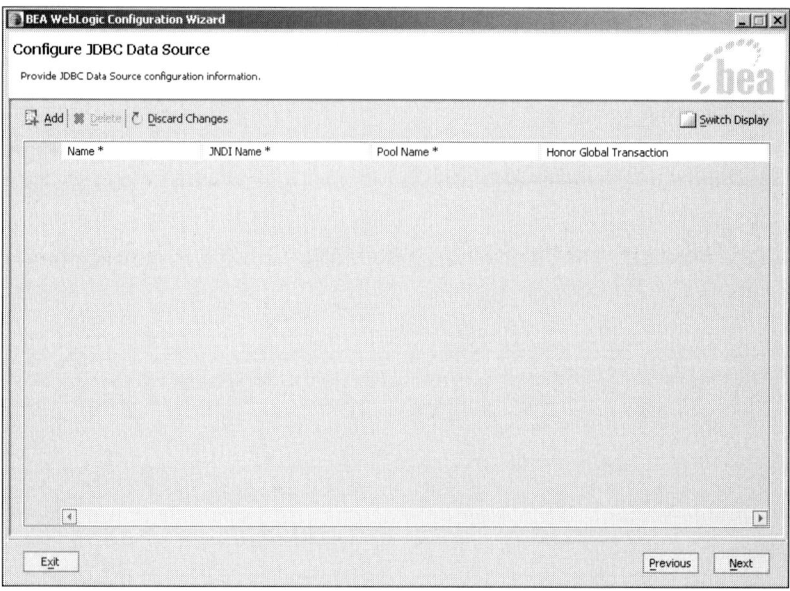

FIGURE A.9 JDBC data source configuration.

11. The next screen enables you to test your database settings. This is shown in Figure A.10. If your database is up and running (PointBase can start it from this user interface), you can test whether the connection is successful. Test your pool if you want to, and then click Next.

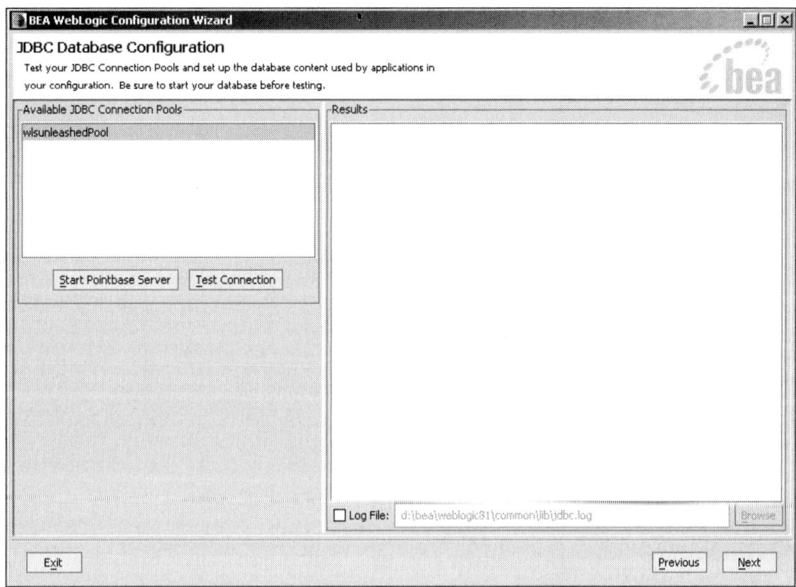

FIGURE A.10 Testing the JDBC connections.

12. The screen shown in Figure A.11 enables you to choose whether you want to configure JMS components. Select Yes and click on Next.

13. Configure a JMS connection factory, as shown in Figure A.12. When you're done, click Next.

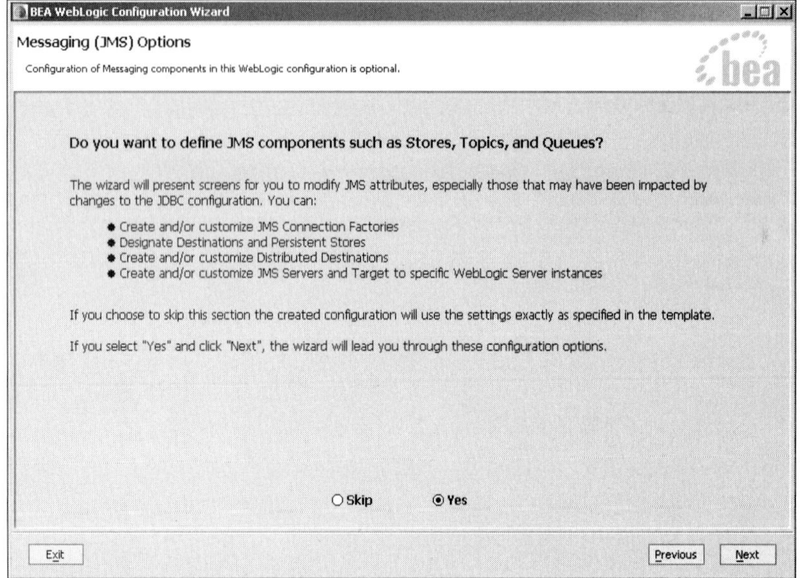

FIGURE A.11 JMS options.

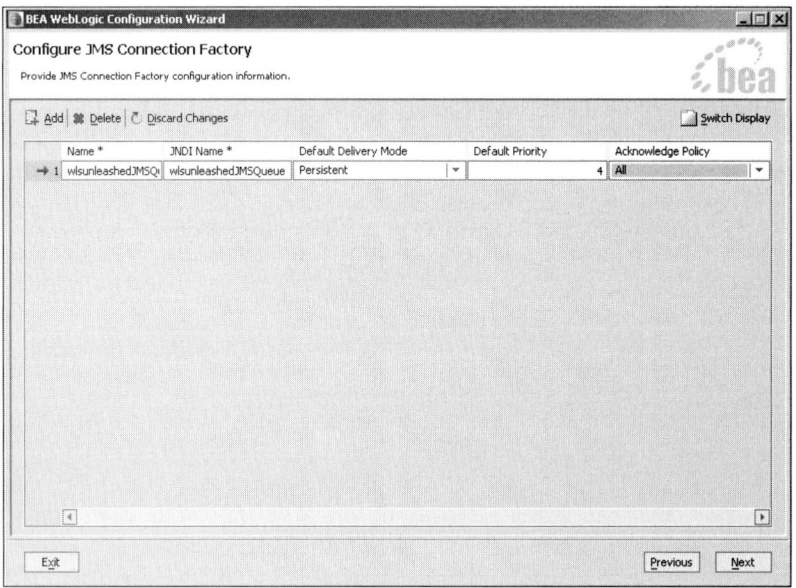

FIGURE A.12 JMS connection factory.

14. Configure a JMS file store if you want. When you're finished, click Next. This is shown in Figure A.13.

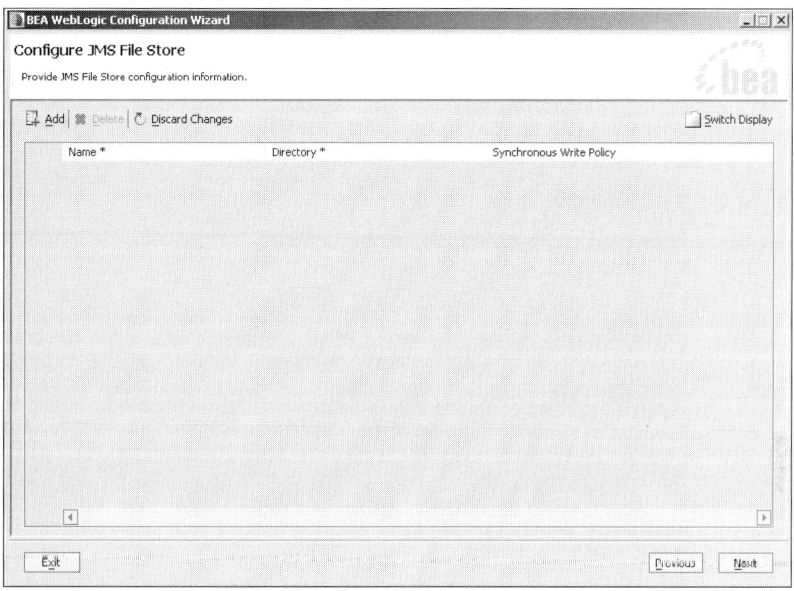

FIGURE A.13 JMS file store options.

15. Configure a JMS JDBC store. I am leaving this as optional for you, because you can always do this later through the administration console. This is shown in Figure A.14. After you're done, click Next.

16. Configure a JMS server (shown in Figure A.15). When you've finished, click Next.

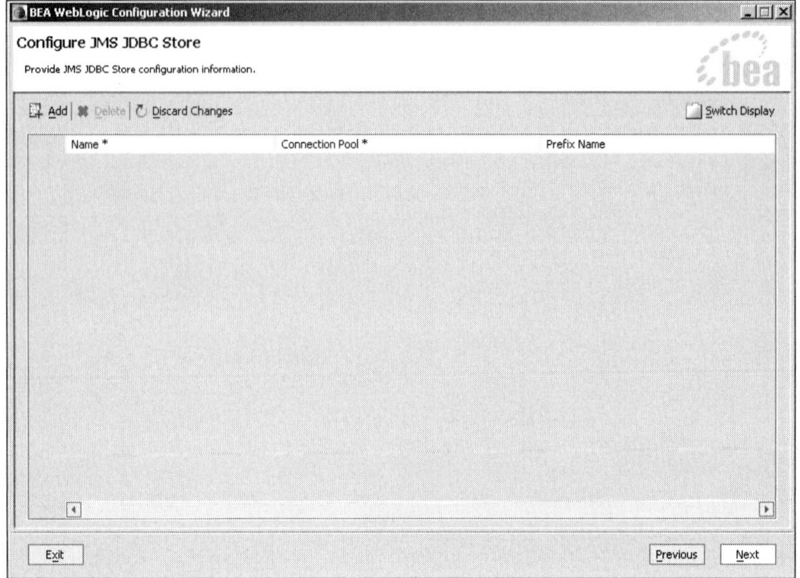

FIGURE A.14 JMS JDBC store.

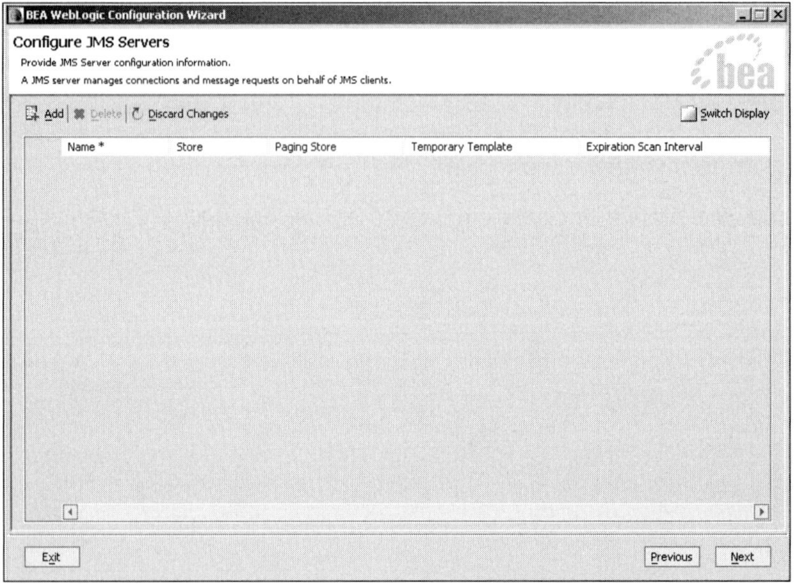

FIGURE A.15 Configure JMS server.

17. Figure A.16 shows the targeting section. It enables you to choose the servers on which each of the JDBC pools, JMS queues, topics, and so on are deployed. Select Yes and click Next.

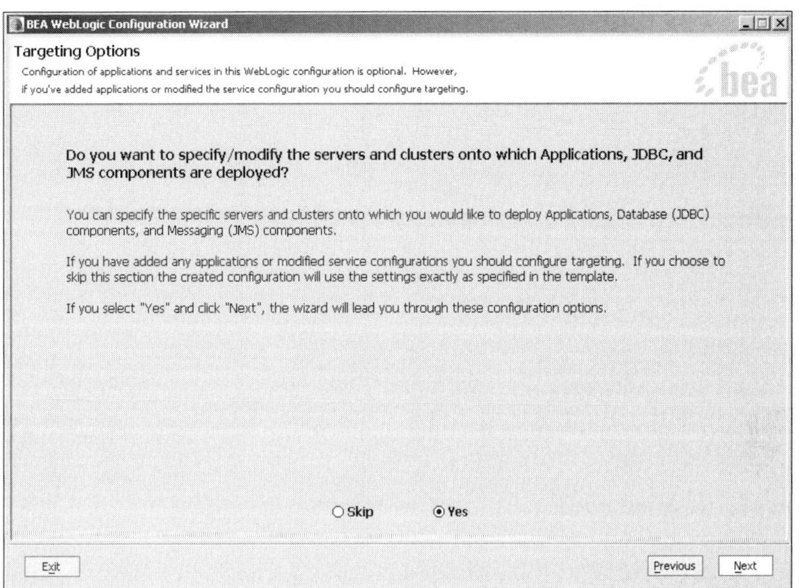

FIGURE A.16 JMS targeting options.

18. Assign a server to each of the JDBC pools and JMS destinations and click on Next as shown in Figure A.17.

19. The screen shown in Figure A.18 enables you to configure advanced security. You can create groups, users, and roles. Feel free to explore this, but for now it is okay if you skip it and click Next.

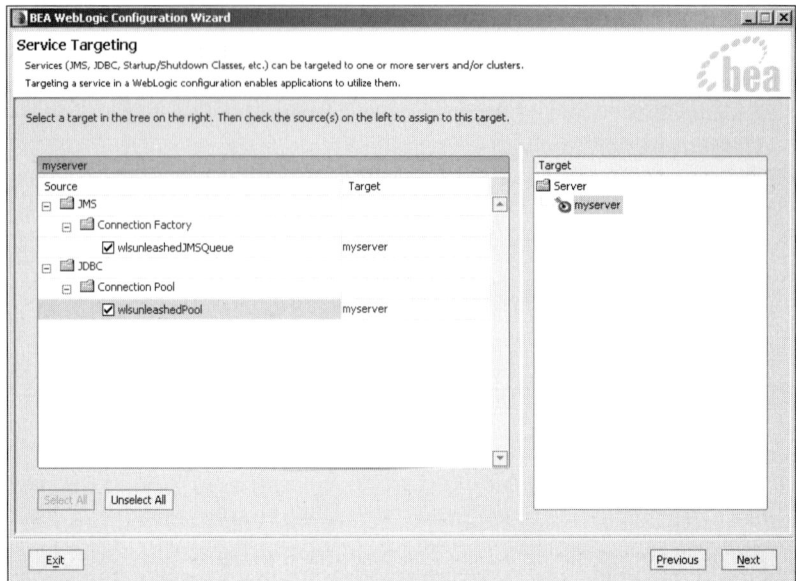

FIGURE A.17 Services targeting.

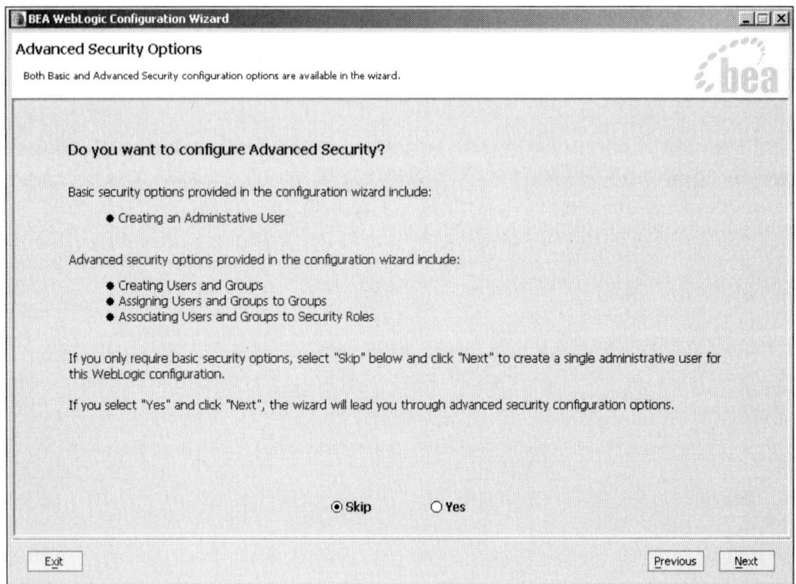

FIGURE A.18 Advanced security options.

20. On the screen in Figure A.19, you must create a WebLogic administrator. For our sample domain, you can use `weblogic/password`. For production environments, you would want to use something less intuitive and more secure. After you enter these details, click Next.

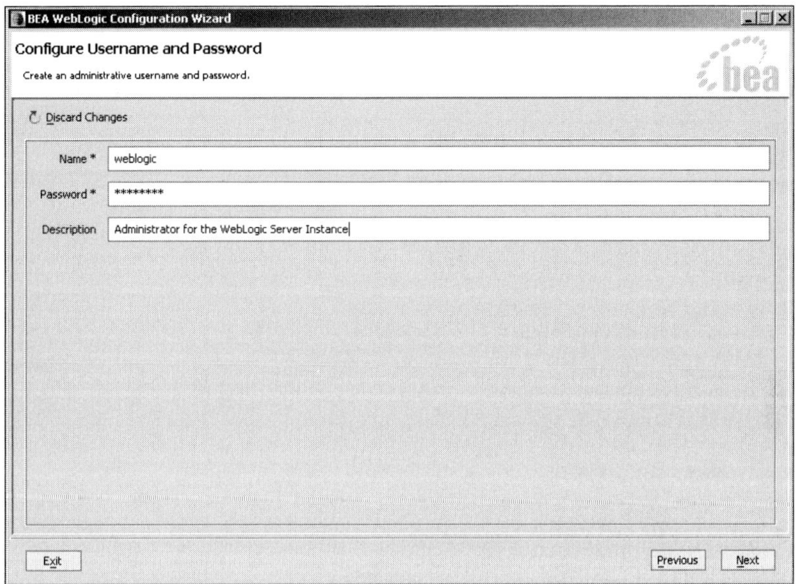

FIGURE A.19 Configure username and password.

21. The screen shown in Figure A.20 enables you to create shortcuts and deploy WebLogic as a service. For now, leave the defaults as shown in the figure and click Next.

22. On the screen in Figure A.21, you define the start scripts and directories. You can leave the defaults for now and click Next.

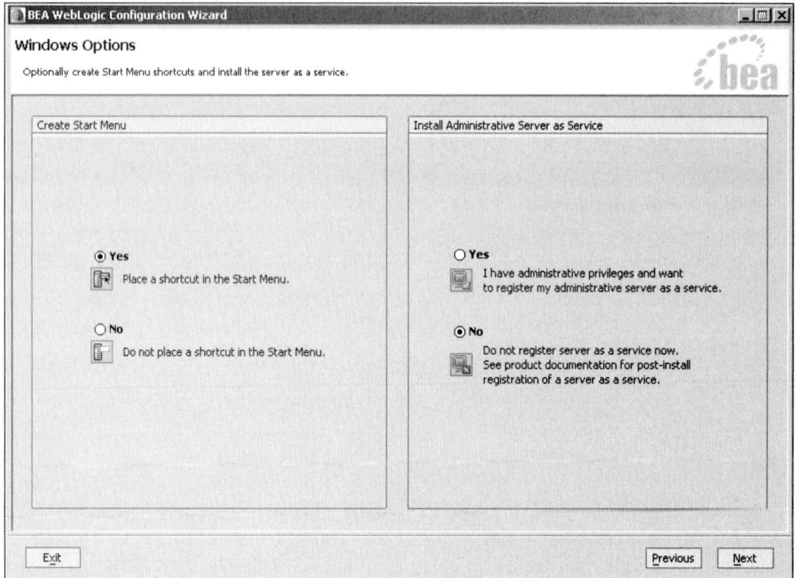

FIGURE A.20 Windows options.

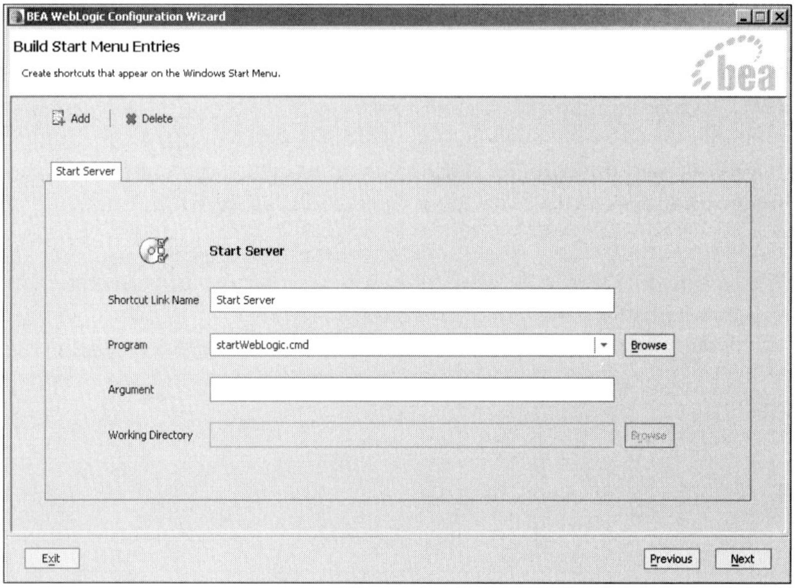

FIGURE A.21 Build Start menu entries.

23. Now you select between development mode and production mode. You can also choose the JDK you want to use. For now, leave the defaults shown in Figure A.22 or change them as you want. Click Next when you're done.

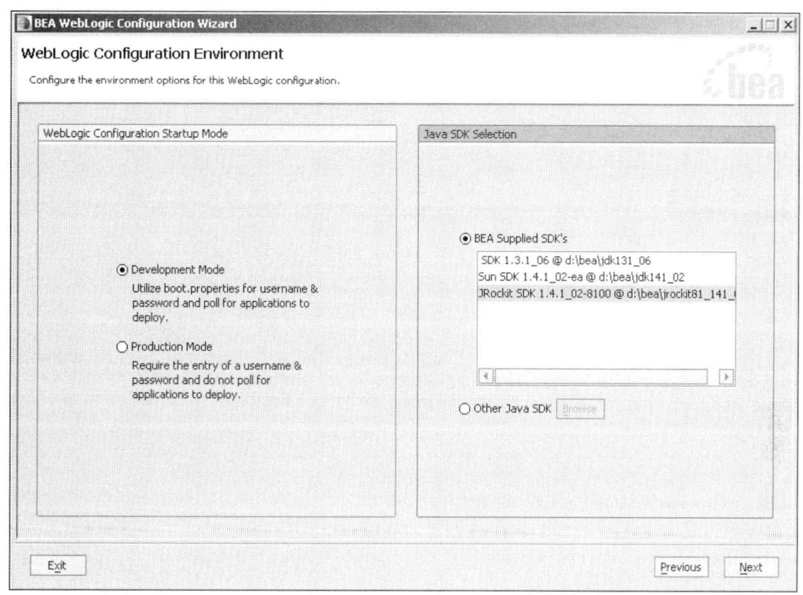

FIGURE A.22 WebLogic configuration environment.

24. You're almost done. Figure A.23 shows the last screen. Choose a name for your domain configuration. The default is `mydomain`. Click Create to create your domain. Click on Done and exit the Configuration Wizard.

Installation can be confirmed by finding the new `/user_projects/mydomain` directory under the BEA installation directory. If you've used WebLogic before, the structure will look familiar. Under the `/mydomain` directory is the `/applications/` directory. Read the `readme.txt` file created in the `applications` directory for details on its purpose. If you elected to install the domain into the Windows Start menu from step 22, you can start the new server from that link. Otherwise, you can start it from a command prompt at

```
C:/bea/user_projects/mydomain/StartWebLogic.cmd
```

Now that a domain environment has been created, we can use it to host our Web and enterprise applications.

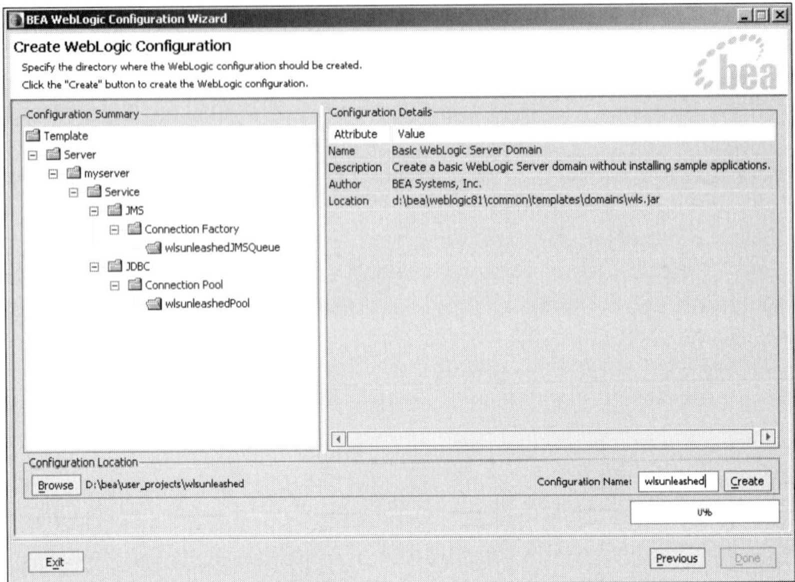

FIGURE A.23 Create a WebLogic configuration.

Deploying an HTML Page

You can create a Web application by creating a new directory under applications; for example, `/applications/DefaultWebApp/`. The quickest way to view an HTML page is to place it in the root directory of the default Web application in your WebLogic Server installation. The following steps will guide you through the deployment of an HTML page:

1. Start the administration server.
2. Copy your HTML file into the default Web application directory of your WebLogic Server installation. For illustrative purposes, we'll name this HTML file `foo.html`. If you haven't done so already, create the directory `c:/bea/user_projects/mydomain/applications/DefaultWebApp`. We'll deploy our HTML file into this directory.
3. Copy all of your supporting files, such as image or media files, into the `/DefaultWebApp` directory. You can create subdirectories (such as `/images/mypic.gif`) to handle any relative links.
4. Deploy the Web application through the console.
5. You can now view the HTML page in a Web browser by using the URL `http://`*`localhost`*`:`*`port`*`/DefaultWebApp/foo.html`.

   where

localhost is the name of the WebLogic Server hosting the HTML page. If you deployed the HTML page on a remote machine, you would substitute the IP address or machine name of the other server for this name.

port is the listening address for the server.

`foo.html` is the name of the HTML file you copied to the server in step 2.

NOTE

If you've installed locally with the default options, you can use `http://127.0.0.1:7001/DefaultWebApp/foo.html` or `http://localhost:7001/DefaultWebApp/foo.html` as the URL.

Deploying a JSP

Deploying a JavaServer Page is much like deploying an HTML page. A JSP will compile to a servlet, but unlike a servlet, it does not require any specific registration. You simply copy it into the root directory of the deployed Web application. The following steps will guide you through the deployment of a JSP:

1. Start the administration server.
2. Copy your JSP file into the default Web application directory of your WebLogic Server installation. You can create a Web Application, and set the default Web Application through the WebLogic Administration Console. For illustrative purposes, we will name this file `bar.jsp`. We'll deploy our JSP file into this directory:

   ```
   C:/bea/user_projects/mydomain/applications/DefaultWebApp
   ```

3. Copy all of your supporting files, such as image or media files, into the `/DefaultWebApp` directory. You can create subdirectories (such as `/images/mypic.gif`) to handle any relative links.
4. You'll now be able to view the HTML page in a Web browser by using the following URL:

   ```
   http://127.0.0.1:7001/DefaultWebApp/bar.jsp
   ```

   where

   localhost is the name of the WebLogic Server hosting the JSP page. If you deployed the JSP page on a remote machine, you would substitute the IP address or machine name of the other server for this name.

   `port` is the listening address for the server.

   bar.jsp is the name of the JSP file you copied to the server in step 2.

Deploying a Servlet

Deploying servlets involves a few more steps than do HTML and JSP pages. Servlets must be defined in the Web application deployment descriptor, `web.xml`, and their deployment structures must match their package structures. The following steps will walk you through the deployment of a servlet:

1. Create a directory to hold your servlet classes, if one isn't already present. Go to the Web application directory `/DefaultWebApp`, and under the `/WEB-INF` directory, create a subdirectory named `/classes`. If you created the domain `mydomain` from the first section in this appendix, your directory structure should resemble the following:

   ```
   C:/bea/user_projects/mydomain/applications/DefaultWebApp/WEB-INF/classes
   ```

2. Copy your compiled servlet into the `/classes` subdirectory. If your servlet has a `package` statement, you'll need to create an additional subdirectory for each level of the package statement. For example, suppose that you have a servlet named `BlackboardServlet`, and it has a `package` statement of `com.pirates`. Your servlet class would be placed in the following location:

   ```
   C:/bea/user_projects/mydomain/applications/DefaultWebApp/WEB-INF/classes/
   ➥com/pirates/BlackboardServlet.class
   ```

3. Before we can start our servlet, we must register it. This is done in the Web application configuration file `web.xml`, which is stored in the `/WEB-INF` directory. That one file holds the registration information for all of your servlets. Check your `/WEB-INF` directory to see whether the `web.xml` file already exists. If so, bring it up in a text editor (or, preferably, an XML editor). If the file doesn't exist, open a text editor, create a new file, and save it as `web.xml` into the `/WEB-INF` directory.

4. Edit the `web.xml` file with the servlet's information between the `<web-app>` and `</web-app>` tags. You can do this using any text or XML editor, or use the WebLogic Builder utility that comes with WebLogic. The format is as follows:

   ```
   <servlet>
    <servlet-name>
     BlackboardServlet
    </servlet-name>
    <servlet-class>
     com.pirates.BlackboardServlet
    </servlet-class>
   </servlet>

   <servlet-mapping>
    <servlet-name>
     BlackboardServlet
   ```

```
  </servlet-name>
  <url-pattern>
   TeachServlet
  </url-pattern>
</servlet-mapping>
```

where

BlackboardServlet is the name of your Servlet class file.

com.pirates.BlackboardServlet is the full package name of your servlet class.

TeachServlet is the name that you type into the browser to access the `BlackboardServlet`. (This *could* also be the same name as the servlet or any other string.)

5. Save the `web.xml` file into the `/WEB-XML` directory.
6. Start the administration server.
7. Call your servlet from a Web browser with the following URL:

```
http:// 127.0.0.1:7001/DefaultWebApp/TeachServlet
```

where

localhost is the name of the WebLogic Server hosting the HTML page. If you deployed the HTML page on a remote machine, you would substitute the IP address or machine name of the other server for this name.

`port` is the listening address for the server.

TeachServlet is the reference to the servlet `BlackboardServlet`, defined between the `<url-pattern>` and `</url-pattern>` tags of the `web.xml` file.

APPENDIX **B**

Migration from Previous Versions

by Kunal Mittal and Joe McGuire

IN THIS APPENDIX

- Migration from Versions 6.0/6.1/7.0 to 8.1
- Migration from Versions 4.5/5.1 to 8.1
- Installation Recommendations for All Migrations
- Application Recommendations for All Migrations

If you're reading this appendix, you probably have an existing WebLogic application on an earlier version of WebLogic Server that you would like to migrate to version 8.1.

Migration involves upgrading two components: the server installation and the applications. The particular migration procedures you'll follow depend on whether you're migrating from versions 6.0/6.1/7.0 or from versions 4.5/5.1.

Prior to version 6.0, the WebLogic installation used a number of proprietary files, such as the `weblogic.properties` file, to configure server and application properties. WebLogic Server also used its own class loader and security files. As J2EE standards began to take shape, version 6.0 was introduced to more closely conform to those standards. Version 6.0 was a radical departure from its predecessor, version 5.1, and wholly changed not only the WebLogic Server configuration, but also application structure and deployment.

This appendix walks you through each of the two migration scenarios: first from the perspective of a version 6.0/6.1/7.0 upgrade, and then from that of versions 4.5/5.1.

CAUTION

If you haven't already done so, make a backup copy of all your existing WebLogic Server domains before installing version 8.1. After you've started the 8.1 administration server, changes are made to the domain using WebLogic Server 8.1 classes that prevent you from being able to revert back if anything should go wrong!

Migration from Versions 6.0/6.1/7.0 to 8.1

If you're upgrading from versions 6.0/6.1/7.0, your migration couldn't be any smoother. Like versions 6.0/6.1/7.0, version 8.1 conforms to the J2EE specification, and does not radically differ in its installation and application configurations.

Upgrading a WebLogic 6.0/6.1/7.0/7.0 Installation to 8.1

The installation structure of version 8.1 is similar to that of versions 6.0/6.1/7.0; however, there are a few changes that you need to take notice of.

The most apparent change is the new domain directory structure. By default, versions 6.0/6.1/7.0 placed domains under the `\config` directory inside the WebLogic Server installation directory. When you create a new domain in version 8.1, you have the option to create a domain to any location on your hard drive. If unspecified, a new domain is created in a default `\user_projects` directory that's installed under `\bea`. However, you're encouraged to create your own directory structure that best suits your application and needs.

When migrating a pre-existing domain into version 8.1, you can still use the same directory structure, but the recommendation is to place it in a new location outside the WebLogic Server installation directory.

If you choose to place your existing domain into a new domain structure, you have to make some adjustments to your startup scripts. In a text editor, open the WebLogic Server startup script for your old domain and make the adjustments shown in Table B.1.

> **TIP**
>
> Make a backup of your domain directory before attempting a migration. This is basic housekeeping.

Table B.1 shows the before and after values of key properties in `startWebLogic.cmd`.

TABLE B.1 Before and After Property Settings

Property Name	Before	After
JAVA_HOME	C:\bea\jdk131_02	C:\bea\jdk141_02
WL_HOME	C:\bea\weblogicXXX	C:\bea\weblogic81
CLASSPATH	%WL_HOME%\lib\weblogic_sp.jar; %WL_HOME%\lib\weblogic.jar	%WL_HOME%\lib\weblogic.jar

1. Modify the `bea.home` property to point to the BEA home directory that contains your `license.bea` file:

   ```
   -Dbea.home=c:\bea
   ```

2. You might need to change any references to relative paths to other files and also change any script that tries to verify a file on a relative path or in the old directory structure. Specifically, look at the start scripts and the `config.xml` file.
3. Decide whether you want to use Cloudscape or PointBase. (those upgrading from 6.0 or 6.1 might have to make this decision). If you're migrating from 7.0 and are already using PointBase, you don't need to worry about this step. Ensure that the path to either database is set up correctly in your `startWeblogic.cmd` file.
4. If you're switching to PointBase, change all references in the start scripts, class path settings, and so on to point to PointBase and not to Cloudscape. You also have to migrate your data from Cloudscape to PointBase: Use Cloudview in Cloudscape to generate a database script and run that script in the PointBase console.
5. Repeat the steps for any additional servers in the domain.

It's important to make sure that all files referenced in your classpath are set correctly. For instance, if you're migrating a domain that makes use of the Cloudscape database incorporated in the version 6 or 7 installation, the classpath will still have to reference those files. This can become a little tricky when you're trying to use relative locations, so you might want to explicitly set the classpath reference from the root directory:

```
set CLASSPATH=%CLASSPATH%;
➥c:\bea\wlserver6.1\samples\eval\cloudscape\lib\cloudscape.jar;
```

CAUTION

When you start your migrated domain in version 8.1, WebLogic reads the `config.xml` file and recognizes that it has been converted from an earlier version. WebLogic then runs in Compatibility mode. Compatibility mode enables version 8.1 to recognize and use users, groups, and ACLs through version 6's legacy files, such as the `fileRealm.properties` file.

Version 8.1 does not support the guest user as the anonymous user (as version 6.*x* did). To use this feature, you must pass the following argument in the `startWeblogic.cmd` script:

```
-Dweblogic.security.anonymousUserName=guest
```

Upgrading Version 6.0/6.1/7.0 WebLogic Applications

Like versions 6.0/6.1/7.0, version 8.1 conforms to the Sun J2EE specification and your existing WebLogic applications will usually require no change whatsoever. That said, there are still a few instances in which you'll either need to make alterations or will want to make alterations to take advantage of new features.

The circumstances in which you absolutely must make alterations are few. One is in the odd chance that your application uses remote relationships among container-managed persistence EJBs. Remote relationships are no longer supported in version 8.1. You can still use your application, but you'll have to combine and deploy all such EJBs into a single bundled JAR file.

Another situation occurs in the remote possibility that you're using `NULL` or `guest` as a username in an application—these names are no longer supported in version 8.1. You should also change the `DOCTYPE`s to point to the new DTDs to resolve any changes.

> **NOTE**
>
> Actually, you can still use the username `guest` by creating it as a valid user within the Administration Console. However, `NULL` is no longer permitted.

The most notable change you might need to make is to any Web service applications (available since version 6.1). Numerous changes were made to the Web service runtime system that make version 6.1 applications incompatible on version 8.1. For detailed information about upgrading your version 6.1 Web services, refer to the BEA documentation on the subject: `http://edocs.bea.com/wls/docs81/webserv/migrate.html`.

Migration from Versions 4.5/5.1 to 8.1

If you're migrating from a version earlier than 6.0, you have a little more work to do. Luckily, WebLogic Server 8.1 includes a number of migration tools to make your upgrade as quick and painless as possible.

Upgrading a WebLogic 4.5/5.1 Installation to 8.1

Assuming that you've backed up all of your WebLogic 4.5/5.1 domains and installed WebLogic Server 8.1, the next thing you need to do is to upgrade your WebLogic Server license files.

Upgrading Your BEA License Files

To upgrade your license file, which is presumably a nonexpiring license file, first check to see which kind of license file format you have. It will be either a `WebLogicLicense.class` license file or a `WebLogicLicense.xml` file.

If it's `WebLogicLicense.class` file, you'll first need to convert it to the XML file `WebLogicLicense.xml`. WebLogic Server 8.1 provides a utility to do this: the `licenseConverter`.

To convert the class file into XML, open a command window and run the `setEnv.cmd` command to set your environment. Then run the following:

```
java utils.licenseConverter -w c:\weblogic
```

where *c:\weblogic* is the location you want the WebLogicLicense.xml file to be written to.

Now that you have a WebLogicLicense.xml file, you can use it to get the license.bea-type file used in WebLogic version 8.1. There are a few steps involved in doing this, and you'll need a little help from the folks at BEA. First, log in to the BEA Customer Service site at http://elicense.bea.com/elicense_webapp/index.jsp.At the left of the page, click on the Upgrade link.

You can submit up to 10 WebLogicLicense.xml files for conversion, as long as they are on your hard drive. BEA will then email you back a converted license_wls81.bea file for each.

Now that you have the license_wls81.bea file, you still have to convert it to a license.bea file. To do this, you use the UpdateLicense utility to merge it with the evaluation license that was installed when you installed WebLogic Server 8.1. This is demonstrated in the following steps:

1. Open a command window and run the setEnv.cmd command to set your environment.
2. Place the license file you received from BEA into the BEA home directory (make sure that it's saved as something other than license.bea).
3. Navigate to the BEA home directory (this is where the target file will be output to). Then run the following:

   ```
   c:\bea\weblogic81>java UpdateLicense license_wls81.bea
   ```

   where *license_wls81.bea* is the name of the file you received from BEA and have in the WebLogic root directory.

   A new license.bea file is created to replace the old one.
4. The last step is a precaution. Save the resulting license.bea file to a floppy disk or back it up somewhere on the network in case you need it for any future reinstallations.

You should now be able to start your WebLogic Server 8.1 installation with the new license.bea file.

Converting the weblogic.properties File

After you've upgraded your license files, you need to convert your old WebLogic Server's weblogic.properties file into a new domain. The weblogic.properties file was used to hold configuration information for both the server installation as well as the applications. Each installation had two weblogic.properties files: a global file to set universal attributes and a server-specific one to override settings on the global file. Beginning in

WebLogic Server version 6.0, domain configuration and application configuration were separated. Domain configurations went into a domain configuration file, `config.xml`, and the application's configurations moved to the application deployment descriptors, such as `web.xml` and `ejb-jar.xml`.

WebLogic Server 8.1 provides utilities to make the conversion process as easy as possible. The following steps walk you through a typical conversion:

1. First, start WebLogic Server 8.1.
2. Next, log in to the Administration Console. In the right panel, click on the Convert `weblogic.properties` link under the Information and Resources - Helpful Tools heading. The GUI conversion utility is displayed in the right panel.
3. Now locate the root directory of your old WebLogic Server installation. This is the directory where the `weblogic.properties` file that you want to convert is located. Navigation is a bit tricky on this page. Click a directory link to move up or down the directories. My legacy WebLogic installation is in the `c:\weblogic` directory, so I want to have `c:\weblogic` displayed and I'm going to click on the little pentagonal icon next to it to select it.

CAUTION

Make sure that you click on the icon on the left, not the directory link!

4. The next page displayed asks you to identify any server-specific or cluster-specific directories for the conversion (this corresponds to the server-specific `weblogic.properties` file). For this example, I'll choose to convert the `myserver` server's specific `weblogic.properties` file.
5. To complete the form, you're also asked to assign an administrative server name and an output directory (where the new `config.xml` file will be written to). I'll name my administration server `oldserver` and use the output directory at `c:\bea\user_projects\OldServer`. Remember, WebLogic Server 8.1 best practices suggest that this new domain directory should be outside the WebLogic Server installation. The subdirectory name `\OldServer` will be the name of the new domain. Enter the WebLogic home directory of your old installation if it was other then the default (`c:\weblogic`). If you're using the default, you can leave this blank. Finally, you must enter a name for the new domain. I'll call mine `OldDomain`.
6. Click Convert to begin the conversion process.

   If everything goes as planned, you should get a successful conversion confirmation page.

NOTE

You can confirm the new domain conversion by starting WebLogic Server for the newly created domain. In my example, I would run the `startOldDomain.cmd` command file, created by the conversion utility, which was created in the `c:\bea\user_projects\OldDomain\` directory.

The username and password required to start the migrated domain correspond to the old installation.

Upgrading Version 4.5/5.1 WebLogic Applications

When migrating existing applications into the WebLogic 8.1 environment, they must be restructured to conform to the J2EE-specified directory structure. Fortunately, the `weblogic.properties` conversion utility handles this for you. The utility separates installation configuration data from application configuration data, and automatically re-creates your previous application structures into the J2EE-compliant 6.*x*/7.0/8.1 format.

For instance, Web applications now have a `\WEB-INF` subdirectory that holds configuration files for the Web application, and EJB applications now have a `\META-INF` subdirectory that hold configuration files for the EJB application. It's recommended that you install this new domain structure outside of the WebLogic 8.1 directory, as suggested during the conversion process.

The conversion utility also creates new startup scripts. Because the structure changed so much between versions 5.1 and 6.0, there isn't much you can use from the original scripts. You should check the classpath variables to ensure that all the libraries are correct. The license file should be removed from the classpath.

You also should double-check the environment variables set using the `-D` tags. The conversion utility is good, but it isn't a magic bullet.

Installation Recommendations for All Migrations

The most apparent difference in version 8.1 is that the domain directory structure lies outside the WebLogic Server installation. When migrating existing domains, it's recommended to take advantage of the new structure by placing it outside of the WebLogic Server installation directory as well. If you create a new domain in version 8.1 using the Configuration Wizard utility, the default output destination is a `\user_projects` directory that's located outside of the WebLogic Server installation. You are, however, encouraged to create your own structure. The independent structure allows for greater maintainability and flexibility. For instance, you could create separate directories for development, test, and production.

In addition, it's recommended to separate the roles and responsibilities of the administrative server and managed servers. This model was first introduced in version 6.0, and version 7 introduces a new deployment process and staging modes that further support that model. Version 8.1 builds on top of the new approach from version 7.

The distributed model is to use the administrative server for administrative purposes and to deploy applications on the managed servers. Even if the administrative and managed servers are running on the same machine, there are advantages to maintenance as well as the instant capability to scale or join a cluster. WebLogic goes on to support this model further in version 8 with its two-phase deployment. When you deployed an application in version 6.0/6.1/7.0, a copy was sent and deployed on all the target servers. If deployment on one of those servers failed, the application would be placed in an inconsistent state. Version 8.1 helps prevent this from happening by splitting deployment into two phases, and it works much like a transaction's two-phase commit:

1. Prepare phase—A copy of the application is sent to all target servers and loaded, but clients cannot yet access the application.
2. Activation phase—If all the servers respond that they've successfully received and loaded the application, they then activate, which allows client access.

If you've moved the application to your managed servers, the two-phase deployment process assures you that the application is deployed and active on all targeted servers. This was introduced in WebLogic 7.0 and enhanced in WebLogic 8.1.

Moving applications to managed servers also enables you to take advantage of version 8.1's application staging modes. By defining a staging mode, you can control how files are copied for deployment. For more information about application staging, refer to the BEA documentation at `http://edocs.bea.com/wls/docs81/deployment/index.html` and Chapter 7, "Deploying Web Applications."

The last major change you might want to implement is to upgrade security. If you upgraded from version 4.5/5.1, the conversion utility converted the security information from the `weblogic.properties` file into a file-based WebLogic Server 6.1–type format (in the `fileRealm.properties` file). When an upgraded domain with file-based security is started in version 8.1, it runs in compatibility mode security. This security level might be fine for your present operation, but you might want to upgrade to WebLogic Server 8.1 security to take advantage of its improved security features, such as JAAS authentication. We showed you earlier in this appendix how to upgrade from compatibility mode security to WebLogic Server 8.1 security.

Application Recommendations for All Migrations

This section brings to light some of the many situations in which you'll want to alter your existing applications to take advantage of the many new features of WebLogic Server version 8.1.

Servlet Recommendations

Version 8.1 is compliant with the Servlet 2.3 specification of the J2EE 1.3 specification. If your Web application is using an older specification, you might want to take advantage of some of the features in the newer specification.

Version 6.1 used the Servlet 2.2 specification, and your servlets should work exactly the same in version 7. However, if you're using WebLogic Server as a proxy to another server or cluster, you might want to use the two new proxy servlets in version 8.1. To do so, make the following changes in your `web.xml` deployment descriptor:

Change

```
weblogic.servlet.internal.Http.ClusterServlet
```

to

```
weblogic.servlet.proxy.Http.ClusterServlet
```

Also change

```
weblogic.t3.srvr.HttpProxyServlet
```

to

```
weblogic.servlet.proxy.HttpProxyServlet
```

EJB Recommendations

Version 8.1 is compliant with the EJB 2.0 specifications of the J2EE 1.3 specification. If you're migrating a 1.0 EJB application, you'll need to recompile it to one of the newer specifications. Also consider recompiling your EJBs to the EJB 2.0 specification and taking advantage of the new local home and local interfaces not found in previous versions. The local interfaces give local clients (on the same VM) quicker access to EJB objects.

If your EJBs still use the WebLogic Query Language (WL QL), consider converting to the new EJB Query Language (EJB-QL), which is compliant with the EJB 2.0 specification. EJB-QL is portable and includes features not found in WL QL. If you used EJB-QL in version 6.1, remember that in version 8.1 queries require a `SELECT` clause. Also new to version 8.1 is the support for dynamic EJB-QL queries. Queries were previously hard-coded into the `ejb-jar.xml` deployment descriptor. With dynamic queries, you can construct your queries programmatically and implement new queries dynamically without having to redeploy the EJB. You'll also need to upgrade the deployment descriptors. You can read about how to upgrade deployment descriptors at `http://edocs.bea.com/wls/docs81/upgrade/upgrade70to81.html#1075478`.

JMS Recommendations

Version 8.1 is compliant with JMS version 1.0.2b of the J2EE 1.3 specification, and includes many new and improved features not found in previous versions. If you're migrating any JMS applications, you might want to take advantage of some of these improvements.

The first is the use of version 8.1's distributed JMS destinations. In a clustered environment, you were previously able to define only one physical JMS destination. By being able to define multiple destinations, you can add failover capability to JMS.

JMS also includes new flow control and message pooling features that can be used to prevent missing messages when the number of messages exceeds JMS server or destination thresholds.

TIP

BEA has really gone out of its way to enable migration with no change or as little change as possible to your existing configuration. Remember though that some manual tweaking will always be needed. Be sure that you have a test suite ready that you can use to test your new application after migration. The hard part will be deciding which of all those new and improved features you want to implement into your existing applications!

APPENDIX C

Using WebLogic Workshop 8.1 with WebLogic Server

by Kunal Mittal

IN THIS APPENDIX

- Workshop 8.1—More Than an IDE
- Workshop 8.1—More Than a Web Services Tool
- What Can You Do with Workshop 8.1?
- Development Using Workshop
- Debugging and Testing Using Workshop
- Compatibility of Workshop 8.1 with Workshop 7.0
- Service Oriented Development in Workshop

According to the research firm Gartner, Inc., there is a need for a tool that simplifies the development of Java applications on the Java platform. Rapid application development (RAD) toolsets will continue to grow in demand and popularity. WebLogic Workshop is the tool from BEA that addresses this requirement of the Java developer community.

If you're considering the BEA WebLogic Platform or even just WebLogic Server 8.1, or talking to anyone from BEA, you've surely heard the buzz around BEA WebLogic Workshop and how it plays a critical role in the BEA WebLogic Platform 8.1 release. The entire release has been closely focused around Workshop. At BEA eWorld 2003, where BEA announced the WebLogic Platform 8.1, the focus on Workshop was extraordinary, as proven by the number of people talking about the tool. The eWorld 2003 theme of "Convergence" describes the new release of Workshop accurately. All the different GUI tools that were packaged with products such as WebLogic Integration, WebLogic Portal, and WebLogic Server as a part of the BEA WebLogic Platform 7.0 have now been integrated into a single, consistent tool—namely, Workshop.

In this appendix, we go over the origins of Workshop and the role it plays in the BEA world. We uncover the positioning and strategy of Workshop and motivate the key features that it provides towards a service-oriented architecture (SOA).

Workshop 8.1—More Than an IDE

WebLogic Workshop consists of two parts:

- An integrated development environment (IDE)
- A standards-based runtime environment

The purpose of the IDE is to remove the complexity in building applications for the entire WebLogic platform. Applications you build in the IDE are constructed from high-level components rather than low-level API calls. Best practices and productivity are built into both the IDE and runtime. We'll expand on this subject later in this appendix.

BEA WebLogic Workshop is a part of the standard BEA WebLogic Platform download. Workshop is available in two editions:

- WebLogic Workshop Application Developer Edition is targeted to be the basic IDE for developers on the BEA WebLogic Platform. It enables developers to build complete J2EE application and Web Services. The general paradigm for Workshop is the use of Java controls, which are covered later in this appendix. The key components that developers would use this edition for are
  - Java controls
  - Web Services
  - Web applications
  - Enterprise JavaBeans (EJBs)
- WebLogic Workshop Platform Edition includes additional extensions to the IDE and runtime framework that enable you to build portal applications and workflows in conjunction with the WebLogic Portal and WebLogic Integration products, respectively. The key components you develop in this edition, in addition to the ones you can create in the Application Developer edition are
  - Portal applications
  - WebLogic Integration components: workflows, data transformations, and application view controls

Workshop 8.1—More Than a Web Services Tool

The first release of BEA WebLogic Workshop concentrated primarily on Web Services. Workshop was seen as an enabler for Web Services development, testing, and orchestration. In the current BEA WebLogic Platform release, Workshop has undergone major revision. The core theme of Web Services enablement has not changed, but the scope has been expanded. Workshop is now the standard, integrated development view into the BEA WebLogic Platform. All WebLogic Integration and WebLogic Portal development can now be done through Workshop.

Goals of Workshop 8.1

The new Workshop tool accomplishes two key goals: simplifying J2EE development and reducing IT complexity. It achieves these goals in numerous different ways that we discuss in this section.

Simplifying J2EE Development

Eighty percent of the application code that's written for an application deals with low-level plumbing, such as a J2EE component. Developers typically spend more time trying to understand what J2EE technologies to use and how to use them than they do writing code to solve a business problem.

Workshop generates a lot of this plumbing code for developers, thus lowering the barrier to entry and enabling them to focus on business requirements and leverage their domain experience. They don't need to worry about the complexities of writing to the J2EE APIs, such as writing an EJB or servlet. The goal of Workshop is to make developers write simple business code and set up different properties and code annotations. Workshop takes care of the complexities of J2EE and the underlying implementation of Web Services.

Reducing IT Complexity

Workshop 8.1 provides developers with a single tool and a single, simplified programming model for building and integrating any type of application using core J2EE, Web Services, Portal, and Integration technologies. This enables developers to leverage the entire BEA WebLogic Platform from one tool and in a unified manner.

Figure C.1 clearly shows the role of BEA WebLogic Workshop in the BEA WebLogic Platform. The components shown in Figure C.1 live on top of J2EE. Workshop provides a powerful, easy-to-use, and unified development environment for all BEA products. It provides the visual development and runtime environment to deliver on the J2EE Made Easy vision of BEA. Many developers view the new Workshop IDE as a Visual Studio for Java programmers.

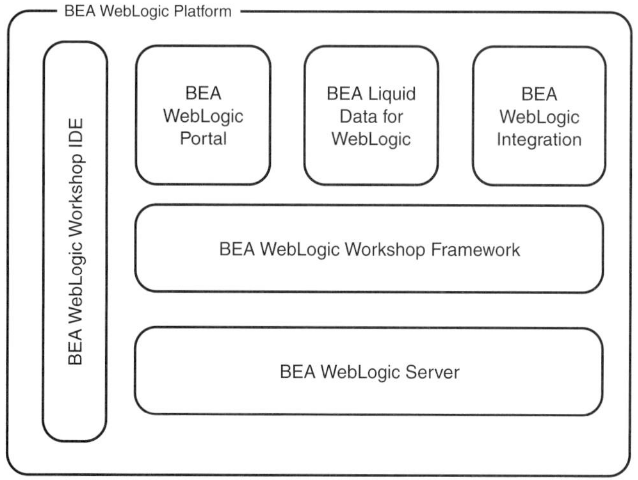

FIGURE C.1 BEA WebLogic Platform.

Key Focal Points of Workshop

To achieve the goals set out in the previous section, Workshop is built around various key focal points.

Javadoc Properties and Code Generation

Workshop uses Java-annotated file formats that enable it to provide a source and graphical view of the application being developed. Workshop provides a What You See Is What You Get (WYSIWYG) approach to Java development. Just as HTML editors such as Dreamweaver and FrontPage enable you to graphically develop HTML pages and make it possible to see the code and output side by side, Workshop provides a Design view and Code view of the Java files.

Design view enables you to set various properties on the components you create, that allow the Workshop framework to generate appropriate code during compile time. These properties can also be edited in the Code view as they get represented as code annotations. *Code annotations* are Javadoc-like comments that store the properties used to determine how the implementation or plumbing code is generated. BEA is promoting various Java Specification Requests (JSRs) to standardize the annotated code definitions.

Application Architecture

Workshop writes much of the plumbing code based on a solid J2EE application architecture that can fully leverage best practice design patterns and the J2EE blueprints. Workshop generates the application leveraging an MVC framework based on Struts, EJBs, and Web Services. It hides the complexity of J2EE applications by providing data binding, navigation management, state management, transaction management, and other architecture services through annotated coding.

Visual Development Environment

The Workshop IDE is a complete development environment for creating J2EE applications and Web Services. It has visual development, testing, and debugging capabilities. This IDE will compete with the other IDEs in the marketplace. Figure C.2 shows a screenshot of a Web Service being developed in Workshop 8.1.

Figure C.2 shows various windows. The window that is most different from other Java IDEs is the Design View section. This is a graphical representation of an underlying Web Service written in Java and J2EE.

Runtime Framework

The runtime framework that comes with BEA WebLogic Workshop provides the loose coupling and the layer of abstraction between business code and the J2EE plumbing code. This framework can generate EJBs (using a tool called EJBGen), Java Message Service (JMS) and JDBC code, as well as code for several other J2EE technologies as required by the application. The framework takes the different code annotations supported in Workshop and generates all the J2EE and Web Services code in the background. It addresses several J2EE design issues and uses best practices, design patterns, and the J2EE blueprints to provide code that is reliable, scalable, and secure.

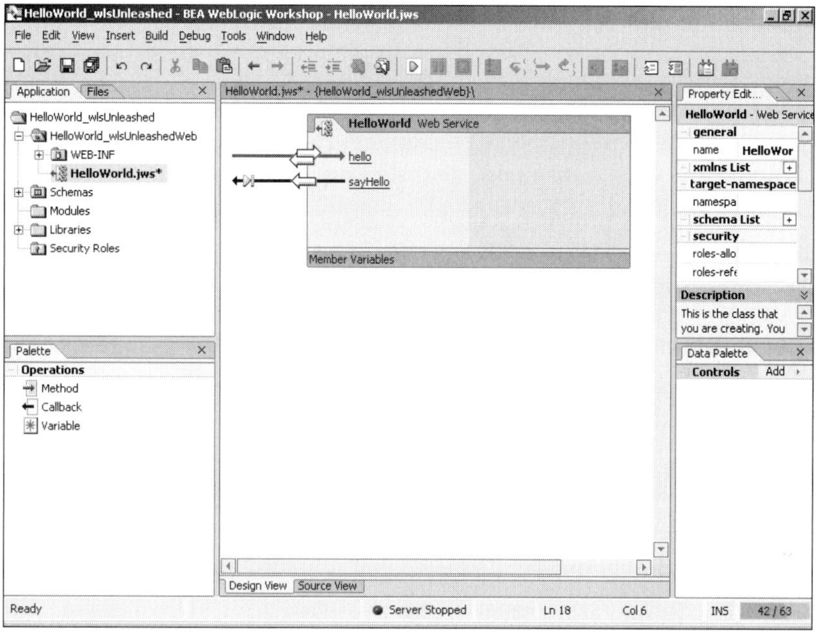

FIGURE C.2 Web Services development in Workshop.

The runtime framework provides an added layer of convergence for the BEA WebLogic Platform by sitting on top of the core BEA WebLogic Server, as well as WebLogic Integration and WebLogic Portal.

Extend Workshop Using Java Controls

Java controls are visually created components that contain all the methods and properties to connect to external systems, applications, and business code. After a Java control has been created, that control can be used easily and consistently from a Web Service, a Web page flow, a portal, a workflow, or another Java control. Files with the extension JCS (Java Control Source) or JCX (Java Control Extension) contain WebLogic Workshop controls. They typically include a collection of method definitions that enable you to easily access a resource such as a database or a Web Service. Workshop 8.1 also provides an extensible Java controls technology to make it easy to leverage existing IT infrastructure such as databases, legacy applications, and other backend resources, which empowers developers to accomplish more in less time.

WebLogic Workshop includes several built-in controls that facilitate access to commonly used enterprise resources. These controls include

- Timer control—Runs code at a given interval
- Database control—Accesses a relational database
- Web Service control—Calls a Web Service from within your application

- EJB control—Accesses an existing Enterprise JavaBean
- JMS control—Sends and receives messages via a Java Message Service queue or topic

You can create custom Java controls to encapsulate any business logic that's required by your application. You can create a Java control in one of two ways:

- Controls for a single project—You use the control's source files directly when you want the convenience of code that can be called from multiple places within a project, but probably won't be reused in additional projects. When you use control sources directly, the control's implementation file and interface file are in the same project as the application that uses them.
- Custom control libraries—You build a control within a control project when you want to end up with a Java library-style JAR file that can also be used in other projects, such as Web application projects, and potentially by other developers. To use the control in another project, that project's developer simply puts the control JAR file into the project's library folder. The control then appears in the palette and menu.

BEA provides a graphical palette and tools to specify the interfaces to custom controls and properties that dictate their runtime behavior. They also write the business code that is exposed by the control. BEA views the use of controls in WebLogic as an enabler for its view of a service-oriented architecture. Controls can be exposed as Web Services in a Web Services architecture. Such controls would fit our definition of an enterprise-class Web Service.

Controls have the following key benefits:

- Visual representation—Controls have a design-time view that gives developers a visual representation of the business logic that they expose.
- Properties—Controls expose simple properties that implement advanced and complex functionality, such as asynchronous messaging, security, state and life cycle management, transaction-based connections to external systems, and so on.
- Package—Controls are packaged in JAR files so that they can be reused.
- Connectivity—Controls are used to connect to remote systems such as databases or custom and legacy applications.
- Extensibility—An open API and wizards enable third parties to create controls for use in their custom applications or for packaging and selling to enhance Workshop or to expose some of the functionality of their tools in Workshop.

What Can You Do with Workshop 8.1?

Web Services development and deployment is just one of the aspects of Workshop. However, as the product evolved from its first release as part of the BEA WebLogic Platform 7.0 to its second release in the BEA WebLogic Platform 8.1, Workshop is now wearing multiple hats.

Enterprise-Class Web Services Development

Workshop goes beyond the synchronous view of Web Services prevalent today. It provides the infrastructure for loosely coupled, asynchronous Web Services with commitments toward enhanced security and reliable messaging that increase the overall interoperability of these services. Built on top of the industry-proven WebLogic Server, these Web Services are highly scalable, available, and reliable. Workshop also provides a rich development environment and various deployment and orchestration environments.

Table C.1 highlights some of the key features within Workshop that enable truly enterprise-class Web Services development and deployment.

TABLE C.1 Web Services Features in Workshop

Feature	Benefit
Asynchronous conversations	Workshop supports seamless message correlation, state management, and conversation lifecycle management.
Business service objects	Business developers deal with a higher abstraction; coarse-grained messages that improve scalability and usability. They worry about writing business code rather than technologies implementation details.
Reliable messaging	Workshop provides the ability to ensure "once and only once" and "specific order" processing of messages.
XQuery	Visual, standards-based transformation of data between Java and XML
XMLBeans	XMLBeans is a technology that enables you to maintain the native XML structure, while providing a JavaBeans interface or view to the data. Therefore, you always have a synchronized version of the XML structure and corresponding JavaBean structure.
Standards support	Workshop supports the SOAP 1.2, WSDL 1.1, and UDDI 2.0 specifications.
Security	Workshop supports the evolving WS-Security specification.
Powerful runtime	Support for synchronous and asynchronous Web Services orchestration, distributed transactions, and security.
Deployment	You can deploy your Web Services and your J2EE applications through the Workshop IDE, on top of the WebLogic Server.
Testing	Workshop generates a complete test environment that allows testing of these Web Services independent of a full application and access to all resources.

Web Application Development

BEA WebLogic Workshop 8.1 introduces a set of visual designers, controls, and framework extensions that enable developers to create powerful server-side applications with dynamic JSP/HTML user interfaces. These visual editors and drag-and-drop tools expose the Java page flow, Worklists, XMLBeans, and control functionality of Workshop that enable the development, assembly, and deployment of Web applications. Much of the J2EE plumbing, such as session and state management, is hidden from the developers by using annotated Java files.

Table C.2 highlights some of the key features within Workshop that simplify Web application development.

TABLE C.2 Application Development Features in Workshop

Feature	Benefit
Architecture	Workshop is standards based, built on blueprints, and leverages the MVC design pattern and the Struts open source framework for Web application development.
Visual development	Workshop provides a rich WYSIWYG interface, two-way editing, drag-and-drop interfaces to write Java code as well as JSP and HTML.
Java Page Flows	Workshop provides tools for developing Web page flows, business logic execution, and data binding.
Data binding	Workshop has drag and drop tools for binding data on a JSP to a backend database, control, or Web Service. Rich tag libraries to provide JSP/HTML support.
Annotated code model	Workshop introduces the concept of annotated coding to support complex functionality such as navigation, state management, validation, security, logging, and other core architecture services.
Reuse	All components developed through Workshop are packaged as JAR files so that components can be reused and leveraged across applications.

Portals and Integration Application Development

In Platform 7.0, no Portal or Integration development was done through Workshop. In the 8.1 release of Platform, Workshop forms the single point of entry into the entire BEA suite. Workshop enables developers to incorporate advanced EAI/BPM and process portal functionality into custom development projects by unifying workflow, presentation, and business logic in a single environment using the same programming model. WebLogic Workshop Platform Edition enables you to create workflows graphically so that you can focus on the application logic rather than on implementation details as you develop. It includes a data mapper to create data transformations graphically. WebLogic Workshop generates a query from the graphical representation of the data transformation.

Table C.3 highlights some of the key features within Workshop that allow Portal and Integration development from this unified IDE.

TABLE C.3 Workshop Leverages the BEA WebLogic Platform

Feature	Benefit
Java controls	Extensible through the creation of controls. These controls are available for use anywhere in the Platform—through Workshop, they are available in Integration, Portal, and Server.
Java Page Flows	A concept from the portal product that allows Struts based page navigation and actions.
Worklists	The business process management tool from the Integration product is now available through Workshop.

Development Using Workshop

In this section, we describe the various technologies and features of Workshop that help in developing applications on the BEA WebLogic Platform. We also cover the key development concepts that an architect needs to know for tool selection.

Code Annotations in Workshop

Using annotated Java code files is a big push toward streamlining and simplifying J2EE development. Basically what this means is that in place of coding everything manually, the developer inserts special Javadoc tags that will be used to add behavior during execution. This is very similar to the notion of generating stubs and skeletons when working with RMI or EJBs. It is a code generation process. When you decide to build the application, Workshop generates all the required underlying code (similar to running the EJB compiler for EJBs) and deploys it to WebLogic Server.

BEA is working within the Java Community Process (JCP) to make this a standard. Workshop incorporates this concept in a big way within the IDE.

NOTE

For details on the Java Specification Request that aims at standardizing code annotations, see JSR 175 at `http://www.jcp.org/en/jsr/detail?id=175`.

C

Workshop JWS

JWS (Java Web Service) is Java code annotation syntax for creating Web Services in WebLogic Workshop. BEA introduced this in the first release of Workshop and has submitted this to the Java Community Process for adoption as a standard.

Workshop leverages Apache Axis as the underlying technology for Web Services. JWS files are created through the Workshop UI and the JWS files are used to generate Apache Axis Web Services at compile time.

NOTE

For details on the Java Specification Request that aims at standardizing JWS files, see JSR 181 at `http://www.jcp.org/en/jsr/detail?id=181`.

A JWS file is a syntactically correct Java file along with several Javadoc type attributes to enable Workshop developers to leverage powerful Web Services functionality. The underlying infrastructure to support the logic defined in the JWS file is generated behind the scenes.

The basic form of a JWS file includes

- Javadoc tags that allow WebLogic Workshop to generate the appropriate infrastructure code for the logic
- A JWS extension that marks this as a Web Service

Java Page Flows

WebLogic Workshop builds on top of the Apache Struts project and introduces what BEA calls *Java Page Flows* (JPF). Developers can visually build Java Page Flows that define their Web application. All the underlying Struts-based code is automatically generated for them at runtime. This is a very similar concept as the Java Web Services files that we talked about in the previous section.

A JPF is a Java class with Javadoc annotations that define the flow of the Web application. It generally includes one or more JSPs and the appropriate flow to connect activities in the JSP (such as a submit) to Struts-like action classes. The action classes are the classes that manage the Web application and perform logic.

The Workshop IDE is used to visually develop these Java Page Flows. The Source view can be used to add some custom code and develop the JSPs. An example of a Page Flow is shown in Figure C.3.

Page Flows in Workshop are a good implementation of the Model-View-Controller (MVC) design pattern. Controls implement the model layer of the MVC architecture. JSPs are used for the view, and Java Page Flows are used as controllers.

Page flows enable developers and architects to quickly and graphically design their Web applications. They can drag and drop JSPs, controls, actions, and conditional logic using a graphical palette. Thus, the first pass through the page flows can enable developers or architects to quickly build skeleton applications. They can then come back and implement the logic for the skeleton pieces that they've created. Page flows also support dynamic binding of database types to the JSP, and have several tag libraries to aid in the development of the JSPs. They also manage state transition and XML–Java mapping of the value objects.

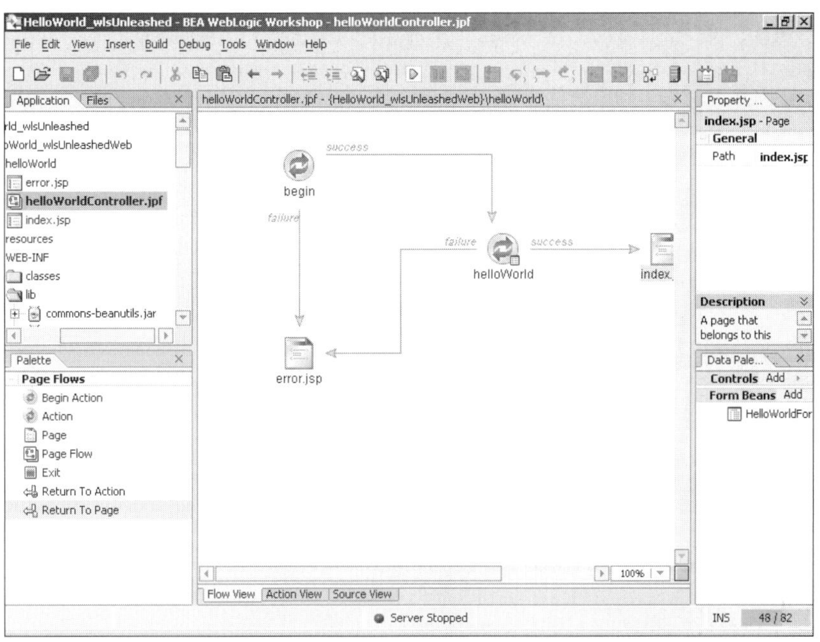

FIGURE C.3 Java Page Flows.

Net UI

The Net UI technology is basically a JSP tag library that provides functionality for Web application development in Workshop. These tags help in HTML processing, data binding, and templating.

Net UI HTML Tags

These tags allow the development of dynamic HTML pages. The tags are related to HTML development such as forms, select boxes, radio buttons, and other HTML controls. In addition, these tags also include support for binding to a data source, formatting data for display, and error and exception handling.

Net UI Data Binding Tags

The data binding tags are very powerful. These tags allow the design of dynamic tables with repeating headers, footers, title columns, rows, and so on. They also allow the invocation of other page flows and controls.

Net UI Template Tags

At first glance, the Net UI template tags look like portals. They basically allow HTML pages to be templatized with repeating sections and attributes that can be shared across pages. You should not confuse these with portals, but they do provide some of the very basic functionality that's currently available only in a portal product, in traditional JSP development.

> **NOTE**
>
> The Workshop help files have a complete list of the NET UI tags and Javadocs on how to use them. These can be found at `http://edocs.bea.com/workshop/docs81/doc/en/core/index.html`.

XMLBeans

XMLBeans is a technology from BEA that allows the manipulation of XML data and files in Java. This is a strongly typed Java object interface for XML data that enables a developer to manipulate raw XML data using the productivity and flexibility benefits of the Java language. Developers see a familiar and convenient JavaBeans-like object-based view of their XML data without losing access to the original native XML structure. Before XMLBeans, developers had to parse XML files using either the DOM or SAX parser to convert the files into Java objects. After manipulation of the Java objects, they would have to be converted back into XML files. As you can imagine, this was a slow and time-consuming process. Using XMLBeans, while developers are manipulating the XML data as if they were Java objects, the XML file underneath is always kept in sync. XMLBeans support technologies such as XML schemas, XQuery, and other XML technologies.

> **NOTE**
>
> You can see the XMLBeans documentation from BEA at `http://workshop.bea.com/xmlbeans/docindex.html`.

WebLogic Workshop has a built-in visual mapping tool that enables you to map XML data to Java objects. XQuery is used to do this mapping. Figure C.4 shows the visual XML-to-Java mapping tool.

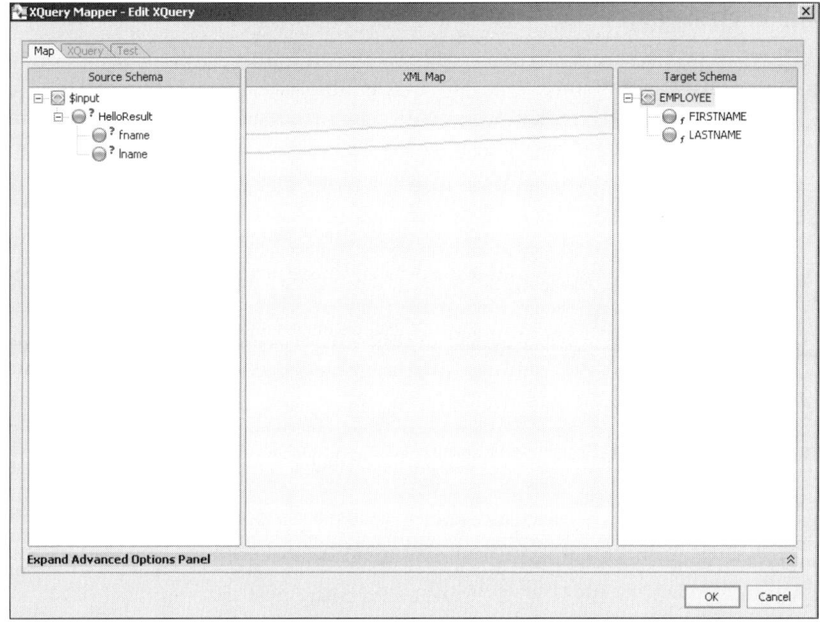

FIGURE C.4 XML-to-Java mapping.

Debugging and Testing Using Workshop

Applications developed in Workshop can be tested with the click of a button. WebLogic Workshop comes with a full debugging and test environment to test J2EE applications and Web Services.

Debugging a Web Application

How many times have you written 100% error-free code? Workshop comes with a debugger that has all the features of a standard debugger that you might be used to—with the ability to set breakpoints, step through your code line-by-line, view local variables, and set flags on variables. This debugger can be used to test Web applications from within Workshop.

Debugging a Web Service

WebLogic Workshop enables you to use the same debugging concepts to debug Web Services that you as a developer are used to for debugging your Java applications. With Workshop, you can set up breakpoints or do a step-by-step execution of your Web Service. This is covered briefly in Chapter 30.

C

Testing a Web Service

After you've written and debugged your Web Service, it's time to see it in action. Workshop automatically generates test JSPs that enable you to walk through the execution of your Web Service and see the SOAP and XML data that is being passed back and forth. You can also double-check the WSDL and SOAP that define the Web Service. The test JSPs support the testing for both synchronous and synchronous Web Services. Figure C.5 shows a sample test view.

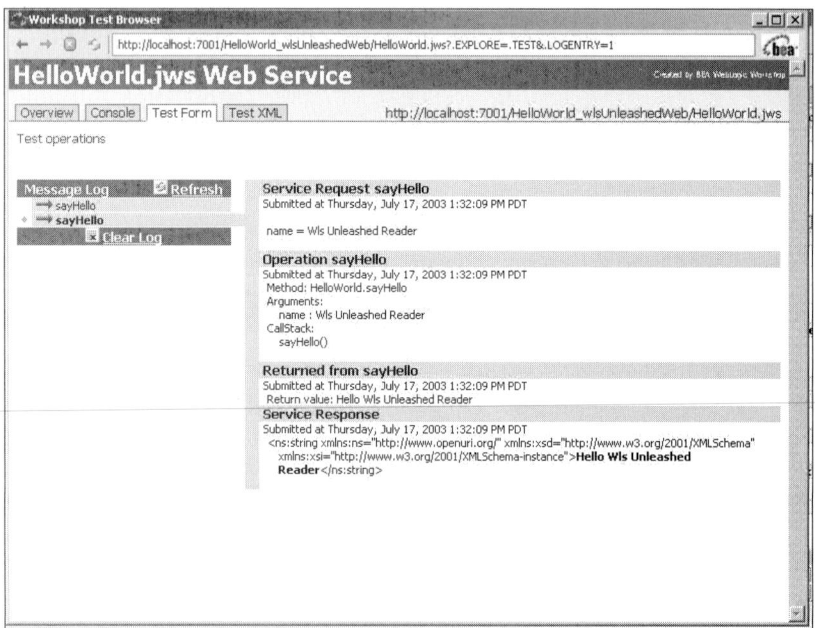

FIGURE C.5 Web Services testing.

Compatibility of Workshop 8.1 with Workshop 7.0

In this section, we talk about how the release of Workshop with BEA WebLogic Platform 7.0 differs from the 8.1 release.

Web Services

Web Services developed in Workshop 7.0 and deployed on WebLogic Server 7.0 are interoperable with Web Services deployed on WebLogic Server 8.1. Web Services built in Workshop 7.0 can be imported into Workshop 8.1. However, BEA has made considerable enhancements to the 8.1 runtime and thus Web Services built in Workshop 8.1 are *not* backward compatible on WebLogic Server 7.0. Applications built in Workshop 8.1 are only deployable on WebLogic Server 8.1 because they enable you to leverage core Web Services support features in WebLogic Server 8.1.

Other Components

Workshop 7.0 primarily focused on Web Services. It did not have an extensible controls API, the concept of page flows, or Worklist. These features are clearly new to 8.1 and thus not backward compatible with the 7.0 release of the BEA WebLogic Platform.

> **NOTE**
>
> For a complete guide on how to upgrade existing Workshop applications to Workshop 8.1, please see the "Upgrading Existing Applications" section in the Workshop help at `http://e-docs.bea.com/workshop/docs81/doc/en/core/index.html`.

Service-Oriented Development in Workshop

Business needs are continuously evolving that demand that technology and business be loosely coupled so that a change in the business does not mean a delay by weeks or months in the software life cycle.

BEA WebLogic Workshop provides a rich framework and a robust development environment for the development of modularized Web Services, which is a special case of a service. Although BEA does not market Workshop as a truly service-oriented platform, the rich features provided by Workshop, such as code annotation and the simplicity in J2EE development, enable us to write applications along service boundaries rather than technology boundaries. The simplicity in writing J2EE code, due to the loose coupling with the underlying plumbing, enables business developers to be more productive and write business services without becoming J2EE experts.

Java controls that encapsulate business logic as independent, reusable modules can be thought of as services in a service-oriented architecture (SOA) world. These are the first steps towards developing a truly service-oriented architecture.

Index

Symbols

A

B

C

How can we make this index more useful? Email us at indexes@samspublishing.com

D

E

F

G

H

I

J

K

L

M

N

O

P

S

T

U

V

W

X – Y

Z

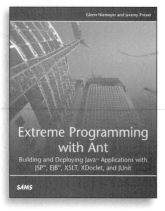